IMPORTANT

HERE IS YOUR REGISTRATION CODE TO ACCESS MCGRAW-h PREMIUM CONTENT AND MCGRAW-HILL ONLINE RESOURCES

For key premium online resources you need THIS CODE to gain access. Once the code is entered, you will be able to use the web resources for the length of your course.

Access is provided only if you have purchased a new book.

If the registration code is missing from this book, the registration screen on our website, and within your WebCT or Blackboard course will tell you how to obtain your new code. Your registration code can be used only once to establish access. It is not transferable

To gain access to these online resources

1. **USE** your web browser to go to: **www.mhhe.com/hill**

2. **CLICK** on "First Time User"

3. **ENTER** the Registration Code printed on the tear-off bookmark on the right

4. After you have entered your registration code, click on "Register"

5. **FOLLOW** the instructions to setup your personal UserID and Password

6. **WRITE** your UserID and Password down for future reference. Keep it in a safe place.

If your course is using WebCT or Blackboard, you'll be able to use this code to access the McGraw-Hill content within your instructor's online course.

To gain access to the McGraw-Hill content in your instructor's WebCT or Blackboard course simply log into the course with the user ID and Password provided by your instructor. Enter the registration code exactly as it appears to the right when prompted by the system. You will only need to use this code the first time you click on McGraw-Hill content.

These instructions are specifically for student access. Instructors are not required to register via the above instructions.

The McGraw-Hill Companies

McGraw-Hill
Irwin

Thank you, and welcome to your
McGraw-Hill/Irwin Online Resources.

Hill
International Business, 6/e
0-07-310260-1
978-0-07-310260-3

W9-CZI-346

9KJ6-9A49-GNAW-CXQP-D

REGISTRATION CODE
REGISTRATION CODE

The McGraw-Hill Companies

McGraw-Hill
Irwin

6 E International
Business

COMPETING IN THE GLOBAL
MARKETPLACE

Charles W. L. Hill
UNIVERSITY OF WASHINGTON

McGraw-Hill
Irwin

Boston   Burr Ridge, IL   Dubuque, IA   Madison, WI   New York   San Francisco   St. Louis
Bangkok   Bogotá   Caracas   Kuala Lumpur   Lisbon   London   Madrid   Mexico City
Milan   Montreal   New Delhi   Santiago   Seoul   Singapore   Sydney   Taipei   Toronto

INTERNATIONAL BUSINESS: COMPETING IN THE GLOBAL MARKETPLACE

Published by McGraw-Hill/Irwin, a business unit of The McGraw-Hill Companies, Inc., 1221 Avenue of the Americas, New York, NY, 10020.

Some ancillaries, including electronic and print components, may not be available to customers outside the United States.

This book is printed on acid-free paper.

1 2 3 4 5 6 7 8 9 0 DOW/DOW 0 9 8 7 6

ISBN-13: 978-0-07-110671-9
ISBN-10: 0-07-110671-5

www.mhhe.com

For **June Hill**
and **Mike Hill,** my parents

about the AUTHOR

Charles W. L. Hill is the Hughes M. Blake Professor of International Business at the School of Business, University of Washington. Professor Hill received his Ph.D. from the University of Manchester's Institute of Science and Technology (UMIST) in Britain. In addition to the University of Washington, he has served on the faculties of UMIST, Texas A&M University, and Michigan State University.

Professor Hill has published over 40 articles in peer-reviewed academic journals, including the *Academy of Management Journal, Academy of Management Review, Strategic Management Journal,* and *Organization Science.* He has also published two college texts: one on strategic management and the other on international business. Professor Hill has served on the editorial boards of several academic journals, including the *Strategic Management Journal* and *Organization Science.* Between 1993 and 1996 he was consulting editor at the *Academy of Management Review.*

Professor Hill teaches in the MBA, Executive MBA, Management, and Ph.D. programs at the University of Washington. He has received awards for teaching excellence in the MBA, Executive MBA, and Management programs. He has also taught customized executive programs.

Professor Hill works on a consulting basis with a number of organizations. His clients have included ATL, Boeing, BF Goodrich, Hexcel, House of Fraser, Microsoft, Seattle City Light, Tacoma City Light, Thompson Financial Services, and Wizards of the Coast.

brief CONTENTS

Part 6   Business Operations

CONTENTS

Part 1
Introduction and Overview

Part 2
Country Differences

Part 3
The Global Trade and Investment
Environment

Part 4
The Global Monetary System

Part 5
The Strategy and Structure of
International Business

CHAPTER 12
The Strategy of International Business   406

CHAPTER 13
The Organization of International
Business   438

Part 6
Business Operations

list of MAPS

PREFACE

It is now almost 15 years since I began work on the first edition of *International Business: Competing in the Global Marketplace*. By the third edition, the book was the most widely used international business text in the world. Since then its market share has only increased. I attribute the success of the book to a number of goals I set out for myself when I embarked on the first edition of the book. Specifically, I wanted to write a book that (1) was comprehensive and up-to-date, (2) went beyond an uncritical presentation and shallow explanation of the body of knowledge, (3) maintained a tight, integrated flow between chapters, (4) focused on managerial implications, and (5) made important theories accessible and interesting to students.

Over the years, and through six editions, I have worked hard to adhere to these goals. It has not always been easy. An enormous amount has happened over the last 15 years, both in the real world of economics, politics, and business, and in the academic world of theory and empirical research. Often I have had to significantly rewrite chapters, scrap old examples, bring in new ones, incorporate new theory and evidence into the book, and phase out older theories that are increasingly less relevant to the modern and dynamic world of international business. That process continues in the current edition. As noted later, there have been significant changes in this edition, and that will no doubt continue to be the case in the future. In deciding what changes to make, I have been guided not only by my own reading, teaching, and research, but also by the invaluable feedback I receive from professors and students around the world who use the book, from reviewers, and from the editorial staff at McGraw-Hill. My thanks go out to all of them.

COMPREHENSIVE AND UP-TO-DATE

To be comprehensive, an international business textbook must:

- Explain how and why the world's countries differ.
- Present a thorough review of the economics and politics of international trade and investment.
- Explain the functions and form of the global monetary system.
- Examine the strategies and structures of international businesses.
- Assess the special roles of an international business's various functions.

I have always endeavored to do all of these things in *International Business*. In my view, many other texts paid insufficient attention to the strategies and structures of international businesses and to the implications of international business for firms' various functions. This omission has been a serious deficiency. Many of the students in these international business courses will soon be working in international businesses, and they will be expected to understand the implications of international business for their organization's strategy, structure, and functions. This book pays close attention to these issues.

Comprehensiveness and relevance also require coverage of the major theories. It has always been my goal to incorporate into the text the insights gleaned from recent academic work. Consistent with this goal, over the last six editions I have added insights from the following research:

- The new trade theory and strategic trade policy.
- The work of Nobel Prize–winning economist Amartya Sen on economic development.
- The work of Hernando de Soto on the link between property rights and economic development.
- Samuel Huntington's influential thesis on the "clash of civilizations."
- The new growth theory of economic development championed by Paul Romer and Gene Grossman.
- Empirical work by Jeffrey Sachs and others on the relationship between international trade and economic growth.
- Michael Porter's theory of the competitive advantage of nations.
- Robert Reich's work on national competitive advantage.
- The work of Nobel Prize winner Douglass North and others on national institutional structures and the protection of property rights.
- The market imperfections approach to foreign direct investment that has grown out of Ronald Coase and Oliver Williamson's work on transaction cost economics.
- Bartlett and Ghoshal's research on the transnational corporation.
- The writings of C. K. Prahalad and Gary Hamel on core competencies, global competition, and global strategic alliances.
- Insights for international business strategy that can be derived from the resource-based view of the firm.

In addition to including leading-edge theory, in light of the fast-changing nature of the international business environment, every effort is being made to ensure that the book is as up-to-date as possible when it goes to press. A significant amount has happened in the world since the first edition of this book was published in 1993. The Uruguay Round of GATT negotiations was successfully concluded and the World Trade Organization was established. In 2001 the WTO embarked upon another major round of talks aimed to reduce barriers to trader, the Doha Round. The European Union moved forward with its post-1992 agenda to achieve a closer economic and monetary union, including the establishment of a common currency in January 1999. The North American Free Trade Agreement passed into law, and Chile indicated its desire to become the next member of the free trade area. The Asian-Pacific Economic Cooperation forum (APEC) emerged as the kernel of a possible future Asia Pacific free trade area. The former Communist states of Eastern Europe and Asia continued on the road to economic and political reform. As they did, the euphoric mood that followed the collapse of communism in 1989 was slowly replaced with a growing sense of realism about the hard path ahead for many of these countries. The global money market continued its meteoric growth. By 2005, more than $1.5 trillion per day was flowing across national borders. The size of such flows fueled concern about the ability of short-term speculative shifts in global capital markets to destabilize the world economy. The World Wide Web emerged from nowhere to become the backbone of an emerging global network for electronic commerce. The world continued to become more global. Several Asian Pacific economies, including most notably China, continued to grow their economies at a rapid rate. Outsourcing of service functions to places such as China and India emerged as a major issue in developed Western nations. New multinationals continued to emerge from developing nations in addition to the world's established industrial powers. Increasingly, the globalization of the world economy affected a wide range of firms of all sizes, from the very large to the very small. And unfortunately, in the wake of the terrorist attacks on the United States on September 11, 2001, global terrorism and the attendant geopolitical risks emerged as a threat to global economic integration and activity.

Reflecting this rapid pace change, in this edition of the book I have tried to ensure that all material and statistics are as up-to-date as possible as of 2005. However, being absolutely up-to-date is impossible since change is always

with us. What is current today may be outdated tomorrow. Accordingly, I have a home page for this book on the World Wide Web at www.mhhe.com/hill.

BEYOND UNCRITICAL PRESENTATION AND SHALLOW EXPLANATION

Many issues in international business are complex and thus necessitate considerations of pros and cons. To demonstrate this to students, I have adopted a critical approach that presents the arguments for and against economic theories, government policies, business strategies, organizational structures, and so on.

Related to this, I have attempted to explain the complexities of the many theories and phenomena unique to international business so the student might fully comprehend the statements of a theory or the reasons a phenomenon is the way it is. I believe that these theories and phenomena are explained in more depth in this book than they are in competing textbooks, the rationale being that a shallow explanation is little better than no explanation. In international business, a little knowledge is indeed a dangerous thing.

INTEGRATED PROGRESSION OF TOPICS

A weakness of many texts is that they lack a tight, integrated flow of topics from chapter to chapter. In this book students are told in Chapter 1 how the book's topics are related to each other. Integration has been achieved by organizing the material so that each chapter builds on the material of the previous ones in a logical fashion.

Part 1

Chapter 1 provides an overview of the key issues to be addressed and explains the plan of the book.

Part 2

Chapters 2 and 3 focus on national differences in political economy and culture, and Chapter 4 on ethical issues in international business. Most international business textbooks place this material at a later point, but I believe it is vital to discuss national differences first. After all, many of the central issues in international trade and investment, the global monetary system, international business strategy and structure, and international business operations arise out of national differences in political economy and culture. To fully understand these issues, students must first appreciate the differences in countries and cultures. Ethical issues are dealt with at this juncture primarily because many ethical dilemmas flow out of national differences in political systems, economic systems, and culture.

Part 3

Chapters 5 through 9 investigate the political economy of international trade and investment. The purpose of this part is to describe and explain the trade and investment environment in which international business occurs.

Part 4

Chapters 10 and 11 describe and explain the global monetary system, laying out in detail the monetary framework in which international business transactions are conducted.

Part 5

In Chapters 12 through 14 attention shifts from the environment to the firm. Here the book examines the strategies and structures that firms adopt to compete effectively in the international business environment.

Part 6

In Chapters 15 through 20 the focus narrows further to investigate business operations. These chapters explain how firms can perform their key functions—manufacturing, marketing, R&D, human resource management, accounting, and finance—in order to compete and succeed in the international business environment.

Throughout the book, the relationship of new material to topics discussed in earlier chapters is pointed out to the students to reinforce their understanding of how the material comprises an integrated whole.

IMPLICATIONS FOR MANAGERS

I have always believed that it is important to show students how the material covered in the text is relevant to the actual practice of international business. This is explicit in the later chapters of the book, which focus on the practice of international business, but it is not always obvious in the first half of the book, which considered many macroeconomic and political issues, from international trade theory and foreign direct investment flows to the IMF and the influence of inflation rates on foreign exchange quotations. Accordingly, at the end of each chapter in Parts 2, 3, and 4—where the focus is on the environment of international business, as opposed to particular firms—is a section titled "Implications for Managers." In this section, the managerial implications

of the material discussed in the chapter are clearly explained. For example, Chapter 5, International Trade Theory, ends with a detailed discussion of the various trade theories' implications for international business management.

In addition, each chapter begins with a <u>case</u> that illustrates the relevance of chapter material for the practice of international business. Chapter 2, National Differences in Political Economy, for example, opens with a case that describes how endemic corruption in Indonesia has raised the costs of doing business in that country.

I have also added a <u>closing case</u> to each chapter. These cases are also designed to illustrate the relevance of chapter material for the practice of international business. The closing case to Chapter 2, for example, looks at the reasons for the persistency of poverty is sub-Saharan Africa and links this to the low level of foreign direct investment by international businesses in the region. The case is also designed to help students think through how the region might pull itself out of the poverty trap, and the opportunities that this might create for international business.

Another tool that I have used to focus on managerial implications is *Management Focus* boxes. There is at least one Management Focus in each chapter. Like the opening case, the purpose of these boxes is to illustrate the relevance of chapter material for the practice of international business. The Management Focus in Chapter 2, for example, looks at the battle against piracy in the global market for video games. This feature illustrates the important role that national differences in the protection of intellectual property rights can play in international business.

Appearing once again in this edition are the GlobalEdge Research Tasks at the end of each chapter. Created by the CIBER group at Michigan State University headed by Tomas Hult and Tunga Kiyak, these application exercises challenge students to research, collect, and analyze data as they act as managers working for international firms. From exploring differences in business etiquette to using data sources such as the *World Investment Dictionary* to identifying tariff restrictions in different countries, these exercises expose students to the types of sources and tools international managers use to make informed business decisions.

ACCESSIBLE AND INTERESTING

The international business arena is fascinating and exciting, and I have tried to communicate my enthusiasm for it to the student. Learning is easier and better if the subject matter is communicated in an interesting, informative, and accessible manner. One technique I have used to achieve this is weaving interesting anecdotes into the narrative of the text—stories that illustrate theory. The opening cases and focus boxes are also used to make the theory being discussed in the text both accessible and interesting.

Each chapter has two kinds of focus boxes—a Management Focus box (described above) and a Country Focus box. Country Focus features provide background on the political, economic, social, or cultural aspects of countries grappling with an international business issue. In Chapter 2, for example, one Country Focus box discusses the steps that India has taken over the last decade to build a dynamic, market-based economic system.

WHAT'S NEW IN THE 6TH EDITION

The success of the first five editions of *International Business* was based in part upon the incorporation of leading-edge research into the text, the use of up-to-date examples and statistics to illustrate global trends and enterprise strategy, and the discussion of current events within the context of the appropriate theory. Building on these strengths, my goals for the sixth edition have been threefold:

1. Incorporate new insights from recent scholarly research wherever appropriate.

2. Make sure the content of the text covers all appropriate issues.

3. Make sure the text is as up-to-date as possible with regard to current events, statistics, and examples.

As part of the revision process, a new chapter has been added on ethics in international business (Chapter 4). Although there has always been significant discussion of ethics in the book, in the wake of the numerous ethical scandals that swept through the business world over the last few years, I felt it was appropriate to place greater emphasis on this vitally important topic.

At the same time, I did not want to add to the overall length of the book, so I made a hard choice to eliminate one chapter. This was a chapter that looked at the rise of the global capital market. Some of the content in this chapter has been relocated to Chapters 10 and 11, and some has been eliminated. I made this decision after reading through feedback from reviewers, which suggested that this was the least used chapter in the book.

As part of the overall revision process, *changes have been made to every chapter in the book*. All statistics have been updated to incorporate the most recently available data. New examples, cases, and boxes have been added and older examples updated to reflect new developments. New material has been inserted wherever appropriate to reflect recent academic work or important current events. For example, Chapter 5 has been updated to discuss progress on the current round of talks sponsored by the WTO aimed at reducing barriers to trade, particularly in agriculture (the Doha Round). Chapter 6 now discusses the slump in foreign direct investment flows that took place in 2001–2004. The section on the European Union in Chapter 8 has been revised to reflect the fact that 10 more member states were admitted on May 1, 2004. At several places in the book, there is extended discussion of the outsourcing of service activities, from software testing and diagnosis of MRI scans to telephone call centers and billing functions, to developing nations such as India, and the implications of this development for international business are explored. And so on.

ACKNOWLEDGMENTS

Numerous people deserve to be thanked for their assistance in preparing this book. First thank you to all the people at McGraw-Hill/Irwin who have worked with me on this project:

John E. Biernat, Editorial Director

Ryan Blankenship, Sponsoring Editor

Natalie Ruffatto, Developmental Editor

Meg Beamer, Associate Marketing Manager

Laura Griffin, Senior Project Manager

Damian Moshak, Media Producer

Sesha Bolisetty, Production Supervisor

Kami Carter, Designer

Susan Lombardi, Media Project Manager

Jeremy Cheshareck, Senior Photo Research Coordinator

Second, my thanks go to the reviewers, who provided good feedback that helped shape this book.

Yequing Bao, University of Alabama in Huntsville

Lawrence A. Beer, Arizona State University

Thomas Cary, City University

Charles Dhanaraj, Indiana University

P. Roberto Garcia, Indiana University

Stuart Graham, Georgia Institute of Technology

Anthony D. Gribble, East Carolina University

Seid Y. Hassan, Murray State University

Antoine Monteils, University of Houston Downtown

H. Lynne Moretz, Central Piedmont Community College

William F. Shuster, Colorado State University

Andrew Spicer, University of California, Riverside

Bala Subramanian, Morgan State University

Yim-Yu Wong, San Francisco State University

International
Business

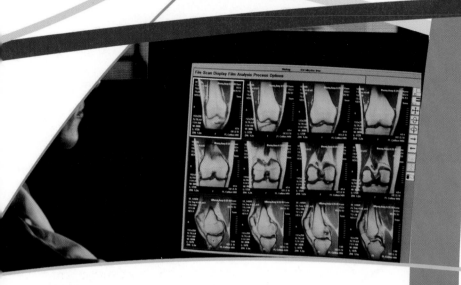

1

Globalization

The Globalization of Health Care

Conventional wisdom holds that health care is one of the industries least vulnerable to dislocation from globalization. After all, like many service businesses, health care is delivered where it is purchased, right? If an American goes to a hospital for an MRI scan, won't that scan be read by a local radiologist? And if the MRI scan shows that surgery is required, surely the surgery will be done at a local hospital in the United States. Until recently, this was true, but we are now witnessing the beginnings of globalization in this traditionally most local of industries.

Consider the MRI scan: The United States has a shortage of radiologists, the doctors who specialize in reading and interpreting diagnostic medical images including X-rays, CT scans, MRI scans, and ultrasound. Demand for radiologists is reportedly growing twice as fast as the rate at which medical schools are graduating radiologists with the skills and qualifications required to read medical images. This imbalance between supply and demand means that radiologists are expensive; an American radiologist can earn as much as $350,000 a year. In 2002, an Indian radiologist working at the prestigious Massachusetts General Hospital, Dr. Sanjay Saini, thought he had found a clever way to deal with the shortage and expense—beam images over the Internet to India where they could be interpreted by radiologists. This would reduce the workload on America's radiologists and also cut costs. A radiologist in India might earn one-tenth of his or her U.S. counterpart. Plus, because India is on the opposite side of the globe, the images could be interpreted while it was nighttime in the United States, and be ready for the attending physician when he or she arrived for work the following morning.

As for the surgery, here too we are witnessing the beginnings of an outsourcing trend. In October 2004, for example, Howard Staab, a 53-year-old uninsured self-employed carpenter from North Carolina had surgery to repair a leaking heart valve—in India! Mr. Staab flew to New Delhi, had the operation, and afterward toured the Taj Mahal, the price of which was bundled with that of the surgery. The cost, including airfare, totaled $10,000. If Mr. Staab's surgery had been performed in the United States, the cost would have been $60,000 and there would have been no visit to the Taj Mahal.

Howard Staab is not alone. Some 170,000 foreigners visited India in 2004 for medical treatments. That number is projected to rise by 15 percent a year for the next several years. According to the management consultancy McKinsey & Co., medical tourism (overseas trips to have medical procedures performed) could be a $2.3 billion industry in India by 2012. In another example, after years of living in pain, Robert Beeney, a 64-year-old from San Francisco, was advised to get his hip joint replaced, but after doing some research on the Internet, Mr. Beeney elected instead for joint resurfacing, which was not covered by his insurance. Instead of going to a nearby hospital, he flew to Hyderabad in southern India and had the surgery done for $6,600, a fraction of the $25,000 the procedure would have cost in the United States.

Mr. Beeney had his surgery performed at a branch of the Apollo hospital chain. Apollo, which was founded by Dr. Prathap C. Reddy, a surgeon trained at Massachusetts General Hospital, runs a chain of 18 state-of-the-art hospitals throughout Asia. Between 2001 and 2004, Apollo treated 43,000 foreigners, mainly from nations in Southeast Asia and the Persian Gulf, although a growing number are from Western Europe and North America. In 2004, 7 percent of its revenue came from foreigners. With 200 U.S.-trained doctors on his staff, Dr. Reddy reckons that he can offer medical care equivalent to that in the United States, but at a fraction of the cost. Nor is he alone; Mr. Staab's surgery was performed by Dr. Naresh Trehan, a cardiac surgeon who was trained at New York University School of Medicine and worked there for a decade. Dr. Trehan returned home to India and opened his own cardiac hospital, which now conducts 4,000 heart surgeries a year, with a 0.8 percent mortality rate and 0.3 percent infection rate, on par with the best of the world's hospitals.

So will demand for American health services soon collapse as work moves offshore to places like India? Hardly! Regulations, personal preferences, and practical considerations mean that the majority of health services will always be performed in the country where the patient resides. Consider the MRI scan—to safeguard patient care, U.S. regulations require that a radiologist be licensed in the state where the image was made and that he or she be certified by the hospital where care is being given. Given that not many radiologists in India have these qualifications, no more than a small fraction of images can be interpreted overseas. Another complication is that the U.S. government-sponsored medical insurance program, Medicare, will not pay for services done outside of the country. Nor will many private insurance plans, or not yet anyway. Moreover, most people would prefer to have care delivered close to home, and only in exceptional cases, such as when the procedure is not covered by their medical plan, are they likely to consider the foreign option. Still, most experts believe that the trends now in place will continue, and that a small but significant percentage of medical service will be performed in a country that is different from the one where the patient resides.

Sources: G. Colvin, "Think Your Job Can't Be Sent to India?" *Fortune,* December 13, 2004, p. 80; A. Pollack, "Who's Reading Your X-Ray," *The New York Times,* November 16, 2003, pp. 1, 9; S. Rai, "Low Costs Lure Foreigners to India for Medical Care," *The New York Times,* April 7, 2005, p. C6; J. Solomon, "Traveling Cure: India's New Coup in Outsourcing," *The Wall Street Journal,* April 26, 2004, p. A1; and J. Slater, "Increasing Doses in India," *Far Eastern Economic Review,* February 19, 2004, pp. 32–35.

Introduction

A fundamental shift is occurring in the world economy. We are moving away from a world in which national economies were relatively self-contained entities, isolated from each other by barriers to cross-border trade and investment; by distance, time zones, and language; and by national differences in government regulation, culture, and business systems. And we are moving toward a world in which barriers to cross-border trade and investment are declining; perceived distance is shrinking due to advances in transportation and telecommunications technology; material culture is starting to look similar the world over; and national economies are merging into an interdependent, integrated global economic system. The process by which this is occurring is commonly referred to as globalization.

In this interdependent global economy, an American might drive to work in a car designed in Germany that was assembled in Mexico by DaimlerChrysler from components made in the United States and Japan that were fabricated from Korean steel and Malaysian rubber. She may have filled the car with gasoline at a BP service station owned by a British multinational company. The gasoline could have been made from oil pumped out of a well off the coast of Africa by a French oil company that transported it to the United States in a ship owned by a Greek shipping line. While driving to work, the American might talk to her stockbroker on a Nokia cell phone that was designed in Finland and assembled in Texas using chip sets produced in Taiwan that were designed by Indian engineers working for Texas Instruments. She could tell the stockbroker to purchase shares in Deutsche Telekom, a German telecommunications firm that was transformed from a former state-owned monopoly into a global company by an energetic Israeli CEO. She may turn on the car radio, which was made in Malaysia by a Japanese firm, to hear a popular hip-hop song composed by a Swede and sung by a group of Danes in English who signed a record contract with a French music company to promote their record in America. The driver might pull into a drive-through coffee stall run by a Korean immigrant and order a "single-tall-non-fat latte" and chocolate-covered biscotti. The coffee beans come from Brazil and the chocolate from Peru, while the biscotti was made locally using an old Italian recipe. After the song ends, a news announcer might inform the American listener that antiglobalization protests at a meeting of heads of state in Davos, Switzerland, have turned violent. One protester has been killed. The announcer then turns to the next item, a story about how fear of interest rate hikes in the United States has sent Japan's Nikkei stock market index down to new lows for the year.

This is the world we live in. It is a world where the volume of goods, services, and investment crossing national borders has expanded faster than world output consistently for more than half a century. It is a world where more than $1.2 billion in foreign exchange transactions are made every day, where $8.88 trillion of goods and $2.10 trillion of services were sold across national borders in 2004.[1] It is a world in which international institutions such as the World Trade Organization and gatherings of leaders from the world's most powerful economies have called for even lower barriers to cross-border trade and investment. It is a world where the symbols of material and popular culture are increasingly global: from Coca-Cola and Starbucks to Sony PlayStations, Nokia cell phones, MTV shows, and Disney films. It is a world in which products are made from inputs that come from all over the world. It is a world in which an economic crisis in Asia can cause a recession in the United States, and the threat of higher interest rates in the United States really did help drive Japan's Nikkei index down in the spring of 2004. It is also a world in which vigorous and vocal groups protest against globalization, which they blame for a list of ills, from unemployment in developed nations to environmental degradation and the Americanization of popular culture. And yes, these protests really have turned violent.

For businesses, this process has produced many opportunities. Firms can expand their revenues by selling around the world and reduce their costs by producing in nations where key inputs, including labor, are cheap. Since the collapse of communism at the end of the 1980s, the pendulum of public policy in nation after nation has swung toward the free market end of the economic spectrum. Regulatory and administrative barriers to doing business in foreign nations have come down, while those nations have often transformed their economies, privatizing state-owned enterprises, deregulating markets, increasing competition, and welcoming investment by foreign businesses. This has allowed businesses both large and small, from both advanced nations and developing nations, to expand internationally.

At the same time, globalization has created new threats for businesses accustomed to dominating their domestic markets. Foreign companies have entered many formerly protected industries in developing nations, increasing competition and driving down prices. For three decades, U.S. automobile companies have been battling foreign enterprises, as Japanese, European, and now Korean companies have taken business from them. General Motors has seen its market share decline from more than 50 percent to about 28 percent, while Japan's Toyota has passed Chrysler, now DaimlerChrysler, to become the third largest automobile company in America behind Ford and GM.

As globalization unfolds, it is transforming industries and creating anxiety among those who believed their jobs were protected from foreign competition. Historically, while many workers in manufacturing industries worried about the impact foreign competition might have on their jobs, workers in service industries felt more secure. Now this too is changing. Advances in technology, lower transportation costs, and the rise of skilled workers in developing countries imply that many services no longer need to be performed where they are delivered. As illustrated by the opening case, the outsourcing trend is even hitting health services. An MRI scan might now be interpreted by a radiologist living in Bangalore, and a North Carolina man might elect to have surgery in Hyderabad, India, rather than his local hospital. Similar trends can be seen in many other service industries. Accounting work is being outsourced from America to India. In 2003, some 25,000 U.S. individual tax returns were done in India; in 2005 the number was expected to be closer to 400,000. Indian accountants, trained in U.S. tax rules, perform work for U.S. accounting firms.[2] They access individual tax returns stored on computers in the United States, perform routine calculations, and save their work so that it can be inspected by a U.S. accountant, who then bills clients. As the best-selling author Thomas Friedman has recently argued, the world is becoming flat.[3] People living in developed nations no longer have the playing field tilted in their favor. Increasingly, enterprising individuals based in India, China, or Brazil have the same opportunities to better themselves as those living in Western Europe, the United States, or Canada.

In this book we will take a close look at the issues introduced here, and at many more besides. We will explore how changes in regulations governing international trade and investment, when coupled with changes in political systems and technology, have dramatically altered the competitive playing field confronting many businesses. We will discuss the resulting opportunities and threats, and review the different strategies that managers can pursue to exploit the opportunities and counter the threats. We will consider whether globalization benefits or harms national economies. We will look at what economic theory has to say about the outsourcing of manufacturing and service jobs to places such as India and China, and at the benefits and costs of outsourcing, not just to business firms and their employees, but also to entire economies. First, though, we need to get a better overview of the nature and process of globalization, and that is the function of the current chapter.

🌐 What is Globalization?

As used in this book, **globalization** refers to the shift toward a more integrated and interdependent world economy. Globalization has several facets, including the globalization of markets and the globalization of production.

BEIJING, CHINA: Chinese shoppers walk through Beijing's main downtown shopping promenade past a Kentucky Fried Chicken (KFC) franchise. KFC is one of the most successful international businesses in China due to its adaptation and appeal to the Chinese market.

THE GLOBALIZATION OF MARKETS

The **globalization of markets** refers to the merging of historically distinct and separate national markets into one huge global marketplace. Falling barriers to cross-border trade have made it easier to sell internationally. It has been argued for some time that the tastes and preferences of consumers in different nations are beginning to converge on some global norm, thereby helping to create a global market.[4] Consumer products such as Citigroup credit cards, Coca-Cola soft drinks, Sony PlayStation video games, McDonald's hamburgers, and Starbucks coffee are frequently held up as prototypical examples of this trend. Firms such as Citigroup, Coca-Cola, McDonald's, Starbucks, and Sony are more than just benefactors of this trend; they are also facilitators of it. By offering the same basic product worldwide, they help to create a global market.

A company does not have to be the size of these multinational giants to facilitate, and benefit from, the globalization of markets. In the United States, for example, nearly 90 percent of firms that export are small businesses that employ less than 100 people, and their share of total U.S. exports has grown steadily over the last decade and now exceeds 20 percent.[5] Firms with less than 500 employees accounted for 97 percent of all U.S. exporters and almost 30 percent of all exports by value.[6] Typical of these is Hytech, a New York–based manufacturer of solar panels that generates 40 percent of its $3 million in annual sales from exports to five countries, or B&S Aircraft Alloys, another New York company whose exports account for 40 percent of its $8 million annual revenues.[7] The situation is similar in several other nations. In Germany, for example, companies with less than 500 employees account for about 30 percent of that nation's exports.[8]

Despite the global prevalence of Citigroup credit cards, McDonald's hamburgers, and Starbucks coffee, it is important not to push too far the view that national markets are giving way to the global market. As we shall see in later chapters, very significant differences still exist among national markets along many relevant dimensions, including consumer tastes and preferences, distribution channels, culturally embedded value systems, business systems, and legal regulations. These differences frequently require that marketing strategies, product features, and operating practices be customized to best match conditions in a country. For example, automobile companies will promote different car models depending on a range of factors such as local fuel costs, income levels, traffic congestion, and cultural values. Similarly, many companies need to vary aspects of their product mix and operations from country to country depending on local tastes and preferences.

The most global markets currently are not markets for consumer products—where national differences in tastes and preferences are still often important enough to act as a brake on globalization—but markets for industrial goods and materials that serve a universal need the world over. These include the markets for commodities such as aluminum, oil, and wheat; the markets for industrial products such as microprocessors, DRAMs (computer memory chips), and commercial jet aircraft; the markets for computer software; and the markets for financial assets from U.S. Treasury bills to eurobonds and futures on the Nikkei index or the Mexican peso.

In many global markets, the same firms frequently confront each other as competitors in nation after nation. Coca-Cola's rivalry with PepsiCo is a global one, as are the rivalries between Ford and Toyota, Boeing and Airbus, Caterpillar and Komatsu in earthmoving equipment, and Sony, Nintendo, and Microsoft in video games. If one firm moves into a nation that is not currently served by its rivals, those rivals are sure to follow to prevent their competitor from gaining an advantage.[9] As firms follow each other around the world, they bring with them many of the assets that served them well in other national markets—including their products, operating strategies, marketing strategies, and brand names—creating some homogeneity across markets. Thus, greater uniformity replaces diversity. In an increasing number of industries, it is no longer meaningful to talk about "the German market," "the American market," "the Brazilian market," or "the Japanese market"; for many firms there is only the global market.

THE GLOBALIZATION OF PRODUCTION

The **globalization of production** refers to the sourcing of goods and services from locations around the globe to take advantage of national differences in the cost and quality of **factors of production** (such as labor, energy, land, and capital). By doing this, companies hope to lower their overall cost structure and/or improve the quality or functionality of their product offering, thereby allowing them to compete more effectively. Consider the Boeing Company's commercial jet airliner, the 777. Eight Japanese suppliers make parts for the fuselage, doors, and wings; a supplier in Singapore makes the doors for the nose landing gear; three suppliers in Italy manufacture wing flaps; and so on.[10] In total, some 30 percent of the 777, by value, is built by foreign companies. For its next jet airliner, the 787, Boeing is pushing this trend even further, with some 65 percent of the total value of the aircraft scheduled to be outsourced to foreign companies, 35 percent of which will go to three major Japanese companies.[11]

Part of Boeing's rationale for outsourcing so much production to foreign suppliers is that these suppliers are the best in the world at their particular activity. A global web of suppliers yields a better final product, which enhances the chances of Boeing winning a greater share of total orders for aircraft than its global rival, Airbus Industrie. Boeing also outsources some production to foreign countries to increase the chance that it will win significant orders from airlines based in that country.

For another example of a global web of activities, consider the IBM ThinkPad X31 laptop computer.[12] This product was designed in the United States by IBM engineers because IBM believed that was the best location in the world to do the basic design work. The case, keyboard, and hard drive were made in Thailand; the display screen and memory were made in South Korea; the built-in wireless card was made in Malaysia; and the microprocessor was manufactured in the United States. In each case, these components were manufactured in the optimal location given an assessment of production costs and transportation costs. These components were shipped to an IBM operation in Mexico, where the product was assembled, before being shipped to the United States for final sale. IBM assembled the ThinkPad in Mexico because IBM's managers calculated that due to low labor costs, the costs of assembly could be minimized there. The marketing and sales strategy for North America was developed by IBM personnel in the United States, primarily because IBM believed that due to their knowledge of the local marketplace, U.S. personnel would add more value to the product through their marketing efforts than personnel based elsewhere. (Interestingly, in another comment on the nature of globalization, in 2005, IBM's personal computer business, including the ThinkPad, was purchased by the Chinese company Lenovo, which promptly moved its headquarters to the United States because it believed that was the best location from which to run this business. See the Management Focus later in this chapter on Lenovo.)

While historically significant outsourcing has been primarily confined to manufacturing enterprises such as Boeing and IBM, increasingly companies take advantage of modern communications technology, particularly the Internet, to outsource service activities to low-cost producers in other nations. As we saw in the opening case, the Internet has allowed hospitals to outsource some radiology work to India, where images from MRI scans and the like are read at night while U.S. physicians sleep and the results are ready for them in the morning. Similarly, in December 2003, IBM

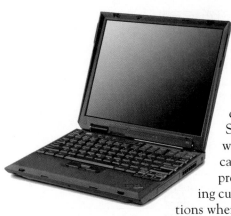

The ThinkPad X31 is ultra-global—its components come from various locations worldwide, but the assembly occurs in Mexico.

announced it would move the work of some 4,300 software engineers from the United States to India and China (software production is counted as a service activity).[13] Many software companies now use Indian engineers to perform maintenance functions on software designed in the United States. Due to the time difference, Indian engineers can run debugging tests on software written in the United States when U.S. engineers sleep, transmitting the corrected code back to the United States over secure Internet connections so it is ready for U.S. engineers to work on the following day. Dispersing value creation activities in this way can compress the time and lower the costs required to develop new software programs. Other companies from computer makers to banks are outsourcing customer service functions, such as customer call centers, to developing nations where labor is cheaper.

Robert Reich, who served as secretary of labor in the Clinton administration, has argued that as a consequence of the trend exemplified by companies such as Boeing, Microsoft, and IBM, in many cases it is becoming irrelevant to talk about American products, Japanese products, German products, or Korean products. Increasingly, according to Reich, the outsourcing of productive activities to different suppliers results in the creation of products that are global in nature; that is, "global products."[14] But as with the globalization of markets, one must be careful not to push the globalization of production too far. As we will see in later chapters, substantial impediments still make it difficult for firms to achieve the optimal dispersion of their productive activities to locations around the globe. These impediments include formal and informal barriers to trade between countries, barriers to foreign direct investment, transportation costs, and issues associated with economic and political risk. For example, government regulations ultimately limit the ability of hospitals to outsource the process of interpreting MRI scans to developing nations where radiologists are cheaper (see the opening case).

Nevertheless, we are traveling down the road toward a future characterized by the increased globalization of markets and production. Modern firms are important actors in this drama, by their very actions fostering increased globalization. These firms, however, are merely responding in an efficient manner to changing conditions in their operating environment—as well they should.

The Emergence of Global Institutions

As markets globalize and an increasing proportion of business activity transcends national borders, institutions are needed to help manage, regulate, and police the global marketplace, and to promote the establishment of multinational treaties to govern the global business system. Over the past half century, a number of important global institutions have been created to help perform these functions. These institutions include the **General Agreement on Tariffs and Trade (the GATT)** and its successor, the World Trade Organization (WTO); the International Monetary Fund (IMF) and its sister institution, the World Bank; and the United Nations (UN). All these institutions were created by voluntary agreement between individual nation-states, and their functions are enshrined in international treaties.

The **World Trade Organization** (like the GATT before it) is primarily responsible for policing the world trading system and making sure nation-states adhere to the rules laid down in trade treaties signed by WTO member states. As of May 2005, 148 nations that collectively accounted for 97 percent of world trade were WTO members, thereby giving the organization enormous scope and influence. The WTO is also responsible for facilitating the establishment of additional multinational agreements between WTO member states. Over its entire history, and that of the GATT before it, the WTO has promoted the lowering of barriers to cross-border trade and investment.

The United Nations has the important goal of improving the well-being of people around the world.

In doing so, the WTO has been the instrument of its member states, which have sought to create a more open global business system unencumbered by barriers to trade and investment between countries. Without an institution such as the WTO, the globalization of markets and production is unlikely to have proceeded as far as it has. However, as we shall see in this chapter and in Chapter 6 when we look closely at the WTO, critics charge that the WTO is usurping the national sovereignty of individual nation-states.

The **International Monetary Fund (IMF)** and the **World Bank** were both created in 1944 by 44 nations that met at **Bretton Woods,** New Hampshire. The task of the IMF was to maintain order in the international monetary system, and that of the World Bank was to promote economic development. In the 60 years since their creation, both institutions have emerged as significant players in the global economy. The World Bank is the less controversial of the two sister institutions. It has focused on making low-interest loans to cash-strapped governments in poor nations that wish to undertake significant infrastructure investments (such as building dams or roads).

The IMF is often seen as the lender of last resort to nation-states whose economies are in turmoil and currencies are losing value against those of other nations. Repeatedly during the past decade, for example, the IMF has lent money to the governments of troubled states, including Argentina, Indonesia, Mexico, Russia, South Korea, Thailand, and Turkey. The IMF loans come with strings attached; in return for loans, the IMF requires nation-states to adopt specific economic policies aimed at returning their troubled economies to stability and growth. These "strings" have generated the most debate, for some critics charge that the IMF's policy recommendations are often inappropriate, while others maintain that by telling national governments what economic policies they must adopt, the IMF, like the WTO, is usurping the sovereignty of nation-states. We shall look at the debate over the role of the IMF in Chapter 11.

The **United Nations** was established October 24, 1945, by 51 countries committed to preserving peace through international cooperation and collective security. Today nearly every nation in the world belongs to the United Nations; membership now totals 191 countries. When states become members of the United Nations, they agree to accept the obligations of the UN Charter, an international treaty that establishes basic principles of international relations. According to the charter, the United Nations has four purposes: to maintain international peace and security, to develop friendly relations among nations, to cooperate in solving international problems and in promoting respect for human rights, and to be a center for harmonizing the actions of nations. Although the UN is perhaps best known for its peacekeeping role, one of the organization's central mandates is the promotion of higher standards of living, full employment, and conditions of economic and social progress and development—all issues that are central to the creation of a vibrant global economy. As much as 70 percent of the work of the UN system is devoted to accomplishing this mandate. To do so, the United Nations works closely with other international institutions such as the World Bank. Guiding the work is the belief that eradicating poverty and improving the well-being of people everywhere are necessary steps in creating conditions for lasting world peace.[15]

Drivers of Globalization

Two macro factors seem to underlie the trend toward greater globalization.[16] The first is the decline in barriers to the free flow of goods, services, and capital that has occurred since the end of World War II. The second factor is technological change, particularly the dramatic developments in recent years in communication, information processing, and transportation technologies.

DECLINING TRADE AND INVESTMENT BARRIERS

During the 1920s and 30s, many of the world's nation-states erected formidable barriers to international trade and foreign direct investment. **International trade** occurs when a firm exports goods or services to consumers in another country. **Foreign direct investment (FDI)** occurs when a firm invests resources in business activities outside its home country. Many of the barriers to international trade took the form of high tariffs on imports of manufactured goods. The typical aim of such tariffs was to protect domestic industries from foreign competition. One consequence, however, was "beggar thy neighbor" retaliatory trade policies with countries progressively raising trade barriers against each other. Ultimately, this depressed world demand and contributed to the Great Depression of the 1930s.

Having learned from this experience, the advanced industrial nations of the West committed themselves after World War II to removing barriers to the free flow of goods, services, and capital between nations.[17] This goal was enshrined in the General Agreement on Tariffs and Trade (GATT). Under the umbrella of GATT, eight rounds of negotiations among member states (now numbering 148) have worked to lower barriers to the free flow of goods and services. The most recent round of negotiations, known as the Uruguay Round, was completed in December 1993. The Uruguay Round further reduced trade barriers; extended GATT to cover services as well as manufactured goods; provided enhanced protection for patents, trademarks, and copyrights; and established the World Trade Organization (WTO) to police the international trading system.[18] Table 1.1 summarizes the impact of GATT agreements on average tariff rates for manufactured goods. As can be seen, average tariff rates have fallen significantly since 1950 and now stand at about 4 percent.

In late 2001, the WTO launched a new round of talks aimed at further liberalizing the global trade and investment framework. For this meeting, it picked the remote location of Doha in the Persian Gulf state of Qatar. At Doha, the member states of the WTO staked out an agenda. The talks were scheduled to last three years, although it now looks as if they may go on significantly longer. The agenda includes cutting tariffs on industrial goods, services, and agricultural products; phasing out subsidies to agricultural producers; reducing barriers to cross-border investment; and limiting the use of antidumping laws.

	1913	1950	1990	2003
France	21%	18%	5.9%	4.0%
Germany	20	26	5.9	4.0
Italy	18	25	5.9	4.0
Japan	30	—	5.3	3.8
Holland	5	11	5.9	4.0
Sweden	20	9	4.4	4.0
Great Britain	—	23	5.9	4.0
United States	44	14	4.8	4.0

TABLE 1.1

Average Tariff Rates on Manufactured Products as Percent of Value

Sources: 1913–1990 data from "Who Wants to Be a Giant?" *The Economist: A Survey of the Multinationals*, June 24, 1995, pp. 3–4. Copyright © The Economist Books, Ltd. The 2003 data are from World Trade Organization, *2004 Annual Report* (Geneva: WTO, 2005).

The biggest gain may come from discussion on agricultural products; average agricultural tariff rates are still about 40 percent, and rich nations spend some $300 billion a year in subsidies to support their farm sectors. The world's poorer nations have the most to gain from any reduction in agricultural tariffs and subsidies; such reforms would give them access to the markets of the developed world.[19]

In addition to reducing trade barriers, many countries have also been progressively removing restrictions to foreign direct investment (FDI). According to the United Nations, some 94 percent of the 1,885 changes made worldwide between 1991 and 2003 in the laws governing foreign direct investment created a more favorable environment for FDI.[20] Governments' desire to facilitate FDI also has been reflected in a dramatic increase in the number of bilateral investment treaties designed to protect and promote investment between two countries. As of 2003, 2,265 such treaties in the world involved more than 160 countries, a 12-fold increase from the 181 treaties that existed in 1980.[21]

Such trends have been driving both the globalization of markets and the globalization of production. The lowering of barriers to international trade enables firms to view the world, rather than a single country, as their market. The lowering of trade and investment barriers also allows firms to base production at the optimal location for that activity. Thus, a firm might design a product in one country, produce component parts in two other countries, assemble the product in yet another country, and then export the finished product around the world.

According to data from the World Trade Organization, the volume of world merchandise trade has grown faster than the world economy since 1950 (see Figure 1.1).[22] From 1970 to 2004, the volume of world merchandise trade expanded almost 26-fold, outstripping the expansion of world production, which grew about 7.5 times in real terms. (World merchandise trade includes trade in manufactured goods, agricultural goods and mining products, but *not* services. World production and trade are measured in real, or inflation-adjusted, dollars.) As suggested by Figure 1.1, due to falling barriers to cross-border trade and investment, the growth in world trade seems to have accelerated since the early 1980s.

The data summarized in Figure 1.1 imply several things. First, more firms are doing what Boeing does with the 777 and 787 and IBM with the ThinkPad: dispersing parts of their production process to different locations around the globe to drive down production costs and increase product quality. Second, the economies of the world's nation-states are becoming more intertwined. As trade expands, nations are becoming increasingly dependent on each other for important goods and services. Third, the world

FIGURE 1.1

Growth in World Trade and World Production, 1950–2004

Source: Calculated by the author from World Trade Organization data accessed May 2005 at www.wto.org/english/res_e/statis_e/statis_e.htm

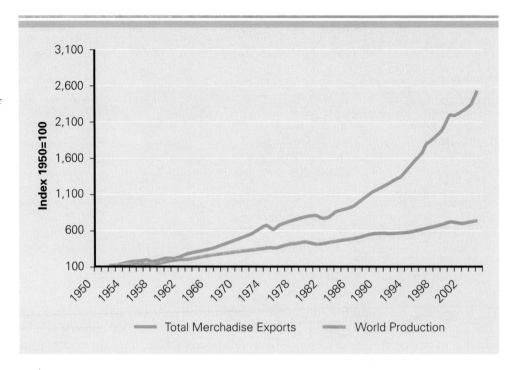

has become significantly wealthier since 1950, and the implication is that rising trade is the engine that has helped to pull the global economy along.

What Figure 1.1 does not show is that since the mid-1980s the value of international trade in services grew robustly. Trade in services now accounts for almost 20 percent of the value of all international trade. Increasingly, international trade in services has been driven by advances in communications, which allow corporations to outsource service activities to different locations around the globe (see the opening case). Thus, as noted earlier, many corporations in the developed world outsource customer service functions, from software maintenance activities to customer call centers, to developing nations where labor costs are lower.

The evidence also suggests that foreign direct investment (FDI) is playing an increasing role in the global economy as firms increase their cross-border investments. The average yearly outflow of FDI increased from $25 billion in 1975 to a record $1.3 trillion in 2000, before falling back to $620 billion in 2004.[23] Despite the slowdown in 2001–04, the flow of FDI not only accelerated over the past quarter century, but also accelerated faster than the growth in world trade. As shown in Figure 1.2, between 1992 and 2004 the total flow of FDI from all countries increased by about 360 percent, while world trade doubled and world output grew by 35 percent.[24] As a result of the strong FDI flow, by 2003 the global stock of FDI exceeded $8.1 trillion. In total, at least 61,000 parent companies had 900,000 affiliates in foreign markets that collectively employed some 54 million people abroad and generated value accounting for about one-tenth of global GDP. The foreign affiliates of multinationals had an estimated $17.6 trillion in global sales, nearly twice as high as the value of global exports of goods and service combined, which stood at $9.2 trillion.[25]

The globalization of markets and production and the resulting growth of world trade, foreign direct investment, and imports all imply that firms are finding their home markets under attack from foreign competitors. This is true in Japan, where U.S. companies such as Kodak, Procter & Gamble, and Merrill Lynch are expanding their presence. It is true in the United States, where Japanese automobile firms have taken market share away from General Motors and Ford. And it is true in Europe, where the once-dominant Dutch company Philips has seen its market share in the consumer electronics industry taken by

FIGURE 1.2

Growth of World Trade, Production, and FDI, 1992–2004

Sources: Calculated by the author from World Trade Organization data accessed May 2005 at www.wto.org/english/res_e/statis_e/statis_e.htm, and from United Nations, *World Investment Report, 2004* (New York and Geneva: United Nations, 2004), and United Nations Conference on Trade and Development, "World FDI Flows Grew and Estimated 6% in 2004," UNCTAD Press Release, January 11, 2005.

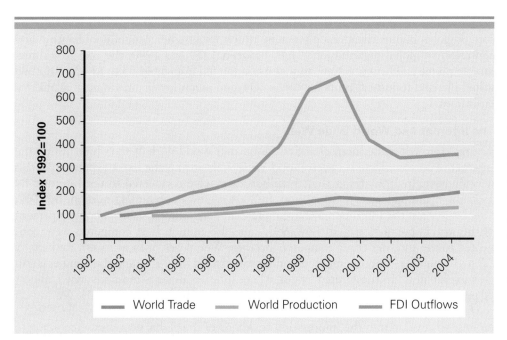

Japan's JVC, Matsushita, and Sony. The growing integration of the world economy into a single, huge marketplace is increasing the intensity of competition in a range of manufacturing and service industries.

However, declining barriers to cross-border trade and investment cannot be taken for granted. As we shall see in subsequent chapters, demands for "protection" from foreign competitors are still often heard in countries around the world, including the United States. Although a return to the restrictive trade policies of the 1920s and 30s is unlikely, it is not clear whether the political majority in the industrialized world favors further reductions in trade barriers. If trade barriers decline no further, at least for the time being, this will put a brake upon the globalization of both markets and production.

THE ROLE OF TECHNOLOGICAL CHANGE

The lowering of trade barriers made globalization of markets and production a theoretical possibility. Technological change has made it a tangible reality. Since the end of World War II, the world has seen major advances in communication, information processing, and transportation technology, including the explosive emergence of the Internet and World Wide Web. Telecommunications is creating a global audience. Transportation is creating a global village. From Buenos Aires to Boston, and from Birmingham to Beijing, ordinary people are watching MTV, they're wearing blue jeans, and they're listening to iPods as they commute to work.

Microprocessors and Telecommunications

Perhaps the single most important innovation has been development of the microprocessor, which enabled the explosive growth of high-power, low-cost computing, vastly increasing the amount of information that can be processed by individuals and firms. The microprocessor also underlies many recent advances in telecommunications technology. Over the past 30 years, global communications have been revolutionized by developments in satellite, optical fiber, and wireless technologies, and now the Internet and the World Wide Web. These technologies rely on the microprocessor to encode, transmit, and decode the vast amount of information that flows along these electronic highways. The cost of microprocessors continues to fall, while their power increases (a phenomenon known as **Moore's Law,** which predicts that the power of microprocessor technology doubles and its cost of production falls in half every 18 months).[26] As this happens, the cost of global communications plummets, which lowers the costs of coordinating and controlling a global organization. Thus, between 1930 and 1990, the cost of a three-minute phone call between New York and London fell from $244.65 to $3.32.[27] By 1998 it had plunged to just 36 cents for consumers, and much lower rates were available for businesses.[28]

The Internet and World Wide Web

The rapid growth of the Internet and the associated World Wide Web (which utilizes the Internet to communicate between World Wide Web sites) is the latest expression of this development. In 1990, fewer than 1 million users were connected to the Internet. By 1995 the figure had risen to 50 million. In 2004 it grew to about 945 million. By 2007, forecasts suggest the Internet may have more than 1.47 billion users, or about 25 percent of the world's population.[29] In July 1993, some 1.8 million host computers were connected to the Internet (host computers host the Web pages of local users). By January 2005, the number of host computers had increased to 317 million, and the number is still growing rapidly.[30] In the United States, where Internet usage is most advanced, almost 60 percent of the population was using the Internet by 2003 (see Figure 1.3). Worldwide the figure was 15 percent and growing fast. The Internet and World Wide Web (WWW) promise to develop into the information backbone of the global economy. According to Forrester Research, the value of Web-based transactions hit $657 billion in 2000, up from virtually nothing in 1994, and was predicted to hit $6.8 trillion in 2004, with the United States accounting for 47 percent of all Web-based transactions.[31] Many of these transactions are not business-to-consumer transactions (e-commerce), but business-to-business (or e-business) transactions. The greatest current potential of the Web seems to be in the business-to-business arena.

Included in the expanding volume of Web-based traffic is a growing percentage of cross-border trade. Viewed globally, the Web is emerging as an equalizer. It rolls back some of the constraints of location, scale, and time zones.[32] The Web makes it much easier for buyers and sellers to find each other, wherever they may be located and whatever their size. The Web allows businesses, both small and large, to expand their global presence at a lower cost than ever before. One example is a small California-based start-up, Cardiac Science, which makes defibrillators and heart monitors. In 1996, Cardiac Science was itching to break into international markets but had little idea of how to establish an international presence. By 1998, the company was selling to customers in 46 countries and foreign sales accounted for $1.02 million of its $1.2 million revenues. By 2002 revenues had surged on the back of product introductions to $50 million, some $17.5 million of which came from sales to customers in 50 countries. Although some of this business was developed through conventional export channels, a good percentage of it came from hits to the company's Web site, which, according to the company's CEO, "attracts international business people like bees to honey."[33] Similarly, 10 years ago no one would have thought that a small British company based in Stafford could have built a global market for its products by utilizing the Internet, but that is exactly what Bridgewater Pottery has done.[34] Bridgewater traditionally sold premium pottery through exclusive distribution channels, but the company found it difficult and laborious to identify new retail outlets. Since establishing an Internet presence in 1997, Bridgewater has conducted a significant amount of business with consumers in other countries who could not be reached through existing distribution channels or could not be reached cost effectively.

Transportation Technology

In addition to developments in communication technology, several major innovations in transportation technology have occurred since World War II. In economic terms, the most important are probably the development of commercial jet aircraft and super-freighters

FIGURE 1.3

Internet Users per
1,000 People,
1990–2003

Source: Constructed by the
author from World Bank, *World
Development Indicators*, 2005.

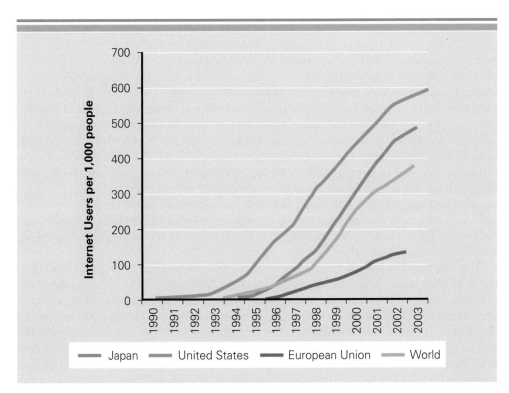

and the introduction of containerization, which simplifies transshipment from one mode of transport to another. The advent of commercial jet travel, by reducing the time needed to get from one location to another, has effectively shrunk the globe. In terms of travel time, New York is now "closer" to Tokyo than it was to Philadelphia in the Colonial days.

Containerization has revolutionized the transportation business, significantly lowering the costs of shipping goods over long distances. Before the advent of containerization, moving goods from one mode of transport to another was very labor intensive, lengthy, and costly. It could take days and several hundred longshoremen to unload a ship and reload goods onto trucks and trains. With the advent of widespread containerization in the 1970s and 1980s, the whole process can be executed by a handful of longshoremen in a couple of days. Since 1980, the world's containership fleet has more than quadrupled, reflecting in part the growing volume of international trade and in part the switch to this mode of transportation. As a result of the efficiency gains associated with containerization, transportation costs have plummeted, making it much more economical to ship goods around the globe, thereby helping to drive the globalization of markets and production. Between 1920 and 1990, the average ocean freight and port charges per ton of U.S. export and import cargo fell from $95 to $29 (in 1990 dollars).[35] The cost of shipping freight per ton-mile on railroads in the United States fell from 3.04 cents in 1985 to 2.3 cents in 2000, largely as a result of efficiency gains from the widespread use of containers.[36] An increased share of cargo now goes by air. Between 1955 and 1999, average air transportation revenue per ton-kilometer fell by more than 80 percent.[37] Reflecting the falling cost of airfreight, by the early 2000s air shipments accounted for 28 percent of the value of U.S. trade, up from 7 percent in 1965.[38]

Implications for the Globalization of Production

As transportation costs associated with the globalization of production declined, dispersal of production to geographically separate locations became more economical. As a result of the technological innovations discussed above, the real costs of information processing and communication have fallen dramatically in the past two decades. These developments make it possible for a firm to create and then manage a globally dispersed production system, further facilitating the globalization of production. A worldwide communications network has become essential for many international businesses. For example, Dell uses the Internet to coordinate and control a globally dispersed production system to such an extent that it holds only three days' worth of inventory at its assembly locations. Dell's Internet-based system records orders for computer equipment as they are submitted by customers via the company's Web site, then immediately transmits the resulting orders for components to various suppliers around the world, which have a real-time look at Dell's order flow and can adjust their production schedules accordingly. Given the low cost of airfreight, Dell can use air transportation to speed up the delivery of critical components to meet unanticipated demand shifts without delaying the shipment of final product to consumers. Dell also has used modern communications technology to outsource its customer service operations to India. When U.S. customers call Dell with a service inquiry, they are routed to Bangalore in India, where English-speaking service personnel handle the call.

The Internet has been a major force facilitating international trade in services. It is the Web that allows hospitals in Chicago to send MRI scans to India for analysis, accounting offices in San Francisco to outsource routine tax preparation work to accountants living in the Philippines, and software testers in India to debug code written by developers in Redmond, Washington, the headquarters of Microsoft. We are probably still in the early stages of this development. As Moore's Law continues to advance and telecommunications bandwidth continues to increase, almost any work processes that can be digitalized will be, and this will allow that work to be performed wherever in the world it is most efficient and effective to do so.

The development of commercial jet aircraft has also helped knit together the worldwide operations of many international businesses. Using jet travel, an American manager need spend a day at most traveling to her firm's European or Asian operations. This enables her to oversee a globally dispersed production system.

Implications for the Globalization of Markets

In addition to the globalization of production, technological innovations have also facilitated the globalization of markets. Low-cost global communications networks such as the World Wide Web are helping to create electronic global marketplaces. As noted above, low-cost transportation has made it more economical to ship products around the world, thereby helping to create global markets. For example, due to the tumbling costs of shipping goods by air, roses grown in Ecuador can be cut and sold in New York two days later while they are still fresh. This has given rise to an industry in Ecuador that did not exist 20 years ago and now supplies a global market for roses (see the accompanying Country Focus). In addition, low-cost jet travel has resulted in the mass movement of people between countries. This has reduced the cultural distance between countries and is bringing about some convergence of consumer tastes and preferences. At the same time, global communication networks and global media are creating a worldwide culture. U.S. television networks such as CNN, MTV, and HBO are now received in many countries, and Hollywood films are shown the world over. In any society, the media are primary conveyors of culture; as global media develop, we must expect the evolution of something akin to a global culture. A logical result of this evolution is the emergence of global markets for consumer products. The first signs of this are already apparent. It is now as easy to find a McDonald's restaurant in Tokyo as it is in New York, to buy an iPod in Rio as it is in Berlin, and to buy Gap jeans in Paris as it is in San Francisco.

Despite these trends, we must be careful not to overemphasize their importance. While modern communication and transportation technologies are ushering in the "global village," very significant national differences remain in culture, consumer preferences, and business practices. A firm that ignores differences between countries does so at its peril. We shall stress this point repeatedly throughout this book and elaborate on it in later chapters.

COUNTRY FOCUS It is 6:20 A.M. February 7, in the Ecuadorean town of Cayambe, and Maria Pacheco has just been dropped off for work by the company bus. She pulls on thick rubber gloves, wraps an apron over her white, traditional embroidered dress, and grabs her clippers, ready for another long day. Any other time of year, Maria would work until 2 P.M., but it's a week before Valentine's Day, and Maria along with her 84 co-workers at the farm are likely to be busy until 5 P.M. By then, Maria will have cut more than 1,000 rose stems.

A few days later, after they have been refrigerated and shipped via aircraft, the roses Maria cut will be selling for premium prices in stores from New York to London. Ecuadorean roses are quickly becoming the Rolls-Royce of roses. They have huge heads and unusually vibrant colors, including 10 different reds, from bleeding heart crimson to a rosy lover's blush.

Most of Ecuador's 460 or so rose farms are located in the Cayambe and Cotopaxi regions, 10,000 feet up in the Andes about an hour's drive from the capital, Quito. The rose bushes are planted in huge flat fields at the foot of snowcapped volcanoes that rise to more than 20,000 feet. The bushes are protected by 20-foot-high canopies of plastic sheeting. The combination of intense sunlight, fertile volcanic soil, an equatorial location, and high altitude makes for ideal growing conditions, allowing roses to flower almost year-round.

Ecuador's rose industry started some 20 years ago and has been expanding rapidly since. Ecuador is now the world's fourth largest producer of roses. Roses are the nation's fifth largest export, with customers all over the world. Rose farms generate $240 million in sales and support tens of thousands of jobs. In Cayambe, the population has increased in 10 years from 10,000 to 70,000, primarily as a result of the rose industry. The revenues and taxes from rose growers have helped to pave roads, build schools, and construct sophisticated irrigation systems. In 2003, construction was to begin on an international airport between Quito and Cayambe from which Ecuadorean roses will begin their journey to flower shops all over the world.

Maria works Monday to Saturday, and earns $210 a month, which she says is an average wage in Ecuador and substantially above the country's $120 a month minimum wage. The farm also provides her with health care and a pension. By employing women such as Maria, the industry has fostered a social revolution in which mothers and wives have more control over their family's spending, especially on schooling for their children.

For all of the benefits that roses have bought to Ecuador, where the gross national income per capita is only $1,080 a year, the industry has come under fire from environmentalists. Large growers have been accused of misusing a toxic mixture of pesticides, fungicides, and fumigants to grow and export unblemished pest-free flowers. Reports claim that workers often fumigate roses in street clothes without protective equipment. Some doctors and scientists claim that many of the industry's 50,000 employees have serious health problems as a result of exposure to toxic chemicals. A 1999 study published by the International Labor Organization claimed that women in the industry had more miscarriages than average and that some 60 percent of all workers suffered from headaches, nausea, blurred vision, and fatigue. Still, the critics acknowledge that their studies have been hindered by a lack of access to the farms, and they do not know what the true situation is. The International Labor Organization has also claimed that some rose growers in Ecuador use child labor, a claim that has been strenuously rejected by both the growers and Ecuadorean government agencies.

In Europe, consumer groups have urged the European Union to press for improved environmental safeguards. In response, some Ecuadorean growers have joined a voluntary program aimed at helping customers identify responsible growers. The certification signifies that the grower has distributed protective gear, trained workers in using chemicals, and hired doctors to visit workers at least weekly. Other environmental groups have pushed for stronger sanctions, including trade sanctions, against Ecuadorean rose growers that are not environmentally certified by a reputable agency. On February 14, however, most consumers are oblivious to these issues; they simply want to show their appreciation to their wives and girlfriends with a perfect bunch of roses.

Sources: G. Thompson, "Behind Roses' Beauty, Poor and Ill Workers," *The New York Times,* February 13, 2003, pp. A1, A27; J. Stuart, "You've Come a Long Way Baby," *The Independent,* February 14, 2003, p. 1; V. Marino, "By Any Other Name, It's Usually a Rosa," *The New York Times,* May 11, 2003, p. A9; and A. DePalma, "In Trade Issue, the Pressure Is on Flowers," *The New York Times,* January 24, 2002, p. 1.

The Changing Demographics of the Global Economy

Hand in hand with the trend toward globalization has been a fairly dramatic change in the demographics of the global economy over the past 30 years. As late as the 1960s, four stylized facts described the demographics of the global economy. The first was U.S. dominance in the world economy and world trade picture. The second was U.S. dominance in world foreign direct investment. Related to this, the third fact was the dominance of large, multinational U.S. firms on the international business scene. The fourth was that roughly half the globe—the centrally planned economies of the Communist world—were off-limits to Western international businesses. As will be explained below, all four of these qualities either have changed or are now changing rapidly.

THE CHANGING WORLD OUTPUT AND WORLD TRADE PICTURE

In the early 1960s, the United States was still by far the world's dominant industrial power. In 1963 the United States accounted for 40.3 percent of world output. By 2004, the United States accounted for nearly 21 percent of world output, still by far the world's largest industrial power but down significantly in relative size since the 1960s (see Table 1.2). Nor was the United States the only developed nation to see its relative standing slip. The same occurred to Germany, France, and the United Kingdom, all nations that were among the first to industrialize. This decline in the U.S. position was not an absolute decline, since the U.S. economy grew at a robust average annual rate of more than 3 percent from 1963 to 2004 (the economies of Germany, France, and the United Kingdom also grew during this time). Rather, it was a relative decline, reflecting the faster economic growth of several other economies, particularly in Asia. For example, as can be seen from Table 1.2, from 1963 to 2004, China's share of world output increased from a trivial amount to 13.2 percent. Other countries that markedly increased their share of world output included Japan, Thailand, Malaysia, Taiwan, and South Korea.

By the end of the 1980s, the U.S. position as the world's leading exporter was threatened. Over the past 30 years, U.S. dominance in export markets has waned as Japan, Germany, and a number of newly industrialized countries such as South Korea and China have taken a larger share of world exports. During the 1960s, the United States routinely accounted for 20 percent of world exports of manufactured goods. But as Table 1.2 shows, the U.S. share of world exports of goods and services had slipped to 10.4 percent by 2004. Despite the fall, the United States still remained the world's largest exporter, ahead of Germany, Japan, France, and the fast-rising economic power, China.

In 1997 and 1998, the dynamic economies of the Asian Pacific region were hit by a serious financial crisis that threatened to slow their economic growth rates for several years. Despite this, their powerful growth may continue over the long run, as will that of several other important emerging economies in Latin America (e.g., Brazil) and Eastern Europe (e.g., Poland). Thus, a further relative decline in the share of world output and world exports accounted for by the United States and other long-established developed nations seems likely. By itself, this is not bad. The relative decline of the United States reflects the growing economic development and industrialization of the world economy, as opposed to any absolute decline in the health of the U.S. economy, which entered the new millennium stronger than ever.

If we look 20 years into the future, most forecasts now predict a rapid rise in the share of world output accounted for by developing nations such as China, India, Indonesia, Thailand, South Korea, Mexico, and Brazil, and a commensurate decline in the share enjoyed by rich industrialized countries such as Great Britain, Germany, Japan, and the United States. The World Bank, for example, has estimated that if current trends continue, by 2020 the Chinese economy could be larger than that of the United States, while

Country	Share of World Output 1963	Share of World Output 2004	Share of World Exports 2004
United States	40.3%	20.9%	10.4%
Germany	9.7	4.3	9.5
France	6.3	3.1	4.8
United Kingdom	6.5	3.1	4.7
Japan	5.5	6.9	5.7
Italy	3.4	2.9	3.8
Canada	3.0	3.5	3.4
China	NA	13.2	5.9

TABLE 1.2

The Changing Pattern of World Output and Trade

Sources: IMF, *World Economic Outlook,* April 2005, and data for 1963 from N. Hood and J. Young, *The Economics of the Multinational Enterprise* (New York: Longman, 1973).

the economy of India will approach that of Germany. The World Bank also estimates that today's developing nations may account for more than 60 percent of world economic activity by 2020, while today's rich nations, which currently account for over 55 percent of world economic activity, may account for only about 38 percent.[39] Forecasts are not always correct, but these suggest that a shift in the economic geography of the world is now under way, although the magnitude of that shift is not totally evident. For international businesses, the implications of this changing economic geography are clear: Many of tomorrow's economic opportunities may be found in the developing nations of the world, and many of tomorrow's most capable competitors will probably also emerge from these regions.

THE CHANGING FOREIGN DIRECT INVESTMENT PICTURE

Reflecting the dominance of the United States in the global economy, U.S. firms accounted for 66.3 percent of worldwide foreign direct investment flows in the 1960s. British firms were second, accounting for 10.5 percent, while Japanese firms were a distant eighth, with only 2 percent. The dominance of U.S. firms was so great that books were written about the economic threat posed to Europe by U.S. corporations.[40] Several European governments, most notably France, talked of limiting inward investment by U.S. firms.

However, as the barriers to the free flow of goods, services, and capital fell, and as other countries increased their shares of world output, non-U.S. firms increasingly began to invest across national borders. The motivation for much of this foreign direct investment by non-U.S. firms was the desire to disperse production activities to optimal locations and to build a direct presence in major foreign markets. Thus, beginning in the 1970s, European and Japanese firms began to shift labor-intensive manufacturing operations from their home markets to developing nations where labor costs were lower. In addition, many Japanese firms invested in North America and Europe—often as a hedge against unfavorable currency movements and the possible imposition of trade barriers. For example, Toyota, the Japanese automobile company, rapidly increased its investment in automobile production facilities in the United States and Europe during the late 1980s and early 1990s. Toyota executives believed that an increasingly strong Japanese yen would price Japanese automobile exports out of foreign markets; therefore, production in the most important foreign markets, as opposed

FIGURE 1.4

Percentage Share of
Total FDI Stock, 1980
and 2003

Source: Calculated by author
from data in United Nations,
World Investment Report, 2004
(New York and Geneva: United
Nations, 2004).

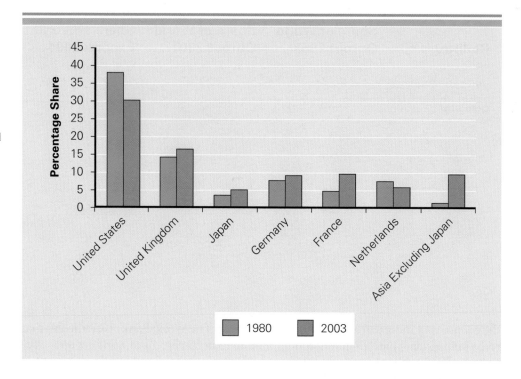

to exports from Japan, made sense. Toyota also undertook these investments to head off growing political pressures in the United States and Europe to restrict Japanese automobile exports into those markets.

One consequence of these developments is illustrated in Figure 1.4, which shows how the stock of foreign direct investment by the world's six most important national sources—the United States, the United Kingdom, Germany, the Netherlands, France, and Japan—changed between 1980 and 2003. (The **stock of foreign direct investment** refers to the total cumulative value of foreign investments.) Figure 1.4 also shows the stock accounted for by firms from Asia, excluding Japan. The share of the total stock accounted for by U.S. firms declined from about 38 percent in 1980 to 30 percent in 2003. Meanwhile, the shares accounted for by France, Japan, and other Asian nations, and the world's developing nations increased markedly. The rise in the share for Asia excluding Japan reflects a growing trend for firms from these countries to invest outside their borders. In 2003, firms based in Asian nations excluding Japan accounted for 9.2 percent of the stock of foreign direct investment, up from only 1.1 percent in 1980. Firms based in Hong Kong, South Korea, Singapore, Taiwan, and mainland China accounted for most of this investment.

Figure 1.5 illustrates two other important trends—the sustained growth in cross-border flows of foreign direct investment that occurred during the 1990s and the emerging importance of developing nations as the destination of foreign direct investment. Throughout the 1990s, the amount of investment directed at both developed and developing nations increased dramatically, a trend that reflects the increasing internationalization of business corporations. A surge in foreign direct investment into developed nations from 1998 to 2000 was followed by a slump from 2001 to 2004 associated with a slowdown in global economic activity after the collapse of the financial bubble of the late 1990s and 2000. Investment directed at developing nations, however, held up relatively well, averaging about $200 billion annually between 1998 and 2004, with China taking the most important share of this. As we shall see later in this book, the sustained flow of foreign investment into developing nations is a very important stimulus for economic growth in those countries, and bodes well for the future of countries such as China, Mexico, and Brazil, all leading beneficiaries of this trend.

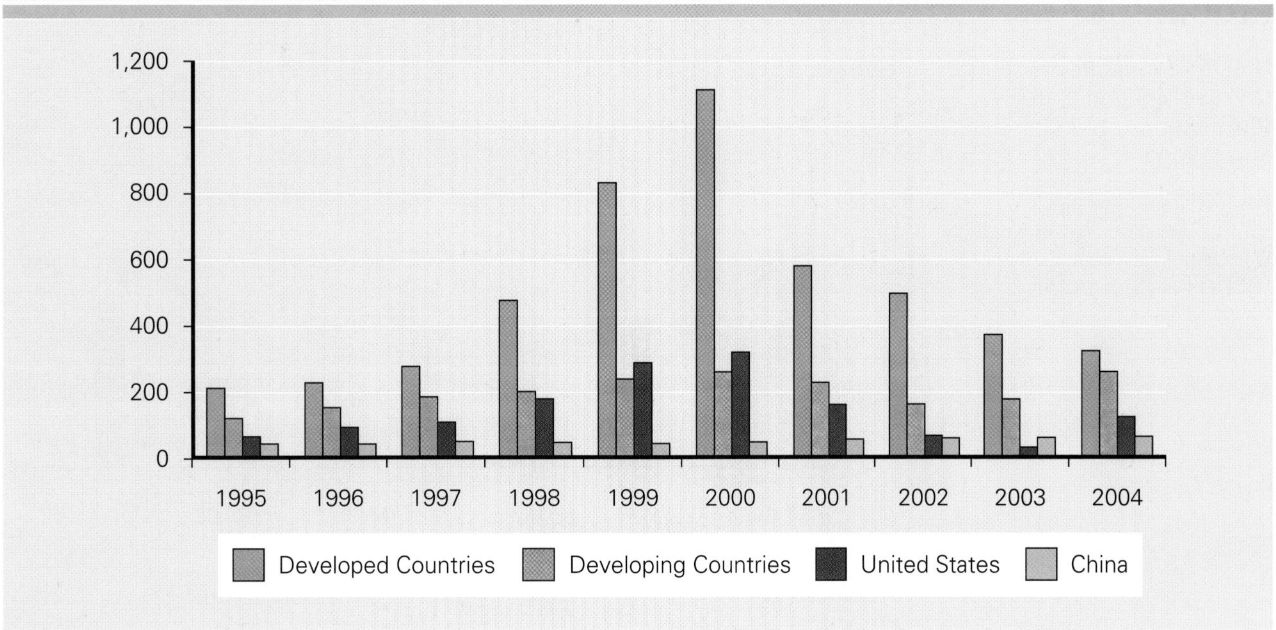

FIGURE 1.5

FDI Inflows, 1995–2004 (in $ billions)

Sources: Calculated by author from data in United Nations, *World Investment Report, 2004* (New York and Geneva: United Nations, 2004), and United Nations Conference on Trade and Development, "World FDI Flows Grew and Estimated 6% in 2004," UNCTAD press release, January 11, 2005.

THE CHANGING NATURE OF THE MULTINATIONAL ENTERPRISE

A **multinational enterprise (MNE)** is any business that has productive activities in two or more countries. Since the 1960s, two notable trends in the demographics of the multinational enterprise have been: (1) the rise of non-U.S. multinationals and (2) the growth of mini-multinationals.

Non-U.S. Multinationals

In the 1960s, global business activity was dominated by large U.S. multinational corporations. With U.S. firms accounting for about two-thirds of foreign direct investment during the 1960s, one would expect most multinationals to be U.S. enterprises. According to the data summarized in Figure 1.6, in 1973, 48.5 percent of the world's 260 largest multinationals were U.S. firms. The second largest source country was the United Kingdom, with 18.8 percent of the largest multinationals. Japan accounted for 3.5 percent of the world's largest multinationals at the time. The large number of U.S. multinationals reflected U.S. economic dominance in the three decades after World War II, while the large number of British multinationals reflected that country's industrial dominance in the early decades of the 20th century.

By 2002 things had shifted significantly. U.S. firms accounted for 28 percent of the world's 100 largest multinationals, followed by France with 14 percent, Germany with 13 percent, and Britain with 12 percent.[41] Although the 1973 data are not strictly comparable with the later data, they illustrate the trend (the 1973 figures are based on the largest 260 firms, whereas the later figures are based on the largest 100 multinationals). The globalization of the world economy has resulted in a relative decline in the dominance of U.S. firms in the global marketplace.

According to UN data, the ranks of the world's largest 100 multinationals are still dominated by firms from developed economies.[42] However, three firms from developing

FIGURE 1.6

National Origin of
Largest Multinational
Corporations, 1973,
1991, 2002

Source: Calculated by author
from data in United Nations,
World Investment Report, 2004
(New York and Geneva: United
Nations, 2004).

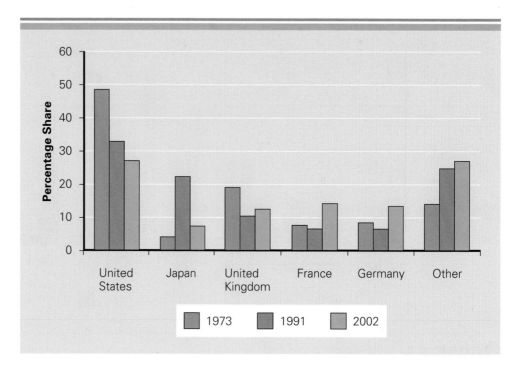

economies entered the UN's list of the 100 largest multinationals. They were Hutchison Whampoa of Hong Kong, China, which ranked 16 in terms of foreign assets; Singtel of Singapore, which was ranked 70; and Cemex of Mexico, which came in at 87.[43] The growth in the number of multinationals from developing economies is evident when we look at smaller firms. In the early 2000s, the largest 50 multinationals from developing economies had foreign sales of $103 billion out of total sales of $453 billion and employed 483,129 people outside of their home countries. Some 22 percent of these companies came from Hong Kong, 16.7 percent from Korea, 8.8 percent from China, and 7.6 percent from Brazil. We can reasonably expect more growth of new multinational enterprises from the world's developing nations. Firms from developing nations can be expected to emerge as important competitors in global markets, further shifting the axis of the world economy away from North America and Western Europe and threatening the long dominance of Western companies. One such rising competitor, Lenovo of China, is profiled in the accompanying Management Focus.

The Rise of Mini-Multinationals

Another trend in international business has been the growth of medium-size and small multinationals (mini-multinationals).[44] When people think of international businesses, they tend to think of firms such as Exxon, General Motors, Ford, Fuji, Kodak, Matsushita, Procter & Gamble, Sony, and Unilever—large, complex multinational corporations with operations that span the globe. Although most international trade and investment is still conducted by large firms, many medium-size and small businesses are becoming increasingly involved in international trade and investment. We have already discussed examples in this chapter—Bridgewater Pottery, and Cardiac Science—and we have noted how the rise of the Internet is lowering the barriers that small firms face in building international sales.

For another example, consider Lubricating Systems, Inc., of Kent, Washington. Lubricating Systems, which manufactures lubricating fluids for machine tools, employs 25 people and generates sales of $6.5 million. It's hardly a large, complex multinational, yet more than $2 million of the company's sales are generated by exports to a score of countries, including Japan, Israel, and the United Arab Emirates. Lubricating Systems also has set up a joint venture with a German company to serve the European market.[45] Consider also Lixi, Inc., a small U.S. manufacturer of industrial X-ray equipment; 70 percent of

MANAGEMENT FOCUS In late 2004, the Chinese personal computer manufacturer Lenovo stunned the business world when it announced that it would acquire IBM's personal computer operations for $1.25 billion. Lenovo, formerly known as Legend, was founded in 1984 by a group of young Chinese scientists with government financing. The company started as a distributor of computers and printers, selling IBM, ACT, and Hewlett-Packard brands. In the late 1980s, however, the company moved into manufacturing and began to design, make, and sell its own personal computers. Taking advantage of China's low labor costs, Lenovo quickly emerged as a low-cost provider.

By 2004, the company led the PC market in China, where it had a 26 percent share. But for Lenovo's founders, this was not enough. They were worried about the entry of efficient foreign competitors, such as Dell, into the Chinese market. Lenovo might have low labor costs, but its 2.3 percent share of global PC sales left it trailing far behind Dell and Hewlett-Packard, which held 18.3 percent and 15.7 percent of the global market, respectively. Dell and HP could realize substantial economies of scale from their global volume. As a result, increasingly they were able to match Lenovo on costs. At the same time, Lenovo's managers wondered whether it was time to expand internationally and turn Lenovo into a global brand. To deal with Dell at home, and expand into the global marketplace, Lenovo's managers realized that they needed to do two things: (1) attain greater scale economies to further lower costs, which meant more sales volume, and (2) match Western companies on product innovation, differentiation, and brand.

Their solution was to acquire IBM's PC business, which held 6 percent of the global market in 2004. The IBM purchase not only gave Lenovo potential scale economies and global reach, but also brought Lenovo IBM's renowned engineering skills, exemplified by the company's best-selling line of ThinkPad laptop computers, and IBM's extensive sales force and long-established customers. Top executives at Lenovo were smart enough to realize that the acquisition would have little value if IBM's managers and engineers left the company, so they made another surprising decision—they moved Lenovo's global headquarters to New York! Moreover, the former head of IBM's PC division, Stephen Ward, was appointed CEO of Lenovo, while Yang Yuanqing, the former CEO of Lenovo, will become chairman, and Lenovo's Mary Ma will be CFO. The 30-member top management team is split down the middle—half Chinese, half American—and boasts more women than men. English has been declared the company's new business language. The goal, according to Yang, is to transform Lenovo into a truly global corporation capable of going head-to-head with Dell in the battle for dominance in the global PC business.

Sources: D. Barboza, "An Unknown Giant Flexes Its Muscles," *The New York Times*, December 4, 2004, pp. B1, B3; D. Roberts and L. Lee, "East Meets West," *BusinessWeek*, May 9, 2005, pp. 1–4; and C. Forelle, "How IBM's Ward Will Lead China's Largest PC Company," *The Wall Street Journal*, April 21, 2005, p. B1.

www.mhhe.com/hill

Lixi's $4.5 million in revenues comes from exports to Japan.[46] Or take G. W. Barth, a manufacturer of cocoa-bean roasting machinery based in Ludwigsburg, Germany. Employing just 65 people, this small company has captured 70 percent of the global market for cocoa-bean roasting machines.[47] International business is conducted not just by large firms but also by medium-size and small enterprises.

THE CHANGING WORLD ORDER

Between 1989 and 1991 a series of remarkable democratic revolutions swept the Communist world. For reasons that are explored in more detail in Chapter 2, in country after country throughout Eastern Europe and eventually in the Soviet Union itself, Communist Party governments collapsed like the shells of rotten eggs. The Soviet Union is now receding into history, having been replaced by 15 independent republics. Czechoslovakia has divided itself into two states, while Yugoslavia dissolved into a bloody civil war, now thankfully over, among its five successor states.

Many of the former Communist nations of Europe and Asia seem to share a commitment to democratic politics and free market economics. If this continues, the opportunities for international businesses may be enormous. For half a century, these countries were essentially closed to Western international businesses. Now they present a host of export and investment opportunities. Just how this will play out over the next 10 to 20 years is difficult to say. The economies of many of the former Communist states are still relatively undeveloped, and their continued commitment to democracy and free market economics cannot be taken for granted. Disturbing signs of growing unrest and totalitarian tendencies continue to be seen in several Eastern European and Central Asian states. Thus, the risks involved in doing business in such countries are high, but so may be the returns.

In addition to these changes, more quiet revolutions have been occurring in China and Latin America. Their implications for international businesses may be just as profound as the collapse of communism in Eastern Europe. China suppressed its own prodemocracy movement in the bloody Tiananmen Square massacre of 1989. Despite this, China continues to move progressively toward greater free market reforms. If what is occurring in China continues for two more decades, China may move from Third World to industrial superpower status even more rapidly than Japan did. If China's gross domestic product (GDP) per capita grows by an average of 6 percent to 7 percent, which is slower than the 8 percent growth rate achieved during the last decade, then by 2020 this nation of 1.273 billion people could boast an average income per capita of about $13,000, roughly equivalent to that of Spain's today.

The potential consequences for international business are enormous. On the one hand, with nearly 1.3 billion people, China represents a huge and largely untapped market. Reflecting this, between 1983 and 2004, annual foreign direct investment in China increased from less than $2 billion to $64 billion. On the other hand, China's new firms are proving to be very capable competitors, and they could take global market share away from Western and Japanese enterprises (for example, see the Management Focus about Lenovo). Thus, the changes in China are creating both opportunities and threats for established international businesses.

As for Latin America, both democracy and free market reforms also seem to have taken hold. For decades, most Latin American countries were ruled by dictators, many of whom seemed to view Western international businesses as instruments of imperialist domination. Accordingly, they restricted direct investment by foreign firms. In addition, the poorly managed economies of Latin America were characterized by low growth, high debt, and hyperinflation—all of which discouraged investment by international businesses. Now much of this seems to be changing. Throughout most of Latin America, debt and inflation are down, governments are selling state-owned enterprises to private investors, foreign investment is welcomed, and the region's economies have expanded. These changes have increased the attractiveness of Latin America, both as a market for exports and as a site for foreign direct investment. At the same time, given the long history of economic mismanagement in Latin America, there is no guarantee that these favorable trends will continue. As in the case of Eastern Europe, substantial opportunities are accompanied by substantial risks.

THE GLOBAL ECONOMY OF THE 21ST CENTURY

As discussed, the past quarter century has seen rapid changes in the global economy. Barriers to the free flow of goods, services, and capital have been coming down. The volume of cross-border trade and investment has been growing more rapidly than global output, indicating that national economies are becoming more closely integrated into a single, interdependent, global economic system. As their economies advance, more nations are joining the ranks of the developed world. A generation ago, South Korea and Taiwan were viewed as second-tier developing nations. Now they boast large economies, and their firms are major players in many global industries from shipbuilding and steel to electronics and chemicals. The move toward a global economy has been further strengthened by the widespread adoption of liberal economic policies by countries that had firmly opposed them for two generations or more. Thus, in keeping with the normative prescriptions of liberal economic ideology, in country after country we are seeing state-owned businesses privatized, widespread deregulation adopted, markets opened to more competition, and commitment increased to removing barriers to cross-border trade and investment. This suggests that over the next few decades, countries such as the Czech Republic, Poland, Brazil, China, India, and South Africa may build powerful market-oriented economies. In short, current trends indicate that the world is moving rapidly toward an economic system that is more favorable for international business.

But it is always hazardous to use established trends to predict the future. The world may be moving toward a more global economic system, but globalization is not inevitable. Countries may pull back from the recent commitment to liberal economic ideology if their experiences do not match their expectations. Periodic signs, for example, indicate a retreat from liberal economic ideology in Russia. Russia has experienced considerable economic pain as it tries to shift from a centrally planned economy to a market economy. If Russia's hesitation were to become more permanent and widespread, the liberal vision of a more prosperous global economy based on free market principles might not occur as quickly as many hope. Clearly, this would be a tougher world for international businesses.

Also, greater globalization brings with it risks of its own. This was starkly demonstrated in 1997 and 1998 when a financial crisis in Thailand spread first to other East Asian nations and then in 1998 to Russia and Brazil. Ultimately the crisis threatened to plunge the economies of the developed world, including the United States, into a recession. We explore the causes and consequences of this and other similar global financial crises in Chapter 11. Even from a purely economic perspective, globalization is not all good. The opportunities for doing business in a global economy may be significantly enhanced, but as we saw in 1997–98, the risks associated with global financial contagion are also greater. Still, as explained later in this book, firms can exploit the opportunities associated with globalization, while at the same time reducing the risks through appropriate hedging strategies.

The Globalization Debate

Is the shift toward a more integrated and interdependent global economy a good thing? Many influential economists, politicians, and business leaders seem to think so.[48] They argue that falling barriers to international trade and investment are the twin engines driving the global economy toward greater prosperity. They say increased international trade and cross-border investment will result in lower prices for goods and services. They believe that globalization stimulates economic growth, raises the incomes of consumers, and helps to create jobs in all countries that participate in the global trading system. The arguments of those who support globalization are covered in detail in Chapters 5, 6, and 7. As we shall see, there are good theoretical reasons for believing that declining barriers to international trade and investment do stimulate economic growth, create jobs, and raise income levels. As described in Chapters 6 and 7, empirical evidence lends support to the predictions of this theory. However, despite the existence of a compelling body of theory and evidence, globalization has its critics.[49] Some of these critics have become increasingly vocal and active, taking to the streets to demonstrate their opposition to globalization. Here we look at the rising tide of protests against globalization and briefly review the main themes of the debate concerning the merits of globalization. In later chapters we elaborate on many of the points mentioned below.

ANTIGLOBALIZATION PROTESTS

Street demonstrations against globalization date to December 1999, when more than 40,000 protesters blocked the streets of Seattle in an attempt to shut down a World Trade Organization meeting being held in the city. The demonstrators were protesting against

Demonstrators at the WTO meeting in Seattle in December 1999 began looting and rioting in the city's downtown area.

a wide range of issues, including job losses in industries under attack from foreign competitors, downward pressure on the wage rates of unskilled workers, environmental degradation, and the cultural imperialism of global media and multinational enterprises, which was seen as being dominated by what some protesters called the "culturally impoverished" interests and values of the United States. All of these ills, the demonstrators claimed, could be laid at the feet of globalization. The World Trade Organization was meeting to try to launch a new round of talks to cut barriers to cross-border trade and investment. As such, it was seen as a promoter of globalization and a legitimate target for the antiglobalization protesters. The protests turned violent, transforming the normally placid streets of Seattle into a running battle between "anarchists" and Seattle's bemused and poorly prepared police department. Pictures of brick-throwing protesters and armored police wielding their batons were duly recorded by the global media, which then circulated the images around the world. Meanwhile, the World Trade Organization meeting failed to reach agreement, and although the protests outside the meeting halls had little to do with that failure, the impression took hold that the demonstrators had succeeded in derailing the meetings.

Emboldened by the experience in Seattle, antiglobalization protesters have turned up at almost every major meeting of a global institution. In February 2000, they demonstrated at the World Economic Forum meetings in Davos, Switzerland, and vented their frustrations against global capitalism by trashing that hated symbol of U.S. imperialism, a McDonald's restaurant. In April 2000, demonstrators disrupted talks being held at the World Bank and International Monetary Fund, and in September 2000, 12,000 demonstrated at the annual meeting of the World Bank and IMF in Prague. In April 2001, demonstrations and police firing tear gas and water cannons overshadowed the Summit of the Americas meeting in Quebec City, Canada. In June 2001, 40,000 protesters marched against globalization at the European Union summit in Göteborg, Sweden. The march was peaceful until a core of masked anarchists wielding cobblestones created bloody mayhem. In July 2001, antiglobalization protests in Genoa, Italy, where the heads of the eight largest economies were meeting (the so-called G8 meetings), turned violent, and in the now familiar ritual of running battles between protesters and police, a protester was killed, giving the antiglobalization movement its first martyr. Smaller scale protests have occurred in several countries, such as France, where antiglobalization protesters destroyed a McDonald's restaurant in August 1999 to protest the impoverishment of French culture by American imperialism (see the Country Focus, "Protesting Globalization in France," for details).

While violent protests may give the antiglobalization effort a bad name, it is clear from the scale of the demonstrations that support for the cause goes beyond a core of anarchists. Large segments of the population in many countries believe that globalization has detrimental effects on living standards and the environment, and the media have often fed on this fear. In 2004 and 2005, for example, CNN news anchor Lou Dobbs ran a series that was highly critical of the trend by American companies to take advantage of globalization and "export jobs" overseas. Both theory and evidence suggest that many of these fears are exaggerated, but this may not have been communicated clearly and both politicians and businesspeople need to do more to counter these fears. Many protests against globalization are tapping into a general sense of loss at the passing of a world in which barriers of time and distance, and vast differences in economic institutions, political institutions, and the level of development of different nations, produced a world rich in the diversity of human cultures. This world is now passing into history. However, while the rich citizens of the developed world may have the luxury of mourning the fact that they can now see McDonald's restaurants and Starbucks coffeehouses on their vacations to exotic locations such as Thailand, fewer complaints are heard from the citizens of those countries, who welcome the higher living standards that progress brings.

GLOBALIZATION, JOBS, AND INCOME

One concern frequently voiced by globalization opponents is that falling barriers to international trade destroy manufacturing jobs in wealthy advanced economies such as the United States and the United Kingdom. The critics argue that falling trade barriers allow firms to move manufacturing activities to countries where wage rates are much lower.[50] D. L. Bartlett and J. B. Steele, two journalists for the *Philadelphia Inquirer* who gained notoriety for their attacks on free trade, cite the case of Harwood Industries, a U.S. clothing manufacturer that closed its U.S. operations, where it paid workers $9 per hour, and shifted manufacturing to Honduras, where textile workers receive 48 cents per hour.[51] Because of moves such as this, argue Bartlett and Steele, the wage rates of poorer Americans have fallen significantly over the past quarter of a century.

In the last few years, the same fears have been applied to services, which have increasingly been outsourced to nations with lower labor costs (see the opening case). The popular feeling is that when corporations such as Dell, IBM, or Citigroup outsource service activities to lower cost foreign suppliers—as all three have done—they are "exporting jobs" to low-wage nations and contributing to higher unemployment and lower living standards in their home nations (in this case the United States). Some lawmakers in the United States have responded by calling for legal barriers to job outsourcing.

Supporters of globalization reply that critics of these trends miss the essential point about free trade—the benefits outweigh the costs.[52] They argue that free trade will result in countries specializing in the production of those goods and services that they can produce most efficiently, while importing goods and services that they cannot produce as efficiently. When a country embraces free trade, there is always some dislocation—lost textile jobs at Harwood Industries, or lost call center jobs at Dell—but the whole economy is better off as a result. According to this view, it makes little sense for the United States to produce textiles at home when they can be produced at a lower cost in Honduras or China (which, unlike Honduras, is a major source of U.S. textile imports). Importing textiles from China leads to lower prices for clothes in the United States, which enables consumers to spend more of their money on other items. At the same time, the increased income generated in China from textile exports increases income levels in that country, which helps the Chinese to purchase more products produced in the United States, such as pharmaceuticals from Amgen, Boeing jets, Intel-based computers, Microsoft software, and Cisco routers.

The same argument can be made to support the outsourcing of services to low-wage countries. By outsourcing its customer service call centers to India, Dell can reduce its cost structure, and thereby its prices for PCs. U.S. consumers benefit from this development. As prices for PCs fall, Americans can spend more of their money on other goods and services. Moreover, the increase in income levels in India allows Indians to purchase more U.S. goods and services, which helps to create jobs in the United States. In this manner, supporters of globalization argue that free trade benefits *all* countries that adhere to a free trade regime.

Nevertheless, some supporters of globalization concede that the wage rate enjoyed by unskilled workers in many advanced economies may have declined in recent years.[53] However, the evidence on this is decidedly mixed.[54] A United States Federal Reserve study found that in the seven years preceding 1996, the earnings of the best-paid 10 percent of U.S. workers rose in real terms by 0.6 percent annually while the earnings of the 10 percent at the bottom of the heap fell by 8 percent. In some areas, the fall was much greater.[55] Another study of long-term trends in income distribution concluded,

> Nationwide, from the late 1970s to the late 1990s, the average income of the lowest-income families fell by over 6 percent after adjustment for inflation, and the average real income of the middle fifth of families grew by about 5 percent. By contrast, the average real income of the highest-income fifth of families increased by over 30 percent.[56]

While globalization critics argue that the decline in unskilled wage rates is due to the migration of low-wage manufacturing jobs offshore and a corresponding reduction in demand for unskilled workers, supporters of globalization see a more complex picture. They maintain that the apparent decline in real wage rates of unskilled workers owes far more to a technology-induced shift within advanced economies away from jobs where the only qualification was a willingness to turn up for work every day and toward jobs that require significant education and skills. They point out that many advanced economies report a shortage of highly skilled workers and an excess supply of unskilled workers. Thus, growing income inequality is a result of the wages for skilled workers being bid up by the labor market and the wages for unskilled workers being discounted. If one agrees with this logic, a solution to the problem of declining incomes is to be found not in limiting free trade and globalization, but in increasing society's investment in education to reduce the supply of unskilled workers.[57]

Some research also suggests that the evidence of growing income inequality may be suspect. Robert Lerman of the Urban Institute believes that the finding of inequality is based on inappropriate calculations of wage rates. Reviewing the data using a different methodology, Lerman has found that far from income inequality increasing, an index of wage rate inequality for all workers actually fell by 5.5 percent between 1987 and 1994.[58] A 2002 study by the Organization for Economic Cooperation and Development, whose members include the 20 richest economies in the world, also suggests a more complex picture. The study noted that while the gap between the poorest and richest segments of society in some OECD countries had widened, this trend was by no means universal.[59] In the United States, for example, the OECD study found that while income inequality increased from the mid-1970s to the mid-1980s, it did not widen further in the next decade. The report also notes that in almost all countries, real income levels rose over the 20-year period looked at in the study, including the incomes of the poorest segment of most OECD societies. To add to the mixed research results, a 2002 U.S. study that included data from 1990 to 2000 concluded that during those years, falling unemployment rates brought gains to low-wage workers and fairly broad-based wage growth, especially in the latter half of the 1990s. The income of the worst-paid 10 percent of the population actually rose twice as fast as that of the average worker during 1998–2000.[60] If such trends continued into the 2000s—and they may not have—the argument that globalization leads to growing income inequality may lose some of its punch.

FIGURE 1.7

Income Levels and
Environmental Pollution

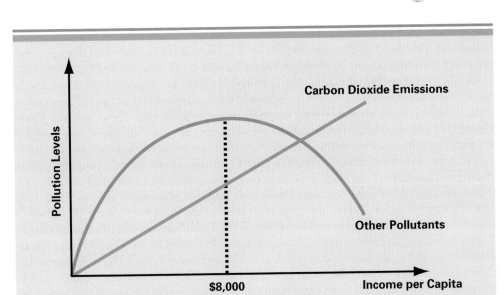

GLOBALIZATION, LABOR POLICIES, AND THE ENVIRONMENT

A second source of concern is that free trade encourages firms from advanced nations to move manufacturing facilities to less developed countries that lack adequate regulations to protect labor and the environment from abuse by the unscrupulous.[61] Globalization critics often argue that adhering to labor and environmental regulations significantly increases the costs of manufacturing enterprises and puts them at a competitive disadvantage in the global marketplace vis-à-vis firms based in developing nations that do not have to comply with such regulations. Firms deal with this cost disadvantage, the theory goes, by moving their production facilities to nations that do not have such burdensome regulations or that fail to enforce the regulations they have.

If this is the case, one might expect free trade to lead to an increase in pollution and result in firms from advanced nations exploiting the labor of less developed nations.[62] This argument was used repeatedly by those who opposed the 1994 formation of the North American Free Trade Agreement (NAFTA) between Canada, Mexico, and the United States. They painted a picture of U.S. manufacturing firms moving to Mexico in droves so that they would be free to pollute the environment, employ child labor, and ignore workplace safety and health issues, all in the name of higher profits.[63]

Supporters of free trade and greater globalization express doubts about this scenario. They argue that tougher environmental regulations and stricter labor standards go hand in hand with economic progress.[64] In general, as countries get richer, they enact tougher environmental and labor regulations.[65] Because free trade enables developing countries to increase their economic growth rates and become richer, this should lead to tougher environmental and labor laws. In this view, the critics of free trade have got it backward—free trade does not lead to more pollution and labor exploitation, it leads to less. By creating wealth and incentives for enterprises to produce technological innovations, the free market system and free trade could make it easier for the world to cope with pollution and population growth. Indeed, while pollution levels are rising in the world's poorer countries, they have been falling in developed nations. In the United States, for example, the concentration of carbon monoxide and sulphur dioxide pollutants in the atmosphere decreased by 60 percent between 1978 and 1997, while lead concentrations decreased by 98 percent—and these reductions have occurred against a background of sustained economic expansion.[66]

A number of econometric studies have found consistent evidence of a hump-shaped relationship between income levels and pollution levels (see Figure 1.7).[67] As an economy grows and income levels rise, initially pollution levels also rise. However, past some point, rising income levels lead to demands for greater environmental protection, and pollution levels then fall. A seminal study by Grossman and Krueger found that the turning point generally occurred before per capita income levels reached $8,000.[68]

While the hump-shaped relationship depicted in Figure 1.7 seems to hold across a wide range of pollutants—from sulphur dioxide to lead concentrations and water quality—carbon dioxide emissions are an important exception, rising steadily with higher income levels. Given that increased atmospheric carbon dioxide concentrations are implicated in global warming, this should be a concern. The solution to the problem, however, is probably not to roll back the trade liberalization efforts that have fostered economic growth and globalization, but to get the nations of the world to agree to tougher standards on limiting carbon emissions. Although United Nations—sponsored talks have had this as a central aim since the 1992 Earth Summit in Rio de Janeiro, there has been little success in moving toward the ambitious goals for reducing carbon emissions laid down in the Earth Summit and subsequent talks in Kyoto, Japan, in part because the largest emitter of carbon dioxide, the United States, has refused to sign global agreements that it claims would unreasonably retard economic growth.

Supporters of free trade also point out that it is possible to tie free trade agreements to the implementation of tougher environmental and labor laws in less developed countries. NAFTA, for example, was passed only after side agreements had been negotiated that committed Mexico to tougher enforcement of environmental protection regulations. Thus, supporters of free trade argue that factories based in Mexico are now cleaner than they would have been without the passage of NAFTA.[69]

They also argue that business firms are not the amoral organizations that critics suggest. While there may be some rotten apples, most business enterprises are staffed by managers who are committed to behave in an ethical manner and would be unlikely to move production offshore just so they could pump more pollution into the atmosphere or exploit labor. Furthermore, the relationship between pollution, labor exploitation, and production costs may not be that suggested by critics. In general, a well-treated labor force is productive, and it is productivity rather than base wage rates that often has the greatest influence on costs. The vision of greedy managers who shift production to low-wage countries to exploit their labor force may be misplaced.

GLOBALIZATION AND NATIONAL SOVEREIGNTY

Another concern voiced by critics of globalization is that today's increasingly interdependent global economy shifts economic power away from national governments and toward supranational organizations such as the World Trade Organization, the European Union, and the United Nations. As perceived by critics, unelected bureaucrats now impose policies on the democratically elected governments of nation-states, thereby undermining the sovereignty of those states and limiting the nation's ability to control its own destiny.[70]

The World Trade Organization (WTO) is a favorite target of those who attack the headlong rush toward a global economy. As noted earlier, the WTO was founded in 1994 to police the world trading system established by the General Agreement on Tariffs and Trade. The WTO arbitrates trade disputes between the 148 states that are signatories to the GATT. The arbitration panel can issue a ruling instructing a member state to change trade policies that violate GATT regulations. If the violator refuses to comply with the ruling, the WTO allows other states to impose appropriate trade sanctions on the transgressor. As a result, according to one prominent critic, U.S. environmentalist, consumer rights advocate, and presidential candidate Ralph Nader:

> Under the new system, many decisions that affect billions of people are no longer made by local or national governments but instead, if challenged by any WTO member nation, would be deferred to a group of unelected bureaucrats sitting behind closed doors in Geneva (which is where the headquarters of the WTO are located). The bureaucrats can decide whether or not people in California can prevent the destruction of the last virgin forests or determine if carcinogenic pesticides can be banned from their foods; or whether European countries have the right to ban dangerous biotech hormones in meat. . . . At risk is the very basis of democracy and accountable decision making.[71]

COUNTRY FOCUS One night in August 1999, 10 men under the leadership of local sheep farmer and rural activist Jose Bove crept into the town of Millau in central France and vandalized a McDonald's restaurant under construction, causing an estimated $150,000 damage. These were no ordinary vandals, however, at least according to their supporters, for the "symbolic dismantling" of the McDonald's outlet had noble aims, or so it was claimed. The attack was initially presented as a protest against unfair American trade policies. The European Union had banned imports of hormone-treated beef from the United States, primarily because of fears that hormone-treated beef might lead to health problems (although EU scientists had concluded there was no evidence of this). After a careful review, the World Trade Organization stated the EU ban was not allowed under trading rules that the EU and United States were party to, and that the EU would have to lift it or face retaliation. The EU refused to comply, so the U.S. government imposed a 100 percent tariff on imports of certain EU products, including French staples such as foie gras, mustard, and Roquefort cheese. On farms near Millau, Bove and others raised sheep whose milk was used to make Roquefort. They felt incensed by the American tariff and decided to vent their frustrations on McDonald's.

Bove and his compatriots were arrested and charged. They quickly became a focus of the antiglobalization movement in France that was protesting everything from a loss of national sovereignty and "unfair" trade policies that were trying to force hormone-treated beef on French consumers, to the invasion of French culture by alien American values, so aptly symbolized by McDonald's. Lionel Jospin, France's prime minister, called the cause of Jose Bove "just." Allowed to remain free pending his trial, Bove traveled to Seattle in December to protest against the World Trade Organization, where he was feted as a hero of the antiglobalization movement. In France, Bove's July 2000 trial drew some 40,000 supporters to the small town of Millau, where they camped outside the courthouse and waited for the verdict. Bove was found guilty and sentenced to three months in jail, far less than the maximum possible sentence of five years. His supporters wore T-shirts claiming, "The world is not merchandise, and neither am I."

About the same time in the Languedoc region of France, California winemaker Robert Mondavi had reached agreement with the mayor and council of the village of Aniane and regional authorities to turn 125 acres of wooded hillside belonging to the village into a vineyard. Mondavi planned to invest $7 million in the project and hoped to produce top-quality wine that would sell in Europe and the United States for $60 a bottle. However, local environmentalists objected to the plan, which they claimed would destroy the area's unique ecological heritage. Jose Bove, basking in sudden fame, offered his support to the opponents, and the protests started. In May 2001, the Socialist mayor who had approved the project was defeated in local elections in which the Mondavi project had become the major issue. He was replaced by a Communist, Manuel Diaz, who denounced the project as a capitalist plot designed to enrich wealthy U.S. shareholders at the cost of his villagers and the environment. Following Diaz's victory, Mondavi announced he would pull out of the project. A spokesman noted, "It's a huge waste, but there are clearly personal and political interests at play here that go way beyond us."

So are the French opposed to foreign investment? The experience of McDonald's and Mondavi seems to suggest so, as does the associated news coverage, but look closer and a different reality seems to emerge. McDonald's has more than 800 restaurants in France and continues to do very well there. In fact, France is one of the most profitable markets for McDonald's. The level of foreign investment in France reached record levels in the late 1990s and early 2000. Between 1998 and 2003 France received $270 billion in inward investment, far more than other large EU nations. In 2000, France recorded 563 major inward investment deals, a record, and American companies accounted for the largest number, some 178. French enterprises are also investing across borders at record levels. Given all of the talk about American cultural imperialism, it is striking that a French company, Vivendi, acquired two of the propagators of American cultural values: Universal Pictures and publisher Houghton Mifflin. And French politicians seem set on removing domestic barriers that make it difficult for French companies to compete effectively in the global economy.

Sources: "Behind the Bluster," *The Economist,* May 26, 2001; "The French Farmers' Anti-global Hero," *The Economist,* July 8, 2000; C. Trueheart, "France's Golden Arch Enemy?" *Toronto Star,* July 1, 2000; J. Henley, "Grapes of Wrath Scare Off U.S. Firm," *The Economist,* May 18, 2001, p. 11; and United Nations, *World Investment Report, 2004* (New York and Geneva: United Nations, 2004).

In contrast to Nader's rhetoric, many economists and politicians maintain that the power of supranational organizations such as the WTO is limited to what nation-states collectively agree to grant. They argue that bodies such as the United Nations and the WTO exist to serve the collective interests of member states, not to subvert those interests. Supporters of supranational organizations point out that the power of these bodies rests largely on their ability to persuade member states to follow a certain action. If these bodies fail to serve the collective interests of member states, those states will withdraw their support and the supranational organization will quickly collapse. In this view, real power still resides with individual nation-states, not supranational organizations.

GLOBALIZATION AND THE WORLD'S POOR

Critics of globalization argue that despite the supposed benefits associated with free trade and investment, over the past hundred years or so the gap between the rich and poor nations of the world has gotten wider. In 1870 the average income per capita in the world's 17 richest nations was 2.4 times that of all other countries. In 1990 the same group was 4.5 times as rich as the rest.[72] While recent history has shown that some of the world's poorer nations are capable of rapid periods of economic growth—witness the transformation that has occurred in some Southeast Asian nations such as South Korea, Thailand, and Malaysia—there appear to be strong forces for stagnation among the world's poorest nations. A quarter of the countries with a GDP per capita of less than $1,000 in 1960 had growth rates of less than zero from 1960 to 1995, and a third had growth rates of less than 0.05 percent.[73] Critics argue that if globalization is such a positive development, this divergence between the rich and poor should not have occurred.

Although the reasons for economic stagnation vary, several factors stand out, none of which have anything to do with free trade or globalization.[74] Many of the world's poorest countries have suffered from totalitarian governments, economic policies that destroyed wealth rather than facilitated its creation, endemic corruption, scant protection for property rights, and war. Such factors help explain why countries such as Afghanistan, Cambodia, Cuba, Haiti, Iraq, Libya, Nigeria, Sudan, Vietnam, and Zaire have failed to improve the economic lot of their citizens during recent decades. A complicating factor is the rapidly expanding populations in many of these countries. Without a major change in government, population growth may exacerbate their problems. Promoters of free trade argue that the best way for these countries to improve their lot is to lower their barriers to free trade and investment and to implement economic policies based on free market economics.[75]

Many of the world's poorer nations are being held back by large debt burdens. Of particular concern are the 40 or so "highly indebted poorer countries" (HIPCs), which are home to some 700 million people. Among these countries, the average government debt burden is equivalent to 85 percent of the value of the economy, as measured by gross domestic product, and the annual costs of serving government debt consumes 15 percent of the country's export earnings.[76] Servicing such a heavy debt load leaves the governments of these countries with little left to invest in important public infrastructure projects, such as education, health care, roads, and power. The result is the HIPCs are trapped in a cycle of poverty and debt that inhibits economic development. Free trade alone, some argue, is a necessary but not sufficient prerequisite to help these countries bootstrap themselves out of poverty. Instead, large-scale debt relief is needed for the world's poorest nations to give them the opportunity to restructure their economies and start the long climb toward prosperity. Supporters of debt relief also argue that new democratic governments in poor nations should not be forced to honor debts that were incurred and mismanaged long ago by their corrupt and dictatorial predecessors.

In the late 1990s, a debt relief movement began to gain ground among the political establishment in the world's richer nations.[77] Fueled by high-profile endorsements from Irish rock star Bono (who has been a tireless and increasingly effective advocate for debt relief), Pope John Paul II, the Dalai Lama, and influential Harvard economist Jeffrey Sachs, the debt relief movement was instrumental in persuading the United States to enact legislation in 2000 that provided $435 million in debt relief for HIPCs. More importantly perhaps, the United States also backed an IMF plan to sell some of its gold reserves and use the proceeds to help with debt relief. The IMF and World Bank have now picked up the banner and have embarked on a systematic debt relief program.

U2's Bono has actively lobbied to have the unpayable debt of poor countries written off.

For such a program to have a lasting effect, however, debt relief must be matched by wise investment in public projects that boost economic growth (such as education), and by the adoption of economic policies that facilitate investment and trade. The rich nations of the world also can help by reducing barriers to the importation of products from the world's poorer nations, particularly tariffs on imports of agricultural products and textiles. High tariff barriers and other impediments to trade make it difficult for poor countries to export more of their agricultural production. The World Trade Organization has estimated that if the developed nations of the world eradicated subsidies to their agricultural producers and removed tariff barriers to trade in agriculture this would raise global economic welfare by $128 billion, with $30 billion of that going to developing nations, many of whom are highly indebted. The faster growth associated with expanded trade in agriculture could reduce the number of people living in poverty by as much as 13 percent by 2015, according to the WTO.[78]

Debt relief is not new; it has been tried before.[79] Too often in the past, however, the short-term benefits were squandered by corrupt governments who used their new-found financial freedom to make unproductive investments in military infrastructure or grandiose projects that did little to foster long-run economic development. Developed nations contributed to past failures by refusing to open their markets to the products of poor nations. If such a scenario can be avoided this time, the entire world will benefit.

🌐 Managing in the Global Marketplace

Much of this book is concerned with the challenges of managing in an international business. An **international business** is any firm that engages in international trade or investment. A firm does not have to become a multinational enterprise, investing directly in operations in other countries, to engage in international business, although multinational enterprises are international businesses. All a firm has to do is export or import products from other countries. As the world shifts toward a truly integrated global economy, more firms, both large and small, are becoming international businesses. What does this shift toward a global economy mean for managers within an international business?

As their organizations increasingly engage in cross-border trade and investment, managers need to recognize that the task of managing an international business differs from that of managing a purely domestic business in many ways. At the most fundamental level, the differences arise from the simple fact that countries are different. Countries differ in their cultures, political systems, economic systems, legal systems, and levels of economic development. Despite all the talk about the emerging global village, and despite the trend toward globalization of markets and production, as we shall see in this book, many of these differences are very profound and enduring.

Differences between countries require that an international business vary its practices country by country. Marketing a product in Brazil may require a different approach from marketing the product in Germany; managing U.S. workers might require different skills than managing Japanese workers; maintaining close relations with a particular level of government may be very important in Mexico and irrelevant in Great Britain; the business strategy pursued in Canada might not work in South Korea; and so on. Managers in an international business must not only be sensitive to these differences, but they must also adopt the appropriate policies and strategies for coping with them. Much of this book is devoted to explaining the sources of these differences and the methods for successfully coping with them.

A further way in which international business differs from domestic business is the greater complexity of managing an international business. In addition to the problems that arise from the differences between countries, a manager in an international business is confronted with a range of other issues that the manager in a domestic business never confronts. The managers of an international business must decide where in the world to site production activities to minimize costs and to maximize value added. They must decide whether it is ethical to adhere to the lower labor and environmental standards found in many less developed nations. Then they must decide how best to coordinate and control globally dispersed production activities (which, as we shall see later in the book, is not a trivial problem). The managers in an international business also must decide which foreign markets to enter and which to avoid. They must choose the appropriate mode for entering a particular foreign country. Is it best to export its product to the foreign country? Should the firm allow a local company to produce its product under license in that country? Should the firm enter into a joint venture with a local firm to produce its product in that country? Or should the firm set up a wholly owned subsidiary to serve the market in that country? As we shall see, the choice of entry mode is critical because it has major implications for the long-term health of the firm.

Conducting business transactions across national borders requires understanding the rules governing the international trading and investment system. Managers in an international business must also deal with government restrictions on international trade and investment. They must find ways to work within the limits imposed by specific governmental interventions. As this book explains, even though many governments are nominally committed to free trade, they often intervene to regulate cross-border trade and investment. Managers within international businesses must develop strategies and policies for dealing with such interventions.

Cross-border transactions also require that money be converted from the firm's home currency into a foreign currency and vice versa. Because currency exchange rates vary in response to changing economic conditions, managers in an international business must develop policies for dealing with exchange rate movements. A firm that adopts a wrong policy can lose large amounts of money, while a firm that adopts the right policy can increase the profitability of its international transactions.

In sum, managing an international business is different from managing a purely domestic business for at least four reasons: (1) countries are different, (2) the range of problems confronted by a manager in an international business is wider and the problems themselves more complex than those confronted by a manager in a domestic business, (3) an international business must find ways to work within the limits imposed by government intervention in the international trade and investment system, and (4) international transactions involve converting money into different currencies.

In this book we examine all these issues in depth, paying close attention to the different strategies and policies that managers pursue to deal with the various challenges created when a firm becomes an international business. Chapters 2 and 3 explore how countries differ from each other with regard to their political, economic, legal, and cultural institutions. Chapter 4 takes a detailed look at the ethical issues that arise in international business. Chapters 5 to 9 look at the international trade and investment environment within which international businesses must operate. Chapters 10 and 11 review the international monetary system. These chapters focus on the nature of the foreign exchange market and the emerging global monetary system. Chapters 12 to 14 explore the strategy and structure of international businesses. Chapters 15 to 20 look at the management of various functional operations within an international business, including production, marketing, human relations, accounting, and finance. By the time you complete this book, you should have a good grasp of the issues that managers working within international business have to grapple with on a daily basis, and you should be familiar with the range of strategies and operating policies available to compete more effectively in today's rapidly emerging global economy.

Chapter Summary

This chapter sets the scene for the rest of the book. It shows how the world economy is becoming more global and reviews the main drivers of globalization, arguing that they seem to be thrusting nation-states toward a more tightly integrated global economy. We looked at how the nature of international business is changing in response to the changing global economy; we discussed some concerns raised by rapid globalization; and we reviewed implications of rapid globalization for individual managers. The chapter made the following points:

1. Over the past two decades, we have witnessed the globalization of markets and production.

2. The globalization of markets implies that national markets are merging into one huge marketplace. However, it is important not to push this view too far.

3. The globalization of production implies that firms are basing individual productive activities at the optimal world locations for the particular activities. As a consequence, it is increasingly irrelevant to talk about American products, Japanese products, or German products, since these are being replaced by "global" products.

4. Two factors seem to underlie the trend toward globalization: declining trade barriers and changes in communication, information, and transportation technologies.

5. Since the end of World War II, barriers to the free flow of goods, services, and capital have been lowered significantly. More than anything else, this has facilitated the trend toward the globalization of production and has enabled firms to view the world as a single market.

6. As a consequence of the globalization of production and markets, in the last decade world trade has grown faster than world output, foreign direct investment has surged, imports have penetrated more deeply into the world's industrial nations, and competitive pressures have increased in industry after industry.

7. The development of the microprocessor and related developments in communication and information processing technology have helped firms link their worldwide operations into sophisticated information networks. Jet air travel, by shrinking travel time, has also helped to link the worldwide operations of international businesses. These changes have enabled firms to achieve tight coordination of their worldwide operations and to view the world as a single market.

8. In the 1960s, the U.S. economy was dominant in the world, U.S. firms accounted for most of the foreign direct investment in the world economy, U.S. firms dominated the list of large multinationals, and roughly half the world—the centrally planned economies of the Communist world—was closed to Western businesses.

9. By the mid-1990s, the U.S. share of world output had been cut in half, with major shares now being accounted for by Western European and Southeast Asian economies. The U.S. share of worldwide foreign direct investment had also fallen, by about two-thirds. U.S. multinationals were now facing competition from a large number of Japanese and European multinationals. In addition, the emergence of mini-multinationals was noted.

10. One of the most dramatic developments of the past 20 years has been the collapse of communism in Eastern Europe, which has created enormous long-run opportunities for international businesses. In addition, the move toward free market economies in China and Latin America is creating opportunities (and threats) for Western international businesses.

11. The benefits and costs of the emerging global economy are being hotly debated among businesspeople, economists, and politicians. The debate focuses on the impact of globalization on jobs, wages, the environment, working conditions, and national sovereignty.

12. Managing an international business is different from managing a domestic business for at least four reasons: (*i*) countries are different, (*ii*) the range of problems confronted by a manager in an international business is wider and the problems themselves more complex than those confronted by a manager in a domestic business, (*iii*) managers in an international business must find ways to work within the limits imposed by governments' intervention in the international trade and investment system, and (*iv*) international transactions involve converting money into different currencies.

Critical Thinking and Discussion Questions

1. Describe the shifts in the world economy over the past 30 years. What are the implications of these shifts for international businesses based in Great Britain? North America? Hong Kong?

2. "The study of international business is fine if you are going to work in a large multinational enterprise, but it has no relevance for individuals who are going to work in small firms." Evaluate this statement.

3. How have changes in technology contributed to the globalization of markets and production? Would the globalization of production and markets have been possible without these technological changes?

4. "Ultimately, the study of international business is no different from the study of domestic business. Thus, there is no point in having a separate course on international business." Evaluate this statement.

5. How might the Internet and the associated World Wide Web affect international business activity and the globalization of the world economy?

6. If current trends continue, China may be the world's largest economy by 2050. Discuss the possible implications of such a development for
   a. The world trading system.
   b. The world monetary system.

   c. The business strategy of today's European and U.S.-based global corporations.
   d. Global commodity prices.

7. Read the Country Focus in this chapter on the Ecuadorean rose industry, then answer the following questions:
   a. How has participation in the international rose trade helped Ecuador's economy and its people? How has the rise of Ecuador as a center for rose growing benefited consumers in developed nations who purchase the roses? What do the answers to these questions tell you about the benefits of international trade?
   b. Why do you think that Ecuador's rose industry only began to take off 20 years ago? Why do you think it has grown so rapidly?
   c. To what extent can the alleged health problems among workers in Ecuador's rose industry be laid at the feet of consumers in the developed world and their desire for perfect Valentine's Day roses?
   d. Do you think governments in the developed world should place trade sanctions on Ecuador roses if reports of health issues among Ecuadorean rose workers are verified? What else might they do to improve the situation in Ecuador?

Research Task   globalEDGE.msu.edu

Use the globalEDGE™ site to complete the following exercises:

1. Your company has developed a new product that is expected to achieve high penetration rates in

all the countries where it is introduced, regardless of the average income status of the local populace. Considering the costs of the product launch, the management team has decided to initially introduce the product only in countries that have a sizable population base. You must prepare a preliminary report with the top 10 countries of the world in terms of population size. Because growth opportunities are another major concern, the average population growth rates should also be listed for management's consideration.

2. You work for a company that is considering investing in a foreign country. Management has requested a report regarding the attractiveness of alternative countries based on the potential return of FDI. Accordingly, a ranking of the top 25 countries is a crucial ingredient for your report. A colleague mentioned a potentially useful tool called the FDI Confidence Index, which is updated periodically. Find this index, and in your report provide additional information regarding how the index is constructed. In addition, discuss the changes that have occurred over the years in the countries ranked in the top 25.

Wipro Ltd.—The New Face of Global Competition

CLOSING CASE Fifteen years ago, Wipro Ltd. of India was a jumbled conglomerate selling everything from cooking oil and personal care products to knockoffs of Dell microcomputers and lightbulbs. Now it is a fast-growing information technology company at the forefront of India's rapidly expanding technology sector. In the year ending March 2005, Wipro generated more than $1.87 billion in sales, the majority from export contracts in information technology services. Its sales have grown by more than 25 percent a year since 1997, and that growth shows no sign of slowing. The company is very profitable, earning $363 million in net income in the year ending March 2005.

Wipro's move into technology began in 1989 when General Electric entered into a joint venture with Wipro, Wipro GE Medical Systems, to make and sell GE ultrasound scanners under license in India. At the time, Wipro's technology revenues were tiny, just $15 million. While sales of GE scanners in India did not take off as quickly as expected, GE quickly realized it had found a cheap source of talented engineers and programmers. India has a solid base of technology-focused universities and colleges that turn out many engineers every year. The vast majority speak English. While software programmers in the United States with two to four years of experience make $64,000 a year, similarly skilled individuals in India can be had for as little as $2 an hour, and programmers at Wipro on average earn $10,000 a year. That might not sound like a lot, but in India, where the annual per capita income is still less than $500, it can translate into a very good living.

GE quickly set aside $5 million a year to hire Wipro software programmers to write code for GE's ultrasound machines and its CT scanners. By the mid-1990s, senior GE managers began to encourage other units to follow the medical division's lead and outsource information technology work to Indian companies. As a result, at one point during the mid-1990s Wipro was getting as much as 50 percent of its revenues from General Electric. However, along the way GE taught Wipro a hard lesson. GE was soon contracting out work to other Indian information technology companies, playing them off against each other in its drive for ever lower costs. To hold onto its GE business, Wipro found that it had to improve its own operating efficiency, so Wipro looked at what GE was doing, and copied it. Wipro's joint venture with GE helped in this regard, since it gave Wipro a window into GE's relentless push for operating efficiencies. Thus, following GE's lead, Wipro was one of the first Indian companies to adopt the Six Sigma process for improving operating efficiency made famous by GE. Today, Wipro executives credit much of their success in the international market to the hard lessons it learned about efficiency as a GE vendor.

By the late 1990s, GE began to turn its attention from simply buying software from India, to using the country as a base for data entry, processing credit card applications, and other clerical tasks that could be performed over the Internet. About this time, other Western companies such as American Express and British Airways began doing the same thing. GE estimates that it cut operating costs $300 million a year by shifting such work to India. Wipro was a major beneficiary.

Today Wipro's 39,000 technology employees write software, integrate back-office solutions, design semiconductors, debug applications, take orders, and field help calls for some of the biggest companies in the world. Its customers still include General Electric along with Hewlett-Packard, Home Depot, Nokia, Sony, and Weyerhaeuser. By using the Internet, Wipro can maintain and manage software applications for companies all over the world in real time. Typical is Wipro's relationship with Weyerhaeuser, one of the world's largest timber companies. Wipro's involvement with Weyerhaeuser began in 1999 when two employees conducted a modest on-site analysis at Weyerhaeuser's U.S. headquarters just south of Seattle. By 2003, Wipro was supporting a broad array of Weyerhaeuser's information systems including logistics, sales, and human resource applications from Bangalore, India. Overall, Wipro estimates it can save clients as much as 40 percent of the cost of maintaining such systems. In a highly competitive global economy, the imperative for companies such as Weyerhaeuser to outsource is compelling.

Wipro, however, is not content to remain in the low-margin end of the software business. The company increasingly is moving upstream into high value-added applications. For example, in 2002, Wipro signed a deal to design and engineer tape storage devices for Storage Technology. In 2004, Wipro took over responsibility for all development work on this product line from 200 employees in Minneapolis. Wipro is also moving rapidly into high value-added software services, such as establishing global supply chain or billing systems for large corporations, a business that is currently dominated by Western consulting outfits such as IBM, EDS, and Accenture.

As Wipro expands its business, it is also taking steps to become a more global company. Around the world, Wipro has been hiring local nationals to lead its sales push. The company now has a direct sales presence in 35 countries, most of which are staffed by local nationals. By 2005, the company hopes that three-quarters of the employees that customers see will be local nationals—in Europe the figure is already 90 percent. According to a Wipro spokesman, using locals "provides the cultural and linguistic ties that make clients smile, and help us build stronger relationships." Wipro is also buying local companies to give it instant industry presence. In November 2002, Wipro paid $26 million for American Management Systems, buying not just credibility but also 90 consultants and 50 existing client relationships in the energy business. While these consultants will manage contact with U.S. customers, much of the software development work will be moved to Bangalore.

In something of a departure from its historic strategy, since 2000 Wipro has also been moving some product development work out of India to developed nations. It now has nine development centers in Europe and the United States. These centers focus on product development work where more communication between Wipro engineers and the client is required than with the typical outsourcing contract, and where language is an issue. In Germany, for example, Wipro has found that it can win more business if not only its salespeople are German, but also some development work is done locally by German engineers.

Sources: K. H. Hammonds, "The New Face of Global Competition," *Fast Company*, February 2003, pp. 90–97; M. Kripalani and P. Engardio, "The Live Wire of Indian High Tech," *BusinessWeek*, January 20, 2003, pp. 70–71; F. Hayes, "Outsourcing Angst," *Computer World*, March 17, 2003, p. 11; J. Solomon and E. Cherney, "Outsourcing to India Sees a Twist," *The Wall Street Journal*, April 1, 2004, p. A2; J. Solomon and K. Kranhold, "Western Exposure: In India's Outsourcing Boom, GE Played a Starring Role," *The Wall Street Journal*, March 23, 2005, p. A1; and A. Campoy, "Think Locally: Indian Outsourcing Companies Have Finally Begun to Crack the European Market," *The Wall Street Journal*, September 27, 2004, p. R8.

Case Discussion Question

1. How did outsourcing work to Wipro improve General Electric's ability to compete in the global economy? Does such outsourcing harm or benefit the American economy?

2. Did General Electric help to create Wipro? How?

3. If India's information technology companies continue to prosper, over time what do you think will happen to the income differential between software programmers in the United States and India? What are the implications for the American economy?

4. Since 2000, Wipro has moved abroad, establishing sales offices in 35 nations and design centers in nine. Why is Wipro doing this? What would happen to the company if it did not follow this strategy?

5. What does the rise of Wipro teach you about the nature of the global economy in the first decade of the 21st century?

Notes

1. World Trade Organization, trade statistics database accessed May 2005 at http://stat.wto.org/Home/WSDBHome.aspx.

2. Thomas L. Friedman, *The World Is Flat* (New York: Farrar, Straus and Giroux, 2005).

3. Ibid.

4. T. Levitt, "The Globalization of Markets," *Harvard Business Review*, May–June 1983, pp. 92–102.

5. U.S. Department of Commerce, "A Profile of U.S. Exporting Companies, 2000–2001," February 2003. Report available at www.census.gov/foreign-trade/aip/index.html#profile.

6. Ibid.

7. C. M. Draffen, "Going Global: Export Market Proves Profitable for Region's Small Businesses," *Newsday*, March 19, 2001, p. C18.

8. W. J. Holstein, "Why Johann Can Export, but Johnny Can't," *BusinessWeek*, November 4, 1991, pp. 64–65.

9. See F. T. Knickerbocker, *Oligopolistic Reaction and Multinational Enterprise* (Boston: Harvard Business School Press, 1973), and R. E. Caves, "Japanese Investment in the U.S.: Lessons for the Economic Analysis of Foreign Investment," *The World Economy* 16 (1993), pp. 279–300.

10. I. Metthee, "Playing a Large Part," *Seattle Post-Intelligencer*, April 9, 1994, p. 13.

11. D. Pritchard, "Are Federal Tax Laws and State Subsidies for Boeing 7E7 Selling America Short?" *Aviation Week*, April 12, 2004, pp. 74–75.

12. D. Barboza, "An Unknown Giant Flexes Its Muscles," *The New York Times*, December 4, 2004, p. B1, B3.

13. W. M. Bulkeley, "IBM to Export Highly Paid Jobs to India," *The Wall Street Journal*, December 15, 2003, pp. B1, B3.

14. R. B. Reich, *The Work of Nations* (New York: A. A. Knopf, 1991).

15. United Nations, "The UN in Brief," www.un.org/Overview/brief.html.

16. J. A. Frankel, "Globalization of the Economy," National Bureau of Economic Research, Working Paper No. 7858, 2000.

17. J. Bhagwati, *Protectionism* (Cambridge, MA: MIT Press, 1989).

18. F. Williams, "Trade Round Like This May Never Be Seen Again," *Financial Times*, April 15, 1994, p. 8.

19. W. Vieth, "Major Concessions Lead to Success for WTO Talks," *Los Angeles Times*, November 14, 2001, p. A1, and "Seeds Sown for Future Growth," *The Economist*, November 17, 2001, pp. 65–66.

20. United Nations, *World Investment Report, 2004* (New York and Geneva: United Nations, 2004).

21. Ibid.

22. World Trade Organization, *International Trade Trends and Statistics, 2003* (Geneva: WTO, 2003), and WTO press release, "World Trade for 2003: Prospects for 2004," April 4, 2004, available at www.wto.org.

23. United Nations, *World Investment Report, 2004,* and United Nations Conference on Trade and Development, "World FDI Flows Grew an Estimated 6% in 2004," UNCTAD press release, January 11, 2005.

24. World Trade Organization, *International Trade Statistics, 2004* (Geneva: WTO, 2004); United Nations, *World Investment Report, 2004;* and United Nations Conference on Trade and Development, "World FDI Flows Grew an Estimated 6% in 2004."

25. United Nations, *World Investment Report, 2004.*

26. Moore's Law is named after Intel founder Gordon Moore.

27. Frankel, "Globalization of the Economy."

28. J. G. Fernald and V. Greenfield, "The Fall and Rise of the Global Economy," *Chicago Fed Letters*, April 2001, pp. 1–4.

29. Data compiled from various sources and listed by CyberAtlas at http://cyberatlas.internet.com/big_picture/.

30. Data on the number of host computers can be found at www.isc.org/index.pl?/ops/ds/.

31. www.forrester.com/ER/Press/ForrFind/0,1768,0,00.html.

32. For a counterpoint, see "Geography and the Net: Putting It in Its Place," *The Economist*, August 11, 2001, pp. 18–20.

33. M. Dickerson, "All Those Inflated Expectations Aside, Many Firms Are Finding the Internet Invaluable in Pursuing International Trade," *Los Angeles Times*, October 14, 1998, p. 10. The company's Web site is www.cardiacscience.com.

34. A. Stewart, "Easier Access to World Markets," *Financial Times*, December 3, 1997, p. 8.

35. Frankel, "Globalization of the Economy."

36. Data from Bureau of Transportation Statistics, 2001.

37. Fernald and Greenfield, "The Fall and Rise of the Global Economy."

38. Data located at www.bts.gov/publications/us_international_trade_and_freight_transportation_trends/2003/index.html.

39. "War of the Worlds," *The Economist: A Survey of the Global Economy*, October 1, 1994, pp. 3–4.

40. Ibid.

41. United Nations, *World Investment Report, 2004.*

42. Ibid.

43. Ibid.

44. S. Chetty, "Explosive International Growth and Problems of Success among Small and Medium Sized Firms," *International Small Business Journal*, February 2003, pp. 5–28.

45. R. A. Mosbacher, "Opening Up Export Doors for Smaller Firms," *Seattle Times*, July 24, 1991, p. A7.

46. "Small Companies Learn How to Sell to the Japanese," *Seattle Times*, March 19, 1992.

47. Holstein, "Why Johann Can Export, but Johnny Can't."

48. J. E. Stiglitz, *Globalization and Its Discontents* (New York: W. W. Norton, 2003); J. Bhagwati, *In Defense of Globalization* (New York: Oxford University Press, 2004); and Friedman, *The World Is Flat*.

49. See, for example, Ravi Batra, *The Myth of Free Trade* (New York: Touchstone Books, 1993); William Greider, *One World, Ready or Not: The Manic Logic of Global Capitalism* (New York: Simon and Schuster, 1997); and D. Radrik, *Has Globalization Gone Too Far?* (Washington, DC: Institution for International Economics, 1997).

50. James Goldsmith, "The Winners and the Losers," in *The Case against the Global Economy*, ed. J. Mander and E. Goldsmith (San Francisco: The Sierra Book Club, 1996). Lou Dobbs, *Exporting America* (New York: Time Warner Books, 2004).

51. D. L. Bartlett and J. B. Steele, "America: Who Stole the Dream," *Philadelphia Inquirer*, September 9, 1996.

52. For example, see Paul Krugman, *Pop Internationalism* (Cambridge, MA: MIT Press, 1996).

53. Peter Gottschalk and Timothy M. Smeeding, "Cross-National Comparisons of Earnings and Income Inequality," *Journal of Economic Literature* 35 (June 1997), pp. 633–87, and Susan M. Collins, *Exports, Imports, and the American Worker* (Washington, DC: Brookings Institution, 1998).

54. B. Milanovic and L. Squire, "Does Tariff Liberalization Increase Wage Inequality?" *National Bureau of Economic Research*, Working Paper No. 11046, January 2005.

55. "A Survey of Pay. Winners and Losers," *The Economist*, May 8, 1999, pp. 5–8.

56. Jared Bernstein, Elizabeth C. McNichol, Lawrence Mishel, and Robert Zahradnik, "Pulling Apart: A State by State Analysis of Income Trends," *Economic Policy Institute*, January 2000.

57. See Krugman, *Pop Internationalism*, and D. Belman and T. M. Lee, "International Trade and the Performance of US Labor Markets," in *U.S. Trade Policy and Global Growth*, ed. R. A. Blecker (New York: Economic Policy Institute, 1996).

58. See Robert Lerman, "Is Earnings Inequality Really Increasing? Economic Restructuring and the Job Market," Brief No. 1 (Washington, DC: Urban Institute, March 1997).

59. M. Forster and M. Pearson, "Income Distribution and Poverty in the OECD Area," *OECD Economic Studies* 34 (2002).

60. Bernstein, McNichol, Mishel, and Zahradnik, "Pulling Apart: A State by State Analysis of Income Trends."

61. E. Goldsmith, "Global Trade and the Environment," in J. Mander and E. Goldsmith, *The Case against the Global Economy* (San Francisco: Sierra Club, 1996).

62. P. Choate, *Jobs at Risk: Vulnerable U.S. Industries and Jobs under NAFTA* (Washington, DC: Manufacturing Policy Project, 1993).

63. Ibid.

64. B. Lomborg, *The Skeptical Environmentalist* (Cambridge: Cambridge University Press, 2001).

65. H. Nordstrom and S. Vaughan, *Trade and the Environment, World Trade Organization Special Studies No. 4* (Geneva: WTO, 1999).

66. Figures are from "Freedom's Journey: A Survey of the 20th Century. Our Durable Planet," *The Economist*, September 11, 1999, p. 30.

67. For an exhaustive review of the empirical literature, see B. R. Copeland and M. Scott Taylor, "Trade, Growth and the Environment," *Journal of Economic Literature*, March 2004, pp. 7–77.

68. G. M. Grossman and A. B. Krueger, "Economic Growth and the Environment," *Quarterly Journal of Economics* 110 (1995), pp. 353–78.

69. Krugman, *Pop Internationalism*.

70. R. Kuttner, "Managed Trade and Economic Sovereignty," in *U.S. Trade Policy and Global Growth*, ed. R. A. Blecker (New York: Economic Policy Institute, 1996).

71. Ralph Nader and Lori Wallach, "GATT, NAFTA, and the Subversion of the Democratic Process," in *US Trade Policy and Global Growth*,

ed. R. A. Blecker (New York: Economic Policy Institute, 1996), pp. 93–94.

72. Lant Pritchett, "Divergence, Big Time," *Journal of Economic Perspectives* 11, no. 3 (Summer 1997), pp. 3–18.

73. Ibid.

74. W. Easterly, "How Did Heavily Indebted Poor Countries Become Heavily Indebted?" *World Development*, October 2002, pp. 1677–96.

75. See D. Ben-David, H. Nordstrom, and L. A. Winters, *Trade, Income Disparity and Poverty. World Trade Organization Special Studies No. 5* (Geneva: WTO, 1999).

76. William Easterly, "Debt Relief," *Foreign Policy,* November–December 2001, pp. 20–26.

77. Jeffrey Sachs, "Sachs on Development: Helping the World's Poorest," *The Economist*, August 14, 1999, pp. 17–20.

78. World Trade Organization, *Annual Report 2003* (Geneva: WTO, 2004).

79. Easterly, "Debt Relief."

DIFFERENT LEGAL SYSTEMS

There are three main types of legal systems—or legal tradition—in use around the world: common law, civil law, and theocratic law.

Common Law

The common law system evolved in England over hundreds of years. It is now found in most of Great Britain's former colonies, including the United States. **Common law** is based on tradition, precedent, and custom. *Tradition* refers to a country's legal history, *precedent* to cases that have come before the courts in the past, and *custom* to the ways in which laws are applied in specific situations. When law courts interpret common law, they do so with regard to these characteristics. This gives a common law system a degree of flexibility that other systems lack. Judges in a common law system have the power to *interpret* the law so that it applies to the unique circumstances of an individual case. In turn, each new interpretation sets a precedent that may be followed in future cases. As new precedents arise, laws may be altered, clarified, or amended to deal with new situations.

Islamic law governs all aspects of the Muslims' lives, even commercial activities.

Civil Law

A **civil law system** is based on a very detailed set of laws organized into codes. When law courts interpret civil law, they do so with regard to these codes. More than 80 countries, including Germany, France, Japan, and Russia, operate with a civil law system. A civil law system tends to be less adversarial than a common law system, since the judges rely upon detailed legal codes rather than interpreting tradition, precedent, and custom. Judges under a civil law system have less *flexibility* than those under a common law system. Judges in a common law system have the power to *interpret* the law, while judges in a civil law system have the power only to *apply* the law.

Theocratic Law

A **theocratic law system** is one in which the law is based on religious teachings. Islamic law is the most widely practiced theocratic legal system in the modern world, although usage of both Hindu and Jewish law persisted into the 20th century. Islamic law is primarily a moral rather than a commercial law, and is intended to govern all aspects of life.[9] The foundation for Islamic law is the holy book of Islam, the Koran; along with the Sunnah, or decisions and sayings of the Prophet Muhammad; and the writings of Islamic scholars who have derived rules by analogy from the principles established in the Koran and the Sunnah. Because the Koran and Sunnah are holy documents, the basic foundations of Islamic law cannot be changed. However, in practice Islamic jurists and scholars are constantly debating the application of Islamic law to the modern world. In reality, many Muslim countries have legal systems that are a blend of Islamic law and a common or civil law system.

Although Islamic law is primarily concerned with moral behavior, it has been extended to cover certain commercial activities. An example is the payment or receipt of interest, which is considered usury and outlawed by the Koran. To the devout Muslim, acceptance of interest payments is seen as a very grave sin; the giver and the taker are equally damned. This is not just a matter of theology; in several Islamic states it has also become a matter of law. In the 1990s, for example, Pakistan's Federal Shariat Court, the highest Islamic lawmaking body in the country, pronounced interest to be un-Islamic and therefore illegal and demanded that the government amend all financial laws accordingly. In 1999, Pakistan's Supreme Court ruled that Islamic banking methods should be used in the country after July 1, 2001.[10] By 2002, some 150 Islamic financial institutions in the world collectively managed more than $200 billion in assets. In addition to Pakistan, Islamic banks are found in many of the Gulf states, Egypt, and Malaysia.[11]

DIFFERENCES IN CONTRACT LAW

The difference between common law and civil law systems can be illustrated by the approach of each to contract law (remember, most theocratic legal systems also have elements of common or civil law). A **contract** is a document that specifies the conditions under which an exchange is to occur and details the rights and obligations of the parties involved. Some form of contract regulates many business transactions. **Contract law** is the body of law that governs contract enforcement. The parties to an agreement normally resort to contract law when one party feels the other has violated either the letter or the spirit of an agreement.

Because common law tends to be relatively ill specified, contracts drafted under a common law framework tend to be very detailed with all contingencies spelled out. In civil law systems, however, contracts tend to be much shorter and less specific because many of the issues are already covered in a civil code. Thus, it is more expensive to draw up contracts in a common law jurisdiction, and resolving contract disputes can be very adversarial in common law systems. But, common law systems have the advantage of greater flexibility and allow for judges to interpret a contract dispute in light of the prevailing situation. International businesses need to be sensitive to these differences; approaching a contract dispute in a state with a civil law system as if it had a common law system may backfire (and vice versa).

When contract disputes arise in international trade, there is always the question of which country's laws to apply. To resolve this issue, a number of countries, including the United States, have ratified the **United Nations Convention on Contracts for the International Sale of Goods (CIGS).** The CIGS establishes a uniform set of rules governing certain aspects of the making and performance of everyday commercial contracts between sellers and buyers who have their places of business in different nations. By adopting the CIGS, a nation signals to other adopters that it will treat the convention's rules as part of its law. The CIGS applies automatically to all contracts for the sale of goods between different firms based in countries that have ratified the convention, unless the parties to the contract explicitly opt out. One problem with the CIGS, however, is that fewer than 70 nations have ratified the convention (the CIGS went into effect in 1988).[12] Many of the world's larger trading nations, including Japan and the United Kingdom, have not ratified the CIGS.

When firms do not wish to accept the CIGS, they often opt for arbitration by a recognized arbitration court to settle contract disputes. The most well known of these courts is the International Court of Arbitration of the International Chamber of Commerce in Paris. In 2004, this court handled some 561 requests for arbitration involving 1,682 parties from 116 countries.[13] Almost 60 percent of disputes involved sums in excess of $1 million.

PROPERTY RIGHTS

In a legal sense, the term *property* refers to a resource over which an individual or business holds a legal title; that is, a resource that it owns. Resources include land, buildings, equipment, capital, mineral rights, businesses, and intellectual property (ideas, which are protected by patents, copyrights, and trademarks). **Property rights** refer to the bundle of legal rights over the use to which a resource is put and over the use made of any income that may be derived from that resource.[14] Countries differ in the extent to which their legal systems define and protect property rights. Although almost all countries have laws on their books that protect property rights, in many countries these laws are not enforced by the authorities and property rights are violated (see the opening case). Property rights can be violated in two ways—through private action and through public action.

Private Action

In this context, **private action** refers to theft, piracy, blackmail, and the like by private individuals or groups. While theft occurs in all countries, a weak legal system allows for a much higher level of criminal action in some than in others. For example, in Russia in the chaotic period following the collapse of communism, an outdated legal system, coupled with a weak police force and judicial system, offered both domestic and foreign businesses scant protection from blackmail by the "Russian Mafia." Successful business owners in Russia often had to pay "protection money" to the Mafia or face violent retribution, including bombings and assassinations (about 500 contract killings of businessmen occurred in 1995 and again in 1996).[15]

Russia is not alone in having Mafia problems (and the situation in Russia has improved significantly since the mid-1990s). The Mafia has a long history in the United States (Chicago in the 1930s was similar to Moscow in the 1990s). In Japan, the local version of the Mafia, known as the *yakuza*, runs protection rackets, particularly in the food and entertainment industries.[16] However, there was a big difference between the magnitude of such activity in Russia in the 1990s and its limited impact in Japan and the United States. This difference arose because the legal enforcement apparatus, such as the police and court system, was so weak in Russia following the collapse of communism. Many other countries from time to time have had problems similar to or even greater than those experienced by Russia.

Public Action and Corruption

Public action to violate property rights occurs when public officials, such as politicians and government bureaucrats, extort income, resources, or the property itself from property holders (see the opening case for an example). This can be done through legal mechanisms such as levying excessive taxation, requiring expensive licenses or permits from property holders, taking assets into state ownership without compensating the owners, or redistributing assets without compensating the prior owners. It can also be done through illegal means, or corruption, by demanding bribes from businesses in return for the rights to operate in a country, industry, or location.[17]

Corruption has been well documented in every society, from the banks of the Congo River to the palace of the Dutch royal family, from Japanese politicians to Brazilian bankers, and from Indonesian government officials to the New York City Police Department. The government of the late Ferdinand Marcos in the Philippines was famous for demanding bribes from foreign businesses wishing to set up operations in that country.[18] The same was true of government officials in Indonesia under the rule of ex-President Suharto (see the opening case). No society is immune to corruption. However, there are systematic differences in the extent of corruption. In some countries, the rule of law minimizes corruption. Corruption is seen and treated as illegal and, when discovered, violators are punished by the full force of the law. In other countries, the rule of law is weak and corruption by bureaucrats and politicians is rife. Corruption is so endemic in some countries that politicians and bureaucrats regard it as a perk of office and openly flout laws against corruption.

According to Transparency International, an independent nonprofit organization dedicated to exposing and fighting corruption, businesses and individuals spend some $400 billion a year worldwide on bribes related to government procurement contracts alone![19] Transparency International has also measured the level of corruption among public officials in different countries.[20] As can be seen in Figure 2.1, the organization rated countries such as Finland and New Zealand as clean, while countries such as Russia, India, Indonesia, and Zimbabwe are seen as corrupt. Bangladesh ranked last out of all 146 countries in the survey, while Finland ranked first.

Economic evidence suggests that high levels of corruption significantly reduce the foreign direct investment, level of international trade, and economic growth rate in a country.[21] By siphoning off profits, corrupt politicians and bureaucrats reduce the returns to business investment and, hence, reduce the incentive of both domestic and foreign businesses to invest in that country. The lower level of investment that results hurts economic growth. Thus, we would expect countries such as Indonesia, Nigeria, and Russia to have a much lower rate of economic growth than might otherwise have been the case. A detailed example of the negative effect that corruption can have on economic progress

FIGURE 2.1

Rankings of Corruption
by Country, 2004

Source: Transparency International, "Global Corruption Report 2005," www.transparency.org. Reprinted with permission.

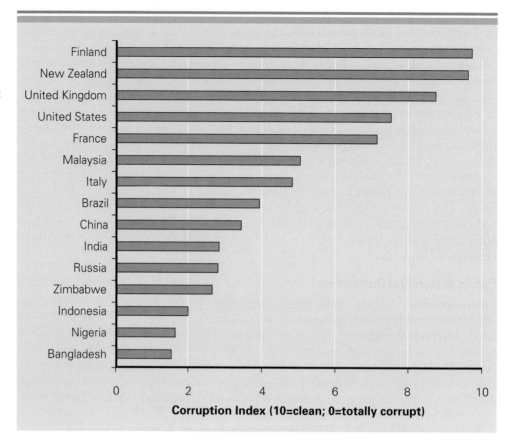

is given in the accompanying Country Focus, which looks at the impact of corruption on economic growth in Nigeria.

Foreign Corrupt Practices Act

In the United States the **Foreign Corrupt Practices Act** was passed during the 1970s following revelations that U.S. companies had bribed government officials in foreign countries in an attempt to win lucrative contracts. This law makes it illegal to bribe a foreign government official to obtain or maintain business over which that foreign official has authority, and it requires all publicly traded companies (whether or not they are involved in international trade) to keep detailed records that would reveal whether a violation of the act has occurred. Along the same lines, in 1997 trade and finance ministers from the member states of the Organization for Economic Cooperation and Development (OECD), an association of the world's 30 most powerful economies, adopted the Convention on Combating Bribery of Foreign Public Officials in International Business Transactions.[22] The convention obliges member states to make the bribery of foreign public officials a criminal offense.

However, both the U.S. law and OECD convention are circumscribed with language that allows for exceptions known as facilitating or expediting payments (also called grease payments or speed money) the purpose of which is to expedite or to secure the performance of a routine governmental action.[23] For example, they allow for small payments made to speed up the issuance of permits or licenses, process paperwork, or just get vegetables off the dock and on their way to market. The explanation for this exception to general antibribery provisions is that while grease payments are, technically, bribes, they are distinguishable from (and, apparently, less offensive than) bribes used to obtain or maintain business, since they merely facilitate performance of duties that the recipients are already obligated to perform.

COUNTRY FOCUS When Nigeria gained independence from Great Britain in 1960, there were hopes that the country might emerge as an economic heavyweight in Africa. Not only was Nigeria Africa's most populous country, but it also was blessed with abundant natural resources, particularly oil, which rose sharply in value in the 1970s following two rounds of oil price increases engineered by the Organization of Petroleum Exporting Countries (OPEC). Between 1970 and 2000, Nigeria earned more than $300 billion from the sale of oil, but at the end of this period it remained one of the poorest countries in the world. In 2000, gross national product per capita was just $300, 40 percent of the adult population was illiterate, life expectancy at birth was only 50 years, and the country was begging for relief on $30 billion in debt. The Human Development Index compiled by the United Nations ranked Nigeria 151 out of 174 countries covered.

What went wrong? Although there is no simple answer, a number of factors seem to have conspired to damage economic activity in Nigeria. The country is composed of several competing ethnic, tribal, and religious groups, and the conflict among them has limited political stability and led to political strife, including a brutal civil war in the 1970s. With the legitimacy of the government always in question, political leaders often purchased support by legitimizing bribes and by raiding the national treasury to reward allies. Civilian rule after independence was followed by a series of military dictatorships, each of which seemed more corrupt and inept than the last (the country returned to civilian rule in 1999).

The most recent military dictator, Sani Abacha, openly and systematically plundered the state treasury for his own personal gain. His most blatant scam was the Petroleum Trust Fund, which he set up in the mid-1990s ostensibly to channel extra revenue from an increase in fuel prices into much-needed infrastructure projects and other investments. The fund was not independently audited, and almost none of the money that passed through it was properly accounted for. It was, in fact, a vehicle for Abacha and his supporters to spend at will a sum that in 1996 was equivalent to some 25 percent of the total federal budget. Abacha, aware of his position as an unpopular and unelected leader, lavished money on personal security and handed out bribes to those whose

support he coveted. With examples like this at the very top of the government, it is not surprising that corruption could be found throughout the political and bureaucratic apparatus.

Some of the excesses were simply astounding. In the 1980s an aluminum smelter was built on the orders of the government, which wanted to industrialize Nigeria. The cost of the smelter was $2.4 billion, some 60 to 100 percent higher than the cost of comparable plants elsewhere in the developed world. This high cost was widely interpreted to reflect the bribes that had to be paid to local politicians by the international contractors that built the plant. The smelter has never operated at more than a fraction of its intended capacity. Another example of corruption in Nigeria was the cement scandal of the early 1980s. At that time, the president announced a grand public housing project. Public officials promptly ordered vast quantities of cement from foreign contractors, taking a percentage of each contract in the form of a kickback. They ordered far more cement than was needed and more than Nigerian ports could cope with. Soon ships loaded with cement formed a line that stretched for several miles outside of Lagos harbor and that took months to unload. Meanwhile, the officials responsible were making a fortune from selling cement import licenses.

Has the situation in Nigeria improved since the country returned to civilian rule in 1999? In 2003, Olusegun Obasanjo was elected president on a platform that included a promise to fight corruption. By some accounts, progress has been seen. His anticorruption chief, Nuhu Ribadu, has claimed that whereas 70 percent of the country's oil revenues were being stolen or wasted in 2002, by 2004 the figure was "only" 40 percent. But in its most recent survey, Transparency International still ranked Nigeria among the most corrupt countries in the world in 2004 (see Figure 2.1), suggesting that the country still has long way to go. Mr. Ribadu has suggested that the problem lies with state governments, who are still riddled with corruption.

Sources: "A Tale of Two Giants," *The Economist,* January 15, 2000, p. 5; J. Coolidge and S. Rose Ackerman, "High Level Rent Seeking and Corruption in African Regimes," World Bank Policy Research Working Paper No. 1780, June 1997; D. L. Bevan, P. Collier, and J. W. Gunning, *Nigeria and Indonesia: The Political Economy of Poverty, Equity and Growth* (Oxford: Oxford University Press, 1999); and "Democracy and Its Discontents," *The Economist,* January 29, 2005, p. 55.

www.mhhe.com/hill

A security guard stands near a pile of pirated CDs and DVDs before they were destroyed at a ceremony in Beijing Saturday, Feb. 26, 2005. Thousands of pirated items were destroyed in the event, one of a number of activities, including an antipiracy pop concert later Saturday, which were staged by China's government to publicize its antipiracy efforts.

THE PROTECTION OF INTELLECTUAL PROPERTY

Intellectual property refers to property that is the product of intellectual activity, such as computer software, a screenplay, a music score, or the chemical formula for a new drug. Patents, copyrights, and trademarks establish ownership rights over intellectual property. A **patent** grants the inventor of a new product or process exclusive rights for a defined period to the manufacture, use, or sale of that invention. **Copyrights** are the exclusive legal rights of authors, composers, playwrights, artists, and publishers to publish and disperse their work as they see fit. **Trademarks** are designs and names, often officially registered, by which merchants or manufacturers designate and differentiate their products (e.g., Christian Dior clothes). In the high-technology "knowledge" economy of the 21st century, intellectual property has become an increasingly important source of economic value for businesses. Protecting intellectual property has also become increasingly problematic, particularly if it can be rendered in a digital form and then copied and distributed at very low cost via pirated CDs or over the Internet (e.g., computer software, music and video recordings).[24]

The philosophy behind intellectual property laws is to reward the originator of a new invention, book, musical record, clothes design, restaurant chain, and the like, for his or her idea and effort. Such laws are a very important stimulus to innovation and creative work. They provide an incentive for people to search for novel ways of doing things, and they reward creativity. For example, consider innovation in the pharmaceutical industry. A patent will grant the inventor of a new drug a 20-year monopoly in production of that drug. This gives pharmaceutical firms an incentive to undertake the expensive, difficult, and time-consuming basic research required to generate new drugs (it can cost $800 million in R&D and take 12 years to get a new drug on the market). Without the guarantees provided by patents, companies would be unlikely to commit themselves to extensive basic research.[25]

The protection of intellectual property rights differs greatly from country to country. While many countries have stringent intellectual property regulations on their books, the enforcement of these regulations has often been lax. This has been the case even among many of the 188 countries that are now members of the **World Intellectual Property Organization,** all of whom have signed international treaties designed to protect intellectual property including the oldest such treaty, the **Paris Convention for the Protection of Industrial Property,** which dates to 1883 and has been signed by some 169 nations as of 2004. Weak enforcement encourages the piracy (theft) of intellectual property. China and Thailand have recently been among the worst offenders in Asia. Pirated computer software is widely available in China. Similarly, the streets of Bangkok, Thailand's capital, are lined with stands selling pirated copies of Rolex watches, Levi Strauss jeans, videotapes, and computer software.

Piracy in music recordings is rampant. The International Federation of the Phonographic Industry claims that about 40 percent of all recorded music products sold worldwide in 2003 were pirated (illegal) copies, suggesting that piracy costs the industry over $4.5 billion annually.[26] The computer software industry also suffers from lax enforcement of intellectual property rights. Estimates suggest that violations of intellectual property rights cost computer software firms revenues equal to $29 billion in 2003.[27] According to the Business Software Alliance, a software industry association, in 2003 some 36 percent of all software applications used in the world were pirated. The worst region was Eastern Europe, where the piracy rate was 71 percent (see Figure 2.2). One of the worst countries was China, where the piracy rate in 2003 ran 92 percent and cost the industry more than $3.8 billion in lost sales, up from $444 million in 1995. Although at 22 percent the piracy

FIGURE 2.2

Regional Piracy Rates
for Software, 2003

Source: Business Software
Alliance, "Seventh Annual
Global Piracy Study," June 2004.

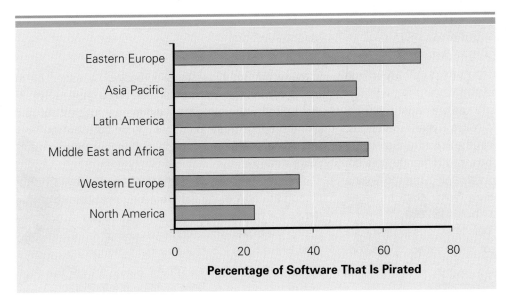

rate was much lower in the United States, the value of sales lost was more significant because of the size of the market, reaching an estimated $6.5 billion in 2003.[28]

International businesses have a number of possible responses to violations of their intellectual property. They can lobby their respective governments to push for international agreements to ensure that intellectual property rights are protected and that the law is enforced. Partly as a result of such actions, international laws are being strengthened. As we shall see in Chapter 6, the most recent world trade agreement, which was signed in 1994, for the first time extends the scope of the General Agreement on Tariffs and Trade (GATT) to cover intellectual property. Under the new agreement, known as the **Trade Related Aspects of Intellectual Property Rights** (or **TRIPS**), as of 1995 a council of the World Trade Organization is overseeing enforcement of much stricter intellectual property regulations. These regulations oblige WTO members to grant and enforce patents lasting at least 20 years and copyrights lasting 50 years. Rich countries had to comply with the rules within a year. Poor countries, in which such protection generally was much weaker, had 5 years of grace, and the very poorest have 10 years.[29] (For further details of the TRIPS agreement, see Chapter 6.)

In addition to lobbying governments, firms can file lawsuits on their own behalf. They may also choose to stay out of countries where intellectual property laws are lax, rather than risk having their ideas stolen by local entrepreneurs. Firms also need to be on the alert to ensure that pirated copies of their products produced in countries with weak intellectual property laws don't turn up in their home market or in third countries. U.S. computer software giant Microsoft, for example, discovered that pirated Microsoft software, produced illegally in Thailand, was being sold worldwide as the real thing.

PRODUCT SAFETY AND PRODUCT LIABILITY

Product safety laws set certain safety standards to which a product must adhere. **Product liability** involves holding a firm and its officers responsible when a product causes injury, death, or damage. Product liability can be much greater if a product does not conform to required safety standards. Both civil and criminal product liability laws exist. Civil laws call for payment and monetary damages. Criminal liability laws result in fines or imprisonment. Both civil and criminal liability laws are probably more extensive in the United States than in any other country, although many other Western nations also have comprehensive liability laws. Liability laws are typically least extensive in less developed nations. A boom in product liability suits and awards in the United States resulted in a dramatic increase in the

MANAGEMENT FOCUS

Over the past decade the video game industry has grown into a global colossus worth more than $25 billion a year in revenues. For the three biggest players in the industry, Sony with PlayStation, Microsoft with Xbox, and Nintendo, this potentially represents a huge growth engine, but the engine is threatened by a rise in piracy, which cost the video game industry an estimated $4 billion in 2004.

The piracy problem is particularly serious in East Asia excluding Japan, where video game consoles are routinely "chipped"—sold with modified chips, called mod chips, that override the console's security system, allowing it to play illegally copied games and CDs. Importers or resellers, who charge a small markup for making the modification, illegally install the mod chips. In some areas, such as Hong Kong, it is almost impossible to find a console that hasn't been modified.

Because they allow users to play illegally copied games, consoles with mod chips offer a gaping gateway for software pirates, and they directly threaten the profitability of console and game makers. The big three in the industry all follow a razor and razor blades business model, where the console (razor) is sold at a loss and profit is made on the sale of the game (razor blades). In the case of Microsoft's Xbox, estimates suggest the company loses as much as $200 on each Xbox it sells. To make profits, Microsoft collects royalties on the sale of games developed under license, in addition to producing and selling some games itself. Games typically retail for about $50 and Microsoft must sell 6 to 12 games to each Xbox user to recoup the $200 loss on the initial sale and start making a profit. If those users purchase pirated games and play them on "chipped" Xbox consoles, Microsoft collects nothing in royalties and may never reach the break-even point. Sony and Nintendo face similar problems. In East Asia, some 70 percent of game software may be pirated thanks to the popularity of "chipped" consoles and the low price of pirated games, which may sell for one-third the price of the legal game.

Historically, all the big video game companies tried to deal with the piracy problem in East Asia by ignoring the market. Sony launched its PlayStation II in East Asia two years after its Japanese launch, and Microsoft delayed its East Asian launch for a year after it launched elsewhere in the world. But this tactic is increasingly questionable in a region where there may soon be more gamers than in the United States. Industry estimates suggest Asian gamers spent more on video game software in 2004 than U.S. gamers, much of it on low-priced pirated games.

Another tactic that both Sony and Microsoft are now using is to regularly alter the hardware specifications of its consoles, rendering the existing mod chips useless. But the companies have found this is just a temporary solution, for within a few weeks mod chips made to override the new specifications are available on the market.

A third tactic is to push local authorities to enforce existing intellectual property rights law that in theory outlaws the mod chip practice. In late 2002, Microsoft, Sony, and Nintendo joined forces to sue the Hong Kong company Lik Sang, which sold mod chips through its Web site and is one of the world's largest distributors of the chips. Some observers question the value of this, however; they argue that if Lik Sang is shut down, many others in Hong Kong may be willing to take its place. What is needed, they argue, is concerted government action to stop the pirates, and so far East Asian governments have not been quick to act.

A final way of dealing with piracy is to change the business model. All three main players in the industry are now starting to push online games where customers pay a subscription fee to play online, as opposed to a onetime fee to purchase a game. This business model makes piracy much less of an issue and it may drive growth in places such as China where piracy is endemic. Indeed, current estimates suggest there are already 29 million gamers in China, most of whom play pirated games, and this figure will increase to 55 million by 2009. If a good percentage switch to online gaming, the revenues could be significant.

Sources: S. Yoon, "The Mod Squad," *East Asian Economic Review*, November 7, 2002, pp. 34–36; R. Cunningham, "Controversy as Sony Loses Mod-Chip Verdict," *Managing Intellectual Property*, September 2002, pp. 15–18; A. Pham, "Video Game Losses Nearly $2 Billion," *Los Angeles Times*, February 18, 2002, p. C8; Andy Holloway, "License to Plunder," *Canadian Business*, November 10, 2003, p. 95; and R. Grover et al., "Game Wars" *BusinessWeek*, February 28, 2005, pp. 60–66.

cost of liability insurance. Many business executives argue that the high costs of liability insurance make American businesses less competitive in the global marketplace.

In addition to the competitiveness issue, country differences in product safety and liability laws raise an important ethical issue for firms doing business abroad. When product safety laws are tougher in a firm's home country than in a foreign country and/or when liability laws are more lax, should a firm doing business in that foreign country follow the more relaxed local standards or should it adhere to the standards of its home country? While the ethical thing to do is undoubtedly to adhere to home-country standards, firms have been known to take advantage of lax safety and liability laws to do business in a manner that would not be allowed at home.

The Determinants of Economic Development

The political, economic, and legal systems of a country can have a profound impact on the level of economic development and hence on the attractiveness of a country as a possible market and/or production location for a firm. Here we look first at how countries differ in their level of development. Then we look at how political economy affects economic progress.

DIFFERENCES IN ECONOMIC DEVELOPMENT

Different countries have dramatically different levels of economic development. One common measure of economic development is a country's gross national income per head of population. GNI is regarded as a yardstick for the economic activity of a country; it measures the total annual income received by residents of a nation (GNI superseded **gross national product,** or **GNP**). Map 2.1 summarizes the GNI per capita of the world's nations in 2003. As can be seen, countries such as Japan, Sweden, Switzerland, and the United States are among the richest on this measure, while the large countries of China and India are among the poorest. Japan, for example, had a 2003 GNI per capita of $34,510, whereas China achieved only $1,100 and India, $530. One of the world's poorest countries, Mozambique, had a GNI per capita of only $210, while one of the world's richest, Switzerland, came in at $39,880.[30]

However, GNI per person figures can be misleading because they don't consider differences in the cost of living. For example, although the 2003 GNI per capita of Switzerland, at $39,880, exceeded that of the United States, which was $37,610, the higher cost of living in Switzerland meant that U.S. citizens could actually afford more goods and services than Swiss citizens. To account for differences in the cost of living, one can adjust GNI per capita by purchasing power. Referred to as a **purchasing power parity (PPP)** adjustment, it allows for a more direct comparison of living standards in different countries. The base for the adjustment is the cost of living in the United States. The PPP for different countries is then adjusted (up or down) depending upon whether the cost of living is lower or higher than in the United States. For example, in 2003 while the GNI per capita for China was $1,100, the PPP per capita was $4,990, suggesting that the cost of living was lower in China and that $1,100 in China would buy as much as $4,990 in the United States. Table 2.1 gives the GNI per capita measured at PPP in 2003 for a selection of countries, along with their GNI per capita and their growth rate in **gross domestic product (GDP)** from 1993 to 2003. Map 2.2 summarizes the GNI PPP per capita in 2003 for the nations of the world.

As can be seen, there are striking differences in the standard of living. Table 2.1 suggests that the average Indian citizen can afford to consume only 7.7 percent of the goods and services consumed by the average U.S. citizen on a PPP basis. Given this, one might conclude that, despite having a population of 1 billion, India is unlikely to be a very lucrative market for the consumer products produced by many Western international businesses. However, this would be incorrect because India has a fairly wealthy middle class of close to 100 million people, despite its large number of very poor.

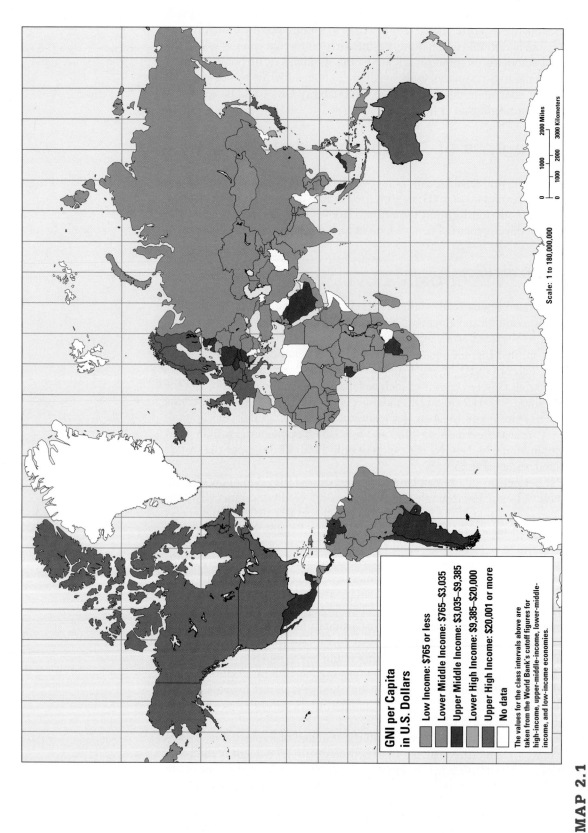

MAP 2.1

Gross National Income per Capita, 2003

**GNI per Capita
in U.S. Dollars**

Low Income: $765 or less
Lower Middle Income: $765–$3,035
Upper Middle Income: $3,035–$9,385
Lower High Income: $9,385–$20,000
Upper High Income: $20,001 or more
No data

The values for the class intervals above are taken from the World Bank's cutoff figures for high-income, upper-middle-income, lower-middle-income, and low-income economies.

Scale: 1 to 180,000,000

0   1000   2000 Miles
0   1000   2000   3000 Kilometers

Source: Data from World Bank, *World Development Indicators Online*, 2003. Reprinted by permission from the International Bank for Reconstruction and Development. © 2001 by the World Bank.

Country	GNI per Capita	GNI PPP per Capita	GDP Growth Rate 1993–2003(%)
Brazil	$2,710	$7,480	2.6%
China	$1,100	$4,990	9.3
Germany	$25,250	$27,460	1.2
India	$530	$2,880	6.1
Japan	$34,510	$28,620	1.2
Nigeria	$320	$900	3.1
Poland	$5,270	$11,450	4.8
Russia	$2,610	$8,920	0.1
Switzerland	$39,880	$32,030	0.9
United Kingdom	$28,350	$27,650	2.8
United States	$37,610	$37,500	3.2

TABLE 2.1

PPP Index and GNI and GDP Data for Selected Countries, 2003

Source: Data from World Bank, *World Development Indicators Online*, 2005.

The GNI and PPP data give a static picture of development. They tell us, for example, that China is much poorer than the United States, but they do not tell us if China is closing the gap. To assess this, we have to look at the economic growth rates achieved by countries. Table 2.1 gives the rate of growth in gross domestic product (GDP) achieved by a number of countries between 1993 and 2003. Map 2.3 summarizes the growth rate in GDP from 1993 to 2003. Although countries such as China and India are currently very poor, their economies are growing more rapidly than those of many advanced nations. Thus, in time they may become advanced nations and be huge markets for the products of international businesses. Given that potential, international businesses might want to get a foothold in these markets now. Even though their current contributions to an international firm's revenues might be small, their future contributions could be much larger.

BROADER CONCEPTIONS OF DEVELOPMENT: AMARTYA SEN

The Nobel Prize–winning economist Amartya Sen has argued that development should be assessed less by material output measures such as GNI per capita and more by the capabilities and opportunities that people enjoy.[31] According to Sen, development should be seen as a process of expanding the real freedoms that people experience. Hence, development requires the removal of major impediments to freedom: poverty as well as tyranny, poor economic opportunities as well as systematic social deprivation, neglect of public facilities as well as the intolerance of repressive states. In Sen's view, development is not just an economic process, but it is a political one too, and to succeed requires the "democratization" of political communities to give citizens a voice in the important decisions made for the community. This perspective leads Sen to emphasize basic health care, especially for children, and basic education, especially for women. Not only are these factors desirable for their instrumental value in helping to achieve higher income levels, but they are also beneficial in their own right. People cannot develop their capabilities if they are chronically ill or woefully ignorant.

Sen's influential thesis has been picked up by the United Nations, which has developed the **Human Development Index (HDI)** to measure the quality of human life in

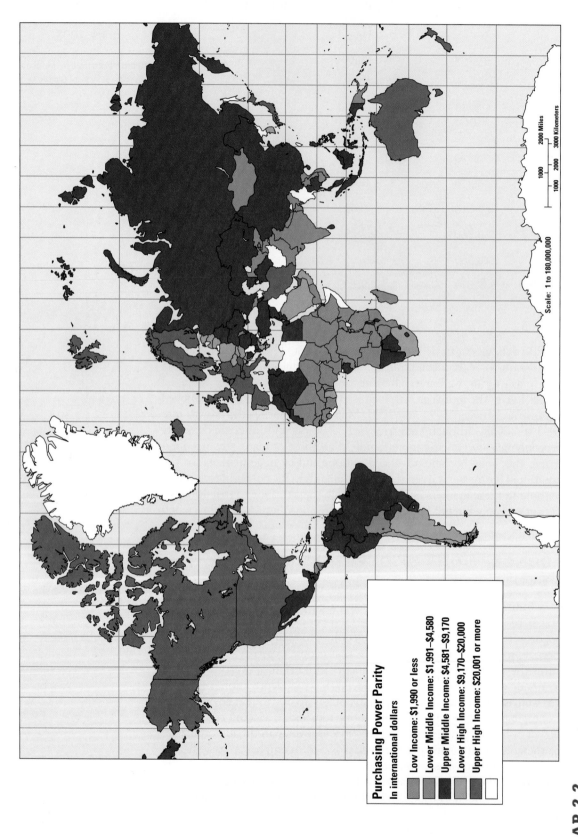

MAP 2.2

Purchasing Power Parity, 2003

Source: Data from World Bank, *World Development Indicators Online*, 2003. Reprinted by permission from the International Bank for Reconstruction and Development. © 2001 by the World Bank.

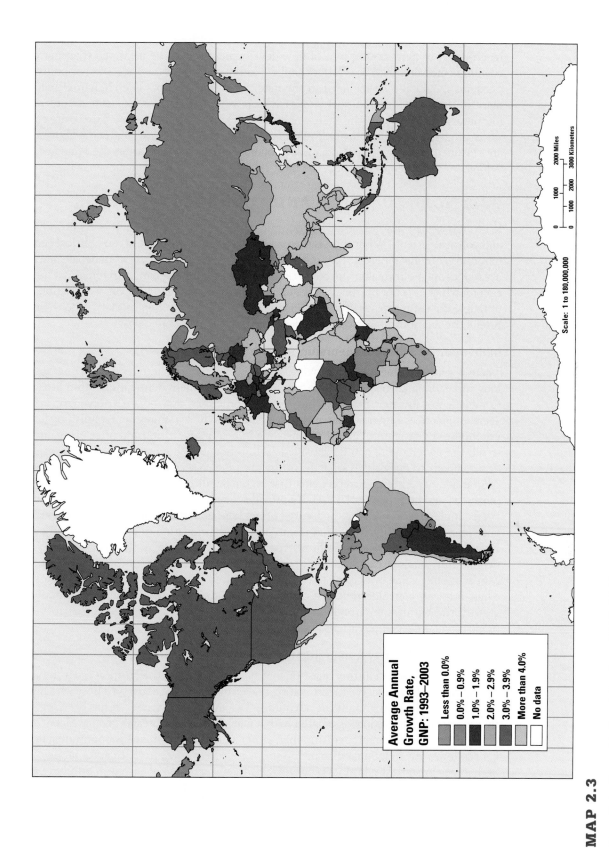

MAP 2.3

Growth in Gross National Product, 1993–2003

Average Annual Growth Rate, GNP: 1993–2003

- Less than 0.0%
- 0.0% – 0.9%
- 1.0% – 1.9%
- 2.0% – 2.9%
- 3.0% – 3.9%
- More than 4.0%
- No data

Scale: 1 to 180,000,000

0   1000   2000   2000 Miles
0   1000   2000   3000 Kilometers

Source: Data from World Bank, *World Development Indicators Online*, 2005. Reprinted by permission from the International Bank for Reconstruction and Development. © 2001 by the World Bank.

different nations. The HDI is based on three measures: life expectancy at birth (which is a function of health care), educational attainment (which is measured by a combination of the adult literacy rate and enrollment in primary, secondary, and tertiary education), and whether average incomes, based on PPP estimates, are sufficient to meet the basic needs of life in a country (adequate food, shelter, and health care). As such, the HDI comes much closer to Sen's conception of how development should be measured than narrow economic measures such as GNI per capita—although Sen's thesis suggests that political freedoms should also be included in the index, and they are not. The Human Development Index is scaled from 0 to 1. Countries scoring less than 0.5 are classified as having low human development (the quality of life is poor), those scoring from 0.5 to 0.8 are classified as having medium human development, while those countries that score above 0.8 are classified as having high human development. Map 2.4 summarizes the Human Development Index scores for 2002, the most recent year for which data are available.

POLITICAL ECONOMY AND ECONOMIC PROGRESS

It is often argued that a country's economic development is a function of its economic and political systems. What then is the nature of the relationship between political economy and economic progress? This question has been the subject of vigorous debate among academics and policymakers for some time. Despite the long debate, this remains a question for which it is not possible to give an unambiguous answer. However, it is possible to untangle the main threads of the arguments and make a few generalizations as to the nature of the relationship between political economy and economic progress.

Innovation and Entrepreneurship Are the Engines of Growth

There is wide agreement that innovation and entrepreneurial activity are the engines of long-run economic growth.[32] Those who make this argument define **innovation** broadly to include not just new products, but also new processes, new organizations, new management practices, and new strategies. Thus, the Toys "R" Us strategy of establishing large warehouse-style toy stores and then engaging in heavy advertising and price discounting to sell the merchandise can be classified as an innovation because Toys "R" Us was the first company to pursue this strategy. Innovation is also seen as the product of entrepreneurial activity. Often, entrepreneurs first commercialize innovative new products and processes, and entrepreneurial activity provides much of the dynamism in an economy. For example, the economy of the United States has benefited greatly from a high level of entrepreneurial activity, which has resulted in rapid innovation in products and process. Firms such as Cisco Systems, Dell, Microsoft, and Oracle were all founded by entrepreneurial individuals to exploit advances in technology, and all these firms created significant economic value by helping to commercialize innovations in products and processes. Thus, one can conclude that if a country's economy is to sustain long-run economic growth, the business environment must be conducive to the consistent production of product and process innovations and to entrepreneurial activity.

Innovation and Entrepreneurship Require a Market Economy

This leads logically to a further question—What is required for the business environment of a country to be conducive to innovation and entrepreneurial activity? Those who have considered this issue highlight the advantages of a market economy.[33] It has been argued that the economic freedom associated with a market economy creates greater incentives for innovation and entrepreneurship than either a planned or a mixed economy. In a market economy, any individual who has an innovative idea is free to try to make money out of that idea by starting a business (by engaging in entrepreneurial activity). Similarly, existing businesses are free to improve their operations through innovation. To the extent that they are successful, both individual entrepreneurs and established businesses can reap rewards in the form of high profits. Thus, market economies contain enormous incentives to develop innovations.

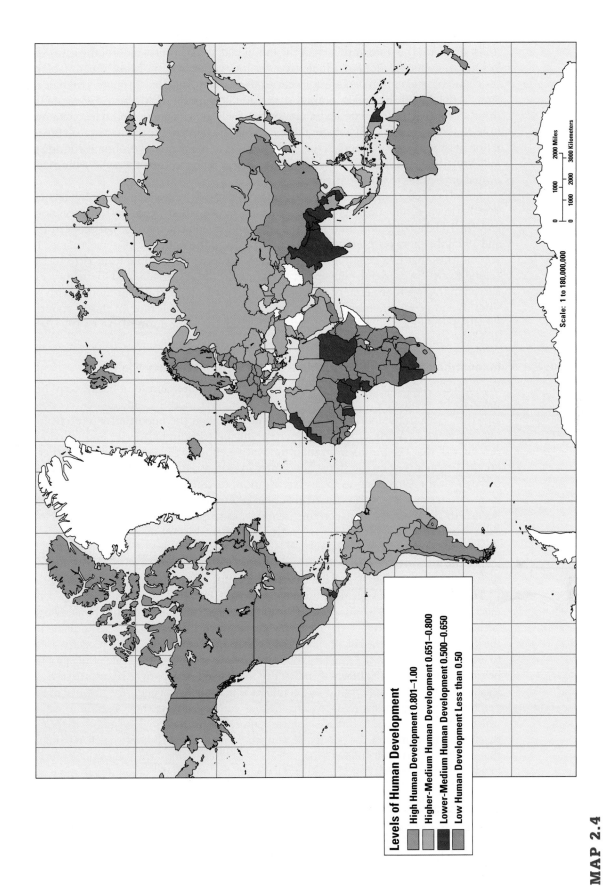

MAP 2.4

The Human Development Index, 2002

Levels of Human Development

High Human Development 0.801–1.00

Higher-Medium Human Development 0.651–0.800

Lower-Medium Human Development 0.500–0.650

Low Human Development Less than 0.50

Scale: 1 to 180,000,000

2000 Miles

3000 Kilometers

Source: Data from United Nations, *Human Development Report, 2004, Human Development Index.*

In a planned economy, the state owns all means of production. Consequently, entre-preneurial individuals have few economic incentives to develop valuable new innovations, since it is the state, rather than the individual, that captures most of the gains. The lack of economic freedom and incentives for innovation was probably a main factor in the economic stagnation of many former communist states and led ultimately to their collapse at the end of the 1980s. Similar stagnation occurred in many mixed economies in those sectors where the state had a monopoly (such as health care and telecommunications in Great Britain). This stagnation provided the impetus for the widespread privatization of state-owned enterprises that we witnessed in many mixed economies during the mid-1980s and is still going on today (privatization refers to the process of selling state-owned enterprises to private investors).

A study of 102 countries over a 20-year period provided evidence of a strong relationship between economic freedom (as provided by a market economy) and economic growth.[34] The study found that the more economic freedom a country had between 1975 and 1995, the more economic growth it achieved and the richer its citizens became. The six countries that had persistently high ratings of economic freedom from 1975 to 1995 (Hong Kong, Switzerland, Singapore, the United States, Canada, and Germany) were also all in the top 10 in terms of economic growth rates. In contrast, no country with persistently low economic freedom achieved a respectable growth rate. In the 16 countries for which the index of economic freedom declined the most during 1975 to 1995, gross domestic product fell at an annual rate of 0.6 percent.

Innovation and Entrepreneurship Require Strong Property Rights

Strong legal protection of property rights is another requirement for a business environment to be conducive to innovation, entrepreneurial activity, and hence economic growth.[35] Both individuals and businesses must be given the opportunity to profit from innovative ideas. Without strong property rights protection, businesses and individuals run the risk that the profits from their innovative efforts will be expropriated, either by criminal elements or by the state. The state can expropriate the profits from innovation through legal means, such as excessive taxation, or through illegal means, such as demands from state bureaucrats for kickbacks in return for granting an individual or firm a license to do business in a certain area (i.e., corruption). According to the Nobel Prize–winning economist Douglass North, throughout history many governments have displayed a tendency to engage in such behavior. Inadequately enforced property rights reduce the incentives for innovation and entrepreneurial activity—since the profits from such activity are "stolen"—and hence reduce the rate of economic growth.

The influential Peruvian development economist Hernando de Soto has argued that much of the developing world will fail to reap the benefits of capitalism until property rights are better defined and protected.[36] De Soto's arguments are interesting because he claims that the key problem is not the risk of expropriation, but the chronic inability of property owners to establish legal title to the property they own. As an example of the scale of the problem, he cites the situation in Haiti where individuals must take 176 steps over 19 years to own land legally. Because most property in poor countries is informally "owned," the absence of legal proof of ownership means that property holders cannot convert their assets into capital, which could then be used to finance business ventures. Banks will not lend money to the poor to start businesses because the poor possess no proof that they own property, such as farmland, that can be used as collateral for a loan. By de Soto's calculations, the total value of real estate held by the poor in Third World and former communist states amounted to more than $9.3 trillion in 2000. If those assets could be converted into capital, the result could be an economic revolution that would allow the poor to bootstrap their way out of poverty.

The Required Political System

Much debate surrounds which kind of political system best achieves a functioning market economy with strong protection for property rights.[37] People in the West tend to associate a representative democracy with a market economic system, strong property rights protection, and economic progress. Building on this, we tend to argue that democracy is good for growth. However, some totalitarian regimes have fostered a market economy and strong property rights protection and have experienced rapid economic growth. Five of the fastest-growing economies of the past 30 years—China, South Korea, Taiwan, Singapore, and Hong Kong—had one thing in common at the start of their economic growth: undemocratic governments! At the same time, countries with stable democratic governments, such as India, experienced sluggish economic growth for long periods. In 1992, Lee Kuan Yew, Singapore's leader for many years, told an audience, "I do not believe that democracy necessarily leads to development. I believe that a country needs to develop discipline more than democracy. The exuberance of democracy leads to undisciplined and disorderly conduct which is inimical to development."[38]

However, those who argue for the value of a totalitarian regime miss an important point: If dictators made countries rich, then much of Africa, Asia, and Latin America should have been growing rapidly during 1960 to 1990, and this was not the case. Only a totalitarian regime that is committed to a free market system and strong protection of property rights is capable of promoting economic growth. Also, there is no guarantee that a dictatorship will continue to pursue such progressive policies. Dictators are rarely so benevolent. Many are tempted to use the apparatus of the state to further their own private ends, violating property rights and stalling economic growth. Given this, it seems likely that democratic regimes are far more conducive to long-term economic growth than are dictatorships, even benevolent ones. Only in a well-functioning, mature democracy are property rights truly secure.[39] Nor should we forget Amartya Sen's arguments that we reviewed earlier. Totalitarian states, by limiting human freedom, also suppress human development and therefore are detrimental to progress.

Economic Progress Begets Democracy

While it is possible to argue that democracy is not a necessary precondition for a free market economy in which property rights are protected, subsequent economic growth often leads to establishment of a democratic regime. Several of the fastest-growing Asian economies adopted more democratic governments during the past two decades, including South Korea and Taiwan. Thus, while democracy may not always be the cause of initial economic progress, it seems to be one consequence of that progress.

A strong belief that economic progress leads to adoption of a democratic regime underlies the fairly permissive attitude that many Western governments have adopted toward human rights violations in China. Although China has a totalitarian government in which human rights are violated, many Western countries have been hesitant to criticize the country too much for fear that this might hamper the country's march toward a free market system. The belief is that once China has a free market system, greater individual freedoms and democracy will follow. Whether this optimistic vision comes to pass remains to be seen.

GEOGRAPHY, EDUCATION, AND ECONOMIC DEVELOPMENT

While a country's political and economic systems are probably the big locomotive driving its rate of economic development, other factors are also important. One that has received attention recently is geography.[40] But the belief that geography can influence economic policy, and hence economic growth rates, goes back to Adam Smith. The influential Harvard University economist Jeffrey Sachs argues

> that throughout history, coastal states, with their long engagements in international trade, have been more supportive of market institutions than landlocked states, which have tended to organize themselves as hierarchical (and often military) societies. Mountainous states, as a result of physical isolation, have often neglected market-based trade. Temperate climes have generally supported higher densities of population and thus a more extensive division of labor than tropical regions.[41]

Sachs's point is that by virtue of favorable geography, certain societies were more likely to engage in trade than others and were thus more likely to be open to and develop market-based economic systems, which in turn would promote faster economic growth. He also argues that, irrespective of the economic and political institutions a country adopts, adverse geographical conditions, such as the high rate of disease, poor soils, and hostile climate that afflict many tropical countries, can have a negative impact on development. Together with colleagues at Harvard's Institute for International Development, Sachs tested for the impact of geography on a country's economic growth rate between 1965 and 1990. He found that landlocked countries grew more slowly than coastal economies and that being entirely landlocked reduced a country's growth rate by roughly 0.7 percent per year. He also found that tropical countries grew 1.3 percent more slowly each year than countries in the temperate zone.

Education emerges as another important determinant of economic development (a point that Amartya Sen emphasizes). The general assertion is that nations that invest more in education will have higher growth rates because an educated population is a more productive population. Anecdotal comparisons suggest this is true. In 1960 Pakistanis and South Koreans were on equal footing economically. However, just 30 percent of Pakistani children were enrolled in primary schools, while 94 percent of South Koreans were. By the mid-1980s, South Korea's GNP per person was three times that of Pakistan's.[42] A survey of 14 statistical studies that looked at the relationship between a country's investment in education and its subsequent growth rates concluded investment in education did have a positive and statistically significant impact on a country's rate of economic growth.[43] Similarly, the work by Sachs discussed above suggests that investments in education help explain why some countries in Southeast Asia, such as Indonesia, Malaysia, and Singapore, have been able to overcome the disadvantages associated with their tropical geography and grow far more rapidly than tropical nations in Africa and Latin America.

States in Transition

The political economy of many of the world's nation-states has changed radically since the late 1980s. Two trends have been evident. First, during the late 1980s and early 1990s, a wave of democratic revolutions swept the world. Totalitarian governments collapsed and were replaced by democratically elected governments that were typically more committed to free market capitalism than their predecessors had been. Second, there has been a strong move away from centrally planned and mixed economies and toward a more free market economic model. We shall look first at the spread of democracy and then turn our attention to the spread of free market economics.

THE SPREAD OF DEMOCRACY

One notable development of the past 15 years has been the spread of democracy (and, by extension, the decline of totalitarianism). Map 2.5 reports on the extent of totalitarianism in the world as determined by Freedom House.[44] This map charts political freedom in 2004, grouping countries into three broad groupings, free, partly free, and not free. In "free" countries, citizens enjoy a high degree of political and civil freedoms. "Partly free" countries are characterized by some restrictions on political rights and civil liberties, often in the context of corruption, weak rule of law, ethnic strife, or civil war. In "not free" countries, the political process is tightly controlled and basic freedoms are denied.

In its 2005 report, Freedom House classified some 89 countries as free, accounting for some 44 percent of the world's population. These countries respect a broad range of political rights. Another 54 countries accounting for 19 percent of the world's population were classified as partly free, while 49 countries representing some 37 percent of the world's population were classified as not free. The number of democracies in the world has increased

MAP 2.5

Political Freedom, 2004

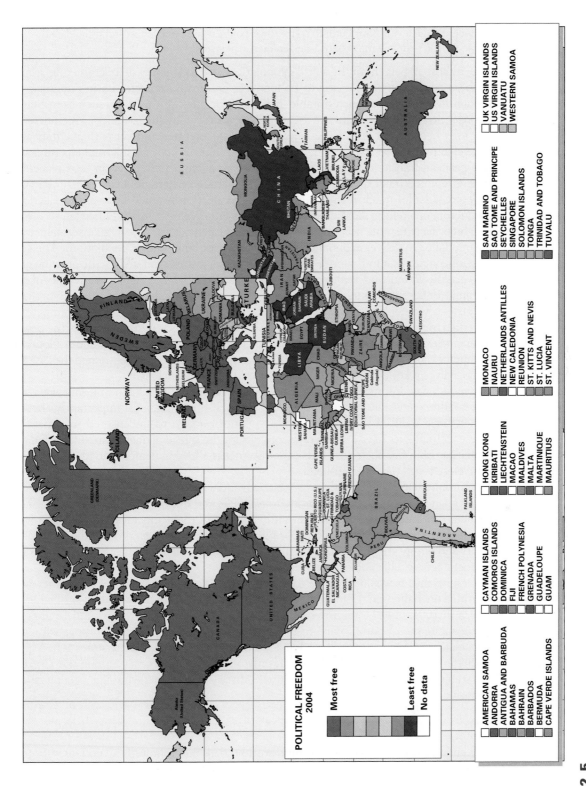

POLITICAL FREEDOM
2004

Most free

Least free

No data

AMERICAN SAMOA
ANDORRA
ANTIGUA AND BARBUDA
BAHAMAS
BAHRAIN
BARBADOS
BERMUDA
CAPE VERDE ISLANDS

CAYMAN ISLANDS
COMOROS ISLANDS
DOMINICA
FIJI
FRENCH POLYNESIA
GRENADA
GUADELOUPE
GUAM

HONG KONG
KIRIBATI
LIECHTENSTEIN
MACAO
MALDIVES
MALTA
MARTINIQUE
MAURITIUS

MONACO
NAURU
NETHERLANDS ANTILLES
NEW CALEDONIA
REUNION
ST. KITTS AND NEVIS
ST. LUCIA
ST. VINCENT

SAN MARINO
SAO TOME AND PRINCIPE
SEYCHELLES
SINGAPORE
SOLOMON ISLANDS
TONGA
TRINIDAD AND TOBAGO
TUVALU

UK VIRGIN ISLANDS
US VIRGIN ISLANDS
VANUATU
WESTERN SAMOA

Source: Map data from Freedom House, *Freedom in the World 2005: The Annual Survey of Political Rights and Civil Liberties.* www.freedomhouse.org. Reprinted with permission.

from 69 nations in 1987 to 119 in 2004. But not all democracies are free, according to Freedom House, because some democracies still restrict certain political and civil liberties. For example, in 2004 Russia was rated "not free." According to Freedom House:

> Russia's step backwards into the Not Free category is the culmination of a growing trend under President Vladimir Putin to concentrate political authority, harass and intimidate the media, and politicize the country's law-enforcement system.[45]

Still, almost 50 percent of the world's population now lives under democratic rule. Many of these newer democracies are to be found in Eastern Europe and Latin America, although there also have been notable gains in Africa during this time, such as in South Africa. Entrants into the ranks of the world's democracies include Mexico, which held its first fully free and fair presidential election in 2000 after free and fair parliamentary and state elections in 1997 and 1998; Senegal, where free and fair presidential elections led to a peaceful transfer of power; Yugoslavia, where a democratic election took place despite attempted fraud by the incumbent; and Ukraine, where popular unrest following widespread ballot fraud in the 2004 presidential election resulted in a second election, the victory of a reform candidate, and a marked improvement in civil liberties.

Three main reasons account for the spread of democracy.[46] First, many totalitarian regimes failed to deliver economic progress to the vast bulk of their populations. The collapse of communism in Eastern Europe, for example, was precipitated by the growing gulf between the vibrant and wealthy economies of the West and the stagnant economies of the Communist East. In looking for alternatives to the socialist model, the populations of these countries could not have failed to notice that most of the world's strongest economies were governed by representative democracies. Today, the economic success of many of the newer democracies, such as Poland and the Czech Republic in the former Communist bloc, the Philippines and Taiwan in Asia, and Chile in Latin America, has strengthened the case for democracy as a key component of successful economic advancement.

Second, new information and communication technologies, including shortwave radio, satellite television, fax machines, desktop publishing, and, most importantly, the Internet, have reduced the state's ability to control access to uncensored information. These technologies have created new conduits for the spread of democratic ideals and information from free societies. Today the Internet is allowing democratic ideals to penetrate closed societies as never before.[47]

Third, in many countries the economic advances of the past quarter century have led to the emergence of increasingly prosperous middle and working classes who have pushed for democratic reforms. This was certainly a factor in the democratic transformation of South Korea. Entrepreneurs and other business leaders, eager to protect their property rights and ensure the dispassionate enforcement of contracts, are another force pressing for more accountable and open government.

Despite this, it would be naive to conclude that the global spread of democracy will continue unchallenged. Democracy is still rare in large parts of the world. In sub-Saharan Africa in 2004, only 11 countries are considered free, 21 are partly free, and 16 are not free. Among the 27 post-Communist countries in Eastern and Central Europe, 8 are still not electoral democracies and Freedom House classifies only 12 of these states as free (primarily in Eastern Europe). And there is only one partial democracy among the 16 Arabic states of the Middle East and North Africa—Iraq—where foreign occupiers are imposing a democratic system.

THE NEW WORLD ORDER AND GLOBAL TERRORISM

The end of the Cold War and the "new world order" that followed the collapse of communism in Eastern Europe and the former Soviet Union, taken together with the demise of many authoritarian regimes in Latin America, have given rise to intense speculation about the future shape of global geopolitics. Author Francis Fukuyama has argued, "We may be witnessing . . . the end of history as such: that is, the end point of mankind's ideological evolution and the universalization of Western liberal democracy as the final form of human government."[48] Fukuyama goes on to say that the war of ideas may be at an end and that liberal democracy has triumphed.

Others question Fukuyama's vision of a more harmonious world dominated by a universal civilization characterized by democratic regimes and free market capitalism. In a controversial book, the influential political scientist Samuel Huntington argues that there is no "universal" civilization based on widespread acceptance of Western liberal democratic ideals.[49] Huntington maintains that while many societies may be modernizing—they are adopting the material paraphernalia of the modern world, from automobiles to Coca-Cola and MTV—they are not becoming more Western. On the contrary, Huntington theorizes that modernization in non-Western societies can result in a retreat toward the traditional, such as the resurgence of Islam in many traditionally Muslim societies. He writes:

> The Islamic resurgence is both a product of and an effort to come to grips with modernization. Its underlying causes are those generally responsible for indigenization trends in non-Western societies: urbanization, social mobilization, higher levels of literacy and education, intensified communication and media consumption, and expanded interaction with Western and other cultures. These developments undermine traditional village and clan ties and create alienation and an identity crisis. Islamist symbols, commitments, and beliefs meet these psychological needs, and Islamist welfare organizations, the social, cultural, and economic needs of Muslims caught in the process of modernization. Muslims feel a need to return to Islamic ideas, practices, and institutions to provide the compass and the motor of modernization.[50]

Thus, the rise of Islamic fundamentalism is portrayed as a response to the alienation produced by modernization.

In contrast to Fukuyama, Huntington sees a world that is split into different civilizations, each of which has its own value systems and ideology. In addition to Western civilization, Huntington predicts the emergence of strong Islamic and Sinic (Chinese) civilizations, as well as civilizations based on Japan, Africa, Latin America, Eastern Orthodox Christianity (Russian), and Hinduism (Indian). Huntington also sees the civilizations as headed for conflict, particularly along the "fault lines" that separate them, such as Bosnia (where Muslims and Orthodox Christians have clashed), Kashmir (where Muslims and Hindus clash), and the Sudan (where a bloody war between Christians and Muslims has persisted for decades). Huntington predicts conflict between the West and Islam and between the West and China. He bases his predictions on an analysis of the different value systems and ideology of these civilizations, which in his view tend to bring them into conflict with each other. While some commentators originally dismissed Huntington's thesis, in the aftermath of the terrorist attacks on the United States on September 11, 2001, Huntington's views received new attention.

If Huntington's views are even partly correct—and there is little doubt that the events surrounding September 11 added more weight to his thesis—they have important implications for international business. They suggest many countries may be increasingly difficult places in which to do business, either because they are shot through with violent conflicts or because they are part of a civilization that is in conflict with an enterprise's home country. Huntington's views are speculative and controversial. It is not clear that his predictions will come to pass. More likely is the evolution of a global political system that is positioned somewhere between Fukuyama's universal global civilization based on liberal democratic ideals and Huntington's vision of a fractured world. That would still be a world, however, in which geopolitical forces periodically limit the ability of business enterprises to operate in certain foreign countries.

In Huntington's thesis, global terrorism is a product of the tension between civilizations and the clash of value systems and ideology. Others point to terrorism's roots in long-standing conflicts that seem to defy political resolution, the Palestinian, Kashmir, and Northern Ireland conflicts being the most obvious examples. It should also be noted that a substantial amount of terrorist activity in some parts of the world, such as Colombia, has been interwoven with the illegal drug trade. In any event, the attacks of September 11, 2001, created the impression that global terror is on the rise. As former U.S. Secretary of State Colin Powell has maintained, terrorism represents one of the major threats to world

FIGURE 2.3

Total International
Terrorist Attacks,
1981–2003

Source: U.S. Department of
State, *Patterns of Global
Terrorism, 2003*, June 2004.

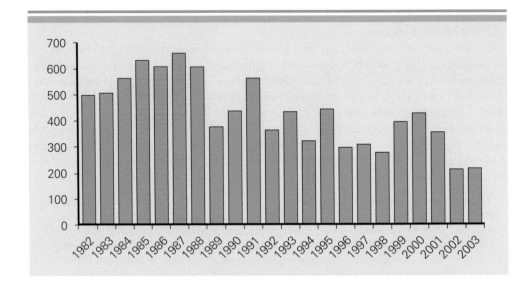

peace and economic progress in the 21st century. However, the vivid and horrific events of September 11, 2001, and the fact that they took place on U.S. soil, may have unduly shaped our perspective of a phenomenon that has long been with us. According to data from the U.S. Department of State, the number of terrorist attacks worldwide was substantially higher in the late 1980s than in recent years (see Figure 2.3). There were, for example, 665 terrorist incidents worldwide in 1987 and 208 in 2004.[54] This is not to deny the psychological and economic shock of the events of September 11, to say nothing of the tragic loss of human life, or the serious threat posed by the combination of determined and sophisticated terrorists, rogue states, and weapons of mass destruction. But it reminds us that global terrorism has long been with us, and it has not yet derailed global trends toward greater political and economic freedom, nor should it.

THE SPREAD OF MARKET-BASED SYSTEMS

Paralleling the spread of democracy since the 1980s has been the transformation from centrally planned command economies to market-based economies. More than 30 countries that were in the former Soviet Union or the Eastern European Communist bloc have changed their economic systems. A complete list of countries where change is now occurring also would include Asian states such as China and Vietnam, as well as African countries such as Angola, Ethiopia, and Mozambique.[52] There has been a similar shift away from a mixed economy. Many states in Asia, Latin America, and Western Europe have sold state-owned businesses to private investors (privatization) and deregulated their economies to promote greater competition.

The rationale for economic transformation has been the same the world over. In general, command and mixed economies failed to deliver the kind of sustained economic performance that was achieved by countries adopting market-based systems, such as the United States, Switzerland, Hong Kong, and Taiwan. As a consequence, even more states have gravitated toward the market-based model. Map 2.6, based on data from the Heritage Foundation, a politically conservative U.S. research foundation, gives some idea of the degree to which the world has shifted toward market-based economic systems. The Heritage Foundation's index of economic freedom is based on 10 indicators, such as the extent to which the government intervenes in the economy, trade policy, the degree to which property rights are protected, foreign investment regulations, and taxation rules. A country can score between 1 (most free) and 5 (least free) on each of these indicators. The lower a country's average score across all 10 indicators, the more closely its economy represents the pure market model. According to the 2005 index, which is summarized in

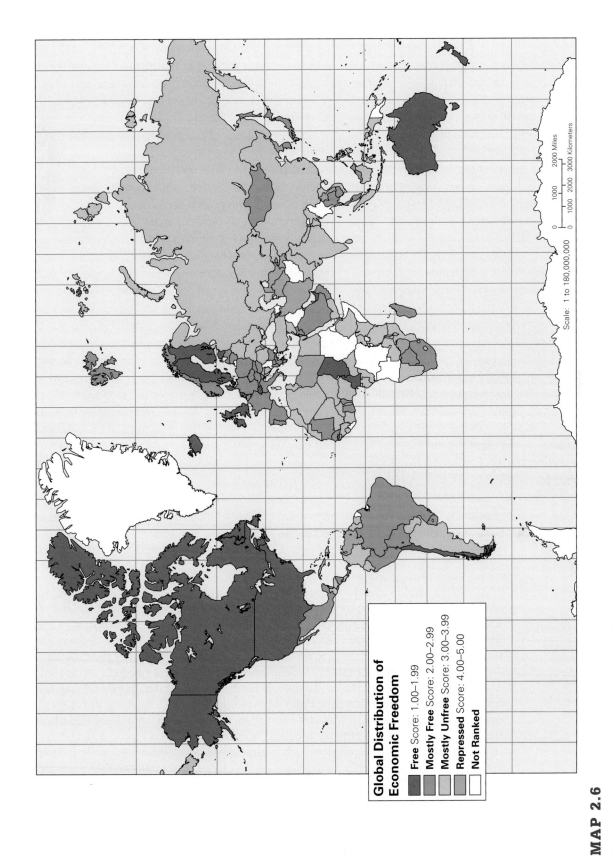

Global Distribution of Economic Freedom

- Free Score: 1.00–1.99
- Mostly Free Score: 2.00–2.99
- Mostly Unfree Score: 3.00–3.99
- Repressed Score: 4.00–5.00
- Not Ranked

Scale: 1 to 180,000,000

0   1000   2000   2000 Miles

0   1000   2000   3000 Kilometers

MAP 2.6

Distribution of Economic Freedom, 2005

Source: Data from Heritage Foundation, 2005 *Index of Economic Freedom*, www.heritage.org. Reprinted with permission.

COUNTRY FOCUS

After gaining independence from Britain in 1947, India adopted a democratic system of government. The economic system that developed in India after 1947 was a mixed economy characterized by a large number of state-owned enterprises (of which there were almost 300 in 1991), centralized planning, and subsidies. This system constrained the growth of the private sector. Private companies could expand only with government permission. Under this system, dubbed the "License Raj," private companies often had to wait months for government approval of routine business activities, such as expanding production or hiring a new director. It could take years to get permission to diversify into a new product. Much of heavy industry, such as auto, chemical, and steel production, was reserved for state-owned enterprises. Production quotas and high tariffs on imports also stunted the development of a healthy private sector, as did restrictive labor laws that made it difficult to fire employees. Access to foreign exchange was limited, investment by foreign firms was severely restricted, land use was strictly controlled, and the government routinely managed prices as opposed to letting them be set by market forces.

By the early 1990s, it was clear that this system was incapable of delivering the kind of economic progress that many Southeastern Asian nations had started to enjoy. In 1994, India's economy was still smaller than Belgium's, despite having a population of 950 million. Its GDP per capita was a paltry $310; less than half the population could read; only 6 million had access to telephones; only 14 percent had access to clean sanitation; the World Bank estimated that some 40 percent of the world's desperately poor lived in India; and only 2.3 percent of the population had a household income in excess of $2,484.

In 1991, the lack of progress led the government to embark on an ambitious economic reform program. Much of the industrial licensing system was dismantled, and several areas once closed to the private sector were opened, including electricity generation, parts of the oil industry, steelmaking, air transport, and some areas of the telecommunications industry. Investment by foreign companies, formerly allowed only grudgingly and subject to arbitrary ceilings, was suddenly welcomed. Approval was made automatic for foreign equity stakes of up to 51 percent in an Indian enterprise, and 100 percent foreign ownership was allowed under certain circumstances. Raw materials and many industrial goods could be freely imported and the maximum tariff that could be levied on imports was reduced from 400 percent to 65 percent. The top income tax rate was also reduced, and corporate tax fell from 57.5 percent to 46 percent in 1994, and then to 35 percent in 1997.

The government also announced plans to start privatizing India's state-owned businesses, some 40 percent of which were losing money in the early 1990s. India's privatization program has had a bumpy record and was often slowed by political opposition; in 1999 some

Map 2.6, the world's freest economies are (in rank order) Hong Kong, Singapore, Luxembourg, Estonia, Ireland, New Zealand, United Kingdom, Denmark, and Iceland. The United States was ranked 12; Japan at 39; France at 44; Mexico, 63; Brazil, 90; China, 112; India, 118; and Russia, 124. The economies of Cuba, Laos, Iraq, Zimbabwe, Turkmenistan, Myanmar; and North Korea are to be found at the bottom of the rankings.[53]

Economic freedom does not necessarily equate with political freedom, as detailed in Map 2.6. For example, 3 of the top 16 states in the Heritage Foundation index, Hong Kong, Singapore, and Bahrain, cannot be classified as politically free. Hong Kong was reabsorbed into Communist China in 1997, and the first thing Beijing did was shut down Hong Kong's freely elected legislature. Singapore is ranked as only partly free on Freedom House's index of political freedom due to practices such as widespread press censorship, while Bahrain is classified as least free due to the monopolization of political power by a hereditary monarchy.

THE NATURE OF ECONOMIC TRANSFORMATION

The shift toward a market-based economic system often entails a number of steps: deregulation, privatization, and creation of a legal system to safeguard property rights.[54]

www.mhhe.com/hill

240 state-owned enterprises were still scattered across many sectors of the economy and accounted for 15 percent of India's gross domestic product. But the program was progressing at a fairly rapid pace in the early 2000s with 30 state-owned enterprises privatized in 2002 alone.

Judged by some measures, the response to these economic reforms has been impressive. The economy expanded at an annual rate of about 6.1 percent from 1994 to 2004. Foreign investment, a key indicator of how attractive foreign companies thought the Indian economy was, jumped from $150 million in 1991 to $4.3 billion in 2003. Some economic sectors have done particularly well, such as the information technology sector where India has emerged as a vibrant global center for software development. The export revenue of India's software services market exceeded $7 billion in 2003, up from less than $500 million in the mid-1990s. In pharmaceuticals, Indian companies are emerging as credible players on the global marketplace, primarily by selling low-cost, generic versions of drugs that have come off patent in the developed world. In 2003, India exported $1.4 billion of pharmaceuticals, up from $330 million in 1998.

However, the country still has a long way to go. Attempts to further reduce import tariffs have been stalled by political opposition from employers, employees, and politicians, who fear that if barriers come down, a flood of inexpensive Chinese products will enter India. The privatization program continues to hit speed bumps—the latest in September 2003 when the Indian Supreme Court ruled that the government could not privatize two state-owned oil companies without explicit approval from the parliament. There has also been strong resistance to reforming many of India's laws that make it difficult for private business to operate efficiently. For example, labor laws make it almost impossible for firms with more than 100 employees to fire workers. Other laws mandate that certain products can be manufactured only by small companies, effectively making it impossible for companies in these industries to attain the scale required to compete internationally.

Also, a decade of reform has done little to solve India's crippling poverty problem. Although the Indian middle class grew richer during the 1990s, some 40 percent of India's nearly 1 billion people still live in abject poverty, earning less than $1 a day. By 2003, the country's gross national income per capita was still only $530; 44 percent of the adult population was illiterate; 19 percent had no access to safe water supplies; 25 percent had no access to health services; 71 percent had no access to sanitation; and 15 percent of the population was not expected to survive to age 40!

Sources: "A Survey of India: The Tiger Steps Out," *The Economist*, January 21, 1995; P. Moore, "Three Steps Forward," *Euromoney*, September 1997, pp. 190–95; "India's Breakthrough Budget?" *The Economist*, March 3, 2001; Shankar Aiyar, "Reforms: Time to Just Do It," *India Today*, January 24, 2000, p. 47; "America's Pain, India's Gain," *The Economist*, January 11, 2003, p. 57; Joanna Slater, "In Once Socialist India, Privatizations Are Becoming More Like Routine Matters," *The Wall Street Journal*, July 5, 2002, p. A8; "India's Economy: Ready to Roll Again?" *The Economist*, September 20, 2003, pp. 39–40; Joanna Slater, "Indian Pirates Turned Partners," *The Wall Street Journal*, November 13, 2003, p. A14; and United Nations, *Human Development Report, 2004*.

Deregulation

Deregulation involves removing legal restrictions to the free play of markets, the establishment of private enterprises, and the manner in which private enterprises operate. Before the collapse of communism, the governments in most command economies exercised tight control over prices and output, setting both through detailed state planning. They also prohibited private enterprises from operating in most sectors of the economy, severely restricted direct investment by foreign enterprises, and limited international trade. Deregulation in these cases involved removing price controls, thereby allowing prices to be set by the interplay between demand and supply; abolishing laws regulating the establishment and operation of private enterprises; and relaxing or removing restrictions on direct investment by foreign enterprises and international trade.

In mixed economies, the role of the state was more limited, but here too, in certain sectors the state set prices, owned businesses, limited private enterprise, restricted investment by foreigners, and restricted international trade (for an example, see the Country Focus on India). For these countries, deregulation has involved the same kind of initiatives that we have seen in former command economies, although the transformation has been easier because these countries often had a vibrant private sector.

Privatization

Hand in hand with deregulation has come a sharp increase in privatization. **Privatization** transfers the ownership of state property into the hands of private individuals, frequently by the sale of state assets through an auction.[55] Privatization is seen as a way to stimulate gains in economic efficiency by giving new private owners a powerful incentive—the reward of greater profits—to search for increases in productivity, to enter new markets, and to exit losing ones.[56]

The privatization movement started in Great Britain in the early 1980s when then Prime Minister Margaret Thatcher started to sell state-owned assets such as the British telephone company, British Telecom (BT). In a pattern that has been repeated around the world, this sale was linked with the deregulation of the British telecommunications industry. By allowing other firms to compete head-to-head with BT, deregulation ensured that privatization did not simply replace a state-owned monopoly with a private monopoly. Since the 1980s, privatization has become a worldwide phenomenon. Perhaps the most dramatic privatization programs have occurred in the economies of the former Soviet Union and its Eastern European satellite states. In the Czech Republic, three-quarters of all state-owned enterprises were privatized between 1989 and 1996, helping to push the share of gross domestic product accounted for by the private sector up from 11 percent in 1989 to 60 percent in 1995. In Russia, where the private sector had been almost completely repressed before 1989, 50 percent of GDP was in private hands by 1995, again much as a result of privatization. And in Poland the private sector accounted for 59 percent of GDP in 1995, up from 20 percent in 1989.[57]

As privatization has proceeded around the world, it has become clear that simply selling state-owned assets to private investors is not enough to guarantee economic growth. Studies of privatization in central Europe have shown that the process often fails to deliver predicted benefits if the newly privatized firms continue to receive subsidies from the state and if they are protected from foreign competition by barriers to international trade and foreign direct investment.[58] In such cases, the newly privatized firms are sheltered from competition and continue acting like state monopolies. When these circumstances prevail, the newly privatized entities often have little incentive to restructure their operations to become more efficient. For privatization to work, it must also be accompanied by a more general deregulation and opening of the economy. Thus, when Brazil decided to privatize the state-owned telephone monopoly, Telebras Brazil, the government also split the company into four independent units that were to compete with each other and removed barriers to foreign direct investment in telecommunications services. This action ensured that the newly privatized entities would face significant competition and thus would have to improve their operating efficiency to survive.

The ownership structure of newly privatized firms also is important.[59] Many former command economies, for example, lack the legal regulations regarding corporate governance that are found in advanced Western economies. In advanced market economies, boards of directors are appointed by shareholders to make sure managers consider the interests of shareholders when making decisions and try to manage the firm in a manner that is consistent with maximizing the wealth of shareholders. However, some former Communist states lack laws requiring corporations to establish effective boards. In such cases, managers with a small ownership stake can often gain control over the newly privatized entity and run it for their own benefit, while ignoring the interests of other shareholders. Sometimes these managers are the same Communist bureaucrats who ran the enterprise before privatization. Because they have been schooled in the old ways of doing things, they often hesitate to take drastic action to increase the efficiency of the enterprise. Instead, they continue to run the firm as a private fiefdom, seeking to extract whatever economic value they can for their own betterment (in the form of perks that are not reported) while doing little to increase the economic efficiency of the enterprise so that shareholders benefit. Such developments seem less likely to occur, however, if a foreign investor takes a stake in the newly privatized entity. The foreign investor, who usually is a major provider of capital, is often able to use control over a critical resource (money) to push through needed change.

Legal Systems

As noted earlier in this chapter, a well-functioning market economy requires laws protecting private property rights and providing mechanisms for contract enforcement. Without a legal system that protects property rights, and without the machinery to enforce that system, the incentive to engage in economic activity can be reduced substantially by private and public entities, including organized crime, that expropriate the profits generated by the efforts of private-sector entrepreneurs. When communism collapsed, many of these countries lacked the legal structure required to protect property rights, all property having been held by the state. Although many nations have made big strides toward instituting the required system, it will be many more years before the legal system is functioning as smoothly as it does in the West. For example, in most Eastern European nations, the title to urban and agricultural property is often uncertain because of incomplete and inaccurate records, multiple pledges on the same property, and unsettled claims resulting from demands for restitution from owners in the pre-Communist era. Also, while most countries have improved their commercial codes, institutional weaknesses still undermine contract enforcement. Court capacity is often inadequate, and procedures for resolving contract disputes out of court are often lacking or poorly developed.[60]

IMPLICATIONS OF CHANGING POLITICAL ECONOMY

The global changes in political and economic systems discussed above have several implications for international business. The long-standing ideological conflict between collectivism and individualism that defined the 20th century is less in evidence today. The West won the Cold War, and Western ideology has never been more widespread than it is now. Although command economies remain and totalitarian dictatorships can still be found around the world, the tide has been running in favor of free markets and democracy.

The implications for business are enormous. For nearly 50 years, half of the world was off-limits to Western businesses. Now all that is changing. Many of the national markets of Eastern Europe, Latin America, Africa, and Asia may still be undeveloped and impoverished, but they are potentially enormous. With a population of more than 1.2 billion, the Chinese market alone is potentially bigger than that of the United States, the European Union, and Japan combined. Similarly India, with its nearly 1 billion people, is a potentially huge future market. Latin America has another 400 million potential consumers. It is unlikely that China, Russia, Vietnam, or any of the other states now moving toward a free market system will attain the living standards of the West soon. Nevertheless, the upside potential is so large that companies need to consider making inroads now.

However, just as the potential gains are large, so are the risks. There is no guarantee that democracy will thrive in many of the world's newer democratic states, particularly if these states have to grapple with severe economic setbacks. Totalitarian dictatorships could return, although they are unlikely to be of the communist variety. Although the bipolar world of the Cold War era has vanished, it may be replaced by a multipolar world dominated by a number of civilizations. In such a world, much of the economic promise inherent in the global shift toward market-based economic systems may stall in the face of conflicts between civilizations. While the long-term potential for economic gain from investment in the world's new market economies is large, the risks associated with any such investment are also substantial. It would be foolish to ignore these.

IMPLICATIONS FOR MANAGERS

The material discussed in this chapter has two broad implications for international business. First, the political, economic, and legal systems of a country raise important ethical issues that have implications for the practice of international business. For example, what ethical implications are associated with doing business in totalitarian countries where citizens are denied basic human rights, corruption is rampant, and bribes are necessary to gain permission to do business? Is it right to operate in such a setting? A full discussion of the ethical implications of country differences in political economy is reserved for Chapter 4, where we explore ethics in international business in much greater depth.

Second, the political, economic, and legal environment of a country clearly influences the attractiveness of that country as a market and/or investment site. The benefits, costs, and risks associated with doing business in a country are a function of that country's political, economic, and legal systems. The overall attractiveness of a country as a market and/or investment site depends on balancing the likely long-term benefits of doing business in that country against the likely costs and risks. Below we consider the determinants of benefits, costs, and risks.

BENEFITS

In the most general sense, the long-run monetary benefits of doing business in a country are a function of the size of the market, the present wealth (purchasing power) of consumers in that market, and the likely future wealth of consumers. While some markets are very large when measured by number of consumers (e.g., China and India), low living standards may imply limited purchasing power and therefore a relatively small market when measured in economic terms. International businesses need to be aware of this distinction, but they also need to keep in mind the likely future prospects of a country. In 1960 South Korea was viewed as just another impoverished Third World nation. By 2003 it was the world's 11th largest economy, measured in terms of GDP. International firms that recognized South Korea's potential in 1960 and began to do business in that country may have reaped greater benefits than those that wrote off South Korea.

By identifying and investing early in a potential future economic star, international firms may build brand loyalty and gain experience in that country's business practices. These will pay back substantial dividends if that country achieves sustained high economic growth rates. In contrast, late entrants may find that they lack the brand loyalty and experience necessary to achieve a significant presence in the market. In the language of business strategy, early entrants into potential future economic stars may be able to reap substantial first-mover advantages, while late entrants may fall victim to late-mover disadvantages.[61] (**First-mover advantages** are the advantages that accrue to early entrants into a market. **Late-mover disadvantages** are the handicap that late entrants might suffer.) This kind of reasoning has been driving significant inward investment into China, which may become the world's largest economy by 2020 if it continues growing at current rates (China is already the world's sixth largest economy). For more than a decade, China has been the largest recipient of foreign direct investment in the developing world as international businesses ranging from General Motors and Volkswagen to Coca-Cola and Unilever try to establish a sustainable advantage in this nation.

A country's economic system and property rights regime are reasonably good predictors of economic prospects. Countries with free market economies in which property rights are protected tend to achieve greater economic growth rates than command economies and/or economies where property rights are poorly protected. It follows that a country's economic system, property rights regime, and market size (in terms of population) probably constitute reasonably good indicators of the potential long-run benefits of doing business in a country. In contrast, countries where property rights are not well respected and where corruption is rampant tend to have lower levels of economic growth.

COSTS

A number of political, economic, and legal factors determine the costs of doing business in a country. With regard to political factors, the costs of doing business in a country can be increased by a need to pay off the politically powerful to be allowed by the government to do business. The need to pay what are essentially bribes is greater in closed totalitarian states than in open democratic societies where politicians are held accountable by the electorate (although this is not a hard-and-fast distinction). Whether a company should actually pay bribes in return for market access should be determined on the basis of the legal and ethical implications of such action. We discuss this consideration in Chapter 4, when we look closely at the issue of business ethics.

With regard to economic factors, one of the most important variables is the sophistication of a country's economy. It may be more costly to do business in relatively primitive or undeveloped economies because of the lack of infrastructure and supporting businesses. At the extreme, an international firm may have to provide its own infrastructure and supporting business, which obviously raises costs. When McDonald's decided to open its first restaurant in Moscow, it found that to serve food and drink indistinguishable from that served in McDonald's restaurants elsewhere, it had to vertically integrate backward to supply its own needs. The quality of Russian-grown potatoes and meat was too poor. Thus, to protect the quality of its product, McDonald's set up its own dairy farms, cattle ranches, vegetable plots, and food processing plants within Russia. This raised the cost of doing business in Russia, relative to the cost in more sophisticated economies where high-quality inputs could be purchased on the open market.

As for legal factors, it can be more costly to do business in a country where local laws and regulations set strict standards with regard to product safety, safety in the workplace, environmental pollution, and the like (since adhering to such regulations is costly). It can also be more costly to do business in a country like the United States, where the absence of a cap on damage awards has meant spiraling liability insurance rates. It can be more costly to do business in a country that lacks well-established laws for regulating business practice (as is the case in many of the former Communist nations). In the absence of a well-developed body of business contract law, international firms may find no satisfactory way to resolve contract disputes and, consequently, routinely face large losses from contract violations. Similarly, local laws that fail to adequately protect intellectual property can lead to the theft of an international business's intellectual property and lost income.

RISKS

As with costs, the risks of doing business in a country are determined by a number of political, economic, and legal factors. **Political risk** has been defined as the likelihood that political forces will cause drastic changes in a country's business environment that adversely affect the profit and other goals of a business enterprise.[62] So defined, political risk tends to be greater in countries experiencing social unrest and disorder or in countries where the underlying nature of a society increases the likelihood of social unrest. Social unrest typically finds expression in strikes, demonstrations, terrorism, and violent conflict. Such unrest is more likely to be found in countries that contain more than one ethnic nationality, in countries where competing ideologies are battling for political control, in countries where economic mismanagement has created high inflation and falling living standards, or in countries that straddle the "fault lines" between civilizations.

Social unrest can result in abrupt changes in government and government policy or, in some cases, in protracted civil strife. Such strife tends to have negative economic implications for the profit goals of business enterprises. For example, in the aftermath of the 1979 Islamic revolution in Iran, the Iranian assets of numerous U.S. companies were seized by the new Iranian government without compensation. Similarly, the violent disintegration of the Yugoslavian federation into warring states, including Bosnia, Croatia, and Serbia, precipitated a collapse in the local economies and in the profitability of investments in those countries.

More generally, a change in political regime can result in the enactment of laws that are less favorable to international business. In Venezuela, for example, the populist socialist politician, Hugo Chavez, won power in 1998, was reelected as president in 2000, and reaffirmed in a 2004 referendum called after the failure of an attempted coup to remove him. Chavez has declared himself to be a "Fidelista," a follower of Cuba's Communist President Fidel Castro. He has pledged to improve the lot of the poor in Venezuela through government intervention in private business, and has frequently railed against American imperialism, all of which is of concern to Western enterprises doing business in the country. While Chavez has taken few concrete actions against foreign businesses, the political risks of operating in the country have arguably increased.

On the economic front, economic risks arise from economic mismanagement by the government of a country. **Economic risks** can be defined as the likelihood that economic mismanagement will cause drastic changes in a country's business environment that hurt the profit and other goals of a particular business enterprise. Economic risks are not independent of political risk. Economic mismanagement may give rise to significant social unrest and hence political risk. Nevertheless, economic risks are worth emphasizing as a separate category because there is not always a one-to-one relationship between economic mismanagement and social unrest. One visible indicator of economic mismanagement tends to be a country's inflation rate. Another tends to be the level of business and government debt in the country.

In Asian states such as Indonesia, Thailand, and South Korea, businesses increased their debt rapidly during the 1990s, often at the bequest of the government, which was encouraging them to invest in industries deemed to be of "strategic importance" to the country. The result was overinvestment, with more industrial (factories) and commercial capacity (office space) being built than could be justified by demand conditions. Many of these investments turned out to be uneconomic. The borrowers failed to generate the profits necessary to service their debt payment obligations. In turn, the banks that had lent money to these businesses suddenly found that they had rapid increases in nonperforming loans on their books. Foreign investors, believing that many local companies and banks might go bankrupt, pulled their money out of these countries, selling local stock, bonds, and currency. This action precipitated the 1997–98 financial crises in Southeast Asia. The crisis included a precipitous decline in the value of Asian stock markets, which in some cases exceeded 70 percent; a similar collapse in the value of many Asian currencies against the U.S. dollar; an implosion of local demand; and a severe economic recession that will affect many Asian countries for years to come. In short, economic risks were rising throughout Southeast Asia during the 1990s. Astute foreign businesses and investors limited their exposure in this part of the world. More naive businesses and investors lost their shirts!

On the legal front, risks arise when a country's legal system fails to provide adequate safeguards in the case of contract violations or to protect property rights. When legal safeguards are weak, firms are more likely to break contracts and/or steal intellectual property if they perceive it as being in their interests to do so. Thus, **legal risks** might be defined as the likelihood that a trading partner will opportunistically break a contract or expropriate property rights. When legal risks in a country are high, an international business might hesitate entering into a long-term contract or joint-venture agreement with a firm in that country. For example, in the 1970s when the Indian government passed a law requiring all foreign investors to enter into joint ventures with Indian companies, U.S. companies such as IBM and Coca-Cola closed their investments in India. They believed that the Indian legal system did not provide for adequate protection of intellectual property rights, creating the very real danger that their Indian partners might expropriate the intellectual property of the American companies—which for IBM and Coca-Cola amounted to the core of their competitive advantage.

OVERALL ATTRACTIVENESS

The overall attractiveness of a country as a potential market and/or investment site for an international business depends on balancing the benefits, costs, and risks associated with doing business in that country (see Figure 2.4). Generally, the costs

FIGURE 2.4

Country Attractiveness

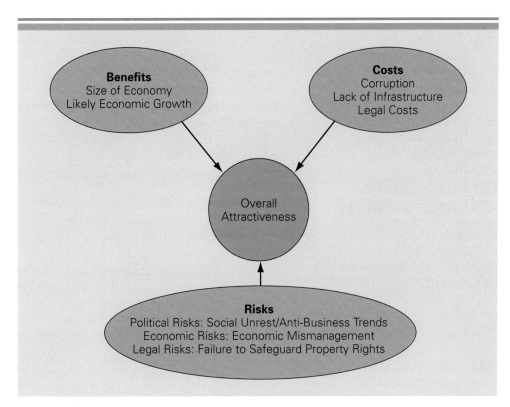

and risks associated with doing business in a foreign country are typically lower in economically advanced and politically stable democratic nations and greater in less developed and politically unstable nations. The calculus is complicated, however, because the potential long-run benefits are dependent not only upon a nation's current stage of economic development or political stability, but also on likely future economic growth rates. Economic growth appears to be a function of a free market system and a country's capacity for growth (which may be greater in less developed nations). This leads one to conclude that, other things being equal, the benefit–cost–risk trade-off is likely to be most favorable in politically stable developed and developing nations that have free market systems and no dramatic upsurge in either inflation rates or private-sector debt. It is likely to be least favorable in politically unstable developing nations that operate with a mixed or command economy or in developing nations where speculative financial bubbles have led to excess borrowing.

Chapter Summary

This chapter has reviewed how the political, economic, and legal systems of countries vary. The potential benefits, costs, and risks of doing business in a country are a function of its political, economic, and legal systems. The chapter made the following points:

1. Political systems can be assessed according to two dimensions: the degree to which they emphasize collectivism as opposed to individualism, and the degree to which they are democratic or totalitarian.

2. Collectivism is an ideology that views the needs of society as being more important than the needs of the individual. Collectivism translates into an advocacy for state intervention in economic activity and, in the case of communism, a totalitarian dictatorship.

3. Individualism is an ideology that is built on an emphasis of the primacy of individual's freedoms in the political, economic, and cultural realms. Individualism translates into an advocacy for democratic ideals and free market economics.

4. Democracy and totalitarianism are at different ends of the political spectrum. In a representative democracy, citizens periodically elect individuals to represent them and political freedoms are guaranteed by a constitution. In a totalitarian state, political power is monopolized by a party, group, or individual, and basic political freedoms are denied to citizens of the state.

5. There are three broad types of economic systems: a market economy, a command economy, and a mixed economy. In a market economy, prices are free of controls and private ownership is predominant. In a command economy, prices are set by central planners, productive assets are owned by the state, and private ownership is forbidden. A mixed economy has elements of both a market economy and a command economy.

6. Differences in the structure of law between countries can have important implications for the practice of international business. The degree to which property rights are protected can vary dramatically from country to country, as can product safety and product liability legislation and the nature of contract law.

7. The rate of economic progress in a country seems to depend on the extent to which that country has a well-functioning market economy in which property rights are protected.

8. Many countries are now in a state of transition. There is a marked shift away from totalitarian governments and command or mixed economic systems and toward democratic political institutions and free market economic systems.

9. The attractiveness of a country as a market and/or investment site depends on balancing the likely long-run benefits of doing business in that country against the likely costs and risks.

10. The benefits of doing business in a country are a function of the size of the market (population), its present wealth (purchasing power), and its future growth prospects. By investing early in countries that are currently poor but are nevertheless growing rapidly, firms can gain first-mover advantages that will pay back substantial dividends in the future.

11. The costs of doing business in a country tend to be greater where political payoffs are required to gain market access, where supporting infrastructure is lacking or underdeveloped, and where adhering to local laws and regulations is costly.

12. The risks of doing business in a country tend to be greater in countries that are (1) politically unstable, (2) subject to economic mismanagement, and (3) lacking a legal system to provide adequate safeguards in the case of contract or property rights violations.

Critical Thinking and Discussion Questions

1. Free market economies stimulate greater economic growth, whereas state-directed economies stifle growth. Discuss.

2. A democratic political system is an essential condition for sustained economic progress. Discuss.

3. What is the relationship between corruption in a country (i.e., bribe taking by government officials) and economic growth? Is corruption always bad?

4. The Nobel Prize–winning economist Amartya Sen argues that the concept of development should be broadened to include more than just economic development. What other factors does Sen think should be included in an assessment of development? How might adoption of Sen's

views influence government policy? Do you think Sen is correct that development is about more than just economic development? Explain.

5. You are the CEO of a company that has to choose between making a $100 million investment in Russia or the Czech Republic. Both investments promise the same long-run return, so your choice is driven by risk considerations. Assess the various risks of doing business in each of these nations. Which investment would you favor and why?

6. Read the Country Focus on India in this chapter and answer the following questions:

    a. What kind of economic system did India operate under during 1947 to 1990? What kind of system is it moving toward today?

What are the impediments to completing this transformation?

b. How might widespread public ownership of businesses and extensive government regulations have impacted (*i*) the efficiency of state and private businesses, and (*ii*) the rate of new business formation in India during the 1947–90 time frame? How do you think these factors affected the rate of economic growth in India during this time frame?

c. How would privatization, deregulation, and the removal of barriers to foreign direct investment affect the efficiency of business, new business formation, and the rate of eco-

nomic growth in India during the post-1990 time period?

d. India now has pockets of strengths in key high-technology industries such as software and pharmaceuticals. Why do you think India is developing strength in these areas? How might success in these industries help to generate growth in the other sectors of the Indian economy?

e. Given what is now occurring in the Indian economy, do you think the country represents an attractive target for inward investment by foreign multinationals selling consumer products? Why?

Research Task   globalEDGE™   globaledge.msu.edu

Use the globalEDGE™ site to complete the following exercises:

1. The Freedom in the World survey evaluates the state of political rights and civil liberties around the world. Provide a description of this survey and a "freedom" ranking of the leaders and laggards of the world. What factors does this survey consider when forming the rankings?

2. Market Potential Indicators (MPI), an indexing study conducted by the Michigan State Univer-

sity Center for International Business Education and Research (MSU-CIBER), compares emerging markets on a variety of dimensions. Describe the indicators used in the indexing procedure. Which of the indicators would have greater importance for a company that markets laptop computers? Considering the MPI rankings, which developing countries would you advise this company to enter first?

The Poorest Continent

CLOSING CASE Sub-Saharan Africa— that part of Africa that lies south of the Sahara Desert—is the poorest region in the world's poorest continent. Half of the area's 700 million people live in dismal poverty, subsisting on $0.65 a day or less. It is the only region of the world to have grown poorer in the past 25 years. A widely used measure of economic wealth, gross domestic product (GDP) per capita, peaked in 1981 at $669, and by 2002, GDP per capita in the region was just $571 (in constant 1995 dollars).

Why is the region so poor? Answers include a harsh tropical climate, disease (three-fourths of the 42 million people in the world afflicted with AIDS live in the region), and perennial wars, often the consequence of illogical national boundaries drawn by former colonial masters that did not respect historic tribal divisions. In addition, the region has a history of bad government and poor economic policies. Since the colonial powers left, much of the region has been cursed by corrupt totalitar-

ian regimes that have enacted economic policies that have retarded growth. In 2004, a year when 46 percent of the world's nation-states were classified as democracies by Freedom House, only 11 of the region's 48 countries had open and fair democratic systems. In many sub-Saharan nations the rule of law is weak, power is concentrated in the hands of the few, and property rights are poorly defined and protected.

Some economists argue that the last point is pivotal in explaining the lack of economic progress. Property ownership is often used as collateral to raise money and finance businesses. In the United States, for example, a common way for an entrepreneur to raise capital for a business venture is to take out a second mortgage on the family home. Raising capital is much harder in Africa. Only one in 10 Africans lives in a house with title deeds or has a legal title to farmland. The inability to establish ownership rights over homes and land means that they cannot be used as collateral to raise money from a bank. For example, a woman living in a $300 home in Malawi wanted to borrow $200 to expand her goat-slaughtering business to meet strong demand for her goat stew, but no bank would accept the house as collateral. The home was built on "customary" land purchased from peasants who had farmed it for generations, and there was no proof of ownership. Without proof of ownership, the banks were unwilling to make the loan. Multiply this example by several million and it is clear that Africans sit on an enormous stock of underexploited assets.

Development economist Hernando de Soto has calculated that the total value of land and houses owned by Africans in the region is roughly $1 trillion, nearly three times as large as the entire GDP of the region. De Soto sees much of this as "dead capital," since it cannot be used to raise funds and start businesses, so economic growth never takes off.

In many countries, uncertainty about future property ownership further complicates the situation. If a farmer has no guarantee that "ownership" of land will be respected, he has scant incentive to invest in improving the land's yield, such as by purchasing farm machinery, so agricultural productivity remains low. In Zimbabwe in the late 1990s, the dictatorial government of President Robert Mugabe started seizing land owned by white farmers and transferring it to black Zimbabweans. At first blush, this might seem like a reasonable way of addressing the historic inequality that arose when white colonialists took land from native populations. Unfortunately, many of the recent seizures in Zimbabwe have been by force and illegal, according to the country's own laws. The seizures frequently turned violent, people lost their lives, and the land was often transferred to members of Mugabe's ZANU-PF Party as a reward for their loyalty, many of whom had scant knowledge of farming. Longtime commercial farmers stopped investing in their land, fearing that it would be expropriated. Many have left the country. Agricultural production in Zimbabwe has collapsed, and food shortages abound because the new landowners have not planted enough maize and wheat to feed the country. Production of Zimbabwe's main cash crop, tobacco, also has tumbled. To make matters worse, the bad publicity arising from violent land seizures has hurt

tourism. In 2002 the tourist trade generated $70 million, down from $700 million in 1999. The Zimbabwean economy is now in a tailspin. Unemployment hit 70 percent in 2003, inflation surged to a staggering 500 percent, and the economy shrunk by one-third between 2000 and 2003.

The region does have hope. Economic growth has been strong in Mozambique since the country's civil war ended in 1992. Once considered the second poorest country in the world, Mozambique has seen real incomes triple in a decade. The economy of this formally Marxist state grew by 14 percent in 2001 and 11 percent in 2002, compared to neighboring Zimbabwe's 8 percent decline in 2001 and 6 percent decline in 2002. One big difference between the two countries is Mozambique now has an elected democracy, which has strengthened property rights. The confidence generated has spurred both domestic and foreign investment. A British mining group has invested $1.3 billion in an aluminum smelter in the country, and tourism is taking off, bringing in much-needed foreign exchange.

Sources: "Breathing Life into Dead Capital," *The Economist*, January 17, 2004, pp. 6–7; "Lion Cubs on a Wire," *The Economist*, August 16, 2003, p. 68; Simon Ndovu, "Zimbabwe: Economy—That Sinking Feeling," *African Business*, January 2004, pp. 46–48; and World Bank, *World Development Indicators Online, 2005*.

Case Discussion Questions

1. What do you think are the three main reasons for the persistence of poverty in sub-Saharan Africa?

2. What steps can be taken by the nations of sub-Saharan Africa to address the causes of poverty? Can the governments of developed nations help in this process? Should they? How?

3. Can international businesses play a role in helping nations in the region to reduce poverty and ignite economic growth?

4. Currently sub-Saharan Africa receives very little in the way of foreign direct investment from firms based in developed nations. If nations in the region start to take the actions you identified in the answer to question 2, what do you think will happen to the flow of foreign direct investment? Will this benefit the region's economies? How?

Notes

1. Although as we shall see, there is not a strict one-to-one correspondence between political systems and economic systems. A. O. Hirschman, "The On-and-Off Again Connection between Political and Economic Progress," *American Economic Review* 84, no. 2 (1994), pp. 343–48.

2. For a discussion of the roots of collectivism and individualism, see H. W. Spiegel, *The Growth of Economic Thought* (Durham, NC: Duke University Press, 1991). A discussion of collectivism and individualism can be found in M. Friedman and R. Friedman, *Free to Choose* (London: Penguin Books, 1980).

3. For a classic summary of the tenets of Marxism details, see A. Giddens, *Capitalism and Modern Social Theory* (Cambridge: Cambridge University Press, 1971).

4. For details see "A Survey of China," *The Economist*, March 18, 1995.

5. J. S. Mill, *On Liberty* (London: Longman's, 1865), p. 6.

6. A. Smith, *The Wealth of Nations, Vol. 1* (London: Penguin Book), p. 325.

7. R. Wesson, *Modern Government—Democracy and Authoritarianism*, 2nd ed. (Englewood Cliffs, NJ: Prentice Hall, 1990).

8. For a detailed but accessible elaboration of this argument, see Friedman and Friedman, *Free to Choose*. Also see P. M. Romer, "The Origins of Endogenous Growth," *Journal of Economic Perspectives* 8, no. 1 (1994), pp. 2–32.

9. T. W. Lippman, *Understanding Islam* (New York: Meridian Books, 1995).

10. "Islam's Interest," *The Economist*, January 18, 1992, pp. 33–34.

11. Rodney Wilson, "Islamic Banking," *Economic Record*, September 2002, pp. 373–74.

12. This information can be found on the UN's Treaty Web site at http://untreaty.un.org/ENGLISH/bible/englishinternetbible/partI/chapterX/treaty17.asp.

13. International Court of Arbitration, www.iccwbo.org/index_court.asp.

14. D. North, *Institutions, Institutional Change, and Economic Performance* (Cambridge: Cambridge University Press, 1991).

15. P. Klebnikov, "Russia's Robber Barons," *Forbes*, November 21, 1994, pp. 74–84; C. Mellow, "Russia: Making Cash from Chaos," *Fortune*, April 17, 1995, pp. 145–51; and "Mr Tatum Checks Out," *The Economist*, November 9, 1996, p. 78.

16. K. van Wolferen, *The Enigma of Japanese Power* (New York: Vintage Books, 1990), pp. 100–05.

17. P. Bardhan, "Corruption and Development: A Review of the Issues," *Journal of Economic Literature*, September 1997, pp. 1320–46.

18. K. M. Murphy, A. Shleifer, and R. Vishny, "Why Is Rent Seeking So Costly to Growth?" *American Economic Review* 83, no. 2 (1993), pp. 409–14.

19. Transparency International, "Global Corruption Report 2005," www.transparency.org, 2005.

20. www.transparency.org.

21. J. Coolidge and S. Rose Ackerman, "High Level Rent Seeking and Corruption in African Regimes," World Bank Policy Research Working Paper No. 1780, June 1997; Murphy, Shleifer, and Vishny, "Why Is Rent Seeking So Costly to Growth?"; M. Habib and L. Zurawicki, "Corruption and Foreign Direct Investment," *Journal of International Business Studies* 33 (2002), pp. 291–307; J. E. Anderson and D. Marcouiller, "Insecurity and the Pattern of International Trade," *Review of Economics and Statistics* 84 (2002), pp. 342–52; and T. S. Aidt, "Economic Analysis of Corruption: A Survey," *The Economic Journal* 113 (November 2003), pp. 632–53.

22. Details can be found at www.oecd.org/EN/home/0,,EN-home-31-nodirectorate-no-nono-31,00.html.

23. Dale Stackhouse and Kenneth Ungar, "The Foreign Corrupt Practices Act: Bribery, Corruption, Record Keeping and More," *Indiana Lawyer*, April 21, 1993.

24. For an interesting discussion of strategies for dealing with the low cost of copying and distributing digital information, see the chapter on rights management in C. Shapiro and H. R. Varian, *Information Rules* (Boston: Harvard Business School Press, 1999).

25. Douglass North has argued that the correct specification of intellectual property rights is one factor that lowers the cost of doing business and, thereby, stimulates economic growth and development. See North, *Institutions, Institutional Change, and Economic Performance*.

26. International Federation of the Phonographic Industry, "Fighting Piracy," 2003, www.ifpi.org.

27. Business Software Alliance, "First Annual BSA and IDC Global Software Piracy Study," June 2004, www.bsa.org.

28. Ibid.

29. "Trade Tripwires," *The Economist*, August 27, 1994, p. 61.

30. World Bank, *World Development Indicators Online, 2004*.

31. A. Sen, *Development as Freedom* (New York: Alfred A. Knopf, 1999).

32. G. M. Grossman and E. Helpman, "Endogenous Innovation in the Theory of Growth," *Journal of Economic Perspectives* 8, no. 1 (1994), pp. 23–44, and Romer, "The Origins of Endogenous Growth."

33. F. A. Hayek, *The Fatal Conceit: Errors of Socialism* (Chicago: University of Chicago Press, 1989).

34. James Gwartney, Robert Lawson, and Walter Block, *Economic Freedom of the World: 1975–1995* (London: Institute of Economic Affairs, 1996).

35. North, *Institutions, Institutional Change, and Economic Performance*. See also Murphy, Shleifer, and Vishny, "Why Is Rent Seeking So Costly to Growth?" Also see K. E. Maskus, "Intellectual Property Rights in the Global Economy," *Institute for International Economics*, 2000.

36. Hernando de Soto, *The Mystery of Capital: Why Capitalism Triumphs in the West and Fails Everywhere Else* (New York: Basic Books, 2000).

37. Hirschman, "The On-and-Off Again Connection between Political and Economic Progress," and A. Przeworski and F. Limongi, "Political Regimes and Economic Growth," *Journal of Economic Perspectives* 7, no. 3 (1993), pp. 51–59.

38. Ibid.

39. For details of this argument, see M. Olson, "Dictatorship, Democracy, and Development," *American Political Science Review*, September 1993.

40. For example, see Jarad Diamond's Pulitzer Prize–winning book, *Guns, Germs, and Steel* (New York: W. W. Norton, 1997). Also see J. Sachs, "Nature, Nurture and Growth," *The Economist*, June 14, 1997, pp. 19–22.

41. Sachs, "Nature, Nurture and Growth."

42. "What Can the Rest of the World Learn from the Classrooms of Asia?" *The Economist*, September 21, 1996, p. 24.

43. J. Fagerberg, "Technology and International Differences in Growth Rates," *Journal of Economic Literature* 32 (September 1994), pp. 1147–75.

44. See The Freedom House Survey Team, "Freedom in the World: 2005" and associated materials, www.freedomhouse.org.

45. "Russia Downgraded to Not Free," Freedom House press release, December 20, 2004, www.freedomhouse.org.

46. Freedom House, "Democracies Century: A Survey of Political Change in the Twentieth Century, 1999," www.freedomhouse.org.

47. L. Conners, "Freedom to Connect," *Wired*, August 1997, pp. 105–06.

48. F. Fukuyama, "The End of History," *The National Interest* 16 (Summer 1989), p. 18.

49. S. P. Huntington, *The Clash of Civilizations and the Remaking of World Order* (New York: Simon & Schuster, 1996).

50. Ibid., p. 116.

51. United States Department of State, *Patterns of Global Terrorism*, June 2004.

52. S. Fisher, R. Sahay, and C. A. Vegh, "Stabilization and the Growth in Transition Economies: the Early Experience," *Journal of Economic Perspectives* 10 (Spring 1996), pp. 45–66.

53. M. Miles, E. Feulner, and M. O'Grady, *2005 Index of Economic Freedom* (Washington, DC: Heritage Foundation, 2005).

54. International Monetary Fund, *World Economic Outlook: Focus on Transition Economies* (Geneva: IMF, October 2000).

55. J. C. Brada, "Privatization Is Transition—Is It?" *Journal of Economic Perspectives*, Spring 1996, pp. 67–86.

56. See S. Zahra et al., "Privatization and Entrepreneurial Transformation," *Academy of Management Review* 3, no. 25 (2000), pp. 509–24.

57. Fischer, Sahay, and Vegh, "Stabilization and the Growth in Transition Economies."

58. J. Sachs, C. Zinnes, and Y. Eilat, "The Gains from Privatization in Transition Economies: Is Change of Ownership Enough?" CAER Discussion Paper No. 63 (Cambridge, MA: Harvard Institute for International Development, 2000).

59. J. Nellis, "Time to Rethink Privatization in Transition Economies?" *Finance and Development* 36, no. 2 (1999), pp. 16–19.

60. M. S. Borish and M. Noel, "Private Sector Development in the Visegrad Countries," *World Bank*, March 1997.

61. For a discussion of first-mover advantages, see M. Liberman and D. Montgomery, "First-Mover Advantages," *Strategic Management Journal* 9 (Summer Special Issue, 1988), pp. 41–58.

62. S. H. Robock, "Political Risk: Identification and Assessment," *Columbia Journal of World Business*, July/August 1971, pp. 6–20.

3

Differences in Culture

Doing Business in Saudi Arabia

Saudi Arabia is not the easiest place in the world for Western enterprises to do business. On the one hand, the oil-rich kingdom offers many opportunities for enterprising businesses. Western construction companies have long played a role in building infrastructure in the kingdom. Western brands from Coca-Cola, Nike, and McDonald's to Body Shop, Next, and Benetton have a significant presence. Western aerospace companies such as Boeing and Lockheed have sold a significant number of aircraft to Saudi Arabia over the years. The Saudi market is one of the larger in the Middle East, with a growing population of 22 million and purchasing power parity per capita of $12,845 in 2003. Since 2000, the government has signaled that it is more open to foreign investment in certain sectors of the economy, although oil and gas extraction is still reserved for state-owned enterprises.

On the other hand, Saudi Arabia is a historically conservative country where a large segment of the population desires to preserve the religious values and ancient traditions of the region, and this can spill over into the business sector. The culture of the country has been shaped by Islam and the Bedouin tradition. The source of law in Saudi Arabia is Islamic law (the Shari'ah), and religious edicts derived from this influence on everyday life. For example, stores and restaurants close at the five daily prayer times, and many restaurants, including Western ones such as McDonald's, have separate dining areas for men and women. Women in Saudi Arabia are not allowed to drive a car, sail a boat, or fly a plane, or to appear outdoors with hair, wrists, or ankles exposed—something that Western companies need to keep in mind when doing business in the country or with Saudis elsewhere.

Saudi adherence to Islamic values has also given rise to anti-American sentiment, which has been increasing since the American-led invasion of another Muslim nation, Iraq. Cultural solidarity has expressed itself in consumer boycotts of American products. More disturbing than consumer boycotts has been a rise in terrorist attacks against Western expatriates in Saudi Arabia, significantly increasing the perceived risks of doing business in the kingdom.

Bedouin traditions have been just as strong as Islamic values in shaping Saudi culture. Less than a hundred years ago, the Arabian Peninsula was populated by nomadic Bedouin tribes. Values that were important to those proud nomads, and enabled them to survive in their harsh desert landscape, are still found in modern Saudi society. They include loyalty, status, an emphasis on interpersonal relationships, the idea of approximate rather than precise time, and an aversion to any behavior that might seem menial or servile (including manual labor).

Reflecting Bedouin traditions, Saudis will often conduct business only after trust has been well established—a process that might require (by Western standards) a large number of face-to-face meetings. Saudis may resent being rushed into a business decision, preferring to let discussions proceed in a more relaxed fashion—something that Westerners with their attachment to precise rather than approximate time might find taxing. Business meetings may be long because many Saudis maintain an "open office" and will interrupt a meeting to conduct other business, which can be traced back to the Bedouin tradition where all tribal members have a right to visit and petition their leaders without an appointment. Given the cultural importance attached to status, Saudi executives will not react well if a foreign company sends a junior executive to transact business.

Loyalty to family and friends is a powerful force, and job security and advancement may be based on family and friendship ties, rather than, or in addition to, demonstrated technical or managerial competence. Westerners might construe this negatively as nepotism, but it reflects a nomadic culture where trust in family and tribe was placed above all else. Saudi executives will also consult with family and friends before making a business decision, and they may place more weight on their opinions than that of experts whom they do not know as well.

The Bedouin aversion to menial work has produced a chronic labor problem in the kingdom, and foreign companies will quickly discover that it is difficult to find Saudi nationals who will undertake manual labor or basic service work. Currently, some 6 million foreign nationals reside in Saudi Arabia. These expatriates, who are primarily from other Muslim nations, undertake many of the menial occupations that Saudis disdain. Although oil revenues have made this social stratification possible, the Saudi government sees it as a potential long-term problem—almost 90 percent of all private-sector jobs in Saudi Arabia are filled by foreign nationals—and has launched a program of "Saudiazation." The aim is to change cultural values toward work perceived as menial, and by doing so, to help build a modern economy. So far success had been halting at best.

Saudi society is starting to change in other important ways. Slowly the rights of Saudi women are being expanded. In 1964, Saudi girls were not allowed to go to school; today 55 percent of university students in the kingdom are women. In 2004, Saudi women were granted the right to hold commercial business licenses, a significant advance considering the women held some $25 billion in deposits in Saudi banks and had little opportunity to use them. As Saudi society evolves, women may come to play a greater role in business.

Sources: G. Rice, "Doing Business in Saudi Arabia," *Thunderbird International Business Review,* January–February 2004, pp. 59–84; A. Kronemer, "Inventing a Working Class in Saudi Arabia," *Monthly Labor Review,* May 1997, pp. 29–30; "Out of the Shadows, into the World—Arab Women," *The Economist,* June 19, 2004, pp. 28–30; and B. Mroue, "Arab Countries Boycott U.S. Goods over Mideast Policies," *Los Angeles Times,* July 29, 2002, p. C3.

Introduction

International business is different from domestic business because countries are different. In Chapter 2, we saw how national differences in political, economic, and legal systems influence the benefits, costs, and risks associated with doing business in different countries. In this chapter, we will explore how differences in culture across and within countries can affect international business. Several themes run through this chapter.

The first theme is that business success in a variety of countries requires cross-cultural literacy. By **cross-cultural literacy,** we mean an understanding of how cultural differences across and within nations can affect the way in which business is practiced. In these days of global communications, rapid transportation, and worldwide markets, when the era of the global village seems just around the corner, it is easy to forget just how different various cultures really are. Underneath the veneer of modernism, deep cultural differences often remain. Westerners in general, and Americans in particular, are quick to conclude that because people from other parts of the world also wear blue jeans, listen to Western popular music, eat at McDonald's, and drink Coca-Cola, they also accept the basic tenets of Western (or American) culture. But this is not true. For example, increasingly, many Saudis are embracing the material products of modern society. Saudi cities in particular seem modern with their office blocks, department stores, malls, and freeways. But as the opening case demonstrates, beneath the veneer of Western modernism, long-standing cultural values that date back to Bedouin traditions have a profound influence on this society. Foreign managers in Saudi Arabia need to be aware of these traditions, and how they might affect the business process in the kingdom.

Another theme developed in this chapter is that a relationship may exist between culture and the cost of doing business in a country or region. Different cultures are more or less supportive of the capitalist mode of production and may increase or lower the costs of doing business. For example, some observers have argued that cultural factors lowered the costs of doing business in Japan and helped to explain Japan's rapid economic ascent during the 1960s, 70s, and 80s.[1] By the same token, cultural factors can sometimes raise the costs of doing business. Historically, class divisions were an important aspect of British culture, and for a long time, firms operating in Great Britain found it difficult to achieve cooperation between management and labor. Class divisions led to a high level of industrial disputes in that country during the 1960s and 1970s and raised the costs of doing business relative to the costs in countries such as Switzerland, Norway, Germany, or Japan, where class conflict was historically less prevalent.

The British example, however, brings us to another theme we will explore in this chapter. Culture is not static. It can and does evolve, although the rate at which culture can change is the subject of some dispute. Important aspects of British culture have changed significantly over the past 20 years, and this is reflected in weaker class distinctions and a lower level of industrial disputes. Between 1993 and 2002, the number of days lost per 1,000 workers due to strikes in the United Kingdom was on average 24 each year, significantly less than in the United States (where the figure was 45), France (where 84 days were lost), and Canada (where 187 were lost).[2] Similarly, there is evidence of changes in the culture of Japan, with the traditional emphasis on group identification giving way to greater emphasis on individualism, and as we saw in the opening case, the culture of Saudi Arabia may be starting to change, particularly with regard to the status and opportunities granted to women.

What Is Culture?

Scholars have never been able to agree on a simple definition of culture. In the 1870s, the anthropologist Edward Tylor defined culture as "that complex whole which includes knowledge, belief, art, morals, law, custom, and other capabilities acquired by man as a member of society."[3] Since then hundreds of other definitions have been offered. Geert Hofstede, an expert on cross-cultural differences and management, defined culture as "the collective programming of the mind which distinguishes the members of one human group from another. . . . Culture, in this sense, includes systems of values; and values are among the building blocks of culture."[4] Another definition of culture comes from sociologists Zvi Namenwirth and Robert Weber who see culture as a system of ideas and argue that these ideas constitute a design for living.[5]

Here we follow both Hofstede and Namenwirth and Weber by viewing **culture** as a system of values and norms that are shared among a group of people and that when taken together constitute a design for living. By **values** we mean abstract ideas about what a group believes to be good, right, and desirable. Put differently, values are shared assumptions about how things ought to be.[6] By **norms** we mean the social rules and guidelines that prescribe appropriate behavior in particular situations. We shall use the term **society** to refer to a group of people who share a common set of values and norms. While a society may be equivalent to a country, some countries harbor several societies (i.e., they support multiple cultures), and some societies embrace more than one country.

VALUES AND NORMS

Values form the bedrock of a culture. They provide the context within which a society's norms are established and justified. They may include a society's attitudes toward such concepts as individual freedom, democracy, truth, justice, honesty, loyalty, social obligations, collective responsibility, the role of women, love, sex, marriage, and so on. Values are not just abstract concepts; they are invested with considerable emotional significance. People argue, fight, and even die over values such as freedom. Values also often are reflected in the political and economic systems of a society. As we saw in Chapter 2, democratic free market capitalism is a reflection of a philosophical value system that emphasizes individual freedom.

Norms are the social rules that govern people's actions toward one another. Norms can be subdivided further into two major categories: folkways and mores. **Folkways** are the routine conventions of everyday life. Generally, folkways are actions of little moral significance. Rather, folkways are social conventions concerning things such as the appropriate dress code in a particular situation, good social manners, eating with the correct utensils, neighborly behavior, and the like. While folkways define the way people are expected to behave, violation of folkways is not normally a serious matter. People who violate folkways may be thought of as eccentric or ill-mannered, but they are not usually considered to be evil or bad. In many countries, foreigners may initially be excused for violating folkways.

A good example of folkways concerns attitudes toward time in different countries. People are keenly aware of the passage of time in the United States and Northern European cultures such as Germany and Britain. Businesspeople are very conscious about scheduling their time and are quickly irritated when their time is wasted because a business associate is late for a meeting or if they are kept waiting. They talk about time as though it were money, as something that can be spent, saved, wasted, and lost.[7] Alternatively, in Arab, Latin, and Mediterranean cultures, time has a more elastic character. Keeping to a schedule is viewed as less important than finishing an interaction with people. While an American businessperson might feel slighted if she is kept waiting for 30 minutes outside the office of a Latin American executive before a meeting, the Latin American may simply be completing an interaction with an associate, and view the information gathered from this as more important than sticking to a rigid schedule. The Latin American executive intends no disrespect, but due to a mutual misunderstanding about the importance of time, the American may see things differently. Similarly, we saw in the opening case how Saudi attitudes to time have been shaped by their nomadic Bedouin heritage, in which precise time played no real role and arriving some-

Understanding rituals and symbolic behaviors is essential to doing business in foreign countries.

where tomorrow might mean next week. Like Latin Americans, many Saudis are unlikely to understand the American obsession with precise time and schedules, and Americans need to adjust their expectations accordingly.

Folkways include rituals and symbolic behavior. Rituals and symbols are the most visible manifestations of a culture and constitute the outward expression of deeper values. For example, upon meeting a foreign business executive, a Japanese executive will hold his business card in both hands and bow while presenting the card to the foreigner.[8] This ritual behavior is loaded with deep cultural symbolism. The card specifies the rank of the Japanese executive, which is a very important piece of information in a hierarchical society such as Japan (Japanese often have business cards with Japanese printed on one side, and English printed on the other). The bow is a sign of respect, and the deeper the angle of the bow, the greater the reverence one person shows for the other. The person receiving the card is expected to examine it carefully, which is a way of returning respect and acknowledging the card giver's position in the hierarchy. The foreigner is also expected to bow when taking the card, and to return the greeting by presenting the Japanese executive with his own card, similarly bowing in the process. To not do so, and to fail to read the card that he has been given, instead casually placing it in his jacket, violates this important folkway and is considered rude.

Mores are norms that are seen as central to the functioning of a society and to its social life. They have much greater significance than folkways. Accordingly, violating mores can bring serious retribution. Mores include such factors as indictments against theft, adultery, incest, and cannibalism. In many societies, certain mores have been enacted into law. Thus, all advanced societies have laws against theft, incest, and cannibalism. However, there are also many differences between cultures. In America, for example, drinking alcohol is widely accepted, whereas in Saudi Arabia the consumption of alcohol is viewed as violating important social mores and is punishable by imprisonment (as some Western citizens working in Saudi Arabia have discovered).

CULTURE, SOCIETY, AND THE NATION-STATE

We have defined a society as a group of people that share a common set of values and norms; that is, people who are bound together by a common culture. There is not a strict one-to-one correspondence between a society and a nation-state. Nation-states are political creations. They may contain a single culture or several cultures. While the French nation can be thought of as the political embodiment of French culture, the nation of Canada has at least three cultures—an Anglo culture, a French-speaking "Quebecois" culture, and a Native American culture. Similarly, many African nations have important cultural differences between tribal groups, as exhibited in the early 1990s when Rwanda dissolved into a bloody civil war between two tribes, the Tutsis and Hutus. Africa is not alone in this regard. India is composed of many distinct cultural groups. During the first Gulf War, the prevailing view presented to Western audiences was that Iraq was a homogenous Arab nation. But over the past 15 years, we have learned several different societies exist within Iraq, each with its own culture. The Kurds in the north do not view themselves as Arabs and have their own distinct history and traditions. There are two Arab societies: the Shiites in the South and the Sunnis who populate the middle of the country and who ruled Iraq under the regime of Saddam Hussein (the terms *Shiites* and *Sunnis* refer to different sects within the religion of Islam). Among the southern Sunnis is another distinct society of 500,000 Marsh Arabs who live at the confluence of the Tigris and Euphrates rivers, pursuing a way of life that dates back 5,000 years.[9]

At the other end of the scale are cultures that embrace several nations. Several scholars argue that we can speak of an Islamic society or culture that is shared by the citizens of many different nations in the Middle East, Asia, and Africa. As you will recall from

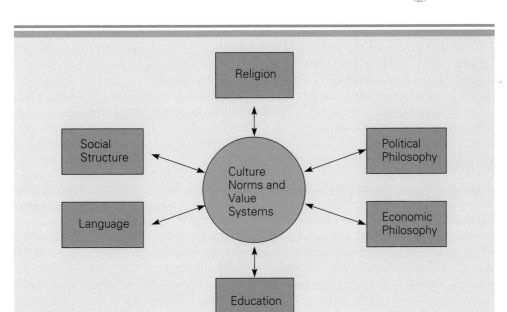

FIGURE 3.1

The Determinants of Culture

the last chapter, this view of expansive cultures that embrace several nations underpins Samuel Huntington's view of a world that is fragmented into different civilizations including Western, Islamic, and Sinic (Chinese).[10]

To complicate things further, it is also possible to talk about culture at different levels. It is reasonable to talk about "American society" and "American culture," but there are several societies within America, each with its own culture. One can talk about Afro-American culture, Cajun culture, Chinese-American culture, Hispanic culture, Indian culture, Irish-American culture, and Southern culture. The relationship between culture and country is often ambiguous. One cannot always characterize a country as having a single homogenous culture, and even when one can, one must also often recognize that the national culture is a mosaic of subcultures.

THE DETERMINANTS OF CULTURE

The values and norms of a culture do not emerge fully formed. They are the evolutionary product of a number of factors, including the prevailing political and economic philosophies, the social structure of a society, and the dominant religion, language, and education (see Figure 3.1). We discussed political and economic philosophies at length in Chapter 2. Such philosophies clearly influence the value systems of a society. For example, the values found in Communist North Korea toward freedom, justice, and individual achievement are clearly different from the values found in the United States, precisely because each society operates according to different political and economic philosophies. Below we will discuss the influence of social structure, religion, language, and education. The chain of causation runs both ways. While factors such as social structure and religion clearly influence the values and norms of a society, the values and norms of a society can influence social structure and religion.

Social Structure

A society's **social structure** refers to its basic social organization. Although social structure consists of many different aspects, two dimensions are particularly important when explaining differences between cultures. The first is the degree to which the basic unit of social organization is the individual, as opposed to the group. In general, Western societies tend to emphasize the primacy of the individual, while groups tend to figure much larger in many other societies. The second dimension is the degree to which a society is stratified into classes or castes. Some societies are characterized by a relatively high degree of social stratification and relatively low mobility between strata (e.g., Indian), while other societies are characterized by a low degree of social stratification and high mobility between strata (e.g., American).

INDIVIDUALS AND GROUPS

A **group** is an association of two or more individuals who have a shared sense of identity and who interact with each other in structured ways on the basis of a common set of expectations about each other's behavior.[11] Human social life is group life. Individuals are involved in families, work groups, social groups, recreational groups, and so on. However, while groups are found in all societies, societies differ according to the degree to which the group is viewed as the primary means of social organization.[12] In some societies, individual attributes and achievements are viewed as being more important than group membership, while in others the reverse is true (in Saudi Arabia, for example, the family group one belongs to is arguably more important than individual attributes and achievements in explaining success—see the opening case).

The Individual

In Chapter 2, we discussed individualism as a political philosophy. However, individualism is more than just an abstract political philosophy. In many Western societies, the individual is the basic building block of social organization. This is reflected not just in the political and economic organization of society, but also in the way people perceive themselves and relate to each other in social and business settings. The value systems of many Western societies, for example, emphasize individual achievement. The social standing of individuals is not so much a function of whom they work for, as of their individual performance in whatever work setting they choose.

The emphasis on individual performance in many Western societies has both beneficial and harmful aspects. In the United States, the emphasis on individual performance finds expression in an admiration of rugged individualism and entrepreneurship. One benefit of this is the high level of entrepreneurial activity in the United States and other Western societies. New products and new ways of doing business (e.g., personal computers, photocopiers, computer software, biotechnology, supermarkets, and discount retail stores) have repeatedly been created in the United States by entrepreneurial individuals. One can argue that the dynamism of the U.S. economy owes much to the philosophy of individualism.

Individualism also finds expression in a high degree of managerial mobility between companies, and this is not always a good thing. While moving from company to company may be good for individual managers, who are trying to build impressive résumés, it is not necessarily a good thing for American companies. The lack of loyalty and commitment to an individual company, and the tendency to move on for a better offer, can result in managers who have good general skills but lack the knowledge, experience, and network of interpersonal contacts that come from years of working within the same company. An effective manager draws on company-specific experience, knowledge, and a network of contacts to find solutions to current problems, and American companies may suffer if their managers lack these attributes. One positive aspect of high managerial mobility is that executives are exposed to different ways of doing business. The ability to compare business practices helps U.S. executives identify how good practices and techniques developed in one firm might be profitably applied to other firms.

The emphasis on individualism may also make it difficult to build teams within an organization to perform collective tasks. If individuals are always competing with each other on the basis of individual performance, it may be difficult for them to cooperate. A study of U.S. competitiveness by the Massachusetts Institute of Technology concluded that U.S. firms are being hurt in the global economy by a failure to achieve cooperation both within a company (e.g., between functions; between management and labor) and between companies (e.g., between a firm and its suppliers). Given the emphasis on individualism in the American value system, this failure is not surprising.[13] The emphasis on individualism in the United States, while helping to create a dynamic entrepreneurial economy, may raise the costs of doing business due to its adverse impact on managerial stability and cooperation.

The Group

In contrast to the Western emphasis on the individual, the group is the primary unit of social organization in many other societies. For example, in Japan, the social status of an individual is determined as much by the standing of the group to which he or she belongs as by his or her individual performance.[14] In traditional Japanese society, the group was the family or village to which an individual belonged. Today the group has frequently come to be associated with the work team or business organization to which an individual belongs. In a now-classic study of Japanese society, Nakane noted how this expresses itself in everyday life:

> When a Japanese faces the outside (confronts another person) and affixes some position to himself socially he is inclined to give precedence to institution over kind of occupation. Rather than saying, "I am a typesetter" or "I am a filing clerk," he is likely to say, "I am from B Publishing Group" or "I belong to S company."[15]

Nakane goes on to observe that the primacy of the group to which an individual belongs often evolves into a deeply emotional attachment in which identification with the group becomes all important in one's life. One central value of Japanese culture is the importance attached to group membership. This may have beneficial implications for business firms. Strong identification with the group is argued to create pressures for mutual self-help and collective action. If the worth of an individual is closely linked to the achievements of the group (e.g., firm), as Nakane maintains is the case in Japan, this creates a strong incentive for individual members of the group to work together for the common good. Some argue that the success of Japanese enterprises in the global economy during the 1970s and 1980s was based partly on their ability to achieve close cooperation between individuals within a company and between companies. This found expression in the widespread diffusion of self-managing work teams within Japanese organizations, the close cooperation among different functions within Japanese companies (e.g., among manufacturing, marketing, and R&D), and the cooperation between a company and its suppliers on issues such as design, quality control, and inventory reduction.[16] In all of these cases, cooperation is driven by the need to improve the performance of the group (i.e., the business firm).

The primacy of the value of group identification also discourages managers and workers from moving from company to company. Lifetime employment in a particular company was long the norm in certain sectors of the Japanese economy (estimates suggest that between 20 and 40 percent of all Japanese employees have formal or informal lifetime employment guarantees). Over the years, managers and workers build up knowledge, experience, and a network of interpersonal business contacts. All these things can help managers perform their jobs more effectively and achieve cooperation with others.

However, the primacy of the group is not always beneficial. Just as U.S. society is characterized by a great deal of dynamism and entrepreneurship, reflecting the primacy of values associated with individualism, some argue that Japanese society is characterized by a corresponding lack of dynamism and entrepreneurship. Although the long-run consequences are unclear, the United States could continue to create more new industries than Japan and continue to be more successful at pioneering radically new products and new ways of doing business.

SOCIAL STRATIFICATION

All societies are stratified on a hierarchical basis into social categories—that is, into **social strata.** These strata are typically defined on the basis of characteristics such as family background, occupation, and income. Individuals are born into a particular stratum. They become a member of the social category to which their parents belong. Individuals born into a stratum toward the top of the social hierarchy tend to have better life chances than individuals born into a stratum toward the bottom of the hierarchy. They are likely to have better education, health, standard of living, and work opportunities. Although all societies are stratified to some degree, they differ in two related ways. First, they differ from each other with regard to the degree of mobility between social strata, and second, they differ with regard to the significance attached to social strata in business contexts.

Social Mobility

The term **social mobility** refers to the extent to which individuals can move out of the strata into which they are born. Social mobility varies significantly from society to society. The most rigid system of stratification is a caste system. A **caste system** is a closed system of stratification in which social position is determined by the family into which a person is born, and change in that position is usually not possible during an individual's lifetime. Often a caste position carries with it a specific occupation. Members of one caste might be shoemakers, members of another might be butchers, and so on. These occupations are embedded in the caste and passed down through the family to succeeding generations. Although the number of societies with caste systems diminished rapidly during the 20th century, one partial example still remains. India has four main castes and several thousand subcastes. Even though the caste system was officially abolished in 1949, two years after India became independent, it is still a force in rural Indian society where occupation and marital opportunities are still partly related to caste.

A **class system** is a less rigid form of social stratification in which social mobility is possible. A class system is a form of open stratification in which the position a person has by birth can be changed through his or her own achievements and/or luck. Individuals born into a class at the bottom of the hierarchy can work their way up, while individuals born into a class at the top of the hierarchy can slip down.

While many societies have class systems, social mobility within a class system varies from society to society. For example, some sociologists have argued that Britain has a more rigid class structure than certain other Western societies, such as the United States.[17] Historically, British society was divided into three main classes: the upper class, which was made up of individuals whose families for generations had wealth, prestige, and occasionally power; the middle class, whose members were involved in professional, managerial, and clerical occupations; and the working class, whose members earned their living from manual occupations. The middle class was further subdivided into the upper-middle class, whose members were involved in important managerial occupations and the prestigious professions (e.g., lawyers, accountants, doctors), and the lower-middle class, whose members were involved in clerical work (e.g., bank tellers) and the less prestigious professions (e.g., schoolteachers).

Historically, the British class system exhibited significant divergence between the life chances of members of different classes. The upper and upper-middle classes typically sent their children to a select group of private schools, where they wouldn't mix with lower-class children, and where they picked up many of the speech accents and social norms that marked them as being from the higher strata of society. These same private schools also had close ties with the most prestigious universities, such as Oxford and Cambridge. Until fairly recently, Oxford and Cambridge guaranteed a certain number of places for the graduates of these private schools. Having been to a prestigious university, the offspring of the upper and upper-middle classes then had an excellent chance of being offered a prestigious job in companies, banks, brokerage firms, and law firms run by members of the upper and upper-middle classes.

In contrast, the members of the British working and lower-middle classes typically went to state schools. The majority left at 16, and those who went on to higher education found it more difficult to get accepted at the best universities. When they did, they found that their lower-class accent and lack of social skills marked them as being from a lower social stratum, which made it more difficult for them to get access to the most prestigious jobs.

Because of this, the class system in Britain perpetuated itself from generation to generation, and mobility was limited. Although upward mobility was possible, it could not normally be achieved in one generation. While an individual from a working-class background may have established an income level that was consistent with membership in the upper-middle class, he or she may not have been accepted as such by others of that class due to accent and background. However, by sending his or her offspring to the "right kind of school," the individual could ensure that his or her children were accepted.

According to many commentators, modern British society is now rapidly leaving this class structure behind and moving toward a classless society. However, sociologists continue to dispute this finding and present evidence that this is not the case. For example, a study reported that in the mid-1990s, state schools in the London suburb of Islington, which has a population of 175,000, had only 79 candidates for university, while one prestigious private school alone, Eton, sent more than that number to Oxford and Cambridge.[18] This, according to the study's authors, implies that "money still begets money." They argue that a good school means a good university, a good university means a good job, and merit has only a limited chance of elbowing its way into this tight little circle.

The class system in the United States is less extreme than in Britain and mobility is greater. Like Britain, the United States has its own upper, middle, and working classes. However, class membership is determined to a much greater degree by individual economic achievements, as opposed to background and schooling. Thus, an individual can, by his or her own economic achievement, move smoothly from the working class to the upper class in a lifetime. Successful individuals from humble origins are highly respected in American society.

Another society where class divisions have historically been of some importance has been China, where there has been a long-standing difference between the life chances of the rural peasantry and urban dwellers. Ironically, this historic division was strengthened during the high point of Communist rule because of a rigid system of household registration that restricted most Chinese to the place of their birth for their lifetime. Bound to collective farming, peasants were cut off from many urban privileges—compulsory education, quality schools, health care, public housing, varieties of foodstuffs, to name only a few, and they largely lived in poverty. Social mobility was thus very limited. This system crumbled following reforms of the late 1970s and early 1980s, and as a consequence, migrant peasant laborers have flooded into China's cities looking for work. Sociologists now hypothesize that a new class system is emerging in China based less on the rural-urban divide and more on urban occupation.[19]

Significance

From a business perspective, the stratification of a society is significant if it affects the operation of business organizations. In American society, the high degree of social mobility and the extreme emphasis on individualism limit the impact of class background on business operations. The same is true in Japan, where most of the population perceives itself to be middle class. In a country such as Great Britain, however, the relative lack of class mobility and the differences between classes have resulted in the emergence of class consciousness. **Class consciousness** refers to a condition where people tend to perceive themselves in terms of their class background, and this shapes their relationships with members of other classes.

This has been played out in British society in the traditional hostility between upper-middle-class managers and their working-class employees. Mutual antagonism and lack of respect historically made it difficult to achieve cooperation between management and labor in many British companies and resulted in a relatively high level of industrial disputes. However, as noted earlier, the last two decades have seen a dramatic reduction in industrial disputes, which bolsters the arguments of those who claim that the country is moving toward a classless society (the level of industrial disputes in the United Kingdom is now lower than in the United States). Alternatively, as noted above, class consciousness may be reemerging in urban China, and may ultimately prove to be significant there.

An antagonistic relationship between management and labor classes, and the resulting lack of cooperation and high level of industrial disruption, tends to raise the costs of production in countries characterized by significant class divisions. In turn, this can make it more difficult for companies based in such countries to establish a competitive advantage in the global economy.

Religious and Ethical Systems

Religion may be defined as a system of shared beliefs and rituals that are concerned with the realm of the sacred.[20] **Ethical systems** refer to a set of moral principles, or values, that are used to guide and shape behavior. Most of the world's ethical systems are the product of religions. Thus, we can talk about Christian ethics and Islamic ethics. However, there is a major exception to the principle that ethical systems are grounded in religion. Confucianism and Confucian ethics influence behavior and shape culture in parts of Asia, yet it is incorrect to characterize Confucianism as a religion.

The relationship among religion, ethics, and society is subtle and complex. Among the thousands of religions in the world today, four dominate in terms of numbers of adherents—Christianity with 1.7 billion adherents, Islam with 1 billion adherents, Hinduism with 750 million adherents (primarily in India), and Buddhism with 350 million adherents (see Map 3.1). Although many other religions have an important influence in certain parts of the modern world (for example, Judaism, which has 18 million adherents), their numbers pale in comparison with these dominant religions (however, as the precursor of both Christianity and Islam, Judaism has an indirect influence that goes beyond its numbers). We will review these four religions, along with Confucianism, focusing on their business implications. Some scholars have argued that the most important business implications of religion center on the extent to which different religions shape attitudes toward work and entrepreneurship and the degree to which the religious ethics affect the costs of doing business in a country.

It is hazardous to make sweeping generalizations about the nature of the relationship between religion and ethical systems and business practice. While some scholars argue that there is a relationship between religious and ethical systems and business practice in a society, in a world where nations with Catholic, Protestant, Muslim, Hindu, and Buddhist majorities all show evidence of entrepreneurial activity and sustainable economic growth, it is important to view such proposed relationships with a degree of skepticism. While the proposed relationships may exist, their impact is probably small compared to the impact of economic policy. Alternatively, recent research by economists Robert Barro and Rachel McCleary does suggest that strong religious beliefs, and particularly beliefs in heaven, hell, and an afterlife, have a positive impact on economic growth rates, irrespective of the particular religion in question.[21] Barro and McCleary looked at religious beliefs and economic growth rates in 59 countries during the 1980s and 1990s. Their conjecture was that higher religious beliefs stimulate economic growth because they help to sustain aspects of individual behavior that lead to higher productivity.

CHRISTIANITY

Christianity is the most widely practiced religion in the world. Approximately 20 percent of the world's people identify themselves as Christians. The vast majority of Christians live in Europe and the Americas, although their numbers are growing rapidly in Africa. Christianity grew out of Judaism. Like Judaism, it is a monotheistic religion

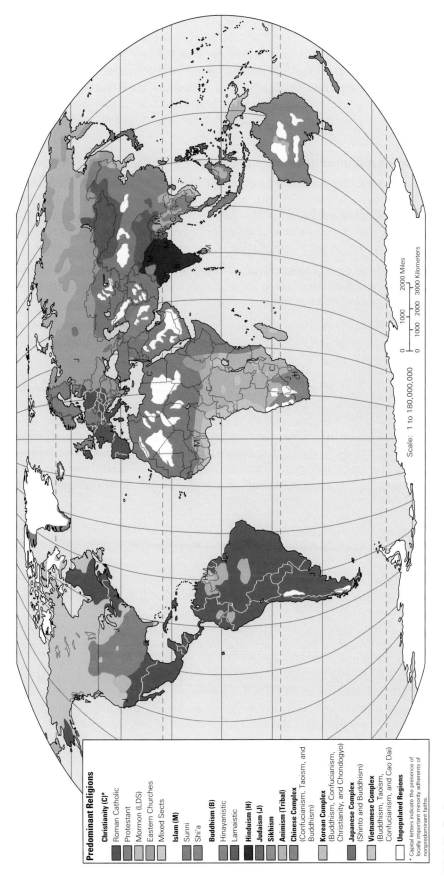

Predominant Religions

Christianity (C)*
Roman Catholic
Protestant
Mormon (LDS)
Eastern Churches
Mixed Sects

Islam (M)
Sunni
Shi'a

Buddhism (B)
Hinayanistic
Lamaistic

Hinduism (H)

Judaism (J)

Sikhism

Animism (Tribal)

Chinese Complex
(Confucianism, Taoism, and
Buddhism)

Korean Complex
(Buddhism, Confucianism,
Christianity, and Chondogyo)

Japanese Complex
(Shinto and Buddhism)

Vietnamese Complex
(Buddhism, Taoism,
Confucianism, and Cao Dai)

Unpopulated Regions

* Capital letters indicate the presence of
locally important minority adherents of
nonpredominant faiths.

Scale: 1 to 180,000,000

0   1000   2000 Miles

0   1000   2000   3000 Kilometers

MAP 3.1

World Religions

Source: From *Student Atlas of World Geography*, Second Edition by John L. Allen. Copyright © 2001 by McGraw-Hill Companies. Reprinted by permission of McGraw-Hill/Dushkin, a division of the McGraw-Hill Companies, Guilford, CT 06437.

(monotheism is the belief in one god). A religious division in the 11th century led to the establishment of two major Christian organizations—the Roman Catholic church and the Orthodox church. Today the Roman Catholic church accounts for more than half of all Christians, most of whom are found in Southern Europe and Latin America. The Orthodox church, while less influential, is still of major importance in several countries (e.g., Greece and Russia). In the 16th century, the Reformation led to a further split with Rome; the result was Protestantism. The nonconformist nature of Protestantism has facilitated the emergence of numerous denominations under the Protestant umbrella (e.g., Baptist, Methodist, Calvinist).

Economic Implications of Christianity: The Protestant Work Ethic

Several sociologists have argued that of the main branches of Christianity—Catholic, Orthodox, and Protestant—the latter has the most important economic implications. In 1904, a German sociologist, Max Weber, made a connection between Protestant ethics and "the spirit of capitalism" that has since become famous.[22] Weber noted that capitalism emerged in Western Europe. He also noted that in Western Europe:

> Business leaders and owners of capital, as well as the higher grades of skilled labor, and even more the higher technically and commercially trained personnel of modern enterprises, are overwhelmingly Protestant.[23]

Weber theorized that there was a relationship between Protestantism and the emergence of modern capitalism. Weber argued that Protestant ethics emphasize the importance of hard work and wealth creation (for the glory of God) and frugality (abstinence from worldly pleasures). According to Weber, this kind of value system was needed to facilitate the development of capitalism. Protestants worked hard and systematically to accumulate wealth. However, their ascetic beliefs suggested that rather than consuming this wealth by indulging in worldly pleasures, they should invest it in the expansion of capitalist enterprises. Thus, the combination of hard work and the accumulation of capital, which could be used to finance investment and expansion, paved the way for the development of capitalism in Western Europe and subsequently in the United States. In contrast, Weber argued that the Catholic promise of salvation in the next world, rather than this world, did not foster the same kind of work ethic.

Protestantism also may have encouraged capitalism's development in another way. By breaking away from the hierarchical domination of religious and social life that characterized the Catholic church for much of its history, Protestantism gave individuals significantly more freedom to develop their own relationship with God. The right to freedom of form of worship was central to the nonconformist nature of early Protestantism. This emphasis on individual religious freedom may have paved the way for the subsequent emphasis on individual economic and political freedoms and the development of individualism as an economic and political philosophy. As we saw in Chapter 2, such a philosophy forms the bedrock on which entrepreneurial free market capitalism is based. Building on this, some scholars claim there is a connection between individualism, as inspired by Protestantism, and the extent of entrepreneurial activity in a nation.[24] Again, one must be careful not to generalize too much from this historical sociological view. While nations with a strong Protestant tradition such as Britain, Germany, and the United States were early leaders in the industrial revolution, nations with Catholic or Orthodox majorities show significant and sustained entrepreneurial activity and economic growth in the modern world.

ISLAM

With nearly 1 billion adherents, Islam is the second largest of the world's major religions. Islam dates back to 610 AD when the prophet Muhammad began spreading the word, although the Muslim calendar begins in 622 AD when, to escape growing opposition,

Despite the rise of radical Islamic fundamentalism, the vast majority of the Muslim population supports peace.

Muhammad left Mecca for the oasis settlement of Yathrib, later known as Madina. Adherents of Islam are referred to as Muslims. Muslims constitute a majority in more than 35 countries and inhabit a nearly contiguous stretch of land from the northwest coast of Africa, through the Middle East, to China and Malaysia in the Far East.

Islam has roots in both Judaism and Christianity (Islam views Jesus Christ as one of God's prophets). Like Christianity and Judaism, Islam is a monotheistic religion. The central principle of Islam is that there is but the one true omnipotent God. Islam requires unconditional acceptance of the uniqueness, power, and authority of God and the understanding that the objective of life is to fulfill the dictates of his will in the hope of admission to paradise. According to Islam, worldly gain and temporal power are an illusion. Those who pursue riches on earth may gain them, but those who forgo worldly ambitions to seek the favor of Allah may gain the greater treasure—entry into paradise. Other major principles of Islam include: (1) honoring and respecting parents, (2) respecting the rights of others, (3) being generous but not a squanderer, (4) avoiding killing except for justifiable causes, (5) not committing adultery, (6) dealing justly and equitably with others, (7) being of pure heart and mind, (8) safeguarding the possessions of orphans, and (9) being humble and unpretentious.[25] Obvious parallels exist with many of the central principles of both Judaism and Christianity.

Islam is an all-embracing way of life governing the totality of a Muslim's being.[26] As God's surrogate in this world, a Muslim is not a totally free agent but is circumscribed by religious principles—by a code of conduct for interpersonal relations—in social and economic activities. Religion is paramount in all areas of life. The Muslim lives in a social structure that is shaped by Islamic values and norms of moral conduct. The ritual nature of everyday life in a Muslim country is striking to a Western visitor. Among other things, orthodox Muslim ritual requires prayer five times a day (business meetings may be put on hold while the Muslim participants engage in their daily prayer ritual), requires that women should be dressed in a certain manner, and forbids the consumption of pork and alcohol.

Islamic Fundamentalism

The past three decades have witnessed the growth of a social movement often referred to as Islamic fundamentalism.[27] In the West, Islamic fundamentalism is associated in the media with militants, terrorists, and violent upheavals, such as the bloody conflict occurring in Algeria, the killing of foreign tourists in Egypt, and the September 11, 2001, attacks on the World Trade Center and Pentagon in the United States. This characterization is at best misleading. Just as Christian fundamentalists are motivated by sincere and deeply held religious values firmly rooted in their faith, so are Islamic fundamentalists. The violence that the Western media associates with Islamic fundamentalism is perpetrated by a very small minority of radical "fundamentalists" who have hijacked the religion to further their own political and violent ends. (Some Christian "fundamentalists" have done exactly the same, including Jim Jones and David Koresh.) The vast majority of Muslims point out that Islam teaches peace, justice, and tolerance, not violence and intolerance, and that Islam explicitly repudiates the violence that a radical minority practices.

The rise of fundamentalism has no one cause. In part, it is a response to the social pressures created in traditional Islamic societies by the move toward modernization and by the influence of Western ideas, such as liberal democracy, materialism, equal rights for women, and attitudes toward sex, marriage, and alcohol. In many Muslim countries, modernization has been accompanied by a growing gap between a rich urban minority and an impoverished urban and rural majority. For the impoverished majority, modernization has offered little in the way of tangible economic progress, while threatening the traditional value system. Thus, for a Muslim who cherishes his traditions and feels that his identity is jeopardized by the encroachment of alien Western values, Islamic fundamentalism has become a cultural anchor.

Fundamentalists demand a rigid commitment to traditional religious beliefs and rituals. The result has been a marked increase in the use of symbolic gestures that confirm Islamic values. In areas where fundamentalism is strong, women have resumed wearing floor-length, long-sleeved dresses and covering their hair; religious studies have increased in universities; the publication of religious tracts has increased; and public religious orations have risen.[28] Also, the sentiments of some fundamentalist groups are increasingly anti-Western. Rightly or wrongly, Western influence is blamed for a range of social ills, and many fundamentalists' actions are directed against Western governments, cultural symbols, businesses, and even individuals.

In several Muslim countries, fundamentalists have gained political power and have used this to try to make Islamic law (as set down in the Koran, the bible of Islam) the law of the land. There are good grounds for this in Islam. Islam makes no distinction between church and state. It is not just a religion; Islam is also the source of law, a guide to statecraft, and an arbiter of social behavior. Muslims believe that every human endeavor is within the purview of the faith—and this includes political activity—because the only purpose of any activity is to do God's will.[29] (Some Christian fundamentalists also share this view.) The Muslim fundamentalists have been most successful in Iran, where a fundamentalist party has held power since 1979, but they also have had an influence in many other countries, such as Algeria, Afghanistan (where the Taliban established an extreme fundamentalist state until removed by the U.S.-led coalition in 2002), Egypt, Pakistan, the Sudan, and Saudi Arabia (see the opening case).

Economic Implications of Islam

The Koran establishes some explicit economic principles, many of which are pro-free enterprise.[30] The Koran speaks approvingly of free enterprise and of earning legitimate profit through trade and commerce (the prophet Mohammed was once a trader). The protection of the right to private property is also embedded within Islam, although Islam asserts that all property is a favor from Allah (God), who created and so owns everything. Those who hold property are regarded as trustees, rather than owners in the Western sense of the word. As trustees they are entitled to receive profits from the property but are admonished to use it in a righteous, socially beneficial, and prudent manner. This reflects Islam's concern with social justice. Islam is critical of those who earn profit through the exploitation of others. In the Islamic view of the world, humans are part of a collective in which the wealthy and successful have obligations to help the disadvantaged. Put simply, in Muslim countries, it is fine to earn a profit, so long as that profit is justly earned and not based on the exploitation of others for one's own advantage. It also helps if those making profits undertake charitable acts to help the poor. Furthermore, Islam stresses the importance of living up to contractual obligations, of keeping one's word, and of abstaining from deception.

Given the Islamic proclivity to favor market-based systems, Muslim countries are likely to be receptive to international businesses as long as those businesses behave in a manner that is consistent with Islamic ethics. Businesses that are perceived as making an unjust profit through the exploitation of others, by deception, or by breaking contractual obligations are unlikely to be welcomed in an Islamic country. In addition, in Islamic countries where fundamentalism is on the rise, hostility toward Western-owned businesses is likely to increase.

In the previous chapter, we noted that one economic principle of Islam prohibits the payment or receipt of interest, which is considered usury. This is not just a matter of theology; in several Islamic states, it is also becoming a matter of law. In 1992, for example, Pakistan's Federal Shariat Court, the highest Islamic law court in the country, pronounced interest to be un-Islamic and therefore illegal and demanded that the government amend all financial laws accordingly. In 1999, Pakistan's Supreme Court ruled that Islamic banking methods should be used in the country after July 1, 2001, but also ruled that Western banking methods could still be used.[31] The accompanying Country Focus takes a closer look at how Islamic banking is being introduced in Pakistan.

HINDUISM

Hinduism has approximately 750 million adherents, most of them on the Indian subcontinent. Hinduism began in the Indus Valley in India more than 4,000 years ago, making it the world's oldest major religion. Unlike Christianity and Islam, its founding is not linked to a particular person. Nor does it have an officially sanctioned sacred book such as the Bible or the Koran. Hindus believe that a moral force in society requires the acceptance of certain responsibilities, called dharma. Hindus believe in reincarnation or rebirth into a different body after death. Hindus also believe in karma, the spiritual progression of each person's soul. A person's karma is affected by the way he or she lives. The moral state of an individual's karma determines the challenges he or she will face in the next life. By perfecting the soul in each new life, Hindus believe that an individual can eventually achieve nirvana, a state of complete spiritual perfection that renders reincarnation no longer necessary. Many Hindus believe that the way to achieve nirvana is to lead a severe ascetic lifestyle of material and physical self-denial, devoting life to a spiritual rather than material quest.

One of the interesting aspects of Hindu culture is the reverence for the cow, which Hindus see as a gift of the gods to the human race. The sacred status of the cow created some unique problems for McDonald's when it entered India in the 1990s, since devout Hindus do not eat beef (and many are also vegetarians). The accompanying Management Focus looks at how McDonald's dealt with that challenge.

Economic Implications of Hinduism

Max Weber, who is famous for expounding on the Protestant work ethic, also argued that the ascetic principles embedded in Hinduism do not encourage the kind of entrepreneurial activity in pursuit of wealth creation that we find in Protestantism.[32] According to Weber, traditional Hindu values emphasize that individuals should not be judged by their material achievements, but by their spiritual achievements. Hindus perceive the pursuit of material well-being as making the attainment of nirvana more difficult. Given

COUNTRY FOCUS The Koran clearly condemns interest, which is called *riba* in Arabic, as exploitative and unjust. For many years, banks operating in Islamic countries conveniently ignored this condemnation, but starting about 30 years ago with the establishment of an Islamic bank in Egypt, Islamic banks started to open in predominantly Muslim countries. By 2005, some 176 Islamic financial institutions worldwide managed over $240 billion in assets, making an average return on capital of more than 16 percent. Even conventional banks are entering the market—both Citigroup and HSBC, two of the world's largest financial institutions, now offer Islamic financial services. While only Iran and the Sudan enforce Islamic banking conventions, in an increasing number of countries customers can choose between conventional banks and Islamic banks. Recently, Pakistan has become one of those countries.

Conventional banks make a profit on the spread between the interest rate they have to pay to depositors and the higher interest rate they charge borrowers. Because Islamic banks cannot pay or charge interest, they must find a different way of making money. Islamic banks have experimented with two different banking methods—the *mudarabah* and the *murabaha*.

A *mudarabah* contract is similar to a profit-sharing scheme. Under *mudarabah,* when an Islamic bank lends money to a business, rather than charging that business interest on the loan, it takes a share in the profits that are derived from the investment. Similarly, when a business (or individual) deposits money at an Islamic bank in a savings account, the deposit is treated as an equity investment in whatever activity the bank uses the capital for. Thus, the depositor receives a share in the profit from the bank's investment (as opposed to interest payments) according to an agreed-on ratio. Some Muslims claim this is a more efficient system than the Western banking system, since it encourages both long-term savings and long-term investment. However, there is no hard evidence of this, and many believe that a *mudarabah* system is less efficient than a conventional Western banking system.

The second Islamic banking method, the *murabaha* contract, is the most widely used among the world's Islamic banks, primarily because it is the easiest to implement. In a *murabaha* contract, when a firm wishes to purchase something using a loan—let's say a piece of equipment that costs $1,000—the firm tells the bank after having negotiated the price with the equipment manufacturer. The bank then buys the equipment for $1,000, and the borrower buys it back from the bank at some later date for, say, $1,100, a price that includes a $100 markup for the bank. A cynic might point out that such a

the emphasis on an ascetic lifestyle, Weber thought that devout Hindus would be less likely to engage in entrepreneurial activity than devout Protestants.

Mahatma Gandhi, the famous Indian nationalist and spiritual leader, was certainly the embodiment of Hindu asceticism. It has been argued that the values of Hindu asceticism and self-reliance that Gandhi advocated had a negative impact on the economic development of postindependence India.[33] But one must be careful not to read too much into Weber's arguments. Modern India is a very dynamic entrepreneurial society and millions of hardworking entrepreneurs form the economic backbone of India's rapidly growing economy.

Historically, Hinduism also supported India's caste system. The concept of mobility between castes within an individual's lifetime makes no sense to traditional Hindus. Hindus see mobility between castes as something that is achieved through spiritual progression and reincarnation. An individual can be reborn into a higher caste in his next life if he achieves spiritual development in this life. In so far as the caste system limits individuals' opportunities to adopt positions of responsibility and influence in society, the economic consequences of this religious belief are somewhat negative. For example, within a business organization, the most able individuals may find their route to the higher levels of the organization blocked simply because they

markup is functionally equivalent to an interest payment, and it is the similarity between this method and conventional banking that makes it so much easier to adopt.

With regard to Pakistan, the development of Islamic banking dates to 1992 when Pakistan's Federal Shariat Court, the highest Islamic law court in the country, pronounced interest to be un-Islamic and therefore illegal. The court demanded that the government amend all financial laws accordingly. In 1999, Pakistan's Supreme Court affirmed that Islamic banking methods should be used in the country, and set a date of July 1, 2001, for their introduction, but in a concession to practical considerations, the higher court agreed that Western banking methods could still be used alongside Islamic banking methods.

Three fears underlay the decision to establish a dual banking system in Pakistan, with Islamic banks operating alongside conventional banks, and some banks offering both Islamic and conventional banking services. One fear was that if there was a mandated shift to Islamic banking methods, it might trigger large-scale withdrawals by depositors worried that they could suffer in the absence of fixed interest rates. Another concern was that the country needed to have a tight regulatory regime to ensure that unscrupulous borrowers using a *mudarabah* contract did not declare themselves bankrupt, even when their businesses were making a profit. That regime did not ex-

ist in 1999. A third concern was that the uncertainty created by the transition would scare off foreign investors, leaving Pakistan starved of capital.

After a slow start, by early 2005 Islamic banks were starting to gain traction in Pakistan. Two full-fledged Islamic banks were operating 25 branches in Pakistan, and a third was scheduled to start operating in early 2005. In addition, nine conventional banks, including Standard Charter and AG Zurich, had opened some 23 branches offering Islamic banking services, and several other major conventional banks, including Citibank and ABN Amro, were negotiating for licensees with the Pakistani banking authorities to start offering Islamic banking services in the country. Estimates now suggest that by 2010, some 20 percent of all assets in the Pakistani banking system will be held by Islamic banks.

Their growth seems assured. As one customer stated, "I never went for conventional banking as it is based on interest, which is prohibited in Islam and amounts to waging war against Allah. Now I have my bank account in an Islamic bank and it satisfies my faith."

Sources: "Forced Devotion," *The Economist,* February 17, 2001, pp. 76–77; "Islamic Banking Marches On," *The Banker,* February 1, 2000; F. Bokhari, "Bankers Fear Introduction of Islamic System Will Prompt Big Withdrawals," *Financial Times,* March 6, 2001, p. 4; and *Agence France Presse,* "Islamic Banking Booms in Pakistan," January 2005 (source of quote).

come from a lower caste. By the same token, individuals may get promoted to higher positions within a firm as much because of their caste background as because of their ability. However, the caste system has been abolished in India and its influence is now fading.

BUDDHISM

Buddhism was founded in India in the sixth century BC by Siddhartha Gautama, an Indian prince who renounced his wealth to pursue an ascetic lifestyle and spiritual perfection. Siddhartha achieved nirvana but decided to remain on earth to teach his followers how they too could achieve this state of spiritual enlightenment. Siddhartha became known as the Buddha (which means "the awakened one"). Today Buddhism has 350 million followers, most of whom are found in Central and Southeast Asia, China, Korea, and Japan. According to Buddhism, suffering originates in people's desires for pleasure. Cessation of suffering can be achieved by following a path for transformation. Siddhartha offered the Noble Eightfold Path as a route for transformation. This emphasizes right seeing, thinking, speech, action, living, effort, mindfulness, and meditation. Unlike Hinduism, Buddhism does not support the caste system. Nor does

MANAGEMENT FOCUS

In many ways, McDonald's Corporation has written the book on global expansion. Every day, on average, somewhere around the world 4.2 new McDonald's restaurants are opened. By 2004, the company had 30,000 restaurants in more than 120 countries that collectively served close to 50 million customers each day.

One of the latest additions to McDonald's list of countries hosting the famous golden arches is India, where McDonald's started to establish restaurants in the late 1990s. Although India is a poor nation, the large and relatively prosperous middle class, estimated to number between 150 million and 200 million, attracted McDonald's. India, however, offered McDonald's unique challenges. For thousands of years, India's Hindu culture has revered the cow. Hindu scriptures state that the cow is a gift of the gods to the human race. The cow represents the Divine Mother that sustains all human beings. Cows give birth to bulls that are harnessed to pull plows, cow milk is highly valued and used to produce yogurt and ghee (a form of butter), cow urine has a unique place in traditional Hindu medicine, and cow dung is used as fuel. Some 300 million of these animals roam India, untethered, revered as sacred providers. They are everywhere, ambling down roads, grazing in rubbish dumps, and resting in temples—everywhere, that is, except on your plate, for Hindus do not eat the meat of the sacred cow.

McDonald's is the world's largest user of beef. Since its founding in 1955, countless animals have died to produce Big Macs. How can a company whose fortunes are built upon beef enter a country where the consumption of beef is a grave sin? Use pork instead? But there are some 140 million Muslims in India, and Muslims don't eat pork. This leaves chicken and mutton. McDonald's responded to this cultural food dilemma by creating an Indian version of its Big Mac—the "Maharaja Mac"—which is made from mutton. Other additions to the menu conform to local sensibilities such as the "McAloo Tikki Burger," which is made from chicken. All foods are strictly segregated into vegetarian and nonvegetarian lines to conform with preferences in a country where many Hindus are vegetarian. According to the head of McDonald's Indian operations, "We had to reinvent ourselves for the Indian palate."

For a while, this seemed to work. Then in 2001 McDonald's was blindsided by a class-action lawsuit brought against it in the United States by three Indian businessmen living in Seattle. The businessmen, all vegetarians and two of whom were Hindus, sued McDonald's for "fraudulently concealing" the existence of beef in McDonald's French fries! McDonald's had said it used only 100 percent vegetable oil to make French fries, but the company soon admitted that it used a "minuscule" amount of beef extract in the oil. McDonald's settled the suit for $10 million and issued an apology, which read, "McDonald's sincerely apologizes to Hindus, vegetarians, and others for failing to provide the kind of information they needed to make informed dietary decisions at our U.S. restaurants." Going forward, the company pledged to do a better job of labeling the ingredients of its food and to find a substitute for the beef extract used in its oil.

However, news travels fast in the global society of the 21st century, and the revelation that McDonald's used beef extract in its oil was enough to bring Hindu nationalists onto the streets in Delhi, where they vandalized one McDonald's restaurant, causing $45,000 in damage; shouted slogans outside of another; picketed the company's headquarters; and called on India's prime minister to close McDonald's stores in the country. McDonald's Indian franchise holders quickly issued denials that they used oil that contained beef extract, and Hindu extremists responded by stating they would submit McDonald's oil to laboratory tests to see if they could detect beef extract.

The negative publicity seemed to have little impact on McDonald's long-term plans in India, however. The company continued to open restaurants, and by 2005 had 65 restaurants in the country with plans to open another 30 or so. When asked why they frequented McDonald's restaurants, Indian customers noted that their children enjoyed the "American" experience, the food was of a consistent quality, and the toilets were always clean!

Sources: Luke Harding, "Give Me a Big Mac—But Hold the Beef," *The Guardian*, December 28, 2000, p. 24; Luke Harding, "Indian McAnger," *The Guardian*, May 7, 2001, p. 1; A. Dhillon, "India Has No Beef with Fast Food Chains," *Financial Times*, March 23, 2002, p. 3; and "McDonald's Plans More Outlets in India," Associated Press Worldstream, December 24, 2004.

Buddhism advocate the kind of extreme ascetic behavior that is encouraged by Hinduism. Nevertheless, like Hindus, Buddhists stress the afterlife and spiritual achievement rather than involvement in this world.

Because of this, the emphasis on wealth creation that is embedded in Protestantism is not found in Buddhism. Thus, in Buddhist societies, we do not see the same kind of historical cultural stress on entrepreneurial behavior that Weber claimed could be found in the Protestant West. But unlike Hinduism, the lack of support for the caste system and extreme ascetic behavior suggests that a Buddhist society may represent a more fertile ground for entrepreneurial activity than a Hindu culture.

CONFUCIANISM

Confucianism was founded in the fifth century BC by K'ung-Fu-tzu, more generally known as Confucius. For more than 2,000 years until the 1949 Communist revolution, Confucianism was the official ethical system of China. While observance of Confucian ethics has been weakened in China since 1949, more than 200 million people still follow the teachings of Confucius, principally in China, Korea, and Japan. Confucianism teaches the importance of attaining personal salvation through right action. Although not a religion, Confucian ideology has become deeply embedded in the culture of these countries over the centuries, and through that, has an impact on the lives of many millions more. Confucianism is built around a comprehensive ethical code that sets down guidelines for relationships with others. High moral and ethical conduct and loyalty to others are central to Confucianism. Unlike religions, Confucianism is not concerned with the supernatural and has little to say about the concept of a supreme being or an afterlife.

Economic Implications of Confucianism

Some scholars maintain that Confucianism may have economic implications as profound as those Weber argued were to be found in Protestantism, although they are of a different nature.[34] Their basic thesis is that the influence of Confucian ethics on the culture of China, Japan, South Korea, and Taiwan, by lowering the costs of doing business in those countries, may help explain their economic success. In this regard, three values central to the Confucian system of ethics are of particular interest—loyalty, reciprocal obligations, and honesty in dealings with others.

In Confucian thought, loyalty to one's superiors is regarded as a sacred duty—an absolute obligation. In modern organizations based in Confucian cultures, the loyalty that binds employees to the heads of their organization can reduce the conflict between management and labor that we find in more class-conscious societies. Cooperation between management and labor can be achieved at a lower cost in a culture where the virtue of loyalty is emphasized in the value systems.

However, in a Confucian culture, loyalty to one's superiors, such as a worker's loyalty to management, is not blind loyalty. The concept of reciprocal obligations is important. Confucian ethics stress that superiors are obliged to reward the loyalty of their subordinates by bestowing blessings on them. If these "blessings" are not forthcoming, then neither will be the loyalty. This Confucian ethic is central to the Chinese concept of *guanxi*, which refers to relationship networks supported by reciprocal obligations.[35] *Guanxi* literally means relationships, although in business settings it can be better understood as connections. Today, Chinese will often cultivate a *guanxiwang*, or "relationship network," for help. Reciprocal obligations are the glue that holds such networks together. If those obligations are not met—if favors done are not paid back or reciprocated—the reputation of the transgressor is tarnished and he or she will be less able to draw on their *guanxiwang* for help in the future. Thus, the implicit threat of social sanctions is often sufficient to ensure that favors are repaid, that obligations are met, and that relationships are honored. In a society that lacks a rule-based legal tradition, and thus legal ways of redressing wrongs such as violations of business agreements, *guanxi* is an important mechanism for building long-term business relationships and getting business done in China (see the following Country Focus for additional details).

COUNTRY FOCUS McDonald's Corporation opened its first restaurant in Beijing, China, in 1992 after a decade of market research. The restaurant, then the largest McDonald's in the world, was located on the corner of Wangfujing Street and the Avenue of Eternal Peace, just two blocks from Tiananmen Square, the very heart of China's capital. The choice of location seemed auspicious, and within two years, sales at the restaurant were surpassing all expectations. Then the Beijing city government dropped a bombshell; officials abruptly informed McDonald's that it would have to vacate the location to make way for a commercial, residential, and office complex planned by Hong Kong developer Li Ka-shing. At the time, McDonald's still had 18 years to run on its 20-year lease. A stunned McDonald's did what any good Western company would do—it took the Beijing city government to court to try to enforce the lease. The court refused to enforce the lease, and McDonald's had to move. Chinese observers had a simple explanation for the outcome. McDonald's, they said, lacked the *guanxi* of Li Ka-shing. Given this, the company could not expect to prevail. Company executives should have accepted the decision in good grace and moved on, but instead, McDonald's filed a lawsuit—a move that would only reduce what *guanxi* McDonald's might have with the city government!

The example illustrates a basic difference between doing business in the West and doing business in China. In the advanced economies of the West, business transactions are conducted and regulated by the centuries-old framework of contract law, which specifies the rights and obligations of parties to a business contract and provides mechanisms for seeking to redress grievances should one party in the exchange fail to live up to the legal agreement. In the West, McDonald's could have relied on the courts to enforce its legal contract with the city government. In China, this approach didn't work. China does not have the same legal infrastructure. Personal power and relationships or connections, rather than the rule of law, have always been the key to getting things done in China. Decades of Communist rule stripped away the basic legal infrastructure that did exist to regulate business transactions. Power, relationships, and connections are an important, and some say necessary, influence on getting things done and enforcing business agreements in China. The key to understanding this process is the concept of *guanxi*.

Guanxi means relationships; McDonald's lost its lease in central Beijing because it lacked the *guanxi* enjoyed by the powerful Li Ka-shing. The concept of *guanxi* is deeply rooted in Chinese culture, particularly the Confucian phi-

losophy of valuing social hierarchy and reciprocal obligations. Confucian ideology has a 2,000-year-old history in China, and more than half a century of Communist rule has done little to dent its influence on everyday life in China. Confucianism stresses the importance of relationships, both within the family and between master and servant. Confucian ideology teaches that people are not created equal. In Confucian thought, loyalty and obligations to one's superiors (or to family) are regarded as a sacred duty, but at the same time, this loyalty has its price. Social superiors are obligated to reward the loyalty of their social inferiors by bestowing "blessings" upon them; thus, the obligations are reciprocal.

As they have come to understand this, many Western businesses have tried to build *guanxi* to grease the wheels required to do business in China. Increasingly, *guanxi* has become a commodity that is for sale to foreigners. Many of the sons and daughters of high-ranking government officials have set up "consulting" firms and offered to mobilize their *guanxiwang* or those of their parents to help Western companies navigate their way through Chinese bureaucracy. Taking advantage of such services, however, requires good ethical judgment. There is a fine line between relationship building, which may require doing favors to meet obligations, and bribery. Consider the case of a lucrative business contract that was under consideration for more than a year between a large Chinese state-owned enterprise and two competing multinational firms. After months of negotiations, the Chinese elected to continue discussions with just one of the competitors—the one that had recently hired the son of the principal Chinese negotiator at a significant salary. This occurred even though the favored firm's equipment was less compatible with Chinese equipment already in place than that offered by the rejected multinational. The clear implication is that the son of the negotiator had mobilized his *guanxiwang* to help his new employer gain an advantage in the contract negotiations. While hiring the son of the principal negotiator may be viewed as good business practice by some in the context of Chinese culture, others might argue that this action was ethically suspect and could be viewed as little more than a thinly concealed bribe.

Sources: S. D. Seligman, "Guanxi: Grease for the Wheels of China," *China Business Review,* September–October 1999, pp. 34–38; L. Dana, "Culture Is the Essence of Asia," *Financial Times,* November 27, 2000, p. 12; L. Minder, "McDonald's to Close Original Beijing Store," *USA Today,* December 2, 1996, p. 1A; and M. W. Peng, *Business Strategies in Transition Economies* (Thousand Oaks, CA: Sage Publications, 2000).

A third concept found in Confucian ethics is the importance attached to honesty. Confucian thinkers emphasize that, although dishonest behavior may yield short-term benefits for the transgressor, dishonesty does not pay in the long run. The importance attached to honesty has major economic implications. When companies can trust each other not to break contractual obligations, the costs of doing business are lowered. Expensive lawyers are not needed to resolve contract disputes. In a Confucian society, people may be less hesitant to commit substantial resources to cooperative ventures than in a society where honesty is less pervasive. When companies adhere to Confucian ethics, they can trust each other not to violate the terms of cooperative agreements. Thus, the costs of achieving cooperation between companies may be lower in societies such as Japan relative to societies where trust is less pervasive.

For example, it has been argued that the close ties between the automobile companies and their component parts suppliers in Japan are facilitated by a combination of trust and reciprocal obligations. These close ties allow the auto companies and their suppliers to work together on a range of issues, including inventory reduction, quality control, and design. The competitive advantage of Japanese auto companies such as Toyota may in part be explained by such factors.[36] Similarly, the Country Focus showed how the combination of trust and reciprocal obligations is central to the workings and persistence of *guanxi* networks in China. Someone seeking and receiving help through a *guanxi* network is then obligated to return the favor and faces social sanctions if that obligation is not reciprocated when it is called upon. If the person does not return the favor, his reputation will be tarnished and he will be unable to draw on the resources of the network in the future. It is claimed that these relationship-based networks can be more important in helping to enforce agreements between businesses than the Chinese legal system. Some claim that *guanxi* networks are a substitute for the legal system.[37]

Language

One obvious way in which countries differ is language. By language, we mean both the spoken and the unspoken means of communication. Language is one of the defining characteristics of a culture.

SPOKEN LANGUAGE

Language does far more than just enable people to communicate with each other. The nature of a language also structures the way we perceive the world. The language of a society can direct the attention of its members to certain features of the world rather than others. The classic illustration of this phenomenon is that whereas the English language has but one word for snow, the language of the Inuit (Eskimos) lacks a general term for it. Instead, because distinguishing different forms of snow is so important in the lives of the Inuit, they have 24 words that describe different types of snow (e.g., powder snow, falling snow, wet snow, drifting snow).[38]

Because language shapes the way people perceive the world, it also helps define culture. In countries with more than one language, one also often finds more than one culture. Canada has an English-speaking culture and a French-speaking culture. Tensions between the two run quite high, with a substantial proportion of the French-speaking minority demanding independence from a Canada "dominated by English speakers." The same phenomenon can be observed in many countries. Belgium is divided into Flemish and French speakers, and tensions between the two groups exist; in Spain, a Basque-speaking minority with its own distinctive culture has been agitating for independence from the Spanish-speaking majority for decades; on the Mediterranean island of Cyprus, the culturally diverse Greek- and Turkish-speaking populations of the island engaged in open conflict in the 1970s, and the island is now partitioned into two parts. While it does not necessarily follow that language differences create differences in culture and, therefore, separatist pressures (e.g., witness the harmony in Switzerland, where four languages are spoken), there certainly seems to be a tendency in this direction.[39]

Chinese is the mother tongue of the largest number of people, followed by English and Hindi, which is spoken in India. However, the most widely spoken language in the world is English, followed by French, Spanish, and Chinese (i.e., many people speak English as a second language). English is increasingly becoming the language of international business. When a Japanese and a German businessperson get together to do business, it is almost certain that they will communicate in English. However, while English is widely used, learning the local language yields considerable advantages. Most people prefer to converse in their own language and being able to speak the local language can build rapport, which may be very important for a business deal. International businesses that do not understand the local language can make major blunders through improper translation. For example, the Sunbeam Corporation used the English words for its "Mist-Stick" mist-producing hair curling iron when it entered the German market, only to discover after an expensive advertising campaign that mist means excrement in German. General Motors was troubled by the lack of enthusiasm among Puerto Rican dealers for its new Chevrolet Nova. When literally translated into Spanish, Nova meant star. However, when spoken it sounded like "no va," which in Spanish means "it doesn't go." General Motors changed the name of the car to Caribe.[40]

UNSPOKEN LANGUAGE

Unspoken language refers to nonverbal communication. We all communicate with each other by a host of nonverbal cues. The raising of eyebrows, for example, is a sign of recognition in most cultures, while a smile is a sign of joy. Many nonverbal cues, however, are culturally bound. A failure to understand the nonverbal cues of another culture can lead to a communication failure. For example, making a circle with the thumb and the forefinger is a friendly gesture in the United States, but it is a vulgar sexual invitation in Greece and Turkey. Similarly, while most Americans and Europeans use the thumbs-up gesture to indicate that "it's all right," in Greece the gesture is obscene.

Another aspect of nonverbal communication is personal space, which is the comfortable amount of distance between you and someone you are talking to. In the United States, the customary distance apart adopted by parties in a business discussion is five to eight feet. In Latin America, it is three to five feet. Consequently, many North Americans unconsciously feel that Latin Americans are invading their personal space and can be seen backing away from them during a conversation. Indeed, the American may feel that the Latin is being aggressive and pushy. In turn, the Latin American may interpret such backing away as aloofness. The result can be a regrettable lack of rapport between two businesspeople from different cultures.

Education

Formal education plays a key role in a society. Formal education is the medium through which individuals learn many of the language, conceptual, and mathematical skills that are indispensable in a modern society. Formal education also supplements the family's role in socializing the young into the values and norms of a society. Values and norms are taught both directly and indirectly. Schools generally teach basic facts about the social and political nature of a society. They also focus on the fundamental obligations of citizenship. Cultural norms are also taught indirectly at school. Respect for others, obedience to authority, honesty, neatness, being on time, and so on, are all part of the "hidden curriculum" of schools. The use of a grading system also teaches children the value of personal achievement and competition.[41]

From an international business perspective, one important aspect of education is its role as a determinant of national competitive advantage.[42] The availability of a pool of skilled and educated workers seems to be a major determinant of the likely economic success of a country. In analyzing the competitive success of Japan since 1945, for example, Michael Porter notes that after the war, Japan had almost nothing except for a pool of skilled and educated human resources.

> With a long tradition of respect for education that borders on reverence, Japan possessed a large pool of literate, educated, and increasingly skilled human resources. . . . Japan has benefited from a large pool of trained engineers. Japanese universities graduate many more engineers per capita than in the United States. . . . A first-rate primary and secondary education system in Japan operates based on high standards and emphasizes math and science. Primary and secondary education is highly competitive. . . . Japanese education provides most students all over Japan with a sound education for later education and training. A Japanese high school graduate knows as much about math as most American college graduates.[43]

Porter's point is that Japan's excellent education system is an important factor explaining the country's postwar economic success. Not only is a good education system a determinant of national competitive advantage, but it is also an important factor guiding the location choices of international businesses. The recent trend to outsource information technology jobs to India, for example, is partly due to the presence of significant numbers of trained engineers in India, which in turn is a result of the Indian education system. By the same token, it would make little sense to base production facilities that require highly skilled labor in a country where the education system was so poor that a skilled labor pool wasn't available, no matter how attractive the country might seem on other dimensions. It might make sense to base production operations that require only unskilled labor in such a country.

The general education level of a country is also a good index of the kind of products that might sell in a country and of the type of promotional material that should be used. For example, a country where more than 70 percent of the population is illiterate is unlikely to be a good market for popular books. Promotional material containing written descriptions of mass-marketed products is unlikely to have an effect in a country where almost three-quarters of the population cannot read. It is far better to use pictorial promotions in such circumstances.

Culture and the Workplace

Of considerable importance for an international business with operations in different countries is how a society's culture affects the values found in the workplace. Management process and practices may need to vary according to culturally determined work-related values. For example, if the cultures of the United States and France result in different work-related values, an international business with operations in both countries should vary its management process and practices to account for these differences.

Probably the most famous study of how culture relates to values in the workplace was undertaken by Geert Hofstede.[44] As part of his job as a psychologist working for IBM, Hofstede collected data on employee attitudes and values for more than 100,000 individuals from 1967 to 1973. These data enabled him to compare dimensions of culture across 40 countries. Hofstede isolated four dimensions that he claimed summarized different cultures—power distance, uncertainty avoidance, individualism versus collectivism, and masculinity versus femininity.

Hofstede's **power distance** dimension focused on how a society deals with the fact that people are unequal in physical and intellectual capabilities. According to Hofstede, high power distance cultures were found in countries that let inequalities grow over time into inequalities of power and wealth. Low power distance cultures were found in societies that tried to play down such inequalities as much as possible.

The **individualism versus collectivism** dimension focused on the relationship between the individual and his or her fellows. In individualistic societies, the ties between individuals were loose and individual achievement and freedom were highly valued. In societies where collectivism was emphasized, the ties between individuals were tight. In such societies, people were born into collectives, such as extended families, and everyone was supposed to look after the interest of his or her collective.

Hofstede's **uncertainty avoidance** dimension measured the extent to which different cultures socialized their members into accepting ambiguous situations and tolerating uncertainty. Members of high uncertainty avoidance cultures placed a premium on job security, career patterns, retirement benefits, and so on. They also had a strong need for rules and regulations; the manager was expected to issue clear instructions, and subordinates' initiatives were tightly controlled. Lower uncertainty avoidance cultures were characterized by a greater readiness to take risks and less emotional resistance to change.

Hofstede's **masculinity versus femininity** dimension looked at the relationship between gender and work roles. In masculine cultures, sex roles were sharply differentiated and traditional "masculine values," such as achievement and the effective exercise of power, determined cultural ideals. In feminine cultures, sex roles were less sharply distinguished, and little differentiation was made between men and women in the same job.

Hofstede created an index score for each of these four dimensions that ranged from 0 to 100 and scored high for high individualism, high power distance, high uncertainty avoidance, and high masculinity. He averaged the score for all employees from a given country. Table 3.1 summarizes these data for 20 selected countries. Western nations such as the United States, Canada, and Britain score high on the individualism scale and low on the power distance scale. At the other extreme are a group of Latin American and Asian countries that emphasize collectivism over individualism and score high on the power distance scale. Table 3.1 also reveals that Japan's culture has strong uncertainty avoidance and high masculinity. This characterization fits the standard stereotype of Japan as a country that is male dominant and where uncertainty avoidance exhibits itself in the institution of lifetime employment. Sweden and Denmark stand out as countries that have both low uncertainty avoidance and low masculinity (high emphasis on "feminine" values).

Hofstede's results are interesting for what they tell us in a very general way about differences between cultures. Many of Hofstede's findings are consistent with standard Western stereotypes about cultural differences. For example, many people believe Americans are more individualistic and egalitarian than the Japanese (they have a lower power distance), who in turn are more individualistic and egalitarian than Mexicans. Similarly, many might agree that Latin countries such as Mexico place a higher emphasis on masculine value—they are machismo cultures—than the Nordic countries of Denmark and Sweden.

However, one should be careful about reading too much into Hofstede's research. It has been criticized on a number of points.[45] First, Hofstede assumes there is a one-to-one correspondence between culture and the nation-state, but as we saw earlier, many countries have more than one culture. Hofstede's results do not capture this distinction. Second, the research may have been culturally bound. The research team was composed of Europeans and Americans. The questions they asked of IBM employees and their analysis of the answers may have been shaped by their own cultural biases and concerns. So it is not surprising that Hofstede's results confirm Western stereotypes, since it was Westerners who undertook the research!

Third, Hofstede's informants worked not only within a single industry, the computer industry, but also within one company, IBM. At the time, IBM was renowned for its own strong corporate culture and employee selection procedures, making it possible that the employees' values were different in important respects from the values of the cultures from which those employees came. Also, certain social classes (such as unskilled manual workers) were excluded from Hofstede's sample. A final caution is that Hofstede's work is now beginning to look dated. Cultures do not stand still; they evolve, albeit slowly. What was a reasonable characterization in the 1960s and 1970s may not be so today.

	Power Distance	Uncertainty Avoidance	Individualism	Masculinity
Argentina	49	86	46	56
Australia	36	51	90	61
Brazil	69	76	38	49
Canada	39	48	80	52
Denmark	18	23	74	16
France	68	86	71	43
Germany (F.R.)	35	65	67	66
Great Britain	35	35	89	66
India	77	40	48	56
Indonesia	78	48	14	46
Israel	13	81	54	47
Japan	54	92	46	95
Mexico	81	82	30	69
Netherlands	38	53	80	14
Panama	95	86	11	44
Spain	57	86	51	42
Sweden	31	29	71	5
Thailand	64	64	20	34
Turkey	66	85	37	45
United States	40	46	91	62

TABLE 3.1

Work-Related Values for 20 Selected Countries

Source: G. Hofstede, *Culture's Consequences.* Copyright 1980 by Sage Publications. Reprinted by permission of Sage Publications. Cited in G. Hofstede, "The Cultural Relativity of Organizational Practices and Theories," *Journal of International Business Studies* 14 (Fall 1983), pp. 75–89. Reprinted by permission of Dr. Geert Hofstede.

    Still, just as it should not be accepted without question, Hofstede's work should not be dismissed either. It represents a starting point for managers trying to figure out how cultures differ and what that might mean for management practices. Also, several other scholars have found strong evidence that differences in culture affect values and practices in the workplace, and Hofstede's basic results have been replicated using more diverse samples of individuals in different settings.[46] Still, managers should use the results with caution, for they are not necessarily accurate.

    Hofstede subsequently expanded his original research to include a fifth dimension that he argued captured additional cultural differences not brought out in his earlier work.[47] He referred to this dimension as "Confucian dynamism" (sometimes called long-term orientation). According to Hofstede, **Confucian dynamism** captures attitudes toward time, persistence, ordering by status, protection of face, respect for tradition, and reciprocation of gifts and favors. The label refers to these "values" being derived from Confucian teachings. As might be expected, East Asian countries such as Japan, Hong Kong, and Thailand scored high on Confucian dynamism, while nations such as the United States and Canada scored low. Hofstede and his associates went on to argue that their evidence suggested that nations with higher economic growth rates scored high on Confucian dynamism and low on individualism—the implication being Confucianism is good for growth. However, subsequent studies have shown that this finding does not hold up under more sophisticated statistical analysis.[48] During the past decade, countries with high individualism and low Confucian dynamics such as the United States have attained high growth rates, while some Confucian cultures such as Japan have had stagnant economic growth. In reality, while culture might influence the economic success of a nation, it is just one of many factors, and while its importance should not be ignored, it should not be overstated either. The factors discussed in Chapter 2—economic, political, and legal systems—are probably more important than culture in explaining differential economic growth rates over time.

🌐 Cultural Change

Culture is not a constant; it evolves over time.[49] Changes in value systems can be slow and painful for a society. In the 1960s, for example, American values toward the role of women, love, sex, and marriage underwent significant changes. Much of the social turmoil of that time reflected these changes. Change, however, does occur and can often be quite profound. For example, at the beginning of the 1960s, the idea that women might hold senior management positions in major corporations was not widely accepted. Many scoffed at the idea. Today, it is a reality and few in the mainstream of American society question the development or the capability of women in the business world. American culture has changed (although it is still more difficult for women to gain senior management positions than men). Similarly, the value systems of many ex-communist states, such as Russia, are undergoing significant changes as those countries move away from values that emphasize collectivism and toward those that emphasize individualism. While social turmoil is an inevitable outcome of such a shift, the shift will still probably occur.

Similarly, some claim that a major cultural shift is occurring in Japan, with a move toward greater individualism.[50] The model Japanese office worker, or "salaryman," is pictured as being loyal to his boss and the organization to the point of giving up evenings, weekends, and vacations to serve the organization, which is the collective of which he is a member. However, a new generation of office workers does not seem to fit this model. An individual from the new generation is more direct than the traditional Japanese. He acts more like a Westerner, a *gaijian*. He does not live for the company and will move on if he gets the offer of a better job. He is not keen on overtime, especially if he has a date. He has his own plans for his free time, and they may not include drinking or playing golf with the boss.[51]

Several studies have suggested that economic advancement and globalization may be important factors in societal change.[52] For example, there is evidence that economic progress is accompanied by a shift in values away from collectivism and toward individualism.[53] Thus, as Japan has become richer, the cultural emphasis on collectivism has declined and greater individualism is being witnessed. One reason for this shift may be that richer societies exhibit less need for social and material support structures built on collectives, whether the collective is the extended family or the paternalistic company. People are better able to take care of their own needs. As a result, the importance attached to collectivism declines, while greater economic freedoms lead to an increase in opportunities for expressing individualism.

The culture of societies may also change as they become richer because economic progress affects a number of other factors, which in turn influence culture. For example, increased urbanization and improvements in the quality and availability of education are both a function of economic progress, and both can lead to declining emphasis on the traditional values associated with poor rural societies. A 25-year study of values in 78 countries, known as the World Values Survey, coordinated by the University of Michigan's Institute for Social Research, has documented how values change, and linked these to changes in a country's level of economic development.[54] According to this research, as countries get richer, a shift occurs away from "traditional values" linked to religion,

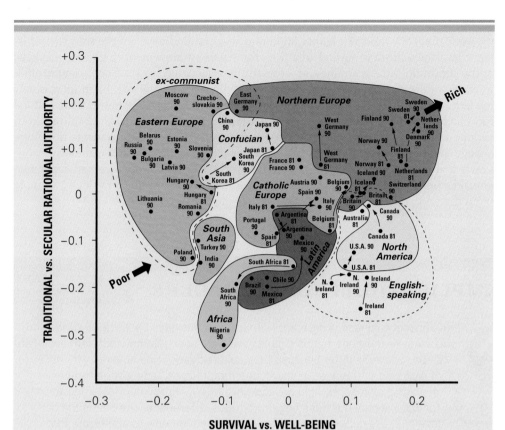

FIGURE 3.2

Changing Values

Source: Reprinted with permission of Ronald Inglehart, "Modernization and Postmodernization," 1997. www.worldvaluessurvey.org.

family, and country, and toward "secular rational" values. Traditionalists say religion is important in their lives. They have a strong sense of national pride, think children should be taught to obey, and that the first duty of a child is to make his or her parents proud. They say abortion, euthanasia, divorce, and suicide are never justified. At the other end of this spectrum are secular rational values.

Another category looked at by the World Values Survey is quality of life attributes. At one end of this spectrum are "survival values," the values people hold when the struggle for survival is of paramount importance. These values tend to stress that economic and physical security are more important than self-expression. People who cannot take food or safety for granted tend to be xenophobic, are wary of political activity, have authoritarian tendencies, and believe that men make better political leaders than women. "Self-expression" or "well-being" values stress the importance of diversity, belonging, and participation in political processes.

As countries get richer, there seems to be a shift from "traditional" to "secular rational" values, and from "survival values" to "well-being" values. The shift, however, takes time, primarily because individuals are socialized into a set of values when they are young and find it difficult to change as they grow older. Substantial changes in values are linked to generations, with younger people typically being in the vanguard of a significant change in values. Figure 3.2 illustrates the position of a number of countries on these dimensions, and shows how they have changed over time.

With regard to globalization, some have argued that advances in transportation and communication technologies, the dramatic increase in trade that we have witnessed since World War II, and the rise of global corporations such as Hitachi, Disney, Microsoft, and Levi Strauss, whose products and operations can be found around the globe, are creating conditions for the merging of cultures.[55] With McDonald's hamburgers in China, The Gap in India, iPods in South Africa, and MTV everywhere helping to foster a ubiquitous youth culture, some argue that the conditions for less cultural variation have been created. At the same time, one must not ignore important countertrends, such as the shift toward Islamic fundamentalism in several countries; the separatist movement in Quebec, Canada; or the continuing ethnic strains and separatist movements in Russia. Such countertrends in many ways are a reaction to the pressures for cultural convergence. In an increasingly modern and materialistic world, some societies are trying to reemphasize their cultural roots and uniqueness. Cultural change is not unidirectional, with national cultures converging toward some homogenous global entity. Also, while some elements of culture change quite rapidly—particularly the use of material symbols—other elements change slowly if at all. Thus, just because people the world over wear blue jeans and eat at McDonald's, one should not assume that they have also adopted American values—for more often than not, they have not.

IMPLICATIONS FOR MANAGERS

International business is different from national business because countries and societies are different. In this chapter, we have seen just how different societies can be. Societies differ because their cultures vary. Their cultures vary because of profound differences in social structure, religion, language, education, economic philosophy, and political philosophy. Three important implications for international business flow from these differences. The first is the need to develop cross-cultural literacy. There is a need not only to appreciate that cultural differences exist, but also to appreciate what such differences mean for international business. A second implication centers on the connection between culture and national competitive advantage. A third implication looks at the connection between culture and ethics in decision making. In this section, we will explore the first two of these issues in depth. The connection between culture and ethics is explored in the next chapter.

CROSS-CULTURAL LITERACY

One of the biggest dangers confronting a company that goes abroad for the first time is the danger of being ill-informed. International businesses that are ill-informed about the practices of another culture are likely to fail. Doing business in different cultures requires adaptation to conform with the value systems and norms of that culture. Adaptation can embrace all aspects of an international firm's operations in a foreign country. The way in which deals are negotiated, the appropriate incentive pay systems for salespeople, the structure of the organization, the name of a product, the tenor of relations between management and labor, the manner in which the product is promoted, and so on, are all sensitive to cultural differences. What works in one culture might not work in another.

To combat the danger of being ill-informed, international businesses should consider employing local citizens to help them do business in a particular culture. They must also ensure that home-country executives are cosmopolitan enough to understand how differences in culture affect the practice of international business. Transferring executives overseas at regular intervals to expose them to different cultures will help build a cadre of cosmopolitan executives. An international business must also be constantly on guard against the dangers of **ethnocentric behavior. Ethnocentrism** is a belief in the superiority of one's own ethnic group or culture. Hand in hand with ethnocentrism goes a disregard or contempt for the culture of other countries. Unfortunately, ethnocentrism is all too prevalent; many Americans are guilty of it, as are many French people, Japanese people, British people, and so on. Ugly as it is, ethnocentrism is a fact of life, one that international businesses must be on guard against.

Simple examples illustrate how important cross-cultural literacy can be. Anthropologist Edward T. Hall has described how Americans, who tend to be informal in nature, react strongly to being corrected or reprimanded in public.[56] This can cause problems in Germany, where a cultural tendency toward correcting strangers can shock and offend most Americans. For their part, Germans can be a bit taken aback by the tendency of Americans to call everyone by their first name. This is uncomfortable enough among executives of the same rank, but it can be seen as insulting when a young and junior American executive addresses an older and more senior German manager by his first name without having been invited to do so. Hall concludes it can take a long time to get on a first-name basis with a German; if you rush the process you will be perceived as overfriendly and rude, and that may not be good for business.

Hall also notes that cultural differences in attitude to time can cause a myriad of problems. He notes that in the United States, giving a person a deadline is a way of increasing the urgency or relative importance of a task. But in the Middle East, giving a deadline can have exactly the opposite effect (see the opening case). The American that insists an Arab business associate make his mind up in a hurry is likely to be perceived as overly demanding and exerting undue pressure. The result may be exactly the opposite of what the American intended, with the Arab going slow as a reaction to the American's arrogance and rudeness. For his part, the American may believe that an Arab associate is being rude if he shows up late to a meeting because he met a friend in the street and stopped to talk. The American, of course, is very concerned about time and scheduling. But for the Arab, who lives in a society where social networks are a major source of information, and maintaining relationships is important, finishing the discussion with a friend is more important than adhering to a strict schedule. Indeed, the Arab may be puzzled as to why the American attaches so much importance to time and schedule.

CULTURE AND COMPETITIVE ADVANTAGE

One theme that continually surfaces in this chapter is the relationship between culture and national competitive advantage. Put simply, the value systems and norms of a country influence the costs of doing business in that country. The costs of doing business in a country influence the ability of firms to establish a competitive advantage in the global marketplace. We have seen how attitudes toward cooperation between management and labor, toward work, and toward the payment of interest are influenced by social structure and religion. It can be argued that the class-based conflict between workers and management in class-conscious societies, when it leads to industrial disruption, raises the costs of doing business in that society. Similarly, we have seen how some sociologists have argued that the ascetic "other-worldly" ethics of Hinduism may not be as supportive of capitalism as the ethics embedded in Protestantism and Confucianism. Also, Islamic laws banning interest payments may raise the costs of doing business by constraining a country's banking system.

Japan presents an interesting example of how culture can influence competitive advantage. Some scholars have argued that the culture of modern Japan lowers the costs of doing business relative to the costs in most Western nations. Japan's emphasis on group affiliation, loyalty, reciprocal obligations, honesty, and education all boost the competitiveness of Japanese companies. The emphasis on group affiliation and loyalty encourages individuals to identify strongly with the companies in which they work. This tends to foster an ethic of hard work and cooperation between management and labor "for the good of the company." Similarly, reciprocal obligations and honesty help foster an atmosphere of trust between companies and their suppliers. This encourages them to enter into long-term relationships with each other to work on inventory reduction, quality control, and design—all of which have been shown to improve an organization's competitiveness. This level of cooperation has often been lacking in the West, where the relationship between a company and its suppliers tends to be a short-term one structured around competitive bidding, rather than one based on long-term mutual commitments. In addition, the availability of a pool of highly skilled labor, particularly engineers, has helped Japanese enterprises develop cost-reducing process innovations that have boosted their productivity.[57] Thus, cultural factors may help explain the competitive advantage enjoyed by many Japanese businesses in the global marketplace. The rise of Japan as an economic power during the second half of the 20th century may be in part attributed to the economic consequences of its culture.

It also has been argued that the Japanese culture is less supportive of entrepreneurial activity than, say, American society. In many ways, entrepreneurial activity is a product of an individualistic mind-set, not a classic characteristic of the Japanese. This may explain why American enterprises, rather than Japanese corporations, dominate industries where entrepreneurship and innovation are highly valued, such as computer software and biotechnology. Of course, obvious and significant exceptions to this generalization exist. Masayoshi Son recognized the potential of software far faster than any of Japan's corporate giants; set up his company, Softbank, in 1981; and has since built it into Japan's top software distributor. Similarly, dynamic entrepreneurial individuals established major Japanese companies such as Sony and Matsushita. But these examples may be the exceptions that prove the rule, for as yet there has been no surge in entrepreneurial high-technology enterprises in Japan equivalent to what has occurred in the United States.

For the international business, the connection between culture and competitive advantage is important for two reasons. First, the connection suggests which countries are likely to produce the most viable competitors. For example, one might argue that U.S. enterprises are likely to see continued growth in aggressive, cost-efficient competitors from those Pacific Rim nations where a combination of free market economics, Confucian ideology, group-oriented social structures, and advanced education systems can all be found (e.g., South Korea, Taiwan, Japan, and, increasingly, China).

Second, the connection between culture and competitive advantage has important implications for the choice of countries in which to locate production facilities and do business. Consider a hypothetical case when a company has to choose between two countries, A and B, for locating a production facility. Both countries are characterized by low labor costs and good access to world markets. Both countries are of roughly the same size (in terms of population) and both are at a similar stage of economic development. In country A, the education system is undeveloped, the society is characterized by a marked stratification between the upper and lower classes, and there are six major linguistic groups. In country B, the education system is well developed, social stratification is lacking, group identification is valued by the culture, and there is only one linguistic group. Which country makes the best investment site?

Country B probably does. In country A, conflict between management and labor, and between different language groups, can be expected to lead to social and industrial disruption, thereby raising the costs of doing business.[58] The lack of a good education system also can be expected to work against the attainment of business goals.

The same kind of comparison could be made for an international business trying to decide where to push its products, country A or B. Again, country B would be the logical choice because cultural factors suggest that in the long run, country B is the nation most likely to achieve the greatest level of economic growth.

But as important as culture is, it is probably less important than economic, political, and legal systems in explaining differential economic growth between nations. Cultural differences are significant, but we should not overemphasize their importance in the economic sphere. For example, earlier we noted that Max Weber argued that the ascetic principles embedded in Hinduism do not encourage entrepreneurial activity. While this is an interesting academic thesis, recent years have seen an increase in entrepreneurial activity in India, particularly in the information technology sector where India is rapidly becoming an important global player. The ascetic principles of Hinduism and caste-based social stratification have apparently not held back entrepreneurial activity in this sector!

Chapter Summary

We have looked at the nature of social culture and studied some implications for business practice. The chapter made the following points:

1. Culture is a complex whole that includes knowledge, beliefs, art, morals, law, customs, and other capabilities acquired by people as members of society.

2. Values and norms are the central components of a culture. Values are abstract ideals about what a society believes to be good, right, and desirable. Norms are social rules and guidelines that prescribe appropriate behavior in particular situations.

3. Values and norms are influenced by political and economic philosophy, social structure, religion, language, and education.

4. The social structure of a society refers to its basic social organization. Two main dimensions along which social structures differ are the individual–group dimension and the stratification dimension.

5. In some societies, the individual is the basic building block of social organization. These societies emphasize individual achievements above all else. In other societies, the group is the basic building block of social organization. These societies emphasize group membership and group achievements above all else.

6. All societies are stratified into different classes. Class-conscious societies are characterized by low social mobility and a high degree of stratification. Less class-conscious societies are characterized by high social mobility and a low degree of stratification.

7. Religion may be defined as a system of shared beliefs and rituals that is concerned with the realm of the sacred. Ethical systems refer to a set of moral principles, or values, that are used to guide and shape behavior. The world's major religions are Christianity, Islam, Hinduism, and Buddhism. Although not a religion, Confucianism has an impact on behavior that is as profound as that of many religions. The value systems of different religious and ethical systems have different implications for business practice.

8. Language is one defining characteristic of a culture. It has both spoken and unspoken dimensions. In countries with more than one spoken language, we tend to find more than one culture.

9. Formal education is the medium through which individuals learn skills and are socialized into the values and norms of a society. Education plays an important role in the determination of national competitive advantage.

10. Geert Hofstede studied how culture relates to values in the workplace. Hofstede isolated four dimensions that he claimed summarized different cultures: power distance, uncertainty avoidance, individualism versus collectivism, and masculinity versus femininity.

11. Culture is not a constant; it evolves. Economic progress and globalization seem to be two important engines of cultural change.

12. One danger confronting a company that goes abroad for the first time is being ill-informed. To develop cross-cultural literacy, international businesses need to employ host-country nationals, build a cadre of cosmopolitan executives, and guard against the dangers of ethnocentric behavior.

13. The value systems and norms of a country can affect the costs of doing business in that country.

Critical Thinking and Discussion Questions

1. Outline why the culture of a country might influence the costs of doing business in that country. Illustrate your answer with examples.

2. Do you think that business practices in an Islamic country are likely to differ from business practices in the United States? If so, how?

3. Reread the opening case on doing business in Saudi Arabia. Has religion been the main factor shaping Saudi culture, or are other factors at work here? What are those factors, and how important do you think they are?

4. What are the implications for international business of differences in the dominant religion and/or ethical system of a country?

5. Choose two countries that appear to be culturally diverse. Compare the cultures of those countries and then indicate how cultural differences influence (*a*) the costs of doing business in each country, (*b*) the likely future economic development of that country, and (*c*) business practices.

Research Task globalEDGE™   globalEDGE.msu.edu

Use the globalEDGE™ site to complete the following exercises:

1. You are preparing for a business trip to Venezuela where you will need to interact extensively with local professionals. Before your departure, you want to collect information regarding local culture and business habits. Prepare a short description of the most striking cultural characteristics that may affect business interactions in this country.

2. Business etiquette varies greatly between Asian cultures and Western cultures. For example, in Thailand it is considered offensive to show the sole of the shoe or foot to another person. Using the globalEDGE™ Web site, find five tips regarding business etiquette in the Asian country of your choice.

Matsushita's and Japan's Changing Culture

CLOSING CASE Established in 1920, the consumer electronics giant Matsushita was at the forefront of the rise of Japan to the status of major economic power during the 1970s and 1980s. Like many other long-standing Japanese businesses, Matsushita was regarded as a bastion of traditional Japanese values based on strong group identification, reciprocal obligations, and loyalty to the company. Several commentators attributed Matsushita's success, and that of the Japanese economy, to the existence of Confucian values in the workplace. At Matsushita, employees were taken care of by the company from "cradle to the grave." Matsushita provided them with a wide range of benefits including cheap housing, guaranteed lifetime employment, seniority-based pay systems, and generous retirement bonuses. In return, Matsushita expected, and got, loyalty and hard work from its employees. To Japan's postwar generation, struggling to recover from the humiliation of defeat, it seemed like a fair bargain. The employees worked hard for the greater good of Matsushita, and Matsushita reciprocated by bestowing "blessings" on employees.

However, culture does not stay constant. According to some observers, the generation born after 1964 lacked the same commitment to traditional Japanese values as their parents. They grew up in a world that was richer, where Western ideas were beginning to make themselves felt, and where the possibilities seemed greater. They did not want to be tied to a company for life, to be a "salaryman." These trends came to the fore in the 1990s, when the Japanese economy entered a prolonged economic slump. As the decade progressed, one Japanese firm after another was forced to change its traditional ways of doing business. Slowly at first, troubled companies started to lay off older workers, effectively abandoning lifetime employment guarantees. As younger people saw this happening, they concluded that loyalty to a company might not be reciprocated, effectively undermining one of the central bargains made in postwar Japan.

Matsushita was one of the last companies to turn its back on Japanese traditions, but in 1998, after years of poor performance, it began to modify traditional practices. The principle agents of change were a group of managers who had extensive experience in Matsushita's overseas operations, and included Kunio Nakamura, who became the chief executive of Matsushita in 2000.

First, Matsushita changed the pay scheme for its 11,000 managers. In the past, the traditional twice-a-year bonuses had been based almost entirely on seniority, but now Matsushita said they would be based on performance. In 1999, Matsushita announced this process would be made transparent; managers would be shown what their performance rankings were and how these fed into pay bonuses. As elementary as this might sound in the West, for Matsushita it represented the beginning of a revolution in human resource practices.

About the same time, Matsushita took aim at the lifetime employment system and the associated perks. Under the new system, recruits were given the choice of three employment options. First, they could sign on to the traditional option. Under this, they were eligible to live in subsidized company housing, go free to company-organized social events, and buy subsidized services such as banking from group companies. They also still would receive a retirement bonus equal to two years' salary. Under a second scheme, employees could forgo the guaranteed retirement bonus in exchange for higher starting salaries and keep perks such as cheap company housing. Under a third scheme, they would lose both the retirement bonus and the subsidized services, but they would start at a still higher salary. In its first two years of operation, only 3 percent of recruits chose the third option—suggesting there is still a hankering for the traditional paternalistic relationship—but 41 percent took the second option.

In other ways Matsushita's designs are grander still. As the company has moved into new industries such as software engineering and network communications technology, it has begun to sing the praises of democratization of employees, and it has sought to encourage individuality, initiative taking, and risk seeking among its younger employees. But while such changes may be easy to articulate, they are hard to implement. For all of its talk, Matsushita has been slow to dismantle its lifetime employment commitment to those hired under the traditional system. This was underlined in early 2001 when, in response to continued poor performance, Matsushita announced it would close 30 factories in Japan, cut 13,000 jobs including 1,000 management jobs, and sell a "huge amount of assets" over the next three years. While this seemed to indicate a final break with the lifetime employment system—it represented the first layoffs in the company's history—the company also said unneeded management staff would not be fired but instead transferred to higher growth areas such as health care.

With so many of its managers a product of the old way of doing things, a skeptic might question the ability of the company to turn its intentions into a reality. As growth has slowed, Matsushita has had to cut back on its hiring, but its continued commitment to longstanding employees means that the average age of its workforce is rising. In the 1960s it was around 25; by the early 2000s it was 35, a trend that might counteract Matsushita's attempts to revolutionize the workplace, for surely those who benefited from the old system will not give way easily to the new. Still, by 2004 it was clear that Matsushita was making progress. After significant losses in 2002, the company broke even in 2003 and started to make profits again in 2004. New growth drivers, such as sales of DVD equipment, certainly helped, but so did the cultural and organizational changes that enabled the company to better exploit these new growth opportunities.

Sources: "Putting the Bounce Back into Matsushita," *The Economist*, May 22, 1999, pp. 67–68; "In Search of the New Japanese Dream," *The Economist*, February 19, 2000, pp. 59–60; P. Landers, "Matsushita to Restructure in Bid to Boost Thin Profits," *The Wall Street Journal*, December 1, 2000, p. A13; and M. Tanikawa, "A Pillar of Japan Inc. Finally Turns Around; Work in Progress," *International Herald Tribune*, August 28, 2004, pp. 17–18.

Case Discussion Questions

1. What were the triggers of cultural change in Japan during the 1990s? How is cultural change starting to affect traditional values in Japan?

2. How might Japan's changing culture influence the way Japanese businesses operate in the future? What are the potential implications of such changes for the Japanese economy?

3. How did traditional Japanese culture benefit Matsushita during the 1950s–1980s? Did traditional values become more of a liability during the 1990s and early 2000s? How so?

4. What is Matsushita trying to achieve with human resource changes it has announced? What are the impediments to successfully implementing these changes? What are the implications for Matsushita if (*a*) the changes are made quickly or (*b*) it takes years or even decades to fully implement the changes?

5. What does the Matsushita case teach you about the relationship between societal culture and business success?

Notes

1. See R. Dore, *Taking Japan Seriously* (Stanford, CA: Stanford University Press, 1987).

2. Data come from J. Monger. "International Comparison of Labor Disputes in 2002," *Labor Market Trends*, April 2004, pp. 145–53.

3. E. B. Tylor, *Primitive Culture* (London: Murray, 1871).

4. Geert Hofstede, *Culture's Consequences: International Differences in Work Related Values* (Beverly Hills, CA: Sage Publications, 1984), p. 21.

5. J. Z. Namenwirth and R. B. Weber, *Dynamics of Culture* (Boston: Allen & Unwin, 1987), p. 8.

6. R. Mead, *International Management: Cross Cultural Dimensions* (Oxford: Blackwell Business, 1994), p. 7.

7. Edward T. Hall and M. R. Hall, *Understanding Cultural Differences* (Yarmouth, ME: Intercultural Press, 1990).

8. Edward T. Hall and M. R. Hall, *Hidden Differences: Doing Business with the Japanese* (New York: Doubleday, 1987).

9. "Iraq: Down But Not Out," *The Economist,* April 8, 1995, pp. 21–23.

10. S. P. Huntington, *The Clash of Civilizations* (New York: Simon & Schuster, 1996).

11. M. Thompson, R. Ellis, and A. Wildavsky, *Cultural Theory* (Boulder, CO: Westview Press, 1990).

12. M. Douglas, "Cultural Bias," in *Active Voice* (London: Routledge, 1982), pp. 183–254.

13. M. L. Dertouzos, R. K. Lester, and R. M. Solow, *Made in America* (Cambridge, MA: MIT Press, 1989).

14. C. Nakane, *Japanese Society* (Berkeley, CA: University of California Press, 1970).

15. Ibid.

16. For details, see M. Aoki, *Information, Incentives, and Bargaining in the Japanese Economy* (Cambridge: Cambridge University Press, 1988); and Dertouzos, Lester, and Solow, *Made in America.*

17. For an excellent historical treatment of the evolution of the English class system, see E. P. Thompson, *The Making of the English Working Class* (London: Vintage Books, 1966). See also R. Miliband, *The State in Capitalist Society* (New York: Basic Books, 1969), especially Chapter 2. For more recent studies of class in British societies, see Stephen Brook, *Class: Knowing Your Place in Modern Britain* (London: Victor Gollancz, 1997); A. Adonis and S. Pollard, *A Class Act: The Myth of Britain's Classless Society* (London: Hamish Hamilton, 1997); and J. Gerteis and M. Savage, "The Salience of Class in Britain and America: A Comparative Analysis," *British Journal of Sociology,* June 1998.

18. Adonis and Pollard, *A Class Act: The Myth of Britain's Classless Society.*

19. Y. Bian, "Chinese Social Stratification and Social Mobility," *Annual Review of Sociology* 28 (2002), pp. 91–117.

20. N. Goodman, *An Introduction to Sociology* (New York: HarperCollins, 1991).

21. R. J. Barro and R. McCleary, "Religion and Economic Growth across Countries," American Sociological Review, October 2003, pp. 760–82.

22. M. Weber, *The Protestant Ethic and the Spirit of Capitalism* (New York: Charles Scribner's Sons, 1958, original 1904–1905). For an excellent review of Weber's work, see A. Giddens, *Capitalism and Modern Social Theory* (Cambridge: Cambridge University Press, 1971).

23. Weber, *The Protestant Ethic and the Spirit of Capitalism,* p. 35.

24. A. S. Thomas and S. L. Mueller, "The Case for Comparative Entrepreneurship," *Journal of International Business Studies* 31, no. 2 (2000), pp. 287–302, and S. A. Shane, "Why Do Some Societies Invent More Than Others?" *Journal of Business Venturing* 7 (1992), pp. 29–46.

25. See S. M. Abbasi, K. W. Hollman, and J. H. Murrey, "Islamic Economics; Foundations and Practices," *International Journal of Social Economics* 16, no. 5 (1990), pp. 5–17, and R. H. Dekmejian, *Islam in Revolution: Fundamentalism in the Arab World* (Syracuse, NY: Syracuse University Press, 1995).

26. T. W. Lippman, *Understanding Islam* (New York: Meridian Books, 1995).

27. Dekmejian, *Islam in Revolution.*

28. M. K. Nydell, *Understanding Arabs* (Yarmouth, ME: Intercultural Press, 1987).

29. Lippman, *Understanding Islam.*

30. The material in this section is based largely on Abbasi, Hollman, and Murrey, "Islamic Economics; Foundations and Practices."

31. "Islam's Interest," *The Economist,* January 18, 1992, pp. 33–34.

32. For details of Weber's work and views, see Giddens, *Capitalism and Modern Social Theory.*

33. See, for example, the views expressed in "A Survey of India: The Tiger Steps Out," *The Economist,* January 21, 1995.

34. See R. Dore, *Taking Japan Seriously,* and C. W. L. Hill, "Transaction Cost Economizing as a Source of Comparative Advantage: The Case of Japan," *Organization Science* 6 (1995).

35. C. C. Chen, Y. R. Chen, and K. Xin, "Guanxi Practices and Trust in Management," *Organization Science* 15, no. 2 (March–April 2004), pp. 200–10.

36. See Aoki, *Information, Incentives, and Bargaining in the Japanese Economy,* and J. P. Womack, D. T. Jones, and D. Roos, *The Machine That Changed the World* (New York: Rawson Associates, 1990).

37. For examples of this line of thinking, see the work by Mike Peng and his associates, M. W. Peng and P. S. Heath, "The Growth of the Firm in Planned Economies in Transition," *Academy of Management Review* 21 (1996), pp. 492–528; M. W. Peng, *Business Strategies in Transition Economies* (Thousand Oaks, CA: Sage, 2000); and M. W. Peng and Y. Luo, "Managerial Ties and Firm Performance in a Transition Economy," *Academy of Management Journal,* June 2000, pp. 486–501.

38. This hypothesis dates back to two anthropologists, Edward Sapir and Benjamin Lee Whorf. See E. Sapir, "The Status of Linguistics as a Science," *Language* 5 (1929), pp. 207–14, and B. L. Whorf, *Language, Thought, and Reality* (Cambridge, MA: MIT Press, 1956).

39. The tendency has been documented empirically. See A. Annett, "Social Fractionalization, Political Instability, and the Size of Government," *IMF Staff Papers* 48 (2001), pp. 561–92.

40. D. A. Ricks, *Big Business Blunders: Mistakes in Multinational Marketing* (Homewood, IL: Dow Jones-Irwin, 1983).

41. N. Goodman, *An Introduction to Sociology.*

42. M. E. Porter, *The Competitive Advantage of Nations* (New York: Free Press, 1990).

43. Ibid., pp. 395–97.

44. G. Hofstede, "The Cultural Relativity of Organizational Practices and Theories," *Journal of International Business Studies,* Fall 1983, pp. 75–89, and G. Hofstede, *Cultures and Organizations: Software of the Mind* (New York: McGraw-Hill, 1997).

45. For a more detailed critique, see R. Mead, *International Management: Cross-Cultural Dimensions* (Oxford: Blackwell, 1994), pp. 73–75.

46. For example, see W. J. Bigoness and G. L. Blakely, "A Cross-National Study of Managerial Values," *Journal of International Business Studies,* December 1996, p. 739; D. H. Ralston, D. H. Holt, R. H. Terpstra, and Y. Kai-Cheng, "The Impact of National Culture and Economic Ideology on Managerial Work Values," *Journal of International Business Studies* 28, no. 1 (1997), pp. 177–208; and P. B. Smith, M. F. Peterson, and Z. Ming Wang, "The Manager as a Mediator of Alternative Meanings," *Journal of International Business Studies* 27, no. 1 (1996), pp. 115–37.

47. G. Hofstede and M. H. Bond, "The Confucius Connection," *Organizational Dynamics* 16, no. 4 (1988), pp. 5–12, and G. Hofstede, *Culture's Consequences: Comparing Values, Behaviors, Institutions and Organizations across Nations* (Thousand Oaks, CA: Sage, 2001).

48. R. S. Yeh and J. J. Lawerence, "Individualism and Confucian Dynamism," *Journal of International Business Studies* 26, no. 3 (1995), pp. 655–66.

49. For evidence of this, see R. Inglehart. "Globalization and Postmodern Values," *The Washington Quarterly,* Winter 2000, pp. 215–28.

50. Mead, *International Management: Cross-Cultural Dimensions,* chap. 17.

51. "Free, Young, and Japanese," *The Economist,* December 21, 1991.

52. Namenwirth and Weber, *Dynamics of Culture,* and Inglehart, "Globalization and Post-modern Values."

53. G. Hofstede, "National Cultures in Four Dimensions," *International Studies of Management and Organization* 13, no. 1, pp. 46–74.

54. See Inglehart, "Globalization and Postmodern Values." For updates, go to http://wvs.isr.umich.edu/index.html.

55. Hofstede, "National Cultures in Four Dimensions."

56. Hall and Hall, *Understanding Cultural Differences.*

57. See Aoki, *Information, Incentives, and Bargaining in the Japanese Economy;* Dertouzos, Lester, and Solow, *Made in America;* and Porter, *The Competitive Advantage of Nations,* pp. 395–97.

58. For empirical work supporting such a view, see Annett, "Social Fractionalization, Political Instability, and the Size of Government."

4

Ethics in International Business

Nike

Nike is in many ways the quintessential global corporation. Established in 1972 by former University of Oregon track star Phil Knight, Nike is now one of the leading marketers of athletic shoes and apparel in the world. The company has $10 billion in annual revenues and sells its products in some 140 countries. Nike does not do any manufacturing. Rather, it designs and markets its products, while contracting for their manufacture from a global network of 600 factories owned by subcontractors that employ some 550,000 people. This huge corporation has made Knight one of the richest people in America. Nike's marketing phrase "Just Do It!" has become as recognizable in popular culture as its "swoosh" logo or the faces of its celebrity sponsors, such as Tiger Woods.

For all of its successes, the company has been dogged for more than a decade by repeated and persistent accusations that its products are made in sweatshops where workers, many of them children, slave away in hazardous conditions for wages that are below subsistence level. Nike's wealth, its detractors claim, has been built upon the backs of the world's poor. Many see Nike as a symbol of the evils of globalization—a rich Western corporation exploiting the world's poor to provide expensive shoes and apparel to the pampered consumers of the developed world. Niketown stores have become standard targets for antiglobalization protesters. Several nongovernmental organizations, such as San Francisco–based Global Exchange, a human rights organization dedicated to promoting environmental, political, and social justice around the world, have targeted Nike for repeated criticism and protests. News programs, such as CBS-TV's *48 Hours,* have run exposés on working conditions in foreign factories that supply Nike. Students on the campuses of several major U.S. universities with which Nike has lucrative sponsorship deals have protested the ties, citing Nike's use of sweatshop labor.

Typical of the allegations were those detailed in *48 Hours* program that aired in 1996. The report painted a picture of young women at a Vietnamese subcontractor who worked with toxic materials six days a week in poor conditions for only 20 cents an hour. The report also stated that a living wage in Vietnam was at least $3 a day, an income that could not be achieved at the subcontractor without working substantial overtime. Nike and its subcontractors were not breaking any laws, but this report, and others like it, raised questions about the ethics of using sweatshop labor to make what were essentially fashion accessories. It may have been legal, but was it ethical to use subcontractors who by Western standards clearly exploited their workforce? Nike's critics thought not, and the company found itself the focus of a wave of demonstrations and consumer boycotts.

Adding fuel to the fire, in November 1997 Global Exchange obtained and leaked a confidential report by Ernst & Young of a Nike-commissioned audit of a Vietnam factory owned by a Nike subcontractor. The factory had 9,200 workers and made 400,000 pairs of shoes a month. The Ernst & Young report painted a dismal picture of thousands of young women, most under age 25, laboring 10 1/2 hours a day, six days a week, in excessive heat and noise and in foul air, for slightly more than $10 a week. The report also found that workers with skin or breathing problems had not been transferred to departments free of chemicals. More than half the workers who dealt with dangerous chemicals did not wear protective masks or gloves. The report stated that in parts of the plant, workers were exposed to carcinogens that exceeded local legal standards by 177 times and that, overall, 77 percent of the employees suffered from respiratory problems.

These exposés surrounding Nike's use of subcontractors forced the company to reexamine its policies. Realizing that, even though it was breaking no law, its subcontracting policies were perceived as unethical, Nike's management took a number of steps. These included establishing a code of conduct for Nike subcontractors and instituting annual monitoring by independent auditors of all subcontractors. Nike's code of conduct included requiring that all employees at footwear factories be at least 18 years old and that exposure to potentially toxic materials does not exceed the permissible exposure limits established by the Occupational Safety and Health Administration (OSHA) for workers in the United States. In short, Nike concluded that behaving ethically required going beyond the requirements of the law. It required the establishment and enforcement of rules that adhere to accepted moral principles of right and wrong.

Sources: CBS News, "Boycott Nike," October 17, 1996; D. Jones, "Critics Tie Sweatshop Sneakers to 'Air Jordan,' " *USA Today,* June 6, 1996, p. 1B; Global Exchange Special Report, "Nike Just Don't Do It," www.globalexchange.org/education/publications/newsltr6.97p2.html#nike; S. Greenhouse, "Nike Shoe Plant in Vietnam Is Called Unsafe for Workers," *The New York Times,* November 8, 1997; and V. Dobnik, "Chinese Workers Abused Making Nikes, Reeboks," *Seattle Times,* September 21, 1997, p. A4.

Introduction

The previous two chapters detail how societies differ in terms of their economic, political, and legal systems, and their culture. We also mapped out some of these implications for the practice of international business. This chapter focuses on the ethical issues that arise when companies do business in different nations. Many of these ethical issues arise precisely because of differences in economic development, politics, legal systems, and culture. The term *ethics* refers to accepted principles of right or wrong that govern the conduct of a person, the members of a profession, or the actions of an organization. **Business ethics** are the accepted principles of right or wrong governing the conduct of businesspeople, and an **ethical strategy** is a strategy, or course of action, that does not violate these accepted principles.

In our society and others, many ethical principles are codified into law—prohibitions against murder, stealing, and incest, for example—but many others are not, such as the principle that an author should not plagiarize another's work. As long as it does not involve word-for-word copying, plagiarism does not technically violate copyright law, but it surely is unethical. Similarly, the history of science is replete with examples of researchers who claim their idea was "stolen" by an unscrupulous colleague for his own personal gain before the originator had the chance to file for a patent or publish the idea himself. Such behavior is not illegal, but it is obviously unethical.

The opening case nicely illustrates the issue. Nike broke no laws when it subcontracted work to factories in Southeast Asia that had very poor working conditions, but many argued that it was acting unethically. Nike no doubt made its decisions regarding subcontracting to drive down its costs and therefore maximize the corporation's long-run profitability. Originally, ethical issues probably did not enter into the company's decision-making calculus. Like managers at many other companies, those at Nike may have reasoned it was the subcontractor's responsibility to make sure local laws were followed, and Nike managers may have naively believed that those laws safeguarded the interests of the subcontractor's employees. In reality, the legal structure in many developing nations is weak and incomplete compared to that found in a developed country. Local laws often do not provide what would be considered adequate safeguards for employees, and even when they do, those laws may not be actively enforced. Given this, the right and proper thing for Nike to do when it decided to subcontract work to firms in developing nations was to establish an ethical code that articulated basic guidelines with regard to the working conditions that subcontractors should meet. Nike ultimately did do this, and then went beyond this, hiring independent auditors to make sure subcontractors adhered to the guidelines. But it took several years of vocal protests before Nike acted. Those protests damaged Nike's reputation, which is one of a corporation's most important intangible assets. One might argue, therefore, that it was in the enlightened self-interest of Nike to proactively insert ethical considerations into its decision-making calculus. More fundamentally, it was just the right thing to do!

This chapter looks at how ethical issues can and should be incorporated into decision making in an international business. We start by looking at the source and nature of ethical issues and dilemmas in an international business. Next, we review the reasons for poor ethical decision making in international businesses. Then we discuss the different philosophical approaches to business ethics. We close the chapter by reviewing the different processes that managers can adopt to make sure that ethical considerations are incorporated into decision making in an international business firm.

Ethical Issues in International Business

Many of the ethical issues and dilemmas in international business are rooted in the fact that political systems, law, economic development, and culture vary significantly from nation to nation. Consequently, what is considered normal practice in one nation may be considered unethical in others. Because they work for an institution that transcends national borders and cultures, managers in a multinational firm need to be particularly sensitive to these differences and able to choose the ethical action in those circumstances where variation across societies creates the potential for ethical problems. In the international business setting, the most common ethical issues involve employment practices, human rights, environmental regulations, corruption, and the moral obligation of multinational corporations.

EMPLOYMENT PRACTICES

As we saw in the opening case, ethical issues may be associated with employment practices in other nations. When work conditions in a host nation are clearly inferior to those in a multinational's home nation, what standards should be applied? Those of the home nation, those of the host nation, or something in between? While few would suggest that pay and work conditions should be the same across nations, how much divergence is acceptable? For example, while 12-hour workdays, extremely low pay, and a failure to protect workers against toxic chemicals may be common in some developing nations, does this mean that it is OK for a multinational to tolerate such working conditions in its subsidiaries there, or to condone it by using local subcontractors?

As the Nike case demonstrates, a strong argument can be made that such behavior is not appropriate. But this still leaves unanswered the question of what standards should be applied. We shall return to and consider this issue in more detail later in the chapter. For now, note that as in the case of Nike, establishing minimal acceptable standards that safeguard the basic rights and dignity of employees, auditing foreign subsidiaries and subcontractors on a regular basis to make sure those standards are met, and taking corrective action if they are not is a good way to guard against ethical abuses. Another apparel company, Levi Strauss, has long taken such an approach. In the early 1990s, the company terminated a long-term contract with one of its large suppliers, the Tan family. The Tans were allegedly forcing 1,200 Chinese and Filipino women to work 74 hours per week in guarded compounds on the Mariana Islands.[1]

HUMAN RIGHTS

Beyond employment issues, questions of human rights can arise in international business. Basic human rights still are not respected in many nations. Rights that we take for granted in developed nations, such as freedom of association, freedom of speech, freedom of assembly, freedom of movement, freedom from political repression, and so on, are by no means universally accepted (see Chapter 2 for details). One of the most obvious examples was South Africa during the days of white rule and apartheid, which did not end until 1994. Among other things, the apartheid system denied basic political rights to the majority nonwhite population of South Africa, mandated segregation between whites and nonwhites, reserved certain occupations exclusively for whites, and prohibited blacks from being placed in positions where they would manage whites. Despite the odious nature of this system, Western businesses operated in South Africa. By the 1980s, however, many questioned the ethics of doing so. They argued that inward investment by foreign multinationals, by boosting the South African economy, supported the repressive apartheid regime.

Several Western businesses started to change their policies in the late 1970s and early 1980s.[2] General Motors, which had significant activities in South Africa, was at the forefront of this trend. GM adopted what came to be called the *Sullivan principles*, named after Leon Sullivan, a black Baptist minister and a member of GM's board of directors. Sullivan argued that it was ethically justified for GM to operate in South Africa so long as two conditions were fulfilled: first, that the company should not obey the apartheid laws in its own South African operations (a form of passive resistance), and second, that the company should do everything within its power to actively promote the abolition of apartheid laws. Sullivan's principles were widely adopted by U.S. firms operating in South Africa. Their violation of the apartheid laws was ignored by the South Africa government, which clearly did not want to antagonize important foreign investors.

However, after 10 years, Leon Sullivan concluded that simply following the principles was not sufficient to break down the apartheid regime and that any American company, even those adhering to his principles, could not ethically justify a continued presence in South Africa. Over the next few years, numerous companies divested their South African operations, including Exxon, General Motors, Kodak, IBM, and Xerox. At the same time, many state pension funds signaled they would no longer hold stock in companies that did business in South Africa, which helped to persuade several companies to divest their South African operations. These divestments, coupled with the imposition of economic sanctions from the U.S. and other governments, contributed to the abandonment of white minority rule and apartheid in South Africa and the introduction of democratic elections in 1994. Thus, adopting an ethical stance was argued to have helped improve human rights in South Africa.[3]

Although change has come in South Africa, many repressive regimes still exist in the world. Is it ethical for multinationals to do business in them? It is often argued that inward investment by a multinational can be a force for economic, political, and social progress that ultimately improves the rights of people in repressive regimes. This position was first discussed in Chapter 2, when we noted that economic progress in a nation can create pressure for democratization. In general, this belief suggests it is ethical for a multinational to do business in nations that lack the democratic structures and human rights records of developed nations. Investment in China, for example, is frequently justified on the grounds that although China's human rights record is often questioned by human rights groups, and although the country is not a democracy, continuing inward investment will help boost economic growth and raise living standards. These developments will ultimately create pressures from the Chinese people for more participative government, political pluralism, and freedom of expression and speech.

But there is a limit to this argument. As in the case of South Africa, some regimes are so repressive that investment cannot be justified on ethical grounds. A current example would be Myanmar (formally known as Burma). Ruled by a military dictatorship for more than 40 years, Myanmar has one of the worst human rights records in the world. Beginning in the mid-1990s, many Western companies exited Myanmar, judging the human rights violations to be so extreme that doing business there cannot be justified on ethical grounds. (In contrast, the accompanying Management Focus looks at the controversy surrounding one company, Unocal, that chose to stay in Myanmar.) However, a cynic might note that Myanmar has a small economy and that divestment carries no great economic penalty for Western firms, unlike, for example, divestment from China.

Nigeria is another country where serious questions have arisen over the extent to which foreign multinationals doing business in the country have contributed to human rights violations. Most notably, the largest foreign oil producer in the country, Royal Dutch/Shell, has been repeatedly criticized.[4] In the early 1990s, several ethnic groups in Nigeria, which was ruled by a military dictatorship, protested against foreign oil companies for causing widespread pollution and failing to invest in the communities from which they extracted oil. Shell reportedly requested the assistance of Nigeria's Mobile Police Force (MPF) to quell the demonstrations. According to the human rights group Amnesty International, the results were bloody. In 1990, the MPF put down protests against Shell in the village of Umuechem, killing 80 people and destroying 495 homes. In 1993, following protests in the Ogoni region of Nigeria that were designed to stop contractors from laying a new pipeline for Shell, the MPF raided the area to quell the unrest. In the chaos that followed, it has been alleged that 27 villages were razed, 80,000 Ogoni people displaced, and 2,000 people killed.

Critics argued that Shell shouldered some of the blame for the massacres. Shell never acknowledged this, and the MPF probably used the demonstrations as a pretext for punishing an ethnic group that had been agitating against the central government for some time. Nevertheless, these events did prompt Shell to look at its own ethics and to set up internal mechanisms to ensure that its subsidiaries acted in a manner that was consistent with basic human rights.[5]

More generally, the question remains, What is the responsibility of a foreign multinational when operating in a country where basic human rights are trampled on? Should the company be there at all, and if it is there, what actions should it take to avoid the situation Shell found itself in?

Nigerian women and children protest Royal Dutch/Shell in April 2004.

ENVIRONMENTAL POLLUTION

Ethical issues arise when environmental regulations in host nations are far inferior to those in the home nation. Many developed nations have substantial regulations governing the emission of pollutants, the dumping of toxic chemicals, the use of toxic materials in the workplace, and so on. Developing nations often lack those regulations, and according to critics, the result can be higher levels of pollution from the operations of multinationals than would be allowed at home. For example, consider again the case of foreign oil companies in Nigeria. According to a 1992 report prepared by environmental activists in Nigeria, in the Niger Delta region,

> Apart from air pollution from the oil industry's emissions and flares day and night, producing poisonous gases that are silently and systematically wiping out vulnerable airborne biota and endangering the life of plants, game, and man himself, we have widespread water pollution and soil/land pollution that results in the death of most aquatic eggs and juvenile stages of the life of fin fish and shell fish on the one hand, whilst, on the other hand, agricultural land contaminated with oil spills becomes dangerous for farming, even where they continue to produce significant yields."[6]

The implication inherent in this description is that pollution controls applied by foreign companies in Nigeria were much laxer than those in developed nations.

Should a multinational feel free to pollute in a developing nation? (To do so hardly seems ethical.) Is there a danger that amoral management might move production to a developing nation precisely because costly pollution controls are not required, and the company is therefore free to despoil the environment and perhaps endanger local people in its quest to lower production costs and gain a competitive advantage? What is the right and moral thing to do in such circumstances? Pollute to gain an economic advantage, or make sure that foreign subsidiaries adhere to common standards regarding pollution controls?

These questions take on added importance because some parts of the environment are a public good that no one owns but anyone can despoil. No one owns the atmosphere or the oceans, but polluting both, no matter where the pollution originates, harms all.[7] The atmosphere and oceans can be viewed as a global commons from which everyone benefits but for which no one is specifically responsible. In such cases, a phenomenon known as the *tragedy of the commons* becomes applicable. The tragedy of the commons occurs when a resource held in common by all, but owned by no one, is overused by individuals, resulting in its degradation. The phenomenon was first named by Garrett Hardin when describing a particular problem in 16th-century England. Large open areas, called commons, were free for all to use as pasture. The poor put out livestock on these commons and supplemented their meager incomes. It was advantageous for each to put out more and more livestock, but the social consequence

MANAGEMENT FOCUS

In 1995, Unocal, an oil and gas enterprise based in California, took a 29 percent stake in a partnership with the French oil company Total and state-owned companies from both Myanmar and Thailand to build a gas pipeline from Myanmar to Thailand. At the time, the $1 billion project was expected to bring Myanmar about $200 million in annual export earnings, a quarter of the country's total. The gas used domestically would increase Myanmar's generating capacity by 30 percent. This investment was made when a number of other American companies were exiting Myanmar. Myanmar's government, a military dictatorship, had a reputation for brutally suppressing internal dissent. Citing the political climate, the apparel companies Levi Strauss and Eddie Bauer had both withdrawn from the country. But as far as Unocal's management was concerned, the giant infrastructure project would generate healthy returns for the company and, by boosting economic growth, a better life for Myanmar's 43 million people. Moreover, while Levi Strauss and Eddie Bauer could easily shift production of clothes to another low-cost location, Unocal argued it had to go where the oil and gas were located.

However, Unocal's investment quickly became highly controversial. Under the terms of the contract, the government of Myanmar was contractually obliged to clear a corridor for the pipeline through Myanmar's tropical forests and to protect the pipeline from attacks by the government's enemies. According to human rights groups, the Myanmar army forcibly moved villages and ordered hundreds of local peasants to work on the pipeline in conditions that were no better than slave labor. Those who refused to comply suffered retaliation. News reports cite the case of one woman who was thrown into a fire, along with her baby, after her husband tried to escape from troops forcing him to work on the project. The baby died and she suffered burns. Other villagers reported being beaten, tortured, raped, and otherwise mistreated when the alleged slave labor conditions were occurring.

In 1996, human rights activists brought a lawsuit against Unocal in the United States on behalf of 13 Myanmar villagers who had fled to refugee camps in Thailand. The suit claimed that Unocal was aware of what was going on, even if it did not participate or condone it, and that awareness was enough to make Unocal in part responsible for the alleged crimes. The presiding judge dismissed the case on the grounds that Unocal could not be held liable for the actions of a foreign government against its own people—although the judge did note that Unocal was aware of what was going on in Myanmar. The plaintiffs appealed, and in late 2003 the case wound up at a superior court. This time, the plaintiffs' legal strategy hinged upon the use of a law that had been on the books since 1792 but was largely ignored for 200 years. Known as the Alien Tort Claims Act (ATCT) of 1792, this law allows foreigners to sue each other in U.S. courts. The ATCT law is being used to allow the foreign plaintiffs to sue the Myanmar subsidiary of Unocal for damages. At the time of this writing, the case is ongoing. Irrespective of the final outcome, however, and most legal scholars believe that Unocal may ultimately be able to dodge any legal liability, there is little doubt that one can question the ethical validity of Unocal's decision to enter into partnership with a brutal military dictatorship for financial gain.

Sources: Jim Carlton, "Unocal Trial for Slave Labor Claims Is Set to Start Today," *The Wall Street Journal,* December 9, 2003, p. A19; Seth Stern, "Big Business Targeted for Rights Abuse," *Christian Science Monitor,* September 4, 2003, p. 2; "Trouble in the Pipeline," *The Economist,* January 18, 1997, p. 39; and Irtani Evelyn, "Feeling the Heat: Unocal Defends Myanmar Gas Pipeline Deal," *Los Angeles Times,* February 20, 1995, p. D1.

was far more livestock than the commons could handle. The result was overgrazing, degradation of the commons, and the loss of this much-needed supplement.[8]

In the modern world, corporations can contribute to the global tragedy of the commons by moving production to locations where they are free to pump pollutants into the atmosphere or dump them in oceans or rivers, thereby harming these valuable global commons. While such action may be legal, is it ethical? Again, such actions seem to violate basic societal notions of ethics and social responsibility.

CORRUPTION

As noted in Chapter 2, corruption has been a problem in almost every society in history, and it continues to be one today. There always have been and always will be corrupt government officials. International businesses can gain and have gained economic advantages by making payments to those officials. A classic example concerns a well-publicized incident in the 1970s. Carl Kotchian, the president of Lockheed, made a $12.5 million payment to Japanese agents and government officials to secure a large order for Lockheed's TriStar jet from Nippon Air. When the payments were discovered, U.S. officials charged Lockheed with falsification of its records and tax violations. Although such payments were supposed to be an accepted business practice in Japan (they might be viewed as an exceptionally lavish form of gift giving), the revelations created a scandal there too. The government ministers in question were criminally charged, one committed suicide, the government fell in disgrace, and the Japanese people were outraged. Apparently, such a payment was not an accepted way of doing business in Japan! The payment was nothing more than a bribe, paid to corrupt officials, to secure a large order that might otherwise have gone to another manufacturer, such as Boeing. Kotchian clearly engaged in unethical behavior, and to argue that the payment was an "acceptable form of doing business in Japan" was self-serving and incorrect.

The Lockheed case was the impetus for the 1977 passage of the **Foreign Corrupt Practices Act** in the United States, which we first discussed in Chapter 2. The act outlawed the paying of bribes to foreign government officials to gain business. Some U.S. businesses immediately objected that the act would put U.S. firms at a competitive disadvantage (there is no evidence that subsequently occurred).[9] The act was subsequently amended to allow for "facilitating payments." Sometimes known as speed money or grease payments, facilitating payments are *not* payments to secure contracts that would not otherwise be secured, nor are they payments to obtain exclusive preferential treatment; rather they are payments to ensure receiving the standard treatment that a business ought to receive from a foreign government but might not due to the obstruction of a foreign official.

In 1997, the trade and finance ministers from the member states of the Organization for Economic Cooperation and Development (OECD) followed the U.S. lead and adopted the **Convention on Combating Bribery of Foreign Public Officials in International Business Transactions.**[10] The convention, which went into force in 1999, obliges member states to make the bribery of foreign public officials a criminal offense. The convention excludes facilitating payments made to expedite routine government action from the convention. To be truly effective, however, the convention must be translated into domestic law by each signatory nation, and that is still in process.

While facilitating payments, or speed money, are excluded from both the Foreign Corrupt Practices Act and the OECD convention on bribery, the ethical implications of making such payments are unclear. In many countries, payoffs to government officials in the form of speed money are a part of life. One can argue that not investing because government officials demand speed money ignores the fact that such investment can bring substantial benefits to the local populace in terms of income and jobs. From a pragmatic standpoint, giving bribes, although a little evil, might be the price that must be paid to do a greater good (assuming the investment creates jobs where none existed and assuming the practice is not illegal). Several economists advocate this reasoning, suggesting that in the context of pervasive and cumbersome regulations in developing countries, corruption may improve efficiency and help growth! These economists theorize that in a country where preexisting political structures distort or limit the workings of the market mechanism, corruption in the form of black-marketeering, smuggling, and side payments to government bureaucrats to "speed up" approval for business investments may enhance welfare.[11] Arguments such as this persuaded the U.S. Congress to exempt facilitating payments from the Foreign Corrupt Practices Act.

In contrast, other economists have argued that corruption reduces the returns on business investment and leads to low economic growth.[12] In a country where corruption is common, unproductive bureaucrats who demand side payments for granting the enterprise permission to operate may siphon off the profits from a business activity. This reduces businesses' incentive to invest and may retard a country's economic growth rate. One study of the connection between corruption and economic growth in 70 countries found that corruption had a significant negative impact on a country's growth rate.[13]

Given the debate and the complexity of this issue, one again might conclude that generalization is difficult and the demand for speed money creates a genuine ethical dilemma. Yes, corruption is bad, and yes, it may harm a country's economic development, but yes, there are also cases where side payments to government officials can remove the bureaucratic barriers to investments that create jobs. However, this pragmatic stance ignores the fact that corruption tends to corrupt both the bribe giver and the bribe taker. Corruption feeds on itself, and once an individual starts down the road of corruption, pulling back may be difficult if not impossible. This argument strengthens the ethical case for never engaging in corruption, no matter how compelling the benefits might seem.

Many multinationals have accepted this argument. The large oil multinational, BP, for example, has a zero-tolerance approach toward facilitating payments. Other corporations have a more nuanced approach. For example, consider the following from the code of ethics at Dow Corning:

> Dow Corning employees will not authorize or give payments or gifts to government employees or their beneficiaries or anyone else in order to obtain or retain business. Facilitating payments to expedite the performance of routine services are strongly discouraged. In countries where local business practice dictates such payments and there is no alternative, facilitating payments are to be for the minimum amount necessary and must be accurately documented and recorded.[14]

This statement allows for facilitating payments when "there is no alternative," although they are strongly discouraged.

MORAL OBLIGATIONS

Multinational corporations have power that comes from their control over resources and their ability to move production from country to country. Although that power is constrained not only by laws and regulations, but also by the discipline of the market and the competitive process, it is nevertheless substantial. Some moral philosophers argue that with power comes the social responsibility for multinationals to give something back to the societies that enable them to prosper and grow. The concept of **social responsibility** refers to the idea that businesspeople should consider the social consequences of economic actions when making business decisions, and that there should be a presumption in favor of decisions that have both good economic and social consequences.[15] In its purest form, social responsibility can be supported for its own sake simply because it is the right way for a business to behave. Advocates of this approach argue that businesses, particularly large successful businesses, need to recognize their *noblesse oblige* and give something back to the societies that have made their success possible. *Noblesse oblige* is a French term that refers to honorable and benevolent behavior considered the responsibility of people of high (noble) birth. In a business setting, it is taken to mean benevolent behavior that is the responsibility of *successful* enterprises. This has long been recognized by many businesspeople, resulting in a substantial and venerable history of corporate giving to society and in businesses making social investments designed to enhance the welfare of the communities in which they operate.

However, some multinationals have abused their power for private gain. The most famous historic example relates to one of the earliest multinationals, the British East India Company. Established in 1600, the East India Company grew to dominate the entire Indian subcontinent in the 19th century. At the height of its power, the company deployed

MANAGEMENT FOCUS

Rupert Murdoch built News Corporation into one of the largest media conglomerates in the world with interests that include newspapers, publishing, and television broadcasting. According to critics, however, Mr. Murdoch abused his power to gain preferential access to the Chinese media market by systematically suppressing media content that was critical of China and publishing material designed to ingratiate the company with the Chinese leadership.

In 1994, News Corporation excluded BBC news broadcasts from Star TV coverage in the region after it had become clear that Chinese politicians were unhappy with the BBC's continual reference to repression in China, and most notably, the 1989 massacre of student protesters for democracy in Beijing's Tiananmen Square. In 1995, News Corporation's book publishing subsidiary, Harper-Collins, published a flattering biography of Deng Xiaoping, the former leader of China, written by his daughter. Then in 1998, HarperCollins dropped plans to publish the memoirs of Chris Patten, the last governor of Hong Kong before its transfer to the Chinese. Mr. Patten, a critic of Chinese leaders, had aroused their wrath by attempting to introduce a degree of democracy into the administration of the old British territory before its transfer back to China in 1997.

In a 1998 interview in *Vanity Fair,* Mr. Murdoch took another opportunity to ingratiate himself with the Chinese leadership when he described the Dalai Lama, the exiled leader of Chinese-occupied Tibet, as "a very political old monk shuffling around in Gucci shoes." On the heels of this, in 2001 Mr. Murdoch's son James, who was in charge of running Star TV, made disparaging remarks about Falun Gong, a spiritual movement involving breathing exercises and meditation that had become so popular in China that the Communist regime regarded it as a political threat, and suppressed its activities. According to James Murdoch, Falun Gong was a "dangerous," "apocalyptic cult" which "clearly does not have the success of China at heart."

Critics argued that these events were all part of a deliberate and unethical effort on the part of News Corporation to curry favor with the Chinese. The company received its reward in 2001 when Star TV struck an agreement with the Chinese government to launch a Mandarin-language entertainment channel for the affluent southern coastal province of Guangdong. Earlier that year, China's leader, Jiang Zemin, had publicly praised Rupert Murdoch and Star TV for their efforts "to present China objectively and to cooperate with the Chinese press."

Source: Daniel Litvin, *Empires of Profit* (New York: Texere, 2003).

more than 40 warships, possessed the largest standing army in the world, was the de facto ruler of India's 240 million people, and even hired its own church bishops, extending its dominance into the spiritual realm.[16]

Power itself is morally neutral. It is how power is used that matters. It can be used in a positive way to increase social welfare, which is ethical, or it can be used in a manner that is ethically and morally suspect. Consider the case of News Corporation, one of the largest media conglomerates in the world, which is profiled in the accompanying Management Focus. The power of media companies derives from their ability to shape public perceptions by the material they choose to publish. News Corporation founder and CEO Rupert Murdoch has long considered China to be one of the most promising media markets in the world and has sought permission to expand News Corporation's operations in China, particularly the satellite broadcasting operations of Star TV. Some critics believe that Murdoch used the power of News Corporation in an unethical way to attain this objective.

Some multinationals have acknowledged a moral obligation to use their power to enhance social welfare in the communities where they do business. BP, one of the world's largest oil companies, has made it part of the company policy to undertake "social investments" in the countries where it does business.[17] In Algeria, BP has been investing in a major project to develop gas fields near the desert town of Salah. When the company noticed the lack of clean water in Salah, it built two desalination plants to provide drinking water for the local community and distributed containers to residents so they could take water from the plants to their homes. There was no economic reason for BP to make this social investment, but the company believes it is morally obligated to use its power in constructive ways. The action, while a small thing for BP, is a very important thing for the local community.

Ethical Dilemmas

The ethical obligations of a multinational corporation toward employment conditions, human rights, corruption, environmental pollution, and the use of power are not always clear cut. There may be no agreement about accepted ethical principles. From an international business perspective, some argue that what is ethical depends upon one's cultural perspective.[18] In the United States, it is considered acceptable to execute murderers, but in many cultures this is not acceptable—execution is viewed as an affront to human dignity and the death penalty is outlawed. Many Americans find this attitude very strange, but many Europeans find the American approach barbaric. For a more business-oriented example, consider the practice of "gift giving" between the parties to a business negotiation. While this is considered right and proper behavior in many Asian cultures, some Westerners view the practice as a form of bribery, and therefore unethical, particularly if the gifts are substantial.

Managers must confront very real ethical dilemmas. For example, imagine that a visiting American executive finds that a foreign subsidiary in a poor nation has hired a 12-year-old girl to work on a factory floor. Appalled to find that the subsidiary is using child labor in direct violation of the company's own ethical code, the American instructs the local manager to replace the child with an adult. The local manager dutifully complies. The girl, an orphan, who is the only breadwinner for herself and her 6-year-old brother, is unable to find another job, so in desperation she turns to prostitution. Two years later she dies of AIDS. Meanwhile, her brother takes up begging. He encounters the American while begging outside the local McDonald's. Oblivious that this was the man responsible for his fate, the boy begs him for money. The American quickens his pace and walks rapidly past the outstretched hand into the McDonald's, where he orders a quarter-pound cheeseburger with fries and cold milk shake. A year later the boy contracts tuberculosis and dies.

Had the visiting American understood the gravity of the girl's situation, would he still have requested her replacement? Perhaps not! Would it have been better, therefore, to stick with the status quo and allow the girl to continue working? Probably not, because that would have violated the reasonable prohibition against child labor found in the company's own ethical code. What then would have been the right thing to do? What was the obligation of the executive given this ethical dilemma?

There is no easy answer to these questions. That is the nature of **ethical dilemmas**—they are situations in which none of the available alternatives seems ethically acceptable.[19] In this case, employing child labor was not acceptable, but given that she was employed, neither was denying the child her only source of income. What the American executive needed, what all managers need, was a moral compass, or perhaps an ethical algorithm, that would guide him through such an ethical dilemma to find an acceptable solution. Later in this chapter we will outline what such a moral compass, or ethical algorithm, might look like. For now, it is enough to note that ethical dilemmas exist because many real-world decisions are complex, difficult to frame, and involve first-, second-, and third-order consequences that are hard to quantify. Doing the right thing, or even knowing what the right thing might be, is often far from easy.

The Roots of Unethical Behavior

Examples abound of managers behaving in a manner that might be judged unethical in an international business setting. A group of American investors became interested in restoring the SS *United States*, at one time a luxurious ocean liner.[20] The first step in the

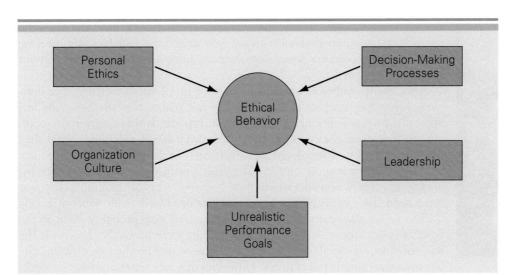

FIGURE 4.1

Determinants of Ethical
Behavior

project involved stripping the ship of its asbestos lining. Asbestos is a highly toxic material that produces a fine dust that when inhaled can cause scarring and result in lung disease, cancer, and death. Accordingly, very tight standards in developed countries govern the removal of asbestos. A bid from a U.S. company, based on the standards established in the United States, priced the job at more than $100 million. A company in the Ukraine offered to do the job for $2 million, so the ship was towed to the Ukrainian port of Sevastopol. Agreeing to do the work for $2 million implied that the Ukrainian company could not have adopted standards even remotely close to those required in the United States. As a consequence, its employees were at a significant risk of developing asbestos-related disease. If this was the case, the desire to limit costs had resulted in the American investors acting in an unethical manner, for they were knowingly rewarding a company that exposed its workers to a significant health risk.

Why do managers behave in a manner that is unethical? There is no simple answer to this question, for the causes are complex, but a few generalizations can be made (see Figure 4.1).[21] First, business ethics are not divorced from *personal ethics*, which are the generally accepted principles of right and wrong governing the conduct of individuals. As individuals, we are typically taught that it is wrong to lie and cheat—it is unethical—and that it is right to behave with integrity and honor, and to stand up for what we believe to be right and true. This is generally true across societies. The personal ethical code that guides our behavior comes from a number of sources, including our parents, our schools, our religion, and the media. Our personal ethical code exerts a profound influence on the way we behave as businesspeople. An individual with a strong sense of personal ethics is less likely to behave in an unethical manner in a business setting. It follows that the first step to establishing a strong sense of business ethics is for a society to emphasize strong personal ethics.

Home-country managers working abroad in multinational firms (expatriate managers) may experience more than the usual degree of pressure to violate their personal ethics. They are away from their ordinary social context and supporting culture, and they are psychologically and geographically distant from the parent company. They may be based in a culture that does not place the same value on ethical norms important in the manager's home country, and they may be surrounded by local employees who have less rigorous ethical standards. The parent company may pressure expatriate managers to meet unrealistic goals that can be fulfilled only by cutting corners or acting unethically. For example, to meet centrally mandated performance goals, expatriate managers might give bribes to win contracts or might implement working conditions and environmental controls that are below minimal acceptable standards. Local managers might encourage the

Former Enron CEO Kenneth Lay was charged with a variety of criminal deeds.

expatriate to adopt such behavior. And due to its geographical distance, the parent company may be unable to see how expatriate managers are meeting goals, or may choose not to see how they are doing so, allowing such behavior to flourish and persist.

Also, many studies of unethical behavior in a business setting have concluded that businesspeople sometimes do not realize they are behaving unethically, primarily because they simply fail to ask, Is this decision or action ethical?[22] Instead, they apply a straightforward business calculus to what they perceive to be a business decision, forgetting that the decision may also have an important ethical dimension. The fault lies in processes that do not incorporate ethical considerations into business decision making. This may have been the case at Nike when managers originally made subcontracting decisions (see the opening case). Those decisions were probably made on the basis of good economic logic. Subcontractors were probably chosen on the basis of business variables such as cost, delivery, and product quality, and the key managers simply failed to ask, How does this subcontractor treat its workforce? If they thought about the question at all, they probably reasoned that it was the subcontractor's concern, not theirs. (For another example of a business decision that may have been unethical, see the accompanying Management Focus describing Pfizer's decision to test an experimental drug on children suffering from meningitis in Nigeria.)

Unfortunately, the climate in some businesses does not encourage people to think through the ethical consequences of business decisions. This brings us to the third cause of unethical behavior in businesses—an organizational culture that deemphasizes business ethics, reducing all decisions to the purely economic. The term **organization culture** refers to the values and norms that are shared among employees of an organization. You will recall from Chapter 3 that values are abstract ideas about what a group believes to be good, right, and desirable, while norms are the social rules and guidelines that prescribe appropriate behavior in particular situations. Just as societies have cultures, so do business organizations. Together, values and norms shape the culture of a business organization, and that culture has an important influence on the ethics of business decision making.

Author Robert Bryce has explained how the organization culture at now-bankrupt multinational energy company Enron was built on values that emphasized greed and deception.[23] According to Bryce, the tone was set by top managers who engaged in self-dealing to enrich themselves and their own families. He tells how former Enron CEO Kenneth Lay made sure his own family benefited handsomely from Enron. Much of Enron's corporate travel business was handled by a travel agency part owned by Lay's sister. When an internal auditor recommended that the company could do better by using another travel agency, he soon found himself out of a job. In 1997, Enron acquired a company owned by Kenneth Lay's son, Mark Lay, which was trying to establish a business trading paper and pulp products. At the time, Mark Lay and another company he controlled were targets of a federal criminal investigation of bankruptcy fraud and embezzlement. As part of the deal, Enron hired Mark Lay as an executive with a three-year contract that guaranteed him at least $1 million in pay over that period, plus options to purchase about 20,000 shares of Enron. Bryce also details how Kenneth Lay's grown daughter used an Enron jet to transport her king-sized bed to France. With Kenneth Lay as an example, it is perhaps not surprising that self-dealing soon became endemic at Enron. The most notable example was Chief Financial Officer Andrew Fastow, who set up "off-balance-sheet" partnerships that not only hid Enron's true financial condition from investors, but also paid tens of millions of dollars directly to Fastow. (Fastow was subsequently indicted by the government for criminal fraud and went to jail.)

The fourth cause of unethical behavior has already been hinted at—it is pressure from the parent company to meet unrealistic performance goals that can be attained only by cutting corners or acting in an unethical manner. Again, Bryce discusses how this may have occurred at Enron. Kenneth Lay's successor as CEO, Jeff Skilling, put a performance

MANAGEMENT FOCUS

The drug development process is long, risky, and expensive. It can take 10 years and cost in excess of $500 million to develop a new drug. Also, between 80 and 90 percent of drug candidates fail in clinical trials. Pharmaceutical companies rely upon a handful of successes to pay for their failures. Among the most successful of the world's pharmaceutical companies is New York–based Pfizer. Given the risks and costs of developing a new drug, pharmaceutical companies will jump at opportunities to reduce them, and in 1996 Pfizer thought it saw one.

Pfizer had been developing a novel antibiotic, Trovan, that was proving to be useful in treating a wide range of bacterial infections. Wall Street analysts were predicting that Trovan could be a blockbuster, one of a handful of drugs capable of generating sales of more than $1 billion a year. In 1996, Pfizer was pushing to submit data on Trovan's efficacy to the Food and Drug Administration (FDA) for review. A favorable review would allow Pfizer to sell the drug in the United States, the world's largest market. Pfizer wanted the drug to be approved for both adults and children, but it was having trouble finding sufficient numbers of sick children in the United States to test the drug on. Then in early 1996, a researcher at Pfizer read about an emerging epidemic of bacterial meningitis in Kano, Nigeria. This seemed like a quick way to test the drug on a large number of sick children.

Within weeks, a team of six doctors had flown to Kano and were administering the drug, in oral form, to children with meningitis. Desperate for help, Nigerian authorities had given the go-ahead for Pfizer to give the drug to children (the epidemic would ultimately kill nearly 16,000 people). Over the next few weeks, Pfizer treated 198 children. The protocol called for half the patients to get Trovan and half to get a comparison antibiotic already approved for the treatment of children. After a few weeks, the Pfizer team left, the experiment complete. Trovan seemed to be about as effective and safe as the already approved antibiotic. The data from the trial were put into a package with data from other trials of Trovan and delivered to the FDA.

Questions were soon raised about the nature of Pfizer's experiment. Allegations charged that the Pfizer team kept children on Trovan even after they failed to show a response to the drug, instead of switching them quickly to another drug. The result, according to critics, was that some children died who might have been saved had they been taken off Trovan sooner. Questions were also raised about the safety of the oral formulation of Trovan, which some doctors feared might lead to arthritis in children. Fifteen children who took Trovan showed signs of joint pain during the experiment, three times the rate of children taking the other antibiotic. Then there were questions about consent. The FDA requires that patient (or parent) consent be given before patients are enrolled in clinical trials, no matter where in the world the trials are conducted. Critics argue that in the rush to get the trial established in Nigeria, Pfizer did not follow proper procedures, and that many parents of the infected children did not know their children were participating in a trial for an experimental drug. Many of the parents were illiterate, could not read the consent forms, and had to rely upon the questionable translation of the Nigerian nursing staff. Pfizer rejected these charges and contends that it did nothing wrong.

Trovan was approved by the FDA for use in adults in 1997, but it was never approved for use in children. It was launched in 1998, and by 1999 there were reports that up to 140 patients in Europe had suffered liver damage after taking Trovan. The FDA subsequently restricted the use of Trovan to those cases where the benefits of treatment outweighed the risk of liver damage. European regulators banned sales of the drug. In 2003, two dozen Nigerian families sued Pfizer in a federal court in New York. The families claim their children either died or were injured because Pfizer did not adequately inform them of the risks and alternatives for treatment with Trovan. The case is still ongoing.

Did Pfizer behave unethically by rushing to take advantage of an epidemic in Nigeria to test an experimental drug on children? Should it have been less opportunistic and proceeded more carefully? Were corners cut with regard to patient consent in the rush to establish a trial? And did doctors keep patients on Trovan too long, when they should have switched them to another medication? Is it ethical to test an experimental drug on children in a crisis setting in the developing world, where the overall standard of health care is so much lower than in the developed world and proper protocols might not be followed? These questions are all raised by the Pfizer case, and they remain unanswered, by the company at least.

Source: Joe Stephens, "Where Profits and Lives Hang in the Balance," *Washington Post,* December 17, 2000, p. A1; Andra Brichacek, "What Price Corruption?" *Pharmaceutical Executive* 21, no. 11 (November 2001), p. 94; and Scott Hensley, "Court Revives Suit against Pfizer on Nigeria Study," *The Wall Street Journal,* October 13, 2004, p. B4.

evaluation system in place that weeded out 15 percent of underperformers every six months. This created a pressure-cooker culture with a myopic focus on short-run performance, and some executives and energy traders responded to that pressure by falsifying their performance—inflating the value of trades, for example—to make it look as if they were performing better than was actually the case.

The lesson from the Enron debacle is that an organizational culture can legitimize behavior that society would judge as unethical, particularly when this is mixed with a focus on unrealistic performance goals, such as maximizing short-term economic performance, no matter what the costs. In such circumstances, there is a greater than average probability that managers will violate their own personal ethics and engage in unethical behavior. By the same token, an organization culture can do just the opposite and reinforce the need for ethical behavior. At Hewlett-Packard, for example, Bill Hewlett and David Packard, the company's founders, propagated a set of values known as The HP Way. These values, which shape the way business is conducted both within and by the corporation, have an important ethical component. Among other things, they stress the need for confidence in and respect for people, open communication, and concern for the individual employee.

The Enron and Hewlett-Packard examples suggest a fifth root cause of unethical behavior—leadership. Leaders help to establish the culture of an organization, and they set the example that others follow. Other employees in a business often take their cue from business leaders, and if those leaders do not behave in an ethical manner, they might not either. It is not what leaders say that matters, but what they do. Enron, for example, had a code of ethics that Kenneth Lay himself often referred to, but Lay's own actions to enrich family members spoke louder than any words.

Philosophical Approaches to Ethics

We shall look at several different approaches to business ethics here, beginning with some that can best be described as straw men, which either deny the value of business ethics or apply the concept in a very unsatisfactory way. Having discussed, and dismissed, the straw men, we then move on to consider approaches that are favored by most moral philosophers and form the basis for current models of ethical behavior in international businesses.

STRAW MEN

Straw men approaches to business ethics are raised by business ethics scholars primarily to demonstrate that they offer inappropriate guidelines for ethical decision making in a multinational enterprise. Four such approaches to business ethics are commonly discussed in the literature. These approaches can be characterized as the Friedman doctrine, cultural relativism, the righteous moralist, and the naive immoralist. All of these approaches have some inherent value, but all are unsatisfactory in important ways. Nevertheless, sometimes companies adopt these approaches.

The Friedman Doctrine

Nobel Prize–winning economist Milton Friedman wrote an article in 1970 that has since become a classic straw man that business ethics scholars outline only to then tear down.[24] Friedman's basic position is that the only social responsibility of business is to increase profits, so long as the company stays within the rules of law. He explicitly rejects the idea that businesses should undertake social expenditures beyond those mandated by the law and required for the efficient running of a business. For example, his arguments suggest that improving working conditions beyond the level required by the law *and* necessary to maximize employee productivity will reduce profits and are therefore not appropriate. His belief is that a firm should maximize its profits because that is the way to maximize the returns that accrue to the owners of the firm, its stockholders. If stockholders then wish to use the proceeds to make social investments, that is their right, according to Friedman, but managers of the firm should not make that decision for them.

Although Friedman is talking about social responsibility, rather than business ethics per se, most business ethics scholars equate social responsibility with ethical behavior, and thus believe Friedman is also arguing against business ethics. However, the assumption that Friedman is arguing against ethics is not quite true, for Friedman does state,

> There is one and only one social responsibility of business—to use its resources and engage in activities designed to increase its profits so long as it stays within the rules of the game, which is to say that it engages in open and free competition without deception or fraud.[25]

In other words, Friedman states that businesses should behave in an ethical manner and not engage in deception and fraud.

Nevertheless, Friedman's arguments do break down under examination. This is particularly true in the realm of international business where the "rules of the game" are not well established or differ substantially from country to county. Consider again the case of sweatshop labor. Child labor may not be against the law in a developing nation, and maximizing productivity may not require that a multinational firm stop using child labor in that country, but it is still immoral to use child labor because the practice conflicts with widely held views about what is the right and proper thing to do. Similarly, there may be no rules against pollution in a developed nation and spending money on pollution control may reduce the profit rate of the firm, but generalized notions of morality would hold that it is still unethical to dump toxic pollutants into rivers or foul the air with gas releases. In addition to the local consequences of such pollution, which may have serious health effects for the surrounding population, there is also a global consequence as pollutants degrade those two global commons so important to us all—the atmosphere and the oceans.

Cultural Relativism

Another straw man often raised by business ethics scholars is **cultural relativism,** which is the belief that ethics are nothing more than the reflection of a culture—all ethics are culturally determined—and that accordingly, a firm should adopt the ethics of the culture in which it is operating.[26] This approach is often summarized by the maxim *when in Rome do as the Romans.* As with Friedman's approach, cultural relativism does not stand up to a closer look. At its extreme, cultural relativism suggests that if a culture supports slavery, it is OK to use slave labor in a country. Clearly it is not. Cultural relativism implicitly rejects the idea that universal notions of morality transcend different cultures, but, as we shall argue later in the chapter, some universal notions of morality are found across cultures.

While dismissing cultural relativism in its most sweeping form, some ethicists argue there is residual value in this approach.[27] As we noted in Chapter 3, societal values and norms do vary from culture to culture, customs do differ, so it might follow that certain business practices are ethical in one country, but not another. Indeed, the facilitating payments allowed in the Foreign Corrupt Practices Act can be seen as an acknowledgment that in some countries, the payment of speed money to government officials is necessary to get business done, and if not ethically desirable, it is at least ethically acceptable.

However, not all ethicists or companies agree with this pragmatic view. As noted earlier, oil company BP explicitly states it will not make facilitating payments, no matter what the prevailing cultural norms are. In 2002, BP enacted a zero-tolerance policy for facilitation payments, primarily on the basis that such payments are a low-level form of corruption, and thus cannot be justified because corruption corrupts both the bribe giver and the bribe taker and perpetuates the corrupt system. As BP notes on its Web site, as a result of its zero-tolerance policy:

> Some oil product sales in Vietnam involved inappropriate commission payments to the managers of customers in return for placing orders with BP. These were stopped during

2002 with the result that BP failed to win certain tenders with potential profit totalling $300k. In addition, two sales managers resigned over the issue. The business, however, has recovered using more traditional sales methods and has exceeded its targets at year-end.

BP in India has been working in an environment where facilitation payments are commonplace. The business unit took measures not only to eliminate direct facilitation payments but also extended the policy application to agents, consultants, sales distributors, and suppliers. Workshops covering suppliers, distributors, and agents were held and key third parties provided signed statements confirming their compliance with our ethics policy. Contracts with three distributors and one freight agent were terminated for unethical behaviour. The main lesson learnt was that perseverance is eventually rewarded despite delays. A plant was connected to the national grid, an office co-location project was approved, and a major income tax refund was received—all without making the facilitation payments that would have been required in the past.[28]

BP's experience suggests that companies should not use cultural relativism as an argument for justifying behavior that is clearly based upon suspect ethical grounds, even if that behavior is both legal and routinely accepted in the country where the company is doing business.

The Righteous Moralist

A **righteous moralist** claims that a multinational's home-country standards of ethics are the appropriate ones for companies to follow in foreign countries. This approach is typically associated with managers from developed nations. While this seems reasonable at first blush, the approach can create problems. Consider the following example: An American bank manager was sent to Italy and was appalled to learn that the local branch's accounting department recommended grossly underreporting the bank's profits for income tax purposes.[29] The manager insisted that the bank report its earnings accurately, American style. When he was called by the Italian tax department to the firm's tax hearing, he was told the firm owed three times as much tax as it had paid, reflecting the department's standard assumption that each firm underreports its earnings by two-thirds. Despite his protests, the new assessment stood. In this case, the righteous moralist has run into a problem caused by the prevailing cultural norms in the country where he is doing business. How should he respond? The righteous moralist would argue for maintaining the position, while a more pragmatic view might be that in this case, the right thing to do is to follow the prevailing cultural norms, since there is a big penalty for not doing so.

The main criticism of the righteous moralist approach is that its proponents go too far. While there are some universal moral principles that should not be violated, it does not always follow that the appropriate thing to do is adopt home-country standards. For example, U.S. laws set down strict guidelines with regard to minimum wage and working conditions. Does this mean it is ethical to apply the same guidelines in a foreign country, paying people the same as they are paid in the United States, providing the same benefits and working conditions? Probably not, because doing so might nullify the reason for investing in that country and therefore deny locals the benefits of inward investment by the multinational. Clearly, a more nuanced approach is needed.

The Naive Immoralist

A **naive immoralist** asserts that if a manager of a multinational sees that firms from other nations are not following ethical norms in a host nation, that manager should not either. The classic example to illustrate the approach is known as the drug lord problem. In one variant of this problem, an American manager in Colombia routinely pays off the local drug lord to guarantee that his plant will not be bombed and that none of his employees will be kidnapped. The manager argues that such payments are ethically defensible because everyone is doing it.

The objection is twofold. First, to simply say that an action is ethically justified if everyone is doing it is not sufficient. If firms in a country routinely employ 12-year-olds and makes them work 10-hour days, is it therefore ethically defensible to do the same?

Obviously not, and the company does have a clear choice. It does not have to abide by local practices, and it can decide not to invest in a country where the practices are particularly odious. Second, the multinational must recognize that it does have the ability to change the prevailing practice in a country. It can use its power for a positive moral purpose. This is what BP is doing by adopting a zero-tolerance policy with regard to facilitating payments. BP is stating that the prevailing practice of making facilitating payments in countries such as India is ethically wrong, and it is incumbent upon the company to use its power to try to change the standard. While some might argue that such an approach smells of moral imperialism and a lack of cultural sensitivity, if it is consistent with widely accepted moral standards in the global community, it may be ethically justified.

To return to the drug lord problem, an argument can be made that it is ethically defensible to make such payments, not because everyone else is doing so but because not doing so would cause greater harm (i.e., the drug lord might seek retribution and engage in killings and kidnappings). Another solution to the problem is to refuse to invest in a country where the rule of law is so weak that drug lords can demand protection money. This solution, however, is also imperfect, for it might mean denying the law-abiding citizens of that country the benefits associated with inward investment by the multinational (i.e., jobs, income, greater economic growth). Clearly, the drug lord problem constitutes one of those intractable ethical dilemmas where there is no obvious right solution, and managers need a moral compass to help them find an acceptable solution to the dilemma.

UTILITARIAN AND KANTIAN ETHICS

In contrast to the straw men just discussed, most moral philosophers see value in utilitarian and Kantian approaches to business ethics. These approaches were developed in the 18th and 19th centuries, and although they have been largely superseded by more modern approaches, they also form part of the tradition upon which newer approaches have been constructed.

The utilitarian approach to business ethics dates to philosophers such as David Hume (1711–1776), Jeremy Bentham (1784–1832), and John Stuart Mill (1806–1873). **Utilitarian approaches** to ethics hold that the moral worth of actions or practices is determined by their consequences.[30] An action is judged to be desirable if it leads to the best possible balance of good consequences over bad consequences. Utilitarianism is committed to the maximization of good and the minimization of harm. It recognizes that actions have multiple consequences, some of which are good in a social sense and some of which are harmful. As a philosophy for business ethics, it focuses attention on the need to carefully weigh all of the social benefits and costs of a business action and to pursue only those actions where the benefits outweigh the costs. The best decisions, from a utilitarian perspective, are those that produce the greatest good for the greatest number of people.

Many businesses have adopted specific tools such as cost–benefit analysis and risk assessment that are firmly rooted in a utilitarian philosophy. Managers often weigh the benefits and costs of an action before deciding whether to pursue it. An oil company considering drilling in the Alaskan wildlife preserve must weigh the economic benefits of increased oil production and the creation of jobs against the costs of environmental degradation in a fragile ecosystem. An agricultural biotechnology company such as Monsanto must decide whether the benefits of genetically modified crops that produce natural pesticides outweigh the risks. The benefits include increased crop yields and reduced need for chemical fertilizers. The risks include the possibility that Monsanto's insect-resistant crops might make matters worse over time if insects evolve a resistance to the natural pesticides engineered into Monsanto's plants, rendering the plants vulnerable to a new generation of super bugs.

For all of its appeal, utilitarian philosophy has some serious drawbacks as an approach to business ethics. One problem is measuring the benefits, costs, and risks of an action before deciding to pursue it. In the case of an oil company considering drilling in Alaska, how does one measure the potential harm done to the region's ecosystem? In the Monsanto example, how can one quantify the risk that genetically engineered crops might ultimately result in the evolution of super bugs that are resistant to the natural pesticide engineered into the crops? In general, utilitarian philosophers recognize that the measurement of benefits, costs, and risks is often not possible due to limited knowledge.

The second problem with utilitarianism is that the philosophy omits the consideration of justice. The action that produces the greatest good for the greatest number of people may result in the unjustified treatment of a minority. Such action cannot be ethical, precisely because it is unjust. For example, suppose that in the interests of keeping down health insurance costs, the government decides to screen people for the HIV virus and deny insurance coverage to those who are HIV positive. By reducing health costs, such action might produce significant benefits for a large number of people, but the action is unjust because it discriminates unfairly against a minority.

Kantian ethics are based on the philosophy of Immanuel Kant (1724–1804). **Kantian ethics** hold that people should be treated as ends and never purely as *means* to the ends of others. People are not instruments, like a machine. People have dignity and need to be respected as such. Employing people in sweatshops, making them work long hours for low pay in poor work conditions, is a violation of ethics, according to Kantian philosophy, because it treats people as mere cogs in a machine and not as conscious moral beings who have dignity. Although contemporary moral philosophers tend to view Kant's ethical philosophy as incomplete—for example, his system has no place for moral emotions or sentiments such as sympathy or caring—the notion that people should be respected and treated with dignity still resonates in the modern world.

RIGHTS THEORIES

Developed in the 20th century, **rights theories** recognize that human beings have fundamental rights and privileges that transcend national boundaries and cultures. Rights establish a minimum level of morally acceptable behavior. One well-known definition of a fundamental right construes it as something that takes precedence over or "trumps" a collective good. Thus, we might say that the right to free speech is a fundamental right that takes precedence over all but the most compelling collective goals and overrides, for example, the interest of the state in civil harmony or moral consensus.[31] Moral theorists argue that fundamental human rights form the basis for the *moral compass* that managers should navigate by when making decisions that have an ethical component. More precisely, they should not pursue actions that violate these rights.

The notion that there are fundamental rights that transcend national borders and cultures was the underlying motivation for the United Nations **Universal Declaration of Human Rights,** which has been ratified by almost every country on the planet and lays down basic principles that should always be adhered to irrespective of the culture in which one is doing business.[32] Echoing Kantian ethics, Article 1 of this declaration states:

> Article 1: All human beings are born free and equal in dignity and rights. They are endowed with reason and conscience and should act towards one another in a spirit of brotherhood.

Article 23 of this declaration, which relates directly to employment, states:

1. Everyone has the right to work, to free choice of employment, to just and favorable conditions of work, and to protection against unemployment.
2. Everyone, without any discrimination, has the right to equal pay for equal work.
3. Everyone who works has the right to just and favorable remuneration ensuring for himself and his family an existence worthy of human dignity, and supplemented, if necessary, by other means of social protection.
4. Everyone has the right to form and to join trade unions for the protection of his interests.

Clearly, the rights to "just and favorable work conditions," "equal pay for equal work," and remuneration that ensures an "existence worthy of human dignity" embodied in Article 23 imply that it is unethical to employ child labor in sweatshop settings and pay less than subsistence wages, even if that happens to be common practice in some countries. These are fundamental human rights that transcend national borders.

It is important to note that along with *rights* come *obligations*. Because we have the right to free speech, we are also obligated to make sure that we respect the free speech of others. The notion that people have obligations is stated in Article 29 of the Universal Declaration of Human Rights:

> Article 29: Everyone has duties to the community in which alone the free and full development of his personality is possible.

Within the framework of a theory of rights, certain people or institutions are obligated to provide benefits or services that secure the rights of others. Such obligations also fall upon more than one class of moral agent (a moral agent is any person or institution that is capable of moral action such as a government or corporation).

For example, to escape the high costs of toxic waste disposal in the West, in the late 1980s several firms shipped their waste in bulk to African nations, where it was disposed of at a much lower cost. In 1987, five European ships unloaded toxic waste containing dangerous poisons in Nigeria. Workers wearing sandals and shorts unloaded the barrels for $2.50 a day and placed them in a dirt lot in a residential area. They were not told about the contents of the barrels.[33] Who bears the obligation for protecting the safety of workers and residents in a case like this? According to rights theorists, the obligation rests not on the shoulders of one moral agent, but on the shoulders of all moral agents whose actions might harm or contribute to the harm of the workers and residents. Thus, it was the obligation not just of the Nigerian government but also of the multinational firms that shipped the toxic waste to make sure it did no harm to residents and workers. In this case, both the government and the multinationals apparently failed to recognize their basic obligation to protect the fundamental human rights of others.

JUSTICE THEORIES

Justice theories focus on the attainment of a just distribution of economic goods and services. A **just distribution** is one that is considered fair and equitable. There is no one theory of justice, and several theories of justice conflict with each other in important ways.[34] Here we shall focus on one particular theory of justice that both is very influential and has important ethical implications. The theory is attributed to philosopher John Rawls.[35] Rawls argues that all economic goods and services should be distributed equally except when an unequal distribution would work to everyone's advantage.

According to Rawls, valid principles of justice are those with which all persons would agree if they could freely and impartially consider the situation. Impartiality is guaranteed by a conceptual device that Rawls calls the *veil of ignorance*. Under the veil of ignorance, everyone is imagined to be ignorant of all of his or her particular characteristics, for example, race, sex, intelligence, nationality, family background, and special talents. Rawls then asks what system people would design under a veil of ignorance. Under these conditions, people would unanimously agree on two fundamental principles of justice.

The first principle is that each person be permitted the maximum amount of basic liberty compatible with a similar liberty for others. Rawls takes these to be political liberty (e.g., the right to vote), freedom of speech and assembly, liberty of conscience and freedom of thought, the freedom and right to hold personal property, and freedom from arbitrary arrest and seizure.

The second principle is that once equal basic liberty is assured, inequality in basic social goods—such as income and wealth distribution, and opportunities—is to be allowed *only* if such inequalities benefit everyone. Rawls accepts that inequalities can be just if the system that produces inequalities is to the advantage of everyone. More precisely, he formulates what he calls the *difference principle*, which is that inequalities are justified if they benefit the position of the least-advantaged person. So, for example, wide variations in income and wealth can be considered just if the market-based system that produces this unequal distribution also benefits the least-advantaged members of society. One can argue that a well-regulated, market-based economy and free trade, by promoting economic growth, benefit the least-advantaged members of society. In principle at least, the inequalities inherent in such systems are therefore just (in other words, the rising tide of wealth created by a market-based economy and free trade lifts all boats, even those of the most disadvantaged).

In the context of international business ethics, Rawls's theory creates an interesting perspective. Managers could ask themselves whether the policies they adopt in foreign operations would be considered just under Rawls's veil of ignorance. Is it just, for example, to pay foreign workers less than workers in the firm's home country? Rawls's theory would suggest it is, so long as the inequality benefits the least-advantaged members of the global society (which is what economic theory suggests). Alternatively, it is difficult to imagine that managers operating under a veil of ignorance would design a system where foreign employees were paid subsistence wages to work long hours in sweatshop conditions and where they were exposed to toxic materials. Such working conditions are clearly unjust in Rawls's framework, and therefore, it is unethical to adopt them. Similarly, operating under a veil of ignorance, most people would probably design a system that imparts some protection from environmental degradation to important global commons, such as the oceans, atmosphere, and tropical rain forests. To the extent that this is the case, it follows that it is unjust, and by extension unethical, for companies to pursue actions that contribute toward extensive degradation of these commons. Thus, Rawls's veil of ignorance is a conceptual tool that contributes to the moral compass that managers can use to help them navigate through difficult ethical dilemmas.

Ethical Decision Making

What then is the best way for managers in a multinational firm to make sure that ethical considerations figure into international business decisions? How do managers decide upon an ethical course of action when confronted with decisions pertaining to working conditions, human rights, corruption, and environmental pollution? From an ethical perspective, how do managers determine the moral obligations that flow from the power of a multinational? In many cases, there are no easy answers to these questions, for many of the most vexing ethical problems arise because there are very real dilemmas inherent in them and no obvious correct action. Nevertheless, managers can and should do many things to make sure that basic ethical principles are adhered to and that ethical issues are routinely inserted into international business decisions.

Here we focus on five things that an international business and its managers can do to make sure ethical issues are considered in business decisions. These are (1) favor hiring and promoting people with a well-grounded sense of personal ethics; (2) build an organizational culture that places a high value on ethical behavior; (3) make sure that leaders within the business not only articulate the rhetoric of ethical behavior, but also act in a manner that is consistent with that rhetoric; (4) implement decision-making processes that require people to consider the ethical dimension of business decisions; and (5) develop moral courage.

HIRING AND PROMOTION

It seems obvious that businesses should strive to hire people who have a strong sense of personal ethics and would not engage in unethical or illegal behavior. Similarly, you would rightly expect a business to not promote people, and perhaps to fire people, whose behavior does not match generally accepted ethical standards. But actually doing so is very difficult. How do you know that someone has a poor sense of personal ethics? People hide a lack of personal ethics from public view because unethical people are no longer trusted.

Some probing questions to ask about a prospective employer:

1. Is there a formal code of ethics? How widely is it distributed? Is it reinforced in other formal ways such as through decision-making systems?

2. Are workers at all levels trained in ethical decision making? Are they also encouraged to take responsibility for their behavior or to question authority when asked to do something they consider wrong?

3. Do employees have formal channels available to make their concerns known confidentially? Is there a formal committee high in the organization that considers ethical issues?

4. Is misconduct disciplined swiftly and justly within the organization?

5. Is integrity emphasized to new employees?

6. How are senior managers perceived by subordinates in terms of their integrity? How do such leaders model ethical behavior?

TABLE 4.1

A Job Seeker's Ethics Audit

Source: Linda K. Trevino, chair of the Department of Management and Organization, Smeal College of Business, Pennsylvania State University. Reported in K. Maher, "Career Journal. Wanted: Ethical Employer," *The Wall Street Journal*, July 9, 2002, p. B1. Copyright 2002 by Dow Jones & Co. Inc. Reproduced with permission of Dow Jones & Co. Inc. via Copyright Clearnace Center.

Is there anything that businesses can do to make sure they do not hire people who subsequently turn out to have poor personal ethics (the unethical person may lie about his or her nature)? Businesses can give potential employees psychological tests to try to discern their ethical predisposition, and they can check with prior employees regarding someone's reputation (e.g., by asking for letters of reference and talking to people who have worked with the prospective employee). The latter is common and does influence the hiring process. Promoting people who have displayed poor ethics should not occur in a company where the organization culture values the need for ethical behavior and where leaders act accordingly.

Not only should businesses strive to identify and hire people with a strong sense of personal ethics, but it also is in the interests of prospective employees to find out as much as they can about the ethical climate in an organization. Who wants to work at a multinational such as Enron, which ultimately entered bankruptcy because unethical executives had established risky partnerships that were hidden from public view and that existed in part to enrich those same executives? Table 4.1 lists questions job seekers might want to ask a prospective employer.

ORGANIZATION CULTURE AND LEADERSHIP

To foster ethical behavior, businesses need to build an organization culture that values ethical behavior. Three things are particularly important in building such a culture. First, the businesses must explicitly articulate values that emphasize ethical behavior. Many companies now do this by drafting a **code of ethics,** which is a formal statement of the ethical priorities a business adheres to. Often, the code of ethics draws heavily upon documents such as the UN Universal Declaration of Human Rights, which is grounded in Kantian and rights-based theories of moral philosophy. Others have incorporated ethical statements into documents that articulate the values or mission of the business. For example, the food and consumer products multinational Unilever has a code of ethics that includes the following points:[36]

> **Employees:** Unilever is committed to diversity in a working environment where there is mutual trust and respect and where everyone feels responsible for the performance and reputation of our company. We will recruit, employ, and promote employees on the sole basis of the qualifications and abilities needed for the work to be performed. We are committed to safe and healthy working conditions for all employees. We will not use any form of forced, compulsory, or child labor. We are committed to working with employees to develop and enhance each individual's skills and capabilities. We respect the dignity of

the individual and the right of employees to freedom of association. We will maintain good communications with employees through company-based information and consultation procedures.

Business Integrity: Unilever does not give or receive, whether directly or indirectly, bribes or other improper advantages for business or financial gain. No employee may offer, give, or receive any gift or payment which is, or may be construed as being, a bribe. Any demand for, or offer of, a bribe must be rejected immediately and reported to management. Unilever accounting records and supporting documents must accurately describe and reflect the nature of the underlying transactions. No undisclosed or un-recorded account, fund, or asset will be established or maintained.

It is clear from these principles, that among other things, Unilever will not tolerate substandard working conditions, use child labor, or give bribes under any circumstances. Note also the reference to respecting the dignity of employees, a statement that is grounded in Kantian ethics. Unilever's principles send a very clear message about appropriate ethics to managers and employees.

Having articulated values in a code of ethics or some other document, leaders in the business must give life and meaning to those words by repeatedly emphasizing their importance *and then acting on them*. This means using every relevant opportunity to stress the importance of business ethics and making sure that key business decisions not only make good economic sense but also are ethical. Many companies have gone a step further, hiring independent auditors to make sure the company is behaving in a manner consistent with its ethical codes. Nike, for example, has hired independent auditors to determine whether subcontractors used by the company are living up to Nike's code of conduct.

Finally, building an organization culture that places a high value on ethical behavior requires incentive and benefit systems, including promotions, that benefit people who engage in ethical behavior and sanction those who do not. At General Electric, for example, the former CEO Jack Welch has described how he reviewed the performance of managers, dividing them into several groups. These included overperformers who displayed the right values and were singled out for advancement and bonuses and overperformers who displayed the wrong values and were let go. Welch was not willing to tolerate leaders within the company who did not act in accordance with the central values of the company, even if they were in all other respects skilled managers.[37]

DECISION-MAKING PROCESSES

In addition to establishing the right kind of ethical culture in an organization, businesspeople must be able to think through the ethical implications of decisions in a systematic way. To do this, they need a moral compass, and both rights theories and Rawls's theory of justice help to provide such a compass. Beyond these theories, some experts on ethics have proposed a straightforward practical guide—or ethical algorithm—to determine whether a decision is ethical.[38] According to these experts, a decision is acceptable on ethical grounds if a businessperson can answer yes to each of these questions:

1. Does my decision fall within the accepted values or standards that typically apply in the organizational environment (as articulated in a code of ethics or some other corporate statement)?
2. Am I willing to see the decision communicated to all stakeholders affected by it—for example, by having it reported in newspapers or on television?
3. Would the people with whom I have a significant personal relationship, such as family members, friends, or even managers in other businesses, approve of the decision?

Others have recommended a five-step process to think through ethical problems (this is another example of an ethical algorithm).[39] In Step 1, businesspeople should identify which stakeholders a decision would affect and in what ways. A firm's **stakeholders** are individuals or groups that have an interest, claim, or stake in the company, in what it does, and in how well it performs.[40] They can be divided into internal stakeholders and external stakeholders. **Internal stakeholders** are individuals or groups who work for or own the business. They include all employees, the board of directors, and stockholders. **External stakeholders** are all other individuals and groups that have some claim on the firm. Typically, this group comprises customers, suppliers, lenders, governments, unions, local communities, and the general public.

All stakeholders are in an exchange relationship with the company. Each stakeholder group supplies the organization with important resources (or contributions), and in exchange each expects its interests to be satisfied (by inducements).[41] For example, employees provide labor, skills, knowledge, and time and in exchange expect commensurate income, job satisfaction, job security, and good working conditions. Customers provide a company with its revenues and in exchange they want quality products that represent value for money. Communities provide businesses with local infrastructure and in exchange they want businesses that are responsible citizens and seek some assurance that the quality of life will be improved as a result of the business firm's existence.

Stakeholder analysis involves a certain amount of what has been called *moral imagination*.[42] This means standing in the shoes of a stakeholder and asking how a proposed decision might impact that stakeholder. For example, when considering outsourcing to subcontractors, managers might need to ask themselves how it might feel to be working under substandard health conditions for long hours.

Step 2 involves judging the ethics of the proposed strategic decision, given the information gained in Step 1. Managers need to determine whether a proposed decision would violate the *fundamental rights* of any stakeholders. For example, we might argue that the right to information about health risks in the workplace is a fundamental entitlement of employees. Similarly, the right to know about potentially dangerous features of a product is a fundamental entitlement of customers (something tobacco companies violated when they did not reveal to their customers what they knew about the health risks of smoking). Managers might also want to ask themselves whether they would allow the proposed strategic decision if they were designing a system under Rawls's veil of ignorance. For example, if the issue under consideration was whether to outsource work to a subcontractor with low pay and poor working conditions, managers might want to ask themselves whether they would allow for such action if they were considering it under a veil of ignorance, where they themselves might ultimately be the ones to work for the subcontractor.

The judgment at this stage should be guided by various moral principles that should not be violated. The principles might be those articulated in a corporate code of ethics or other company documents. In addition, certain moral principles that we have adopted as members of society—for instance, the prohibition on stealing—should not be violated. The judgment at this stage will also be guided by the decision rule that is chosen to assess the proposed strategic decision. Although maximizing long-run profitability is the decision rule that most businesses stress, it should be applied subject to the constraint that no moral principles are violated—that the business behaves in an ethical manner.

Step 3 requires managers to establish moral intent. This means the business must resolve to place moral concerns ahead of other concerns in cases where either the fundamental rights of stakeholders or key moral principles have been violated. At this stage, input from top management might be particularly valuable. Without the proactive encouragement of top managers, middle-level managers might tend to place the narrow economic interests of the company before the interests of stakeholders. They might do so in the (usually erroneous) belief that top managers favor such an approach.

Step 4 requires the company to engage in ethical behavior. Step 5 requires the business to audit its decisions, reviewing them to make sure they were consistent with ethical principles, such as those stated in the company's code of ethics. This final step is critical and often overlooked. Without auditing past decisions, businesspeople may not know if their decision process is working and if changes should be made to ensure greater compliance with a code of ethics.

ETHICS OFFICERS

To make sure that a business behaves in an ethical manner, a number of firms now have ethics officers. These individuals are responsible for making sure that all employees are trained to be ethically aware, that ethical considerations enter the business decision-making process, and that the company's code of ethics is adhered to. Ethics officers may also be responsible for auditing decisions to make sure they are consistent with this code. In many businesses, ethics officers act as an internal ombudsperson with responsibility for handling confidential inquiries from employees, investigating complaints from employees or others, reporting findings, and making recommendations for change.

For example, United Technologies, a multinational aerospace company with worldwide revenues of more than $28 billion, has had a formal code of ethics since 1990.[43] Some 160 business practice officers within United Technologies (this is the company's name for ethics officers) are responsible for making sure the code is followed. United Technologies also established an ombudsperson program in 1986 that lets employees inquire anonymously about ethics issues. The program has received some 56,000 inquiries since 1986, and 8,000 cases have been handled by an ombudsperson.

MORAL COURAGE

Finally, it is important to recognize that employees in an international business may need significant *moral courage*. Moral courage enables managers to walk away from a decision that is profitable, but unethical. Moral courage gives an employee the strength to say no to a superior who instructs her to pursue actions that are unethical. And moral courage gives employees the integrity to go public to the media and blow the whistle on persistent unethical behavior in a company. This moral courage does not come easily; individuals have lost their jobs because they blew the whistle on corporate behaviors they thought unethical, telling the media about what was occurring.[44]

However, companies can strengthen the moral courage of employees by committing themselves to not retaliate against employees who exercise moral courage, say no to superiors, or otherwise complain about unethical actions. For example, consider the following extract from Unilever's code of ethics:

> Any breaches of the Code must be reported in accordance with the procedures specified by the Joint Secretaries. The Board of Unilever will not criticize management for any loss of business resulting from adherence to these principles and other mandatory policies and instructions. The Board of Unilever expects employees to bring to their attention, or to that of senior management, any breach or suspected breach of these principles. Provision has been made for employees to be able to report in confidence and no employee will suffer as a consequence of doing so.[45]

Clearly this statement gives permission to employees to exercise moral courage. Companies can also set up ethics hotlines, which allow employees to anonymously register a complaint with a corporate ethics officer.

SUMMARY OF DECISION-MAKING STEPS

All of the steps discussed here—hiring and promoting people based upon ethical considerations as well as more traditional metrics of performance, establishing an ethical culture in the organization, instituting ethical decision-making processes, appointing ethics officers, and creating an environment that facilitates moral courage—can help to make sure that when deciding business issues, managers are cognizant of the ethical implications and do not violate basic ethical prescripts. But not all ethical dilemmas have a clean and obvious solution—that is why they are dilemmas. In these cases, a premium is placed on managers' ability to make sense out of complex situations and make balanced decisions that are as just as possible.

Chapter Summary

This chapter has discussed the source and nature of ethical issues in international businesses, the different philosophical approaches to business ethics, and the steps managers can take to ensure that ethical issues are respected in international business decisions. The chapter made the following points:

1. The term *ethics* refers to accepted principles of right or wrong that govern the conduct of a person, the members of a profession, or the actions of an organization. Business ethics are the accepted principles of right or wrong governing the conduct of businesspeople, and an ethical strategy is one that does not violate these accepted principles.

2. Ethical issues and dilemmas in international business are rooted in the variations among political systems, law, economic development, and culture from nation to nation.

3. The most common ethical issues in international business involve employment practices, human rights, environmental regulations, corruption, and the moral obligation of multinational corporations.

4. Ethical dilemmas are situations in which none of the available alternatives seems ethically acceptable.

5. Unethical behavior is rooted in poor personal ethics, the psychological and geographical distances of a foreign subsidiary from the home office, a failure to incorporate ethical issues into strategic and operational decision making, a dysfunctional culture, and failure of leaders to act in an ethical manner.

6. Moral philosophers contend that approaches to business ethics such as the Friedman doctrine, cultural relativism, the righteous moralist, and the naive immoralist are unsatisfactory in important ways.

7. The Friedman doctrine states that the only social responsibility of business is to increase profits, as long as the company stays within the rules

of law. Cultural relativism contends that one should adopt the ethics of the culture in which one is doing business. The righteous moralist monolithically applies home-country ethics to a foreign situation, while the naive immoralist believes that if a manager of a multinational sees that firms from other nations are not following ethical norms in a host nation, that manager should not either.

8. Utilitarian approaches to ethics hold that the moral worth of actions or practices is determined by their consequences, and the best decisions are those that produce the greatest good for the greatest number of people.

9. Kantian ethics state that people should be treated as ends and never purely as *means* to the ends of others. People are not instruments, like a machine. People have dignity and need to be respected as such.

10. Rights theories recognize that human beings have fundamental rights and privileges that transcend national boundaries and cultures. These rights establish a minimum level of morally acceptable behavior.

11. The concept of justice developed by John Rawls suggests that a decision is just and ethical if people would allow for it when designing a social system under a veil of ignorance.

12. To make sure that ethical issues are considered in international business decisions, managers should (*a*) favor hiring and promoting people with a well-grounded sense of personal ethics; (*b*) build an organization culture that places a high value on ethical behavior; (*c*) make sure that leaders within the business not only articulate the rhetoric of ethical behavior, but also act in a manner that is consistent with that rhetoric; (*d*) put decision-making processes in place that require people to consider the ethical dimension of business decisions; and (*e*) be morally courageous and encourage others to do the same.

Critical Thinking and Discussion Questions

1. Review the Management Focus on testing drugs in the developing world and discuss the following questions:

   a. Did Pfizer behave unethically by rushing to take advantage of a Nigerian epidemic to test an experimental drug on sick children? Should the company have proceeded more carefully?

   b. Is it ethical to test an experimental drug on children in emergency settings in the developing world where the overall standard of health care is much lower than in the developed world, and where proper protocols might not be followed?

2. A visiting American executive finds that a foreign subsidiary in a poor nation has hired a 12-year-old girl to work on a factory floor, in violation of the company's prohibition on child labor. He tells the local manager to replace the child and tell her to go back to school. The local manager tells the American executive that the child is an orphan with no other means of support, and she will probably become a street child if she is denied work. What should the American executive do?

3. Drawing upon John Rawls's concept of the veil of ignorance, develop an ethical code that will (a) guide the decisions of a large oil multinational toward environmental protection, and (b) influence the policies of a clothing company outsourcing its manufacturing.

4. Under what conditions is it ethically defensible to outsource production to the developing world where labor costs are lower when such actions also involve laying off long-term employees in the firm's home country?

5. Are facilitating payments ethical?

Research Task   globalEDGE™   globaledge.msu.edu

Use the globalEDGE™ site to complete the following exercises:

1. Promoting respect for universal human rights is a central dimension of foreign policy for many countries. Begun in 1977, the U.S. State Department's annual Country Reports on Human Rights Practices are designed to assess the state of democracy and human rights around the world, call attention to violations, and prompt needed changes in policies toward particular countries. Find the most recent annual Country Reports on Human Rights Practices, and compare conditions in three Western Hemisphere countries of your choice.

2. The Corruption Perceptions Index (CPI) is a comparative assessment of a country's integrity performance regarding corruption. Provide a description of this index and its ranking. Identify the five countries with the lowest as well as the five with the highest CPI scores.

Mired in Corruption—Kellogg Brown & Root in Nigeria

CLOSING CASE In 1998 the large Texas-based oil and gas service firm, Halliburton, acquired Dresser Industries. At the time the CEO of Halliburton was Dick Cheney, who subsequently became the vice president of the United States under George W. Bush. Among other businesses, Dresser owned M. W. Kellogg, one of the world's largest general contractors for construction projects in distant parts of the globe. After the acquisition, Kellogg was combined with an existing Halliburton business and renamed Kellogg Brown & Root, or KBR. At the time it looked like a good deal for Halliburton. Among other things, Kellogg was involved in a four-firm consortium that was building a series of liquefied natural gas (LNG) plants in Nigeria. By early 2004, the total value of the contracts associated with these plants had exceeded $8 billion.

In early 2005, however, Halliburton put KBR up for sale. The sale was seen as an attempt by Halliburton to distance itself from several scandals that had engulfed KBR. One of these concerned allegations that KBR had systematically overcharged the Pentagon for services it provided to the U.S. military in Iraq. Another scandal centered on the Nigerian LNG plants and involved KBR employees, several former officials of the Nigeria government, and a mysterious British lawyer called Jeffrey Tesler.

The roots of the Nigerian scandal date to 1994 when Kellogg and its consortium partners were trying to win an initial contract from the Nigerian government to build two LNG plants. The contract was valued at about $2 billion. Each of the four firms held a 25 percent stake in the consortium, and each had veto power over its decisions. Kellogg employees held many of the top positions at the consortium, and two of the other members, Technip of France and JGC of Japan, have claimed that Kellogg managed the consortium (the fourth member, ENI of Italy, has not made any statement regarding management).

The Kellogg consortium was one of two to submit a bid on the initial contract, and its bid was the lower of the two. By early 1995, the consortium was deep in final negotiations on the contract when Nigeria's oil minister had a falling out with the country's military dictator, General Abacha, and was replaced by Dan Etete. Etete proved to be far less accommodating to the Kellogg group, and suddenly the entire deal looked to be in jeopardy. According to some observers, Dan Etete was a tough customer who immediately began to use his influence over the LNG project for personal gain. The consortium quickly entered into a contract with the British lawyer, Jeffery Tesler. The contract, signed by a Kellogg executive, called on Tesler to obtain government permits for the LNG project, maintain good relations with government officials, and provide advice on sales strategy. Tesler's fee for these services was $60 million.

Tesler had long-standing relations with some 20 to 30 senior Nigeria government and military officials. For years he had handled their London legal affairs, helping them to purchase real estate and set up financial accounts. Kellogg had a relationship with Tesler that dated back to the mid-1980s, when it had employed him to broker the sale of Kellogg's minority interest in a Nigerian fertilizer plant to the Nigerian government.

What happened next is currently the subject of government investigations in France, Nigeria, and the United States. The suspicion is that Tesler promised to funnel big sums to Nigerian government officials if the deal was done. Investigators base these suspicions on a number of factors, including the known corruption of General Abacha's government, the size of the payment to Tesler, which seemed out of proportion to the services he was contracted to provide, and a series of notes turned up by internal investigators at Halliburton. The handwritten notes, taken by Wojciech Chodan, a Kellogg executive, document a meeting between Chodan and Tesler in which they discussed the possibility of channeling $40 million of Tesler's $60 million payment to General Abacha.

It is not known whether a bribe was actually paid. What is known is that in December 1995, Nigeria awarded the $2 billion contract to the Kellogg consortium. The LNG plant soon became a success. Nigeria contracted to build a second plant in 1999, two more in 2002, and a sixth in July 2004. KBR rehired Tesler in 1999 and again in 2001 to help secure the new contracts, all of which it won. In total, Tesler was paid some $132.3 million from 1994 through to early 2004 by the consortium.

Tesler's involvement in the project might have remained unknown were it not for an unrelated event. Georges Krammer, an employee of the consortium member Technip, was charged by the French government with embezzlement. When Technip refused to defend Krammer, he turned around and aired what he perceived to be Technip's dirty linen. This included the payments to Tesler to secure the Nigeria LNG contracts.

This led French and Swiss officials to investigate Tesler's Swiss bank accounts. They discovered that Tesler was "kicking back" some of the funds he received to executives in the consortium and at subcontractors. One of the alleged kickbacks was a transfer of $5 million from Tesler's account to that of Albert J. "Jack" Stanley, who was head of M. W. Kellogg and then Halliburton's KBR unit. Tesler also transferred some $2.5 million into Swiss bank accounts held under a false name by the Nigerian oil minister, Dan Etete. Other payments include a $1 million transfer into an account controlled by Wojciech Chodan, the former Kellogg executive whose extensive handwritten notes suggest the payment of a bribe to General Abacha, and $5 million to a German subcontractor on the LNG project in exchange for "information and advice."

After this came out in June 2004, Halliburton fired Jack Stanley and severed its long-standing relationship with Tesler, asking its three partners in the Nigeria consortium to do the same. The United States Justice Department took things further, establishing a grand jury investigation to determine if Halliburton, through its KBR subsidiary, had violated the Foreign Corrupt Practices Act. In November 2004, the Justice Department widened its investigation to include payments in connection with the Nigeria fertilizer plant that Kellogg had been involved with during the 1980s under the leadership of Jack Stanley. In March 2005, the Justice Department also stated it was looking at whether Jack Stanley had tried to coordinate bidding with rivals and fix prices on certain foreign construction projects.

Sources: R. Gold and C. Flemming, "Out of Africa: In Halliburton Nigeria Inquiry, a Search for Bribes to a Dictator," *The Wall Street Journal*, September 29, 2004, p. A1; R. Gold, "Halliburton to Put KBR Unit on Auction Block," *The New York Times*, January 31, 2005, p. A2; T. Sawyer, "Citing Violations, Halliburton Cuts Off Former KBR Chairman," *ENR*, June 28, 2004, p. 16; and D. Ivanovich, "Halliburton: Contracts Investigated," *Houston Chronicle*, March 2, 2005, p. 1.

Case Discussion Questions

1. Could the alleged payment of bribes to Nigerian government officials by Jeffrey Tesler be considered "facilitating payments" or "speed money" under the terms of the Foreign Corrupt Practices Act?

2. Irrespective of the legality of any payments that may have been made by Tesler, do you think it was reasonable for KBR to hire him as an intermediary?

3. Given the known corruption of the Abacha government in Nigeria, should Kellogg and its successor, KBR, have had a policy in place to deal with bribery and corruption? What might that policy have looked like?

4. Should Kellogg have walked away from the Nigerian LNG project once it became clear that the payment of bribes might be required to secure the contract?

5. There is evidence that Jack Stanley, the former head of M. W. Kellogg and KBR, may have taken kickback payments from Tesler. At least one other former Kellogg employee, Wojciech Chodan, may have taken kickback payments. What does this tell you about the possible nature of the ethical climate at Kellogg and then KBR?

6. Should Halliburton be called into account if it is shown that its KBR unit used bribery to gain business in Nigeria? To what extent should a corporation and its officers be held accountable for ethically suspect activities by the managers in a subsidiary, particularly given that many of those activities were initiated before the subsidiary was owned by Halliburton?

Notes

1. Thomas Donaldson, "Values in Tension: Ethics Away from Home," *Harvard Business Review*, September–October 1996.

2. Robert Kinloch Massie, *Loosing the Bonds: The United States and South Africa in the Apartheid Years* (Doubleday, 1997).

3. Not everyone agrees that the divestment trend had much influence on the South African economy. For a counterview see Siew Hong Teoh, Ivo Welch, and C. Paul Wazzan, "The Effect of Socially Activist Investing on the Financial Markets: Evidence from South Africa," *The Journal of Business* 72, no. 1 (January 1999), pp. 35–60.

4. Andy Rowell, "Trouble Flares in the Delta of Death; Shell Has Polluted More Than Ken Saro Wiwa's Oroniland in Nigeria," *The Guardian*, November 8, 1995, p. 6.

5. H. Hamilton, "Shell's New World Wide View," *Washington Post*, August 2, 1998, p. H1.

6. Rowell, "Trouble Flares in the Delta of Death."

7. Peter Singer, *One World: The Ethics of Globalization*. (New Haven, CT: Yale University Press, 2002).

8. Garrett Hardin, "The Tragedy of the Common," *Science* 162, no. 1, pp. 243–48.

9. Richard T. De George, *Competing with Integrity in International Business* (Oxford: Oxford University Press, 1993).

10. Details can be found at www.oecd.org/EN/home/0,,EN-home-31-nodirectorate-no-nono-31,00.html.

11. Bardhan Pranab, "Corruption and Development," *Journal of Economic Literature* 36 (September 1997), pp. 1320–46.

12. A. Shleifer and R. W. Vishny, "Corruption," *Quarterly Journal of Economics*, no. 108 (1993), pp. 599–617, and I. Ehrlich and F. Lui, "Bureaucratic Corruption and Endogenous Economic Growth," *Journal of Political Economy* 107 (December 1999), pp. 270–92.

13. P. Mauro, "Corruption and Growth," *Quarterly Journal of Economics*, no. 110 (1995), pp. 681–712.

14. Detailed at www.iit.edu/departments/csep/PublicWWW/codes/coe/Bus_Conduct_Dow_Corning(1996).html.

15. S. A. Waddock and S. B. Graves, "The Corporate Social Performance-Financial Performance Link," *Strategic Management Journal* 8 (1997), pp. 303–19.

16. Daniel Litvin, *Empires of Profit* (New York: Texere, 2003).

17. Details can be found at BP's Web site, www.bp.com.

18. This is known as the "when in Rome perspective." Donaldson, "Values in Tension: Ethics Away from Home."

19. De George, *Competing with Integrity in International Business*.

20. Donaldson, "Values in Tension: Ethics Away from Home."

21. Saul W. Gellerman, "Why Good Managers Make Bad Ethical Choices," in *Ethics in Practice:*

Managing the Moral Corporation, ed. Kenneth R. Andrews (Cambridge, MA: Harvard Business School Press, 1989).

22. David Messick and Max H. Bazerman, "Ethical Leadership and the Psychology of Decision Making," *Sloan Management Review* 37 (Winter 1996), pp. 9–20.

23. Robert Bryce, *Pipe Dreams: Greed, Ego and the Death of Enron* (New York: Public Affairs, 2002).

24. Milton Friedman, "The Social Responsibility of Business Is to Increase Profits," *The New York Times Magazine*, September 13, 1970. Reprinted in Tom L. Beauchamp and Norman E. Bowie, *Ethical Theory and Business*, 7th ed. (Upper Saddle River, NJ: Prentice Hall, 2001).

25. Friedman, "The Social Responsibility of Business Is to Increase Profits," p. 55.

26. For example, see Donaldson, "Values in Tension: Ethics Away from Home." See also Norman Bowie, "Relativism and the Moral Obligations of Multination Corporations," in Beauchamp and Bowie, *Ethical Theory and Business*.

27. For example, see De George, *Competing with Integrity in International Business*.

28. Details can be found at www.bp.com/sectiongenericarticle.do?category1d=79&contentId=2002369#2014689.

29. This example is often repeated in the literature on international business ethics. It was first outlined by Arthur Kelly in "Case Study—Italian Style Mores." Printed in Thomas Donaldson and Patricia Werhane, *Ethical Issues in Business* (Englewood Cliffs, NJ: Prentice Hall, 1979).

30. See Beauchamp and Bowie, *Ethical Theory and Business*.

31. Thomas Donaldson, *The Ethics of International Business* (Oxford: Oxford University Press, 1989).

32. Found at www.un.org/Overview/rights.html.

33. Donaldson, *The Ethics of International Business*.

34. See Chapter 10 in Beauchamp and Bowie, *Ethical Theory and Business*.

35. John Rawls, *A Theory of Justice*, rev. ed. (Cambridge, MA: Belknap Press, 1999).

36. Found on Unilever's Web site at www.unilever.com/company/ourprinciples/.

37. Joseph Bower and Jay Dial, "Jack Welch: General Electric's Revolutionary," Harvard Business School Case No. 9-394-065, April 1994.

38. For example, see R. Edward Freeman and Daniel Gilbert, *Corporate Strategy and the Search for Ethics* (Englewood Cliffs, NJ: Prentice Hall, 1988); Thomas Jones, "Ethical Decision Making by Individuals in Organizations," *Academy of Management Review* 16 (1991), pp. 366–95; and J. R. Rest, *Moral Development: Advances in Research and Theory* (New York: Praeger, 1986).

39. Ibid.

40. See E. Freeman, *Strategic Management: A Stakeholder Approach* (Boston: Pitman Press, 1984); C. W. L. Hill and T. M. Jones, "Stakeholder-Agency Theory," *Journal of Management Studies* 29 (1992), pp. 131–54; and J. G. March and H. A. Simon, *Organizations* (New York: Wiley, 1958).

41. Hill and Jones, "Stakeholder-Agency Theory," and March and Simon, *Organizations*.

42. De George, *Competing with Integrity in International Business*.

43. The code can be accessed at the United Technologies Web site, www.utc.com/profile/ethics/index.htm.

44. Colin Grant, "Whistle Blowers: Saints of Secular Culture," *Journal of Business Ethics*, September 2002, pp. 391–400.

45. Found on Unilever's Web site, www.unilever.com/company/ourprinciples/.

Cases

Western Drug Companies and the AIDS Epidemic in South Africa

In December 1997, the government of South Africa passed a law that authorized two controversial practices. One, called parallel importing, allowed importers in South Africa to purchase drugs from the cheapest source available, regardless of whether the patent holders had given their approval or not. Thus, South Africa asserted its right to import "generic versions" of drugs that are still patent protected. The government did this because it claimed to be unable to afford the high cost of medicines that were patent protected. The other practice, called compulsory licensing, permitted the South African government to license local companies to produce cheaper versions of drugs whose patents are held by foreign companies, irrespective of whether the patent holder agreed.

The law seemed to violate international agreements to protect property rights, including a World Trade Organization agreement on patents to which South Africa is a signatory. South Africa, however, insisted the law was necessary given the country's health crisis and the high cost of patented medicines. By 1997, South Africa was wrestling with an AIDS crisis of enormous proportions. It was estimated that over 3 million of the country's 45 million people were infected with the virus at the time, more than in any other country. However, although the AIDS epidemic in South Africa was seen as the primary reason for the new law, the law itself was applied to "communicable diseases" (of which AIDS is just one, albeit a devastating one).

Foreign drug manufacturers saw the law as an unbridled attempt to expropriate their intellectual property rights, and 39 foreign companies quickly filed a lawsuit in the country to try to block implementation of the law. Drug manufacturers were particularly concerned about the applicability of the law to all "communicable diseases." They feared that South Africa was the thin end of the wedge, and if the law was allowed to stand, other countries would follow suit. Many Western companies also feared that if poor countries such as South Africa were allowed to buy low-priced generic versions of patent-protected drugs, in violation of intellectual property laws, American and European consumers would soon demand the same.

In defense of their patents, the drug companies argued that because drug development is a very expensive, time-consuming, and risky process, they need the protection of intellectual property laws to maintain the incentive to innovate. It can take $800 million and 12 years to develop a drug and bring it to market. Less than one in five compounds that enter clinical trials actually become marketed drugs—the rest fail in trials due to poor efficacy or unfavorable side effects—and of those that make

it to market, only 3 out of 10 earn profits that exceed their costs of capital. If drug companies could not count on high prices for their few successful products, the drug development process would dry up.

The drug companies have long recognized that countries such as South Africa face special health challenges and lack the money to pay developed world prices. Accordingly, the industry has priced drugs low in the developing world or given them away. For example, many AIDS drugs were already being sold to developing nations at large discounts to their prices in the United States. The South African government thought this was not good enough. The government was quickly supported by various human rights and AIDS organizations, which cast the case as an attempt by the prosperous multinational drug companies of the West to maintain their intellectual property rights in the face of desperate attempts by an impoverished government to stem a deadly crisis. For their part, the drug companies stated that the case had little to do with AIDS and was really about the right of South Africa to break international law.

While the drug companies may have had international law on their side, the tie-in with the AIDS epidemic clearly put them on the public relations defensive. After a blizzard of negative publicity, and little support from Western governments that were keen not to touch this political "hot potato," several leading manufacturers of AIDS drugs, while still opposing the South African law, started to change their policies. In May 2000, five large manufacturers of AIDS medicines—Merck, Bristol-Myers Squibb, Roche, Glaxo, and Boehringer Ingelheim—announced that they would negotiate lower priced AIDS drugs in developing countries, primarily in sub-Saharan Africa (some 25 million of the 36 million people infected with the HIV virus in 2000 lived in that region). Still the protests continued.

In February 2001, an Indian drug company, Cipla Ltd., offered to sell a cocktail of three AIDS drugs to poor African nations for $600 per patient per year, and for $350 a year to Doctors without Borders (AIDS is commonly treated with a cocktail that combines up to 10 antiviral drugs). The patents for these drugs were held by Western companies, but Indian law allowed local companies to produce generic versions of patent-protected drugs.

The Cipla announcement seemed to galvanize Western drug companies into further action. In March 2001, Merck announced that it would cut the prices of its two AIDS drugs, Crixivan and Stocrin. Crixivan, which sold for $6,016 per year in the United States, would be sold in developing countries for $600 a year. Stocrin, which cost $4,730 a year in the United States, would be sold for $500. Both drugs were often used together as part of an AIDS cocktail. Officials at Doctors without Borders, the Nobel Peace Prize–winning relief agency, welcomed the announcement, but pointed out that in a region where many people lived on less than a dollar a day, the price was still out of reach of many AIDS patients.

A few days later, Bristol-Myers Squibb went further, announcing it would sell its AIDS drug Zerit to poor nations in Africa for just $0.15 a day, or $54 a patient per year, which was below Zerit's production costs. In the United States and Europe, Zerit was selling for $3,589 per patient per year. This was followed by an announcement from Abbott Laboratories that it would sell two of its AIDS drugs at "no profit" in sub-Saharan Africa.

None of these moves, however, were enough to satisfy critics. In April 2001, the drug companies seemed to conclude that they were losing the public relations war, and they agreed to drop their suit against the South African government. This opened the way for South Africa to start importing cheap generic versions of patented medicines from producers such as Cipla of India. The decision to drop the suit was widely interpreted in the media as a defeat for the drug companies and a reaffirmation of the ability of the South African government to enforce compulsory licensing. At the same time, the pharmaceutical companies appear to have gotten assurances from South Africa that locally produced generic versions of patented drugs would be sold only in sub-Saharan Africa, and not exported to other regions of the world.

In 2003, Aspen Pharmaceuticals, a South African drugmaker, took advantage of the 1997 law to introduce a generic version of Stavudine, and it asked South African authorities for permission to produce up to six more AIDS drugs. Aspen had licensed the rights to produce these drugs from Bristol-Myers Squibb and Glaxo, the large British company. Bristol and Glaxo had waived their rights to royalties from sales of the drugs in sub-Saharan Africa. At the same, the companies noted that Aspen was able to sell the drugs only within the sub-Sahara region.

Despite these moves, critics still urged Western drug companies to do more to fight the global AIDS epidemic, which by 2003 was estimated to afflict some 50 million people. For example, in a 2003 *New York Times* op-ed article, noted playwright and AIDS activist Larry Kramer stated, "It is incumbent upon every manufacturer of every HIV drug to contribute its patents or its drugs free for the salvation of these people. . . . I believe it is evil for drug companies to possess a means of saving lives and then not provide it to the desperate people who need it. What kind of hideous people have we become? It is time to throw out the selfish notion that these companies have the right not to share their patents."

Meanwhile in South Africa, the AIDS epidemic continued on its relentless course. By 2004 some 5.3 million South Africans were estimated to have been infected with HIV, and 600 people a day were dying from AIDS-related complications. In 2003, the South African government had committed itself to offering at low or no cost antiviral drugs to everyone with AIDS. By working with pharmaceutical companies such as Aspen and three Indian producers of generic drugs, the government was able to purchase a cocktail of antiviral HIV drugs for $65 per patient per month. However, by late 2004, only one out of 50 AIDS patients who were ready for the drugs was getting them, according to news reports. The problem now was distribution and a chronic shortage of clinics, doctors, and nurses. Estimates suggested that it would still be years before cheap AIDS drugs were available to all those who needed them in South Africa.

Case Discussion Questions

1. Why is it so important for the drug companies to protect their patents?

2. What should the policy of drug companies be toward the pricing of patent-protected drugs for AIDS in poor developing nations such as South Africa?

3. What should the policy be in developed nations? Is it ethical to charge a high price for drugs that treat a life-threatening condition, such as AIDS?

4. In retrospect, could the large Western pharmaceuticals have responded differently to the 1997 South African law? How might they have better taken the initiative?

5. Is AIDS a special case, or should large drug companies make it normal practice to price low or give away patent-protected medicines to those who cannot afford them in poor nations?

Sources

1. Block, R. "Big Drug Firms Defend Right to Patent on AIDS Drugs in South African Courts." *The Wall Street Journal*, March 6, 2001, p. A3.

2. Cooper, H., R. Zimmerman, and L. McGinley. "Patents Pending—AIDS Epidemic Traps Drug Firms in a Vise." *The Wall Street Journal*, March 2, 2001, p. A1.

3. Jeter, J. "Trial Opens in South Africa AIDS Drug Suit." *Washington Post*, March 6, 2001, p. A1.

4. Kramer, L. "The Plague We Can't Escape." *The New York Times*, March 15, 2003, p. A17.

5. Nurton, J. "Overcoming the AIDS Hurdle." *Managing Intellectual Property*, June 2002, pp. 39–40.

6. Smith, T. "Mixed View of a Pact for Generic Drugs." *The New York Times*, August 29, 2003, p. C3.

7. Timberg, C. "South Africans with AIDS See a Ray of Hope." *Washington Post*, November 30, 2004, p. A1.

KFC in India—Ethical Issues

"Each bird whom KFC puts into a box or a bucket had a miserable life and a frightening death. People would be shocked to see our footage of a KFC supplier's employee who walks through a barn, carelessly lighting lamps and letting flames fall on the terrified birds. The air inside these filthy barns reeks of ammonia fumes, making it difficult for the birds to breathe. No one with a grain of compassion should set foot in KFC."[1]

Ingrid Newkirk, Director
PETA[2]

"The chicken they serve is full of chemicals, and the birds are given hormones, antibiotics, and arsenic chemicals to fatten them quickly."[3]

Nanjundaswamy[4]

PROTEST AGAINST KFC

On August 20, 2003, a five-foot-tall chicken complete with an ensemble of feathers and beak hobbled on a pair of crutches outside Kentucky Fried Chicken's (KFC) Indian outlet in Bangalore. The chicken was brought by PETA (People for the Ethical Treatment of Animals) activists,

who carried placards reading, "Quit India" and "Stop Playing Fowl" (a pun on "Foul"). The chicken was placed at the center and a peaceful protest was held against the alleged ill treatment of birds in KFC's poultry farms. Media persons were called to give the demonstration wide coverage.

Explaining the rationale behind the protest, Bijal Vachcharajani, special projects coordinator of PETA, said, "Ours is the land of Gandhi. Just as 61 years back our leaders gave a call for colonizers to quit India, we too are saying we will not tolerate cruel multinationals."[5] On the 61st anniversary of the "Quit India" movement,[6] PETA India wrote a letter to the managing director of Tricon Restaurant International, the parent company of KFC, asking it to close its sole KFC outlet in India. They got no reply. PETA activists decided to protest against KFC by carrying a crippled chicken, which represented the birds suffering in the KFC's farms.

PETA claimed that after two years of intensive campaigning to increase animal welfare standards in poultry farms, other foreign fast-food restaurants operating in India like McDonald's[7] and Burger King[8] had improved the treatment of animals specially raised and slaughtered for food. Only KFC had not acted. Though PETA had organized other protests earlier, the crippled chicken campaign became the precursor for more intensive protests. PETA's was one of the many shows of protest against KFC's Indian outlet.

BACKGROUND

KFC was founded by Harland Sanders in the early 1930s, when he started cooking and serving food for hungry travelers who stopped by his service station in Corbin,

[1] "PETA Reveals Shocking Cruelty to Animals at KFC Factory Chicken Farm," Bijal Vachcharajani, www.petaindia.com, October 9, 2003.
[2] Founded in the United States in 1980, with more than 800,000 members and offices in the United States, England, Italy, Germany, and Mumbai, PETA is the largest animal rights organization in the world. It focuses primarily on areas where the greatest numbers of animals suffer the most: in the food and leather industries, in laboratories, and in the entertainment industry. PETA undertakes investigative work, public education, research, animal rescue, legislation, special events, celebrity involvement, and international media coverage for the protection and improvement of the quality of animal lives. PETA India, based in Mumbai, was launched in January 2000.
[3] Shakuntala Narasimhan, "Tandoori vs. Kentucky Fried," *Multinational Monitor*, January/February 1996.
[4] Prof. Nanjundaswamy is the founder-leader of the Karnataka Rajya Ryota Sangha (KRRS). Apart from his campaign against KFC, he also organized a campaign in South India against global seed patenting provisions of the Uruguay Round of the General Agreement on Tariffs and Trade (GATT).

[5] "Crippled Chicken Alleges Cruelty, Asks KFC to Quit India," www.newindpress.com, August 20, 2003.
[6] The Quit India Movement, which started on August 9, 1942, is an important milestone in the history of India's struggle for freedom from British rule.
[7] With revenues of $17.1 billion in the fiscal year 2003, McDonald's is the world's largest food service company with more than 30,000 restaurants in 100 countries, serving more than 46 million customers every day. McDonald's entered India in October 1996. It has restaurants in Mumbai, Delhi, Pune, Ahmedabad, Vadodara, Ludhiana, Jaipur, Noida, Faridabad, Doraha, Manesar, and Gurgaon.
[8] The U.S.-based Burger King is an international fast-food chain founded by James W. McLamore and David Edgerton in Miami in 1954. It was renamed Burger King Corporation in 1972. In 2004, the company had more than 11,220 restaurants in 61 countries worldwide.

Kentucky. He did not own a restaurant then, but served people on his own dining table in the living quarters of his service station. His chicken delicacies became popular and people started coming just for food. Kentucky Fried Chicken was born. Soon, Sanders moved across the street to a motel-cum-restaurant, later named "Sanders Court & Cafe," that seated around 142 people.

Over the next nine years, he perfected his secret blend of 11 herbs and spices and the basic cooking technique of chicken. Sanders's fame grew and he was given the title Kentucky Colonel by the governor in 1935 for his contribution to the state's cuisine.

Sanders's restaurant business witnessed an unexpected halt in the early 1950s, when a new interstate highway was planned bypassing the town of Corbin. His restaurant flourished mainly due to the patronage of highway travelers. The new development meant the end of this. Sanders sold his restaurant operations. After settling all his bills, he was reduced to living on a meager $105 Social Security check.

But Sanders did not lose hope. Banking on the popularity of his product and confident of his unique recipe for fried chicken, Sanders started franchising his chicken business in 1952. He called it Kentucky Fried Chicken. He traveled the length and breadth of the country by car, visiting as many restaurants as possible and cooking batches of chicken. If the restaurant owners liked his chicken, he entered into a handshake agreement that stipulated payment of a nickel[9] for each plate of chicken sold by the restaurant.

By 1964, Sanders franchised more than 600 chicken outlets in the United States and Canada. The same year, he sold his interest in his company in the United States for $2 million to a group of investors. However, he remained the public spokesperson for the company. KFC grew rapidly under the new owners and issued shares to the public on March 17, 1966. In July 1971, KFC was acquired by Heublein Inc. for $285 million. By then, KFC had over 3,500 franchised and company-owned restaurants in the world.

Heublein Inc. was acquired by Reynolds Industries Inc. (now RJR Nabisco Inc.) in 1982. In October 1986, the company again changed hands, and was acquired by PepsiCo Inc. for $840 million. PepsiCo had other quick-service restaurants too—Taco Bell and Pizza Hut. PepsiCo moved all of them into an independent restaurant company called Tricon Global Restaurants in January 1997. In May 2002, Tricon's name was changed to Yum! Brands Inc.[10] to reflect its expanding portfolio of brands.

By 2004, KFC emerged as one of the world's most popular chicken restaurant chains. With more than 11,000 restaurants in nearly 80 countries, KFC enjoyed the patronage of nearly 8 million customers every day all over the world. KFC specialties included Original Recipe, Extra Crispy, Chunky Chicken Pot Pie, Twister, and Colonel's Crispy Strips chicken with home-style sides.

KFC'S ENTRY INTO INDIA

Foreign fast-food companies were allowed to enter India during the early 1990s due to the economic liberalization policy of the Indian government. KFC was among the first fast-food multinationals to enter India. On receiving permission to open 30 new outlets across the country, KFC opened its first fast-food outlet in Bangalore in June 1995.

Bangalore was chosen as the launch pad because it had a substantial upper-middle-class population, with a trend of families eating out. It was considered India's fastest growing metropolis in the 1990s. Apart from Bangalore, PepsiCo planned to open 60 KFC and Pizza Hut outlets in the country in the next seven years. However, KFC got embroiled in various controversies even before it started full-fledged business in India.

When the issue of granting permission to multinational food giants to set up business in the country came up for discussion in the Indian parliament, some members from the opposition parties were vocal in their displeasure. They criticized the government's decision saying that in India, where millions of people could not afford one meal per day, the government was inviting multinationals to establish fast-food chains, which only the upper middle and affluent classes could afford. They pointed out that a piece of chicken was sold for the equivalent of a little more than $1 at KFC, more than the daily per-capita income in India.

Leading economists vigorously opposed the idea of multinationals in the food business entering India as they posed a threat to domestic business. Nationalists feared a cultural invasion; environmentalists and farmers felt grain consumption by cattle for meat production would be detrimental; and nutritionists highlighted the high rates of obesity, hypertension, heart disease, and cancer (which were relatively low in India so far) in the United States caused by consumption of meat, processed and fried foods which were high in sodium and cholesterol. All activists were unanimous in their opposition to foreign fast-food joints. They argued that traditional Indian recipes such as "tandoori chicken"[11] were more nutritious than the junk-food alternatives.

---

[9] Nickel is a colloquial term used for "five cents" in the United States. The coin is worth one-twentieth of a dollar.

[10] In 2004, the businesses owned by Yum! Brands Inc. included A&W All-American Food Restaurants, KFC, Long John Silvers, Pizza Hut, and Taco Bell restaurants. With these, Yum! Brands owned nearly 32,500 outlets in more than 100 countries in the world.

---

[11] Popular in India, it is called "tandoori chicken" because it is cooked in a "tandoor," a clay oven. The meat is marinated in a spice mixture and threaded onto skewers and placed in the hot oven. In the tandoor, the meat cooks by a combination of convected and radiated heat. The distinct flavor of food cooked in a tandoor is a result from the oils and fats dripping from the marinated meats onto the hot charcoal producing smoky flavors. It does not contain any artificial flavoring agents and is prepared according to centuries-old traditional recipes, using natural ingredients.

PROBLEMS FOR KFC

From the very first day of opening its restaurant, KFC faced problems in the form of protests by angry farmers led by the Karnataka Rajya Ryota Sangha (KRRS).[12] The farmers' leader, Nanjundaswamy, who led these protests, vehemently condemned KFC's entry into India, saying that it was unethical to promote highly processed "junk food" in a poor country like India with severe malnutrition problems. Nanjundaswamy expressed concern that the growing number of foreign fast-food chains would deplete India's livestock, which would adversely affect its agriculture and the environment. He argued that nonvegetarian fast-food restaurants like KFC would encourage Indian farmers to shift from production of basic crops to more lucrative varieties like animal feed and meat, leaving poorer sections of society with no affordable food.

KRRS held a convention on November 1, 1995, to protest the entry of fast-food multinationals and the Westernization of local agriculture. National banks, insurance companies, political parties, and nongovernmental organizations supported the convention. All parties attending the convention agreed that India needed a new "Quit India" movement against junk-food companies.

Amidst these vociferous protests, the Indian government tried to justify its actions by saying that economic liberalization policies would attract multinationals and their opening of businesses would create employment and develop infrastructure. However, Nanjundaswamy differed with the government's contentions. He argued that fast-food companies brought jobs only for a handful of educated people and displaced the poor majority. He cited the example of Venkateshwara Hatcheries,[13] which supplied KFC with broilers after closing down its restaurants in Mumbai and Pune as part of a deal with KFC.

On January 30, 1996, KFC's Bangalore outlet again witnessed protesting farmers carrying "Boycott KFC" signs. Media reports stated that around 100 irate farmers entered the restaurant, smashed windows, broke furniture, and ransacked the cash box, demanding that KFC should leave India. KFC's billboards were destroyed across the state by agitators. Following the violence, several farmers were imprisoned. On February 3, 1996, Nanjundaswamy was also jailed on charges of looting, attempt to murder, and other offenses.

Despite these setbacks, KRRS did not relent and continued its protests against Western fast-food joints in general and KFC in particular. KRRS maintained that the entry of Western fast-food chains in India would threaten the livelihood of more than 70 percent of the Indian population, which depended on agriculture. They regarded multinational food companies as the first step toward the destruction of India's food security.

Nanjundaswamy also said that apart from the threat to local agriculture, another negative aspect of fast-food chains like KFC was large-scale factory farming of chickens. He maintained that the chicken served by KFC was full of chemicals because the birds were reportedly being given hormones, antibiotics, and arsenic to fatten them quickly. He called the chickens "chemically poisoned."

KRRS got a boost when Maneka Gandhi, former environment minister and animal activist, attacked KFC stating that they served overpriced processed chicken, which was artificially raised and refried several times. Ecologists also joined the farmers' protests by saying that the opening of fast-food joints meant more trash, including plastic lids, paper cups, bags, and extra condiments, on the highways and sidewalks.

NONCONFORMITY WITH FOOD PRODUCTS REGULATIONS

In August 1995, just a couple of months after launch, KFC's Bangalore outlet faced a major crisis when municipal food inspectors visited the restaurant and found that KFC's "hot & spicy" seasoning contained nearly three times more monosodium glutamate (MSG, popularly known as ajinomoto, a flavor-enhancing ingredient) than allowed by the Indian Prevention of Food Adulteration Act, 1954 (IPFAA).[14] (Refer to Exhibit I for the definition of adulterated food).

Used in a wide range of fast foods, MSG had been associated with behavioral disorders, hyperactivity, severe brain damage in rats, nausea and headache among adults, and worst, its teratogenic effects. Intake by pregnant women leads to retardation and birth defects in offspring. Unborn children were considered to be at grave risk as MSG concentrated in the placenta. Children under 12 were are also advised against taking MSG as it retarded brain development. The IPFAA fixed an MSG ceiling in fast foods at 1 percent. The food inspectors' examination, followed by laboratory tests and analysis, found that KFC's chicken contained 2.8 percent of MSG.

The MSG controversy reached a crescendo on September 13, 1995. The Bangalore City Corporation revoked the restaurant's license and directed the police to close it on

---

[12] KRRS is the Karnataka State Farmers' Association representing 10 million farmers in Karnataka.
[13] With its registered office in Mumbai, Venkateshwara Hatcheries is a leading company in the Indian poultry market. It supplies poultry/cattle feed supplements and poultry equipment.

[14] IPFAA aims at making provisions for the prevention of adulteration of food. The act extends to the whole of India and came into force on June 1, 1955. It discusses in detail what is adulterated food, when food can be considered adulterated or misbranded, the prohibitions and restrictions with regard to the use of certain ingredients, flavoring agents, preservatives and their quantities, analysis of food products under certain circumstances, offenses, and punishments under the act.

EXHIBIT I

Definition of
Adulterated Food

Source: www.helplinelaw.com.

According to the Prevention of Food Adulteration Act, 1954, an article of food shall be deemed to be adulterated:

- If the article sold by a vendor is not of the nature, substance, or quality demanded by the purchaser or which it purports to be;

- If the article contains any substance affecting its quality or if it is so processed as to injuriously affect its nature, substance, or quality;

- If any inferior or cheaper substance has been substituted wholly or partly for the article, or any constituent of the article has been wholly or partly abstracted from it, so as to affect its quality or if it is so processed as to injuriously affect its nature, substance, or quality;

- If the article had been prepared, packed, or kept under insanitary conditions whereby it has become contaminated or injurious to health;

- If the article consists wholly or in part of any filthy, putrid, disgusting, rotten, decomposed, or diseased animal or vegetable substance or being insect-infested, or is otherwise unfit for human consumption;

- If the article is obtained from a diseased animal;

- If the article contains any poisonous or other ingredient which is injurious to health;

- If the container of the article is composed of any poisonous or deleterious substance which renders its contents injurious to health;

- If the article contains any prohibited coloring matter or preservative, or any permitted coloring matter or preservative in excess of the prescribed limits;

- If the quality or purity of the article falls below the prescribed standard, or its constituents are present in proportions other than standard, or its constituents are present in proportions other than those prescribed, whether or not rendering it injurious to health.

As per the above clauses, even addition of water to milk is considered adulteration within the meaning of the Act.

the ground that KFC not only exceeded the legal MSG limits but had also failed to disclose what seasoning it used in its preparations. It charged KFC with serving food that was "adulterated, misbranded, and unfit for human consumption." Refuting the charges, Sandeep Kohli, managing director of KFC India, said, "We serve the same product in Bangalore as we do in our over 9,000 restaurants in 78 countries. And we know for a fact that the level of MSG is what is within permissible norms."[15] He further added that the health standards followed by KFC were among the best compared to other restaurants in Bangalore.

The closure orders enraged both the local management of KFC and their U.S. bosses. PepsiCo's Senior Research Department argued that India lacked the laboratory equipment needed to accurately test the level of MSG in food products. Meanwhile, to test MSG levels, an Indian business weekly—*Outlook*—bought samples of fried chicken from KFC and took them to the Food Research and Analysis Centre of the Federation of Indian Cham-

bers of Commerce. The analysis showed that KFC had the highest level of MSG, much above the permitted levels. However, PepsiCo refused to accept the result of the tests and put forth the same argument that Indian labs were not well-equipped to measure the additive accurately.

KFC's management approached the Karnataka State High Court and obtained a stay order against the closure orders issued by the Bangalore City Corporation. The judge said the restaurant could operate as usual till full court hearings. After securing the stay order, KFC's management announced at a press conference that all they wanted was to let customers decide and if the latter did not like the company's products, it would have to close the shop. But, soon after reopening, KFC had to face the wrath of farmers who attacked the restaurant and destroyed the billboards of the company. KFC had to then run its business under police protection.

Undeterred by the problems at Bangalore, PepsiCo opened a second KFC outlet in Delhi, the national capital, in October 1995. KFC's management also announced that six more outlets would be opened in Delhi by the end of 1996. However, in a couple of weeks, the Delhi outlet too

[15] "KFC Takes On India over MSG," Ashis Ray, www.cnn.com, September 21, 1995.

faced protests by a coalition of farmers, vegetarians, and environmentalists. Within a couple of weeks of launch, the Delhi restaurant had to stop its business as health officials canceled its license on November 6, 1995, on the grounds that the coating mix imported from the United States contained sodium aluminium phosphate (SAP),[16] which was hazardous to human health. KFC sought redress from the Delhi High Court and argued that the food contained no harmful chemicals and that the amount of SAP, an ingredient in baking powder, was within the limits approved by the World Health Organization and the U.S. Food and Drug Administration. The charges were withdrawn as KFC proved that SAP was used in small quantities in the baking powder and was not harmful. The restaurant then resumed business.

KFC won a favorable order from the Delhi High Court, but this did not deter farmers' associations from resuming their protests. In December 1995, the government of India permitted higher levels of MSG in Indian food,[17] which meant that KFC could continue its business. The activists retaliated by taking up other issues against KFC. The Swadeshi Jagran Manch (National Awakening Forum)[18] began a probe into the hygiene conditions at the restaurant. An inspection by food inspectors found flies buzzing around the kitchen and garbage cans just outside the restaurant premises. The Municipal Corporation of Delhi served a closure order on grounds of hygiene and sanitation. Thus, the Delhi KFC outlet was closed within 23 days of reopening.

Later, KFC's management decided to close the outlet permanently citing high rentals as the prime reason. They said that the outlet was hit by high rents and the

cost of doing business in Delhi was not in line with its worldwide standards. Apart from this, the main ingredient—chicken—was easily available in the south, east, and west parts of India, but not in the north. So, procuring chicken also became an expensive proposition for KFC. Thus, the Bangalore restaurant remained the sole KFC outlet in India for many years. However, it had to face continuous protests from PETA against the alleged cruel treatment of chickens by KFC staff and suppliers.

CAMPAIGNS BY PETA

By the late 1990s, the MSG controversy and the protests by nationalists and farmers subsided. However, KFC faced a new problem in the form of PETA. PETA had been protesting for a long time against KFC at the international level on the grounds that KFC was extremely cruel to chickens and did not care to provide even minimum hygiene for the birds at its factories. It ran a special Web site called www.kfcfriedcruelty.com, which detailed the inhuman treatment of the birds in KFC poultry farms and the slaughterhouses of the suppliers.

PETA India also launched an extensive protest program against KFC's Indian outlet. It said that despite repeated appeals to the management, KFC had not cared to improve either the conditions or the treatment of birds. PETA urged the Indian public not to go to KFC's restaurant and asked them to demand its closure in India. The protests grew rampant from 2003 onwards as the company did not budge. However, unlike the previous violent protests by the farmers, PETA demonstrations were peaceful.

PETA then started a mass education program stating that it wanted to enlighten people about the cruelty suffered by chickens at KFC poultry farms. "KFC stands for cruelty" was the slogan of PETA. Pamphlets with a graphic description of the cruelty were distributed. KFC's spokespersons denied the charges and said the company was committed to the well-being and humane treatment of chickens.

To substantiate its allegations regarding KFC's cruelty, PETA released a video documenting the daily suffering of thousands of chickens in a factory farm in Venkateshwara Hatcheries in Pune that supplied chickens to KFC. The 10-minute video gave a telling description of the plight of the birds with visuals. This was premiered at a news conference at Bangalore on October 9, 2003. It showed chickens stuffed into overcrowded warehouses, pushing each other for food, a barn littered with carcasses of chickens that had died of disease, dirty and injured chickens that never received any medication, and chickens suffering at the hands of indifferent staff.

The video showed thousands of chickens crammed into sheds that stank of ammonia fumes from accumulated waste. The birds were forced to live for whatever time they were alive in the amount of a space equivalent to a standard sheet of paper. They had barely enough room to move.

---

[16]SAP, technically known as E541 compound, is mainly used in the food industry as a leavening agent or acid for mixing baking powders. It has an excellent buffering action for flour mixes, enhancing the properties of formula ingredients. When SAP is used in food products, it becomes crunchy and has fine texture. With high levels of aluminium, SAP has been linked with Alzheimer's and osteoporosis because of its tendency to accumulate in the brain and in bones. Its ill effects are manifested only in the long run and by then it could be too late for treatment. Pregnant and lactating women, children, and the elderly are considered more prone to these ill effects.

[17]Following the furor caused by the KFC controversy on MSG levels in food products, the government of India raised permitted levels of MSG in food in December 1995. The National Health Standards were rewritten to allow higher amounts of MSG in Indian food. The government was apprehensive that driving away KFC, one of the first multinational food companies to set up business in India, would deter further investment in India by foreign food processing companies and fast-food chains like McDonald's, which planned to open around 60 outlets in India in 1996.

[18]Some nationalists felt that even decades after the country's independence, India was not economically independent. They felt that for total economic freedom it is essential to make Swadeshi (Nationalism) a way of life. To make people aware of the ongoing economic imperialism, some organizations like the Bharatiya Mazdoor Sangh, Bharatiya Kisan Sangh, and Akhil Bharatiya Vidyarthi Parishad started a massive campaign for Swadeshi in the 1980s and the National Awakening Forum (NAF) came into existence on November 22, 1991, at Nagpur, a city in western India. NAF's motto is self-reliance for India, equitable world order, and fight against economic imperialism of multinationals. The organization has an all-India network of subunits up to the district level across the country.

KFC's chickens each have less space than a standard-sized sheet of paper.

Chickens are stuffed by the tens of thousands into overcrowded sheds, where they have no space to stretch their wings or move about freely. Owing to the lack of space in the shed, chickens stamp and climb on each other to get from one place to another. Chickens can be seen struggling and pushing other chickens aside to get to their food. The air in these sheds is heavy with ammonia fumes, making it difficult to breathe.

KFC's chickens suffer from crippling leg deformities for their entire lives.

Birds are fed genetically modified feed in order to accelerate their growth rate, making them top-heavy. Ailments such as extreme obesity and fatty livers and kidneys, heart attacks, septicaemia, and deformities caused by arthritis are a common sight. This abnormal weight gain, along with other ailments, causes stress to young bones, making the chickens' legs crumple beneath them to the extent that they cannot even get to their feed. These crippling leg deformities then lead to diseases like arthritis and osteoporosis.

KFC's chickens suffer from fatal heart attacks resulting from poor breeding.

Because of unsanitary living conditions along with increased growth rate, chickens die an early death. These chickens fall prey to ailments like heart attacks, fatty livers and kidneys, arthritis. According to the UK-based Animal Aid Organisation, "Many broiler chickens also die from ascites: Their growth rate is so rapid that their heart, lungs, and circulatory system struggle to maintain sufficient oxygen levels. This results in breathlessness and distended abdomens." In chickens, this disease is believed to be caused by the fact that the birds' heart and lung capacity cannot keep up with their rapid growth rate.

KFC's chickens are slaughtered before they are six weeks old.

When living in their natural surroundings, chickens live up to 10 years. However, at KFC factory farms, they are fed a steady dose of growth promoters, and they are slaughtered at 35 to 45 days. The reason behind this accelerated growth is a high-protein diet and a steady diet of growth promoters.

KFC's chickens receive little to no veterinary care.

Owing to human negligence, the chickens have to suffer throughout their lives. Unhygienic conditions, growth-promoting feed, and improper care on the part of the handlers lead to the rapid spread of dangerous diseases among chickens. The consequences of such diseases are usually fatal.

KFC's chickens suffer at the hands of callous workers.

These birds routinely suffer broken bones from callous handling. The workers roughly grab them by their legs and stuff them into crates. It seems to be a common occurrence for workers at KFC supply farms to walk through an overcrowded shed bursting at the seams with chickens and nonchalantly stamp on a few who dare get in the way. A worker carelessly lights lamps and lets flames fall on the terrified birds. The air inside these filthy barns reeks of ammonia fumes, making it difficult for the birds even to breathe. These birds lie unattended at the farms, writhing in pain because of the carelessness of workers.

KFC's chickens suffer during transport.

All chickens are subjected to the ordeal of catching, transportation, and slaughter. The birds are typically grabbed by the feet and thrust into crates before being loaded onto lorries or are caught, three chickens in one hand and two in the other, and slammed into the lorry. Many suffer additional injuries at this time, and hundreds of chickens can die from a panic-induced crush each time the catching gang enters the shed. Others die during the journey to the killing plants, often from heart attacks. Injuries and wounds account for the other fatalities. The most common injury is dislocation of the femur (the bone between the hip and the knee). This is almost certainly the result of rough handling by catching teams. Soft young bones break, and joints (often already painfully deformed) become dislocated when birds are caught.

EXHIBIT II

PETA's Fact Sheet of KFC's Cruelty

Source: www.petaindia.com.

When the birds were killed, they were barely two months old.[19] They were genetically engineered and overfed to get fat faster. Being abnormally top-heavy, the birds suffered from limited mobility, leg deformities, broken bones, and heart attacks. But the birds received no treatment. The beaks were cut off using a hot blade without giving anesthesia (Refer to Exhibit II for PETA's detailed fact sheet of cruelty).

Apart from these inhuman conditions, the young chicks also suffered the callousness of the staff, who grabbed them by their legs and stuffed them into crates for being transported to the slaughterhouse by lorry. The

_____
[19] Chickens have a natural life span of 10 to 15 years.

EXHIBIT III

Relevant Provision of
the Animal Welfare
Legislation

Source: www.helplinelaw.com.

SECTION II

According to the Prevention of Cruelty to Animals Act, 1960, it is an offence to do the following:

- Convey or carry, whether in or upon any vehicle or not, any animal in such a manner or position as to subject him or her to unnecessary pain or suffering.
- Keep or confine any animal in any cage or other receptacle which does not measure sufficiently in height, length, and breadth to permit the animal a reasonable opportunity for movement.
- Fail to provide [one's] animal with sufficient food, drink, or shelter.

The Transport of Animals (Amendment) Rules, 2001.
Chapter VII: TRANSPORT OF POULTRY BY RAIL, ROAD, AND AIR.
RULES (77–80)

- General requirement—In transport of poultry by rail, road, or air, the poultry shall not be exposed to the sunlight, rain, and direct blast of air during transport.
- Day-old chicks and turkey poultry—In transport of day-old chicks and poultry by rail, road, and air personal attention shall be given by the consignor or the forwarding agent to ensure that all consignments are kept out of direct sunlight, rain, and heat.
- Poultry other than day-old chicks and turkey poultry—In transport of poultry other than day-old chicks and turkey poultry by rail, road, or air, the poultry to be transported shall be healthy and in good condition and shall be examined and certified by a veterinary doctor for freedom from infectious diseases and fitness to undertake the journey.
- Poultry shall be properly fed and watered before it is placed in containers for transportation and extra feed and water shall be provided in suitable troughs fixed in the containers.
- Road travel—In transport of poultry by road the container shall not be placed one on the top of the other and shall be covered properly in order to provide light, ventilation, and to protect from rain, heat, and cold air.

mode of transportation violated the legislative provisions regarding animal transportation (Refer to Exhibit III for the relevant provisions). Many birds died during transport. The birds were shackled upside down at the slaughterhouses. They were often fully conscious when their throats were cut or when they were dumped into tanks of scalding hot water to remove their feathers.

The video contradicted KFC's statements to the media that its supply farms strictly adhered to animal welfare standards. PETA reiterated that "KFC stands for cruelty and we do not need this cruel outlet in India. This cruelty must be stopped. All we are asking for is for reasonable improvement on our list of demands or get out. I hope the people of India will join us."[20]

THE AFTERMATH

By late 2003, PETA further intensified its campaign against the cruel treatment meted out to chickens by KFC through protests at regular intervals. Celebrities like Anoushka Shankar, daughter of the legendary sitar maestro Ravi Shankar, directly supported the cause of PETA. Anoushka, a sitarist herself, wrote a letter to the top management of PepsiCo condemning the continued cruelty of KFC in spite of repeated requests of PETA. The organization also had the support of other celebrities like the famous cricket player Anil Kumble (based in Bangalore), popular Indian models like Aditi Govitrikar, the late Nafisa Joseph and John Abraham, who promoted vegetarianism. Film actresses like Raveena Tandon and Ameesha Patel also took up the cause of animal abuse.

Undeterred by the continued protests, KFC added three more outlets[21] to its existing one at Bangalore. KFC also announced a major expansion program for 2005. Sharanita Keswani, KFC's marketing director, said that as the retail business was poised for a boom in India, they considered it the right time for expansion. Feeling positive about the flourishing malls in all big cities,

[20] "Video of Chicken Cruelty Revealed," www.bday.co.za, October 14, 2003.

[21] The other outlets are located at Indira Nagar junction, at a Bangalore's posh suburb hosting many IT and business process outsourcing companies, and at the International Technology Park in Whitefield on the outskirts of the city.

Keswani revealed that this time KFC planned to have a presence in prime locations or in a mall where turnout would be assured.

The company aimed at targeting cosmopolitan cities like Chandigarh, Pune, Kolkata, Chennai, and Hyderabad, where mall culture was fast developing. PepsiCo also decided to concentrate on the expansion of KFC since its other brand, Pizza Hut, had successfully established a strong foothold in India.

Vegetarianism was predominant and was a way of life in India. Many people ate nonvegetarian food only occasionally and avoided it during festivals or religious occasions. KFC did not want to alienate the vegetarian community, which was a majority in India. It decided to add more vegetarian and Indian items to the menu, in an effort to become attractive to both vegetarian and nonvegetarian customers. Rather than affecting chicken sales, the presence of vegetarian dishes in the menu was expected to make the brand more appealing to a wider section of consumers. The diversification into vegetarian food was considered inevitable by the management to establish itself as a universal brand across the country.

While KFC was busy planning extensive expansion, PETA conducted another demonstration at Bangalore on February 17, 2004. The protesters held placards reading, "KFC quit India" and "Don't let KFC roost in India." They also distributed pamphlets stating that apart from the abuse of chickens raised for food, PETA was targeting KFC because the company killed more chickens, more than 750 million per annum, compared to any other food company. PETA said, "As the world's leading killer of chickens, KFC had the responsibility to take the lead in eliminating at least the worst abuse, but had done nothing to address them."

In response to this protest, Pankaj Batra, director of marketing for the Indian subcontinent, Yum! Restaurants International, observed that KFC was committed to the "well-being and humane treatment of chickens" and that they required their suppliers to follow the welfare guidelines developed by Yum! Restaurants International, along with leading experts, on their Animal Welfare Advisory Council (Refer to Exhibit IV for KFC's Poultry Welfare Guidelines). He emphasized that they respected Indian law and that KFC guidelines completely adhered to them.

However, PETA was not convinced and announced that it would continue its protests against the multinational until it changed its cruel practices or left India. The battle between KFC and PETA in India continued.

Case Discussion Questions

1. Since its entry into India in 1995, KFC has been facing protests by cultural and economic activists and farmers. What are the reasons for these protests and do you think these reasons are justified? Explain.

2. PETA has been protesting against KFC in India since the late 1990s. What are the reasons for PETA's protests against KFC and how did KFC's management react to them? Do you agree with PETA that KFC has been cruel toward the birds and hence it should leave India?

3. What is the importance of ethics in doing business? Do you think in the face of fierce competition, business organizations are justified not to support ethical values at the cost of making profits? Why or why not? Justify your answer giving examples.

Additional Readings and References

1. Spaeth, Anthony, and Dick Thompson. "Battle of the Chickens," www.times.com, 1995.

2. Ray, Ashis. "KFC Takes On India over MSG," www.cnn.com, September 21, 1995.

3. Dahlburg, John-Thor, and Amitabh Sharma. "The Feathers Fly over Chicken Eatery in India." *Los Angeles Times*, September 22, 1995.

4. "Delhi's Fried Chicken Blues," www.theasiaweek.com, November 24, 1995.

5. "Kentucky Fried Chicken Protests in India." *The Ecologist*, November/December 1995.

6. "KFC Finds a Foe," www.hinduism-today.com, January 1996.

7. Narasimhan, Shakuntala. "Tandoori vs. Kentucky Fried." *Multinational Monitor*, January/February 1996.

8. Davis, A. Elizabeth. "Protesters Reveal Fast Food Disappointments," January 31, 1996.

9. Vandana, Shiva. "More Than a Matter of Two Flies: Why KFC Is an Ecological Issue," www.mcsspotlight.org, January 1996.

10. "US Fast Food Giants Rock India." *The Earth Island Journal*, Spring 1996.

11. Bhatnagar, Mohini. "An All American Accepts Indian Palate," www.domain-b.com, January 4, 2002.

12. Mishra, Richa. "Tricon to Refresh Pizza Hut Brand Equity—Plans 60 Restaurants by 2002," www.blonnet.com, June 29, 2002.

13. "PETA Stages Demo against KFC." *The Deccan Herald*, August 19, 2003.

14. "Crippled Chicken Alleges Cruelty, Asks KFC to Quit India," www.newindpress.com, August 20, 2003.

In 2000, KFC adopted specific, comprehensive welfare performance standards for processing chickens and audits its suppliers against the standards. KFC's processing guidelines and audits are designed to manage and monitor each step of the process to determine whether the birds supplied to KFC are handled humanely and that any suffering is minimized. KFC audits its suppliers for compliance, and noncompliance could result in termination of the supplier's contract. KFC's policies for its suppliers apply to all chickens intended to be sold to KFC. KFC's guidelines for its suppliers include:

PROCESSING GUIDELINES

General: Suppliers must have a documented program for animal welfare including a designated program leader, formal employee training, and a system of regular self-audits and record keeping. Corrective action for suppliers' deviations from KFC's poultry welfare guidelines should be clearly stated and effective. Birds arriving at the plant should be clean and in good health. If an audit reveals dirty or sick birds, corrective action at the grow-out house must be taken by the supplier.

Comfort and Shelter: KFC's guidelines call for its suppliers to house birds in shelters that are clean, well ventilated, and protective. Temperature, humidity, ammonia levels, lighting, and litter conditions should be continually monitored and maintained to maximize the comfort level of the birds. Birds should be free to roam throughout the shelters.

Catching: KFC's guidelines also provide that every reasonable precaution should be taken to minimize injury to birds arriving at supplier's plants. KFC recommends that its suppliers implement an incentive program that rewards catching crews for minimizing injury if KFC's audit reveals that birds are being injured during the catching process.

Transport: KFC's guidelines call for transport crates to be in good repair. KFC recommends that there be no crate damage that would allow injury to birds or allow crates to accidentally open. Transport crates should not be over-filled and enough space should be provided to allow all birds to lie down.

Holding: Birds held in storage sheds by suppliers should be provided adequate ventilation and climate control such as fans or curtains.

Stunning: Suppliers' stunning equipment should be maintained to confirm that birds are insensible prior to slaughter, and that the time between stunning and slaughter should be limited to minimize any likelihood that a bird may regain consciousness prior to slaughter.

Humane Slaughter: Slaughter equipment at all supply facilities should be properly maintained to confirm that the birds are slaughtered quickly.

KFC's FARM LEVEL GUIDELINES

In May 2003, KFC committed itself to the adoption of comprehensive industry-leading guidelines and audits for the humane raising and handling of poultry at the farm level. KFC does not own or operate any poultry farms or processing facilities. Instead, it purchases chickens from, at any given time, approximately 16 different suppliers who collectively operate up to 52 facilities around the country. The new standards adopted by KFC address the breeding, hatching, and raising of poultry at the farm level. The standards were developed by leading animal welfare experts at the direction of the National Council of Chain Restaurants and the Food Marketing Institute. The standards address:

Education and Training of Poultry Supplier Personnel: Suppliers must have a documented program for animal welfare including a designated program leader, formal employee training, and a system of regular self-audits and record keeping. Corrective action for suppliers' deviations from KFC's poultry welfare guidelines should be clearly stated and effective.

Breeding: Birds used to produce hatching eggs must be treated in a humane manner including access to feed and water. Suppliers must provide adequate space for the birds.

Hatchery Operations: Climate and sanitation must be monitored by suppliers to promote chick health and comfort. All processing systems must be designed, maintained, and operated in a manner that minimizes injury to the chicks. Beak trimming is not allowed for poultry that will be sold in KFC restaurants.

Raising: Consistent with federal (U.S.) law, it is KFC's policy that its suppliers must not use hormones or steroids for any purpose, including to promote growth in their chickens, and suppliers tell KFC that they are complying with this policy. Suppliers say that in order to promote the health and well-being of the chickens in their care, some chickens may, from time to time, be given medications (including antibiotics) under veterinary supervision to cure or prevent disease in the flocks. KFC's policy prohibits suppliers from using antibiotics to promote the growth of healthy chickens where such antibiotics are significant to human health. Suppliers assure KFC that they are complying with this KFC policy.

Proper Nutrition and Feeding: KFC's guidelines recommend that suppliers should formulate feed to deliver proper nutrition and promote the health of the birds.

Appropriate Comfort and Shelter: KFC's guidelines call for a program to be in place at poultry farms to monitor climate control systems as well as have emergency procedures in the event of a power failure.

EXHIBIT IV

KFC'S Poultry Welfare Guidelines

Source: www.kfc.com.

15. "Giving a Future Shock," www.economictimes. indiatimes.com, December 26, 2003.

16. "Protest against KFC," www.hindu.com, February 18, 2004.

17. Desmaris, Martin. "Shankar Rails against KFC, Indian Chicken Suppliers," www.indusbisinessjournal. com, June 15, 2004.

18. Prashanth, GN. "Chicken and More." *The Hindu*, June 15, 2004.

19. John, Sujith. "Baking News! Veggie Wonders from KFC," www.timesofindia.com, October 7, 2004.

20. Balaji, Fakir. "KFC to Open More Outlets in India," www.southasiamonitor.org, November 4, 2004.

21. www.swadeshi.org.

22. www.chemtrailcentral.com.

23. www.worldoffoodindianews.com.

24. www.indiatimes.com.

25. www.kfc.com.

26. www.indiainfoline.com.

27. www.kfccruelty.com.

28. www.unh.edu.

29. www.yum.com.

30. www.petaindia.com.

31. www.veg.ca.

32. www.dd-b.net.

Related Case Studies

1. Reebok—Managing Human Rights Issues "Ethically"? Reference No. 703–005–1.

2. Coke—Ethical Issues, Reference No. 702–020–1.

3. Nike's Labor Practices, Reference No. 702–021–1.

Anne Burns's Personal Jihad

ABSTRACT

An American expatriate is assigned to work in a nonprofit organization in Jordan that sought to promote Jordanian exports, especially those produced and sold by female entrepreneurs. She experienced difficulties as she attempted to promote the economic standing of women in Jordan, and became involved in organizational politics she did not understand.

Anne Burns, a 45-year-old American woman who started a number of businesses in the United States, was hired by a recently established nonprofit organization called ExportJordan. Working with a grant from USAID, ExportJordan's mission was to further develop local businesses in Jordan in order to capitalize on the recently signed free trade agreement with the United States. Having just sold her last business, and having her two grown children out of the house, Anne and her husband, Don, decided to forgo their empty nest and strike out on a new adventure in the Middle East.

Anne and Don did not need to work since the businesses they had created, and sold, provided more than a comfortable living for them. Having many productive years ahead of them, they sought out a unique challenge. Jordan was to be that new challenge.

JORDAN

Jordan is a constitutional monarchy based on heredity. Male descendants of the dynasty of King Abdullah bin al Hussein inherit the throne and rule the country without

opposition. The country now called Jordan was created at the end of World War I when the League of Nations gave the territory to the United Kingdom to rule. The UK created a semiautonomous jurisdiction called the Emirate of Transjordan. In 1946 Transjordan became an independent country and changed its name in 1950 to the Hashemite Kingdom of Jordan. The country is presently ruled by King Abdullah II, a Western-educated and progressive leader who has strong ties to the United States. King Abdullah has moved for a free press, democratic reform, and women's rights. King Abdullah's father ruled Jordan through much of its independence. As King Abdullah has moved for even more reforms than his father, both the United States and the European Union have rewarded Jordan with free trade agreements. Jordan is a member of the World Trade Organization. The close ties between Jordan and Western nations coupled with the king and his wife's desire to advance the status of women helped create ExportJordan. ExportJordan was charged with helping to create an entrepreneurial spirit among Jordan's female citizens, and to help them develop and export products. Currently Jordan is successful in exporting clothing, food products, phosphate, and some pharmaceuticals. With the new free trade agreements it was hoped that additional areas could be developed for export.

TROUBLE FROM THE START

It was a spirit of adventure and a genuine desire to help others that led Anne and her husband to Jordan. They were both impressed with the young king and his views for leading his country into the 21st century. They had hoped to find a cooperative environment, but that hope was somewhat challenged from the start.

When Anne arrived at the offices of ExportJordan for the first time, she met Hayat Maani. Hayat was a Western-educated young woman with passion. She was deeply concerned with the plight of women in her country and was involved in a number of social causes throughout Jordan. She welcomed Anne and gave her a tour of the offices, explaining what the organization did and what Anne's role would be in the new venture. Anne would work closely with Hayat in helping small businesses owned by Jordanian women to find international buyers for their products. The mission of ExportJordan was to promote all Jordanian products, but Anne would mainly be involved in helping female entrepreneurs. On the initial office tour and series of introductions, Anne met Jafar Faqir, a middle-aged man who worked in the export finance division of the organization. Hayat introduced Jafar to Anne. Jafar did not extend his hand when Anne initiated a handshake and she thought this a bit odd, but quickly forgot about it when Jafar asked her "how do you find Jordan." Anne explained that she had only been in the country a short time but that she was very impressed with the king and his approach to the advancement of women. The look on Jafar's face told Anne that he did not like her response. Hayat told Jafar that Anne would be responsible for promoting women entrepreneurs and Jafar told her to remember these words, "The eye cannot raise above the eyebrow." Hayat shouted to Jafar something in Arabic and Jafar left without saying another word. When Anne asked what had just happened, Hayat simply said that unfortunately not all Jordanian men were supportive of equality for women. Anne would find that this would not be her only negative encounter with Jafar.

The rest of the day went smoothly for Anne as she continued to meet more people associated with the organization. She noticed that all of the women in the offices wore a hejab or head scarf, except for Hayat. Anne noticed other interesting cultural dimensions, such as the common response "Inshallah" or "God willing." Many of the people she met seemed very interested in her and asked many questions, such as how many children she and her husband had, especially boys. Anne and her husband had two girls and when she told this to one of her male colleagues, he responded with "Oh, I'm so sorry." Anne knew that it was going to be a very different and interesting experience living in the Middle East.

PROGRESS BEGINS

Anne and Don settled into their life in Jordan, and apart from the normal difficulties of living abroad, the couple didn't feel as if they experienced too much difficulty ad-

justing. Although there were no other Westerners at ExportJordan, Anne and Don met other American and British expatriates and enjoyed their company and they all enjoyed sharing their experiences living in Jordan. Don kept busy looking for business opportunities for himself and helping Anne with her assignment.

After two months it became clear to Anne that she was in need of an assistant to help her with the preliminary analytical work she was doing. Anne suggested to Hayat that Don be hired to help her. Hayat told her that she didn't think that would be possible; however, she would find someone else to help her. After a few days, Hayat introduced Anne to Karim Dabbas, a young Jordanian man who was hired as her assistant. Karim spoke English well, yet his youth and inexperience gave Anne some concern.

With the help of Karim, Anne completed her initial analysis and was ready to begin to do her fieldwork. Anne had planned on hosting seminars for women around Jordan explaining the possibilities of the export market and finding women with whom she could personally consult about their businesses. Karim would be helpful in the fieldwork, acting as both a driver and interpreter.

The first seminar was planned for Amman and was heavily promoted. Although Anne and Hayat had hoped for a very large audience, they were not unhappy with the few women who attended, because among the attendees were some good prospects for the export market. With Anne's expertise in creating business plans and her knowledge of the U.S. market, Anne and Hayat began helping three women who produced crafts which were felt had international appeal. Additional seminars were planned for other cities in Jordan in the future, and Anne was convinced that she would be able to make a contribution to ExportJordan.

WARNINGS FROM JAFAR

During the next two weeks Anne and Karim worked with the three women from the seminar on their business plans and creating ways of making their products more appealing to the global marketplace. Anne had not seen Hayat for a few days, but she and Karim were busy, and she really didn't need any help from Hayat at that time. One of the female entrepreneurs introduced Anne to two other women who were seeking help with their businesses, and so Anne now had five clients to assist. With the increasing workload, Anne began to turn more responsibility over to Karim. Karim was not confident that he could do the work requested by Anne, but she tried to reassure him that he was capable and there would not be any problems.

Karim made slow progress and frequently asked Anne for help with his work. Anne became increasingly frustrated by the slow pace of Karim's work and his constant need for assurances. She developed a nickname for him, "worn sole," meaning that he was wearing out the bottom of his shoes running back and forth from his office to hers asking questions. His nickname appeared appropriate as well to her in that Karim was constantly worried and thus was developing a "worn soul." Karim took the puns in stride but, nevertheless, didn't seem to change his behavior.

One particular incident involving Karim produced difficulties for Anne. She was standing in the hallway talking to another ExportJordan employee when Karim came running down the hall, again looking for her. She mentioned to her co-worker "here comes old worn sole again." She continued to tell the co-worker about Karim's weaknesses and as she discussed these weaknesses she noticed that Jafar was near and listening. Anne and Jafar did not have much contact with each other, yet the relationship between the two was strained. When they passed in the hall Jafar would not even look at Anne. After once again giving Karim clarification on his task, Anne turned to Jafar and asked him if he needed anything from her. He stared at her for what seemed like a very long time and then muttered, "Just remember this—the family knife does not cut." At this point Anne had had enough with Jafar and his sayings and so she decided to confront him. Jafar turned and went back to his office and Anne followed him. Anne asked Jafar, in a loud voice, "What is it with you and all of these bullshit sayings." Jafar's eyes got big as he pointed his finger towards her and told her that she should be very careful in her "American ways." With no intention of letting this go, Anne sat down in the chair in front of Jafar's desk and propped her feet up on his desk. She told Jafar to sit down, as they needed to talk. Jafar refused to sit down and asked her to leave. Anne began to explain to Jafar that she was in Jordan to help the Jordanian people and that by helping women to develop their businesses she was helping all people in Jordan. It appeared to Anne that Jafar was not listening to a word she was saying. After a long silence Anne stood up and walked out of the office. As she was leaving Jafar said to her "Don't you want to know what happened to your friend, Hayat?" When she turned in surprise, Jafar closed and locked the door.

Anne hadn't seen Hayat for a number of days and was curious where she was but now she was concerned. Anne immediately found Karim and asked him if he knew where Hayat was, and he responded that he didn't. He also didn't know if she still worked at ExportJordan. Anne began to ask others in the offices if they knew what happened to Hayat, and it seemed that no one did. One of her colleagues, Mania, told her that she thought that Hayat had been fired and that Jafar had something to do with it. Already upset with Jafar, Anne decided that it was time to confront him again. She went to his office and found the door unlocked this time. She barged in and demanded to know what he meant by his statement about Hayat and what happened to her. At first Jafar denied knowing much about the situation and told her that he was only in charge of financing arrangements and that he had no authority over Hayat. Anne, losing her temper, shouted to Jafar, "Goddamn it, Jafar, tell me the truth about Hayat." At that moment it appeared that a calm had come over Jafar. He put his head down and stared at the floor. He then raised his head and told Anne that he wanted her to tell him about "the truth of America's plan to eliminate Palestine." Anne could see that this conversation was not going well and decided just to leave Jafar's office. Before she could go, Jafar approached her, stood very close, and looking into her eyes announced, "Muslim Brotherhood will prevail." Anne felt frightened and threatened as she left the office.

MEETING WITH THE DIRECTOR

Anne went straight to her office and felt comfort there. She composed herself and began thinking about what she should do. The organizational structure of ExportJordan was very unstructured and Anne really did not have a supervisor. Hayat acted in some ways as her manager; however, Hayat really did not have formal authority over Anne, and Anne also was not sure whom Jafar reported to as well. Anne decided that perhaps she should schedule an appointment with Dr. Massimi, director of ExportJordan. She felt a bit uncomfortable approaching him directly, but since there really wasn't any formal organizational structure (at least that she knew), she reasoned that it would not be improper. She had met Dr. Massimi on a number of occasions and he appeared to be a very kind and understanding man. She hoped that a meeting with him would clear up what happened to Hayat and resolve the tensions with Jafar.

Anne asked Karim to call and schedule an appointment for her with Dr. Massimi. Karim appeared very nervous and didn't appear to want to talk. He said he would do it as soon as he returned from a meeting. Anne wasn't aware of any meeting involving Karim, and he wasn't forthcoming about the details. Anne decided to do some work to get her mind off the Jafar incident. Later in the afternoon Anne came out of her office to check on Karim. He was nowhere to be found. Anne asked if anyone knew where Karim was and was told by one of her colleagues that he was with Jafar. Surprised by this information, Anne went back in her office and decided to call Dr. Massimi herself. Dr. Massimi answered the telephone directly and Anne told him that she needed to see him as soon as possible. He told her that she could come to his office immediately.

Anne entered the office and asked Dr. Massimi what happened to Hayat. Dr. Massimi sat in his chair and, without answering her question, asked her how she was enjoying Jordan. Anne told him that she liked most of the people, but that she was having a problem with Jafar. At that moment an assistant brought a tray of tea into the office and offered a cup to Anne. She was too upset to drink tea, she told the assistant. Dr. Massimi took a cup and told Anne to take a cup and that it would calm her. Anne still refused the tea. As Dr. Massimi enjoyed his tea, Anne began to tell him about Jafar. He listened a bit and then asked Anne about her family. Anne told him that they were fine and then preceded to again explain her situation with Jafar. Dr. Massimi listened a bit more and then interrupted Anne again by telling her about his family and told her that his son was studying in the United States. He explained that his son had some difficulties adjusting to American culture. Anne told Dr. Massimi that she and her husband were adjusting well but that she was having problems with her job. Dr. Massimi then began telling a story about his first international job in Iran. He went into great detail about the problems he experienced. Anne listened but wondered if Dr. Massimi was just avoiding her questions.

Anne decided to take another approach. When Dr. Massimi finished his story, Anne told him how happy she was to be able to help Jordanian women and that she was hoping that she could be more successful in her job. Dr. Massimi told her that she was providing a very important service to Jordan and that her work was appreciated. When Anne started to mention Jafar again Dr. Massimi interrupted her to ask if she had visited Petra. When she said that she had planned a visit but had not yet had time, Dr. Massimi began to tell her the history of this ancient city and its importance. Visitors to the office interrupted the history lesson. Three men from the Jordanian Ministry of Tourism stopped by to see Dr. Massimi. He invited them in and introduced them to Anne. Dr. Massimi told the men that he was just talking about Petra and the four men began a discussion about tourist sites in Jordan, and more tea was brought in the office. The four men discussed many things, sometimes in Arabic and sometimes in English, as Anne sat looking at her watch. Getting impatient Anne got up and told Dr. Massimi that she would come back and talk to him "when he could give her his full attention."

Returning to her office, Anne decided that she should compose an e-mail message to Dr. Massimi explaining what she was not able to explain in his office. She explained the situation with Jafar, asked for clarification on Hayat, and told him that she was confused by the structure of the organization.

As Anne was ready to leave for home she checked her e-mail one last time. There was a response from Dr. Massimi. As she anxiously opened the message expecting to get clarification on all the issues, she was shocked to see the response was "Yes, Mrs. Burns, Jordan is a complex country." He did invite her to come to see him again so that they could discuss her situation. As she turned off her computer, Anne muttered, "What's the use." She set out for home with the intention of telling her husband that they should look for another opportunity, one not in the Middle East.

Sources

1. Kelly, R. (2003). *Countrywatch Jordan Report*.
2. Nydell, M. (2003). *Understanding Arabs*. Yarmouth, ME: International Press.
3. www.countrywatch.com.
4. www.odci/cia/publications/factbook/geos/jo.html.
5. www.state.gov.

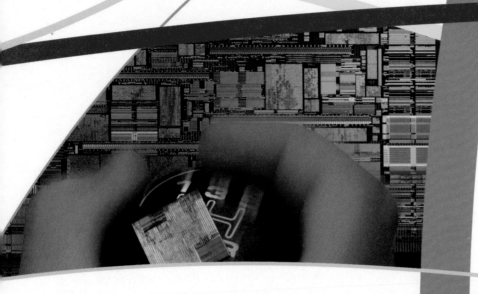

The Global Trade
and Investment Environment part 3

5

International Trade
Theory

International Trade in Information Technology Hardware and U.S. Economic Growth

Entrepreneurial enterprises in the United States invented most of the information technology that we use today, including computer and communications hardware, software, and services. In the 1960s and 1970s, the information technology sector was led by companies such as IBM and DEC, which developed first mainframe and then midrange computers. In the 1980s, the locus of growth in the sector shifted to personal computers, and the innovations of companies like Intel, which introduced the first microprocessor in 1971; MITS, which made the first personal computer; Apple and IBM, which drove the initial commercialization of PCs; and then Dell and Compaq, which made "IBM compatible" PCs and helped to develop the mass market for the product. Along the way, however, something happened to this uniquely American industry—it started to move the production of hardware offshore.

In the early 1980s, production of "commodity components" for computers such as DRAMs (memory chips) migrated to low-cost producers in Japan, and then later to Taiwan and Korea. Intel, once the largest manufacturer of DRAMs in the world, pulled out of the market in the mid-1980s to focus on making microprocessors. Soon hard disk drives, display screens, keyboards, computer mice, and a host of other components were outsourced to foreign manufacturers. By the early 2000s, American factories were specializing in making the highest value components, such as the microprocessors made by Intel, and in final assembly (Dell for example, assembles PCs in two North American facilities). Almost every other component was made overseas—because it cost less to do so.

During the 1980s and early 1990s, politicians and journalists did much hand-wringing about the possible negative implication for the U.S. economy of this trend. According to the critics, high-paying manufacturing jobs in the information technology sector were being exported to foreign producers. The collective political angst reached such a pitch that in 1986 U.S. trade officials brokered an agreement with Japan, then the largest producer of DRAMs, that limited the ability of Japanese producers to lower their prices of DRAMs. But then offshore production migrated to Korea and Taiwan instead, where producers undercut the Japanese on price, and manufacturing job losses in the U.S. continued.

Was this trend bad for the U.S. economy, as the critics claimed? The evidence suggests not. According to recent research, the globalization of production made information technology hardware about 20 percent less expensive than it would otherwise have been. The price declines supported additional investments in information technology by businesses and households. Because they were getting cheaper, computers diffused throughout the United States faster. In turn, the rapid diffusion of information technology translated into faster productivity growth in the United States as businesses used computers to streamline processes. Between 1995 and 2002, productivity grew by 2.8 percent annually in the United States, well above the historic norm. According to recent calculations, some 0.3 percent annually of this growth could be attributed directly to the reduced prices of information technology hardware made possible by the move to offshore production. In turn, the 0.3 percent annual gain in productivity from 1995 to 2002 resulted in an additional $230 billion in accumulated gross domestic product in the United States. In short, the American economy grew at a faster rate precisely because production of information technology hardware was shifted to foreigners.

Also, ample evidence suggests that the reduced price for hardware made possible by international trade created a boom in jobs in two related information technology industries—computer software and services. During the 1990s, the number of information technology jobs in the United States grew by 22 percent, twice the rate of job creation in the economy as a whole, and this at a time when manufacturing information technology jobs were moving offshore. The growth could partly be attributed to robust demand for computer software and services within the United States and partly due to demand for software and services from foreigners, including those same foreigners who were now making much of the hardware. In sum, buying computer hardware from foreigners, as opposed to making it in the United States, had a significant *positive* impact upon the U.S. economy that outweighed any adverse effects from job losses in the manufacturing sector.

Sources: C. L. Mann, "Globalization of IT Services and White Collar Jobs," International Economic Policy Briefs, *Institute of International Economics,* December 2003; A. Bernstein, "Shaking Up Trade Theory," *BusinessWeek,* December 6, 2004, pp. 116–20; "Semiconductor Trade: A Wafer Thin Case," *The Economist,* July 27, 1996, pp. 53–54; and K. J. Stiroh, "Information Technology and the U.S. Productivity Revival," *Federal Reserve Bank of New York,* January 2001.

Introduction

The opening case goes to the heart of a debate that has been played out many times over the past half century. Some argue that free trade leads to a migration of jobs overseas and will ultimately create higher unemployment and lower living standards. To these people, the trend for U.S. information technology companies to shift manufacturing jobs to other nations where goods can be produced more cheaply has been a disturbing development, and represents the "hollowing out" of America. However, economists schooled in international trade theory argue that free trade ultimately benefits *all* countries that participate in a free trade system. Those who take this position concede that some individuals lose as a result of a shift to free trade, but in the aggregate, they argue, the gains outweigh the losses.

The opening case provides some evidence in support of this position. The trend by information technology companies to shift production of hardware offshore had tangible benefits for the U.S. economy. Due to globalization, costs of information technology hardware in the United States fell by 20 percent more than would have been the case had the transfer of production to other countries not occurred. Lower prices for hardware speeded up the diffusion of information technology in the United States, boosted productivity, and added some $230 billion to the nation's GDP between 1995 and 2002. Also, the availability of cheap information technology helped to create additional jobs in the computer software and service sectors, where employment grew at twice the national average during 1995–2002.

The arguments surrounding the benefits and costs of free trade are not abstract academic ones. International trade theory has shaped the economic policy of many nations for the past 50 years and is the driver behind the formation of the World Trade Organization and regional trade blocs such as the European Union and the North American Free Trade Agreement (NAFTA). The 1990s, in particular, saw a global move toward greater free trade. It is crucially important to understand, therefore, what these theories are and why they have been so successful in shaping the economic policy of so many nations and the competitive environment that international businesses must compete in.

This chapter has two goals that go to the heart of this debate. The first is to review a number of theories that explain why it is beneficial for a country to engage in international trade. The second goal is to explain the pattern of international trade that we observe in the world economy. With regard to the pattern of trade, we will be primarily concerned with explaining the pattern of exports and imports of goods and services between countries. The pattern of foreign direct investment between countries is discussed in Chapter 7.

An Overview of Trade Theory

We open this chapter with a discussion of mercantilism. Propagated in the 16th and 17th centuries, mercantilism advocated that countries should simultaneously encourage exports and discourage imports. Although mercantilism is an old and largely discredited doctrine, its echoes remain in modern political debate and in the trade policies of many countries. Next we will look at Adam Smith's theory of absolute advantage. Proposed in 1776, Smith's theory was the first to explain why unrestricted free trade is beneficial to a country. **Free trade** refers to a situation where a government does not attempt to influence through quotas or duties what its citizens can buy from another country, or what they can produce and sell to another country. Smith argued that the invisible hand of the market mechanism, rather than government policy, should determine what a country imports and what it exports. His arguments imply that such a laissez-faire stance toward trade was in the best interests of a country. Building on Smith's work are two additional theories. One is the theory of comparative advantage, advanced by the 19th-century English economist David Ricardo. This theory is the intellectual basis of the modern argument for unrestricted free trade. In the 20th century, Ricardo's work was refined by two Swedish economists, Eli Heckscher and Bertil Ohlin, whose theory is known as the Heckscher-Ohlin theory.

THE BENEFITS OF TRADE

The great strength of the theories of Smith, Ricardo, and Heckscher-Ohlin is that they identify with precision the specific benefits of international trade. Common sense suggests that some international trade is beneficial. For example, nobody would suggest that Iceland should grow its own oranges. Iceland can benefit from trade by exchanging some of the products that it can produce at a low cost (fish) for some products that it cannot produce at all (oranges). Thus, by engaging in international trade, Icelanders are able to add oranges to their diet of fish. The theories of Smith, Ricardo, and Heckscher-Ohlin go beyond this commonsense notion, however, to show why it is beneficial for a country to engage in international trade *even for products it is able to produce for itself*. This is a difficult concept for people to grasp. For example, many people in the United States believe that American consumers should buy products produced in the United States by American companies whenever possible to help save American jobs from foreign competition. Such thinking apparently underlay a 2002 decision by President George W. Bush to protect American steel producers from competition from lower-cost foreign producers (a decision that the Bush administration reversed a year later).

The same kind of nationalistic sentiments can be observed in many other countries. However, the theories of Smith, Ricardo, and Heckscher-Ohlin tell us that a country's economy may gain if its citizens buy certain products from other nations that could be produced at home. The gains arise because international trade allows a country to specialize in the manufacture and export of products that can be produced most efficiently in that country, while importing products that can be produced more efficiently in other countries. So it may make sense for the United States to specialize in the production and export of commercial jet aircraft, since the efficient production of commercial jet aircraft requires resources that are abundant in the United States, such as a highly skilled labor force and cutting-edge technological know-how. On the other hand, it may make sense for the United States to import textiles from China since the efficient production of textiles requires a relatively cheap labor force—and cheap labor is not abundant in the United States.

Of course, this economic argument is often difficult for segments of a country's population to accept. With their future threatened by imports, U.S. textile companies and their employees have tried hard to persuade the government to limit the importation of textiles by demanding quotas and tariffs. Although such import controls may benefit particular groups, such as textile businesses and their employees or unprofitable steel mills and their employees, the theories of Smith, Ricardo, and Heckscher-Ohlin suggest that such action hurts the economy as a whole. Limits on imports are often in the interests of domestic producers, but not domestic consumers.

THE PATTERN OF INTERNATIONAL TRADE

The theories of Smith, Ricardo, and Heckscher-Ohlin help to explain the pattern of international trade that we observe in the world economy. Some aspects of the pattern are easy to understand. Climate and natural-resource endowments explain why Ghana exports cocoa, Brazil exports coffee, Saudi Arabia exports oil, and China exports crawfish. But much of the observed pattern of international trade is more difficult to explain. For example, why does Japan export automobiles, consumer electronics, and machine tools? Why does Switzerland export chemicals, pharmaceuticals, watches, and jewelry? David Ricardo's theory of comparative advantage offers an explanation in terms of international differences in labor productivity. The more sophisticated Heckscher-Ohlin theory emphasizes the interplay between the proportions in which the factors of production (such as land, labor, and capital) are available in different countries and the proportions in which they are needed for producing particular goods. This explanation rests on the assumption that countries have varying endowments of the various factors of production. Tests of this theory, however, suggest that it is a less powerful explanation of real-world trade patterns than once thought.

One early response to the failure of the Heckscher-Ohlin theory to explain the observed pattern of international trade was the product life-cycle theory. Proposed by Raymond Vernon, this theory suggests that early in their life cycle, most new products are produced in and exported from the country in which they were developed. As a new product becomes widely accepted internationally, however, production starts in other countries. As a result, the theory suggests, the product may ultimately be exported back to the country of its original innovation.

In a similar vein, during the 1980s economists such as Paul Krugman of the Massachusetts Institute of Technology developed what has come to be known as the **new trade theory.** New trade theory stresses that in some cases countries specialize in the production and export of particular products not because of underlying differences in factor endowments, but because in certain industries the world market can support only a limited number of firms. (This is argued to be the case for the commercial aircraft industry.) In such industries, firms that enter the market first build a competitive advantage that is subsequently difficult to challenge. Thus, the observed pattern of trade between nations may be due in part to the ability of firms within a given nation to capture first-mover advantages. The United States is a major exporter of commercial jet aircraft because American firms such as Boeing were first movers in the world market. Boeing built a competitive advantage that has subsequently been difficult for firms from countries with equally favorable factor endowments to challenge (although Europe's Airbus Industrie has succeeded in doing that).

In a work related to the new trade theory, Michael Porter of the Harvard Business School developed a theory, referred to as the theory of national competitive advantage. This attempts to explain why particular nations achieve international success in certain industries. In addition to factor endowments, Porter points out the importance of country factors such as domestic demand and domestic rivalry in explaining a nation's dominance in the production and export of particular products.

TRADE THEORY AND GOVERNMENT POLICY

Although all these theories agree that international trade is beneficial to a country, they lack agreement in their recommendations for government policy. Mercantilism makes a crude case for government involvement in promoting exports and limiting imports. The theories of Smith, Ricardo, and Heckscher-Ohlin form part of the case for unrestricted free trade. The argument for unrestricted free trade is that both import controls and export incentives (such as subsidies) are self-defeating and result in wasted resources. Both the new trade theory and Porter's theory of national competitive advantage can be interpreted as justifying some limited government intervention to support the development of certain export-oriented industries. We will discuss the pros and cons of this argument, known as strategic trade policy, as well as the pros and cons of the argument for unrestricted free trade, in Chapter 6.

Mercantilism

The first theory of international trade emerged in England in the mid-16th century. Referred to as *mercantilism,* its principal assertion was that gold and silver were the mainstays of national wealth and essential to vigorous commerce. At that time, gold and silver were the currency of trade between countries; a country could earn gold and silver by exporting goods. By the same token, importing goods from other countries would result in an outflow of gold and silver to those countries. The main tenet of **mercantilism** was that it was in a country's best interests to maintain a trade surplus, to export more than it imported. By doing so, a country would accumulate gold and silver and, consequently, increase its national wealth, prestige, and power. As the English mercantilist writer Thomas Mun put it in 1630:

> The ordinary means therefore to increase our wealth and treasure is by foreign trade, wherein we must ever observe this rule: to sell more to strangers yearly than we consume of theirs in value.[1]

Consistent with this belief, the mercantilist doctrine advocated government intervention to achieve a surplus in the balance of trade. The mercantilists saw no virtue in a large volume of trade. Rather, they recommended policies to maximize exports and minimize imports. To achieve this, imports were limited by tariffs and quotas, while exports were subsidized.

The classical economist David Hume pointed out an inherent inconsistency in the mercantilist doctrine in 1752. According to Hume, if England had a balance-of-trade surplus with France (it exported more than it imported), the resulting inflow of gold and silver would swell the domestic money supply and generate inflation in England. In France, however, the outflow of gold and silver would have the opposite effect. France's money supply would contract, and its prices would fall. This change in relative prices between France and England would encourage the French to buy fewer English goods (because they were becoming more expensive) and the English to buy more French goods (because they were becoming cheaper). The result would be a deterioration in the English balance of trade and an improvement in France's trade balance, until the English surplus was eliminated. Hence, according to Hume, in the long run no country could sustain a surplus in the balance of trade and so accumulate gold and silver as the mercantilists had envisaged.

The flaw with mercantilism was that it viewed trade as a zero-sum game. (A **zero-sum game** is one in which a gain by one country results in a loss by another.) It was left to Adam Smith and David Ricardo to show the shortsightedness of this approach and to demonstrate that trade is a **positive-sum game,** or a situation in which all countries can benefit. The mercantilist doctrine is by no means dead.[2] For example, Jarl Hagelstam, a former director at the Finnish Ministry of Finance, observed that in most trade negotiations:

> The approach of individual negotiating countries, both industrialized and developing, has been to press for trade liberalization in areas where their own comparative competitive advantages are the strongest, and to resist liberalization in areas where they are less competitive and fear that imports would replace domestic production.[3]

Hagelstam attributes this strategy by negotiating countries to a neo-mercantilist belief held by the politicians of many nations. This belief equates political power with economic power and economic power with a balance-of-trade surplus. Thus, the trade strategy of many nations is designed to simultaneously boost exports and limit imports.[4]

🌐 Absolute Advantage

In his 1776 landmark book *The Wealth of Nations*, Adam Smith attacked the mercantilist assumption that trade is a zero-sum game. Smith argued that countries differ in their ability to produce goods efficiently. In his time, the English, by virtue of their superior manufacturing processes, were the world's most efficient textile manufacturers. Due to the combination of favorable climate, good soils, and accumulated expertise, the French had the world's most efficient wine industry. The English had an *absolute advantage* in the production of textiles, while the French had an *absolute advantage* in the production of wine. Thus, a country has an **absolute advantage** in the production of a product when it is more efficient than any other country in producing it.

FIGURE 5.1

The Theory of Absolute
Advantage

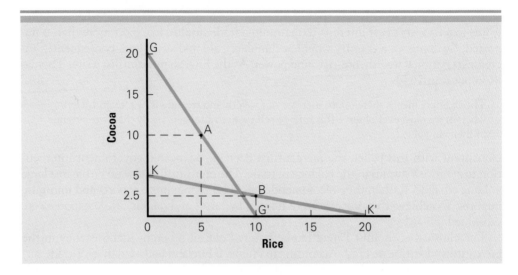

According to Smith, countries should specialize in the production of goods for which they have an absolute advantage and then trade these for goods produced by other countries. In Smith's time, this suggested that the English should specialize in the production of textiles while the French should specialize in the production of wine. England could get all the wine it needed by selling its textiles to France and buying wine in exchange. Similarly, France could get all the textiles it needed by selling wine to England and buying textiles in exchange. Smith's basic argument, therefore, is that a country should never produce goods at home that it can buy at a lower cost from other countries. Smith demonstrates that, by specializing in the production of goods in which each has an absolute advantage, both countries benefit by engaging in trade.

Consider the effects of trade between two countries, Ghana and South Korea. The production of any good (output) requires resources (inputs) such as land, labor, and capital. Assume that Ghana and South Korea both have the same amount of resources and that these resources can be used to produce either rice or cocoa. Assume further that 200 units of resources are available in each country. Imagine that in Ghana it takes 10 resources to produce one ton of cocoa and 20 resources to produce one ton of rice. Thus, Ghana could produce 20 tons of cocoa and no rice, 10 tons of rice and no cocoa, or some combination of rice and cocoa between these two extremes. The different combinations that Ghana could produce are represented by the line GG' in Figure 5.1. This is referred to as Ghana's production possibility frontier (PPF). Similarly, imagine that in South Korea it takes 40 resources to produce one ton of cocoa and 10 resources to produce one ton of rice. Thus, South Korea could produce 5 tons of cocoa and no rice, 20 tons of rice and no cocoa, or some combination between these two extremes. The different combinations available to South Korea are represented by the line KK' in Figure 5.1, which is South Korea's PPF. Clearly, Ghana has an absolute advantage in the production of cocoa. (More resources are needed to produce a ton of cocoa in South Korea than in Ghana.) By the same token, South Korea has an absolute advantage in the production of rice.

Now consider a situation in which neither country trades with any other. Each country devotes half of its resources to the production of rice and half to the production of cocoa. Each country must also consume what it produces. Ghana would be able to produce 10 tons of cocoa and 5 tons of rice (point A in Figure 5.1), while South Korea would be able to produce 10 tons of rice and 2.5 tons of cocoa. Without trade, the combined production of both countries would be 12.5 tons of cocoa (10 tons in Ghana plus 2.5 tons in South Korea) and 15 tons of rice (5 tons in Ghana and 10 tons in South Korea). If each country were to specialize in producing the good for which it had an absolute advantage

TABLE 5.1

Absolute Advantage and the Gains from Trade

Resources Required to Produce 1 Ton of Cocoa and Rice		
	Cocoa	**Rice**
Ghana	10	20
South Korea	40	10
Production and Consumption without Trade		
	Cocoa	**Rice**
Ghana	10.0	5.0
South Korea	2.5	10.0
Total production	12.5	15.0
Production with Specialization		
	Cocoa	**Rice**
Ghana	20.0	0.0
South Korea	0.0	20.0
Total production	20.0	20.0
Consumption After Ghana Trades 6 Tons of Cocoa for 6 Tons of South Korean Rice		
	Cocoa	**Rice**
Ghana	14.0	6.0
South Korea	6.0	14.0
Increase in Consumption as a Result of Specialization and Trade		
	Cocoa	**Rice**
Ghana	4.0	1.0
South Korea	3.5	4.0

and then trade with the other for the good it lacks, Ghana could produce 20 tons of cocoa, and South Korea could produce 20 tons of rice. Thus, by specialization, the production of both goods could be increased. Production of cocoa would increase from 12.5 tons to 20 tons, while production of rice would increase from 15 tons to 20 tons. The increase in production that would result from specialization is therefore 7.5 tons of cocoa and 5 tons of rice. Table 5.1 summarizes these figures.

By engaging in trade and swapping one ton of cocoa for one ton of rice, producers in both countries could consume more of both cocoa and rice. Imagine that Ghana and South Korea swap cocoa and rice on a one-to-one basis; that is, the price of one ton of cocoa is equal to the price of one ton of rice. If Ghana decided to export 6 tons of cocoa to South Korea and import 6 tons of rice in return, its final consumption after trade would be 14 tons of cocoa and 6 tons of rice. This is 4 tons more cocoa than it could have consumed before specialization and trade and 1 ton more rice. Similarly, South Korea's final consumption after trade would be 6 tons of cocoa and 14 tons of rice. This is 3.5 tons more cocoa than it could have consumed before specialization and trade and 4 tons more rice. Thus, as a result of specialization and trade, output of both cocoa and rice would be increased, and consumers in both nations would be able to consume more. Thus, we can see that trade is a positive-sum game; it produces net gains for all involved.

Comparative Advantage

David Ricardo took Adam Smith's theory one step further by exploring what might happen when one country has an absolute advantage in the production of all goods.[5] Smith's theory of absolute advantage suggests that such a country might derive no benefits from international trade. In his 1817 book *Principles of Political Economy*, Ricardo showed that this was not the case. According to Ricardo's theory of **comparative advantage,** it makes sense for a country to specialize in the production of those goods that it produces most efficiently and to buy the goods that it produces less efficiently from other countries, even if this means buying goods from other countries that it could produce more efficiently itself.[6] While this may seem counterintuitive, the logic can be explained with a simple example.

Assume that Ghana is more efficient in the production of both cocoa and rice; that is, Ghana has an absolute advantage in the production of both products. In Ghana it takes 10 resources to produce one ton of cocoa and 13 1/3 resources to produce one ton of rice. Thus, given its 200 units of resources, Ghana can produce 20 tons of cocoa and no rice, 15 tons of rice and no cocoa, or any combination in between on its PPF (the line GG' in Figure 5.2). In South Korea it takes 40 resources to produce one ton of cocoa and 20 resources to produce one ton of rice. Thus, South Korea can produce 5 tons of cocoa and no rice, 10 tons of rice and no cocoa, or any combination on its PPF (the line KK' in Figure 5.2). Again assume that without trade, each country uses half of its resources to produce rice and half to produce cocoa. Thus, without trade, Ghana will produce 10 tons of cocoa and 7.5 tons of rice (point A in Figure 5.2), while South Korea will produce 2.5 tons of cocoa and 5 tons of rice (point B in Figure 5.2).

In light of Ghana's absolute advantage in the production of both goods, why should it trade with South Korea? Although Ghana has an absolute advantage in the production of both cocoa and rice, it has a comparative advantage only in the production of cocoa: Ghana can produce 4 times as much cocoa as South Korea, but only 1.5 times as much rice. Ghana is *comparatively* more efficient at producing cocoa than it is at producing rice.

Without trade the combined production of cocoa will be 12.5 tons (10 tons in Ghana and 2.5 in South Korea), and the combined production of rice will also be 12.5 tons (7.5 tons in Ghana and 5 tons in South Korea). Without trade each country must consume what it produces. By engaging in trade, the two countries can increase their combined production of rice and cocoa, and consumers in both nations can consume more of both goods.

THE GAINS FROM TRADE

Imagine that Ghana exploits its comparative advantage in the production of cocoa to increase its output from 10 tons to 15 tons. This uses up 150 units of resources, leaving the remaining 50 units of resources to use in producing 3.75 tons of rice (point C in Figure 5.2). Meanwhile, South Korea specializes in the production of rice, producing 10 tons. The combined output of both cocoa and rice has now increased. Before specialization, the combined output was 12.5 tons of cocoa and 12.5 tons of rice. Now it is 15 tons of cocoa and 13.75 tons of rice (3.75 tons in Ghana and 10 tons in South Korea). The source of the increase in production is summarized in Table 5.2.

Not only is output higher, but both countries also can now benefit from trade. If Ghana and South Korea swap cocoa and rice on a one-to-one basis, with both countries choosing to exchange 4 tons of their export for 4 tons of the import, both countries are able to consume more cocoa and rice than they could before specialization and trade (see Table 5.2). Thus, if Ghana exchanges 4 tons of cocoa with South Korea for 4 tons of rice, it is still left with 11 tons of cocoa, which is 1 ton more than it had before trade. The 4 tons of rice it gets from South Korea in exchange for its 4 tons of cocoa, when added to the 3.75 tons it now produces domestically, leaves it with a total of 7.75 tons of rice, which is .25 of a ton more than it had before specialization. Similarly, after swapping

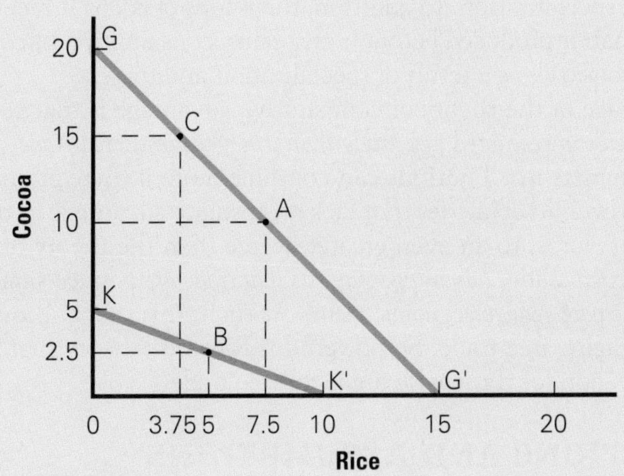

FIGURE 5.2

The Theory of
Comparative Advantage

TABLE 5.2

Comparative Advantage
and the Gains from
Trade

Resources Required to Produce 1 Ton of Cocoa and Rice		
	Cocoa	Rice
Ghana	10	13.33
South Korea	40	20
Production and Consumption without Trade		
	Cocoa	Rice
Ghana	10.0	7.5
South Korea	2.5	5.0
Total production	12.5	12.5
Production with Specialization		
	Cocoa	Rice
Ghana	15.0	3.75
South Korea	0.0	10.0
Total production	15.0	13.75
Consumption After Ghana Trades 4 Tons of Cocoa for 4 Tons of South Korean Rice		
	Cocoa	Rice
Ghana	11.0	7.75
South Korea	4.0	6.0
Increase in Consumption as a Result of Specialization and Trade		
	Cocoa	Rice
Ghana	1.0	0.25
South Korea	1.5	1.0

4 tons of rice with Ghana, South Korea still ends up with 6 tons of rice, which is more than it had before specialization. In addition, the 4 tons of cocoa it receives in exchange is 1.5 tons more than it produced before trade. Thus, consumption of cocoa and rice can increase in both countries as a result of specialization and trade.

The basic message of the theory of comparative advantage is that *potential world production is greater with unrestricted free trade than it is with restricted trade*. Ricardo's theory suggests that consumers in all nations can consume more if there are no restrictions on trade. This occurs even in countries that lack an absolute advantage in the production of any good. In other words, to an even greater degree than the theory of absolute advantage, *the theory of comparative advantage suggests that trade is a positive-sum game in which all countries that participate realize economic gains*. As such, this theory provides a strong rationale for encouraging free trade. So powerful is Ricardo's theory that it remains a major intellectual weapon for those who argue for free trade.

QUALIFICATIONS AND ASSUMPTIONS

The conclusion that free trade is universally beneficial is a rather bold one to draw from such a simple model. Our simple model includes many unrealistic assumptions:

1. We have assumed a simple world in which there are only two countries and two goods. In the real world, there are many countries and many goods.
2. We have assumed away transportation costs between countries.
3. We have assumed away differences in the prices of resources in different countries. We have said nothing about exchange rates, simply assuming that cocoa and rice could be swapped on a one-to-one basis.
4. We have assumed that resources can move freely from the production of one good to another within a country. In reality, this is not always the case.
5. We have assumed constant returns to scale; that is, that specialization by Ghana or South Korea has no effect on the amount of resources required to produce one ton of cocoa or rice. In reality, both diminishing and increasing returns to specialization exist. The amount of resources required to produce a good might decrease or increase as a nation specializes in production of that good.
6. We have assumed that each country has a fixed stock of resources and that free trade does not change the efficiency with which a country uses its resources. This static assumption makes no allowances for the dynamic changes in a country's stock of resources and in the efficiency with which the country uses its resources that might result from free trade.
7. We have assumed away the effects of trade on income distribution within a country.

Given these assumptions, can the conclusion that free trade is mutually beneficial be extended to the real world of many countries, many goods, positive transportation costs, volatile exchange rates, immobile domestic resources, nonconstant returns to specialization, and dynamic changes? Although a detailed extension of the theory of comparative advantage is beyond the scope of this book, economists have shown that the basic result derived from our simple model can be generalized to a world composed of many countries producing many different goods.[7] Despite the shortcomings of the Ricardian model, research suggests that the basic proposition that countries will export the goods that they are most efficient at producing is borne out by the data.[8]

However, once all the assumptions are dropped, the case for unrestricted free trade, while still positive, has been argued by some economists associated with the "new trade theory" to lose some of its strength.[9] We return to this issue later in this chapter and in the next when we discuss the new trade theory. In a recent and widely discussed analysis, the Nobel Prize–winning economist Paul Samuelson argued that contrary to the standard interpretation, in certain circumstances the theory of comparative advantage predicts that a rich country might actually be *worse* off by switching to a free trade regime with a poor nation.[10] We will consider Samuelson's critique in the next section.

EXTENSIONS OF THE RICARDIAN MODEL

Let us explore the effect of relaxing three of the assumptions identified above in the simple comparative advantage model. Below we relax the assumption that resources move freely from the production of one good to another within a country and the assumption that trade does not change a country's stock of resources or the efficiency with which those resources are utilized.

Immobile Resources

In our simple comparative model of Ghana and South Korea, we assumed that producers (farmers) could easily convert land from the production of cocoa to rice, and vice versa. While this assumption may hold for some agricultural products, resources do not always shift quite so easily from producing one good to another. A certain amount of friction is involved. For example, embracing a free trade regime for an advanced economy such as the United States often implies that the country will produce less of some labor-intensive goods, such as textiles, and more of some knowledge-intensive goods, such as computer software or biotechnology products. Although the country as a whole will gain from such a shift, textile producers will lose. A textile worker in South Carolina is probably not qualified to write software for Microsoft. Thus, the shift to free trade may mean that she becomes unemployed or has to accept another less attractive job, such as working at a fast-food restaurant. For an example of how the shift toward free trade can impact an individual enterprise and its employees, look at the Management Focus profiling how the outdoor equipment cooperative REI is adjusting its own production activities to deal with a move toward greater free trade in textiles.

Resources do not always move easily from one economic activity to another. The process creates friction and human suffering too. While the theory predicts that the benefits of free trade outweigh the costs by a significant margin, this is of cold comfort to those who bear the costs. Accordingly, political opposition to the adoption of a free trade regime typically comes from those whose jobs are most at risk. In the United States, for example, textile workers and their unions have long opposed the move toward free trade precisely because this group has much to lose from free trade. Governments often ease the transition toward free trade by helping to retrain those who lose their jobs as a result. The pain caused by the movement toward a free trade regime is a short-term phenomenon, while the gains from trade once the transition has been made are both significant and enduring.

Diminishing Returns

The simple comparative advantage model developed above assumes constant returns to specialization. By **constant returns to specialization** we mean the units of resources required to produce a good (cocoa or rice) are assumed to remain constant no matter where one is on a country's production possibility frontier (PPF). Thus, we assumed that it always took Ghana 10 units of resources to produce one ton of cocoa. However, it is more realistic to assume diminishing returns to specialization. **Diminishing returns to specialization** occurs when more units of resources are required to produce each additional unit. While 10 units of resources may be sufficient to increase Ghana's output of cocoa from 12 tons to 13 tons, 11 units of resources may be needed to increase output from 13 to 14 tons, 12 units of resources to increase output from 14 tons to 15 tons, and so on. Diminishing returns implies a convex PPF for Ghana (see Figure 5.3), rather than the straight line depicted in Figure 5.2.

It is more realistic to assume diminishing returns for two reasons. First, not all resources are of the same quality. As a country tries to increase its output of a certain good,

FIGURE 5.3

Ghana's PPF under
Diminishing Returns

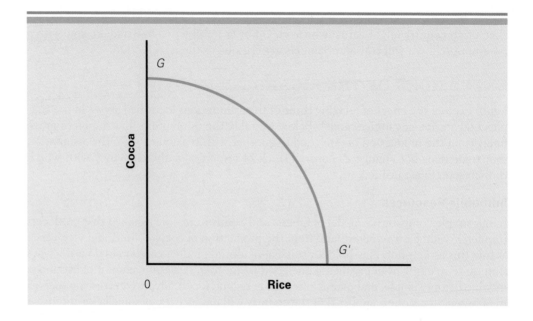

it is increasingly likely to draw on more marginal resources whose productivity is not as great as those initially employed. The result is that it requires ever more resources to produce an equal increase in output. For example, some land is more productive than other land. As Ghana tries to expand its output of cocoa, it might have to utilize increasingly marginal land that is less fertile than the land it originally used. As yields per acre decline, Ghana must use more land to produce one ton of cocoa.

A second reason for diminishing returns is that different goods use resources in different proportions. For example, imagine that growing cocoa uses more land and less labor than growing rice, and that Ghana tries to transfer resources from rice production to cocoa production. The rice industry will release proportionately too much labor and too little land for efficient cocoa production. To absorb the additional resources of labor and land, the cocoa industry will have to shift toward more labor-intensive methods of production. The effect is that the efficiency with which the cocoa industry uses labor will decline, and returns will diminish.

Diminishing returns show that it is not feasible for a country to specialize to the degree suggested by the simple Ricardian model outlined earlier. Diminishing returns to specialization suggest that the gains from specialization are likely to be exhausted before specialization is complete. In reality, most countries do not specialize but, instead, produce a range of goods. However, the theory predicts that it is worthwhile to specialize until that point where the resulting gains from trade are outweighed by diminishing returns. Thus, the basic conclusion that unrestricted free trade is beneficial still holds, although because of diminishing returns, the gains may not be as great as suggested in the constant returns case.

Dynamic Effects and Economic Growth

The simple comparative advantage model assumed that trade does not change a country's stock of resources or the efficiency with which it utilizes those resources. This static assumption makes no allowances for the dynamic changes that might result from trade. If we relax this assumption, it becomes apparent that opening an economy to trade is likely to generate dynamic gains of two sorts.[11] First, free trade might increase a country's stock of resources as increased supplies of labor and capital from abroad become available for use within the country. For example, this has been occurring in Eastern Europe since the early 1990s, with many Western businesses have been investing significant capital in the former Communist countries.

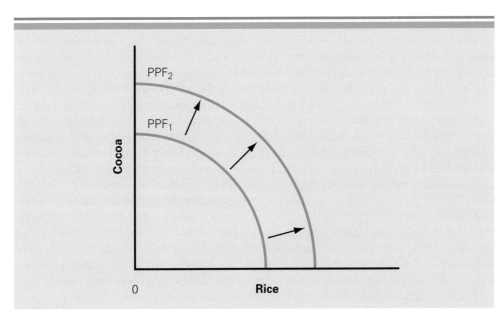

FIGURE 5.4

The Influence of Free Trade on the PPF

Second, free trade might also increase the efficiency with which a country uses its resources. Gains in the efficiency of resource utilization could arise from a number of factors. For example, economies of large-scale production might become available as trade expands the size of the total market available to domestic firms. Trade might make better technology from abroad available to domestic firms; better technology can increase labor productivity or the productivity of land. (The so-called green revolution had this effect on agricultural outputs in developing countries.) Also, opening an economy to foreign competition might stimulate domestic producers to look for ways to increase their efficiency. Again, this phenomenon has arguably been occurring in the once-protected markets of Eastern Europe, where many former state monopolies are increasing the efficiency of their operations to survive in the competitive world market.

Dynamic gains in both the stock of a country's resources and the efficiency with which resources are utilized will cause a country's PPF to shift outward. This is illustrated in Figure 5.4, where the shift from PPF$_1$ to PPF$_2$ results from the dynamic gains that arise from free trade. As a consequence of this outward shift, the country in Figure 5.4 can produce more of both goods than it did before introduction of free trade. The theory suggests that opening an economy to free trade not only results in static gains of the type discussed earlier, but also results in dynamic gains that stimulate economic growth. If this is so, then one might think that the case for free trade becomes stronger still, and in general it does. However, as noted above, in a recent article one of the leading economic theorists of the 20th century, Paul Samuelson, argued that in some circumstances, dynamic gains can lead to an outcome that is not so beneficial.

The Samuelson Critique

Samuelson's critique looks at what happens when a rich country—the United States—enters into a free trade agreement with a poor country—China—that rapidly improves its productivity after the introduction of a free trade regime (i.e., there is a dynamic gain in the efficiency with which resources are used in the poor country). The Samuelson model suggests that in such cases, the lower prices that U.S. consumers pay for goods imported from China following the introduction of a free trade regime *may* not be enough to produce a net gain for the U.S. economy if the dynamic effect of free trade is to lower real wage rates in the United States. As he stated in a *New York Times* interview, "Being able to purchase groceries 20 percent cheaper at Wal-Mart (due to international trade) does not necessarily make up for the wage losses (in America)."[12]

Samuelson notes that he is particularly concerned about the ability to send offshore service jobs that traditionally were not internationally mobile, such as software debugging, call center jobs, accounting jobs, and even medical diagnosis of MRI scans (see the accompanying Country Focus for details). Recent advances in communications technology have made this possible, effectively expanding the labor market for these jobs to include educated people in places such as India, the Philippines, and China. When coupled with rapid advances in the productivity of foreign labor due to better education, the effect on middle-class wages in the United States, according to Samuelson, may be similar to mass inward migration into the United States—it will lower the market clearing wage rate, *perhaps* by enough to outweigh the positive benefits of international trade.

Samuelson concedes that free trade has historically benefited rich counties (as data discussed below seem to confirm). Also, he notes that introducing protectionist measures (e.g., trade barriers) to guard against the theoretical possibility that free trade may harm the United States in the future may produce a situation that is worse than the disease they are trying to prevent. To quote Samuelson: "Free trade may turn out pragmatically to be still best for each region in comparison to lobbyist-induced tariffs and quotas which involve both a perversion of democracy and nonsubtle deadweight distortion losses."[13]

Some economists have been quick to dismiss Samuelson's fears.[14] While not questioning his analysis, they note that as a practical matter developing nations are unlikely to be able to upgrade the skill level of their workforce rapidly enough to give rise to the situation in Samuelson's model. In other words, they will quickly run into diminishing returns. To quote one such rebuttal: "The notion that India and China will quickly educate 300 million of their citizens to acquire sophisticated and complex skills at stake borders on the ludicrous. The educational sectors in these countries face enormous difficulties."[15] Notwithstanding such rebuttals, however, Samuelson's stature is such that his work will undoubtedly be debated for some time to come.

Evidence for the Link between Trade and Growth

Many economic studies have looked at the relationship between trade and economic growth.[16] In general, these studies suggest that, as predicted by the standard theory of comparative advantage, countries that adopt a more open stance toward international trade enjoy higher growth rates than those that close their economies to trade (the opening case provides us with an example of the link between trade and growth). Jeffrey Sachs and Andrew Warner created a measure of how "open" to international trade an economy was and then looked at the relationship between "openness" and economic growth for a sample of more than 100 countries from 1970 to 1990.[17] Among other findings, they reported:

> We find a strong association between openness and growth, both within the group of developing and the group of developed countries. Within the group of developing countries, the open economies grew at 4.49 percent per year, and the closed economies grew at 0.69 percent per year. Within the group of developed economies, the open economies grew at 2.29 percent per year, and the closed economies grew at 0.74 percent per year.[18]

A study by Wacziarg and Welch updated the Sachs and Warner data through the late 1990s. They found that over the period 1950–1998, countries that liberalized their trade regimes experienced, on average, increases in their annual growth rates of 1.5 percent compared to preliberalization times.[19]

The message of these studies seems clear: Adopt an open economy and embrace free trade, and over time your nation will be rewarded with higher economic growth rates. Higher growth will raise income levels and living standards. This last point has been confirmed by a study that looked at the relationship between trade and growth in incomes. The study, undertaken by Jeffrey Frankel and David Romer, found that on average, a one percentage point increase in the ratio of a country's trade to its gross domestic product increases income per person by at least one-half percent.[20] For every 10 percent increase in

COUNTRY FOCUS Economists have long argued that free trade produces gains for all countries that participate in a free trading system, but as the next wave of globalization sweeps through the U.S. economy, many people are wondering if this is true, particularly those who stand to lose their jobs as a result of this wave of globalization. In the popular imagination for much of the past quarter century, free trade was associated with the movement of low-skill, blue-collar manufacturing jobs out of rich countries such as the United States and toward low-wage countries—textiles to Costa Rica, athletic shoes to the Philippines, steel to Brazil, electronic products to Malaysia, and so on. While many observers bemoaned the "hollowing out" of U.S. manufacturing, economists stated that high-skilled and high-wage, white-collar jobs associated with the knowledge-based economy would stay in the United States. Computers might be assembled in Malaysia, so the argument went, but they would continue to be designed in Silicon Valley by high-skilled U.S. engineers.

Recent developments have some people questioning this assumption. As the global economy slowed after 2000 and corporate profits slumped, many American companies responded by moving white-collar "knowledge-based" jobs to developing nations where they could be performed for a fraction of the cost. During the long economic boom of the 1990s, Bank of America had to compete with other organizations for the scarce talents of information technology specialists, driving annual salaries to more than $100,000. But with business under pressure, between 2002 and early 2003 the bank cut nearly 5,000 jobs from its 25,000-strong, U.S.-based information technology workforce. Some of these jobs are being transferred to India, where work that costs $100 an hour in the United States can be done for $20 an hour.

One beneficiary of Bank of America's downsizing is Infosys Technologies Ltd., a Bangalore, India, information technology firm where 250 engineers now develop information technology applications for the bank. Other Infosys employees are busy processing home loan applications for Greenpoint Mortgage of Novato, California. Nearby in the offices of another Indian firm, Wipro Ltd., five radiologists interpret 30 CT scans a day for

Massachusetts General Hospital that are sent over the Internet. At yet another Bangalore business, engineers earn $10,000 a year designing leading-edge semiconductor chips for Texas Instruments. Nor is India the only beneficiary of these changes. Accenture, a large U.S. management consulting and information technology firm, recently moved 5,000 jobs in software development and accounting to the Philippines. Also in the Philippines, Procter & Gamble employs 650 professionals who prepare the company's global tax returns. The work used to be done in the United States, but now it is done in Manila, with just final submission to local tax authorities in the United States and other countries handled locally.

Some architectural work also is being outsourced to lower-cost locations. Flour Corp., a California-based construction company, employs some 1,200 engineers and draftsmen in the Philippines, Poland, and India to turn layouts of industrial facilities into detailed specifications. For a Saudi Arabian chemical plant Flour is designing, 200 young engineers based in the Philippines earning less than $3,000 a year collaborate in real time over the Internet with elite U.S. and British engineers who make up to $90,000 a year. Why does Flour do this? According to the company, the answer is simple. Doing so reduces the prices of a project by 15 percent, giving the company a cost-based competitive advantage in the global market for construction design.

The companies that outsource such skilled jobs clearly benefit from lower costs, enhanced competitiveness in the global economy, and greater profits. American consumers benefit from the lower prices made possible by global outsourcing. Developing nations such as India and the Philippines with a good supply of well-educated, skilled, and (by global standards) low-cost labor also benefit. However, some observers wonder whether the United States will suffer from the loss of highly skilled and high-paying jobs, and whether this trend will not ultimately depress the salaries of white-color employees nationwide. And if that happens, might not this have negative implications for the entire U.S. economy?

Sources: P. Engardio, A. Bernstein, and M. Kripalani, "Is Your Job Next?" *BusinessWeek*, February 3, 2003, pp. 50–60; "America's Pain, India's Gain," *The Economist*, January 11, 2003, p. 57; M. Schroeder and T. Aeppel, "Skilled Workers Mount Opposition to Free Trade, Swaying Politicians," *The Wall Street Journal*, October 10, 2003, p. A1, A11.

www.mhhe.com/hill

MANAGEMENT FOCUS

Recreational Equipment Inc. (REI) is a buyers' cooperative that has grown into one of the major suppliers of outdoor equipment in the United States and has a rapidly growing international business. Started in Seattle in 1938 by Lloyd Anderson, the company provided high-quality climbing gear at a low price to members of the cooperative. For its first 37 years, REI operated a single store in Seattle, but in 1975 the cooperative started opening stores in other cities. Today REI has become a $800 million-a-year business with 76 stores, 6,500 employees, revenue growth of 6 to 8 percent annually, and a goal of opening three to six retail outlets per year. Despite the growth, REI is still organized as a cooperative with 1.7 million active members. All members receive a dividend check at the end of each year that amounts to about 10 percent of the value of their purchases during the year (one does not have to be a member to shop at REI).

To supply some of its own product needs, REI long had a manufacturing subsidiary, Thaw, which for 33 years supplied REI with a range of gear, including tents, backpacks, sleeping bags, and clothing. In the 1990s, Thaw concentrated on producing fleece clothing items for REI's stores. Unfortunately for Thaw's 200 employees, the economics of manufacturing garments in the United States have been changing for several years. Following passage of the North American Free Trade Agreement (NAFTA) in 1993, all tariffs on trade in textile garments between the United States and Mexico were dropped. In the following years, an increasing number of textile operations shut down in the United States and moved to Mexico, attracted by lower labor costs. Wage rates for textile workers in Mexico run about $5 to $10 a day, compared to $8 to $10 an hour at Thaw's operation. For a labor-intensive operation such as garment production, these wage differentials are significant.

Given these economics, in mid-2000, REI announced it would be closing its Thaw subsidiary and sourcing its fleece products from Mexico. By shifting its production to Mexico, REI expected to reduce the cost of its fleece items by 20 percent. That means lower prices for REI's members and other customers and bigger profits for REI, which translates into larger dividend checks for REI's members. It also means that its Thaw employees will be out of a job. To assist its former employees at Thaw, REI added funds to federal money to assist with job retraining, unemployment benefits, and health insurance.

The events at Thaw are being repeated across the country. According to industry data, employment in apparel manufacturing in the United States has fallen from more than 929,000 in 1990 to just 316,000 in June 2003. As painful as this has been for textile workers, the U.S. consumer has gained from lower prices, and U.S. companies in many other industries have seen their sales to Mexico boom as trade barriers have come down. Thus, while a strong case can be made that NAFTA has benefited the majority of U.S. citizens and Mexicans alike, it has inflicted pain on some groups, such as U.S. textile workers, and forced some companies, such as REI, to make difficult managerial decisions.

Sources: R. T. Nelson, "REI's Globalization," *Seattle Times,* May 14, 2000, pp. D1, D2; E. Chabrow, "REI Gets Head Start in Clicks and Mortar Race," *Information Week,* May 1, 2000; J. Ozretich, "Largest 100 Private Companies: REI Climbs Back into Prominence after Down Years," *Puget Sound Business Journal,* June 14, 2002, p. 59; and American Apparel and Footware Association Trends, Annual 2004, available at www.apparelandfootwear.org/data/Trends2003Q3.pdf.

www.mhhe.com/hill

the importance of international trade in an economy, average income levels will rise by at least 5 percent. Despite the short-term adjustment costs associated with adopting a free trade regime, trade would seem to produce greater economic growth and higher living standards in the long run, just as the theory of Ricardo would lead us to expect.[21]

Heckscher-Ohlin Theory

Ricardo's theory stresses that comparative advantage arises from differences in productivity. Thus, whether Ghana is more efficient than South Korea in the production of cocoa depends on how productively it uses its resources. Ricardo stressed labor productivity and argued that differences in labor productivity between nations underlie the notion of comparative advantage. Swedish economists Eli Heckscher (in 1919) and Bertil Ohlin (in 1933) put forward a different explanation of comparative advantage. They argued that comparative advantage arises from differences in national factor endowments.[22] By **factor endowments** they meant the extent to which a country is endowed with such resources as land, labor, and capital. Nations have varying factor endowments, and different factor endowments explain differences in factor costs; specifically, the more abundant a factor, the lower its cost. The **Heckscher-Ohlin theory** predicts that countries will export those goods that make intensive use of factors that are locally abundant, while importing goods that make intensive use of factors that are locally scarce. Thus, the Heckscher-Ohlin theory attempts to explain the pattern of international trade that we observe in the world economy. Like Ricardo's theory, the Heckscher-Ohlin theory argues that free trade is beneficial. Unlike Ricardo's theory, however, the Heckscher-Ohlin theory argues that the pattern of international trade is determined by differences in factor endowments, rather than differences in productivity.

The Heckscher-Ohlin theory has commonsense appeal. For example, the United States has long been a substantial exporter of agricultural goods, reflecting in part its unusual abundance of arable land. In contrast, China excels in the export of goods produced in labor-intensive manufacturing industries, such as textiles and footwear. This reflects China's relative abundance of low-cost labor. The United States, which lacks abundant low-cost labor, has been a primary importer of these goods. Relative, not absolute, endowments are important; a country may have larger absolute amounts of land and labor than another country, but be relatively abundant in one of them.

THE LEONTIEF PARADOX

The Heckscher-Ohlin theory has been one of the most influential theoretical ideas in international economics. Most economists prefer the Heckscher-Ohlin theory to Ricardo's theory because it makes fewer simplifying assumptions. Because of its influence, the theory has been subjected to many empirical tests. Beginning with a famous study published in 1953 by Wassily Leontief (winner of the Nobel Prize in economics in 1973), many of these tests have raised questions about the validity of the Heckscher-Ohlin theory.[23] Using the Heckscher-Ohlin theory, Leontief postulated that since the United States was relatively abundant in capital compared to other nations, the United States would be an exporter of capital-intensive goods and an importer of labor-intensive goods. To his surprise, however, he found that U.S. exports were less capital intensive than U.S. imports. Since this result was at variance with the predictions of the theory, it has become known as the **Leontief paradox.**

No one is quite sure why we observe the Leontief paradox. One possible explanation is that the United States has a special advantage in producing new products or goods made with innovative technologies. Such products may be less capital intensive than products whose technology has had time to mature and become suitable for mass production. Thus, the United States may be exporting goods that heavily use skilled labor and innovative entrepreneurship, such as computer software, while importing heavy manufacturing products that use large amounts of capital. Some empirical studies tend to confirm this.[24] Tests of the Heckscher-Ohlin theory using data for a large number of countries tend to confirm the existence of the Leontief paradox.[25]

This leaves economists with a difficult dilemma. They prefer the Heckscher-Ohlin theory on theoretical grounds, but it is a relatively poor predictor of real-world international trade patterns. But the theory they regard as being too limited, Ricardo's theory of comparative advantage, actually predicts trade patterns with greater accuracy. The best solution to this dilemma may be to return to the Ricardian idea that trade patterns are largely driven by international differences in productivity. Thus, one might argue that the United States exports commercial aircraft and imports textiles not because its factor endowments are especially suited to aircraft manufacture and not suited to textile manufacture, but because the United States is relatively more efficient at producing aircraft than textiles. A key assumption in the Heckscher-Ohlin theory is that technologies are the same across countries. This may not be the case. Differences in technology may lead to differences in productivity, which in turn, drives international trade patterns.[26] Thus, Japan's success in exporting automobiles in the 1970s and 1980s was based not just on the relative abundance of capital, but also on its development of innovative manufacturing technology that enabled it to achieve higher productivity levels in automobile production than other countries that also had abundant capital. More recent empirical work strongly suggests that this theoretical explanation may be correct.[27] The new research shows that once differences in technology across countries are controlled for, countries do indeed export those goods that make intensive use of factors that are locally abundant, while importing goods that make intensive use of factors that are locally scarce. In other words, after accounting for the impact of technology on productivity, the Heckscher-Ohlin seems to gain predictive power.

The Product Life-Cycle Theory

Raymond Vernon initially proposed the **product life-cycle theory** in the mid-1960s.[28] Vernon's theory was based on the observation that for most of the 20th century a very large proportion of the world's new products had been developed by U.S. firms and sold first in the U.S. market (e.g., mass-produced automobiles, televisions, instant cameras, photocopiers, personal computers, and semiconductor chips). To explain this, Vernon argued that the wealth and size of the U.S. market gave U.S. firms a strong incentive to develop new consumer products. In addition, the high cost of U.S. labor gave U.S. firms an incentive to develop cost-saving process innovations.

Just because a new product is developed by a U.S. firm and first sold in the U.S. market, it does not follow that the product must be produced in the United States. It could be produced abroad at some low-cost location and then exported back into the United States. However, Vernon argued that most new products were initially produced in America. Apparently, the pioneering firms believed it was better to keep production facilities close to the market and to the firm's center of decision making, given the uncertainty and risks inherent in introducing new products. Also, the demand for most new products tends to be based on nonprice factors. Consequently, firms can charge relatively high prices for new products, which obviates the need to look for low-cost production sites in other countries.

Vernon went on to argue that early in the life cycle of a typical new product, while demand is starting to grow rapidly in the United States, demand in other advanced countries is limited to high-income groups. The limited initial demand in other advanced countries does not make it worthwhile for firms in those countries to start producing the new product, but it does necessitate some exports from the United States.

Over time, demand for the new product grows in other advanced countries (e.g., Great Britain, France, Germany, and Japan). As it does, it becomes worthwhile for foreign producers to begin producing for their home markets. In addition, U.S. firms might set up production facilities in those advanced countries where demand is growing. Consequently, production within other advanced countries begins to limit the potential for exports from the United States.

As the market in the United States and other advanced nations matures, the product becomes more standardized, and price becomes the main competitive weapon. As this occurs, cost considerations start to play a greater role in the competitive process. Producers based in advanced countries where labor costs are lower than in the United States (e.g., Italy, Spain) might now be able to export to the United States. If cost pressures become intense, the process might not stop there. The cycle by which the United States lost its advantage to other advanced countries might be repeated once more, as developing countries (e.g., Thailand) begin to acquire a production advantage over advanced countries. Thus, the locus of global production initially switches from the United States to other advanced nations and then from those nations to developing countries.

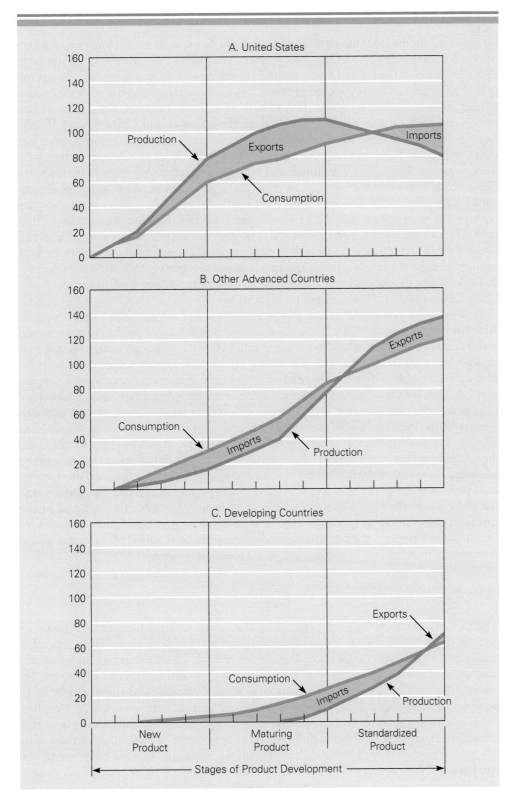

FIGURE 5.5

The Product Life-Cycle Theory

Source: Adapted from R. Vernon and L. T. Wells, *The Economic Environment of International Business.* 4th ed., © 1986. Reprinted by permission of Pearson Education, Inc. Upper Saddle River, N.J.

The consequence of these trends for the pattern of world trade is that over time the United States switches from being an exporter of the product to an importer of the product as production becomes concentrated in lower-cost foreign locations. Figure 5.5 shows the growth of production and consumption over time in the United States, other advanced countries, and developing countries.

EVALUATING THE PRODUCT LIFE-CYCLE THEORY

Historically, the product life-cycle theory seems to be an accurate explanation of international trade patterns. Consider photocopiers; the product was developed in the early 1960s by Xerox in the United States and sold initially to U.S. users. Originally Xerox exported photocopiers from the United States, primarily to Japan and the advanced countries of Western Europe. As demand began to grow in those countries, Xerox entered into joint ventures to set up production in Japan (Fuji-Xerox) and Great Britain (Rank-Xerox). In addition, once Xerox's patents on the photocopier process expired, other foreign competitors began to enter the market (e.g., Canon in Japan, Olivetti in Italy). As a consequence, U.S. exports declined, and U.S. users began to buy some of their photocopiers from lower-cost foreign sources, particularly Japan. More recently, Japanese companies have found that manufacturing costs are too high in their own country, so they have begun to switch production to developing countries such as Singapore and Thailand. Thus, initially the United States and now other advanced countries (e.g., Japan and Great Britain) have switched from being exporters of photocopiers to importers. This evolution in the pattern of international trade in photocopiers is consistent with the predictions of the product life-cycle theory that mature industries tend to go out of the United States and into low-cost assembly locations.

However, the product life-cycle theory is not without weaknesses. Viewed from an Asian or European perspective, Vernon's argument that most new products are developed and introduced in the United States seems ethnocentric. Although it may be true that during U.S. dominance of the global economy (1945–1975), most new products were introduced in the United States, there have always been important exceptions. These exceptions appear to have become more common in recent years. Many new products are now introduced in Japan (e.g., video game consoles) or Europe (new wireless phones). Also, with the increased globalization and integration of the world economy discussed in Chapter 1, a growing number of new products (e.g., laptop computers, compact disks, and digital cameras) are now introduced simultaneously in the United States, Japan, and the advanced European nations. This may be accompanied by globally dispersed production, with particular components of a new product being produced in those locations around the globe where the mix of factor costs and skills is most favorable (as predicted by the theory of comparative advantage). In sum, although Vernon's theory may be useful for explaining the pattern of international trade during the brief period of American global dominance, its relevance in the modern world seems more limited.

New Trade Theory

The new trade theory began to emerge in the 1970s when a number of economists pointed out that the ability of firms to attain economies of scale might have important implications for international trade. **Economies of scale** are unit cost reductions associated with a large volume of output. Economies of scale have a number of sources, including the ability to spread fixed costs over a large volume, and the ability of large producers to utilize specialized employees and equipment that are more productive than less specialized employees and equipment. Economies of scale are a major source of cost reductions in many industries, including computer software, automobiles, pharmaceuticals, and aerospace. For example, Microsoft realizes economies of scale by spreading the fixed costs of developing new versions of its Windows operating system, which runs to about $1 billion, over the 100 million or so personal computers upon which each new system is ultimately installed. Similarly, automobile companies realize economies of scale by producing a high volume of automobiles from an assembly line where each employee has a specialized task.

New trade theory makes two important points: First, through its impact on economies of scale, trade can increase the variety of goods available to consumers and decrease the average costs of those goods. Second, in those industries when the output required to attain economies of scale represents a significant proportion of total world demand, the global market may only be able to support a small number of enterprises. Thus, world trade in certain products may be dominated by countries whose firms were first movers in their production.

INCREASING PRODUCT VARIETY AND REDUCING COSTS

Imagine first a world without trade. In industries where economies of scale are important, both the variety of goods that a country can produce and the scale of production are limited by the size of the market. If a national market is small, there may not be enough demand to enable producers to realize economies of scale for certain products. Accordingly, those products may not be produced, thereby limiting the variety of products available to consumers. Alternatively, they may be produced, but at such low volumes that unit costs and prices are considerably higher than they might be if economies of scale could be realized.

Now consider what happens when nations trade with each other. Individual national markets are combined into a larger world market. As the size of the market expands due to trade, individual firms may be able to better attain economies of scale. The implication, according to new trade theory, is that each nation may be able to specialize in producing a narrower range of products than it would in the absence of trade, yet by buying goods from other countries, each nation can simultaneously increase the *variety* of goods available to its consumers and *lower the costs* of those goods—thus trade offers an opportunity for mutual gain even when countries do not differ in their resource endowments or technology.

Suppose there are two countries, each with an annual market for 1 million automobiles. By trading with each other, these countries can create a combined market for 2 million cars. In this combined market, due to the ability to better realize economies of scale, more varieties (models) of cars can be produced, and cars can be produced at a lower average cost, than in either market alone. For example, demand for a sports car may be limited to 55,000 units in each national market, while a total output of at least 100,000 per year may be required to realize significant scale economies. Similarly, demand for a minivan may be 80,000 units in each national market, and again a total output of at least 100,000 per year may be required to realize significant scale economies. Faced with limited domestic market demand, firms in each nation may decide not to produce a sports car, since the costs of doing so at such low volume are too great. Although they may produce minivans, the cost of doing so will be higher, as will prices, than if significant economies of scale had been attained. Once the two countries decide to trade, however, a firm in one nation may specialize in producing sports cars, while a firm in the other nation may produce minivans. The combined demand for 110,000 sports cars and 160,000 minivans allows each firm to realize scale economies. Consumers benefit from having access to a product (sports cars) that was not available before international trade and from the lower price for a product (minivans) that could not be produced at the most efficient scale before international trade. Trade is thus mutually beneficial because it allows for the specialization of production, the realization of scale economies, the production of a greater variety of products, and lower prices.

ECONOMIES OF SCALE, FIRST-MOVER ADVANTAGES AND THE PATTERN OF TRADE

A second theme in new trade theory is that the pattern of trade we observe in the world economy may be the result of economies of scale and first-mover advantages. **First-mover advantages** are the economic and strategic advantages that accrue to early entrants into an industry.[29] The ability to capture scale economies ahead of later entrants, and thus benefit from a lower cost structure, is an important first-mover advantage. New trade theory argues that for those products where economies of scale are significant and represent a substantial proportion of world demand, the first movers in an industry can gain a scale-based cost advantage that later entrants find almost impossible to match. Thus, the pattern of trade that we observe for such products may reflect first-mover advantages. Countries may dominate in the export of certain goods because economies of scale are important in their production and because firms located in those countries were the first to capture scale economies, giving them a first-mover advantage.

For example, consider the commercial aerospace industry, which benefits from substantial scale economies that come from the ability to spread the fixed costs of developing a new jet aircraft over a large number of sales. It is costing Airbus Industrie some $14 billion to develop its new super-jumbo jet, the 550-seat A380. To recoup those costs and break even, Airbus will have to sell at least 250 A380 planes. However, total demand over the next 20 years for this class of aircraft is estimated to be somewhere between 400 and 600 units. Thus, the global market can probably profitably support only one producer of jet aircraft in the super-jumbo category. The European Union might come to dominate in the export of very large jet aircraft, primarily because a European-based firm, Airbus, was the first to produce a 550-seat jet aircraft and realize scale economies. Other potential producers, such as Boeing, might be shut out of the market because they will lack the scale economies that Airbus will enjoy. By pioneering this market category, Airbus may have captured a first-mover advantage based on scale economies that will be difficult for rivals to match, and that will result in the European Union becoming the leading exporter of very large jet aircraft.

IMPLICATIONS OF NEW TRADE THEORY

New trade theory has important implications. The theory suggests that nations may benefit from trade even when they do not differ in resource endowments or technology. Trade allows a nation to specialize in the production of certain products, attaining scale economies and lowering the costs of producing those products, while buying products that it does not produce from other nations that specialize in the production of other products. By this mechanism, the variety of products available to consumers in each nation is increased, while the average costs of those products should fall, as should their price, freeing resources to produce other goods and services.

The theory also suggests that a country may dominate in the export of a good simply because it was lucky enough to have one or more firms among the first to produce that good. Because they are able to gain economies of scale, the first movers in an industry may get a lock on the world market that discourages subsequent entry. First movers' ability to benefit from increasing returns creates a barrier to entry. In the commercial aircraft industry, the fact that Boeing and Airbus are already in the industry and have the benefits of economies of scale discourages new entry and reinforces the dominance of America and Europe in the trade of midsize and large jet aircraft. This dominance is further reinforced because global demand may not be sufficient to profitably support another producer of midsize and large jet aircraft. So although Japanese firms might be able to compete in the market, they have decided not to enter the industry but to ally themselves as major subcontractors with primary producers (e.g., Mitsubishi Heavy Industries is a major subcontractor for Boeing on the 777 and 7E7 programs).

New trade theory is at variance with the Heckscher-Ohlin theory, which suggests that a country will predominate in the export of a product when it is particularly well endowed with those factors used intensively in its manufacture. New trade theorists argue that the United States is a major exporter of commercial jet aircraft not because it is better endowed with the factors of production required to manufacture aircraft, but because one of the first movers in the industry, Boeing, was a U.S. firm. The new trade theory is not at variance with the theory of comparative advantage. Economies of scale increase productivity. Thus, the new trade theory identifies an important source of comparative advantage.

This theory is quite useful in explaining trade patterns. Empirical studies seem to support the predictions of the theory that trade increases the specialization of production within an industry, increases the variety of products available to consumers, and results in lower average prices.[30] With regard to first-mover advantages and international trade, a study by Harvard business historian Alfred Chandler suggests the existence of first-mover advantages is an important factor in explaining the dominance of firms from certain nations in specific industries.[31] The number of firms is very limited in many global industries, including the chemical industry, the heavy construction-equipment industry, the heavy truck industry, the tire industry, the consumer electronics industry, the jet engine industry, and the computer software industry.

Perhaps the most contentious implication of the new trade theory is the argument that it generates for government intervention and strategic trade policy.[32] New trade theorists stress the role of luck, entrepreneurship, and innovation in giving a firm first-mover advantages. According to this argument, the reason Boeing was the first mover in commercial jet aircraft manufacture—rather than firms such as Great Britain's De-Havilland and Hawker Siddley, or Holland's Fokker, all of which could have been— was that Boeing was both lucky and innovative. One way Boeing was lucky is that DeHavilland shot itself in the foot when its Comet jet airliner, introduced two years earlier than Boeing's first jet airliner, the 707, was found to be full of serious technological flaws. Had DeHavilland not made some serious technological mistakes, Great Britain might have become the world's leading exporter of commercial jet aircraft. Boeing's innovativeness was demonstrated by its independent development of the technological know-how required to build a commercial jet airliner. Several new trade theorists have pointed out, however, that Boeing's research and development cost was largely paid for by the U.S. government; the 707 was a spin-off from a government-funded military program (the entry of Airbus into the industry was also supported by significant government subsidies). Herein is a rationale for government intervention; by the sophisticated and judicious use of subsidies, could a government increase the chances of its domestic firms becoming first movers in emerging industries, as the U.S. government apparently did with Boeing (and the European Union did with Airbus)? If this is possible, and the new trade theory suggests it might be, we have an economic rationale for a proactive trade policy that is at variance with the free trade prescriptions of the trade theories we have reviewed so far. We will consider the policy implications of this issue in Chapter 6.

National Competitive Advantage: Porter's Diamond

In 1990 Michael Porter of the Harvard Business School published the results of an intensive research effort that attempted to determine why some nations succeed and others fail in international competition.[33] Porter and his team looked at 100 industries in 10 nations. Like the work of the new trade theorists, Porter's work was driven by a belief that existing theories of international trade told only part of the story. For Porter, the essential task was to explain why a nation achieves international success in a particular industry. Why does Japan do so well in the automobile industry? Why does Switzerland excel in the production and export of precision instruments and pharmaceuticals? Why do Germany and the United States do so well in the chemical industry? These questions cannot be answered easily by the Heckscher-Ohlin theory, and the theory of comparative advantage offers only a partial explanation. The theory of comparative advantage would say that Switzerland excels in the production and export of precision instruments because it uses its resources very productively in these industries. Although this may be correct, this does not explain why Switzerland is more productive in this industry than Great Britain, Germany, or Spain. Porter tries to solve this puzzle.

FIGURE 5.6

Determinants of
National Competitive
Advantage: Porter's
Diamond

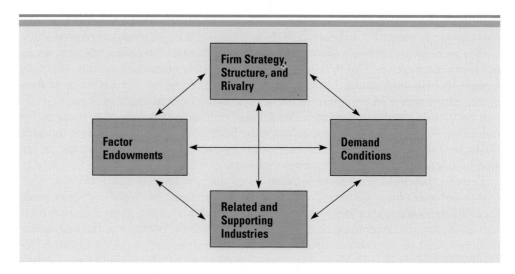

Porter theorizes that four broad attributes of a nation shape the environment in which local firms compete, and these attributes promote or impede the creation of competitive advantage (see Figure 5.6). These attributes are

- *Factor endowments*—a nation's position in factors of production such as skilled labor or the infrastructure necessary to compete in a given industry.
- *Demand conditions*—the nature of home demand for the industry's product or service.
- *Relating and supporting industries*—the presence or absence of supplier industries and related industries that are internationally competitive.
- *Firm strategy, structure, and rivalry*—the conditions governing how companies are created, organized, and managed and the nature of domestic rivalry.

Porter speaks of these four attributes as constituting the *diamond*. He argues that firms are most likely to succeed in industries or industry segments where the diamond is most favorable. He also argues that the diamond is a mutually reinforcing system. The effect of one attribute is contingent on the state of others. For example, Porter argues favorable demand conditions will not result in competitive advantage unless the state of rivalry is sufficient to cause firms to respond to them.

Porter maintains that two additional variables can influence the national diamond in important ways: chance and government. Chance events, such as major innovations, can reshape industry structure and provide the opportunity for one nation's firms to supplant another's. Government, by its choice of policies, can detract from or improve national advantage. For example, regulation can alter home demand conditions, antitrust policies can influence the intensity of rivalry within an industry, and government investments in education can change factor endowments.

FACTOR ENDOWMENTS

Factor endowments lie at the center of the Heckscher-Ohlin theory. While Porter does not propose anything radically new, he does analyze the characteristics of factors of production. He recognizes hierarchies among factors, distinguishing between *basic factors* (e.g., natural resources, climate, location, and demographics) and *advanced factors* (e.g., communication infrastructure, sophisticated and skilled labor, research facilities, and technological know-how). He argues that advanced factors are the most significant for competitive advantage. Unlike the naturally endowed basic factors, advanced factors are a product of investment by individuals, companies, and governments. Thus, government investments in basic and higher education, by improving the general skill and knowledge level of the population and by stimulating advanced research at higher education institutions, can upgrade a nation's advanced factors.

The relationship between advanced and basic factors is complex. Basic factors can provide an initial advantage that is subsequently reinforced and extended by investment in advanced factors. Conversely, disadvantages in basic factors can create pressures to invest in advanced factors. An obvious example of this phenomenon is Japan, a country that lacks arable land and mineral deposits and yet through investment has built a substantial endowment of advanced factors. Porter notes that Japan's large pool of engineers (reflecting a much higher number of engineering graduates per capita than almost any other nation) has been vital to Japan's success in many manufacturing industries.

DEMAND CONDITIONS

Porter emphasizes the role home demand plays in upgrading competitive advantage. Firms are typically most sensitive to the needs of their closest customers. Thus, the characteristics of home demand are particularly important in shaping the attributes of domestically made products and in creating pressures for innovation and quality. Porter argues that a nation's firms gain competitive advantage if their domestic consumers are sophisticated and demanding. Such consumers pressure local firms to meet high standards of product quality and to produce innovative products. Porter notes that Japan's sophisticated and knowledgeable buyers of cameras helped stimulate the Japanese camera industry to improve product quality and to introduce innovative models. A similar example can be found in the wireless telephone equipment industry, where sophisticated and demanding local customers in Scandinavia helped push Nokia of Finland and Ericsson of Sweden to invest in cellular phone technology long before demand for cellular phones took off in other developed nations. The case of Nokia is reviewed in more depth in the accompanying Management Focus.

RELATED AND SUPPORTING INDUSTRIES

The third broad attribute of national advantage in an industry is the presence of suppliers or related industries that are internationally competitive. The benefits of investments in advanced factors of production by related and supporting industries can spill over into an industry, thereby helping it achieve a strong competitive position internationally. Swedish strength in fabricated steel products (e.g., ball bearings and cutting tools) has drawn on strengths in Sweden's specialty steel industry. Technological leadership in the U.S. semiconductor industry provided the basis for U.S. success in personal computers and several other technically advanced electronic products. Similarly, Switzerland's success in pharmaceuticals is closely related to its previous international success in the technologically related dye industry.

One consequence of this process is that successful industries within a country tend to be grouped into clusters of related industries. This was one of the most pervasive findings of Porter's study. One such cluster Porter identified was in the German textile and apparel sector, which included high-quality cotton, wool, synthetic fibers, sewing machine needles, and a wide range of textile machinery. Such clusters are important, because valuable knowledge can flow between the firms within a geographic cluster, benefiting all within that cluster. Knowledge flows occur when employees move between firms within a region and when national industry associations bring employees from different companies together for regular conferences or workshops.[34]

FIRM STRATEGY, STRUCTURE, AND RIVALRY

The fourth broad attribute of national competitive advantage in Porter's model is the strategy, structure, and rivalry of firms within a nation. Porter makes two important points here. First, nations are characterized by different management ideologies, which

MANAGEMENT FOCUS The wireless phone market is one of the great growth stories of the last decade. Starting from a very low base in 1990, annual global sales of wireless phones surged to 440 million units in 2003. By the end of 2003, there were more than 1.2 billion wireless subscribers worldwide, up from less than 10 million in 1990. Nokia is a dominant player in the market for mobile telephone sales. Nokia's roots are in Finland, not normally a country that comes to mind when one talks about leading-edge technology companies. In the 1980s, Nokia was a rambling Finnish conglomerate with activities that embraced tire manufacturing, paper production, consumer electronics, and telecommunication equipment. By 2004 it had transformed itself into a focused telecommunications equipment manufacturer with a global reach, sales of over $30 billion, earnings of more than $5 billion, and a 38 percent share of the global market for wireless phones. How has this former conglomerate emerged to take a global leadership position in wireless telecommunication equipment? Much of the answer lies in the history, geography, and political economy of Finland and its Nordic neighbors.

The story starts in 1981 when the Nordic nations got together to create the world's first international wireless telephone network. Sparsely populated and inhospitably cold, they had good reason to become pioneers: It cost far too much to lay down a traditional wire line telephone service. Yet the same features that made it difficult make telecommunications all the more valuable there: People driving through the Arctic winter and owners of remote northern houses needed a telephone to summon help if things go wrong. As a result, Sweden, Norway, and Finland became the first nations in the world to take wireless telecommunications seriously. They found, for example, that although it cost up to $800 per subscriber to bring a traditional landline service to remote locations, the same locations could be linked by wireless cellular for only $500 per person. As a consequence, 12 percent of people in Scandinavia owned cellular phones by 1994, compared with less than 6 percent in the United States, the world's second most developed market. This lead continued over the next decade. By the end of 2003, 85 percent of the population in Finland owned a wireless phone, compared with 55 percent in the United States.

Nokia, a longtime telecommunications equipment supplier, was well positioned to take advantage of this development from the start, but other forces were also either help them or do not help them to build national competitive advantage. For example, Porter noted the predominance of engineers in top management at German and Japanese firms. He attributed this to these firms' emphasis on improving manufacturing processes and product design. In contrast, Porter noted a predominance of people with finance backgrounds leading many U.S. firms. He linked this to U.S. firms' lack of attention to improving manufacturing processes and product design. He argued that the dominance of finance led to an overemphasis on maximizing short-term financial returns. According to Porter, one consequence of these different management ideologies was a relative loss of U.S. competitiveness in those engineering-based industries where manufacturing processes and product design issues are all-important (e.g., the automobile industry).

Porter's second point is that a strong association exists between vigorous domestic rivalry and the creation and persistence of competitive advantage in an industry. Vigorous domestic rivalry induces firms to look for ways to improve efficiency, which makes them better international competitors. Domestic rivalry creates pressures to innovate, to improve quality, to reduce costs, and to invest in upgrading advanced factors. All this helps to create world-class competitors. Porter cites the case of Japan:

> Nowhere is the role of domestic rivalry more evident than in Japan, where it is all-out warfare in which many companies fail to achieve profitability. With goals that stress market share, Japanese companies engage in a continuing struggle to outdo each other.

at work to help Nokia develop its competitive edge. Unlike virtually every other developed nation, Finland has never had a national telephone monopoly. Instead, the country's telephone services have long been provided by about 50 or so autonomous local telephone companies whose elected boards set prices by referendum (which naturally means low prices). This army of independent and cost-conscious telephone service providers prevented Nokia from taking anything for granted in its home country. With typical Finnish pragmatism, its customers were willing to buy from the lowest cost supplier, whether that was Nokia, Ericsson, Motorola, or some other company. This situation contrasted sharply with that prevailing in most developed nations until the late 1980s and early 1990s, where domestic telephone monopolies typically purchased equipment from a dominant local supplier or made it themselves. Nokia responded to this competitive pressure by doing everything possible to drive down its manufacturing costs while staying at the leading edge of wireless technology.

The consequences of these forces are clear. Nokia is now the leader in digital wireless technology, which is the wave of the future. Many now regard Finland as the lead market for wireless telephone services. If you want to see the future of wireless, you don't go to New York or San Francisco, you go to Helsinki, where Finns use their wireless handsets not just to talk to each other, but also to browse the Web, execute e-commerce transactions, control household heating and lighting systems, or purchase Coke from a wireless-enabled vending machine. Nokia has gained this lead because Scandinavia started switching to digital technology five years before the rest of the world. Spurred on by its cost-conscious Finnish customers, Nokia now has the lowest cost structure of any cellular phone equipment manufacturer in the world, making it a more profitable enterprise than Motorola, its leading global rival. It cost Nokia an average of $114 to make and sell each phone in 2002, compared with about $131 a year earlier. Its closest rival, Motorola Inc. of Schaumburg, Illinois, spent an average of $139 to make and sell each phone.

Sources: "Lessons from the Frozen North," *The Economist*, October 8, 1994, pp. 76–77; G. Edmondson, "Grabbing Markets from the Giants," *BusinessWeek*, Special Issue: 21st Century Capitalism, 1995, p. 156; Q. Hardy, "Bypassing the Bells—A Wireless World," *The Wall Street Journal*, September 21, 1998, p. R16; Q. Hardy and G. Naik, "Nokia Takes the Lead as Wireless Makers Sell 162.9 Million Phones in 1998," *The Wall Street Journal*, February 8, 1999, p. A1; "A Finnish Fable," *The Economist*, October 14, 2000; M. Newman, "The U.S. Starts to Catch Up," *The Wall Street Journal*, September 23, 2002, p. R6; D. Pringle, "How Nokia Thrives by Breaking the Rules," *The Wall Street Journal*, January 3, 2003, p. A7; and Nokia Web site at www.nokia.com.

Shares fluctuate markedly. The process is prominently covered in the business press. Elaborate rankings measure which companies are most popular with university graduates. The rate of new product and process development is breathtaking.[35]

A similar point about the stimulating effects of strong domestic competition can be made with regard to the rise of Nokia of Finland to global preeminence in the market for cellular telephone equipment. For details, see the Management Focus.

EVALUATING PORTER'S THEORY

Porter contends that the degree to which a nation is likely to achieve international success in a certain industry is a function of the combined impact of factor endowments, domestic demand conditions, related and supporting industries, and domestic rivalry. He argues that the presence of all four components is usually required for this diamond to boost competitive performance (although there are exceptions). Porter also contends that government can influence each of the four components of the diamond—either positively or negatively. Factor endowments can be affected by subsidies, policies toward capital markets, policies toward education, and so on. Government can shape domestic demand through local product standards or with regulations that mandate or influence buyer needs. Government policy can influence supporting and related industries through regulation and influence firm rivalry through such devices as capital market regulation, tax policy, and antitrust laws.

If Porter is correct, we would expect his model to predict the pattern of international trade that we observe in the real world. Countries should be exporting products from those industries where all four components of the diamond are favorable, while importing in those areas where the components are not favorable. Is he correct? We simply do not know. Porter's theory has not been subjected to detailed empirical testing. Much about the theory rings true, but the same can be said for the new trade theory, the theory of comparative advantage, and the Heckscher-Ohlin theory. It may be that each of these theories, which complement each other, explains something about the pattern of international trade.

IMPLICATIONS FOR MANAGERS

Why does all this matter for business? Three main implications for international businesses of the material discussed in this chapter are location implications, first-mover implications, and policy implications.

LOCATION

Underlying most of the theories we have discussed is the notion that different countries have particular advantages in different productive activities. Thus, from a profit perspective, it makes sense for a firm to disperse its productive activities to those countries where, according to the theory of international trade, they can be performed most efficiently. If design can be performed most efficiently in France, that is where design facilities should be located; if the manufacture of basic components can be performed most efficiently in Singapore, that is where they should be manufactured; and if final assembly can be performed most efficiently in China, that is where final assembly should be performed. The result is a global web of productive activities, with various activities being performed in different locations around the globe depending on considerations of comparative advantage, factor endowments, and the like. If the firm does not do this, it may find itself at a competitive disadvantage relative to firms that do.

Consider the production of a laptop computer, a process with four major stages: (1) basic research and development of the product design, (2) manufacture of standard electronic components (e.g., memory chips), (3) manufacture of advanced components (e.g., flat-top color display screens and microprocessors), and (4) final assembly. Basic R&D requires a pool of highly skilled and educated workers with backgrounds in microelectronics. The two countries with a comparative advantage in basic microelectronics R&D and design are Japan and the United States, so most producers of laptop computers locate their R&D facilities in one, or both, of these countries. (Apple, IBM, Motorola, Texas Instruments, Toshiba, and Sony all have major R&D facilities in both Japan and the United States.)

The manufacture of standard electronic components is a capital-intensive process requiring semiskilled labor, and cost pressures are intense. The best locations for such activities today are places such as Taiwan, Malaysia, and South Korea. These countries have pools of relatively skilled, moderate-cost labor. Thus, many producers of laptop computers have standard components, such as memory chips, produced at these locations.

The manufacture of advanced components such as microprocessors is a capital-intensive process requiring skilled labor. Because cost pressures are not so intense at this stage, these components can be—and are—manufactured in countries with high labor costs that also have pools of highly skilled labor (e.g., Japan and the United States).

Finally, assembly is a relatively labor-intensive process requiring only low-skilled labor, and cost pressures are intense. As a result, final assembly may be carried out in a country such as Mexico, which has an abundance of low-cost, low-skilled labor. A laptop computer produced by a U.S. manufacturer may be designed in California, have its standard components produced in Taiwan and Singapore, its advanced components produced in Japan and the United States, its final assembly in Mexico, and be sold in the United States or elsewhere in the world. By dispersing production activities to different locations around the globe, the U.S. manufacturer is taking advantage of the differences between countries identified by the various theories of international trade.

FIRST-MOVER ADVANTAGES

According to the new trade theory, firms that establish a first-mover advantage with regard to the production of a particular new product may subsequently dominate global trade in that product. This is particularly true in industries where the global market can profitably support only a limited number of firms, such as the aerospace market, but early commitments also seem to be important in less concentrated industries such as the market for cellular telephone equipment (see the Management Focus on Nokia). For the individual firm, the clear message is that it pays to invest substantial financial resources in trying to build a first-mover, or early-mover, advantage, even if that means several years of substantial losses before a new venture becomes profitable—the idea being to preempt the available demand, gain cost advantages related to volume, build an enduring brand ahead of later competitors, and, consequently, establish a long-term sustainable competitive advantage. Although the details of how to achieve this are beyond the scope of this book, many publications offer strategies for exploiting first-mover advantages, and for avoiding the traps associated with pioneering a market (first-mover disadvantages).[36]

GOVERNMENT POLICY

The theories of international trade also matter to international businesses because firms are major players on the international trade scene. Business firms produce exports, and business firms import the products of other countries. Because of their pivotal role in international trade, businesses can exert a strong influence on government trade policy, lobbying to promote free trade or trade restrictions. The theories of international trade claim that promoting free trade is generally in the best interests of a country, although it may not always be in the best interest of an individual firm. Many firms recognize this and lobby for open markets.

For example, when the U.S. government announced in 1991 its intention to place a tariff on Japanese imports of liquid crystal display (LCD) screens, IBM and Apple Computer protested strongly. Both IBM and Apple pointed out that (1) Japan was the lowest cost source of LCD screens, (2) they used these screens in their own laptop computers, and (3) the proposed tariff, by increasing the cost of LCD screens, would increase the cost of laptop computers produced by IBM and Apple, thus making them less competitive in the world market. In other words, the tariff, designed to protect U.S. firms, would be self-defeating. In response to these pressures, the U.S. government reversed its posture.

Unlike IBM and Apple, however, businesses do not always lobby for free trade. In the United States, for example, restrictions on steel imports are the result of direct pressure by U.S. firms on the government. In some cases, the government has responded to pressure by getting foreign companies to agree to "voluntary" restrictions on their imports, using the implicit threat of more comprehensive formal trade barriers to get them to adhere to these agreements (historically, this has occurred in the automobile industry). In other cases, the government used what are called "antidumping" actions to justify tariffs on imports from other nations (these mechanisms will be discussed in detail in the next chapter).

As predicted by international trade theory, many of these agreements have been self-defeating, such as the voluntary restriction on machine tool imports agreed to in 1985. Due to limited import competition from more efficient foreign suppliers, the prices of machine tools in the United States rose to higher levels than would have prevailed under free trade. Because machine tools are used throughout the manufacturing industry, the result was to increase the costs of U.S. manufacturing in general, creating a corresponding loss in world market competitiveness. Shielded from international competition by import barriers, the U.S. machine tool industry had no incentive to increase its efficiency. Consequently, it lost many of its export markets to more efficient foreign competitors. As a consequence of this misguided action, the U.S. machine tool industry shrank during the period when the agreement was in force. For anyone schooled in international trade theory, this was not surprising.[37] A similar scenario unfolded in the U.S. steel industry, where tariff barriers erected by the government in 2001 raised the cost of steel to important U.S. users, such as automobile companies and appliance makers, making their products more uncompetitive.

Finally, Porter's theory of national competitive advantage also contains policy implications. Porter's theory suggests that it is in the best interest of business for a firm to invest in upgrading advanced factors of production; for example, to invest in better training for its employees and to increase its commitment to research and development. It is also in the best interests of business to lobby the government to adopt policies that have a favorable impact on each component of the national diamond. Thus, according to Porter, businesses should urge government to increase investment in education, infrastructure, and basic research (since all these enhance advanced factors) and to adopt policies that promote strong competition within domestic markets (since this makes firms stronger international competitors, according to Porter's findings).

Chapter Summary

This chapter has reviewed a number of theories that explain why it is beneficial for a country to engage in international trade and has explained the pattern of international trade observed in the world economy. We have seen how the theories of Smith, Ricardo, and Heckscher-Ohlin all make strong cases for unrestricted free trade. In contrast, the mercantilist doctrine and, to a lesser extent, the new trade theory can be interpreted to support government intervention to promote exports through subsidies and to limit imports through tariffs and quotas. In explaining the pattern of international trade, the second objective of this chapter, we have seen that with the exception of mercantilism, which is silent on this issue, the different theories offer largely complementary explanations. Although no one theory may explain the apparent pattern of international trade, taken together, the theory of comparative advantage, the Heckscher-Ohlin theory, the product life-cycle theory, the new trade theory, and Porter's theory of national competitive advantage do suggest which factors are important. Comparative advantage tells us that productivity differences are important; Heckscher-Ohlin tells us that factor endowments matter; the product life-cycle theory tells us that where a new product is introduced is

important; the new trade theory tells us that increasing returns to specialization and first-mover advantages matter; and Porter tells us that all these factors may be important insofar as they impact the four components of the national diamond. The chapter made these following points:

1. Mercantilists argued that it was in a country's best interests to run a balance-of-trade surplus. They viewed trade as a zero-sum game, in which one country's gains cause losses for other countries.

2. The theory of absolute advantage suggests that countries differ in their ability to produce goods efficiently. The theory suggests that a country should specialize in producing goods in areas where it has an absolute advantage and import goods in areas where other countries have absolute advantages.

3. The theory of comparative advantage suggests that it makes sense for a country to specialize in producing those goods that it can produce most efficiently, while buying goods that it can produce relatively less efficiently from other

countries—even if that means buying goods from other countries that it could produce more efficiently itself.

4. The theory of comparative advantage suggests that unrestricted free trade brings about increased world production; that is, that trade is a positive-sum game.

5. The theory of comparative advantage also suggests that opening a country to free trade stimulates economic growth, which creates dynamic gains from trade. The empirical evidence seems to be consistent with this claim.

6. The Heckscher-Ohlin theory argues that the pattern of international trade is determined by differences in factor endowments. It predicts that countries will export those goods that make intensive use of locally abundant factors and will import goods that make intensive use of factors that are locally scarce.

7. The product life-cycle theory suggests that trade patterns are influenced by where a new product is introduced. In an increasingly integrated global economy, the product life-cycle theory seems to be less predictive than it once was.

8. New trade theory states that trade allows a nation to specialize in the production of certain goods, attaining scale economies and lowering the costs of producing those goods, while buying goods that it does not produce from other nations that are similarly specialized. By this mech-

anism, the variety of goods available to consumers in each nation is increased, while the average costs of those goods should fall.

9. New trade theory also states that in those industries where substantial economies of scale imply that the world market will profitably support only a few firms, countries may predominate in the export of certain products simply because they had a firm that was a first mover in that industry.

10. Some new trade theorists have promoted the idea of strategic trade policy. The argument is that government, by the sophisticated and judicious use of subsidies, might be able to increase the chances of domestic firms becoming first movers in emerging industries.

11. Porter's theory of national competitive advantage suggests that the pattern of trade is influenced by four attributes of a nation: (*a*) factor endowments, (*b*) domestic demand conditions, (*c*) relating and supporting industries, and (*d*) firm strategy, structure, and rivalry.

12. Theories of international trade are important to an individual business firm primarily because they can help the firm decide where to locate its various production activities.

13. Firms involved in international trade can and do exert a strong influence on government policy toward trade. By lobbying government, business firms can promote free trade or trade restrictions.

Critical Thinking and Discussion Questions

1. Mercantilism is a bankrupt theory that has no place in the modern world. Discuss.

2. Is free trade fair? Discuss!

3. Unions in developed nations often oppose imports from low-wage countries and advocate trade barriers to protect jobs from what they often characterize as "unfair" import competition. Is such competition "unfair"? Do you think that this argument is in the best interests of (*a*) the unions, (*b*) the people they represent, and/or (*c*) the country as a whole?

4. What are the potential costs of adopting a free trade regime? Do you think governments should do anything to reduce these costs? What?

5. Reread the Country Focus on outsourcing service jobs. Is there a difference between the transference of high-paying, white-collar jobs, such as computer programming and accounting, to developing nations, and low-paying, blue-collar

jobs? If so, what is the difference, and should government do anything to stop the flow of white-collar jobs to countries such as India?

6. Drawing upon the new trade theory and Porter's theory of national competitive advantage, outline the case for government policies that would build national competitive advantage in biotechnology. What kinds of policies would you recommend that the government adopt? Are these policies at variance with the basic free trade philosophy?

7. The world's poorest countries are at a competitive disadvantage in every sector of their economies. They have little to export. They have no capital; their land is of poor quality; they often have too many people given available work opportunities; and they are poorly educated. Free trade cannot possibly be in the interests of such nations! Discuss.

Research Task globalEDGE™   globaledge.msu.edu

Use the globalEDGE™ site to complete the following exercises:

1. The WTO's annual International Trade Statistics report provides comprehensive, comparable, and up-to-date statistics on trade in merchandise and commercial services. This report allows for an assessment of world trade flows by country, region, and main product groups or service categories. Using the most recent statistics available, identify the top five countries that lead in the export and import of merchandise, respectively.

2. Your company is interested in importing Australian wine. As part of the initial analysis, you want to identify the strengths of the Australian wine industry. Provide a short description of the current status of Australian wine exports and also a list of the top importing countries of Australian wine. Then compare the current state of Australian wine exports with both Russian and Chinese wine exports. From the information available, which country provides the best opportunities for your company? Include information to support your decision.

Logitech

CLOSING CASE Best known as one of the world's largest producers of computer mice, Logitech is in many ways the epitome of the modern global corporation. Founded in 1981 in Apples, Switzerland, by two Italians and a Swiss, the company now generates annual sales of more than $1 billion, most from products such as mice, keyboards, and low-cost video cameras that cost under $100. Logitech made its name as a technological innovator in the highly competitive business of personal computer peripherals. Among other things, it was the first company to introduce a mouse that used infrared tracking, rather than a tracking ball, and the first to introduce wireless mice and keyboards. Logitech is differentiated from competitors by its continuing innovation—in 2003 it introduced 91 new products—its high brand recognition, and its strong retail presence. Less obvious to consumers, but equally important, has been the way the company has configured its global value chain to lower production costs while maintaining the value of those assets that lead to differentiation.

Logitech still undertakes basic R&D work (primarily software programming) in Switzerland where it has 200 employees. The company is still legally Swiss, but the corporate headquarters are in Fremont, California, close to many of America's high-technology enterprises, where it has 450 employees. Some R&D work (again, primarily software programming) is also carried out in Fremont. Most significantly, though, Fremont is the headquarters for the company's global marketing, finance, and logistics operations. The ergonomic design of Logitech's products—their look and feel—is done in Ireland by an outside design firm. Most of Logitech's products are manufactured in Asia.

Logitech's expansion into Asian manufacturing began in the late 1980s when it opened a factory in Taiwan. At the time, most of its mice were produced in the United States. Logitech was trying to win two of the most prestigious OEM customers—Apple Computer and IBM. Both bought their mice from Alps, a large Japanese firm that supplied Microsoft. To attract discerning customers such as Apple, Logitech not only needed the capacity to produce at high volume and low cost, but it also had to offer a better designed product. The solution: manufacture in Taiwan. Cost was a factor in the decision, but it was not as significant as might be expected, since direct labor accounted for only 7 percent of the cost of Logitech's mouse. Taiwan offered a well-developed supply base for parts, qualified people, and a rapidly expanding local computer industry. As an inducement to fledgling innovators, Taiwan provided space in its science-based industrial park in Hsinchu for the modest fee of $200,000. Sizing this up as a deal that was too good to pass up, Logitech signed the lease. Shortly afterward, Logitech won the OEM contract with Apple. The Taiwanese factory was soon outproducing Logitech's U.S. facility. After the Apple contract, Logitech's other OEM business started being served from Taiwan; the plant's total capacity increased to 10 million mice per year.

By the late 1990s, Logitech needed more production capacity. This time it turned to China. A wide variety of the company's retail products are now made there. Take one of Logitech's biggest sellers, a wireless infrared mouse called Wanda. The mouse itself is assembled in Suzhou, China, in a factory that Logitech owns. The factory employs 4,000 people, mostly young women such as Wang Yan, an 18-year-old employee from the impoverished rural province of Anhui. She is paid $75 a month to sit all day at a conveyer belt plugging three tiny bits of metal into circuit boards. She does this about 2,000 times each day. The mouse Wang Yan helps assemble sells to American consumers for about $40. Of this, Logitech takes about $8, which is used to fund R&D, marketing, and corporate overhead. What remains of the $8 after that is the profit attributable to Logitech's shareholders. Distributors and retailers around the world take a further $15. Another $14 goes to the suppliers who make Wanda's parts. For example, a Motorola plant in Malaysia makes the mouse's chips and another American company, Agilent Technologies, supplies the optical sensors from a plant in the Philippines. That leaves just $3 for the Chinese factory, which is used to cover wages, power, transport, and other overhead costs.

Logitech is not alone in exploiting China to manufacture products. According to China's Ministry of Commerce, foreign companies account for three-quarters of China's high-tech exports. China's top 10 exporters include American companies with Chinese operations, such as Motorola and Seagate Technologies, a maker of disk drives for computers. Intel now produces some 50 million chips a year in China, the majority of which end up in computers and other goods that are exported to other parts of Asia or back to the United States. Yet Intel's plant in Shanghai doesn't really make chips; it tests and assembles chips from silicon wafers made in Intel plants abroad, mostly in the United States. China adds less than 5 percent of the value. The U.S. operations of Intel generate the bulk of the value and profits.

Sources: V. K. Jolly and K. A. Bechler, "Logitech: The Mouse That Roared," *Planning Review* 20 no. 6 (1992), pp. 20–34; K. Guerrino, "Lord of the Mice," *Chief Executive*, July 2003, pp. 42–44; A. Higgins,

"As Chin Surges, It Also Proves a Buttress to American Strength," *The Wall Street Journal*, January 30, 2004, pp. A1, A8; and J. Fox, "Where Is Your Job Going?" *Fortune*, November 24, 2003, pp. 84–88.

Case Discussion Questions

1. In a world without trade, what would American consumers have to pay for Logitech's products?

2. Explain how trade lowers the costs of making computer peripherals such as mice and keyboards.

3. Use the theory of comparative advantage to explain the way in which Logitech has configured its global operations. Why does the company manufacture in China and Taiwan, undertake basic R&D in California and Switzerland, design products in Ireland, and coordinate marketing and operations from California?

4. Who creates more value for Logitech, the 650 people it employs in Fremont and Switzerland or the 4,000 employees at its Chinese factory? What are the implications of this observation for the argument that free trade is beneficial?

5. Why do you think the company decided to shift its corporate headquarters from Switzerland to Fremont?

6. To what extent can Porter's diamond help explain the choice of Taiwan as a major manufacturing site for Logitech?

7. Why do you think China is now a favored location for so much high-technology manufacturing activity? How will China's increasing involvement in global trade help that country? How will it help the world's developed economies? What potential problems are associated with moving work to China?

Notes

1. H. W. Spiegel, *The Growth of Economic Thought* (Durham, NC: Duke University Press, 1991).

2. G. de Jonquieres, "Mercantilists Are Treading on Thin Ice," *Financial Times*, July 3, 1994, p. 16.

3. Jarl Hagelstam, "Mercantilism Still Influences Practical Trade Policy at the End of the Twentieth Century," *Journal of World Trade*, 1991, pp. 95–105.

4. M. Solis, "The Politics of Self-Restraint: FDI Subsidies and Japanese Mercantilism," *The World Economy* 26 (February 2003), pp. 153–70.

5. S. Hollander, *The Economics of David Ricardo* (Buffalo, NY: The University of Toronto Press, 1979).

6. D. Ricardo, *The Principles of Political Economy and Taxation* (Homewood, IL: Irwin, 1967, first published in 1817).

7. For example, R. Dornbusch, S. Fischer, and P. Samuelson, "Comparative Advantage: Trade and Payments in a Ricardian Model with a Continuum of Goods," *American Economic Review* 67 (December 1977), pp. 823–39.

8. B. Balassa, "An Empirical Demonstration of Classic Comparative Cost Theory," *Review of Economics and Statistics*, 1963, pp. 231–38.

9. See P. R. Krugman, "Is Free Trade Passé?" *Journal of Economic Perspectives* 1 (Fall 1987), pp. 131–44.

10. P. Samuelson, "Where Ricardo and Mill Rebut and Confirm Arguments of Mainstream Economists Supporting Globalization," *Journal of Economic Perspectives* 18, no. 3 (Summer 2004), pp. 135–46.

11. P. Samuelson, "The Gains from International Trade Once Again," *Economic Journal* 72 (1962), pp. 820–29.

12. S. Lohr, "An Elder Challenges Outsourcing's Orthodoxy," *The New York Times*, September 9, 2004, p. C1.

13. Samuelson, "Where Ricardo and Mill Rebut and Confirm Arguments of Mainstream Economists Supporting Globalization," p. 143.

14. See A. Dixit and G. Grossman, "Samuelson Says Nothing about Trade Policy," Princeton University, 2004, accessed from www.princeton.edu/~dixitak/home/.

15. J. Bhagwati, A. Panagariya and T. N. Sirinivasan, "The Muddles over Outsourcing," *Journal of Economic Perspectives* 18, no. 4 (Fall 2004), pp. 93–114.

16. For example, J. D. Sachs and A. Warner, "Economic Reform and the Process of Global Integration," *Brookings Papers on Economic Activity*, 1995, pp. 1–96; J. A. Frankel and D. Romer, "Does Trade Cause Growth?" *American Economic Review* 89, no. 3 (June 1999), pp. 379–99; and D. Dollar and A. Kraay, "Trade, Growth and Poverty," Working Paper, Development Research Group, World Bank, June 2001. Also, for an accessible discussion of the relationship between free trade and economic growth, see T. Taylor, "The Truth about Globalization," *Public Interest*, Spring 2002, pp. 24–44.

17. Sachs and Warner, "Economic Reform and the Process of Global Integration."

18. Ibid., pp. 35–36.

19. R. Wacziarg and K. H. Welch, "Trade Liberalization and Growth: New Evidence," *NBER Working Paper Series*, Working Paper No. 10152, December 2003.

20. Frankel and Romer, "Does Trade Cause Growth?"

21. A recent skeptical review of the empirical work on the relationship between trade and growth questions these results. See Francisco Rodriguez and Dani Rodrik, "Trade Policy and Economic Growth: A Skeptic's Guide to the Cross-National Evidence," *National Bureau of Economic Research*, Working Paper No. 7081, April 1999. Even these authors, however, cannot find any evidence that trade hurts economic growth or income levels.

22. B. Ohlin, *Interregional and International Trade* (Cambridge: Harvard University Press, 1933). For a summary, see R. W. Jones and J. P. Neary, "The Positive Theory of International Trade," in *Handbook of International Economics*, R. W. Jones and P. B. Kenen, eds. (Amsterdam: North Holland, 1984).

23. W. Leontief, "Domestic Production and Foreign Trade: The American Capital Position Re-Examined," *Proceedings of the American Philosophical Society* 97 (1953), pp. 331–49.

24. R. M. Stern and K. Maskus, "Determinants of the Structure of U.S. Foreign Trade," *Journal of International Economics* 11 (1981), pp. 207–44.

25. See H. P. Bowen, E. E. Leamer, and L. Sveikayskas, "Multicountry, Multifactor Tests of the Factor Abundance Theory," *American Economic Review* 77 (1987), pp. 791–809.

26. D. Trefler, "The Case of the Missing Trade and Other Mysteries," *American Economic Review* 85 (December 1995), pp. 1029–46.

27. D. R. Davis and D. E. Weinstein, "An Account of Global Factor Trade," *American Economic Review*, December 2001, pp. 1423–52.

28. R. Vernon, "International Investments and International Trade in the Product Life Cycle," *Quarterly Journal of Economics*, May 1966, pp. 190–207, and R. Vernon and L. T. Wells, *The Economic Environment of International Business*, 4th ed. (Englewood Cliffs, NJ: Prentice Hall, 1986).

29. M. B. Lieberman and D. B. Montgomery, "First-Mover Advantages," *Strategic Management Journal* 9 (Summer 1988), pp. 41–58, and W. T. Robinson and Sungwook Min, "Is the First to Market the First to Fail?" *Journal of Marketing Research* 29 (2002), pp. 120–28.

30. J. R. Tybout, "Plant and Firm Level Evidence on New Trade Theories," *National Bureau of Economic Research*, Working Paper Series No. 8418, August 2001. Paper available at www.nber.org. And S. Deraniyagala and B. Fine, "New Trade Theory versus Old Trade Policy: A Continuing Enigma." *Cambridge Journal of Economics*, November 2001, pp. 809–25.

31. A. D. Chandler, *Scale and Scope* (New York: Free Press, 1990).

32. Krugman, "Does the New Trade Theory Require a New Trade Policy?"

33. M. E. Porter, *The Competitive Advantage of Nations* (New York: Free Press, 1990). For a good review of this book, see R. M. Grant, "Porter's Competitive Advantage of Nations: An Assessment," *Strategic Management Journal* 12 (1991), pp. 535–48.

34. B. Kogut, ed., *Country Competitiveness: Technology and the Organizing of Work* (New York: Oxford University Press, 1993).

35. Porter, *The Competitive Advantage of Nations*, p. 121.

36. Lieberman and Montgomery, "First-Mover Advantages." See also Robinson and Min, "Is the First to Market the First to Fail?"; W. Boulding and M. Christen, "First Mover Disadvantage," *Harvard Business Review,* October 2001, pp. 20–21; and R. Agarwal and M. Gort, "First Mover Advantage and the Speed of Competitive Entry," *Journal of Law and Economics* 44 (2001), pp. 131–59.

37. C. A. Hamilton, "Building Better Machine Tools," *Journal of Commerce,* October 30, 1991, p. 8, and "Manufacturing Trouble," *The Economist,* October 12, 1991, p. 71.

6

The Political Economy of International Trade

Trade in Textiles—The Chinese Juggernaut

Since 1974, international trade in textiles has been governed by a system of quotas known as the Multi-Fiber Agreement (MFA). Designed to protect textile producers in developed nations from foreign competition, the MFA assigned countries quotas that specified the amount of textiles they could export. The quotas restrained textile exports from some countries, such as China, but in other cases created a textile industry that might not have existed. Countries such as Bangladesh, Sri Lanka, and Cambodia were able to take advantage of favorable quota allocations to build significant textile industries that generated substantial exports. In 2003, textiles accounted for more than 70 percent of exports from Bangladesh and Cambodia and 50 percent of those from Sri Lanka.

This is now changing. When the World Trade Organization was created in 1995, member countries agreed to let the MFA expire on December 31, 2004. At the time, many textile exporters in the developing world expected to gain from the elimination of the quota system. What they did not anticipate, however, was that China would join the WTO in 2001 and that Chinese textile exports would surge. By 2003, China was making 17 percent of the world's textiles, but this may only be a start. The WTO forecasts that China's share may rise to 50 percent by 2007 as the country's producers take advantage of the removal of quotas to expand their exports to the United States and European Union, displacing exports from many other developing nations. China's gains are due to its comparative advantage in the manufacture of textiles. Not only does the country benefit from low wages and a productive labor force, but China's huge factories also enable its producers to attain economies of scale unimaginable in most developing nations. Also, the country's good infrastructure ensures quick transport of products and a timely turnaround of ships at ports, a critical asset in the clothing industry where fashion trends can result in rapid changes in demand. Chinese producers have been able to reduce the order-to-shipment cycle to as low as 60 days, far below the 90 to 120 days achieved by many other producers in the developing world. In addition, Chinese textile producers have garnered a reputation for reliably delivering on commitments, unlike those in some other countries. Producers in Bangladesh, for example, have a reputation for low quality and poor delivery that offsets their low prices.

Fearful that they will lose market share to China, trade associations from more than 50 other textile-producing nations, many of them low- and middle-income nations, signed the "Istanbul declaration" in 2004 asking the WTO to delay the removal of quotas, but to no avail. Many developing nations now fear that they will lose substantial market share to China. This could conceivably cripple the economies of countries such as Bangladesh, where some 2 million people, most of them women, are employed in the textile industry. Other developing nations, however, think that they might benefit from the removal of the MFA. They believe that buyers in developed nations will need to diversify their supply base as a hedge against disruption in China. Among this second group are Vietnam, India, and Pakistan, all of whom expect rising textile exports after 2004. The Indian textile manufacturers group expects Indian textile exports to grow by 18 percent a year after 2004, reaching $40 billion in 2010, or one-third of the country's exports.

In developing nations, too, the prospect of surging imports from China causes unease. In the United States, textile producers lobbied the government to impose quotas on Chinese imports after the MFA expired. Under the terms of China's entry into the WTO, the United States and other major trading nations reserved the right until 2008 to impose annual quotas on Chinese textile imports if they are deemed to be "disruptive."

China tried to head off protectionist pressures in December 2004 by announcing it would impose a tariff on textile exports. By raising the costs of Chinese textiles, the tariff was designed to reduce overseas demand. However, the tariffs are modest, ranging from 2.4 to 6 cents per item, with most at the low end of the range. Many observers see them as little more than a token gesture.

The first three months of 2005 provided a glimpse of what may be to come. Imports of Chinese textiles into the United States surged 62 percent compared with the same period in 2004. Chinese textile imports into the EU also rose. The increase in imports resulted in renewed calls in the United States for quotas on Chinese textile imports. However, others noted that total textile imports into the United States remained flat, and that the surge represented a shift from other producers to China, rather than an absolute increase in the volume of imports. Even so, in April 2005 the U.S. Department of Commerce announced it was investigating the need to reimpose trade quotas on China. Similar moves are expected in the EU. Meanwhile, Chinese producers complained that just the threat of reintroducing quotas has led buyers to start switching orders from China to producers elsewhere.

Sources: "The Looming Revolution—The Textile Industry," *The Economist,* November 13, 2004, pp. 92–96; "A New Knot in Textile Trade," *The Economist,* December 18, 2004, p. 138; "Textile Disruption," *The Wall Street Journal,* April 11, 2005, p. A21; and M. Fong and W. Echikson, "China Bristles at U.S. Inquiry on Textiles Trade," *The Wall Street Journal,* April 6, 2005, p. A9.

Introduction

Our review of the classical trade theories of Smith, Ricardo, and Heckscher-Ohlin in Chapter 5 showed us that in a world without trade barriers, trade patterns are determined by the relative productivity of different factors of production in different countries. Countries will specialize in products that they can make most efficiently, while importing products that they can produce less efficiently. Chapter 5 also laid out the intellectual case for free trade. Remember, **free trade** refers to a situation where a government does not attempt to restrict what its citizens can buy from another country or what they can sell to another country. As we saw in Chapter 5, the theories of Smith, Ricardo, and Heckscher-Ohlin predict that the consequences of free trade include both static economic gains (because free trade supports a higher level of domestic consumption and more efficient utilization of resources) and dynamic economic gains (because free trade stimulates economic growth and the creation of wealth).

In this chapter, we look at the political reality of international trade. While many nations are nominally committed to free trade, they tend to intervene in international trade to protect the interests of politically important groups. The opening case illustrates the nature of such political realities. To protect jobs in the textile industries of developed nations, for three decades international trade in textiles was governed by the Multi-Fiber Agreement (MFA). The MFA "managed" international trade by allocating production quotas to different nations. The formal end of the MFA in December 2004 implies that production should now migrate toward the most efficient producers, many of which happen to be located in China. In theory, this should result in reduced prices for consumers. The losers are the less efficient producers, both in the developed world and in other developing nations. As the opening case explains, now confronted by the possibility that the Chinese juggernaut will gain share in the global textile market, textile producers in many other nations are lobbying their respective governments for protection. In return for their support of China's entry into the World Trade Organization in 2001, major trading nations including the United States and the EU reserved the right until 2008 to reimpose quotas on textile imports from China. In light of surging Chinese textile imports in early 2005, it now seems likely that some renewed protection will occur. If so, the prices of textile products will be higher than would otherwise have been the case and relatively inefficient producers will continue in business.

In this chapter, we explore the political and economic reasons that governments have for intervening in international trade. When governments intervene, they often do so by restricting imports of goods and services into their nation, while adopting policies that promote exports. Normally their motives are to protect domestic producers and jobs from foreign competition while increasing the foreign market for products of domestic producers. However, in recent years, "social" issues have intruded into the decision-making calculus. In the United States, for example, a movement is growing to ban imports of goods from countries that do not abide by the same labor, health, and environmental regulations as the United States.

We start this chapter by describing the range of policy instruments that governments use to intervene in international trade. This is followed by a detailed review of the various political and economic motives that governments have for intervention. In the third section of this chapter, we consider how the case for free trade stands up in view of the various justifications given for government intervention in international trade. Then we look at the emergence of the modern international trading system, which is based on the General Agreement on Tariffs and Trade (GATT) and its successor, the WTO. The GATT and WTO are the creations of a series of multinational treaties. The most recent was completed in 1995, involved more than 120 countries, and resulted in the creation of the WTO. The purpose of these treaties has been to lower barriers to the free flow of goods and services between nations. Like the GATT before it, the WTO promotes free trade by limiting the ability of national governments to adopt policies that restrict imports into their nations. In the final section of this chapter, we discuss the implications of this material for business practice.

Instruments of Trade Policy

Trade policy uses seven main instruments: tariffs, subsidies, import quotas, voluntary export restraints, local content requirements, administrative policies, and antidumping duties. Tariffs are the oldest and simplest instrument of trade policy. As we shall see later in this chapter, they are also the instrument that the GATT and WTO have been most successful in limiting. A fall in tariff barriers in recent decades has been accompanied by a rise in nontariff barriers, such as subsidies, quotas, voluntary export restraints, and antidumping duties.

TARIFFS

A **tariff** is a tax levied on imports (or exports). Tariffs fall into two categories. **Specific tariffs** are levied as a fixed charge for each unit of a good imported (for example, $3 per barrel of oil). **Ad valorem tariffs** are levied as a proportion of the value of the imported good. In most cases, tariffs are placed on imports to protect domestic producers from foreign competition by raising the price of imported goods. However, tariffs also produce revenue for the government. Until the income tax was introduced, for example, the U.S. government received most of its revenues from tariffs.

The important thing to understand about an import tariff is who suffers and who gains. The government gains, because the tariff increases government revenues. Domestic producers gain, because the tariff affords them some protection against foreign competitors by increasing the cost of imported foreign goods. Consumers lose because they must pay more for certain imports. For example, in March 2002 the U.S. government placed an ad valorem tariff of 8 percent to 30 percent on imports of foreign steel. The idea was to protect domestic steel producers from cheap imports of foreign steel. The effect, however, was to raise the price of steel products in the United States by between 30 percent and 50 percent. A number of U.S. steel consumers, ranging from appliance makers to automobile companies, objected that the steel tariffs would raise their costs of production and make it more difficult for them to compete in the global marketplace. Whether the gains to the government and domestic producers exceed the loss to consumers depends on various factors such as the amount of the tariff, the importance of the imported good to domestic consumers, the number of jobs saved in the protected industry, and so on. In the steel case, many argued that the losses to steel consumers apparently outweighed the gains to steel producers. (In November 2003 the World Trade Organization declared that the tariffs represented a violation of the WTO treaty, and the United States removed them in December of that year).

In general, two conclusions can be derived from economic analysis of the effect of import tariffs.[1] First, tariffs are unambiguously pro-producer and anti-consumer. While they protect producers from foreign competitors, this restriction of supply also raises domestic prices. For example, a study by Japanese economists calculated that tariffs on imports of foodstuffs, cosmetics, and chemicals into Japan in 1989 cost the average Japanese consumer about $890 per year in the form of higher prices.[2] Almost all studies find that import tariffs impose significant costs on domestic consumers in the form of higher prices.[3]

Second, import tariffs reduce the overall efficiency of the world economy. They reduce efficiency because a protective tariff encourages domestic firms to produce products at home that, in theory, could be produced more efficiently abroad. The consequence is an inefficient utilization of resources. For example, tariffs on the importation of rice into South Korea have caused the land of South Korean rice farmers to be used in an unproductive manner. It would make more sense for the South Koreans to purchase their rice from lower-cost foreign producers and to utilize the land now employed in rice production in some other way, such as growing foodstuffs that cannot be produced more efficiently elsewhere or for residential and industrial purposes.

Sometimes tariffs are levied on exports of a product from a country. Export tariffs are far less common than import tariffs. In general, export tariffs have two objectives; first, to raise revenue for the government, and second, to reduce exports from a sector, often for political reasons. We saw an example in the opening case, where China imposed a tariff on textile exports. The primary objective was to moderate the growth in exports of textiles from China, thereby alleviating tensions with other trading partners.

SUBSIDIES

A **subsidy** is a government payment to a domestic producer. Subsidies take many forms including cash grants, low-interest loans, tax breaks, and government equity participation in domestic firms. By lowering production costs, subsidies help domestic producers in two ways: (1) competing against foreign imports, and (2) gaining export markets.

Agriculture tends to be one of the largest beneficiaries of subsidies in most countries. In 2002, the European Union was paying $43 billion annually in farm subsidies. Not to be outdone, in May 2002 President George W. Bush signed into law a bill that contained subsidies of more than $180 billion for U.S. farmers spread out over 10 years. The Japanese have a long history of supporting inefficient domestic producers with farm subsidies. The accompanying Country Focus looks at subsidies to wheat producers in Japan.

Nonagricultural subsidies are much lower, but they are still significant. For example, subsidies historically were given to Boeing and Airbus to help them lower the cost of developing new commercial jet aircraft. In Boeing's case, subsides came in the form of tax credits for R&D spending or Pentagon money that was used to develop military technology, which then was transferred to civil aviation projects. In the case of Airbus, subsidies took the form of EU loans at below-market interest rates.

The main gains from subsidies accrue to domestic producers, whose international competitiveness is increased as a result. Advocates of strategic trade policy (which, as you will recall from Chapter 5, is an outgrowth of the new trade theory) favor subsidies to help domestic firms achieve a dominant position in those industries where economies of scale are important and the world market is not large enough to profitably support more than a few firms (e.g., aerospace, semiconductors). According to this argument, subsidies can help a firm achieve a first-mover advantage in an emerging industry (just as U.S. government subsidies, in the form of substantial R&D grants, allegedly helped Boeing). If this is achieved, further gains to the domestic economy arise from the employment and tax revenues that a major global company can generate. However, subsidies must be paid for. Governments typically pay for subsidies by taxing individuals.

Whether subsidies generate national benefits that exceed their national costs is debatable. In practice, many subsidies are not that successful at increasing the international competitiveness of domestic producers. Rather, they tend to protect the inefficient and promote excess production. For example, agricultural subsidies (1) allow inefficient farmers to stay in business, (2) encourage countries to overproduce heavily subsidized agricultural products, (3) encourage countries to produce products that could be grown more cheaply elsewhere and imported, and, therefore, (4) reduce international trade in agricultural products. One study estimated that if advanced countries abandoned subsidies to farmers, global trade in agricultural products would be 50 percent higher and the world as a whole would be better off by $160 billion.[4] This increase in wealth arises from the more efficient use of agricultural land. For a specific example, see the Country Focus on wheat subsidies in Japan.

IMPORT QUOTAS AND VOLUNTARY EXPORT RESTRAINTS

An **import quota** is a direct restriction on the quantity of some good that may be imported into a country. The restriction is usually enforced by issuing import licenses to a group of individuals or firms. For example, the United States has a quota on cheese

COUNTRY FOCUS Japan is not a particularly good environment for growing wheat. Wheat produced on large fields in the dry climates of North America, Australia, and Argentina is far cheaper and of much higher quality than anything produced in Japan. Indeed, Japan imports some 80 percent of its wheat from foreign producers. Yet tens of thousands of farmers in Japan still grow wheat, usually on small fields where yields are low and costs high, and production is rising. The reason is government subsidies designed to keep inefficient Japanese wheat producers in business. In 2004, Japanese farmers were selling their output at market prices, which were running at $9 per bushel, but they received an average of at least $35 per bushel for their 2004 production! The difference—$26 a bushel—was government subsidies paid to producers. The estimated costs of these subsidies were more than $700 million in 2004.

To finance its production subsidy, Japan operates a tariff rate quota on wheat imports in which a higher tariff rate is imposed once wheat imports exceed the quota level. The in-quota rate tariff is zero, while the over-quota tariff rate for wheat is $500 a ton. The tariff raises the cost so much that it deters over-quota imports, essentially restricting supply and raising the price for wheat inside Japan. The Japanese Ministry of Agriculture, Forestry and Fisheries (MAFF) has the sole right to purchase wheat imports within the quota (and since there are very few over-quota imports, the MAFF is a monopoly buyer on wheat imports into Japan). The MAFF buys wheat at world prices, then resells it to millers in Japan at the artificially high prices that arise due to the restriction on supply engineered by the tariff rate quota. Estimates suggest that in 2003, the world market price for wheat was $5.96 per bushel, but within Japan the average price for imported wheat was $10.23 a bushel. The markup of $4.27 a bushel yielded the MAFF in excess of $450 million in profit. This "profit" was then used to help cover the $700 million cost of subsidies to inefficient wheat farmers, with the rest of the funds coming from general government tax revenues.

Thanks to these policies, the price of wheat in Japan can be anything from 80 to 120 percent higher than the world price, and Japanese wheat production, which exceeded 850,000 tons in 2004, is significantly greater than it would be if a free market was allowed to operate. Indeed, under free market conditions, there would be virtually no wheat production in Japan since the costs of production are simply too high. The beneficiaries of this policy are the thousands of small farmers in Japan who grow wheat. The losers include Japanese consumers, who must pay more for products containing wheat and who must finance wheat subsidies through taxes, and foreign producers, who are denied access to a chunk of the Japanese market by the over-quota tariff rate. Why then does the Japanese government continue to pursue this policy? It continues because small farmers are an important constituency and Japanese politicians want their votes.

Sources: J. Dyck and H. Fukuda, "Taxes on Imports Subsidize Wheat Production in Japan," *Amber Waves*, February 2005, p. 2, and H. Fukuda, J. Dyck, and J. Stout, "Wheat and Barley Policies in Japan," *United States Department of Agriculture Research Report*, WHS-04i-01, November 2004.

www.mhhe.com/hill

imports. The only firms allowed to import cheese are certain trading companies, each of which is allocated the right to import a maximum number of pounds of cheese each year. In some cases, the right to sell is given directly to the governments of exporting countries. Historically this is the case for sugar and textile imports in the United States. As discussed in the opening case, however, the international agreement governing the imposition of import quotas on textiles, the Multi-Fiber Agreement, expired in December 2004.

A common hybrid of a quota and a tariff is known as a tariff rate quota. Under a **tariff rate quota,** a lower tariff rate is applied to imports within the quota than those over the quota. For example, as illustrated in Figure 6.1, an *ad valorem* tariff rate of 10 percent might be levied on rice imports into South Korea of 1 million tons, after which an out-of-quota rate of 80 percent might be applied. Thus, South Korea might import 2 million tons of rice, 1 million at a 10 percent tariff rate and another 1 million at an 80 percent tariff. Tariff rate quotas are very common in agriculture, where

FIGURE 6.1

Hypothetical Tariff Rate
Quote

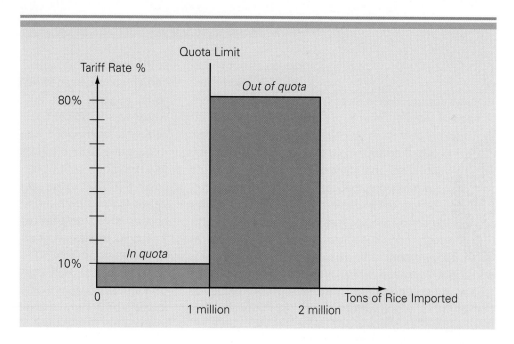

their goal is to limit imports over quota. An example is given in the Country Focus that looks at how Japan uses the combination of a tariff rate quota and subsidies to protect inefficient Japanese wheat farmers from foreign competition.

A variant on the import quota is the voluntary export restraint. A **voluntary export restraint (VER)** is a quota on trade imposed by the exporting country, typically at the request of the importing country's government. One of the most famous examples is the limitation on auto exports to the United States enforced by Japanese automobile producers in 1981. A response to direct pressure from the U.S. government, this VER limited Japanese imports to no more than 1.68 million vehicles per year. The agreement was revised in 1984 to allow 1.85 million Japanese vehicles per year. The agreement was allowed to lapse in 1985, but the Japanese government indicated its intentions at that time to continue to restrict exports to the United States to 1.85 million vehicles per year.[5]

Foreign producers agree to VERs because they fear more damaging punitive tariffs or import quotas might follow if they do not. Agreeing to a VER is seen as a way to make the best of a bad situation by appeasing protectionist pressures in a country.

As with tariffs and subsidies, both import quotas and VERs benefit domestic producers by limiting import competition. As with all restrictions on trade, quotas do not benefit consumers. An import quota or VER always raises the domestic price of an imported good. When imports are limited to a low percentage of the market by a quota or VER, the price is bid up for that limited foreign supply. In the case of the automobile industry, for example, the VER increased the price of the limited supply of Japanese imports. According to a study by the U.S. Federal Trade Commission, the automobile industry VER cost U.S. consumers about $1 billion per year between 1981 and 1985. That $1 billion per year went to Japanese producers in the form of higher prices.[6] The extra profit that producers make when supply is artificially limited by an import quota is referred to as a **quota rent.**

If a domestic industry lacks the capacity to meet demand, an import quota can raise prices for *both* the domestically produced and the imported good. This happened in the U.S. sugar industry, where a tariff rate quota system has long limited the amount foreign producers can sell in the U.S. market. According to one study, as a result of import quotas the price of sugar in the United States has been as much as 40 percent greater than the world price.[7] These higher prices have translated into greater profits for U.S. sugar producers, which have lobbied politicians to keep the lucrative agreement. They argue U.S. jobs in the sugar industry will be lost to foreign producers if the quota system is scrapped.

LOCAL CONTENT REQUIREMENTS

A **local content requirement** is a requirement that some specific fraction of a good be produced domestically. The requirement can be expressed either in physical terms (e.g., 75 percent of component parts for this product must be produced locally) or in value terms (e.g., 75 percent of the value of this product must be produced locally). Local content regulations have been widely used by developing countries to shift their manufacturing base from the simple assembly of products whose parts are manufactured elsewhere into the local manufacture of component parts. They have also been used in developed countries to try to protect local jobs and industry from foreign competition. For example, a little-known law in the United States, the Buy America Act, specifies that government agencies must give preference to American products when putting contracts for equipment out to bid unless the foreign products have a significant price advantage. The law specifies a product as "American" if 51 percent of the materials by value are produced domestically. This amounts to a local content requirement. If a foreign company, or an American one for that matter, wishes to win a contract from a U.S. government agency to provide some equipment, it must ensure that at least 51 percent of the product by value is manufactured in the United States.

Local content regulations provide protection for a domestic producer of parts in the same way an import quota does: by limiting foreign competition. The aggregate economic effects are also the same; domestic producers benefit, but the restrictions on imports raise the prices of imported components. In turn, higher prices for imported components are passed on to consumers of the final product in the form of higher final prices. So as with all trade policies, local content regulations tend to benefit producers and not consumers.

ADMINISTRATIVE POLICIES

In addition to the formal instruments of trade policy, governments of all types sometimes use informal or administrative policies to restrict imports and boost exports. **Administrative trade policies** are bureaucratic rules designed to make it difficult for imports to enter a country. Some would argue that the Japanese are the masters of this trade barrier. In recent years, Japan's formal tariff and nontariff barriers have been among the lowest in the world. However, critics charge that the country's informal administrative barriers to imports more than compensate for this. For example, the Netherlands exports tulip bulbs to almost every country in the world except Japan. In Japan, customs inspectors insist on checking every tulip bulb by cutting it vertically down the middle, and even Japanese ingenuity cannot put them back together. Federal Express has had a tough time expanding its global express shipping services into Japan because Japanese customs inspectors insist on opening a large proportion of express packages to check for pornography, a process that can delay an "express" package for days. Japan is not the only country that engages in such policies. France required that all imported videotape recorders arrive through a small customs entry point that was both remote and poorly staffed. The resulting delays kept Japanese VCRs out of the French market until a VER agreement was negotiated.[8] As with all instruments of trade policy, administrative instruments benefit producers and hurt consumers, who are denied access to possibly superior foreign products.

ANTIDUMPING POLICIES

In the context of international trade, **dumping** is variously defined as selling goods in a foreign market at below their costs of production, or as selling goods in a foreign market at below their "fair" market value. There is a difference between these two definitions; the "fair" market value of a good is normally judged to be greater than the costs of producing that good because the former includes a "fair" profit margin. Dumping is viewed as a method by which firms unload excess production in foreign markets. Some dumping may be the result of predatory behavior, with producers using substantial profits from their home markets to subsidize prices in a foreign market with a view to driving indigenous competitors out of that market. Once this has been achieved, so the argument goes, the predatory firm can raise prices and earn substantial profits.

An alleged example of dumping occurred in 1997, when two South Korean manufacturers of semiconductors, LG Semicon and Hyundai Electronics, were accused of selling dynamic random access memory chips (DRAMs) in the U.S. market at below their costs of production. This action occurred in the middle of a worldwide glut of chip-making capacity. It was alleged that the firms were trying to unload their excess production in the United States.

Antidumping policies are designed to punish foreign firms that engage in dumping. The ultimate objective is to protect domestic producers from "unfair" foreign competition. Although antidumping policies vary somewhat from country to country, the majority are similar to the policies used in the United States. If a domestic producer believes that a foreign firm is dumping production in the U.S. market, it can file a petition with two government agencies, the Commerce Department and the International Trade Commission. In the Korean DRAM case, Micron Technology, a U.S. manufacturer of DRAMs, filed the petition. The government agencies then investigate the complaint. If a complaint has merit, the Commerce Department may impose an antidumping duty on the offending foreign imports (antidumping duties are often called **countervailing duties**). These duties, which represent a special tariff, can be fairly substantial and stay in place for up to five years. For example, after reviewing Micron's complaint, the Commerce Department imposed 9 percent and 4 percent countervailing duties on LG Semicon and Hyundai DRAM chips, respectively. Another example of a firm using antidumping legislation to gain protection from unfair foreign competitors is discussed in the accompanying Management Focus, which looks at how U.S. Magnesium has gained protection from foreign producers.

The Case for Government Intervention

Now that we have reviewed the various instruments of trade policy that governments can use, it is time to look at the case for government intervention in international trade. Arguments for government intervention take two paths—political and economic. Political arguments for intervention are concerned with protecting the interests of certain groups within a nation (normally producers), often at the expense of other groups (normally consumers). Economic arguments for intervention are typically concerned with boosting the overall wealth of a nation (to the benefit of all, both producers and consumers).

POLITICAL ARGUMENTS FOR INTERVENTION

Political arguments for government intervention cover a range of issues including preserving jobs, protecting industries deemed important for national security, retaliating against unfair foreign competition, protecting consumers from "dangerous" products, furthering the goals of foreign policy, and advancing the human rights of individuals in exporting countries.

Protecting Jobs and Industries

Perhaps the most common political argument for government intervention is that it is necessary for protecting jobs and industries from "unfair" foreign competition. The tariffs placed on imports of foreign steel by President George W. Bush in March 2002 were designed to do this. (Many steel producers were located in states that Bush needed to win reelection in 2004.) A political motive also underlay establishment of the Common Agricultural Policy (CAP) by the European Union. The CAP was designed to protect the jobs of Europe's politically powerful farmers by restricting imports and guaranteeing prices.

MANAGEMENT FOCUS

In February 2004, U.S. Magnesium, the sole surviving U.S. producer of magnesium, a metal that is primarily used in the manufacture of certain automobile parts and aluminum cans, filed a petition with the U.S. International Trade Commission (ITC) contending that a surge in imports had caused material damage to the U.S. industry's employment, sales, market share, and profitability. According to U.S. Magnesium, Russian and Chinese producers had been selling the metal at prices significantly below market value. During 2002 and 2003, imports of magnesium into the United States rose 70 percent, while prices fell by 40 percent and the market share accounted for by imports jumped to 50 percent from 25 percent.

"The United States used to be the largest producer of magnesium in the world," a U.S. Magnesium spokesman said at the time of the filing. "What's really sad is that you can be state of the art and have modern technology, and if the Chinese, who pay people less than 90 cents an hour, want to run you out of business, they can do it. And that's why we are seeking relief."

During a yearlong investigation the ITC solicited input from various sides in the dispute. Foreign producers and consumers of magnesium in the United States argued that falling prices for magnesium during 2002 and 2003 simply reflected an imbalance between supply and demand due to additional capacity coming on stream not from Russia or China, but from a new Canadian plant that opened in 2001 and from a planned Australian plant. The Canadian plant shut down in 2003, the Australian plant never came on stream, and prices for magnesium rose again in 2004.

Magnesium consumers in the United States also argued to the ITC that imposing antidumping duties on foreign imports of magnesium would raise prices in the United States significantly above world levels. A spokesman for Alcoa, which mixes magnesium with aluminum to make alloys for cans, predicted that if antidumping duties were imposed, high magnesium prices in the United States would force Alcoa to move some production out of the United States. Alcoa also noted that in 2003, U.S. Magnesium was unable to supply all of Alcoa's needs, forcing the company to turn to imports. Consumers of magnesium in the automobile industry asserted that high prices in the United States would drive engineers to design magnesium out of automobiles, or force manufacturing elsewhere, which would ultimately hurt everyone.

The six members of the ITC were not convinced by these arguments. In March 2005, the ITC ruled that both China and Russia had been dumping magnesium in the United States. The government decided to impose duties ranging from 50 percent to more than 140 percent on imports of magnesium from China. Russian producers face duties ranging from 19 percent to 22 percent. The duties will be levied for five years, after which the ITC will revisit the situation.

According to U.S. Magnesium, the favorable ruling will now allow the company to reap the benefits of nearly $50 million in investments made in its manufacturing plant during the last few years and enable the company to boost its capacity by 28 percent by the end of 2005. Commenting on the favorable ruling, a U.S. Magnesium spokesman noted, "Once unfair trade is removed from the marketplace we'll be able to compete with anyone." U.S. Magnesium's customers and competitors, however, did not view the situation in 2002–2003 as one of unfair trade. While the imposition of antidumping duties no doubt will help to protect U.S. Magnesium and the 400 people it employs from foreign competition, magnesium consumers in the United States are left wondering if they will be the ultimate losers.

Sources: D. Anderton, "US Magnesium Lands Ruling on Unfair Imports," *Desert News*, October 1, 2004, p. D10; "US Magnesium and Its Largest Consumers Debate before US ITC," *Platt's Metals Week*, February 28, 2005, p. 2; and S. Oberbeck, "U.S. Magnesium Plans Big Utah Production Expansion," *Salt Lake Tribune*, March 30, 2005.

www.mhhe.com/hill

However, the higher prices that resulted from the CAP have cost Europe's consumers dearly. This is true of most attempts to protect jobs and industries through government intervention. For example, the imposition of steel tariffs in 2002 raised steel prices for American consumers, such as automobile companies, making them less competitive in the global marketplace.

National Security

Countries sometimes argue that it is necessary to protect certain industries because they are important for national security. Defense-related industries often get this kind of attention (e.g., aerospace, advanced electronics, semiconductors, etc.). Although not as common as it used to be, this argument is still made. Those in favor of protecting the U.S. semiconductor industry from foreign competition, for example, argue that semiconductors are now such important components of defense products that it would be dangerous to rely primarily on foreign producers for them. In 1986, this argument helped persuade the federal government to support Sematech, a consortium of 14 U.S. semiconductor companies that accounted for 90 percent of the U.S. industry's revenues. Sematech's mission was to conduct joint research into manufacturing techniques that can be parceled out to members. The government saw the venture as so critical that Sematech was specially protected from antitrust laws. Initially, the U.S. government provided Sematech with $100 million per year in subsidies. By the mid-1990s, however, the U.S. semiconductor industry had regained its leading market position, largely through the personal computer boom and demand for microprocessor chips made by Intel. In 1994, the consortium's board voted to seek an end to federal funding, and since 1996 the consortium has been funded entirely by private money.[9]

Retaliation

Some argue that governments should use the threat to intervene in trade policy as a bargaining tool to help open foreign markets and force trading partners to "play by the rules of the game." The U.S. government has used the threat of punitive trade sanctions to try to get the Chinese government to enforce its intellectual property laws. Lax enforcement of these laws had given rise to massive copyright infringements in China that had been costing U.S. companies such as Microsoft hundreds of millions of dollars per year in lost sales revenues. After the United States threatened to impose 100 percent tariffs on a range of Chinese imports, and after harsh words between officials from the two countries, the Chinese agreed to tighter enforcement of intellectual property regulations.[10]

If it works, such a politically motivated rationale for government intervention may liberalize trade and bring with it resulting economic gains. It is a risky strategy, however. A country that is being pressured may not back down and instead may respond to the imposition of punitive tariffs by raising trade barriers of its own. This is exactly what the Chinese government threatened to do when pressured by the United States, although it ultimately did back down. If a government does not back down, however, the results could be higher trade barriers all around and an economic loss to all involved.

Protecting Consumers

Many governments have long had regulations to protect consumers from "unsafe" products. The indirect effect of such regulations often is to limit or ban the importation of such products. In 1998, the U.S. government decided to permanently ban imports of 58 types of military-style assault weapons. (The United States already prohibited the sale of such weapons in the United States by U.S.-based firms.) The ban was motivated by a desire to increase public safety. It followed on the heels of a rash of random and deadly shootings by deranged individuals using such weapons, including one in President Clinton's home state of Arkansas that left four children and a schoolteacher dead.[11]

The accompanying Country Focus describes how the European Union banned the sale and importation of hormone-treated beef. The ban was motivated by a desire to protect European consumers from the possible health consequences of eating meat from animals treated with growth hormones. The conflict over the importation of hormone-treated beef into the European Union may prove to be a taste of things to come. In addition to the use of hormones to promote animal growth and meat production, biotechnology has made it possible to genetically alter many crops so that they resist common herbicides, produce proteins that are natural insecticides, grow dramatically improved yields, or withstand inclement weather conditions. A new breed of genetically modified tomatoes has an antifreeze gene inserted into its genome and can thus be grown in colder climates than hitherto possible. Another example is a genetically engineered cotton seed produced by Monsanto. The seed has been engineered to express a protein that protects against three common insect pests: the cotton bollworm, tobacco budworm, and pink bollworm. Use of this seed reduces or eliminates the need for traditional pesticide applications for these pests.

As enticing as such innovations sound, they have met with intense resistance from consumer groups, particularly in Europe. The fear is that the widespread use of genetically altered seed corn could have unanticipated and harmful effects on human health and may result in "genetic pollution." (An example of genetic pollution would be when the widespread use of crops that produce "natural pesticides" stimulates the evolution of "superbugs" that are resistant to those pesticides.) Such concerns have led Austria and Luxembourg to outlaw the importation, sale, or use of genetically altered organisms. Sentiment against genetically altered organisms also runs strong in several other European countries, most notably Germany and Switzerland. It seems likely, therefore, that the World Trade Organization will be drawn into the conflict between those that want to expand the global market for genetically altered organisms, such as Monsanto, and those that want to limit it, such as Austria and Luxembourg.[12]

Furthering Foreign Policy Objectives

Governments sometimes use trade policy to support their foreign policy objectives.[13] A government may grant preferential trade terms to a country it wants to build strong relations with. Trade policy has also been used several times to pressure or punish "rogue states" that do not abide by international law or norms. Iraq labored under extensive trade sanctions after the UN coalition defeated the country in the 1991 Gulf War until the 2003 invasion of Iraq by U.S.-led forces. The theory is that such pressure might persuade the "rogue state" to mend its ways or it might hasten a change of government. In the case of Iraq, the sanctions were seen as a way of forcing that country to comply with several UN resolutions. The United States has maintained long-running trade sanctions against Cuba. Their principal function is to impoverish Cuba in the hope that the resulting economic hardship will lead to the downfall of Cuba's Communist government and its replacement with a more democratically inclined (and pro-U.S.) regime. The United States also has had trade sanctions in place against Libya and Iran, both of which it accuses of supporting terrorist action against U.S. interests and building weapons of mass destruction. In late 2003, the sanctions against Libya seemed to yield some returns when that country announced it would terminate a program to build nuclear weapons, and the U.S. government responded by relaxing those sanctions.

Other countries can undermine unilateral trade sanctions. The U.S. sanctions against Cuba, for example, have not stopped other Western countries from trading with Cuba. The U.S. sanctions have done little more than help create a vacuum into which other trading nations, such as Canada and Germany, have stepped. In an attempt to halt this and further tighten the screws on Cuba, in 1996 the U.S. Congress passed the **Helms-Burton Act.** This act allows Americans to sue foreign firms that use property in Cuba confiscated from them after the 1959 revolution. A similar act, the **D'Amato Act,** aimed at Libya and Iran was also passed that year.

The passage of Helms-Burton elicited protests from America's trading partners, including the European Union, Canada, and Mexico, all of which claim the law violates their sovereignty and is illegal under World Trade Organization rules. For example, Canadian companies that have been doing business in Cuba for years see no reason they should suddenly be sued in U.S. courts when Canada does not restrict trade with Cuba. They are not violating Canadian law and they are not U.S. companies, so why should

Even though the United States holds trade sanctions with Cuba, other Western countries continue to trade with the island nation.

they be subject to U.S. law? Despite such protests, the law is still on the books in the United States, although the U.S. government has not enforced this act—probably because it is unenforceable.

Protecting Human Rights

Protecting and promoting human rights in other countries is an important element of foreign policy for many democracies. Governments sometimes use trade policy to try to improve the human rights policies of trading partners. For years the most obvious example of this was the annual debate in the United States over whether to grant most favored nation (MFN) status to China. MFN status allows countries to export goods to the United States under favorable terms. Under MFN rules, the average tariff on Chinese goods imported into the United States was 8 percent. If China's MFN status were rescinded, tariffs could have risen to about 40 percent. Trading partners who are signatories of the World Trade Organization, as most are, automatically receive MFN status. However, China did not join the WTO until 2001, so historically the decision of whether to grant MFN status to China was a real one. The decision was made more difficult by the perception that China had a poor human rights record. As indications of the country's disregard for human rights, critics of China often point to the 1989 Tiananmen Square massacre, China's continuing subjugation of Tibet (which China occupied in the 1950s), and the squashing of political dissent in China.[14] These critics argued that it was wrong for the United States to grant MFN status to China, and that instead, the United States should withhold MFN status until China showed measurable improvement in its human rights record. The critics argued that trade policy should be used as a political weapon to force China to change its internal policies toward human rights.

Others contend that limiting trade with such countries would make matters worse, not better. They argue that the best way to change the internal human rights stance of a country is to engage it through international trade. At its core, the argument is simple: Growing bilateral trade raises the income levels of both countries, and as a state becomes richer, its people begin to demand—and generally receive—better treatment with regard to their human rights. This is a variant of the argument in Chapter 2 that economic progress begets political progress (if political progress is measured by the adoption of a democratic government that respects human rights). This argument ultimately won the day in 1999 when the Clinton administration blessed China's application to join the WTO and announced that trade and human rights issues should be decoupled.

ECONOMIC ARGUMENTS FOR INTERVENTION

With the development of the new trade theory and strategic trade policy (see Chapter 5), the economic arguments for government intervention have undergone a renaissance in recent years. Until the early 1980s, most economists saw little benefit in government intervention and strongly advocated a free trade policy. This position has changed at the margins with the development of strategic trade policy, although as we will see in the next section, there are still strong economic arguments for sticking to a free trade stance.

The Infant Industry Argument

The **infant industry argument** is by far the oldest economic argument for government intervention. Alexander Hamilton proposed it in 1792. According to this argument, many developing countries have a potential comparative advantage in manufacturing, but new manufacturing industries cannot initially compete with established industries in

COUNTRY FOCUS   In the 1970s, scientists discovered how to synthesize certain hormones and use them to accelerate the growth rate of livestock animals, reduce the fat content of meat, and increase milk production. Bovine somatotropin (BST), a growth hormone produced by cattle, was first synthesized by the biotechnology firm Genentech. Injections of BST could be used to supplement an animal's own hormone production and increase its growth rate. These hormones soon became popular among farmers, who found that they could cut costs and help satisfy consumer demands for leaner meat. Although these hormones occurred naturally in animals, consumer groups in several countries soon raised concerns about the practice. They argued that the use of hormone supplements was unnatural and that the health consequences of consuming hormone-treated meat were unknown but might include hormonal irregularities and cancer.

The European Union responded to these concerns in 1989 by banning the use of growth-promoting hormones in the production of livestock and the importation of hormone-treated meat. The ban was controversial because a reasonable consensus existed among scientists that the hormones posed no health risk. Before the ban, a number of these hormones had passed licensing procedures in several EU countries. As part of this process, research had been assembled that appeared to show that consuming hormone-treated meat had no effect on human health. Although the EU banned hormone-treated meat, many other countries did not, including big meat-producing countries such as Australia, Canada, New Zealand, and the United States. The use of hormones soon became widespread in these countries. According to trade officials outside the EU, the European ban constituted an unfair restraint on trade. As a result of this ban, exports of meat to the EU fell. For example, U.S. red meat exports to the EU declined from $231 million in 1988 to $98 million in 1994. The complaints of meat exporters were bolstered in 1995 when Codex Alimentarius, the international food standards body of the UN's Food and Agriculture Organization and the World Health Organization, approved the use of growth hormones. In making this decision, Codex reviewed the scientific literature and found no evidence of a link between the consumption of hormone-treated meat and human health problems, such as cancer.

Fortified by such decisions, in 1995 the United States pressed the EU to drop the import ban on hormone-treated beef. The EU refused, citing "consumer concerns about food safety." In response, both Canada and the United States independently filed formal complaints with the World Trade Organization. The United States was joined in its complaint by a number of other countries, including Australia and New Zealand. The WTO created a trade panel of three independent experts. After reviewing evidence and hearing from a range of experts and representatives of both parties, the panel in May 1997 ruled that the EU ban on hormone-treated beef was illegal because it had no scientific justification. The panel also noted that the EU was inconsistent in its application of the ban. The EU takes a very strict view on the use of growth-promoting hormones in the beef sector, where it has a substantial surplus and is not internationally competitive, while it still allows the use of some growth hormones for pork production, where the EU has no substantial surplus and does not compete in international markets. The EU immediately indicated it would appeal the finding to the WTO court of appeals. The WTO court heard the appeal in November 1997 and in February 1998 agreed with the findings of the trade panel that the EU had not presented any scientific evidence to justify the hormone ban.

This ruling left the EU in a difficult position. Legally, the EU had to lift the ban or face punitive sanctions, but the ban had wide public support in Europe. The EU feared that lifting the ban could produce a consumer backlash. Instead the EU did nothing, so in February 1999 the United States asked the WTO for permission to impose punitive sanctions on the EU. The WTO responded by allowing the United States to impose punitive tariffs valued at $120 million on EU exports to the United States. The EU decided to accept these tariffs, rather than lift the ban on hormone-treated beef, and as of 2005, the ban and punitive tariffs were still in place.

Sources: C. Southey, "Hormones Fuel a Meaty EU Row," *Financial Times,* September 7, 1995, p. 2; E. L. Andrews, "In Victory for U.S., European Ban on Treated Beef Is Ruled Illegal," *The New York Times,* May 9, 1997, p. A1; F. Williams and G. de Jonquieres, "WTO's Beef Rulings Give Europe Food for Thought," *Financial Times,* February 13, 1998, p. 5; R. Baily, "Food and Trade: EU Fear Mongers' Lethal Harvest," *Los Angeles Times,* August 18, 2002, p. M3; "The US-EU Dispute over Hormone Treated Beef," *The Kiplinger Agricultural Letter,* January 10, 2003; and Scott Miller, "EU Trade Sanctions Have Duel Edge," *The Wall Street Journal,* February 26, 2004, p. A3.

www.mhhe.com/hill

developed countries. To allow manufacturing to get a toehold, the argument is that governments should temporarily support new industries (with tariffs, import quotas, and subsidies) until they have grown strong enough to meet international competition.

This argument has had substantial appeal for the governments of developing nations during the past 50 years, and the GATT has recognized the infant industry argument as a legitimate reason for protectionism. Nevertheless, many economists remain very critical of this argument for two main reasons. First, protection of manufacturing from foreign competition does no good unless the protection helps make the industry efficient. In case after case, however, protection seems to have done little more than foster the development of inefficient industries that have little hope of ever competing in the world market. Brazil, for example, built the world's 10th largest auto industry behind tariff barriers and quotas. Once those barriers were removed in the late 1980s, however, foreign imports soared, and the industry was forced to face up to the fact that after 30 years of protection, the Brazilian industry was one of the world's most inefficient.[15]

Second, the infant industry argument relies on an assumption that firms are unable to make efficient long-term investments by borrowing money from the domestic or international capital market. Consequently, governments have been required to subsidize long-term investments. Given the development of global capital markets over the past 20 years, this assumption no longer looks as valid as it once did. Today, if a developing country has a potential comparative advantage in a manufacturing industry, firms in that country should be able to borrow money from the capital markets to finance the required investments. Given financial support, firms based in countries with a potential comparative advantage have an incentive to endure the necessary initial losses in order to make long-run gains without requiring government protection. Many Taiwanese and South Korean firms did this in industries such as textiles, semiconductors, machine tools, steel, and shipping. Thus, given efficient global capital markets, the only industries that would require government protection would be those that are not worthwhile.

Strategic Trade Policy

Some new trade theorists have proposed the strategic trade policy argument.[16] We reviewed the basic argument in Chapter 5 when we considered the new trade theory. The new trade theory argues that in industries where the existence of substantial scale economies implies that the world market will profitably support only a few firms, countries may predominate in the export of certain products simply because they had firms that were able to capture first-mover advantages. The long-term dominance of Boeing in the commercial aircraft industry has been attributed to such factors.

The **strategic trade policy** argument has two components. First, it is argued that by appropriate actions, a government can help raise national income if it can somehow ensure that the firm or firms to gain first-mover advantages in such an industry are domestic rather than foreign enterprises. Thus, according to the strategic trade policy argument, a government should use subsidies to support promising firms that are active in newly emerging industries. Advocates of this argument point out that the substantial R&D grants that the U.S. government gave Boeing in the 1950s and 60s probably helped tilt the field of competition in the newly emerging market for passenger jets in Boeing's favor. (Boeing's 707 jet airliner was derived from a military plane.) Similar arguments are now made with regard to Japan's dominance in the production of liquid crystal display screens (used in laptop computers). Although these screens were invented in the United States, the Japanese government, in cooperation with major electronics companies, targeted this industry for research support in the late 1970s and early 80s. The result was that Japanese firms, not U.S. firms, subsequently captured first-mover advantages in this market.

The second component of the strategic trade policy argument is that it might pay government to intervene in an industry if it helps domestic firms overcome the barriers to entry created by foreign firms that have already reaped first-mover advantages. This argument underlies government support of Airbus Industrie, Boeing's major competitor. Formed in 1966 as a consortium of four companies from Great Britain, France, Germany, and Spain, Airbus had less than 5 percent of the world commercial aircraft market when it began production in the mid-1970s. By 2004 it had increased its share to more than 50 percent, threatening Boeing's long-term dominance of the market. How did Airbus achieve this? According to the U.S. government, the answer is a $13.5 billion subsidy from the governments of Great Britain, France, Germany, and Spain.[17] Without this subsidy, Airbus would never have been able to break into the world market. In another example, the rise to dominance of the Japanese semiconductor industry, despite the first-mover advantages enjoyed by U.S. firms, is attributed to intervention by the Japanese government. In this case the government did not subsidize the costs of domestic manufacturers. Rather, it protected the Japanese home market while pursuing policies that ensured Japanese companies got access to the necessary manufacturing and product know-how.

If these arguments are correct, they support a rationale for government intervention in international trade. Governments should target technologies that may be important in the future and use subsidies to support development work aimed at commercializing those technologies. Furthermore, government should provide export subsidies until the domestic firms have established first-mover advantages in the world market. Government support may also be justified if it can help domestic firms overcome the first-mover advantages enjoyed by foreign competitors and emerge as viable competitors in the world market (as in the Airbus and semiconductor examples). In this case, a combination of home-market protection and export-promoting subsidies may be needed.

The Revised Case for Free Trade

The strategic trade policy arguments of the new trade theorists suggest an economic justification for government intervention in international trade. This justification challenges the rationale for unrestricted free trade found in the work of classic trade theorists such as Adam Smith and David Ricardo. In response to this challenge to economic orthodoxy, a number of economists—including some of those responsible for the development of the new trade theory, such as Paul Krugman—point out that although strategic trade policy looks appealing in theory, in practice it may be unworkable. This response to the strategic trade policy argument constitutes the revised case for free trade.[18]

RETALIATION AND TRADE WAR

Krugman argues that a strategic trade policy aimed at establishing domestic firms in a dominant position in a global industry is a beggar-thy-neighbor policy that boosts national income at the expense of other countries. A country that attempts to use such policies will probably provoke retaliation. In many cases, the resulting trade war between two or more interventionist governments will leave all countries involved worse off than if a hands-off approach had been adopted in the first place. If the U.S. government were to respond to the Airbus subsidy by increasing its own subsidies to Boeing, for example, the result might be that the subsidies would cancel each other out. In the process, both European and U.S. taxpayers would end up supporting an expensive and pointless trade war, and both Europe and the United States would be worse off.

Krugman may be right about the danger of a strategic trade policy leading to a trade war. The problem, however, is how to respond when one's competitors are already being supported by government subsidies; that is, how should Boeing and the United States respond to the subsidization of Airbus? According to Krugman, the answer is probably not to engage in retaliatory action, but to help establish rules of the game that minimize the use of trade-distorting subsidies. This is what the World Trade Organization seeks to do.

DOMESTIC POLITICS

Governments do not always act in the national interest when they intervene in the economy; politically important interest groups often influence them. The European Union's support for the Common Agricultural Policy (CAP), which arose because of the political power of French and German farmers, is an example. The CAP benefited inefficient farmers and the politicians who relied on the farm vote, but not consumers in the EU, who end up paying more for their foodstuffs. Thus, a further reason for not embracing strategic trade policy, according to Krugman, is that such a policy is almost certain to be captured by special-interest groups within the economy, who will distort it to their own ends. Krugman concludes that in the United States:

> To ask the Commerce Department to ignore special-interest politics while formulating detailed policy for many industries is not realistic: To establish a blanket policy of free trade, with exceptions granted only under extreme pressure, may not be the optimal policy according to the theory but may be the best policy that the country is likely to get.[19]

🌐 Development of the World Trading System

Strong economic arguments support unrestricted free trade. While many governments have recognized the value of these arguments, they have been unwilling to unilaterally lower their trade barriers for fear that other nations might not follow suit. Consider the problem that two neighboring countries, say, Brazil and Argentina, face when deciding whether to lower trade barriers between them. In principle, the government of Brazil might favor lowering trade barriers, but it might be unwilling to do so for fear that Argentina will not do the same. Instead, the government might fear that the Argentineans will take advantage of Brazil's low barriers to enter the Brazilian market, while at the same time continuing to shut Brazilian products out of their market through high trade barriers. The Argentinean government might believe that it faces the same dilemma. The essence of the problem is a lack of trust. Both governments recognize that their respective nations will benefit from lower trade barriers between them, but neither government is willing to lower barriers for fear that the other might not follow.[20]

Such a deadlock can be resolved if both countries negotiate a set of rules to govern cross-border trade and lower trade barriers. But who is to monitor the governments to make sure they are playing by the trade rules? And who is to impose sanctions on a government that cheats? Both governments could set up an independent body to act as a referee. This referee could monitor trade between the countries, make sure that no side cheats, and impose sanctions on a country if it does cheat in the trade game.

While it might sound unlikely that any government would compromise its national sovereignty by submitting to such an arrangement, since World War II an international trading framework has evolved that has exactly these features. For its first 50 years, this framework was known as the General Agreement on Tariffs and Trade. Since 1995, it has been known as the World Trade Organization. Here we look at the evolution and workings of the GATT and WTO.

FROM SMITH TO THE GREAT DEPRESSION

As noted in Chapter 5, the theoretical case for free trade dates to the late 18th century and the work of Adam Smith and David Ricardo. Free trade as a government policy was first officially embraced by Great Britain in 1846, when the British Parliament repealed the Corn Laws. The Corn Laws placed a high tariff on imports of foreign corn. The objectives of the Corn Laws tariff were to raise government revenues and to protect British corn producers. There had been annual motions in Parliament in favor of free trade since the 1820s when David Ricardo was a member. However, agricultural protection was withdrawn only as a result of a protracted debate when the effects of a harvest failure in Great

Britain were compounded by the imminent threat of famine in Ireland. Faced with considerable hardship and suffering among the populace, Parliament narrowly reversed its long-held position.

During the next 80 years or so, Great Britain, as one of the world's dominant trading powers, pushed the case for trade liberalization; but the British government was a voice in the wilderness. Its major trading partners did not reciprocate the British policy of unilateral free trade. The only reason Britain kept this policy for so long was that as the world's largest exporting nation, it had far more to lose from a trade war than did any other country.

By the 1930s, however, the British attempt to stimulate free trade was buried under the economic rubble of the Great Depression. The Great Depression had roots in the failure of the world economy to mount a sustained economic recovery after the end of World War I in 1918. Things got worse in 1929 with the U.S. stock market collapse and the subsequent run on the U.S. banking system. Economic problems were compounded in 1930 when the U.S. Congress passed the Smoot-Hawley tariff. Aimed at avoiding rising unemployment by protecting domestic industries and diverting consumer demand away from foreign products, the **Smoot-Hawley Act** erected an enormous wall of tariff barriers. Almost every industry was rewarded with its "made-to-order" tariff. A particularly odd aspect of the Smoot-Hawley tariff-raising binge was that the United States was running a balance-of-payment surplus at the time and it was the world's largest creditor nation. The Smoot-Hawley tariff had a damaging effect on employment abroad. Other countries reacted to the U.S. action by raising their own tariff barriers. U.S. exports tumbled in response, and the world slid further into the Great Depression.[21]

1947–1979: GATT, TRADE LIBERALIZATION, AND ECONOMIC GROWTH

Economic damage caused by the beggar-thy-neighbor trade policies that the Smoot-Hawley Act ushered in exerted a profound influence on the economic institutions and ideology of the post-World War II world. The United States emerged from the war both victorious and economically dominant. After the debacle of the Great Depression, opinion in the U.S. Congress had swung strongly in favor of free trade. Under U.S. leadership, the GATT was established in 1947.

The GATT was a multilateral agreement whose objective was to liberalize trade by eliminating tariffs, subsidies, import quotas, and the like. From its foundation in 1947 until it was superseded by the WTO, the GATT's membership grew from 19 to more than 120 nations. The GATT did not attempt to liberalize trade restrictions in one fell swoop; that would have been impossible. Rather, tariff reduction was spread over eight rounds. The last, the Uruguay Round, was launched in 1986 and completed in December 1993. In these rounds, mutual tariff reductions were negotiated among all members, who then committed themselves not to raise import tariffs above negotiated rates. GATT regulations were enforced by a mutual monitoring mechanism. If a country believed that one of its trading partners was violating a GATT regulation, it could ask the Geneva-based bureaucracy that administered the GATT to investigate. If GATT investigators found the complaints to be valid, member countries could be asked to pressure the offending party to change its policies. In general, such pressure was sufficient to get an offending country to change its policies. If it were not, the offending country could be expelled from the GATT.

In its early years, the GATT was by most measures very successful. For example, the average tariff declined by nearly 92 percent in the United States between the Geneva Round of 1947 and the Tokyo Round of 1973–79. Consistent with the theoretical arguments first advanced by Ricardo and reviewed in Chapter 5, the move toward free trade under the GATT appeared to stimulate economic growth. From 1953 to 1963, world trade grew at an annual rate of 6.1 percent, and world income grew at an annual rate of 4.3 percent. Performance from 1963 to 1973 was even better; world trade grew at 8.9 percent annually, and world income grew at 5.1 percent annually.[22]

1980–1993: PROTECTIONIST TRENDS

During the 1980s and early 1990s, the world trading system erected by the GATT came under strain as pressures for greater protectionism increased around the world. Three reasons caused the rise in such pressures during the 1980s. First, the economic success of Japan strained the world trading system. Japan was in ruins when the GATT was created. By the early 1980s, however, it had become the world's second largest economy and its largest exporter. Japan's success in such industries as automobiles and semiconductors might have been enough to strain the world trading system. Things were made worse by the widespread perception in the West that despite low tariff rates and subsidies, Japanese markets were closed to imports and foreign investment by administrative trade barriers.

Second, the world trading system was strained by the persistent trade deficit in the world's largest economy, the United States. Although the deficit peaked in 1987 at more than $170 billion, by the end of 1992 the annual rate was still running about $80 billion. From a political perspective, the matter was worsened in 1992 by the $45 billion U.S. trade deficit with Japan, a country perceived as not playing by the rules. The consequences of the U.S. deficit included painful adjustments in industries such as automobiles, machine tools, semiconductors, steel, and textiles, where domestic producers steadily lost market share to foreign competitors. The resulting unemployment gave rise to renewed demands in the U.S. Congress for protection against imports.

A third reason for the trend toward greater protectionism was that many countries found ways to get around GATT regulations. Bilateral voluntary export restraints (VERs) circumvent GATT agreements, because neither the importing country nor the exporting country complain to the GATT bureaucracy in Geneva—and without a complaint, the GATT bureaucracy can do nothing. Exporting countries agreed to VERs to avoid more damaging punitive tariffs. One of the best-known examples is the VER between Japan and the United States, under which Japanese producers promised to limit their auto imports into the United States as a way of defusing growing trade tensions. According to a World Bank study, 13 percent of the imports of industrialized countries in 1981 were subjected to nontariff trade barriers such as VERs. By 1986, this figure had increased to 16 percent. The most rapid rise was in the United States, where the value of imports affected by nontariff barriers (primarily VERs) increased by 23 percent between 1981 and 1986.[23]

THE URUGUAY ROUND AND THE WORLD TRADE ORGANIZATION

Against the background of rising pressures for protectionism, in 1986 GATT members embarked on their eighth round of negotiations to reduce tariffs, the Uruguay Round (so named because it occurred in Uruguay). This was the most difficult round of negotiations yet, primarily because it was also the most ambitious. Until then, GATT rules had applied only to trade in manufactured goods and commodities. In the Uruguay Round, member countries sought to extend GATT rules to cover trade in services. They also sought to write rules governing the protection of intellectual property, to reduce agricultural subsidies, and to strengthen the GATT's monitoring and enforcement mechanisms.

The Uruguay Round dragged on for seven years before an agreement was reached December 15, 1993. The agreement was formally signed by member states at a meeting in Marrakech, Morocco, on April 15, 1994. It went into effect July 1, 1995. The Uruguay Round contained the following provisions:

1. Tariffs on industrial goods were to be reduced by more than one-third, and tariffs were to be scrapped on over 40 percent of manufactured goods.
2. Average tariff rates imposed by developed nations on manufactured goods were to be reduced to less than 4 percent of value, the lowest level in modern history.

3. Agricultural subsidies were to be substantially reduced.
4. GATT fair trade and market access rules were to be extended to cover a wide range of services.
5. GATT rules also were to be extended to provide enhanced protection for patents, copyrights, and trademarks (intellectual property).
6. Barriers on trade in textiles were to be significantly reduced over 10 years.
7. The World Trade Organization (WTO) was to be created to implement the GATT agreement.

Services and Intellectual Property

In the long run, the extension of GATT rules to cover services and intellectual property may be particularly significant. Until 1995, GATT rules applied only to industrial goods (i.e., manufactured goods and commodities). In 2004, world trade in services amounted to $2,100 billion (compared to world trade in goods of $8,880 billion).[24] Ultimately, extension of GATT rules to this important trading arena could significantly increase both the total share of world trade accounted for by services and the overall volume of world trade. The extension of GATT rules to cover intellectual property will make it much easier for high-technology companies to do business in developing nations where intellectual property rules historically have been poorly enforced (see Chapter 2 for details).

The World Trade Organization

The clarification and strengthening of GATT rules and the creation of the World Trade Organization also hold out the promise of more effective policing and enforcement of GATT rules. The WTO acts as an umbrella organization that encompasses the GATT along with two new sister bodies, one on services and the other on intellectual property. The WTO's General Agreement on Trade in Services (GATS) has taken the lead to extending free trade agreements to services. The WTO's Agreement on Trade Related Aspects of Intellectual Property Rights (TRIPS) is an attempt to narrow the gaps in the way intellectual property rights are protected around the world, and to bring them under common international rules. WTO has taken over responsibility for arbitrating trade disputes and monitoring the trade policies of member countries. While the WTO operates on the basis of consensus as the GATT did, in the area of dispute settlement, member countries are no longer able to block adoption of arbitration reports. Arbitration panel reports on trade disputes between member countries are automatically adopted by the WTO unless there is a consensus to reject them. Countries that have been found by the arbitration panel to violate GATT rules may appeal to a permanent appellate body, but its verdict is binding. If offenders fail to comply with the recommendations of the arbitration panel, trading partners have the right to compensation or, in the last resort, to impose (commensurate) trade sanctions. Every stage of the procedure is subject to strict time limits. Thus, the WTO has something that the GATT never had—teeth.[25]

WTO: EXPERIENCE TO DATE

By 2005, the WTO had 148 members, including China, which joined at the end of 2001. Another 25 countries, including the Russian Federation and Saudi Arabia, were negotiating for membership into the organization. Since its formation, the WTO has remained at the forefront of efforts to promote global free trade. Its creators expressed the hope that the enforcement mechanisms granted to the WTO would make it more effective at policing global trade rules than the GATT had been. The great hope was that the WTO might emerge as an effective advocate and facilitator of future trade deals, particularly in areas such as services. The experience so far has been encouraging, although the collapse of WTO talks in Seattle in late 1999 raised a number of questions about the future direction of the WTO.

WTO as Global Police

The first decade in the life of the WTO suggests that its policing and enforcement mechanisms are having a positive effect.[26] Between 1995 and early 2005, more than 325 trade disputes between member countries were brought to the WTO.[27] This record compares with a total of 196 cases handled by the GATT over almost half a century. Of the cases brought to the WTO, three-fourths had been resolved by late 2004 following informal consultations between the disputing countries. Resolving the remainder has involved more formal procedures, but these have been largely successful. In general, countries involved have adopted the WTO's recommendations. The fact that countries are using the WTO represents an important vote of confidence in the organization's dispute resolution procedures.

Expanding Trade Agreements

As explained above, the Uruguay Round of GATT negotiations extended global trading rules to cover trade in services. The WTO was given the role of brokering future agreements to open up global trade in services. The WTO was also encouraged to extend its reach to encompass regulations governing foreign direct investment, something the GATT had never done. Two of the first industries targeted for reform were the global telecommunication and financial services industries.

In February 1997, the WTO brokered a deal to get countries to agree to open their telecommunication markets to competition, allowing foreign operators to purchase ownership stakes in domestic telecommunication providers and establishing a set of common rules for fair competition. Under the pact, 68 countries accounting for more than 90 percent of world telecommunication revenues pledged to start opening their markets to foreign competition and to abide by common rules for fair competition in telecommunications. Most of the world's biggest markets, including the United States, European Union, and Japan, were fully liberalized by January 1, 1998, when the pact went into effect. All forms of basic telecommunication service are covered, including voice telephony, data and fax transmissions, and satellite and radio communications. Many telecommunication companies responded positively to the deal, pointing out that it would give them a much greater ability to offer their business customers "one-stop shopping"—a global, seamless service for all their corporate needs and a single bill.[28]

This was followed in December 1997 with an agreement to liberalize cross-border trade in financial services.[29] The deal covers more than 95 percent of the world's financial services market. Under the agreement, which took effect at the beginning of March 1999, 102 countries pledged to open to varying degrees their banking, securities, and insurance sectors to foreign competition. In common with the telecommunication deal, the accord covers not just cross-border trade but also foreign direct investment. Seventy countries agreed to dramatically lower or eradicate barriers to foreign direct investment in their financial services sector. The United States and the European Union, with minor exceptions, are fully open to inward investment by foreign banks, insurance, and securities companies. As part of the deal, many Asian countries made important concessions that allow significant foreign participation in their financial services sectors for the first time.

The WTO in Seattle: A Watershed?

At the end of November 1999, representatives from the WTO's member states met in Seattle, Washington. The goal of the meeting was to launch a new round of talks—dubbed "the millennium round"—aimed at further reducing barriers to cross-border trade and investment. Prominent on the agenda was an attempt to get the assembled countries to agree to work toward the reduction of barriers to cross-border trade in agricultural products and trade and investment in services.

These expectations were dashed on the rocks of a hard and unexpected reality. The talks ended December 3, 1999, without any agreement being reached. Inside the meeting rooms, the problem was an inability to reach consensus on the primary goals for the next round of talks. A major stumbling block was friction between the United States and

WTO protesters gather in front of the Niketown store at Fifth Avenue and Pike Street in downtown Seattle before the opening of the WTO sessions in Seattle.

the European Union over whether to endorse the aim of ultimately eliminating subsidies to agricultural exporters. The United States wanted the elimination of such subsidies to be a priority. The EU, with its politically powerful farm lobby and long history of farm subsidies, was unwilling to take this step. Another stumbling block was related to efforts by the United States to write "basic labor rights" into the law of the world trading system. The United States wanted the WTO to allow governments to impose tariffs on goods imported from countries that did not abide by what the United States saw as fair labor practices. Representatives from developing nations reacted angrily to this proposal, suggesting it was simply an attempt by the United States to find a legal way of restricting imports from poorer nations.

While the disputes inside the meeting rooms were acrimonious, it was events outside that captured the attention of the world press. The WTO talks proved to be a lightning rod for a diverse collection of organizations from environmentalists and human rights groups to labor unions. For various reasons, these groups oppose free trade. All these organizations argued that the WTO is an undemocratic institution that was usurping the national sovereignty of member states and making decisions of great importance behind closed doors. They took advantage of the Seattle meetings to voice their opposition, which the world press recorded. Environmentalists expressed concern about the impact that free trade in agricultural products might have on the rate of global deforestation. They argued that lower tariffs on imports of lumber from developing nations will stimulate demand and accelerate the rate at which virgin forests are logged, particularly in nations such as Malaysia and Indonesia. They also pointed to the adverse impact that some WTO rulings have had on environmental policies. For example, the WTO had recently blocked a U.S. rule that ordered shrimp nets be equipped with a device that allows endangered sea turtles to escape. The WTO found the rule discriminated against foreign importers who lacked such nets.[30] Environmentalists argued that the rule was necessary to protect the turtles from extinction.

Human rights activists see WTO rules as outlawing the ability of nations to stop imports from countries where child labor is used or working conditions are hazardous. Similarly, labor unions oppose trade laws that allow imports from low-wage countries and result in a loss of jobs in high-wage countries. They buttress their position by arguing that American workers are losing their jobs to imports from developing nations that do not have adequate labor standards.

Supporters of the WTO and free trade dismiss these concerns. They have repeatedly pointed out that the WTO exists to serve the interests of its member states, not subvert them. The WTO lacks the ability to force any member nation to take an action that it is opposed to. The WTO can allow member nations to impose retaliatory tariffs on countries that do not abide by WTO rules, but that is the limit of its power. Furthermore, supporters argue, it is rich countries that pass strict environmental laws and laws governing labor standards, not poor ones. In their view, free trade, by raising living standards in developing nations, will be followed by the passage of such laws in these nations. Using trade regulations to try to impose such practices on developing nations, they believe, will produce a self-defeating backlash.

Many representatives from developing nations, which make up about 110 of the WTO's 148 members, also reject the position taken by environmentalists and advocates of human and labor rights. Poor countries, which depend on exports to boost their economic growth rates and work their way out of poverty, fear that rich countries will use environmental concerns, human rights, and labor-related issues to erect barriers to the products of the developing world. They believe that attempts to incorporate language about the environment or labor standards in future trade agreements will amount to little more than trade barriers by another name.[31] If this were to occur, they argue that the effect would be to trap the developing nations of the world in a grinding cycle of poverty and debt.

These pro-trade arguments fell on deaf ears. As the WTO representatives gathered in Seattle, environmentalists, human rights activists, and labor unions marched in the streets. Some of the more radical elements in these organizations, together with groups of anarchists who were philosophically opposed to "global capitalism" and "the rape of the world by multinationals," succeeded not only in shutting down the opening ceremonies of the WTO, but also in sparking violence in the normally peaceful streets of Seattle. A number of demonstrators damaged property and looted; and the police responded with tear gas, rubber bullets, pepper spray, and baton charges. When it was over, 600 demonstrators had been arrested, millions of dollars in property had been damaged in downtown Seattle, and the global news media had their headline: "WTO Talks Collapse amid Violent Demonstrations."

What happened in Seattle is notable because it may have been a watershed of sorts. In the past, previous trade talks were pursued in relative obscurity with only interested economists, politicians, and businesspeople paying much attention. Seattle demonstrated that the issues surrounding the global trend toward free trade have moved to center stage in the popular consciousness. The debate on the merits of free trade and globalization has become mainstream. Whether further liberalization occurs, therefore, may depend on the importance that popular opinion in countries such as the United States attaches to issues such as human rights and labor standards, job security, environmental policies, and national sovereignty. It will also depend on the ability of advocates of free trade to articulate in a clear and compelling manner the argument that, in the long run, free trade is the best way of promoting adequate labor standards, of providing more jobs, and of protecting the environment.

THE FUTURE OF THE WTO: UNRESOLVED ISSUES AND THE DOHA ROUND

Much remains to be done on the international trade front. Four issues at the forefront of the current agenda of the WTO are the increase in antidumping policies, the high level of protectionism in agriculture, the lack of strong protection for intellectual property rights in many nations, and continued high tariff rates on nonagricultural goods and services in many nations. We shall look at each in turn before discussing the latest round of talks between WTO members aimed at reducing trade barriers, the Doha Round, which began in 2001.

Antidumping Actions

Antidumping actions proliferated during the 1990s. WTO rules allow countries to impose antidumping duties on foreign goods that are being sold cheaper than at home, or below their cost of production, when domestic producers can show that

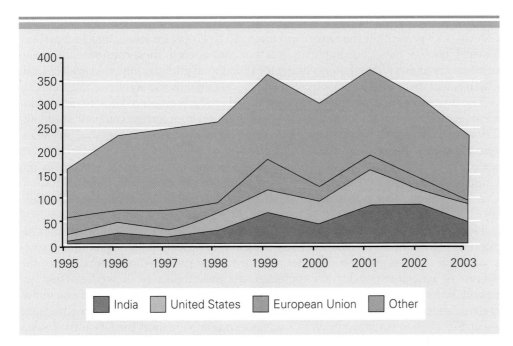

FIGURE 6.2

The Rise (and Fall?) of Antidumping Actions (number of actions per year by reporting country)

Source: Data from WTO, www.wto.org/english/tratop_e/adp_e/adp_e.htm

they are being harmed. Unfortunately, the rather vague definition of what constitutes "dumping" has proved to be a loophole that many countries are exploiting to pursue protectionism.

Between January 1995 and June 2004, WTO members had reported implementation of some 2,537 antidumping actions to the WTO. India initiated the largest number of antidumping actions, some 383; the EU initiated 287 over the same period, and the United States 356 (see Figure 6.2). Antidumping actions seem to be concentrated on certain sectors of the economy. Basic metal industries (e.g., aluminum and steel) accounted for 770 of the 2,537 antidumping cases between 1995 and 2004, followed by chemicals (495), plastics (315), and machinery and electrical equipment (210).[32] In sum, four sectors account for some 70 percent of all antidumping actions reported to the WTO. These four sectors since 1995 have been characterized by periods of intense competition and excess productive capacity, which have led to low prices and profits (or losses) for firms in those industries. It is not unreasonable, therefore, to hypothesize that the high level of antidumping actions in these industries represents an attempt by beleaguered manufacturers to use the political process in their nations to seek protection from foreign competitors, who they claim are engaging in unfair competition. While some of these claims may have merit, the process can become very politicized as representatives of businesses and their employees lobby government officials to "protect domestic jobs from unfair foreign competition," and government officials, mindful of the need to get votes in future elections, oblige by pushing for antidumping actions. The WTO is clearly worried by this trend, suggesting that it reflects persistent protectionist tendencies and pushing members to strengthen the regulations governing the imposition of antidumping duties. On the other hand, since the WTO signaled that antidumping would be a focus of the Doha Round, the number of antidumping actions has declined somewhat (see Figure 6.2).

Protectionism in Agriculture

Another recent focus of the WTO has been the high level of tariffs and subsidies in the agricultural sector of many economies. Tariff rates on agricultural products are generally much higher than tariff rates on manufactured products or services. In 2003, for example, the average tariff rates on nonagricultural products were 4.2 percent for Canada, 3.8 percent for the European Union, 3.9 percent for Japan, and 4.4 percent for the United

States. On agricultural products, however, the average tariff rates were 21.2 percent for Canada, 15.9 percent for the European Union, 18.6 percent for Japan, and 10.3 percent for the United States.[33] The implication is that consumers in these countries are paying significantly higher prices than necessary for agricultural products imported from abroad, which leaves them with less money to spend on other goods and services.

The historically high tariff rates on agricultural products reflect a desire to protect domestic agriculture and traditional farming communities from foreign competition. In addition to high tariffs, agricultural producers also benefit from substantial subsidies. According to estimates from the OECD, government subsidies on average account for some 17 percent of the cost of agricultural production in Canada, 21 percent in the United States, 35 percent in the European Union, and 59 percent in Japan.[34] In total, OECD countries spent more than $300 billion a year in subsidies to agricultural producers in 2003.

Not surprisingly, the combination of high tariff barriers and significant subsidies introduces significant distortions into the production of agricultural products and international trade of those products. The net effect is to raise prices to consumers, reduce the volume of agricultural trade, and encourage the overproduction of products that are heavily subsidized (with the government typically buying the surplus). Because global trade in agriculture currently amounts to 10.5 percent of total merchandized trade, or about $700 billion per year, the WTO argues that removing tariff barriers and subsidies could significantly boost the overall level of trade, lower prices to consumers, and raise global economic growth by freeing consumption and investment resources for more productive uses. According to estimates from the International Monetary Fund, removal of tariffs and subsidies on agricultural products would raise global economic welfare by $128 billion annually.[35]

The biggest defenders of the existing system have been the advanced nations of the world, which want to protect their agricultural sectors from competition by low-cost producers in developing nations. In contrast, developing nations have been pushing hard for reforms that would allow their producers greater access to the protected markets of the developed nations. Estimates suggest that removing all subsidies on agricultural production alone in OECD countries could return to the developing nations of the world three times more than all the foreign aid they currently receive from the OECD nations.[36] In other words, free trade in agriculture could help to jump-start economic growth among the world's poorer nations and alleviate global poverty.

Protecting Intellectual Property

Another issue that has become increasingly important to the WTO has been protecting intellectual property. As noted earlier, the 1995 Uruguay agreement that established the WTO also contained an agreement to protect intellectual property (the Trade Related Aspects of Intellectual Property Rights, or TRIPS, agreement). The TRIPS regulations oblige WTO members to grant and enforce patents lasting at least 20 years and copyrights lasting 50 years. Rich countries had to comply with the rules within a year. Poor countries, in which such protection generally was much weaker, had 5 years' grace, and the very poorest had 10 years. The basis for this agreement was a strong belief among signatory nations that the protection of intellectual property through patents, trademarks, and copyrights must be an essential element of the international trading system. Inadequate protections for intellectual property reduce the incentive for innovation. Because innovation is a central engine of economic growth and rising living standards, the argument has been that a multilateral agreement is needed to protect intellectual property.

Without such an agreement it is feared that producers in a country, let's say India, might market imitations of patented innovations pioneered in a different country, let's say the United States. This can affect international trade in two ways. First, it reduces the export opportunities in India for the original innovator in the United States. Second, to the extent that the Indian producer is able to export its pirated imitation to additional countries, it also reduces the export opportunities in those countries for the U.S. inven-

TABLE 6.1

Bound Tariffs on Select
Industrial Products
(simple averages)

Source: World Trade Report
2005, WTO, Geneva, 2005.

Country	Metals	Transportation Equipment	Electric Machinery
Canada	2.8%	6.8%	5.2%
United States	1.8	2.7	2.1
Brazil	33.4	33.6	31.9
Mexico	34.7	35.8	34.1
European Union	1.6	4.8	3.3
Australia	4.5	15.1	13.3
Japan	0.9	0.0	0.2
South Korea	7.7	24.6	16.1

tor. Also, one can argue that because the size of the total world market for the innovator is reduced, its incentive to pursue risky and expensive innovations is also reduced. The net effect would be less innovation in the world economy and less economic growth.

Something very similar to this has been occurring in the pharmaceutical industry, with Indian drug companies making copies of patented drugs discovered elsewhere. In 1970, the Indian government stopped recognizing product patents on drugs, but elected to continue respecting process patents. This permitted Indian companies to reverse-engineer Western pharmaceuticals without paying licensing fees. As a result, foreigners' share of the Indian drug market fell from 75 percent in 1970 to 30 percent in 2000. For example, an Indian company sells a version of Bayer's patented antibiotic Cipro for $0.12 a pill, versus the $5.50 it costs in the United States. Under the WTO TRIPS agreement, India has agreed to adopt and enforce the international drug patent regime by 2005.[37]

As noted in Chapter 2, intellectual property rights violation is also an endemic problem in several other industries, most notably computer software and music. The WTO believes that reducing piracy rates in areas such as drugs, software, and music recordings would have a significant impact on the volume of world trade and increase the incentive for producers to invest in the creation of intellectual property. A world without piracy would have more new drugs, computer software, and music recordings produced every year. In turn, this would boost economic and social welfare, and global economic growth rates. It is thus in the interests of WTO members to make sure that intellectual property rights are respected and enforced. While the 1995 Uruguay agreement that created the WTO did make headway with the TRIPS agreement, some believe these requirements do not go far enough and further commitments are necessary.

Market Access for Nonagricultural Goods and Services

Although the WTO and the GATT have made huge strides in reducing the tariff rates on nonagricultural products, much work remains. While most developed nations have brought their tariff rates on industrial products down to an *average* of 3.8 percent of value, exceptions still remain. In particular, while average tariffs are low, high tariff rates persist on certain imports into developed nations, which limit market access and economic growth. For example, Australia and South Korea, both OECD countries, still have bound tariff rates of 15.1 percent and 24.6 percent, respectively, on imports of transportation equipment ("bound tariff rates" are the highest rate that can be charged, which is often, but not always, the rate that is charged). In contrast, the bound tariff rates on imports of transportation equipment into the United States, EU, and Japan are 2.7 percent, 4.8 percent, and 0 percent, respectively (see Table 6.1). A particular area for concern is high tariff rates on imports of selected goods from developing nations into developed nations.

COUNTRY FOCUS A recent study published by the Institute for International Economics has tried to estimate the gains to the American economy from free trade. According to the study, due to reductions in tariff barriers under the GATT and WTO since 1947, by 2003 the GDP of the United States was 7.3 percent higher than would otherwise be the case. The benefits of that amount to roughly $1 trillion a year, or $9,000 extra income for each American household per year!

The same study tried to estimate what would happen if America concluded free trade deals with all its trading partners, reducing tariff barriers on all goods and services to zero. Using several methods to estimate the impact, the study concluded that additional annual gains of between $450 billion and $1.3 trillion could be realized. This final march to free trade, according to the authors of the study, could safely be expected to raise incomes of the average American household by an additional $4,500 per year.

The authors also tried to estimate the scale and cost of employment disruption that would be caused by a move to universal free trade. Jobs would be lost in certain sectors and gained in others if the country abolished all tariff barriers. Using historical data as a guide, they estimated that 226,000 jobs would be lost every year due to expanded trade, although some two-thirds of those losing jobs would find reemployment after a year. Reemployment, however, would be at a wage that was 13 to 14 percent lower. The study concluded that the disruption costs would total some $54 billion annually, primarily in the form of lower lifetime wages to those whose jobs were disrupted as a result of free trade. Offset against this, however, must be the higher economic growth resulting from free trade, which creates many new jobs and raises household incomes, creating another $450 billion to $1.3 trillion annually in *net* gains to the economy. In other words, the estimated annual gains from trade are far greater than the estimated annual costs associated with job disruption, and more people benefit than lose as result of shift to a universal free trade regime.

Source: S. C. Bradford, P. L. E. Grieco, and G. C. Hufbauer, "The Payoff to America from Global Integration," in *The United States and the World Economy: Foreign Policy for the Next Decade,* C. F. Bergsten, ed. (Washington, DC: Institute for International Economics, 2005).

In addition, tariffs on services remain higher than on industrial goods. The average tariff on business and financial services imported into United States, for example, is 8.2 percent, into the EU it is 8.5 percent, and into Japan it is 19.7 percent.[38] Given the rising value of cross-border trade in services, reducing these figures can be expected to yield substantial gains.

The WTO would like to bring down tariff rates still further, and reduce the scope for the selective use of high tariff rates. The ultimate aim is to reduce tariff rates to zero. While this might sound ambitious, 40 nations have already moved to zero tariffs on information technology goods, so a precedent exists. Empirical work suggests that further reductions in average tariff rates toward zero would yield substantial gains. One estimate by economists at the World Bank suggests that a broad global trade agreement coming out of the current Doha negotiations could increase world income by $263 billion annually by 2015, of which $109 billion would go to poor countries.[39] See the accompanying Country Focus for estimates of the benefits to the American economy from free trade.

Looking further out, the WTO would like to bring down tariff rates on imports of nonagricultural goods into developing nations. While many of these nations use the infant industry argument to justify the continued imposition of high tariff rates, ultimately these rates need to come down for these nations to reap the full benefits of international trade. For example, the bound tariff rates of 53.9 percent on imports of transportation equipment into India and 33.6 percent on imports into Brazil, by raising domestic prices, help to protect inefficient domestic producers and limit economic growth by reducing the real income of consumers who must pay more for transportation equipment and related services.

www.mhhe.com/hill

A New Round of Talks: Doha

Antidumping actions, trade in agricultural products, better enforcement of intellectual property laws, and expanded market access were four of the issues the WTO wanted to tackle at the 1999 meetings in Seattle, but those meetings were derailed. In late 2001, the WTO tried again to launch a new round of talks between member states aimed at further liberalizing the global trade and investment framework. For this meeting, it picked the remote location of Doha in the Persian Gulf state of Qatar, no doubt with an eye on the difficulties that antiglobalization protesters would have in getting there. Unlike the Seattle meetings, at Doha, the member states of the WTO agreed to launch a new round of talks and staked out an agenda. The talks were originally scheduled to last three years, although they have already gone on longer and may not be concluded for a while.

The agenda agreed upon at Doha should be seen as a game plan for negotiations over the next few years. The agenda includes cutting tariffs on industrial goods and services, phasing out subsidies to agricultural producers, reducing barriers to cross-border investment, and limiting the use of antidumping laws. Some difficult compromises were made to reach agreement on this agenda. The EU and Japan had to give significant ground on the issue of agricultural subsidies, which are used extensively by both entities to support politically powerful farmers. The United States bowed to pressure from virtually every other nation to negotiate revisions of antidumping rules, which the United States has used extensively to protect its steel producers from foreign competition. Europe had to scale back its efforts to include environmental policy in the trade talks, primarily because of pressure from developing nations that see environmental protection policies as trade barriers by another name. Excluded from the agenda was any language pertaining to attempts to tie trade to labor standards in a country.

Countries with big pharmaceutical sectors acquiesced to demands from African, Asian, and Latin American nations on the issue of drug patents. Specifically, the language in the agreement declares that WTO regulation on intellectual property "does not and should not prevent members from taking measures to protect public health." This language was meant to assure the world's poorer nations that they can make or buy generic equivalents to fight such killers as AIDS and malaria.

Clearly, it is one thing to agree to an agenda and quite another to reach a consensus on a new treaty. Nevertheless, this agreement yields some potential winners. These include low-cost agricultural producers in the developing world and developed nations such as Australia and the United States. If the talks are successful, agricultural producers in these nations will ultimately see the global markets for their goods expand. Developing nations also gain from the lack of language on labor standards, which many saw as an attempt by rich nations to erect trade barriers. The sick and poor of the world also benefit from guaranteed access to cheaper medicines. There are also clear losers in this agreement, including EU and Japanese farmers, U.S. steelmakers, environmental activists, and pharmaceutical firms in the developed world. These losers can be expected to lobby their governments hard during the ensuing years to make sure that the final agreement is more in their favor.[40] In general, though, if successful, the Doha Round of negotiations could significantly raise global economic welfare. The World Bank has estimated that a successful Doha Round would raise global incomes by more than $500 billion a year by 2015, with 60 percent of the gain going to the world's poorer nations, which would help to pull 144 million people out of poverty.[41]

The talks are currently ongoing, and as seems normal in these cases, they are characterized by halting progress punctuated by significant setbacks and missed deadlines. A September 2003 meeting in Cancun, Mexico, broke down, primarily because there was no agreement on how to proceed with reducing agricultural subsidies and tariffs; the EU, United States, and India, among others, proved less than willing to reduce subsidies and tariffs to their politically important farmers, while countries such as Brazil and certain

West African nations wanted free trade as quickly as possible. However, in early 2004, both the United States and the EU made a determined push to start the talks again, and in mid-2004 both seemed to commit themselves to sweeping reductions in agricultural tariffs and subsidies. It remains to be seen if and when the Doha Round of talks will be completed.

IMPLICATIONS FOR MANAGERS

What are the implications of all this for business practice? Why should the international manager care about the political economy of free trade or about the relative merits of arguments for free trade and protectionism? There are two answers to this question. The first concerns the impact of trade barriers on a firm's strategy. The second concerns the role that business firms can play in promoting free trade and/or trade barriers.

TRADE BARRIERS AND FIRM STRATEGY

To understand how trade barriers affect a firm's strategy, consider first the material in Chapter 5. Drawing on the theories of international trade, we discussed how it makes sense for the firm to disperse its various production activities to those countries around the globe where they can be performed most efficiently. Thus, it may make sense for a firm to design and engineer its product in one country, to manufacture components in another, to perform final assembly operations in yet another country, and then export the finished product to the rest of the world.

Clearly, trade barriers constrain a firm's ability to disperse its productive activities in such a manner. First and most obviously, tariff barriers raise the costs of exporting products to a country (or of exporting partly finished products between countries). This may put the firm at a competitive disadvantage to indigenous competitors in that country. In response, the firm may then find it economical to locate production facilities in that country so that it can compete on an even footing. Second, quotas may limit a firm's ability to serve a country from locations outside of that country. Again, the response by the firm might be to set up production facilities in that country—even though it may result in higher production costs. Such reasoning was one of the factors behind the rapid expansion of Japanese automaking capacity in the United States during the 1980s and 1990s. This followed the establishment of a VER agreement between the United States and Japan that limited U.S. imports of Japanese automobiles.

Third, to conform to local content regulations, a firm may have to locate more production activities in a given market than it would otherwise. Again, from the firm's perspective, the consequence might be to raise costs above the level that could be achieved if each production activity was dispersed to the optimal location for that activity. And finally, even when trade barriers do not exist, the firm may still want to locate some production activities in a given country to reduce the threat of trade barriers being imposed in the future.

All these effects are likely to raise the firm's costs above the level that could be achieved in a world without trade barriers. The higher costs that result need not translate into a significant competitive disadvantage relative to other foreign firms, however, if the countries imposing trade barriers do so to the imported products of all foreign firms, irrespective of their national origin. But when trade barriers are targeted at exports from a particular nation, firms based in that nation are at a competitive disadvantage to firms of other nations. The firm may deal with such targeted trade barriers by moving production into the country imposing barriers. Another strategy may be to move production to countries whose exports are not targeted by the specific trade barrier.

Finally, the threat of antidumping action limits the ability of a firm to use aggressive pricing to gain market share in a country. Firms in a country also can make strategic use of antidumping measures to limit aggressive competition from low-cost foreign producers. For example, the U.S. steel industry has been very aggressive in bringing antidumping actions against foreign steelmakers, particularly in times of weak global demand for steel and excess capacity. In 1998 and 1999, the United States faced a surge in low-cost steel imports as a severe recession in Asia left producers there with excess capacity. The U.S. producers filed several complaints with the International Trade Commission. One argued that Japanese producers of hot rolled steel were selling it at below cost in the United States. The ITC agreed and levied tariffs ranging from 18 percent to 67 percent on imports of certain steel products from Japan (these tariffs are separate from the steel tariffs discussed earlier).[42]

POLICY IMPLICATIONS

As noted in Chapter 5, business firms are major players on the international trade scene. Because of their pivotal role in international trade, firms can and do exert a strong influence on government policy toward trade. This influence can encourage protectionism or it can encourage the government to support the WTO and push for open markets and freer trade among all nations. Government policies with regard to international trade can have a direct impact on business.

Consistent with strategic trade policy, examples can be found of government intervention in the form of tariffs, quotas, antidumping actions, and subsidies helping firms and industries establish a competitive advantage in the world economy. In general, however, the arguments contained in this chapter and in Chapter 5 suggest that government intervention has three drawbacks. Intervention can be self-defeating because it tends to protect the inefficient rather than help firms become efficient global competitors. Intervention is dangerous; it may invite retaliation and trigger a trade war. Finally, intervention is unlikely to be well executed, given the opportunity for such a policy to be captured by special-interest groups. Does this mean that business should simply encourage government to adopt a laissez-faire free trade policy?

Most economists would probably argue that the best interests of international business are served by a free trade stance, but not a laissez-faire stance. It is probably in the best long-run interests of the business community to encourage the government to aggressively promote greater free trade by, for example, strengthening the WTO. Business probably has much more to gain from government efforts to open protected markets to imports and foreign direct investment than from government efforts to support certain domestic industries in a manner consistent with the recommendations of strategic trade policy.

This conclusion is reinforced by a phenomenon we touched on in Chapter 1—the increasing integration of the world economy and internationalization of production that has occurred over the past two decades. We live in a world where many firms of all national origins increasingly depend for their competitive advantage on globally dispersed production systems. Such systems are the result of freer trade. Freer trade has brought great advantages to firms that have exploited it and to consumers who benefit from the resulting lower prices. Given the danger of retaliatory action, business firms that lobby their governments to engage in protectionism must realize that by doing so they may be denying themselves the opportunity to build a competitive advantage by constructing a globally dispersed production system. By encouraging their governments to engage in protectionism, their own activities and sales overseas may be jeopardized if other governments retaliate. This does not mean a firm should never seek protection in the form of antidumping actions and the like, but it should review its options carefully and think through the larger consequences.

Chapter Summary

The objective of this chapter was to describe how the reality of international trade deviates from the theoretical ideal of unrestricted free trade reviewed in Chapter 5. In this chapter we have reported the various instruments of trade policy, reviewed the political and economic arguments for government intervention in international trade, reexamined the economic case for free trade in light of the strategic trade policy argument, and looked at the evolution of the world trading framework. While a policy of free trade may not always be the theoretically optimal policy (given the arguments of the new trade theorists), in practice it is probably the best policy for a government to pursue. In particular, the long-run interests of business and consumers may be best served by strengthening international institutions such as the WTO. Given the danger that isolated protectionism might escalate into a trade war, business probably has far more to gain from government efforts to open protected markets to imports and foreign direct investment (through the WTO) than from government efforts to protect domestic industries from foreign competition. The chapter made the following points:

1. The effect of a tariff is to raise the cost of imported products. Gains accrue to the government (from revenues) and to producers (who are protected from foreign competitors). Consumers lose because they must pay more for imports.

2. By lowering costs, subsidies help domestic producers to compete against low-cost foreign imports and to gain export markets. However, subsidies must be paid for by taxpayers. They also tend to be captured by special interests that use them to protect the inefficient.

3. An import quota is a direct restriction imposed by an importing country on the quantity of some good that may be imported. A voluntary export restraint (VER) is a quota on trade imposed from the exporting country's side. Both import quotas and VERs benefit domestic producers by limiting import competition, but they result in higher prices, which hurt consumers.

4. A local content requirement calls for some specific fraction of a good to be produced domesti-

cally. Local content requirements benefit the producers of component parts, but they raise prices of imported components, which hurts consumers.

5. An administrative policy is an informal instrument or bureaucratic rule that can be used to restrict imports and boost exports. Such policies benefit producers but hurt consumers, who are denied access to possibly superior foreign products.

6. There are two types of arguments for government intervention in international trade: political and economic. Political arguments for intervention are concerned with protecting the interests of certain groups, often at the expense of other groups, or with promoting goals with regard to foreign policy, human rights, consumer protection, and the like. Economic arguments for intervention are about boosting the overall wealth of a nation.

7. The most common political argument for intervention is that it is necessary to protect jobs. However, political intervention often hurts consumers and it can be self-defeating.

8. Countries sometimes argue that it is important to protect certain industries for reasons of national security.

9. Some argue that government should use the threat to intervene in trade policy as a bargaining tool to open foreign markets. This can be a risky policy; if it fails, the result can be higher trade barriers.

10. The infant industry argument for government intervention contends that to let manufacturing get a toehold, governments should temporarily support new industries. In practice, however, governments often end up protecting the inefficient.

11. Strategic trade policy suggests that with subsidies, government can help domestic firms gain first-mover advantages in global industries where economies of scale are important. Government subsidies may also help domestic firms overcome barriers to entry into such industries.

12. The problems with strategic trade policy are twofold: (a) such a policy may invite retaliation, in which case all will lose, and (b) strategic trade policy may be captured by special-interest groups, which will distort it to their own ends.

13. The Smoot-Hawley Act, introduced in 1930, erected an enormous wall of tariff barriers to imports. Other countries responded by adopting similar tariffs, and the world slid further into the Great Depression.

14. The GATT was a product of the postwar free trade movement. The GATT was successful in lowering trade barriers on manufactured goods and commodities. The move toward greater free trade under the GATT appeared to stimulate economic growth.

15. The completion of the Uruguay Round of GATT talks and the establishment of the World Trade Organization have strengthened the world trading system by extending GATT rules to services, increasing protection for intellectual property, reducing agricultural subsidies, and enhancing monitoring and enforcement mechanisms.

16. Trade barriers act as a constraint on a firm's ability to disperse its various production activities to optimal locations around the globe. One response to trade barriers is to establish more production activities in the protected country.

17. Business may have more to gain from government efforts to open protected markets to imports and foreign direct investment than from government efforts to protect domestic industries from foreign competition.

Critical Thinking and Discussion Questions

1. Do you think governments should consider human rights when granting preferential trading rights to countries? What are the arguments for and against taking such a position?

2. Whose interests should be the paramount concern of government trade policy—the interests of producers (businesses and their employees) or those of consumers?

3. Given the arguments relating to the new trade theory and strategic trade policy, what kind of trade policy should business be pressuring government to adopt?

4. You are an employee of a U.S. firm that produces personal computers in Thailand and then exports them to the United States and other countries for sale. The personal computers were originally produced in Thailand to take advantage of relatively low labor costs and a skilled workforce. Other possible locations considered at the time were Malaysia and Hong Kong. The U.S. government decides to impose punitive 100 percent ad valorem tariffs on imports of computers from Thailand to punish the country for administrative trade barriers that restrict U.S. exports to Thailand. How should your firm respond? What does this tell you about the use of targeted trade barriers?

Research Task   globalEDGE™   globaledge.msu.edu

Use the globalEDGE™ site to complete the following exercises:

1. Your company is considering exporting its products to Egypt. Yet, management's current knowledge of this country's trade policies and barriers is limited. Conduct some Web research to identify Egypt's current import policies with respect to fundamental issues such as tariffs and restrictions. Prepare an executive summary of your findings.

2. The number of member nations of the World Trade Organization is increasing constantly. Additionally, some of the non-member countries have observer status, which requires accession negotiations to begin within five years of attaining the preliminary position. Identify the current total number of WTO members. Also, prepare a list of the observer countries.

CLOSING CASE In December 2003, Boeing announced it would go ahead with the development of its latest commercial jetliner, the 7E7, which Boeing will position against Airbus's popular A330 aircraft. The "E" in the Boeing 7E7 stands for 'efficient.' By making extensive use of new composite and engine technology, Boeing hopes to reduce the aircraft's operating costs by as much as 20 percent compared to a traditional design. If it is successful, this will make the plane a potent competitor against the best-selling A330.

However, the 7E7, now renamed the 787, is a risky project for Boeing. The aircraft will cost about $7 billion to develop, according to industry estimates, and demand is uncertain. To share the costs and risks of development Boeing has taken on several partners who will help to design and build the 787. Most important among these are a trio of three Japanese companies, Mitsubishi Heavy Industries, Kawasaki Heavy Industries, and Fuji Heavy Industries. Collectively, these three companies will probably build as much as 35 percent of the 787 by value, including parts of the fuselage, wings, and landing gear. They will ship the finished components to Everett, Washington, for final assembly. These three companies are longtime Boeing partners. They contributed about 21 percent by value to Boeing's last new jetliner, the Boeing 777.

Although there has been a long history of development subsidies in the commercial aerospace industry, a 1992 agreement between Boeing and Airbus limits the state aid either company can get from their respective governments. Airbus, now a private company, is limited to repayable launch aid that must not exceed one-third of the development costs of a new aircraft. The launch aid has to be repaid only if aircraft sales are high enough for Airbus to turn a profit on the investment in a new plane. As for Boeing, indirect aid from U.S. government agencies such as R&D contracts from the Pentagon and NASA are capped at 4 percent of its total revenues.

It is unclear if the 1992 agreement extends to other parties in the projects. The Japanese Aircraft Development Corporation, an association of Japanese aircraft makers, has asked the Japanese government for help with the 787 project. The country's Ministry of Economy, Trade, and Industry has submitted a budget request that would make the 787 a "national project." Newspaper reports put the request at about $1.5 billion.

Upon hearing this, Airbus officials were quick to claim that the arrangement could violate several inter-national agreements, including a 1994 WTO prohibition against subsidies that can harm competitors. Behind the scenes, Airbus executives started to urge the European Union to look at the issue and possibly file a case on their behalf. They also noted that Boeing received aid from the states of Washington and Kansas, where its factories are located, and that also constituted an unfair subsidy that was outside the scope of the 1992 agreement.

In mid-2004, the issue became even more contentious when the U.S. government demanded an end to Airbus's launch aid. Airbus had already been granted loans of $3.7 billion to develop its latest aircraft, the A380 super-jumbo, but what really got attention in America were signs from Airbus that it would also build a direct competitor to the 787, the A350, and ask for launch aid to help cover the development costs of that plane. Estimates suggested the launch aid for the A350 could total $1.3 billion. Furthermore, in 2004 Airbus surpassed Boeing in global market share. American officials felt that given the strength of the company, subsidies were no longer appropriate.

In late 2004, the EU and U.S. government entered into negotiations to try to resolve the dispute, but talks ended in March 2005 with no agreement. The dispute now goes to the World Trade Organization, which must rule on the legality of the various subsidies. Meanwhile, Boeing is starting to pile up orders for the 787, and industry observers speculate that the longer launch aid for an Airbus competitor is stalled in legal limbo, the less likely Airbus will be to go ahead with the plane.

Sources: D. Michaels and J. L. Lunsford, "Airbus Contends That Boeing's Plan to Fund Plane Breaks Trade Rules," *The Wall Street Journal*, December 11, 2003, p. A3; M. Mecham, "Overseas Shipments Alenia and the Japanese Heavies Will Play Major Roles in the Design and Manufacture of the 7E7's Structure," *Aviation Week*, November 24, 2003, p. 36–37; and M. Lander, "A Dogfight between Jetliners," *The New York Times*, April 13, 2005, pp. C1, 18.

Case Discussion Questions

1. How might the repayable launch aid for Airbus change its decision making on launching a new aircraft? What are the potential consequences for (*a*) Boeing, (*b*) airlines, and (*c*) the profitability of both Boeing and Airbus?

2. When Airbus originally received government aid in the 1960s, it was a new enterprise. Today it is the global market share leader in the commercial aero-

space business. How do gains in market share affect the legitimacy of claims for subsidies?

3. Do you think that R&D contracts from NASA and the Pentagon benefit Boeing's commercial aerospace business? How?

4. If the EU does file a complaint with the WTO protesting Japanese launch aid on the Boeing 787

aircraft, how might the Japanese retaliate? Given this, what should Airbus urge the EU to do?

5. What do you think is the most equitable solution to the long-running battle between the United States and EU on subsidies for commercial aircraft development?

Notes

1. For a detailed welfare analysis of the effect of a tariff, see P. R. Krugman and M. Obstfeld, *International Economics: Theory and Policy* (New York: HarperCollins, 2000), chap. 8.

2. Y. Sazanami, S. Urata, and H. Kawai, *Measuring the Costs of Protection in Japan* (Washington, DC: Institute for International Economics, 1994).

3. J. Bhagwati, *Protectionism* (Cambridge, MA: MIT Press, 1988), and "Costs of Protection," *Journal of Commerce*, September 25, 1991, p. 8A.

4. The study was undertaken by Kym Anderson of the University of Adelaide. See "A Not So Perfect Market," *The Economist; Survey of Agriculture and Technology*, March 25, 2000, pp. 8–10.

5. R. W. Crandall, *Regulating the Automobile* (Washington, DC: Brookings Institution, 1986).

6. Quoted in Krugman and Obstfeld, *International Economics*.

7. G. Hufbauer and Z. A. Elliott, *Measuring the Costs of Protectionism in the United States* (Washington, DC: Institute for International Economics, 1993).

8. Bhagwati, *Protectionism*, and "Japan to Curb VCR Exports," *The New York Times*, November 21, 1983, p. D5.

9. Alan Goldstein, "Sematech Members Facing Dues Increase; 30% Jump to Make Up for Loss of Federal Funding," *Dallas Morning News*, July 27, 1996, p. 2F.

10. N. Dunne and R. Waters, "U.S. Waves a Big Stick at Chinese Pirates," *Financial Times*, January 6, 1995, p. 4.

11. John Broder, "Clinton to Impose Ban on 58 Types of Imported Guns," *The New York Times*, April 6, 1998, p. A1.

12. Bill Lambrecht, "Monsanto Softens Its Stance on Labeling in Europe," *St. Louis Post-Dispatch*, March 15, 1998, p. E1.

13. Peter S. Jordan, "Country Sanctions and the International Business Community," *American Society of International Law Proceedings of the Annual Meeting* 20, no. 9 (1997), pp. 333–42.

14. "Waiting for China; Human Rights and International Trade," *Commonwealth*, March 11, 1994, and "China: The Cost of Putting Business First," *Human Rights Watch*, July 1996.

15. "Brazil's Auto Industry Struggles to Boost Global Competitiveness," *Journal of Commerce*, October 10, 1991, p. 6A.

16. For reviews, see J. A. Brander, "Rationales for Strategic Trade and Industrial Policy," in *Strategic Trade Policy and the New International Economics*, ed. P. R. Krugman (Cambridge, MA: MIT Press, 1986); P. R. Krugman, "Is Free Trade Passé?" *Journal of Economic Perspectives* 1 (1987), pp. 131–44; and P. R. Krugman, "Does the New Trade Theory Require a New Trade Policy?" *World Economy* 15, no. 4 (1992), pp. 423–41.

17. "Airbus and Boeing: The Jumbo War," *The Economist*, June 15, 1991, pp. 65–66.

18. For details see Krugman, "Is Free Trade Passé?" and Brander, "Rationales for Strategic Trade and Industrial Policy."

19. Krugman, "Is Free Trade Passé?"

20. This dilemma is a variant of the famous prisoner's dilemma, which has become a classic metaphor for the difficulty of achieving cooperation between self-interested and mutually suspicious entities. For a good general introduction, see A. Dixit and B. Nalebuff, *Thinking Strategically: The Competitive Edge in Business, Politics, and Everyday Life* (New York: W. W. Norton & Co., 1991).

21. Note that the Smoot-Hawley Act did not cause the Great Depression. However, the beggar-thy-neighbor trade policies that it ushered in certainly made things worse. See Bhagwati, *Protectionism*.

22. Ibid.

23. World Bank, *World Development Report* (New York: Oxford University Press, 1987).

24. World Trade Organization, "World Trade 2004, Prospects 2005," WTO press release, April 14, 2005.

25. Frances Williams, "WTO—New Name Heralds New Powers," *Financial Times*, December 16, 1993, p. 5, and Frances Williams, "Gatt's Successor to Be Given Real Clout," *Financial Times*, April 4, 1994, p. 6.

26. W. J. Davey, "The WTO Dispute Settlement System: The First Ten Years," *Journal of International Economic Law*, March 2005, pp. 17–28.

27. Information provided on WTO Web site at www.wto.org/english/tratop_e/dispu_e/dispu_status_e.htm.

28. Frances Williams, "Telecoms: World Pact Set to Slash Costs of Calls," *Financial Times*, February 17, 1997.

29. G. De Jonquieres, "Happy End to a Cliff Hanger," *Financial Times*, December 15, 1997, p. 15.

30. Jim Carlton, "Greens Target WTO Plan for Lumber," *The Wall Street Journal*, November 24, 1999, p. A2.

31. Kari Huus, "WTO Summit Leaves Only Discontent," MSNBC, December 3, 1999 (www.msnbc.com).

32. Data at www.wto.org/english/tratop_e/adp_e/adp_e.htm.

33. *Annual Report by the Director General 2003* (Geneva: World Trade Organization, 2003).

34. Ibid.

35. Ibid.

36. World Trade Organization, *Annual Report 2002* (Geneva: WTO, 2002).

37. A. Tanzer, "Pill Factory to the World," *Forbes*, December 10, 2001, pp. 70–72.

38. S. C. Bradford, P. L. E. Grieco, and G. C. Hufbauer, "The Payoff to America from Global Integration," in *The United States and the World Economy: Foreign Policy for the Next Decade*, C. F. Bergsten, ed. (Washington, DC: Institute for International Economics, 2005).

39. World Bank, *Global Economic Prospects 2005* (Washington, DC: World Bank, 2005).

40. W. Vieth, "Major Concessions Lead to Success for WTO Talks," *Los Angeles Times*, November 14, 2001, p. A1, and "Seeds Sown for Future Growth," *The Economist*, November 17, 2001, pp. 65–66.

41. "The WTO under Fire—The Doha Round," *The Economist*, September 20, 2003, pp. 30–32.

42. "Punitive Tariffs Are Approved on Imports of Japanese Steel," *The New York Times*, June 12, 1999, p. A3.

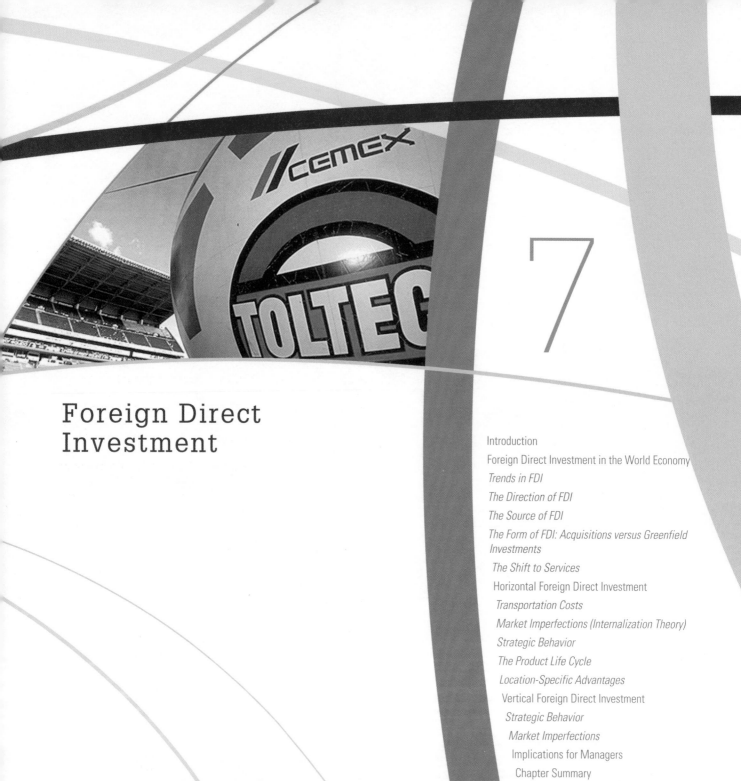

Foreign Direct Investment

7

Cemex's Foreign Direct Investment

In little more than a decade, Mexico's largest cement manufacturer, Cemex, has transformed itself from a primarily Mexican operation into the third largest cement company in the world behind Holcim of Switzerland and Lafarge Group of France with 2004 sales of $7.1 billion and more than $2 billion in cash flow. Cemex has long been a powerhouse in Mexico and currently controls more than 60 percent of the market for cement in that country. Cemex's domestic success has been based in large part on an obsession with efficient manufacturing and a focus on customer service that is tops in the industry.

Cemex is a leader in using information technology to match production with consumer demand. The company sells ready-mixed cement that can survive for only about 90 minutes before solidifying, so precise delivery is important. But Cemex can never predict with total certainty what demand will be on any given day, week, or month. To better manage unpredictable demand patterns, Cemex developed a system of seamless information technology, including truck-mounted global positioning systems, radio transmitters, satellites, and computer hardware, that allows Cemex to control the production and distribution of cement like no other company can, responding quickly to unanticipated changes in demand and reducing waste. The results are lower costs and superior customer service, both differentiating factors for Cemex.

The company also pays lavish attention to its distributors—some 5,000 in Mexico alone—who can earn points toward rewards for hitting sales targets. Those points can then be converted into Cemex stock. High-volume distributors can purchase trucks and other supplies through Cemex at significant discounts. Cemex also is known for its marketing drives that focus on end users, the builders themselves. For example, Cemex trucks drive around Mexican building sites, and if Cemex cement is being used, the construction crews win soccer balls, caps, and T-shirts.

Cemex's international expansion strategy was driven by a number of factors. First, the company wished to reduce its reliance on the Mexican construction market, which was characterized by very volatile demand. Second, the company realized there was tremendous demand for cement in many developing countries, where significant construction was being undertaken or needed. Third, the company believed that it understood the needs of construction businesses in developing nations better than the established multinational cement companies, all of which were from developed nations. Fourth, Cemex believed that it could create significant value by acquiring inefficient cement companies in other

markets and transferring its skills in customer service, marketing, information technology, and production management to those units.

The company embarked in earnest on its international expansion strategy in the early 1990s. Initially Cemex targeted other developing nations, acquiring established cement makers in Venezuela, Colombia, Indonesia, the Philippines, Egypt, and several other countries. It also purchased two stagnant companies in Spain and turned them around. Bolstered by the success of its Spanish ventures, Cemex began to look for expansion opportunities in developed nations. In 2000, Cemex purchased Houston-based Southland, one of the largest cement companies in the United States, for $2.5 billion. Following the Southland acquisition, Cemex had 56 cement plants in 30 countries, most of which were gained through acquisitions. In all cases, Cemex devoted great attention to transferring its technological, management, and marketing know-how to acquired units, thereby improving their performance.

The benefits of this strategy flowed through to the bottom line. From 1991 to 2003, the company's earnings before interest, tax, and depreciation when measured in U.S. dollars grew by more than 18 percent annually. Cash earnings per share also grew by 20 percent a year, while sales grew by 15 percent. Since profits have grown faster than sales, the company must be realizing significant efficiency gains in its acquired units. By 2002, Cemex was number one among the world's four largest cement manufacturers on most measures of financial performance, suggesting that its strategy of entering foreign markets through acquisitions was paying dividends, and it was more profitable than its major competitors.

In 2004, Cemex made another major foreign investment move, purchasing RMC of Great Britain for $5.8 billion. RMC was a huge multinational cement firm with sales of $8.0 billion, only 22 percent of which were in the United Kingdom, and operations in more than 20 other nations, including many European nations where Cemex had no presence. Finalized in March 2005, the RMC acquisition has transformed Cemex into a global powerhouse in the cement industry with more than $15 billion in annual sales and operations in 50 countries. Only about 15 percent of the company's sales are now generated in Mexico.

Sources: C. Piggott, "Cemex's Stratospheric Rise," *Latin Finance*, March 2001, p. 76; J. F. Smith, "Making Cement a Household Word," *Los Angeles Times*, January 16, 2000, p. C1; D. Helft, "Cemex Attempts to Cement Its Future," *The Industry Standard*, November 6, 2000; Diane Lindquist, "From Cement to Services," *Chief Executive*, November 2002, pp. 48–50; "Cementing Global Success," *Strategic Direct Investor*, March 2003, p. 1; M. T. Derham, "The Cemex Surprise," *Latin Finance*, November 2004, pp. 1–2; and "Holcim Seeks to Acquire Aggregate," *The Wall Street Journal*, January 13, 2005, p. 1.

Introduction

Foreign direct investment (FDI) occurs when a firm invests directly in facilities to produce and/or market a product in a foreign country. According to the U.S. Department of Commerce, FDI occurs whenever a U.S. citizen, organization, or affiliated group takes an interest of 10 percent or more in a foreign business entity. Once a firm undertakes FDI, it becomes a **multinational enterprise.** An example of FDI is given in the opening case. Between the early 1990s and 2005, the Mexican cement maker Cemex made foreign direct investments totaling some $16 billion to establish operations in 50 countries. By 2005, this FDI had transformed Cemex from a Mexican operation into a multinational powerhouse in the cement industry with annual sales in excess of $15 billion, only 15 percent of which were generated in Mexico.

FDI takes on two main forms. The first is a **greenfield investment,** which involves the establishment of a new operation in a foreign country. The second involves acquiring or merging with an existing firm in the foreign country (most of Cemex's expansion has been in the form of acquisition). Acquisitions can be a minority (where the foreign firm takes a 10 percent to 49 percent interest in the firm's voting stock), majority (foreign interest of 50 percent to 99 percent), or full outright stake (foreign interest of 100 percent).[1]

In Chapter 5, we considered several theories that sought to explain the pattern of trade between countries. These theories focus on why countries export some products and import others. None of these theories addresses why a firm might decide to invest directly in production facilities in a foreign country, rather than exporting its domestic production to that country or licensing a foreign entity to produce its product in return for licensing fees. The theories we reviewed in Chapter 5 do not explain the pattern of foreign direct investment between countries. They do not explain, for example, why Cemex chose to acquire Southland in the United States, rather than simply exporting cement to the country. The theories we explore in this chapter seek to do just this.

Our central objective will be to identify the economic rationale that underlies foreign direct investment. Firms often view exports and FDI as substitutes for each other. For example, when deciding to serve the North American market, the Japanese car manufacturer Toyota had to choose between exporting and foreign direct investment in North American production facilities. Although Toyota initially served the North American market through exports, increasingly it has turned to FDI. Toyota now has the capability to produce 1.45 million cars a year in North America. This chapter attempts to understand the conditions under which firms such as Toyota prefer FDI to exporting. We will review various theories regarding these conditions.

These theories also need to explain why a firm might prefer to engage in FDI rather than licensing. **Licensing** occurs when a domestic firm, the licensor, licenses to a foreign firm, the licensee, the right to produce its product, to use its production processes, or to use its brand name or trademark. In return for giving the licensee these rights, the licensor collects royalty fees on every unit the licensee sells or on total licensee revenues. The advantage claimed for licensing over FDI is that the licensor does not have to pay for opening a foreign market; the licensee does that. Nor does the licensor have to bear the risks associated with opening a foreign market. However, despite these attractions, many firms are reluctant to engage in straight licensing arrangements, preferring to make some kind of foreign direct investment. What is the theoretical rationale for such a decision? We shall answer this question, and as we shall see, the need for control is an important factor in explaining the decision.

In the remainder of the chapter, we first look at the growing importance of FDI in the world economy. Next we look at the theories that have been used to explain horizontal foreign direct investment. **Horizontal foreign direct investment** is FDI in the same industry in which a firm operates at home. Cemex's acquisition of RMC in Britain is an example of horizontal FDI. After reviewing horizontal FDI, we consider the theories that help to explain vertical foreign direct investment. **Vertical foreign direct investment** is

FDI in an industry that provides inputs for a firm's domestic operations, or it may be FDI in an industry abroad that sells the outputs of a firm's domestic operations. Finally, we review the implications of these theories for business practice.

Foreign Direct Investment in the World Economy

When discussing foreign direct investment, it is important to distinguish between the flow of FDI and the stock of FDI. The **flow of FDI** refers to the amount of FDI undertaken over a given time period (normally a year). The **stock of FDI** refers to the total accumulated value of foreign-owned assets at a given time. We also talk of **outflows of FDI,** meaning the flow of FDI out of a country, and **inflows of FDI,** meaning the flow of FDI into a country.

TRENDS IN FDI

The past 30 years have seen a marked increase in both the flow and stock of FDI in the world economy. The average yearly outflow of FDI increased from $25 billion in 1975 to a record $1.2 trillion in 2000, before falling back to an estimated $620 billion in 2004 (see Figure 7.1).[2] Over this period, the flow of FDI accelerated faster than the growth in world trade and world output. For example, between 1992 and 2004, the total flow of FDI from all countries increased about 260 percent while world trade by value grew by some 100 percent and world output by 32 percent.[3] As a result of the strong FDI flow, by 2003 the global stock of FDI exceeded $8.1 trillion. At least 61,000 parent companies had 900,000 affiliates in foreign markets that collectively employed some 54 million people abroad and generated value accounting for about one-tenth of global GDP. The foreign affiliates of multinationals had an estimated $17.6 trillion in global sales, nearly twice as high as the value of global exports which stood at $9.2 trillion.[4]

FDI has grown more rapidly than world trade and world output for several reasons. Despite the general decline in trade barriers over the past 30 years, business firms still fear protectionist pressures. Executives see FDI as a way of circumventing future trade barriers. Also, much of the recent increase in FDI is being driven by the political and economic changes that have been occurring in many of the world's developing nations. The general shift toward democratic political institutions and free market economies that we discussed in Chapter 2 has encouraged FDI. Across much of Asia, Eastern Europe, and Latin America, economic growth, economic deregulation, privatization programs that are open to foreign investors, and removal of many restrictions on FDI have made these countries more attractive to foreign multinationals. According to the United Nations, some 94 percent of the 1,885 changes made between 1991 and 2003 worldwide in the laws governing foreign direct investment created a more favorable environment for FDI. The desire of governments to facilitate FDI also has been reflected in a dramatic increase in the number of bilateral investment treaties designed to protect and promote investment between two countries. As of 2003, 2,265 such treaties involved more than 160 countries, a 12-fold increase from the 181 treaties that existed in 1980.[5]

The globalization of the world economy is also having a positive impact on the volume of FDI. Firms such as Cemex now see the whole world as their market, and they are undertaking FDI in an attempt to make sure they have a significant presence in many regions of the world. For reasons that we shall explore later in this book, many firms now believe it is important to have production facilities based close to their major customers. This, too, creates pressure for greater FDI.

Slumping FDI: 2001–2004

In contrast to the long-term trend, between 2000 and 2004 the value of FDI slumped almost 50 percent from $1.2 trillion to about $620 billion (see Figure 7.1). The most notable decline was in the levels of cross-border mergers and acquisitions, which have been

FIGURE 7.1

FDI Outflows,
1982–2004 ($ billions)

Notes: Figures for 1982–86 and 1987–91 are annual averages. The 2004 data represent preliminary estimates.
Sources: United Nations, *World Investment Report, 2004* (New York and Geneva: United Nations, 2004), and United Nations Conference on Trade and Development, "World FDI Flows Grew an Estimated 6% in 2004," UNCTAD press release, January 11, 2005.

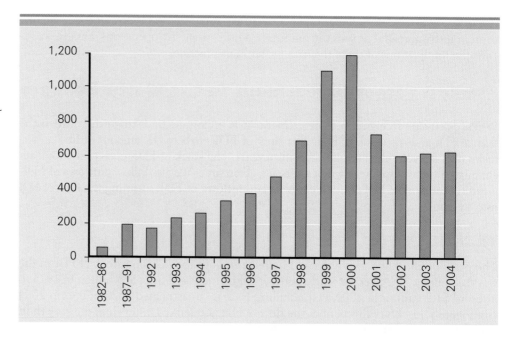

major drivers of global FDI flows since the 1980s. In 2000, the peak year, 7,900 cross-border deals totaled $1.1 trillion. The total number and value of deals fell in each of the next three years. In 2003, 4,200 cross-border merger and acquisition deals valued at $241 billion were executed. The overall decline in FDI has been most pronounced in developed nations.[6]

The slowdown in FDI flows observed in 2001–2004 probably will be temporary. It appears to reflect three developments: (1) the general slowdown in the growth rate of the world economy; (2) the heightened geopolitical uncertainty following the September 11, 2001, attack on the United States; and (3) the bursting of the stock market bubble in the United States, which limited the ability of many companies to raise additional capital to finance aggressive FDI activity, particularly mergers and acquisitions. The surge in FDI during 1999 and 2000 was a product of the late 1990s stock market bubble, and in retrospect represented an unsustainable short-term peak in FDI activity. As noted, much of the FDI activity during this period took the form of mergers and acquisitions, and many of these were financed by issuing new shares on world stock markets. With global stock markets in a depressed state, this seems unlikely to be repeated soon.

Nevertheless, surveys undertaken by the United Nations and other institutions suggest that most corporations plan to continue with their foreign investment plans over the next few years. The fundamental drivers of the long-term FDI trend still exist. Multinationals have been making foreign direct investments to get access to national markets or to establish low-cost manufacturing locations from which to serve regional or global markets, and these motives will surely be important going forward. Among the nations that are likely to benefit from increased FDI inflows during the next decade, China may see the largest percentage increase. China has been the largest recipient of FDI among developed nations for nearly a decade, a trend that continued in 2004 when the country received a record $62 billion in FDI from multinationals.[7]

THE DIRECTION OF FDI

Historically, most FDI has been directed at the developed nations of the world as firms based in advanced countries invested in the others' markets (see Figure 7.2). The United States has often been the favorite target for FDI inflows. This trend continued in the late

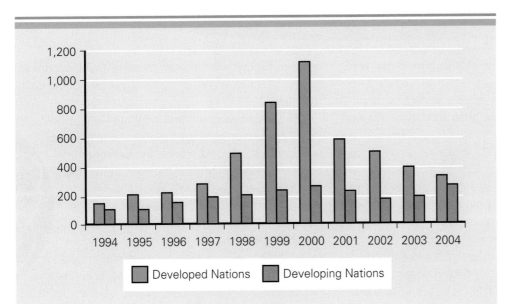

FIGURE 7.2

FDI Flows by Region ($ billion)

Note: 2004 data represent preliminary estimates.
Sources: Complied by the author from data in United Nations, *World Investment Report, 2004* (New York and Geneva: United Nations, 2004), and United Nations Conference on Trade and Development, "World FDI Flows Grew an Estimated 6% in 2004," UNCTAD press release, January 11, 2005.

1990s, when the United States remained the largest recipient of foreign direct investment.[8] In 2000, the United States was again the largest national recipient of FDI, accounting for $314 billion of the $1.2 trillion in global FDI, while the European Union was the largest single regional recipient of FDI, with $671 billion in inflows.[9] However, by 2004 the totals for the United States and the EU dropped to $121 billion and $165 billion, respectively, reflecting the drop in economic activity.[10] Historically, the United States has been an attractive target for FDI because of its large and wealthy domestic markets, its dynamic and stable economy, a favorable political environment, and the openness of the country to FDI. Investors include firms based in Great Britain, Japan, Germany, Holland, and France. Inward investment into the United States rose to $121 billion in 2004 and seems likely to continue to rebound.

Even though developed nations still account for the largest share of FDI inflows, FDI into developing nations has increased (see Figure 7.2). From 1985 to 1990, the annual inflow of FDI into developing nations averaged $27.4 billion, or 17.4 percent of the total global flow. In the mid- to late 1990s, the inflow into developing nations was generally between 35 and 40 percent of the total, before falling back to account for about 25 percent of the total in 2000–2002 and then rising to 44 percent in 2004. Most recent inflows into developing nations have been targeted at the emerging economies of South, East, and Southeast Asia. Driving much of the increase has been the growing importance of China as a recipient of FDI.[11] The reasons for the strong flow of investment into China are discussed in the accompanying Country Focus.

Latin America emerged as the next most important region in the developing world for FDI inflows. In 2000, total inward investments into this region reached about $86 billion, and it remained at that level during 2001 before dropping to $53 billion in 2002, $44 billion in 2003, and rising back to $69 billion in 2004. Much of this investment was concentrated in Mexico and Brazil and was a response to reforms in the region, including the privatization of industries, the liberalization of regulations governing FDI, and the growing importance of regional free trade areas such as MERCOSUR and NAFTA (which will be discussed in Chapter 9). At the other end of the scale, Africa received the smallest amount of inward investment, about $20 billion in 2004. The inability of Africa to attract greater investment is in part a reflection of the political unrest, armed conflict, and frequent changes in economic policy in the region.[12]

Another way of looking at the importance of FDI inflows is to express them as a percentage of gross fixed capital formation. **Gross fixed capital formation** summarizes the

COUNTRY FOCUS

Beginning in late 1978, China's leadership decided to move the economy away from a centrally planned system to one that was more market driven, while still maintaining the rigid political framework of Communist Party control. The strategy had a number of key elements, including a switch to household responsibility in agriculture instead of the old collectivization, increases in the authority of local officials and plant managers in industry, establishment of small- to medium-scale private enterprises in services and light manufacturing, and increased foreign trade and investment. The result has been two and a half decades of sustained high economic growth rates of between 10 and 11 percent annually compounded.

Starting from a tiny base, foreign investment increased to an annual average rate of $2.7 billion between 1985 and 1990 and then surged to $40 billion annually in the late 1990s, making China the second biggest recipient of FDI inflows in the world after the United States. Although world FDI flows slumped in 2001–2003, China still attracted increasing FDI each year, including a record $62 billion in 2004. Over the past 20 years, this inflow has resulted in establishment of 170,000 foreign-funded enterprises in China. The total stock of FDI in China had grown to $501 billion in 2003 ($876 billion if Hong Kong is added to this figure), amounting to about 30 percent of China's total GDP and 11 to 12 percent of annualized gross fixed capital formation between 1998 and 2003. FDI inflows have been a major source of investment and economic growth in China since liberalization began, accounting for perhaps as much as 30 percent of the country's growth.

The reasons for the investment are fairly obvious. With a population of nearly 1.3 billion people, China represents the largest market in the world. Import tariffs have made it difficult to serve this market via exports, so FDI was required if a company wanted to tap into the country's huge potential. Although China joined the World Trade Organization in 2001, which will ultimately mean a reduction in import tariffs, this will occur slowly, so this motive for investing in China will persist. Also, many foreign firms believe that doing business in China requires a substantial presence in the country to build *guanxi*, the crucial relationship networks (see Chapter 3 for details). Furthermore, a combination of cheap labor and tax incentives, particularly for enterprises that establish themselves in special economic zones, makes China an attractive base from which to serve Asian or world markets with exports. By 2001, foreign affiliates were accounting for some 50 percent of all exports from China, with rapid growth in exports of high-technology products from China made by the Chinese subsidiaries of companies such as Samsung, Nokia, and Motorola.

Less obvious, at least to begin with, was how difficult it would be for foreign firms to do business in China. Blinded by the size and potential of China's market, many firms have paid scant attention to the complexities

total amount of capital invested in factories, stores, office buildings, and the like. Other things being equal, the greater the capital investment in an economy, the more favorable its future growth prospects are likely to be. Viewed this way, FDI can be seen as an important source of capital investment and a determinant of the future growth rate of an economy. Figure 7.3 summarizes inward flows of FDI as a percentage of gross fixed capital formation for developed and developing economies for 1992–2003. During 1992–1997, FDI accounted for about 4 percent of gross fixed capital formation in developed nations, and 8 percent in developing nations. By the 1998–2003 period, the figure was 12.5 percent worldwide, suggesting that FDI had become an increasingly important source of investment in the world's economies.

These gross figures hide important individual country differences. For example, in 2003, inward FDI accounted for some 75 percent of gross fixed capital formation in Ireland and 20 percent in Chile, but only 4 percent in India and 0.6 percent in Japan—suggesting that FDI is an important source of investment capital, and thus economic

of operating a business in this country until after the investment has been made. China may have a huge population, but despite two decades of rapid growth, it is still a poor country where the average income is little more than $1,100 per year. The lack of purchasing power translates into a weak market for many Western consumer goods from automobiles to household appliances. Another problem is the lack of a well-developed transportation infrastructure or distribution system. PepsiCo discovered this problem at its subsidiary in Chongqing. Perched above the Yangtze River in southwest Sichuan province, Chongqing lies at the heart of China's massive hinterland. The Chongqing municipality, which includes the city and its surrounding regions, contains more than 30 million people, but according to Steve Chen, the manager of the PepsiCo subsidiary, the lack of well-developed road and distribution systems means he can reach only about half of this population with his product.

Other problems include a highly regulated environment, which can make it problematic to conduct business transactions, and shifting tax and regulatory regimes. For example, in 1997, the Chinese government suddenly scrapped a tax credit scheme that had made it attractive to import capital equipment into China. This immediately made it more expensive to set up operations in the country. Then there are problems with local joint-venture partners who are inexperienced, opportunistic, or simply operate according to different goals. One U.S. manager explained that when he laid off 200 people to reduce costs, his Chinese partner hired them all back the next day. When he inquired why they had been hired back, the executive of the Chinese partner, which was government owned, explained that as an agency of the government, it had an "obligation" to reduce unemployment.

To continue to attract foreign investment, the Chinese government has committed itself to invest more than $800 billion in infrastructure projects over the next 10 years. This should improve the nation's poor highway system. By giving preferential tax breaks to companies that invest in special regions, such as that around Chongqing, the Chinese have created incentives for foreign companies to invest in China's vast interior where markets are underserved. They have been pursuing a macroeconomic policy that includes an emphasis on maintaining steady economic growth, low inflation, and a stable currency, all of which are attractive to foreign investors. Given these developments, it seems likely that the country will continue to be an important magnet for foreign investors well into the future.

Sources: Interviews by the author while in China, March 1998; L. Sly, "China Losing Its Golden Glow," *Chicago Tribune,* September 15, 1997, p. 1; M. Miller, "Search for Fresh Capital Widens," *South China Morning Post,* April 9, 1998, p. 1; S. Mufson, "China Says Asian Crisis Will Have an Impact," *Washington Post,* March 8, 1998, p. A27; United Nations, *World Investment Report, 2004* (New York and Geneva: United Nations, 2004); and Linda Ng and C. Tuan, "Building a Favorable Investment Environment: Evidence for the Facilitation of FDI in China," *The World Economy,* 2002, pp. 1095–114.

growth, in the first two countries, but not the latter two. These differences can be explained by several factors, including the perceived ease and attractiveness of investing in a nation. To the extent that burdensome regulations limit the opportunities for foreign investment in countries such as Japan and India, these nations may be hurting themselves by limiting their access to needed capital investments.

THE SOURCE OF FDI

Since World War II, the United States has been the largest source country for FDI, a position it retained during the late 1990s and early 2000s (see Figure 7.4). Other important source countries include the United Kingdom, France, Germany, the Netherlands, and Japan. Collectively, these six countries accounted for 60 percent of all FDI outflows for 1998–2003 and 63 percent of the total global stock of FDI in 2003. As might be expected, these countries also predominate in rankings of the world's largest multinationals.

FIGURE 7.3

Inward FDI as a Percent of Gross Fixed Capital Formation, 1992–2003

Note: 1992–1997 figures are annual averages.
Sources: Compiled by the author from data in United Nations, *World Investment Report, 2004* (New York and Geneva: United Nations, 2004).

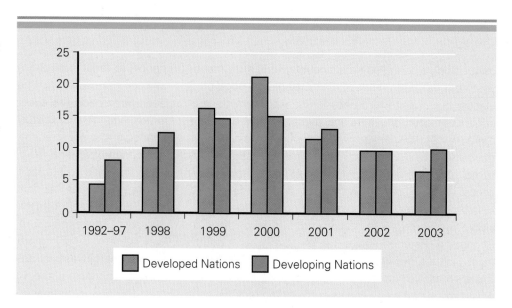

FIGURE 7.4

Cumulative FDI Outflows, 1998–2003 ($ billions)

Source: Compiled by the author from data in United Nations, *World Investment Report, 2004* (New York and Geneva: United Nations, 2004).

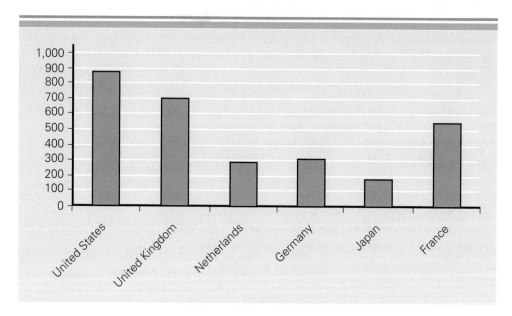

As of 2003, 27 percent of the world's 100 largest multinationals were U.S. enterprises; 14 percent were French; 12 percent, German; 12 percent, British; and 7 percent, Japanese. In terms of the global stock of FDI, 25 percent belonged to U.S. firms, 14 percent to British, 8 percent to French firms, 8 percent to German firms, 5 percent to Dutch firms, and 4 percent to Japanese.[13] These nations dominate primarily because they were the most developed nations with the largest economies during much of the postwar period, and therefore home to many of the largest and best-capitalized enterprises. Many of these countries also had a long history as trading nations and naturally looked to foreign markets to fuel their economic expansion. Thus, it is no surprise that enterprises based there have been at the forefront of foreign investment trends.

THE FORM OF FDI: ACQUISITIONS VERSUS GREENFIELD INVESTMENTS

FDI can take the form of a greenfield investment in a new facility or an acquisition of or a merger with an existing local firm. The data suggest the majority of cross-border investment is in the form of mergers and acquisitions rather than greenfield investments.

UN estimates indicate that some 40 to 80 percent of all FDI inflows were in the form of mergers and acquisitions between 1998 and 2003. In 2001, for example, mergers and acquisitions accounted for some 78 percent of all FDI inflows. In 2003 the figure was 49 percent.[14] However, FDI flows into developed nations differ markedly from those into developing nations. In the case of developing nations, only about one-third of FDI is in the form of cross-border mergers and acquisitions. The lower percentage of mergers and acquisitions may simply reflect the fact that there are fewer target firms to acquire in developing nations.

When contemplating FDI, why do firms apparently prefer to acquire existing assets rather than undertake greenfield investments? We shall consider it in greater depth in Chapter 14, so for now we will make only a few basic observations. First, mergers and acquisitions are quicker to execute than greenfield investments. This is an important consideration in the modern business world where markets evolve very rapidly. Many firms apparently believe that if they do not acquire a desirable target firm, then their global rivals will. The case of Cemex illustrates this (see the opening case). Cemex is the world's third largest cement company and Mexico's largest multinational. Cemex's rise to global status took less than a decade and has been driven primarily by acquisitions. If Cemex had relied on greenfield investments, it could not have become so large so fast.

Second, foreign firms are acquired because those firms have valuable strategic assets, such as brand loyalty, customer relationships, trademarks or patents, distribution systems, production systems, and the like. It is easier and perhaps less risky for a firm to acquire those assets than to build them from the ground up through a greenfield investment. Cemex's acquisition of Houston-based cement maker Southland for $2.5 billion is a good example. Cemex wanted quick entry to the growing U.S. construction market, and Southland's production and distribution assets enabled Cemex to achieve this.

Third, firms make acquisitions because they believe they can increase the efficiency of the acquired unit by transferring capital, technology, or management skills. For example, Cemex has developed the best information systems in the global cement industry, which has enabled it to better meet customer needs (see the opening case for details). Cemex can increase the efficiency of its acquired units, such as Southland, by transferring its technological know-how to those units after the acquisition. Thus, some fairly compelling arguments favor mergers and acquisitions over greenfield investments. But many mergers and acquisitions fail to realize their anticipated gains.[15] Chapter 14 further studies this issue.

THE SHIFT TO SERVICES

In the past two decades, the sector composition of FDI has shifted sharply away from extractive industries and manufacturing and toward services. In 1990, some 47 percent of outward FDI stock was in service industries; by 2003 this figure had increased to 67 percent. Similar trends can be seen in the composition of cross-border mergers and acquisitions, in which services are playing a much larger role (see Figure 7.5). The composition of FDI in services has also changed. Until recently it was concentrated in trade and financial services. However, industries such as electricity, water, telecommunications, and business services (such as information technology consulting services) are becoming more prominent.

The shift to services is being driven by four factors that will probably stay in place for some time. First, the shift reflects the general move in many developed economies away from manufacturing and toward service industries. By the early 2000s, services accounted for 72 percent of the GDP in developed economies and 52 percent in developing economies. Second, many services cannot be traded internationally. They need to be produced where they are consumed. Starbucks, which is a service business, cannot sell hot lattes to Japanese consumers from its Seattle stores—it has to set up shops in Japan. FDI is the principal way to bring services to foreign markets. Third, many countries have liberalized their regimes governing FDI in services (Chapter 6 revealed that the WTO engineered global deals to remove barriers to cross-border investment in

FIGURE 7.5

Cross-Border Mergers and Acquisitions by Sector of Seller, 1998–2003 ($ millions)

Source: Compiled by the author from data in United Nations, *World Investment Report, 2004* (New York and Geneva: United Nations, 2004).

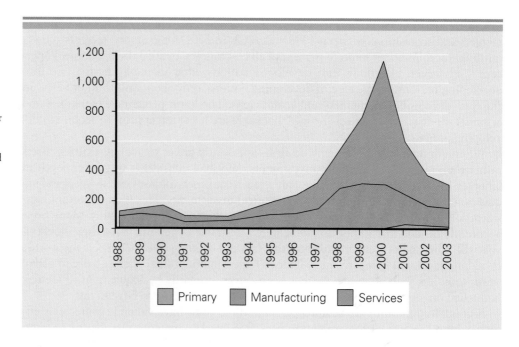

telecommunications and financial services during the late 1990s). This liberalization has made large inflows possible. After Brazil privatized its telecommunications company in the late 1990s and removed restrictions on investment by foreigners in this sector, FDI surged into the Brazilian telecommunications sector.

Finally, the rise of Internet-based global telecommunications networks has allowed some service enterprises to relocate some of their value creation activities to different nations to take advantage of favorable factor costs. Procter & Gamble, for example, has shifted some of its back-office accounting functions to the Philippines where accountants trained in U.S. accounting rules can be hired at a much lower salary. Dell has call answering centers in India for the same reason. Similarly, both Microsoft and IBM now have some software development and testing facilities located in India. Software code written at Microsoft during the day can now be transmitted instantly to India, and tested while the code writers in Microsoft sleep. By the time they arrive for work the next morning, the code has been tested, bugs have been identified, and they can start working on corrections. By locating testing facilities in India, Microsoft can work on its code 24 hours a day, reducing the time it takes to develop new software products.

🌐 Horizontal Foreign Direct Investment

Horizontal FDI is investment in the same industry abroad as a firm operates in at home. We need to understand why firms go to the trouble of acquiring or establishing operations abroad, when the alternatives of exporting and licensing are available. Other things being equal, FDI is expensive and risky compared to exporting or licensing. FDI is expensive because a firm must bear the costs of establishing production facilities in a foreign country or of acquiring a foreign enterprise. FDI is risky because of the problems associated with doing business in another culture where the "rules of the game" may be very different. Relative to firms native to a culture, a firm in a foreign culture has a greater probability of making costly mistakes due to ignorance. When a firm exports, it need not bear the costs of FDI, and the risks associated with selling abroad can be reduced by using a native sales agent. Similarly, when a firm licenses its know-how, it need not bear the costs or risks of FDI. So why do so many firms apparently prefer FDI over either exporting or licensing?

The quick answer is that other things are not equal! A number of factors can alter the relative attractiveness of exporting, licensing, and FDI. We will consider these factors: transportation costs, market imperfections, competitions, strategic behavior, and location advantages.

TRANSPORTATION COSTS

When transportation costs are added to production costs, it becomes unprofitable to ship some products a long distance. This is particularly true of products that have a low value-to-weight ratio and can be produced in almost any location (e.g., cement, soft drinks, etc.). For such products, relative to either FDI or licensing, the attractiveness of exporting decreases. Thus, transportation costs alone help explain why Cemex has undertaken FDI rather than exporting (see the opening case). For products with a high value-to-weight ratio, however, transport costs are normally a very minor component of total landed cost (e.g., electronic components, personal computers, medical equipment, computer software, etc.). In such cases, transportation costs have little impact on the relative attractiveness of exporting, licensing, and FDI.

MARKET IMPERFECTIONS (INTERNALIZATION THEORY)

Market imperfections provide a major explanation of why firms may prefer FDI to either exporting or licensing. **Market imperfections** are factors that inhibit markets from working perfectly. The market imperfections explanation of FDI is the one favored by most economists.[16] In the international business literature, the marketing imperfection approach to FDI is typically referred to as **internalization theory.**

With regard to horizontal FDI, market imperfections arise in two circumstances: when there are impediments to the free flow of products between nations, and when there are impediments to the sale of know-how. (Licensing is a mechanism for selling know-how.) Impediments to the free flow of products between nations decrease the profitability of exporting, relative to FDI and licensing. Impediments to the sale of know-how increase the profitability of FDI relative to licensing. Thus, the market imperfections explanation predicts that FDI will be preferred whenever there are impediments that make both exporting and the sale of know-how difficult and/or expensive.

Impediments to Exporting

Governments are the main source of impediments to the free flow of products between nations. By placing tariffs on imported goods, governments increase the cost of exporting relative to FDI and licensing. Similarly, by limiting imports through the imposition of quotas, governments increase the attractiveness of FDI and licensing. For example, the wave of FDI by Japanese auto companies in the United States during the 1980s was partly driven by protectionist threats from Congress and by quotas on the importation of Japanese cars. For Japanese auto companies, these factors have decreased the profitability of exporting and increased the profitability of FDI. Similarly, investments by Western automobile companies in Russia in the early 2000s were in part driven by high tariff barriers on imports of cars into the country (see the next Management Focus).

Impediments to the Sale of Know-How

The competitive advantage that many firms enjoy comes from their technological, marketing, or management know-how. Technological know-how can enable a company to build a better product; for example, Nokia's technological know-how has given it a strong competitive position in the global market for wireless telephone equipment. Alternatively, technological know-how can improve a company's production process vis-á-vis competitors. For example, many claim that Toyota's competitive advantage comes from its superior production system. Marketing know-how can enable a company to better position its products in the marketplace; the competitive advantage of such companies as

Kellogg, H. J. Heinz, and Procter & Gamble seems to come from superior marketing know-how. Management know-how with regard to factors such as organizational structure, human relations, control systems, planning systems, inventory management, and so on, can enable a company to manage its assets more efficiently than competitors. Cemex has used its technological know-how to better manage customer demand and improve operating efficiencies and its marketing knowledge to build a well-earned reputation for being very customer focused (see the opening case).

If we view know-how (expertise) as a competitive asset, it follows that the larger the market in which that asset is applied, the greater the profits that can be earned from the asset. Nokia can earn greater returns on its know-how by selling its wireless telephone equipment worldwide than by selling it only in its native Finland. However, this alone does not explain why Nokia undertakes FDI (the company has production locations around the world). For Nokia to favor FDI, two conditions must hold. First, transportation costs and/or impediments to exporting must rule out exporting as an option. Second, there must be some reason Nokia cannot sell its wireless know-how to foreign producers. Because licensing is the main mechanism by which firms sell their know-how, there must be some reason Nokia is not willing to license a foreign firm to manufacture and market its cellular telephone equipment. Other things being equal, licensing might look attractive to such a firm, since it would not have to bear the costs and risks associated with FDI yet it could still earn a good return from its know-how in the form of royalty fees.

Economic theory supports three reasons the market often does not work well as a mechanism for selling know-how, or why licensing is not as attractive as it initially appears. First, licensing may result in a firm's giving away its know-how to a potential foreign competitor. For example, in the 1960s, RCA licensed its leading-edge color television technology to a number of Japanese companies, including Matsushita and Sony. At the time, RCA saw licensing as a way to earn a good return from its technological know-how in the Japanese market without the costs and risks associated with FDI. However, Matsushita and Sony quickly assimilated RCA's technology and used it to enter the U.S. market to compete directly against RCA. As a result, RCA is now a minor player in its home market, while Matsushita and Sony have a much bigger market share.

Second, licensing does not give a firm the tight control over manufacturing, marketing, and strategy in a foreign country that may be required to profitably exploit its advantage in know-how. With licensing, control over production, marketing, and strategy is granted to a licensee in return for a royalty fee. However, for both strategic and operational reasons, a firm may want to retain control over these functions. For example, a firm might want its foreign subsidiary to price and market very aggressively, to keep a global competitor in check, but the licensee, which has to make a profit, may be unwilling to do this for the greater good of the licensor. Kodak has used its Japanese subsidiary to launch aggressive attacks against its global competitor, Fuji Film. The idea has been to keep Fuji busy defending its home market, which limits Fuji's ability to launch aggressive attacks in the United States. While Kodak's Japanese subsidiary, which is wholly owned, has to accept such strategic direction, a licensee would be unlikely to accept such an imposition because such a strategy would allow the licensee to make only a low profit or even take a loss.

In addition, a firm may want control over the operations of a foreign entity to take advantage of differences in factor costs among countries, producing only part of its final product in a given country, while importing other parts from where they can be produced at lower cost. Again, a licensee would be unlikely to accept such an arrangement because it would limit the licensee's autonomy. When tight control over a foreign entity is desirable, horizontal FDI is preferable to licensing.

Third, a firm's know-how may not be amenable to licensing. This is particularly true of management and marketing know-how. It is one thing to license a foreign firm to manufacture a particular product, but quite another to license the way a firm does business—how it manages its process and markets its products. Consider Toyota, a company whose competitive advantage in the global auto industry is acknowledged to come from its superior ability to manage the overall process of designing, engineering, manufacturing, and selling automobiles; that is, from its management and organizational know-how. Toyota is credited with pioneering the development of a new production process, known as lean production, that enables it to produce higher-quality automobiles at a lower cost than its global rivals.[17] Although Toyota has certain products that can be licensed, its real competitive advantage comes from its management and process know-how. These kinds of skills are difficult to articulate or codify; they cannot be written down in a simple licensing contract. They are organizationwide and have been developed over years. They are not embodied in any one individual, but instead are widely dispersed throughout the company. Toyota's skills are embedded in its organizational culture, and culture is something that cannot be licensed. Thus, as Toyota moves away from its traditional exporting strategy, it has increasingly pursued a strategy of FDI, rather than licensing foreign enterprises to produce its cars. The same is true of Cemex. Because it is embedded in organizational processes and managerial skills, Cemex's know-how with regard to management, marketing, and technology might all be difficult to transfer via a licensing contract. Thus, FDI became the logical way for Cemex to expand internationally.

All of this suggests that when one or more of the following conditions holds, markets fail as a mechanism for selling know-how and FDI is more profitable than licensing: (1) when the firm has valuable know-how that cannot be adequately protected by a licensing contract, (2) when the firm needs tight control over a foreign entity to maximize its market share and earnings in that country, and (3) when a firm's skills and know-how are not amenable to licensing.

STRATEGIC BEHAVIOR

Another theory used to explain FDI is based on the idea that FDI flows are a reflection of strategic rivalry between firms in the global marketplace. An early variant of this argument was expounded by F. T. Knickerbocker, who looked at the relationship between FDI and rivalry in oligopolistic industries.[18] An **oligopoly** is an industry composed of a limited number of large firms (e.g., an industry in which four firms control 80 percent of a domestic market would be defined as an oligopoly). A critical competitive feature of such industries is *interdependence* of the major players: What one firm does can have an immediate impact on the major competitors, forcing a response in kind. If one firm in an oligopoly cuts prices, this can take market share away from its competitors, forcing them to respond with similar price cuts to retain their market share. Thus, the interdependence between firms in an oligopoly leads to imitative behavior; rivals often quickly imitate what a firm does in an oligopoly.

Imitative behavior can take many forms in an oligopoly. One firm raises prices, the others follow; someone expands capacity, and the rivals imitate lest they be left at a disadvantage in the future. Knickerbocker argued that the same kind of imitative behavior characterizes FDI. Consider an oligopoly in the United States in which three firms—A, B and C—dominate the market. Firm A establishes a subsidiary in France. Firms B and C decide that if this investment is successful, it may knock out their export business to France and give firm A a first-mover advantage. Furthermore, firm A might discover some competitive asset in France that it could repatriate to the United States to torment firms B and C on their native soil. Given these possibilities, firms B and C decide to follow firm A and establish operations in France.

Studies that looked at FDI by U.S. firms during the 1950s and 60s show that firms based in oligopolistic industries tended to imitate each other's FDI.[19] The same phenomenon has been observed with regard to FDI undertaken by Japanese firms during the 1980s.[20] For example, Toyota and Nissan responded to investments by Honda in the United States and Europe by undertaking their own FDI in the United States and Europe. More recently, research has shown that models of strategic behavior in a global oligopoly can explain the pattern of FDI in the global tire industry.[21] As the accompanying Management Focus suggests, recent investments in Russia by GM and Ford might also be viewed in this way.

MANAGEMENT FOCUS In July 2002, Ford Motor Company officially opened its first Russian car factory near Saint Petersburg. The factory, which cost some $150 million to build, is 100 percent owned by Ford and represents the first wholly owned investment by a foreign carmaker in Russia. The factory is small; it will employ 800 people and initially will produce 10,000 Ford Focus cars a year. By comparison, a typical auto plant in the developed world produces 200,000 cars a year. If things go well, Ford plans to increase production to 25,000 cars a year by 2007, and if things go really well, the plant may ultimately produce 100,000 vehicles a year. If these plans come to fruition, it could be a boon for the region. Assembly-line workers at the Ford factory will make approximately $220 a month, significantly more than the $134 average wage in Russia, and skilled engineers at the factory may make as much as $600 a month.

Ford was motivated in part by a desire to gain a foothold in the Russian car market. Although car ownership levels in Russia are very low by international standards—120 cars per 1,000 people compared to 580 per 1,000 in Western Europe—car sales have been rising by 7 to 8 percent a year. In 2002, about 1.5 million new and used cars were bought in Russia, about 1 million of which were Russian cars. New Russian models sell for $5,000 to $8,000. Ford intends to sell its locally produced Ford Focus for about $10,900, a price premium that Ford believes is justified given the poor reputation of Russian cars. An imported Ford Focus currently sells for $14,000 due to transportation costs, import duties, and higher wages at Ford's Western European factories. With the Russian government increasing import tariffs on finished cars to about 35 percent, and the political climate stabilizing, Ford thought it was time to establish local production.

Three months after Ford's announcement, General Motors became the second Western company to invest in Russian car factories. Rather than go it alone, however, GM opted to enter a joint venture with Avto-VAZ, Russia's largest auto company, to produce a new version of its popular SUV, the Niva. Avto-VAZ was reportedly looking for a venture partner to both invest capital and provide much-needed technical expertise to help the company upgrade product quality and lower production costs. In recent years, AvtoVAZ has been losing market share to imported used cars. In late 2002, it halted production in its factories for three weeks, despite strong car sales in Russia, while it attempted to move unsold inventory of 60,000 cars. GM will reportedly invest some $141 million in the AvtoVAZ venture for a 41.5 percent ownership stake. The joint venture plans to produce 75,000 Nivas a year, each selling for about $8,000. In addition to selling the car locally, there are plans to export the Nivas to the Middle East, Asia, and Latin America. In total, the venture expects to create some 3,500 new jobs.

Not wishing to be left out, in mid-2003, Renault became the third Western company to set up operations in Russia. Renault announced it would invest $250 million in an auto plant 62 percent owned by Renault and 38 percent by the Moscow City government. Renault's plan is to use the plant to design and build an entirely new model, the X90, which will be priced less than $10,000 and targeted at emerging markets including Russia.

Sources: B. Aris, "Ford Drives under the Barrier," *Euromoney,* August 2002, pp. 20–22; J. Daniszewski, "GM Rolls Out Joint Venture with Russia," *Los Angeles Times,* September 24, 2002, p. A3; and G. Chazan, "Russians Want Foreign Wheels," *The Wall Street Journal,* December 24, 2002, p. A8; and "Russian Company: Renault's Big Gamble," EIU Views Wire, March 20, 2003.

Knickerbocker's theory can be extended to embrace the concept of multipoint competition. **Multipoint competition** arises when two or more enterprises encounter each other in different regional markets, national markets, or industries.[22] Economic theory suggests that rather like chess players jockeying for advantage, firms will try to match each other's moves in different markets to try to hold each other in check. The idea is to ensure that a rival does not gain a commanding position in one market and then use the profits generated there to subsidize competitive attacks in other markets. Kodak and Fuji Photo Film Co., for example, compete against each other around the world. If Kodak enters a particular foreign market, Fuji will not be far behind. Fuji feels compelled to follow

Kodak to ensure that Kodak does not gain a dominant position in the foreign market that it could then leverage to gain a competitive advantage elsewhere. The converse also holds, with Kodak following Fuji when the Japanese firm is the first to enter a foreign market.

Although Knickerbocker's theory and its extensions can help to explain imitative FDI behavior by firms in oligopolistic industries, it does not explain why the first firm in an oligopoly decides to undertake FDI, rather than to export or license. The market imperfections explanation addresses this phenomenon. The imitative theory also does not address the issue of whether FDI is more efficient than exporting or licensing for expanding abroad. Again, the market imperfections approach addresses the efficiency issue. For these reasons, many economists favor the market imperfections explanation for FDI, although most would agree that the imitative explanation tells an important part of the story.

THE PRODUCT LIFE CYCLE

Raymond Vernon's product life-cycle theory, described in Chapter 5, also is used to explain FDI. Vernon argued that often the same firms that pioneer a product in their home markets undertake FDI to produce a product for consumption in foreign markets. Thus, Xerox introduced the photocopier in the United States, and it was Xerox that set up production facilities in Japan (Fuji-Xerox) and Great Britain (Rank-Xerox) to serve those markets. Vernon's view is that firms undertake FDI at particular stages in the life cycle of a product they have pioneered. They invest in other advanced countries when local demand in those countries grows large enough to support local production (as Xerox did). They subsequently shift production to developing countries when product standardization and market saturation give rise to price competition and cost pressures. Investment in developing countries, where labor costs are lower, is seen as the best way to reduce costs.

Vernon's theory has merit. Firms do invest in a foreign country when demand in that country will support local production, and they do invest in low-cost locations (e.g., developing countries) when cost pressures become intense.[23] However, Vernon's theory fails to explain why it is profitable for a firm to undertake FDI at such times, rather than continuing to export from its home base and rather than licensing a foreign firm to produce its product. Just because demand in a foreign country is large enough to support local production, it does not necessarily follow that local production is the most profitable option. It may still be more profitable to produce at home and export to that country (to realize the scale economies that arise from serving the global market from one location). Alternatively, it may be more profitable for the firm to license a foreign company to produce its product for sale in that country. The product life-cycle theory ignores these options and, instead, simply argues that once a foreign market is large enough to support local production, FDI will occur. This limits its explanatory power and its usefulness to business in that it fails to identify when it is profitable to invest abroad.

LOCATION-SPECIFIC ADVANTAGES

The British economist John Dunning has argued that in addition to the various factors discussed above, location-specific advantages can help explain the nature and direction of FDI.[24] By **location-specific advantages,** Dunning means the advantages that arise from using resource endowments or assets that are tied to a particular foreign location and that a firm finds valuable to combine with its own unique assets (such as the firm's technological, marketing, or management know-how). Dunning accepts the internalization argument that market failures make it difficult for a firm to license its own unique assets (know-how). Therefore, he argues that combining location-specific assets or resource endowments and the firm's own unique assets often requires FDI. It requires the firm to establish production facilities where those foreign assets or resource endowments are located (Dunning refers to this argument as the **eclectic paradigm**).

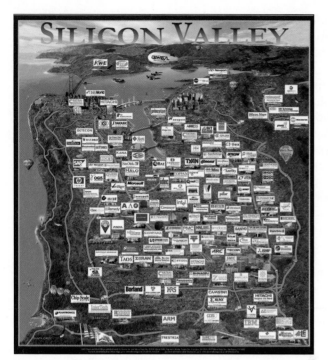

Silicon Valley has long been known as the epicenter of the computer and semiconductor industry.

An obvious example of Dunning's arguments is natural resources, such as oil and other minerals, which are specific to certain locations. Dunning suggests that a firm must undertake FDI to exploit such foreign resources. This explains the FDI undertaken by many of the world's oil companies, which have to invest where oil is located to combine their technological and managerial knowledge with this valuable location-specific resource. Another example is valuable human resources, such as low-cost highly skilled labor. The cost and skill of labor varies from country to country. Since labor is not internationally mobile, according to Dunning it makes sense for a firm to locate production facilities where the cost and skills of local labor are most suited to its particular production processes.

However, the implications of Dunning's theory go beyond basic resources such as minerals and labor. Consider Silicon Valley, which is the world center for the computer and semiconductor industry. Many of the world's major computer and semiconductor companies, such as Apple Computer, Applied Materials, and Intel, are located close to each other in the Silicon Valley region of California. As a result, much of the cutting-edge research and product development in computers and semiconductors occurs here. According to Dunning's arguments, knowledge being generated in Silicon Valley with regard to the design and manufacture of computers and semiconductors is available nowhere else in the world. As it is commercialized, that knowledge diffuses throughout the world, but the leading edge of knowledge generation in the computer and semiconductor industries is to be found in Silicon Valley. In Dunning's language, this means Silicon Valley has a location-specific advantage in the generation of knowledge related to the computer and semiconductor industries. In part, this advantage comes from the sheer concentration of intellectual talent in this area, and in part it arises from a network of informal contacts that allows firms to benefit from each other's knowledge generation. Economists refer to such knowledge "spillovers" as **externalities,** and one well-established theory suggests that firms can benefit from such externalities by locating close to their source.[25]

In so far as this is the case, it makes sense for foreign computer and semiconductor firms to invest in research and (perhaps) production facilities so they too can learn about and utilize valuable new knowledge before those based elsewhere, thereby giving them a competitive advantage in the global marketplace.[26] Evidence suggests that European, Japanese, South Korean, and Taiwanese computer and semiconductor firms are investing in the Silicon Valley region, precisely because they wish to benefit from the externalities that arise there.[27] Others have argued that direct investment by foreign firms in the U.S. biotechnology industry has been motivated by desires to gain access to the unique location-specific technological knowledge of U.S. biotechnology firms.[28] Dunning's theory, therefore, seems to be a useful addition to those outlined above, for it helps explain how location factors affect the direction of FDI.[29]

Vertical Foreign Direct Investment

Vertical FDI takes two forms. **Backward vertical FDI** is an investment in an industry abroad that provides inputs for a firm's domestic production processes. Historically, most backward vertical FDI has been in extractive industries (e.g., oil extraction, bauxite mining, tin mining, and copper mining). The objective has been to provide inputs into a firm's downstream operations (e.g., oil refining, aluminum smelting and fabrication, tin smelting and fabrication). Firms such as Royal Dutch/Shell, British Petroleum (BP), RTZ, Consolidated Gold Field, and Alcoa are among the classic examples of such vertically integrated multinationals.

A second form of vertical FDI is **forward vertical FDI** in which an industry abroad sells the outputs of a firm's domestic production processes. Forward vertical FDI is less common than backward vertical FDI. For example, when Volkswagen entered the U.S. market, it acquired a large number of dealers rather than distribute its cars through independent U.S. dealers.

With both horizontal and vertical FDI, the question that must be answered is why would a firm go to all the trouble and expense of setting up operations in a foreign country? Why, for example, did petroleum companies such as BP and Royal Dutch/Shell vertically integrate backward into oil production abroad? The location-specific advantages argument helps explain the direction of such FDI; vertically integrated multinationals in extractive industries invest where the raw materials are. However, this argument does not clarify why they did not simply import raw materials extracted by local producers. And why do companies such as Volkswagen feel it is necessary to acquire their own dealers in foreign markets, when in theory it might seem less costly to rely on foreign dealers? There are two basic answers to these kinds of questions. The first is a strategic behavior argument, and the second draws on the market imperfections approach.

STRATEGIC BEHAVIOR

According to economic theory, by vertically integrating backward to gain control over the source of raw material, a firm can raise entry barriers and shut new competitors out of an industry.[30] Such strategic behavior involves vertical FDI if the raw material is found abroad. A famous example occurred in the 1930s when North American firms such as Alcoa pioneered commercial smelting of aluminum, which is derived from bauxite. Although bauxite is a common mineral, the percentage of aluminum in bauxite is typically so low that it is not economical to mine and smelt. During the 1930s, only one large-scale deposit of bauxite with an economical percentage of aluminum had been discovered, and it was on the Caribbean island of Trinidad. Alcoa and Alcan vertically integrated backward and acquired ownership of the deposit. This action created a **barrier to entry** into the aluminum industry. Potential competitors were deterred because they could not get access to high-grade bauxite—it was all owned by Alcoa and Alcan. Those that did enter the industry had to use lower-grade bauxite than Alcan and Alcoa and found themselves at a cost disadvantage. This situation persisted until the 1950s and 1960s, when new high-grade deposits were discovered in Australia and Indonesia.

However, the opportunities for barring entry through vertical FDI seem far too limited to explain the incidence of vertical FDI among the world's multinationals. In most extractive industries, mineral deposits are not as concentrated as in the case of bauxite in the 1930s; new deposits are constantly being discovered. Consequently, any attempt to monopolize all viable raw material deposits is bound to prove very expensive if not impossible.

Another strand of the strategic behavior explanation of vertical FDI sees such investment not as an attempt to build entry barriers, but as an attempt to circumvent the barriers established by firms already doing business in a country. This may explain Volkswagen's decision to establish its own dealer network when it entered the North American auto market. GM, Ford, and Chrysler then dominated the market. Each firm had its own network of dealers. Volkswagen felt that the only way to get quick access to the United States was to promote its cars through company-owned dealerships.

MARKET IMPERFECTIONS

As in the case of horizontal FDI, a more general explanation of vertical FDI can be found in the market imperfections approach.[31] The market imperfections approach offers two explanations for vertical FDI. As with horizontal FDI, the first explanation revolves around the idea that there are impediments to the sale of know-how through the market mechanism. The second explanation is based on the idea that investments in specialized assets expose the investing firm to hazards that can be reduced only through vertical FDI.

Impediments to the Sale of Know-How

Consider the case of oil refining companies such as British Petroleum and Royal Dutch/Shell. Historically, these firms pursued backward vertical FDI to supply their British and Dutch oil refining facilities with crude oil. When this occurred in the early decades of the 20th century, neither Great Britain nor the Netherlands had domestic oil supplies. Why did these firms not just import oil from firms in oil-rich countries such as Saudi Arabia and Kuwait?

Originally, there were no Saudi Arabian or Kuwaiti firms with the technological expertise for finding and extracting oil. BP and Royal Dutch/Shell had to develop this know-how to get access to oil. This alone does not explain FDI, however, for once BP and Shell had developed the necessary know-how, they could have licensed it to Saudi Arabian or Kuwaiti firms. However, as we saw in the case of horizontal FDI, licensing can be self-defeating as a mechanism for the sale of know-how. If the oil refining firms had licensed their prospecting and extraction know-how to Saudi Arabian or Kuwaiti firms, they would have risked giving away their technological know-how to those firms, creating future competitors in the process. Once they had the know-how, the Saudi and Kuwaiti firms might have gone prospecting for oil in other parts of the world, competing directly against BP and Royal Dutch/Shell. Thus, it made more sense for these firms to undertake backward vertical FDI and extract the oil themselves instead of licensing their hard-earned technological expertise to local firms.

By generalization from this example, backward vertical FDI will occur when a firm has the knowledge and the ability to extract raw materials in another country and there is no efficient producer in that country that can supply raw materials to the firm.

Investment in Specialized Assets

Another strand of the market imperfections argument predicts that vertical FDI will occur when a firm must invest in specialized assets whose value depends on inputs provided by a foreign supplier. In this context, a specialized asset is an asset designed to perform a specific task and whose value is significantly reduced in its next-best use. Consider the case of an aluminum refinery, which is designed to refine bauxite ore and produce aluminum. Bauxite ores vary in content and chemical composition from deposit to deposit. Each type of ore requires a different type of refinery. Running one type of bauxite through a refinery designed for another type increases production costs by 20 to 100 percent.[32] Thus, the value of an investment in an aluminum refinery depends on the availability of the desired kind of bauxite ore.

Imagine that a U.S. aluminum company must decide whether to invest in an aluminum refinery designed to refine a certain type of ore. Assume further that this ore is available only through an Australian mining firm at a single bauxite mine. Using a different type of ore in the refinery would raise production costs by at least 20 percent. Therefore, the value of the U.S. company's investment depends on the price it must pay the Australian firm for this bauxite. Recognizing this, once the U.S. company has invested in a new refinery, what is to stop the Australian firm from raising bauxite prices? Absolutely nothing, and once it has made the investment, the U.S. firm is locked into its relationship with the Australian supplier. The Australian firm can increase bauxite prices, secure in the knowledge that as long as the increase in the total production costs is less than 20 percent, the U.S. firm will continue to buy from it. (It would become economical for the U.S. firm to buy from another supplier only if total production costs increased by more than 20 percent.)

The U.S. firm can reduce the risk of the Australian firm opportunistically raising prices in this manner by buying out the Australian firm. If the U.S. firm can buy the Australian firm, or its bauxite mine, it need no longer fear that bauxite prices will be increased after it has invested in the refinery. In other words, it would make economic sense for the U.S. firm to engage in vertical FDI. In practice, these kinds of considerations have driven aluminum firms to pursue vertical FDI to such a degree that a large percentage of the total volume of bauxite is transferred within vertically integrated firms.[33]

IMPLICATIONS FOR MANAGERS

The implications of the theories of horizontal and vertical FDI for business practice are relatively straightforward. First, the location-specific advantages argument associated with John Dunning helps explain the direction of FDI, with regard to both horizontal and vertical FDI. However, the argument does not explain why firms prefer FDI to licensing or to exporting. In this regard, from both an explanatory and a business perspective, perhaps the most useful theory is the market imperfections approach. With regard to horizontal FDI, this approach identifies with some precision how the relative rates of return associated with horizontal FDI, exporting, and licensing vary with circumstances. The theory suggests that exporting is preferable to licensing and horizontal FDI as long as transport costs are minor and tariff barriers are trivial. As transport costs and/or tariff barriers increase, exporting becomes unprofitable, and the choice is between horizontal FDI and licensing. Since horizontal FDI is more costly and more risky than licensing, other things being equal, the theory argues that licensing is preferable to horizontal FDI. Other things are seldom equal, however. Although licensing may work, it is not an attractive option when one or more of the following conditions exist: (*a*) the firm has valuable know-how that cannot be adequately protected by a licensing contract, (*b*) the firm needs tight control over a foreign entity to maximize its market share and earnings in that country, and (*c*) a firm's skills and know-how are not amenable to licensing. Figure 7.6 presents these considerations as a decision tree.

Firms for which licensing is not a good option tend to be clustered in three types of industries:

1. High-technology industries where protecting firm-specific expertise is of paramount importance and licensing is hazardous.
2. Global oligopolies, where competitive interdependence requires that multinational firms maintain tight control over foreign operations so that they have the ability to launch coordinated attacks against their global competitors (as Kodak has done with Fuji).
3. Industries where intense cost pressures require that multinational firms maintain tight control over foreign operations (so they can disperse manufacturing to locations around the globe where factor costs are most favorable to minimize costs).

The majority of the evidence seems to support these conjectures.[34] In addition, licensing is not a good option if the competitive advantage of a firm is based upon managerial or marketing knowledge that is embedded in the routines of the firm, and/or the skills of its managers, and is difficult to codify in a "book of blueprints." This would seem to be the case for firms based in a fairly wide range of industries, and as we have seen from examples in this chapter, includes the likes of Toyota and Cemex.

Firms for which licensing is a good option tend to be in industries whose conditions are opposite to those specified above. Licensing tends to be more common (and more profitable) in fragmented, low-technology industries in which globally dispersed manufacturing is not an option. Licensing is also easier if the knowledge to be transferred is relatively easy to codify. A good example of an industry where these conditions seem to exist is the

FIGURE 7.6

A Decision Framework

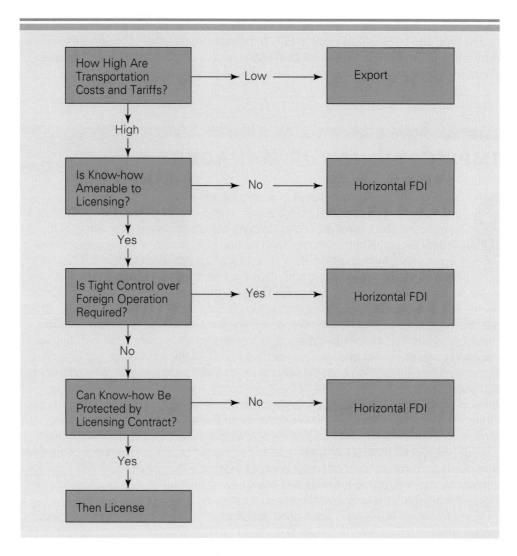

fast-food industry. McDonald's has expanded globally by using a franchising strategy. Franchising is essentially the service-industry version of licensing—although it normally involves much longer-term commitments than licensing. With franchising, the firm licenses its brand name to a foreign firm in return for a percentage of the franchisee's profits. The franchising contract specifies the conditions that the franchisee must fulfill if it is to use the franchisor's brand name. Thus, McDonald's allows foreign firms to use its brand name as long as they agree to run their restaurants on exactly the same lines as McDonald's restaurants elsewhere in the world. This strategy makes sense for McDonald's because (a) like many services that are performed where they are delivered, fast food cannot be exported, (b) franchising economizes the costs and risks associated with opening foreign markets, (c) unlike technological know-how, brand names are relatively easy to protect using a contract, (d) there is no compelling reason for McDonald's to have tight control over franchisees, and (e) McDonald's know-how, in terms of how to run a fast-food restaurant, is amenable to being specified in a written contract (e.g., the contract specifies the details of how to run a McDonald's restaurant). But McDonald's does undertake some FDI to establish "master franchisors" in each country in which it does business. These master franchisors are normally joint ventures with local companies, and their task is to manage McDonald's franchisees within a particular country.

In contrast to the market imperfections approach, the product life-cycle theory and Knickerbocker's theory of horizontal FDI are less useful from a business perspective.

These two theories are descriptive rather than analytical. They do a good job of describing the historical pattern of FDI, but they do a relatively poor job of identifying the factors that influence the relative profitability of FDI, licensing, and exporting. The issue of licensing as an alternative to FDI is ignored by both these theories.

Finally, with regard to vertical FDI, both the market imperfections approach and the strategic behavior approach have some useful implications for business practice. The strategic behavior approach points out that vertical FDI may be a way of building barriers to entry into an industry. The strength of the market imperfections approach is that it points out the conditions under which vertical FDI might be preferable to the alternatives. Most importantly, the market imperfections approach points to the importance of investments in specialized assets and imperfections in the market for know-how as factors that increase the relative attractiveness of vertical FDI.

Chapter Summary

This chapter reviewed theories that attempt to explain the pattern of FDI between countries. This objective takes on added importance in light of the expanding volume of FDI in the world economy. As we saw early in the chapter, the volume of FDI has grown more rapidly than the volume of world trade in recent years. We also noted that any theory seeking to explain FDI must explain why firms go to the trouble of acquiring or establishing operations abroad when the alternatives of exporting and licensing are available.

We reviewed a number of theories that attempt to explain horizontal and vertical FDI. With regard to horizontal FDI, it was argued that the market imperfections and location-specific advantages approaches might have the greatest explanatory power and therefore be most useful for business practice. This is not to belittle the explanations for horizontal FDI put forward by Vernon and Knickerbocker, since these theories also have value in explaining the pattern of FDI in the world economy. Still, both theories are weakened by their failure to explicitly consider the factors that drive the choice among exporting, licensing, and FDI. Finally, with regard to vertical FDI, it was argued that the strategic behavior and market imperfections approaches both have a certain amount of explanatory power. The chapter made the following points:

1. Foreign direct investment occurs when a firm invests directly in facilities to produce a product in a foreign country. It also occurs when a firm buys an existing enterprise in a foreign country.

2. Horizontal FDI is FDI in the same industry abroad as a firm operates at home. Vertical FDI is FDI in an industry abroad that provides inputs into or sells outputs from a firm's domestic operations.

3. Any theory seeking to explain FDI must explain why firms go to the trouble of acquiring or establishing operations abroad when the alternatives of exporting and licensing are available.

4. Several factors characterized FDI trends over the past 20 years: (a) the total volume of FDI undertaken has increased; (b) the relative importance of the United States as a source for FDI has declined, while several other countries have increased their share of total FDI outflows; (c) an increasing share of FDI seems to be directed at the developing nations of Asia and Eastern Europe, while the United States has become a major recipient of FDI; and (d) the amount of FDI undertaken by firms based in developing nations has increased.

5. High transportation costs and/or tariffs imposed on imports help explain why many firms prefer horizontal FDI or licensing over exporting.

6. Impediments to the sale of know-how explain why firms prefer horizontal FDI to licensing. These impediments arise when: (a) a firm has valuable know-how that cannot be adequately protected by a licensing contract, (b) a firm needs tight control over a foreign entity to maximize its market share and earnings in that country, and (c) a firm's skills and know-how are not amenable to licensing.

7. Knickerbocker's theory suggests that much FDI is explained by imitative strategic behavior by

rival firms in an oligopolistic industry. However, this theory does not address the issue of whether FDI is more efficient than exporting or licensing for expanding abroad.

8. Vernon's product life-cycle theory suggests that firms undertake FDI at particular stages in the life cycle of products they have pioneered. However, Vernon's theory does not address the issue of whether FDI is more efficient than exporting or licensing for expanding abroad.

9. Dunning has argued that location-specific advantages are of considerable importance in explaining the nature and direction of FDI. According to Dunning, firms undertake FDI to exploit resource endowments or assets that are location-specific.

10. Backward vertical FDI may be explained as an attempt to create barriers to entry by gaining control over the source of material inputs into the downstream stage of a production process. Forward vertical FDI may be seen as an attempt to circumvent entry barriers and gain access to a national market.

11. The market imperfections approach suggests that vertical FDI is a way of reducing a firm's exposure to the risks that arise from investments in specialized assets.

12. From a business perspective, the most useful theory is probably the market imperfections approach, because it identifies how the relative profit rates associated with horizontal FDI, exporting, and licensing vary with circumstances.

Critical Thinking and Discussion Questions

1. In 2003, inward FDI accounted for some 78 percent of gross fixed capital formation in Ireland, but only 0.6 percent in Japan. What do you think explains this difference in FDI inflows into the two countries?

2. Compare and contrast these explanations of horizontal FDI: the market imperfections approach, Vernon's product life-cycle theory, and Knickerbocker's theory of FDI. Which theory do you think offers the best explanation of the historical pattern of horizontal FDI? Why?

3. Read the opening case on Cemex. What kind of FDI is Cemex pursuing? Which theoretical explanation of FDI best explains Cemex's FDI?

4. Compare and contrast these explanations of vertical FDI: the strategic behavior approach and the market imperfections approach. Which theory do you think offers the better explanation of the historical pattern of vertical FDI? Why?

5. You are the international manager of a U.S. business that has just developed a revolutionary new personal computer that can perform the same functions as existing PCs but costs only half as much to manufacture. Several patents protect the unique design of this computer. Your CEO has asked you to formulate a recommendation for how to expand into Western Europe. Your options are (*a*) to export from the United States, (*b*) to license a European firm to manufacture and market the computer in Europe, and (*c*) to set up a wholly owned subsidiary in Europe. Evaluate the pros and cons of each alternative and suggest a course of action to your CEO.

6. Read the Management Focus on recent investments by Western automobile firms in Russia. Which theory best explains these investments? Why?

Research Task   globalEDGE™   globaledge.msu.edu

Use the globalEDGE™ site to complete the following exercises:

1. The *World Investment Report* published annually by UNCTAD provides quick electronic access to comprehensive statistics on foreign direct investment (FDI) and the operations of transnational corporations (TNCs). Gather a list of the top transnational corporations in terms of their foreign direct investment. Also, identify their home country (i.e., headquarters country). Provide a commentary about the characteristics of countries that have the greatest number of transnational firms.

2. Your company is considering opening a new factory in Latin America, and management is in the process of evaluating the specific country locations for this direct investment. The pool of candidate countries has been narrowed down to Argentina, Mexico, and Brazil. Prepare a short report comparing the foreign direct investment environment and regulations of these three countries.

Starbucks' FDI

CLOSING CASE Thirty years ago Starbucks was a single store in Seattle's Pike Place Market selling premium roasted coffee. Today it is a global roaster and retailer of coffee with over 8,400 stores, more than 2,000 of which are to be found in 31 foreign countries. Starbucks Corporation set out on its current course in the 1980s when the company's director of marketing, Howard Schultz, came back from a trip to Italy enchanted with the Italian coffeehouse experience. Schultz, who later became CEO, persuaded the company's owners to experiment with the coffeehouse format—and the Starbucks experience was born. The basic strategy was to sell the company's own premium roasted coffee, along with freshly brewed espresso-style coffee beverages, a variety of pastries, coffee accessories, teas, and other products, in a tastefully designed coffeehouse setting. The company also stressed providing superior customer service. Reasoning that motivated employees provide the best customer service, Starbucks' executives devoted a lot of attention to employee hiring and training programs and progressive compensation policies that gave even part-time employees stock option grants and medical benefits. The formula met with spectacular success in the United States, where Starbucks went from obscurity to one of the best known brands in the country in a decade.

In 1995, with almost 700 stores across the United States, Starbucks began exploring foreign opportunities. Its first target market was Japan. Although Starbucks had resisted a franchising strategy in North America, where its stores are company owned, Starbucks initially decided to license its format in Japan. However, the company also realized that a pure licensing agreement would not give Starbucks the control needed to ensure that the Japanese licensees closely followed Starbucks' successful formula. So the company established a joint venture with a local retailer, Sazaby Inc. Each company held a 50 percent stake in the venture, Starbucks Coffee of Japan. Starbucks initially invested $10 million in this venture, its first foreign direct investment. The Starbucks format was then licensed to the venture, which was charged with taking over responsibility for growing Starbucks' presence in Japan.

To make sure the Japanese operations replicated the "Starbucks experience" in North America, Starbucks transferred some employees to the Japanese operation. The licensing agreement required all Japanese store managers and employees to attend training classes similar to those given to U.S. employees. The agreement also required that stores adhere to the design parameters established in the United States. In 2001, the company in-

troduced a stock option plan for all Japanese employees, making it the first company in Japan to do so. Skeptics doubted that Starbucks would be able to replicate its North American success overseas, but by early 2005, Starbucks had almost 550 stores in Japan and plans to continue opening them at a brisk pace.

After getting its feet wet in Japan, the company embarked on an aggressive foreign investment program. In 1998, it purchased Seattle Coffee, a British coffee chain with 60 retail stores, for $84 million. An American couple, originally from Seattle, had started Seattle Coffee with the intention of establishing a Starbucks-like chain in Britain. In the late 1990s, Starbucks opened stores in Taiwan, China, Singapore, Thailand, New Zealand, South Korea, and Malaysia.

In Asia, Starbucks' most common strategy was to license its format to a local operator in return for initial licensing fees and royalties on store revenues. Starbucks also sold coffee and related products to the local licensees, which then resold them to customers. As in Japan, Starbucks insisted on an intensive employee training program and strict specifications regarding the format and layout of the store. However, Starbucks became disenchanted with some of the straight licensing arrangements and converted several into joint-venture arrangements or wholly owned subsidiaries. In Thailand, for example, Starbucks initially entered into a licensing agreement with Coffee Partners, a local Thai company. Under the terms of the licensing agreement, Coffee Partners was required to open at least 20 Starbucks coffee stores in Thailand within five years. However, Coffee Partners found it difficult to raise funds from Thai banks to finance this expansion. In July 2000, Starbucks acquired Coffee Partners for about $12 million. Its goal was to gain tighter control over the expansion strategy in Thailand. A similar development occurred in South Korea, where Starbucks initially licensed its format to ESCO Korea Ltd. in 1999. Although ESCO soon had 10 very successful stores open, Starbucks felt that ESCO would not be able to achieve the company's aggressive growth targets, so in December 2000 it converted its licensing arrangement into a joint venture with Shinsegae, the parent company of ESCO. The joint venture enabled Starbucks to exercise greater control over the growth strategy in South Korea and to help fund that operation, while gaining the benefits of a local operating partner. By October 2000, Starbucks had invested some $52 million in foreign joint ventures.

By the end of 2002, Starbucks had more than 1,200 stores in 27 countries outside of North America and was initiating aggressive expansion plans into mainland Europe. The company's plans called for opening stores in six European countries, including the coffee cultures of France and Italy. As its first entry point on the European mainland (Starbucks had 150 stores in Great Britain), Starbucks chose Switzerland. Drawing on its experience in Asia, the company entered into a joint venture with a Swiss company, Bon Appetit Group, Switzerland's largest food service company. Bon Appetit was to hold a majority stake in the venture, and Starbucks would license its format to the Swiss company using a similar agreement to those it had used successfully in Asia. This was followed by a joint venture in Germany with KarstadtQuelle, one of the country's largest retailers. Under the agreement, Starbucks held 18 percent of the equity in the venture, and Karstadt the remainder. In early 2005, with more than 2,000 international stores, Starbucks announced that it believed there was the potential for up to 15,000 stores outside of the United States.

Sources: Starbucks 10K, various years; C. McLean, "Starbucks Set to Invade Coffee-Loving Continent," *Seattle Times*, October 4, 2000, p. E1; J. Ordonez, "Starbucks to Start Major Expansion in Overseas Market," *The Wall Street Journal*, October 27, 2000, p. B10; S. Homes and D. Bennett, "Planet Starbucks," *BusinessWeek*, September 9, 2002, pp. 99–110; and "Starbucks Outlines International Growth Strategy," *Business Wire*, October 14, 2004.

Case Discussion Questions

1. Initially Starbucks expanded internationally by licensing its format to foreign operators. It soon became disenchanted with this strategy. Why?

2. Why do you think Starbucks has now elected to expand internationally primarily through local joint ventures, to whom it licenses its format, as opposed to a pure licensing strategy?

3. What are the advantages of a joint-venture entry mode for Starbucks over entering through wholly owned subsidiaries? On occasion, Starbucks has chosen a wholly owned subsidiary to control its foreign expansion (e.g., in Britain and Thailand). Why?

4. Which theory of FDI best explains the international expansion strategy adopted by Starbucks?

Notes

1. United Nations, *World Investment Report, 2000* (New York and Geneva: United Nations, 2001).

2. United Nations, *World Investment Report, 2004*, and United Nations Conference on Trade and Development, "World FDI Flows Grew an Estimated 6% in 2004," UNCTAD press release, January 11, 2005.

3. World Trade Organization, *International Trade Statistics, 2004* (Geneva: WTO, 2004), and United Nations, *World Investment Report, 2004*.

4. United Nations, *World Investment Report, 2004*.

5. Ibid.

6. United Nations Conference on Trade and Development, "Global FDI Decline Bottoms Out in 2003."

7. United Nations Conference on Trade and Development, "World FDI Flows Grew an Estimated 6% in 2004."

8. United Nations, *World Investment Report, 2003* (New York and Geneva: United Nations, 2004).

9. United Nations, *World Investment Report, 2002* (New York and Geneva: United Nations, 2003).

10. United Nations Conference on Trade and Development, "Global FDI Decline Bottoms Out in 2003."

11. United Nations, *World Investment Report, 2003*, and United Nations Conference on Trade and Development, "Global FDI Decline Bottoms Out in 2003."

12. United Nations Conference on Trade and Development, "World FDI Flows Grew an Estimated 6% in 2004."

13. United Nations, *World Investment Report, 2004*.

14. Ibid.

15. See D. J. Ravenscraft and F. M. Scherer, *Mergers, Selloffs and Economic Efficiency* (Washington, DC: The Brookings Institution, 1987). Also A. Seth, K. P. Song, and R. R. Pettit, "Value Creation and Destruction in Cross Border Acquisitions," *Strategic Management Journal* 23 (2002), pp. 921–40.

16. For example, see S. H. Hymer, *The International Operations of National Firms: A Study of Direct Foreign Investment* (Cambridge, MA: MIT Press, 1976); A. M. Rugman, *Inside the Multinationals: The Economics of Internal Markets* (New York: Columbia University Press, 1981); D. J. Teece, "Multinational Enterprise, Internal Governance, and Industrial Organization," *American Economic Review* 75 (May 1983), pp. 233–38; and C. W. L. Hill and W. C. Kim, "Searching for

a Dynamic Theory of the Multinational Enterprise: A Transaction Cost Model," *Strategic Management Journal* (special issue) 9 (1988), pp. 93–104.

17. J. P. Womack, D. T. Jones, and D. Roos, *The Machine That Changed the World* (New York: Rawson Associates, 1990).

18. The argument is most often associated with F. T. Knickerbocker, *Oligopolistic Reaction and Multinational Enterprise* (Boston: Harvard Business School Press, 1973).

19. The studies are summarized in R. E. Caves, *Multinational Enterprise and Economic Analysis*, 2nd ed. (Cambridge, UK: Cambridge University Press, 1996).

20. See R. E. Caves, "Japanese Investment in the US: Lessons for the Economic Analysis of Foreign Investment," *The World Economy* 16 (1993), pp. 279–300; B. Kogut and S. J. Chang, "Technological Capabilities and Japanese Direct Investment in the United States," *Review of Economics and Statistics* 73 (1991), pp. 401–43; and J. Anand and B. Kogut, "Technological Capabilities of Countries, Firm Rivalry, and Foreign Direct Investment," *Journal of International Business Studies*, Third Quarter (1997), pp. 445–65.

21. K. Ito and E. L. Rose, "Foreign Direct Investment Location Strategies in the Tire Industry," *Journal of International Business Studies* 33 (2002), pp. 593–602.

22. H. Haveman and L. Nonnemaker, "Competition in Multiple Geographical Markets," *Administrative Science Quarterly*, 45 (2000), pp. 232–67.

23. For the use of Vernon's theory to explain Japanese direct investment in the United States and Europe, see S. Thomsen, "Japanese Direct Investment in the European Community," *The World Economy* 16 (1993), pp. 301–15.

24. J. H. Dunning, *Explaining International Production* (London: Unwin Hyman, 1988).

25. P. Krugman, "Increasing Returns and Economic Geography," *Journal of Political Economy* 99, no. 3 (1991), pp. 483–99.

26. J. M. Shaver and F. Flyer, "Agglomeration Economies, Firm Heterogeneity, and Foreign Direct Investment in the United States," *Strategic Management Journal* 21 (2000), pp. 1175–93.

27. J. H. Dunning and R. Narula, "Transpacific Foreign Direct Investment and the Investment Development Path," *South Carolina Essays in International Business* 10 (May 1995).

28. W. Shan and J. Song, "Foreign Direct Investment and the Sourcing of Technological Advantage: Evidence from the Biotechnology Industry," *Journal of International Business Studies*, Second Quarter 1997, pp. 267–84.

29. For additional evidence, see L. E. Brouthers, K. D. Brouthers, and S. Warner, "Is Dunning's Eclectic Framework Descriptive or Normative?" *Journal of International Business Studies* 30 (1999), pp. 831–44.

30. Caves, *Multinational Enterprise and Economic Analysis*.

31. J. F. Hennart, "Upstream Vertical Integration in the Aluminum and Tin Industries," *Journal of Economic Behavior and Organization* 9 (1988), pp. 281–99, and O. E. Williamson, *The Economic Institutions of Capitalism* (New York: Free Press, 1985). See also G. M. Grossman and E. Helpman, "Outsourcing versus FDI in Industry Equilibrium," NBER Working Paper No. 9300, October 2002.

32. Hennart, "Upstream Vertical Integration."

33. Ibid.

34. See Caves, *Multinational Enterprise and Economic Analysis*.

The Political Economy of Foreign Direct Investment

8

Foreign Direct Investment in India

Along with China, India is often viewed as one of the emerging economic superpowers in the developing world. Both countries have moved to embrace market-based economic reforms over the last decade. Both countries have enjoyed economic growth, although China has grown substantially faster. Both countries have large populations that could potentially evolve into enormous markets for consumer products. And both nations have vibrant entrepreneurial activity that is giving rise to homegrown enterprises that are starting to compete on the world stage. But there is also a big difference between the two countries; China has attracted a far higher level of foreign direct investment than India. From 1998 to 2004, China attracted some $342 billion in FDI, India just $24 billion. While FDI in China has stimulated economic growth—much of it in the form of exports from the Chinese operations of foreign firms—the lack of FDI in India may help explain the country's lower economic growth.

The differences in FDI inflows between the two nations are in part driven by differences in government policy. China is rapidly dismantling restrictions on FDI and welcoming foreigners with open arms. The Indian position is more complex. At one time, India had very strict prohibitions against inward FDI, but beginning in the early 1990s, regulations have been progressively relaxed. Still, some schizophrenia is evident in the Indian position, and the country still has significant regulations in place that inhibit FDI. This has its roots in strong nationalist tendencies and a desire not to be dominated by foreigners—a reaction to Indian's long rule by the British.

For example, after initially opening the retailing sector to FDI in the early 1990s, in 1997 the Indian government reversed course and banned FDI by foreign retailers. The reason was the strong opposition to foreign investment from the enormous number of small retailers that dominate India's retailing sector. At last count, India had as many as 10.7 million small retailers, 98 percent of whom employed fewer than six workers. It was feared that large foreign retailers would drive small Indian retailers out of business, with serious repercussions for employment. Currently foreign retailers are limited to setting up franchise operations in India.

In a similar vein, in 2004 the Reserve Bank of India, India's central bank, issued new regulations that limited foreign investors to stakes of no more than 5 to 10 percent in Indian banks. While this does not bar foreign banks from setting up shop in India, it does restrict them from doing that via the acquisition of an Indian bank, which happens to be the favored mode for large-scale entry into a market.

Sometimes restrictions have been more subtle. A government guideline, known as *Press Note 18*, issued in 1998, states that any foreign investor with previous or existing joint-venture agreements cannot seek automatic approval for additional direct investments in the same field or a related field. The rule was put in place after protests from some Indian industrialists, who argued that foreign companies tend to exit joint ventures once they have acquired locals' knowledge and experience, to the detriment of the Indian partner. Foreign investors see the regulation as a hurdle. For example, Honeywell, which has a 50/50 joint venture in India with RKKR Infotech to produce products using amorphous metals, wanted to set up a wholly owned subsidiary in India to manufacture transformer cores and laminations of amorphous metal alloys, primarily for export to other countries. RKKR argued that the proposed investment would seriously harm the joint venture and used *Press Note 18* to request that Honeywell's application be denied.

Recognizing the detrimental effect such policies can have on FDI and economic growth, in 2004 the government committed itself to removing barriers to FDI in the hope that FDI would double or triple from recent levels. It made a start on this in January 2005 by abolishing *Press Note 18*.

Sources: United Nations, *World Investment Report 2004* (New York and Geneva: United Nations, 2004); "Indian Industry: Foreign Retailers Get Cold Shoulder," *EIU Views Wire,* October 27, 2003; "Curious Welcome: Banking in India," *The Economist,* July 21, 2004, p. 74; "Government Scraps Press Note 18," *Indian Express,* January 13, 2005.

Introduction

Chapter 7 looked at the phenomenon of foreign direct investment (FDI) and reviewed several theories that attempt to explain the economic rationale for FDI, but it did not discuss the role of governments. Through their choice of policies and their statements and actions, governments can both encourage and restrict FDI. Host governments can encourage FDI by dismantling regulations that inhibit FDI and providing incentives for foreign firms to invest in their economies. They can restrict or discourage FDI through a variety of laws, policies, and statements. The opening case reported how India has discouraged FDI inflows through rules and regulations, such as *Press Note 18*. The current Indian government, recognizing the beneficial effect that inward FDI can have on economic growth, has committed itself to removing such restrictions.

The government of a source country for FDI also can encourage or restrict FDI by domestic firms. In the 1980s and 1990s, the Japanese government pressured many Japanese firms to undertake FDI. The Japanese government saw FDI as a substitute for exporting and thus as a way of reducing Japan's politically embarrassing balance of payments surplus. In contrast, the U.S. government has, for political reasons, from time to time restricted FDI by domestic firms. For example, in response to a belief that the Iranian government actively supports terrorist organizations, the U.S. government has prohibited American firms from investing in or exporting to Iran.

Historically, one important determinant of a government's policy toward FDI has been its political ideology. Accordingly, this chapter opens with a discussion of how political ideology influences government policy. To a greater or lesser degree, the officials of many governments tend to be pragmatic nationalists who weigh the benefits and costs of FDI and vary their stated policy on a case-by-case basis. After discussing political ideology, we will consider the benefits and costs of FDI. Then we will look at the various policies home and host governments adopt to encourage and/or restrict FDI. The chapter closes with a detailed discussion of the implications of government policy for the business firm. In this closing section, we examine the factors that determine the relative bargaining strengths of a host government and a firm contemplating FDI. We will look at how the negotiations between firm and government are sometimes played out and at how firms can use this knowledge to their advantage.

Political Ideology and Foreign Direct Investment

Historically, ideology toward FDI has ranged from a dogmatic radical stance that is hostile to all FDI at one extreme to an adherence to the noninterventionist principle of free market economics at the other. Between these two extremes is an approach that might be called pragmatic nationalism.

THE RADICAL VIEW

The radical view traces its roots to Marxist political and economic theory. Radical writers argue that the multinational enterprise (MNE) is an instrument of imperialist domination. They see the MNE as a tool for exploiting host countries to the exclusive benefit of their capitalist-imperialist home countries. They argue that MNEs extract profits from the host country and take them to their home country, giving nothing of value to the host country in exchange. They note, for example, that key technology is tightly controlled by the MNE, and that important jobs in the foreign subsidiaries of MNEs go to home-country nationals rather than to citizens of the host country. Because of this, according to the radical view, FDI by the MNEs of advanced capitalist nations keeps the less developed countries of the world relatively backward and dependent on advanced capitalist nations for investment, jobs, and technology. Thus, according to the extreme version of this view, no country should ever permit foreign corporations to undertake FDI, since they can never be instruments of economic development, only of economic domination. Where MNEs already exist in a country, they should be immediately nationalized.[1]

From 1945 until the 1980s, the radical view was very influential in the world economy. Until the collapse of communism between 1989 and 1991, the countries of Eastern Europe were opposed to FDI. Similarly, communist countries elsewhere, such as China, Cambodia, and Cuba, were all opposed in principle to FDI (although in practice the Chinese started to allow FDI in mainland China in the 1970s). Many socialist countries, particularly in Africa where one of the first actions of many newly independent states was to nationalize foreign-owned enterprises, also embraced the radical position. Countries whose political ideology was more nationalistic than socialistic further embraced the radical position. This was true in Iran and India, for example, both of which adopted tough policies restricting FDI and nationalized many foreign-owned enterprises. Iran is a particularly interesting case because its Islamic government, while rejecting Marxist theory, has essentially embraced the radical view that FDI by MNEs is an instrument of imperialism.

By the end of the 1980s, however, the radical position was in retreat almost everywhere. There seem to be three reasons for this: (1) the collapse of communism in Eastern Europe; (2) the generally abysmal economic performance of those countries that embraced the radical position, and a growing belief by many of these countries that FDI can be an important source of technology and jobs and can stimulate economic growth; and (3) the strong economic performance of those developing countries that embraced capitalism rather than radical ideology (e.g., Singapore, Hong Kong, and Taiwan).

THE FREE MARKET VIEW

The free market view traces its roots to classical economics and the international trade theories of Adam Smith and David Ricardo (see Chapter 5). The intellectual case for this view has been strengthened by the market imperfections explanation of horizontal and vertical FDI that we reviewed in Chapter 7. The free market view argues that international production should be distributed among countries according to the theory of comparative advantage. Countries should specialize in the production of those goods and services that they can produce most efficiently. Within this framework, the MNE is an instrument for dispersing the production of goods and services to the most efficient locations around the globe. Viewed this way, FDI by the MNE increases the overall efficiency of the world economy.

Consider a well-publicized decision by IBM in the mid-1980s to move assembly operations for many of its personal computers from the United States to Guadalajara, Mexico. IBM invested about $90 million in an assembly facility with the capacity to produce 100,000 PCs per year, 75 percent of which were exported back to the United States.[2] According to the free market view, moves such as this can be seen as increasing the overall efficiency of resource utilization in the world economy. Mexico, due to its low labor costs, has a comparative advantage in the assembly of PCs. According to the free market view, by moving the production of PCs from the United States to Mexico, IBM frees resources for use in activities in which the United States has a comparative advantage (e.g., the design of computer software, the manufacture of high-value-added components such as microprocessors, or basic R&D). Also, consumers benefit because the PCs cost less than they would if they were produced domestically. In addition, Mexico gains from the technology, skills, and capital that IBM transfers with its FDI. Contrary to the radical view, the free market view stresses that such resource transfers benefit the host country and stimulate its economic growth. Thus, the free market view argues that FDI is a benefit to both the source country and the host country. (In early 2005, IBM's PC operations, including the Mexican assembly operations, were sold to the Chinese firm Lenovo.)

For reasons explored earlier in this book (see Chapter 2), the free market view has been ascendant worldwide in recent years, spurring a global move toward the removal of restrictions on inward and outward foreign direct investment. An example is South

Korea, which started dismantling its restrictive regulations governing inward FDI in the mid-1990s. As described in the accompanying Management Focus, foreign firms are starting to affect competition in certain sectors of the South Korean economy.

As noted in the last chapter, according to the United Nations, some 94 percent of the 1,885 changes made worldwide between 1991 and 2003 in the laws governing foreign direct investment created a more favorable environment for FDI.[3] The tide is clearly running strongly in favor of the free market view. However, in practice no country has adopted the free market view in its pure form (just as no country has adopted the radical view in its pure form). Countries such as Great Britain and the United States are among the most open to FDI, but the governments of these countries both have still reserved the right to intervene. Britain does so by reserving the right to block foreign takeovers of domestic firms if the takeovers are seen as "contrary to national security interests" or if they have the potential for "reducing competition." (In practice this right is rarely exercised.) U.S. controls on FDI are more limited and largely informal. For political reasons, the United States will occasionally restrict U.S. firms from undertaking FDI in certain countries (e.g., Cuba and Iran). In addition, inward FDI meets some limited restrictions. For example, foreigners are prohibited from purchasing more than 25 percent of any U.S. airline or from acquiring a controlling interest in a U.S. television broadcast network. Since 1988, the government has had the right to review the acquisition of a U.S. enterprise by a foreign firm on the grounds of "national security." However, of the 1,500 bids reviewed by the Committee on Foreign Investment in the U.S. under this law by 2005, only one has been nullified based on its recommendation—the sale of a Seattle-based aircraft parts manufacturer to a Chinese enterprise in the early 1990s.[4]

PRAGMATIC NATIONALISM

In practice, many countries have adopted neither a radical policy nor a free market policy toward FDI, but instead a policy that can best be described as pragmatic nationalism.[5] The pragmatic nationalist view is that FDI has both benefits and costs. FDI can benefit a host country by bringing capital, skills, technology, and jobs, but those benefits come at a cost. When a foreign company rather than a domestic company produces products, the profits from that investment go abroad. Many countries are also concerned that a foreign-owned manufacturing plant may import many components from its home country, which has negative implications for the host country's balance-of-payments position.

Recognizing this, countries adopting a pragmatic stance pursue policies designed to maximize the national benefits and minimize the national costs. According to this view, FDI should be allowed only if the benefits outweigh the costs. Japan offers an example of pragmatic nationalism. Until the 1980s, Japan's policy was probably one of the most restrictive among countries adopting a pragmatic nationalist stance. This was due to Japan's perception that direct entry of foreign (especially U.S.) firms with ample managerial resources into the Japanese markets could hamper the development and growth of the nation's own industry and technology.[6] This belief led Japan to block the majority of applications to invest in Japan. However, there were always exceptions to this policy. Firms that had important technology were often permitted to undertake FDI if they insisted that they would neither license their technology to a Japanese firm nor enter into a joint venture with a Japanese enterprise. IBM and Texas Instruments were able to set up wholly owned subsidiaries in Japan by adopting this negotiating position. From the perspective of the Japanese government, the benefits of FDI in such cases—the stimulus that these firms might impart to the Japanese economy— outweighed the perceived costs.

Another aspect of pragmatic nationalism is the tendency to aggressively court FDI believed to be in the national interest by, for example, offering subsidies to foreign MNEs in the form of tax breaks or grants. The countries of the European Union often seem to be competing with each other to attract U.S. and Japanese FDI by offering large tax breaks and subsidies. Britain has been the most successful at attracting Japanese invest-

MANAGEMENT FOCUS

Historically, South Korea has been largely closed to foreign direct investment. During its 30-year dash from one of the world's poorest nations to one of its richest, South Korea closely adhered to the Japanese model of development, severely restricting foreign ownership of industrial and commercial activities. However, in 1997 South Korea's long period of economic expansion came to an abrupt end when a financial crisis swept across Asia. This produced a sharp drop in economic activity in the country. The Korean currency slumped against the dollar, requiring the government to seek $58 billion in aid from the International Monetary Fund. As demand for their products plummeted, dozens of highly leveraged South Korean companies found themselves unable to service the debt that they had taken on during the boom years to finance their expansion. Many teetered on the edge of bankruptcy. The government responded by removing many of the restrictions to foreign direct investment, including regulations that prohibited foreign firms from making hostile takeovers of South Korean enterprises.

The impact was dramatic. FDI surged from $3 billion in 1997 to $9.3 billion in 2000. The total stock of foreign investment in South Korea soared from $5.2 billion in 1990 to $62.7 billion by the end of the decade. While many Koreans initially viewed the new wave of foreign investment with deep suspicion, and the radical press demonized foreign companies as unwelcome guests feeding off the local market like leeches, it quickly became apparent that the reality was something else. An example was the acquisition of Samsung's unprofitable construction equipment division by Sweden's Volvo in February 1998 for $572 million. This was South Korea's first major sale of a distressed company to a foreign investor, and both the public and Samsung employees greeted the sale with deep apprehension. Two years later, however, most of those fears had been put to rest.

Volvo immediately launched an ambitious investment program, committing another $200 million to the plant in an attempt to turn the ex-Samsung facility into its main global base for excavators and other construction equipment. The company transferred leading-edge manufacturing technology to the plant, moved in some of its very best managers to oversee the operations, and made the facility its global center for R&D in excavators. Volvo even closed its excavator plant in Sweden, signaling the company's commitment to the Korean facility. Although some 13 percent of the 1,655 employees at the plant left after the Volvo acquisition, these job reductions were achieved through attrition and not layoffs. Volvo refocused the production of the plant, emphasizing higher-quality and higher-priced machines that promise better profit margins. The old Korean emphasis on sales volume and market share has been replaced by a focus on product quality, operating efficiency, and profitability. The management hierarchy was significantly reduced, much of the bureaucracy was removed, and decision-making responsibilities were pushed down the line to self-managing work teams.

By 2002, the plant was once more making a profit and production had increased from 3,543 units in 1998 to 6,331. Also, exports from the plant had surged from 34 percent of output in 1997 to 68 percent in 2002. Volvo now has a 7 percent share of the global market for large excavators, and plans to increase this to between 10 and 15 percent by 2006–2007 with production from the Korean plant.

Sources: Charles, S. Lee. "Foreign Affair," *Far Eastern Economic Review*, April 29, 1999, pp. 58–60; S. W. Park, "Foreign Retail Chains Take Root in Korea," *Business Korea*, December 1999, pp. 42–43; M. Schuman, "South Korea Enjoys Foreign Investment Boom," *The Wall Street Journal*, November 26, 1999, p. A8; H. Ilbo, "Volvo Helps Korea Secure Global Strength," *Korea Times*, November 24, 2001; and L. Stewart, "Volvo Excavators Take On the World," *Construction Equipment*, December 2003, p. 19.

www.mhhe.com/hill

ment in the automobile industry. Nissan, Toyota, and Honda now have major assembly plants in Britain and use the country as their base for serving the rest of Europe—with obvious employment and balance-of-payments benefits for Britain.

SUMMARY

The three main ideological positions regarding FDI are summarized in Table 8.1. Recent years have seen a marked decline in the number of countries that adhere to a radical ideology. Although few countries have adopted a pure free market policy stance, an in-

TABLE 8.1

Political Ideology
toward FDI

Ideology	Characteristics	Host-Government Policy Implications
Radical	Marxist roots Views the MNE as an instrument of imperialist domination	Prohibit FDI Nationalize subsidiaries of foreign-owned MNEs
Free market	Classical economic roots (Smith) Views the MNE as an instrument for allocating production to most efficient locations	No restrictions on FDI
Pragmatic nationalism	Views FDI as having both benefits and costs	Restrict FDI Where costs outweigh benefits Bargain for greater benefits and fewer costs Aggressively court beneficial FDI by offering incentives

creasing number of countries are gravitating toward the free market end of the spectrum and have liberalized their foreign investment regime. This includes many countries that less than two decades ago were firmly in the radical camp (e.g., the former communist countries of Eastern Europe and many of the socialist countries of Africa) and several countries that until recently could best be described as pragmatic nationalists with regard to FDI (e.g., Japan, South Korea, Italy, Spain, and most Latin American countries). One result has been the surge in the volume of FDI worldwide, which, as we noted in Chapter 7, has been growing twice as fast as the growth in world trade. Another result has been an increase in the volume of FDI directed at countries that have recently liberalized their FDI regimes, such as China, India, and Vietnam.

The Benefits of FDI to Host Countries

In this section, we explore the four main benefits of FDI for a **host country:** the resource-transfer effect, the employment effect, the balance-of-payments effect, and the effect on competition and economic growth. In the next section, we will explore the costs of FDI to host countries. Economists who favor the free market view argue that the benefits of FDI to a host country so outweigh the costs that pragmatic nationalism is a misguided policy. According to the free market view, in a perfect world the best policy would be for all countries to forgo intervening in the investment decisions of MNEs.[7]

RESOURCE-TRANSFER EFFECTS

Foreign direct investment can make a positive contribution to a host economy by supplying capital, technology, and management resources that would otherwise not be available and thus boost that country's economic growth rate.[8] The accompanying Country Focus describes how the Irish government has been encouraging FDI in a largely successful attempt to benefit from resource-transfer effects. The transfer of capital, technology, and management resources was also an important feature of Volvo's acquisition of Samsung's excavation business (see the Management Focus).

Capital

Many MNEs, by virtue of their large size and financial strength, have access to financial resources not available to host-country firms. These funds may be available from internal company sources, or, because of their reputation, large MNEs may find it easier to borrow money from capital markets than host-country firms would. This consideration was a factor in the proactive policy of the Irish government toward FDI during the 1990s (see the Country Focus).

Technology

As we saw in Chapter 2, the crucial role played by technological progress in economic growth is now widely accepted.[9] Technology can stimulate economic development and industrialization. It can take two forms, both of which are valuable. Technology can be incorporated in a production process (e.g., the technology for discovering, extracting, and refining oil) or it can be incorporated in a product (e.g., personal computers). However, many countries lack the resources and skills required to develop their own indigenous product and process technology. This is particularly true of the world's less developed nations. Such countries must rely on advanced industrialized nations for much of the technology required to stimulate economic growth, and FDI can provide it. In addition, even developed nations can benefit from the inflow of technology that accompanies FDI. For example, the technological base of Ireland has been enhanced as a result of inward investment by technology-based multinationals such as Microsoft, Intel, and Dell (see the Country Focus).

FDI is not the only way to access advanced technology. Another option is to license that technology from foreign MNEs. The Japanese government, in particular, long favored this strategy. The Japanese government believed that, with FDI, the technology is still ultimately controlled by the foreign MNE. Consequently, it is difficult for indigenous Japanese firms to develop their own, possibly better, technology because they are denied access to the basic technology. With this in mind, the Japanese government has insisted in the past that technology be transferred to Japan through licensing agreements, rather than through FDI. The advantage of licensing is that in return for royalty payments, host-country firms are given direct access to valuable technology.

The licensing option is generally less attractive to the MNE, however. By licensing its technology to foreign companies, an MNE risks creating a future competitor—as many U.S. firms have learned at great cost in Japan. Given this tension, the mode for transferring technology—licensing or FDI—can be a major negotiating point between an MNE and a host government. Whether the MNE gets its way depends on the relative bargaining powers of the MNE and the host government. In addition to this issue, it can be difficult to transfer technology using a licensing agreement, particularly when the technology is complex and making the technology operational requires substantial experience. In such cases, direct investment is usually preferred to licensing (this issue is discussed in more detail in Chapter 7).

A fairly large body of research evidence supports the view that multinational firms often do transfer significant technology when they invest in a foreign country.[10] For example, a study of FDI in Sweden found that foreign firms increased both the labor and total productivity of Swedish firms that they acquired, suggesting that significant technology transfers had occurred (technology typically boosts productivity).[11] Also, a study of FDI by the Organization for Economic Cooperation and Development (OECD) found that foreign investors invested significant amounts of capital in R&D in the countries in which they had invested, suggesting that not only were they transferring technology to those countries, but they may also have been upgrading existing technology or creating new technology in those countries.[12]

Management

Foreign management skills acquired through FDI may also produce important benefits for the host country. Foreign managers trained in the latest management techniques can often help to improve the efficiency of operations in the host country, whether those operations are acquired or greenfield developments. This was a factor in Volvo's acquisition of Samsung's excavation business, when Volvo's managers took actions to improve the operations and efficiency of the acquired unit (see the Management Focus). Beneficial spin-off effects may also arise when local personnel who are trained to occupy managerial, financial, and

COUNTRY FOCUS During the 1990s and early 2000s, Ireland registered one of the fastest economic growth rates in the developed world. Long an economic backwater in Western Europe famed only for its export of people and its relative poverty, between 1990 and 2001 Ireland's GDP grew at an average annual rate of 7.24 percent. At the start of this period, the GDP per capita in Ireland on a purchasing power parity basis was $12,687. By the end of the period it had reached $32,133, putting it ahead of countries such as Great Britain ($24,421), Germany ($25,715), and France ($25,074). Driving much of this growth was a rapid expansion in exports from Ireland. In 1985, Ireland exported $10 billion of goods and services. By 2001 the figure had risen to $82.8 billion. Plus, the mix of exports from Ireland had changed dramatically, with exports of primary products (agricultural goods) falling from 20.5 percent to 6 percent of the total, while exports of high-technology manufactured products rose from 23 percent to 36 percent.

Driving this export-led boom was an inflow of foreign direct investment. Inward FDI grew from $164 million in 1985 to a record $24 billion in 2000, before dropping off to $9.78 billion in 2001 (the 2001 decline reflected a general slump in global FDI activity). Much of this FDI was undertaken by large multinationals that saw Ireland as a desirable base for exporting to the rest of Europe. Among the major investors were a raft of large American high-technology multinationals, including Intel, Dell, Microsoft, Gateway, Apple, IBM, and EMC, and several major pharmaceutical firms including Johnson & Johnson, Bristol-Myers Squibb, and Eli Lilly. By the early 2000s, the Irish subsidiaries of foreign multinationals were accounting for over 80 percent of Ireland's exports, with Intel and Dell both exporting more than $4 billion each from Irish factories, Microsoft almost $2.5 billion, and Eli Lilly and Johnson & Johnson more than $1 billion apiece. Indeed, two-thirds of Ireland's top exporters are the Irish subsidiaries of foreign multinationals.

How did Ireland become so successful at attracting FDI? First, Ireland benefited from a number of favorable location factors. With Ireland a member of the European Union, subsidiaries based in Ireland have preferential access to EU markets. In addition, Ireland was blessed with a highly educated workforce, including many engineers, relatively low wage rates, low corporate tax rates, good basic infrastructure (e.g., roads, water, electricity, telecommunications), English as the main language (important for American multinationals), and a government that was friendly toward foreign businesses.

The last item became perhaps the linchpin in Ireland's success. Since the 1980s, Ireland has implemented an industrialization strategy that relies on FDI to promote dynamic export-led growth. The centerpiece of this strategy has been the country's Investment and Development Agency (IDA), which has been endowed with a large budget to be directed at attracting FDI (in 2000 this included $160 million in grant money that could be used to attract foreign multinationals). The IDA has helped to coordinate a combination of tax breaks and outright grants that, when put together with other location-specific factors, have helped to attract many multinationals to Ireland. The IDA has been very proactive in seeking out investors from the high-technology sector, realizing early that Ireland was a good location for centralized call centers. Companies such as Dell now have important customer service call centers in Ireland.

More importantly perhaps, the IDA was instrumental in persuading Intel to open its first plant in Ireland in 1990. Subsequently, Intel's investment helped to encourage many other high-technology firms to locate facilities in Ireland. High-technology investments have also been stimulated by an Irish government policy that all royalty income from products developed in Ireland is tax-free. This has created an incentive for foreign multinationals to establish R&D centers in Ireland. By the mid-1990s, the process had become self-sustaining, with the concentration of high-technology enterprises in Ireland attracting other high-technology enterprises so they could benefit from being close to suppliers, providers of complementary products, and even rivals.

Sources: United Nations, *World Investment Report, 2002.* (New York and Geneva: United Nations, 2002); L. Bowman, "Irish Revival," *Strategic Direct Investor,* April 2002, pp. 30–32; World Bank Online database; and E. R. E. O'Higgins, "Government and the Creation of the Celtic Tiger," *Academy of Management Executive* 16 (2002), pp. 104–20.

www.mhhe.com/hill

technical posts in the subsidiary of a foreign MNE leave the firm and help to establish indigenous firms. Similar benefits may arise if the superior management skills of a foreign MNE stimulate local suppliers, distributors, and competitors to improve their own management skills.

The benefits may be considerably reduced if most management and highly skilled jobs in the subsidiaries are reserved for home-country nationals. The percentage of management and skilled jobs that go to citizens of the host country can be a major negotiating point between an MNE wishing to undertake FDI and a potential host government. In recent years, most MNEs have responded to host-government pressures on this issue by agreeing to reserve a large proportion of management and highly skilled jobs for citizens of the host country.

Job creation is a result of FDI. These French workers assemble cars at Toyota's Valenciennes manufacturing plant.

EMPLOYMENT EFFECTS

Another beneficial employment effect claimed for FDI is that it brings jobs to a host country that would otherwise not be created there. The effects of FDI on employment are both direct and indirect. Direct effects arise when a foreign MNE employs a number of host-country citizens. Indirect effects arise when jobs are created in local suppliers as a result of the investment and when jobs are created because of increased local spending by employees of the MNE. The indirect employment effects are often as large as, if not larger than, the direct effects. For example, when Toyota decided to open a new auto plant in France in 1997, estimates suggested that the plant would create 2,000 direct jobs and perhaps another 2,000 jobs in support industries.[13]

Cynics argue that not all the "new jobs" created by FDI represent net additions in employment. In the case of FDI by Japanese auto companies in the United States, some argue that the jobs created by this investment have been more than offset by the jobs lost in U.S.-owned auto companies, which have lost market share to their Japanese competitors. As a consequence of such substitution effects, the net number of new jobs created by FDI may not be as great as initially claimed by an MNE. The issue of the likely net gain in employment may be a major negotiating point between an MNE wishing to undertake FDI and the host government.

When FDI takes the form of an acquisition of an established enterprise in the host economy as opposed to a greenfield investment (as in the case of Volvo's acquisition of Samsung's excavation division), the immediate effect may be to reduce employment as the multinational restructures the operations of the acquired unit to improve its operating efficiency (this was the case in Volvo's acquisition of the Samsung division; see the Management Focus). However, even in such cases, research suggests that once the initial restructuring is over, enterprises acquired by foreign firms tend to increase their employment base at a faster rate than domestic rivals. For example, an OECD study found that between 1989 and 1996, foreign firms created new jobs at a faster rate than their domestic counterparts.[14] In America, the workforce of foreign firms grew by 1.4 percent per year, compared to 0.8 percent per year for domestic firms. In Britain and France, the workforce of foreign firms grew at 1.7 percent per year, while employment at domestic firms fell by 2.7 percent. The same study found that foreign firms tended to pay higher wage rates than domestic firms, suggesting that the quality of employment was better. Another study looking at FDI in Eastern European transition economies found that although employment fell after the acquisition of an enterprise by a foreign firm, often those enterprises were in competitive difficulties and would not have survived if they had not been acquired. Moreover, after an initial period of adjustment and retrenchment, employment downsizing was often followed by new investments, and employment either remained stable or increased.[15]

TABLE 8.2

U.S. Balance of Payments Accounts for 2004 ($ millions)

Source: U.S. Department of Commerce.

Current Account	Credits	Debits
Exports of Goods, Services, and Income	$1,516,169	
Merchandise Goods	807,610	
Services	339,571	
Income Receipts on Investments	368,988	
Imports of Goods, Services, and Income		$−1,764,256
Merchandise Goods		−1,473,087
Services		−291,169
Income Payments on Investments		−344,925
Unilateral Transfers		−72,928
Balance of Current Account		−665,940
Capital Account		
U.S. Assets Abroad		−817,676
Foreign Assets in U.S.	1,433,171	
Statistical Discrepancy	51,922	

BALANCE-OF-PAYMENTS EFFECTS

FDI's effect on a country's **balance-of-payments** accounts is an important policy issue for most host governments. To understand this concern, we must first familiarize ourselves with balance-of-payments accounting. Then we will examine the link between FDI and the balance-of-payments accounts.

Balance-of-Payments Accounts

A country's **balance-of-payments accounts** keep track of both its payments to and its receipts from other countries. A summary copy of the U.S. balance-of-payments accounts for 2004 is given in Table 8.2. Any transaction resulting in a payment to other countries is entered in the balance-of-payments accounts as a debit and given a negative (−) sign. Any transaction resulting in a receipt from other countries is entered as a credit and given a positive (+) sign.

Balance-of-payments accounts are divided into two main sections: the current account and the capital account. The **current account** records transactions that pertain to three categories, all of which can be seen in Table 8.2. The first category, *merchandise goods*, refers to the export or import of physical goods (e.g., autos, computers, chemicals). The second category is the export or import of *services* (e.g., intangible products such as banking and insurance services). The third category, *investment income*, refers to income from foreign investments and payments that have to be made to foreigners investing in a country. For example, if a U.S. citizen owns a share of a Finnish company and receives a dividend payment of $5, that payment shows up on the U.S. current account as the receipt of $5 of investment income.

A **current account deficit** occurs when a country imports more goods, services, and income than it exports. A **current account surplus** occurs when a country exports more goods, services, and income than it imports. In recent years, the United States has run a persistent trade deficit. Table 8.2 shows that in 2004 the current account deficit was $665,940 million.

The **capital account** records transactions that involve the purchase or sale of assets. Thus, when a German firm purchases stock in a U.S. company, the transaction enters the U.S. balance of payments as a credit on the capital account. This is because capital is flowing into the country. When capital flows out of the United States, it enters the capital account as a debit.

A basic principle of balance-of-payments accounting is double-entry bookkeeping. Every international transaction automatically enters the balance of payments twice—once as a credit and once as a debit. Imagine that you purchase a car produced in Japan by Toyota for $20,000. Since your purchase represents a payment to another country for goods, it will enter the balance of payments as a debit on the current account. Toyota now has the $20,000 and must do something with it. If Toyota deposits the money at a U.S. bank, the transaction will show up as a $20,000 credit on the capital account. Or Toyota might deposit the cash in a Japanese bank in return for Japanese yen. Now the Japanese bank must decide what to do with the $20,000. Any action that it takes will ultimately result in a credit for the U.S. balance of payments. For example, if the bank lends the $20,000 to a Japanese firm that uses it to import personal computers from the United States, then the $20,000 must be credited to the U.S. balance-of-payments current account. Or the Japanese bank might use the $20,000 to purchase U.S. government bonds, in which case it will show up as a credit on the U.S. balance-of-payments capital account.

Thus, any international transaction automatically gives rise to two offsetting entries in the balance of payments. Because of this, the current account balance and the capital account balance should always add up to zero. (In practice, this does not always occur due to the existence of statistical discrepancies that need not concern us here.)

Governments normally are concerned when the country is running a deficit on the current account of the balance of payments.[16] When a country runs a current account deficit, the money that flows to other countries is then used by those countries to purchase assets in the deficit country. Thus, when the United States runs a trade deficit with Japan, the Japanese use the money that they receive from U.S. consumers to purchase U.S. assets such as stocks, bonds, and the like. Put another way, a deficit on the current account is financed by selling assets to other countries; that is, by a surplus on the capital account. Thus, the U.S. current account deficit during the 1980s, 1990s, and early 2000s was financed by a steady sale of U.S. assets (stocks, bonds, real estate, and whole corporations) to other countries. Countries that run current account deficits become net debtors.

For example, as a result of financing its current account deficit through asset sales, the United States must deliver a stream of interest payments to foreign bondholders, rents to foreign landowners, and dividends to foreign stockholders. Such payments to foreigners drain resources from a country and limit the funds available for investment within the country. Since investment within a country is necessary to stimulate economic growth, a persistent current account deficit can choke off a country's future economic growth.

FDI and the Balance of Payments

Given the concern about current account deficits, the balance-of-payments effects of FDI can be an important consideration for a host government. There are three potential balance-of-payments consequences of FDI. First, when an MNE establishes a foreign subsidiary, the capital account of the host country benefits from the initial capital inflow. (A debit will be recorded in the capital account of the MNE's home country, since capital is flowing out of the home country.) However, this is a one-time-only effect. Set against this must be the outflow of earnings to the foreign parent company, which will be recorded as a debit on the current account of the host country.

Second, if the FDI is a substitute for imports of goods or services, it can improve the current account of the host country's balance of payments. Much of the FDI by Japanese automobile companies in the United States and United Kingdom, for example, can be seen as substituting for imports from Japan. Thus, the current account of the U.S. balance of payments has improved somewhat because many Japanese companies are now supplying the U.S. market from production facilities in the United States, as opposed to facilities in Japan. Insofar as this has reduced the need to finance a current account deficit by asset sales to foreigners, the United States has clearly benefited.

A third potential benefit to the host country's balance-of-payments position arises when the MNE uses a foreign subsidiary to export goods and services to other countries. There are some striking examples of this phenomenon. In the Czech Republic, Skoda, the national automobile company, was a well-established producer and exporter. After its sale to Volkswagen in 1992, however, exports boomed as the new owners redirected the company's sales efforts toward the European Union. The share of exports in Skoda's sales increased from 34 percent in 1990 to 52 percent in 1995 and 80 percent in 1999. The Management Focus feature provides another example of this phenomenon. After acquiring Samsung's excavation division, Volvo made it the global center for its excavation business and redirected its attention toward exports. In addition, as we saw in the Country Focus, much of the FDI into Ireland has spurred rising exports from Ireland as foreign multinationals have used the country as a base for exporting to the rest of the European Union.

According to a recent United Nations report, inward FDI by foreign multinationals has been a major driver of export-led economic growth in a number of developing and developed nations over the last decade.[17] An example is China, where exports of goods increased from $26 billion in 1985 to more than $438 billion by 2003. According to UN data, much of this export growth was due to the presence of foreign multinationals that invested heavily in China during the 1990s. The subsidiaries of foreign multinationals accounted for about 50 percent of all exports from that country in 2003, up from 17 percent in 1991. In mobile phones, for example, the Chinese subsidiaries of foreign multinationals—primarily Nokia, Motorola, Ericsson, and Siemens—accounted for 95 percent of China's exports.

EFFECT ON COMPETITION AND ECONOMIC GROWTH

Economic theory tells us that the efficient functioning of markets depends on an adequate level of competition between producers. When FDI takes the form of a greenfield investment, a new enterprise is established, increasing the number of players in a market and thus consumer choice. In turn, this can increase the level of competition in a national market, thereby driving down prices and increasing the economic welfare of consumers. Increased competition tends to stimulate capital investments by firms in plant, equipment, and R&D as they struggle to gain an edge over their rivals. The long-term results may include increased productivity growth, product and process innovations, and greater economic growth.[18] Such beneficial effects seem to have occurred in the South Korean retail sector following the liberalization of FDI regulations in 1996. FDI by large Western discount stores, including Wal-Mart, Costco, Carrefour, and Tesco, seems to have encouraged indigenous Korean discounters such as E-Mart to improve the efficiency of their own operations. The results have included more competition and lower prices, which benefits Korean consumers.

FDI's impact on competition in domestic markets may be particularly important in the case of services, such as telecommunications, retailing, and many financial services, where exporting is often not an option because the service has to be produced where it is delivered.[19] For example, under a 1997 agreement sponsored by the World Trade Organization, 68 countries accounting for more than 90 percent of world telecommunications revenues pledged to start opening their markets to foreign investment and competition and to abide by common rules for fair competition in telecommunications. Before this agreement, most of the world's telecommunications markets were closed to foreign competitors, and in most countries the market was monopolized by a single carrier, which was often a state-owned enterprise. The agreement has dramatically increased the level of competition in many national telecommunications markets. Three benefits from this agreement have started to occur. First, inward investment has increased competition and stimulated investment in the modernization of telephone networks around the world, leading to better service. Second, the increased competition has resulted in lower prices. Third, trade in other goods and services depends upon flows of information matching buyers to sellers. As telecommunications service improves in quality and declines in price, international trade increases in volume and becomes less costly for traders. Telecommunications reform, therefore, should promote cross-border trade in other goods and services.

The Costs of FDI to Host Countries

Three costs of FDI concern host countries. They arise from possible adverse effects on competition within the host nation, adverse effects on the balance of payments, and the perceived loss of national sovereignty and autonomy.

ADVERSE EFFECTS ON COMPETITION

Although we have just outlined in the previous section how foreign direct investment can boost competition, host governments sometimes worry that the subsidiaries of foreign MNEs may have greater economic power than indigenous competitors. If it is part of a larger international organization, the foreign MNE may be able to draw on funds generated elsewhere to subsidize its costs in the host market, which could drive indigenous companies out of business and allow the firm to monopolize the market. (Once the market was monopolized, the foreign MNE could raise prices above those that would prevail in competitive markets, with harmful effects on the economic welfare of the host nation.) This concern tends to be greater in countries that have few large firms of their own (generally less developed countries). For example, this concern was a major factor in India's 1997 decision to ban further investment by foreign retailers (see the opening case). It tends to be a relatively minor concern in most advanced industrialized nations.

In general, while FDI in the form of greenfield investments should increase competition, it is less clear that this is the case when the FDI takes the form of acquisition of an established enterprise in the host nation, as was the case when Volvo acquired Samsung's excavation division (see the Management Focus). Because an acquisition does not result in a net increase in the number of players in a market, the effect on competition may be neutral. Indeed, when a foreign investor acquires two or more firms in a host country, and subsequently merges them, the effect may be to reduce the level of competition in that market, create monopoly power for the foreign firm, reduce consumer choice, and raise prices. For example, in India, Hindustan Lever Ltd., the Indian subsidiary of Unilever, acquired its main local rival, Tata Oil Mills, to assume a dominant position in the bath soap (75 percent) and detergents (30 percent) markets. Hindustan Lever also acquired several local companies in other markets, such as the ice cream makers Dollops, Kwality, and Milkfood. By combining these companies, Hindustan Lever's share of the Indian ice cream market went from zero in 1992 to 74 percent in 1997.[20] However, while such cases are of obvious concern, such developments are not widespread. In many nations, domestic competition authorities have the right to review and block any mergers or acquisitions that they view as having a detrimental impact on competition. If such institutions are operating effectively, this should assure that foreign entities do not monopolize a country's markets.

ADVERSE EFFECTS ON THE BALANCE OF PAYMENTS

The possible adverse effects of FDI on a host country's balance-of-payments position have been hinted at earlier. There are two main areas of concern with regard to the balance of payments. First, set against the initial capital inflow that comes with FDI must be the subsequent outflow of earnings from the foreign subsidiary to its parent company. Such outflows show up as a debit on the capital account. Some governments have responded to such outflows by restricting the amount of earnings that can be repatriated to a foreign subsidiary's home country.

A second concern arises when a foreign subsidiary imports a substantial number of its inputs from abroad, which results in a debit on the current account of the host country's balance of payments. One criticism leveled against Japanese-owned auto assembly operations in the United States, for example, is that they tend to import many component parts from Japan. Because of this, the favorable impact of this FDI on the current account of the U.S. balance-of-payments position may not be as great as initially supposed. The Japanese auto companies have responded to these criticisms by pledging to purchase 75 percent of their component parts from U.S.-based manufacturers (but not necessarily U.S.-owned manufacturers). When the Japanese auto company Nissan invested in the United Kingdom, Nissan responded to concerns about local content by pledging to increase the proportion of local content to 60 percent, and by subsequently raising it to more than 80 percent.

NATIONAL SOVEREIGNTY AND AUTONOMY

Some host governments worry that FDI is accompanied by some loss of economic independence. The concern is that key decisions that can affect the host country's economy will be made by a foreign parent that has no real commitment to the host country, and over which the host country's government has no real control. A quarter of a century ago this concern was expressed by several European countries, who feared that FDI by U.S. MNEs was threatening their national sovereignty. The same concerns surfaced in the United States with regard to European and Japanese FDI during the 1980s and early 1990s. The main fear seems to be that if foreigners own assets in the United States, they can somehow "hold the country to economic ransom." Twenty-five years ago when officials in the French government were making similar complaints about U.S. investments in France, many U.S. politicians dismissed the charge as silly, but when the shoe was on the other foot, some American politicians did not think the notion was silly. However, most economists dismiss such concerns as groundless and irrational. Political scientist Robert Reich has noted that such concerns are the product of outmoded thinking because they fail to account for the growing interdependence of the world economy.[21] In a world where firms from all advanced nations are increasingly investing in each other's markets, it is not possible for one country to hold another to "economic ransom" without hurting itself.

The Benefits and Costs of FDI to Home Countries

FDI also produces costs and benefits to the **home** (or source) **country.** Does the U.S. economy benefit or lose from investments by its firms in foreign markets? Does the Swedish economy lose or gain from Volvo's investment in South Korea? Some argue that FDI is not always in the home country's national interest and should be restricted. Others argue that the benefits far outweigh the costs and any restrictions would be contrary to national interests. To understand why people take these positions, let us look at the benefits and costs of FDI to the home (source) country.[22]

BENEFITS OF FDI TO THE HOME COUNTRY

The benefits of FDI to the home country arise from three sources. First, and perhaps most important, the capital account of the home country's balance of payments benefits from the inward flow of foreign earnings. Thus, one benefit to Sweden from Volvo's investment in South Korea are the earnings that are subsequently repatriated to Sweden. FDI can also benefit the current account of the home country's balance of payments if the foreign subsidiary creates demands for home-country exports of capital equipment, intermediate goods, complementary products, and the like.

Second, benefits to the home country from outward FDI arise from employment effects. As with the balance of payments, positive employment effects arise when the foreign subsidiary creates demand for home-country exports of capital equipment, intermediate goods, complementary products, and the like. Thus, Toyota's investment in auto assembly operations in Europe has benefited both the Japanese balance-of-payments position and employment in Japan, because Toyota imports some component parts for its European-based auto assembly operations directly from Japan.

Third, benefits arise when the home-country MNE learns valuable skills from its exposure to foreign markets that can subsequently be transferred back to the home country. This amounts to a reverse resource-transfer effect. Through its exposure to a foreign market, an MNE can learn about superior management techniques and superior product and process technologies. These resources can then be transferred back to the home country, contributing to its economic growth rate.[23] For example, one reason General Motors and Ford invested in Japanese automobile companies (GM owns part of Isuzu, and Ford owns part of Mazda) was to learn about their production processes. If GM and Ford are successful in transferring this know-how back to their American operations, the result may be a net gain for the U.S. economy.

COSTS OF FDI TO THE HOME COUNTRY

Against these benefits must be set the apparent costs of FDI for the home (source) country. The most important concerns center around the balance-of-payments and employment effects of outward FDI. The home country's balance of payments may suffer in three ways. First, the capital account of the balance of payments suffers from the initial capital outflow required to finance the FDI. This effect, however, is usually more than offset by the subsequent inflow of foreign earnings. Second, the current account of the balance of payments suffers if the purpose of the foreign investment is to serve the home market from a low-cost production location. Third, the current account of the balance of payments suffers if the FDI is a substitute for direct exports. Thus, insofar as Toyota's assembly operations in the United States are intended to substitute for direct exports from Japan, the current account position of Japan will deteriorate.

With regard to employment effects, the most serious concerns arise when FDI is seen as a substitute for domestic production. This was the case with Volvo's investment in South Korea and Toyota's investments in Europe. One obvious result of such FDI is reduced home-country employment. If the labor market in the home country is already very tight, with little unemployment, this concern may not be that great. However, if the home country is suffering from unemployment, concern about the export of jobs may arise. For example, one objection frequently raised by U.S. labor leaders to the free trade pact between the United States, Mexico, and Canada (see the next chapter) is that the United States will lose hundreds of thousands of jobs as U.S. firms invest in Mexico to take advantage of cheaper labor and then export back to the United States.[24]

INTERNATIONAL TRADE THEORY AND FDI

When assessing the costs and benefits of FDI to the home country, keep in mind the lessons of international trade theory (see Chapter 5). International trade theory tells us that home-country concerns about the negative economic effects of offshore production may be misplaced. The term **offshore production** refers to FDI undertaken to serve the home market. Far from reducing home-country employment, such FDI may actually stimulate economic growth (and hence employment) in the home country by freeing home-country resources to concentrate on activities where the home country has a comparative advantage. In addition, home-country consumers benefit if the price of the particular product falls as a result of the FDI. Also, if a company were prohibited from making such investments on the grounds of negative employment effects while its international competitors reaped the benefits of low-cost production locations, it

would undoubtedly lose market share to its international competitors. Under such a scenario, the adverse long-run economic effects for a country would probably outweigh the relatively minor balance-of-payments and employment effects associated with off-shore production.

Government Policy Instruments and FDI

Before tackling the important issue of bargaining between the MNE and the host government, we need to discuss the policy instruments that governments use to regulate FDI activity by MNEs. Both home (source) countries and host countries have a range of policy instruments that they can use. We will look at each in turn.

HOME-COUNTRY POLICIES

Through their choice of policies, home countries can both encourage and restrict FDI by local firms. We look at policies designed to encourage outward FDI first. These include foreign risk insurance, capital assistance, tax incentives, and political pressure. Then we will look at policies designed to restrict outward FDI.

Encouraging Outward FDI

Many investor nations now have government-backed insurance programs to cover major types of foreign investment risk. The types of risks insurable through these programs include expropriation (nationalization), war losses, and the inability to transfer profits back home. Such programs are particularly useful in encouraging firms to undertake investments in politically unstable countries.[25] In addition, several advanced countries also have special funds or banks that make government loans to firms wishing to invest in developing countries. As a further incentive to encourage domestic firms to undertake FDI, many countries have eliminated double taxation of foreign income (i.e., taxation of income in both the host country and the home country). Last, and perhaps most significant, a number of investor countries (including the United States) have used their political influence to persuade host countries to relax their restrictions on inbound FDI. For example, in response to direct U.S. pressure, Japan relaxed many of its formal restrictions on inward FDI in the 1980s. Now, in response to further U.S. pressure, Japan moved toward relaxing its informal barriers to inward FDI. One beneficiary of this trend was Toys "R" Us, which, after five years of intensive lobbying by company and U.S. government officials, opened its first retail stores in Japan in December 1991. By 2000, Toys "R" Us had more than 150 stores in Japan, and its Japanese operation, in which the company retained a controlling stake, had a listing on the Japanese stock market.

Restricting Outward FDI

Virtually all investor countries, including the United States, have exercised some control over outward FDI from time to time. One common policy has been to limit capital outflows out of concern for the country's balance of payments. From the early 1960s until 1979, for example, Britain had exchange-control regulations that limited the amount of capital a firm could take out of the country. Although the main intent of such policies was to improve the British balance of payments, an important secondary intent was to make it more difficult for British firms to undertake FDI.

In addition, countries have occasionally manipulated tax rules to try to encourage their firms to invest at home. The objective behind such policies is to create jobs at home rather than in other nations. At one time these policies were also adopted by Great Britain. The British advanced corporation tax system taxed British companies' foreign earnings at a higher rate than their domestic earnings. This tax code created an incentive for British companies to invest at home.

Finally, countries sometimes prohibit national firms from investing in certain countries for political reasons. Such restrictions can be formal or informal. For example, formal rules prohibited U.S. firms from investing in countries such as Cuba and Iran, whose political ideology and actions are judged to be contrary to American interests. Similarly, during the 1980s, informal pressure was applied to dissuade U.S. firms from investing in South Africa. In this case, the objective was to pressure South Africa to change its apartheid laws, which occurred during the early 1990s.

HOST-COUNTRY POLICIES

Host countries adopt policies designed both to restrict and to encourage inward FDI. As noted earlier in this chapter, political ideology has determined the type and scope of these policies in the past. In the last decade of the 20th century, many countries moved quickly away from adherence to some version of the radical stance, prohibiting much FDI, and toward a combination of free market objectives and pragmatic nationalism.

Because Japan was willing to relax some obstacles to FDI, Toys "R" Us was able to open stores there

Encouraging Inward FDI

It is increasingly common for governments to offer incentives to foreign firms to invest in their countries. Such incentives take many forms, but the most common are tax concessions, low-interest loans, and grants or subsidies. Incentives are motivated by a desire to gain from the resource-transfer and employment effects of FDI. They are also motivated by a desire to capture FDI away from other potential host countries. For example, in the mid-1990s, the governments of Britain and France competed with each other on the incentives they offered Toyota to invest in their respective countries. In the United States, state governments often compete with each other to attract FDI. Kentucky offered Toyota an incentive package worth $112 million to persuade it to build its U.S. automobile assembly plants there. The package included tax breaks, new state spending on infrastructure, and low-interest loans.[26]

Restricting Inward FDI

Host governments use a wide range of controls to restrict FDI in one way or another. The two most common are ownership restraints and performance requirements. Ownership restraints can take several forms. In some countries, foreign companies are excluded from specific fields. For example, they are excluded from tobacco and mining in Sweden and from the development of certain natural resources in Brazil, Finland, and Morocco. In other industries, foreign ownership may be permitted although a significant proportion of the equity of the subsidiary must be owned by local investors. Foreign ownership is restricted to 25 percent or less of an airline in the United States. In India, foreign firms were prohibited from owning media businesses until 2001, when the rules were relaxed allowing foreign firms to purchase up to 26 percent of a foreign newspaper.[27]

The rationale underlying ownership restraints seems to be twofold. First, foreign firms are often excluded from certain sectors on the grounds of national security or competition. Particularly in less developed countries, the feeling seems to be that local firms might not be able to develop unless foreign competition is restricted by a combination of import tariffs and controls on FDI. This is a variant of the infant industry argument discussed in Chapter 6.

Second, ownership restraints seem to be based on a belief that local owners can help to maximize the resource-transfer and employment benefits of FDI for the host country. Until the early 1980s, the Japanese government prohibited most FDI but allowed joint ventures between Japanese firms and foreign MNEs if the MNE had a valuable technology. The Japanese government clearly believed such an arrangement would speed up the subsequent diffusion of the MNE's valuable technology throughout the Japanese economy.

Performance requirements can also take several forms. Performance requirements are controls over the behavior of the MNE's local subsidiary. The most common performance requirements are related to local content, exports, technology transfer, and local participation in top management. As with certain ownership restrictions, the logic underlying performance requirements is that such rules help to maximize the benefits and minimize the costs of FDI for the host country. Virtually all countries employ some form of performance requirements when it suits their objectives. However, performance requirements tend to be more common in less developed countries than in advanced industrialized nations.[28] For example, one study found that some 30 percent of the affiliates of U.S. MNEs in less developed countries were subject to performance requirements, while only 6 percent of the affiliates in advanced countries were faced with such requirements.[29]

INTERNATIONAL INSTITUTIONS AND THE LIBERALIZATION OF FDI

Until the 1990s, multinational institutions were not consistently involved in the governing of FDI. This changed with the formation of the World Trade Organization in 1995. As noted in Chapter 6, the WTO embraces the promotion of international trade in services. Because many services have to be produced where they are sold, exporting is not an option (for example, one cannot export McDonald's hamburgers or consumer banking services). Given this, the WTO has become involved in regulations governing FDI. As might be expected for an institution created to promote free trade, the thrust of the WTO's efforts has been to push for the liberalization of regulations governing FDI, particularly in services. Under the auspices of the WTO, two extensive multinational agreements were reached in 1997 to liberalize trade in telecommunications and financial services. Both these agreements contained detailed clauses that require signatories to liberalize their regulations governing inward FDI, essentially opening their markets to foreign telecommunications and financial services companies.

However, the WTO has had less success trying to initiate talks aimed at establishing a universal set of rules designed to promote the liberalization of FDI. Led by Malaysia and India, developing nations have so far rejected any attempts by the WTO to start such discussions. In an attempt to make some progress on this issue, the **Organization for Economic Cooperation and Development (OECD)** in 1995 initiated talks between its members. (The OECD is a Paris-based intergovernmental organization of "wealthy" nations whose purpose is to provide its 29 member states with a forum in which governments can compare their experiences, discuss the problems they share, and seek solutions that can then be applied within their own national contexts. The members include most European Union countries, the United States, Canada, Japan, and South Korea.) The aim of the talks was to draft the **Multilateral Agreement on Investment (MAI)** that would make it illegal for signatory states to discriminate against foreign investors. This would liberalize rules governing FDI between OECD states. Unfortunately for those promoting the agreement, the talks broke down in early 1998, primarily because the United States refused to sign the agreement. According to the United States, the proposed agreement contained too many exceptions that would weaken its powers. For example, the proposed agreement would not have barred discriminatory taxation of foreign-owned companies, and it would have allowed countries to restrict foreign television programs and music in the name of preserving culture. Also campaigning against the MAI were environmental and labor groups, who criticized the proposed agreement on the grounds that it contained no binding environmental or labor agreements. Despite these problems, negotiations on a revised MAI treaty could restart. As noted earlier, individual nations have continued to unilaterally remove restrictions to inward FDI as a wide range of countries from South Korea to South Africa try to encourage foreign firms to invest in their economies.[30]

IMPLICATIONS FOR MANAGERS

There are a number of fairly obvious implications for business in the material discussed in this chapter. For a start, a host government's attitude toward FDI should be an important variable in deciding where to locate foreign production facilities and where to make a foreign direct investment. Other things being equal, investing in countries that have permissive policies toward FDI is clearly preferable to investing in countries that restrict FDI.

Generally, however, the issue is not this straightforward. Despite the move toward a free market stance in recent years, many countries still have a rather pragmatic stance toward FDI.[31] In such cases, a firm considering FDI may have to negotiate the specific terms of the investment with the host country's government. Such negotiations often center on two broad issues. If the host government is trying to attract FDI, the central issue is likely to be the kind of incentives the host government is prepared to offer to the MNE and what the firm will commit in exchange. If the host government is uncertain about the benefits of FDI and might restrict access, the central issue is likely to be the concessions that the firm must make to go forward with a proposed investment.

In the remainder of this section, we will focus on negotiating with a host government. Increasingly, negotiations between MNEs and host governments are occurring within the framework of broad multilateral agreements to which the host and home countries are signatories.[32] For example, when an American firm is considering investment in the Brazilian telecommunications sector, the 1997 WTO telecommunications agreement sets the parameters under which negotiations can proceed. Because the agreement has removed most impediments to cross-border investments in telecommunications, the scope for bargaining between the MNE and the host government is significantly reduced. The same is true of much cross-border investment in financial services, again due to the establishment of a WTO agreement. In addition, extensive regional agreements such as the European Union (EU) and the North American Free Trade Agreement (NAFTA) now govern FDI flows between countries that are members of the same regional bloc (we discuss these agreements in depth in the next chapter). The NAFTA agreement, for example, sets the parameters that govern the conditions under which firms from Canada, Mexico, and the United States can invest in each other's markets. These parameters, which are generally very liberal and remove most restrictions on FDI flows between member states, significantly limit the scope for bargaining. Still, given the failure of both the WTO and the OECD to establish extensive multilateral agreements governing FDI, negotiation between MNEs and host governments remains an important issue in many instances.

THE NATURE OF NEGOTIATION

The objective of any negotiation is to reach an agreement that benefits both parties. Negotiation is both an art and a science. The science of it requires analyzing the relative bargaining strengths of each party and the different strategic options available and assessing how the other party might respond to various bargaining ploys.[33] The art of negotiation incorporates "interpersonal skills, the ability to convince and be convinced, the ability to employ a basketful of bargaining ploys, and the wisdom to know when and how to use them."[34] In the context of international business, the art of negotiation also includes understanding the influence of national norms, value systems, and culture on the approach and likely negotiating tactics of the other party as well as sensitivity to such factors in shaping a firm's approach to negotiations with a foreign government. For example, negotiating with the Japanese government for access is likely to be very different from negotiating with the British government.

Consequently, it requires different interpersonal skills and bargaining ploys. We discussed national differences in society and culture in Chapter 3; these are important at this juncture.

The negotiation process has been characterized as occurring within the context of "the four Cs": common interests, conflicting interests, compromise, and criteria (see Figure 8.1).[35] To explore this concept, consider the negotiations between IBM and Mexico that occurred in 1984 and 1985 when IBM tried to get permission to establish a facility to manufacture personal computers in Guadalajara, Mexico. At that time, Mexican law required foreign investors to agree to a minimum of 51 percent local ownership of any production facilities they established in Mexico (the law was repealed as part of the 1994 North American Free Trade Agreement). The rationale for this law was Mexico's desire to reduce its economic dependence on foreign-owned enterprises, thereby preserving its national sovereignty. As with many such laws, it was used as a bargaining chip by the Mexican government to extract concessions from foreign firms wishing to establish production facilities in Mexico. The government was often willing to waive the 51 percent ownership requirement if a foreign firm would make concessions that increased the beneficial impact of its investment on the Mexican economy.

IBM proposed to invest about $40 million in a state-of-the-art production facility with the capacity to produce 100,000 PCs per year, 75 percent of which would be exported (primarily to the United States). IBM's objective was to take advantage of Mexico's low labor costs to reduce the cost of manufacturing PCs. Given the proprietary nature of the product and process technology involved in the design and manufacture of PCs, IBM wanted to maintain 100 percent ownership of the Guadalajara facility. IBM felt that if it entered into a joint venture with a Mexican firm to produce PCs, as required under Mexican law, it would risk giving away valuable technology to a potential future competitor. When presenting its case to the Mexican government, IBM stressed the benefits of the proposed investment for the Mexican economy. These included the creation of 80 direct jobs and 800 indirect ones, the transfer of high-technology job skills to Mexico, new direct investment of $7 million (the remaining $33 million required to finance the investment would be raised from the Mexican capital market), and exports of 75,000 personal computers per year. The Mexican government rejected the proposal on the grounds that IBM did not propose to use sufficient local content in the plant and would thus be importing too many parts and materials. IBM twice resubmitted its proposal. Maintaining its insistence on 100 percent ownership, IBM with each proposal increased its commitment to purchase local parts, increased the level of its direct investment, and raised its planned level of exports. The Mexican government agreed to the third proposal, which had extracted significant concessions from IBM. The final agreement required IBM to invest $91 million (up from $40 million). This money was distributed among expansion of the Guadalajara plant ($7 million), investment in local R&D ($35 million), development of local part suppliers ($20 million), expansion of its purchasing and distribution network ($13 million), contributions to a Mexican government-sponsored semiconductor technology center ($12 million), and various other minor investments. In addition, IBM agreed to achieve 82 percent local content by the fourth year of operation and to export 92 percent of the PCs produced. In exchange, the Mexican government waived its 51 percent local ownership requirement and allowed IBM to maintain 100 percent control.[36]

In this example, the common interest of both IBM and Mexico is establishing a new enterprise in Mexico. Conflicting interests arise from such issues as the proportion of component parts that will be procured locally rather than imported, the total amount of investment, the total number of jobs created, and the proportion of output that will be exported. Compromise involves reaching a decision that brings benefits to both parties, even though neither will get all of what it wants. IBM's criteria or objectives are to achieve satisfactory profits and to maintain 100 percent ownership. Mexico's criteria are to achieve satisfactory net benefits from the resource-transfer, employment, and balance-of-payments effects of the investment.

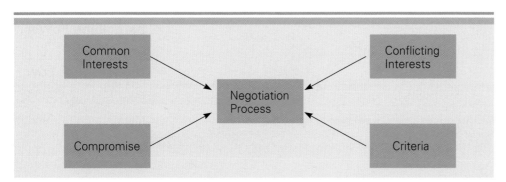

FIGURE 8.1

The Context of
Negotiation—
The Four Cs

BARGAINING POWER

The outcome of any negotiated agreement depends on the relative bargaining power of both parties. Each side's bargaining power depends on three factors (see Table 8.3):

- The value each side places on what the other has to offer.
- The number of comparable alternatives available to each side.
- Each party's time horizon.

From the perspective of a firm negotiating the terms of an investment with a host government, the firm's bargaining power is high when the host government places a high value on what the firm has to offer, the number of comparable alternatives open to the firm is great, and the firm has a long time in which to complete the negotiations. The converse also holds. The firm's bargaining power is low when the host government places a low value on what the firm has to offer, few comparable alternatives are open to the firm, and the firm has a short time in which to complete the negotiations.

To see how this plays out in practice, consider again the case of IBM and Mexico. IBM was in a fairly strong bargaining position, primarily because Mexico was suffering from a flight of capital out of the country at the time (1985 and 1986), which made the government eager to attract new foreign investment. But IBM's bargaining power was moderated somewhat by three things. First, despite its symbolic importance, the size of the proposed investment was unlikely to have more than a marginal impact on the Mexican economy, so the economic value placed by Mexico on the investment was not that great. Second, IBM was looking for a low-labor-cost, politically stable location close to the United States. Mexico was obviously the most desirable location given these criteria. Greater distance and higher transportation costs made alternative low-labor-cost locations, such as Taiwan or Singapore, relatively less attractive, while other potential locations in Central America were ruled out by political instability. Third, given the profusion of low-cost competitors moving into the U.S. personal computer market during the mid-1980s, IBM probably felt it needed to move quickly to establish its own low-cost production facilities. But there was no compelling reason for Mexico to close a deal quickly. Due to all these factors, the Mexican government also held some bargaining power in the negotiations and was able to extract some concessions from IBM. On the other hand, IBM's strong position allowed it to insist that it maintain 100 percent ownership of its Mexican subsidiary. This represented a significant concession from the Mexican government; IBM was the first major company for which Mexico waived its prohibition of majority ownership.

In a similar case during the 1960s, IBM was one of the few firms to get the Japanese government to waive the restriction on FDI that would allow it to establish a wholly owned subsidiary in Japan. IBM was able to do this because it was the only major source of mainframe computer technology at the time, and numerous Japanese companies needed that technology for data processing. The lack of comparable alternatives available to the Japanese enabled IBM to pry open the Japanese market. Similarly,

TABLE 8.3

Determinants of
Bargaining Power

	Bargaining Power of Firm	
	High	**Low**
Firm's time horizon	Long	Short
Comparable alternatives open to firm	Many	Few
Value placed by host government on investment	High	Low

during the 1980s, Toyota extracted significant concessions from the state of Kentucky in the form of tax breaks, low-interest loans, and grants, and Honda received similar concessions from the state of Ohio. At that time, both states were suffering from high unemployment, and the proposed auto assembly plants promised to have a substantial impact on employment. Also, both companies had a number of states from which to choose. Thus, the high value placed by state governments on the proposed investment and the number of comparable alternatives open to each company considerably strengthened the bargaining power of both companies relative to that of the state governments.

Chapter Summary

This chapter examined governments' influence on firms' decisions to invest in foreign countries. By their choice of policies, both host-country and home-country governments encourage and restrict FDI. We also explored the factors that influence negotiations between a host-country government and a firm contemplating FDI. The chapter made the following points:

1. An important determinant of government policy toward FDI is political ideology. Political ideology ranges from a radical stance that is hostile to FDI to a noninterventionist, free market stance. Between the two extremes is an approach best described as pragmatic nationalism.

2. The radical view sees the MNE as an imperialist tool for exploiting host countries. According to this view, no country should allow FDI. Due to the collapse of communism, the radical view was in retreat everywhere by the end of the 1990s.

3. The free market view sees the MNE as an instrument for increasing the overall efficiency of resource utilization in the world economy. FDI can be viewed as a way of dispersing the production of goods and services to those locations around the globe where they can be produced most efficiently.

4. Pragmatic nationalism views FDI as having both benefits and costs. Countries adopting a pragmatic stance pursue policies designed to maximize the benefits and minimize the costs of FDI.

5. The benefits of FDI to a host country arise from resource-transfer effects, employment effects, balance-of-payments effects, and its ability to promote competition.

6. FDI can make a positive contribution to a host economy by supplying capital, technology, and management resources that would otherwise not be available. Such resource transfers can stimulate the economic growth of the host economy.

7. Employment effects arise from the direct and indirect creation of jobs by FDI.

8. Balance-of-payments effects arise from the initial capital inflow to finance FDI, from import substitution effects, and from subsequent exports by the new enterprise.

9. By increasing consumer choice, foreign direct investment can help to increase the level of competition in national markets, thereby driving down prices and increasing the economic welfare of consumers.

10. The costs of FDI to a host country include adverse effects on competition and balance of payments and a perceived loss of national sovereignty.

11. Host governments are concerned that foreign MNEs may have greater economic power than indigenous companies and that they may be able to monopolize the market.

12. Adverse effects on the balance of payments arise from the outflow of a foreign subsidiary's earnings and from the import of inputs from abroad.

13. National sovereignty concerns are raised by FDI because key decisions that affect the host country will be made by a foreign parent that may have no real commitment to the host country and the host government will have no control over them.

14. The benefits of FDI to the home (source) country include improvement in the balance of payments as a result of the inward flow of foreign earnings, positive employment effects when the foreign subsidiary creates demand for home-country exports, and benefits from a reverse resource-transfer effect. A reverse resource-transfer effect arises when the foreign subsidiary learns valuable skills abroad that can be transferred back to the home country.

15. The costs of FDI to the home country include adverse balance-of-payments effects that arise from the initial capital outflow and from the export substitution effects of FDI. Costs also arise when FDI exports jobs abroad.

16. Home countries can adopt policies designed to both encourage and restrict FDI. Host countries try to attract FDI by offering incentives and try to restrict FDI by dictating ownership restraints and requiring that foreign MNEs meet specific performance requirements.

17. A firm considering FDI usually must negotiate the terms of the investment with the host government. The object of any negotiation is to reach an agreement that benefits both parties. Negotiation inevitably involves compromise.

18. The outcome of negotiation is typically determined by the relative bargaining powers of the foreign MNE and the host government. Bargaining power depends on the value each side places on what the other has to offer, the number of comparable alternatives available to each side, and each party's time horizon.

Critical Thinking and Discussion Questions

1. Read the Country Focus on FDI in Ireland. How important has FDI been to the health of the Irish economy?

2. Explain how the political ideology of a host government might influence the negotiations with a foreign MNE.

3. Under what circumstances is an MNE in a powerful negotiating position vis-à-vis a host government? What kind of concessions is a firm likely to win in such situations?

4. Under what circumstances is an MNE in a weak negotiating position vis-à-vis a host government? What kind of concessions is a host government likely to win in such situations?

5. Inward FDI is bad for (i) a developing economy and (ii) a developed economy and should be subjected to strict controls Discuss.

6. Firms should not be investing abroad when there is a need for investment to create jobs at home Discuss.

7. Do you think the successful conclusion of a multilateral agreement to liberalize regulations governing FDI will benefit the world economy? Why?

Research Task globaledge.msu.edu

Use the globalEDGE™ site to complete the following exercises:

1. The top management of your company wants an analysis of the current position of the United States in world trade. Using what you have learned about the dynamics of the balance of payments, prepare the analysis of the latest state of U.S. trade.

2. The Bureau of Economic Analysis, an agency of the U.S. Department of Commerce, lists data about the U.S. International Accounts, including current investment positions and the amount of direct investment by multinational corporations. Prepare a brief report based on the most recent information regarding the direct investments of other countries in the United States. What Middle Eastern country is leading in a foreign direct investment position on a historical-cost basis for the real estate, rental, and leasing industries? Is this the same Middle Eastern country that leads for the information industry?

Foreign Direct Investment in Venezuela's Petroleum Industry

CLOSING CASE In 1976, Venezuela nationalized its oil industry, effectively closing the sector to foreign investors. The stated goal at the time was to control this important natural resource for the benefit of Venezuela, as opposed to foreign oil companies. The results, however, fell short of expectations. The country's state-owned oil monopoly, Petroleos de Venezuela SA (PDVSA), failed to develop new oil fields to replace the depletion of existing reserves, and the country's oil output was falling by the mid-1980s.

Faced with the prospect of declining export revenues from oil, in 1991 Venezuela opened its oil industry to foreign investors. The Venezuelan government turned to foreign investors for three reasons. First, it recognized that PDVSA did not have the capital required to undertake the investment alone. Second, it realized that PDVSA lacked the technological resources and skills of many of the world's major oil companies, particularly in the areas of oil exploration, oil field development, and sophisticated refining. The government understood that if PDVSA was to develop many of Venezuela's oil fields in a timely fashion, it had no alternative but to turn to foreign companies for help. Third, the government believed that PDVSA would be able to use joint ventures with foreign oil companies as a vehicle for learning about modern management techniques in the industry. PDVSA could then use this knowledge to improve the efficiency of its own operations.

The original plan called for the investment of $73 billion in the oil industry to develop a crude oil production of 7 million barrels per day by 2007 (the country produced about 2.6 million barrels per day in 1991). Of the $73 billion in projected capital spending, $45 billion was to come from PDVSA while foreign oil companies were expected to supply $28 billion. The first FDI agreement was signed in 1992 with British Petroleum (BP). BP agreed to invest $60 million by 1995 to develop a marginal oil field that it would then be given the rights to for 20 years. Using a BP study, PDVSA identified sectors in eastern Venezuela with strong prospects for large discoveries of crude oil and entered into several joint ventures with other foreign partners to develop these zones. PDVSA took a minority stake in these ventures, typically about 35 percent. If commercial quantities of oil are discovered, PDVSA will share future production with its partners. Under the terms of most agreements, PDVSA will receive 35 percent of the earnings from its stake in the venture. In addition, the Venezuelan government was to collect 1 percent royalties on oil production.

By 1997, more than 40 development projects were under way in Venezuela involving joint ventures between PDVSA and foreign oil companies. Almost all of the world's major oil companies had some activities in the country by 1999, compared to none before 1991. The country's oil output was also expanding, reaching 3.5 million barrels per day in 1997, up from a low of 1.7 million barrels per day in 1985. By 1999, PDVSA earned record profits of $2.4 billion, boosted in part by higher oil prices and in part by a 20 percent reduction in operating costs due to productivity gains.

Buoyed by this success, in 2000, PDVSA launched another 10-year plan. The plan called for the investment of another $53 billion between 2000 and 2010, with some $31 billion coming from the private sector, and the majority of that from foreign investors. Then everything changed! Hugo Chavez, a radical politician, was elected president of Venezuela. In 2003, Chavez installed one of his political allies as the head of PDVSA. Some 18,000 PDVSA employees walked out on strike in protest, shutting down the company. Chavez responded by firing them all and hiring inexperienced employees. The damage has been considerable. By 2004, the country's oil production was down to 2.6 million barrels a day. However, due to high oil prices PDVSA was making record profits, which Chavez was investing in social projects designed to help the poor. Noble perhaps, but the result is that PDVSA has been starved of investment funds, making Venezuela more reliant on foreign investors to develop its oil industry. But here too, Chavez may be killing the goose that laid the golden egg. In October 2004 he hiked royalties due the government to 16.7 percent. He also changed the terms on any new joint ventures with foreign oil companies. For new ventures, royalties payable to the government will be 30 percent and PDVSA will take a 51 percent stake, effectively giving PDVSA control.

Sources: J. Mann, "A Little Help from Their Friends," *Financial Times*, November 10, 1993, p. 28; "Venezuela: A Survey," *The Economist*, October 14, 1994; E. Luce, "Oil: Foreign Investment: Finding a Balanced Approach," *Financial Times*, October 21, 1997, p. 6; "PDVSA Projects $53 Billion in Outlays for 10-Year Plan," *Oil & Gas Journal*, April 17, 2000, pp. 26–27; and G. Smith, "Killing the Golden Goose?" *BusinessWeek*, March 14, 2005, p. 52.

Case Discussion Questions

1. What do you think underlay Venezuela's decision to close its oil industry to foreign investment in 1976?

2. Why did the Venezuelan government reverse course in 1991 and open its arms to foreign investment? What were the potential benefits it saw for the Venezuelan economy?

3. What political ideology probably governed Venezuela's approach to inward FDI during the 1990s? How do you think this ideology changed following the election of Hugo Chavez to the presidency?

4. Under the terms of the new regulations announced in late 2004 governing FDI in Venezuela's oil sector, what are the potential implications for (*a*) oil production in Venezuela, (*b*) the long-term profitability of PDVSA, and (*c*) economic growth in Venezuela?

Notes

1. For elaboration see S. Hood and S. Young, *The Economics of the Multinational Enterprise* (London: Longman, 1979), and P. M. Sweezy and H. Magdoff, "The Dynamics of U.S. Capitalism," *Monthly Review Press,* 1972.

2. S. Weiss, "The Long Path to the IBM-Mexico Agreement: An Analysis of Micro-Computer Investment Decisions," Working Paper No. 3, NYU School of Business, 1989.

3. Ibid.

4. C. Forelle and G. Hitt, "IBM Discusses Security Measure in Lenovo Deal," *The Wall Street Journal,* February 25, 2005, p. A2.

5. For an example of this policy as practiced in China, see L. G. Branstetter and R. C. Freenstra, "Trade and Foreign Direct Investment in China: A Political Economy Approach," *Journal of International Economics,* December 2002, pp. 335–58.

6. M. Itoh and K. Kiyono, "Foreign Trade and Direct Investment," in *Industrial Policy of Japan,* ed. R. Komiya, M. Okuno, and K. Suzumura (Tokyo: Academic Press, 1988).

7. See S. Hood and S. Young, *The Economics of the Multinational Enterprise* (London: Longman, 1979). Also, Chapter 6 in United Nations, *World Investment Report 2000* (New York and Geneva: United Nations, 2000).

8. R. E. Lipsey, "Home and Host Country Effects of FDI," National Bureau of Economic Research, Working Paper No. 9293, October 2002; and X. Li and X. Liu, "Foreign Direct Investment and Economic Growth," *World Development* 33 (March 2005), pp. 393–413.

9. P. M. Romer, "The Origins of Endogenous Growth," *Journal of Economic Perspectives* 8, no. 1 (1994), pp. 3–22.

10. X. J. Zhan, and T. Ozawa, *Business Restructuring in Asia: Cross Border M&As in Crisis Affected Countries* (Copenhagen: Copenhagen Business School, 2000); I. Costa, S. Robles, and R. de Queiroz, "Foreign Direct Investment and Technological Capabilities," *Research Policy* 31 (2002), pp. 1431–43; B. Potterie and F. Lichtenberg, "Does Foreign Direct Investment Transfer Technology across Borders?" *Review of Economics and Statistics* 83 (2001), pp. 490–97; and K. Saggi, "Trade, Foreign Direct Investment and International Technology Transfer," *World Bank Research Observer* 17 (2002), pp. 191–235.

11. K. M. Moden, "Foreign Acquisitions of Swedish Companies: Effects on R&D and Productivity," Stockholm: Research Institute of International Economics, mimeo, 1998.

12. "Foreign Friends," *The Economist,* January 8, 2000, pp. 71–72.

13. A. Jack, "French Go into Overdrive to Win Investors," *Financial Times,* December 10, 1997, p. 6.

14. "Foreign Friends."

15. G. Hunya and K. Kalotay, *Privatization and Foreign Direct Investment in Eastern and Central Europe* (Geneva: UNCTAD, 2001).

16. P. Krugman, *The Age of Diminished Expectations* (Cambridge, MA: MIT Press, 1990).

17. United Nations, *World Investment Report, 2002.*

18. R. Ram and K. H. Zang, "Foreign Direct Investment and Economic Growth," *Economic Development and Cultural Change* 51 (2002), pp. 205–25.

19. United Nations, *World Investment Report, 1998* (New York and Geneva: United Nations, 1997).

20. United Nations, *World Investment Report, 2000* (New York and Geneva: United Nations, 2000).

21. R. B. Reich, *The Work of Nations: Preparing Ourselves for the 21st Century* (New York: Alfred A. Knopf, 1991).

22. For a review, see J. H. Dunning, "Re-Evaluating the Benefits of Foreign Direct Investment," *Transnational Corporations* 3, no. 1 (February 1994), pp. 23–51.

23. This idea has recently been articulated, although not quite in this form, by C. A. Bartlett and S. Ghoshal, *Managing across Borders: The Transnational Solution* (Boston: Harvard Business School Press, 1989).

24. P. Magnusson, "The Mexico Pact: Worth the Price?" *BusinessWeek*, May 27, 1991, pp. 32–35.

25. C. Johnston, "Political Risk Insurance," in *Assessing Corporate Political Risk*, ed. D. M. Raddock (Totowa, NJ: Rowan & Littlefield, 1986).

26. M. Tolchin and S. Tolchin, *Buying into America: How Foreign Money Is Changing the Face of Our Nation* (New York: Times Books, 1988).

27. S. Rai, "India to Ease Limits on Foreign Ownership of Media and Tea," *The New York Times*, June 26, 2002, p. W1.

28. L. D. Qiu and Z. Tao, "Export, Foreign Direct Investment and Local Content Requirements," *Journal of Development Economics*, October 2001, pp. 101–25.

29. J. Behrman and R. E. Grosse, *International Business and Government: Issues and Institutions* (Columbia, SC: University of South Carolina Press, 1990).

30. G. De Jonquiers and S. Kuper, "Push to Keep Alive Effort to Draft Global Investment Rules," *Financial Times*, April 29, 1988, p. 5.

31. J. H. Dunning, "An Overview of Relations with National Governments," *New Political Economy* 3, no. 2 (1998), pp. 280–84.

32. R. Ramamurti, "The Obsolescing Bargaining Model? MNC-Host Developing Country Relations Revisited," *Journal of International Business Studies* 32, no. 1, (2001), pp. 23–39.

33. For a good introduction, see M. H. Bazerman, *Negotiating Rationally* (New York: Free Press, 1997), and A. Dixit and B. Nalebuff, *Thinking Strategically: The Competitive Edge in Business, Politics, and Everyday Life* (New York: W. W. Norton, 1991).

34. H. Raiffa, *The Art and Science of Negotiation* (Cambridge, MA: Harvard University Press, 1982).

35. J. Fayerweather and A. Kapoor, *Strategy and Negotiation for the International Corporation* (Cambridge, MA: Ballinger, 1976).

36. Behrman and Grosse, *International Business and Government: Issues and Institutions*, and S. Weiss, "The Long Path to the IBM-Mexico Agreement: An Analysis of Microcomputer Investment Negotiations, 1983–1986," Working Paper No. 3, NYU School of Business, 1989.

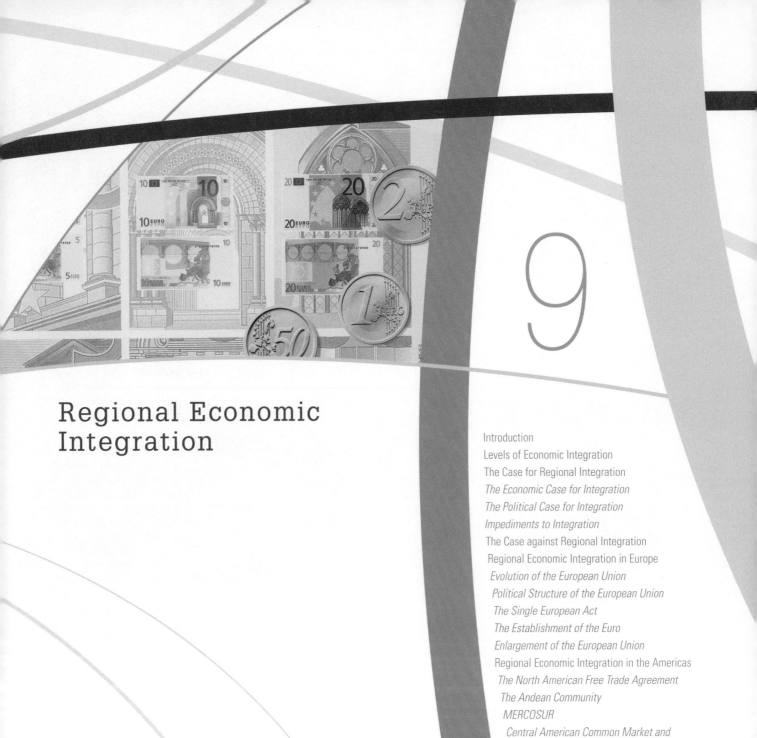

Regional Economic
Integration

Creating a Single European Market in Financial Services

The European Union (EU) in 1999 embarked upon an ambitious action plan to create a single market in financial services by January 1, 2005. Launched a few months after the euro, the EU's single currency, the goal was to dismantle barriers to cross-border activity in financial services, creating a continentwide market for banking service, insurance services, and investment products. In this vision of a single Europe, a citizen of France might use a German firm for basic banking services, borrow a home mortgage from an Italian institution, buy auto insurance from a Dutch enterprise, and keep her savings in mutual funds managed by a British company. Similarly, an Italian firm might raise capital from investors across Europe, using a German firm as its lead underwriter to issue stock for sale through stock exchanges in London and Frankfurt.

One main benefit of a single market, according to its advocates, would be greater competition for financial services, which would give consumers more choices, lower prices, and require financial service firms in the EU to become more efficient, thereby increasing their global competitiveness. Another major benefit would be the creation of a single European capital market. The increased liquidity of a larger capital market would make it easier for firms to borrow funds, lowering their cost of capital (the price of money) and stimulating business investment in Europe, which would create more jobs. A European Commission study suggested that the creation of a single market in financial services would increase the EU's gross domestic product by 1.1 percent a year, creating an additional 130 billion euros (€) in wealth over a decade. Total business investment would increase by 6 percent annually in the long run, private consumption by 0.8 percent, and total employment by 0.5 percent a year.

Creating a single market, however, has been anything but easy. The financial markets of different EU member states have historically been segmented from each other, and each has its own regulatory framework. In the past, EU financial services firms rarely did business across national borders because of a host of different national regulations with regard to taxation, oversight, accounting information, cross-border takeovers, and the like, all of which had to be harmonized. To complicate matters, long-standing cultural and linguistic barriers complicated the move toward a single market. While in theory an Italian might benefit by being able to purchase homeowners' insurance from a British company, in practice he might be predisposed to purchase it from a local enterprise, even if the price were higher.

By January 2005, the EU had made significant progress. Of 42 measures in the original action plan, some 39 had become EU law. The new rules embraced issues as diverse as the conduct of business by investment firms, stock exchanges, and banks; disclosure standards for listing companies on public exchanges; and the harmonization of accounting standards across nations. However, there had also been some significant setbacks. Most notably, legislation designed to make it easier for firms to make hostile cross-border acquisitions was defeated, primarily due to opposition from German members of the European Parliament, making it more difficult for financial service firms to build pan-European operations. In addition, national governments have still reserved the right to block even friendly cross-border mergers between financial service firms. For example, Italian banking law still requires the governor of the Bank of Italy to give permission to any foreign enterprise that wishes to purchase more than 5 percent of an Italian bank—and no foreigners have yet to acquire a majority position in an Italian bank, primarily, say critics, due to nationalistic concerns on the part of the Italians.

The critical issue now is enforcement of the rules that have been put in place. Some believe that it will be at least another decade before the benefits of the new regulations become apparent. In the meantime, the changes may impose significant costs on financial institutions as they attempt to deal with the new raft of regulations.

Sources: C. Randzio-Plath, "Europe Prepares for a Single Financial Market," *Intereconomic,* May–June 2004, pp. 142–46; T. Buck, D. Hargreaves, and P. Norman, "Europe's Single Financial Market," *Financial Times,* January 18, 2005, p. 17; *Anonymous,* "The Gatekeeper," *The Economist,* February 19, 2005, p. 79; P. Hofheinz, "A Capital Idea: The European Union Has a Grand Plan to Make Its Financial Markets More Efficient," *The Wall Street Journal,* October 14, 2002, p. R4; and "European Disunion," *The Economist,* May 24, 2003, p. 76.

One notable trend in the global economy in recent years has been the accelerated move-ment toward regional economic integration. **Regional economic integration** refers to agreements among countries in a geographic region to reduce, and ultimately remove, tariff and nontariff barriers to the free flow of goods, services, and factors of production between each other. The last few years have witnessed an unprecedented proliferation of regional trade arrangements. World Trade Organization members are required to notify the WTO of any regional trade agreements in which they participate. By 2005, nearly all of the WTO's members had notified the organization of participation in one or more re-gional trade agreements. From 1948 to 1994, there were 124 notifications to the GATT of regional trade agreements. Since the creation of the WTO in 1995, more than 130 ad-ditional arrangements covering trade in goods or services have been created. Not all re-gional trade agreements of the past 50 years are still in force. Most of the discontinued agreements, however, have been superseded by redesigned agreements among the same signatories. Out of the more than 250 agreements or enlargements so far notified to the GATT and the WTO, some 170 are deemed to be currently in force. By the end of 2005, if regional trade agreements reportedly planned or already under negotiation are con-cluded, the total number of agreements in force might approach 300.[1]

Consistent with the predictions of international trade theory, particularly the theory of comparative advantage (see Chapter 5), agreements designed to promote freer trade within regions are believed to produce gains from trade for all member countries. As we saw in Chapter 6, the General Agreement on Tariffs and Trade and its successor, the World Trade Organization, also seek to reduce trade barriers. With more than 148 mem-ber states, the WTO has a worldwide perspective. By entering into regional agreements, groups of countries aim to reduce trade barriers more rapidly than can be achieved under the auspices of the WTO.

Nowhere has the movement toward regional economic integration been more suc-cessful than in Europe. On January 1, 1993, the European Union (EU) formally removed many barriers to doing business across borders within the EU in an attempt to create a single market with 340 million consumers. But the EU is not stopping there. The mem-ber states of the EU have launched a single currency, the euro; they are moving toward a closer political union; and on May 1, 2004, the EU expanded from 15 to 25 countries with a population of 450 million consumers and a gross domestic product approaching that of the United States. However, as the opening case illustrates, progress toward a unified pan-European market has not always been smooth. It wasn't until January 1, 2005, that the EU finally enacted legislation creating a single market in financial services. Even af-ter that, cultural, linguistic, and remaining regulatory barriers may mean that a true sin-gle market in financial services is some way off. Nevertheless, the trend is clear; within the boundaries of the EU a persistent movement toward greater economic integration is in place.

Similar moves toward regional integration are being pursued elsewhere in the world. Canada, Mexico, and the United States have implemented the North American Free Trade Agreement (NAFTA). This promises to ultimately remove all barriers to the free flow of goods and services between the three countries. In 1991, Argentina, Brazil, Paraguay, and Uruguay implemented an agreement known as MERCOSUR to start re-ducing barriers to trade between each other, and although progress within MERCOSUR has been halting, the institution is still in place. Moves are also under way to establish a hemispherewide Free Trade Agreement of the Americas (FTAA). Negotiations between 34 countries in the Americas began in 2001 and are ongoing. Along similar lines, 21 Pa-cific Rim countries, including the NAFTA member states, Japan, and China, have been discussing a possible pan-Pacific free trade area under the auspices of the Asia-Pacific Economic Cooperation forum (APEC). There are also active attempts at regional eco-nomic integration in Central America, the Andean region of South America, Southeast Asia, and parts of Africa.

While the move toward regional economic integration is generally seen as a good thing, some observers worry that it will lead to a world in which regional trade blocs compete against each other. In this possible future scenario, free trade will exist within each bloc, but each bloc will protect its market from outside competition with high tariffs. The specter of the EU and NAFTA turning into economic fortresses that shut out foreign producers with high tariff barriers is worrisome to those who believe in unrestricted free trade. If such a situation were to materialize, the resulting decline in trade between blocs could more than offset the gains from free trade within blocs.

With these issues in mind, this chapter will explore the economic and political debate surrounding regional economic integration, paying particular attention to the economic and political benefits and costs of integration; review progress toward regional economic integration around the world; and map the important implications of regional economic integration for the practice of international business. But before tackling these objectives, we first need to examine the levels of integration that are theoretically possible.

Levels of Economic Integration

Several levels of economic integration are possible in theory (see Figure 9.1). From least integrated to most integrated, they are a free trade area, a customs union, a common market, an economic union, and, finally, a full political union.

In a **free trade area,** all barriers to the trade of goods and services among member countries are removed. In the theoretically ideal free trade area, no discriminatory tariffs, quotas, subsidies, or administrative impediments are allowed to distort trade between members. Each country, however, is allowed to determine its own trade policies with regard to nonmembers. Thus, for example, the tariffs placed on the products of nonmember countries may vary from member to member. Free trade agreements are the most popular form of regional economic integration, accounting for almost 90 percent of regional agreements.[2]

The most enduring free trade area in the world is the **European Free Trade Association (EFTA).** Established in January 1960, EFTA currently joins four countries—Norway, Iceland, Liechtenstein, and Switzerland—down from seven in 1995 (three EFTA members, Austria, Finland, and Sweden, joined the EU on January 1, 1996). EFTA was founded by those Western European countries that initially decided not to be part of the European Community (the forerunner of the EU). Its original members included Austria, Great Britain, Denmark, Finland, and Sweden, all of which are now members of the EU. The emphasis of EFTA has been on free trade in industrial goods. Agriculture was left out of the arrangement, each member being allowed to determine its own level of support. Members are also free to determine the level of protection applied to goods coming from outside EFTA. Other free trade areas include the North American Free Trade Agreement, which we shall discuss in depth later in the chapter.

The customs union is one step farther along the road to full economic and political integration. A **customs union** eliminates trade barriers between member countries and adopts a common external trade policy. Establishment of a common external trade policy necessitates significant administrative machinery to oversee trade relations with nonmembers. Most countries that enter into a customs union desire even greater economic integration down the road. The EU began as a customs union and has moved beyond this stage. Other customs unions around the world include the current version of the Andean Pact (between Bolivia, Colombia, Ecuador, and Peru). The Andean Pact established free trade between member countries and imposes a common tariff, of 5 to 20 percent, on products imported from outside.[3]

The next level of economic integration, a **common market** has no barriers to trade between member countries, includes a common external trade policy, and allows factors of production to move freely between members. Labor and capital are free to move because there are no restrictions on immigration, emigration, or cross-border flows of

FIGURE 9.1

Levels of Economic
Integration

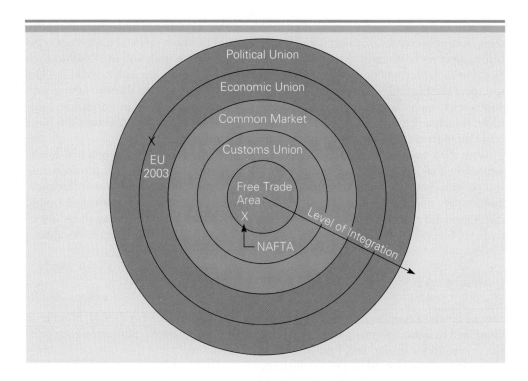

capital between member countries. Establishing a common market demands a significant degree of harmony and cooperation on fiscal, monetary, and employment policies. Achieving this degree of cooperation has proven very difficult. For years, the European Union functioned as a common market, although it has now moved beyond this stage. MERCOSUR, the South American grouping of Argentina, Brazil, Paraguay, and Uruguay, hopes to eventually establish itself as a common market.

An economic union entails even closer economic integration and cooperation than a common market. Like the common market, an **economic union** involves the free flow of products and factors of production between member countries and the adoption of a common external trade policy, but it also requires a common currency, harmonization of members' tax rates, and a common monetary and fiscal policy. Such a high degree of integration demands a coordinating bureaucracy and the sacrifice of significant amounts of national sovereignty to that bureaucracy. The EU is an economic union, although an imperfect one since not all members of the EU have adopted the euro, the currency of the EU, and differences in tax rates and regulations across countries still remain.

The move toward economic union raises the issue of how to make a coordinating bureaucracy accountable to the citizens of member nations. The answer is through **political union** in which a central political apparatus coordinates the economic, social, and foreign policy of the member states. The EU is on the road toward at least partial political union. The European Parliament, which is playing an ever more important role in the EU, has been directly elected by citizens of the EU countries since the late 1970s. In addition, the Council of Ministers (the controlling, decision-making body of the EU) is composed of government ministers from each EU member. The United States provides an example of even closer political union; in the United States, independent states are effectively combined into a single nation. Ultimately, the EU may move toward a similar federal structure.

The Case for Regional Integration

The case for regional integration is both economic and political. The case for integration is typically not accepted by many groups within a country, which explains why most attempts to achieve regional economic integration have been contentious and halting. In this section, we examine the economic and political cases for integration and two impediments to integration. In the next section, we look at the case against integration.

THE ECONOMIC CASE FOR INTEGRATION

The economic case for regional integration is straightforward. We saw in Chapter 5 how economic theories of international trade predict that unrestricted free trade will allow countries to specialize in the production of goods and services that they can produce most efficiently. The result is greater world production than would be possible with trade restrictions. That chapter also revealed how opening a country to free trade stimulates economic growth, which creates dynamic gains from trade. Chapter 7 detailed how foreign direct investment (FDI) can transfer technological, marketing, and managerial knowhow to host nations. Given the central role of knowledge in stimulating economic growth, opening a country to FDI also is likely to stimulate economic growth. In sum, economic theories suggest that free trade and investment is a positive-sum game, in which all participating countries stand to gain.

Given this, the theoretical ideal is an absence of barriers to the free flow of goods, services, and factors of production among nations. However, as we saw in Chapters 6 and 8, a case can be made for government intervention in international trade and FDI. Because many governments have accepted part or all of the case for intervention, unrestricted free trade and FDI have proved to be only an ideal. Although international institutions such as GATT and the WTO have been moving the world toward a free trade regime, success has been less than total. In a world of many nations and many political ideologies, it is very difficult to get all countries to agree to a common set of rules.

Against this background, regional economic integration can be seen as an attempt to achieve additional gains from the free flow of trade and investment between countries beyond those attainable under international agreements such as the WTO. It is easier to establish a free trade and investment regime among a limited number of adjacent countries than among the world community. Coordination and policy harmonization problems are largely a function of the number of countries that seek agreement. The greater the number of countries involved, the more perspectives that must be reconciled, and the harder it will be to reach agreement. Thus, attempts at regional economic integration are motivated by a desire to exploit the gains from free trade and investment.

THE POLITICAL CASE FOR INTEGRATION

The political case for regional economic integration also has loomed large in most attempts to establish free trade areas, customs unions, and the like. Linking neighboring economies and making them increasingly dependent on each other creates incentives for political cooperation between the neighboring states and reduces the potential for violent conflict. In addition, by grouping their economies, the countries can enhance their political weight in the world.

These considerations underlay the 1957 establishment of the European Community (EC), the forerunner of the EU. Europe had suffered two devastating wars in the first half of the 20th century, both arising out of the unbridled ambitions of nation-states. Those who have sought a united Europe have always had a desire to make another war in Europe unthinkable. Many Europeans also believed that after World War II, the European nation-states were no longer large enough to hold their own in world markets and politics. The need for a united Europe to deal with the United States and the politically alien Soviet Union loomed large in the minds of many of the EC's founders.[4] A long-standing joke in Europe is that the European Commission should erect a statue to Joseph Stalin, for without the aggressive policies of the former dictator of the old Soviet Union, the countries of Western Europe may have lacked the incentive to cooperate and form the EC.

COUNTRY FOCUS   When the North American Free Trade Agreement went into effect in 1994, many expressed fears that large job losses in the U.S. textile industry would occur as companies moved production from the United States to Mexico. NAFTA opponents argued passionately, but unsuccessfully, that the treaty should not be adopted because of the negative impact it would have on U.S. employment.

A quick glance at the data available 10 years after the passage of NAFTA suggests the critics had a point. Between 1994 and 2004, production of apparel fell by 40 percent and production of textiles by 20 percent and this during a period when overall U.S. demand for apparel grew by almost 60 percent. During the same time frame, employment in textile mills in the United Stated dropped from 478,000 to 239,000, and employment in apparel plummeted from 858,000 to 296,000. During the same period, exports of apparel from Mexico to the United States surged $1.88 billion, to $6.94 billion. Such data seem to indicate that the job losses have been due to apparel production migrating from the United States to Mexico. Anecdotal examples are plentiful. In 1995, Fruit of the Loom Inc., the largest manufacturer of underwear in the United States, said it would close six of its domestic plants and cut back operations at two others, laying off

about 3,200 workers, or 12 percent of its U.S. workforce. The company announced the closures were part of its drive to move its operations to cheaper plants abroad, particularly in Mexico. Before the closures, less than 30 percent of its sewing was done outside the United States, but Fruit of the Loom planned to move the majority of that work to Mexico. Similarly, fabric makers have been moving production to Mexico. Cone Mills of South Carolina, one of the country's largest producers of denim fabric, has reduced its U.S. employment by one-third since 1994, while investing $200 million in two new factories in Mexico. Burlington Industries in 1999 eliminated 2,900 jobs in its North Carolina fabric plants, or 17 percent of its total workforce, while investing heavily in Mexican manufacturing capability.

For textile manufacturers, the advantages of locating in Mexico include cheap labor and inputs. Labor rates in Mexico average between $10 and $20 a day, compared to $10 to $12 an hour for U.S. textile workers. Another advantage for denim makers such as Cone Mills is cheap water (water is essential for dyeing cotton yarn with indigo). In Mexico, Cone Mills pays about 30 cents per cubic meter for water, about one-fifth of the rate in South Carolina. In addition, Cone Mills and other fabric makers have been locating in Mexico because many of their customers—

IMPEDIMENTS TO INTEGRATION

Despite the strong economic and political arguments in support, integration has never been easy to achieve or sustain for two main reasons. First, although economic integration aids the majority, it has its costs. While a nation as a whole may benefit significantly from a regional free trade agreement, certain groups may lose. Moving to a free trade regime involves painful adjustments. For example, as a result of the 1994 establishment of NAFTA, some Canadian and U.S. workers in such industries as textiles, which employ low-cost, low-skilled labor, lost their jobs as Canadian and U.S. firms moved production to Mexico. The promise of significant net benefits to the Canadian and U.S. economies as a whole is little comfort to those who lose as a result of NAFTA. Such groups have been at the forefront of opposition to NAFTA and will continue to oppose any widening of the agreement (see the accompanying Country Focus).

A second impediment to integration arises from concerns over national sovereignty. For example, Mexico's concerns about maintaining control of its oil interests resulted in an agreement with Canada and the United States to exempt the Mexican oil industry from any liberalization of foreign investment regulations achieved under NAFTA. Concerns about national sovereignty arise because close economic integration demands that countries give up some degree of control over such key issues as monetary policy, fiscal policy (e.g., tax policy), and trade policy. This has been a major stumbling block in the EU. To achieve full economic union, the EU introduced a common currency, the euro, controlled

garment makers—have already located there and being in the same region reduces transportation costs.

However, job losses in the U.S. textile industry do not mean that the overall effects of NAFTA have been negative. Clothing prices in the United States have also fallen since 1994 as textile production shifted from high-cost U.S. producers to lower-cost Mexican producers. This benefits consumers, who now have more money to spend on other items. Denim fabric, which used to sell for $3.20 per yard, now sells for $2.40 per yard. The cost of a typical pair of designer jeans, for example, fell from $55 in 1994 to about $48 today. In 1994, blank T-shirts wholesaled for $24 a dozen. Now they sell for $14 a dozen.

In addition to lower prices, the shift in textile production to Mexico also has benefited the U.S. economy in other ways. First, despite the move of fabric and apparel production to Mexico, exports have surged for U.S. fabric and yarn makers, many of which are in the chemical industry. Before the passage of NAFTA, U.S. yarn producers, such as E. I. du Pont, supplied only small amounts of fabric and yarn to Asian producers. However, as apparel production moved from Asia to Mexico, exports of fabric and yarn to that country have surged. U.S. producers supply 70 percent of the raw material going to Mexican sewing shops. Between 1993 and 2004, U.S. textile and yarn exports to Mexico, mostly in the form of cut pieces ready for sewing, grew from $794 million to $3.42 billion. In addition, U.S. manufacturers of textile equipment have also seen an increase in their sales as apparel factories in Mexico order textile equipment. Exports of textile equipment to Mexico grew from $153 million in 1994 to $320 million in 2000, before falling back to $157 million in 2004.

Although the U.S. textile industry has lost jobs, advocates of NAFTA argue that the U.S. economy has benefited in the form of lower clothing prices and an increase in exports from fabric and yarn producers and from producers of textile machinery, to say nothing of the gains in other sectors of the U.S. economy. Trade has been created as a result of NAFTA. The gains from trade are being captured by U.S. consumers and by producers in certain sectors. As always, the establishment of a free trade area creates winners and losers—and the losers have been employees in the textile industry—but advocates argue that the gains outweigh the losses.

Sources: C. Burritt, "Seven Years into NAFTA, Textile Makers Seek a Payoff in Mexico," *Atlanta Journal-Constitution,* December 17, 2000, p. Q1; I. McAllister, "Trade Agreements: How They Affect U.S. Textile," *Textile World,* March 2000, pp. 50–54; J. Millman, "Mexico Weaves More Ties," *The Wall Street Journal,* August 21, 2000, p. A12; J. R. Giermanski, "A Fresh Look at NAFTA: What Really Happened?" *Logistics,* September 2002, pp. 43–46; American Textile Manufactures Institute at www.atmi.org/index.asp; and U.S. Department of Commerce Trade Stat Express Web site at http://tse.export.gov/.

by a central EU bank. Although most member states have signed on, Great Britain remains an important holdout. A politically important segment of public opinion in that country opposes a common currency on the grounds that it would require relinquishing control of the country's monetary policy to the EU, which many British perceive as a bureaucracy run by foreigners. In 1992, the British won the right to opt out of any single currency agreement, and as of 2005, the British government had yet to reverse its decision.

The Case against Regional Integration

Although the tide has been running strongly in favor of regional free trade agreements in recent years, some economists have expressed concern that the benefits of regional integration have been oversold, while the costs have often been ignored.[5] They point out that the benefits of regional integration are determined by the extent of trade creation, as opposed to trade diversion. **Trade creation** occurs when high-cost domestic producers are replaced by low-cost producers within the free trade area. It may also occur when higher-cost external producers are replaced by lower-cost external producers within the free trade area (see the accompanying Country Focus for an example). **Trade diversion** occurs when lower-cost external suppliers are replaced by higher-cost suppliers within the free trade area. A regional free trade agreement will benefit the world only if the amount of trade it creates exceeds the amount it diverts.

Suppose the United States and Mexico imposed tariffs on imports from all countries, and then they set up a free trade area, scrapping all trade barriers between themselves but maintaining tariffs on imports from the rest of the world. If the United States began to import textiles from Mexico, would this change be for the better? If the United States previously produced all its own textiles at a higher cost than Mexico, then the free trade agreement has shifted production to the cheaper source. According to the theory of comparative advantage, trade has been created within the regional grouping, and there would be no decrease in trade with the rest of the world. Clearly, the change would be for the better. If, however, the United States previously imported textiles from Costa Rica, which produced them more cheaply than either Mexico or the United States, then trade has been diverted from a low-cost source—a change for the worse.

In theory, WTO rules should ensure that a free trade agreement does not result in trade diversion. These rules allow free trade areas to be formed only if the members set tariffs that are not higher or more restrictive to outsiders than the ones previously in effect. However, as we saw in Chapter 6, GATT and the WTO do not cover some nontariff barriers. As a result, regional trade blocs could emerge whose markets are protected from outside competition by high nontariff barriers. In such cases, the trade diversion effects might outweigh the trade creation effects. The only way to guard against this possibility, according to those concerned about this potential, is to increase the scope of the WTO so it covers nontariff barriers to trade. There is no sign that this is going to occur anytime soon, however; so the risk remains that regional economic integration will result in trade diversion.

Regional Economic Integration in Europe

Europe has two trade blocs—the European Union and the European Free Trade Association. Of the two, the EU is by far the more significant, not just in terms of membership (the EU currently has 25 members; the EFTA has 4), but also in terms of economic and political influence in the world economy. Many now see the EU as an emerging economic and political superpower of the same order as the United States and Japan. Accordingly, we will concentrate our attention on the EU.[6]

EVOLUTION OF THE EUROPEAN UNION

The **European Union** (EU) is the product of two political factors: (1) the devastation of Western Europe during two world wars and the desire for a lasting peace, and (2) the European nations' desire to hold their own on the world's political and economic stage. In addition, many Europeans were aware of the potential economic benefits of closer economic integration of the countries.

The forerunner of the EU, the European Coal and Steel Community, was formed in 1951 by Belgium, France, West Germany, Italy, Luxembourg, and the Netherlands. Its objective was to remove barriers to intragroup shipments of coal, iron, steel, and scrap metal. With the signing of the **Treaty of Rome** in 1957, the European Community was established. The name changed again in 1994 when the European Community became the European Union following the ratification of the Maastricht Treaty (discussed later).

The Treaty of Rome provided for the creation of a common market. Article 3 of the treaty laid down the key objectives of the new community, calling for the elimination of internal trade barriers and the creation of a common external tariff and requiring member states to abolish obstacles to the free movement of factors of production among the members. To facilitate the free movement of goods, services, and factors of production, the treaty provided for any necessary harmonization of the member states' laws. Furthermore, the treaty committed the EC to establish common policies in agriculture and transportation.

The community grew in 1973, when Great Britain, Ireland, and Denmark joined. These three were followed in 1981 by Greece, in 1986 by Spain and Portugal, and in 1996 by Austria, Finland, and Sweden, bringing the total membership to 15 (East Germany became part of the EC after the reunification of Germany in 1990). Another 10 countries joined the EU

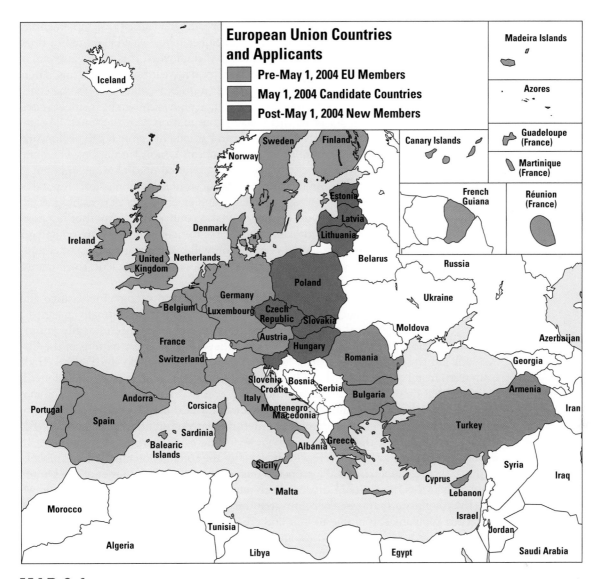

European Union Countries and Applicants

- Pre-May 1, 2004 EU Members
- May 1, 2004 Candidate Countries
- Post-May 1, 2004 New Members

MAP 9.1

European Union Members in 2005

Source: www.europarl.org.uk.

on May 1, 2004, 8 of them from Eastern Europe plus the small Mediterranean nations of Malta and Cyprus (see Map 9.1; the name of each country in Map 9.1 is given in the local language). With a population of 450 million and a GDP of $11 trillion, similar to that of the United States, the EU through these enlargements has become a global superpower.[7] Three more countries are currently considered applicants for entry into the EU—Romania, Bulgaria, and Turkey—with Romania and Bulgaria set to join in 2007.

POLITICAL STRUCTURE OF THE EUROPEAN UNION

The economic policies of the EU are formulated and implemented by a complex and still-evolving political structure. The four main institutions in this structure are the European Commission, the Council of the European Union, the European Parliament, and the Court of Justice.[8]

The **European Commission** is responsible for proposing EU legislation, implementing it, and monitoring compliance with EU laws by member states. Headquartered in Brussels, Belgium, the commission has more than 24,000 employees. It is run by a group of commissioners appointed by each member country for five-year renewable terms. There are 25 commissioners, one from each member state (until November 2004, some countries had two commissioners). A president of the commission is chosen by member states, and the president then chooses other members in consultation with the states. The entire commission has to be approved by the European Parliament before it can begin work. The commission has a monopoly in proposing European Union legislation. The commission makes a proposal, which goes to the Council of the European Union and then to the European Parliament. The council cannot legislate without a commission proposal in front of it. The commission is also responsible for implementing aspects of EU law, although in practice much of this must be delegated to member states. Another responsibility of the commission is to monitor member states to make sure they are complying with EU laws. In this policing role, the commission will normally ask a state to comply with any EU laws that are being broken. If this persuasion is not sufficient, the commission can refer a case to the Court of Justice.

The European Commission's role in competition policy has become increasingly important to business in recent years. Since 1990 when the office was formally assigned a role in competition policy, the EU's competition commissioner has been steadily gaining influence as the chief regulator of competition policy in the member nations of the EU. As with antitrust authorities in the United States, which include the Federal Trade Commission and the Department of Justice, the role of the competition commissioner is to ensure that no one enterprise uses its market power to drive out competitors and monopolize markets. The commissioner also reviews proposed mergers and acquisitions to make sure they do not create a dominant enterprise with substantial market power.[9] Between 1990 and 2003, the commission reviewed some 2,387 merger cases. Of these, 18 were rejected, and another 20 were withdrawn after the commission raised substantial objections.[10] For example, in 2000 a proposed merger between Time Warner of the United States and EMI of the United Kingdom, both music recording companies, was withdrawn after the commission expressed concerns that the merger would reduce the number of major record companies from five to four and create a dominant player in the $40 billion global music industry. Similarly, the commission blocked a proposed merger between two U.S. telecommunication companies, WorldCom and Sprint, because their combined holdings of Internet infrastructure in Europe would give the merged companies so much market power that the commission argued the combined company would dominate that market. Another example of the commission's influence over business combinations is given in the accompanying Management Focus, which looks at the commission's role in shaping mergers and joint ventures in the media industry.

The **Council of the European Union** represents the interests of member states. It is clearly the ultimate controlling authority within the EU since draft legislation from the commission can become EU law only if the council agrees. The council is composed of one representative from the government of each member state. The membership, however, varies depending on the topic being discussed. When agricultural issues are being discussed, the agriculture ministers from each state attend council meetings; when transportation is being discussed, transportation ministers attend, and so on. Before 1993, all council issues had to be decided by unanimous agreement between member states. This often led to marathon council sessions and a failure to make progress or reach agreement on commission proposals. In an attempt to clear the resulting logjams, the Single European Act formalized the use of majority voting rules on issues "which have as their object the establishment and functioning of a single market." Most other issues, however, such as tax regulations and immigration policy, still require unanimity among council members if they are to become law. The votes that a country gets in the council are related to the size of the country. For example, Britain, a large country, has 29 votes, whereas Denmark, a much smaller state, has 7 votes.

The **European Parliament,** which now has 732 members, is directly elected by the populations of the member states. The parliament, which meets in Strasbourg, France, is primarily a consultative rather than legislative body. It debates legislation proposed by the commission and forwarded to it by the council. It can propose amendments to that legislation, which the commission and ultimately the council are not obliged to take up but often will. The power of the parliament recently has been increasing, although not by as much as parliamentarians would like. The European Parliament now has the right to vote on the appointment of commissioners as well as veto some laws (such as the EU budget and single-market legislation). One major debate now being waged in Europe is whether the council or the parliament should ultimately be the most powerful body in the EU. Some in Europe express concern over the democratic accountability of the EU bureaucracy. One side thinks the answer to this apparent democratic deficit lies in increasing the power of the parliament, while others think that true democratic legitimacy lies with elected governments, acting through the Council of the European Union.[11]

The **Court of Justice,** which is comprised of one judge from each country, is the supreme appeals court for EU law. Like commissioners, the judges are required to act as independent officials, rather than as representatives of national interests. The commission or a member country can bring other members to the court for failing to meet treaty obligations. Similarly, member countries, companies, or institutions can bring the commission or council to the court for failure to act according to an EU treaty.

THE SINGLE EUROPEAN ACT

Two revolutions occurred in Europe in the late 1980s. The first was the collapse of communism in Eastern Europe. The second revolution was much quieter, but its impact on Europe and the world may have been just as profound as the first. It was the adoption of the **Single European Act** by the member nations of the European Community (EC) in 1987. This act committed member countries to work toward establishment of a single market by December 31, 1992.

The Single European Act was born of a frustration among members that the community was not living up to its promise. By the early 1980s, it was clear that the EC had fallen short of its objectives to remove barriers to the free flow of trade and investment between member countries and to harmonize the wide range of technical and legal standards for doing business. Against this background, many of the EC's prominent businesspeople mounted an energetic campaign in the early 1980s to end the EC's economic divisions. The EC responded by creating the Delors Commission. Under the chairmanship of Jacques Delors, the commission proposed that all impediments to the formation of a single market be eliminated by December 31, 1992. The result was the Single European Act, which was independently ratified by the parliaments of each member country and became EC law in 1987.

The Objectives of the Act

The purpose of the Single European Act was to have one market in place by December 31, 1992. The act proposed the following changes:[12]

- Remove all frontier controls between EC countries, thereby abolishing delays and reducing the resources required for complying with trade bureaucracy.
- Apply the principle of "mutual recognition" to product standards. A standard developed in one EC country should be accepted in another, provided it meets basic requirements in such matters as health and safety.
- Open public procurement to nonnational suppliers, reducing costs directly by allowing lower-cost suppliers into national economies and indirectly by forcing national suppliers to compete.
- Lift barriers to competition in the retail banking and insurance businesses, which should drive down the costs of financial services, including borrowing, throughout the EC.

- Remove all restrictions on foreign exchange transactions between member countries by the end of 1992.
- Abolish restrictions on cabotage—the right of foreign truckers to pick up and deliver goods within another member state's borders—by the end of 1992. Estimates suggested this would reduce the cost of haulage within the EC by 10 to 15 percent.

All those changes were predicted to lower the costs of doing business in the EC, but the single-market program was also expected to have more complicated supply-side effects. For example, the expanded market was predicted to give EC firms greater opportunities to exploit economies of scale. In addition, it was thought that the increase in competitive intensity brought about by removing internal barriers to trade and investment would force EC firms to become more efficient. To signify the importance of the Single European Act, the European Community also decided to change its name to the European Union once the act took effect.

Impact

The Single European Act has had a significant impact on the EU economy.[13] The act provided the impetus for the restructuring of substantial sections of European industry. Many firms have shifted from national to pan-European production and distribution systems in an attempt to realize scale economies and better compete in a single market. The results have included faster economic growth than would otherwise have been the case.

However, 13 years after the formation of a single market, the reality still falls short of the ideal. As documented in the opening case, as of 2005 there was still not a fully functioning single market for financial services in the EU (although the groundwork is now in place for one to emerge). Thus, although the EU is undoubtedly moving toward a single marketplace, established legal, cultural, and language differences between nations mean that implementation has been uneven. As in the case of the automobile industry, however, progress is being made toward the adoption of a single market.

THE ESTABLISHMENT OF THE EURO

In December 1991, EC members signed a treaty (the **Maastricht Treaty**) that committed them to adopting a common currency by January 1, 1999.[14] The euro is now used by 12 of the 25 member states of the European Union; these 12 states are members of what is often referred to as the euro zone. The 10 countries that joined the EU on May 1, 2004, will adopt the euro when they fulfill certain economic criteria—a high degree of price stability, a sound fiscal situation, stable exchange rates, and converged long-term interest rates. The current members had to meet the same criteria.

Establishment of the euro has rightly been described as an amazing political feat with few historical precedents. Establishing the euro required participating national governments not only to give up their own currencies, but also to give up control over monetary policy. Governments do not routinely sacrifice national sovereignty for the greater good, indicating the importance that the Europeans attach to the euro. By adopting the euro, the EU has created the second largest currency zone in the world after that of the U.S. dollar. Some believe that ultimately the euro could come to rival the dollar as the most important currency in the world.

Three long-term EU members, Great Britain, Denmark, and Sweden, are still sitting on the sidelines. The 12 countries agreeing to the euro locked their exchange rates against each other January 1, 1999. Euro notes and coins were not actually issued until January 1, 2002. In the interim, national currencies circulated in each of the 12 countries. However, in each participating state, the national currency stood for a defined amount of euros. After January 1, 2002, euro notes and coins were issued and the national currencies were taken out of circulation. By mid-2002, all prices and routine economic transactions within the euro zone were in euros.

MANAGEMENT FOCUS

In late 1999, U.S. Internet giant AOL announced it would merge with the music and publishing conglomerate Time Warner. Both the U.S. companies had substantial operations in Europe. The European commissioner for competition, Mario Monti, announced the commission would investigate the impact of the merger on competition in Europe.

The investigation took on a new twist when Time Warner subsequently announced it would form a joint venture with British-based EMI. Time Warner and EMI are two of the top five music publishing companies in the world. The proposed joint venture would have been three times as large as its nearest global competitor. The European Commission now had two concerns. The first was that the joint venture between EMI and Time Warner would reduce the level of competition in the music publishing industry. The second was that a combined AOL–Time Warner would dominate the emerging market for downloading music over the Internet, particularly given the fact that AOL would be able to gain preferential access to the music libraries of both Warner and EMI. This would potentially put other online service providers at a disadvantage. The commission was also concerned that AOL Europe was a joint venture between AOL and Bertelsmann, a German media company that also had considerable music publishing interests. Accordingly, the commission announced it would undertake a separate investigation of the proposed deal between Time Warner and EMI.

Yet another twist occurred in mid-2000 while the AOL, Time Warner, EMI combinations were still under investigation. Vivendi, a French media conglomerate with significant music publishing, television, and Internet activities, announced it was in talks to acquire Seagram, a Canadian company that owned Universal Studios and Polygram Records, along with an alcoholic beverage business. Vivendi's plan was to sell the beverage business and hold on to Universal. Vivendi announced that its proposed acquisition would be a competitive answer to the AOL–Time Warner combination. The European Commission, however, was concerned that Vivendi, which owned Europe's largest pay-television service, Canal Plus, and had a 20 percent ownership stake in British Sky Broadcasting, a satellite TV venture, would use its power to dominate the pay-television market and dictate the use of Universal films and music, thereby putting competitors in the film and music business at a disadvantage. Thus, Monti announced that the European Commission would also investigate this deal.

These investigations continued into late 2000 and were resolved by a series of concessions extracted by the European Commission from the various players. First, under pressure from the commission, Time Warner and EMI agreed to drop their proposed joint venture, thereby maintaining the level of competition in the music publishing business. Second, AOL and Time Warner agreed to allow rival Internet service providers access to online music on the same terms as AOL would receive from Warner Music Group for the next five years. Third, AOL agreed to sever all ties with Bertelsmann, and the German company agreed to withdraw from AOL Europe. These developments alleviated the commission's concern that the AOL–Time Warner combination would dominate the emerging market for the digital download of music. With these concessions in hand, the commission approved the AOL–Time Warner merger in early October 2000.

The commission then turned its attention to the proposed deal between Vivendi and Seagram. The commission appeared to buy the argument that the Vivendi–Universal combination was a competitive response to the AOL–Time Warner action, but still it extracted several concessions from Vivendi to ensure that the enlarged company did not abuse its market power. Most importantly, the commission agreed that the proposed acquisition could proceed as long as Vivendi agreed to sell its 20 percent ownership stake in British Sky Broadcasting, a condition to which Vivendi readily agreed.

By late 2000, all these transactions had been completed. The shape of the media business, both in Europe and worldwide, now looked very different, and the European Commission had played a pivotal role in determining the outcome. Its demand for concessions altered the strategy of several of the players, led to somewhat different combinations from those originally planned, and, the commission believed, preserved competition in the global media business.

Sources: W. Drozdiak, "EU Allows Vivendi Media Deal," *Washington Post*, October 14, 2000, p. E2; D. Hargreaves, "Business as Usual in the New Economy," *Financial Times*, October 6, 2000, p. 1; and D. Hargreaves, "Brussels Clears AOL-Time Warner Deal," *Financial Times*, October 12, 2000, p. 12.

www.mhhe.com/hill

Benefits of the Euro

Europeans decided to establish a single currency in the EU for a number of reasons. First, they believe that businesses and individuals will realize significant savings from having to handle one currency, rather than many. These savings come from lower foreign exchange and hedging costs. For example, people going from Germany to France will no longer have to pay a commission to a bank to change German deutsche marks into French francs. Instead, they will be able to use euros. According to the European Commission, such savings should amount to 0.5 percent of the European Union's GDP, or about $45 billion a year.

Second, and perhaps more importantly, the adoption of a common currency will make it easier to compare prices across Europe. This should increase competition because it will be much easier for consumers to shop around. For example, if a German finds that cars sell for less in France than Germany, he may be tempted to purchase from a French car dealer rather than his local car dealer. Alternatively, traders may engage in arbitrage to exploit such price differentials, buying cars in France and reselling them in Germany. The only way that German car dealers will be able to hold on to business in the face of such competitive pressures will be to reduce the prices they charge for cars. As a consequence of such pressures, the introduction of a common currency should lead to lower prices. This should translate into substantial gains for European consumers.

Third, faced with lower prices, European producers will be forced to look for ways to reduce their production costs to maintain their profit margins. The introduction of a common currency, by increasing competition, should ultimately produce long-run gains in the economic efficiency of European companies.

Fourth, the introduction of a common currency should give a strong boost to the development of a highly liquid pan-European capital market (see the opening case). The development of such a capital market should lower the cost of capital and lead to an increase in both the level of investment and the efficiency with which investment funds are allocated. This could be especially helpful to smaller companies that have historically had difficulty borrowing money from domestic banks. For example, the capital market of Portugal is very small and illiquid, which makes it extremely difficult for bright Portuguese entrepreneurs with a good idea to borrow money at a reasonable price. However, in theory, such companies should soon be able to tap a much more liquid pan-European capital market. Currently Europe has no continentwide capital market, such as the NASDAQ market in the United States, that funnels investment capital to dynamic young growth companies. The euro's introduction could facilitate establishment of such a market, particularly when coupled with regulations designed to create a single market in financial services (see the opening case). The long-run benefits of such a development should not be underestimated.

Finally, the development of a pan-European, euro-denominated capital market will increase the range of investment options open to both individuals and institutions. For example, it will now be much easier for individuals and institutions based in, let's say, Holland to invest in Italian or French companies. This will enable European investors to better diversify their risk, which again lowers the cost of capital, and should also increase the efficiency with which capital resources are allocated.[15]

Costs of the Euro

The drawback, for some, of a single currency is that national authorities have lost control over monetary policy. Thus, it is crucial to ensure that the EU's monetary policy is well managed. The Maastricht Treaty called for establishment of the independent European Central Bank (ECB), similar in some respects to the U.S. Federal Reserve, with a clear mandate to manage monetary policy so as to ensure price stability. The ECB, based in Frankfurt, is meant to be independent from political pressure—although critics question this. Among other things, the ECB sets interest rates and determines monetary policy across the euro zone.

The implied loss of national sovereignty to the ECB underlies the decision by Great Britain, Denmark, and Sweden to stay out of the euro zone for now. Many in these countries are suspicious of the ECB's ability to remain free from political pressure and to keep inflation under tight control.

In theory, the design of the ECB should ensure that it remains free of political pressure. The ECB is modeled on the German Bundesbank, which historically has been the most independent and successful central bank in Europe. The Maastricht Treaty prohibits the ECB from taking orders from politicians. The executive board of the bank, which consists of a president, vice president, and four other members, carries out policy by issuing instructions to national central banks. The policy itself is determined by the governing council, which consists of the executive board plus the central bank governors from the 12 euro zone countries. The governing council votes on interest rate changes. Members of the executive board are appointed for eight-year nonrenewable terms, insulating them from political pressures to get reappointed. Nevertheless, the jury is still out on the issue of the ECB's independence, and it will take some time for the bank to establish its credentials.

According to critics, another drawback of the euro is that the EU is not what economists would call an optimal currency area. In an **optimal currency area,** similarities in the underlying structure of economic activity make it feasible to adopt a single currency and use a single exchange rate as an instrument of macroeconomic policy. Many of the European economies in the euro zone, however, are very dissimilar. For example, Finland and Portugal have different wage rates, tax regimes, and business cycles, and they may react very differently to external economic shocks. A change in the euro exchange rate that helps Finland may hurt Portugal. Obviously, such differences complicate macroeconomic policy. For example, when euro economies are not growing in unison, a common monetary policy may mean that interest rates are too high for depressed regions and too low for booming regions. It will be interesting to see how the EU copes with the strains caused by such divergent economic performance.

One way of dealing with such divergent effects within the euro zone might be for the EU to engage in fiscal transfers, taking money from prosperous regions and pumping it into depressed regions. Such a move, however, would open a political can of worms. Would the citizens of Germany forgo their "fair share" of EU funds to create jobs for underemployed Portuguese workers?

Several critics believe that the euro puts the economic cart before the political horse. In their view, a single currency should follow, not precede, political union. They argue that the euro will unleash enormous pressures for tax harmonization and fiscal transfers from the center, both policies that cannot be pursued without the appropriate political structure. The most apocalyptic vision that flows from these negative views is that far from stimulating economic growth, as its advocates claim, the euro will lead to lower economic growth and higher inflation within Europe. To quote one critic:

> Imposing a single exchange rate and an inflexible exchange rate on countries that are characterized by different economic shocks, inflexible wages, low labor mobility, and separate national fiscal systems without significant cross-border fiscal transfers will raise the overall level of cyclical unemployment among EMU members. The shift from national monetary policies dominated by the (German) Bundesbank within the European Monetary System to a European Central Bank governed by majority voting with a politically determined exchange rate policy will almost certainly raise the average future rate of inflation.[16]

The Early Experience

Since its establishment January 1, 1999, the euro has had a volatile trading history against the world's major currency, the U.S. dollar. After starting life in 1999 at $1.17, the euro steadily fell until it reached a low of 83 cents to the dollar in October 2000, leading critics to claim the euro was a failure. A major reason for the fall in the euro's value was that international investors were investing money in booming U.S. stocks and bonds and taking money out of Europe to finance this investment. In other words, they were selling euros to buy dollars so that they could invest in dollar-denominated assets. This increased the demand for dollars and decreased the demand for the euro, driving the value of the euro down against the dollar.

The fortunes of the euro began improving in late 2001 when the dollar weakened, and the currency stood at a robust five-year high of $1.33 in early March 2005. One reason for the rise in the value of the euro was that the flow of capital into the United States had stalled as the U.S. financial markets fell.[17] Many investors were now taking money out of the United States, selling dollar-denominated assets such as U.S. stocks and bonds, and purchasing euro-denominated assets. Falling demand for U.S. dollars and rising demand for euros translated into a fall in the value of the dollar against the euro. Furthermore, in a vote of confidence in both the euro and the ability of the ECB to manage monetary policy within the euro zone, many foreign central banks added more euros to their supply of foreign currencies during 2002–2004. In the first three years of its life, the euro never reached the 13 percent of global reserves made up by the deutsche mark and other former euro zone currencies. The euro didn't jump that hurdle until early 2002, but by 2003 it made up 15 percent of global reserves. Currency specialists expected the growing U.S. current account deficit, at 5 percent in 2004, to drive the dollar down further, and the euro still higher, over the next two to four years.[18] However, this is a mixed blessing for the EU. A strengthening euro, while a source of pride, will make it harder for euro zone exporters to sell their goods abroad.

ENLARGEMENT OF THE EUROPEAN UNION

One major issue facing the EU over the past few years has been that of enlargement. Enlargement of the EU into Eastern Europe has been a possibility since the collapse of communism at the end of the 1980s, and by the end of the 1990s, 13 countries had applied to become EU members. To qualify for EU membership the applicants had to privatize state assets, deregulate markets, restructure industries, and tame inflation. They also had to enshrine complex EU laws into their own systems, establish stable democratic governments, and respect human rights.[19] In December 2002, the EU formally agreed to accept the applications of 10 countries, and they joined on May 1, 2004. The new members include the Baltic countries, the Czech Republic, and the larger nations of Hungary and Poland. The only new members not in Eastern Europe are the Mediterranean island nations of Malta and Cyprus. Their inclusion in the EU expanded the union to 25 states, stretching from the Atlantic to the borders of Russia; added 23 percent to the landmass of the EU; brought 75 million new citizens into the EU, building an EU with a population of 450 million people; and created a single continental economy with a GDP of close to €11 trillion.

The new members will not be able to adopt the euro until 2007, and free movement of labor between the new and existing members will not be allowed until then. Consistent with theories of free trade, the enlargement should create added benefits for all members. However, given the small size of the Eastern European economies (together they amount to only 5 percent of the GDP of current EU members) the initial impact will probably be small. The biggest notable change might be in the EU bureaucracy and decision-making processes, where budget negotiations among 25 nations are bound to prove more problematic than negotiations among 15 nations.

Left standing at the door were Turkey, Romania, and Bulgaria. Turkey, which has long lobbied to join the union, presents the EU with some difficult issues. The country has had a customs union with the EU since 1995, and about half of its international trade is already with the EU. However, full membership has been denied because of concerns over human rights issues (particularly Turkish policies toward its Kurdish minority). In addition, some on the Turk side suspect the EU is not eager to let a primarily Muslim nation of 66 million people, which has one foot in Asia, join the EU. The EU formally indicated in December 2002 that it would allow the Turkish application to proceed with no further delay in December 2004 if the country improved its human rights record to the satisfaction of the EU. In December the EU agreed to allow Turkey to start accession talks in October 2005. It now looks as if Romania and Bulgaria could join the EU by 2007, and Turkey by 2009, bringing the total number of nations to 28.

🌐 Regional Economic Integration in the Americas

No other attempt at regional economic integration comes close to the EU in its boldness or its potential implications for the world economy, but regional economic integration is on the rise in the Americas. The most significant attempt is the North American Free Trade Agreement. In addition to NAFTA, several other trade blocs are in the offing in the Americas (see Map 9.2), the most significant of which appear to be the Andean Group and MERCOSUR. Also, negotiations are under way to establish a hemispherewide Free Trade Area of the Americas (FTAA), although currently they seem to be stalled.

THE NORTH AMERICAN FREE TRADE AGREEMENT

The governments of the United States and Canada in 1988 agreed to enter into a free trade agreement, which took effect January 1, 1989. The goal of the agreement was to eliminate all tariffs on bilateral trade between Canada and the United States by 1998. This was followed in 1991 by talks among the United States, Canada, and Mexico aimed at establishing a **North American Free Trade Agreement** for the three countries. The talks concluded in August 1992 with an agreement in principle, and the following year the agreement was ratified by the governments of all three countries. The agreement became law January 1, 1994.[20]

NAFTA'S Contents

The contents of NAFTA include the following:

- Abolition within 10 years of tariffs on 99 percent of the goods traded between Mexico, Canada, and the United States.
- Removal of most barriers on the cross-border flow of services, allowing financial institutions, for example, unrestricted access to the Mexican market by 2000.
- Protection of intellectual property rights.
- Removal of most restrictions on foreign direct investment between the three member countries, although special treatment (protection) will be given to Mexican energy and railway industries, American airline and radio communications industries, and Canadian culture.
- Application of national environmental standards, provided such standards have a scientific basis. Lowering of standards to lure investment is described as being inappropriate.
- Establishment of two commissions with the power to impose fines and remove trade privileges when environmental standards or legislation involving health and safety, minimum wages, or child labor are ignored.

The Case for NAFTA

Proponents of NAFTA have argued that the free trade area should be viewed as an opportunity to create an enlarged and more efficient productive base for the entire region. Advocates acknowledge that one effect of NAFTA would be that some U.S. and Canadian firms would move production to Mexico to take advantage of lower labor costs. (In 2004, the average hourly labor cost in Mexico was still one-tenth of that in the United States and Canada.) Movement of production to Mexico, they argued, was most likely to occur in low-skilled, labor-intensive manufacturing industries where Mexico might have

MAP 9.2

Economic Integration in
the Americas

Continental Commerce
- NAFTA
- MERCOSUR
- Andean community
- Central America
- Caribbean community

a comparative advantage (e.g., textiles; see the Country Focus). Advocates of NAFTA argued that many would benefit from such a trend. Mexico would benefit from much-needed inward investment and employment. The United States and Canada would benefit because the increased incomes of the Mexicans would allow them to import more U.S. and Canadian goods, thereby increasing demand and making up for the jobs lost in industries that moved production to Mexico. U.S. and Canadian consumers would benefit from the lower prices of products made in Mexico. In addition, the international competitiveness of U.S. and Canadian firms that move production to Mexico to take advantage of lower labor costs would be enhanced, enabling them to better compete with Asian and European rivals.

The Case against NAFTA

Those who opposed NAFTA claimed that ratification would be followed by a mass exodus of jobs from the United States and Canada into Mexico as employers sought to profit from Mexico's lower wages and less strict environmental and labor laws. According to one extreme opponent, Ross Perot, up to 5.9 million U.S. jobs would be lost to Mexico after NAFTA in what he famously characterized as a "giant sucking sound." Most economists, however, dismissed these numbers as being absurd and alarmist. They argued that

Mexico would have to run a bilateral trade surplus with the United States of close to $300 billion for job loss on such a scale to occur—and $300 billion was the size of Mexico's GDP. In other words, such a scenario seemed implausible.

More sober estimates of the impact of NAFTA ranged from a net creation of 170,000 jobs in the United States (due to increased Mexican demand for U.S. goods and services) and an increase of $15 billion per year to the joint U.S. and Mexican GDP, to a net loss of 490,000 U.S. jobs. To put these numbers in perspective, employment in the U.S. economy was predicted to grow by 18 million from 1993 to 2003. As most economists repeatedly stressed, NAFTA would have a small impact on both Canada and the United States. It could hardly be any other way, since the Mexican economy was only 5 percent of the size of the U.S. economy. Signing NAFTA required the largest leap of economic faith from Mexico rather than Canada or the United States. Falling trade barriers would expose Mexican firms to highly efficient U.S. and Canadian competitors that, when compared to the average Mexican firm, had far greater capital resources, access to highly educated and skilled workforces, and much greater technological sophistication. The short-run outcome was likely to be painful economic restructuring and unemployment in Mexico. But advocates of NAFTA claimed there would be long-run dynamic gains in the efficiency of Mexican firms as they adjusted to the rigors of a more competitive marketplace. To the extent that this occurred, they argued, Mexico's economic growth rate would accelerate, and Mexico might become a major market for Canadian and U.S. firms.[21]

Environmentalists also voiced concerns about NAFTA. They pointed to the sludge in the Rio Grande River and the smog in the air over Mexico City and warned that Mexico could degrade clean air and toxic waste standards across the continent. They pointed out that the lower Rio Grande was the most polluted river in the United States, and that with NAFTA, chemical waste and sewage would increase along its course from El Paso, Texas, to the Gulf of Mexico.

There was also opposition in Mexico to NAFTA from those who feared a loss of national sovereignty. Mexican critics argued that their country would be dominated by U.S. firms that would not really contribute to Mexico's economic growth, but instead would use Mexico as a low-cost assembly site, while keeping their high-paying, high-skilled jobs north of the border.

NAFTA: The First Decade

Studies of NAFTA's early impact suggest its initial effects were at best muted, and both advocates and detractors may have been guilty of exaggeration.[22] The most comprehensive early study was undertaken by researchers at the University of California–Los Angeles and funded by various departments of the U.S. government.[23] This study focused on the effects of NAFTA in its first three and a half years. The authors concluded that the growth in trade between Mexico and the United States began to change nearly a decade before the implementation of NAFTA when Mexico unilaterally started to liberalize its own trade regime to conform with GATT standards. The initial period since NAFTA took effect had little impact on trends already in place. The study found that trade growth in those sectors that underwent tariff liberalization in the first two and a half years of NAFTA was only marginally higher than trade growth in sectors not yet liberalized. For example, between 1993 and 1996, U.S. exports to Mexico in sectors liberalized under NAFTA grew by 5.83 percent annually, while exports in sectors not liberalized under NAFTA grew by 5.35 percent. In short, the authors argue that NAFTA had only a marginal impact on the level of trade between the United States and Mexico.

As for NAFTA's much-debated impact on jobs in the United States, the study concluded the impact was positive but very small. The study found that while NAFTA created 31,158 new jobs in the United States, 28,168 jobs were lost due to imports from Mexico, for a net job gain of about 3,000 in the first two years of the NAFTA regime. However, as the report's authors point out, trade flows and employment in 1995 and 1996 were significantly affected by an economic crisis that gripped Mexico in early 1995. Given this, it may have been too early to draw conclusions about the true impact of NAFTA on trade flows and employment.

More recent surveys indicate that NAFTA's overall impact has been small but positive.[24] From 1993 to 2004, trade between NAFTA's partners grew by 250 percent.[25] Canada and Mexico are now the number one and two trade partners of the United States, suggesting the economies of the three NAFTA nations have become more closely integrated. In 1990, U.S. trade with Canada and Mexico accounted for about a quarter of total U.S. trade. By 2004, the figure was one-third. Canada's trade with its NAFTA partners increased from about 70 percent to more than 80 percent of all Canadian foreign trade between 1993 and 2004, while Mexico's trade with NAFTA increased from 66 percent to 80 percent over the same period. All three countries also experienced strong productivity growth over this period. In Mexico, labor productivity has increased by 50 percent since 1993, and the passage of NAFTA may have contributed to this. However, estimates suggest that employment effects of NAFTA have been small. The most pessimistic estimates suggest the United States lost 110,000 jobs per year due to NAFTA between 1994 and 2000—and many economists dispute this figure—which is tiny compared to the more than 2 million jobs a year created in the United States during the same period. Perhaps the most significant impact of NAFTA has not been economic, but political. Many observers credit NAFTA with helping to create the background for increased political stability in Mexico. Mexico is now viewed as a stable democratic nation with a steadily growing economy, something that is beneficial to the United States, which shares a 2,000-mile border with the country.[26]

Enlargement

One issue confronting NAFTA is that of enlargement. A number of other Latin American countries have indicated their desire to eventually join NAFTA. The governments of both Canada and the United States are adopting a wait-and-see attitude with regard to most countries. Getting NAFTA approved was a bruising political experience, and neither government is eager to repeat the process soon. Nevertheless, the Canadian, Mexican, and U.S. governments began talks in 1995 regarding Chile's possible entry into NAFTA. As of 2005, however, these talks had yielded little progress, partly because of political opposition in the U.S. Congress to expanding NAFTA. In December 2002, however, the United States and Chile did sign a bilateral free trade pact.

THE ANDEAN COMMUNITY

Bolivia, Chile, Ecuador, Colombia, and Peru signed an agreement in 1969 to create the Andean Pact. The **Andean Pact** was largely based on the EU model, but was far less successful at achieving its stated goals. The integration steps begun in 1969 included an internal tariff reduction program, a common external tariff, a transportation policy, a common industrial policy, and special concessions for the smallest members, Bolivia and Ecuador.

By the mid-1980s, the Andean Pact had all but collapsed and had failed to achieve any of its stated objectives. There was no tariff-free trade between member countries, no common external tariff, and no harmonization of economic policies. Political and economic problems seem to have hindered cooperation between member countries. The countries of the Andean Pact have had to deal with low economic growth, hyperinflation, high unemployment, political unrest, and crushing debt burdens. In addition, the dominant political ideology in many of the Andean countries during this period tended toward the radical/socialist end of the political spectrum. Since such an ideology is hostile to the free market economic principles on which the Andean Pact was based, progress toward closer integration could not be expected.

The tide began to turn in the late 1980s when, after years of economic decline, the governments of Latin America began to adopt free market economic policies. In 1990, the heads of the five current members of the Andean Pact—Bolivia, Ecuador, Peru,

Colombia, and Venezuela—met in the Galápagos Islands. The resulting Galápagos Declaration effectively relaunched the Andean Pact, which was renamed the Andean Community in 1997. The declaration's objectives included the establishment of a free trade area by 1992, a customs union by 1994, and a common market by 1995. This last milestone has not been reached. A customs union was implemented in 1995, although until 2003 Peru opted out and Bolivia received preferential treatment. The Andean Community now operates as a customs union. In December 2003, it signed an agreement with MERCOSUR to restart stalled negotiations on the creation of a free trade area between the two trading blocs. Those negotiations are currently proceeding at a slow pace.

MERCOSUR

MERCOSUR originated in 1988 as a free trade pact between Brazil and Argentina. The modest reductions in tariffs and quotas accompanying this pact reportedly helped bring about an 80 percent increase in trade between the two countries in the late 1980s.[27] This success encouraged the expansion of the pact in March 1990 to include Paraguay and Uruguay. The initial aim was to establish a full free trade area by the end of 1994 and a common market sometime thereafter. The four countries of MERCOSUR have a combined population of 200 million. With a market of this size, MERCOSUR could have a significant impact on the economic growth rate of the four economies. In December 1995, MERCOSUR's members agreed to a five-year program under which they hoped to perfect their free trade area and move toward a full customs union—something that has yet to be achieved.[28]

For its first eight years or so, MERCOSUR seemed to be making a positive contribution to the economic growth rates of its member states. Trade between MERCOSUR's four core members quadrupled between 1990 and 1998. The combined GDP of the four member states grew at an annual average rate of 3.5 percent between 1990 and 1996, a performance that is significantly better than the four attained during the 1980s.[29]

However, MERCOSUR has its critics, including Alexander Yeats, a senior economist at the World Bank, who wrote a stinging critique of MERCOSUR that was "leaked" to the press in October 1996.[30] According to Yeats, the trade diversion effects of MERCOSUR outweigh its trade creation effects. Yeats points out that the fastest growing items in intra-MERCOSUR trade are cars, buses, agricultural equipment, and other capital-intensive goods that are produced relatively inefficiently in the four member countries. In other words, MERCOSUR countries, insulated from outside competition by tariffs that run as high as 70 percent of value on motor vehicles, are investing in factories that build products that are too expensive to sell to anyone but themselves. The result, according to Yeats, is that MERCOSUR countries might not be able to compete globally once the group's external trade barriers come down. In the meantime, capital is being drawn away from more efficient enterprises. In the near term, countries with more efficient manufacturing enterprises lose because MERCOSUR's external trade barriers keep them out of the market.

The leak of the Yeats report caused a storm at the World Bank, which typically does not release reports that are critical of member states (the MERCOSUR countries are members of the World Bank). It also drew strong protests from Brazil, one of the primary targets of the critique. Still, in tacit admission that at least some of the arguments have merit, a senior MERCOSUR diplomat let it be known that external trade barriers will gradually be reduced, forcing member countries to compete globally. Many external MERCOSUR tariffs, which average 14 percent, are lower than they were before the group's creation, and there are plans for a hemispheric Free Trade Area of the Americas (which will combine MERCOSUR, NAFTA, and other American nations). If that occurs, MERCOSUR will have no choice but to reduce its external tariffs further.

MERCOSUR hit a significant roadblock in 1998, when its member states slipped into recession and intrabloc trade slumped. Trade fell further in 1999 following a financial crisis in Brazil that led to the devaluation of the Brazilian real, which immediately made the goods of other MERCOSUR members 40 percent more expensive in Brazil, their largest export market. At this point, progress toward establishing a full customs union all but stopped. Things deteriorated further in 2001 when Argentina, beset by economic stresses, suggested the customs union be temporarily suspended. Argentina wanted to suspend MERCOSUR's tariff so that it could abolish duties on imports of capital equipment, while raising those on consumer goods to 35 percent (MERCOSUR had established a 14 percent import tariff on both sets of goods). Brazil agreed to this request, effectively halting MERCOSUR's quest to become a fully functioning customs union.[31] Hope for a revival arose in 2003 when new Brazilian President Lula da Silva announced his support for a revitalized and expanded MERCOSUR modeled after the EU with a larger membership, a common currency, and a democratically elected MERCOSUR parliament.[32] As of 2005, however, no tangible progress had been made in moving MERCOSUR down that road, and critics felt that the customs union was if anything becoming more imperfect over time.[33]

CENTRAL AMERICAN COMMON MARKET AND CARICOM

Two other trade pacts in the Americas have not made much progress. In the early 1960s, Costa Rica, El Salvador, Guatemala, Honduras, and Nicaragua attempted to set up a Central American Common Market. It collapsed in 1969 when war broke out between Honduras and El Salvador after a riot at a soccer match between teams from the two countries. Since then the five countries have made some progress toward reviving their agreement, and the proposed common market was given a boost in 2003 when the United States signaled its intention to enter into bilateral free trade negotiations with the group.

A customs union was to have been created in 1991 between the English-speaking Caribbean countries under the auspices of the Caribbean Community. Referred to as **CARICOM,** it was established in 1973. However, it has repeatedly failed to progress toward economic integration. A formal commitment to economic and monetary union was adopted by CARICOM's member states in 1984, but since then little progress has been made. In October 1991, the CARICOM governments failed, for the third consecutive time, to meet a deadline for establishing a common external tariff.

FREE TRADE AREA OF THE AMERICAS

At a hemispherewide Summit of the Americas in December 1994, a Free Trade Area of the Americas (FTAA) was proposed. It took more than three years for the talks to start, but in April 1998, 34 heads of state traveled to Santiago, Chile, for the second Summit of the Americas where they formally inaugurated talks to establish an FTAA by January 1, 2005, which didn't occur. The continuing talks have addressed a wide range of economic, political, and environmental issues related to cross-border trade and investment. Although both the United States and Brazil were early advocates of the FTAA, support from both countries seems to be mixed at this point. Because the United States and Brazil have the largest economies in North and South America, respectively, strong U.S. and Brazilian support is a precondition for establishment of the free trade area.

The major stumbling blocks so far have been twofold. First, the United States wants its southern neighbors to agree to tougher enforcement of intellectual property rights and lower manufacturing tariffs, which they do not seem to be eager to embrace. Second, Brazil and Argentina want the United States to reduce its subsidies to U.S. agricultural producers and scrap tariffs on agricultural imports, which the U.S. government does not seem inclined to do. For progress to be made, most observers agree that the United States and Brazil have to first reach an agreement on these crucial issues.[34] If the FTAA is eventually established, it will have major implications for cross-border trade and investment flows within the hemisphere. The FTAA would open a free trade umbrella over 850 million people who accounted for some $13.5 trillion in GDP in 2003. Currently, however, it is very much a work in progress, and the progress has been slow.

🌐 Regional Economic Integration Elsewhere

Numerous attempts at regional economic integration have been tried throughout Asia and Africa. However, few exist in anything other than name. Perhaps the most significant is the Association of Southeast Asian Nations (ASEAN). In addition, the Asia-Pacific Economic Cooperation (APEC) forum has recently emerged as the seed of a potential free trade region.

ASSOCIATION OF SOUTHEAST ASIAN NATIONS

Formed in 1967, the **Association of Southeast Asian Nations (ASEAN)** includes Brunei, Cambodia, Indonesia, Laos, Malaysia, Myanmar, Philippines, Singapore, Thailand, and Vietnam. Laos, Myanmar, Vietnam, and Cambodia have all joined recently, creating a regional grouping of 500 million people with a combined GDP of some $740 billion (see Map 9.3). The basic objective of ASEAN is to foster freer trade between member countries and to achieve cooperation in their industrial policies. Progress so far has been limited, however.

Until recently only 5 percent of intra-ASEAN trade consisted of goods whose tariffs had been reduced through an ASEAN preferential trade arrangement. This may be changing. In 2003 an ASEAN Free Trade Area (AFTA) between the six original members of ASEAN came into full effect. The AFTA has cut tariffs on manufacturing and agricultural products to less than 5 percent. However, there are some significant exceptions to this tariff reduction. Malaysia, for example, refused to bring down tariffs on imported cars until 2005, and then will only lower the tariff to 20 percent, not the 5 percent called for under the AFTA. Malaysia wants to protect Proton, and inefficient local carmakers, from foreign competition. Similarly, the Philippines has refused to lower tariff rates on petrochemicals, and rice, the largest agricultural product in the region, will remain subject to higher tariff rates until at least 2020.[35]

Notwithstanding such issues, ASEAN and AFTA are at least progressing toward establishing a free trade zone. Vietnam will join the AFTA in 2006, Laos and Myanmar in 2008, and Cambodia in 2010. The goal is to reduce import tariffs among the six original members to zero by 2010, and to do so by 2015 for the newer members (although important exceptions to that goal, such as tariffs on rice, will no doubt persist). ASEAN is also pushing for free trade agreements with China, Japan, and South Korea.

ASIA-PACIFIC ECONOMIC COOPERATION

Asia-Pacific Economic Cooperation (APEC) was founded in 1990 at the suggestion of Australia. APEC currently has 21 member states including such economic powerhouses as the United States, Japan, and China (see Map 9.4). Collectively, the member states account for about 60 percent of the world's GNP, 47 percent of world trade, and much of the growth in the world economy. The stated aim of APEC is to increase multilateral cooperation in view of the economic rise of the Pacific nations and the growing interdependence within the region. U.S. support for APEC was also based on the belief that it might prove a viable strategy for heading off any moves to create Asian groupings from which it would be excluded.

Interest in APEC was heightened considerably in November 1993 when the heads of APEC member states met for the first time at a two-day conference in Seattle. Debate before the meeting speculated on the likely future role of APEC. One view was that APEC should commit itself to the ultimate formation of a free trade area. Such a move would transform the Pacific Rim from a geographical expression into the world's largest free trade area. Another view was that APEC would produce no more than hot air and lots of photo opportunities for the leaders involved. As it turned out, the APEC meeting produced little more than some vague commitments from member states to work together

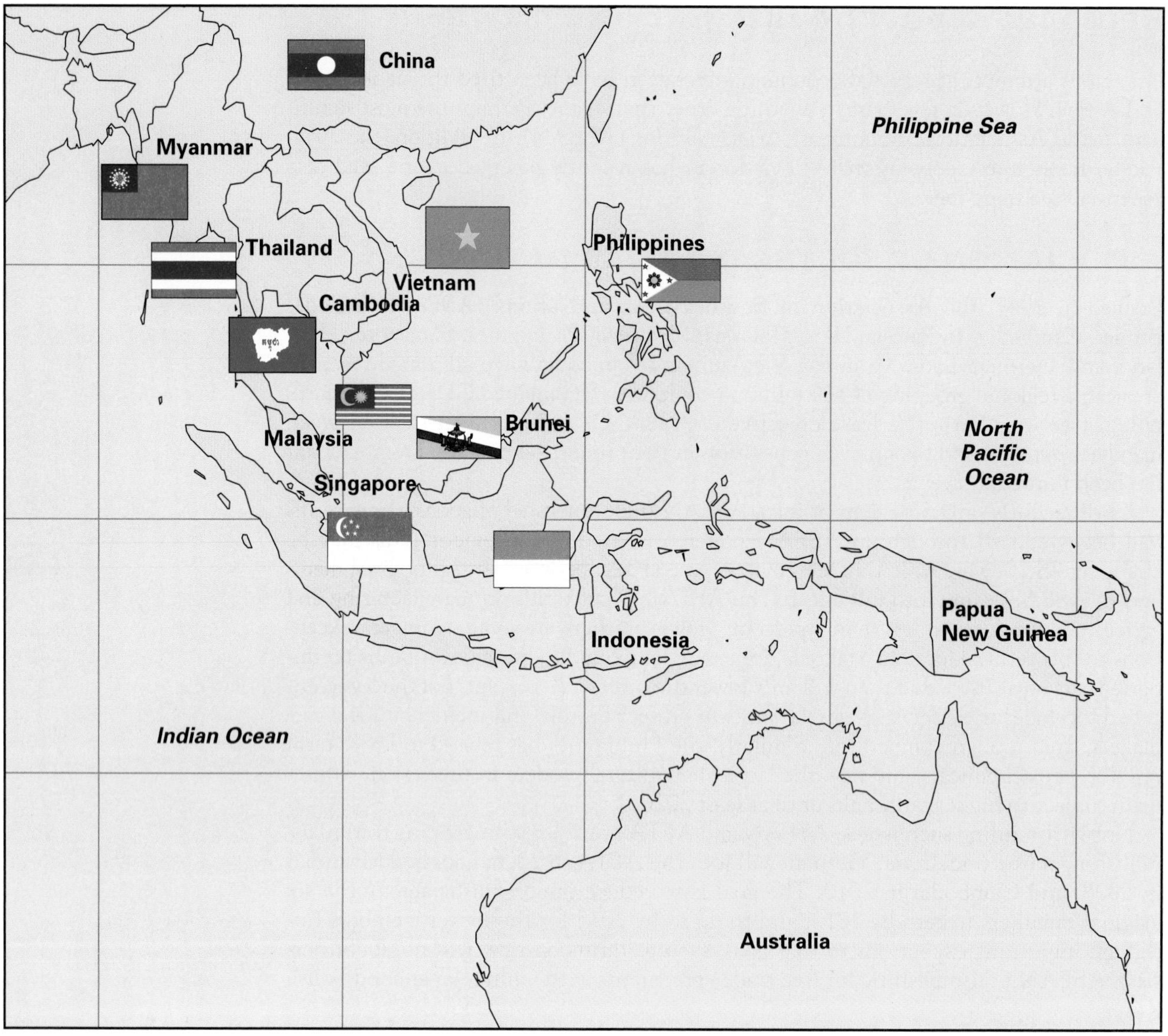

MAP 9.3

ASEAN Countries

Source: www.aseansec.org/
69.htm.

for greater economic integration and a general lowering of trade barriers. However, significantly, member states did not rule out the possibility of closer economic cooperation in the future.[36]

The heads of state have met again on a number of occasions. They have formally committed APEC's industrialized members to remove their trade and investment barriers by 2010 and for developing economies to do so by 2020. They also called for a detailed blueprint charting how this might be achieved. At a 1997 meeting, member states formally endorsed proposals designed to remove trade barriers in 15 sectors, ranging from fish to toys. However, the vague plan committed APEC to doing no more than holding further talks. Commenting on the vagueness of APEC pronouncements, the influential Brookings Institution, a U.S.-based economic policy institution, noted that APEC "is in grave danger of shrinking into irrelevance as a serious forum." Despite the slow progress, APEC is worth watching. If it eventually does transform itself into a free trade area, it will probably be the world's largest.[37]

REGIONAL TRADE BLOCS IN AFRICA

African countries have been experimenting with regional trade blocs for half a century. There are now nine trade blocs on the African continent. Many countries are members

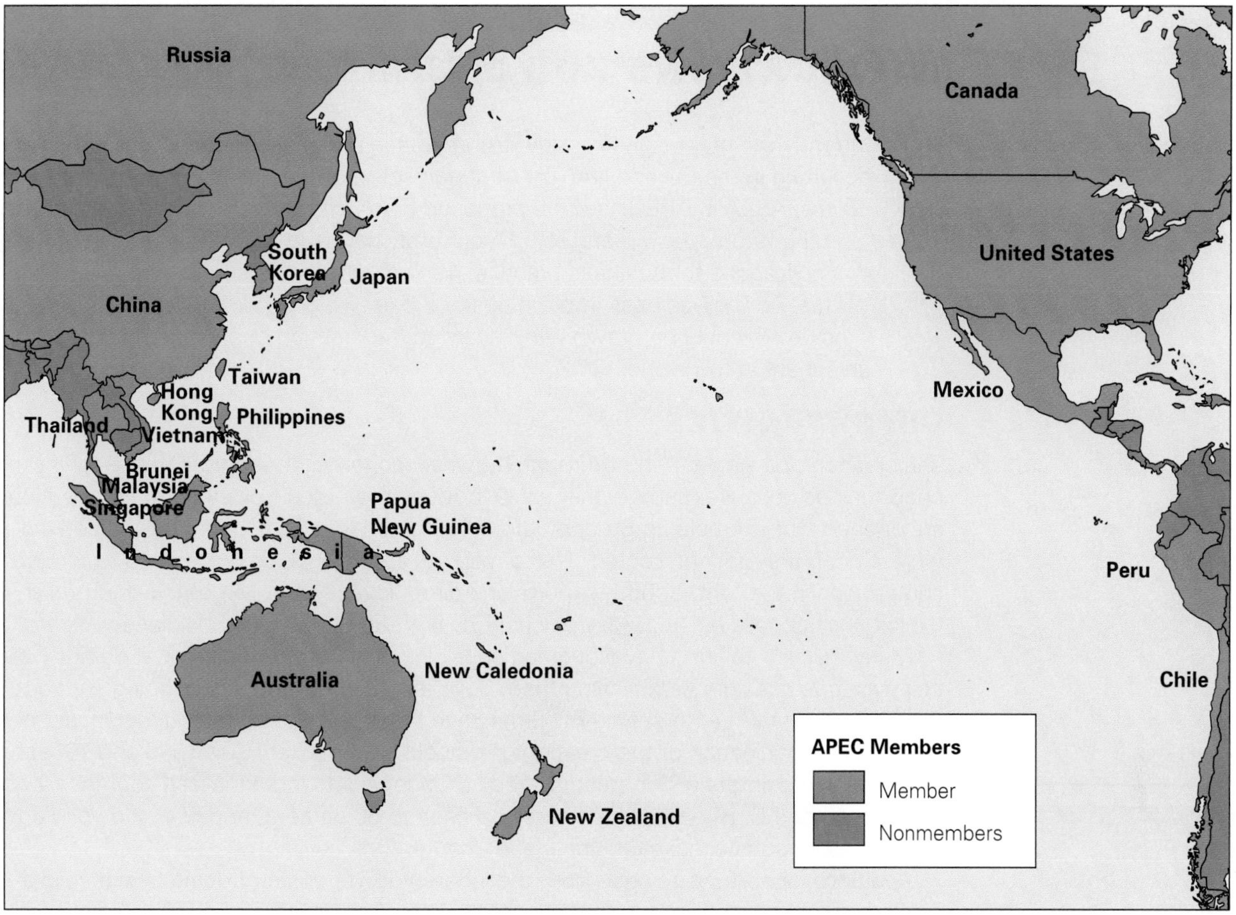

MAP 9.4

APEC Members

Source: APEC Website.

of more than one group. Although the number of trade groups is impressive, progress toward the establishment of meaningful trade blocs has been slow.

Many of these groups have been dormant for years. Significant political turmoil in several African nations has persistently impeded any meaningful progress. Also, deep suspicion of free trade exists in several African countries. The argument most frequently heard is that because these countries have less developed and less diversified economies, they need to be "protected" by tariff barriers from unfair foreign competition. Given the prevalence of this argument, it has been hard to establish free trade areas or customs unions.

The most recent attempt to reenergize the free trade movement in Africa occurred in early 2001, when Kenya, Uganda, and Tanzania, member states of the East African Community (EAC), committed themselves to relaunching their bloc, 24 years after it collapsed. The three countries, with 80 million inhabitants, intend to establish a customs union, regional court, legislative assembly, and, eventually, a political federation.

Their program includes cooperation on immigration, road and telecommunication networks, investment, and capital markets. However, while local business leaders welcomed the relaunch as a positive step, they were critical of the EAC's failure in practice to make progress on free trade. At the EAC treaty's signing in November 1999, members gave themselves four years to negotiate a customs union, with a draft slated for the end of 2001. But that fell far short of earlier plans for an immediate free trade zone, shelved after Tanzania and Uganda, fearful of Kenyan competition, expressed concerns that the zone could create imbalances similar to those that contributed to the breakup of the first community.[38] It remains to be seen if these countries can succeed this time, but if history is any guide, it will be an uphill road.

IMPLICATIONS FOR MANAGERS

Currently the most significant developments in regional economic integration are occurring in the EU and NAFTA. Although some of the Latin American trade blocs, ASEAN, APEC, and the proposed FTAA, may have economic significance in the future, the EU and NAFTA currently have more profound and immediate implications for business practice. Accordingly, in this section we will concentrate on the business implications of those two groups. Similar conclusions, however, could be drawn with regard to the creation of a single market anywhere in the world.

OPPORTUNITIES

The creation of a single market through regional economic integration offers significant opportunities because markets that were formerly protected from foreign competition are opened. For example, in Europe before 1992 the large French and Italian markets were among the most protected. These markets are now much more open to foreign competition in the form of both exports and direct investment. Nonetheless, to fully exploit such opportunities, it may pay non-EU firms to set up EU subsidiaries.

Many major U.S. firms have long had subsidiaries in Europe. Those that do not would be advised to consider establishing them now, lest they run the risk of being shut out of the EU by nontariff barriers. Non-EU firms have rapidly increased their direct investment in the EU in anticipation of the creation of a single market. Between 1985 and 1989, for example, approximately 37 percent of the FDI inflows into industrialized countries was directed at the EC. By 1991, this figure had risen to 66 percent, and FDI inflows into the EU have been substantial ever since (see Chapter 7).[39]

Additional opportunities arise from the inherent lower costs of doing business in a single market—as opposed to 25 national markets in the case of the EU or 3 national markets in the case of NAFTA. Free movement of goods across borders, harmonized product standards, and simplified tax regimes make it possible for firms based in the EU and the NAFTA countries to realize potentially significant cost economies by centralizing production in those EU and NAFTA locations where the mix of factor costs and skills is optimal. Rather than producing a product in each of the 25 EU countries or the 3 NAFTA countries, a firm may be able to serve the whole EU or North American market from a single location. This location must be chosen carefully, of course, with an eye on local factor costs and skills.

For example, in response to the changes created by EU after 1992, the St. Paul–based 3M Company consolidated its European manufacturing and distribution facilities to take advantage of economies of scale. Thus, a plant in Great Britain now produces 3M's printing products and a German factory its reflective traffic control materials for all of the EU. In each case, 3M chose a location for centralized production after carefully considering the likely production costs in alternative locations within the EU. The ultimate goal of 3M is to dispense with all national distinctions, directing R&D, manufacturing, distribution, and marketing for each product group from an EU headquarters.[40] Similarly, Unilever, one of Europe's largest companies, began rationalizing its production in advance of 1992 to attain scale economies. Unilever concentrated its production of dishwashing powder for the EU in one plant, bath soap in another, and so on.[41]

Even after the removal of barriers to trade and investment, enduring differences in culture and competitive practices often limit the ability of companies to realize cost economies by centralizing production in key locations and producing a standardized product for a single multicountry market. Consider the case of Atag Holdings NV, a Dutch maker of kitchen appliances.[42] Atag thought it was well placed to benefit from the single market, but found it tough going. Atag's plant is just one mile from the

German border and near the center of the EU's population. The company thought it could cater to both the "potato" and "spaghetti" belts—marketers' terms for consumers in Northern and Southern Europe—by producing two main product lines and selling these standardized "euro-products" to "euro-consumers." The main benefit of doing so is the economy of scale derived from mass production of a standardized range of products. Atag quickly discovered that the "euro-consumer" was a myth. Consumer preferences vary much more across nations than Atag had thought. Consider ceramic cooktops; Atag planned to market just 2 varieties throughout the EU but has found it needs 11. Belgians, who cook in huge pots, require extra-large burners. Germans like oval pots and burners to fit. The French need small burners and very low temperatures for simmering sauces and broths. Germans like oven knobs on the top; the French want them on the front. Most Germans and French prefer black and white ranges; the British demand a range of colors including peach, pigeon blue, and mint green.

THREATS

Just as the emergence of single markets creates opportunities for business, it also presents a number of threats. For one thing, the business environment within each grouping will become more competitive. The lowering of barriers to trade and investment between countries is likely to lead to increased price competition throughout the EU and NAFTA. For example, before 1992 a Volkswagen Golf cost 55 percent more in Great Britain than in Denmark and 29 percent more in Ireland than in Greece.[43] Over time, such price differentials will vanish in a single market. This is a direct threat to any firm doing business in EU or NAFTA countries. To survive in the tougher single-market environment, firms must take advantage of the opportunities offered by the creation of a single market to rationalize their production and reduce their costs. Otherwise, they will be at a severe disadvantage.

A further threat to firms outside these trading blocs arises from the likely long-term improvement in the competitive position of many firms within the areas. This is particularly relevant in the EU, where many firms have historically been limited by a high cost structure in their ability to compete globally with North American and Asian firms. The creation of a single market and the resulting increased competition in the EU is beginning to produce serious attempts by many EU firms to reduce their cost structure by rationalizing production. This is transforming many EU companies into efficient global competitors. The message for non-EU businesses is that they need to prepare for the emergence of more capable European competitors by reducing their own cost structures.

Another threat to firms outside of trading areas is the threat of being shut out of the single market by the creation of a "trade fortress." The charge that regional economic integration might lead to a fortress mentality is most often leveled at the EU. Although the free trade philosophy underpinning the EU theoretically argues against the creation of any fortress in Europe, occasional signs indicate the EU may raise barriers to imports and investment in certain "politically sensitive" areas, such as autos. Non-EU firms might be well advised, therefore, to set up their own EU operations. This could also occur in the NAFTA countries, but it seems less likely.

Finally, the emerging role of the European Commission in competition policy suggests the EU is increasingly willing and able to intervene and impose conditions on companies proposing mergers and acquisitions. This is a threat insofar as it limits the ability of firms to pursue the corporate strategy of their choice. As we saw in the Management Focus on the media industry mergers, the commission may require significant concessions from businesses as a precondition for allowing proposed mergers and acquisitions to proceed. While this constrains the strategic options for firms, it should be remembered that in taking such action, the commission is trying to maintain the level of competition in Europe's single market, which should benefit consumers.

Chapter Summary

This chapter pursued three main objectives: to examine the economic and political debate surrounding regional economic integration; to review the progress toward regional economic integration in Europe, the Americas, and elsewhere; and to distinguish the important implications of regional economic integration for the practice of international business. The chapter made the following points:

1. A number of levels of economic integration are possible in theory. In order of increasing integration, they include a free trade area, a customs union, a common market, an economic union, and full political union.

2. In a free trade area, barriers to trade between member countries are removed, but each country determines its own external trade policy. In a customs union, internal barriers to trade are removed and a common external trade policy is adopted. A common market is similar to a customs union, except that a common market also allows factors of production to move freely between countries. An economic union involves even closer integration, including the establishment of a common currency and the harmonization of tax rates. A political union is the logical culmination of attempts to achieve ever closer economic integration.

3. Regional economic integration is an attempt to achieve economic gains from the free flow of trade and investment between neighboring countries.

4. Integration is not easily achieved or sustained. Although integration brings benefits to the majority, it is never without costs for the minority. Concerns over national sovereignty often slow or stop integration attempts.

5. Regional integration will not increase economic welfare if the trade creation effects in the free trade area are outweighed by the trade diversion effects.

6. The Single European Act sought to create a true single market by abolishing administrative barriers to the free flow of trade and investment between EU countries.

7. Twelve EU members now use a common currency, the euro. The economic gains from a common currency come from reduced exchange costs, reduced risk associated with currency fluctuations, and increased price competition within the EU.

8. Increasingly, the European Commission is taking an activist stance with regard to competition policy, intervening to restrict mergers and acquisitions that it believes will reduce competition in the EU.

9. Although no other attempt at regional economic integration comes close to the EU in terms of potential economic and political significance, various other attempts are being made in the world. The most notable include NAFTA in North America, the Andean Pact and MERCOSUR in Latin America, ASEAN in Southeast Asia, and perhaps APEC.

10. The creation of single markets in the EU and North America means that many markets that were formerly protected from foreign competition are now more open. This creates major investment and export opportunities for firms within and outside these regions.

11. The free movement of goods across borders, the harmonization of product standards, and the simplification of tax regimes make it possible for firms based in a free trade area to realize potentially enormous cost economies by centralizing production in those locations within the area where the mix of factor costs and skills is optimal.

12. The lowering of barriers to trade and investment between countries within a trade group will probably be followed by increased price competition.

Critical Thinking and Discussion Questions

1. NAFTA has produced significant net benefits for the Canadian, Mexican, and U.S. economies. Discuss.

2. What are the economic and political arguments for regional economic integration? Given these arguments, why don't we see more substantial examples of integration in the world economy?

3. What effect is creation of a single market and a single currency within the EU likely to have on competition within the EU? Why?

4. Do you think it is correct for the European Commission to restrict mergers between American companies that do business in Europe? (For example, the European Commission vetoed the proposed merger between WorldCom and Sprint, both U.S. companies, and it carefully reviewed the merger between AOL and Time Warner, again both U.S. companies.)

5. How should a U.S. firm that currently exports only to ASEAN countries respond to the creation of a single market in this regional grouping?

6. How should a firm with self-sufficient production facilities in several ASEAN countries respond to the creation of a single market? What are the constraints on its ability to respond in a manner that minimizes production costs?

7. After a promising start, MERCOSUR, the major Latin American trade agreement, has faltered and made little progress since 2000. What problems are hurting MERCOSUR? What can be done to solve these problems?

8. Would establishment of a Free Trade Area of the Americas (FTAA) be good for the two most advanced economies in the hemisphere, the United States and Canada? How might the establishment of the FTAA impact the strategy of North American firms?

Research Task   globalEDGE™   globaledge.msu.edu

Use the globalEDGE™ site to complete the following exercises:

1. Your company is considering expanding by opening new representative offices in the European Union (EU). Nevertheless, the size of the investment is significant and top management wishes to have a clearer picture of the current and probable future economic status of the EU. Prepare an executive summary describing the features you consider as crucial in making such a decision.

2. The establishment of the Free Trade Area of the Americas can be a threat, as well as an opportunity for your company. Using the globalEDGE™ Web site, identify the countries participating in the negotiations for the FTAA. What are the main themes of the negotiation process?

Car Price Differentials in the European Union

CLOSING CASE The Single European Act became law among the member states of the European Union on January 1, 1993. The goal of the act was to remove barriers to cross-border trade and investment within the confines of the EU, thereby creating a single market instead of a collection of distinct national markets. Among the benefits claimed for this act were an increase in competition and a corresponding reduction in prices. The move toward a single market received another boost January 1, 1999, when the majority of the EU's member states formally adopted the euro as a common currency. As of 2005, 12 of the 25 member states of the EU used the euro as their currency (these 12 countries are referred to as members of the euro zone). It was claimed that the euro would benefit European consumers by making it easier to compare prices across nations, and should in theory lead to the harmonization of prices within the euro zone. For example, due to the adoption of a common currency within a single market, a car sold in Germany should in theory be priced the same as a car sold in France.

In the automobile market, the reality has been somewhat different. By the end of 2004, significant variations remained between the prices of the same automobiles in different countries. According to the European Commission, in November 2004 there was a 28.3 percent differential between the price of a Volkswagen Golf in the cheapest and the most expensive national markets in the euro zone. There was also a 20.8 percent differential in the price of a Ford Focus, a 14 percent differential in the price of a Peugeot 206, and a 10.2 percent differential in the price of an Audi A4 Opel Vectra. However, these differentials with regard to certain models hid the fact that on average, prices have been converging on EU wide norms. As of late 2004, the average price differential of cars across countries in the euro zone was just 4.4 percent, a marked improvement from November 1999, when the average price differential was 17.5 percent. The average price differential of cars across all EU member states was 6.6 percent in November 2004.

Within the euro zone, Germany was the most expensive car market. In Germany, 38 car models were sold to consumers at the highest prices in the euro zone in November 2004, and 21 of these were 20 percent more expensive than the cheapest national market within the euro zone. Within the euro zone countries, cars are cheapest in Greece and Finland. A VW Passat, for example, cost €18,664 in Germany and €14,269 in Greece. The United Kingdom is perennially among the most expensive car markets within the EU, with the average new car costing British consumers €800 more than comparable models sold in cheaper EU markets. The widest price differential found by the European Commission was for the Opel Astra which cost almost 50 percent more in Germany than neighboring Denmark!

One reason for the persistence of price differentials within the EU is that since 1985, regulations have allowed automobile manufacturers to restrict competition between car dealers. The "block exemption" clause in EU competition policy allowed automakers to dictate where a dealership could be located, to limit the number of brands that a dealer could sell, and to prohibit a dealer from selling vehicles outside of its home country. For example, Volkswagen might tell a dealer in Belgium that if it wanted to become (or remain) a Volkswagen dealer, it (a) could not sell models made by other car companies, and (b) could not sell Volkswagen cars on its lot to consumers in Germany. This practice effectively allowed automobile companies to restrict competition, segment the European market, and price cars differently in various countries to reflect underlying demand conditions.

In response to persistent complaints from consumers, the European Commission in late 2002 scrapped the block exemption clause and issued a new set of regulations designed to encourage competition within the EU car market. Under the new rules, dealers will be allowed to sell anywhere they want to, open new locations where

they choose, and sell more than one brand of car. Thus, a Belgium car dealer now will be able to sell Volkswagen cars to German consumers. In a concession to automobile companies, which lobbied against the proposed revisions, the new rules will be phased in over three years and take full effect in September 2005.

Sources: K. Kelly, "Global Politics Shift Auto Industry Focus," *Ward's Auto World*, November 2002, pp. 39–40; S. Miller, "Benefits of EU Car Sales Rules Are Questionable," *The Wall Street Journal*, July 17, 2002, p. A14; and European Commission, "Competition: Car Prices Converge in an Enlarged European Union," European Commission press release DN: IP/05/267, March 8, 2005.

Case Discussion Questions

1. What are the sources of significant price differentials in the EU automobile market?

2. In a pure single market would these price differentials exist? By what process might price differentials be eradicated?

3. Why do you think the United Kingdom is one of the most expensive car markets in Europe?

4. What do you think will happen to price differentials in the EU automobile market under the new regulations set to take effect in September 2005?

5. What will the impact of these new regulations be on (a) competitive intensity in the EU automobile market, and (b) the profitability of automobile operations in the EU?

6. Which automobile companies will do best in the post-2005 environment?

Notes

1. Information taken from World Trade Organization Web site and current as of March 2005, www.wto.org.

2. Ibid.

3. The Andean Pact has been through a number of changes since its inception. The latest version was established in 1991. See "Free-Trade Free for All," *The Economist*, January 4, 1991, p. 63.

4. D. Swann, *The Economics of the Common Market*, 6th ed. (London: Penguin Books, 1990).

5. See J. Bhagwati, "Regionalism and Multilateralism: An Overview," Columbia University Discussion Paper 603, Department of Economics, Columbia University, New York; A. de la Torre and M. Kelly, "Regional Trade Arrangements," Occasional Paper 93, Washington, DC: International Monetary Fund, March 1992; J. Bhagwati, "Fast Track to Nowhere," *The Economist*, October 18, 1997, pp. 21–24; Jagdish Bhagwati, *Free Trade Today* (Princeton and Oxford: Princeton

   University Press, 2002); and B. K. Gordon, "A High Risk Trade Policy," *Foreign Affairs* 82 no. 4 (July/August 2003), pp. 105–15.

6. N. Colchester and D. Buchan, *Europower: The Essential Guide to Europe's Economic Transformation in 1992* (London: The Economist Books, 1990), and Swann, *Economics of the Common Market*.

7. A. S. Posen, "Fleeting Equality, The Relative Size of the EU and US Economies in 2020," The Brookings Institution, September 2004.

8. Swann, *Economics of the Common Market*; Colchester and Buchan, *Europower: The Essential Guide to Europe's Economic Transformation in 1992*; "The European Union: A Survey," *The Economist*, October 22, 1994; "The European Community: A Survey," *The Economist*, July 3, 1993; and the European Union Web site at http://europa.eu.int.

9. E. J. Morgan, "A Decade of EC Merger Control," *International Journal of Economics and Business*, November 2001, pp. 451–73.

10. European Commission, *XXXIII Report on Competition Policy, 2003* (Brussels: European Commission, 2004).

11. "The European Community: A Survey."

12. "One Europe, One Economy," *The Economist*, November 30, 1991, pp. 53–54, and "Market Failure: A Survey of Business in Europe," *The Economist*, June 8, 1991, pp. 6–10.

13. Alan Riley, "The Single Market Ten Years On," *European Policy Analyst*, December 2002, pp. 65–72.

14. See C. Wyploze, "EMU: Why and How It Might Happen," *Journal of Economic Perspectives* 11 (1997), pp. 3–22, and M. Feldstein, "The Political Economy of the European Economic and Monetary Union," *Journal of Economic Perspectives* 11 (1997), pp. 23–42.

15. "One Europe, One Economy," and Feldstein, "The Political Economy of the European Economic and Monetary Union."

16. Feldstein, "The Political Economy of the European Economic and Monetary Union."

17. "Time for Europhoria?" *The Economist*, January 4, 2003, p. 58.

18. "The Passing of the Buck?" *The Economist*, December 4, 2004, pp. 78–80.

19. Details regarding conditions of membership and the progression of enlargement negotiations can be found at http:europa.eu.int/comm/enlargement/index.htm.

20. "What Is NAFTA?" *Financial Times*, November 17, 1993, p. 6, and S. Garland, "Sweet Victory," *BusinessWeek*, November 29, 1993, pp. 30–31.

21. "NAFTA: The Showdown," *The Economist*, November 13, 1993, pp. 23–36.

22. N. C. Lustog, "NAFTA: Setting the Record Straight," *The World Economy*, 1997, pp. 605–14.

23. R. H. Ojeda, C. Dowds, R. McCleery, S. Robinson, D. Runsten, C. Wolff, and G. Wolff, "NAFTA—How Has It Done? North American Integration Three Years after NAFTA," North American Integration and Development Center at UCLA, December 1996.

24. W. Thorbecke and C. Eigen-Zucchi, "Did NAFTA Cause a Giant Sucking Sound?" *Journal of Labor Research*, Fall 2002, pp. 647–58; G. Gagne, "North American Free Trade, Canada, and U.S. Trade Remedies: An Assessment after Ten Years," *The World Economy*, 2000, pp. 77–91; and "Free Trade on Trial," *The Economist*, January 3, 2004, pp. 13–16.

25. All trade figures from U.S. Department of Commerce Trade Stat Express Web site at http://tse.export.gov/.

26. J. Cavanagh et al., "Happy Ever NAFTA?" *Foreign Policy*, September–October 2002, pp. 58–65.

27. "The Business of the American Hemisphere," *The Economist*, August 24, 1991, pp. 37–38.

28. "NAFTA Is Not Alone," *The Economist*, June 18, 1994, pp. 47–48.

29. "Murky MERCOSUR," *The Economist*, July 26, 1997, pp. 66–67.

30. See M. Philips, "South American Trade Pact under Fire," *The Wall Street Journal*, October 23, 1996, p. A2; A. J. Yeats, *Does MERCOSUR's Trade Performance Justify Concerns about the Global Welfare-Reducing Effects of Free Trade Arrangements? Yes!* (Washington, DC: World Bank, 1996); and D. M. Leipziger et al., "MERCOSUR: Integration and Industrial Policy," *The World Economy*, 1997, pp. 585–604.

31. "Another Blow to MERCOSUR," *The Economist*, March 31, 2001, pp. 33–34.

32. "Lula Lays Out MERCOSUR Rescue Mission," *Latin America Newsletters*, February 4, 2003, p. 7.

33. "A Free Trade Tug of War," *The Economist*, December 11, 2004, p. 54.

34. M. Esterl, "Free Trade Area of the Americas Stalls," *The Economist*, January 19, 2005, p. 1.

35. "Every Man for Himself: Trade in Asia," *The Economist*, November 2, 2002, pp. 43–44.

36. "Aimless in Seattle," *The Economist*, November 13, 1993, pp. 35–36.

37. G. de Jonquieres, "APEC Grapples with Market Turmoil," *Financial Times*, November 21, 1997, p. 6, and G. Baker, "Clinton Team Wins Most of the APEC Tricks," *Financial Times*, November 27, 1997, p. 5.

38. M. Turner, "Trio Revives East African Union," *Financial Times*, January 16, 2001, p. 4.

39. United Nations, *World Investment Report*, various issues (New York and Geneva: United Nations).

40. P. Davis, "A European Campaign: Local Companies Rush for a Share of EC Market While Barriers Are Down," *Minneapolis-St. Paul City Business*, January 8, 1990, p. 1.

41. "The Business of Europe," *The Economist*, December 7, 1991, pp. 63–64.

42. T. Horwitz, "Europe's Borders Fade," *The Wall Street Journal*, May 18, 1993, pp. A1, A12; "A Singular Market," *The Economist*, October 22, 1994, pp. 10–16; and "Something Dodgy in Europe's Single Market," *The Economist*, May 21, 1994, pp. 69–70.

43. E. G. Friberg, "1992: Moves Europeans Are Making," *Harvard Business Review*, May–June 1989, pp. 85–89.

Cases

Agricultural Subsidies and Development

For decades the rich countries of the developed world have lavished subsidies on their farmers, typically guaranteeing them a minimum price for the products they produce. The aim has been to protect farmers in the developed world from the potentially devastating effects of low commodity prices. Although they are small in numbers, farmers tend to be politically active, and winning their support is important for many politicians. The politicians often claim that their motive is to preserve a historic rural lifestyle, and they see subsidies as a way of doing this.

This logic has resulted in financial support estimated to exceed $300 billion a year for farmers in rich nations. The European Union, for example, has set a minimum price for butter of 3,282 euros per ton. If the world price for butter falls below that amount, the EU will make up the difference to farmers in the form of a direct payment or subsidy. In total, EU dairy farmers receive roughly $15 billion a year in subsidies to produce milk and butter, or about $2 a day for every cow in the EU—a figure that is more than the daily income of half the world's population. Overall, EU farmers receive $53 billion a year in subsidies.

The EU is not alone in this practice. In the United States, subsidies are given to a wide range of crop and dairy farmers. Typical is the guarantee that U.S. cotton farmers will receive at least $0.70 for every pound of cotton they harvest. If world cotton prices fall below this level, the government makes up the difference, writing a check to the farmers. Some 25,000 U.S. cotton farmers received some $3.4 billion in annual subsidy checks. Total agricultural subsidies in the United States amount to some $19 billion a year.

One consequence of such subsidies is to create surplus production. That surplus is sold on world markets, where the extra supply depresses prices, making it much harder for producers in the developing world to sell their output at a profit. For example, EU subsidies to sugar beet producers amount to more than $4,000 an acre. With a minimum price guarantee that exceeds their costs of production, EU farmers plant more sugar beet than the EU market can absorb. The surplus, some 6 million tons per year, is dumped on the world market, where it depresses world prices. Estimates suggest that if the EU stopped dumping its surplus production on world markets, sugar prices would increase by 20 percent. That would make a big difference for developing nations such as South Africa, which exports roughly half of its 2.6 million tons of annual sugar production. With a 20 percent rise in world prices, the South African economy would reap about $40 million more from sugar exports.

American subsidies to cotton farmers have a similar effect. Brazilian officials contend that by creating surplus production in the United States that is then dumped on the world market, U.S. cotton subsidies have depressed world prices for cotton by more than 50 percent since the mid-1990s. Low cotton prices cost Brazil some $600 million in lost export earnings in 2001–2002. India, another big cotton producer, has estimated that U.S. cotton subsidies reduced its export revenue from cotton by some $1 billion in 2001. According to the charitable organization Oxfam, the U.S. government spends about three times as much on cotton subsidies as it does on foreign aid for all of Africa. In 2001, the African nation of Mali lost about $43 million in export revenues due to plunging cotton prices, significantly more than the $37 million in foreign aid it received from the United States that year.

Overall, the United Nations has estimated that while developed nations give about $50 billion a year in foreign aid to the developing world, agricultural subsidies cost producers in the developing world some $50 billion in lost export revenues, effectively canceling out the effect of the aid. As one UN official has noted, "It's no good building up roads, clinics, and infrastructure in poor areas if you don't give them access to markets and engines for growth." Similarly, Oxfam has taken the unusual position for a charity of coming out strongly in support of the elimination of agricultural subsidies and price supports. If world prices were increased and production was shifted from high-cost, protected producers in Europe and America to lower-cost producers in the developing world, Oxfam claims that consumers in rich nations would benefit from lower domestic prices and the elimination of taxes required to pay for the subsidies, while producers in the developing world would gain from fairer competition, expanded markets, and higher world prices. In the long run, the greater economic growth that would occur in agriculturally dependent developing nations would be to everyone's benefit.

Although subsidies have been against the spirit of World Trade Organization rules, under the terms of a 1995 "peace agreement," WTO members agreed not to take each other to court over agricultural subsidies. However, that agreement expired December 31, 2004. Signs are growing that unless rich countries take steps to cut their subsidies soon, a number of efficient agricultural exporting countries will launch an assault on farm subsidies. Brazil did not even wait for the "peace agreement" to expire; in late 2003 it filed a complaint with the World Trade Organization, claiming that the United States had retained its position as the second largest cotton grower in the world, and the largest exporter, by paying $12.5 billion in subsidies to its cotton farmers between August 1999 and July 2003. Brazil argued that in 2001–2002, the U.S. funneled nearly $4 billion in subsidies to its cotton farmers for a crop worth just $3 billion, which depressed world prices and cost Brazil $600 million in lost sales. In an interim ruling issued in mid-2004, the WTO agreed that U.S. subsidies, by encouraging surplus production, had lowered cotton prices and harmed Brazilian exporters. The United States appealed, and it may be two more years before the issue is resolved.

Case Discussion Questions

1. If agricultural tariffs and subsidies to producers were removed overnight, what would the impact be on the average consumer in developed nations such as the United States and the EU countries? What would be the impact on the average farmer? Do you think the total benefits outweigh the total costs, or vice versa?

2. Which do you think would help the citizens of the world's poorest nations more, increasing foreign aid or removing all agricultural tariffs and subsidies?

3. Why do you think governments in developed nations continue to lavish extensive support on agricultural producers, even though those producers constitute a very small segment of the population?

4. The current Doha Round of talks organized by the World Trade Organization is trying to reduce barriers to free trade in agriculture. So far, however, the talks have made little concrete progress on this issue. Why do you think this is the case? What other solutions can you think of for the problems created by barriers to trade in agriculture?

Sources

1. Andrews, E. L. "Rich Nations Are Criticized for Enforcing Trade Barriers." *The New York Times*, September 30, 2002, p. A1.

2. King, N. "WTO Rules against U.S. Cotton Aid." *The Wall Street Journal*, April 27, 2004, p. A2.

3. Oxfam. "Milking the CAP." Oxfam Briefing Paper No. 34, 2002, www.maketradefair.com/assets/english/DairyPaper.pdf.

4. Thurrow, R., and G. Winestock. "Bittersweet: How an Addiction to Sugar Subsidies Hurts Development." *The Wall Street Journal*, September 16, 2002, p. A1.

Drug Development in the European Union

Europe has long produced some of the world's most successful drug companies. However, many of them in recent years have complained that European Union regulations are hurting their ability to develop new proprietary (brand-name) drugs and compete in the global marketplace against companies from the United States. Developing innovative new drugs is a very expensive, risky, and time-consuming business. In both the United States and EU it can take as long as 12 years to move a drug from the laboratory, through human clinical trials, and into the marketplace. The failure rate is high, with as many as 85 percent of all drugs entering clinical trials not reaching the market, either because they did not show the predicted efficacy in clinical trials, or because they had safety problems due to adverse side effects. Furthermore, it can cost more than $500 million to bring a new drug to market. Given the costs and risks, drug companies rely upon a small number of successful new drugs to pay for all of their failures, fund future research, and provide a return to their shareholders. Many European drug companies now believe that EU regulations have made it very difficult for them to earn a sufficient return on their new drugs to do this.

One problem is that extensive price controls on brand-name drugs exist throughout the EU. Prices are set by national health care providers, often by negotiation between the providers and drug companies. Because the providers have the objective of reducing health care costs, and thus the tax burden on their citizens, they tend to push for lower drug prices than those found in the United States, where the prices of new brand-name drugs are not regulated. This results in a lower return to drug companies in Europe. Also, the extent of price controls varies from country to country. This allows for arbitrage, whereby distributors buy drugs in countries where prices are low and resell them where they are high. For example, price controls on new drugs are much more stringent in France, Italy, and Spain than they are in Germany or the United Kingdom. This has led to the reexporting of drugs sold for a low price in Spain to Germany where they are sold for less than the price prevailing in that market. Such arbitrage reduces the profits that a pharmaceutical firm can earn from developing a successful new drug. According to industry data, some €6 billion in sales every year can be attributed to arbitrage, with the profits being captured by the distributors who practice arbitrage, not the drug companies.

Another issue concerns regulations governing the introduction of a generic version of a brand-name drug, which historically have varied from country to country within the EU. Drug companies have been given 6 to 10 years of protection from generic competition, depending on the country. The drug companies have long argued that six years is not sufficient to recoup the investment required to bring a new drug to market. (The price of a brand-name drug can fall by as much as 80 percent once a generic competitor is introduced.)

The enlargement of the EU from 15 to 25 countries added urgency to this complaint, since eight of the new EU members are in Eastern Europe where protection from generic competition historically lasted for only three years. This led to fears that cheap generic versions of brand-name drugs from new EU members would flood the rest of the EU, further reducing returns to drug companies and making it extremely difficult to fund research to develop new drugs. Furthermore, the expansion of the EU into Eastern Europe is also increasing the opportunities for arbitrage, since prices for drugs are as much as 70 percent lower in some Eastern European countries than in Germany or Great Britain.

Recognizing how serious these issues had become, in 2001 the European Union started to look at the rules governing generic competition. In late December 2003, the European Parliament approved a new set of regulations that established a uniform period of eight years after market introduction before allowing generic drug producers access to data that would help them to develop generic versions of brand-name pharmaceuticals, and an additional two years before allowing the sale of generic drugs. This was widely seen as a victory for European pharmaceutical companies, who would now be protected from generic competition for 10 years after market introduction of a drug.

Drug companies are attempting to deal with the arbitrage problem through the EU legal system. In 1996, the European Commission found the German drugmaker Bayer guilty of restricting the arbitrage of Adalat, a brand-name heart medicine. Bayer had struck agreements with French and Spanish wholesalers to dissuade them from taking advantage of price differentials to resell Adalat in Britain, where prices were higher. The European Commission stated that Bayer's actions restricted competition. Bayer appealed the decision, and in early 2004 the European Court of Justice ruled that the European Commission failed to prove there were anticompetitive agreements between Bayer and the wholesalers. In a statement released after the judgment, Bayer interpreted the ruling as meaning that pharmaceutical manufacturers are under no obligation to supply the entire EU market from the member state with the lowest state-regulated price. If this ruling is not overturned by legislation in the European Parliament, it might reduce the scope of arbitrage

in the European Union, boosting the returns to developing new brand-name drugs, and increasing the competitiveness of Europe's drug companies in the global economy.

However, the legal issues surrounding arbitrage have not yet been resolved. On the heels of the Bayer decision, another large EU drug company, GlaxoSmithKline (GSK), took steps to restrict the supply of three drugs to Greece. Historically, GSK had supplied substantially more drugs than were required to Greek wholesalers, only to see the excess being reexported to the United Kingdom and other countries where prices were higher. GSK's decision to limit supplies to Greece was challenged by Greek wholesalers, who brought the case before the Greek competition authorities. They in turn referred the case to the European Court of Justice. However, in June 2005 Europe's highest court ruled that it did not have the authority to rule in the case, and referred the issue back to the Greek competition authorities—an action that was widely seen as plunging the industry once more into legal uncertainty.

Case Discussion Questions

1. To what extent have regulations and institutional arrangements in the EU put European drug companies at a disadvantage with their U.S. competitors?

2. What would the EU have to do to put European companies on an equal footing with drug companies based in the United States?

3. Who is likely to oppose any attempt to outlaw arbitrage of drugs within the EU? What do you think the arguments will be? How successful might they be?

4. What does this case tell you about the efficacy of the attempt to establish a single market for goods and services within the European Union?

5. If arbitrage in the EU is allowed to continue, what do you think the response of EU drug companies will be?

Sources

1. Cowell, A. "European Union Expansion Has Drug Makers Worried." *The New York Times*, November 20, 2003, pp. W1, W7.

2. "EU Extends Data Exclusivity." *Chemical Market Reporter*, December 22, 2003, p. 5.

3. Meller, P. "Europe Effort to Control Pricing Is Set Back." *The New York Times*, January 7, 2004, p. W1.

4. Timmons, H. "Drug Firms Lose Appeal on Sales Trading Dispute." *International Herald Tribune*, June 1, 2005, p. 11.

	1970–80	1981–85	1986–90	1991–95	1996–00	1981–00
India	455	295	835	4,018	13,122	18,270
China	0	3,983	14,263	112,673	205,320	336,239
India as a % of China	—	7.4%	5.9%	3.6%	6.4%	5.4%

TABLE I

Flow of FDI (in $ million)

Source: World Bank, World Development Indicators Online Database, 2002 (www.worldbank.org)

FDI: India versus China

INTRODUCTION

India and China, the world's two biggest nations and the fastest growing among the emerging economies of the world, have a number of similarities ranging from huge population to being colonies and socialist legacies in policies in the 1950s and the 1960s. Similarities aside, the two countries have many differences. In 2002, India's per capital income was $440 per year against China's $990. While in China, 3 percent of the population were below the poverty line, in India it was between 30 and 40 percent.[1] China received foreign direct investment (FDI) of $52.7 billion in 2002, while India received $4.67 billion.[2] Since the opening up of the economy in 1978, China witnessed increased FDI inflows (Table I). China had a share of 40 percent of the total FDI that the developing countries received and was the second largest recipient of FDI in the world, topped only by the United States.[3] Cumulative FDI in China in the reform period exceeded $400 billion at the start of 2003, much higher than the cumulative FDI in India during the last decade.

China was able to surge ahead of India in attracting FDI, considered to be a prime input for the progress of developing economies, as it embraced reforms much earlier and eventually established itself as "workshop of the world." India, on the other hand, was slow to open its markets and had initiated reform only in 1991. Even after more than a decade of reforms, India did not have much to show except for its achievements in the software industry and to some extent in the pharmaceutical sector. The performance of the manufacturing sector had been lackluster and even in the much-talked-about software industry, companies limited themselves to low-end work such as outsourcing compared to Chinese companies, which involved more high-end work such as hardware manufacturing, telecommunication, and broadband infrastructure building. According to the *World Competitiveness Report*, 2002 prepared by IMD, Switzerland,[4] among the 49 countries surveyed, India ranked 47th in terms of overall technological competitiveness compared to China's 35th. However, some economists believed that India had a potential to achieve 10 percent growth if reforms are pursued vigorously.

BACKGROUND NOTE

After being ruled by a foreign power (East India Company), India seemed to have developed an aversion to foreign investment. For a long time after independence, domestic enterprises were protected from foreign companies through licensing, import barriers, and investment restrictions. As a result, instead of creating a lobby for foreign investment, development policy framework created bureaucratic mechanisms that acted as a barrier to a competitive business environment.

In contrast to India, China opened up its economy in late 1978, and FDI was authorized in 1979. FDI was considered as one of the best ways to introduce foreign capital and bring in modern technology and management skills. On the one hand, China provided incentives for export promotion and on the other hand it introduced strong import protection measures. But import protection measures began to hamper exports by increasing the cost of capital goods and of intermediate inputs required to produce goods for export. To overcome this problem, China insulated the exporting companies by allowing them to import goods outside the normal custom regime through duty-free export promotion zones that later turned out to be a major hub of development in China.

In China, while the large state-owned companies enjoyed protection, the private sector was subjected to

---

© ICFAI University Press & ICFAI Business School Case Development Centre, 2005. Reprinted with permission. www.icfaipress.org/ www.icfaipress.org/books.

[1] J. Srinivasan. "Playing Catch with China," *Business Line*, www.thehindubusinessline.com, May 14, 2002.

[2] Anupam Goswami, "FDI Filler," *Business India, www.businessIndia.com*, July 7–20, 2003. The figure for India was calculated according to new estimations of FDI using methodology recommended by IMF.

[3] C. Srikanth, "Foreign Direct Investment: Prescription for Growth," *Chartered Financial Analyst*, October 2000.

[4] Roy Anindya, "Going High Tech: India vs. China," *EffectiveExecutive*, April 2003.

TABLE II

India and China—
Selected Indicators

Source: International Financial
Statistics and China Statistical
Yearbook.

	1978		2000	
	China	**India**	**China**	**India**
GDP per capita (in constant U.S. dollars)	225.1	196.8	855.0	467.4
	(In percent of GDP)			
External trade and investment:				
Current account balance	0.3	0.1	1.9	−0.7
Exports of goods	4.6	5.1	19.1	9.2
Imports of goods	5.2	6.8	23.1	12.4
Net inward FDI flows	0.0	0.0	3.6	0.4
Net inward FDI flows (in percent of total investment)	0.0	0.1	9.8	1.9
Comparison of output:				
Primary sector value added	28.1	38.6	15.9	25.9
Secondary sector value added	48.2	25.6	50.9	26.1
Tertiary sector value added	23.7	35.7	33.2	48.0

strong market forces. China could levy lower taxes because it was able to keep the government spending at considerably low level of 14 percent of GDP compared to 33 percent in India. For example, in China, an individual taxpayer earning $4,000 paid a 10 percent marginal tax rate, compared to a 30 percent marginal tax rate on the same income in India.[5]

China's labor markets were highly flexible in the private sector. While workers in the state sector were accorded generous job guarantees, workers in the nonstate sector did not receive guaranteed employment. Employment in China grew at a rapid pace as firms could hire workers without fear of being stuck with unwanted labor in the future.

ENCOURAGING FDI—
THE CHINESE WAY

In the formative years of the reform process, China followed a selective approach towards FDI. While the sectors in which investments were sought received incentives like tariff exemptions and fiscal reductions, other sectors were subjected to severe constraints. However, since the mid-90s the level of protection has been progressively lowered. The average tariff rate came down from 43 percent in 1992 to 23 percent in 1996. In 1997, the average tariff on industrial products was reduced to 17 percent and the country had plans to bring it down to 10 percent in 2005.[6] In contrast India's average tariff rate

of 27 percent exceeded the average tariff rates of most other economies.[7] Also China established foreign exchange centers in the late 1980s and currency convertibility for current account operations in 1996, which made it easier for foreign firms to handle their operations in foreign currencies.

China's emergence as the world's largest manufacturer of consumer durables such as color TVs, washing machines, and refrigerators and its dominance in the hardware sector was possible largely because of large FDI inflows. Since 1998, China had focused on foreign investments in technology development and innovation aimed at transforming industries from low- to high-tech. Several tax incentives have been offered to lure foreign investors. Foreign companies that transferred advanced technology to China were exempted from both business and income tax. Foreign firms that increased their technology spending in China by more than 10 percent over the previous year were allowed to deduct 50 percent of the funds actually spent on technological development from their income-tax dues. In addition, if companies imported the technology, equipment, and components to upgrade industries that were on the priority list of the government, exemption from import duty was provided. In contrast, such incentives were not provided in India, and companies had to face many hurdles even for transfer of technology.

China's success in attracting FDI was attributed by many to its authoritarian political structure that allowed it to make policy changes more easily than the democratic set-up that prevailed in India. China could easily

[5] Bajpai Nirupam, "Two Versions of Openness," Center for International Development, www.cid.harvard.edu.
[6] Françoise Lemoline, "FDI and the Opening Up of China's Economy," www.cepii.fr.

[7] "Two Versions of Openness."

create a policy framework that was investor-friendly. Export processing zones set up with the sole purpose of facilitating production by multinationals for export from China into their home markets met with huge success.

Apart from being a big market and a source of skilled manpower, there were many aspects that gave China an edge over other developing economies. Many transnational companies (TNCs), while evaluating investment opportunities and locations, typically looked for the stability of the domestic currency because any depreciation of the currency increased their cost of debt servicing. China, because of its limited integration with global markets, could provide a stable currency and resisted the depreciation of its currency, the yuan, against currencies like the U.S. dollar.

Another favorable factor for China was the existence of more than 100,000 state-owned undertakings, which were earmarked for privatization. For many of these units, China looked for foreign capital that was expected to bring credibility to the venture and help them to secure loans from international agencies. These state-owned units were for sale at a low price and so were able to attract foreign capital.

However, many economists questioned the efficacy of the FDI figures that China had made public over the years. According to them, FDI figures that China claimed as flowing into the country were not foreign capital but China's own money coming in the form of foreign investment, through a process popularly called round-tripping.[8] The process was made possible through the holding companies that did not have any operating assets, except their mainland-registered ventures. These ventures were typically located in Hong Kong followed by British Virgin Islands, Cayman Islands, and Bermuda. In 2002, Hong Kong accounted for $19.2 billion of China's $52 billion in utilized FDI. Virgin Islands was the second largest source of FDI in China, with $6.15 billion. By including these investments as FDI, China, it was estimated had overstated its FDI figures by one-quarter to one-third.

THE INDIAN SCENARIO

Renowned Harvard economist Jeffrey Sachs once commented, "The fact that India trails China so much in attracting FDI is a matter of significant policy concern for India, because India is missing a lot of markets and a lot of capital investment that should be going there and losing it to China."[9]

India seemed to have realized the need to attract a much higher level of FDI especially in the context of achieving the 8 percent average annual GDP growth rate that it set itself in the Tenth Plan. But most of the economists, policymakers, and industry leaders expressed doubts about achieving this target considering the slowdown in investment, particularly in agriculture and manufacturing industry. According to a survey conducted[10] on the theme at the "India Economic Summit 2002—8% Growth for 20 Years. How?", as many as 59 percent of businessmen had forecast a 6 percent annual growth over the next five years and 37 percent expect the growth to be a mere 5 percent. Only 4 percent of the respondents were optimistic of achieving 8 percent growth rate. And 94 percent of the respondents felt that India might not be able to match China's competitive edge by 2007.

In countries like Taiwan and Korea the share of TNCs in exports was around 15 percent and in China it was 50 percent. However, in India TNC affiliates accounted for a mere 3 percent of its exports. Some attributed it to the existence of a large domestic market, but even China shared the same characteristic with India. China was able to push up TNCs' share in exports from 17 percent in 1991 to 50 percent in 2001. As UNCTAD's *World Investment Report, 2002* mentioned, the degree of success of a host country in attracting and upgrading export-oriented FDI depends critically on its ability to develop domestic capabilities. To benefit fully from export-oriented FDI, it advised the host countries to encourage linkages between foreign affiliates and local suppliers. The report mentioned, "Simply opening up the economy is no longer enough. There is a need to develop attractive configuration of locational advantages."

In a "Foreign Direct Investment Confidence Audit: India" (2001) organized by AT Kearney, a management consulting subsidiary of global technology services leader EDS, it was pointed out that[11] bureaucracy, slow pace in reforms, corruption, poor infrastructure, rigid labor laws, and the Indian government's role in the economy were the main reasons behind less FDI flow into India. The Indian government is yet to change its archaic labor laws that would give more flexibility in recruiting and firing employees. Also the basic infrastructure in the areas of power, ports, roads, or civil aviation remained in a poor state. While China built the required infrastructure to attract FDI for export production, India looked for FDI in infrastructure development. That was considered to be difficult to get because of the large investments, long gestation period, and complicated policies.

In India, economic reforms faced many roadblocks. Even in cases where approvals were granted, the

---

[8] Through this process, capital that originated from China went through another country, often an offshore tax haven, before re-entering the country as "foreign" investment. Such money could be from state and private-owned mainland firms, Chinese individuals or China-based Hong Kong, Taiwan, and foreign firms recycling earnings from their mainland operations.

[9] As told to in a videoconference on UNCTAD's annual World Investment Report, www.rediff.com, September 19, 2001.

[10] S. D. Nalk, "Turning the FDI Tide," *Business Line, www.thehindubusinessline.com*, December 13, 2002.

[11] "Going High Tech: India vs. China."

bureaucracy hampered implementation. As a result, only about 25 percent of FDI approvals translated into investments. There were cases where companies withdrew, even after the setting up of joint ventures. While China and other Asian countries were going all out to attract FDI, India seemed in no hurry to remove the hurdles. Large numbers of products were reserved for the small-scale sector, allowing only 24 percent FDI. Even the retail sector that offered opportunities to attract huge foreign investments was not opened up.

The World Bank's *World Business Environment Survey* noted that in India managements spend as much as 16 percent of their time dealing with government officials. Amit Mitra, secretary-general of the Federation of Indian Chambers of Commerce and Industry, cited[12] six issues that weigh more heavily on Indian companies than on their competitors: the cost of power, which was "two to three times higher" than elsewhere, "the cost of borrowing, red tape, and the corruption that went with it," onerous sales and local taxes, "slow and expensive transport," and inflexible labor markets. Paul O'Neill, who visited India as the U.S. Treasury Secretary to attend the Conference of Finance Ministers of Group of 20 countries, felt that India's English language skills and democracy should have made it a preferred destination for investors over China. However, while U.S. investments in China had gone up from $1.25 billion in 1997 to $1.6 billion in 2000, in India they declined from $737 million to $336 million over the same period. He said, "No one wants to spend time and capital fighting a system that is unfriendly to success and fears competition."[13]

In 2001 McKinsey, in its report "Achieving a Quantum Leap in India's Foreign Direct Investment" prepared for the American Chamber of Commerce in India, mentioned that India had the potential to attract $100 billion FDI in the next five years, at the rate of $20 billion

a year, and thereby enhance its GDP growth rate to over 8 percent per annum. To achieve this, the report suggested that the government remove sector-specific barriers, relax foreign ownership restrictions, and reduce red tape. McKinsey projected that another $49 billion FDI could come through the privatization programs.

Some differences between the performances of India and China could be attributed to the Chinese entrepreneurs in Hong Kong and Taiwan, who in order to escape rising wages in their respective home economies moved to China. But the difference in composition of GDP of the two economies was also considered to be a critical factor in determining the FDI flows. In 1980, the proportion of GDP originating in manufacturing industry was 48.5 percent in China whereas in India it was 24.2 percent. In India, services contributed 37.2 percent to GDP and the figure for China was 21.4 percent. In the next 20 years, despite considerable growth, the share of manufacturing did not rise in India. Instead, the entire decline in the share of agriculture was absorbed by services, unlike other countries where the decline in the share of agriculture in GDP was accompanied by a substantial expansion of manufacturing industry.

Typically for a developing country, it was believed that imports and exports would take off if a large portion of their output originated from the manufacturing sector rather than services. In India, neither the domestic nor foreign investments have taken off in the manufacturing sector. At the same time, the capacity of the formal services sector to absorb foreign investment was limited. Though the information technology sector showed some promise, the investments still remained small. It was felt that to improve FDI inflows, it is required to stimulate growth in the manufacturing sector. It was widely accepted that to increase the flow of FDI it is necessary to rationalize the tariffs, remove the small-scale industries reservation, reframe the exit policy and bankruptcy laws, and give a thrust to the privatization of public-sector undertakings. But the question that remains is: Will the government act?

---

[12] "The China Syndrome," *www.economist.com*, December 7, 2000.
[13] "Turning the FDI Tide."

Mergers and Acquisitions in the Russian Oil Sector— The FDI Factor

"Russia has become the world's largest oil producer and has taken a firm grip of global leadership in the export of hydrocarbon products."[1]

Russian Energy Minister Igor Yusufov

---

[1] Douglas Stinemetz, "Russian Oil Sector Rebound in Full Swing," www.haynesboone.com, 2003.

INTRODUCTION

Oil was found to be one of the important resources for strengthening Russia's presence in international relations.[2] Russia held the world's largest natural gas reserves. It had the second largest coal reserves and eighth largest oil reserves in the world. Russia was also the

---

[2] Ken Koyama, "The Energy Dimension in Russian Global Strategy," www.rice.edu/energy/publications.

world's largest exporter of natural gas, the second largest exporter of oil, and the third largest energy consumer.[3] Russia's vast natural resources drew immense interest from major players in the international market, including the United States, Europe, Asia, and OPEC. This resulted in a continued flow of foreign currency into the country. Russia accounted for 11.4 percent of the total oil production in 2003 and emerged seventh on estimations of the world's oil reserves.[4] Since the oil industry of Russia had been more privatized than that of the Persian Gulf states, the Russian oil industry had an entrepreneurial outlook in attracting foreign players for mergers, acquisitions, and joint ventures.[5]

EVOLVING PHASE FOR INVESTMENTS SINCE 1991

For the then Soviet Union, the Baku oil reserves of the Caspian and the oil fields of the North Caucasus remained the center for oil production till the Second World War. Thereafter, the Soviet planners began to accelerate the development of the Volga-Urals region. The fields in this region had access to transportation services and by the 1950s they accounted for 45 percent of the Soviet oil production. It was notable that the investments in this region paid off largely, allowing for a huge hike in Soviet oil production. The early years of the 1960s witnessed a series of discoveries in the Western Siberian region, culminating in the discovery of the super-giant Samotlor field in 1965. This rapid growth in oil production paved the way for the Soviet Union to begin ramping up the exports of oil. By the late 1960s the Soviet Union had replaced Venezuela as the second largest oil producer in the world. The arrival of low-cost Soviet oil in the market posed a threat to many Western oil companies.

Production from the Volga-Urals region peaked at close to 4.5 million barrels per day (bpd) in 1975 and the oil production at Western Siberian region underpinned an increase in total Soviet production from 7.6 million bpd in 1971 to 9.9 million bpd in 1975. This phenomenal growth in oil production from these fields was achieved by improper reservoir management practices, by drilling too many wells, and by injecting too much water. In 1988, Russia was the leading producer of oil, pumping 11.4 million bpd.[6] However, in mid-1988, production began to decline and the Soviet Union was forced to either reduce the oil consumption or to switch to other alternative sources of energy. This sudden "oil crisis" was mainly due to the excessive exploration of oil fields in Western Siberia during the 1970s and the employment of obsolete extraction techniques, which led to depletion of the oil wells. Even the Soviet technology was not capable of extracting oil as efficiently as the Western technology and lacked innovation.[7]

Moreover, a stable investment climate was also necessary for FDI flow into Russia as a continuum. The economic reforms of the late 1980s permitted limited foreign investments in the Soviet Union in the form of joint ventures (JVs). The first Joint Venture Law was enacted in 1987 and it restricted foreign ownership to 49 percent in Russia. However, the law was made flexible in 1991 and, since then, the foreign entities were allowed 100 percent ownership of subsidiaries in Russia. This Joint Venture Law did serve as a door to foreign direct investment in the Soviet Union, providing Russia wider access to Western capital, technology, and management know-how. However, with the collapse of the Soviet Union in December 1991, oil production in Russia fell precipitously, reaching an all-time low of 6 million barrels per day or around one-half of the Soviet-era peak. Following the downfall of the Soviet Union, the Law on Foreign Investments was passed. This law promised to treat foreign investments as favorably as domestic investments. In order to meet the rising demands from foreign oil investors for stronger legal guarantees, the Law on Oil and Gas, passed in July 1995, provided a basic framework for other laws and regulations pertaining to exploration, production, transportation, and security of oil and gas.[8]

Russia's oil production fell nearly 23 percent from 1992 to 1998 after the Soviet Union collapse, but made a remarkable comeback in 1999 and 2000 (Exhibits I and II). From 7.86 million bpd in 1992, production fell drastically to 6.07 million bpd in 1998 reflecting a substantial decline in oil drilling activities in Russia. However, the financial crisis in August 1998 led to a sharp devaluation of the ruble, which in turn reduced the production costs for Russian oil companies and boosted production from 1999 onwards. Russia, all of a sudden, looked very attractive to foreign investors.[9]

Late 1995 witnessed the promulgation of the Production-Sharing-Agreement Bill,[10] which provided opportunity for practical implementation of large-scale projects by foreign investors, mainly in the energy sector.

---

[3] "Russia—Country Analysis Briefs," www.eia.doc.gov, May 2004.
[4] "BP's Statistical Review of World Energy," www.bp.com, June 2004.
[5] Kiesling Lyne and Joseph Becker, "Russia's Role in Shifting the World Oil Market," www.bcsia.ksg.harvard.edu, May 2002.
[6] "History of Oil in Russia," www.sibneft.com.

[7] "Soviet Union Oil Field Mismanagement," http://reference.allrefer.com/county-guide/story/Russia.
[8] David Johnson, "Foreign Investment," www.reference.allefer.com.
[9] "Russia's Boost in Oil Production Grabs World Attention," www.cdi.org/russia, March 27, 2002.
[10] A PSA allows an oil company to develop fields and produce oil according to detailed agreements between the oil company and the host government.

EXHIBIT I

Russian Oil Production
and Consumption,
1992–2000

Source: www.eia.doe.gov.

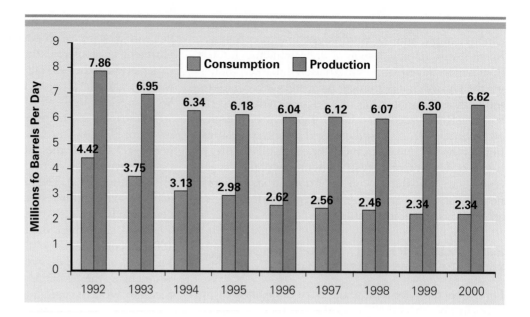

EXHIBIT II

Russian Oil Production
and Consumption,
1992–2004

Source: www.eia.doe.gov.

Russian government drops its oil
production growth forecast for
2004 from around 10 percent
(December 2003) to as low as
2.5 percent (early January 2004)
following the Yukos Affair, the
December Duma elections, and
talk of a new oil taxation policy.
In late January 2004, Minenergo
estimated growth of 6–8 percent.

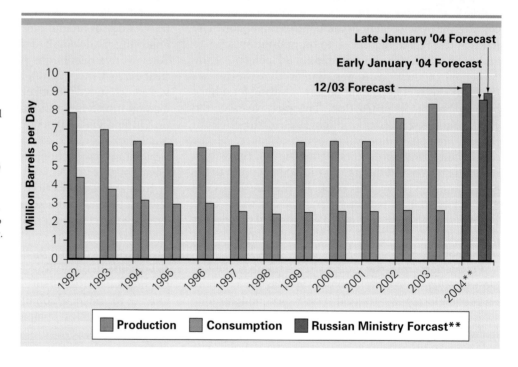

This bill lifted many financial impediments to investments by dismantling excise and customs duty on oil exports by joint ventures. Meanwhile, several state-owned oil enterprises were already converted into different categories of oil companies by early 1993. The formation was followed by domestic acquisitions of medium-to-small-size companies by the Russian oil majors, resulting in the emergence of 10 vertically integrated companies by 2003—Lukoil, Yukos, Surgutneftgas, Rosneft, Tyumen oil, Sibneft, Slavneft, Sidanco, Bashneft, and Tatneft.

These oil majors also introduced transparency in their corporate governance laws and showed signs of adapting to the Western management culture. In the early 1990s there was imposition of high tax rates, which deterred investments by foreign companies in the oil sector. This tax rate was slashed to a flat income tax rate of 13 percent in 2001, and rapid reforms in the legal and administrative environment of Russia attracted the European Union and the United States. In 2002, Russia was granted "market economy" status.

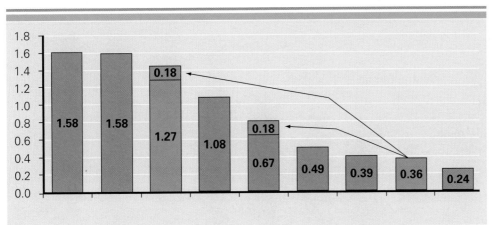

EXHIBIT III

Average Daily Crude Oil Production (million barrels in 2003)

Source: "Russia and Europe," Policy Summit, Brussels, May 14, 2004.

Analysts believe that foreign countries invest their funds in Russia mainly in search of natural resources, new markets, or for obtaining higher efficiency levels. According to studies by UNCTAD, the natural resources of Russia hold considerable potential for foreign investments.[12] The surge in oil production from late 1998 followed by the lifting of several restrictions on investment served as key drivers in increasing foreign direct investments in subsequent years.

THE FDI WAVE TAKES OFF

Since 1999, the increase in crude oil output along with low production costs in Russia had not escaped the attention of major international oil companies. The greatest achievement for Russia was in 2002 when U.K.-based British Petroleum announced its plans of acquiring a 50 percent stake in Russian Tyumen oil, TNK. This joint venture marked the beginning of the FDI era in Russia, and the TNK-BP merger was viewed as a case that tested the viability of "strategic partnerships" between Russian and European oil companies. TNK was originally formed in 1995 by a Russian governmental consolidation of eight Russian oil production enterprises, which were subsequently privatized, via a number of auctions, in 1998. TNK, prior to this merger, was ranked among the top 15 oil companies in the world and its holdings stretched from Sakhlain in the east to Lesycahnsk, Ukraine, in the west. This joint venture would make the Russian oil company technologically more sound and financially supportive for large-scale investments.

This merger move was approved by the antitrust ministry of Russia on August 25, 2003, laying the foundation

stone for the creation of the third largest oil producer in Russia and the 10th largest oil company in terms of global oil production (Exhibit III).[13] British Petroleum agreed to pay $ 6.15 billion for the 50 percent stake in TNK, and in September 2003, the assets of TNK and BP were merged into one company. The combined firm was expected to produce 1.2 million barrels of crude oil per day, mainly in western Siberia.[14]

This merger approval sent a positive signal to the West about the Russian oil sector, which had immense potential. This also symbolized the combinative control over management in the Russian oil counterparts by the foreign stakeholders. BP believed that Russia was a key source to the world's oil supply and by utilizing Russia's natural resources to the fullest it would be possible to penetrate into international markets. Sir John Brown, BP president, said that foreign investors would now express "greater trust in Russia than before."[15] TNK-BP owned five oil refineries with the overall processing capacity of 50 million tons annually and the new holding company took control over a chain of filling stations in Russia and Ukraine (Exhibit IV).[16] In 2003, TNK-BP posted growth of 14 percent and TNK-BP's five year strategy set forth the company's overall objectives from 2004 to 2008—including aggressive growth in crude oil production combined with active reserve replenishment, increased investment in technology across business, and improvement of the quality of oil field services.[17]

---

[12] "Foreign Investment in Russia—Is It Taking Off?" www.unctad.org, May 2003.

[13] Robert Dudly, "Doing Business in Russia," Russia and Europe Policy Summit, May 14, 2004.
[14] www.tnk-bp.com/press/media, August 26, 2003.
[15] BP President, "Merger with TNK Will Provide Stability on World Energy Markets," Pravda®, September 2003.
[16] "TNK-BP Profits Steeply Increase," PRAVDA.RU, June 2004.
[17] "Insight TNK-BP," www.tnk-bp.com/press/insight, September 2004.

EXHIBIT IV

TNK-BP Asset
Overview

Source: "Russia and Europe,"
Policy Summit, Brussels, May 14,
2004.

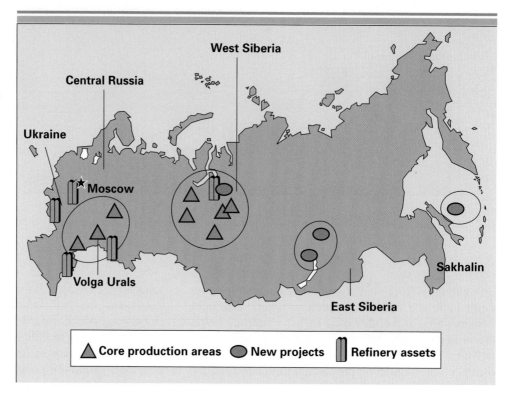

YUKOS—ITS DOOM

Around the same time when the TNK-BP merger took place, Yukos oil, the second largest Russian oil company in terms of production, was gradually spreading its investment net and was engaged in merger talks with Sibneft in early 2003. It would be another mega-merger of two renowned oil companies. Yukos was originally formed by the Russian state in 1993 from the combination of the two Soviet-era companies, Yuganskneftgas and Kuibyshevnefteorgsintez. Later in 1995–96 it underwent privatization and the reins of this company were passed to Mikhail Khodorkovsky.

From 1996 till 1999, Yukos had a poor reputation among other companies listed in the stock exchange, and the market capitalization was below $200 million. However, in the course of a few years, Yukos was transformed into the largest and most efficient company in the Russian oil sector, and this position would be reemphasized once it acquired Sibneft.[18] On August 14, 2003, Russian authorities finally approved the $11 billion merger of Yukos and Sibneft, creating the world's fourth largest private oil company worth $ 35billion (Exhibit V). The competitive advantage for both the companies was their operating efficiency in terms of

reduction of costs, which acted as a precursor to become the largest integrated oil company in terms of crude oil exports in Russia after the merger approval (Exhibit VI).[19]

However, Sibneft withdrew from the merger plan in the latter half of the same year after the onset of tax investigations into Yukos, which was followed by the detention of the CEO, Mikhail Khodorkovsky, in October 2003. The ministry even announced its plans to sell the company's core production unit, Yuganskeneftgaz,[20] to cover the tax claims. The merger, which could have created an oil colossus (Exhibit VII), was called off and this unexpected fate of Yukos was seen as the outcome of the conflict between the government and business class of Russia.[21] The sudden news of the merger dismissal at an early stage also had substantial impact on the world energy markets. Another major setback, immediately after the fallout of Yukos, was the immediate closure of one of the biggest proposed deals in Russia—the acquisition of a stake in Yukos Sibneft by Exxon Mobil in order to pose a challenge to the one BP had in TNK-BP.

---

[18] "Yukos Oil: A Corporate Governance Success Story?"
www.gsb.columbia.edu/journals, *The Chazen Web Journal of International Business 2003*.

[19] "Integration and Consolidation in Russian Oil Industry—Mikhail Khordorkovsky," June 2, 2003.
[20] The authorities claim back taxes amounting to $3 billion for the year 2000, $6 billion for 2001, and $2 billion on Yuganskeneftegaz production unit.
[21] "Russian Economy: The Conoco Two-Step," www.viewswire.com, October 1, 2004.

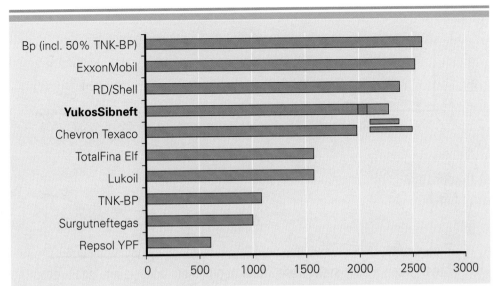

EXHIBIT V

Major Private
International Oil
Companies (Crude oil
production in 2002,
thousand bpd)

Source: Yukos—Integration and
consolidation in Russian oil
industry.

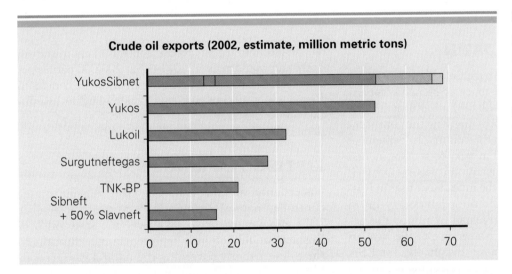

EXHIBIT VI

Russia's Crude Oil
Exports (2002,
estimate, million metric
tons)

Source: Yukos—Integration and
consolidation in Russian oil
industry.

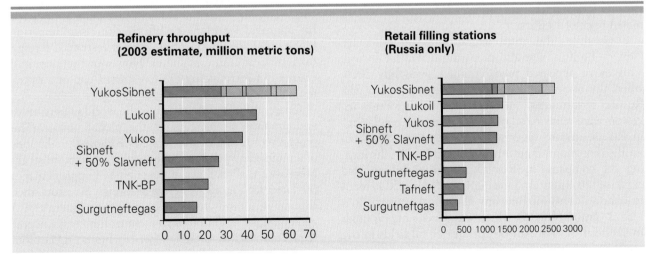

EXHIBIT VII

Russia's Refinery Throughput (2003 estimate, million metric tons)

Source: Yukos—Integration and consolidation in Russian oil industry.

EXHIBIT VIII

Russia's FDI Inflows
($ billions)

Russia's FDI Stock
($ billions)

Source: "The Great Transformation: Russia's Return to the World Economy," www.som.hw.ac.uk, January 2004.

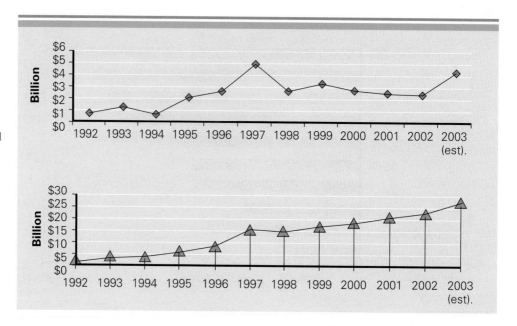

BREAK OF A NEW DAWN

Though the Yukos affair did create a cloud of uncertainty regarding FDI in Russia, the move of French company Total SA (formerly TotalFinaElf SA) into Russia in early 2004 was a noteworthy incident, marking the consistent flow of foreign currency into the country. In September 2004, Total SA was engaged in talks to acquire its first stake in a Russian oil company, an acquisition well planned taking into account the investment risks in Russia and guided by the 50 percent acquisition of BP in TNK in 2003. Apprehension remained around this acquisition, which would be a reassurance to the Russian economy after the Yukos failure. Eventually, Total SA announced it would acquire a 25 percent stake in the Russian independent gas producer Novatek for an estimated price of 1 billion.[22]

Meanwhile, the third largest U.S. oil company, Conoco-Phillips, was also preparing to bid for Lukoil. This move appeared predetermined since July 2004, when the two companies sought the approval of the Russian government.[23] It was a signal that foreign investors were ready to adapt to the changing regulations in Russia, despite several political conflicts. Conoco-Phillips bought a 7.6 percent stake into Lukoil (the leading oil company in Russia) for $1.99 billion and expressed its intention of acquiring a further 20 percent in Lukoil.[24] This oil company also bought a stake in a Lukoil venture, Russco, which was developing oil fields in Western Siberia. Russco operates 16 oil fields in the

Timan-Pechora region; production was likely to start in 2007 and would peak in 2011–12 at 200,000 barrels per day.[25] Analysts observed that the investment climate in Russia was "really positive" and Conoco-Phillips and Total's move did exercise an "affirmative" vote of confidence after the Yukos crisis (Exhibit VIII).

LIFTING THE RING FENCE

Uncertainty around Gazprom, the Russian state-controlled natural gas monopoly, as to its September 2004 announcement to take over the state oil firm Rosneft, would certainly represent a modification to the rules currently governing the natural gas sector in Russia. Another astonishing move came September 14, 2004, when the Russian president announced his approval for plans to lift the long-standing ring fence on shares in Gazprom, which restricted foreign ownership of Gazprom shares. However, there are still chances of introducing an investment cap of a maximum of 49 percent.

Gazprom holds 20 percent of the world's gas reserves and produces 16 percent of the global output. The prospective lifting of this fence encourages predictions of a multibillion-dollar demand for the Gazprom stock. Moreover, this takeover of Rosneft by Gazprom makes the latter look more attractive to foreign investors since this move intends to increase the government's 39.3 percent stake in Gazprom to a controlling stake, a prerequisite to loosen foreign ownership limits on Gazprom shares. Takeover of Rosneft would transform Gazprom into a dominant integrated energy supplier in the inter-

---

[22] "Total Makes a Move in Russia's Oil Patch," *BusinessWeek* online.
[23] "Russia Economy: The Conoco Two Step."
[24] Ibid.

[25] Ibid.

national market and some analysts even view this move as a precursor to a dramatic step in Russian history—the takeover of the Yukos core production unit by a Gazprom to create a new conglomerate under Kremlin control.

MOVING AHEAD

The Russian oil majors were engaged in giving themselves a new look by adopting US GAAP in financial planning and acquiring technology from foreign companies via mergers and takeovers. The oil exports in Russia trended upwards since 1998 and by 2000 had surpassed 4 million bpd. The projections indicated that Russian total oil transport capacity needs would increase to at least 7 million bpd by 2012.[26] The increase in oil production was noteworthy, showing a 38 percent increase from 1999 reaching 8.43 million bpd in 2003. The restructuring undertaken by the privatized vertically integrated Russian companies was chiefly responsible for such a striking achievement in this oil production pattern.

Russia's refusal to meet OPEC's demand to cut oil production, and its focus on increasing market share, would aid in repositioning the Russian oil majors as important players in the future global oil markets. Andrei Illarionov, an economic advisor to the Russian president, stated that OPEC would be "historically doomed" and that markets would overcome "price fixing agreements." Analysts believed that the Russian oil sector could destabilize OPEC once it regained the status of being the world's key oil exporter. This incident was likely to undermine OPEC's influence on world oil pricing. If the productivity in Russia increases in such leaps and bounds through foreign assistance, then there could be chances of the widening of the price differential between OPEC and Russia. This in turn would lead to the ineffectiveness of OPEC in controlling worldwide oil production.

The headline deals were mostly seen in the energy sector, and it is expected that Russia would offer massive opportunities in this sector even in the future. Indeed, analysts contend that these foreign ventures were only the first of the several waves of the merger and acquisition activity.[27]

---

[26] Peter Baker, "Russia State Gas, Oil Firms Merge," Washington-postcom, September 15, 2004.

[27] "Russia Economy: Opening Gazprom on the State's Terms," E??? Views wire, September 16, 2004.

Ireland in 2004

INTRODUCTION

In the early 2000s, Ireland was considered one of the most globally competitive economies in the world. Despite its small size (population of just 3.7 million), Ireland had emerged as an attractive investment destination. A combination of factors had turned the Irish economy into a "Celtic Tiger." These included tough cuts in government spending since the late 1980s, "National Wage Partnership Programs"[1] which fostered cooperative industrial relations, reduction in taxes, targeted government programs to attract foreign direct investment (FDI), and financial support from the European Union (EU). One of the most open economies in Europe, Ireland had also developed a solid reputation for its quality of life.

BACKGROUND NOTE

Early History

From 1800 to 1921, Ireland was an integral part of the United Kingdom. During the period 1846–48, the Irish economy was overshadowed by a severe economic depression. Mass famine spawned the first wave of Irish emigration to the United States. In 1858, the Irish Republican Brotherhood was founded as a secret society dedicated to armed rebellion against the British. A political counterpart, the Home Rule Movement,[2] was created in 1874, advocating constitutional change for independence. Galvanized by the leadership of Charles Stewart Parnell,[3] the party was able to force the British government to introduce several home rule bills after

---

[1] One of the most significant moves by the Irish government was designing the "National Partnership," a short-term agreement signed by the government, employers, and employees to put national interests above individual gains. Launched in 1987 and renewed every three years, the first national partnership agreement put the cap on wage increases at 3 percent but also sharply cut personal income taxes. Left with more take-home pay, employees were relatively satisfied. At the same time, Ireland's comparatively low wages worked as a powerful tool in the government's efforts to attract FDI.

[2] In 1870, Isaac Butt (a prominent Unionist lawyer interested in land reform) founded the Home Government Association (Home Rule League) as a constitutional movement. In the election of 1874, it returned about 60 members to Parliament. The movement was tolerated rather than encouraged by various groups of Irish nationalists. It was not fully supported by the Roman Catholic clergy until the 1880s.
[3] Charles Stewart Parnell, the squire of Avondale, County Wicklow, made two attempts to get elected to Parliament—one in Wicklow, another in Dublin, and was on both occasions defeated. Then in 1875, he replaced John Martin in Meath. He was regarded as a nice gentleman, who would create no sensation in the House of Commons.

Annual Data	2003	Historical Averages (%)	1999–2003
Population (million)	3.9	Population growth	1.4
GDP (US$ billion; market exchange rate)	149.4	Real GDP growth	7.1
GDP (US$ billion; PPP)	129.7	Real domestic demand growth	5.3
GDP per head (US$; market exchange rate)	37,911	Inflation	4.0
GDP per head (US$; purchasing power parity)	32,916	Current-account balance/GDP	−0.7
Exchange rate (av) £:US$	0.9	FDI inflows/GDP	18.0

EXHIBIT I

Fact Sheet

Source: Economist Intelligence Unit, June 11, 2004.

1885. The turn of the century witnessed a surge of interest in Irish nationalism, including the founding of Sinn Féin (meaning "We Ourselves") political party. British attempts to smash Sinn Féin ignited the Anglo-Irish War of 1919–21.

The war resulted in the Anglo-Irish treaty of 1921, leading to Ireland's independence from Britain. In 1932, Eamon de Valera, the political leader of the forces, which were initially opposed to the treaty, became the president of Ireland. A new Irish constitution was enacted in 1937. The government formally declared Ireland a republic in 1948. Subsequently, two parties, namely Fianna Fáil and Fine Gael, became the country's largest political parties.

The Irish economy was in bad shape at the time of independence. Protectionism discouraged foreign trade and foreign investment. As exports fell, living standards declined. Per capita income growth lagged far behind other countries in Western Europe.

During World War II, 99 percent of Irish exports went to the United Kingdom. Heavily dependent on British markets, the Irish economy relied on agriculture, which the British government actively encouraged. But the government's unimaginative economic policies worsened Ireland's plight.

From the 1950s, Ireland's economic recovery began as restrictions on foreign ownership were removed. In 1956, tax-free status was granted to export-oriented firms. The signing of the Anglo-Irish Trade Agreement in 1965[4] led to rapid growth in foreign investment. By the late 1960s, Ireland had become an industrialized nation, largely due to foreign investments. Growing com-

petition led to a shakeout and many Irish firms collapsed. Car assembly was wiped out and the clothing, textile, and chemical industries suffered badly, leading to thousands of job losses.

Recent History

The Irish economy went from strength to strength in the 1970s, with the gradual freeing of trade and the diversification of Irish exports away from the United Kingdom, towards other European countries. In 1973, Ireland became a member of the European Economic Community (EEC).[5] This gave Ireland access to European markets, agricultural subsidies, and capital. The surge of inward investment that followed Ireland's EU membership had a dramatic impact on the Irish economy.

The early 1980s marked a period of retrenchment. Employment in public services was frozen. Ireland did not make some of the costly political errors of continental Europe at that time, such as making unrealistic pension commitments and creating an overprotected labor market. In the late 1980s, social partnership agreements among employees, employers, and government kept the wage increase well below the European average while productivity grew at a rate significantly above the European average.

---

[4] The Anglo-Irish Free Trade Area (AIFTA) agreement of 1965 was an arrangement between Ireland and the United Kingdom. It symbolized a growing maturity in the historic ties between the two countries. It also prepared the way for both countries to join the European Economic Community (EEC) in 1973.

[5] Ireland became a member of the European Economic Community (EEC) in January 1973 following almost a decade of unsuccessful attempts to gain entry. The Irish application to the EEC commenced as early as 1961 at the time when United Kingdom sought to gain membership. The process stalled, however, in 1963 due to strong French opposition to British membership. Since Ireland was heavily dependent on Britain economically, the Irish government felt that it should remain outside the Community until Britain was admitted. Ireland's application was reactivated a second time in 1967, but the French again blocked negotiations. In the late 1960s, the application was accepted and negotiations commenced. Ireland acceded to the EEC on January 1, 1973, after holding a constitutional referendum.

Most of the labor reforms introduced in the 1980s were by left-wing parties. It was during this time that labor parties started finding their place in government, leaving behind Fianna Fail and Fine Gael, which had dominated the government since Ireland's independence.

In the early 2000s, a new industrial policy was introduced with a focus on new sectors like pharmaceuticals, financial services, and electronics. Government subsidies of unprofitable units were reduced. In the economic policy of 2002, the country encouraged competition in telecommunications, electricity, gas, and transport. A Communications Regulation Act was enacted in April 2002, followed by the establishment of a commission to regulate the telecommunications sector.

The return of the Fianna Fail (Soldiers of Destiny) and Progressive Democrats to the coalition government after the May 2002 parliamentary election was seen by many as a vote of confidence in the center-right policies of the previous administration. But some cynical observers believed it was more to do with a lack of alternatives. The election saw an increasing number of independent candidates being elected to the 166-member Dail Eireann (House of Representatives), indicating significant levels of dissatisfaction among the electorate on various issues. Rather than rely on the support of these independents, Fianna Fail, which won 80 seats in the Dail, again opted for the Progressive Democrats to make up a parliamentary majority. This provided an element of policy continuity as well as political stability.

Economic growth slowed in the first nine months of 2003, compared with 2002. Investment, exports, and imports showed negative growth. The manufacturing sector was the hardest hit. Wage and price inflation continued to be moderate. Irish equities rebounded strongly in 2003, in line with developments elsewhere in Europe and North America.

The 2003 budget saw significant cuts in public spending. Although income taxes were not increased, there were increases in stamp duty and levies on financial institutions, as well as increases in tax on diesel, cigarettes, and alcohol. An increase in government spending of 5.7 percent was projected. In order to keep to this, spending cuts across a broad range of public services were announced with health and capital spending programs being heavily hit.

A surge in revenue towards the end of 2003, combined with stricter expenditure control, ensured that the budget almost balanced for the full year. The 2004 budget did not have major surprises except for the announcement of a radical decentralization plan for the civil service. An insurance claims board was established to reduce insurance costs for businesses. The proposed liberalization of the transport sector threatened to provoke industrial action in state-owned monopolies.

ECONOMIC POLICIES

In the 1980s, the Irish government pursued a cautious fiscal policy to ensure compliance with the criteria for Economic and Monetary Union (EMU) prescribed by the Maastricht Treaty.[6] By lowering the annual budget deficit and the level of national debt, the government attempted to create a macroeconomic climate favorable to foreign direct investment (FDI) and private-sector growth. The government received broad political support for privatization. The country made a significant break from the past when protectionism through tariffs and subsidies had been important in key sectors like energy, communication, and transportation.

By the early 2000s, the government's direct role in the economy was sharply reduced and limited to a few key industries, like the state-owned airline Aer Lingus, the state-owned electricity distributor ESB, and Bord Gas, the state-owned natural-gas distributor. The government intended to privatize all the companies in the next few years.

Irish GDP grew at 9.9 percent per annum over the five-year period 1996–2000. In 2001, U.S.-owned companies provided 5 percent of Ireland's total employment, and half of all exports. Thirteen percent of Irish GDP depended on exports to the United States, a figure five times the euro-zone average. The £20 billion ($17.6 billion) chemicals and bulk pharmaceuticals sector also depended heavily on the U.S. market. With exports making up 95 percent of GDP and heavily concentrated in the technology sector, the economy was hard hit by the global slowdown in the demand for information and communication technology in 2001.[7]

GDP growth slowed in 2003 against a backdrop of weak global demand, reduced corporate profitability, much lower public spending, and sharply contracting investment. Private consumption fell in the first half of 2003 as a result of more moderate wage increases and higher household savings ratio. In 2004–05, a more optimistic international outlook and stronger jobs and incomes growth was expected to boost private spending growth. Government consumption growth was expected to slow further from the high rates of recent years, due to expenditure cuts and freezes on public-sector recruitment. Following a fall in fixed capital formation in 2003, investment was expected to pick up in 2004 as business confidence rose, driven by still low interest rates and larger inflows of foreign capital.

[6] In December 1991, in the small town of Maastricht in the Netherlands, the EU established the Maastricht Treaty, which provided for a single European currency, common citizenship, common foreign and security policy, a more effective European Parliament, and a common labor policy.
[7] Industrial Development Agency of Ireland, August 2002.

EXHIBIT II

Ireland: Macro
Economic Indicators

Source: Economist Intelligence
Unit, June 11, 2004.

	2000	2001	2002	2003
GDP per head ($ at PPP)	28,400	30,231	32,220	33,120
GDP (% real change pa)	10.08	6.19	6.92	2.20
Government consumption (% of GDP)	12.61	13.43	13.64	13.90
Budget balance (% of GDP)	4.50	1.70	−0.30	−0.20
Consumer prices (% change pa; av)	5.57	4.86	4.65	3.50
Public debt (% of GDP)	39.30	36.70	33.70	32.40
Labor costs per hour (USD)	12.50	13.28	15.09	18.80
Recorded unemployment (%)	4.30	3.93	4.43	4.70
Current-account balance/GDP	−0.37	−0.66	−0.74	−1.30
Foreign-exchange reserves (US$ million)	5,360	5,587	5,415	4,079

EXHIBIT III

GDP Growth: A
Comparative Analysis

Source: IMD World Competi-
tiveness Yearbook 2002; OECD
Economic Outlook No. 72,
December 2002.

Country	Real GDP Growth, 2001	Real GDP Growth, 2002	2003 (Estimated)
Ireland	**6.8%**	**3.6%**	**3.6%**
UK	2.3	1.5	2.2
France	2.0	1.0	1.9
Germany	0.7	0.4	1.5
Netherlands	1.4	0.1	1.6
Spain	2.7	1.8	2.5
Portugal	1.9	0.4	1.5
USA	1.1	2.3	2.6
Japan	−0.7	−0.7	0.8

Fiscal stability had become a major concern, after a large budget surplus disappeared owing to a period of laxity before the 2002 general election. Following the sharp budgetary deterioration in 2000–02, when a surplus of 4.5 percent of GDP in 2000 turned to a deficit of 0.3 percent in 2002, the general budget balance stabilized in 2003, owing to stronger revenue and lower spending growth.

While Ireland was experiencing much higher inflation rates than the other members of the European Union, its ability to deal with price rise was severely limited by the membership of the euro zone. The European Central Bank (ECB) set the interest rate for the 12 euro-zone countries. While the ECB favored a low interest rate policy to stimulate growth in countries like Germany, such policies created inflationary pressures in Ireland. The ECB interest rate stood at 2.5 percent in March 2003, while Irish inflation was around 5 percent.

INDUSTRY

Irish industry accounted for 24 percent of the country's GDP, 80 percent of the value of annual exports, and approximately 27 percent of employment.

Ireland's indigenous manufacturing base was relatively small. Traditionally, industries such as food and beverages, textiles, paper, nonmetallic minerals, and machinery had dominated. More recently there had been rapid growth in new export-oriented chemicals as well as electronics engineering industries. Most of the new capital and skill-intensive companies were subsidiaries of large U.S. and European multinationals and were heavily dependent on imported inputs.

Since Ireland's accession to the European Union, the structure of its industry had changed dramatically, with the growing dominance of high-technology, foreign-owned industries. Pharmaceuticals accounted for 25 percent of Ireland's total exports. In 2003, nine out of the world's top 10 pharmaceutical companies operated in Ireland. Ireland was a major exporter of computer software. The country was also emerging as an important center for back-office processing and financial services.

The government's stated policy was to respond quickly to the problems of businesses. When Microsoft had decided not to locate a key Web hosting operation in Ireland in 1998 because of insufficient connectivity, the government responded by a speedy deregulation of the telecom sector. Subsequently, Ireland had become a very important country in Microsoft's global network.

The software industry in Ireland consisted of about 800 companies employing over 25,000 people. Software production was estimated to be in excess of €9 billion. The people involved in the industry were employed in a broad range of activities—development and customization, translation, production and distribution, and technical support. The estimated breakdown of the different sectors was: digital media/e-learning (33 percent), software tools/system software (26 percent), banking and finance (19 percent), telecommunications (13 percent), and the Internet (9 percent). The industry was concentrated mainly in the Dublin area with smaller clusters in Limerick, Galway, and Cork.

The software industry was made up of three categories of companies; MNCs, Irish companies that were engaged in exporting, and Irish companies that served the domestic market. Contrary to the popular view, many of the successful indigenous software companies did not result from spin-offs from multinationals but had evolved from finance/insurance companies.

MNCs accounted for almost 90 percent of industry output and were using Ireland as a European localization and translation base. They not only republished and distributed software from their Irish base but were also involved in software localization, translating applications into the major European languages and packaging these products for sale. As a result, some 60 percent of all PC package software sold in Europe each year was produced in Ireland.

The MNCs in the Irish software sector included most of the top independent software companies in the world, the top package software vendors in Europe, and the top computer service groups in Europe. The famous names included Microsoft, IBM, Oracle, Hitachi, and Siemens Nixdorf, Berlitz, Modus Media, and SAP.

Ireland's IT industry received a big boost when in 1999, it was selected by the prestigious Massachusetts Institute of Technology as the European location for its famous Media Lab research center. Nicholas Negroponte, the center's director and a widely acclaimed expert in digital technology, explained that he had been impressed by Ireland's "great respect for madness" and its "seamless, anti-establishment and chaotic" attitude to innovation.

Ireland was one of the top three manufacturers of pharmaceuticals and nonbulk chemicals in the world, with virtually all the 20 largest multinational pharmaceutical companies operating within its borders. The industry accounted for export sales equivalent to approximately one-third of GDP, 1.5 percent of total employment, and corporation tax payments of over €700 million in 2001. The government's ethical dilemma over stem cell research highlighted the difficulties of marrying economic imperatives with moral concerns in Ireland, where a strong pro-life lobby remained influential. A ban on research on stem cells harvested from embryos was likely to slow down the development of the biotechnology industry in Ireland. Recognizing this, the government had released funding for the creation of a €15 million gene therapy research institute—the Regenerative Medicine Institute—to be based in Galway in western Ireland.

Despite its tremendous success in attracting high-tech industries, Ireland lagged behind in cutting edge R&D. In 2002, industry spending on R&D in Ireland stood at 1.01 percent, below the European average of 1.19 percent and well below the United States (1.98 percent) and Japan (2.18 percent).[8] The share of venture capital invested in early stage development and expansion in Ireland was lower than the European average and significantly less than that of the United States.

Business in Ireland faced a structural cost disadvantage in relation to competitors in both Europe and the United States. Europe favored heavy regulation to protect consumers' interests. In the United States, consumers were encouraged to sue firms to enforce their rights. Irish business faced the worst of both worlds. It had to bear the high cost of EU-level regulation and the Irish law, while also absorbing very high insurance costs owing to the highest litigation rates in Europe. In an effort to lower insurance costs, parliament had enacted legislation to create a Personal Injuries Assessment Board (PIAB). The board would decide the size of damages in claims where the insurers accepted liability—allowing all parties to avoid the expense of going to court—thus cutting insurance companies' costs and lowering premiums for businesses and consumers. Although the board was due to be up and running in 2004, it was likely to be challenged in the courts on the grounds that it limited a constitutional right to due process.

---

[8] Stephanie, Gordon. "Ireland Sets Up Committee to Boost Industry R&D Spend," *EE Times UK*, February 26, 2003.

Ireland was still short of broadband capacity, according to a recently released report by the Information Society Commission, a body established by the government to provide independent advice. Although Internet use had increased by 75 percent during 2000–03 (more than 10 percent of the population used the Internet on a daily basis and over 30 percent used it at least once a week), Ireland remained a broadband laggard. Broadband penetration stood at only 0.25 percent of the population, compared with an EU average of 4.65 percent and 10.44 percent in the case of broadband leaders such as Denmark. Two in every five small to medium-sized companies[9] that tried to upgrade their Internet connections could not—either because the costs were prohibitive or service so poor as not to warrant the extra spending. However, there were signs that costs might come down. In December 2003, Eircom, the former state monopoly which maintained ownership of the infrastructure, dropped its wholesale connection fee to the three other existing broadband providers. At the same time, the government announced it would spend €140 million on an initiative to increase broadband use in areas likely to be ignored by commercial providers—specifically smaller towns and villages outside Dublin to prevent a "digital divide" within the country.

Ireland continued to face difficulties in liberalizing the transport sector. Plans to introduce greater competition in the airport and Dublin bus market had provoked the trade unions. The unions threatened strike action at Dublin airport to coincide with an informal meeting of EU justice ministers, in an attempt to force the government to back down. Although the strike action was suspended, the threat remained. In addition to these concerns, major infrastructure projects continued to slip even further behind schedule. The long-awaited Luas light-rail system in the capital, originally due to be operational by the end of 2003, again missed its deadline and looked unlikely to run before June 2004. Major motorway extensions and upgrades, as set out in the National Development Plan in 2000, had seen their completion date slip to 2007.

Tourism was one of Ireland's fastest growing sectors, accounting for an estimated 7 percent of annual GNP and revenues of over $2 million per annum. The sector supported an estimated 125,000 jobs in 2001. There were more than 270 golf courses in Ireland. Ireland's tourism sector received substantial financial assistance from the EU.

FOREIGN TRADE

Ireland was far more dependent on the United Kingdom and the United States for trade than its euro-zone counterparts. When combined, the United States and the United Kingdom accounted for 34.7 percent of Irish exports in 2001, compared with 39.8 percent for the EU (excluding the United Kingdom).

Exports consisted mainly of live cattle, meat, dairy produce, textiles, machinery and transport equipment, and more recently chemicals and electronics. Main destinations were the United Kingdom (22 percent of 2001 total), United States (16.8 percent), Germany (12.7 percent), France (6.1 percent), and Belgium (4.8 percent).

Imports consisted mainly of petroleum and petroleum products, foodstuffs, chemicals, manufactured goods and components, machinery and transport equipment. Quantitative restrictions applied to the import of some clothing, textiles, and tableware products from certain non-EU countries. Quantitive restrictions also applied to unprocessed foodstuffs. Main sources were the United Kingdom (37.4 percent of 2001 total), the United States (15 percent), Germany (6.3 percent), France (4.8 percent), and the Netherlands (3.8 percent).

Ireland's current-account deficit was expected to widen in 2004, as savings rates fell. Despite particularly strong growth in services exports (Ireland became the largest exporter in the world of services per head in 2002), a larger deficit on the income account would more than offset the growth of the trade surplus.

The seasonally adjusted cumulative value of Ireland's exports in the first three quarters of 2003 was €60.9 billion, a decrease of 15.8 percent over the same period in 2002. The value of exports overstated the extent of the slump, as it reflected price decreases caused by the appreciation of the euro. 2003 was one of the worst years for Irish exports in decades. The last year in which an annual decline in exports was recorded was 1962.

Significant year-on-year export declines were recorded across the key high-tech sectors. Exports of electrical machinery were down year on year by 58.7 percent to €3.8 billion, but decreases were also recorded on organic chemicals (down 18.5 percent to £11.2 billion), medical and pharmaceutical equipment (down 9.9 percent to €10.2 billion) and computer equipment (down 18 percent to 10.5 billion).

Exports to the United Kingdom totaled €11 billion in the first three quarters of 2003 (down year on year by 39.5 percent), while those to the United States increased by 1.5 percent, to reach €12.7 billion. Exports to the euro area fell in value by 13.8 percent during the same period, in part a reflection of a deeper slump in exports to Belgium (the third largest market), which were down by 23.3 percent.

Patterns in imports tended to mirror those of exports, reflecting the import intensity of Ireland's high-tech exporters. Accordingly, the seasonally adjusted level of imports in the first nine months of 2003 was down considerably on the same period a year earlier. The cumulative import bill for this period was €35.2 billion, a

---

[9] Irish Chamber of Commerce.

Major Exports (2003)	% of Total	Major Imports (2003)	% of Total
Machinery & transport	28.5%	Machinery & transport	43.6%
Chemicals	43.5	Chemicals	14.4
Food and live animals	7.0	Food and live animals	6.5
Misc. Manufactures	11.3	Mineral fuels	3.8

EXHIBIT IV

International Trade: Major Exports and Imports

Source: Economist Intelligence Unit, August 7, 2004.

Leading Markets (2002)	% of Total	Leading Suppliers (2002)	% of Total
United Kingdom	24.0%	United Kingdom	35.9%
United States	17.5	United States	15.4
Germany	7.2	Germany	6.4
France	5.0	France	4.1
Netherlands	3.6	Netherlands	3.3

EXHIBIT V

International Trade: Major Markets and Suppliers

Source: Economist Intelligence Unit, March 1, 2004.

year-on-year decline of 18.3 percent. In volume terms, the drop was less precipitous owing to falling import prices. In addition to the reduced input requirements of a struggling export sector, this reduction in imports also reflected the fall in personal consumption. As with exports, the rate of decline of imports had shown signs of easing since the first half of the year.

FOREIGN INVESTMENTS

Foreign private investment had been a major driver of Irish economic growth. In 2000, overseas companies located in Ireland accounted for 65 percent of manufacturing output, 47 percent of manufacturing employment, and 82 percent of manufactured exports. Foreign firms in manufacturing generated about one-quarter of GDP. Of the approximately 1,500 international companies operating in Ireland in 2001, around 600 firms (more than one-third) were from the United States. These firms mostly operated in chemicals, pharmaceuticals and healthcare, computer hardware and software, electronics, and financial services.

Producing on a global scale, foreign firms were generally well managed and paid their workers higher compensation. Though they sourced less of their inputs locally than indigenous firms, they provided valuable managerial experience. In some cases (computer software, for example) they led to the spin-off of many start-ups. Their marketing networks also helped Ireland to penetrate new markets.

Four state organizations promoted foreign investments. The Industrial Development Agency of Ireland

(IDA Ireland) had overall responsibility for promoting and facilitating foreign direct investment in all areas of the country, except the Shannon free zone. IDA Ireland was also responsible for attracting foreign companies to Dublin's International Financial Services Center (IFSC). IDA Ireland maintained offices in New York, Boston, Chicago, Los Angeles, San Jose, and Atlanta, as well as locations in Europe and Asia. Enterprise Ireland promoted joint ventures and strategic alliances between indigenous and foreign companies. SFADCO handled investment in the Shannon free zone. Udaras was responsible for economic development in those areas of Ireland where Irish (Gaelic) was the predominant language, and worked with IDA Ireland to promote overseas investment in these regions.

The Mergers, Takeovers and Monopolies Control Act of 1978 set out rules governing mergers and takeovers by foreign and domestic companies. The Competition (Amendment) Act of 1996 amended and extended the Competition Act of 1991 and the Mergers and Takeovers (Control) Acts of 1978 and 1987, and set out the rules governing competitive behavior. The Companies Act of 1963 contained the basic requirements for incorporation in Ireland (amended in 1990). In addition, there were numerous laws and regulations pertaining to employment, social security, environmental protection and taxation, many of them determined at EU level.

Ireland offered one of the most attractive corporate tax environments in the world. The English-speaking workforce was another major plus. Existing foreign companies had also contributed to higher foreign direct investment by pulling in new players.

The rapid decline in unemployment in the late 1990s, as well as the success in attracting high-tech foreign investment, had prompted the Irish government to pursue a more selective approach to foreign investment and to provide targeted assistance to foreign investors. Grants were conditional on companies located in less-developed regions in the west of the country where unemployment was higher and infrastructure was less developed. Irish authorities were also encouraging companies to move into higher-value-adding businesses and to deepen the value chain activities in the existing Irish operations.

Ireland's competitive advantages such as a quality workforce, a favorable business environment, and lower costs had been somewhat eroded in recent years. Addressing infrastructure shortcomings, skills shortage, and remaining cost competitive held the key to Ireland's continuing attractiveness as an investment destination.

LABOR MARKETS

Compared to the United States, there was greater government regulation of the workplace and labor relations in Ireland. Labor markets worked within a social frame-

EXHIBIT VI

General Government Receipts and Expenditures

Source: Ireland Department of Finance, *Monthly Economic Bulletin*, January 2004.

	2001 (€ million)	2002 (Projected) (€ million)	2003 (Estimated) (€ million)
GG receipts	39,127	42,292	45,674
GG expenditure	38,112	42,537	45,832
GG balance	1,014	−246	−158
—as a % of GDP	0.9	−0.2	−0.1
Financing of GG balance			
Currency and deposits	*−241.83*	*−81.18*	
Securities other than shares (excl. derivatives)	*2,079.60*	*412.60*	
Short-term	5,003.30	−1,170.70	
Long-term	−2,923.70	1,583.30	
Loans	*138.04*	*106.88*	
Short-term	201.53	53.00	
Long-term	−63.49	53.88	
Other movements	*−961.81*	*−684.30*	
Total	1,014	−246	−158

EXHIBIT VII

Balance of Payments— Current Account (in € million)

Source: Ireland Department of Finance, *Monthly Economic Bulletin*, January 2004.

	Q1	Q2	Q3	Q4	Total
1998	−€173	€271	€512	€20	€627
1999	€63	−€6	−€31	€199	€226
2000	−€432	€505	−€238	−€214	−€379
2001	−€508	−€26	€126	−€349	−€757
2002	€45	−€471	−€310	−€218	−€954
2003	−€1,039	−€389	−€316		

work, like in most parts of continental Europe but were considered more flexible than a typical EU nation. Social partnership agreements between the government, labor, and employers held down wage costs. A centralized wage agreement, "Program for Prosperity and Fairness,"[10] was entered into by representatives of government, labor unions, employers, and farmers in April 2000.

The Irish constitution gave workers the right to form and join labor unions. But employers in Ireland were not compelled to recognize unions and could deal with employees individually. Strikes in the Irish private sector were relatively rare, having declined sharply since the late 1970s and early 1980s.

Since 1987, collective bargaining had taken place under the framework of national economic programs, negotiated by representatives of employers, trade unions, the government, farmers, and other social partners. The Program for Prosperity and Fairness traded off pay moderation by trade unions in return for generous income tax cuts by the government. But there was some worker resentment because the benefits of increased income were nullified by a higher inflation rate in the late 1990s. Meanwhile, employers strongly opposed trade union demands for greater partnership between employees and employers at an enterprise level, including worker participation in managerial decisions through German-style work councils.

In 1998, a government commission projected that 2,200 more technical specialists would be needed in each of the next five years to fill shortages of skilled labor in the high-tech sectors of the economy. The government had established a $330 million Education in Science and Technology Fund that encouraged Irish students, from secondary level education upwards, to pursue careers in science and technology.

Jobs Ireland, run by FAS (the state training and employment authority), aimed at meeting the growing need for skilled labor in Ireland's booming economy. Irish emigration had peaked around 1989, with far fewer people leaving the country in the 1990s than in the previous decade. The government believed people who had been away for 10 years or longer were unlikely to return. As a result, the authorities targeted non-Irish nationals for jobs. Top Irish politicians had been leading delegations abroad.

The IDA provided grants for training employees in new industries. The grant generally covered the full payroll cost during the employees' training period and sometimes also covered traveling expenses, management training costs, and the cost of instructors. FAS worked closely with applicant companies in devising training programs and in ensuring that companies complied with IDA's grant requirements.

Many observers felt that much more had to be done to develop Irish human resources. An international comparison of adult literacy levels in 1999 revealed the country's weaknesses. While the average initial

Ireland	**0.15**
France	0.11
Netherlands	0.11
Finland	0.29
Belgium	0.15
Italy	0.26
Germany	0.21
UK	0.16

EXHIBIT VIII

Cost of International Calls: A Comparative Analysis (100-line business customer, avg cost per call minute in euros)

Source: *Analysis Publications*, December 2002.

Ireland	**15,839**
France	10,940
Germany	18,854
Netherlands	20,157
Finland	19,944
Sweden	25,851
UK	31,848
Italy	24,759

EXHIBIT IX

Cost of 64kbit/s International Half Circuit (€): A Comparative Analysis USA (avg cost per line per year)

Source: *Analysis Publications*, December 2002.

---

[10] Since 1987, Ireland had developed five "social partnership" agreements, with the latest launched in February 2000 called the "Program for Prosperity and Fairness."[10] This program outlined a comprehensive set of economic and social objectives finalized after extensive consultations among the government and a range of civil society organizations from November 1999 to February 2000. The idea evolved in the late 80s when Ireland was going through a tough recession (1980–87), aggravated by high inflation, heavy public borrowing and deficit, and decline in manufacturing.

Country	US$ (per kilowatt hour)
Ireland	0.057
UK	0.064
France	0.047
Netherlands	0.061
USA	0.039
Germany	0.057
Spain	0.056

EXHIBIT X

International Industrial Electricity Prices:
A Comparative Analysis

Source: *Energy Prices & Taxes—Quarterly Statistics*, National Energy
Information Center, 2001.

Country	Total
Ireland	12.50
United Kingdom	15.88
France	16.38
Germany (Unified)	22.99
Netherlands	19.08
Spain	10.85
USA	19.86
Japan	22.00

EXHIBIT XII

Total Hourly Compensation Costs in (€), 2002:
A Comparative Analysis

Source: U.S. Department of Labor, 2002.

Ireland	0.63
USA	0.51
Spain	0.57
UK	1.18
France	1.23
Netherlands	1.25
Germany	1.91

EXHIBIT XI

Cost of Water (per cubic meter) in $: A Comparative
Analysis

Source: National Utility Services Ltd., International Water Price
Survey, 2002.

educational attainment was improving, not much had been done about education and training, especially for the unemployed. The initial education system, too, had room for improvement. The school-leaving age remained unusually low. Some educationalists felt that a greater emphasis on natural sciences, foreign languages, and vocational and technical programs was required.

Labor market data, relating to the third quarter of 2003, provided one of the least rosy pictures of labor market conditions in some time. While the economy continued to generate jobs at a rate broadly in line with that registered during the previous two years, an uptick in the growth in the labor force caused unemployment to jump. A third-quarter year-on-year increase of 2 percent in the size of the labor force was the result of those formerly in full-time education entering the labor market. The year-on-year rate of employment growth was down to 1.4 percent, from 1.6 percent in the previous quarter. As a result of supply outstripping demand, the level of joblessness rose to 5.2 percent of the workforce, from 4.6 percent in the same period in 2002.

The hotels and restaurants sector recorded one of the highest levels of job creation, with a year-on-year increase of 6.6 percent. The only sector to record a higher rate of growth was health, where the numbers in employment were up by 8.9 percent. This reflected the ongoing effects of significant government investment in the public health service. Increases were also recorded in other predominantly public-service sectors. Employment in education was up by 3.7 percent and in public administration by 2.7 percent. The building sector recorded impressive job creation, with an increase of 4.7 percent, reflecting the still strong growth in housing and infrastructure construction. Slower growth was recorded in the "other services" sector (up by 2.4 percent), the wholesale and retail sector (up by 1.1 percent) and the financial sector (up by 0.4 percent). A decrease was recorded in industrial employment (down 3.1 percent) owing to much lower rates of output growth combined with strong productivity increases. In line with long-term trends, agricultural employment continued to shrink, falling by 3.8 percent, while em-

EXHIBIT XIII

Labor Hours and
Wages: A Comparative
Analysis

Source: Incomes Data Services
UK, December 2002.

Country	Legal Maximum Working Hours per Week	Actual Average Working Hours per Week	Statutory Holidays	Typical Holidays
Ireland	48	39	20 days	20–25 days
UK	48	35–40	20 days	20–30 days
France	10 per day	35	25 days	25–30
Germany	8 per day	35–38 West 37–40 East	20 days	30
Netherlands	9 per day	35–38	4 × days worked p/w	23–30 days
Spain	9 per day	34–38	20 days	22–25 days
Portugal	8 per day	35–40	22 days	22–25 days
USA	No limit	30–35 for union members; 40 for clerical staff	Nil	10 days
Japan	40	N/A	10–20 days	N/A

EXHIBIT XIV

Population by Age
Group, April 2002 (000s)

Source: Population & Migration
Estimates, September 2002,
CSO.

Age	Total	% of Total
00–14	822.4	21%
15–24	664.7	17
25–44	1,151.7	30
45+	1,258.2	32
Total	3,897.0	100

ployment in the transport, storage and communications sector decreased by 2.7 percent.

FUTURE OUTLOOK

Ireland had been highly successful in attracting foreign investments. Overseas companies continued to play a critical role in Irish economic development. Ireland had a good mix of high-quality global businesses in various sectors. Hundreds of overseas companies had chosen Ireland as their European base and were involved in a wide range of activities. However, future investments were linked to how well the country handled key infrastructural issues such as telecommunications, electricity supply and education.

The Irish policy of lower corporation tax had proved successful in attracting investment and won the back-

ing of the OECD. But Ireland's EU partners saw it as giving the country an unfair competitive advantage. The prospect of tax harmonization, favored by higher-tax EU members, could strain Ireland's future relationship with the EU. Other proposed changes in EU policies had already raised eyebrows. Irish farmers had made it clear to the government that any agreement with the EU on Common Agricultural Policy (CAP) reform that resulted in a cut in producer subsidies would be strongly resisted. Similarly, Irish fishermen had expressed considerable concern about the opening of Irish fishing waters to European trawlers under EU fishery reforms.

The governing parties, Fianna Fail and the Progressive Democrats (PDs), were expected to stay in power despite some differences over the pace of economic reforms. These reforms would also continue to provoke strong opposition from public-sector trade unions that were adversely affected by them. The most significant electoral challenge the government would face was a referendum on the EU constitution. Although a vote in favor (in late 2005 or 2006) was not a foregone conclusion, a majority in favor was expected.

Country	% Population
Ireland	29.0
United Kingdom	12.5
France	25.0
Netherlands	23.0
Portugal	21.0
Germany	19.0
Spain	15.6
USA	30.8
Japan	19.0

EXHIBIT XV

Future Workforce Availability: A Comparative Analysis (% of population under 25 in the year 2050)

Source: *World Population Prospectus, the 2000 Revision*, United Nations.

Sources

1. Barry, Frank, and John Bradley. "Foreign Direct Investment and Trade: The Irish Host-Country Experience." *Economic Journal*, November 1997, Vol. 107, Issue 445, p. 1798.
2. "A Missed Opportunity." *The Economist*, March 8, 1997, Vol. 342, Issue 8007, p. 64.
3. "Greener." *The Economist*, May 10, 1997, Vol. 343, Issue 8016, p. 55.
4. "Full Speed Ahead." *The Economist*, July 26, 1997, Vol. 344, Issue 8027, p. 49.
5. "Musical Chairs." *The Economist*, August 30, 1997, Vol. 344, Issue 8032, pp. 42–43.
6. "Edging Forward." *The Economist*, September 20, 1997, Vol. 344, Issue 8035, pp. 63–64.
7. "Treading Carefully." *The Economist*, October 18, 1997, Vol. 345, Issue 8039, pp. 56–57.
8. "End of the Line." *The Economist*, February 14, 1998, Vol. 346, Issue 8055, pp. 80–81.
9. "Thirty Troubled Years." *The Economist*, April 18, 1998, Vol. 346, Issue 8064, p. 20.
10. Hyland, Julie. "What Makes Celtic Tiger Run." *World Socialist Web site*, June 16, 1998.
11. Sweeney, Paul. "Ireland's Economic Miracle Explained." *www.wsws.org*, June 16, 1998.
12. "Roadblock." *The Economist*, November 7, 1998, Vol. 349, Issue 8093, pp. 60–61.

EXHIBIT XVI

Education as % of Total Public Expenditure: A Comparative Analysis

Source: OECD, *Education at a Glance, 2002*.

Country	Total % All Levels	Primary and Secondary %	Tertiary %
Ireland	13.2	9.4	3.6
UK	11.8	8.1	2.6
France	11.5	8.0	2.0
Germany	9.7	6.2	2.3
Netherlands	10.4	6.8	2.9
Spain	11.3	8.2	2.3
Portugal	13.1	9.7	2.4
Belgium	11.0	6.3	3.0
Italy	9.4	6.6	1.7

13. "Interesting Dilemma." *The Economist,* November 14, 1998, Vol. 349, Issue 8094, pp. 56–57.

14. Crowley, E., and J. MacLaughlin. "Under the Belly of the Celtic Tiger: Class, Race, Identity and Culture in the Global Ireland," *Dublin: Irish Reporter Silicon Isle Time-Digital,* 1999.

15. "Last Chance?" *The Economist,* June 26, 1999, Vol. 351, Issue 8125, p. 65.

16. "Honey Pot." *The Economist,* August 28, 1999, Vol. 352, Issue 8134, pp. 39–40.

17. "Converging by Diverging." *The Economist,* October 2, 1999, Vol. 353, Issue 8139, p. 84.

18. Brien, Tim O. "High-Tech Industry Clusters Hard to Generate in the Regions." *Irish Times,* October 14, 1999.

19. Norton, Rob. "The Luck of the Irish." *Fortune,* October 25, 1999, Vol. 140, Issue 8, pp. 194–205.

20. Baker, Stephen. "Mary Harney/Ireland: High-Tech Hibernia." *BusinessWeek,* November 9, 1999.

21. *World Population Prospectus: The 2000 Revision, Vol. III.* United Nations Population Division, 2000.

22. Kieran, Allen. "The Celtic Tiger? The Myth of Social Partnership." *Manchester University Press,* 2000.

23. MacSharry, Ray, and Padraic White. "The Making of the Celtic Tiger: the Inside Story of Ireland's Boom Economy." www.res.org.uk.

24. Kerry, Capel; Carol Craig; and David R. Fairlamb. "Ireland: Burning Too Bright." *BusinessWeek,* April 10, 2000.

25. Bruton, John. "Ireland's Economic Miracle." *Montreal Economic Institute,* May 10, 2000.

26. "A New Route." *The Economist,* July 15, 2000, Vol. 356, Issue 8179, p. 51.

27. Brady, Mick. "Ireland's High-Tech Jig." *E-Commerce Times,* September 5, 2000.

28. "Come Back!" *The Economist,* October 28, 2000, Vol. 357, Issue 8194, p. 50.

29. Humphreys, Joe. "Digital District." *Irish Times,* December 12, 2000.

30. Black, Jane. "Irish Eyes Turn in a New Direction," *BusinessWeek,* July 30, 2001.

31. ESRI Manpower Forecasting Studies, 2002.

32. "Going Through the Roof." *The Economist,* March 30, 2002, Vol. 362, Issue 8266, pp. 59–61.

33. IDA Ireland, August 2002.

34. Kim, Mi-hui. "Ireland Rises from Rags to Riches on Sheer Will and a Little Luck." *Korea Herald,* September 12, 2002.

35. "Why Irish Eyes Aren't Smiling." *BusinessWeek,* October 28, 2002.

36. Creevy, Charlie. "The Tiger Tamed." *The Economist,* December 14, 2002, Vol. 365, Issue 8303, p. 44.

37. James, Steve. "Social Tension Deepens as 'Celtic Tiger' Staggers." www.wsws.org, November 7, 2002.

38. Census 2002, *Central Statistics Office Ireland,* July 2002.

39. Concagh, Geraldine. "Report of Ireland Economic Outlook." *Economic Outlook and Business Review,* June 2002.

40. Rourke, Breffni O. "How Ireland Unleashed Its 'Celtic Tiger' Economy." www.rferl.org/nca/features.

41. Moskowitz, Milton, and Robert Levering. "10 Great Companies to Work for in Europe: Intel." *Fortune,* January 7, 2003.

42. Economic Overview, *Estates Gazette,* January 25, 2003.

43. Hanley, Mike. "Feeding the Celtic Tiger: Ireland's Strong Economy Wants Imports,"

44. "A History of the Irish Race." *Old Ireland.*

45. Ireland Tax Data 2003, Price Waterhouse Coopers, www.pwcglobal.com.

46. Gordon, Stephanie. "Ireland Sets Up Committee to Boost Industry R&D Spend," *EE Times UK,* February 26, 2003.

47. Ireland-Department of Finance, *Monthly Economic Bulletin,* January 2004.

48. www.irish-trade.ic.

49. www.usembassy.ie.

50. www.onbusiness.ie/ndm/home.html.

51. www.irlgov.ie/taoiseach/publication/prosperityandfairness.htm.

10

The Foreign Exchange Market

Volkswagen's Hedging Strategy

In January 2004, Volkswagen, Europe's largest carmaker and until recently one of its most successful, reported a 95 percent drop in 2003 fourth-quarter profits, which slumped from €1.05 billion to a mere €50 million. For all of 2003, Volkswagen's operating profit fell by 50 percent from the record levels attained in 2002. Although the profit slump had multiple causes, two factors were the focus of much attention—the unprecedented rise in the value of the euro against the dollar during 2003, and Volkswagen's decision to hedge only 30 percent of its foreign currency exposure, as opposed to the 70 percent it had traditionally hedged. In total, currency losses due to the dollar's rise are estimated to have reduced Volkswagen's operating profits by some €1.2 billion ($1.5 billion).

The rise in the value of the euro during 2003 took many companies by surprise. Since its introduction January 1, 1999, when it became the currency unit of 12 members of the European Union, the euro had recorded a volatile trading history against the U.S. dollar. In early 1999 the exchange rate stood at €1 = $1.17, but by October 2000 it had slumped to €1 = $0.83. Although it recovered, reaching parity of €1 = $1.00 in late 2002, few analysts predicted a rapid rise in the value of the euro against the dollar during 2003. As so often happens in the foreign exchange markets, the experts were wrong; by late 2003 the exchange rate stood at €1 = $1.25.

One cause of this reversal in the value of the euro against the dollar was a record U.S. foreign trade deficit in 2003. The U.S. economy grew rapidly during 2003, sucking in imports from foreign nations while generating anemic export growth. The result was a flow of dollars out of the United States into the hands of foreigners. Historically, foreigners had reinvested those dollars in the United States, and the return flow had kept the dollar strong despite persistent trade deficits. This didn't happen to the same extent in 2003. Instead, many foreigners sold the dollars they received for other currencies, such as the euro, Japanese yen, or British pound. They did this because they had become increasingly pessimistic about the future value of the dollar and were reducing their dollar holdings accordingly. Their pessimism was itself a function of two factors. First, U.S. government officials stated that they would prefer a weaker dollar in order to increase the competitiveness of U.S. companies in the global marketplace (the theory being that a falling dollar would make U.S. exports more competitive). With the government talking the dollar down, many foreigners decided to reduce their dollar holdings. Second, the U.S. government ran a record budget deficit in 2003, and this was projected to remain high for some time. Looking at this, some foreigners concluded that the U.S. government might be forced to finance its spending by expanding the supply of dollars (i.e., by printing money), which would lead to inflation and reduce the value of the

dollar even further. Thus, they sold dollars and purchased currencies thought to be less inflation prone.

For Volkswagen, which made cars in Germany and exported them to the United States, the fall in the value of the dollar against the euro during 2003 was devastating. To understand what happened, consider a Volkswagen Jetta built in Germany for export to the United States. The Jetta costs €14,000 to make in Germany and ship to a dealer in the United States, where it sells for $15,000. With the exchange rate standing at around €1 = $1.00, the $15,000 earned from the sale of a Jetta in the U.S. could be converted into €15,000, giving Volkswagen a profit of €1,000 on every Jetta sold. But if the exchange rate changes during the year, ending up at €1 = $1.25 as it did during 2003, each dollar of revenue will now buy only €0.80 (€1/$1.25 = €0.80), and Volkswagen is squeezed. At an exchange rate of €1 = $1.25, the $15,000 Volkswagen gets for the Jetta is now only worth €12,000 when converted back into euros, meaning the company will lose €2,000 on every Jetta sold (when the exchange rate is €1 = $1.25, $15,000/1.25 = €12,000).

Volkswagen could have insured against this adverse movement in exchange rates by entering the foreign exchange market in late 2002 and buying a *forward contract* for dollars at an exchange rate of around $1 = €1 (a *forward contract* gives the holder the right to exchange one currency for another at some point in the future at a predetermined exchange rate). Called *hedging,* the financial strategy of buying forward guarantees that at some future point, such as 180 days, Volkswagen would have been able to exchange the dollars it got from selling Jettas in the United States into euros at $1 = €1, *irrespective of what the actual exchange rate was at that time.* In 2003 such a strategy would have been good for Volkswagen. However, hedging is not without its costs. If the euro had declined in value against the dollar, instead of appreciating as it did, Volkswagen would have made even more profit per car in euros by not hedging (a dollar at the end of 2003 would have bought more euros than a dollar at the end of 2002). Also, hedging is expensive because foreign exchange dealers will charge a high commission for selling currency forward. For whatever reason, Volkswagen decided to hedge just 30 percent of its anticipated U.S. sales in 2003 though forward contracts, rather than the 70 percent it had historically hedged. The decision cost the company more than a €1 billion. For 2004, the company announced that it would revert back to hedging 70 percent of its foreign currency exposure!

Sources: Mark Landler, "As Exchange Rates Swing, Car Makers Try to Duck," *The New York Times,* January 17, 2004, pp. B1, B4; N. Boudette, "Volkswagen Posts 95% Drop in Net," *The Wall Street Journal,* Februray 19, 2004, p. A3; and "Volkswagen's Financial Mechanic," *Corporate Finance,* June 2003, p. 1.

Introduction

This chapter has three main objectives. The first is to explain how the foreign exchange market works. The second is to examine the forces that determine exchange rates, and to discuss the degree to which it is possible to predict future exchange rate movements. The third objective is to map the implications for international business of exchange rate movements and the foreign exchange market. This chapter is the first of two that deal with the international monetary system and its relationship to international business. In the next chapter, we will explore the institutional structure of the international monetary system. The institutional structure is the context within which the foreign exchange market functions. As we shall see, changes in the institutional structure of the international monetary system can exert a profound influence on the development of foreign exchange markets.

The **foreign exchange market** is a market for converting the currency of one country into that of another country. An **exchange rate** is simply the rate at which one currency is converted into another. For example, Volkswagen uses the foreign exchange market to convert the dollars it earns from selling cars in the United States into euros. Without the foreign exchange market, international trade and international investment on the scale that we see today would be impossible; companies would have to resort to barter. The foreign exchange market is the lubricant that enables companies based in countries that use different currencies to trade with each other.

We know from earlier chapters that international trade and investment have their risks. As the opening case illustrates, some of these risks exist because future exchange rates cannot be perfectly predicted. The rate at which one currency is converted into another can change over time. In January 1999, for example, the U.S. dollar/European euro exchange rate stood at €1 = $1.17, by October 2000 it stood at €1 = $0.82, by December 2002 it was up to €1 = $1.00, and in early January 2005 it stood at €1 = $1.30. One function of the foreign exchange market is to provide some insurance against the risks that arise from such volatile changes in exchange rates, commonly referred to as foreign exchange risk. Although the foreign exchange market offers some insurance against foreign exchange risk, it cannot provide complete insurance. It is not unusual for international businesses to suffer losses because of unpredicted changes in exchange rates. Currency fluctuations can make seemingly profitable trade and investment deals unprofitable, and vice versa. The opening case on Volkswagen contains an example.

We begin this chapter by looking at the functions and the form of the foreign exchange market. This includes distinguishing among spot exchanges, forward exchanges, and currency swaps. Then we will consider the factors that determine exchange rates. We will also look at how foreign trade is conducted when a country's currency cannot be exchanged for other currencies; that is, when its currency is not convertible. The chapter closes with a discussion of these things in terms of their implications for business.

The Functions of the Foreign Exchange Market

The foreign exchange market serves two main functions. The first is to convert the currency of one country into the currency of another. The second is to provide some insurance against **foreign exchange risk,** by which we mean the adverse consequences of unpredictable changes in exchange rates.[1]

CURRENCY CONVERSION

Each country has a currency in which the prices of goods and services are quoted. In the United States, it is the dollar ($); in Great Britain, the pound (£); in France, Germany, and other members of the euro zone it is the euro (€); in Japan, the yen (¥); and so on. In general, within the borders of a particular country, one must use the national currency.

The foreign exchange market enables companies based in countries that use different currencies to trade with each other.

A U.S. tourist cannot walk into a store in Edinburgh, Scotland, and use U.S. dollars to buy a bottle of Scotch whisky. Dollars are not recognized as legal tender in Scotland; the tourist must use British pounds. Fortunately, the tourist can go to a bank and exchange her dollars for pounds. Then she can buy the whisky.

When a tourist changes one currency into another, she is participating in the foreign exchange market. The exchange rate is the rate at which the market converts one currency into another. For example, an exchange rate of €1 = $1.30 specifies that one euro buys 1.30 U.S. dollars. The exchange rate allows us to compare the relative prices of goods and services in different countries. Our U.S. tourist wishing to buy a bottle of Scotch whisky in Edinburgh may find that she must pay £30 for the bottle, knowing that the same bottle costs $45 in the United States. Is this a good deal? Imagine the current pound/dollar exchange rate is £1.00 = $1.80. Our intrepid tourist takes out her calculator and converts £30 into dollars. (The calculation is 30 × 1.8). She finds that the bottle of Scotch costs the equivalent of $54. She is surprised that a bottle of Scotch whisky could cost less in the United States than in Scotland (alcohol is taxed heavily in Great Britain).

Tourists are minor participants in the foreign exchange market; companies engaged in international trade and investment are major ones. International businesses have four main uses of foreign exchange markets. First, the payments a company receives for its exports, the income it receives from foreign investments, or the income it receives from licensing agreements with foreign firms may be in foreign currencies. To use those funds in its home country, the company must convert them to its home country's currency. Consider the Scotch distillery that exports its whisky to the United States. The distillery is paid in dollars, but since those dollars cannot be spent in Great Britain, they must be converted into British pounds. Similarly, as we saw in the opening case, when Volkswagen sells cars in the United States for dollars, it must convert those dollars into euros to use them in Germany.

Second, international businesses use foreign exchange markets when they must pay a foreign company for its products or services in its country's currency. For example, Dell buys many of the components for its computers from Malaysian firms. The Malaysian companies must be paid in Malaysia's currency, the ringgit, so Dell must convert money from dollars into ringgit to pay them.

Third, international businesses use foreign exchange markets when they have spare cash that they wish to invest for short terms in money markets. For example, consider a

U.S. company that has $10 million it wants to invest for three months. The best interest rate it can earn on these funds in the United States may be 2 percent. Investing in a South Korean money market account, however, may earn 12 percent. Thus, the company may change its $10 million into Korean won and invest it in South Korea. Note, however, that the rate of return it earns on this investment depends not only on the Korean interest rate, but also on the changes in the value of the Korean won against the dollar in the intervening period.

Finally, **currency speculation** is another use of foreign exchange markets. Currency speculation typically involves the short-term movement of funds from one currency to another in the hopes of profiting from shifts in exchange rates. Consider again a U.S. company with $10 million to invest for three months. Suppose the company suspects that the U.S. dollar is overvalued against the Japanese yen. That is, the company expects the value of the dollar to *depreciate* (fall) against that of the yen. Imagine the current dollar/yen exchange rate is $1 = ¥120. The company exchanges its $10 million into yen, receiving ¥1.2 billion ($10 million × 120 = ¥1.2 billion). Over the next three months, the value of the dollar depreciates against the yen until $1 = ¥100. Now the company exchanges its ¥1.2 billion back into dollars and finds that it has $12 million. The company has made a $2 million profit on currency speculation in three months on an initial investment of $10 million! In general, however, companies should beware that speculation is a very risky business. The company cannot know for sure what will happen to exchange rates. While a speculator may profit handsomely if his speculation about future currency movements turns out to be correct, he can also lose vast amounts of money if it turns out to be wrong.

INSURING AGAINST FOREIGN EXCHANGE RISK

A second function of the foreign exchange market is to provide insurance against foreign exchange risk, which is the possibility that unpredicted changes in future exchange rates will have adverse consequences for the firm. To explain how the market performs this function, we must first distinguish among spot exchange rates, forward exchange rates, and currency swaps.

Spot Exchange Rates

When two parties agree to exchange currency and execute the deal immediately, the transaction is referred to as a spot exchange. Exchange rates governing such "on the spot" trades are referred to as spot exchange rates. The **spot exchange rate** is the rate at which a foreign exchange dealer converts one currency into another currency on a particular day. Thus, when our U.S. tourist in Edinburgh goes to a bank to convert her dollars into pounds, the exchange rate is the spot rate for that day.

Spot exchange rates are reported daily in the financial pages of newspapers. Table 10.1 shows the dollar exchange rates for currencies traded in the New York foreign exchange market as of noon January 11, 2005. An exchange rate can be quoted in two ways: as the amount of foreign currency one U.S. dollar will buy, or as the value of a dollar for one unit of foreign currency. Thus, one U.S. dollar bought €0.759821 on January 11, 2005, and one euro bought $1.3161.

Spot rates change continually, often on a day-by-day basis (although the magnitude of changes over such short periods is usually small). The value of a currency is determined by the interaction between the demand and supply of that currency relative to the demand and supply of other currencies. For example, if lots of people want U.S. dollars and dollars are in short supply, and few people want British pounds and pounds are in plentiful supply, the spot exchange rate for converting dollars into pounds will change. The dollar is likely to appreciate against the pound (or, the pound will depreciate against the dollar). Imagine the spot exchange rate is £1 = $1.50 when the market opens. As the day progresses, dealers demand more dollars and fewer pounds. By the end of the day, the spot exchange rate might be £1 = $1.48. Each pound now buys fewer dollars than at the start of the day. The dollar has appreciated, and the pound has depreciated.

TABLE 10.1

Foreign Exchange
Quotations for One U.S.
Dollar, January 11, 2005

Source: www.x-rates.com.

	Foreign Currency per 1USD	Dollars per Unit of Foreign Currency
Australian dollar	1.30856	0.764199
Brazilian real	2.712	0.368732
British pound	0.532028	1.8796
Canadian dollar	1.2142	0.823588
Chinese yuan	8.2765	0.120824
Danish krone	5.653	0.176897
Euro	0.759821	1.3161
Hong Kong dollar	7.7955	0.128279
Indian rupee	43.68	0.0228938
Japanese yen	103.42	0.00966931
Malaysian ringgit	3.8	0.263158
Mexican peso	11.217	0.0891504
New Zealand dollar	1.42816	0.700202
Norwegian kroner	6.2278	0.16057
Singapore dollar	1.6363	0.611135
South African rand	5.955	0.167926
South Korean won	1045	0.000956938
Sri Lanka rupee	98.1	0.0101937
Swedish krona	6.8616	0.145739
Swiss franc	1.1758	0.850485
Taiwan dollar	31.98	0.0312695
Thai baht	39	0.025641
Venezuelan bolivar	1915.2	0.000522139

Forward Exchange Rates

As we saw in the opening case, changes in spot exchange rates can be problematic for an international business. For example, a U.S. company that imports laptop computers from Japan knows that in 30 days it must pay yen to a Japanese supplier when a shipment arrives. The company will pay the Japanese supplier ¥200,000 for each laptop computer, and the current dollar/yen spot exchange rate is $1 = ¥120. At this rate, each computer costs the importer $1,667 (i.e., 1,667 = 200,000/120). The importer knows she can sell the computers the day they arrive for $2,000 each, which yields a gross profit of $333 on each computer ($2,000 − $1,667). However, the importer will not have the funds to pay the Japanese supplier until the computers have been sold. If over the next 30 days the dollar unexpectedly depreciates against the yen, say, to $1 = ¥95, the importer will still have to pay the Japanese company ¥200,000 per computer, but in dollar terms that would be equivalent to $2,105 per computer, which is more than she can sell the computers for. A depreciation in the value of the dollar against the yen from $1 = ¥120 to $1 = ¥95 would transform a profitable deal into an unprofitable one.

To avoid this risk, the U.S. importer might want to engage in a forward exchange. A **forward exchange** occurs when two parties agree to exchange currency and execute the deal at some specific date in the future. Exchange rates governing such future transactions are referred to as **forward exchange rates.** For most major currencies, forward exchange rates are quoted for 30 days, 90 days, and 180 days into the future. In some cases, it is possible to get forward exchange rates for several years into the future. Returning to our computer importer example, let us assume the 30-day forward exchange rate for converting dollars into yen is $1 = ¥110. The importer enters into a 30-day forward exchange transaction with a foreign exchange dealer at this rate and is guaranteed that she will have to pay no more than $1,818 for each computer (1,818 = 200,000/110). This guarantees her a profit of $182 per computer ($2,000 − $1,818). She also insures herself against the possibility that an unanticipated change in the dollar/yen exchange rate will turn a profitable deal into an unprofitable one.

In this example, the spot exchange rate ($1 = ¥120) and the 30-day forward rate ($1 = ¥110) differ. Such differences are normal; they reflect the expectations of the foreign exchange market about future currency movements. In our example, the fact that $1 bought more yen with a spot exchange than with a 30-day forward exchange indicates foreign exchange dealers expected the dollar to depreciate against the yen in the next 30 days. When this occurs, we say the dollar is selling at a *discount* on the 30-day forward market (i.e., it is worth less than on the spot market). Of course, the opposite can also occur. If the 30-day forward exchange rate were $1 = ¥130, for example, $1 would buy more yen with a forward exchange than with a spot exchange. In such a case, we say the dollar is selling at a *premium* on the 30-day forward market. This reflects the foreign exchange dealers' expectations that the dollar will appreciate against the yen over the next 30 days.

In sum, when a firm enters into a forward exchange contract, it is taking out insurance against the possibility that future exchange rate movements will make a transaction unprofitable by the time that transaction has been executed. Although many firms routinely enter into forward exchange contracts to hedge their foreign exchange risk, there are some spectacular examples of what happens when firms don't take out this insurance. One such example was given in the opening case, which looked at the case of Volkswagen. Another is given in the accompanying Management Focus, which explains how a failure to fully insure against foreign exchange risk cost South African Airlines $1.05 billion.

Currency Swaps

The above discussion of spot and forward exchange rates might lead you to conclude that the option to buy forward is very important to companies engaged in international trade—and you would be right. By 2004 forward instruments accounted for some 65 percent of all foreign exchange transactions, while spot exchanges accounted for 35 percent.[2] However, the vast majority of these forward exchanges were not forward exchanges of the type we have been discussing, but rather a more sophisticated instrument known as currency swaps.

A **currency swap** is the simultaneous purchase and sale of a given amount of foreign exchange for two different value dates. **Swaps** are transacted between international businesses and their banks, between banks, and between governments when it is desirable to move out of one currency into another for a limited period without incurring foreign exchange risk. A common kind of swap is spot against forward. Consider a company such as Apple Computer. Apple assembles laptop computers in the United States, but the screens are made in Japan. Apple also sells some of the finished laptops in Japan. So, like many companies, Apple both buys from and sells to Japan. Imagine Apple needs to change $1 million into yen to pay its supplier of laptop screens today. Apple knows that

MANAGEMENT FOCUS The management of South African Airlines in 2002 decided to enter into forward exchange contracts valued at $1.3 billion to protect against a possible drop in the value of South Africa's currency, the rand, against the U.S. dollar. The contracts were designed to ensure that South African Airlines could lock in the price that it would have to pay for future purchases of jet fuel and 41 new aircraft from Airbus Industrie, both of which are priced in U.S. dollars. For several years the rand had been weak against the dollar, and management felt that further declines were likely. The contracts, which extended out over 10 years, assumed that the rand would average 10.80 to one U.S. dollar.

This hedge seemed logical. It was certainly a conservative thing to do. However, management declined to hedge against the possibility that the rand might appreciate against the dollar. Apparently, such a possibility seemed so remote that they decided to forgo the costs of entering into additional forward exchange contracts to guard against a possible rise in the value of the rand against the dollar. They were wrong. In 2002 and early 2003, the South African rand appreciated against the U.S. dollar by almost 30 percent, to 6.09 rand to the dollar. For South African Airlines, this was an unmitigated disaster. In March 2003, the company announced it had recorded $1.05 billion in unrealized foreign exchange losses. This wiped out the airline's profit and pushed its loss for the year to $808 million. In the aftermath, the CFO resigned, followed later by the CEO. The company also announced that its financial difficulties meant it had to cancel orders for 15 Airbus planes.

Sources: D. Robertson, "SAA Up against Rand Hedge," *Business Day*, August 27, 2003, p. 3; J. Flottau, "SAA under Duress," *Aviation Week*, July 12, 2004, p. 40; and J. Wallace, "Order Cancellations a Hard Hit to Airbus," *Seattle Post Intelligencer*, August 28, 2004, p. E6.

in 90 days it will be paid ¥120 million by the Japanese importer that buys its finished laptops. It will want to convert these yen into dollars for use in the United States. Let us say today's spot exchange rate is $1 = ¥120 and the 90-day forward exchange rate is $1 = ¥110. Apple sells $1 million to its bank in return for ¥120 million. Now Apple can pay its Japanese supplier. At the same time, Apple enters into a 90-day forward exchange deal with its bank for converting ¥120 million into dollars. Thus, in 90 days Apple will receive $1.09 million (¥120 million/ 110 = $1.09 million). Since the yen is trading at a premium on the 90-day forward market, Apple ends up with more dollars than it started with (although the opposite could also occur). The swap deal is just like a conventional forward deal in one important respect: It enables Apple to insure itself against foreign exchange risk. By engaging in a swap, Apple knows today that the ¥120 million payment it will receive in 90 days will yield $1.09 million.

The Nature of the Foreign Exchange Market

The foreign exchange market is not located in any one place. It is a global network of banks, brokers, and foreign exchange dealers connected by electronic communications systems. When companies wish to convert currencies, they typically go through their own banks rather than entering the market directly. The foreign exchange market has been growing at a rapid pace, reflecting a general growth in the volume of cross-border trade and investment (see Chapter 1). In March 1986, the average total value of global foreign exchange trading was about $200 billion per day. By April 1995, it was more than $1,200 billion per day, and by April 1998, it reached $1,490 billion per day. While it fell back to $1,200 billion per day in April 2001, largely due to the introduction of the euro, which reduced the number of major trading currencies in the world, by April 2004 it had grown to $1.88 trillion.[3] The most important trading centers are London (31 percent of activity), New York (19 percent of activity), Tokyo (8 percent of activity), and Singapore (5 percent of activity).[4] Major secondary trading centers include Zurich, Frankfurt, Paris, Hong Kong, and Sydney.

London's dominance in the foreign exchange market is due to both history and geography. As the capital of the world's first major industrial trading nation, London had become the world's largest center for international banking by the end of the 19th century, a position it has retained. Today London's central position between Tokyo and Singapore to the east and New York to the west has made it the critical link between the East Asian and New York markets. Due to the particular differences in time zones, London opens soon after Tokyo closes for the night and is still open for the first few hours of trading in New York.

Two features of the foreign exchange market are of particular note. The first is that the market never sleeps. Tokyo, London, and New York are all shut for only 3 hours out of every 24. During these three hours, trading continues in a number of minor centers, particularly San Francisco and Sydney, Australia. The second feature of the market is the integration of the various trading centers. High-speed computer linkages between trading centers around the globe have effectively created a single market. The integration of financial centers implies there can be no significant difference in exchange rates quoted in the trading centers. For example, if the yen/dollar exchange rate quoted in London at 3 P.M. is ¥120 = $1, the yen/dollar exchange rate quoted in New York at the same time (10 A.M. New York time) will be identical. If the New York yen/dollar exchange rate were ¥125 = $1, a dealer could make a profit through **arbitrage**, buying a currency low and selling it high. For example, if the prices differed in London and New York as given, a dealer in New York could take $1 million and use that to purchase ¥125 million. She could then immediately sell the ¥125 million for dollars in London, where the transaction would yield $1.046666 million, allowing the trader to book a profit of $46,666 on the transaction. If all dealers tried to cash in on the opportunity, however, the demand for yen in New York would rise, resulting in an appreciation of the yen against the dollar such that the price differential between New York and London would quickly disappear. Because foreign exchange dealers are always watching their computer screens for arbitrage opportunities, the few that arise tend to be small, and they disappear in minutes.

Another feature of the foreign exchange market is the important role played by the U.S. dollar. Although a foreign exchange transaction can involve any two currencies, most transactions involve dollars on one side. This is true even when a dealer wants to sell a nondollar currency and buy another. A dealer wishing to sell Korean won for Brazilian real, for example, will usually sell the won for dollars and then use the dollars to buy real. Although this may seem a roundabout way of doing things, it is actually cheaper than trying to find a holder of real who wants to buy won. Because the volume of international transactions involving dollars is so great, it is not hard to find dealers who wish to trade dollars for won or real.

Due to its central role in so many foreign exchange deals, the dollar is a vehicle currency. In 2004, 89 percent of all foreign exchange transactions involved dollars on one side of the transaction. After the dollar, the most important vehicle currencies were the euro, the Japanese yen, and the British pound—reflecting the importance of these trading entities in the world economy. The euro has replaced the Germany mark as the world's second most important vehicle currency. The British pound used to be second in importance to the dollar as a vehicle currency, but its importance has diminished in recent years. Despite this, London has retained its leading position in the global foreign exchange market.

Economic Theories of Exchange Rate Determination

At the most basic level, exchange rates are determined by the demand and supply of one currency relative to the demand and supply of another. For example, if the demand for dollars outstrips the supply of them and if the supply of Japanese yen is greater than the demand for them, the dollar/yen exchange rate will change. The dollar will appreciate against the yen (or the yen will depreciate against the dollar). However, while differences in relative demand and supply explain the determination of exchange rates, they do so only in a superficial sense. This simple explanation does not tell us what factors underlie the demand for and supply of a currency. Nor does it tell us when the demand for dollars will exceed the supply (and vice versa) or when the supply of Japanese yen will exceed demand for them (and vice versa). Neither does it tell us under what conditions a currency is in demand or under what conditions it is not demanded. In this section, we will review economic theory's answers to these questions. This will give us a deeper understanding of how exchange rates are determined.

If we understand how exchange rates are determined, we may be able to forecast exchange rate movements. Because future exchange rate movements influence export opportunities, the profitability of international trade and investment deals, and the price competitiveness of foreign imports, this is valuable information for an international business. Unfortunately, there is no simple explanation. The forces that determine exchange rates are complex, and no theoretical consensus exists, even among academic economists who study the phenomenon every day. Nonetheless, most economic theories of exchange rate movements seem to agree that three factors have an important impact on future exchange rate movements in a country's currency: the country's price inflation, its interest rate, and market psychology.[5]

PRICES AND EXCHANGE RATES

To understand how prices are related to exchange rate movements, we first need to discuss an economic proposition known as the law of one price. Then we will discuss the theory of purchasing power parity (PPP), which links changes in the exchange rate between two countries' currencies to changes in the countries' price levels.

The Law of One Price

The **law of one price** states that in competitive markets free of transportation costs and barriers to trade (such as tariffs), identical products sold in different countries must sell for the same price when their price is expressed in terms of the same currency.[6] For example, if the exchange rate between the British pound and the dollar is £1 = $1.50, a jacket that retails for $75 in New York should sell for £50 in London (since $75/1.50 = £50). Consider what would happen if the jacket cost £40 in London ($60 in U.S. currency). At this price, it would pay a trader to buy jackets in London and sell them in New York (an example of arbitrage). The company initially could make a profit of $15 on each jacket by purchasing it for £40 ($60) in London and selling it for $75 in New York (we are assuming away transportation costs and trade barriers). However, the increased demand for jackets in London would raise their price in London, and the increased supply of jackets in New York would lower their price there. This would continue until prices were equalized. Thus, prices might equalize when the jacket cost £44 ($66) in London and $66 in New York (assuming no change in the exchange rate of £1 = $1.50).

Purchasing Power Parity

If the law of one price were true for all goods and services, the purchasing power parity (PPP) exchange rate could be found from any individual set of prices. By comparing the prices of identical products in different currencies, it would be possible to determine the "real" or PPP exchange rate that would exist if markets were efficient. (An **efficient market** has no impediments to the free flow of goods and services, such as trade barriers.)

A less extreme version of the PPP theory states that given relatively efficient markets—that is, markets in which few impediments to international trade exist—the price of a "basket of goods" should be roughly equivalent in each country. To express the PPP theory in symbols, let $P_\$$ be the U.S. dollar price of a basket of particular goods and P_Y be the price of the same basket of goods in Japanese yen. The PPP theory predicts that the dollar/yen exchange rate, $E_{\$/\yen}$, should be equivalent to:

$$E_{\$/\yen} = P_\$/P_\yen$$

Thus, if a basket of goods costs \$200 in the United States and ¥20,000 in Japan, PPP theory predicts that the dollar/yen exchange rate should be \$200/¥20,000 or \$0.01 per Japanese yen (i.e. \$1 = ¥100).

Every year, the newsmagazine *The Economist* publishes its own version of the PPP theorem, which it refers to as the "Big Mac Index." *The Economist* has selected McDonald's Big Mac as a proxy for a "basket of goods" because it is produced according to more or less the same recipe in about 120 countries. The Big Mac PPP is the exchange rate that would have hamburgers costing the same in each country. According to *The Economist*, comparing a country's actual exchange rate with the one predicted by the PPP theorem based on relative prices of Big Macs is a test on whether a currency is undervalued or not. This is not a totally serious exercise, as *The Economist* admits, but it does provide us with a useful illustration of the PPP theorem.

The Big Mac index for June 2005 is reproduced in Table 10.2. To calculate the index *The Economist* converts the price of a Big Mac in a country into dollars at current exchange rates and divides that by the average price of a Big Mac in America (which is \$3). According to the PPP theorem, the prices should be the same. If they are not, it implies that the currency is either overvalued against the dollar or undervalued. For example, the average price of a Big Mac in the euro area was \$3.58 at the euro/dollar exchange rate prevailing in June 2005. Dividing this by the average price of a Big Mac in the United States gives 1.17 (i.e., 3.58/3.06), which suggests that the euro was overvalued by 17 percent against the U.S. dollar in June 2005.

The next step in the PPP theory is to argue that the exchange rate will change if relative prices change. For example, imagine there is no price inflation in the United States, while prices in Japan are increasing by 10 percent a year. At the beginning of the year, a basket of goods costs \$200 in the United States and ¥20,000 in Japan, so the dollar/yen exchange rate, according to PPP theory, should be \$1 = ¥100. At the end of the year, the basket of goods still costs \$200 in the United States, but it costs ¥22,000 in Japan. PPP theory predicts that the exchange rate should change as a result. More precisely, by the end of the year:

$$E_{\$/\yen} = \$200/\yen22,000$$

Thus, ¥1 = \$0.0091 (or \$1 = ¥110). Because of 10 percent price inflation, the Japanese yen has *depreciated* by 10 percent against the dollar. One dollar will buy 10 percent more yen at the end of the year than at the beginning.

Money Supply and Price Inflation

In essence, PPP theory predicts that changes in relative prices will result in a change in exchange rates. Theoretically, a country in which price inflation is running wild should expect to see its currency depreciate against that of countries in which inflation rates are lower. If we can predict what a country's future inflation rate is likely to be, we can also predict how the value of its currency relative to other currencies—its exchange rate—is likely to change. The growth rate of a country's money supply determines its likely future inflation rate.[7] Thus, in theory at least, we can use information about the growth in money supply to forecast exchange rate movements.

Inflation is a monetary phenomenon. It occurs when the quantity of money in circulation rises faster than the stock of goods and services; that is, when the money supply increases faster than output increases. Imagine what would happen if everyone in the country was suddenly given \$10,000 by the government. Many people would rush out to spend their extra money on those things they had always wanted—new cars, new furniture, better clothes, and so on. There would be a surge in demand for goods and services. Car dealers, department stores, and other providers of goods and services would respond to this upsurge in demand by raising prices. The result would be price inflation.

	Big Mac Price in Dollars*	Implied PPP† of the Dollar	Under (–)/ Over (+) Valuation against the Dollar, %		Big Mac Price in Dollars*	Implied PPP† of the Dollar	Under (–)/ Over (+) Valuation against the Dollar, %
United States	3.06	—	—	Aruba	2.77	1.62	−10
Argentina	1.64	1.55	−46	Bulgaria	1.88	0.98	−39
Australia	2.50	1.06	−18	Colombia	2.79	2124	−9
Brazil	2.39	1.93	−22	Costa Rica	2.38	369	−22
Britain	3.44	1.63§	+12	Croatia	2.50	4.87	−18
Canada	2.63	1.07	−14	Dominican Republic	2.12	19.6	−31
Chile	2.53	490	−17	Estonia	2.31	9.64	−24
China	1.27	3.43	−59	Fiji	2.50	1.39	−18
Czech Republic	2.30	18.4	−25	Georgia	2.00	1.19	−34
Denmark	4.58	9.07	+50	Guatemala	2.20	5.47	−28
Egypt	1.55	2.94	−49	Honduras	1.91	11.7	−38
Euro area	3.58**	1.17††	+17	Iceland	6.67	143	+118
Hong Kong	1.54	3.92	−50	Jamaica	2.70	53.9	−12
Hungary	2.60	173	−15	Jordan	3.66	0.85	+19
Indonesia	1.53	4,771	−50	Latvia	1.92	0.36	−37
Japan	2.34	81.7	−23	Lebanon	2.85	1405	−7
Malaysia	1.38	1.72	−55	Lithuania	2.31	2.12	−24
Mexico	2.58	9.15	−16	Macau	1.40	3.66	−54
New Zealand	3.17	1.45	+4	Macedonia	1.90	31.0	−38
Peru	2.76	2.94	−10	Moldova	1.84	7.52	−40
Philippines	1.47	26.1	−52	Morocco	2.73	8.02	−11
Poland	1.96	2.12	−36	Nicaragua	2.11	11.3	−31
Russia	1.48	13.7	−52	Norway	6.06	12.7	+98
Singapore	2.17	1.18	−29	Pakistan	2.18	42.5	−29
South Africa	2.10	4.56	−31	Paraguay	1.44	2941	−53
South Korea	2.49	817	−19	Qatar	0.68	0.81	−78
Sweden	4.17	10.1	+36	Saudi Arabia	2.40	2.94	−22
Switzerland	5.05	2.06	+65	Serbia & Montenegro	2.08	45.8	−32
Taiwan	2.41	24.5	−21	Slovakia	2.09	21.6	−32
Thailand	1.48	19.6	−52	Slovenia	2.56	163	−16
Turkey	2.92	1.31	−5	Sri Lanka	1.75	57.2	−43
Venezuela	2.13	1,830	−30	Ukraine	1.43	2.37	−53
				UAE	2.45	2.94	−20
				Uruguay	1.82	14.4	−40

TABLE 10.2

The Big Mac Index, June 2005

*At current exchange rates †Purchasing-power parity ‡Average of New York, Chicago, San Francisco and Atlanta §Dollars per pound
**Weighted average of member countries ††Dollars per euro

A government increasing the money supply is analogous to giving people more money. An increase in the money supply makes it easier for banks to borrow from the government and for individuals and companies to borrow from banks. The resulting increase in credit causes increases in demand for goods and services. Unless the output of goods and services is growing at a rate similar to that of the money supply, the result will be inflation. This relationship has been observed time after time in country after country.

So now we have a connection between the growth in a country's money supply, price inflation, and exchange rate movements. Put simply, when the growth in a country's money supply is faster than the growth in its output, price inflation is fueled. The PPP theory tells us that a country with a high inflation rate will see depreciation in its currency exchange rate. In one of the clearest historical examples, in the mid-1980s, Bolivia experienced hyperinflation—an explosive and seemingly uncontrollable price inflation in which money loses value very rapidly. Table 10.3 presents data on Bolivia's money supply, inflation rate, and its peso's exchange rate with the U.S. dollar during the period of hyperinflation. The exchange rate is actually the "black market" exchange rate, as the Bolivian government prohibited converting the peso to other currencies during the period. The data show that the growth in money supply, the rate of price inflation, and the depreciation of the peso against the dollar all moved in step with each other. This is just what PPP theory and monetary economics predict. Between April 1984 and July 1985, Bolivia's money supply increased by 17,433 percent, prices increased by 22,908 percent, and the value of the peso against the dollar fell by 24,662 percent! In October 1985, the Bolivian government instituted a dramatic stabilization plan—which included the introduction of a new currency and tight control of the money supply—and by 1987 the country's annual inflation rate was down to 16 percent.[8]

Another way of looking at the same phenomenon is that an increase in a country's money supply, which increases the amount of currency available, changes the relative demand and supply conditions in the foreign exchange market. If the U.S. money supply is growing more rapidly than U.S. output, dollars will be relatively more plentiful than the currencies of countries where monetary growth is closer to output growth. As a result of this relative increase in the supply of dollars, the dollar will depreciate on the foreign exchange market against the currencies of countries with slower monetary growth.

Government policy determines whether the rate of growth in a country's money supply is greater than the rate of growth in output. A government can increase the money supply simply by telling the country's central bank to issue more money. Governments tend to do this to finance public expenditure (building roads, paying government workers, paying for defense, etc.). A government could finance public expenditure by raising taxes, but since nobody likes paying more taxes and since politicians do not like to be unpopular, they have a natural preference for expanding the money supply. Unfortunately, there is no magic money tree. The inevitable result of excessive growth in money supply is price inflation. However, this has not stopped governments around the world from expanding the money supply, with predictable results. If an international business is attempting to predict future movements in the value of a country's currency on the foreign exchange market, it should examine that country's policy toward monetary growth. If the government seems committed to controlling the rate of growth in money supply, the country's future inflation rate may be low (even if the current rate is high) and its currency should not depreciate too much on the foreign exchange market. If the government seems to lack the political will to control the rate of growth in money supply, the future inflation rate may be high, which is likely to cause its currency to depreciate. Historically, many Latin American governments have fallen into this latter category, including Argentina, Bolivia, and Brazil. More recently, many of the newly democratic states of Eastern Europe made the same mistake.

Empirical Tests of PPP Theory

PPP theory predicts that exchange rates are determined by relative prices, and that changes in relative prices will result in a change in exchange rates. A country in which price inflation is running wild should expect to see its currency depreciate against that of

TABLE 10.3

Macroeconomic Data for Bolivia, April 1984–October 1985

Source: Juan-Antino Morales, "Inflation Stabilization in Bolivia," in *Inflation Stabilization: The Experience of Israel, Argentina, Brazil, Bolivia, and Mexico,* ed. Michael Bruno et al. (Cambridge, MA: MIT Press, 1988).

Month	Money Supply (billions of pesos)	Price Level Relative to 1982 (average = 1)	Exchange Rate (pesos per dollar)
1984			
April	270	21.1	3,576
May	330	31.1	3,512
June	440	32.3	3,342
July	599	34.0	3,570
August	718	39.1	7,038
September	889	53.7	13,685
October	1,194	85.5	15,205
November	1,495	112.4	18,469
December	3,296	180.9	24,515
1985			
January	4,630	305.3	73,016
February	6,455	863.3	141,101
March	9,089	1,078.6	128,137
April	12,885	1,205.7	167,428
May	21,309	1,635.7	272,375
June	27,778	2,919.1	481,756
July	47,341	4,854.6	885,476
August	74,306	8,081.0	1,182,300
September	103,272	12,647.6	1,087,440
October	132,550	12,411.8	1,120,210

countries with lower inflation rates. This is intuitively appealing, but is it true in practice? There are several good examples of the connection between a country's price inflation and exchange rate position (such as Bolivia). However, extensive empirical testing of PPP theory has yielded mixed results.[9] While PPP theory seems to yield relatively accurate predictions in the long run, it does not appear to be a strong predictor of short-run movements in exchange rates covering time spans of five years or less.[10] In addition, the theory seems to best predict exchange rate changes for countries with high rates of inflation and underdeveloped capital markets. The theory is less useful for predicting short-term exchange rate movements between the currencies of advanced industrialized nations that have relatively small differentials in inflation rates.

The failure to find a strong link between relative inflation rates and exchange rate movements has been referred to as the purchasing power parity puzzle. Several factors may explain the failure of PPP theory to predict exchange rates more accurately.[11] PPP theory assumes away transportation costs and barriers to trade. In practice, these factors are significant and they tend to create significant price differentials between countries.

Transportation costs are certainly not trivial for many goods. Moreover, as we saw in Chapter 6, governments routinely intervene in international trade, creating tariff and nontariff barriers to cross-border trade. Barriers to trade limit the ability of traders to use arbitrage to equalize prices for the same product in different countries, which is required for the law of one price to hold. Government intervention in cross-border trade, by violating the assumption of efficient markets, weakens the link between relative price changes and changes in exchange rates predicted by PPP theory.

In addition, the PPP theory may not hold if many national markets are dominated by a handful of multinational enterprises that have sufficient market power to be able to exercise some influence over prices, control distribution channels, and differentiate their product offerings between nations.[12] In fact, this situation seems to prevail in a number of industries. In the detergent industry, two companies, Unilever and Procter & Gamble, dominate the market in nation after nation. In heavy earthmoving equipment, Caterpillar Inc. and Komatsu are global market leaders. In the market for semiconductor equipment, Applied Materials has a commanding market share lead in almost every important national market. Microsoft dominates the market for personal computer operating systems and applications systems around the world, and so on. In such cases, dominant enterprises may be able to exercise a degree of pricing power, setting different prices in different markets to reflect varying demand conditions. This is referred to as price discrimination. For price discrimination to work, arbitrage must be limited. According to this argument, enterprises with some market power may be able to control distribution channels and therefore limit the unauthorized resale (arbitrage) of products purchased in another national market. They may also be able to limit resale (arbitrage) by differentiating otherwise identical products among nations along some line, such as design or packaging.

For example, even though the version of Microsoft Office sold in China may be less expensive than the version sold in the United States, the use of arbitrage to equalize prices may be limited because few Americans would want a version that was based on Chinese characters. The design differentiation between Microsoft Office for China and for the United States means that the law of one price would not work for Microsoft Office, even if transportation costs were trivial and tariff barriers between the United States and China did not exist. If the inability to practice arbitrage were widespread enough, it would break the connection between changes in relative prices and exchange rates predicted by the PPP theorem and help explain the limited empirical support for this theory.

Another factor of some importance is that governments also intervene in the foreign exchange market in attempting to influence the value of their currencies. We will look at why and how they do this in Chapter 11. For now, the important thing to note is that governments regularly intervene in the foreign exchange market, and this further weakens the link between price changes and changes in exchange rates. One more factor explaining the failure of PPP theory to predict short-term movements in foreign exchange rates is the impact of investor psychology and other factors on currency purchasing decisions and exchange rate movements. We will discuss this issue in more detail later in this chapter.

INTEREST RATES AND EXCHANGE RATES

Economic theory tells us that interest rates reflect expectations about likely future inflation rates. In countries where inflation is expected to be high, interest rates also will be high, because investors want compensation for the decline in the value of their money. This relationship was first formalized by economist Irvin Fisher and is referred to as the Fisher Effect. The **Fisher Effect** states that a country's "nominal" interest rate (i) is the sum of the required "real" rate of interest (r) and the expected rate of inflation over the period for which the funds are to be lent (I). More formally,

$$i = r + I$$

For example, if the real rate of interest in a country is 5 percent and annual inflation is expected to be 10 percent, the nominal interest rate will be 15 percent. As predicted by the Fisher Effect, a strong relationship seems to exist between inflation rates and interest rates.[13]

We can take this one step further and consider how it applies in a world of many countries and unrestricted capital flows. When investors are free to transfer capital between countries, real interest rates will be the same in every country. If differences in real interest rates did emerge between countries, arbitrage would soon equalize them. For example, if the real interest rate in Japan was 10 percent and only 6 percent in the United States, it would pay investors to borrow money in the United States and invest it in Japan. The resulting increase in the demand for money in the United States would raise the real interest rate there, while the increase in the supply of foreign money in Japan would lower the real interest rate there. This would continue until the two sets of real interest rates were equalized.

It follows from the Fisher Effect that if the real interest rate is the same worldwide, any difference in interest rates between countries reflects differing expectations about inflation rates. Thus, if the expected rate of inflation in the United States is greater than that in Japan, U.S. nominal interest rates will be greater than Japanese nominal interest rates.

Since we know from PPP theory that there is a link (in theory at least) between inflation and exchange rates, and since interest rates reflect expectations about inflation, it follows that there must also be a link between interest rates and exchange rates. This link is known as the International Fisher Effect (IFE). The **International Fisher Effect** states that for any two countries, the spot exchange rate should change in an equal amount but in the opposite direction to the difference in nominal interest rates between the two countries. Stated more formally, the change in the spot exchange rate between the United States and Japan, for example, can be modeled as follows:

$$[(S_1 - S_2)/S_2] \times 100 = i_\$ - i_¥$$

where $i_\$$ and $i_¥$ are the respective nominal interest rates in the United States and Japan, S_1 is the spot exchange rate at the beginning of the period, and S_2 is the spot exchange rate at the end of the period. If the U.S. nominal interest rate is higher than Japan's, reflecting greater expected inflation rates, the value of the dollar against the yen should fall by that interest rate differential in the future. So if the interest rate in the United States is 10 percent and in Japan it is 6 percent, we would expect the value of the dollar to depreciate by 4 percent against the Japanese yen.

Do interest rate differentials help predict future currency movements? The evidence is mixed; as in the case of PPP theory, in the long run, there seems to be a relationship between interest rate differentials and subsequent changes in spot exchange rates. However, considerable short-run deviations occur. Like PPP, the International Fisher Effect is not a good predictor of short-run changes in spot exchange rates.[14]

INVESTOR PSYCHOLOGY AND BANDWAGON EFFECTS

Empirical evidence suggests that neither PPP theory nor the International Fisher Effect are particularly good at explaining short-term movements in exchange rates. One reason may be the impact of investor psychology on short-run exchange rate movements. Evidence accumulated over the last decade reveals that various psychological factors play an important role in determining the expectations of market traders as to likely future exchange rates.[15] In turn, expectations have a tendency to become self-fulfilling prophecies.

A good example of this mechanism occurred in September 1992 when the famous international financier George Soros made a huge bet against the British pound. Soros borrowed billions of pounds, using the assets of his investment funds as collateral, and immediately sold those pounds for German deutschmarks (this was before the advent of the euro). This technique, known as **short selling,** can earn the speculator enormous profits if he can subsequently buy back the pounds he sold at a much better exchange rate, and then use those pounds, purchased cheaply, to repay his loan. By selling pounds and buying deutschmarks, Soros helped to start pushing down the value of the pound on the foreign exchange markets. More importantly, when Soros started shorting the British pound, many foreign exchange traders, knowing Soros's reputation, jumped on the bandwagon and did likewise. This triggered a classic *bandwagon effect* with traders moving as a herd in the same

George Soros, whose Quantum Fund has been fantastically successful in managing **hedge funds,** has been criticized by world leaders for being able to cause huge changes in currency markets by his actions.

COUNTRY FOCUS In early 1997, South Korea could look back with pride on a 30-year "economic miracle" that had raised the country from the ranks of the poor and given it the world's 11th largest economy. By the end of 1997, the Korean currency, the won, had lost a staggering 67 percent of its value against the U.S. dollar, the South Korean economy lay in tatters, and the International Monetary Fund was overseeing a $55 billion rescue package. This sudden turn of events had its roots in investments made by South Korea's large industrial conglomerates, or *chaebol,* during the 1990s, often at the bequest of politicians. In 1993, Kim Young-Sam, a populist politician, became president of South Korea. Mr. Kim took office during a mild recession and promised to boost economic growth by encouraging investment in export-oriented industries. He urged the *chaebol* to invest in new factories. South Korea enjoyed an investment-led economic boom in 1994–1995, but at a cost. The *chaebol,* always reliant on heavy borrowing, built up massive debts that were equivalent, on average, to four times their equity.

As the volume of investments ballooned during the 1990s, the quality of many of these investments declined significantly. The investments often were made on the basis of unrealistic projections about future demand conditions. This resulted in significant excess capacity and falling prices. An example is investments made by South Korean *chaebol* in semiconductor factories. Investments in such facilities surged in 1994 and 1995 when a temporary global shortage of dynamic random access memory chips (DRAMs) led to sharp price increases for this product. However, supply shortages had disappeared by 1996 and excess capacity was beginning to make itself felt, just as the South Koreans started to bring new DRAM factories on stream. The results were predictable; prices for DRAMs plunged and the earnings of South Korean DRAM manufacturers fell by 90 percent, which meant it was difficult for them to make scheduled payments on the debt they had acquired to build the extra capacity. The risk of corporate bankruptcy increased significantly, and not just in the semiconductor industry. South Korean companies were also investing heavily in a wide range of other industries, including automobiles and steel.

Matters were complicated further because much of the borrowing had been in U.S. dollars, as opposed to Korean won. This had seemed like a smart move at the time. The dollar/won exchange rate had been stable at around $1 = won850. Interest rates on dollar borrowings were two to three percentage points lower than rates on borrowings in Korean won. Much of this borrowing was in the form of short-term, dollar-denominated debt that had to be paid back to the lending institution within one year. While the borrowing strategy seemed to make sense, it involved risk. If the won were to depreciate against the dollar, the size of the debt burden that South Korean companies would have to service would increase when measured in the local currency. Currency depreciation would raise borrowing costs, depress corporate earnings, and increase the risk of bankruptcy. This is exactly what happened.

direction at the same time. As the bandwagon effect gained momentum, with more traders selling British pounds and purchasing deutsche marks in expectation of a decline in the pound, their expectations became a self-fulfilling prophecy. Massive selling forced down the value of the pound against the deutsch mark. In other words, the pound declined in value not so much because of any major shift in macroeconomic fundamentals, but because investors followed a bet placed by a major speculator, George Soros.

According to a number of studies, investor psychology and bandwagon effects play a major role in determining short-run exchange rate movements.[16] However, these effects can be hard to predict. Investor psychology can be influenced by political factors and by microeconomic events, such as the investment decisions of individual firms, many of which are only loosely linked to macroeconomic fundamentals, such as relative inflation rates. Also, bandwagon effects can be both triggered and exacerbated by the idiosyncratic behavior of politicians. Something like this seems to have occurred in Southeast Asia during 1997 when, one after another, the currencies of Thailand, Malaysia, South Korea, and Indonesia lost between 50 percent and 70 percent of their value against the U.S. dol-

By mid-1997, foreign investors had become alarmed at the rising debt levels of South Korean companies, particularly given the emergence of excess capacity and plunging prices in several areas where the companies had made huge investments, including semiconductors, automobiles, and steel. Given increasing speculation that many South Korean companies would not be able to service their debt payments, foreign investors began to withdraw their money from the Korean stock and bond markets. In the process, they sold Korean won and purchased U.S. dollars. The selling of won accelerated in mid-1997 when two of the smaller *chaebol* filed for bankruptcy, citing their inability to meet scheduled debt payments. The increased supply of won and the increased demand for U.S. dollars pushed down the price of won in dollar terms from around won 840 = $1 to won 900 = $1.

At this point, the South Korean central bank stepped into the foreign exchange market to try to keep the exchange rate above won 1,000 = $1. It used dollars that it held in reserve to purchase won. The idea was to try to push up the price of the won in dollar terms and restore investor confidence in the stability of the exchange rate. This action, however, did not address the underlying debt problem faced by South Korean companies. Against a backdrop of more corporate bankruptcies in South Korea, and the government's stated intentions to take some troubled companies into state ownership, Standard & Poor's, the U.S. credit rating agency, downgraded South Korea's sovereign debt. This caused the Korean stock market to plunge 5.5 percent, and the Korean won to fall to won 930 = $1. According to S&P, "The downgrade of

. . . ratings reflects the escalating cost to the government of supporting the country's ailing corporate and financial sectors."

The S&P downgrade triggered a sharp sale of the Korean won. In an attempt to protect the won against what was fast becoming a classic bandwagon effect, the South Korean central bank raised short-term interest rates to over 12 percent, more than double the inflation rate. The bank also stepped up its intervention in the currency exchange markets, selling dollars and purchasing won in an attempt to keep the exchange rate above won 1,000 = $1. The main effect of this action, however, was to rapidly deplete South Korea's foreign exchange reserves. These stood at $30 billion on November 1, but fell to only $15 billion two weeks later. With its foreign exchange reserves almost exhausted, the South Korean central bank gave up its defense of the won November 17. Immediately, the price of won in dollars plunged to around won 1,500 = $1, effectively increasing by 60 to 70 percent the amount of won heavily indebted Korean companies had to pay to meet scheduled payments on their dollar-denominated debt. These losses, due to adverse changes in foreign exchange rates, depressed the profits of many firms. South Korean firms suffered foreign exchange losses of more than $15 billion in 1997.

Sources: J. Burton and G. Baker, "The Country That Invested Its Way into Trouble," *Financial Times*, January 15, 1998, p. 8; J. Burton, "South Korea's Credit Rating Is Lowered," *Financial Times*, October 25, 1997, p. 3; J. Burton, "Currency Losses Hit Samsung Electronics," *Financial Times*, March 20, 1998, p. 24; and "Korean Firms' Foreign Exchange Losses Exceed US $15 Billion," *Business Korea*, February 1998, p. 55.

lar in a few months. For a detailed look at what occurred in South Korea, see the accompanying Country Focus. The collapse in the value of the Korean currency did not occur because South Korea had a higher inflation rate than the United States. It occurred because of an excessive buildup of dollar-denominated debt among South Korean firms. By mid-1997 it was clear that these companies were having trouble servicing this debt. Foreign investors, fearing a wave of corporate bankruptcies, took their money out of the country, exchanging won for U.S. dollars. As this began to depress the exchange rate, currency traders jumped on the bandwagon and speculated against the won (selling it short), and it was this that produced a collapse in the value of the won.

SUMMARY

Relative monetary growth, relative inflation rates, and nominal interest rate differentials are all moderately good predictors of long-run changes in exchange rates. They are poor predictors of short-run changes in exchange rates, however, perhaps because of the impact of psychological factors, investor expectations, and bandwagon effects on short-term currency movements. This information is useful for an international business. Insofar as the long-term profitability of foreign investments, export opportunities, and the price competitiveness of foreign imports are all influenced by long-term movements in exchange rates, international businesses would be advised to pay attention to countries' differing monetary growth, inflation, and interest rates. International businesses that engage in foreign exchange transactions on a day-to-day basis could benefit by knowing some predictors of short-term foreign exchange rate movements. Unfortunately, short-term exchange rate movements are difficult to predict.

🌐 Exchange Rate Forecasting

A company's need to predict future exchange rate variations raises the issue of whether it is worthwhile for the company to invest in exchange rate forecasting services to aid decision making. Two schools of thought address this issue. The efficient market school argues that forward exchange rates do the best possible job of forecasting future spot exchange rates, and, therefore, investing in forecasting services would be a waste of money. The other school of thought, the inefficient market school, argues that companies can improve the foreign exchange market's estimate of future exchange rates (as contained in the forward rate) by investing in forecasting services. In other words, this school of thought does not believe the forward exchange rates are the best possible predictors of future spot exchange rates.

THE EFFICIENT MARKET SCHOOL

Forward exchange rates represent market participants' collective predictions of likely spot exchange rates at specified future dates. If forward exchange rates are the best possible predictor of future spot rates, it would make no sense for companies to spend additional money trying to forecast short-run exchange rate movements. Many economists believe the foreign exchange market is efficient at setting forward rates.[17] An **efficient market** is one in which prices reflect all available public information. (If forward rates reflect all available information about likely future changes in exchange rates, a company cannot beat the market by investing in forecasting services.)

If the foreign exchange market is efficient, forward exchange rates should be unbiased predictors of future spot rates. This does not mean the predictions will be accurate in any specific situation. It means inaccuracies will not be consistently above or below future spot rates; they will be random. Many empirical tests have addressed the efficient market hypothesis. Although most of the early work seems to confirm the hypothesis (suggesting that companies should not waste their money on forecasting services) some recent studies have challenged it.[18] There is some evidence that forward rates are not unbiased predictors of future spot rates, and that more accurate predictions of future spot rates can be calculated from publicly available information.[19]

THE INEFFICIENT MARKET SCHOOL

Citing evidence against the efficient market hypothesis, some economists believe the foreign exchange market is inefficient. An **inefficient market** is one in which prices do not reflect all available information. In an inefficient market, forward exchange rates will not be the best possible predictors of future spot exchange rates.

If this is true, it may be worthwhile for international businesses to invest in forecasting services (as many do). The belief is that professional exchange rate forecasts might provide better predictions of future spot rates than forward exchange rates do. However, the track record of professional forecasting services is not that good.[20] For example, forecasting services did not predict the 1997 currency crisis that swept through Southeast Asia.

APPROACHES TO FORECASTING

Assuming the inefficient market school is correct that the foreign exchange market's estimate of future spot rates can be improved, on what basis should forecasts be prepared? Here again, there are two schools of thought. One adheres to fundamental analysis, while the other uses technical analysis.

Fundamental Analysis

Fundamental analysis draws on economic theory to construct sophisticated econometric models for predicting exchange rate movements. The variables contained in these models typically include those we have discussed, such as relative money supply growth rates, inflation rates, and interest rates. In addition, they may include variables related to balance-of-payments positions.

Running a deficit on a balance-of-payments current account (a country is importing more goods and services than it is exporting) creates pressures that may result in the depreciation of the country's currency on the foreign exchange market.[21] Consider what might happen if the United States was running a persistent current account balance-of-payments deficit. Since the United States would be importing more than it was exporting, people in other countries would be increasing their holdings of U.S. dollars. If these people were willing to hold their dollars, the dollar's exchange rate would not be influenced. However, if these people converted their dollars into other currencies, the supply of dollars in the foreign exchange market would increase (as would demand for the other currencies). This shift in demand and supply would create pressures that could lead to the depreciation of the dollar against other currencies.

This argument hinges on whether people in other countries are willing to hold dollars. This depends on such factors as U.S. interest rates, the return on holding other dollar-denominated assets such as stocks in U.S. companies, and, most importantly, inflation rates. So, in a sense, the balance-of-payments situation is not a fundamental predictor of future exchange rate movements. For example, between 1998 and 2001, the U.S. dollar appreciated against most major currencies despite a growing balance-of-payments deficit. Relatively high real interest rates in the United States, coupled with low inflation and a booming U.S. stock market that attracted inward investment from foreign capital, made the dollar very attractive to foreigners, so they did not convert their dollars into other currencies. On the contrary, they converted other currencies into dollars to invest in U.S. financial assets, such as bonds and stocks, because they believed they could earn a high return by doing so. Capital flows into the United States fueled by foreigners who wanted to buy U.S. stocks and bonds kept the dollar strong despite the current account deficit. But what makes financial assets such as stocks and bonds attractive? The answer is prevailing interest rates and inflation rates, both of which affect underlying economic growth and the real return to holding U.S. financial assets. Given this, we are back to the argument that the fundamental determinants of exchange rates are monetary growth, inflation rates, and interest rates.

Technical Analysis

Technical analysis uses price and volume data to determine past trends, which are expected to continue into the future. This approach does not rely on a consideration of economic fundamentals. Technical analysis is based on the premise that there are analyzable market trends and waves and that previous trends and waves can be used to predict future trends and waves. Since there is no theoretical rationale for this assumption of predictability, many economists compare technical analysis to fortune-telling. Despite this skepticism, technical analysis has gained favor in recent years.[22]

Currency Convertibility

Until this point we have invalidly assumed that the currencies of various countries are freely convertible into other currencies. Due to government restrictions, a significant number of currencies are not freely convertible into other currencies. A country's currency is said to be **freely convertible** when the country's government allows both residents and nonresidents to purchase unlimited amounts of a foreign currency with it. A currency is said to be **externally convertible** when only nonresidents may convert it into a foreign currency without any limitations. A currency is **nonconvertible** when neither residents nor nonresidents are allowed to convert it into a foreign currency.

Free convertibility is not universal. Many countries place some restrictions on their residents' ability to convert the domestic currency into a foreign currency (a policy of external convertibility). Restrictions range from the relatively minor (such as restricting the amount of foreign currency they may take with them out of the country on trips) to the major (such as restricting domestic businesses' ability to take foreign currency out of the country). External convertibility restrictions can limit domestic companies' ability to invest abroad, but they present few problems for foreign companies wishing to do business in that country. For example, even if the Japanese government tightly controlled the ability of its residents to convert the yen into U.S. dollars, all U.S. businesses with deposits in Japanese banks may at any time convert all their yen into dollars and take them out of the country. Thus, a U.S. company with a subsidiary in Japan is assured that it will be able to convert the profits from its Japanese operation into dollars and take them out of the country.

Serious problems arise, however, under a policy of nonconvertibility. This was the practice of the former Soviet Union, and it continued to be the practice in Russia until recently. When strictly applied, nonconvertibility means that although a U.S. company doing business in a country such as Russia may be able to generate significant ruble profits, it may not convert those rubles into dollars and take them out of the country. Obviously this is not desirable for international business.

Governments limit convertibility to preserve their foreign exchange reserves. A country needs an adequate supply of these reserves to service its international debt commitments and to purchase imports. Governments typically impose convertibility restrictions on their currency when they fear that free convertibility will lead to a run on their foreign exchange reserves. This occurs when residents and nonresidents rush to convert their holdings of domestic currency into a foreign currency—a phenomenon generally referred to as **capital flight.** Capital flight is most likely to occur when the value of the domestic currency is depreciating rapidly because of hyperinflation, or when a country's economic prospects are shaky in other respects. Under such circumstances, both residents and nonresidents tend to believe that their money is more likely to hold its value if it is converted into a foreign currency and invested abroad. Not only will a run on foreign exchange reserves limit the country's ability to service its international debt and pay for imports, but it will also lead to a precipitous depreciation in the exchange rate as residents and nonresidents unload their holdings of domestic currency on the foreign exchange markets (thereby increasing the market supply of the country's currency). Governments fear that the rise in import prices resulting from currency depreciation will lead to further increases in inflation. This fear provides another rationale for limiting convertibility.

Companies can deal with the nonconvertibility problem by engaging in countertrade. Countertrade is discussed in detail in Chapter 15, so we will merely introduce the concept here. Countertrade refers to a range of barterlike agreements by which goods and services can be traded for other goods and services. Countertrade can make sense when a country's currency is nonconvertible. For example, consider the deal that General Electric struck with the Romanian government in 1984, when that country's currency was nonconvertible. When General Electric won a contract for a $150 million generator project in Romania, it agreed to take payment in the form of Romanian goods that could be sold for $150 million on international markets. In a similar case, the Venezuelan government negotiated a contract with Caterpillar in 1986 under which Venezuela would trade 350,000 tons of iron ore for Caterpillar heavy construction equipment. Caterpillar subsequently traded the iron ore to Romania in exchange for Romanian farm products, which it then sold on international markets for dollars.[23] More recently, in a 2003 deal the government of Indonesia entered into a countertrade with Libya under which Libya agreed to purchase $540 million in Indonesian goods, including textiles, tea, coffee, electronics, plastics, and auto parts, in exchange for 50,000 barrels per day of Libyan crude oil.[24]

How important is countertrade? Twenty years ago, a large number of nonconvertible currencies existed in the world, and countertrade was quite significant. However, in recent years many governments have made their currencies freely convertible, and the percentage of world trade that involves countertrade is probably below 10 percent.[25]

IMPLICATIONS FOR MANAGERS

This chapter contains a number of clear implications for business. First, it is critical that international businesses understand the influence of exchange rates on the profitability of trade and investment deals. Adverse changes in exchange rates can make apparently profitable deals unprofitable. As noted, the risk introduced into international business transactions by changes in exchange rates is referred to as foreign exchange risk. Foreign exchange risk is usually divided into three main categories: transaction exposure, translation exposure, and economic exposure.

TRANSACTION EXPOSURE

Transaction exposure is the extent to which the income from individual transactions is affected by fluctuations in foreign exchange values. Such exposure includes obligations for the purchase or sale of goods and services at previously agreed prices and the borrowing or lending of funds in foreign currencies. For example, suppose in 2001 an American airline agrees to purchase 10 Airbus 330 aircraft for €120 million each for a total price of €1.20 billion, with delivery scheduled for 2005 and payment due then. When the contract was signed in 2001 the dollar/euro exchange rate stood at $1 = €1.10 so the American airline anticipates paying $1.09 billion for the 10 aircraft when they are delivered (€1.2 billion/1.1 = $1.09 billion). However, imagine that the value of the dollar depreciates against the euro over the intervening period, so that one dollar only buys €0.80 in 2005 when payment is due ($1 = €0.80). Now the total cost in U.S. dollars is $1.5 billion (€1.2 billion/0.80 = $1.5 billion), an increase of $0.41 billion! The *transaction exposure* here is $0.41 billion, which is the money lost due to an adverse movement in exchange rates between the time when the deal was signed and when the aircraft were paid for.

TRANSLATION EXPOSURE

Translation exposure is the impact of currency exchange rate changes on the reported financial statements of a company. Translation exposure is basically concerned with the present measurement of past events. The resulting accounting gains or losses are said to be unrealized—they are "paper" gains and losses—but they are still important. Consider a U.S. firm with a subsidiary in Mexico. If the value of the Mexican peso depreciates significantly against the dollar this would substantially reduce the dollar value of the Mexican subsidiary's equity. In turn, this would reduce the total dollar value of the firm's equity reported in its consolidated balance sheet. This would raise the apparent leverage of the firm (its debt ratio), which could increase the firm's cost of borrowing and potentially limit its access to the capital market. Similarly, if an American firm has a subsidiary in the European Union, and if the value of the euro depreciates rapidly against that of the dollar over a year, this will reduce the dollar value of the euro profit made by the European subsidiary, resulting in negative translation exposure. In fact, many U.S. firms suffered from significant translation exposure in Europe during 2000, precisely because the euro did depreciate rapidly against the dollar. The experience of one such firm, Baxter International, is given in the accompanying Management Focus. But in 2002–2004, the euro rose in value against the dollar, boosting the dollar profits of American multinationals with significant operations in Europe.

ECONOMIC EXPOSURE

Economic exposure is the extent to which a firm's future international earning power is affected by changes in exchange rates. Economic exposure is concerned with the long-run effect of changes in exchange rates on future prices, sales, and costs. This is distinct from transaction exposure, which is concerned with the effect of exchange rate changes on individual transactions, most of which are short-term affairs that will be executed within a few weeks or months. Consider the effect of wide swings in the value of the dollar on many U.S. firms' international competitiveness. The rapid rise in the value of the dollar on the foreign exchange market in the 1990s hurt the price competitiveness of many U.S. producers in world markets. U.S. manufacturers that relied heavily on exports (such as Caterpillar) saw their export volume and world market share decline. The reverse phenomenon occurred in 2000–2004, when the dollar declined against most major currencies. The fall in the value of the dollar helped increase the price competitiveness of U.S. manufacturers in world markets.

REDUCING TRANSLATION AND TRANSACTION EXPOSURE

A number of tactics can help firms minimize their transaction and translation exposure. These tactics primarily protect short-term cash flows from adverse changes in exchange rates. We have already discussed two of these tactics at length in the chapter, *entering into forward exchange rate contracts* and *buying swaps*. In addition to buying forward and using swaps, firms can minimize their foreign exchange exposure through leading and lagging payables and receivables—that is, paying suppliers and collecting payment from customers early or late depending on expected exchange rate movements. A **lead strategy** involves attempting to collect foreign currency receivables (payments from customers) early when a foreign currency is expected to depreciate and paying foreign currency payables (to suppliers) before they are due when a currency is expected to appreciate. A **lag strategy** involves delaying collection of foreign currency receivables if that currency is expected to appreciate and delaying payables if the currency is expected to depreciate. Leading and lagging involves accelerating payments from weak-currency to strong-currency countries and delaying inflows from strong-currency to weak-currency countries.

Lead and lag strategies can be difficult to implement, however. The firm must be in a position to exercise some control over payment terms. Firms do not always have this kind of bargaining power, particularly when they are dealing with important customers who are in a position to dictate payment terms. Also, because lead and lag strategies can put pressure on a weak currency, many governments limit leads and lags. For example, some countries set 180 days as a limit for receiving payments for exports or making payments for imports.

MANAGEMENT FOCUS On July 20, 2000, the CEO of Baxter International, a U.S. producer of medical products, announced that the company's second-quarter results were better than expected due to strong global sales. The CEO confidently predicted that the company would hit its earnings and sales targets for all of 2000, and, due to continuing strong global sales, would grow revenues and earnings by a figure in the mid-teens for 2001.

Three months later when the company released its third-quarter results, the CEO had a less optimistic story to tell. Year 2000 earnings and revenues were still on track, but the company now expected much slower growth in 2001, which would reduce the projected increase in operating income by some $100 million. The main culprit, according to the CEO, was the continuing weakness of the euro against the U.S. dollar. At €1 = $0.83 the euro had depreciated by 10 percent since July, and 30 percent since the beginning of 1999. The continued weakness meant that the dollar value of Baxter's European revenues and earnings, which accounted for about 27 percent of the company's 2000 revenues, would decline significantly. Baxter was not alone—a host of other U.S. companies also announced that due to negative translation exposure to the euro, their financial results for late 2000 and probably much of 2001 would be lower than previously thought. According to one estimate, the decline in the value of the euro between June and September 2000 reduced the value of earnings for the Standard & Poor's index of 500 large U.S. companies by 3 percent.

In the aftermath, many wondered why companies such as Baxter hadn't hedged their European earnings against a fall in the value of the euro by entering the foreign exchange market and buying forward, locking in a more favorable dollar/euro exchange rate? The answer was that the costs of hedging had risen dramatically during 2000 due to the high volatility of the euro against the dollar. The high volatility meant that foreign exchange dealers were worried about the risk associated with selling forward contracts. It was very difficult for them to predict where the dollar/euro exchange rate might be in a few months, so they demanded a high premium from companies in return for selling a forward contract or writing a currency option. The costs of hedging an exchange rate are related to the volatility of that exchange rate (i.e., how much the value of currencies fluctuate against each other), with a doubling in volatility often tripling the cost of hedging as foreign exchange dealers demand a higher premium for writing increasingly risky forward contracts or other derivative contracts such as currency options. The average annual volatility between two currencies over a year is about 8 to 10 percent, but the volatility of the dollar/euro exchange rate had risen to 18 to 20 percent, tripling the cost of hedging. For Baxter, that volatility meant the costs of hedging the euro against the dollar would run into tens of millions of dollars. So in mid-2000, Baxter decided to take a risk, and not hedge, effectively betting that the euro would stabilize against the dollar. It didn't, and Baxter lost the gamble.

Source: S. McMurray, "The Lost Art of Hedging," *Institutional Investor,* December 2000, pp. 63–69.

REDUCING ECONOMIC EXPOSURE

Reducing economic exposure requires strategic choices that go beyond the realm of financial management. The key to reducing economic exposure is to distribute the firm's productive assets to various locations so the firm's long-term financial well-being is not severely affected by adverse changes in exchange rates. The post-1985 trend by Japanese automakers to establish productive capacity in North America and Western Europe can partly be seen as a strategy for reducing economic exposure (it is also a strategy for reducing trade tensions). Before 1985, most Japanese automobile companies concentrated their productive assets in Japan. However, the rise in the value of the yen on the foreign exchange market transformed Japan from a low-cost to a high-cost manufacturing location. In response, Japanese auto firms have moved many of their productive assets overseas to ensure their car prices will not be unduly affected by further rises in the value of the yen. In general, reducing economic exposure necessitates that the firm ensure its assets are not too concentrated in countries where likely rises in currency values will lead to damaging increases in the foreign prices of the goods and services they produce.

OTHER STEPS FOR MANAGING FOREIGN EXCHANGE RISK

The firm needs to develop a mechanism for ensuring it maintains an appropriate mix of tactics and strategies for minimizing its foreign exchange exposure. Although there is no universal agreement as to the components of this mechanism, a number of common themes stand out.[26] First, central control of exposure is needed to protect resources efficiently and ensure that each subunit adopts the correct mix of tactics and strategies. Many companies have set up in-house foreign exchange centers. Although such centers may not be able to execute all foreign exchange deals—particularly in large, complex multinationals where myriad transactions may be pursued simultaneously— they should at least set guidelines for the firm's subsidiaries to follow.

Second, firms should distinguish between, on one hand, transaction and translation exposure and, on the other, economic exposure. Many companies seem to focus on reducing their transaction and translation exposure and pay scant attention to economic exposure, which may have more profound long-term implications.[27] Firms need to develop strategies for dealing with economic exposure. For example, Black & Decker, the maker of power tools, has a strategy for actively managing its economic risk. The key to Black & Decker's strategy is flexible sourcing. In response to foreign exchange movements, Black & Decker can move production from one location to another to offer the most competitive pricing. Black & Decker manufactures in more than a dozen locations around the world—in Europe, Australia, Brazil, Mexico, and Japan. More than 50 percent of the company's productive assets are based outside North America. Although each of Black & Decker's factories focuses on one or two products to achieve economies of scale, there is considerable overlap. On average, the company runs its factories at no more than 80 percent capacity, so most are able to switch rapidly from producing one product to producing another or to add a product. This allows a factory's production to be changed in response to foreign exchange movements. For example, if the dollar depreciates against other currencies, the amount of imports into the United States from overseas subsidiaries can be reduced and the amount of exports from U.S. subsidiaries to other locations can be increased.[28]

Third, the need to forecast future exchange rate movements cannot be overstated, though, as we saw earlier in the chapter, this is a tricky business. No model comes close to perfectly predicting future movements in foreign exchange rates. The best that can be said is that in the short run, forward exchange rates provide the best predictors of exchange rate movements, and in the long run, fundamental economic factors— particularly relative inflation rates—should be watched because they influence exchange rate movements. Some firms attempt to forecast exchange rate movements in-house; others rely on outside forecasters. However, all such forecasts are imperfect attempts to predict the future.

Fourth, firms need to establish good reporting systems so the central finance function (or in-house foreign exchange center) can regularly monitor the firm's exposure positions. Such reporting systems should enable the firm to identify any exposed accounts, the exposed position by currency of each account, and the time periods covered.

Finally, on the basis of the information it receives from exchange rate forecasts and its own regular reporting systems, the firm should produce monthly foreign exchange exposure reports. These reports should identify how cash flows and balance sheet elements might be affected by forecasted changes in exchange rates. The reports can then be used by management as a basis for adopting tactics and strategies to hedge against undue foreign exchange risks.

Surprisingly, some of the largest and most sophisticated firms don't take such precautionary steps, exposing themselves to very large foreign exchange risks. As we have seen in this chapter, Volkswagen, South African Airlines, and Baxter International all suffered significant losses during the early 2000s due to a failure to hedge their foreign exchange exposure.

Chapter Summary

This chapter explained how the foreign exchange market works, examined the forces that determine exchange rates, and then discussed the implications of these factors for international business. Given that changes in exchange rates can dramatically alter the profitability of foreign trade and investment deals, this is an area of major interest to international business. The chapter made the following points:

1. One function of the foreign exchange market is to convert the currency of one country into the currency of another. A second function of the foreign exchange market is to provide insurance against foreign exchange risk.

2. The spot exchange rate is the exchange rate at which a dealer converts one currency into another currency on a particular day.

3. Foreign exchange risk can be reduced by using forward exchange rates. A forward exchange rate is an exchange rate governing future transactions. Foreign exchange risk can also be reduced by engaging in currency swaps. A swap is the simultaneous purchase and sale of a given amount of foreign exchange for two different value dates.

4. The law of one price holds that in competitive markets that are free of transportation costs and barriers to trade, identical products sold in different countries must sell for the same price when their price is expressed in the same currency.

5. Purchasing power parity (PPP) theory states the price of a basket of particular goods should be roughly equivalent in each country. PPP theory predicts that the exchange rate will change if relative prices change.

6. The rate of change in countries' relative prices depends on their relative inflation rates. A country's inflation rate seems to be a function of the growth in its money supply.

7. The PPP theory of exchange rate changes yields relatively accurate predictions of long-term trends in exchange rates, but not of short-term movements. The failure of PPP theory to predict exchange rate changes more accurately may be due to transportation costs, barriers to trade and investment, and the impact of psychological factors such as bandwagon effects on market movements and short-run exchange rates.

8. Interest rates reflect expectations about inflation. In countries where inflation is expected to be high, interest rates also will be high.

9. The International Fisher Effect states that for any two countries, the spot exchange rate should change in an equal amount but in the opposite direction to the difference in nominal interest rates.

10. The most common approach to exchange rate forecasting is fundamental analysis. This relies on variables such as money supply growth, inflation rates, nominal interest rates, and balance-of-payments positions to predict future changes in exchange rates.

11. In many countries, the ability of residents and nonresidents to convert local currency into a foreign currency is restricted by government policy. A government restricts the convertibility of its currency to protect the country's foreign exchange reserves and to halt any capital flight.

12. Problematic for international business is a policy of nonconvertibility, which prohibits residents and nonresidents from exchanging local currency for foreign currency. Nonconvertibility makes it very difficult to engage in international trade and investment in the country. One way of coping with the nonconvertibility problem is to engage in countertrade—to trade goods and services for other goods and services.

13. The three types of exposure to foreign exchange risk are transaction exposure, translation exposure, and economic exposure.

14. Tactics that insure against transaction and translation exposure include buying forward, using currency swaps, leading and lagging payables and receivables, manipulating transfer prices, using local debt financing, accelerating dividend payments, and adjusting capital budgeting to reflect foreign exchange exposure.

15. Reducing a firm's economic exposure requires strategic choices about how the firm's productive assets are distributed around the globe.

16. To manage foreign exchange exposure effectively, the firm must exercise centralized oversight over its foreign exchange hedging activities, recognize the difference between transaction exposure and economic exposure, forecast future exchange rate movements, establish good reporting systems within the firm to monitor exposure positions, and produce regular foreign exchange exposure reports that can be used as a basis for action.

Critical Thinking and Discussion Questions

1. The interest rate on South Korean government securities with one-year maturity is 4 percent, and the expected inflation rate for the coming year is 2 percent. The interest rate on U.S. government securities with one-year maturity is 7 percent, and the expected rate of inflation is 5 percent. The current spot exchange rate for Korean won is $1 = W1,200. Forecast the spot exchange rate one year from today. Explain the logic of your answer.

2. Two countries, Great Britain and the United States, produce just one good: beef. Suppose the price of beef in the United States is $2.80 per pound and in Britain it is £3.70 per pound.

   a. According to PPP theory, what should the dollar/pound spot exchange rate be?

   b. Suppose the price of beef is expected to rise to $3.10 in the United States and to £4.65 in Britain. What should the one-year forward dollar/pound exchange rate be?

   c. Given your answers to parts a and b, and given that the current interest rate in the United States is 10 percent, what would you expect the current interest rate to be in Britain?

3. You manufacture wine goblets. In mid-June you receive an order for 10,000 goblets from Japan. Payment of ¥400,000 is due in mid-December. You expect the yen to rise from its present rate of $1 = ¥130 to $1 = ¥100 by December. You can borrow yen at 6 percent a year. What should you do?

4. You are the CFO of a U.S. firm whose wholly owned subsidiary in Mexico manufactures component parts for your U.S. assembly operations. The subsidiary has been financed by bank borrowings in the United States. One of your analysts told you that the Mexican peso is expected to depreciate by 30 percent against the dollar on the foreign exchange markets over the next year. What actions, if any, should you take?

Research Task   globalEDGE™   globaledge.msu.edu

Use the globalEDGE™ site to complete the following exercises:

1. You must ensure the availability of 100,000 euros for a payment scheduled for next month, but your company possesses only Indian rupees. Identify the spot and forward exchange rates. What factors affect your decision of utilizing spot versus forward exchange rates? Which one would you choose? How many rupees must you spend to acquire the needed euros?

2. The Big Mac Index compares the purchasing power parity of 120 countries based on the price of an identical item. Locate the latest edition of this index. Identify at least five Middle Eastern countries (and their currencies). Which Middle Eastern country has the lowest purchasing power parity according to this classification. Which currencies, if any, are overvalued?

The Rising Euro Hammers Auto Parts Manufacturers

CLOSING CASE Udo Pfeiffer, the CEO of SMS Elotherm, a German manufacturer of machine tools to engineer crankshafts for cars, signed a deal in late November 2004, to supply the U.S. operations of DaimlerChrysler with $1.5 million worth of machines. The machines would be manufactured in Germany and exported to the United States. When the deal was signed, Pfeiffer calculated that at the agreed price, the machines would yield a profit of €30,000 each. Within three days that profit had declined by €8,000! The dollar had slid precipitously against the euro. SMS would be paid in dollars by DaimlerChrysler, but when translated back into euros, the price had declined. Since the company's costs were in euros, the declining revenues when expressed in euros were squeezing profit margins.

With the exchange rate standing at €1 = $1.33 in early December 2004, Pfeiffer was deeply worried. He knew that if the dollar declined further to around €1 = $1.50, SMS would be losing money on its sales to America. He could try to raise the dollar price of his products to compensate for the fall in the value of the dollar, but he knew that was unlikely to work. The market for machine tools was very competitive, and manufacturers were constantly pressuring machine tool companies to lower prices, not raise them.

Another small German supplier to U.S. automobile companies, Keiper, was faring somewhat better. In 2001 Keiper, which manufactures metal frames for automobile seats, opened a plant in London, Ontario, to supply the U.S. operations of DaimlerChrysler. At the time the investment was made, the exchange rate was €1 = $1. Management at Keiper had agonized over whether the investment made sense. Some in the company felt that it was better to continue exporting from Germany. Others argued that Keiper would benefit from being close to a major customer. Now with the euro appreciating every day, it looked like a smart move. Keiper had a real hedge against the rising value of the euro. But the advantages of being based in Canada were tempered by two things; first, the U.S. dollar had also depreciated against the Canadian dollar, although not by as much as its depreciation against the euro. Second, Keiper was still importing parts from Germany, and the euro had also appreciated against the Canadian dollar, raising the costs at Keiper's Ontario plant.

Sources: Adapted from M. Landler, "Dollar's Fall Drains Profit of European Small Business," *The New York Times*, December 2, 2004, p. C1.

Case Discussion Questions

1. Could SMS Elotherm have taken steps to avoid the position it now found itself in? What were those steps? Why do you think the company did not take these steps?

2. Why was Keiper weathering the rise of the euro better than SMS?

3. In retrospect, what might Keiper have done differently to improve the value of its "real hedge" against a rise in the value of the euro?

4. If the U.S. dollar had appreciated against the euro and Canadian dollar, instead of depreciating, which company would have done better? Why?

Notes

1. For a good general introduction to the foreign exchange market, see R. Weisweiller, *How the Foreign Exchange Market Works* (New York: New York Institute of Finance, 1990). A detailed description of the economics of foreign exchange markets can be found in P. R. Krugman and M. Obstfeld, *International Economics: Theory and Policy* (New York: HarperCollins, 1994).

2. Bank for International Settlements, *Central Bank Survey of Foreign Exchange and Derivatives Market Activity, April 2004* (Basle, Switzerland: BIS, 2004).

3. Ibid.

4. Ibid.

5. For a comprehensive review see M. Taylor, "The Economics of Exchange Rates," *Journal of Economic Literature* 33 (1995), pp. 13–47.

6. Krugman and Obstfeld, *International Economics: Theory and Policy.*

7. M. Friedman, *Studies in the Quantity Theory of Money* (Chicago: University of Chicago Press, 1956). For an accessible explanation, see M. Friedman and R. Friedman, *Free to Choose* (London: Penguin Books, 1979), chap. 9.

8. Juan-Antino Morales, "Inflation Stabilization in Bolivia," in *Inflation Stabilization: The Experience of Israel, Argentina, Brazil, Bolivia, and Mexico,* ed. Michael Bruno et al. (Cambridge, MA: MIT Press, 1988), and The Economist, *World Book of Vital Statistics* (New York: Random House, 1990).

9. For reviews and recent articles see, H. J. Edison, J. E. Gagnon, and W. R. Melick, "Understanding the Empirical Literature on Purchasing Power Parity," *Journal of International Money and Finance* 16 (February 1997), pp. 1–18; J. R. Edison, "Multi-Country Evidence on the Behavior of Purchasing Power Parity under the Current Float," *Journal of International Money and Finance* 16 (February 1997), pp. 19–36; K. Rogoff, "The Purchasing Power Parity Puzzle," *Journal of Economic Literature* 34 (1996), pp. 647–68; D. R. Rapach and M. E. Wohar, "Testing the Monetary Model of Exchange Rate Determination: New Evidence from a Century of Data," *Journal of International Economics,* December 2002, pp. 359–85; and M. P. Taylor, "Purchasing Power Parity," *Review of International Economics,* August 2003, pp. 436–456.

10. M. Obstfeld and K. Rogoff, "The Six Major Puzzles in International Economics," National Bureau of Economic Research Working Paper No. 7777, July 2000.

11. Ibid.

12. See M. Devereux and C. Engel, "Monetary Policy in the Open Economy Revisited: Price Setting and Exchange Rate Flexibility," National Bureau of Economic Research Working Paper No. 7665, April 2000. Also P. Krugman, "Pricing to Market When the Exchange Rate Changes," in *Real Financial Economics,* ed. S. Arndt and J. Richardson (Cambridge, MA: MIT Press, 1987).

13. For a summary of the evidence, see the survey by Taylor, "The Economics of Exchange Rates."

14. R. E. Cumby and M. Obstfeld, "A Note on Exchange Rate Expectations and Nominal Interest Differentials: A Test of the Fisher Hypothesis," *Journal of Finance,* June 1981, pp. 697–703; and L. Coppock and M. Poitras, "Evaluating the Fisher Effect in Long Term Cross Country Averages," *International Review of Economics and Finance* 9 (2000), pp. 181–203.

15. Taylor, "The Economics of Exchange Rates." See also R. K. Lyons, *The Microstructure Approach to Exchange Rates* (Cambridge, MA: MIT Press, 2002).

16. See H. L. Allen and M. P. Taylor, "Charts, Noise, and Fundamentals in the Foreign Exchange Market," *Economic Journal* 100 (1990), pp. 49–59, and T. Ito, "Foreign Exchange Rate Expectations: Micro Survey Data," *American Economic Review* 80 (1990), pp. 434–49.

17. For example, see E. Fama, "Forward Rates as Predictors of Future Spot Rates," *Journal of Financial Economics,* October 1976, pp. 361–77.

18. L. Kilian and M. P. Taylor, "Why Is It so Difficult to Beat the Random Walk Forecast of Exchange Rates?" *Journal of International Economics* 20 (May 2003), pp. 85–103, and R. M. Levich, "The Efficiency of Markets for Foreign Exchange," in *International Finance,* ed. G. D. Gay and R. W. Kold (Richmond, VA: Robert F. Dane, Inc., 1983).

19. J. Williamson, *The Exchange Rate System* (Washington, DC: Institute for International Economics, 1983), and R. H. Clarida, L. Sarno, M. P. Taylor, and G. Valente, "The Out of Sample Success of Term Structure Models as Exchange Rate Predictors," *Journal of International Economics* 60 (May 2003), pp. 61–84.

20. Kilian and Taylor, "Why Is It So Difficult to Beat the Random Walk Forecast of Exchange Rates."

21. Rogoff, "The Purchasing Power Parity Puzzle."

22. C. Engel and J. D. Hamilton, "Long Swings in the Dollar: Are They in the Data and Do Markets Know It?" *American Economic Review,* September 1990, pp. 689–713.

23. J. R. Carter and J. Gagne, "The Do's and Don'ts of International Countertrade," *Sloan Management Review,* Spring 1988, pp. 31–37.

24. "Where There Is a Will," *Trade Finance*, October 2003, pp. 1–2.

25. D. S. Levine, "Got a Spare Destroyer Lying Around?" *World Trade* 10 (June 1997), pp. 34–35, and Dan West, "Countertrade," *Business Credit*, April 2001, pp. 64–67.

26. For details on how various firms manage their foreign exchange exposure, see the articles contained in the special foreign exchange issue of *Business International Money Report*, December 18, 1989, pp. 401–12.

27. Ibid.

28. S. Arterian, "How Black & Decker Defines Exposure," *Business International Money Report*, December 18, 1989, pp. 404, 405, 409.

11

The International Monetary System

Rescuing Brazil

The International Monetary Fund on August 7, 2002, agreed to provide Brazil with $30 billion in funds to help the country come to grips with a financial crisis that had driven its currency, the real, down to all-time lows against the U.S. dollar. This was not the first time the IMF had stepped in to help Brazil. The IMF had provided assistance to Brazil since 1998, when it gave $41.5 billion in financial commitments to the country to help it ride out a financial crisis that was driving down the value of the real on foreign exchange markets. Four years later the country was back at the IMF asking for more money.

There were several reasons for the 2002 crisis. First, a global economic slowdown had hurt the economies of South America, slowing exports, reducing foreign direct investment inflows, and leading to an economic recession. Second, earlier in the year Brazil's neighbor and largest trading partner, Argentina, had defaulted on its government debt. In the first half of 2002, Argentina's economy shrunk by almost 20 percent and unemployment surged to 22 percent. With financial chaos in Argentina, Brazilian exports to its neighbor slumped, helping to drive Brazil into a recession.

Third, in October 2002 Brazil was scheduled to hold presidential elections. Foreign investors were nervous that a populist left-wing candidate, Luiz Inacio Lula da Silva (known as "Lula"), would win, replacing President Fernando Henrique Cardoso. As finance minister in the early 1990s, Cardoso had been the mastermind of Brazil's "real plan," which conquered hyperinflation, a long-term problem in Brazil, and put the country on a stable growth track. Cardoso had won high marks from the international financial community for adhering rigorously to conditions imposed by the IMF in 1998 in return for its loans. An important part of that plan called for Brazil's government to run a budget surplus and use that to pay down government debt. If Cardoso was replaced by Lula, foreign investors feared that the Brazilian government's commitment to maintain IMF targets on Brazilian government debt levels would be shattered. Publicly, Lula had stated that he favored increasing government spending in times of economic crisis. To many, this seems like a recipe for more government debt—debt that in all probability would be financed by printing money and lead to a resurgence of hyperinflation. Foreign investors feared that this would be unsustainable, and that Brazil would ultimately follow the example of Argentina and default on its government debt. History provided little comfort for the foreign investment community; Brazil had defaulted on its government debt in the 1980s.

Rather than wait for the outcome of the October 2002 election, in early 2002 foreign investors began to pull money out of Brazil, while inflows of foreign capital started to dry up. This led to a fall in the value of the real against the dollar on foreign exchange markets. Sensing a currency crisis, traders began to sell the Brazilian currency short (effectively betting that it would go down). This put more pressure on the currency, and its decline against the dollar accelerated, falling by 25 percent by early August from its January levels.

To protect the real from further depreciation, the Brazilian central bank started to use its foreign exchange reserves (mainly U.S. dollars) to buy *real* on the foreign exchange markets. The central bank also raised interest rates—but this increased the costs of serving government debt—and implied that to meet IMF-mandated debt targets, the Brazilian government would have to further reduce government spending, taking money out of an economy that was already on the ropes.

It soon became clear that Brazil was in a very difficult position. The country's foreign exchange reserves were limited and high interest rates could be self-defeating. Without further assistance from the IMF the currency could collapse, plunging Brazil into a financial crisis. If this happened, it could destabilize the entire region, and perhaps throw the global financial system into chaos.

It was against this background that the IMF decided to extend further loans to Brazil. The $30 billion loan package would be spread out over 15 months. In return for the loans, the Brazilian government agreed to maintain a budget surplus of at least 3.75 percent of GDP, using the surplus to continue retiring Brazilian government debt. However, the IMF did not seek agreement from election candidates, such as Lula, to abide by the terms of the agreement. This led to some skepticism on the part of investors, and the real declined by another 15 percent against the dollar by late September. At this point, Lula stated that if he won the presidential election in October, he would abide by the IMF-mandated debt targets in 2003. The statement helped the currency to stabilize.

Lula won the presidential election, and his administration was quick to state that it would continue to pursue the free market policies of the prior administration, and grant operational autonomy to the Brazilian central bank, effectively removing politics from decisions about monetary policy. The new government also indicated that it would adhere to the terms of the IMF rescue package. Two years later, Lula's government had been as good as its word. In 2004, the government ran a budget surplus of greater than 5 percent of GDP and used the proceeds to pay down the national debt. Economic growth was running at 4 percent a year, the country racked up a $30 billion trade surplus, inflation remained relatively subdued by historic standards at 7 percent annually, and the *real* had rallied against the U.S. dollar.

Sources: "Stopping the Rot in Brazil," *The Economist,* August 3, 2002, pp. 11–12; "A Matter of Faith: Brazil and the IMF," *The Economist,* August 17, 2002, pp. 56–57; "Race against Time: Brazil," *The Economist,* September 28, 2002, p. 69; and K. G. Hall, "New Leftist Brazilian President Moves to Calm Investors," Knight Ridder/Tribune News Service, January 3, 2003.

Introduction

The **international monetary system** refers to the institutional arrangements that govern exchange rates. In Chapter 10 we assumed the foreign exchange market was the primary institution for determining exchange rates, and the impersonal market forces of demand and supply determined the relative value of any two currencies (i.e., their exchange rate). Furthermore, we explained that the demand and supply of currencies is influenced by their respective countries' relative inflation rates and interest rates. When the foreign exchange market determines the relative value of a currency, we say that the country is adhering to a **floating exchange rate** regime. The world's four major trading currencies—the U.S. dollar, the European Union's euro, the Japanese yen, and the British pound—are all free to float against each other. Thus, their exchange rates are determined by market forces and fluctuate against each other day to day, if not minute to minute. However, the exchange rates of many currencies are not determined by the free play of market forces; other institutional arrangements are adopted.

Many of the world's developing nations peg their currencies, primarily to the dollar or the euro. A **pegged exchange rate** means the value of the currency is fixed relative to a reference currency, such as the U.S. dollar, and then the exchange rate between that currency and other currencies is determined by the reference currency exchange rate. For example, China pegs its currency to the dollar, and the exchange rate between the Chinese yuan and the euro is determined by the U.S. dollar/euro exchange rate.

Other countries, while not adopting a formal pegged rate, try to hold the value of their currency within some range against an important reference currency such as the U.S. dollar. This is often referred to as a **dirty float.** It is a float because in theory, the value of the currency is determined by market forces, but it is a dirty float (as opposed to a clean float) because the central bank of a country will intervene in the foreign exchange market to try to maintain the value of its currency if it depreciates too rapidly against an important reference currency. This was the case with Brazil in the early 2000s, which tried to keep its currency, from depreciating too rapidly against the U.S. dollar (see the opening case).

Still other countries have operated with a **fixed exchange rate,** in which the values of a set of currencies are fixed against each other at some mutually agreed on exchange rate. Before the introduction of the euro in 2000, several member states of the European Union operated with fixed exchange rates within the context of the **European Monetary System (EMS).** For a quarter of a century after World War II, the world's major industrial nations participated in a fixed exchange rate system. Although this system collapsed in 1973, some still argue that the world should attempt to reestablish it.

In this chapter, we will explain how the international monetary system works and point out its implications for international business. To understand how the system works, we must review its evolution. We will begin with a discussion of the gold standard and its breakup during the 1930s. Then we will discuss the 1944 Bretton Woods conference. This established the basic framework for the post–World War II international monetary system. The Bretton Woods system called for fixed exchange rates against the U.S. dollar. Under this fixed exchange rate system, the value of most currencies in terms of U.S. dollars was fixed for long periods and allowed to change only under a specific set of circumstances. The Bretton Woods conference also created two major international institutions that play a role in the international monetary system—the International Monetary Fund (IMF) and the World Bank. The IMF was given the task of maintaining order in the international monetary system; the World Bank's role was to promote development.

Today, both these institutions continue to play major roles in the world economy and in the international monetary system. In 1997 and 1998, for example, the IMF helped several Asian countries deal with the dramatic decline in the value of their currencies that occurred during the Asian financial crisis that started in 1997. As discussed in the opening case, in 2002 the IMF stepped in to help Brazil weather a financial crisis and support the value of its currency on the foreign exchange markets. By 2004, the IMF had programs in 49 countries, the majority in the developing world, and had committed some $97 billion in loans to these nations.[1] However, debate is growing about the role of the IMF and to a lesser extent the World Bank and the appropriateness of their policies for many developing nations. Several prominent critics claim that in some cases, IMF policies make things worse, not better. The debate over the role of the IMF took on new urgency given the institution's extensive involvement in the economies of developing countries during the late 1990s and early 2000s. Accordingly, we shall discuss the issue in some depth.

The Bretton Woods system of fixed exchange rates collapsed in 1973. Since then, the world has operated with a mixed system in which some currencies are allowed to float freely, but many are either managed by government intervention or pegged to another currency. We will explain the reasons for the failure of the Bretton Woods system as well as the nature of the present system. We will also discuss how pegged exchange rate systems work. Three decades after the breakdown of the Bretton Woods system, the debate continues over what kind of exchange rate regime is best for the world. Some economists advocate a system in which major currencies are allowed to float against each other. Others argue for a return to a fixed exchange rate regime similar to the one established at Bretton Woods. This debate is intense and important, and we will examine the arguments of both sides.

Finally, we will discuss the implications of all this material for international business. We will see how the exchange rate policy adopted by a government can have an important impact on the outlook for business operations in a given country. If government exchange rate policies result in a currency devaluation, for example, exporters based in that country may benefit as their products become more price competitive in foreign markets. Alternatively, importers will suffer from an increase in the price of their products. We will also look at how the policies adopted by the IMF can have an impact on the economic outlook for a country and, accordingly, on the costs and benefits of doing business in that country.

The Gold Standard

The gold standard had its origin in the use of gold coins as a medium of exchange, unit of account, and store of value—a practice that dates to ancient times. When international trade was limited in volume, payment for goods purchased from another country was typically made in gold or silver. However, as the volume of international trade expanded in the wake of the Industrial Revolution, a more convenient means of financing international trade was needed. Shipping large quantities of gold and silver around the world to finance international trade seemed impractical. The solution adopted was to arrange for payment in paper currency and for governments to agree to convert the paper currency into gold on demand at a fixed rate.

MECHANICS OF THE GOLD STANDARD

Pegging currencies to gold and guaranteeing convertibility is known as the **gold standard.** By 1880, most of the world's major trading nations, including Great Britain, Germany, Japan, and the United States, had adopted the gold standard. Given a common gold standard, the value of any currency in units of any other currency (the exchange rate) was easy to determine.

For example, under the gold standard, one U.S. dollar was defined as equivalent to 23.22 grains of "fine" (pure) gold. Thus, one could, in theory, demand that the U.S. government convert that one dollar into 23.22 grains of gold. Since there are 480 grains in an ounce, one ounce of gold cost $20.67 (480/23.22). The amount of a currency needed to purchase one ounce of gold was referred to as the **gold par value.** The British pound was valued at 113 grains of fine gold. In other words, one ounce of gold cost £4.25 (480/113). From the gold par values of pounds and dollars, we can calculate what the exchange rate was for converting pounds into dollars; it was £1 = $4.87 (i.e., $20.67/£4.25).

STRENGTH OF THE GOLD STANDARD

The great strength claimed for the gold standard was that it contained a powerful mechanism for achieving balance-of-trade equilibrium by all countries.[2] A country is said to be in **balance-of-trade equilibrium** when the income its residents earn from exports is equal to the money its residents pay to other countries for imports (the current account of its balance of payments is in balance). Suppose there are only two countries in the world, Japan and the United States. Imagine Japan's trade balance is in surplus because it exports more to the United States than it imports from the United States. Japanese exporters are paid in U.S. dollars, which they exchange for Japanese yen at a Japanese bank. The Japanese bank submits the dollars to the U.S. government and demands payment of gold in return. (This is a simplification of what would occur, but it will make our point.)

Under the gold standard, when Japan has a trade surplus, there will be a net flow of gold from the United States to Japan. These gold flows automatically reduce the U.S. money supply and swell Japan's money supply. As we saw in Chapter 10, there is a close connection between money supply growth and price inflation. An increase in money supply will raise prices in Japan, while a decrease in the U.S. money supply will push U.S. prices downward. The rise in the price of Japanese goods will decrease demand for these goods, while the fall in the price of U.S. goods will increase demand for these goods. Thus, Japan will start to buy more from the United States, and the United States will buy less from Japan, until a balance-of-trade equilibrium is achieved.

This adjustment mechanism seems so simple and attractive that even today, almost 70 years after the final collapse of the gold standard, some people believe the world should return to a gold standard.

THE PERIOD BETWEEN THE WARS: 1918–1939

The gold standard worked reasonably well from the 1870s until the start of World War I in 1914, when it was abandoned. During the war, several governments financed part of their massive military expenditures by printing money. This resulted in inflation, and by the war's end in 1918, price levels were higher everywhere. The United States returned to the gold standard in 1919, Great Britain in 1925, and France in 1928.

Great Britain returned to the gold standard by pegging the pound to gold at the prewar gold parity level of £4.25 per ounce, despite substantial inflation between 1914 and 1925. This priced British goods out of foreign markets, which pushed the country into a deep depression. When foreign holders of pounds lost confidence in Great Britain's commitment to maintaining its currency's value, they began converting their holdings of pounds into gold. The British government saw that it could not satisfy the demand for gold without seriously depleting its gold reserves, so it suspended convertibility in 1931.

The United States followed suit and left the gold standard in 1933 but returned to it in 1934, raising the dollar price of gold from $20.67 per ounce to $35 per ounce. Since more dollars were needed to buy an ounce of gold than before, the implication was that the dollar was worth less. This effectively amounted to a devaluation of the dollar relative to other currencies. Thus, before the devaluation, the pound/dollar exchange rate was £1 = $4.87, but after the devaluation it was £1 = $8.24. By reducing the price of U.S. exports and increasing the price of imports, the government was trying to create employment in the United States by boosting output (the U.S. government was basically using the exchange rate as an instrument of trade policy). However, a number of other countries adopted a similar tactic, and in the cycle of competitive devaluations that soon emerged, no country could win.

The net result was the shattering of any remaining confidence in the system. With countries devaluing their currencies at will, one could no longer be certain how much gold a currency could buy. Instead of holding onto another country's currency, people often tried to change it into gold immediately, lest the country devalue its currency in the intervening period. This put pressure on the gold reserves of various countries, forcing them to suspend gold convertibility. By the start of World War II in 1939, the gold standard was dead.

The Bretton Woods System

In 1944, at the height of World War II, representatives from 44 countries met at Bretton Woods, New Hampshire, to design a new international monetary system. With the collapse of the gold standard and the Great Depression of the 1930s fresh in their minds, these statesmen were determined to build an enduring economic order that would facilitate postwar economic growth. There was general consensus that fixed exchange rates were desirable. In addition, the conference participants wanted to avoid the senseless competitive devaluations of the 1930s, and they recognized that the gold standard would not assure this. The major problem with the gold standard as previously constituted was that no multinational institution could stop countries from engaging in competitive devaluations.

The agreement reached at Bretton Woods established two multinational institutions—the International Monetary Fund (IMF) and the World Bank. The task of the IMF would be to maintain order in the international monetary system and that of the World Bank would be to promote general economic development. The Bretton Woods agreement also called for a system of fixed exchange rates that would be policed by the IMF. Under the agreement, all countries were to fix the value of their currency in terms of gold but were not required to exchange their currencies for gold. Only the dollar remained convertible into gold—at a price of $35 per ounce. Each country decided what it wanted its exchange rate to be vis-à-vis the dollar and then calculated the gold par value of the currency based on that selected dollar exchange rate. All participating countries agreed to try to maintain the value of their currencies within 1 percent of the par value by buying or selling currencies (or gold) as needed. For example, if foreign exchange dealers were selling more of a country's currency than demanded, that country's government would intervene in the foreign exchange markets, buying its currency in an attempt to increase demand and maintain its gold par value.

Another aspect of the Bretton Woods agreement was a commitment not to use devaluation as a weapon of competitive trade policy. However, if a currency became too weak to defend, a devaluation of up to 10 percent would be allowed without any formal approval by the IMF. Larger devaluations required IMF approval.

THE ROLE OF THE IMF

The IMF Articles of Agreement were heavily influenced by the worldwide financial collapse, competitive devaluations, trade wars, high unemployment, hyperinflation in Germany and elsewhere, and general economic disintegration that occurred between the two world wars. The aim of the Bretton Woods agreement, of which the IMF was the main custodian, was to try to avoid a repetition of that chaos through a combination of discipline and flexibility.

Discipline

A fixed exchange rate regime imposes discipline in two ways. First, the need to maintain a fixed exchange rate puts a brake on competitive devaluations and brings stability to the world trade environment. Second, a fixed exchange rate regime imposes monetary discipline on countries, thereby curtailing price inflation. For example, consider what would happen under a fixed exchange rate regime if Great Britain rapidly increased its money supply by printing pounds. As explained in Chapter 10, the increase in money supply would lead to price inflation. Given fixed exchange rates, inflation would make British goods uncompetitive in world markets, while the prices of imports would become more attractive in Great Britain. The result would be a widening trade deficit in Great Britain, with the country importing more than it exports. To correct this trade imbalance under a fixed exchange rate regime, Great Britain would be required to restrict the rate of growth in its money supply to bring price inflation back under control. Thus, fixed exchange rates are seen as a mechanism for controlling inflation and imposing economic discipline on countries.

Flexibility

Although monetary discipline was a central objective of the Bretton Woods agreement, it was recognized that a rigid policy of fixed exchange rates would be too inflexible. It would probably break down just as the gold standard had. In some cases, a country's attempts to reduce its money supply growth and correct a persistent balance-of-payments deficit could force the country into recession and create high unemployment. The architects of the Bretton Woods agreement wanted to avoid high unemployment, so they built limited flexibility into the system. Two major features of the IMF Articles of Agreement fostered this flexibility: IMF lending facilities and adjustable parities.

The IMF stood ready to lend foreign currencies to members to tide them over during short periods of balance-of-payments deficits, when a rapid tightening of monetary or fiscal policy would hurt domestic employment. A pool of gold and currencies contributed by IMF members provided the resources for these lending operations. A persistent balance-of-payments deficit can lead to a depletion of a country's reserves of foreign currency, forcing it to devalue its currency. By providing deficit-laden countries with short-term foreign currency loans, IMF funds would buy time for countries to bring down their inflation rates and reduce their balance-of-payments deficits. The belief was that such loans would reduce pressures for devaluation and allow for a more orderly and less painful adjustment.

Countries were to be allowed to borrow a limited amount from the IMF without adhering to any specific agreements. However, extensive drawings from IMF funds would require a country to agree to increasingly stringent IMF supervision of its macroeconomic policies. Heavy borrowers from the IMF must agree to monetary and fiscal conditions set down by the IMF, which typically included IMF-mandated targets on domestic money supply growth, exchange rate policy, tax policy, government spending, and so on.

The system of adjustable parities allowed for the devaluation of a country's currency by more than 10 percent if the IMF agreed that a country's balance of payments was in "fundamental disequilibrium." The term *fundamental disequilibrium* was not defined in the IMF's Articles of Agreement, but it was intended to apply to countries that had suffered permanent adverse shifts in the demand for their products. Without devaluation, such a country would experience high unemployment and a persistent trade deficit until the domestic price level had fallen far enough to restore a balance-of-payments equilibrium. The belief was that devaluation could help sidestep a painful adjustment process in such circumstances.

THE ROLE OF THE WORLD BANK

The official name for the World Bank is the International Bank for Reconstruction and Development (IBRD). When the Bretton Woods participants established the World Bank, the need to reconstruct the war-torn economies of Europe was foremost in their minds. The bank's initial mission was to help finance the building of Europe's economy by providing low-interest loans. As it turned out, the World Bank was overshadowed in this role by the Marshall Plan, under which the United States lent money directly to European nations to help them rebuild. So the bank turned its attention to "development" and began lending money to Third World nations. In the 1950s, the bank concentrated on public-sector projects. Power stations, road building, and other transportation investments were much in favor. During the 1960s, the bank also began to lend heavily in support of agriculture, education, population control, and urban development.

The bank lends money under two schemes. Under the IBRD scheme, money is raised through bond sales in the international capital market. Borrowers pay what the bank calls a market rate of interest—the bank's cost of funds plus a margin for expenses. This "market" rate is lower than commercial banks' market rate. Under the IBRD scheme, the bank offers low-interest loans to risky customers whose credit rating is often poor, such as the governments of underdeveloped nations.

A second scheme is overseen by the International Development Agency (IDA), an arm of the bank created in 1960. Resources to fund IDA loans are raised through subscriptions from wealthy members such as the United States, Japan, and Germany. IDA loans go only to the poorest countries. Borrowers have 50 years to repay at an interest rate of 1 percent a year.

The Collapse of the Fixed Exchange Rate System

The system of fixed exchange rates established at Bretton Woods worked well until the late 1960s, when it began to show signs of strain. The system finally collapsed in 1973, and since then we have had a managed-float system. To understand why the system collapsed, one must appreciate the special role of the U.S. dollar in the system. As the only currency that could be converted into gold, and as the currency that served as the reference point for all others, the dollar occupied a central place in the system. Any pressure on the dollar to devalue could wreak havoc with the system, and that is what occurred.

Most economists trace the breakup of the fixed exchange rate system to the U.S. macroeconomic policy package of 1965–1968.[3] To finance both the Vietnam conflict and his welfare programs, President Lyndon Johnson backed an increase in U.S. government spending that was not financed by an increase in taxes. Instead, it was financed by an increase in the money supply, which led to a rise in price inflation from less than 4 percent in 1966 to close to 9 percent by 1968. At the same time, the rise in government spending had stimulated the economy. With more money in their pockets, people spent more—particularly on imports—and the U.S. trade balance began to deteriorate. (The perceptive reader will note that there are parallels here with the situation prevailing in America in 2002–2004 where once again a government expanded spending to pay for a foreign war and financed that spending through monetary expansion—in essence, more government borrowing—that stimulated the economy and led to a surge in imports. Some observers worry that the implied expansion in the U.S. money supply may ultimately lead to acceleration in the inflation rate in the United States.)

The increase in inflation and the worsening of the U.S. foreign trade position gave rise to speculation in the foreign exchange market that the dollar would be devalued. Things came to a head in the spring of 1971 when U.S. trade figures showed that for the first time since 1945, the United States was importing more than it was exporting. This set off massive purchases of German deutsche marks in the foreign exchange market by speculators who guessed that the mark would be revalued against the dollar. On a single day, May 4, 1971, the Bundesbank (Germany's central bank) had to buy $1 billion to hold the dollar/deutsche mark exchange rate at its fixed exchange rate given the great demand for deutsche marks. On the morning of May 5, the Bundesbank purchased another $1 billion during the first hour of foreign exchange trading! At that point, the Bundesbank faced the inevitable and allowed its currency to float.

In the weeks following the decision to float the deutsche mark, the foreign exchange market became increasingly convinced that the dollar would have to be devalued. However, devaluation of the dollar was no easy matter. Under the Bretton Woods provisions, any other country could change its exchange rates against all currencies simply by fixing its dollar rate at a new level. But as the key currency in the system, the dollar could be devalued only if all countries agreed to simultaneously revalue against the dollar. And many countries did not want this, because it would make their products more expensive relative to U.S. products.

To force the issue, President Nixon announced in August 1971 that the dollar was no longer convertible into gold. He also announced that a new 10 percent tax on imports would remain in effect until U.S. trading partners agreed to revalue their currencies against the dollar. This brought the trading partners to the bargaining table, and in December 1971 an agreement was reached to devalue the dollar by about 8 percent against foreign currencies. The import tax was then removed.

The problem was not solved, however. The U.S. balance-of-payments position continued to deteriorate throughout 1972, while the nation's money supply continued to expand at an inflationary rate. Speculation continued to grow that the dollar was still overvalued and that a second devaluation would be necessary. In anticipation, foreign exchange dealers began converting dollars to deutsche marks and other currencies. After a massive wave of speculation in February 1972, which culminated with European central banks spending $3.6 billion on March 1 to try to prevent their currencies from appreciating against the dollar, the foreign exchange market was closed. When the foreign exchange market reopened March 19, the currencies of Japan and most European countries were floating against the dollar, although many developing countries continued to peg their currency to the dollar, and many do to this day. At that time, the switch to a floating system was viewed as a temporary response to unmanageable speculation in the foreign exchange market. But it is now more than 30 years since the Bretton Woods system of fixed exchange rates collapsed, and the temporary solution looks permanent.

The Bretton Woods system had an Achilles' heel: The system could not work if its key currency, the U.S. dollar, was under speculative attack. The Bretton Woods system could work only as long as the U.S. inflation rate remained low and the United States did not run a balance-of-payments deficit. Once these things occurred, the system soon became strained to the breaking point.

The Floating Exchange Rate Regime

The floating exchange rate regime that followed the collapse of the fixed exchange rate system was formalized in January 1976 when IMF members met in Jamaica and agreed to the rules for the international monetary system that are in place today.

THE JAMAICA AGREEMENT

The Jamaica meeting revised the IMF's Articles of Agreement to reflect the new reality of floating exchange rates. The main elements of the Jamaica agreement include the following:

1. Floating rates were declared acceptable. IMF members were permitted to enter the foreign exchange market to even out "unwarranted" speculative fluctuations.
2. Gold was abandoned as a reserve asset. The IMF returned its gold reserves to members at the current market price, placing the proceeds in a trust fund to help poor nations. IMF members were permitted to sell their own gold reserves at the market price.
3. Total annual IMF quotas—the amount member countries contribute to the IMF—were increased to $41 billion. (Since then they have been increased to $311 billion while the membership of the IMF has been expanded to include 184 countries.) Non-oil-exporting, less developed countries were given greater access to IMF funds.

After Jamaica, the IMF continued its role of helping countries cope with macroeconomic and exchange rate problems, albeit within the context of a radically different exchange rate regime.

EXCHANGE RATES SINCE 1973

Since March 1973, exchange rates have become much more volatile and less predictable than they were between 1945 and 1973.[4] This volatility has been partly due to a number of unexpected shocks to the world monetary system, including:

1. The oil crisis in 1971, when the Organization of Petroleum Exporting Countries (OPEC) quadrupled the price of oil. The harmful effect of this on the U.S. inflation rate and trade position resulted in a further decline in the value of the dollar.
2. The loss of confidence in the dollar that followed a sharp rise in the U.S. inflation rate in 1977–1978.
3. The oil crisis of 1979, when OPEC once again increased the price of oil dramatically—this time it was doubled.
4. The unexpected rise in the dollar between 1980 and 1985, despite a deteriorating balance-of-payments picture.
5. The rapid fall of the U.S. dollar against the Japanese yen and German deutsche mark between 1985 and 1987, and against the yen between 1993 and 1995.
6. The partial collapse of the European Monetary System in 1992.
7. The 1997 Asian currency crisis, when the Asian currencies of several countries, including South Korea, Indonesia, Malaysia, and Thailand, lost between 50 percent and 80 percent of their value against the U.S. dollar in a few months.

Figure 11.1 summarizes how the value of the U.S. dollar has fluctuated against an index of major trading currencies between 1973 and 2004. (The index, which was set equal to 100 in March 1973, is a weighted average of the foreign exchange values of the U.S. dollar against currencies that circulate widely outside the country of issue). An interesting phenomenon in Figure 11.1 is the rapid rise in the value of the dollar between 1980 and 1985 and its subsequent fall between 1985 and 1988. A similar, though less pronounced, rise and fall in the value of the dollar occurred between 1995 and 2005. We will briefly discuss the rise and fall of the dollar during these periods, since this tells us something about how the international monetary system has operated in recent years.[5]

The rise in the value of the dollar between 1980 and 1985 occurred when the United States was running a large and growing trade deficit, importing substantially more than it exported. Conventional wisdom would suggest that the increased supply of dollars in the foreign exchange market as a result of the trade deficit should lead to a reduction in the value of the dollar, but as shown in Figure 11.1 it increased in value. Why?

A number of favorable factors overcame the unfavorable effect of a trade deficit. Strong economic growth in the United States attracted heavy inflows of capital from foreign investors seeking high returns on capital assets. High real interest rates attracted foreign investors seeking high returns on financial assets. At the same time, political turmoil in other parts of the world, along with relatively slow economic growth in the developed countries of Europe, helped create the view that the United States was a good place to invest. These inflows of capital increased the demand for dollars in the foreign exchange market, which pushed the value of the dollar upward against other currencies.

The fall in the value of the dollar between 1985 and 1988 was caused by a combination of government intervention and market forces. The rise in the dollar, which priced U.S. goods out of foreign markets and made imports relatively cheap, had contributed to a dismal trade picture. In 1985, the United States posted a record-high trade deficit of

FIGURE 11.1

Major Currencies Dollar Index, 1973–2004

Source: Constructed by the author from Federal Reserve statistics at www.federalreserve.gov/releases/ H10/summary/.

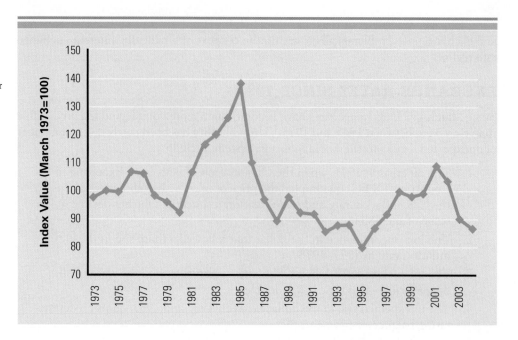

more than $160 billion. This led to growth in demands for protectionism in the United States. In September 1985, the finance ministers and central bank governors of the so-called Group of Five major industrial countries (Great Britain, France, Japan, Germany, and the United States) met at the Plaza Hotel in New York and reached what was later referred to as the Plaza Accord. They announced that it would be desirable for most major currencies to appreciate vis-à-vis the U.S. dollar and pledged to intervene in the foreign exchange markets, selling dollars, to encourage this objective. The dollar had already begun to weaken in the summer of 1985, and this announcement further accelerated the decline.

The dollar continued to decline until 1987. The governments of the Group of Five began to worry that the dollar might decline too far, so the finance ministers of the Group of Five met in Paris in February 1987 and reached a new agreement known as the Louvre Accord. They agreed that exchange rates had been realigned sufficiently and pledged to support the stability of exchange rates around their current levels by intervening in the foreign exchange markets when necessary to buy and sell currency. Although the dollar continued to decline for a few months after the Louvre Accord, the rate of decline slowed, and by early 1988 the decline had ended.

Except for a brief speculative flurry around the time of the Persian Gulf War in 1991, the dollar was relatively stable for the first half of the 1990s. However, in the late 1990s the dollar again began to appreciate against most major currencies, including the euro after its introduction, even though the United States was still running a significant balance-of-payments deficit. Once again, the driving force for the appreciation in the value of the dollar was that foreigners continued to invest in U.S. financial assets, primarily stocks and bonds, and the inflow of money drove up the value of the dollar on foreign exchange markets. The inward investment was due to a belief that U.S. financial assets offered a favorable rate of return.

By 2002, however, foreigners had started to lose their appetite for U.S. stocks and bonds, and the inflow of money into the United States slowed. Instead of reinvesting dollars earned from exports to the United States in U.S. financial assets, they exchanged those dollars for other currencies, particularly euros, to invest them in nondollar-denominated assets. One reason for this was the continued growth in the U.S. trade deficit, which hit a record $600 billion in 2004. Although the U.S. trade deficits had been hitting records for decades, this deficit was the largest ever when measured as a percentage of the country's GDP (6 percent of GDP in 2004).

The record deficit meant that ever more dollars were flowing out of the United States into foreign hands, and those foreigners were less inclined to reinvest those dollars in the United States at a rate required to keep the dollar stable. This growing reluctance of foreigners to invest in the United States was in turn due to several factors. First, there was a slowdown in U.S. economic activity during 2001–2002, and a sluggish recovery thereafter, which made U.S. assets less attractive. Second, the U.S. government's budget deficit expanded rapidly after 2001. This led to fears that ultimately the budget deficit would be financed by an expansionary monetary policy that could lead to higher price inflation. Since inflation would reduce the value of the dollar, foreigners decided to hedge against this risk by holding fewer dollar assets in their investment portfolios. Third, from 2003 onward U.S. government officials began to "talk down" the value of the dollar, in part because the administration believed that a cheaper dollar would increase exports and reduce imports, thereby improving the U.S. balance of trade position.[6] Foreigners saw this as a signal that the U.S. government would not intervene in the foreign exchange markets to prop up the value of the dollar, which increased their reluctance to reinvest dollars earned from export sales in U.S. financial assets. As a result of these factors, demand for dollars weakened and the value of the dollar slid on the foreign exchange markets, hitting an index value of 80.19 in December 2004, its lowest value since the index began in 1973.

Thus, we see that in recent history the value of the dollar has been determined by both market forces and government intervention. Under a floating exchange rate regime, market forces have produced a volatile dollar exchange rate. Governments have sometimes responded by intervening in the market—buying and selling dollars—in an attempt to limit the market's volatility and to correct what they see as overvaluation (in 1985) or potential undervaluation (in 1987) of the dollar. In addition to direct intervention, the value of the dollar has frequently been influenced by statements from government officials. The dollar may not have declined by as much as it did in 2004, for example, had not U.S. government officials publicly ruled out any action to stop the decline. Paradoxically, a signal not to intervene can affect the market. The frequency of government intervention in the foreign exchange market explains why the current system is sometimes thought of as a **managed-float system** or a dirty-float system.

Fixed versus Floating Exchange Rates

The breakdown of the Bretton Woods system has not stopped the debate about the relative merits of fixed versus floating exchange rate regimes. Disappointment with the system of floating rates in recent years has led to renewed debate about the merits of fixed exchange rates. In this section, we review the arguments for fixed and floating exchange rate regimes.[7] We will discuss the case for floating rates before discussing why many commentators are disappointed with the experience under floating exchange rates and yearn for a system of fixed rates.

THE CASE FOR FLOATING EXCHANGE RATES

The case in support of floating exchange rates has two main elements: monetary policy autonomy and automatic trade balance adjustments.

Monetary Policy Autonomy

It is argued that under a fixed system, a country's ability to expand or contract its money supply as it sees fit is limited by the need to maintain exchange rate parity. Monetary expansion can lead to inflation, which puts downward pressure on a fixed exchange rate (as predicted by the PPP theory; see Chapter 10). Similarly, monetary contraction requires high interest rates (to reduce the demand for money). Higher interest rates lead to an inflow of money from abroad, which puts upward pressure on a fixed exchange rate. Thus, to maintain exchange rate parity under a fixed system, countries were limited in their ability to use monetary policy to expand or contract their economies.

Advocates of a floating exchange rate regime argue that removal of the obligation to maintain exchange rate parity would restore monetary control to a government. If a government faced with unemployment wanted to increase its money supply to stimulate domestic demand and reduce unemployment, it could do so unencumbered by the need to maintain its exchange rate. While monetary expansion might lead to inflation, this would lead to a depreciation in the country's currency. If PPP theory is correct, the resulting currency depreciation on the foreign exchange markets should offset the effects of inflation. Although under a floating exchange rate regime, domestic inflation would have an impact on the exchange rate, it should have no impact on businesses' international cost competitiveness due to exchange rate depreciation. The rise in domestic costs should be exactly offset by the fall in the value of the country's currency on the foreign exchange markets. Similarly, a government could use monetary policy to contract the economy without worrying about the need to maintain parity.

Trade Balance Adjustments

Under the Bretton Woods system, if a country developed a permanent deficit in its balance of trade (importing more than it exported) that could not be corrected by domestic policy, this would require the IMF to agree to a currency devaluation. Critics of this system argue that the adjustment mechanism works much more smoothly under a floating exchange rate regime. They argue that if a country is running a trade deficit, the imbalance between the supply and demand of that country's currency in the foreign exchange markets (supply exceeding demand) will lead to depreciation in its exchange rate. In turn, by making its exports cheaper and its imports more expensive, an exchange rate depreciation should correct the trade deficit.

THE CASE FOR FIXED EXCHANGE RATES

The case for fixed exchange rates rests on arguments about monetary discipline, speculation, uncertainty, and the lack of connection between the trade balance and exchange rates.

Monetary Discipline

We have already discussed the nature of monetary discipline inherent in a fixed exchange rate system when we discussed the Bretton Woods system. The need to maintain a fixed exchange rate parity ensures that governments do not expand their money supplies at inflationary rates. While advocates of floating rates argue that each country should be allowed to choose its own inflation rate (the monetary autonomy argument), advocates of fixed rates argue that governments all too often give in to political pressures and expand the monetary supply far too rapidly, causing unacceptably high price inflation. A fixed exchange rate regime would ensure that this does not occur.

Speculation

Critics of a floating exchange rate regime also argue that speculation can cause fluctuations in exchange rates. They point to the dollar's rapid rise and fall during the 1980s, which they claim had nothing to do with comparative inflation rates and the U.S. trade deficit, but everything to do with speculation. They argue that when foreign exchange dealers see a currency depreciating, they tend to sell the currency in the expectation of future depreciation regardless of the currency's longer-term prospects. As more traders jump on the bandwagon, the expectations of depreciation are realized. Such destabilizing speculation tends to accentuate the fluctuations around the exchange rate's long-run value. It can damage a country's economy by distorting export and import prices. Thus, advocates of a fixed exchange rate regime argue that such a system will limit the destabilizing effects of speculation.

Uncertainty

Speculation also adds to the uncertainty surrounding future currency movements that characterizes floating exchange rate regimes. The unpredictability of exchange rate movements in the post–Bretton Woods era has made business planning difficult, and it adds risk to exporting, importing, and foreign investment activities. Given a volatile exchange rate, international businesses do not know how to react to the changes—and often they do not react. Why change plans for exporting, importing, or foreign investment after a 6 percent fall in the dollar this month, when the dollar may rise 6 percent next month? This uncertainty, according to the critics, dampens the growth of international trade and investment. They argue that a fixed exchange rate, by eliminating such uncertainty, promotes the growth of international trade and investment. Advocates of a floating system reply that the forward exchange market insures against the risks associated with exchange rate fluctuations (see Chapter 10), so the adverse impact of uncertainty on the growth of international trade and investment has been overstated.

Trade Balance Adjustments

Those in favor of floating exchange rates argue that floating rates help adjust trade imbalances. Critics question the closeness of the link between the exchange rate and the trade balance. They claim trade deficits are determined by the balance between savings and investment in a country, not by the external value of its currency.[8] They argue that depreciation in a currency will lead to inflation (due to the resulting increase in import prices). This inflation will wipe out any apparent gains in cost competitiveness that arise from currency depreciation. In other words, a depreciating exchange rate will not boost exports and reduce imports, as advocates of floating rates claim; it will simply boost price inflation. In support of this argument, those who favor floating rates point out that the 40 percent drop in the value of the dollar between 1985 and 1988 did not correct the U.S. trade deficit. In reply, advocates of a floating exchange rate regime argue that between 1985 and 1992, the U.S. trade deficit fell from more than $160 billion to about $70 billion, and they attribute this in part to the decline in the value of the dollar.

WHO IS RIGHT?

Which side is right in the vigorous debate between those who favor a fixed exchange rate and those who favor a floating exchange rate? Economists cannot agree. Business, as a major player on the international trade and investment scene, has a large stake in the resolution of the debate. Would international business be better off under a fixed regime, or are flexible rates better? The evidence is not clear.

We do, however, know that a fixed exchange rate regime modeled along the lines of the Bretton Woods system will not work. Speculation ultimately broke the system, a phenomenon that advocates of fixed rate regimes claim is associated with floating exchange rates! Nevertheless, a different kind of fixed exchange rate system might be more enduring and might foster the stability that would facilitate more rapid growth in international trade and investment. In the next section, we look at potential models for such a system and the problems with such systems.

Exchange Rate Regimes in Practice

Governments around the world pursue a number of different exchange rate policies. These range from a pure "free float" where the exchange rate is determined by market forces to a pegged system that has some aspects of the pre-1973 Bretton Woods system of

FIGURE 11.2

Exchange Rate Policies, IMF Members, 2004

Source: *IMF Annual Report, 2004*, Table 11.13 (Washington, DC: IMF, 2004). Reprinted with permission.

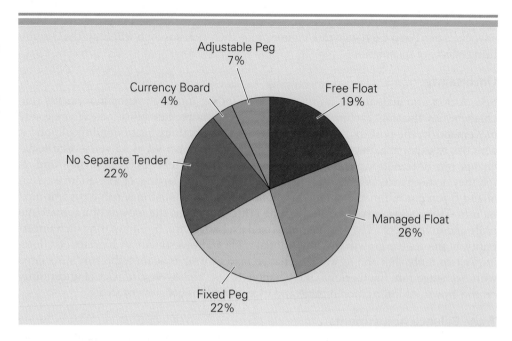

fixed exchange rates. Figure 11.2 summarizes the exchange rate policies adopted by member states of the IMF in 2004. Some 19 percent of the IMF's members allow their currency to float freely. Another 26 percent intervene in only a limited way (the so-called managed float). A further 22 percent of IMF members now have no separate legal tender of their own. These include the 12 European Union countries that have adopted the euro, and effectively given up their own currencies, along with 29 smaller states mostly in Africa or the Caribbean that have no domestic currency and have adopted a foreign currency as legal tender within their borders, typically the U.S. dollar or the euro. The remaining countries use more inflexible systems, including a fixed peg arrangement (22 percent) under which they peg their currencies to other currencies, such as the U.S. dollar or the euro, or to a basket of currencies. Other countries have adopted a somewhat more flexible system under which their exchange rate is allowed to fluctuate against other currencies within a target zone (an adjustable peg system). In this section, we will look more closely at the mechanics and implications of exchange rate regimes that rely on a currency peg or target zone.

PEGGED EXCHANGE RATES

Under a pegged exchange rate regime, a country will peg the value of its currency to that of a major currency so that, for example, as the U.S. dollar rises in value, its own currency rises too. For example, China has pegged the value of its currency, the yuan, to that of the U.S. dollar since 1994. Pegged exchange rates are popular among many of the world's smaller nations (China is obviously an exception to this). As with a full fixed exchange rate regime, the great virtue claimed for a pegged exchange rate is that it imposes monetary discipline on a country and leads to low inflation. For example, if Belize pegs the value of the Belizean dollar to that of the U.S. dollar so that US$1 = B$1.97 (the peg as of 2005), then the Belizean government must make sure the inflation rate in Belize is similar to that in the United States. If the Belizean inflation rate is greater than the U.S. inflation rate, this will lead to pressure to devalue the Belizean dollar (i.e., to alter the peg). To maintain the peg, the Belizean government would be required to rein in inflation. Of course, for a pegged exchange rate to impose monetary discipline on a country, the country whose currency is chosen for the peg must also pursue sound monetary policy.

Evidence shows that adopting a pegged exchange rate regime moderates inflationary pressures in a country. An IMF study concluded that countries with pegged exchange rates had an average annual inflation rate of 8 percent, compared with 14 percent for intermediate regimes and 16 percent for floating regimes.[9] However, many countries operate with only a nominal peg and in practice are willing to devalue their currency rather than pursue a tight monetary policy. It can be very difficult for a smaller country to maintain a peg against another currency if capital is flowing out of the country and foreign exchange traders are speculating against the currency. Something like this occurred in 1997 when a combination of adverse capital flows and currency speculation forced several Asian countries, including Thailand and Malaysia, to abandon pegs against the U.S. dollar and let their currencies float freely. Malaysia and Thailand would not have been in this position had they dealt with a number of problems that began to arise in their economies during the 1990s, including excessive private-sector debt and expanding current account trade deficits.

CURRENCY BOARDS

Hong Kong's experience during the 1997 Asian currency crisis added a new dimension to the debate over how to manage a pegged exchange rate. During late 1997 when other Asian currencies were collapsing, Hong Kong maintained the value of its currency against the U.S. dollar at about HK$15 = $7.8 despite several concerted speculative attacks. Hong Kong's currency board has been given credit for this success. A country that introduces a **currency board** commits itself to converting its domestic currency on demand into another currency at a fixed exchange rate. To make this commitment credible, the currency board holds reserves of foreign currency equal at the fixed exchange rate to at least 100 percent of the domestic currency issued. The system used in Hong Kong means its currency must be fully backed by the U.S. dollar at the specified exchange rate. This is still not a true fixed exchange rate regime, because the U.S. dollar, and by extension the Hong Kong dollar, floats against other currencies, but it has some features of a fixed exchange rate regime.

Under this arrangement, the currency board can issue additional domestic notes and coins only when there are foreign exchange reserves to back it. This limits the ability of the government to print money and, thereby, create inflationary pressures. Under a strict currency board system, interest rates adjust automatically. If investors want to switch out of domestic currency into, for example, U.S. dollars, the supply of domestic currency will shrink. This will cause interest rates to rise until it eventually becomes attractive for investors to hold the local currency again. In the case of Hong Kong, the interest rate on three-month deposits climbed as high as 20 percent in late 1997, as investors switched out of Hong Kong dollars and into U.S. dollars. The dollar peg held, however, and interest rates declined again.

Since its establishment in 1983, the Hong Kong currency board has weathered several storms, including the latest. This success persuaded several other countries in the developing world to consider a similar system. Argentina introduced a currency board in 1991, and Bulgaria, Estonia, and Lithuania have all gone down this road in recent years (seven IMF members had currency boards in 2004). Despite growing interest in the arrangement, however, critics are quick to point out that currency boards have their drawbacks.[10] If local inflation rates remain higher than the inflation rate in the country to which the currency is pegged, the currencies of countries with currency boards can become uncompetitive and overvalued. Also, under a currency board system, government lacks the ability to set interest rates. Interest rates in Hong Kong, for example, are effectively set by the U.S. Federal Reserve. In addition, economic collapse in Argentina in 2001 and the subsequent decision to abandon its currency board dampened much of the enthusiasm for this mechanism of managing exchange rates (see the accompanying Country Focus).

COUNTRY FOCUS During the 1990s, Argentina was often held up as an example of a country that was on the fast track to economic prosperity. Between 1991 and 1998, inflation, long the scourge of Argentina, was vanquished, foreign capital poured into the country, and the economy grew at an annual average rate of 5.7 percent, the highest growth rate in the region. Much of the credit for this performance was laid at the feet of President Carlos Menem and his finance minister, Domingo Cavallo. Under their leadership, Argentina in 1991 adopted a currency board that pegged the Argentinean peso at parity to the dollar ($1 = 1 peso). They also opened the economy to foreign investment and international trade, and they privatized numerous state-owned enterprises.

By 2002, the glory days of the 1990s were a distant memory. In early 2002, after a brutal four-year recession that had pushed unemployment up to 25 percent, Argentina defaulted on its $155 billion public-sector debt, the largest such default by any country in history. The currency board arrangement was abandoned, and the peso fell from parity to 3.5 pesos to the dollar by mid-2002.

Why did the Argentinean economy go so badly astray? According to some critics, the currency board was partly to blame. By adopting a currency board, Argentina renounced both exchange rate and monetary policy (interest rates were in effect set by the U.S. Federal Reserve). This limited the ability of the government to respond to external shocks, and Argentina was hit by several of them. First, prices for commodities stopped rising, depriving the Argentinean economy of a major source of export earnings. Then, the dollar appreciated against other major currencies, and since it was pegged to the dollar, so did the Argentinean peso, pricing many Argentinean goods out of world export markets while making imports cheaper. Finally, Brazil, Argentina's largest trading partner, devalued its currency, making Ar-

www.mhhe.com/hill

Crisis Management by the IMF

Many observers initially believed that the collapse of the Bretton Woods system in 1973 would diminish the role of the IMF within the international monetary system. The IMF's original function was to provide a pool of money from which members could borrow, short term, to adjust their balance-of-payments position and maintain their exchange rate. Some believed the demand for short-term loans would be considerably diminished under a floating exchange rate regime. A trade deficit would presumably lead to a decline in a country's exchange rate, which would help reduce imports and boost exports. No temporary IMF adjustment loan would be needed. Consistent with this, after 1973, most industrialized countries tended to let the foreign exchange market determine exchange rates in response to demand and supply. No major industrial country has borrowed funds from the IMF since the mid-1970s, when Great Britain and Italy did. Since the early 1970s, the rapid development of global capital markets has allowed developed countries such as Great Britain and the United States to finance their deficits by borrowing private money, as opposed to drawing on IMF funds. Despite these developments, the activities of the IMF have expanded over the past 30 years. By 2004, the IMF had 184 members, 49 of which had some kind of IMF program in place. In 1997, the institution implemented its largest rescue packages, committing more than $110 billion in short-term

gentinean exports prohibitively expensive in Brazil. These factors conspired to dramatically slow Argentina's export-led growth and contributed to rapidly rising unemployment.

To make matters worse, from 1996 onward the Argentinean government expanded public-sector spending without increasing taxes. At the same time, the pace of economic reform started to slow. The inevitable result was rising public-sector debt. Investors began to fear that the government would not be able to finance its growing debt, particularly in light of the slowdown in Argentinean exports. Capital started to leave the country, and foreign investors limited their lending to the Argentinean government. In late 2000, Argentina applied to the IMF for help and was granted a $14 billion loan in January 2001 to support the peso and maintain the dollar peg. In return for the IMF loan, the government agreed to reduce public spending. But with Argentinean exports still priced out of world markets, conditions failed to improve. Ordinary Argentineans began to lose confidence in the government and the ability of the banking system to finance spiraling public-sector debts. Between July and November 2001, Argentineans withdrew some $15 billion from local banks. With their asset base shrinking, the banks could no longer finance government debt, and with foreign financial institutions unwilling to lend more money to the government, the stage was set for Ar-

gentina's decision to default on payment of its public-sector debt. The government simply did not have enough money left to finance the debt that it had taken on in the late 1990s, and could not borrow any more.

Shortly afterward, the government abandoned the currency board arrangement, and the peso plunged, reaching a low of 3.5 to the dollar in mid-2002 before rising to about 2.90 to the dollar in early 2004. In 2002, exports started to pick up, imports declined, the economy expanded for the first time since 1998, albeit by a small amount, unemployment started to fall (it was down to 18 percent by late 2002), and consumer confidence rose. While prices increased by 40 percent in 2002, reflecting the impact of currency devaluation on inflation rates, the rise was less than the depreciation in the currency, and held in check by weak internal demand. The economy improved further in 2003 and 2004, with growth increasing to about 8 percent and inflation falling to below 5 percent. By abandoning the currency board, Argentina may have started on the road to economic recovery.

Sources: "Down and Almost Out in Buenos Aires," *The Economist*, November 3, 2001, pp. 43–44; "A Decline without Parallel," *The Economist*, March 2, 2002, pp. 26–28; "Storm Abated, Outlook Still Unsettled," *The Economist*, January 11, 2003, pp. 26–27; "Which Is the Victim? Argentina and the IMF," *The Economist*, March 6, 2004, p. 82; and F. J. Gurtner, "Why Did Argentina's Currency Board Collapse?" *The World Economy*, May 2004, pp. 697–704.

loans to three troubled Asian countries—South Korea, Indonesia, and Thailand. This was followed by additional IMF rescue packages in Turkey, Russia, Argentina, and Brazil (see the opening case).

The IMF's activities have expanded because periodic financial crises have continued to hit many economies in the post–Bretton Woods era, particularly among the world's developing nations. The IMF has repeatedly lent money to nations experiencing financial crises, requesting in return that the governments enact certain macroeconomic policies. Critics of the IMF claim these policies have not always been as beneficial as the IMF might have hoped and in some cases may have made things worse. Following the IMF loans to several Asian economies, these criticisms reached new levels and a vigorous debate is under way as to the appropriate role of the IMF. In this section, we shall discuss some of the main challenges the IMF has had to deal with over the past quarter of a century and review the ongoing debate over the role of the IMF.

FINANCIAL CRISES IN THE POST–BRETTON WOODS ERA

A number of broad types of financial crises have occurred over the past 30 years, many of which have required IMF involvement. A **currency crisis** occurs when a speculative attack on the exchange value of a currency results in a sharp depreciation in the value of the

FIGURE 11.3

Incidence of Currency and Banking Crises, 1975–1997

Source: International Monetary Fund, *World Economic Outlook, 1998* (Washington, DC: IMF, May 1998), p. 77. Reprinted with permission.

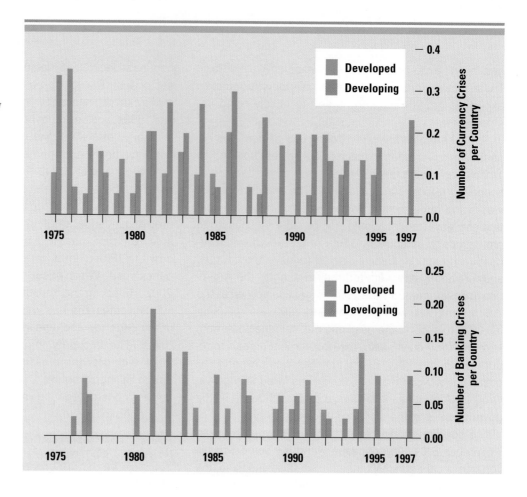

currency or forces authorities to expend large volumes of international currency reserves and sharply increase interest rates to defend the prevailing exchange rate. This is what happened in Brazil in 2002, and the IMF stepped in to help stabilize the value of the Brazilian currency on foreign exchange markets (see the opening case). A **banking crisis** refers to a loss of confidence in the banking system that leads to a run on banks, as individuals and companies withdraw their deposits. A **foreign debt crisis** is a situation in which a country cannot service its foreign debt obligations, whether private-sector or government debt.

These crises tend to have common underlying macroeconomic causes: high relative price inflation rates, a widening current account deficit, excessive expansion of domestic borrowing, and asset price inflation (such as sharp increases in stock and property prices).[11] At times, elements of currency, banking, and debt crises may be present simultaneously, as in the 1997 Asian crisis and the 2000–2002 Argentinean crisis (see the Country Focus).

To assess the frequency of financial crises, the IMF looked at the macroeconomic performance of a group of 53 countries from 1975 to 1997 (22 of these countries were developed nations, and 31 were developing countries).[12] The IMF found there had been 158 currency crises, including 55 episodes in which a country's currency declined by more than 25 percent. There were also 54 banking crises. The IMF's data, which are summarized in Figure 11.3, suggest that developing nations were more than twice as likely to experience currency and banking crises as developed nations. It is not surprising, therefore, that most of the IMF's loan activities since the mid-1970s have been targeted toward developing nations.

Here we look at two crises that have been of particular significance in terms of IMF involvement since the early 1990s—the 1995 Mexican currency crisis and the 1997 Asian financial crisis. These crises were the result of excessive foreign borrowings, a weak or poorly regulated banking system, and high inflation rates. These factors came together to trigger simultaneous debt and currency crises. Checking the resulting crises required IMF involvement.

MEXICAN CURRENCY CRISIS OF 1995

The Mexican peso had been pegged to the dollar since the early 1980s when the International Monetary Fund made it a condition for lending money to the Mexican government to help bail the country out of a 1982 financial crisis. Under the IMF-brokered arrangement, the peso had been allowed to trade within a tolerance band of plus or minus 3 percent against the dollar. The band was also permitted to "crawl" down daily, allowing for an annual peso depreciation of about 4 percent against the dollar. The IMF believed that the need to maintain the exchange rate within a fairly narrow trading band would force the Mexican government to adopt stringent financial policies to limit the growth in the money supply and contain inflation.

Until the early 1990s, it looked as if the IMF policy had worked. However, the strains were beginning to show by 1994. Since the mid-1980s, Mexican producer prices had risen 45 percent more than prices in the United States, and yet there had not been a corresponding adjustment in the exchange rate. By late 1994, Mexico was running a $17 billion trade deficit, which amounted to some 6 percent of the country's gross domestic product, and there had been an uncomfortably rapid expansion in public- and private-sector debt. Despite these strains, Mexican government officials had been stating publicly that they would support the peso's dollar peg at around $1 = 3.5 pesos by adopting appropriate monetary policies and by intervening in the currency markets if necessary. Encouraged by such statements, $64 billion of foreign investment money poured into Mexico between 1990 and 1994 as corporations and money managers sought to take advantage of the booming economy.

However, many currency traders concluded the peso would have to be devalued, and they began to dump pesos on the foreign exchange market. The government tried to hold the line by buying pesos and selling dollars, but it lacked the foreign currency reserves required to halt the speculative tide (Mexico's foreign exchange reserves fell from $6 billion at the beginning of 1994 to less than $3.5 billion at the end of the year). In mid-December 1994, the Mexican government abruptly announced a devaluation. Immediately, much of the short-term investment money that had flowed into Mexican stocks and bonds over the previous year reversed its course, as foreign investors bailed out of peso-denominated financial assets. This exacerbated the sale of the peso and contributed to the rapid 40 percent drop in its value.

The IMF stepped in again, this time arm in arm with the U.S. government and the Bank for International Settlements. Together the three institutions pledged close to $50 billion to help Mexico stabilize the peso and to redeem $47 billion of public- and private-sector debt that was set to mature in 1995. Of this amount, $20 billion came from the U.S. government and another $18 billion came from the IMF (which made Mexico the largest recipient of IMF aid up to that point). Without the aid package, Mexico would probably have defaulted on its debt obligations, and the peso would have gone into free fall. As is normal in such cases, the IMF insisted on tight monetary policies and further cuts in public spending, both of which helped push the country into a deep recession. However, the recession was relatively short-lived, and by 1997 the country was once more on a growth path, had pared down its debt, and had paid back the $20 billion borrowed from the U.S. government ahead of schedule.[13]

THE ASIAN CRISIS

The financial crisis that erupted across Southeast Asia during the fall of 1997 emerged as the biggest challenge to date for the IMF. Holding the crisis in check required IMF loans to help the shattered economies of Indonesia, Thailand, and South Korea stabilize their currencies. In addition, although they did not request IMF loans, the economies of Japan, Malaysia, Singapore, and the Philippines were also hurt by the crisis.

The seeds of this crisis were sown during the previous decade when these countries were experiencing unprecedented economic growth. Although there were and remain important differences between the individual countries, a number of elements were common to most. Exports had long been the engine of economic growth in these countries. From 1990 to 1996, the value of exports from Malaysia had grown by 18 percent annually, Thai exports had grown by 16 percent per year, Singapore's by 15 percent, Hong Kong's by 14 percent, and those of South Korea and Indonesia by 12 percent annually.[14] The nature of these exports had also shifted in recent years from basic materials and products such as textiles to complex and increasingly high-technology products, such as automobiles, semiconductors, and consumer electronics.

The Investment Boom

The wealth created by export-led growth helped fuel an investment boom in commercial and residential property, industrial assets, and infrastructure. The value of commercial and residential real estate in cities such as Hong Kong and Bangkok started to soar. This fed a building boom the likes of which had never been seen in Asia. Heavy borrowing from banks financed much of this construction. As for industrial assets, the success of Asian exporters encouraged them to make bolder investments in industrial capacity. This was exemplified most clearly by South Korea's giant diversified conglomerates, or *chaebol*, many of which had ambitions to build a major position in the global automobile and semiconductor industries.

An added factor behind the investment boom in most Southeast Asian economies was the government. In many cases, the governments had embarked on huge infrastructure projects. In Malaysia, for example, a new government administrative center was being constructed in Putrajaya for M$20 billion (U.S. $8 billion at the pre-July 1997 exchange rate), and the government was funding the development of a massive high-technology communications corridor and the huge Bakun dam, which at a cost of M$13.6 billion was to be the most expensive power-generation plant in the country.[15] Throughout the region, governments also encouraged private businesses to invest in certain sectors of the economy in accordance with "national goals" and "industrialization strategy." In South Korea, long a country where the government played a proactive role in private-sector investments, President Kim Young-Sam urged the *chaebol* to invest in new factories as a way of boosting economic growth. South Korea enjoyed an investment-led economic boom in 1994–1995, but at a cost. The *chaebol*, always reliant on heavy borrowings, built up massive debts that were equivalent, on average, to four times their equity.[16]

In Indonesia, President Suharto had long supported investments in a network of an estimated 300 businesses owned by his family and friends in a system known as "crony capitalism." Many of these businesses were granted lucrative monopolies by the president. For example, Suharto announced in 1995 that he had decided to manufacture a national car, built by a company owned by one of his sons, Hutomo Mandala Putra, in association with Kia Motors of South Korea. To support the venture, a consortium of Indonesian banks was "ordered" by the government to offer almost $700 million in start-up loans to the company.[17]

By the mid-1990s, Southeast Asia was in the grips of an unprecedented investment boom, much of it financed with borrowed money. Between 1990 and 1995, gross domestic investment grew by 16.3 percent annually in Indonesia, 16 percent in Malaysia, 15.3 percent in Thailand, and 7.2 percent in South Korea. By comparison, investment grew by 4.1 percent annually over the same period in the United States and 0.8 percent in all high-income economies.[18] And the rate of investment accelerated in 1996. In Malaysia, for example, spending on investment accounted for a remarkable 43 percent of GDP in 1996.[19]

Excess Capacity

As the volume of investments ballooned during the 1990s, often at the bequest of national governments, the quality of many of these investments declined significantly. The investments often were made on the basis of unrealistic projections about future demand conditions. The result was significant excess capacity. For example, South Korean *chaebol* investments in semiconductor factories surged in 1994 and 1995 when a temporary global shortage of dynamic random access memory chips (DRAMs) led to sharp price increases for this product. However, supply shortages had disappeared by 1996 and excess capacity was beginning to make itself felt, just as the South Koreans started to bring new DRAM factories on stream. The results were predictable; prices for DRAMs plunged, and the earnings of South Korean DRAM manufacturers fell by 90 percent, which meant it was difficult for them to make scheduled payments on the debt they had taken on to build the extra capacity.[20]

The boom in commercial and residential real estate in Asia in the early 1990s was fueled by export-led growth.

In another example, a building boom in Thailand resulted in excess capacity in residential and commercial property. By early 1997, an estimated 365,000 apartment units were unoccupied in Bangkok. With another 100,000 units scheduled to be completed in 1997, years of excess demand in the Thai property market had been replaced by excess supply. By one estimate, Bangkok's building boom had produced enough excess space by 1997 to meet its residential and commercial needs for five years.[21]

The Debt Bomb

By early 1997 what was happening in the South Korean semiconductor industry and the Bangkok property market was being played out elsewhere in the region. Massive investments in industrial assets and property had created excess capacity and plunging prices, while leaving the companies that had made the investments groaning under huge debt burdens that they were now finding it difficult to service.

To make matters worse, much of the borrowing had been in U.S. dollars, as opposed to local currencies. This had originally seemed like a smart move. Throughout the region, local currencies were pegged to the dollar, and interest rates on dollar borrowings were generally lower than rates on borrowings in domestic currency. Thus, it often made economic sense to borrow in dollars if the option was available. However, if the governments could not maintain the dollar peg and their currencies started to depreciate against the dollar, this would increase the size of the debt burden when measured in the local currency. Currency depreciation would raise borrowing costs and could result in companies defaulting on their debt obligations.

Expanding Imports

A final complicating factor was that by the mid-1990s, although exports were still expanding across the region, imports were too. The investments in infrastructure, industrial capacity, and commercial real estate were sucking in foreign goods at unprecedented rates. To build infrastructure, factories, and office buildings, Southeast Asian countries were purchasing capital equipment and materials from America, Europe, and Japan. Many Southeast Asian states saw the current accounts of their balance of payments shift strongly into the red during the mid-1990s. By 1995, Indonesia was running a current account deficit that was equivalent to 3.5 percent of its GDP, Malaysia's was 5.9 percent, and Thailand's was 8.1 percent.[22] With deficits like these, it was increasingly difficult for the governments of these countries to maintain their currencies against the U.S. dollar. If that peg could not be held, the local currency value of dollar-denominated debt would increase, raising the specter of large-scale default on debt service payments. The scene was now set for a potentially rapid economic meltdown.

The Crisis

The Asian meltdown began in mid-1997 in Thailand when it became clear that several key Thai financial institutions were on the verge of default. These institutions had been borrowing dollars from international banks at low interest rates and lending Thai baht at higher interest rates to local property developers. However, due to speculative over-building, these developers could not sell their commercial and residential property, forcing them to default on their debt obligations. In turn, the Thai financial institutions seemed increasingly likely to default on their dollar-denominated debt obligations to international banks. Sensing the beginning of the crisis, foreign investors fled the Thai stock market, selling their positions and converting them into U.S. dollars. The increased demand for dollars and increased supply of Thai baht, pushed down the dollar/Thai baht exchange rate, while the stock market plunged.

Seeing these developments, foreign exchange dealers and hedge funds started speculating against the baht, selling it short. For the previous 13 years, the Thai baht had been pegged to the U.S. dollar at an exchange rate of about $1 = Bt25. The Thai government tried to defend the peg, but only succeeded in depleting its foreign exchange reserves. On July 2, 1997, the Thai government abandoned its defense and announced it would allow the baht to float freely against the dollar. The baht started a slide that would bring the exchange rate down to $1 = Bt55 by January 1998. As the baht declined, the Thai debt bomb exploded. The 55 percent decline in the value of the baht against the dollar doubled the amount of baht required to serve the dollar-denominated debt commitments taken on by Thai financial institutions and businesses. This increased the probability of corporate bankruptcies and further pushed down the battered Thai stock market. The Thailand Set stock market index ultimately declined from 787 in January 1997 to a low of 337 in December of that year, on top of a 45 percent decline in 1996.

On July 28, the Thai government called in the International Monetary Fund. With its foreign exchange reserves depleted, Thailand lacked the foreign currency needed to finance its international trade and service debt commitments and desperately needed the capital the IMF could provide. It also needed to restore international confidence in its currency and needed the credibility associated with gaining access to IMF funds. Without IMF loans, the baht likely would increase its free fall against the U.S. dollar and the whole country might go into default. The IMF agreed to provide the Thai government with $17.2 billion in loans, but the conditions were restrictive.[23] The IMF required the Thai government to increase taxes, cut public spending, privatize several state-owned businesses, and raise interest rates—all steps designed to cool Thailand's overheated economy. The IMF also required Thailand to close illiquid financial institutions. In December 1997, the government shut 56 financial institutions, laying off 16,000 people and further deepening the recession that now gripped the country.

Following the devaluation of the Thai baht, wave after wave of speculation hit other Asian currencies. One after another in a period of weeks, the Malaysian ringgit, Indonesian rupiah, and the Singaporean dollar were all marked sharply lower. With its foreign exchange reserves down to $28 billion, Malaysia let the ringgit float on July 14, 1997. Before the devaluation, the ringgit was trading at $1 = 2.525 ringgit. Six months later it had declined to $1 = 4.15 ringgit. Singapore followed on July 17, and the Singaporean dollar quickly dropped in value from $1 = S$1.495 before the devaluation to $1 = S$2.68 a few days later. Next up was Indonesia, whose rupiah was allowed to float August 14. For Indonesia, this was the beginning of a precipitous decline in the value of its currency, which was to fall from $1 = 2,400 rupiah in August 1997 to $1 = 10,000 rupiah on January 6, 1998, a loss of 76 percent.

With the exception of Singapore, whose economy is probably the most stable in the region, these devaluations were driven by factors similar to those behind the earlier devaluation of the Thai baht—a combination of excess investment; high borrowings, much of it in dollar-denominated debt; and a deteriorating balance-of-payments position. Although both Malaysia and Singapore were able to halt the slide in their currencies and stock markets without the help of the IMF, Indonesia was not. Indonesia was struggling with a private-sector, dollar-denominated debt of close to $80 billion. With the rupiah sliding precipitously almost every day, the cost of servicing this debt was exploding, pushing more Indonesian companies into technical default.

On October 31, 1997, the IMF announced it had assembled a $37 billion rescue deal for Indonesia in conjunction with the World Bank and the Asian Development Bank. In return, the Indonesian government agreed to close a number of troubled banks, reduce public spending, remove government subsidies on basic foodstuffs and energy, balance the budget, and unravel the crony capitalism that was so widespread in Indonesia. But the government of President Suharto appeared to backtrack several times on commitments made to the IMF. This precipitated further declines in the Indonesian currency and stock markets. Ultimately, Suharto removed costly government subsidies, only to see the country dissolve into chaos as the populace took to the streets to protest the resulting price increases. This unleashed a chain of events that led to Suharto's removal from power in May 1998.

The final domino to fall was South Korea (for further details, see the Country Focus in Chapter 10). During the 1990s, South Korean companies had built up huge debt loads as they invested heavily in new industrial capacity. Now they found they had too much industrial capacity and could not generate the income required to service their debt. South Korean banks and companies had also made the mistake of borrowing in dollars, much of it in the form of short-term loans that would come due within a year. Thus, when the Korean won started to decline in the fall of 1997 in sympathy with the problems elsewhere in Asia, South Korean companies saw their debt obligations balloon. Several large companies were forced to file for bankruptcy. This triggered a decline in the South Korean currency and stock market that was difficult to halt. The South Korean central bank tried to keep the dollar/won exchange rate above $1 = W1,000 but found that this only depleted its foreign exchange reserves. On November 17, the South Korean central bank gave up the defense of the won, which quickly fell to $1 = W1,500.

With its economy on the verge of collapse, the South Korean government on November 21 requested $20 billion in standby loans from the IMF. As the negotiations progressed, it became apparent that South Korea was going to need far more than $20 billion. Among other problems, the country's short-term foreign debt was found to be twice as large as previously thought at close to $100 billion, while the country's foreign exchange reserves were down to less than $6 billion. On December 3, 1997, the IMF and South Korean government reached a deal to lend $55 billion to the country. The agreement with the IMF called for the South Koreans to open their economy and banking system to foreign investors. South Korea also pledged to restrain the *chaebol* by reducing their share of bank financing and requiring them to publish consolidated financial statements and undergo annual independent external audits. On trade liberalization, the IMF said South Korea would comply with its commitments to the World Trade Organization to eliminate trade-related subsidies and restrictive import licensing and would streamline its import certification procedures, all of which should open the South Korean economy to greater foreign competition.[24]

EVALUATING THE IMF'S POLICY PRESCRIPTIONS

By 2005, the IMF was committing loans to some 49 countries that were struggling with economic and currency crises. A detailed example of one such program is given in the next Country Focus, which looks at IMF loans to Turkey. All IMF loan packages come with conditions attached. In general, the IMF insists on a combination of tight macroeconomic policies, including cuts in public spending, higher interest rates, and tight monetary policy. It also often pushes for the deregulation of sectors formerly protected from domestic and foreign competition, privatization of state-owned assets, and better financial reporting from the banking sector. These policies are designed to cool overheated economies by reining in inflation and reducing government spending and debt. Recently, this set of policy prescriptions has come in for tough criticisms from many observers.[25]

COUNTRY FOCUS In May 2001, the International Monetary Fund (IMF) agreed to lend $8 billion to Turkey to help the country stabilize its economy and halt a sharp slide in the value of its currency. This was the third time in two years that the international lending institution had put together a loan program for Turkey, and it was the 18th program since Turkey became a member of the IMF in 1958.

Many of Turkey's problems stemmed from a large and inefficient state sector and heavy subsidies to various private sectors of the economy such as agriculture. Although the Turkish government started to privatize state-owned companies in the late 1980s, the programs proceeded at a glacial pace, hamstrung by political opposition within Turkey. Instead of selling state-owned assets to private investors, successive governments increased support to unprofitable state-owned industries and raised the wage rates of state employees. Nor did the government cut subsidies to politically powerful private sectors of the economy, such as agriculture. To support state industries and finance subsidies, Turkey issued significant amounts of government debt. To limit the amount of debt, the government expanded the money supply to finance spending. The result, predictably, was rampant inflation and high interest rates. During the 1990s, inflation averaged over 80 percent a year while real interest rates rose to more than 50 percent on a number of occasions. Despite this, the Turkish economy continued to grow at a healthy pace of 6 percent annually in real terms, a remarkable achievement given the high inflation rates and interest rates.

By the late 1990s the "Turkish miracle" of sustained growth in the face of high inflation and interest rates was running out of steam. Government debt had risen to 60 percent of gross domestic product, government borrowing was leaving little capital for private enterprises, and the cost of financing government debt was spiraling out of control. Rampant inflation was putting pressure on the Turkish currency, the lira, which at the time was pegged in value to a basket of other currencies. Realizing that it needed to drastically reform its economy, the Turkish government sat down with the IMF in late 1999 to work out a recovery program, adopted in January 2000.

As with most IMF programs, the focus was on bringing down the inflation rate, stabilizing the value of the Turkish currency, and restructuring the economy to reduce government debt. The Turkish government committed itself to reducing government debt by taking a number of steps. These included an accelerated privatization program, using the proceeds to pay down debt; the reduction of agricultural subsidies; reform to make it more difficult for people to qualify for public pension programs; and tax increases. The government also agreed to rein in the growth in the money supply to better control inflation. To limit the possibility of speculative attacks on the Turkish currency in the foreign exchange markets, the Turkish government and IMF announced that Turkey would peg the value of the lira against a basket of currencies and devalue the lira by a predetermined amount each month throughout 2000, bringing the total devaluation for the year to 25 percent. To ease the pain, the IMF agreed to provide the Turkish government with $5 billion in loans that could be used to support the value of the lira.

Initially the program seemed to be working. Inflation fell to 35 percent in 2000, while the economy grew by 6 percent. By the end of 2000, however, the program was in trouble. Burdened with nonperforming loans, a number of Turkish banks faced default and had been taken into public ownership by the government. When a criminal fraud investigation uncovered evidence that several of these banks had been pressured by politicians into providing loans at below-market interest rates, foreign investors, worried that more banks might be involved, started to pull their money out of Turkey. This sent the

Inappropriate Policies

One criticism is that the IMF's "one-size-fits-all" approach to macroeconomic policy is inappropriate for many countries. In the case of the Asian crisis, critics argue that the tight macroeconomic policies imposed by the IMF are not well suited to countries that are suffering not from excessive government spending and inflation, but from a private-sector debt crisis with deflationary undertones.[26] In South Korea, for example, the government had been running a budget surplus for years (it was 4 percent of South Korea's GDP in 1994–1996) and inflation was low at about 5 percent. South Korea had the sec-

Turkish stock market into a tailspin and put enormous pressure on the Turkish lira as foreign investors took their money out of the country. The government raised Turkish overnight interbank lending rates to as high as 1,950 percent to try to stem the outflow of capital, but it was clear that Turkey alone could not halt the flow.

The IMF stepped once more into the breach, December 6, 2000, announcing a quickly arranged $7.5 billion loan program for the country. In return for the loan, the IMF required the Turkish government to close 10 insolvent banks, speed up its privatization plans (which had once more stalled), and cap any pay increases for government workers. The IMF also reportedly urged the Turkish government to let its currency float freely in the foreign exchange markets, but the government refused, arguing that the result would be a rapid devaluation in the lira, which would raise import prices and fuel price inflation. The government insisted that reducing inflation should be its first priority.

This plan started to come apart in February 2001. A surge in inflation and a rapid slowdown in economic growth once more spooked foreign investors. Into this explosive mix waded Turkey's prime minister and president, who engaged in a highly public argument about economic policy and political corruption. This triggered a rapid outflow of capital. The government raised the overnight interbank lending rate to 7,500 percent to try to persuade foreigners to leave their money in the country, but to no avail. Realizing that it would be unable to keep the lira within its planned monthly devaluation range without raising interest rates to absurd levels or seriously depleting the country's foreign exchange reserves, on February 23, 2001, the Turkish government decided to let the lira float freely. The lira immediately dropped 50 percent in value against the U.S. dollar, but ended the day down some 28 percent.

Over the next two months, the Turkish economy continued to weaken as a global economic slowdown affected the nation. Inflation stayed high, and progress at reforming the country's economy remained bogged down by political considerations. By early April, the lira had fallen 40 percent against the dollar since February 23, and the country was teetering on the brink of an economic meltdown. For the third time in 18 months, the IMF stepped in, arranging for another $8 billion in loans. Once more, the IMF insisted that the Turkish government accelerate privatization, close insolvent banks, deregulate its market, and cut government spending. Critics of the IMF, however, claimed this "austerity program" would only slow the Turkish economy and make matters worse, not better. These critics advocated a mix of sound monetary policy and tax cuts to boost Turkey's economic growth.

By late 2004 significant progress had been made. Initially the Turkish government failed to fully comply with IMF mandates on economic policy, causing the institution to hold back a scheduled $1.6 billion in IMF loans until the government passed an "austerity budget," which it did reluctantly in March 2003 after months of public handwringing. Since then, things have improved. Inflation fell from a peak of 65 percent in December 2000 to about 10.5 percent for 2004. Economic growth increased to a robust 9 percent in 2004. The pace of the privatization program has increased, with the government raising $4 billion from asset sales in 2003. The government also generated budget surpluses of 6.5 percent of GDP in 2003 and 2004. Can Turkey finally be counted as an IMF success?

Sources: P. Blustein, "Turkish Crisis Weakens the Case for Intervention," *Washington Post,* March 2, 2001, p. E1; H. Pope, "Can Turkey Finally Mend Its Economy?" *The Wall Street Journal,* May 22, 2001, p. A18; "Turkish Bath," *The Wall Street Journal,* February 23, 2001, p. A14; E. McBride, "Turkey—Fingers Crossed," *The Economist,* June 10, 2000, p. SS16–SS17; "Turkey and the IMF," *The Economist,* December 9, 2000, pp. 81–82; G. Chazan, "Turkey's Decision on Aid Is Sinking In," *The Wall Street Journal,* March 6, 2003, p. A11; S. Fittipaldi, "Markets Keep a Wary Eye on Ankara," *Global Finance,* October 2003, p. 88; and "Plumper: Turkey," *The Economist,* December 18, 2004, p. 141.

ond strongest financial position of any country in the Organization for Economic Cooperation and Development. Despite this, critics say, the IMF insisted on applying the same policies that it applies to countries suffering from high inflation. The IMF required South Korea to maintain an inflation rate of 5 percent. However, given the collapse in the value of its currency and the subsequent rise in price for imports such as oil, critics claimed inflationary pressures would inevitably increase in South Korea. So to hit a 5 percent inflation rate, the South Koreans would be forced to apply an unnecessarily tight monetary policy. Short-term interest rates in South Korea did jump from 12.5 percent to 21 percent immediately after the country signed its initial deal with the IMF. Increasing interest rates made it even more difficult for companies to service their already excessive short-term debt obligations, and critics used this as evidence to argue that the cure prescribed by the IMF may actually increase the probability of widespread corporate defaults, not reduce them.

The IMF rejected this criticism. According to the IMF, the central task was to rebuild confidence in the won. Once this was achieved, the won would recover from its oversold levels, reducing the size of South Korea's dollar-denominated debt burden when expressed in won, making it easier for companies to service their debt. The IMF also argued that by requiring South Korea to remove restrictions on foreign direct investment, foreign capital would flow into the country to take advantage of cheap assets. This, too, would increase demand for the Korean currency and help to improve the dollar/won exchange rate.

Korea did recover fairly quickly from the crisis, supporting the position of the IMF. While the economy contracted by 7 percent in 1998, by 2000 it had rebounded and grew at a 9 percent rate (measured by growth in GDP). Inflation, which peaked at 8 percent in 1998, fell to 2 percent by 2000, and unemployment fell from 7 percent to 4 percent over the same period. The won hit a low of $1 = W1,812 in early 1998, but by 2000 was back to an exchange rate of around $1 = W1,200, at which it seems to have stabilized.

Moral Hazard

A second criticism of the IMF is that its rescue efforts are exacerbating a problem known to economists as moral hazard. **Moral hazard** arises when people behave recklessly because they know they will be saved if things go wrong. Critics point out that many Japanese and Western banks were far too willing to lend large amounts of capital to overleveraged Asian companies during the boom years of the 1990s. These critics argue that the banks should now be forced to pay the price for their rash lending policies, even if that means some banks must close.[27] Only by taking such drastic action, the argument goes, will banks learn the error of their ways and not engage in rash lending in the future. By providing support to these countries, the IMF is reducing the probability of debt default and in effect bailing out the banks whose loans gave rise to this situation.

This argument ignores two critical points. First, if some Japanese or Western banks with heavy exposure to the troubled Asian economies were forced to write off their loans due to widespread debt default, the impact would have been difficult to contain. The failure of large Japanese banks, for example, could have triggered a meltdown in the Japanese financial markets. That would almost inevitably lead to a serious decline in stock markets around the world, which was the very risk the IMF was trying to avoid by stepping in with financial support. Second, it is incorrect to imply that some banks have not had to pay the price for rash lending policies. The IMF has insisted on the closure of banks in South Korea, Thailand, and Indonesia. Foreign banks with short-term loans outstanding to South Korean enterprises have been forced by circumstances to reschedule those loans at interest rates that do not compensate for the extension of the loan maturity.

Lack of Accountability

The final criticism of the IMF is that it has become too powerful for an institution that lacks any real mechanism for accountability.[28] The IMF has determined macroeconomic policies in those countries, yet according to critics such as noted economist Jeffrey Sachs, the IMF, with a staff of less than 1,000, lacks the expertise required to do a good job. Evidence of this, according to Sachs, can be found in the fact that the IMF was singing the praises of the Thai and South Korean governments only months before both countries lurched into crisis. Then the IMF put together a draconian program for South Korea without having deep knowledge of the country. Sachs's solution to this problem is to reform the IMF so it makes greater use of outside experts and its operations are open to greater outside scrutiny.

Observations

As with many debates about international economics, it is not clear which side has the winning hand about the appropriateness of IMF policies. There are cases where one can argue that IMF policies have been counterproductive, or only had limited success. For example, one might question the success of the IMF's involvement in Turkey given that the country has had to implement some 18 IMF programs since 1958 (see the accompanying Country Focus)! But the IMF can also point to some notable accomplishments, including its success in containing the Asian crisis, which could have rocked the global international monetary system to its core. Similarly, many observers give the IMF credit for its deft handling of politically difficult situations, such as the Mexican peso crisis, and for successfully promoting a free market philosophy.

Several years after the IMF's intervention, the economies of Asia and Mexico recovered. Certainly they all averted the kind of catastrophic implosion that might have occurred had the IMF not stepped in, and although some countries still faced considerable problems, it is not clear that the IMF should take much blame for this. The IMF cannot force countries to adopt the policies required to correct economic mismanagement. While a government may commit to taking corrective action in return for an IMF loan, internal political problems may make it difficult for a government to act on that commitment. In such cases, the IMF is caught between a rock and a hard place, for if it decided to withhold money, it might trigger financial collapse and the kind of contagion that it seeks to avoid.

IMPLICATIONS FOR MANAGERS

The implications for international businesses of the material discussed in this chapter fall into three main areas: currency management, business strategy, and corporate–government relations.

CURRENCY MANAGEMENT

An obvious implication with regard to currency management is that companies must recognize that the foreign exchange market does not work quite as depicted in Chapter 10. The current system is a mixed system in which a combination of government intervention and speculative activity can drive the foreign exchange market. Companies engaged in significant foreign exchange activities need to be aware of this and to adjust their foreign exchange transactions accordingly. For example, the currency management unit of Caterpillar claims it made millions of dollars in the hours following the announcement of the Plaza Accord by selling dollars and buying currencies that it expected to appreciate on the foreign exchange market following government intervention.

Under the present system, speculative buying and selling of currencies can create very volatile movements in exchange rates (as exhibited by the rise and fall of the dollar during the 1980s and the Asian currency crisis of the late 1990s). Contrary to the predictions of the purchasing power parity theory (see Chapter 10), exchange rate movements during the 1980s and 1990s often did not seem to be strongly influenced by relative inflation rates. Insofar as volatile exchange rates increase foreign exchange risk, this is not good news for business. On the other hand, as we saw in Chapter 10, the foreign exchange market has developed a number of instruments, such as the forward market and swaps, that can help to insure against foreign exchange risk. Not surprisingly, use of these instruments has increased markedly since the breakdown of the Bretton Woods system in 1973.

BUSINESS STRATEGY

The volatility of the present global exchange rate regime presents a conundrum for international businesses. Exchange rate movements are difficult to predict, and yet their movement can have a major impact on a business's competitive position. For a detailed example, see the accompanying Management Focus on Airbus. Faced with uncertainty about the future value of currencies, firms can utilize the forward exchange market, which Airbus has done. However, the forward exchange market is far from perfect as a predictor of future exchange rates (see Chapter 10). It is also difficult if not impossible to get adequate insurance coverage for exchange rate changes that might occur several years in the future. The forward market tends to offer coverage for exchange rate changes a few months—not years—ahead. Given this, it makes sense to pursue strategies that will increase the company's strategic flexibility in the face of unpredictable exchange rate movements—that is, to pursue strategies that reduce the economic exposure of the firm (which we first discussed in Chapter 10).

Maintaining strategic flexibility can take the form of dispersing production to different locations around the globe as a real hedge against currency fluctuations (this seems to be what Airbus is now considering). Consider the case of Daimler-Benz (now Daimler-Chrysler), Germany's export-oriented automobile and aerospace company. In June 1995, the company stunned the German business community when it announced it expected to post a severe loss in 1995 of about $720 million. The cause was Germany's strong currency, which had appreciated by 4 percent against a basket of major currencies since the beginning of 1995 and had risen by more than 30 percent against the U.S. dollar since late 1994. By mid-1995, the exchange rate against the dollar stood at $1 = DM1.38. Daimler's management believed it could not make money with an exchange rate under $1 = DM1.60. Daimler's senior managers concluded that the appreciation of the mark against the dollar was probably permanent, so they decided to move substantial production outside of Germany and increase purchasing of foreign components. The idea was to reduce the vulnerability of the company to future exchange rate movements. The Mercedes-Benz division has begun to implement this move. Even before its acquisition of Chrysler Corporation in 1998, Mercedes planned to produce 10 percent of its cars outside of Germany by 2000, mostly in the United States.[29] Similarly, the move by Japanese automobile companies to expand their productive capacity in the United States and Europe can be seen in the context of the increase in the value of the yen between 1985 and 1995, which raised the price of Japanese exports. For the Japanese companies, building production capacity overseas is a hedge against continued appreciation of the yen (as well as against trade barriers).

Another way of building strategic flexibility and reducing economic exposure involves contracting out manufacturing. This allows a company to shift suppliers from country to country in response to changes in relative costs brought about by exchange rate movements. However, this kind of strategy may work only for low-value-added manufacturing (e.g., textiles), in which the individual manufacturers have few if any firm-specific skills that contribute to the value of the product. It may be less appropriate for high-value-added manufacturing, in which firm-specific technology and skills add significant value to the product (e.g., the heavy equipment industry) and in which switching costs are correspondingly high. For high-value-added manufacturing, switching suppliers will lead to a reduction in the value that is added, which may offset any cost gains arising from exchange rate fluctuations.

The roles of the IMF and the World Bank in the present international monetary system also have implications for business strategy. Increasingly, the IMF has been acting as the macroeconomic police of the world economy, insisting that countries seeking significant borrowings adopt IMF-mandated macroeconomic policies. These policies typically include anti-inflationary monetary policies and reductions in government spending. In the short run, such policies usually result in a sharp contraction of demand. International businesses selling or producing in such countries need to be

MANAGEMENT FOCUS Airbus had reason to celebrate in 2003; for the first time in the company's history it delivered more commercial jet aircraft than longtime rival Boeing. Airbus delivered 305 planes in 2003, compared to Boeing's 281. The celebration, however, was muted, for the strength of the euro against the U.S. dollar was casting a cloud over the company's future. Airbus, which is based in Toulouse, France, prices planes in dollars, just as Boeing has always done. But more than half of Airbus's costs are in euros. So as the dollar drops in value against the euro, and it dropped by over 50 percent between 2002 and the end of 2004, Airbus's costs rise in proportion to its revenue, squeezing profits in the process.

In the short run, the fall in the value of the dollar against the euro will not hurt Airbus. The company fully hedged its dollar exposure until 2005 and was mostly hedged for 2006. However, anticipating that the dollar will stay weak against the euro, Airbus is taking other steps to reduce its economic exposure to a strong European currency. Recognizing that raising prices is not an option given the strong competition from Boeing, Airbus has decided to focus on reducing its costs by some 15 percent by 2006. As a step toward doing this, Airbus is giving U.S. suppliers a greater share of work on new aircraft models, such as the A380 super-jumbo. It is also shifting supply work on some of its older models from European to American-based suppliers. This will increase the proportion of its costs that are in dollars, making profits less vulnerable to a rise in the value of the euro and reducing the costs of building an aircraft when they are converted back into euros.

In addition, Airbus is pushing its European-based suppliers to start pricing in U.S. dollars. Because the costs of many of these supplier are in euros, the suppliers are finding that to comply with Airbus's wishes, they too have to move more work to the United States, or to countries whose currency is pegged to the U.S. dollar. Thus, one large French-based supplier, Zodiac, has announced that it was considering acquisitions in the United States. Not only is Airbus pushing suppliers to price components for commercial jet aircraft in dollars, but the company is also requiring suppliers to its A400M program, a military aircraft that will be sold to European governments and priced in euros, to price components in U.S. dollars. Beyond these steps, the CEO of EADS, Airbus's parent company, has publicly stated that it might be prepared to assemble aircraft in the United States if that helps to win important U.S. contracts.

Sources: D. Michaels, "Airbus Deliveries Top Boeing's; But Several Obstacles Remain," *The Wall Street Journal,* January 16, 2004, p. A9; J. L. Gerondeau, "Airbus Eyes U.S. Suppliers as Euro Gains," *Seattle Times,* February 21, 2004, p. C4; and "Euro's Gains Create Worries in Europe," *Houston Chronicle.com,* January 13, 2004, p. 3.

www.mhhe.com/hill

aware of this and plan accordingly. In the long run, the kind of policies imposed by the IMF can promote economic growth and an expansion of demand, which create opportunities for international business.

CORPORATE–GOVERNMENT RELATIONS

As major players in the international trade and investment environment, businesses can influence government policy toward the international monetary system. For example, intense government lobbying by U.S. exporters helped convince the U.S. government that intervention in the foreign exchange market was necessary. With this in mind, business can and should use its influence to promote an international monetary system that facilitates the growth of international trade and investment. Whether a fixed or floating regime is optimal is a subject for debate. However, exchange rate volatility such as the world experienced during the 1980s and 1990s creates an environment less conducive to international trade and investment than one with more stable exchange rates. Therefore, it would seem to be in the interests of international business to promote an international monetary system that minimizes volatile exchange rate movements, particularly when those movements are unrelated to long-run economic fundamentals.

Chapter Summary

This chapter explained the workings of the international monetary system and pointed out its implications for international business. The chapter made the following points:

1. The gold standard is a monetary standard that pegs currencies to gold and guarantees convertibility to gold. It was thought that the gold standard contained an automatic mechanism that contributed to the simultaneous achievement of a balance-of-payments equilibrium by all countries. The gold standard broke down during the 1930s as countries engaged in competitive devaluations.

2. The Bretton Woods system of fixed exchange rates was established in 1944. The U.S. dollar was the central currency of this system; the value of every other currency was pegged to its value. Significant exchange rate devaluations were allowed only with the permission of the IMF. The role of the IMF was to maintain order in the international monetary system (i) to avoid a repetition of the competitive devaluations of the 1930s and (ii) to control price inflation by imposing monetary discipline on countries.

3. The fixed exchange rate system collapsed in 1973, primarily due to speculative pressure on the dollar following a rise in U.S. inflation and a growing U.S. balance-of-trade deficit.

4. Since 1973 the world has operated with a floating exchange rate regime, and exchange rates have become more volatile and far less predictable. Volatile exchange rate movements have helped reopen the debate over the merits of fixed and floating systems.

5. The case for a floating exchange rate regime claims (i) such a system gives countries autonomy regarding their monetary policy and (ii) floating exchange rates facilitate smooth adjustment of trade imbalances.

6. The case for a fixed exchange rate regime claims (i) the need to maintain a fixed exchange rate imposes monetary discipline on a country, (ii) floating exchange rate regimes are vulnerable to speculative pressure, (iii) the uncertainty that accompanies floating exchange rates dampens the growth of international trade and investment, and (iv) far from correcting trade imbalances, depreciating a currency on the foreign exchange market tends to cause price inflation.

7. In today's international monetary system, some countries have adopted floating exchange rates, some have pegged their currency to another currency such as the U.S. dollar, and some have pegged their currency to a basket of other currencies, allowing their currency to fluctuate within a zone around the basket.

8. In the post–Bretton Woods era, the IMF has continued to play an important role in helping countries navigate their way through financial crises by lending significant capital to embattled governments and by requiring them to adopt certain macroeconomic policies.

9. An important debate is occurring over the appropriateness of IMF-mandated macroeconomic policies. Critics charge that the IMF often imposes inappropriate conditions on developing nations that are the recipients of its loans.

10. The present managed-float system of exchange rate determination has increased the importance of currency management in international businesses.

11. The volatility of exchange rates under the present managed-float system creates both opportunities and threats. One way of responding to this volatility is for companies to build strategic flexibility and limit their economic exposure by dispersing production to different locations around the globe by contracting out manufacturing (in the case of low-value-added manufacturing) and other means.

Critical Thinking and Discussion Questions

1. Why did the gold standard collapse? Is there a case for returning to some type of gold standard? What is it?

2. What opportunities might current IMF lending policies to developing nations create for international businesses? What threats might they create?

3. Do you think the standard IMF policy prescriptions of tight monetary policy and reduced government spending are always appropriate for developing nations experiencing a currency crisis? How might the IMF change its approach? What would the implications be for international businesses?

4. Debate the relative merits of fixed and floating exchange rate regimes. From the perspective of an international business, what are the most important criteria in a choice between the systems? Which system is the more desirable for an international business?

5. Imagine that Canada, the United States, and Mexico decide to adopt a fixed exchange rate system. What would be the likely consequences of such a system for (*a*) international businesses and (*b*) the flow of trade and investment among the three countries?

Research Task globalEDGE™ globaledge.msu.edu

Use the globalEDGE™ site to complete the following exercises:

1. The *Global Financial Stability Report* is a semi-annual report published by the International Capital Markets division of IMF. The report aims to provide a regular assessment of global financial markets and to identify potential systemic weaknesses that could lead to crises. Locate and download the latest report to prepare a summary of what IMF sees as the developments and vulnerabilities facing emerging market countries.

2. The biz/ed Web site presents a "Trade Balance and Exchange Rate Simulation" which helps you understand how a change in exchange rates influences the trade balance. Locate the online simulator (check under the Academy section of globalEDGE) and identify what the trade balance is assumed to be a function of. Run the simulation to identify how exchange rate changes affect exports, imports, and the trade balance.

China's Pegged Exchange Rate

CLOSING CASE Since 1994 China has pegged the value of its currency, the yuan, to the U.S. dollar at an exchange rate of $1 = 8.28 yuan. Consequently, the value of the yuan has moved in lockstep with the value of the U.S. dollar against other currencies. As the dollar rose in the 1990s, so did the yuan, and as the dollar fell in 2002–2004, so did the yuan. To maintain the exchange rate of the yuan against the dollar, the Chinese central bank regularly bought or sold dollars. China also has much stricter currency controls than most countries, which makes it very difficult for private citizens or companies in China to move money out of the country and exchange it for foreign currency. This too, helps to preserve the value of the yuan against the dollar. By early 2005, however, pressure was building for China to alter its exchange rate policy and let the yuan float freely against the dollar.

Many claim that after years of rapid economic growth and foreign capital inflows, the pegged exchange rate undervalues the yuan by as much as 40 percent. In turn, the cheap yuan is helping to fuel a boom in Chinese exports to the West, particularly the United States where the trade deficit with China expanded to a record $160 billion in 2004. Job losses among American manufacturing companies have created political pressures in the United States for the government to push the Chinese to let the yuan float freely against the dollar. Some American manufacturers complain that they cannot compete against "artificially cheap" Chinese imports. In mid-2003, 16 U.S. senators from both parties sent a letter to the George W. Bush administration complaining that the cheap yuan was harming American manufacturers, leading to job losses and threatening the case for free trade. Others have painted the Chinese policy as a kind of neo-mercantilism, whereby an artificially cheap currency is used to boost exports and limit imports.

Keeping the yuan pegged to the dollar is also becoming increasingly problematic for the Chinese, too. The trade surplus with the United States and strong inflows of foreign investment have led to a surge of dollars into China. To maintain the exchange rate, the Chinese central bank regularly buys dollars from commercial banks, issuing them yuan at the official exchange rate. As a result, China's foreign exchange reserves had risen to more than $600 billion in early 2005, and the Chinese were reportedly buying some $15 billion each month in an

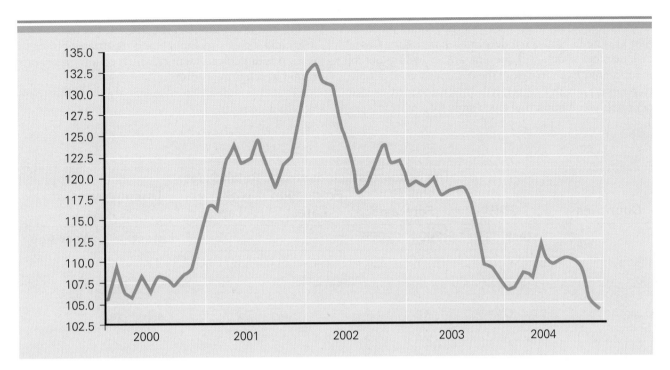

EXHIBIT 2

Japanese Yen versus U.S. Dollar

Note: Average exchange rates are calculated over a 12-month period, and available on December 31 and June 30 each year.

Source: *Pacific Exchange Rate Service*, fx.sauder.ubc.ca.

In the early 1990s, after the dollar's previous long slide, the greenback's preeminence had survived. But then there had been no alternative to the dollar. Since 1999, the euro had emerged as a potential rival to the greenback. Moreover, in 2004, the situation seemed significantly different from the late 1980s and early 1990s. The current-account deficit was running at close to 6 percent of GDP, almost twice as big as at its peak in the late 1980s. In the 1980s, America had been a net foreign creditor. In 2004, it had net foreign liabilities and these were expected to reach $3.3 trillion, or 28 percent of GDP. By the end of 2004, America's budget deficit had also reached astronomical proportions.

Dipankar concluded: "It looks as though the dollar will lose its reserve currency status. The dollar's share of global foreign-exchange reserves has already fallen from 80 percent in the mid-1970s to around 65 percent in late 2004."

At that point, a student in the class spoke up: "I don't quite agree with the views expressed so far. We seem to be missing the woods for the trees. I feel a currency represents a country's global competitiveness. If the economy is strong, the currency will continue to be credible. So what if the U.S. runs a big trade deficit or a budget deficit? More than macroeconomic factors, we need to see how competitive U.S. industries are globally. I recently read Michael Porter's book, *The Competitive Advantage of Nations*. He emphasizes that macroeconomic parameters do not convey the full story. The U.S. remains the center of innovation for most high-tech industries. We say that this is the age of services. Name any advanced service. The U.S. is the global leader. The U.S. has also shown a remarkable ability to restructure itself from time to time. Take outsourcing. U.S. companies are getting things done in India at a much lower cost. In countries like Germany and France, such a possibility evokes strong negative sentiments from the public. I believe the competitiveness of the U.S. can never be equaled by Europe. How many European companies have succeeded in software, biotech, or microprocessors? Why is it that the best people in the world want to migrate to the U.S., not to Europe or Japan? There is no way the euro can replace the dollar."

Another student added: "Even the macroeconomic picture in the U.S. is far healthier than projected. The U.S. can afford a big budget deficit. That is because with so much excess capacity, there is little likelihood of inflation. The U.S. also has deep, well-functioning financial markets which will prevent any crowding out of investments. Even in case of the current account deficit, the fears are largely exaggerated. True, no country can indefinitely go on importing much more than what it is ex-porting. But if Toyota USA imports engines from South Africa and exports to Europe and repatriates profits to Japan, it is difficult to identify which country is exporting and which is importing."

As the class ended, Dipankar wondered whether these students were right.

Countries	GDP			The Economist Poll GDP Forecasts		Industrial Production Latest		Retail Sales (volume) Latest		Unemployment % Rate		
	Latest		Qtr*	2004	2005					Latest		Year Ago
Britain	+3.1	Q3	+1.8	+3.2	+2.4	1.9	Oct	+6.1	Nov	4.7	Oct	5
Canada	+3.3	Q3	+3.2	+2.9	+3.1	3.6	Oct	+5.0	Oct	7.3	Nov	7.5
Japan	+2.6	Q3	+0.2	+3.9	+1.9	4.3	Nov	−2.2	Oct	4.5	Nov	5.1
Switzerland	+1.8	Q3	+1.4	+1.8	+1.8	+3.5	Q3	−1.0	Oct	3.9	Nov	4.0
United States	+4.0	Q3	+4.0	+4.4	+3.5	3.8	Nov	+4.3	Nov	5.4	Nov	5.9
Euro area	+1.8	Q3	+1.2	+1.8	+1.7	1	Oct	−0.2	Oct	8.9	Oct	8.9

EXHIBIT 3

Output, Demand, and Jobs (% change on year ago)

*% change on previous quarter at an annual rate.
Not seasonally adjusted.
New series.
Aug-Oct; claimant count rate 2.7% in Nov.
EU harmonized rate 9.9% in Oct.
**Sep-Nov.

Source: *www.economist.com*, January 1, 2005.

Countries	Trade Balance* ($bn latest 12 months)		Current Account Balance				Exchange Rate							Budget Balance % of GDP, 2004
			$bn latest 12 months		The Economist poll % of GDP, Forecast		Trade Weighted, 1990-100		Currency Units					
					2004	2005	Dec. 28	Year ago	Per $		Per £	Per euro	Per ¥100	
									Dec. 28	Year ago				
Britain	−103.2	Oct	−47.4	Q3	−2.5	−2.7	102.3	100.3	0.52	0.56	–	0.7	0.5	−3.2
Canada	+49.6	Oct	+26.7	Q3	+2.7	+2.3	92.6	87.7	1.23	1.31	2.37	1.66	1.19	+1.1
Japan	+135.8	Oct	+169.9	Oct	+1.5	+3.4	136.0	136.8	104	107	200	140	–	−6.5
Switzerland	+7.9	Oct	+45.9	Q2	+11.7	+11.2	114.1	111.8	1.14	1.25	2.2	1.55	1.1	−1.6
United States	−634.0	Oct	−603.2	Q3	−5.5	−5.6	89.5	95.3	–	–	1.93	1.35	0.97	−4.4
Euro area	+94.7	Oct	+47.3	Oct	+0.5	+0.5	94.8	92.4	0.74	0.8	1.42	–	0.71	−2.9

EXHIBIT 4

Trade, Exchange Rates, and Budgets

Source: *www.economist.com*, January 1, 2005.

Countries	Consumer Prices			The Economist Poll Consumer Prices Forecast		Producer Prices			Wages/Earnings		
	Latest		Year Ago	2004	2005	Latest		Year Ago	Latest		Year Ago
Britain	+1.5	Nov*	+1.3	+1.5	+1.7	+3.5	Nov	+1.7	+4.1	Oct	+3.6
Canada	+2.4	Nov	+1.6	+1.9	+2.1	+5.4	Oct	−4	+2.6	Sep	+3
Japan	+0.8	Nov	−0.5	−0.1	nil	+2	Nov	−0.5	+1.4	Nov	+0.1
Switzerland	+1.5	Nov	+0.5	+0.8	+1.2	+1.9	Nov	−0.2	+1.4	2003	+1.8
United States	+3.5	Nov	+1.8	+2.7	+2.3	+5.1	Nov	+3.4	+2.4	Nov	+2.2
Euro area	+2.2	Nov	+2.2	+2.1	+1.8	+4	Oct	+0.8	+2	Q3	+2.8

EXHIBIT 5

Prices and Wages (*% change on year ago*)

*New series RPI inflation rate 3.4% in November.

Source: *www.economist.com*, January 1, 2005.

EXHIBIT 6

The U.S. Economy at a Glance

Source: *Economist Intelligence Unit, Country Data,* May 26, 2004.

	2000	2001	2002	2003
GDP per head ($ at PPP)	34,770	35,438	36,432	37,831
GDP (% real change pa)	3.66	0.51	2.19	3.12
Government consumption (% of GDP)	17.54	17.97	18.44	18.72
Budget balance (% of GDP)	2.44	1.27	−1.52	−3.46
Consumer prices (% change pa; av)	3.37	2.83	1.58	2.28
Public debt (% of GDP)	57.98	57.47	59.75	62.43
Labor costs per hour (USD)	19.76	20.60	21.33	21.83
Recorded unemployment (%)	3.98	4.76	5.78	5.99
Current-account balance/GDP	−4.19	−3.90	−4.59	−4.90
Foreign-exchange reserves (mUS$)	56,600	57,633	67,962	74,894

12

The Strategy of International Business

Wal-Mart's Global Expansion

Established in Arkansas in 1962 by Sam Walton, over the last four decades Wal-Mart has grown rapidly to become the largest retailer in the world with 2004 sales of $280 billion, 1.5 million associates (Wal-Mart's term for employees), and more than 4,500 stores. Until 1991, Wal-Mart's operations were confined to the United States. There it established a competitive advantage based upon a combination of efficient merchandising, buying power, and human relations policies. Among other things, Wal-Mart was a leader in the implementation of information systems to track product sales and inventory, developed one of the most efficient distribution systems in the world, and was one of the first companies to promote widespread stock ownership among employees. These practices led to high productivity that enabled Wal-Mart to drive down its operating costs, which it passed on to consumers in the form of everyday low prices, a strategy that enabled the company to gain market share first in general merchandising, where it now dominates, and later in food retailing, where it is taking market share from established supermarkets.

By 1990, however, Wal-Mart realized that its opportunities for growth in the United States were becoming more limited. Management calculated that by the early 2000s, domestic growth opportunities would be constrained due to market saturation. So the company decided to expand globally. Initially, the critics scoffed. Wal-Mart, they said, was too American a company. While its retailing practices were well suited to America, they would not work in other countries where infrastructure was different, consumer tastes and preferences vary, and where established retailers already dominated.

Unperturbed, in 1991 Wal-Mart started to expand internationally with the opening of its first stores in Mexico. The Mexican operation was established as a joint venture with Cifera, the largest local retailer. Initially, Wal-Mart made a number of missteps that seemed to prove the critics right. Wal-Mart had problems replicating its efficient distribution system in Mexico. Poor infrastructure, crowded roads, and a lack of leverage with local suppliers, many of which could not or would not deliver directly to Wal-Mart's stores or distribution centers, resulted in stocking problems and raised costs and prices. Initially, prices at Wal-Mart in Mexico were some 20 percent above prices for comparable products in the company's U.S. stores, which limited Wal-Mart's ability to gain market share. There were also problems with merchandise selection. Many of the stores in Mexico carried items that were popular in the United States. These included ice skates, riding lawn mowers, leaf blowers, and fishing tackle. Not surprisingly, these items did not sell well in Mexico, so managers would slash prices to move inventory, only to find that the company's automated information systems would immediately order more inventory to replenish the depleted stock.

By the mid-1990s, however, Wal-Mart had learned from its early mistakes and adapted its Mexican operations to match the local environment. A partnership with a Mexican trucking company dramatically improved the distribution system, while more careful stocking practices meant that the Mexican stores sold merchandise that appealed more to local tastes and preferences. As Wal-Mart's presence grew, many of Wal-Mart's suppliers built factories near its Mexican distribution centers so that they could better serve the company, which helped to further drive down inventory and logistics costs. Today, Mexico is a leading light in Wal-Mart's international operations. In 1998, Wal-Mart acquired a controlling interest in Cifera. By 2004, Wal-Mart was more than twice the size of its nearest rival in Mexico with 670 stores and revenues of more than $11 billion.

The Mexican experience proved to Wal-Mart that it could compete outside of the United States. It has subsequently expanded into nine other countries. Wal-Mart entered Canada, Great Britain, Germany, Japan, and South Korea, by acquiring existing retailers and then transferring its information systems, logistics, and management expertise. In Puerto Rico, Brazil, Argentina, and China, Wal-Mart established its own stores. As a result of these moves, by 2004 the company had over 1,500 stores outside the United States, employed 330,000 associates, and generated international revenues of more than $50 billion.

In addition to greater growth, expanding internationally has bought Wal-Mart two other major benefits. First, Wal-Mart has also been able to reap significant economies of scale from its global buying power. Many of Wal-Mart's key suppliers have long been international companies; for example, GE (appliances), Unilever (food products), and Procter & Gamble (personal care products) are all major Wal-Mart suppliers that have long had their own global operations. By building international reach, Wal-Mart has used its enhanced size to demand deeper discounts from the local operations of its global suppliers, increasing the company's ability to lower prices to consumers, gain market share, and ultimately earn greater profits. Second, Wal-Mart has found that it is benefiting from the flow of ideas across the 11 countries in which it now competes. For example, a two-level store in New York State came about because of the success of multilevel stores in South Korea. Other ideas, such as wine departments in its stores in Argentina, have now been integrated into layouts worldwide.

Wal-Mart realized that if it didn't expand internationally, other global retailers would beat it to the punch. Wal-Mart faces significant global competition from Carrefour of France, Ahold of Holland, and Tesco from the United Kingdom. Carrefour, the world's second largest retailer, is perhaps the most global of the lot. The pioneer of the hypermarket concept now operates in 26 countries and generates more than 50 percent of its sales outside France. Compared to this, Wal-Mart is a laggard with less than 20 percent of its sales in 2004 generated from international operations. However, there is room for significant global expansion. The global retailing market is still very fragmented. The top 25 retailers controlled less than

20 percent of worldwide retail sales in 2004, although forecasts suggest the figure could reach 40 percent by 2009, with Latin America, Southeast Asia, and Eastern Europe being the main battlegrounds.

Sources: A. Lillo, "Wal-Mart Says Global Going Good," *Home Textiles Today,* September 15, 2003, p. 12–13; A. de Rocha and L. A. Dib, "The Entry of Wal-Mart into Brazil," *International Journal of Retail and Distribution Management,* 30 (2002), pp. 61–73; "Wal-Mart: Mexico's Biggest Retailer," *Chain Store Age,* June 2001, pp. 52–54; M. N. Hamilton, "Global Food Fight," *Washington Post,* November 19, 2000, p. H1; "Global Strategy—Why Tesco Will Beat Carrefour," *Retail Week,* April 6, 2001, p. 14; "Shopping all over the World," *The Economist,* June 19, 1999, pp. 59–61; M. Flagg, "In Asia, Going to the Grocery Increasingly Means Heading for a European Retail Chain," *The Wall Street Journal,* April 24, 2001, p. A21; and Wal-Mart Web site.

Introduction

Our primary concern thus far in this book has been with aspects of the larger environment in which international businesses compete. As we have described it in the preceding chapters, this environment has included the different political, economic, and cultural institutions found in nations, the international trade and investment framework, and the international monetary system. Now our focus shifts from the environment to the firm itself and, in particular, to the actions managers can take to compete more effectively as an international business. In this chapter, we look at how managers can increase the performance of their firm by expanding into foreign markets. We discuss the different strategies that firms pursue when competing internationally. We consider the pros and cons of these strategies, and we discuss the various factors that affect the choice of strategy. In subsequent chapters we shall build on the framework established here to discuss a variety of topics including the design of organization structures and control systems for international businesses, strategies for entering foreign markets, the use and misuse of strategic alliances, strategies for exporting, and the various manufacturing, marketing, R&D, human resource, accounting, and financial strategies that are pursued by international businesses.

Wal-Mart, profiled in the opening case, gives us a preview of some issues that we will explore in this chapter. Like many other companies, Wal-Mart moved into other countries for three reasons: (1) its growth opportunities at home were becoming constrained, (2) it thought it could create value by transferring its business model to foreign markets, and (3) it wished to preempt other retailers that were also starting to expand globally. Wal-Mart initially treated foreign markets much like the United States, but it soon found that this was not the correct approach. Differences in customer tastes and preferences, and in local infrastructure, required Wal-Mart to change some store location, store layout, and stocking practices. In other words, to succeed abroad Wal-Mart has had to customize its offering to local conditions. At the same time, the company's core strategies and operations remain the same in every market in which it competes. Wal-Mart continues to emphasize everyday low prices and to focus on the attainment of operating efficiencies from world-class logistics management and information systems. Like many other companies, Wal-Mart has also found that going global has yielded additional benefits, including enhanced bargaining power with suppliers and the ability to transfer valuable ideas from one country to another. By striving to strike the right balance between the global standardization of operating practices and strategy, and local customization of store layout and stocking practices, and by focusing on the transfer of ideas across national borders, Wal-Mart is on the way to becoming what we shall refer to as a **transnational corporation.**

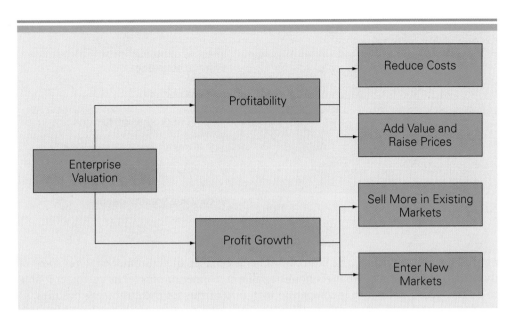

FIGURE 12.1

Determinates of Enterprise Value

Strategy and the Firm

Before we discuss the strategies that managers in the multinational enterprise can pursue, we need to review some basic principles of strategy. A firm's **strategy** can be defined as the actions that managers take to attain the goals of the firm. For most firms, the preeminent goal is to maximize the value of the firm for its owners, its shareholders (subject to the very important constraint that this is done in a legal, ethical, and socially responsible manner—see Chapter 5 for details). To maximize the value of a firm, managers must pursue strategies that increase the *profitability* of the enterprise and its rate of *profit growth* over time (see Figure 12.1). **Profitability** can be measured in a number of ways, but for consistency, we shall define it as the rate of return that the firm makes on its invested capital (ROIC), which is calculated by dividing the net profits of the firm by total invested capital.[1] **Profit growth** is measured by the percentage increase in net profits over time. In general, higher profitability and a higher rate of profit growth will increase the value of an enterprise and thus the returns garnered by its owners, the shareholders.[2] For a formal exposition of this, see the appendix at the end of this chapter.

Managers can increase the profitability of the firm by pursuing strategies that lower costs or by pursuing strategies that add value to the firm's products, which enables the firm to raise prices. Managers can increase the rate at which the firm's profits grow over time by pursuing strategies to sell more products in existing markets or by pursuing strategies to enter new markets. As we shall see, expanding internationally can help managers boost the firm's profitability *and* increase the rate of profit growth over time. For example, by expanding into foreign markets, Wal-Mart has been able to increase its rate of profit growth. Also, Wal-Mart's increased size has enhanced its bargaining power with suppliers, enabling it to drive down the price it pays for the goods it sells in its stores. Lowering Wal-Mart's cost structure has helped to increase the company's profitability.

VALUE CREATION

The way to increase the profitability of a firm is to create more value. The amount of value a firm creates is measured by the difference between its costs of production and the value that consumers perceive in its products. In general, the more value customers place on a firm's products, the higher the price the firm can charge for those products. However, the price a firm charges for a good or service is typically less than the value placed

FIGURE 12.2

Value Creation

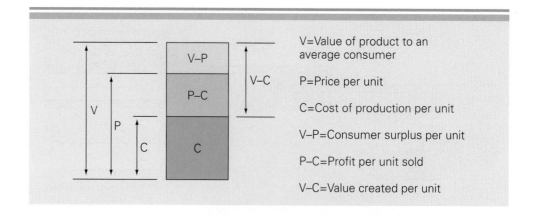

on that good or service by the customer. This is because the customer captures some of that value in the form of what economists call a consumer surplus.[3] The customer is able to do this because the firm is competing with other firms for the customer's business, so the firm must charge a lower price than it could were it a monopoly supplier. Also, it is normally impossible to segment the market to such a degree that the firm can charge each customer a price that reflects that individual's assessment of the value of a product, which economists refer to as a customer's reservation price. For these reasons, the price that gets charged tends to be less than the value placed on the product by many customers.

Figure 12.2 illustrates these concepts. The value of a product to an average consumer is V; the average price that the firm can charge a consumer for that product given competitive pressures and its ability to segment the market is P; and the average unit cost of producing that product is C (C comprises all relevant costs, including the firm's cost of capital). The firm's profit per unit sold (π) is equal to P − C, while the consumer surplus per unit is equal to V − P (another way of thinking of the consumer surplus is as "value for the money"; the greater the consumer surplus, the greater the value for the money the consumer gets). The firm makes a profit so long as P is greater than C, and its profit will be greater the lower C is *relative* to P. The difference between V and P is in part determined by the intensity of competitive pressure in the marketplace; the lower the intensity of competitive pressure, the higher the price charged relative to V.[4] In general, the higher the firm's profit per unit sold is, the greater its profitability will be, all else being equal.

The firm's **value creation** is measured by the difference between V and C (V − C); a company creates value by converting inputs that cost C into a product on which consumers place a value of V. A company can create more value (V − C) either by lowering production costs, C, or by making the product more attractive through superior design, styling, functionality, features, reliability, after-sales service, and the like, so that consumers place a greater value on it (V increases) and, consequently, are willing to pay a higher price (P increases). This discussion suggests that *a firm has high profits when it creates more value for its customers and does so at a lower cost.* We refer to a strategy that focuses primarily on lowering production costs as a *low-cost strategy.* We refer to a strategy that focuses primarily on increasing the attractiveness of a product as a *differentiation strategy.*[5]

Michael Porter has argued that *low cost* and *differentiation* are two basic strategies for creating value and attaining a competitive advantage in an industry.[6] According to Porter, superior profitability goes to those firms that can create superior value, and the way to create superior value is to drive down the cost structure of the business and/or differentiate the product in some way so that consumers value it more and are prepared to pay a premium price. Superior value creation relative to rivals does not necessarily require a firm to have the lowest cost structure in an industry, or to create the most valuable product in the eyes of consumers. However, it does require that the gap between value (V) and cost of production (C) be greater than the gap attained by competitors.

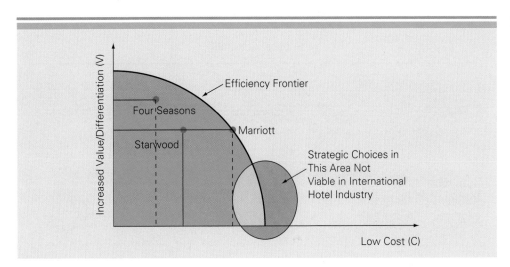

FIGURE 12.3

Strategic Choice in the International Hotel Industry

STRATEGIC POSITIONING

Porter notes that it is important for a firm to be explicit about its choice of strategic emphasis with regard to value creation (differentiation) and low cost, and to configure its internal operations to support that strategic emphasis.[7] Figure 12.3 illustrates his point. The convex curve in Figure 12.3 is what economists refer to as an efficiency frontier. The efficiency frontier shows all of the different positions that a firm can adopt with regard to adding value to the product (V) and low cost (C) assuming that its internal operations are configured efficiently to support a particular position (note that the horizontal axis in Figure 12.3 is reverse scaled—moving along the axis to the right implies lower costs). The efficiency frontier has a convex shape because of diminishing returns. Diminishing returns imply that when a firm already has significant value built into its product offering, increasing value by a relatively small amount requires significant additional costs. The converse also holds, when a firm already has a low-cost structure, it has to give up a lot of value in its product offering to get additional cost reductions.

Three hotel firms with a global presence are plotted on Figure 12.3, Four Seasons, Marriott International, and Starwood (Starwood owns the Sheraton and Westin chains). Four Seasons positions itself as a luxury chain and emphasizes the value of its product offering, which drives up its costs of operations. Marriott and Starwood are positioned more in the middle of the market. Both emphasize sufficient value to attract international business travelers, but are not luxury chains like Four Seasons. In Figure 12.3, Four Seasons and Marriott are shown to be on the efficiency frontier, indicating that their internal operations are well configured to their strategy and run efficiently. Starwood is inside the frontier, indicating that its operations are not running as efficiently as they might be, and that its costs are too high. This implies that Starwood is less profitable than Four Seasons and Marriott, and that its managers must take steps to improve the company's performance.

Porter emphasizes that it is very important for management to decide where the company wants to be positioned with regard to value (V) and cost (C), to configure operations accordingly, and to manage them efficiently to make sure the firm is operating on the efficiency frontier. However, not all positions on the efficiency frontier are viable. In the international hotel industry, for example, there might not be enough demand to support a chain that emphasizes very low cost and strips all the value out of its product offering (see Figure 12.3). International travelers are relatively affluent and expect a degree of comfort (value) when they travel away from home.

A central tenet of the basic strategy paradigm is that to maximize its profitability, a firm must do three things: (*a*) pick a position on the efficiency frontier that is viable in the sense that there is enough demand to support that choice; (*b*) configure its internal

FIGURE 12.4

The Value Chain

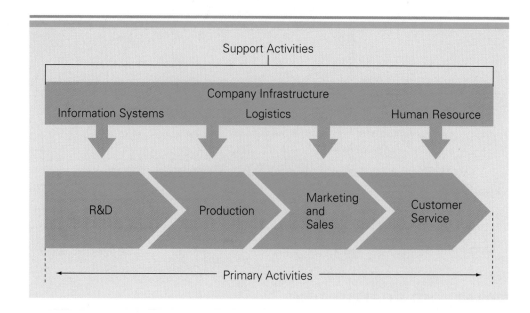

operations, such as manufacturing, marketing, logistics, information systems, human resources, and so on, so that they support that position; and (c) make sure that the firm has the right organization structure in place to execute its strategy. *The strategy, operations, and organization of the firm must all be consistent with each other if it is to attain a competitive advantage and garner superior profitability.* Operations refers to the different value creation activities a firm undertakes, which we shall review next.

OPERATIONS: THE FIRM AS A VALUE CHAIN

The operations of a firm can be thought of as a value chain composed of a series of distinct value creation activities including production, marketing and sales, materials management, R&D, human resources, information systems, and the firm infrastructure. We can categorize these value creation activities, or operations, as primary activities and support activities (see Figure 12.4).[8] As noted above, if a firm is to implement its strategy efficiently, and position itself on the efficiency frontier shown in Figure 12.3, it must manage these activities effectively and in a manner that is consistent with its strategy.

Primary Activities

Primary activities have to do with the design, creation, and delivery of the product; its marketing; and its support and after-sale service. Following normal practice, in the value chain illustrated in Figure 12.4, the primary activities are divided into four functions: research and development, production, marketing and sales, and customer service.

Research and development (R&D) is concerned with the design of products and production processes. Although we think of R&D as being associated with the design of physical products and production processes in manufacturing enterprises, many service companies also undertake R&D. For example, banks compete with each other by developing new financial products and new ways of delivering those products to customers. Online banking and smart debit cards are two examples of product development in the banking industry. Earlier examples of innovation in the banking industry included automated teller machines, credit cards, and debit cards. Through superior product design, R&D can increase the functionality of products, which makes them more attractive to consumers (raising V). Alternatively, R&D may result in more efficient production processes, thereby cutting production costs (lowering C). Either way, the R&D function can create value.

Production is concerned with the creation of a good or service. For physical products, when we talk about production we generally mean manufacturing. Thus, we can talk about

Perception is everything! Even though the Ford Expedition (left) and the Lincoln Navigator (right) share many of the same attributes such as the body and engine, customers are willing to pay about $10,000 more for the Navigator's "little extras."

the production of an automobile. For services such as banking or health care, "production" typically occurs when the service is delivered to the customer (for example, when a bank originates a loan for a customer it is engaged in "production" of the loan). For a retailer such as Wal-Mart, "production" is concerned with selecting the merchandise, stocking the store, and ringing up the sale at the cash register. The production activity of a firm creates value by performing its activities efficiently so lower costs result (lower C) or by performing them in such a way that a higher-quality product is produced (which results in higher V).

The marketing and sales functions of a firm can help to create value in several ways. Through brand positioning and advertising, the marketing function can increase the value (V) that consumers perceive to be contained in a firm's product. If these create a favorable impression of the firm's product in the minds of consumers, they increase the price that can be charged for the firm's product. For example, Ford has produced a high-value version of its Ford Expedition SUV. Sold as the Lincoln Navigator and priced around $10,000 higher, the Navigator has the same body, engine, chassis, and design as the Expedition, but through skilled advertising and marketing, supported by some fairly minor features changes (e.g., more accessories and the addition of a Lincoln-style engine grille and nameplate), Ford has fostered the perception that the Navigator is a "luxury SUV." This marketing strategy has increased the perceived value (V) of the Navigator relative to the Expedition, and enables Ford to charge a higher price for the car (P).

Marketing and sales can also create value by discovering consumer needs and communicating them back to the R&D function of the company, which can then design products that better match those needs. For example, the allocation of research budgets at Pfizer, the world's largest pharmaceutical company, is determined by the marketing function's assessment of the potential market size associated with solving unmet medical needs. Thus, Pfizer is currently directing significant monies to R&D efforts aimed at finding treatments for Alzheimer's disease, principally because marketing has identified the treatment of Alzheimer's as a major unmet medical need.

The role of the enterprise's service activity is to provide after-sale service and support. This function can create a perception of superior value (V) in the minds of consumers by solving customer problems and supporting customers after they have purchased the product. Caterpillar, the U.S.-based manufacturer of heavy earthmoving equipment, can get spare parts to any point in the world within 24 hours, thereby minimizing the amount of downtime its customers have to suffer if their Caterpillar equipment malfunctions. This is an extremely valuable capability in an industry where downtime is very expensive. It has helped to increase the value that customers associate with Caterpillar products and thus the price that Caterpillar can charge.

Support Activities

The support activities of the value chain provide inputs that allow the primary activities to occur (see Figure 12.4). In terms of attaining a competitive advantage, they can be as important as, if not more important than, the "primary" activities of the firm. The logistics function controls the transmission of physical materials through the value chain, from procurement through production and into distribution. The efficiency with which this is carried out can significantly reduce cost (lower C), thereby creating more value. As noted in the opening case, logistics is a major source of Wal-Mart's competitive advantage.

The human resource function can help create more value in a number of ways. It ensures that the company has the right mix of skilled people to perform its value creation activities effectively. Wal-Mart, for example, is increasingly using local managers to run stores and logistics operations in countries outside of the United States. The thinking behind this is that local nationals will have a better feel for the tastes and preferences of local customers than expatriate managers from the United States. In so far as this improves the fit between Wal-Mart's merchandising and local tastes, it should result in higher sales. The human resource function also ensures that people are adequately trained, motivated, and compensated to perform their value creation tasks.

Information systems refer to the electronic systems for managing inventory, tracking sales, pricing products, selling products, dealing with customer service inquiries, and so on. Information systems, when coupled with the communications features of the Internet, can alter the efficiency and effectiveness with which a firm manages its other value creation activities. As we shall see, good information systems are very important in the global arena. Again, Wal-Mart's competitive advantage is based in large part on its pioneering use of information systems to track in-store sales. This tracking capability means that Wal-Mart is almost never caught with too much of a certain item, or too little of that item. This reduces Wal-Mart's need to hold an extensive stock of buffer inventory, which reduces inventory costs (lowers C), and makes sure that Wal-Mart never has to hold sales to shift excess inventory (keeping price, P, from having to be reduced).

The final support activity is the company infrastructure, or the context within which all the other value creation activities occur. The infrastructure includes the organizational structure, control systems, and culture of the firm. Because top management can exert considerable influence in shaping these aspects of a firm, top management should also be viewed as part of the firm's infrastructure. Through strong leadership, top management can consciously shape the infrastructure of a firm and through that the performance of all its value creation activities.

Global Expansion, Profitability, and Profit Growth

Expanding globally allows firms to increase their profitability and rate of profit growth in ways not available to purely domestic enterprises.[9] Firms that operate internationally are able to:

1. Expand the market for their domestic product offerings by selling those products in international markets.

2. Realize location economies by dispersing individual value creation activities to those locations around the globe where they can be performed most efficiently and effectively.

3. Realize greater cost economies from experience effects by serving an expanded global market from a central location, thereby reducing the costs of value creation.

4. Earn a greater return by leveraging any valuable skills developed in foreign operations and transferring them to other entities within the firm's global network of operations.

As we will see, however, a firm's ability to increase its profitability and profit growth by pursuing these strategies is constrained by the need to customize its product offering, marketing strategy, and business strategy to differing national conditions; that is, by the imperative of localization.

EXPANDING THE MARKET: LEVERAGING PRODUCTS AND COMPETENCIES

A company can increase its growth rate by taking goods or services developed at home and selling them internationally. Almost all multinationals started out doing just this. Procter and Gamble, for example, developed most of its best-selling products such as Pampers disposable diapers and Ivory soap in the United States, and subsequently then sold them around the world. Similarly, although Microsoft developed its software in the United States, from its earliest days the company has always focused on selling that software in international markets. Automobile companies such as Volkswagen and Toyota also grew by developing products at home and then selling them in international markets. The returns from such a strategy are likely to be greater if indigenous competitors in the nations a company enters lack comparable products. Thus, Toyota has increased its profits by entering the large automobile markets of North America and Europe, offering products that are different from those offered by local rivals (Ford and GM) by their superior quality and reliability.

The success of many multinational companies that expand in this manner is based not just upon the goods or services that they sell in foreign nations, but also upon the core competencies that underlie the development, production, and marketing of those goods or services. The term **core competence** refers to skills within the firm that competitors cannot easily match or imitate.[10] These skills may exist in any of the firm's value creation activities—production, marketing, R&D, human resources, logistics, general management, and so on. Such skills are typically expressed in product offerings that other firms find difficult to match or imitate. Core competencies are the bedrock of a firm's competitive advantage. They enable a firm to reduce the costs of value creation and/or to create perceived value in such a way that premium pricing is possible. For example, Toyota has a core competence in the production of cars. It is able to produce high-quality, well-designed cars at a lower delivered cost than any other firm in the world. The competencies that enable Toyota to do this seem to reside primarily in the firm's production and logistics functions.[11] McDonald's has a core competence in managing fast-food operations (it seems to be one of the most skilled firms in the world in this industry); Procter & Gamble has a core competence in developing and marketing name brand consumer products (it is one of the most skilled firms in the world in this business); Wal-Mart has a core competence in the information systems and logistics required to efficiently manage a large-scale retail operation. Starbucks has a core competence in the management of retail outlets selling high volumes of freshly brewed coffee-based drinks.

Since core competencies are by definition the source of a firm's competitive advantage, the successful global expansion by manufacturing companies such as Toyota and P&G was based not just on leveraging products and selling them in foreign markets, but also on the transfer of core competencies to foreign markets where indigenous competitors lacked them. The same can be said of companies engaged in the service sectors of an economy, such as financial institutions, retailers, restaurant chains, and hotels. Expanding the market for their services often means replicating their business model in foreign nations (albeit with some changes to account for local differences, which we will discuss in more detail shortly). Starbucks, for example, is expanding rapidly outside of the United States by taking the basic business model it developed at home and using that as a blueprint for establishing international operations. As explained in the opening case, Wal-Mart has done the same thing, establishing stores in nine other nations since 1992 following the model it developed in the United States. Similarly, McDonald's is famous for its international expansion strategy, which has taken the company into more than 120 nations that collectively generate over half of the company's revenues.

LOCATION ECONOMIES

We know from earlier chapters that countries differ along a range of dimensions, including the economic, political, legal, and cultural, and that these differences can either raise or lower the costs of doing business in a country. The theory of international trade also teaches us that due to differences in factor costs, certain countries have a comparative advantage in the production of certain products. Japan might excel in the production of automobiles and consumer electronics; the United States in the production of computer software, pharmaceuticals, biotechnology products, and financial services; Switzerland in the production of precision instruments and pharmaceuticals; South Korea in the production of semiconductors; and China in the production of apparel.[12]

For a firm that is trying to survive in a competitive global market, this implies that *trade barriers and transportation costs* permitting, the firm will benefit by basing each value creation activity it performs at that location where economic, political, and cultural conditions, including relative factor costs, are most conducive to the performance of that activity. Thus, if the best designers for a product live in France, a firm should base its design operations in France. If the most productive labor force for assembly operations is in Mexico, assembly operations should be based in Mexico. If the best marketers are in the United States, the marketing strategy should be formulated in the United States. And so on.

Firms that pursue such a strategy can realize what we refer to as **location economies,** which are the economies that arise from performing a value creation activity in the optimal location for that activity, wherever in the world that might be (transportation costs and trade barriers permitting). Locating a value creation activity in the optimal location for that activity can have one of two effects. *It can lower the costs of value creation and help the firm to achieve a low-cost position, and/or it can enable a firm to differentiate its product offering from those of competitors.* In terms of Figure 12.2, it can lower C and/or increase V (which in general supports higher pricing), both of which boost the profitability of the enterprise.

For an example of how this works in an international business, consider Clear Vision, a manufacturer and distributor of eyewear. Started in the 1980s by David Glassman, the firm now generates annual gross revenues of more than $100 million. Not exactly small, but no corporate giant either, Clear Vision is a multinational firm with production facilities on three continents and customers around the world. Clear Vision began its move toward becoming a multinational in the 1980s. The strong dollar at that time made U.S.-based manufacturing very expensive. Low-priced imports were taking an ever-larger share of the U.S. eyewear market, and Clear Vision realized it could not survive unless it also began to import. Initially the firm bought from independent overseas manufacturers, primarily in Hong Kong. However, the firm became dissatisfied with these suppliers' product quality and delivery. As Clear Vision's volume of imports increased, Glassman decided the best way to guarantee quality and delivery was to set up Clear Vision's own manufacturing operation overseas. Accordingly, Clear Vision found a Chinese partner, and together they opened a manufacturing facility in Hong Kong, with Clear Vision being the majority shareholder.

The choice of the Hong Kong location was influenced by its combination of low labor costs, a skilled workforce, and tax breaks given by the Hong Kong government. The firm's objective at this point was to lower production costs by locating value creation activities at an appropriate location. After a few years, however, the increasing industrialization of Hong Kong and a growing labor shortage had pushed up wage rates to the extent that it was no longer a low-cost location. In response, Glassman and his Chinese partner moved part of their manufacturing to a plant in mainland China to take advantage of the lower wage rates there. Again, the goal was to lower production costs. The parts for eyewear

frames manufactured at this plant are shipped to the Hong Kong factory for final assembly and then distributed to markets in North and South America. The Hong Kong factory now employs 80 people and the China plant between 300 and 400.

At the same time, Clear Vision was looking for opportunities to invest in foreign eyewear firms with reputations for fashionable design and high quality. Its objective was not to reduce production costs but to launch a line of high-quality differentiated, "designer" eyewear. Clear Vision did not have the design capability in-house to support such a line, but Glassman knew that certain foreign manufacturers did. As a result, Clear Vision invested in factories in Japan, France, and Italy, holding a minority shareholding in each case. These factories now supply eyewear for Clear Vision's Status Eye division, which markets high-priced designer eyewear.[13]

Thus, to deal with a threat from foreign competition, Clear Vision adopted a strategy intended to lower its cost structure (lower C): shifting its production from a high-cost location, the United States, to a low-cost location, first Hong Kong and later China. Then Clear Vision adopted a strategy intended to increase the perceived value of its product (increase V) so it could charge a premium price (P). Reasoning that premium pricing in eyewear depended on superior design, its strategy involved investing capital in French, Italian, and Japanese factories that had reputations for superior design. In sum, Clear Vision's strategies included some actions intended to reduce its costs of creating value and other actions intended to add perceived value to its product through differentiation. The overall goal was to increase the value created by Clear Vision and thus the profitability of the enterprise. To the extent that these strategies were successful, the firm should have attained a higher profit margin and greater profitability than if it had remained a U.S.-based manufacturer of eyewear.

Creating a Global Web

Generalizing from the Clear Vision example, one result of this kind of thinking is the creation of a **global web** of value creation activities, with different stages of the value chain being dispersed to those locations around the globe where perceived value is maximized or where the costs of value creation are minimized.[14] Consider IBM's ThinkPad X31 laptop computer.[15] This product was designed in the United States by IBM engineers because IBM believed that the United States was the best location in the world to do the basic design work. The case, keyboard, and hard drive were made in Thailand; the display screen and memory were made in South Korea; the built-in wireless card was made in Malaysia; and the microprocessor was manufactured in the United States. In each case, these components were manufactured in the optimal location given current factor costs. These components were shipped to an IBM operation in Mexico, where the product was assembled, before being shipped to the United States for final sale. IBM assembled the ThinkPad in Mexico because IBM's managers calculated that due to low labor costs, the costs of assembly could be minimized there. The marketing and sales strategy for North America was developed by IBM personnel in the United States, primarily because IBM believed that due to their knowledge of the local marketplace, U.S. personnel would add more value to the product through their marketing efforts than personnel based elsewhere.

In theory, a firm that realizes location economies by dispersing each of its value creation activities to its optimal location should have a competitive advantage vis-à-vis a firm that bases all of its value creation activities at a single location. It should be able to better differentiate its product offering (thereby raising perceived value, V) and lower its cost structure (C) than its single-location competitor. In a world where competitive pressures are increasing, such a strategy may become an imperative for survival.

Some Caveats

Introducing transportation costs and trade barriers complicates this picture. Due to favorable factor endowments, New Zealand may have a comparative advantage for automobile assembly operations, but high transportation costs would make it an uneconomical location from which to serve global markets. Another caveat concerns the importance of assessing political and economic risks when making location decisions. Even if a country looks very attractive as a production location when measured against all the standard criteria, if its government is unstable or totalitarian, the firm might be advised not to base production there. (Political risk is discussed in Chapter 2.) Similarly, if the government appears to be pursuing inappropriate economic policies that could lead to foreign exchange risk, that might be another reason for not basing production in that location, even if other factors look favorable.

EXPERIENCE EFFECTS

The **experience curve** refers to systematic reductions in production costs that have been observed to occur over the life of a product.[16] A number of studies have observed that a product's production costs decline by some quantity about each time *cumulative* output doubles. The relationship was first observed in the aircraft industry, where each time cumulative output of airframes was doubled, unit costs typically declined to 80 percent of their previous level.[17] Thus, production cost for the fourth airframe would be 80 percent of production cost for the second airframe, the eighth airframe's production costs 80 percent of the fourth's, the sixteenth's 80 percent of the eighth's, and so on. Figure 12.5 illustrates this experience curve relationship between unit production costs and *cumulative* output (the relationship is for *cumulative* output over time, and *not* output in any one period, such as a year). Two things explain this: learning effects and economies of scale.

Learning Effects

Learning effects refer to cost savings that come from learning by doing. Labor, for example, learns by repetition how to carry out a task, such as assembling airframes, most efficiently. Labor productivity increases over time as individuals learn the most efficient ways to perform particular tasks. Equally important, in new production facilities management typically learns how to manage the new operation more efficiently over time. Hence, production costs decline due to increasing labor productivity and management efficiency, which increases the firm's profitability.

Learning effects tend to be more significant when a technologically complex task is repeated, because there is more that can be learned about the task. Thus, learning effects will be more significant in an assembly process involving 1,000 complex steps than in one of only 100 simple steps. No matter how complex the task, however, learning effects typically disappear after a while. It has been suggested that they are important only during the start-up period of a new process and that they cease after two or three years.[18] Any decline in the experience curve after such a point is due to economies of scale.

Economies of Scale

Economies of scale refer to the reductions in unit cost achieved by producing a large volume of a product. Attaining economies of scale lowers a firm's unit costs and increases its profitability. Economies of scale have a number of sources. One is the ability to spread fixed costs over a large volume.[19] Fixed costs are the costs required to set up a production facility, develop a new product, and the like. They can be substantial. For example, the fixed cost of establishing a new production line to manufacture semiconductor chips now exceeds $1 billion. Similarly, according to one estimate, developing a new drug and bringing it to market costs about $800 million and takes about 12 years.[20] The only way to recoup such high fixed costs may be to sell the product worldwide, which reduces average unit costs by spreading fixed costs over a larger volume. The more rapidly that cumulative sales volume is built up, the more rapidly fixed costs can be amortized over a large production volume, and the more rapidly unit costs will fall.

Second, a firm may not be able to attain an efficient scale of production unless it serves global markets. In the automobile industry, for example, an efficiently scaled factory is one designed to produce about 200,000 units a year. Automobile firms would pre-

FIGURE 12.5

The Experience Curve

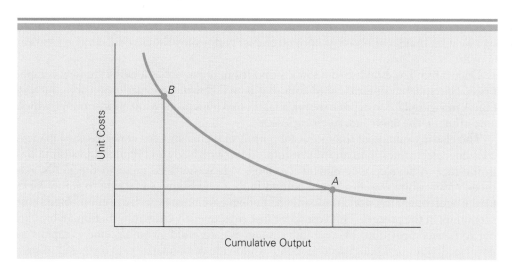

fer to produce a single model from each factory since this eliminates the costs associated with switching production from one model to another. If domestic demand for a particular model is only 100,000 units a year, the inability to attain a 200,000-unit output will drive up average unit costs. By serving international markets as well, however, the firm may be able to push production volume up to 200,000 units a year, thereby reaping greater scale economies, lowering unit costs, and boosting profitability. By serving domestic and international markets from its production facilities a firm may be able to utilize those facilities more intensively. For example, if Intel sold microprocessors only in the United States, it may only be able to keep its factories open for one shift, five days a week. By serving international markets from the same factories, Intel can utilize its productive assets more intensively, which translates into higher capital productivity and greater profitability.

Finally, as global sales increase the size of the enterprise, so its bargaining power with suppliers increases, which may allow it to attain economies of scale in purchasing, bargaining down the cost of key inputs and boosting profitability that way. For example, Wal-Mart has been able to use its enormous sales volume as a lever to bargain down the price it pays suppliers for merchandise sold through its stores.

Strategic Significance

The strategic significance of the experience curve is clear. Moving down the experience curve allows a firm to reduce its cost of creating value (to lower C in Figure 12.2) and increase its profitability. The firm that moves down the experience curve most rapidly will have a cost advantage vis-à-vis its competitors. Firm A in Figure 12.5, because it is farther down the experience curve, has a clear cost advantage over firm B.

Many of the underlying sources of experience-based cost economies are plant based. This is true for most learning effects as well as for the economies of scale derived by spreading the fixed costs of building productive capacity over a large output, attaining an efficient scale of output, and utilizing a plant more intensively. Thus, one key to progressing downward on the experience curve as rapidly as possible is to increase the volume produced by a single plant as rapidly as possible. Because global markets are larger than domestic markets, a firm that serves a global market from a single location is likely to build accumulated volume more quickly than a firm that serves only its home market or that serves multiple markets from multiple production locations. Thus, serving a global market from a single location is consistent with moving down the experience curve and establishing a low-cost position. In addition, to get down the experience curve rapidly, a firm may need to price and market aggressively so demand will expand rapidly. It will also need to build sufficient production capacity for serving a global market. Also, the cost advantages of serving the world market from a single location will be even more significant if that location is the optimal one for performing the particular value creation activity.

Once a firm has established a low-cost position, it can act as a barrier to new competition. Specifically, an established firm that is well down the experience curve, such as firm A in Figure 12.5, can price so that it is still making a profit while new entrants, which are farther up the curve, are suffering losses.

The classic example of the successful pursuit of such a strategy concerns the Japanese consumer electronics company Matsushita. Along with Sony and Philips, Matsushita was in the race to develop a commercially viable videocassette recorder in the 1970s. Although Matsushita initially lagged behind Philips and Sony, it was able to get its VHS format accepted as the world standard and to reap enormous experience curve–based cost economies in the process. This cost advantage subsequently constituted a formidable barrier to new competition. Matsushita's strategy was to build global volume as rapidly as possible. To ensure it could accommodate worldwide demand, the firm increased its production capacity 33-fold from 205,000 units in 1977 to 6.8 million units by 1984. By serving the world market from a single location in Japan, Matsushita was able to realize significant learning effects and economies of scale. These allowed Matsushita to drop its prices 50 percent within five years of selling its first VHS-format VCR. As a result, Matsushita was the world's major VCR producer by 1983, accounting for about 45 percent of world production and enjoying a significant cost advantage over its competitors. The next largest firm, Hitachi, accounted for only 11.1 percent of world production in 1983.[21] Today, firms such as Intel are the masters of this kind of strategy. The costs of building a state-of-the-art facility to manufacture microprocessors are so large (easily in excess of $1 billion) that to make this investment pay Intel *must* pursue experience curve effects, serving world markets from a limited number of plants to maximize the cost economies that derive from scale and learning effects.

LEVERAGING SUBSIDIARY SKILLS

Implicit in our earlier discussion of core competencies is the idea that valuable skills are developed first at home and then transferred to foreign operations. Thus, Wal-Mart developed its retailing skills in the United States before transferring them to foreign locations. However, for more mature multinationals that have already established a network of subsidiary operations in foreign markets, the development of valuable skills can just as well occur in foreign subsidiaries.[22] Skills can be created anywhere within a multinational's global network of operations, wherever people have the opportunity and incentive to try new ways of doing things. The creation of skills that help to lower the costs of production, or to enhance perceived value and support higher product pricing, is not the monopoly of the corporate center.

Leveraging the skills created within subsidiaries and applying them to other operations within the firm's global network may create value. For example, McDonald's increasingly is finding that its foreign franchisees are a source of valuable new ideas. Faced with slow growth in France, its local franchisees have begun to experiment not only with the menu, but also with the layout and theme of restaurants. Gone are the ubiquitous golden arches, gone too are many of the utilitarian chairs and tables and other plastic features of the fast-food giant. Many McDonald's restaurants in France now have hardwood floors, exposed brick walls, and even armchairs. Half of the 930 or so outlets in France have been upgraded to a level that would make them unrecognizable to an American. The menu, too, has been changed to include premier sandwiches, such as chicken on focaccia bread, priced some 30 percent higher than the average hamburger. In France at least, the strategy seems to be working. Following the change, increases in same-store sales rose from 1 percent annually to 3.4 percent. Impressed with the impact, McDonald's executives are now considering adopting similar changes at other McDonald's restaurants in markets where same-store sales growth is sluggish, including the United States.[23]

In another example, Hewlett-Packard has decentralized authority for the design and production of many of its leading-edge ink-jet printers to its operation in Singapore. Hewlett-Packard made this decision after employees in Singapore distinguished themselves by finding ways to reduce production costs through better product design. Hewlett-Packard now views its Singapore subsidiary as an important source for valuable new knowledge about production and product design that can be applied to other activities within the firm's global network of operations.[24]

For the managers of the multinational enterprise, this phenomenon creates important new challenges. First, they must have the humility to recognize that valuable skills that lead to competencies can arise anywhere within the firm's global network, not just at the corporate center. Second, they must establish an incentive system that encourages local employees to acquire new skills. This is not as easy as it sounds. Creating new skills involves a degree of risk. Not all new skills add value. For every valuable idea created by a McDonald's subsidiary in a foreign country, there may be several failures. The management of the multinational must install incentives that encourage employees to take the necessary risks. The company must reward people for successes and not sanction them unnecessarily for taking risks that did not pan out. Third, managers must have a process for identifying when valuable new skills have been created in a subsidiary. And finally, they need to act as facilitators, helping to transfer valuable skills within the firm.

SUMMARY

We have seen how firms that expand globally can increase their profitability and profit growth by entering new markets where indigenous competitors lack similar competencies, by lowering costs and adding value to their product offering through the attainment of location economies, by exploiting experience curve effects, and by transferring valuable skills between their global network of subsidiaries. For completeness it should be noted that strategies that increase profitability may also expand a firm's business, and thus enable it to attain a higher rate of profit growth. For example, by simultaneously realizing location economies and experience effects a firm may be able to produce a more highly valued product at a lower unit cost, thereby boosting profitability. The increase in the perceived value of the product may also attract more customers, thereby growing revenues and profits as well. Furthermore, rather than raising prices to reflect the higher perceived value of the product, the firm's managers may elect to hold prices low in order to increase global market share and attain greater scale economies (in other words, they may elect to offer consumers better "value for money"). Such a strategy could increase the firm's rate of profit growth even further, since consumers will be attracted by prices that are low relative to value. The strategy might also increase profitability if the scale economies that result from market share gains are substantial. In sum, managers need to keep in mind the complex relationship between profitability and profit growth when making strategic decisions about pricing.

Cost Pressures and Pressures for Local Responsiveness

Firms that compete in the global marketplace typically face two types of competitive pressure that effect their ability to realize location economies and experience effects, to leverage products and transfer competencies and skills within the enterprise. They face *pressures for cost reductions* and *pressures to be locally responsive* (see Figure 12.6).[25] These competitive pressures place conflicting demands on a firm. Responding to pressures for cost reductions requires that a firm try to minimize its unit costs. But responding to pressures to be locally responsive requires that a firm differentiate its product offering and marketing strategy from country to country in an effort to accommodate the diverse demands arising from national differences in consumer tastes and preferences, business practices, distribution channels, competitive conditions, and

FIGURE 12.6

Pressures for Cost
Reductions and Local
Responsiveness

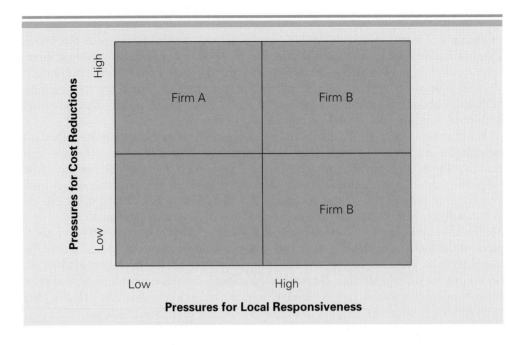

Pressures for Local Responsiveness

government policies. Because differentiation across countries can involve significant duplication and a lack of product standardization, it may raise costs.

While some enterprises, such as firm A in Figure 12.6, face high pressures for cost reductions and low pressures for local responsiveness, and others, such as firm B, face low pressures for cost reductions and high pressures for local responsiveness, many companies are in the position of firm C. They face high pressures for *both* cost reductions and local responsiveness. Dealing with these conflicting and contradictory pressures is a difficult strategic challenge, primarily because being locally responsive tends to raise costs.

PRESSURES FOR COST REDUCTIONS

In competitive global markets, international businesses often face pressures for cost reductions. Responding to pressures for cost reduction requires a firm to try to lower the costs of value creation. A manufacturer, for example, might mass-produce a standardized product at the optimal location in the world, wherever that might be, to realize economies of scale, learning effects, and location economies. Alternatively, a firm might outsource certain functions to low-cost foreign suppliers in an attempt to reduce costs. Thus, many computer companies have outsourced their telephone-based customer service functions to India, where qualified technicians who speak English can be hired for a lower wage rate than in the United States. In the same manner, a retailer such as Wal-Mart might push its suppliers (manufacturers) to do the same. (The pressure that Wal-Mart has placed on its suppliers to reduce prices has been cited as a major cause of the trend among North American manufacturers to shift production to China.)[26] A service business such as a bank might respond to cost pressures by moving some back-office functions, such as information processing, to developing nations where wage rates are lower.

Pressures for cost reduction can be particularly intense in industries producing commodity-type products where meaningful differentiation on nonprice factors is difficult and price is the main competitive weapon. This tends to be the case for products that serve universal needs. **Universal needs** exist when the tastes and preferences of consumers in different nations are similar if not identical. This is the case for conventional commodity products such as bulk chemicals, petroleum, steel, sugar, and the like. It also tends to be the case for many industrial and consumer products; for example, handheld calculators, semiconductor chips, personal computers, and liquid crystal display screens.

Pressures for cost reductions are also intense in industries where major competitors are based in low-cost locations, where there is persistent excess capacity, and where consumers are powerful and face low switching costs. The liberalization of the world trade and investment environment in recent decades, by facilitating greater international competition, has generally increased cost pressures.[27]

PRESSURES FOR LOCAL RESPONSIVENESS

Pressures for local responsiveness arise from national differences in consumer tastes and preferences, infrastructure, accepted business practices, and distribution channels, and from host-government demands. Responding to pressures to be locally responsive requires a firm to differentiate its products and marketing strategy from country to country to accommodate these factors, all of which tends to raise the firm's cost structure.

Differences in Customer Tastes and Preferences

Strong pressures for local responsiveness emerge when customer tastes and preferences differ significantly between countries, as they often do for deeply embedded historic or cultural reasons. In such cases, a multinational's products and marketing message have to be customized to appeal to the tastes and preferences of local customers. This typically creates pressure to delegate production and marketing responsibilities and functions to a firm's overseas subsidiaries.

For example, the automobile industry in the 1980s and early 1990s moved toward the creation of "world cars." The idea was that global companies such as General Motors, Ford, and Toyota would be able to sell the same basic vehicle the world over, sourcing it from centralized production locations. If successful, the strategy would have enabled automobile companies to reap significant gains from global scale economies. However, this strategy frequently ran aground upon the hard rocks of consumer reality. Consumers in different automobile markets seem to have different tastes and preferences, and demanded different types of vehicles. North American consumers show a strong demand for pickup trucks. This is particularly true in the South and West where many families have a pickup truck as a second or third car. But in European countries, pickup trucks are seen purely as utility vehicles and are purchased primarily by firms rather than individuals. As a consequence, the product mix and marketing message needs to be tailored to consider the different nature of demand in North America and Europe. Another example that illustrates the need to respond to national differences in tastes and preferences appears in the accompanying Management Focus, which looks at the experience of MTV Networks in foreign markets.

Some commentators have argued that customer demands for local customization are on the decline worldwide.[28] According to this argument, modern communications and transport technologies have created the conditions for a convergence of the tastes and preferences of consumers from different nations. The result is the emergence of enormous global markets for standardized consumer products. The worldwide acceptance of McDonald's hamburgers, Coca-Cola, Gap clothes, Nokia cell phones, and Sony PlayStations, all of which are sold globally as standardized products, are often cited as evidence of the increasing homogeneity of the global marketplace.

However, as illustrated by the case of MTV, this argument seems somewhat naive. Significant differences in consumer tastes and preferences still exist across nations and cultures. Managers in international businesses do not yet have the luxury of being able to ignore these differences, and they may not for a long time to come. Even in a modern industry such as the cell phone business, important national differences in consumer usage patterns can be observed. Americans, for example, tend to think of cell phones primarily as devices for talking, and not as devices that can also send e-mails and browse the Web. Consequently, when selling to U.S. consumers, cell phone manufacturers focus more on slim good looks and less on advanced functions and features. This is in direct contrast to Asia and Europe, where text messaging and Web browsing functions have been much more widely embraced. A cultural issue seems to be at work here. People in Europe and Asia often have more time

MANAGEMENT FOCUS

MTV Networks has become a symbol of globalization. Established in 1981, the U.S.-based music TV network has been expanding outside of its North American base since 1987 when it opened MTV Europe. Now owned by media conglomerate Viacom, MTV Networks, which includes siblings Nickelodeon and VH1, the music station for the aging baby boomers, generates more than $1 billion in revenues outside the United States. Since 1987, MTV has become the most ubiquitous cable programmer in the world. By 2004 the network had 72 channels, or distinct feeds, that reached a combined total of 321 million households in 140 countries.

While the United States still leads in number of households, with 70 million, the most rapid growth is elsewhere, particularly in Asia, where nearly two-thirds of the region's 3 billion people are under 35, the middle class is expanding quickly, and TV ownership is spreading rapidly. MTV Networks figures that every second of every day almost 2 million people are watching MTV around the world, the majority outside the United States.

Despite its international success, MTV's global expansion got off to a weak start. In 1987, it piped a single feed across Europe almost entirely composed of American programming with English-speaking veejays. Naively, the network's U.S. managers thought Europeans would flock to the American programming. But while viewers in Europe shared a common interest in a handful of global superstars, who at the time included Madonna and Michael Jackson, their tastes turned out to be surprisingly local. What was popular in Germany might not be popular in Great Britain. Many staples of the American music scene left Europeans cold. MTV suffered as a result. Soon local copycat stations were springing up in Europe that focused on the music scene in individual countries. They took viewers and advertisers away from MTV. As explained by Tom Freston, chairman of MTV Networks, "We were going for the most shallow layer of what united viewers and brought them together. It didn't go over too well."

In 1995, MTV changed its strategy and broke Europe into regional feeds, of which there are now eight: one for the United Kingdom and Ireland; another for Germany, Austria, and Switzerland; one for Scandinavia; one for Italy; one for France; one for Spain; one for Holland; and a feed for other European nations including Belgium and Greece. The network adopted the same localization strategy elsewhere in the world. For example, in Asia it has an English-Hindi channel for India, separate Mandrine

to browse the Web on their phones because they spend more time commuting on trains, while Americans tend to spend more time in cars, where their hands are occupied.[29]

Differences in Infrastructure and Traditional Practices

Pressures for local responsiveness arise from differences in infrastructure or traditional practices among countries, creating a need to customize products accordingly. Fulfilling this need may require the delegation of manufacturing and production functions to foreign subsidiaries. For example, in North America, consumer electrical systems are based on 110 volts, whereas in some European countries, 240-volt systems are standard. Thus, domestic electrical appliances have to be customized for this difference in infrastructure. Traditional practices also often vary across nations. For example, in Britain, people drive on the left-hand side of the road, creating a demand for right-hand-drive cars, whereas in France (and the rest of Europe), people drive on the right-hand side of the road and therefore want left-hand-drive cars. Obviously, automobiles have to be customized to accommodate this difference in traditional practice.

Although many national differences in infrastructure are rooted in history, some are quite recent. For example, in the wireless telecommunications industry different technical standards exist in different parts of the world. A technical standard known as GSM is

feeds for China and Taiwan, a Korean feed for South Korea, a Bahasa-language feed for Indonesia, Japanese feed for Japan, and so on. Digital and satellite technology have made the localization of programming cheaper and easier. MTV Networks can now beam half a dozen feeds off one satellite transponder.

While MTV Networks exercises creative control over these different feeds, and while all the channels have the same familiar frenetic look and feel of MTV in the United States, a significant share of the programming and content is now local. When MTV opens a local station now, it begins with expatriates from elsewhere in the world to do a "gene transfer" of company culture and operating principles. Once these are established, however, the network switches to local employees and the expatriates move on. The idea is to "get inside the heads" of the local population and produce programming that matches their tastes. Although as much as 60 percent of the programming still originates in the United States, with staples such as "The Real World" having equivalents in different countries, an increasing share of programming is local in conception. In Italy, "MTV Kitchen" combines cooking with a music countdown. "Erotica" airs in Brazil and features a panel of youngsters discussing sex. The Indian channel produces 21 homegrown shows hosted by local veejays who speak "Hinglish," a city-bred breed of Hindi and English. Hit shows include "MTV Cricket in Control," appropriate for a land where cricket is a national obsession, "MTV Housefull," which hones in on Hindi film stars (India has the biggest film industry outside of Hollywood), and "MTV Bakra," which is modeled after "Candid Camera."

This localization push has reaped big benefits for MTV, capturing viewers back from local imitators. In India, ratings increased by more than 700 percent between 1996 when the localization push began and 2000. In turn, localization helps MTV to capture more of those all-important advertising revenues, even from other multinationals such as Coca-Cola, whose own advertising budgets are often locally determined. In Europe, MTV's advertising revenues increased by 50 percent between 1995 and 2000. While the total market for pan-European advertising is valued at just $200 million, the total market for local advertising across Europe is a much bigger pie, valued at $12 billion. MTV now gets 70 percent of its European advertising revenue from local spots, up from 15 percent in 1995. Similar trends are evident elsewhere in the world.

Sources: M. Gunther, "MTV's Passage to India," *Fortune,* August 9, 2004, pp. 117–122; B. Pulley and A. Tanzer, "Sumner's Gemstone," *Forbes,* February 21, 2000, pp. 107–11; K. Hoffman, "Youth TV's Old Hand Prepares for the Digital Challenge," *Financial Times,* February 18, 2000, p. 8; presentation by Sumner M. Redstone, chairman and CEO, Viacom Inc., delivered to Salomon Smith Barney 11th Annual Global Entertainment Media, Telecommunications Conference, Scottsdale, AZ, January 8, 2001; archived at www.viacom.com; and Viacom 10K Statement, 2003.

common in Europe, and an alternative standard, CDMA, is more common in the United States and parts of Asia. Equipment designed for GSM will not work on a CDMA network, and vice versa. Thus, companies such as Nokia, Motorola, and Ericsson, which manufacture wireless handsets and infrastructure such as switches, need to customize their product offering according to the technical standard prevailing in a given country.

Differences in Distribution Channels

A firm's marketing strategies may have to be responsive to differences in distribution channels among countries, which may necessitate the delegation of marketing functions to national subsidiaries. In the pharmaceutical industry, for example, the British and Japanese distribution systems are radically different from the U.S. system. British and Japanese doctors will not accept or respond favorably to a U.S.-style high-pressure sales force. Thus, pharmaceutical companies have to adopt different marketing practices in Britain and Japan compared with the United States—soft sell versus hard sell.

Host Government Demands

Economic and political demands imposed by host-country governments may require local responsiveness. For example, pharmaceutical companies are subject to local clinical testing, registration procedures, and pricing restrictions, all of which make it necessary that the manufacturing and marketing of a drug should meet local requirements. Because governments and government agencies control a significant proportion of the health care budget in most countries, they are in a powerful position to demand a high level of local responsiveness.

More generally, threats of protectionism, economic nationalism, and local content rules (which require that a certain percentage of a product should be manufactured locally) dictate that international businesses manufacture locally. For example, consider Bombardier, the Canadian-based manufacturer of railcars, aircraft, jet boats, and snowmobiles. Bombardier has 12 railcar factories across Europe. Critics of the company argue that the resulting duplication of manufacturing facilities leads to high costs and helps explain why Bombardier makes lower profit margins on its railcar operations than on its other business lines. In reply, managers at Bombardier argue that in Europe, informal rules with regard to local content favor people who use local workers. To sell railcars in Germany, they claim, you must manufacture in Germany. The same goes for Belgium, Austria, and France. To try to address its cost structure in Europe, Bombardier has centralized its engineering and purchasing functions, but it has no plans to centralize manufacturing.[30]

Choosing a Strategy

Pressures for local responsiveness imply that it may not be possible for a firm to realize the full benefits from economies of scale, learning effects, and location economies. It may not be possible to serve the global marketplace from a single low-cost location, producing a globally standardized product, and marketing it worldwide to attain the cost reductions associated with experience effects. The need to customize the product offering to local conditions may work against the implementation of such a strategy. For example, automobile firms have found that Japanese, American, and European consumers demand different kinds of cars, and this necessitates producing products that are customized for local markets. In response, firms such as Honda, Ford, and Toyota are pursuing a strategy of establishing top-to-bottom design and production facilities in each of these regions so that they can better serve local demands. Although such customization brings benefits, it also limits the ability of a firm to realize significant scale economies and location economies.

In addition, pressures for local responsiveness imply that it may not be possible to leverage skills and products associated with a firm's core competencies wholesale from one nation to another. Concessions often have to be made to local conditions. Despite being depicted as "poster boy" for the proliferation of standardized global products, even McDonald's has found that it has to customize its product offerings (i.e., its menu) to account for national differences in tastes and preferences.

How do differences in the strength of pressures for cost reductions versus those for local responsiveness affect the firm's choice of strategy? Firms typically choose among four main strategic postures when competing internationally. These can be characterized as a global standardization strategy, a localization strategy, a transnational strategy, and an international strategy.[31] The appropriateness of each strategy varies given the extent of pressures for cost reductions and local responsiveness. Figure 12.7 illustrates the conditions under which each of these strategies is most appropriate.

GLOBAL STANDARDIZATION STRATEGY

Firms that pursue a **global standardization strategy** focus on increasing profitability and profit growth by reaping the cost reductions that come from economies of scale, learning effects, and location economies; that is, their strategic goal is to pursue a low-cost strategy on a global scale. The production, marketing, and R&D activities of firms pursuing a global standardization strategy are concentrated in a few favorable locations. Firms pursuing a global standardization strategy try not to customize their product offering and

FIGURE 12.7

Four Basic Strategies

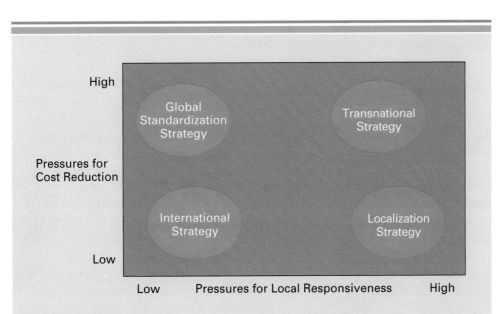

marketing strategy to local conditions because customization involves shorter production runs and the duplication of functions, which tends to raise costs. Instead, they prefer to market a standardized product worldwide so that they can reap the maximum benefits from economies of scale and learning effects. They also tend to use their cost advantage to support aggressive pricing in world markets.

This strategy makes most sense when there are strong pressures for cost reductions and demands for local responsiveness are minimal. Increasingly, these conditions prevail in many industrial goods industries, whose products often serve universal needs. In the semiconductor industry, for example, global standards have emerged, creating enormous demands for standardized global products. Accordingly, companies such as Intel, Texas Instruments, and Motorola all pursue a global standardization strategy. However, these conditions are not yet found in many consumer goods markets, where demands for local responsiveness remain high. The strategy is inappropriate when demands for local responsiveness are high.

LOCALIZATION STRATEGY

A **localization strategy** focuses on increasing profitability by customizing the firm's goods or services so that they provide a good match to tastes and preferences in different national markets. Localization is most appropriate when there are substantial differences across nations with regard to consumer tastes and preferences, and where cost pressures are not too intense. By customizing the product offering to local demands, the firm increases the value of that product in the local market. On the downside, because it involves some duplication of functions and smaller production runs, customization limits the ability of the firm to capture the cost reductions associated with mass-producing a standardized product for global consumption. The strategy may make sense, however, if the added value associated with local customization supports higher pricing, which enables the firm to recoup its higher costs, or if it leads to substantially greater local demand, enabling the firm to reduce costs through the attainment of some scale economies in the local market.

MTV is a good example of a company that has had to pursue a localization strategy (see the Management Focus). If MTV had not localized its programming to match the demands of viewers in different nations, it would have lost market share to local competitors, its advertising revenues would have fallen, and its profitability would have declined. Thus, even though it raised costs, localization was a strategic imperative at MTV.

MANAGEMENT FOCUS

General Motors is one of the oldest multinational corporations in the world. Founded in 1908, GM established its first international operations in the 1920s. General Motors is now the world's largest industrial corporation and full-line automobile manufacturer with annual revenues in 2003 of $185 billion. The company sells 8.5 million vehicles per year, 3.2 million of which are produced and marketed outside of its North American base. In 2003, GM had a 15 percent share of the world automobile market.

Historically, most of GM's foreign operations have been concentrated in Western Europe. Local brand names such as Opel, Vauxhall, Saab, and Holden helped the company to capture a 12 percent market share in 2002, second only to that of Ford. Although GM has long had a presence in Latin America and Asia, until recently sales there accounted for only a relatively small fraction of the company's total international business. However, GM's plans call for this to change. Sensing that Asia, Latin America, and Eastern Europe may be the automobile industry's growth markets, in 1997 GM embarked on ambitious plans to invest $2.2 billion in four new manufacturing facilities in Argentina, Poland, China, and Thailand. This expansion goes hand in hand with a change in GM's philosophy toward the management of its international operations.

Traditionally, GM saw the developing world as a dumping ground for obsolete technology and outdated models. Just a few years ago, for example, GM's Brazilian factories were churning out U.S.-designed Chevy Chevettes that hadn't been produced in North America for years. GM's Detroit-based executives saw this as a way of squeezing the maximum cash flow from the company's investments in aging technology. GM managers in the developing world, however, took it as an indication that the center did not view developing world operations as being significant. This feeling was exacerbated by the fact that most operations in the developing world were instructed to carry out manufacturing and marketing plans formulated in the company's Detroit headquarters, rather than being trusted to develop their own.

In contrast, GM's European operations were traditionally managed on an arm's-length basis, with the company's national operations often being allowed to design their own cars and manufacturing facilities and formulate their own marketing strategies. This regional and national autonomy allowed GM's European operations to produce vehicles that were closely tailored to the needs of local customers. However, it also led to costly duplication in design and manufacturing operations and to a failure to share valuable technology, skills, and practices among subsidiaries. Thus, while General Motors exerted tight control over its operations in the developing world, its control over operations in Europe was perhaps too lax.

At the same time, firms such as MTV still have to keep an eye on costs. Firms pursuing a localization strategy still need to be efficient and, whenever possible, to capture some scale economies from their global reach. As noted earlier, many automobile companies have found that they have to customize some of their product offerings to local market demands—for example, producing large pickup trucks for U.S. consumers and small fuel-efficient cars for Europeans and Japanese. At the same time, these multinationals try to get some scale economies from their global volume by using common vehicle platforms and components across many different models, and manufacturing those platforms and components at efficiently scaled factories that are optimally located. By designing their products in this way, these companies have been able to localize their product offering, yet simultaneously capture some scale economies, learning effects, and location economies.

TRANSNATIONAL STRATEGY

We have argued that a global standardization strategy makes most sense when cost pressures are intense, and demands for local responsiveness limited. Conversely, a localization strategy makes most sense when demands for local responsiveness are high, but cost pressures are moderate or low. What happens, however, when the firm simultaneously faces

The result was a company whose international operations lacked overall strategic coherence.

GM has been trying to change this since the late 1990s by switching from its Detroit-centric view of the world to a philosophy that centers of excellence may reside anywhere in the company's global operations. The company is trying to tap these centers of excellence to provide its global operations with the very latest technology. The four new manufacturing plants in the developing world are an embodiment of this new approach. Each is identical, each incorporates state-of-the-art technology, and each has been designed not by Americans, but by a team of Brazilian and German engineers. By building identical plants, GM hopes to mimic Toyota, whose plants are so much alike that a change in a car in Japan can be quickly replicated around the world. The plants are modeled after GM's Eisenach facility in Germany, which is managed by the company's Opel subsidiary. It was at the Eisenach plant that GM figured out how to implement the lean production system pioneered by Toyota. The plant is now the most efficient auto-manufacturing operation in Europe and the best within GM. Its productivity is at least twice that of most North American assembly operations. Each of the new plants produces state-of-the-art vehicles for local consumption.

To realize scale economies, GM is also trying to design and build vehicles that share a common global platform. Engineering teams located in Germany, Detroit, South America, and Australia are designing these common vehicle platforms. Local plants are allowed to customize certain features of these vehicles to match the tastes and preferences of local customers. At the same time, adhering to a common global platform enables the company to spread its costs of designing a car over greater volume and to realize scale economies in the manufacture of shared components—both of which should help GM lower its overall cost structure. The first fruits of this effort include the 1998 Cadillac Seville, which was designed to be sold in more than 40 countries. GM's family of front-wheel-drive minivans was also designed around a common platform that allows the vehicles to be produced in multiple locations around the globe, as was the 1998 Opel Astra, which is GM's best-selling car in Europe. Ultimately, GM hopes this coordinated global approach to designing cars will reduce the costs of developing a new vehicle by 15 to 25 percent. GM also hopes that sharing of common parts between GM cars will reduce by $3.5 billion its annual bill of $100 billion for component parts.

Sources: R. Blumenstein, "GM Is Building Plants in Developing Nations to Woo New Markets," *The Wall Street Journal,* August 4, 1997, p. A1; Haig Simonian, "GM Hopes to Turn Corner with New Astra," *Financial Times,* November 29, 1997, p. 15; D. Howes, "GM, Ford Play for Keeps Abroad," *Detroit News,* March 8, 1998, p. D1; "The Global Gambles of General Motors," *The Economist,* June 24, 2000, pp. 67–68; and J. Fahey, "Would You Buy a Chevy Saab?" *Forbes,* December 9, 2002, pp. 82–84.

both strong cost pressures and strong pressures for local responsiveness? How can managers balance the competing and inconsistent demands such divergent pressures place on the firm? According to some researchers, the answer is to pursue what has been called a transnational strategy.

Two of these researchers, Christopher Bartlett and Sumantra Ghoshal, argue that in today's global environment, competitive conditions are so intense that to survive, firms must do all they can to respond to pressures for cost reductions and local responsiveness. They must try to realize location economies and experience effects, to leverage products internationally, to transfer core competencies and skills within the company, and to simultaneously pay attention to pressures for local responsiveness.[32] Bartlett and Ghoshal note that in the modern multinational enterprise, core competencies and skills do not reside just in the home country but can develop in any of the firm's worldwide operations. Thus, they maintain that the flow of skills and product offerings should not be all one way, from home country to foreign subsidiary. Rather, the flow should also be from foreign subsidiary to home country and from foreign subsidiary to foreign subsidiary. Transnational enterprises, in other words, must also focus on leveraging subsidiary skills.

In essence, firms that pursue a **transnational strategy** are trying to simultaneously achieve low costs through location economies, economies of scale, and learning effects;

differentiate their product offering across geographic markets to account for local differences; and foster a multidirectional flow of skills between different subsidiaries in the firm's global network of operations. As attractive as this may sound in theory, the strategy is not an easy one to pursue since it places conflicting demands on the company. Differentiating the product to respond to local demands in different geographic markets raises costs, which runs counter to the goal of reducing costs. Companies such as Ford and ABB (one of the world's largest engineering conglomerates) have tried to embrace a transnational strategy and found it difficult to implement.

How best to implement a transnational strategy is one of the most complex questions that large multinationals are grappling with today. Few if any enterprises have perfected this strategic posture. But some clues as to the right approach can be derived from a number of companies. The example of General Motors is given in the accompanying Management Focus. For another example, consider the case of Caterpillar. The need to compete with low-cost competitors such as Komatsu of Japan forced Caterpillar to look for greater cost economies. However, variations in construction practices and government regulations across countries mean that Caterpillar also has to be responsive to local demands. Therefore, Caterpillar confronted significant pressures for cost reductions *and* for local responsiveness.

To deal with cost pressures, Caterpillar redesigned its products to use many identical components and invested in a few large-scale component manufacturing facilities, sited at favorable locations, to fill global demand and realize scale economies. At the same time, the company augments the centralized manufacturing of components with assembly plants in each of its major global markets. At these plants, Caterpillar adds local product features, tailoring the finished product to local needs. Thus, Caterpillar is able to realize many of the benefits of global manufacturing while reacting to pressures for local responsiveness by differentiating its product among national markets.[33] Caterpillar started to pursue this strategy in 1979 and by 1997 had succeeded in doubling output per employee, significantly reducing its overall cost structure in the process. Meanwhile, Komatsu and Hitachi, which are still wedded to a Japan-centric global strategy, have seen their cost advantages evaporate and have been steadily losing market share to Caterpillar.

Changing a firm's strategic posture to build an organization capable of supporting a transnational strategy is a complex and challenging task. Some would say it is too complex, because the strategy implementation problems of creating a viable organizational structure and control systems to manage this strategy are immense. This is an issue that we shall return to and discuss in Chapter 13.

INTERNATIONAL STRATEGY

Sometimes it is possible to identify multinational firms that find themselves in the fortunate position of being confronted with low cost pressures and low pressures for local responsiveness. Many of these enterprises have pursued an **international strategy,** taking products first produced for their domestic market and selling them internationally with only minimal local customization. The distinguishing feature of many such firms is that they are selling a product that serves universal needs, but they do not face significant competitors, and thus unlike firms pursuing a global standardization strategy, they are not confronted with pressures to reduce their cost structure. Xerox found itself in this position in the 1960s after its invention and commercialization of the photocopier. The technology underlying the photocopier was protected by strong patents, so for several years Xerox did not face competitors—it had a monopoly. The product serves universal needs, and it was highly valued in most developed nations. Thus, Xerox was able to sell the same basic product the world over, charging a relatively high price for that product. Since Xerox did not face direct competitors, it did not have to deal with strong pressures to minimize its cost structure.

Enterprises pursuing an international strategy have followed a similar developmental pattern as they expanded into foreign markets. They tend to centralize product development functions such as R&D at home. However, they also tend to establish manufactur-

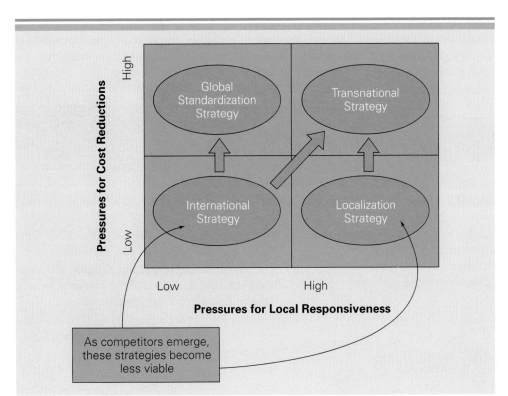

FIGURE 12.8

Changes in Strategy over Time

ing and marketing functions in each major country or geographic region in which they do business. The resulting duplication can raise costs, but this is less of an issue if the firm does not face strong pressures for cost reductions. Although they may undertake some local customization of product offering and marketing strategy, this tends to be rather limited in scope. Ultimately, in most firms that pursue an international strategy, the head office retains fairly tight control over marketing and product strategy.

Other firms that have pursued this strategy include Procter & Gamble and Microsoft. Historically, Procter & Gamble developed innovative new products in Cincinnati and then transferred them wholesale to local markets. Similarly, the bulk of Microsoft's product development work takes place in Redmond, Washington, where the company is headquartered. Although some localization work is undertaken elsewhere, this is limited to producing foreign-language versions of popular Microsoft programs.

THE EVOLUTION OF STRATEGY

The Achilles' heel of the international strategy is that over time, competitors inevitably emerge, and if managers do not take proactive steps to reduce their firm's cost structure, it will be rapidly outflanked by efficient global competitors. This is exactly what happened to Xerox. Japanese companies such as Canon ultimately invented their way around Xerox's patents, produced their own photocopiers in very efficient manufacturing plants, priced them below Xerox's products, and rapidly took global market share from Xerox. In the final analysis, Xerox's demise was not due to the emergence of competitors, for ultimately that was bound to occur, but due to its failure to proactively reduce its cost structure in advance of the emergence of efficient global competitors. The message in this story is that an international strategy may not be viable in the long term, and to survive, firms need to shift toward a global standardization strategy or a transnational strategy in advance of competitors (see Figure 12.8).

The same can be said about a localization strategy. Localization may give a firm a competitive edge, but if it is simultaneously facing aggressive competitors, the company will also have to reduce its cost structure, and the only way to do that may be to shift toward a transnational strategy. Thus, as competition intensifies, international and localization strategies tend to become less viable, and managers need to orientate their companies toward either a global standardization strategy or a transnational strategy.

Chapter Summary

In this chapter we reviewed basic principles of strategy and the various ways in which firms can profit from global expansion, and we looked at the strategies that firms that compete globally can adopt. The chapter made the following points:

1. A firm's strategy can be defined as the actions that managers take to attain the goals of the firm. For most firms, the preeminent goal is to maximize shareholder value. Maximizing shareholder value requires firms to focus on increasing their profitability and the growth rate of profits over time.

2. International expansion may enable a firm to earn greater returns by transferring the product offerings derived from its core competencies to markets where indigenous competitors lack those product offerings and competencies.

3. Due to national differences, it may pay a firm to base each value creation activity it performs at that location where factor conditions are most conducive to the performance of that activity. We refer to this strategy as focusing on the attainment of location economies.

4. By rapidly building sales volume for a standardized product, international expansion can assist a firm in moving down the experience curve by realizing learning effects and economies of scale.

5. A multinational firm can create additional value by identifying valuable skills created within its

foreign subsidiaries and leveraging those skills within its global network of operations.

6. The best strategy for a firm to pursue often depends on a consideration of the pressures for cost reductions and for local responsiveness.

7. Pressures for cost reductions are greatest in industries producing commodity-type products where price is the main competitive weapon.

8. Pressures for local responsiveness arise from differences in consumer tastes and preferences, national infrastructure and traditional practices, distribution channels, and from host-government demands.

9. Firms pursuing an international strategy transfer the products derived from core competencies to foreign markets, while undertaking some limited local customization.

10. Firms pursuing a localization strategy customize their product offering, marketing strategy, and business strategy to national conditions.

11. Firms pursuing a global standardization strategy focus on reaping the cost reductions that come from experience curve effects and location economies.

12. Many industries are now so competitive that firms must adopt a transnational strategy. This involves a simultaneous focus on reducing costs, transferring skills and products, and boosting local responsiveness. Implementing such a strategy may not be easy.

Critical Thinking and Discussion Questions

1. In a world of zero transportation costs, no trade barriers, and nontrivial differences between nations with regard to factor conditions, firms must expand internationally if they are to survive. Discuss.

2. Plot the position of the following firms on Figure 12.6: Procter & Gamble, Boeing, Coca-Cola, Dow Chemical, Intel, McDonald's. In each case justify your answer.

3. Read the Management Focus on General Motors contained in this chapter, then answer the following questions:
   - How would you characterize the strategy pursued by GM in the (*a*) developing world and (*b*) Europe before 1997?
   - What do you think were the likely competitive effects of the pre-1997 strategy?

   - How would you characterize the strategy that GM has been pursuing since 1997? How should this strategy affect GM's ability to create value in the global automobile market?

4. What do you see as the main organizational problems that are likely to be associated with implementation of a transnational strategy?

Research Task globalEDGE™ globaledge.msu.edu

Use the globalEDGE™ site to complete the following exercises:

1. Several classifications and rankings of multinational corporations are prepared by a variety of sources. Find one such ranking system and identify the criteria that are used in ranking the top global companies. Although some of these rankings require subscriptions, find a freely available ranking and extract the list of the highest ranked 25 companies paying particular attention to the home countries of the companies.

2. The top management of your company, a manufacturer and marketer of laptop computers, has decided to pursue international expansion opportunities in Eastern Europe. In order to achieve some economies of scale, your management is aiming toward a strategy of minimum local adaptation. Focusing on an Eastern European country of your choice, prepare an executive summary that features those aspects of the product where standardization will simply not work, and adaptation to local conditions will be essential.

The Evolution of Strategy at Procter & Gamble

CLOSING CASE Founded in 1837, Cincinnati-based Procter & Gamble has long been one of the world's most international of companies. Today P&G is a global colossus in the consumer products business with annual sales in excess of $50 billion, some 54 percent of which are generated outside of the United States. P&G sells more than 300 brands—including Ivory soap, Tide, Pampers, IAM pet food, Crisco, and Folgers—to consumers in 160 countries. It has operations in 80 countries and employs close to 100,000 people globally. P&G established its first foreign factory in 1915 when it opened a plant in Canada to produce Ivory soap and Crisco. This was followed in 1930 by the establishment of the company's first foreign subsidiary in Britain. The pace of international expansion quickened in the 1950s and 1960s as P&G expanded rapidly in Western Europe, and then again in the 1970s when the company entered Japan and other Asian nations. Sometimes P&G entered a nation by acquiring an established competitor and its brands, as occurred in the case of Great Britain and Japan, but more typically the company set up operations from the ground floor.

By the late 1970s, the strategy at P&G was well established. The company developed new products in Cincinnati and then relied on semiautonomous foreign subsidiaries to manufacture, market, and distribute those products in different nations. In many cases, foreign subsidiaries had their own production facilities and tailored the packaging, brand name, and marketing message to local tastes and preferences. For years this strategy delivered a steady stream of new products and reliable growth in sales and profits. By the 1990s, however, profit growth at P&G was slowing.

The essence of the problem was simple; P&G's costs were too high because of extensive duplication of manufacturing, marketing, and administrative facilities in different national subsidiaries. The duplication of assets made sense in the world of the 1960s, when national markets were segmented from each other by barriers to cross-border trade. Products produced in Great Britain, for example, could not be sold economically in Germany due to high tariff duties levied on imports into Germany. By the 1980s, however, barriers to cross-border trade were falling rapidly worldwide and fragmented national markets were merging into larger regional or global markets. Also, the retailers through which P&G distributed its products were growing larger and more global, such as Wal-Mart, Tesco from the United Kingdom, and Carrefour from France. These emerging global retailers were demanding price discounts from P&G.

In 1993, P&G embarked on a major reorganization in an attempt to control its cost structure and recognize the new reality of emerging global markets. The company shut down some 30 manufacturing plants around the globe, laid off 13,000 employees, and concentrated production in fewer plants that could better realize economies of scale and serve regional markets. These actions cut some $600 million a year out of P&G's cost structure. It wasn't enough! Profit growth remained sluggish.

In 1998, P&G launched its second reorganization of the decade. Named "Organization 2005," the goal was to transform P&G into a truly global company. The company tore up its old organization, which was based on countries and regions, and replaced it with one based on seven self-contained global business units, ranging from baby care to food products. Each business unit was given complete responsibility for generating profits from its products, and for manufacturing, marketing, and product development. Each business unit was told to rationalize production, concentrating it in fewer larger facilities; to try to build global brands wherever possible, thereby eliminating marketing difference between countries; and to accelerate the development and launch of new products. In 1999, P&G announced that as a result of this initiative, it would close another 10 factories and lay off 15,000 employees, mostly in Europe where there was still extensive duplication of assets. The annual cost savings were estimated to be about $800 million. P&G planned to use the savings to cut prices and increase marketing spending in an effort to gain market share, and thus further lower costs through the attainment of scale economies.

This time the strategy seemed to be working. In 2003 and again in 2004, P&G reported strong growth in both sales and profits. Between 2002 and 2004 revenues surged 28 percent from $40.2 billion to $51.4 billion, while profits increased an impressive 46 percent from $4.35 billion to $6.34 billion. Significantly, P&G's global competitors, such as Unilever, Kimberly-Clark, and Colgate-Palmolive, were struggling in 2003 and 2004.

Source: J. Neff, "P&G Outpacing Unilever in Five-Year Battle," *Advertising Age*, November 3, 2003, pp. 1–3; G. Strauss, "Firm Restructuring into Truly Global Company," *USA Today*, September 10, 1999, p. B2; *Procter & Gamble 10K Report, 2004*; and M. Kolbasuk McGee, "P&G Jump-Starts Corporate Change," *Information Week*, November 1, 1999, pp. 30–34.

Case Discussion Questions

1. What strategy was Procter & Gamble pursuing when it first entered foreign markets in the period up until the 1980s?

2. Why do you think this strategy became less viable in the 1990s?

3. What strategy does P&G appear to be moving toward? What are the benefits of this strategy? What are the potential risks associated with it?

Notes

1. More formally, ROIC = Net profit after tax/Capital, where capital includes the sum of the firm's equity and debt. This way of calculating profitability is highly correlated with return on assets. For details, see the appendix to this chapter.

2. T. Copeland, T. Koller, and J. Murrin. *Valuation: Measuring and Managing the Value of Companies* (New York: John Wiley & Sons, 2000).

3. The concept of consumer surplus is an important one in economics. For a more detailed exposition, see D. Besanko, D. Dranove, and M. Shanley, *Economics of Strategy* (New York: John Wiley & Sons, 1996).

4. However, P = V only in the special case where the company has a perfect monopoly, and where it can charge each customer a unique price that reflects the value of the product to that customer (i.e., where perfect price discrimination is possible). More generally, except in the limiting case of perfect price discrimination, even a monopolist will see most consumers capture some of the value of a product in the form of a consumer surplus.

5. This point is central to the work of Michael Porter, *Competitive Advantage* (New York: Free Press, 1985). See also chap. 4 in P. Ghemawat, *Commitment: The Dynamic of Strategy* (New York: Free Press, 1991).

6. M. E. Porter, *Competitive Strategy* (New York: Free Press, 1980).

7. M. E. Porter, "What Is Strategy?" *Harvard Business Review*, On-point Enhanced Edition article, February 1, 2000.

8. Porter, *Competitive Advantage*.

9. Empirical evidence does seem to indicate that, on average, international expansion is linked

to greater firm profitability. For some recent examples, see M. A. Hitt, R. E. Hoskisson, and H. Kim, "International Diversification, Effects on Innovation and Firm Performance," *Academy of Management Journal* 40, no. 4 (1997), pp. 767–98, and S. Tallman and J. Li, "Effects of International Diversity and Product Diversity on the Performance of Multinational Firms," *Academy of Management Journal* 39, no. 1 (1996), pp. 179–96.

10. This concept has been popularized by G. Hamel and C. K. Prahalad, *Competing for the Future* (Boston: Harvard Business School Press, 1994). The concept is grounded in the resource-based view of the firm; for a summary, see J. B. Barney, "Firm Resources and Sustained Competitive Advantage," *Journal of Management* 17 (1991), pp. 99–120, and K. R. Conner, "A Historical Comparison of Resource-Based Theory and Five Schools of Thought within Industrial Organization Economics: Do We Have a New Theory of the Firm?" *Journal of Management* 17 (1991), pp. 121–54.

11. J. P. Womack, D. T. Jones, and D. Roos, *The Machine That Changed the World* (New York: Rawson Associates, 1990).

12. M. E. Porter, *The Competitive Advantage of Nations* (New York: Free Press, 1990).

13. Example is based on C. S. Trager, "Enter the Mini-Multinational," *Northeast International Business,* March 1989, pp. 13–14.

14. See: R. B. Reich, *The Work of Nations* (New York: Alfred A. Knopf, 1991), and P. J. Buckley and N. Hashai, "A Global System View of Firm Boundaries," *Journal of International Business Studies,* January 2004, pp. 33–50.

15. D. Barboza, "An Unknown Giant Flexes Its Muscles," *The New York Times,* December 4, 2004, pp. B1, B3.

16. G. Hall and S. Howell, "The Experience Curve from an Economist's Perspective," *Strategic Management Journal* 6 (1985), pp. 197–212.

17. A. A. Alchain, "Reliability of Progress Curves in Airframe Production," *Econometrica* 31 (1963), pp. 697–93.

18. Hall and Howell, "The Experience Curve from an Economist's Perspective."

19. For a full discussion of the source of scale economies, see D. Besanko, D. Dranove, and M. Shanley, *Economics of Strategy* (New York: John Wiley & Sons, 1996).

20. This estimate was provided by the Pharmaceutical Manufacturers Association.

21. "Matsushita Electrical Industrial in 1987," in *Transnational Management,* eds. C. A. Bartlett and S. Ghoshal (Homewood, IL: Richard D. Irwin, 1992).

22. See J. Birkinshaw and N. Hood, "Multinational Subsidiary Evolution: Capability and Charter Change in Foreign Owned Subsidiary Companies," *Academy of Management Review* 23 (October 1998), pp. 773–95; A. K. Gupta and V. J. Govindarajan, "Knowledge Flows within Multinational Corporations," *Strategic Management Journal* 21 (2000), pp. 473–96; V. J. Govindarajan and A. K. Gupta, *The Quest for Global Dominance* (San Francisco: Jossey Bass, 2001); T. S. Frost, J. M. Birkinshaw, and P. C. Ensign, "Centers of Excellence in Multinational Corporations," *Strategic Management Journal* 23 (2002), pp. 997–1018; and U. Andersson, M. Forsgren, and U. Holm, "The Strategic Impact of External Networks," *Strategic Management Journal* 23 (2002), pp. 979–96.

23. S. Leung, "Armchairs, TVs and Espresso: Is It McDonald's?" *The Wall Street Journal,* August 30, 2002, pp. A1, A6.

24. K. Ferdows, "Making the Most of Foreign Factories," *Harvard Business Review,* March–April 1997, pp. 73–88.

25. C. K. Prahalad and Yves L. Doz, *The Multinational Mission: Balancing Local Demands and Global Vision* (New York: Free Press, 1987). Also see J. Birkinshaw, A. Morrison, and J. Hulland, "Structural and Competitive Determinants of a Global Integration Strategy," *Strategic Management Journal* 16 (1995), pp. 637–55.

26. J. E. Garten, "Wal-Mart Gives Globalization a Bad Name," *BusinessWeek,* March 8, 2004, p. 24.

27. Prahalad and Doz, *The Multinational Mission: Balancing Local Demands and Global Vision.* Prahalad and Doz actually talk about local responsiveness rather than local customization.

28. T. Levitt, "The Globalization of Markets," *Harvard Business Review,* May–June 1983, pp. 92–102.

29. K. Belson, "In U.S., Cell Phone Users Are Often All Talk," *The New York Times,* December 13, 2004, pp. C1, C4.

30. C. J. Chipello, "Local Presence Is Key to European Deals," *The Wall Street Journal,* June 30, 1998, p. A15.

31. Bartlett and Ghoshal, *Managing across Borders.*

32. Ibid.

33. T. Hout, M. E. Porter, and E. Rudden, "How Global Companies Win Out," *Harvard Business Review,* September–October 1982, pp. 98–108.

Appendix: Profitability, Growth, and Valuation

The ultimate goal of strategy is to maximize the value of a company to its shareholders (subject to the important constraints that this is done in a legal, ethical, and socially responsible manner). The two main drivers of enterprise valuation are profitability, as measured by the company's return on invested capital (**ROIC**) and the growth rate of profits, **g.***

ROIC is defined as net operating profits less adjusted taxes (NOPLAT) over the invested capital of the enterprise (IC), where IC is the sum of the company's equity and debt (the method for calculating adjusted taxes need not concern us here). That is:

$$ROIC = NOPLAT/IC$$

Where:

$$NOPLAT = Revenues - Cost\ of\ goods\ sold - Operating\ expenses$$
$$- Depreciation\ charges - Adjusted\ taxes$$
$$IC = Value\ of\ shareholders\ equity + Value\ of\ debt$$

The growth rate of profits, **g,** can be defined as the percentage increase in net operating profits (NOPLAT) over a given time period. More precisely:

$$g = [(NOPLAT_{t+1} - NOPLAT_t)/NOPLAT_t] \times 100$$

The valuation of a company can be calculated using discounted cash flow analysis and applying it to future expected free cash flows (free cash flow in a period is defined as NOPLAT − Net investments). It can be shown that the valuation of a company so calculated is related to the company's weighted average cost of capital (WACC), which is the cost of the equity and debt that the firm uses to finance its business, and the company's ROIC. Specifically:

- If ROIC > WACC, the company is earning more than its cost of capital and it is creating value.
- If ROIC = WACC, the company is earning its cost of capital and its valuation will be stable.
- If ROIC < WACC, the company is earning less than its cost of capital and it is therefore destroying value.

A company that earns more than its cost of capital is even more valuable if it can grow its net operating profits less adjusted taxes (NOPLAT) over time. Conversely, a firm that is not earning its cost of capital destroys value if it grows its NOPLAT. This critical relationship between ROIC, **g,** and value is shown in Table 12.A1.

In Table 12.A1, the figures in the cells of the matrix represent the discounted present values of future free cash flows for a company that has a starting NOPLAT of $100, invested capital of $1,000, cost of capital equal to 10 percent, and a 25-year time horizon after which ROIC = Cost of capital.

The important points revealed by this exercise are as follows:

- A company with an already high ROIC can create more value by increasing its profit growth rate rather than pushing for an even higher ROIC. Thus, a company with an ROIC of 15 percent and a 3 percent growth rate can create

---

*C. Y. Baldwin, *Fundamental Enterprise Valuation: Return on Invested Capital,* Harvard Business School Note 9-801-125, July 3, 2004, and T. Copeland et al., *Valuation: Measuring and Managing the Value of Companies* (New York: Wiley, 2000).

NOPLAT Growth g	ROIC 7.5%	ROIC 10.0%	ROIC 12.5%	ROIC 15.0%	ROIC 20%
3%	887	1,000	1,058	1,113	1,170
6%	708	1,000	1,117	1,295	1,442
9%	410	1,000	1,354	1,591	1,886

TABLE 12.A1

ROIC, Growth, and Valuation

more value by increasing its profit growth rate from 3 percent to 9 percent than it can by increasing ROIC to 20 percent.

- A company with a low ROIC destroys value if it grows. Thus, if ROIC equals 7.5 percent, a 9 percent growth rate for 25 years will produce less value than a 3 percent growth rate. This is because unprofitable growth requires capital investments, the cost of which cannot be covered.
- Unprofitable growth destroys value.

The best of both worlds is high ROIC and high growth.

Very few companies are able to maintain an ROIC > WACC and grow NOPLAT over time, but there are some notable examples including Dell, Microsoft, and Wal-Mart—all of which have increased their profitability and their growth rates by expanding internationally. Because these companies have generally been able to fund their capital investment needs from internally generated cash flows, they have not had to issue more shares to raise capital. Thus, growth in NOPLAT has translated directly into higher earnings per share for these companies, making their shares more attractive to investors and leading to substantial share price appreciation. By successfully pursuing strategies that result in a high ROIC and growing NOPLAT, these firms have maximized shareholder value.

The Organization of International Business

A Decade of Organizational Change at Unilever

Unilever is one of the world's oldest multinational corporations with extensive product offerings in the food, detergent, and personal care businesses. It generates annual revenues in excess of $50 billion and a wide range of branded products in virtually every country. Detergents, which account for about 25 percent of corporate revenues, include well-known names such as Omo, which is sold in more than 50 countries. Personal care products, which account for about 15 percent of sales, include Calvin Klein Cosmetics, Pepsodent toothpaste brands, Faberge hair care products, and Vaseline skin lotions. Food products account for the remaining 60 percent of sales and include strong offerings in margarine (where Unilever's market share in most countries exceeds 70 percent), tea, ice cream, frozen foods, and bakery products.

Historically, Unilever was organized on a decentralized basis. Subsidiary companies in each major national market were responsible for the production, marketing, sales, and distribution of products in that market. In Western Europe, for example, the company had 17 subsidiaries in the early 1990s, each focused on a different national market. Each was a profit center and each was held accountable for its own performance. This decentralization was viewed as a source of strength. The structure allowed local managers to match product offerings and marketing strategy to local tastes and preferences and to alter sales and distribution strategies to fit the prevailing retail systems. To drive the localization, Unilever recruited local managers to run local organizations; the U.S. subsidiary (Lever Brothers) was run by Americans, the Indian subsidiary by Indians, and so on.

By the mid-1990s, this decentralized structure was increasingly out of step with a rapidly changing competitive environment. Unilever's global competitors, which include the Swiss firm Nestlé and Procter & Gamble from the United States, had been more successful than Unilever on several fronts—building global brands, reducing cost structure by consolidating manufacturing operations at a few choice locations, and executing simultaneous product launches in several national markets. Unilever's decentralized structure worked against efforts to build global or regional brands. It also meant lots of duplication, particularly in manufacturing; a lack of scale economies; and a high-cost structure. Unilever also found that it was falling behind rivals in the race to bring new products to market. In Europe, for example, while Nestlé and Procter & Gamble moved toward pan-European product launches, it could take Unilever four to five years to "persuade" its 17 European operations to adopt a new product.

Unilever began to change all this in the mid-1990s. In 1996, it introduced a new structure based on regional business groups. Within each business group were a number of divisions, each focusing on a specific category of products. Thus, in the European Business Group, a division focused on detergents, another on ice cream and frozen foods, and so on. These groups and divisions coordinated the activities of national subsidiaries within their region to drive down operating costs and speed up the process of developing and introducing new products.

For example, Lever Europe was established to consolidate the company's detergent operations. The 17 European companies reported directly to Lever Europe. Using its newfound organizational clout, Lever Europe consolidated the production of detergents in Europe in a few key locations to reduce costs and speed up new product introduction. Implicit in this new approach was a bargain: the 17 companies relinquished autonomy in their traditional markets in exchange for opportunities to help develop and execute a unified pan-European strategy. The number of European plants manufacturing soap was cut from 10 to 2, and some new products were manufactured at only one site. Product sizing and packaging were harmonized to cut purchasing costs and to accommodate unified pan-European advertising. By taking these steps, Unilever estimated it saved as much as $400 million a year in its European detergent operations.

By 2000, however, Unilever found that it was still lagging its competitors, so the company embarked upon another reorganization. This time the goal was to cut the number of brands that Unilever sold from 1,600 to just 400 that could be marketed on a regional or global scale. To support this new focus, the company planned to reduce the number of manufacturing plants from 380 to about 280 by 2004. The company also established a new organization based on just two global product divisions—a food division, and a home personal care division. Within each division are a number of regional business groups that focus on developing, manufacturing, and marketing either food or personal care products within a given region. For example, Unilever Bestfoods Europe, which is headquartered in Rotterdam, focuses on selling food brands across Western and Eastern Europe, while Unilever Home and Personal Care Europe does the same for home and personal care products. A similar structure can be found in North America, Latin America, and Asia. Thus, Bestfoods North America, headquartered in New Jersey, has a similar charter to Bestfoods Europe, but in keeping with differences in local history, many of the food brands marketed by Unilever in North America are different from those marketed in Europe.

H. Connon, "Unilever's Got the Nineties Licked," *The Guardian*, May 24, 1998, p. 5; "Unilever: A Networked Organization," *Harvard Business Review*, November–December 1996, p. 138; C. Christensen and J. Zobel, "Unilever's Butter Beater: Innovation for Global Diversity," Harvard Business School Case No. 9-698-017, March 1998; M. Mayer, A. Smith, and R. Whittington, "Restructuring Roulette," *Financial Times*, November 8, 2002, p. 8; and Unilever's Web site at www.unilever.com

Introduction

This chapter identifies the organizational architecture that international businesses use to manage and direct their global operations. By **organizational architecture** we mean the totality of a firm's organization, including formal organization structure, control systems and incentives, processes, organizational culture, and people. The core argument outlined in this chapter is that superior enterprise profitability requires three conditions to be fulfilled. First, the different elements of a firm's organizational architecture must be internally consistent. For example, the control and incentive systems used in the firm must be consistent with the structure of the enterprise. Second, the organizational architecture must match or fit the strategy of the firm—strategy and architecture must be consistent. For example, if a firm is pursuing a global standardization strategy but it has the wrong kind of organization architecture in place, it is unlikely that it will be able to execute that strategy effectively and poor performance may result. Third, the strategy and architecture of the firm must not only be consistent with each other, but they also must be consistent with competitive conditions prevailing in the firm's markets—strategy, architecture, and competitive environment must all be consistent. For example, a firm pursuing a localization strategy might have the right kind of organizational architecture in place for that strategy. However, if it competes in markets where cost pressures are intense and demands for local responsiveness are low, it will still have inferior performance because a global standardization strategy is more appropriate in such an environment. The opening case on Unilever touches on some of the important issues here. Historically Unilever has competed in markets where local responsiveness has been very important. The production and marketing of food, detergent, and personal care products have traditionally been tailored to the tastes and preferences of consumers in different nations. Unilever satisfied this environmental demand for local responsiveness by pursuing a localization strategy. Its organizational architecture reflected this strategy. Unilever operated with a decentralized structure that delegated responsibility for production, marketing, sales, and distribution decisions to autonomous national operating companies. This allowed local managers to configure product offerings, and marketing and sales activities, to the conditions prevailing in a particular nation. For a long time, this fit between strategy and architecture served Unilever well, helping it to become a dominant consumer products enterprise.

However, by the early 1990s the competitive environment was changing. Trade barriers between countries were falling, particularly in the European Union following the creation of a single market in 1992. This made it possible to manufacture certain items such as detergents and margarine at favorable central locations to realize the benefits associated with location and experience curve economies. Also, new products in areas such as frozen foods and margarine were gaining regional or even global acceptance. Unfortunately for Unilever, some of its global competitors moved more rapidly to exploit this change in the competitive environment. Unilever found itself disadvantaged by a high-cost structure (caused by the duplication of manufacturing operations) and an inability to introduce new products in several national markets at once. In other words, the competitive environment changed, but Unilever did not change with it.

By the mid-1990s, Unilever had recognized its problems and changed both its strategy and its organizational architecture so that it better matched the new competitive realities. Unilever began to shift toward more of a transnational strategic orientation, seeking to balance local responsiveness in marketing and sales with the centralization of manufacturing and product development activities to realize scale economies and execute pan-regional product launches. To implement this strategy, Unilever introduced a new organizational architecture based on regional business groups, each of which contained product divisions. These divisions were given the responsibility for centralizing manufacturing and product development activities, which implied a reduction in the autonomy traditionally granted to operating subsidiaries. By 2000, Unilever concluded that this process had not gone far enough, so it reorganized again, this time creating two worldwide divisions—one for food products and one for home and personal care products. The divisions were made responsible for reducing Unilever's brands from 1,600 to just 400, and for consolidating manufacturing in fewer, more efficient factories. However, recognizing that localization is still important in its markets, Unilever maintained a regional structure under its two divisions. What Unilever was trying to do through these reorganizations was to reestablish a fit between strategy, architecture, and environment by reconfiguring its organization and operations to match new competitive realities.

To explore the issues illustrated by cases such as Unilever's, we open the current chapter by discussing in more detail the concepts of organizational architecture and fit. Next we turn to a more detailed exploration of various components of architecture—structure, control systems and incentives, organization culture, and processes—and explain how these components must be internally consistent. (We discuss the "people" component of architecture in Chapter 18, when we discuss human resource strategy in the multinational firm.) After reviewing the various components of architecture, we look at the ways in which architecture can be matched to strategy and the competitive environment to achieve high performance. The chapter closes with a discussion of organizational change, for as the Unilever case illustrates, periodically firms have to change their organization so that it matches new strategic and competitive realities.

Organizational Architecture

As noted in the introduction, the term *organizational architecture* refers to the totality of a firm's organization, including formal organizational structure, control systems and incentives, organizational culture, processes, and people.[1] Figure 13.1 illustrates these different elements. By **organizational structure,** we mean three things: First, the formal division of the organization into subunits such as product divisions, national operations, and functions (most organizational charts display this aspect of structure); second, the location of decision-making responsibilities within that structure (e.g., centralized or decentralized); and third, the establishment of integrating mechanisms to coordinate the activities of subunits including cross-functional teams and or pan-regional committees.

Control systems are the metrics used to measure the performance of subunits and make judgments about how well managers are running those subunits. For example, historically Unilever measured the performance of national operating subsidiary companies according to profitability—profitability was the metric. **Incentives** are the devices used to reward appropriate managerial behavior. Incentives are very closely tied to performance metrics. For example, the incentives of a manager in charge of a national operating subsidiary might be linked to the performance of that company. Specifically, she might receive a bonus if her subsidiary exceeds its performance targets.

Processes are the manner in which decisions are made and work is performed within the organization. Examples are the processes for formulating strategy, for deciding how to allocate resources within a firm, or for evaluating the performance of managers and giving feedback. Processes are conceptually distinct from the location of decision-making responsibilities within an organization, although both involve decisions. While the CEO might have ultimate responsibility for deciding what the strategy of the firm should be (i.e., the decision-making responsibility is centralized), the process he or she uses to make that decision might include the solicitation of ideas and criticism from lower-level managers.

Organizational culture refers to the norms and value systems that are shared among the employees of an organization. Just as societies have cultures (see Chapter 3 for details), so do organizations. Organizations are societies of individuals who come together to perform collective tasks. They have their own distinctive patterns of culture and subculture.[2] As we shall see, organizational culture can have a profound impact on how a firm performs. Finally, by **people** we mean not just the employees of the organization, but

FIGURE 13.1

Organization
Architecture

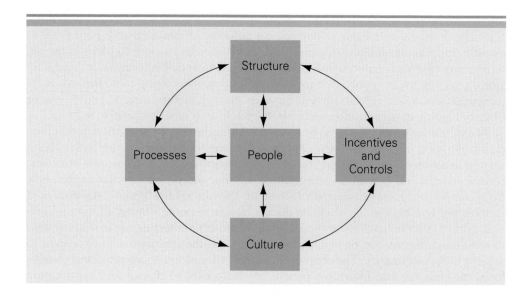

also the strategy used to recruit, compensate, and retain those individuals and the type of people that they are in terms of their skills, values, and orientation (discussed in depth in Chapter 18).

As illustrated by the arrows in Figure 13.1, the various components of an organization's architecture are not independent of each other: Each component shapes, and is shaped by, other components of architecture. An obvious example is the strategy regarding people. This can be used proactively to hire individuals whose internal values are consistent with those that the firm wishes to emphasize in its organization culture. Thus, the people component of architecture can be used to reinforce (or not) the prevailing culture of the organization. For example, Unilever has historically made an effort to hire managers who were sociable and placed a high value on consensus and cooperation, values that the enterprise wished to emphasize in its own culture.[3]

If a firm is going to maximize its profitability, it must pay close attention to achieving internal consistency between the various components of its architecture. Let us look at how structure and control systems might be inconsistent with each other. Figure 13.2 shows an organizational chart for how Unilever's European operations might have been structured following its mid-1990s reorganization (this chart is hypothetical). Note that there are several country subsidiaries, one for France, one for Germany, one for Spain, and so on, each reporting to the European Business Group. There are also several pan-European product divisions, one for detergents, one for frozen food, one for margarine, and so on, again each reporting to the European Business Group. Within this structure, responsibility for marketing, sales, and distribution decisions might be given to the country subsidiaries, while responsibility for product manufacturing might be given to the product divisions. As for control systems, imagine that profitability is the metric used to evaluate the performance of the country subsidiaries.

One problem with this set of arrangements is that the profitability of the country subsidiaries depends on manufacturing costs and new-product development, and yet the managers running the various country subsidiaries are not responsible for those important functions—responsibility resides in the product divisions! Thus, if the managers of the product divisions do not do their job properly, production costs may rise and the profitability of the country subsidiaries might fall. In other words, the managers of the country subsidiaries are being evaluated according to a metric over which they do not have total control. If the performance of a subsidiary declines, they may argue that this is not their fault; it was due to the inability of the managers in the pan-European product divisions to drive down manufacturing costs. Thus, there is a potential conflict between structure and the control systems used; they are potentially inconsistent.

FIGURE 13.2

Fictional Organizational
Structure at Unilever

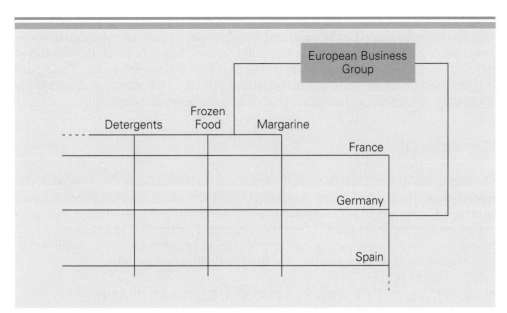

Some inconsistency is a fact of life in organizations. Perfection in the design of organization architecture is very difficult to achieve. Nevertheless, the inconsistency between different components of an organization's architecture can be minimized through intelligent design. In the example just given, if the performance of each product division were assessed on the basis of manufacturing costs, it would give the managers of the product division the incentive to optimize manufacturing efficiency. The problem might be further alleviated if the heads of both the country subsidiaries and the European product divisions were rewarded according to the profitability of the *entire* European Business Group (for example, by having their bonus pay linked to the profitability of the entire group). This would give the heads of the divisions a further reason to reduce manufacturing costs, and it would create an incentive for the heads of each subsidiary and division to share any best practices developed in their operation with colleagues across Europe to the betterment of the entire European Business Group.

Internal consistency is a necessary but not a sufficient condition for high performance. Consistency between architecture and the strategy of the organization is also required; architecture must fit strategy. When Unilever began to emphasize cost reduction as a major strategic goal, the firm had to change its architecture to match this new strategic reality. It had to move away from a structure based primarily on stand-alone national operating subsidiaries in each country and toward one based more on regional and global units. That structure was necessary to push through Unilever's plans to reduce operating costs, close factories, consolidate production in fewer, more efficient facilities, and reduce the number of brands from 1,600 to 400.

Change, such as that implemented by Unilever, is much easier said than done. It is relatively easy for senior managers to announce a radical change in strategy, but it is much harder to actually put that change into action. Doing so requires a change in architecture. Strategy is implemented through architecture, and changing architecture is much more difficult than announcing a change in strategy. We shall discuss why it is hard to change architecture later in this chapter. As we shall see, a prime reason is that organizations tend to be relative inert; they are by nature difficult to change.

Even with internal consistency and a fit between strategy and architecture, high performance is not guaranteed. The firm must also ensure that the fusion between its strategy and architecture is consistent with the competitive demands of the market, or markets, in which the firm competes. In the 1980s Unilever had a good fit between its strategy and architecture—it was pursuing a localization strategy. A decentralized architecture composed of self-contained country subsidiaries was well suited to implementing this strategy. However, by the 1990s the strategy no longer made much sense due to a change in the competitive environment. Trade barriers between nations had fallen and more efficient global competitors were emerging. Unilever's strategy no longer fit the environment in which it competed, so it had to change both its strategy and its architecture to match the new reality. This type of organizational challenge is not unusual; markets rarely stand still, and firms often have to adjust their strategy and architecture to match new competitive realities.

Organizational Structure

Organizational structure can be thought of in terms of three dimensions: (1) **vertical differentiation,** which refers to the location of decision-making responsibilities within a structure; (2) **horizontal differentiation,** which refers to the formal division of the organization into subunits; and (3) the establishment of **integrating mechanisms,** which are mechanisms for coordinating subunits. We begin by discussing vertical differentiation, then horizontal differentiation, and then integrating mechanisms.

VERTICAL DIFFERENTIATION: CENTRALIZATION AND DECENTRALIZATION

A firm's vertical differentiation determines where in its hierarchy the decision-making power is concentrated.[4] Are production and marketing decisions centralized in the offices of upper-level managers, or are they decentralized to lower-level managers? Where does the responsibility for R&D decisions lie? Are important strategic and financial decisions pushed down to operating units, or are they concentrated in the hands of top management? And so on. There are arguments for centralization and other arguments for decentralization.

Arguments for Centralization

There are four main arguments for centralization. First, centralization can facilitate coordination. For example, consider a firm that has a component manufacturing operation in Taiwan and an assembly operation in Mexico. The activities of these two operations may need to be coordinated to ensure a smooth flow of products from the component operation to the assembly operation. This might be achieved by centralizing production scheduling at the firm's head office. Second, centralization can help ensure that decisions are consistent with organizational objectives. When decisions are decentralized to lower-level managers, those managers may make decisions at variance with top management's goals. Centralization of important decisions minimizes the chance of this occurring.

Third, by concentrating power and authority in one individual or a management team, centralization can give top-level managers the means to bring about needed major organizational changes. Fourth, centralization can avoid the duplication of activities that occurs when similar activities are carried on by various subunits within the organization. For example, many international firms centralize their R&D functions at one or two locations to ensure that R&D work is not duplicated. Production activities may be centralized at key locations for the same reason.

Arguments for Decentralization

There are five main arguments for decentralization. First, top management can become overburdened when decision-making authority is centralized, and this can result in poor decisions. Decentralization gives top management time to focus on critical issues by delegating more routine issues to lower-level managers. Second, motivational research favors decentralization. Behavioral scientists have long argued that people are willing to give more to their jobs when they have a greater degree of individual freedom and control over their work. Third, decentralization permits greater flexibility—more rapid response to environmental changes—because decisions do not have to be "referred up the hierarchy" unless they are exceptional in nature. Fourth, decentralization can result in better decisions. In a decentralized structure, decisions are made closer to the spot by individuals who (presumably) have better information than managers several levels up in a hierarchy (for an example of decentralization to achieve this goal, see the Management Focus on Wal-Mart's international division). Fifth, decentralization can increase control. Decentralization can be used to establish relatively autonomous, self-contained subunits within an organization. Subunit managers can then be held accountable for subunit performance. The more responsibility subunit managers have for decisions that impact subunit performance, the fewer excuses they have for poor performance.

Strategy and Centralization in an International Business

The choice between centralization and decentralization is not absolute. Frequently it makes sense to centralize some decisions and to decentralize others, depending on the type of decision and the firm's strategy. Decisions regarding overall firm strategy, major financial expenditures, financial objectives, and legal issues are typically centralized at the firm's headquarters. However, operating decisions, such as those relating to production, marketing, R&D, and human resource management, may or may not be centralized depending on the firm's strategy.

Consider firms pursuing a global standardization strategy. They must decide how to disperse the various value creation activities around the globe so location and experience economies can be realized. The head office must make the decisions about where to locate R&D, production, marketing, and so on. In addition, the globally dispersed web of value creation activities that facilitates a global strategy must be coordinated. All of this creates pressures for centralizing some operating decisions.

In contrast, the emphasis on local responsiveness in firms pursuing a localization strategy creates strong pressures for decentralizing operating decisions to foreign subsidiaries. Firms pursuing an international strategy also tend to maintain centralized control over their core competency and to decentralize other decisions to foreign subsidiaries. Typically, such firms centralize control over R&D in their home country, but decentralize operating decisions to foreign subsidiaries. For example, Microsoft Corporation, which fits the international mode, centralizes its product development activities (where its core competencies lie) at its Redmond, Washington, headquarters and decentralizes marketing activity to various foreign subsidiaries. Thus, while products are developed at home, managers in the various foreign subsidiaries have significant latitude for formulating strategies to market those products in their particular settings.[5]

The situation in firms pursuing a transnational strategy is more complex. The need to realize location and experience curve economies requires some degree of centralized control over global production centers. However, the need for local responsiveness dictates the decentralization of many operating decisions, particularly for marketing, to foreign subsidiaries. Thus, in firms pursuing a transnational strategy, some operating decisions are relatively centralized, while others are relatively decentralized. In addition, global learning based on the multidirectional transfer of skills between subsidiaries, and between subsidiaries and the corporate center, is a central feature of a firm pursuing a transnational strategy. The concept of global learning is predicated on the notion that foreign subsidiaries within a multinational firm have significant freedom to develop their own skills and competencies. Only then can these be leveraged to benefit other parts of the organization. A substantial degree of decentralization is required if subsidiaries are going to have the freedom to do this. For this reason too, the pursuit of a transnational strategy requires a high degree of decentralization.[6]

HORIZONTAL DIFFERENTIATION: THE DESIGN OF STRUCTURE

Horizontal differentiation is concerned with how the firm decides to divide itself into subunits.[7] The decision is normally made on the basis of function, type of business, or geographical area. In many firms, just one of these predominates, but more complex solutions

FIGURE 13.3

A Typical Functional Structure

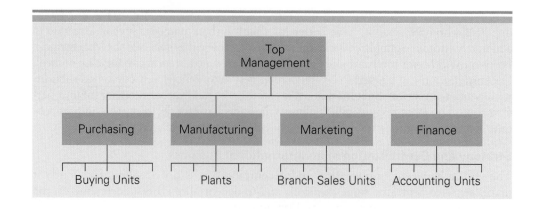

are adopted in others. This is particularly likely in the case of multinational firms, where the conflicting demands to organize the company around different products (to realize location and experience curve economies) and different national markets (to remain locally responsive) must be reconciled.

The Structure of Domestic Firms

Most firms begin with no formal structure and are run by a single entrepreneur or a small team of individuals. As they grow, the demands of management become too great for one individual or a small team to handle. At this point the organization is split into functions reflecting the firm's value creation activities (e.g., production, marketing, R&D, sales). These functions are typically coordinated and controlled by top management (see Figure 13.3). Decision making in this functional structure tends to be centralized.

Further horizontal differentiation may be required if the firm significantly diversifies its product offering, which takes the firm into different business areas. For example, Dutch multinational Philips NV began as a lighting company, but diversification took the company into consumer electronics (e.g., visual and audio equipment), industrial electronics (integrated circuits and other electronic components), and medical systems (MRI scanners and ultrasound systems). In such circumstances, a functional structure can be too clumsy. Problems of coordination and control arise when different business areas are managed within the framework of a functional structure.[8] For one thing, it becomes difficult to identify the profitability of each distinct business area. For another, it is difficult to run a functional department, such as production or marketing, if it is supervising the value creation activities of several business areas.

To solve the problems of coordination and control, at this stage most firms switch to a product divisional structure (see Figure 13.4). With a product divisional structure, each division is responsible for a distinct product line (business area). Thus, Philips created divisions for lighting, consumer electronics, industrial electronics, and medical systems. Each product division is set up as a self-contained, largely autonomous entity with its own functions. The responsibility for operating decisions is typically decentralized to product divisions, which are then held accountable for their performance. Headquarters is responsible for the overall strategic development of the firm and for the financial control of the various divisions.

The International Division

When firms initially expand abroad, they often group all their international activities into an **international division.** This has tended to be the case for firms organized on the basis of functions and for firms organized on the basis of product divisions. Regardless of the firm's domestic structure, its international division tends to be organized on geography. Figure 13.5 illustrates this for a firm whose domestic organization is based on product divisions.

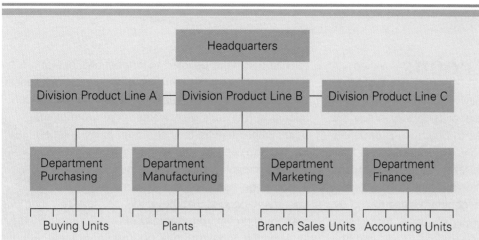

FIGURE 13.4

A Typical Product Divisional Structure

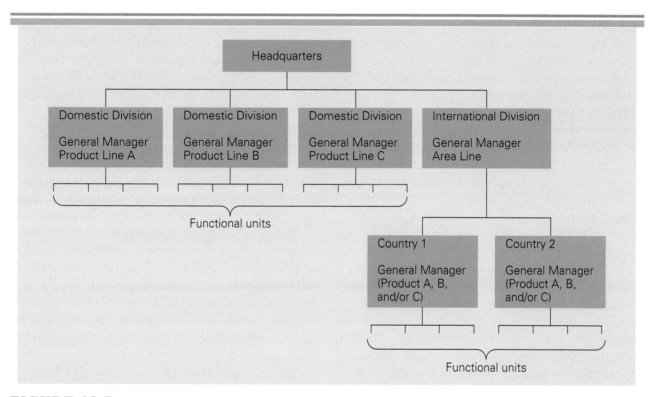

FIGURE 13.5

One Company's International Divisional Structure

Many manufacturing firms expanded internationally by exporting the product manufactured at home to foreign subsidiaries to sell. Thus, in the firm illustrated in Figure 13.5, the subsidiaries in countries 1 and 2 would sell the products manufactured by divisions A, B, and C. In time, however, it might prove viable to manufacture the product in each country, and so production facilities would be added on a country-by-country basis. For firms with a functional structure at home, this might mean replicating the functional structure in every country in which the firm does business. For firms with a divisional structure, this might mean replicating the divisional structure in every country in which the firm does business.

MANAGEMENT FOCUS

When Wal-Mart started to expand internationally in the early 1990s, it decided to set up an international division to oversee the process (see the opening case to Chapter 12 for details of Wal-Mart's global expansion). The International Division was based in Bentonville, Arkansas, at the company headquarters. Today the division oversees operations in nine countries that collectively generate close to $50 billion in sales. In terms of reporting structure, the division is divided into three regions—Europe, Asia, and the Americas, with the CEO of each region reporting to the CEO of the International Division, who in turn reports to the CEO of Wal-Mart.

Initially, the senior management of the International Division exerted tight centralized control over merchandising strategy and operations in different countries. The reasoning was straightforward; Wal-Mart's managers wanted to make sure that international stores copied the format for stores, merchandising, and operations that had served the company so well in the United States. They believed, naively perhaps, that centralized control over merchandising strategy and operations was the way to make sure this was the case.

By the late 1990s, with the international division approaching $20 billion in sales, Wal-Mart's managers concluded that this centralized approach was not serving them well. Country managers had to get permission from their superiors in Bentonville before changing strategy and operations, and this was slowing decision making. Centralization also produced information overload at the headquarters, and led to some poor decisions. Wal-Mart found that managers in Bentonville were not necessarily the best ones to decide on store layout in Mexico, merchandising strategy in Argentina, or compensation policy in the United Kingdom. The need to adapt merchandising strategy and operations to local conditions argued strongly for greater decentralization.

The pivotal event that led to a change in policy at Wal-Mart was the company's 1999 acquisition of Britain's ASDA supermarket chain. The ASDA acquisition added a mature and successful $14 billion operation to Wal-Mart's international division. The company realized that it was not appropriate for managers in Bentonville to be making all important decisions for ASDA. Accordingly, over the next few months, John Menzer, CEO of the International Division, reduced the number of staff located in Bentonville that were devoted to international operations by 50 percent. Country leaders were given greater responsibility, especially in the area of merchandising and operations. In Menzer's own words, "We were at the point where it was time to break away a little bit. . . . You can't run the world from one place. The countries have to drive the business. . . . The change has sent a strong message [to country managers] that they no longer have to wait for approval from Bentonville."

Although Wal-Mart has now decentralized decisions within the International Division, it is still struggling to find the right formula for managing global procurement. Ideally, the company would like to centralize procurement in Bentonville so that it could use its enormous purchasing power to bargain down the prices it pays suppliers. As a practical matter, however, this has not been easy to attain given that the product mix in Wal-Mart stores has to be tailored to conditions prevailing in the local market. Currently, significant responsibility for procurement remains at the country and regional level. However, Wal-Mart would like to have a global procurement strategy such that it can negotiate on a global basis with key suppliers and can simultaneously introduce new merchandise into its stores around the world.

As merchandising and operating decisions have been decentralized, the International Division has increasingly taken on a new role—that of identifying best practices and transferring them between countries. For example, the division has developed a knowledge management system whereby stores in one country, let's say Argentina, can quickly communicate pictures of items, sales data, and ideas on how to market and promote products to stores in another country, such as South Korea. The division is also starting to move personnel between stores in different countries as a way of facilitating the flow of best practices across national borders. Finally, the division is at the cutting edge of moving Wal-Mart away from its U.S.-centric mentality, and showing the organization that ideas implemented in foreign operations might also be used to improve the efficiency and effectiveness of Wal-Mart's operations at home.

Sources: M. Troy, "Wal-Mart Braces for International Growth with Personnel Moves," *DSN Retailing Today,* February 9, 2004, pp. 5–7; "Division Heads Let Numbers Do the Talking," *DSN Retailing Today,* June 21, 2004, pp. 26–28; and "The Division That Defines the Future," *DSN Retailing Today,* June 2001, pp. 4–7.

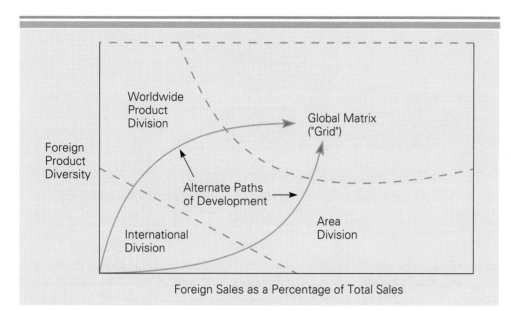

FIGURE 13.6

The International
Structural Stages Model

Source: Adapted from John
M. Stopford and Louis T. Wells,
Strategy and Structure of the Multi-national Enterprise (New York:
Basic Books, 1972).

This structure has been widely used; according to a Harvard study, 60 percent of all firms that have expanded internationally have initially adopted it. A good recent example of a company that uses this structure is Wal-Mart, which created an international division in 1991 to manage its global expansion (Wal-Mart's international division is profiled in the accompanying Management Focus). Despite its popularity, an international division structure can give rise to problems.[9] The dual structure it creates contains inherent potential for conflict and coordination problems between domestic and foreign operations. One problem with the structure is that the heads of foreign subsidiaries are not given as much voice in the organization as the heads of domestic functions (in the case of functional firms) or divisions (in the case of divisional firms). Rather, the head of the international division is presumed to be able to represent the interests of all countries to headquarters. This effectively relegates each country's manager to the second tier of the firm's hierarchy, which is inconsistent with a strategy of trying to expand internationally and build a true multinational organization.

Another problem is the implied lack of coordination between domestic operations and foreign operations, which are isolated from each other in separate parts of the structural hierarchy. This can inhibit the worldwide introduction of new products, the transfer of core competencies between domestic and foreign operations, and the consolidation of global production at key locations so as to realize location and experience curve economies.

As a result of such problems, many firms that continue to expand internationally abandon this structure and adopt one of the worldwide structures we discuss next. The two initial choices are a worldwide product divisional structure, which tends to be adopted by diversified firms that have domestic product divisions, and a worldwide area structure, which tends to be adopted by undiversified firms whose domestic structures are based on functions. These two alternative paths of development are illustrated in Figure 13.6. The model in the figure is referred to as the international structural stages model and was developed by John Stopford and Louis Wells.[10]

Worldwide Area Structure

A **worldwide area structure** tends to be favored by firms with a low degree of diversification and a domestic structure based on functions (see Figure 13.7). Under this structure, the world is divided into geographic areas. An area may be a country (if the market is large enough) or a group of countries. Each area tends to be a self-contained, largely

FIGURE 13.7

A Worldwide Area
Structure

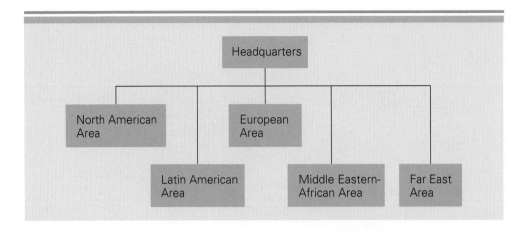

autonomous entity with its own set of value creation activities (e.g., its own production, marketing, R&D, human resources, and finance functions). Operations authority and strategic decisions relating to each of these activities are typically decentralized to each area, with headquarters retaining authority for the overall strategic direction of the firm and financial control.

This structure facilitates local responsiveness. Because decision-making responsibilities are decentralized, each area can customize product offerings, marketing strategy, and business strategy to the local conditions. However, this structure encourages fragmentation of the organization into highly autonomous entities. This can make it difficult to transfer core competencies and skills between areas and to realize location and experience curve economies. In other words, the structure is consistent with a localization strategy, but may make it difficult to realize gains associated with global standardization. Firms structured on this basis may encounter significant problems if local responsiveness is less critical than reducing costs or transferring core competencies for establishing a competitive advantage.

Worldwide Product Divisional Structure

A **worldwide product division structure** tends to be adopted by firms that are reasonably diversified and, accordingly, originally had domestic structures based on product divisions. As with the domestic product divisional structure, each division is a self-contained, largely autonomous entity with full responsibility for its own value creation activities. The headquarters retains responsibility for the overall strategic development and financial control of the firm (see Figure 13.8).

Underpinning the organization is a belief that the value creation activities of each product division should be coordinated by that division worldwide. Thus, the worldwide product divisional structure is designed to help overcome the coordination problems that arise with the international division and worldwide area structures. This structure provides an organizational context that enhances the consolidation of value creation activities at key locations necessary for realizing location and experience curve economies. It also facilitates the transfer of core competencies within a division's worldwide operations and the simultaneous worldwide introduction of new products. The main problem with the structure is the limited voice it gives to area or country managers, since they are seen as subservient to product division managers. The result can be a lack of local responsiveness, which, as we saw in Chapter 12, can lead to performance problems.

Global Matrix Structure

Both the worldwide area structure and the worldwide product divisional structure have strengths and weaknesses. The worldwide area structure facilitates local responsiveness, but it can inhibit the realization of location and experience curve economies and the

FIGURE 13.8

A Worldwide Product
Divisional Structure

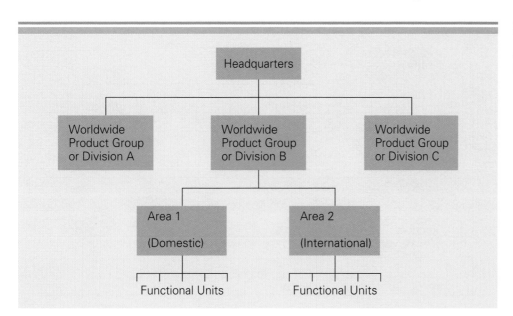

transfer of core competencies between areas. The worldwide product division structure provides a better framework for pursuing location and experience curve economies and for transferring core competencies, but it is weak in local responsiveness. Other things being equal, this suggests that a worldwide area structure is more appropriate if the firm is pursuing a localization strategy, while a worldwide product divisional structure is more appropriate for firms pursuing global standardization or international strategies. However, as we saw in Chapter 12, other things are not equal. As Bartlett and Ghoshal have argued, to survive in some industries, firms must adopt a transnational strategy. That is, they must focus simultaneously on realizing location and experience curve economies, on local responsiveness, and on the internal transfer of core competencies (worldwide learning).[11]

Some firms have attempted to cope with the conflicting demands of a transnational strategy by using a matrix structure. In the classic **global matrix structure,** horizontal differentiation proceeds along two dimensions: product division and geographic area (see Figure 13.9). The philosophy is that responsibility for operating decisions pertaining to a particular product should be shared by the product division and the various areas of the firm. Thus, the nature of the product offering, the marketing strategy, and the business strategy to be pursued in area 1 for the products produced by division A are determined by conciliation between division A and area 1 management. It is believed that this dual decision-making responsibility should enable the firm to simultaneously achieve its particular objectives. In a classic matrix structure, giving product divisions and geographical areas equal status within the organization reinforces the idea of dual responsibility. Individual managers thus belong to two hierarchies (a divisional hierarchy and an area hierarchy) and have two bosses (a divisional boss and an area boss).

The reality of the global matrix structure is that it often does not work as well as the theory predicts. In practice, the matrix often is clumsy and bureaucratic. It can require so many meetings that it is difficult to get any work done. The need to get an area and a product division to reach a decision can slow decision making and produce an inflexible organization unable to respond quickly to market shifts or to innovate. The dual-hierarchy structure can lead to conflict and perpetual power struggles between the areas and the product divisions, catching many managers in the middle. To make matters worse, it can prove difficult to ascertain accountability in this structure. When all critical decisions are the product of negotiation between divisions and areas, one side can always blame the other when things go wrong. As a manager in one global matrix

FIGURE 13.9

A Global Matrix
Structure

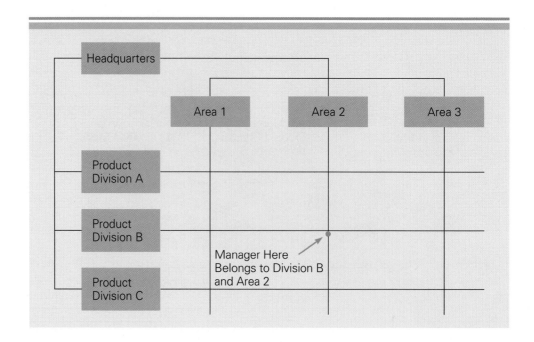

structure, reflecting on a failed product launch, said to the author, "Had we been able to do things our way, instead of having to accommodate those guys from the product division, this would never have happened." (A manager in the product division expressed similar sentiments.) The result of such finger-pointing can be that accountability is compromised, conflict is enhanced, and headquarters loses control over the organization. (See the Management Focus on Dow Chemical for an example of the problems associated with a matrix structure.)

In light of these problems, many firms that pursue a transnational strategy have tried to build "flexible" matrix structures based more on enterprisewide management knowledge networks, and a shared culture and vision, than on a rigid hierarchical arrangement. Within such companies the informal structure plays a greater role than the formal structure. We discuss this issue when we consider informal integrating mechanisms in the next section.

INTEGRATING MECHANISMS

In the previous section, we explained that firms divide themselves into subunits. Now we need to examine some means of coordinating those subunits. One way of achieving coordination is through centralization. If the coordination task is complex, however, centralization may not be very effective. Higher-level managers responsible for achieving coordination can soon become overwhelmed by the volume of work required to coordinate the activities of various subunits, particularly if the subunits are large, diverse, and/or geographically dispersed. When this is the case, firms look toward integrating mechanisms, both formal and informal, to help achieve coordination. In this section, we introduce the various integrating mechanisms that international businesses can use. Before doing so, however, let us explore the need for coordination in international firms and some impediments to coordination.

Strategy and Coordination in the International Business

The need for coordination between subunits varies with the strategy of the firm. The need for coordination is lowest in firms pursuing a localization strategy, is higher in international companies, higher still in global companies, and highest of all in transnational companies. Firms pursuing a localization strategy are primarily concerned with local responsiveness. Such firms are likely to operate with a worldwide area structure in which each area has considerable autonomy and its own set of value creation functions. Because each area is established as a stand-alone entity, the need for coordination between areas is minimized.

The need for coordination is greater in firms pursuing an international strategy and trying to profit from the transfer of core competencies and skills between units at home and abroad. Coordination is necessary to support the transfer of skills and product offerings between units. The need for coordination is also great in firms trying to profit from location and experience curve economies; that is, in firms pursuing global standardization strategies. Achieving location and experience economies involves dispersing value creation activities to various locations around the globe. The resulting global web of activities must be coordinated to ensure the smooth flow of inputs into the value chain, the smooth flow of semifinished products through the value chain, and the smooth flow of finished products to markets around the world.

The need for coordination is greatest in transnational firms, which simultaneously pursue location and experience curve economies, local responsiveness, and the multidirectional transfer of core competencies and skills among all of the firm's subunits (referred to as global learning). As with a global standardization strategy, coordination is required to ensure the smooth flow of products through the global value chain. As with an international strategy, coordination is required for ensuring the transfer of core competencies to subunits. However, the transnational goal of achieving multidirectional transfer of competencies requires much greater coordination than in firms pursuing an international strategy. In addition, a transnational strategy requires coordination between foreign subunits and the firm's globally dispersed value creation activities (e.g., production, R&D, marketing) to ensure that any product offering and marketing strategy is sufficiently customized to local conditions.

Impediments to Coordination

Managers of the various subunits have different orientations, partly because they have different tasks. For example, production managers are typically concerned with production issues such as capacity utilization, cost control, and quality control, whereas marketing managers are concerned with marketing issues such as pricing, promotions, distribution, and market share. These differences can inhibit communication between the managers. Quite simply, these managers often do not even "speak the same language." There may also be a lack of respect between subunits (e.g., marketing managers "looking down on" production managers, and vice versa), which further inhibits the communication required to achieve cooperation and coordination.

Differences in subunits' orientations also arise from their differing goals. For example, worldwide product divisions of a multinational firm may be committed to cost goals that require global production of a standardized product, whereas a foreign subsidiary may be committed to increasing its market share in its country, which will require a nonstandard product. These different goals can lead to conflict.

Such impediments to coordination are not unusual in any firm, but they can be particularly problematic in the multinational enterprise with its profusion of subunits at home and abroad. Differences in subunit orientation are often reinforced in multinationals by the separations of time zone, distance, and nationality between managers of the subunits.

For example, until recently the Dutch company Philips had an organization comprising worldwide product divisions and largely autonomous national organizations. The company has long had problems getting its product divisions and national organizations to cooperate on such things as new-product introductions. When Philips developed a VCR format, the V2000 system, it could not get its North American subsidiary to introduce the product. Rather, the North American unit adopted the rival VHS format pro-

MANAGEMENT FOCUS A handful of major players compete head-to-head around the world in the chemical industry. These companies are Dow Chemical and Du Pont of the United States, Great Britain's ICI, and the German trio of BASF, Hoechst AG, and Bayer. The barriers to the free flow of chemical products between nations largely disappeared in the 1970s. This along with the commodity nature of most bulk chemicals and a severe recession in the early 1980s ushered in a prolonged period of intense price competition. In such an environment, the company that wins the competitive race is the one with the lowest costs. Dow Chemicals was long among the cost leaders.

For years, Dow's managers insisted that part of the credit should be placed at the feet of its "matrix" organization. Dow's organizational matrix had three interacting elements: functions (e.g., R&D, manufacturing, marketing), businesses (e.g., ethylene, plastics, pharmaceuticals), and geography (e.g., Spain, Germany, Brazil). Managers' job titles incorporated all three elements—for example, plastics marketing manager for Spain—and most managers reported to at least two bosses. The plastics marketing manager in Spain might report to both the head of the worldwide plastics business and the head of the Spanish operations. The intent of the matrix was to make Dow operations responsive to both local market needs and corporate objectives. Thus, the plastics business might be charged with minimizing Dow's global plastics production costs, while the Spanish operation might be charged with determining how best to sell plastics in the Spanish market.

When Dow introduced this structure, the results were less than promising; multiple reporting channels led to confusion and conflict. The large number of bosses made for an unwieldy bureaucracy. The overlapping responsibilities resulted in turf battles and a lack of accountability. Area managers disagreed with managers overseeing business sectors about which plants should be built and where. In short, the structure didn't work. Instead of abandoning the structure, however, Dow decided to see if it could be made more flexible.

Dow's decision to keep its matrix structure was prompted by its move into the pharmaceuticals industry. The company realized that the pharmaceutical business is very different from the bulk chemicals business. In bulk chemicals, the big returns come from achieving economies of scale in production. This dictates establishing large plants in key locations from which regional or global markets can be served. But in pharmaceuticals, regulatory and marketing requirements for drugs vary so

duced by Philip's global competitor, Matsushita. Unilever experienced a similar problem in its detergents business. The need to resolve disputes between Unilever's many national organizations and its product divisions extended the time necessary for introducing a new product across Europe to several years. This denied Unilever the first-mover advantage crucial to building a strong market position.

Formal Integrating Mechanisms

The formal mechanisms used to integrate subunits vary in complexity from simple direct contact and liaison roles, to teams, to a matrix structure (see Figure 13.10). In general, the greater the need for coordination, the more complex the formal integrating mechanisms need to be.[12]

Direct contact between subunit managers is the simplest integrating mechanism. By this "mechanism," managers of the various subunits simply contact each other whenever they have a common concern. Direct contact may not be effective if the managers have differing orientations that act to impede coordination, as pointed out in the previous subsection.

Liaison roles are a bit more complex. When the volume of contacts between subunits increases, coordination can be improved by giving a person in each subunit responsibility for coordinating with another subunit on a regular basis. Through these roles, the peo-

much from country to country that local needs are far more important than reducing manufacturing costs through scale economies. A high degree of local responsiveness is essential. Dow realized its pharmaceutical business would never thrive if it were managed by the same priorities as its mainstream chemical operations.

Accordingly, instead of abandoning its matrix, Dow decided to make it more flexible so it could better accommodate the different businesses, each with its own priorities, within a single management system. A small team of senior executives at headquarters helped set the priorities for each type of business. After priorities were identified for each business sector, one of the three elements of the matrix—function, business, or geographic area—was given primary authority in decision making. Which element took the lead varied according to the type of decision and the market or location in which the company was competing. Such flexibility required that all employees understand what was occurring in the rest of the matrix. Although this may seem confusing, for years Dow claimed this flexible system worked well and credited much of its success to the quality of the decisions it facilitated

By the mid-1990s, however, Dow had refocused its business on the chemicals industry, divesting itself of its pharmaceutical activities where the company's performance had been unsatisfactory. Reflecting the change in corporate strategy, in 1995 Dow decided to abandon its matrix structure in favor of a more streamlined structure based on global business divisions. The change was also driven by realization that the matrix structure was just too complex and costly to manage in the intense competitive environment of the 1990s, particularly given the company's renewed focus on its commodity chemicals where competitive advantage often went to the low-cost producer. As Dow's then CEO put it in a 1999 interview, "We were an organization that was matrixed and depended on teamwork, but there was no one in charge. When things went well, we didn't know whom to reward; and when things went poorly, we didn't know whom to blame. So we created a global divisional structure, and cut out layers of management. There used to be 11 layers of management between me and the lowest level employees, now there are five." In short, Dow ultimately found that a matrix structure was unsuited to a company that was competing in very cost-competitive global industries, and it had to abandon its matrix to drive down operating costs.

Source: "Dow Draws Its Matrix Again, and Again, and Again," *The Economist,* August 5, 1989, pp. 55–56; "Dow Goes for Global Structure," *Chemical Marketing Reporter,* December 11, 1995, pp. 4–5; and R. M. Hodgetts, "Dow Chemical CEO William Stavropoulos on Structure and Decision Making," *Academy of Management Executive,* November 1999, pp. 29–35.

ple involved establish a permanent relationship. This helps attenuate the impediments to coordination discussed in the previous subsection.

When the need for coordination is greater still, firms tend to use temporary or permanent teams composed of individuals from the subunits that need to achieve coordination. They typically coordinate product development and introduction, but they are useful when any aspect of operations or strategy requires the cooperation of two or more subunits. Product development and introduction teams are typically composed of personnel from R&D, production, and marketing. The resulting coordination aids the development of products that are tailored to consumer needs and that can be produced at a reasonable cost (design for manufacturing).

When the need for integration is very high, firms may institute a matrix structure, in which all roles are viewed as integrating roles. The structure is designed to facilitate maximum integration among subunits. The most common matrix in multinational firms is based on geographical areas and worldwide product divisions. This achieves a high level of integration between the product divisions and the areas so that, in theory, the firm can pay close attention to both local responsiveness and the pursuit of location and experience curve economies.

In some multinationals, the matrix is more complex still, structuring the firm into geographical areas, worldwide product divisions, and functions, all of which report directly

FIGURE 13.10

Formal Integrating
Mechanisms

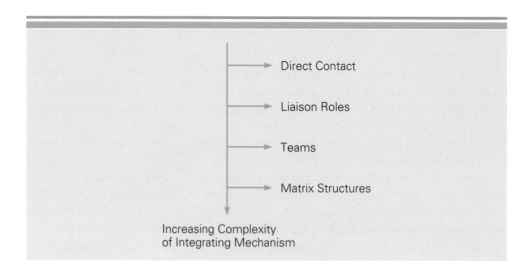

to headquarters. Thus, within a company such as Dow Chemical before it abandoned its matrix in the mid-1990s (see the Management Focus), each manager belonged to three hierarchies (e.g., a plastics marketing manager in Spain was a member of the Spanish subsidiary, the plastics product division, and the marketing function). In addition to facilitating local responsiveness and location and experience curve economies, such a matrix fosters the transfer of core competencies within the organization. This occurs because core competencies tend to reside in functions (e.g., R&D, marketing). A structure such as this in theory facilitates the transfer of competencies existing in functions from division to division and from area to area.

However, as discussed earlier, such matrix solutions to coordination problems in multinational enterprises can quickly become bogged down in a bureaucratic tangle that creates as many problems as it solves. Matrix structures tend to be bureaucratic, inflexible, and characterized by conflict rather than the hoped-for cooperation. For such a structure to work it needs to be somewhat flexible and to be supported by informal integrating mechanisms.[13]

Informal Integrating Mechanism: Knowledge Networks

In attempting to alleviate or avoid the problems associated with formal integrating mechanisms in general, and matrix structures in particular, firms with a high need for integration have been experimenting with an informal integrating mechanism: knowledge networks that are supported by an organization culture that values teamwork and cross-unit cooperation.[14] A **knowledge network** is a network for transmitting information within an organization that is based not on formal organization structure, but on informal contacts between managers within an enterprise and on distributed information systems.[15] The great strength of such a network is that it can be used as a nonbureaucratic conduit for knowledge flows within a multinational enterprise.[16] For a network to exist, managers at different locations within the organization must be linked to each other at least indirectly. For example, Figure 13.11 shows the simple network relationships between seven managers within a multinational firm. Managers A, B, and C all know each other personally, as do managers D, E, and F. Although manager B does not know manager F personally, they are linked through common acquaintances (managers C and D). Thus, we can say that managers A through F are all part of the network, and also that manager G is not.

Imagine manager B is a marketing manager in Spain and needs to know the solution to a technical problem to better serve an important European customer. Manager F, an R&D manager in the United States, has the solution to manager B's problem. Manager

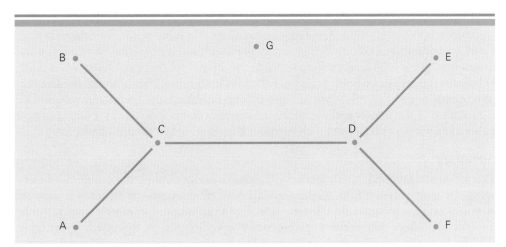

FIGURE 13.11

A Simple Management Network

B mentions her problem to all of her contacts, including manager C, and asks if they know of anyone who might be able to provide a solution. Manager C asks manager D, who tells manager F, who then calls manager B with the solution. In this way, coordination is achieved informally through the network, rather than by formal integrating mechanisms such as teams or a matrix structure.

For such a network to function effectively, however, it must embrace as many managers as possible. For example, if manager G had a problem similar to manager B's, he would not be able to utilize the informal network to find a solution; he would have to resort to more formal mechanisms. Establishing firmwide knowledge networks is difficult, and although network enthusiasts speak of networks as the "glue" that binds multinational companies together, it is far from clear how successful firms have been at building companywide networks. Two techniques being used to establish networks are information systems and management development policies.

Firms are using their distributed computer and telecommunications information systems to provide the foundation for informal knowledge networks.[17] Electronic mail, videoconferencing, high-bandwidth data systems, and Web-based search engines make it much easier for managers scattered over the globe to get to know each other, to identify contacts that might help to solve a particular problem, and to publicize and share best practices within the organization. Wal-Mart, for example, now uses its intranet system to communicate ideas about merchandising strategy between stores located in different countries.

Firms are also using their management development programs to build informal networks. Tactics include rotating managers through various subunits on a regular basis so they build their own informal network and using management education programs to bring managers of subunits together in a single location so they can become acquainted.

Knowledge networks by themselves may not be sufficient to achieve coordination if subunit managers persist in pursuing subgoals that are at variance with firmwide goals. For a knowledge network to function properly—and for a formal matrix structure to work also—managers must share a strong commitment to the same goals. To appreciate the nature of the problem, consider again the case of manager B and manager F. As before, manager F hears about manager B's problem through the network. However, solving manager B's problem would require manager F to devote considerable time to the task. Insofar as this would divert manager F away from his own regular tasks—and the pursuit of subgoals that differ from those of manager B—he may be unwilling to do it. Thus, manager F may not call manager B, and the informal network would fail to provide a solution to manager B's problem.

To eliminate this flaw, organization's managers must adhere to a common set of norms and values that override differing subunit orientations.[18] In other words, the firm must have a strong organizational culture that promotes teamwork and cooperation. When this is the case, a manager is willing and able to set aside the interests of his own subunit when doing so benefits the firm as a whole. If manager B and manager F are committed to the same organizational norms and value systems, and if these organizational norms and values place the interests of the firm as a whole above the interests of any individual subunit, manager F should be willing to cooperate with manager B on solving her subunit's problems.

Summary

The message contained in this section is crucial to understanding the problems of managing the multinational firm. Multinationals need integration—particularly if they are pursuing global standardization, international, or transnational strategies—but it can be difficult to achieve due to the impediments to coordination we discussed. Firms traditionally have tried to achieve coordination by adopting formal integrating mechanisms. These do not always work, however, since they tend to be bureaucratic and do not necessarily address the problems that arise from differing subunit orientations. This is particularly likely with a complex matrix structure, and yet, a complex matrix structure is required for simultaneously achieving location and experience curve economies, local responsiveness, and the multidirectional transfer of core competencies within the organization. The solution to this dilemma seems twofold. First, the firm must try to establish an informal knowledge network that can do much of the work previously undertaken by a formal matrix structure. Second, the firm must build a common culture. Neither of these partial solutions, however, is easy to achieve.[19]

Control Systems and Incentives

A major task of a firm's leadership is to control the various subunits of the firm—whether they be defined on the basis of function, product division, or geographic area—to ensure their actions are consistent with the firm's overall strategic and financial objectives. Firms achieve this with various control and incentive systems. In this section, we first review the various types of control systems firms use to control their subunits. Then we briefly discuss incentive systems. Then we will look at how the appropriate control and incentive systems vary according to the strategy of the multinational enterprise.

TYPES OF CONTROL SYSTEMS

Four main types of control systems are used in multinational firms: personal controls, bureaucratic controls, output controls, and cultural controls. In most firms, all four are used, but their relative emphasis varies with the strategy of the firm.

Personal Controls

Personal control is control by personal contact with subordinates. This type of control tends to be most widely used in small firms, where it is seen in the direct supervision of subordinates' actions. However, it also structures the relationships between managers at different levels in multinational enterprises. For example, the CEO may use a great deal of personal control to influence the behavior of his or her immediate subordinates, such as the heads of worldwide product divisions or major geographic areas. In turn, these heads may use personal control to influence the behavior of their subordinates, and so on down through the organization. Jack Welch, the longtime CEO of General Electric who retired in 2001, had regular one-on-one meetings with the heads of all of GE's major businesses (most of which are international).[20] He used these meetings to probe the managers about the strategy, structure, and financial performance of their operations. In doing so, he essentially exercised personal control over these managers and, undoubtedly, over the strategies that they favored.

Bureaucratic Controls

Bureaucratic control is control through a system of rules and procedures that directs the actions of subunits. The most important bureaucratic controls in subunits within multinational firms are budgets and capital spending rules. Budgets are essentially a set of rules for allocating a firm's financial resources. A subunit's budget specifies with some precision how much the subunit may spend. Headquarters uses budgets to influence the behavior of subunits. For example, the R&D budget normally specifies how much cash the R&D unit may spend on product development. R&D managers know that if they spend too much on one project, they will have less to spend on other projects, so they modify their behavior to stay within the budget. Most budgets are set by negotiation between headquarters management and subunit management. Headquarters management can encourage the growth of certain subunits and restrict the growth of others by manipulating their budgets.

Capital spending rules require headquarters management to approve any capital expenditure by a subunit that exceeds a certain amount. A budget allows headquarters to specify the amount a subunit can spend in a given year, and capital spending rules give headquarters additional control over how the money is spent. Headquarters can be expected to deny approval for capital spending requests that are at variance with overall firm objectives and to approve those that are congruent with firm objectives.

Output Controls

Output controls involve setting goals for subunits to achieve and expressing those goals in terms of relatively objective performance metrics such as profitability, productivity, growth, market share, and quality. The performance of subunit managers is then judged by their ability to achieve the goals.[21] If goals are met or exceeded, subunit managers will be rewarded. If goals are not met, top management will normally intervene to find out why and take appropriate corrective action. Thus, control is achieved by comparing actual performance against targets and intervening selectively to take corrective action. Subunits' goals depend on their role in the firm. Self-contained product divisions or national subsidiaries are typically given goals for profitability, sales growth, and market share. Functions are more likely to be given goals related to their particular activity. Thus, R&D will be given product development goals, production will be given productivity and quality goals, marketing will be given market share goals, and so on.

As with budgets, goals are normally established through negotiation between subunits and headquarters. Generally, headquarters tries to set goals that are challenging but realistic, so subunit managers are forced to look for ways to improve their operations but are not so pressured that they will resort to dysfunctional activities to do so (such as short-run profit maximization). Output controls foster a system of "management by exception," in that so long as subunits meet their goals, they are left alone. If a subunit fails to attain its goals, however, headquarters managers are likely to ask some tough questions. If they don't get satisfactory answers, they are likely to intervene proactively in a subunit, replacing top management and looking for ways to improve efficiency.

Cultural Controls

Cultural controls exist when employees "buy into" the norms and value systems of the firm. When this occurs, employees tend to control their own behavior, which reduces the need for direct supervision. In a firm with a strong culture, self-control can reduce the need for other control systems. We shall discuss organizational culture later. McDonald's actively promotes organizational norms and values, referring to its franchisees and suppliers as partners and emphasizing its long-term commitment to them. This commitment is not just a public relations exercise; it is backed by actions, including a willingness to help suppliers and franchisees improve their operations by providing capital and/or management assistance when needed. In response, McDonald's franchisees and suppliers are integrated into the firm's culture and thus become committed to helping McDonald's succeed. One result is that McDonald's can devote less time than would otherwise be necessary to controlling its franchisees and suppliers.

INCENTIVE SYSTEMS

Incentives refer to the devices used to reward appropriate employee behavior. Many employees receive incentives in the form of annual bonus pay. Incentives are usually closely tied to the performance metrics used for output controls. For example, setting targets linked to profitability might be used to measure the performance of a subunit, such as a global product division. To create positive incentives for employees to work hard to exceed those targets, they may be given a share of any profits above those targeted. If a subunit has set a goal of attaining a 15 percent return on investment and it actually attains a 20 percent return, unit employees may be given a share in the profits generated in excess of the 15 percent target in the form of bonus pay. We shall return to the topic of incentive systems in Chapter 18 when we discuss human resource strategy in the multinational firm. For now, however, several important points need to be made. First, the type of incentive used often varies depending on the employees and their tasks. Incentives for employees working on the factory floor may be very different from the incentives used for senior managers. The incentives used must be matched to the type of work being performed. The employees on the factory floor of a manufacturing plant may be broken into teams of 20 to 30 individuals, and they may have their bonus pay tied to the ability of their team to hit or exceed targets for output and product quality. In contrast, the senior managers of the plant may be rewarded according to metrics linked to the output of the entire operation. The basic principle is to make sure the incentive scheme for an individual employee is linked to an output target that he or she has some control over and can influence. The individual employees on the factory floor may not be able to exercise much influence over the performance of the entire operation, but they can influence the performance of their team, so incentive pay is tied to output at this level.

Second, the successful execution of strategy in the multinational firm often requires significant cooperation between managers in different subunits. For example, as noted earlier, some multinational firms operate with matrix structures where a country subsidiary might be responsible for marketing and sales in a nation, while a global product division might be responsible for manufacturing and product development. The managers of these different units need to cooperate closely with each other if the firm is to be successful. One way of encouraging the managers to cooperate is to link incentives to performance at a higher level in the organization. Thus, the senior managers of the country subsidiaries and global product divisions might be rewarded according to the profitability of the entire firm. The thinking here is that boosting the profitability of the entire firm requires managers in the country subsidiaries and product divisions to cooperate with each other on strategy implementation, and linking incentive systems to the next level up in the hierarchy encourages this. Most firms use a formula for incentives that links a portion of incentive pay to the performance of the subunit in which a manager or employee works and a portion to the performance of the entire firm, or some other higher-level organizational unit. The goal is to encourage employees to improve the efficiency of their unit and to cooperate with other units in the organization.

Third, the incentive systems used within a multinational enterprise often have to be adjusted to account for national differences in institutions and culture. Incentive systems that work in the United States might not work, or even be allowed, in other countries. For example, Lincoln Electric, a leader in the manufacture of arc welding equipment, has used an incentive system for its employees based on piecework rates in its American factories (under a piecework system, employees are paid according to the amount they produce). While this system has worked very well in the United States, Lincoln has found that the system is difficult to introduce in other countries. In some countries, such as Germany, piecework systems are illegal, while in others the prevailing national culture is antagonistic to a system where performance is so closely tied to individual effort. For further details, see the accompanying Management Focus.

MANAGEMENT FOCUS

Lincoln Electric is one of the leading companies in the global market for arc welding equipment. Lincoln's success has been based on extremely high levels of employee productivity. The company attributes its productivity to a strong organizational culture and an incentive scheme based on piecework. Lincoln's organizational culture dates back to James Lincoln, who in 1907 joined the company that his brother had established a few years earlier. Lincoln had a strong respect for the ability of the individual and believed that, correctly motivated, ordinary people could achieve extraordinary performance. He emphasized that Lincoln should be a meritocracy where people were rewarded for their individual effort. Strongly egalitarian, Lincoln removed barriers to communication between "workers" and "managers," practicing an open-door policy. He made sure that all who worked for the company were treated equally; for example, everyone ate in the same cafeteria, there were no reserved parking places for "managers," and so on. Lincoln also believed that any gains in productivity should be shared with consumers in the form of lower prices, with employees in the form of higher pay, and with shareholders in the form of higher dividends.

The organizational culture that grew out of James Lincoln's beliefs was reinforced by the company's incentive system. Production workers receive no base salary but are paid according to the number of pieces they produce. The piecework rates at the company enable an employee working at a normal pace to earn an income equivalent to the average wage for manufacturing workers in the area where a factory is based. Workers have responsibility for the quality of their output and must repair any defects spotted by quality inspectors before the pieces are included in the piecework calculation. Since 1934, production workers have been awarded a semiannual bonus based on merit ratings. These ratings are based on objective criteria (such as an employee's level and quality of output) and subjective criteria (such as an employee's attitudes toward cooperation and his or her dependability). These systems give Lincoln's employees an incentive to work hard and to generate innovations that boost productivity, for doing so influences their level of pay. Lincoln's factory workers have been able to earn a base pay that often exceeds the average manufacturing wage in the area by more than 50 percent and receive a bonus on top of this that in good years could double their base pay. Despite high employee compensation, the workers are so productive that Lincoln has a lower cost structure than its competitors.

While this organizational culture and set of incentives works well in the United States, where it is compatible with the individualistic culture of the country, it did not translate easily into foreign operations. In the 1980s and early 1990s, Lincoln expanded aggressively into Europe and Latin America, acquiring a number of local arc welding manufacturers. Lincoln left local managers in place, believing that they knew local conditions better than Americans. However, the local managers had little working knowledge of Lincoln's strong organizational culture and were unable or unwilling to impose that culture on their units, which had their own long-established organizational cultures. Nevertheless, Lincoln told local managers to introduce its incentive systems in acquired companies. They frequently ran into legal and cultural roadblocks.

In many countries, piecework is viewed as an exploitive compensation system that forces employees to work ever harder. In Germany, where Lincoln made an acquisition, it is illegal. In Brazil, a bonus paid for more than two years becomes a legal entitlement! In many other countries, both managers and workers were opposed to the idea of piecework. Lincoln found that many European workers valued extra leisure more highly than extra income and were not prepared to work as hard as their American counterparts. Many of the acquired companies were also unionized, and the local unions vigorously opposed the introduction of piecework. As a result, Lincoln was not able to replicate the high level of employee productivity that it had achieved in the United States, and its expansion pulled down the performance of the entire company.

Sources: J. O'Connell, "Lincoln Electric: Venturing Abroad," Harvard Business School Case No. 9-398-095, April 1998, and www.lincolnelectric.com.

www.mhhe.com/hill

461

Finally, it is important for managers to recognize that incentive systems can have unintended consequences. Managers need to carefully think through exactly what behavior certain incentives encourage. For example, if employees in a factory are rewarded solely on the basis of how many units of output they produce, with no attention paid to the quality of that output, they may produce as many units as possible to boost their incentive pay, but the quality of those units may be poor.

CONTROL SYSTEMS, INCENTIVES, AND STRATEGY IN THE INTERNATIONAL BUSINESS

The key to understanding the relationship between international strategy, control systems, and incentive systems is the concept of performance ambiguity.

Performance Ambiguity

Performance ambiguity exists when the causes of a subunit's poor performance are not clear. This is not uncommon when a subunit's performance is partly dependent on the performance of other subunits; that is, when there is a high degree of interdependence between subunits within the organization. Consider the case of a French subsidiary of a U.S. firm that depends on another subsidiary, a manufacturer based in Italy, for the products it sells. The French subsidiary is failing to achieve its sales goals, and the U.S. management asks the managers to explain. They reply that they are receiving poor-quality goods from the Italian subsidiary. The U.S. management asks the managers of the Italian operation what the problem is. They reply that their product quality is excellent—the best in the industry, in fact—and that the French simply don't know how to sell a good product. Who is right, the French or the Italians? Without more information, top management cannot tell. Because they are dependent on the Italians for their product, the French have an alibi for poor performance. U.S. management needs to have more information to determine who is correct. Collecting this information is expensive and time consuming and will divert attention away from other issues. In other words, performance ambiguity raises the costs of control.

Consider how different things would be if the French operation were self-contained, with its own manufacturing, marketing, and R&D facilities. The French operation would lack a convenient alibi for its poor performance; the French managers would stand or fall on their own merits. They could not blame the Italians for their poor sales. The level of performance ambiguity, therefore, is a function of the interdependence of subunits in an organization.

Strategy, Interdependence, and Ambiguity

Now let us consider the relationships between strategy, interdependence, and performance ambiguity. In firms pursuing a localization strategy, each national operation is a stand-alone entity and can be judged on its own merits. The level of performance ambiguity is low. In an international firm, the level of interdependence is somewhat higher. Integration is required to facilitate the transfer of core competencies and skills. Since the success of a foreign operation is partly dependent on the quality of the competency transferred from the home country, performance ambiguity can exist.

In firms pursuing a global standardization strategy, the situation is still more complex. Recall that in a pure global firm the pursuit of location and experience curve economies leads to the development of a global web of value creation activities. Many of the activities in a global firm are interdependent. A French subsidiary's ability to sell a product does depend on how well other operations in other countries perform their value creation activities. Thus, the levels of interdependence and performance ambiguity are high in global companies.

The level of performance ambiguity is highest of all in transnational firms. Transnational firms suffer from the same performance ambiguity problems that global firms do. In addition, since they emphasize the multidirectional transfer of core competencies, they also suffer from the problems characteristic of firms pursuing an international strategy.

Strategy	Interdependence	Performance Ambiguity	Costs of Control
Localization	Low	Low	Low
International	Moderate	Moderate	Moderate
Global	High	High	High
Transnational	Very High	Very High	Very High

TABLE 13.1

Interdependence, Performance Ambiguity, and the Costs of Control for the Four International Business Strategies

The extremely high level of integration within transnational firms implies a high degree of joint decision making, and the resulting interdependencies create plenty of alibis for poor performance. There is lots of room for finger-pointing in transnational firms.

Implications for Control and Incentives

The arguments of the previous section, along with the implications for the costs of control, are summarized in Table 13.1. The costs of control can be defined as the amount of time top management must devote to monitoring and evaluating subunits' performance. This is greater when the amount of performance ambiguity is greater. When performance ambiguity is low, management can use output controls and a system of management by exception; when it is high, managers have no such luxury. Output controls do not provide totally unambiguous signals of a subunit's efficiency when the performance of that subunit is dependent on the performance of another subunit within the organization. Thus, management must devote time to resolving the problems that arise from performance ambiguity, with a corresponding rise in the costs of control.

Table 13.1 reveals a paradox. We saw in Chapter 12 that a transnational strategy is desirable because it gives a firm more ways to profit from international expansion than do localization, international, and global standardization strategies. But now we see that due to the high level of interdependence, the costs of controlling transnational firms are higher than the costs of controlling firms that pursue other strategies. Unless there is some way of reducing these costs, the higher profitability associated with a transnational strategy could be canceled out by the higher costs of control. The same point, although to a lesser extent, can be made with regard to firms pursuing a global standardization strategy. Although firms pursuing a global standardization strategy can reap the cost benefits of location and experience curve economies, they must cope with a higher level of performance ambiguity, and this raises the costs of control (in comparison with firms pursuing an international or localization strategy).

This is where control systems and incentives come in. When we survey the systems that corporations use to control their subunits, we find that irrespective of their strategy, multinational firms all use output and bureaucratic controls. However, in firms pursuing either global or transnational strategies, the usefulness of output controls is limited by substantial performance ambiguities. As a result, these firms place greater emphasis on cultural controls. Cultural control—by encouraging managers to want to assume the organization's norms and value systems—gives managers of interdependent subunits an incentive to look for ways to work out problems that arise between them. The result is a reduction in finger-pointing and, accordingly, in the costs of control. The development of cultural controls may be a precondition for the successful pursuit of a transnational strategy and perhaps of a global strategy as well.[22] As for incentives, the material discussed earlier suggests that the conflict between different subunits can be reduced and the potential for cooperation enhanced, if incentive systems are tied in some way to a higher level in the hierarchy. When performance ambiguity makes it difficult to judge the performance of subunits as stand-alone entities, linking the incentive pay of senior managers to the entity to which both subunits belong can reduce the resulting problems.

We defined processes as the manner in which decisions are made and work is performed within the organization.[23] Processes can be found at many different levels within an organization. There are processes for formulating strategy, processes for allocating resources, processes for evaluating new-product ideas, processes for handling customer inquiries and complaints, processes for improving product quality, processes for evaluating employee performance, and so on. Often, the core competencies or valuable skills of a firm are embedded in its processes. Efficient and effective processes can lower the costs of value creation and add additional value to a product. For example, the global success of many Japanese manufacturing enterprises in the 1980s was based in part on their early adoption of processes for improving product quality and operating efficiency, including total quality management and just-in-time inventory systems. Today, the competitive success of General Electric can in part be attributed to a number of processes that have been widely promoted within the company. These include the company's Six Sigma process for quality improvement, its process for "digitalization" of business (using corporate intranets and the Internet to automate activities and reduce operating costs), and its process for idea generation, referred to within the company as "workouts," where managers and employees get together for intensive sessions over several days to identify and commit to ideas for improving productivity.

An organization's processes can be summarized by means of a flow chart, which illustrates the various steps and decision points involved in performing work. Many processes cut across functions, or divisions, and require cooperation between individuals in different subunits. For example, product development processes require employees from R&D, manufacturing, and marketing to work together in a cooperative manner to make sure new products are developed with market needs in mind and designed in such a way that they can be manufactured at a low cost. Because they cut across organizational boundaries, performing processes effectively often requires the establishment of formal integrating mechanisms and incentives for cross-unit cooperation (see above).

A detailed consideration of the nature of processes and strategies for process improvement and reengineering is beyond the scope of this book. However, it is important to make two basic remarks about managing processes, particularly in the context of an international business.[24] The first is that in a multinational enterprise, many processes cut not only across organizational boundaries, embracing several different subunits, but also across national boundaries. Designing a new product may require the cooperation of R&D personnel located in California, production people located in Taiwan, and marketing located in Europe, America, and Asia. The chances of pulling this off are greatly enhanced if the processes are embedded in an organizational culture that promotes cooperation between individuals from different subunits and nations, if the incentive systems of the organization explicitly reward such cooperation, and if formal and informal integrating mechanisms are used to facilitate coordination between subunits.

Second, it is particularly important for a multinational enterprise to recognize that valuable new processes that might lead to a competitive advantage can be developed anywhere within the organization's global network of operations.[25] New processes may be developed by a local operating subsidiary in response to conditions pertaining to its market. Those processes might then have value to other parts of the multinational enterprise. For example, in response to competition in Japan and a local obsession with product quality, Japanese firms were at the leading edge of developing processes for total quality management (TQM) in the 1970s. Because few American firms had Japanese subsidiaries at the time, they were relatively ignorant of the trend until the 1980s when high-quality Japanese products began to make big inroads into the United States. An exception to this generalization was Hewlett-Packard, which had a very successful operating company in Japan, Yokogwa Hewlett-Packard (YHP). YHP was a pioneer of the total quality management process in Japan and won the prestigious Deming Prize for its achievements in improving product quality. Through YHP, Hewlett-Packard learned about the quality movement ahead of many of its U.S. peers and was one of the first Western companies to introduce TQM processes into its worldwide operations. Not only did Hewlett-Packard's Japanese operation give the company access to a valuable process, but the company also transferred this knowledge within its global network of operations, raising the performance of the entire company. The ability to create valuable processes matters, but it is also important to leverage those processes. This requires both formal and informal integrating mechanisms such as knowledge networks.

Organizational Culture

Chapter 3 applied the concept of culture to nation-states. Culture, however, is a social construct ascribed to societies, including organizations.[26] Thus, we can speak of organizational culture and organizational subculture. The basic definition of culture remains the same, whether we are applying it to a large society such as a nation-state or a small society such as an organization or one of its subunits. Culture refers to a system of values and norms that are shared among people. Values are abstract ideas about what a group believes to be good, right, and desirable. Norms mean the social rules and guidelines that prescribe appropriate behavior in particular situations. Values and norms express themselves as the behavior patterns or style of an organization that new employees are automatically encouraged to follow by their fellow employees. Although an organization's culture is rarely static, it tends to change relatively slowly.

CREATING AND MAINTAINING ORGANIZATIONAL CULTURE

An organization's culture comes from several sources. First, there seems to be wide agreement that founders or important leaders can have a profound impact on an organization's culture, often imprinting their own values on the culture.[27] This was certainly the case with Lincoln Electric where the values of James Lincoln became the core values of Lincoln Electric (see the Management Focus). Another famous example of a strong founder effect concerns the Japanese firm Matsushita. Konosuke Matsushita's almost Zen-like personal business philosophy was codified in the "Seven Spiritual Values" of Matsushita that all new employees still learn today. These values are (1) national service through industry, (2) fairness, (3) harmony and cooperation, (4) struggle for betterment, (5) courtesy and humility, (6) adjustment and assimilation, and (7) gratitude. A leader does not have to be the founder to have a profound influence on organizational culture. Jack Welch is widely credited with having changed the culture of GE, primarily by emphasizing when he first became CEO a countercultural set of values, such as risk taking, entrepreneurship, stewardship, and boundaryless behavior. It is more difficult for a leader, however forceful, to change an established organizational culture than it is to create one from scratch in a new venture.

Another important influence on organizational culture is the broader social culture of the nation where the firm was founded. In the United States, for example, the competitive ethic of individualism looms large and there is enormous social stress on producing winners. Many American firms find ways of rewarding and motivating individuals so that they see themselves as winners.[28] The values of American firms often reflect the values of American culture. Similarly, the cooperative values found in many Japanese firms have been argued to reflect the values of traditional Japanese society, with its emphasis on group cooperation, reciprocal obligations, and harmony.[29] Thus, although it may be a generalization, there may be something to the argument that organizational culture is influenced by national culture.

A third influence on organizational culture is the history of the enterprise, which over time may come to shape the values of the organization. In the language of historians, organizational culture is the path-dependent product of where the organization has been through time. For example, Philips NV, the Dutch multinational, long operated with a culture that placed a high value on the independence of national operating companies. This culture was shaped by the history of the company. During World War II, Holland was occupied by the Germans. With the head office in occupied territories, power was devolved by default to various foreign operating companies, such as Philips subsidiaries in the United States and Great Britain. After the war ended, these subsidiaries continued to operate in a highly autonomous fashion. A belief that this was the right thing to do became a core value of the company.

Decisions that subsequently result in high performance tend to become institutionalized in the values of a firm. In the 1920s, 3M was primarily a manufacturer of sandpaper. Richard Drew, who was a young laboratory assistant at the time, came up with what he thought would be a great new product—a glue-covered strip of paper, which he called "sticky tape." Drew saw applications for the product in the automobile industry, where it could be used to mask parts of a vehicle during painting. He presented the idea to the company's president, William McKnight. An unimpressed McKnight suggested that Drew drop the research. Drew didn't; instead he developed the "sticky tape" and then went out and got endorsements from potential customers in the auto industry. Armed with this information, he approached McKnight again. A chastened McKnight reversed his position and gave Drew the go-ahead to start developing what was to become one of 3M's main product lines—sticky tape—a business it dominates to this day.[30] From then on, McKnight emphasized the importance of giving researchers at 3M free rein to explore their own ideas and experiment with product offerings. This soon became a core value at 3M and was enshrined in the company's famous "15 percent rule," which stated that researchers could spend 15 percent of the company time working on ideas of their own choosing. Today, new employees are often told the Drew story, which is used to illustrate the value of allowing individuals to explore their own ideas.

Culture is maintained by a variety of mechanisms. These include: (1) hiring and promotional practices of the organization, (2) reward strategies, (3) socialization processes, and (4) communication strategy. The goal is to recruit people whose values are consistent with those of the company. Lincoln Electric, for example, hires individuals who are very self-reliant, which is necessary in the company's individualistic culture. To further reinforce values, a company may promote individuals whose behavior is consistent with the core values of the organization. Merit review processes may also be linked to a company's values, which further reinforces cultural norms. Thus, at Lincoln Electric, the merit review process rewards people for behavior that is consistent with the attainment of high productivity.

Socialization can be formal, such as training programs for employees that educate them in the core values of the organization. Informal socialization may be friendly advice from peers or bosses or may be implicit in the actions of peers and superiors toward new employees. As for communication strategy, many companies with strong cultures devote a lot of attention to framing their key values in corporate mission statements, communicating them often to employees, and using them to guide difficult decisions. Stories and symbols are often used to reinforce important values (e.g., the Drew and McKnight story at 3M).

ORGANIZATIONAL CULTURE AND PERFORMANCE IN THE INTERNATIONAL BUSINESS

Management authors often talk about "strong cultures."[31] In a strong culture, almost all managers share a relatively consistent set of values and norms that have a clear impact on the way work is performed. New employees adopt these values very quickly, and employees that do not fit in with the core values tend to leave. In such a culture, a new ex-

3M's famous Post-it note was an idea that stuck. Innovation continues to be a hallmark of the company to this day.

ecutive is just as likely to be corrected by his subordinates as by his superiors if he violates the values and norms of the organizational culture. Firms with a strong culture are normally seen by outsiders as having a certain style or way of doing things. Lincoln Electric, profiled in the Management Focus, is an example of a firm with a strong culture. Lincoln's organizational culture places a high value on individual achievements, meritocracy, and egalitarian behavior. Unilever, profiled in the opening case, is another example of a firm with a strong culture. Unilever places a high value on sociability, cooperation, and consensus-building behavior among its employees.

Strong does not necessarily mean good. A culture can be strong but bad. The culture of the Nazi Party in Germany was certainly strong, but it was most definitely not good. Nor does it follow that a strong culture leads to high performance. One study found that in the 1980s General Motors had a "strong culture," but it was a strong culture that discouraged lower-level employees from demonstrating initiative and taking risks, which the authors argued was dysfunctional and led to low performance at GM.[32] Also, a strong culture might be beneficial at one point, leading to high performance, but inappropriate at another time. The appropriateness of the culture depends on the context. In the 1980s, when IBM was performing very well, several management authors sang the praises of its strong culture, which among other things placed a high value on consensus-based decision making.[33] These authors argued that such a decision-making process was appropriate given the substantial financial investments that IBM routinely made in new technology. However, this process turned out to be a weakness in the fast-moving computer industry of the late 1980s and 1990s. Consensus-based decision making was slow, bureaucratic, and not particularly conducive to corporate risk taking. While this was fine in the 1970s, IBM needed rapid decision making and entrepreneurial risk taking in the 1990s, but its culture discouraged such behavior. IBM found itself outflanked by thensmall enterprises such as Microsoft.

One academic study concluded that firms that exhibited high performance over a prolonged period tended to have strong but adaptive cultures. According to this study, in an adaptive culture most managers care deeply about and value customers, stockholders, and employees. They also strongly value people and processes that create useful change in a firm.[34] While this is interesting, it does reduce the issue to a very high level of abstraction; after all, what company would say that it doesn't care deeply about customers, stockholders, and employees? A somewhat different perspective is to argue that the culture of the firm must match the rest of the architecture of the organization, the firm's strategy, and the demands of the competitive environment, for superior performance to be attained. All these elements must be consistent with each other. Lincoln Electric provides another useful example. Lincoln competes in a business that is very competitive, where cost minimization is a key source of competitive advantage. Lincoln's culture and incentive systems both encourage employees to strive for high levels of productivity, which translates into the low costs that are critical for Lincoln's success. The Lincoln example also demonstrates another important point for international businesses: A culture that leads to high performance in the firm's home nation may not be easy to impose on foreign subsidiaries! Lincoln's culture has clearly helped the firm to achieve superior performance in the U.S. market, but this same culture is very "American" in its form and difficult to implement in other countries. The managers and employees of several of Lincoln's European subsidiaries found the culture to be alien to their own values and were reluctant to adopt it. The result was that Lincoln found it very difficult to replicate in foreign markets the success it has had in the United States. Lincoln compounded the problem by acquiring established enterprises that already had their own organizational culture. Thus, in trying to impose its culture on foreign operating subsidiaries, Lincoln had to deal with two problems: how to change the established organizational culture of those units, and how to introduce an organizational culture whose key values might be alien to the values held by members of that society. These problems are not unique to Lincoln; many international businesses have to deal with exactly the same problems.

The solution Lincoln has adopted is to establish new subsidiaries, rather than acquiring and trying to transform an enterprise with its own culture. It is much easier to establish a set of values in a new enterprise than it is to change the values of an established enterprise. A second solution is to devote a lot of time and attention to transmitting the firm's organizational culture to its foreign operations. This was something Lincoln originally omitted. Other firms make this an important part of their strategy for internationalization. When MTV Networks opens an operation in a new country, it initially staffs that operation with several expatriates. The job of these expatriates is to hire local employees whose values are consistent with the MTV culture and to socialize those individuals into values and norms that underpin MTV's unique way of doing things. Once this has been achieved, the expatriates move on to their next assignment, and local employees run the operation. A third solution is to recognize that it may be necessary to change some aspects of a firm's culture so that it better fits the culture of the host nation. For example, many Japanese firms use symbolic behavior, such as company songs and morning group exercise sessions, to reinforce cooperative values and norms. However, such symbolic behavior is seen as odd in Western cultures, so many Japanese firms have not used such practices in Western subsidiaries.

The need for a common organizational culture that is the same across a multinational's global network of subsidiaries probably varies with the strategy of the firm. Shared norms and values can facilitate coordination and cooperation between individuals from different subunits.[35] A strong common culture may lead to goal congruence and can attenuate the problems that arise from interdependence, performance ambiguities, and conflict among managers from different subsidiaries. As noted earlier, a shared culture may help informal integrating mechanisms such as knowledge networks to operate more effectively. As such, a common culture may be of greater value in a multinational that is pursuing a strategy that requires cooperation and coordination between globally dispersed subsidiaries. This suggests that it is more important to have a common culture in firms employing a transnational strategy than a localization strategy, with global and international strategies falling between these two extremes.

Synthesis: Strategy and Architecture

In Chapter 12, we identified four basic strategies that multinational firms pursue: localization, international, global, and transnational. So far in this chapter we have looked at several aspects of organization architecture, and we have discussed the interrelationships between these dimensions and strategies. Now it is time to synthesize this material.

LOCALIZATION STRATEGY

Firms pursuing a localization strategy focus on local responsiveness. Table 13.2 shows that such firms tend to operate with worldwide area structures, within which operating decisions are decentralized to functionally self-contained country subsidiaries. The need for coordination between subunits (areas and country subsidiaries) is low. This suggests that firms pursuing a localization strategy do not have a high need for integrating mechanisms, either formal or informal, to knit together different national operations. The lack of interdependence implies that the level of performance ambiguity in such enterprises is low, as (by extension) are the costs of control. Thus, headquarters can manage foreign operations by relying primarily on output and bureaucratic controls and a policy of management by exception. Incentives can be linked to performance metrics at the level of country subsidiaries. Since the need for integration and coordination is low, the need for common processes and organization culture is also quite low. Were it not for the fact that these firms are unable to profit from the realization of location and experience curve economies, or from the transfer of core competencies, their organizational simplicity would make this an attractive strategy.

Structure and Controls	Strategy			
	Localization	**International**	**Global Standardization**	**Transnational**
Vertical Differentiation	Decentralized	Core competency more centralized; Rest decentralized	Some centralization	Mixed centralization and decentralization
Horizontal Differentiation	Worldwide area structure	Worldwide product divisions	Worldwide product divisions	Informal matrix
Need for Coordination	Low	Moderate	High	Very high
Integrating Mechanisms	None	Few	Many	Very many
Performance Ambiguity	Low	Moderate	High	Very high
Need for Cultural Controls	Low	Moderate	High	Very high

TABLE 13.2

A Synthesis of Strategy, Structure, and Control Systems

INTERNATIONAL STRATEGY

Firms pursuing an international strategy attempt to create value by transferring core competencies from home to foreign subsidiaries. If they are diverse, as most of them are, these firms operate with a worldwide product division structure. Headquarters typically maintains centralized control over the source of the firm's core competency, which is most typically found in the R&D and/or marketing functions of the firm. All other operating decisions are decentralized within the firm to subsidiary operations in each country (which in diverse firms report to worldwide product divisions).

The need for coordination is moderate in such firms, reflecting the need to transfer core competencies. Thus, although such firms operate with some integrating mechanisms, they are not that extensive. The relatively low level of interdependence that results translates into a relatively low level of performance ambiguity. These firms can generally get by with output and bureaucratic controls and with incentives that are focused on performance metrics at the level of country subsidiaries. The need for a common organizational culture and common processes is not that great. An important exception to this is when the core skills or competencies of the firm are embedded in processes and culture, in which case the firm needs to pay close attention to transferring those processes and associated culture from the corporate center to country subsidiaries. Overall, although the organization required for an international strategy is more complex than that of firms pursuing a localization strategy, the increase in the level of complexity is not that great.

GLOBAL STANDARDIZATION STRATEGY

Firms pursuing a global standardization strategy focus on the realization of location and experience curve economies. If they are diversified, as many of them are, these firms operate with a worldwide product division structure. To coordinate the firm's globally dispersed web of value creation activities, headquarters typically maintains ultimate control over most operating decisions. In general, such firms are more centralized than enterprises pursuing a localization or international strategy. Reflecting the need for coordination of the various stages of the firms' globally dispersed value chains, the need for integration in these firms also is high. Thus, these firms tend to operate with an array of formal and informal integrating mechanisms. The resulting interdependencies can lead to significant performance ambiguities. As a result, in addition to output and bureaucratic controls, firms pursuing a global standardization strategy tend to stress the need to build a strong organizational culture that can facilitate coordination and cooperation. They also tend to use incentive systems that are linked to performance metrics at the corporate level, giving the managers of different operations a strong incentive to cooperate with each other to increase the performance of the entire corporation. On average, the organization of such firms is more complex than that of firms pursuing a localization or international strategy.

TRANSNATIONAL STRATEGY

Firms pursuing a transnational strategy focus on the simultaneous attainment of location and experience curve economies, local responsiveness, and global learning (the multidirectional transfer of core competencies or skills). These firms may operate with matrix-type structures in which both product divisions and geographic areas have significant influence. The need to coordinate a globally dispersed value chain and to transfer core competencies creates pressures for centralizing some operating decisions (particularly production and R&D). At the same time, the need to be locally responsive creates pressures for decentralizing other operating decisions to national operations (particularly marketing). Consequently, these firms tend to mix relatively high degrees of centralization for some operating decisions with relative high degrees of decentralization for other operating decisions.

The need for coordination is high in transnational firms. This is reflected in the use of an array of formal and informal integrating mechanisms, including formal matrix structures and informal management networks. The high level of interdependence of subunits implied by such integration can result in significant performance ambiguities, which raise the costs of control. To reduce these, in addition to output and bureaucratic controls, firms pursuing a transnational strategy need to cultivate a strong culture and to establish incentives that promote cooperation between subunits.

ENVIRONMENT, STRATEGY, ARCHITECTURE, AND PERFORMANCE

Underlying the scheme outlined in Table 13.2 is the notion that a "fit" between strategy and architecture is necessary for a firm to achieve high performance. For a firm to succeed, two conditions must be fulfilled. First, the firm's strategy must be consistent with the environment in which the firm operates. We discussed this issue in Chapter 12 and noted that in some industries a global standardization strategy is most viable, in others an international or transnational strategy may be most viable, and in still others a localization strategy may be most viable. Second, the firm's organization architecture must be consistent with its strategy.

If the strategy does not fit the environment, the firm is likely to experience significant performance problems. If the architecture does not fit the strategy, the firm is also likely to experience performance problems. Therefore, to survive, a firm must strive to achieve a fit of its environment, its strategy, and its organizational architecture. You will recall that we saw the importance of this concept in the opening case. Philips NV, the Dutch electronics firm, provides another illustration of the need for this fit. For reasons rooted in the history of the firm, Philips operated until recently with an organization typical of an enterprise pursuing localization; operating decisions were decentralized to largely autonomous foreign subsidiaries. Historically, electronics markets were segmented from each other by high trade barriers, so an organization consistent with a localization strategy made sense. However, by the mid-1980s, the industry in which Philips competed had been revolutionized by declining trade barriers, technological change, and the emergence of low-cost Japanese competitors that utilized a global strategy. To survive, Philips needed to adopt a global standardization strategy itself. The firm recognized this and tried to adopt a global posture, but it did little to change its organizational architecture. The firm nominally adopted a matrix structure based on worldwide product divisions and national areas. In reality, however, the national areas continued to dominate the organization, and the product divisions had little more than an advisory role. As a result, Philips' architecture did not fit the strategy, and by the early 1990s Philips was losing money. It was only after four years of wrenching change and large losses that Philips was finally able to tilt the balance of power in its matrix toward the product divisions. By the mid-1990s, the fruits of this effort to realign the company's strategy and architecture with the demands of its operating environment were beginning to show up in improved financial performance.[36]

Organizational Change

Multinational firms periodically have to alter their architecture so that it conforms to the changes in the environment in which they are competing and the strategy they are pursuing. To be profitable, Philips NV had to alter its strategy and architecture in the 1990s so that both matched the demands of the competitive environment in the electronics industry, which had shifted from localization and toward a global industry. While a detailed consideration of organizational change is beyond the scope of this book, a few comments are warranted regarding the sources of organization inertia and the strategies and tactics for implementing organizational change.

ORGANIZATIONAL INERTIA

Organizations are difficult to change. Within most organizations are strong inertia forces. These forces come from a number of sources. One source of inertia is the existing distribution of power and influence within an organization.[37] The power and influence enjoyed by individual managers is in part a function of their role in the organizational hierarchy, as defined by structural position. By definition, most substantive changes in an organization require a change in structure and, by extension, a change in the distribution of power and influence within the organization. Some individuals will see their power and influence increase as a result of organizational change, and some will see the converse. For example, in the 1990s, Philips NV increased the roles and responsibilities of its global product divisions and decreased the roles and responsibilities of its foreign subsidiary companies. This meant the managers running the global product divisions saw their power and influence increase, while the managers running the foreign subsidiary companies saw their power and influence decline. As might be expected, some managers of foreign subsidiary companies did not like this change and resisted it, which slowed the pace of change. Those whose power and influence are reduced as a consequence of organizational change can be expected to resist it, primarily by arguing that the change might not work. To the extent that they are successful, this constitutes a source of organizational inertia that might slow or stop change.

Another source of organizational inertia is the existing culture, as expressed in norms and value systems. Value systems reflect deeply held beliefs, and as such, they can be very hard to change. If the formal and informal socialization mechanisms within an organization have been emphasizing a consistent set of values for a prolonged period, and if hiring, promotion, and incentive systems have all reinforced these values, then suddenly announcing that those values are no longer appropriate and need to be changed can produce resistance and dissonance among employees. For example, Philips NV historically placed a very high value on local autonomy. The changes of the 1990s implied a reduction in the autonomy enjoyed by foreign subsidiaries, which was counter to the established values of the company and thus resisted.

Organizational inertia might also derive from senior managers' preconceptions about the appropriate business model or paradigm. When a given paradigm has worked well in the past, managers might have trouble accepting that it is no longer appropriate. At Philips, granting considerable autonomy to foreign subsidiaries had worked very well in the past, allowing local managers to tailor product and business strategy to the conditions prevailing in a given country. Since this paradigm had worked so well, it was difficult for many managers to understand why it no longer applied. Consequently, they had difficulty accepting a new business model and tended to fall back on their established paradigm and ways of doing things. This change required managers to let go of long-held assumptions about what worked and what didn't work, which was something many of them couldn't do.

Institutional constraints might also act as a source of inertia. National regulations including local content rules and policies pertaining to layoffs might make it difficult for a multinational to alter its global value chain. As with Unilever (see the opening case), a multinational might wish to take control for manufacturing away from local subsidiaries, transfer that control to global product divisions, and consolidate manufacturing at a few choice locations. However, if local content rules (see Chapter 5) require some degree of local production and if regulations regarding layoffs make it difficult or expensive for a multinational to close operations in a country, a multinational may find that these constraints make it very difficult to adopt the most effective strategy and architecture.

IMPLEMENTING ORGANIZATIONAL CHANGE

Although all organizations suffer from inertia, the complexity and global spread of many multinationals might make it particularly difficult for them to change their strategy and architecture to match new organizational realities. Yet at the same time, the trend toward globalization in many industries has made it more critical than ever that many multinationals do just that. In industry after industry, declining barriers to cross-border trade and investment have led to a change in the nature of the competitive environment. Cost pressures have increased, requiring multinationals to respond by streamlining their operations to realize economic benefits associated with location and experience curve economies and with the transfer of competencies and skills within the organization. At the same time, local responsiveness remains an important source of differentiation. To survive in this emerging competitive environment, multinationals must change not only their strategy but also their architecture so that it matches strategy in discriminating ways. The basic principles for successful organizational change can be summarized as follows: (1) unfreeze the organization through shock therapy, (2) move the organization to a new state through proactive change in the architecture, and (3) refreeze the organization in its new state.

Unfreezing the Organization

Because of inertia forces, incremental change is often no change. Those whose power is threatened by change can too easily resist incremental change. This leads to the big bang theory of change, which maintains that effective change requires taking bold action early to "unfreeze" the established culture of an organization and to change the distribution of power and influence. Shock therapy to unfreeze the organization might include the closure of plants deemed uneconomic or the announcement of a dramatic structural reorganization. It is also important to realize that change will not occur unless senior managers are committed to it. Senior managers must clearly articulate the need for change so employees understand both why it is being pursued and the benefits that will flow from successful change. Senior managers must also practice what they preach and take the necessary bold steps. If employees see senior managers preaching the need for change but not changing their own behavior or making substantive changes in the organization, they will soon lose faith in the change effort, which then will flounder.

Moving to the New State

Once an organization has been unfrozen, it must be moved to its new state. Movement requires taking action—closing operations; reorganizing the structure; reassigning responsibilities; changing control, incentive, and reward systems; redesigning processes; and letting people go who are seen as an impediment to change. In other words, movement requires a substantial change in the form of a multinational's organization architecture so that it matches the desired new strategic posture. For movement to be successful, it must be done with sufficient speed. Involving employees in the change effort is an excellent way to get them to appreciate and buy into the needs for change and to help with rapid movement. For example, a firm might delegate substantial responsibility for designing operating processes to lower-level employees. If enough of their recommendations are then acted on, the employees will see the consequences of their efforts and consequently buy into the notion that change is really occurring.

Jack Welch, General Electric's legendary former CEO, is an individual who set a benchmark for embracing change.

Refreezing the Organization

Refreezing the organization takes longer. It may require that a new culture be established, while the old one is being dismantled. Thus, refreezing requires that employees be socialized into the new way of doing things. Companies will often use management education programs to achieve this. At General Electric, where longtime CEO Jack Welch instituted a major change in the culture of the company, management education programs were used as a proactive tool to communicate new values to organization members. On their own, however, management education programs are not enough. Hiring policies must be changed to reflect the new realities, with an emphasis on hiring individuals whose own values are consistent with that of the new culture the firm is trying to build. Similarly, control and incentive systems must be consistent with the new realities of the organization, or change will never take. Senior management must recognize that changing culture takes a long time. Any letup in the pressure to change may allow the old culture to reemerge as employees fall back into familiar ways of doing things. The communication task facing senior managers, therefore, is a long-term endeavor that requires managers to be relentless and persistent in their pursuit of change. One striking feature of Jack Welch's two-decade tenure at GE, for example, is that he never stopped pushing his change agenda. It was a consistent theme of his tenure. He was always thinking up new programs and initiatives to keep pushing the culture of the organization along the desired trajectory.

Chapter Summary

This chapter identified the organizational architecture that can be used by multinational enterprises to manage and direct their global operations. A central theme of the chapter was that different strategies require different architectures; strategy is implemented through architecture. To succeed, a firm must match its architecture to its strategy in discriminating ways. Firms whose architecture does not fit their strategic requirements will experience performance problems. It is also necessary for the different components of architecture to be consistent with each other. The chapter made the following points:

1. Organizational architecture refers to the totality of a firm's organization, including formal organizational structure, control systems and incentives, processes, organizational culture, and people.

2. Superior enterprise profitability requires three conditions to be fulfilled: the different elements of a firm's organizational architecture must be internally consistent, the organizational architecture must fit the strategy of the firm, and the strategy and architecture of the firm must be consistent with competitive conditions prevailing in the firm's markets.

3. Organizational structure means three things: the formal division of the organization into subunits (horizontal differentiation), the location of decision-making responsibilities within that structure (vertical differentiation), and the establishment of integrating mechanisms.

4. Control systems are the metrics used to measure the performance of subunits and make judgments about how well managers are running those subunits.

5. Incentives refer to the devices used to reward appropriate employee behavior. Many employees receive incentives in the form of annual bonus pay. Incentives are usually closely tied to the performance metrics used for output controls.

6. Processes refer to the manner in which decisions are made and work is performed within the organization. Processes can be found at many different levels within an organization. The core competencies or valuable skills of a firm are often embedded in its processes. Efficient and effective processes can help to lower the costs of value creation and to add additional value to a product.

7. Organizational culture refers to a system of values and norms that is shared among employees. Values and norms express themselves as the behavior patterns or style of an organization that new employees are automatically encouraged to follow by their fellow employees.

8. Firms pursuing different strategies must adopt a different architecture to implement those strategies successfully. Firms pursuing localization, global, international, and transnational strategies all must adopt an organizational architecture that matches their strategy.

9. While all organizations suffer from inertia, the complexity and global spread of many multinationals might make it particularly difficult for them to change their strategy and architecture to match new organizational realities. At the same time, the trend toward globalization in many industries has made it more critical than ever that many multinationals do just that.

Critical Thinking and Discussion Questions

1. "The choice of strategy for a multinational firm must depend on a comparison of the benefits of that strategy (in terms of value creation) with the costs of implementing it (as defined by organizational architecture necessary for implementation). On this basis, it may be logical for some firms to pursue a localization strategy, others a global or international strategy, and still others a transnational strategy." Is this statement correct?

2. Discuss this statement: "An understanding of the causes and consequences of performance ambiguity is central to the issue of organizational design in multinational firms."

3. Describe the organizational architecture a transnational firm might adopt to reduce the costs of control.

4. What is the most appropriate organizational architecture for a firm that is competing in an industry where a global strategy is most appropriate?

5. If a firm is changing its strategy from an international to a transnational strategy, what are the most important challenges it is likely to face in implementing this change? How can the firm overcome these challenges?

Research Task globalEDGE™ globaledge.msu.edu

Use the globalEDGE™ site to complete the following exercises:

1. The Financial Times newspaper and the auditing firm PricewaterhouseCoopers conduct an

annual survey and publish the rankings of World's Most Respected Companies. PricewaterhouseCoopers provides the whole report downloadable as a PDF file. Locate the most recent ranking available and focus on the introductory analysis. Prepare an executive summary of the strategic and organizational success factors that make a company "most respected".

2. The globalEDGE™ presents selected articles from the business print media under its *Knowledge Room* section. Locate the Selected Articles section and find an article that provides insights about the four key challenges facing firms in the globalization process. Prepare a description of these challenges and the solutions that the authors recommend.

Strategic and Organization Change at Black & Decker

CLOSING CASE Known primarily for its power tools, Black & Decker is one of the world's older multinational corporations. The company was founded in Baltimore, Maryland, in 1910, and by the end of the 1920s had become a small multinational company with operations in Canada and Britain. Today the company has two well-known brands, Black & Decker consumer power tools and its DeWalt brand of professional power tools. It sells its products in over 100 nations, and has revenues in excess of $5 billion, more than half of which are generated outside of the United States.

The company grew rapidly during the 1950s and 1960s due to its strong brand name and near monopoly share of the consumer and professional power tools markets. This monopoly was based on Black & Decker's pioneering development of handheld power tools. It was during this period that Black & Decker expanded rapidly in international markets, typically by setting up wholly owned subsidiaries in a nation and giving them the right to develop, manufacture, and market the company's power tools. As a result, by the early 1980s, the company had 23 wholly owned subsidiaries in foreign nations and two joint ventures.

During its period of rapid international expansion, Black & Decker operated with a decentralized organization. In its 1979 annual report, the company described how, "In order to be effective in the market place, Black & Decker follows a decentralized organizational approach. All business functions (marketing, engineering, manufacturing, etc.) are kept as close as possible to the market to be served." In effect, each wholly owned subsidiary was granted considerable autonomy to run its own business.

By the mid-1980s, however, this structure was starting to become untenable. New competitors had emerged in the power tool business, including Bosch, Makita, and Panasonic. As a result, Black & Decker's monopoly position had eroded. Throughout the 1980s, the company pursued a strategy of rationalization. Factories were

closed and the company consolidated production in fewer, more efficient production facilities. This process was particularly evident in Europe, where different national operating companies had traditionally had their own production facilities. As the company noted in its 1985 annual report, "Globalization remains a key strategic objective. In 1985, sound progress was made in designing and marketing products for a worldwide market, rather than just regional ones. Focused design centers will ensure a greater number of global products for the future. . . . Global purchasing programs have been established, and cost benefits are being realized."

During this period, while the company maintained a number of design centers, it cut the number of basic R&D centers from eight to just two. The autonomy of individual factories also started to decrease. The factories that remained after the round of closures had to compete with each other for the right to produce a product for the world market. Major decisions about where to produce products to serve world markets were now being made by managers at the corporate headquarters. Even so, national subsidiaries still maintained a fair degree of autonomy. For example, if a national subsidiary developed a new product, it was still likely that it would get the mandate to produce that product for the world market. Also, if a national subsidiary performed well, it was likely to be left alone by corporate management.

By the 1990s, however, it was clear that this change had not gone far enough. The rise of powerful retailers such as Home Depot and Lowe's in the United States had further pressured prices in the power tools market. Blacker & Decker responded by looking for ways to garner additional manufacturing efficiencies. During this period, Black & Decker shut down several more factories in its long-established subsidiaries and started to shift production to new facilities that it opened in Mexico and China. As this process proceeded, any remaining autonomy enjoyed by the managers of local factories was virtually eliminated. Corporate managers become much more aggressive about allocating products to different factories based on a consideration of operating costs. In effect, Black & Decker's factories now had to compete with each other for the right to make products, and those factories that did not do well in this process were shut down.

In 2001, Black & Decker announced yet another restructuring initiative. Among other things, the initiative involved reducing the workforce by 700 people, to 4,500, shutting long-established factories in the United States and Britain, and shifting production to low-cost facilities. By 2004 this process reached a logical conclusion when the company reorganized its power tools business into two separate global divisions—one that was charged with the global development, manufacture, and marketing of Black & Decker power tools, and another that was charged with the same for the company's professional DeWalt brand. At this point, the company operated some 36 manufacturing facilities, 18 outside of the United States in Mexico, China, the Czech Republic, Germany, Italy, and Britain. It had seven design centers, and two basic R&D centers, one in the United States and one in Britain. Increasingly, the design and R&D centers in the United States and Britain took on responsibility for new-product development for the global market. Throughout the early 2000s, successively larger shares of production were allocated to factories in just three nations, China, Mexico, and the Czech Republic, and in its 2004 annual report, Blacker & Decker indicated that this process was likely to continue.

Sources: N. A. Phelps and P. Waley, "Capital versus the Districts: A Tale of One Multinational Company's Attempt to Disembed Itself," *Economic Geography* 80 (2004), pp. 191–214; T. Walton, "The Black & Decker Corporation," *Design Management Institute Case Study*, October 1997; "Black & Decker Reorganizes Power Tools and Accessories Business," Black & Decker press release, March 1, 2004; and *Black & Decker 10K Report*, 2003.

Case Discussion Questions

1. How would you characterize Black & Decker's international expansion during the 1950s and 1960s? What strategy was the company pursuing? What was the key feature of the international organization structure that Black & Decker operated with at this time? Did Black & Decker's strategy and structure make sense given the competitive environment at that time?

2. How did the competitive environment confronting Black & Decker change during the 1980s and 1990s? What changes did Black & Decker make in its (*a*) strategy and (*b*) structure to compete more effectively in this new environment?

3. By the 2000s, what strategy was Black & Decker pursuing in the global market place? How would you characterize its structure? Did the structure fit the strategy and environment?

4. Why do you think it took nearly two decades for Black & Decker to effect a change in strategy and structure?

Notes

1. D. Naidler, M. Gerstein, and R. Shaw, *Organization Architecture* (San Francisco: Jossey-Bass, 1992).

2. G. Morgan, *Images of Organization* (Beverly Hills, CA: Sage Publications, 1986).

3. "Unilever: A Networked Organization," *Harvard Business Review*, November–December 1996, p. 138.

4. The material in this section draws on John Child, *Organizations* (London: Harper & Row, 1984).

5. Allan Cane, "Microsoft Reorganizes to Meet Market Challenges," *Financial Times*, March 16, 1994, p. 1. Interviews by Charles Hill.

6. For research evidence that is related to this issue, see J. Birkinshaw, "Entrepreneurship in the Multinational Corporation: The Characteristics of Subsidiary Initiatives," *Strategic Management Journal* 18 (1997), pp. 207–29; J. Birkinshaw, N. Hood, and S. Jonsson, "Building Firm Specific Advantages in Multinational Corporations: The Role of Subsidiary Initiatives," *Strategic Management Journal* 19 (1998), pp. 221–41; and I. Bjorkman, W. Barner-Rasussen, and L. Li, "Managing Knowledge Transfer in MNCs: The Impact of Headquarters Control mechanisms," *Journal of International Business* 35 (2004), pp. 443–60.

7. For more detail, see S. M. Davis, "Managing and Organizing Multinational Corporations," in C. A. Bartlett and S. Ghoshal, *Transnational Management* (Homewood, IL: Richard D. Irwin, 1992). Also see J. Wolf and W. G. Egelhoff, "A Reexamination and Extension of International Strategy-Structure Theory," *Strategic Management Journal* 23 (2002), pp. 181–89.

8. A. D. Chandler, *Strategy and Structure: Chapters in the History of the Industrial Enterprise* (Cambridge, MA: MIT Press, 1962).

9. Davis, "Managing and Organizing Multinational Corporations."

10. J. M. Stopford and L. T. Wells, *Strategy and Structure of the Multinational Enterprise* (New York: Basic Books, 1972).

11. C. A. Bartlett and S. Ghoshal, *Managing across Borders* (Boston: Harvard Business School Press, 1989).

12. See J. R. Galbraith, *Designing Complex Organizations* (Reading, MA: Addison-Wesley, 1977).

13. M. Goold and A. Campbell, "Structured Networks: Towards the Well Designed Matrix," *Long Range Planning*, October 2003, pp. 427–60.

14. Bartlett and Ghoshal, *Managing across Borders*; F. V. Guterl, "Goodbye, Old Matrix," *Business Month*, February 1989, pp. 32–38; and Bjorkman, Barner-Rasussen, and Li, "Managing Knowledge Transfer in MNCs".

15. M. S. Granovetter, "The Strength of Weak Ties," *American Journal of Sociology* 78 (1973), pp. 1360–80.

16. A. K. Gupta and V. J. Govindarajan, "Knowledge Flows within Multinational Corporations," *Strategic Management Journal* 21, no. 4 (2000), pp. 473–96; V. J. Govindarajan and A. K. Gupta, *The Quest for Global Dominance*. (San Francisco: Jossey-Bass, 2001), and U. Andersson, M. Forsgren, and U. Holm, "The Strategic Impact of External Networks: Subsidiary Performance and Competence Development in the Multinational Corporation," *Strategic Management Journal* 23 (2002), pp. 979–96.

17. For examples, see W. H. Davidow and M. S. Malone, *The Virtual Corporation* (New York: HarperCollins, 1992).

18. W. G. Ouchi, "Markets, Bureaucracies, and Clans," *Administrative Science Quarterly* 25 (1980), pp. 129–44.

19. For some empirical work that addresses this issue, see T. P. Murtha, S. A. Lenway, and R. P. Bagozzi, "Global Mind Sets and Cognitive Shift in a Complex Multinational Corporation," *Strategic Management Journal* 19 (1998), pp. 97–114.

20. J. Welch and J. Byrne, *Jack: Straight from the Gut* (Warner Books: New York, 2001).

21. C. W. L. Hill, M. E. Hitt, and R. E. Hoskisson, "Cooperative versus Competitive Structures in Related and Unrelated Diversified Firms," *Organization Science* 3 (1992), pp. 501–21.

22. Murtha, Lenway, and Bagozzi, "Global Mind Sets."

23. M. Hammer and J. Champy, *Reengineering the Corporation* (New York: Harper Business, 1993).

24. T. Kostova, "Transnational Transfer of Strategic Organizational Practices: A Contextual Perspective," *Academy of Management Review* 24, no. 2 (1999), pp. 308–24.

25. Andersson, Forsgren, and Holm, "The Strategic Impact of External Networks: Subsidiary Performance and Competence Development in the Multinational Corporation."

26. E. H. Schein, "What Is Culture?" in P. J. Frost et al., *Reframing Organizational Culture* (Newbury Park, CA: Sage, 1991).

27. E. H. Schein, *Organizational Culture and Leadership*, 2nd ed. (San Francisco: Jossey-Bass, 1992).

28. G. Morgan, *Images of Organization* (Beverly Hills, CA: Sage, 1986).

29. R. Dore, *British Factory, Japanese Factory* (London: Allen & Unwin, 1973).

30. M. Dickson, "Back to the Future," *Financial Times*, May 30, 1994, p. 7.

31. See J. P. Kotter and J. L. Heskett, *Corporate Culture and Performance* (New York: Free Press, 1992), and M. L. Tushman and C. A. O'Reilly, *Winning through Innovation* (Boston: Harvard Business School Press, 1997).

32. Kotter and Heskett, *Corporate Culture and Performance*.

33. The classic song of praise was produced by T. Peters and R. H. Waterman, *In Search of Excellence* (New York: Harper & Row, 1982). Ironically, IBM's decline began shortly after Peters and Waterman's book was published.

34. Kotter and Heskett, *Corporate Culture and Performance*.

35. Bartlett and Ghoshal, *Managing across Borders*.

36. See F. J. Aguilar and M. Y. Yoshino, "The Philips Group: 1987," Howard Business School Case No. 388-050, 1987; "Philips Fights Flab," *The Economist*, April 7, 1990, pp. 73–74; and R. Van de Krol, "Philips Wins Back Old Friends," *Financial Times*, July 14, 1995, p. 14.

37. J. Pfeffer, *Managing with Power: Politics and Influence within Organizations* (Boston: Harvard Business School Press, 1992).

14

Entry Strategy and Strategic Alliances

Tesco Goes Global

Tesco is the largest grocery retailer in the United Kingdom, with a 25 percent share of the local market. In its home market, the company's strengths are reputed to come from strong competencies in marketing and store site selection, logistics and inventory management, and its own label product offerings. By the early 1990s, these competencies had already given the company a leading position in the United Kingdom. The company was generating strong free cash flows, and senior management had to decide how to use that cash. One strategy they settled on was overseas expansion. As they looked at international markets, they soon concluded that the best opportunities were not in established markets, such as those in North America and Western Europe, where strong local competitors already existed, but in the emerging markets of Eastern Europe and Asia where there were few capable competitors but strong underlying growth trends.

Tesco's first international foray was into Hungary in 1994, when it acquired an initial 51 percent stake in Global, a 43-store, state-owned grocery chain. By 2004, Tesco was the market leader in Hungary, with some 60 stores and a 14 percent market share. In 1995, Tesco acquired 31 stores in Poland from Stavia; a year later it added 13 stores purchased from Kmart in the Czech Republic and Slovakia, and the following year it entered the Republic of Ireland.

Tesco's Asian expansion began in 1998 in Thailand when it purchased 75 percent of Lotus, a local food retailer with 13 stores. Building on that base, Tesco had 64 stores in Thailand by 2004. In 1999, the company entered South Korea when it partnered with Samsung to develop a chain of hypermarkets. This was followed by entry into Taiwan in 2000, Malaysia in 2002, and China in 2004. The move into China came after three years of careful research and discussions with potential partners. Like many other Western companies, Tesco was attracted to the Chinese market by its large size and rapid growth. In the end, Tesco settled on a 50/50 joint venture with Hymall, a hypermarket chain that is controlled by Ting Hsin, a Taiwanese group, which had been operating in China for six years. Currently, Hymall has 25 stores in China, and it plans to open another 10 each year. Ting Hsin is a well-capitalized enterprise in its own right, and will match Tesco's investments, reducing the risks Tesco faces in China.

As a result of these moves, by early 2004 Tesco had 261 stores in Europe outside the United Kingdom that generated £3,385 million in annual revenues, and 179 stores in Asia that generated £2,665 million in annual revenues. In the United Kingdom, Tesco had some 1,878 stores that generated £24,760 million in annual revenues. The addition of international stores has helped to make Tesco the fourth largest company in the global grocery market behind Wal-Mart, Carrefore of France, and Ahold of Holland. Of the four, however, Tesco may be the most successful internationally. By 2003, all of its foreign ventures were making money with the exception of Taiwan, which was expected to do so in 2004.

In explaining the company's success, Tesco's managers have stated that a number of things are important. First, the company devotes considerable attention to transferring its core capabilities in retailing to its new ventures. At the same time, it does not send in an army of expatriate managers to run local operations, preferring to hire local managers and support them with a few operational experts from the United Kingdom. Second, the company believes that its partnering strategy in Asia has been a great asset. Tesco has teamed up with good companies that have a deep understanding of the markets they are participating in, but which lack Tesco's financial strength and retailing capabilities. Consequently, both Tesco and its partners have brought useful assets to the venture, which have increased the probability of success. As the venture becomes established, Tesco has typically increased its ownership stake in its partner. Thus, under current plans, by 2011 Tesco will own 99 percent of Homeplus, its South Korean hypermarket chain. When the venture was established, Tesco owned 51 percent. Third, the company has focused on markets with good growth potential, but that lack strong indigenous competitors, which provides Tesco with ripe ground for expansion.

Sources: P. N. Child, "Taking Tesco Global," *The McKenzie Quarterly*, no. 3 (2002); H. Keers, "Global Tesco Sets Out Its Stall in China," *Daily Telegraph*, July 15, 2004, p. 31; K. Burgess, "Tesco Spends Pounds 140m on Chinese Partnership," *Financial Times*, July 15, 2004, p. 22; and Tesco's annual reports, archived at www.tesco.com.

Introduction

This chapter is concerned with two closely related topics: (1) the decision of which foreign markets to enter, when to enter them, and on what scale; and (2) the choice of entry mode. Any firm contemplating foreign expansion must first struggle with the issue of which foreign markets to enter and the timing and scale of entry. The choice of which markets to enter should be driven by an assessment of relative long-run growth and profit potential. In the opening case, for example, we saw that in the 1990s and early 2000s, the British grocer Tesco decided to enter a number of emerging markets in Eastern Europe and Asia, primarily because it concluded that these markets offered the best opportunities for profit growth given demand trends in those nations and the lack of strong indigenous competitors.

The choice of mode for entering a foreign market is another major issue with which international businesses must wrestle. The various modes for serving foreign markets are exporting, licensing or franchising to host-country firms, establishing joint ventures with a host-country firm, setting up a new wholly owned subsidiary in a host country to serve its market, or acquiring an established enterprise in the host nation to serve that market. Each of these options has advantages and disadvantages. The magnitude of the advantages and disadvantages associated with each entry mode is determined by a number of factors, including transport costs, trade barriers, political risks, economic risks, business risks, costs, and firm strategy. The optimal entry mode varies by situation, depending on these factors. Thus, whereas some firms may best serve a given market by exporting, other firms may better serve the market by setting up a new wholly owned subsidiary or by acquiring an established enterprise.

As we saw in the opening case, in Asia Tesco has chosen to enter new markets through joint ventures with local enterprises. The logic is that local enterprises already have an infrastructure of stores in place that Tesco can use as a springboard for growth. These venture partners have been well-run companies with a good understanding of local conditions, including, most importantly, customer needs. By matching its financial resources and retailing capabilities with the local knowledge of its partners, Tesco has tried to increase the probability of success. So far, this approach appears to have served the company well. Tesco has displayed a preference for joint ventures in which it has a majority stake, and thus ultimate control. An exception is its recent joint venture in China, but even here, observers speculate that in keeping with its standard practice, Tesco will increase its ownership stake over time. By taking a majority stake, Tesco has perhaps avoided some of the problems that can emerge in 50/50 joint ventures, where divergent goals and battles for control can lead to failure.

Basic Entry Decisions

There are three basic decisions that a firm contemplating foreign expansion must make: which markets to enter, when to enter those markets, and on what scale.[1]

WHICH FOREIGN MARKETS?

There are more than 200 nation-states in the world. They do not all hold the same profit potential for a firm contemplating foreign expansion. Ultimately, the choice must be based on an assessment of a nation's long-run profit potential. This potential is a function of several factors, many of which we have studied in earlier chapters. In Chapter 2, we looked in detail at the economic and political factors that influence the potential attractiveness of a foreign market. There we noted that the attractiveness of a country as a potential market for an international business depends on balancing the benefits, costs, and risks associated with doing business in that country.

Chapter 2 also noted that the long-run economic benefits of doing business in a country are a function of factors such as the size of the market (in terms of demographics), the present wealth (purchasing power) of consumers in that market, and the likely future wealth of consumers, which depends upon economic growth rates. While some markets are very large when measured by number of consumers (e.g., China, India, and Indonesia) one must also look at living standards and economic growth. On this basis, China and, to a lesser extent, India, while relatively poor, are growing so rapidly that they are attractive targets for inward investment. Alternatively, weak growth in Indonesia implies that this populous nation is a far less attractive target for inward investment. As we saw in Chapter 2, likely future economic growth rates appear to be a function of a free market system and a country's capacity for growth (which may be greater in less developed nations). We also argued in Chapter 2 that the costs and risks associated with doing business in a foreign country are typically lower in economically advanced and politically stable democratic nations, and they are greater in less developed and politically unstable nations.

The discussion in Chapter 2 suggests that, other things being equal, the benefit–cost–risk trade-off is likely to be most favorable in politically stable developed and developing nations that have free market systems, and where there is not a dramatic upsurge in either inflation rates or private-sector debt. The trade-off is likely to be least favorable in politically unstable developing nations that operate with a mixed or command economy or in developing nations where speculative financial bubbles have led to excess borrowing (see Chapter 2 for further details).

Another important factor is the value an international business can create in a foreign market. This depends on the suitability of its product offering to that market and the nature of indigenous competition.[2] If the international business can offer a product that has not been widely available in that market and that satisfies an unmet need, the value of that product to consumers is likely to be much greater than if the international business simply offers the same type of product that indigenous competitors and other foreign entrants are already offering. Greater value translates into an ability to charge higher prices and/or to build sales volume more rapidly.

By considering such factors, a firm can rank countries in terms of their attractiveness and long-run profit potential. Preference is then given to entering markets that rank highly. For example, in the case of Tesco, entering emerging markets in Eastern Europe and Asia made sense given the lack of strong local competitors in these markets, the strong underlying growth trends, and Tesco's ability to add value by transferring its core competencies in retailing to those markets (see the opening case).

TIMING OF ENTRY

Once attractive markets have been identified, it is important to consider the **timing of entry.** We say that entry is early when an international business enters a foreign market before other foreign firms and late when it enters after other international businesses have already established themselves. The advantages frequently associated with entering a market early are commonly known as **first-mover advantages.**[3] One first-mover advantage is the ability to preempt rivals and capture demand by establishing a strong brand name. A second advantage is the ability to build sales volume in that country and ride down the experience curve ahead of rivals, giving the early entrant a cost advantage over later entrants. This cost advantage may enable the early entrant to cut prices below that of later entrants, thereby driving them out of the market. A third advantage is the ability of early entrants to create switching costs that tie customers into their products or services. Such switching costs make it difficult for later entrants to win business.

There can also be disadvantages associated with entering a foreign market before other international businesses. These are often referred to as **first-mover disadvantages.**[4] These disadvantages may give rise to **pioneering costs,** costs that an early entrant has to bear that

MANAGEMENT FOCUS

ING Group was formed in 1991 from the merger between the third largest bank in the Netherlands and the country's largest insurance company. Since then, the company has grown rapidly to become one of the top 10 financial services firms in the world, with operations in 65 countries and a wide range of products in banking, insurance, and asset management. ING's strategy has been to expand rapidly across national borders, primarily through a series of careful acquisitions. Its formula has been to pick a target that has good managers and a strong local presence, take a small stake in the company, win the trust of managers, and then propose a takeover. After the deal, the management and products of the acquired companies have been left largely intact, but ING has required them to sell ING products alongside their own. ING's big push has been the selling of insurance, banking, and investment products, something it has been doing in Holland since the original 1991 merger (in Holland, some 20 percent of ING's insurance products are sold through banks).

Two changes in the regulatory environment have helped ING pursue this strategy. One has been a trend to remove regulatory barriers that traditionally kept different parts of the financial services industry separate. In the United States, for example, a Depression-era law known as the Glass-Steagall Act disallowed insurance companies, banks, and asset managers such as mutual fund companies from selling each other's products. The U.S. Congress repealed this act in 1999, opening the way for the consolidation of the U.S. financial services industry. Many other countries that had similar regulations removed them in the 1990s. ING's native Holland was one of the first countries to remove barriers between different areas of the financial services industry. ING took advantage of this to become a pioneer of banking and insurance combinations in Europe. Another significant regulatory development occurred in 1997 when the World Trade Organization struck a deal between its member nations that effectively removed barriers to cross-border investment in financial services. This made it much easier for a company such as ING to build a global financial services business.

ING's expansion was initially centered on Europe where its largest acquisitions have included banks in Germany and Belgium. However, in recent years the centerpiece of ING's strategy has been its aggressive moves into the United States. While ING's Dutch insurance predecessor, Nationale-Nederlanden, had owned several small, regional U.S. insurance companies since the 1970s, the big push into the United States began with the 1997 acquisition of Equitable Life Insurance Company of Iowa. This was followed by the acquisitions of Furman Selz, a New York investment bank, whose activities complement those of Barings, a British-based investment bank with significant U.S. activities that ING acquired in 1995. In 2000, ING acquired ReliaStar Financial Services and the nonhealth insurance units of Aetna Financial Services. These acquisitions combined to make ING one of the top 10 financial services companies in the United States.

ING was attracted to the United States by several factors. The United States is by far the world's largest financial services market, so any company aspiring to be a global player must have a significant presence there.

a later entrant can avoid. Pioneering costs arise when the business system in a foreign country is so different from that in a firm's home market that the enterprise has to devote considerable effort, time, and expense to learning the rules of the game. Pioneering costs include the costs of business failure if the firm, due to its ignorance of the foreign environment, makes some major mistakes. A certain liability is associated with being a foreigner, and this liability is greater for foreign firms that enter a national market early.[5] Research seems to confirm that the probability of survival increases if an international business enters a national market after several other foreign firms have already done so.[6] The late entrant may benefit by observing and learning from the mistakes made by early entrants.

Deregulation made ING's strategy of cross-selling financial service products feasible in the United States. Despite some state-by-state regulation of insurance, ING says it is easier to do business in the United States than in the European Union, where the patchwork of languages and cultures makes it difficult to build a pan-European business with a single identity. Another lure is that with more and more Americans responsible for managing their own retirement with 401k plans and the like rather than traditional pensions, the personal investment business in the United States is booming, which has increased ING's appetite for U.S. financial services firms. In contrast, pensions are still primarily taken care of by national governments in Europe. Furthermore, in recent years U.S. insurance companies have traded at relatively low price–earnings ratios, making them seem like bargains compared to their European counterparts, which trade at higher valuations. Building a substantial U.S. presence also brings with it the benefits of geographic diversification, allowing ING to offset any revenue or profit shortfalls in one region with earnings elsewhere in the world.

Finally, ING has found it somewhat easier to make acquisitions in the United States than in Europe, where national pride has made it difficult for ING to acquire local companies. ING's initial attempt to acquire a Belgium bank in 1992 was rebuffed, primarily due to nationalistic concerns, and it took ING until 1997 to make the acquisition. Similarly, a 1999 attempt to acquire a major French bank, Credit Commercial de France, in which it already held a 19 percent stake, was turned down. According to news reports, French regulators had expressed concerns over what would have been the first foreign acquisition of a French bank, and

the board of CCF believed the acquisition should not proceed without the regulators' blessing.

With ING's major U.S. presence established, its strategy has been to push forward with the cross selling of its various insurance, banking, and asset management products. In mid-2000, the company announced the establishment of ING Direct, an online banking concept the company introduced in Canada, Australia, Spain, and France, where it has performed well. The online bank features a savings account paying above-market interest rates, which ING Direct can afford due to its low-cost structure. Although ING Direct does not offer checking accounts, which are money losers for traditional banks, it can electronically link an ING account to checking accounts that customers have at other banks, allowing them to easily transfer money. In addition to a savings account, ING Direct also offers consumer loans, mortgages, life insurance, and mutual funds. In an interesting move, instead of bank branches the company is setting up a scattering of cyber cafés where customers can drop in, buy a cup of coffee and a muffin, browse the Web, and access their online account. Despite initial skepticism, the concept seems to be doing well in the United States. By late 2004, ING Direct had attracted more than 2 million customers and over $30 billion.

Sources: J. Carreyrou, "Dutch Financial Giant Maps Its U.S. Invasion," *The Wall Street Journal*, June 22, 2000, p. A17; J. B. Treaster, "ING Group Makes Its Move in Virtual Banking and Insurance," *The New York Times*, August 26, 2000, p. C1; "The Lion's Friendly Approach," *The Economist*, December 18, 2000; S. Kirsner, "Would You Like a Mortgage with Your Mocha?" *Fast Company*, March 2003, pp. 110–14; O. O'Sullivan, "Tough Love Bank Thrives," *ABA Banking Journal*, December 2003, p. 12; and L. Bielski, "Bucking the Back to Bricks Trend," *ABA Banking Journal*, November 2004, pp. 25–32.

Pioneering costs also include the costs of promoting and establishing a product offering, including the costs of educating customers. These can be significant when the product being promoted is unfamiliar to local consumers. In contrast, later entrants may be able to ride on an early entrant's investments in learning and customer education by watching how the early entrant proceeded in the market, by avoiding costly mistakes made by the early entrant, and by exploiting the market potential created by the early entrant's investments in customer education. For example, KFC introduced the Chinese to American-style fast food, but a later entrant, McDonald's, has capitalized on the market in China.

An early entrant may be put at a severe disadvantage, relative to a later entrant, if regulations change in a way that diminishes the value of an early entrant's investments. This is a serious risk in many developing nations where the rules that govern business practices are still evolving. Early entrants can find themselves at a disadvantage if a subsequent change in regulations invalidates prior assumptions about the best business model for operating in that country.

SCALE OF ENTRY AND STRATEGIC COMMITMENTS

Another issue that an international business needs to consider when contemplating market entry is the scale of entry. Entering a market on a large scale involves the commitment of significant resources. Entering a market on a large scale implies rapid entry. Consider the entry of the Dutch insurance company ING into the U.S. insurance market in 1999 (described in detail in the accompanying Management Focus). ING had to spend several billion dollars to acquire its U.S. operations. Not all firms have the resources necessary to enter on a large scale, and even some large firms prefer to enter foreign markets on a small scale and then build slowly as they become more familiar with the market.

The consequences of entering on a significant scale—entering rapidly—are associated with the value of the resulting strategic commitments.[7] A strategic commitment has a long-term impact and is difficult to reverse. Deciding to enter a foreign market on a significant scale is a major strategic commitment. Strategic commitments, such as rapid large-scale market entry, can have an important influence on the nature of competition in a market. For example, by entering the U.S. financial services market on a significant scale, ING has signaled its commitment to the market (see the Management Focus). This will have several effects. On the positive side, it will make it easier for the company to attract customers and distributors (such as insurance agents). The scale of entry gives both customers and distributors reasons for believing that ING will remain in the market for the long run. The scale of entry may also give other foreign institutions considering entry into the United States pause; now they will have to compete not only against indigenous institutions in the United States, but also against an aggressive and successful European institution. On the negative side, by committing itself heavily to the United States, ING may have fewer resources available to support expansion in other desirable markets, such as Japan. The commitment to the United States limits the company's strategic flexibility.

As suggested by the ING example, significant strategic commitments are neither unambiguously good nor bad. Rather, they tend to change the competitive playing field and unleash a number of changes, some of which may be desirable and some of which will not be. It is important for a firm to think through the implications of large-scale entry into a market and act accordingly. Of particular relevance is trying to identify how actual and potential competitors might react to large-scale entry into a market. Also, the large-scale entrant is more likely than the small-scale entrant to be able to capture first-mover advantages associated with demand preemption, scale economies, and switching costs.

The value of the commitments that flow from rapid large-scale entry into a foreign market must be balanced against the resulting risks and lack of flexibility associated with significant commitments. But strategic inflexibility can also have value. A famous example from military history illustrates the value of inflexibility. When Hernán Cortés landed in Mexico, he ordered his men to burn all but one of his ships. Cortés reasoned that by eliminating their only method of retreat, his men had no choice but to fight hard to win against the Aztecs—and ultimately they did.[8]

Balanced against the value and risks of the commitments associated with large-scale entry are the benefits of a small-scale entry. Small-scale entry allows a firm to learn about a foreign market while limiting the firm's exposure to that market. Small-scale entry is a way to gather information about a foreign market before deciding whether to enter on a significant scale and how best to enter. By giving the firm time to collect information, small-scale entry reduces the risks associated with a subsequent large-scale entry. But the lack of commitment associated with small-scale entry may make it more difficult for the small-scale entrant to build market share and to capture first-mover or early-mover advantages. The risk-averse firm that enters a foreign market on a small scale may limit its potential losses, but it may also miss the chance to capture first-mover advantages.

Being the first in an industry to enter a developing nation such as India is risky, but potentially rewarding.

SUMMARY

There are no "right" decisions here, just decisions that are associated with different levels of risk and reward. Entering a large developing nation such as China or India before most other international businesses in the firm's industry, and entering on a large scale, will be associated with high levels of risk. In such cases, the liability of being foreign is increased by the absence of prior foreign entrants whose experience can be a useful guide. At the same time, the potential long-term rewards associated with such a strategy are great. The early large-scale entrant into a major developing nation may be able to capture significant first-mover advantages that will bolster its long-run position in that market.[9] In contrast, entering developed nations such as Australia or Canada after other international businesses in the firm's industry, and entering on a small scale to first learn more about those markets, will be associated with much lower levels of risk. However, the potential long-term rewards are also likely to be lower because the firm is essentially forgoing the opportunity to capture first-mover advantages and because the lack of commitment signaled by small-scale entry may limit its future growth potential.

This section has been written largely from the perspective of a business based in a developed country considering entry into foreign markets. Christopher Bartlett and Sumantra Ghoshal have pointed out the ability that businesses based in developing nations have to enter foreign markets and become global players.[10] Although such firms tend to be late entrants into foreign markets, and although their resources may be limited, Bartlett and Ghoshal argue that such late movers can still succeed against well-established global competitors by pursuing appropriate strategies. In particular, Bartlett and Ghoshal argue that companies based in developing nations should use the entry of foreign multinationals as an opportunity to learn from these competitors by benchmarking their operations and performance against them. Furthermore, they suggest that the local company may be able to find ways to differentiate itself from a foreign multinational, for example, by focusing on market niches that the multinational ignores or is unable to serve effectively if it has a standardized global product offering. Having improved its performance through learning and differentiated its product offering, the firm from a developing nation may then be able to pursue its own international expansion strategy. Even though the firm may be a late entrant into many countries, by benchmarking and then differentiating itself from early movers in global markets, the firm from the developing nation may still be able to build a strong international business presence. A good example of how this can work is given in the accompanying Management Focus, which looks at how Jollibee, a Philippines-based fast-food chain, has started to build a global presence in a market dominated by U.S. multinationals such as McDonald's and KFC.

MANAGEMENT FOCUS

Jollibee is one of the Philippines' phenomenal business success stories. Jollibee, which stands for "Jolly Bee," began operations in 1975 as a two-branch ice cream parlor. It later expanded its menu to include hot sandwiches and other meals. Encouraged by early success, Jollibee Foods Corporation was incorporated in 1978, with a network that had grown to seven outlets. In 1981, when Jollibee had 11 stores, McDonald's began to open stores in Manila. Many observers thought Jollibee would have difficulty competing against McDonald's. However, Jollibee saw this as an opportunity to learn from a very successful global competitor. Jollibee benchmarked its performance against that of McDonald's and started to adopt operational systems similar to those used at McDonald's to control its quality, cost, and service at the store level. This helped Jollibee to improve its performance.

As it came to better understand McDonald's business model, Jollibee began to look for a weakness in McDonald's global strategy. Jollibee executives concluded that McDonald's fare was too standardized for many locals, and that the local firm could gain share by tailoring its menu to local tastes. Jollibee's hamburgers were set apart by a secret mix of spices blended into the ground beef to make the burgers sweeter than those produced by McDonald's, appealing more to Philippine tastes. It also offered local fare including various rice dishes, pineapple burgers, and banana *langka* and peach mango pies for desserts. By pursuing this strategy, Jollibee maintained a leadership position over the global giant. By 2003, Jollibee had 467 stores in the Philippines, a market share of more than 50 percent, and revenues of about $500 million. McDonald's, in contrast, had 237 stores.

In the mid-1980s, Jollibee had gained enough confidence to expand internationally. Its initial ventures were into neighboring Asian countries such as Indonesia, where it pursued the strategy of localizing the menu to better match local tastes, thereby differentiating itself from McDonald's. In 1987, Jollibee entered the Middle East, where a large contingent of expatriate Filipino workers provided a ready-made market for the company. The strategy of focusing on expatriates worked so well that in the late 1990s Jollibee decided to enter another foreign market where there was a large Filipino population—the United States. Between 1999 and 2003, Jollibee opened 10 stores in the United States, all in California. Even though many believe the U.S. fast-food market is saturated, the stores have performed well. While the initial clientele was strongly biased toward the expatriate Filipino community, where Jollibee's brand awareness is high, non-Filipinos increasingly are coming to the restaurant. In the

Entry Modes

Once a firm decides to enter a foreign market, the question arises as to the best mode of entry. Firms can use six different modes to enter foreign markets: exporting, turnkey projects, licensing, franchising, establishing joint ventures with a host-country firm, or setting up a new wholly owned subsidiary in the host country. Each entry mode has advantages and disadvantages. Managers need to consider these carefully when deciding which to use.[11]

EXPORTING

Many manufacturing firms begin their global expansion as exporters and only later switch to another mode for serving a foreign market. We take a close look at the mechanics of exporting in the next chapter. Here we focus on the advantages and disadvantages of exporting as an entry mode.

Advantages

Exporting has two distinct advantages. First, it avoids the often substantial costs of establishing manufacturing operations in the host country. Second, exporting may help a firm achieve experience curve and location economies (see Chapter 12). By manufacturing the

San Francisco store, which has been open the longest, more than half the customers are now non-Filipino. Today Jollibee has 33 international stores and a potentially bright future as a niche player in a market that has historically been dominated by U.S. multinationals.

Sources: Christopher Bartlett and Sumantra Ghoshal, "Going Global: Lessons from Late Movers," *Harvard Business Review,* March–April 2000, pp. 132–45; "Jollibee Battles Burger Giants in US Market," *Philippine Daily Inquirer,* July 13, 2000; www.jollibee.com.ph; M. Ballon, "Jollibee Struggling to Expand in U.S.," *Los Angeles Times,* September 16, 2002, p. C1; and J. Hookway, "Burgers and Beer," *Far Eastern Economic Review,* December 2003, pp. 72–74.

Jollibee may be heading your way! Unlike many fast-food chains that have their roots within the United States, the Jollibee chain originated in the Philippines using McDonald's as a role model.

product in a centralized location and exporting it to other national markets, the firm may realize substantial scale economies from its global sales volume. This is how Sony came to dominate the global TV market, how Matsushita came to dominate the VCR market, how many Japanese automakers made inroads into the U.S. market, and how South Korean firms such as Samsung gained market share in computer memory chips.

Disadvantages

Exporting has a number of drawbacks. First, exporting from the firm's home base may not be appropriate if lower-cost locations for manufacturing the product can be found abroad (i.e., if the firm can realize location economies by moving production elsewhere). Thus, particularly for firms pursuing global or transnational strategies, it may be preferable to manufacture where the mix of factor conditions is most favorable from a value creation perspective and to export to the rest of the world from that location. This is not so much an argument against exporting as an argument against exporting from the firm's home country. Many U.S. electronics firms have moved some of their manufacturing to the Far East because of the availability of low-cost, highly skilled labor there. They then export from that location to the rest of the world, including the United States.

A second drawback to exporting is that high transport costs can make exporting uneconomical, particularly for bulk products. One way of getting around this is to manufacture bulk products regionally. This strategy enables the firm to realize some economies from large-scale production and at the same time to limit its transport costs. For example, many multinational chemical firms manufacture their products regionally, serving several countries from one facility.

Another drawback is that tariff barriers can make exporting uneconomical. Similarly, the threat of tariff barriers by the host-country government can make it very risky. A fourth drawback to exporting arises when a firm delegates its marketing, sales, and service in each country where it does business to another company. This is a common approach for manufacturing firms that are just beginning to expand internationally. The other company may be a local agent, or it may be another multinational with extensive international distribution operations. Local agents often carry the products of competing firms and so have divided loyalties. In such cases, the local agent may not do as good a job as the firm would if it managed its marketing itself. Similar problems can occur when another multinational takes on distribution.

The way around such problems is to set up wholly owned subsidiaries in foreign nations to handle local marketing, sales, and service. By doing this, the firm can exercise tight control over marketing and sales in the country while reaping the cost advantages of manufacturing the product in a single location, or a few choice locations.

TURNKEY PROJECTS

Firms that specialize in the design, construction, and start-up of turnkey plants are common in some industries. In a **turnkey project,** the contractor agrees to handle every detail of the project for a foreign client, including the training of operating personnel. At completion of the contract, the foreign client is handed the "key" to a plant that is ready for full operation—hence, the term *turnkey*. This is a means of exporting process technology to other countries. Turnkey projects are most common in the chemical, pharmaceutical, petroleum refining, and metal refining industries, all of which use complex, expensive production technologies.

Advantages

The know-how required to assemble and run a technologically complex process, such as refining petroleum or steel, is a valuable asset. Turnkey projects are a way of earning great economic returns from that asset. The strategy is particularly useful where FDI is limited by host-government regulations. For example, the governments of many oil-rich countries have set out to build their own petroleum refining industries, so they restrict FDI in their oil and refining sectors. But because many of these countries lack petroleum-refining technology, they gain it by entering into turnkey projects with foreign firms that have the technology. Such deals are often attractive to the selling firm because without them, they would have no way to earn a return on their valuable know-how in that country. A turnkey strategy can also be less risky than conventional FDI. In a country with unstable political and economic environments, a longer-term investment might expose the firm to unacceptable political and/or economic risks (e.g., the risk of nationalization or of economic collapse).

Disadvantages

Three main drawbacks are associated with a turnkey strategy. First, the firm that enters into a turnkey deal will have no long-term interest in the foreign country. This can be a disadvantage if that country subsequently proves to be a major market for the output of the process that has been exported. One way around this is to take a minority equity interest in the operation. Second, the firm that enters into a turnkey project with a foreign enterprise may inadvertently create a competitor. For example, many of the Western firms that sold oil-refining technology to firms in Saudi Arabia, Kuwait, and other Gulf states now find themselves competing with these firms in the world oil market. Third, if the firm's process technology is a source of competitive advantage, then selling this technology through a turnkey project is also selling competitive advantage to potential and/or actual competitors.

LICENSING

A **licensing agreement** is an arrangement whereby a licensor grants the rights to intangible property to another entity (the licensee) for a specified period, and in return, the licensor receives a royalty fee from the licensee.[12] Intangible property includes patents, inventions, formulas, processes, designs, copyrights, and trademarks. For example, to enter the Japanese market, Xerox, inventor of the photocopier, established a joint venture with Fuji Photo that is known as Fuji Xerox. Xerox then licensed its xerographic know-how to Fuji Xerox. In return, Fuji Xerox paid Xerox a royalty fee equal to 5 percent of the net sales revenue that Fuji Xerox earned from the sales of photocopiers based on Xerox's patented know-how. In the Fuji Xerox case, the license was originally granted for 10 years, and it has been renegotiated and extended several times since. The licensing agreement between Xerox and Fuji Xerox also limited Fuji Xerox's direct sales to the Asian Pacific region (although Fuji Xerox does supply Xerox with photocopiers that are sold in North America under the Xerox label).[13]

Advantages

In the typical international licensing deal, the licensee puts up most of the capital necessary to get the overseas operation going. Thus, a primary advantage of licensing is that the firm does not have to bear the development costs and risks associated with opening a foreign market. Licensing is very attractive for firms lacking the capital to develop operations overseas. In addition, licensing can be attractive when a firm is unwilling to commit substantial financial resources to an unfamiliar or politically volatile foreign market. Licensing is also often used when a firm wishes to participate in a foreign market but is prohibited from doing so by barriers to investment. This was one of the original reasons for the formation of the Fuji–Xerox joint venture in 1962. Xerox wanted to participate in the Japanese market but was prohibited from setting up a wholly owned subsidiary by the Japanese government. So Xerox set up the joint venture with Fuji and then licensed its know-how to the joint venture.

Finally, licensing is frequently used when a firm possesses some intangible property that might have business applications, but it does not want to develop those applications itself. For example, Bell Laboratories at AT&T originally invented the transistor circuit in the 1950s, but AT&T decided it did not want to produce transistors, so it licensed the technology to a number of other companies, such as Texas Instruments. Similarly, Coca-Cola has licensed its famous trademark to clothing manufacturers, which have incorporated the design into clothing.

Disadvantages

Licensing has three serious drawbacks. First, it does not give a firm the tight control over manufacturing, marketing, and strategy that is required for realizing experience curve and location economies. Licensing typically involves each licensee setting up its own production operations. This severely limits the firm's ability to realize experience curve and location economies by producing its product in a centralized location. When these economies are important, licensing may not be the best way to expand overseas.

Second, competing in a global market may require a firm to coordinate strategic moves across countries by using profits earned in one country to support competitive attacks in another. By its very nature, licensing limits a firm's ability to do this. A licensee is unlikely to allow a multinational firm to use its profits (beyond those due in the form of royalty payments) to support a different licensee operating in another country.

A third problem with licensing is one that we encountered in Chapter 7 when we reviewed the economic theory of FDI. This is the risk associated with licensing technological know-how to foreign companies. Technological know-how constitutes the basis of many multinational firms' competitive advantage. Most firms wish to maintain control over how their know-how is used, and a firm can quickly lose control over its technology by licensing it. Many firms have made the mistake of thinking they could maintain control over their know-how within the framework of a licensing agreement. RCA Corporation, for example, once licensed its color TV technology to Japanese firms including Matsushita and Sony. The Japanese firms quickly assimilated the technology, improved on it, and used it to enter the U.S. market, taking substantial market share away from RCA.

There are ways of reducing this risk. One way is by entering into a cross-licensing agreement with a foreign firm. Under a cross-licensing agreement, a firm might license some valuable intangible property to a foreign partner, but in addition to a royalty payment, the firm might also request that the foreign partner license some of its valuable know-how to the firm. Such agreements are believed to reduce the risks associated with licensing technological know-how, since the licensee realizes that if it violates the licensing contract (by using the knowledge obtained to compete directly with the licensor), the licensor can do the same to it. Cross-licensing agreements enable firms to hold each other hostage, which reduces the probability that they will behave opportunistically toward each other.[14] Such cross-licensing agreements are increasingly common in high-technology industries. For example, the U.S. biotechnology firm Amgen licensed one of its key drugs, Nuprogene, to Kirin, the Japanese pharmaceutical company. The license gives Kirin the right to sell Nuprogene in Japan. In return, Amgen receives a royalty payment and, through a licensing agreement, gained the right to sell some of Kirin's products in the United States.

Another way of reducing the risk associated with licensing is to follow the Fuji Xerox model and link an agreement to license know-how with the formation of a joint venture in which the licensor and licensee take important equity stakes. Such an approach aligns the interests of licensor and licensee, because both have a stake in ensuring that the venture is successful. Thus, the risk that Fuji Photo might appropriate Xerox's technological know-how, and then compete directly against Xerox in the global photocopier market, was reduced by the establishment of a joint venture in which both Xerox and Fuji Photo had an important stake.

FRANCHISING

Franchising is similar to licensing, although franchising tends to involve longer-term commitments than licensing. **Franchising** is basically a specialized form of licensing in which the franchiser not only sells intangible property (normally a trademark) to the franchisee, but also insists that the franchisee agree to abide by strict rules as to how it does business. The franchiser will also often assist the franchisee to run the business on an ongoing basis. As with licensing, the franchiser typically receives a royalty payment, which amounts to some percentage of the franchisee's revenues. Whereas licensing is pursued primarily by manufacturing firms, franchising is employed primarily by service firms.[15] McDonald's is a good example of a firm that has grown by using a franchising strategy. McDonald's strict rules as to how franchisees should operate a restaurant extend to control over the menu, cooking methods, staffing policies, and design and location. McDonald's also organizes the supply chain for its franchisees and provides management training and financial assistance.[16]

Advantages

The advantages of franchising as an entry mode are very similar to those of licensing. The firm is relieved of many of the costs and risks of opening a foreign market on its own. Instead, the franchisee typically assumes those costs and risks. This creates a good incentive for the franchisee to build a profitable operation as quickly as possible. Thus, using a franchising strategy, a service firm can build a global presence quickly and at a relatively low cost and risk, as McDonald's has.

Disadvantages

The disadvantages are less pronounced than in the case of licensing. Since franchising is often used by service companies, there is no reason to consider the need for coordination of manufacturing to achieve experience curve and location economies. But franchising may inhibit the firm's ability to take profits out of one country to support competitive attacks in another. A more significant disadvantage of franchising is quality control. The foundation of franchising arrangements is that the firm's brand name conveys a message to consumers about the quality of the firm's product. Thus, a business traveler checking in at a Four Seasons hotel in Hong Kong can reasonably expect the same quality of room, food, and service that she would receive in New York. The Four Seasons name is supposed to guarantee consistent product quality. This presents a problem in that foreign franchisees may not be as concerned about quality as they are supposed to be, and the result of poor quality can extend beyond lost sales in a particular foreign market to a decline in the firm's worldwide reputation. For example, if the business traveler has a bad experience at the Four Seasons in Hong Kong, she may never go to another Four Seasons hotel and may urge her colleagues to do likewise. The geographical distance of the firm from its foreign franchisees can make poor quality difficult to detect. In addition, the sheer numbers of franchisees—in the case of McDonald's, tens of thousands—can make quality control difficult. Due to these factors, quality problems may persist.

Curves is the largest fitness franchise in the world, with fitness centers in the United States, Europe, Mexico, and Canada, and was ranked the number two franchise in 2004 by *Entrepreneur* magazine.

One way around this disadvantage is to set up a subsidiary in each country in which the firm expands. The subsidiary might be wholly owned by the company or a joint venture with a foreign company. The subsidiary assumes the rights and obligations to establish franchises throughout the particular country or region. McDonald's, for example, establishes a master franchisee in many countries. Typically, this master franchisee is a joint venture between McDonald's and a local firm. The proximity and the smaller number of franchises to oversee reduce the quality control challenge. In addition, because the subsidiary (or master franchisee) is at least partly owned by the firm, the firm can place its own managers in the subsidiary to help ensure that it is doing a good job of monitoring the franchises. This organizational arrangement has proven very satisfactory for McDonald's, KFC, and others.

JOINT VENTURES

A **joint venture** entails establishing a firm that is jointly owned by two or more otherwise independent firms. Fuji Xerox, for example, was set up as a joint venture between Xerox and Fuji Photo. Establishing a joint venture with a foreign firm has long been a popular mode for entering a new market. As we saw in the opening case, Tesco has used joint ventures to expand into foreign markets. The most typical joint venture is a 50/50 venture, in which there are two parties, each of which holds a 50 percent ownership stake and contributes a team of managers to share operating control (this was the case with the Fuji–Xerox joint venture until 2001; it is now a 25/75 venture with Xerox holding 25 percent). Some firms, however, have sought joint ventures in which they have a majority share and thus tighter control.[17] This has been the case with Tesco.

Advantages

Joint ventures have a number of advantages. First, a firm benefits from a local partner's knowledge of the host country's competitive conditions, culture, language, political systems, and business systems. Thus, for many U.S. firms, joint ventures have involved the U.S. company providing technological know-how and products and the local partner providing the marketing expertise and the local knowledge necessary for competing in that country. Second, when the development costs and/or risks of opening a foreign market are high, a firm might gain by sharing these costs and or risks with a local partner. Third, in many countries, political considerations make joint ventures the only feasible entry mode. Research suggests joint ventures with local partners face a low risk of being subject to nationalization or other forms of adverse government interference.[18] This appears to be because local equity partners, who may have some influence on host-government policy, have a vested interest in speaking out against nationalization or government interference.

Disadvantages

Despite these advantages, there are major disadvantages with joint ventures. First, as with licensing, a firm that enters into a joint venture risks giving control of its technology to its partner. Thus, a proposed joint venture in 2002 between Boeing and Mitsubishi Heavy Industries to build a new wide-body jet, raised fears that Boeing might unwittingly give away its commercial airline technology to the Japanese. However, joint-venture agreements can be constructed to minimize this risk. One option is to hold majority ownership in the venture. This allows the dominant partner to exercise greater control over its technology. But it can be difficult to find a foreign partner who is willing to settle for minority ownership. Another option is to "wall off" from a partner technology that is central to the core competence of the firm, while sharing other technology.

A second disadvantage is that a joint venture does not give a firm the tight control over subsidiaries that it might need to realize experience curve or location economies. Nor does it give a firm the tight control over a foreign subsidiary that it might need for engaging in coordinated global attacks against its rivals. Consider the entry of Texas Instruments (TI) into the Japanese semiconductor market. When TI established semiconductor facilities in Japan, it did so for the dual purpose of checking Japanese manufacturers' market share and limiting their cash available for invading TI's global market. In other words, TI was engaging in global strategic coordination. To implement this strategy, TI's subsidiary in Japan had to be prepared to take instructions from corporate headquarters regarding competitive strategy. The strategy also required the Japanese subsidiary to run at a loss if necessary. Few if any potential joint-venture partners would have been willing to accept such conditions, since it would have necessitated a willingness to accept a negative return on investment. Indeed, many joint ventures establish a degree of autonomy that would make such direct control over strategic decisions all but impossible to establish.[19] Thus, to implement this strategy, TI set up a wholly owned subsidiary in Japan.

A third disadvantage with joint ventures is that the shared ownership arrangement can lead to conflicts and battles for control between the investing firms if their goals and objectives change or if they take different views as to what the strategy should be. This was apparently not a problem with the Fuji–Xerox joint venture. According to Yotaro Kobayashi, currently the chairman of Fuji Xerox, a primary reason is that both Xerox and Fuji Photo adopted an arm's-length relationship with Fuji Xerox, giving the venture's management considerable freedom to determine its own strategy.[20] However, much research indicates that conflicts of interest over strategy and goals often arise in joint ventures. These conflicts tend to be greater when the venture is between firms of different nationalities, and they often end in the dissolution of the venture.[21] Such conflicts tend to be triggered by shifts in the relative bargaining power of venture partners. For example, in the case of ventures between a foreign firm and a local firm, as a foreign partner's knowledge about local market conditions increases, it depends less on the expertise of a local partner. This increases the bargaining power of the foreign partner and ultimately leads to conflicts over control of the venture's strategy and goals.[22] Some firms have sought to limit such problems by entering into joint ventures in which one partner has a controlling interest. For example, when it first entered South Korea, Tesco set up a joint venture with Samsung under which it had a 51 percent stake, and thus control (see the opening case).

WHOLLY OWNED SUBSIDIARIES

In a **wholly owned subsidiary,** the firm owns 100 percent of the stock. Establishing a wholly owned subsidiary in a foreign market can be done two ways. The firm either can set up a new operation in that country, often referred to as a greenfield venture, or it can acquire an established firm in that host nation and use that firm to promote its products.[23] For example, as we saw in the Management Focus, ING's strategy for entering the U.S. market was to acquire established U.S. enterprises, rather than try to build an operation from the ground floor.

Advantages

There are several clear advantages of wholly owned subsidiaries. First, when a firm's competitive advantage is based on technological competence, a wholly owned subsidiary will often be the preferred entry mode because it reduces the risk of losing control over that competence. (See Chapter 7 for more details.) Many high-tech firms prefer this entry mode for overseas expansion (e.g., firms in the semiconductor, electronics, and pharmaceutical industries). Second, a wholly owned subsidiary gives a firm tight control over operations in different countries. This is necessary for engaging in global strategic coordination (i.e., using profits from one country to support competitive attacks in another).

Third, a wholly owned subsidiary may be required if a firm is trying to realize location and experience curve economies (as firms pursuing global and transnational strategies try to do). As we saw in Chapter 11, when cost pressures are intense, it may pay a firm to configure its value chain in such a way that the value added at each stage is maximized. Thus, a national subsidiary may specialize in manufacturing only part of the product line or certain components of the end product, exchanging parts and products with other subsidiaries in the firm's global system. Establishing such a global production system requires a high degree of control over the operations of each affiliate. The various operations must be prepared to accept centrally determined decisions as to how they will produce, how much they will produce, and how their output will be priced for transfer to the next operation. Because licensees or joint-venture partners are unlikely to accept such a subservient role, establishing wholly owned subsidiaries may be necessary. Finally, establishing a wholly owed subsidiary gives the firm a 100 percent share in the profits generated in a foreign market.

Disadvantages

Establishing a wholly owned subsidiary is generally the most costly method of serving a foreign market from a capital investment standpoint. Firms doing this must bear the full capital costs and risks of setting up overseas operations. The risks associated with learning to do business in a new culture are less if the firm acquires an established host-country enterprise. However, acquisitions raise additional problems, including those associated with trying to marry divergent corporate cultures. These problems may more than offset any benefits derived by acquiring an established operation. Because the choice between greenfield ventures and acquisitions is such an important one, we shall discuss it in more detail later in the chapter.

Selecting an Entry Mode

As the preceding discussion demonstrated, all the entry modes have advantages and disadvantages, as summarized in Table 14.1. Thus, trade-offs are inevitable when selecting an entry mode. For example, when considering entry into an unfamiliar country with a track record for discriminating against foreign-owned enterprises when awarding government contracts, a firm might favor a joint venture with a local enterprise. Its rationale might be that the local partner will help it establish operations in an unfamiliar environment and will help the company win government contracts. However, if the firm's core competence is based on proprietary technology, entering a joint venture might risk losing control of that technology to the joint-venture partner, in which case the strategy may seem unattractive. Despite the existence of such trade-offs, it is possible to make some generalizations about the optimal choice of entry mode.[24]

Entry Mode	Advantages	Disadvantages
Exporting	Ability to realize location and experience curve economies	High transport costs Trade barriers Problems with local marketing agents
Turnkey contracts	Ability to earn returns from process technology skills in countries where FDI is restricted	Creating efficient competitors Lack of long-term market presence
Licensing	Low development costs and risks	Lack of control over technology Inability to realize location and experience curve economies Inability to engage in global strategic coordination
Franchising	Low development costs and risks	Lack of control over quality Inability to engage in global strategic coordination
Joint ventures	Access to local partner's knowledge Sharing development costs and risks Politically acceptable	Lack of control over technology Inability to engage in global strategic coordination Inability to realize location and experience economies
Wholly owned subsidiaries	Protection of technology Ability to engage in global strategic coordination Ability to realize location and experience economies	High costs and risks

TABLE 14.1

Advantages and Disadvantages of Entry Modes

CORE COMPETENCIES AND ENTRY MODE

We saw in Chapter 12 that firms often expand internationally to earn greater returns from their core competencies, transferring the skills and products derived from their core competencies to foreign markets where indigenous competitors lack those skills. The optimal entry mode for these firms depends to some degree on the nature of their core competencies. A distinction can be drawn between firms whose core competency is in technological know-how and those whose core competency is in management know-how.

Technological Know-how

As was observed in Chapter 7, if a firm's competitive advantage (its core competence) is based on control over proprietary technological know-how, licensing and joint-venture arrangements should be avoided if possible to minimize the risk of losing control over that technology. Thus, if a high-tech firm sets up operations in a foreign country to profit from a core competency in technological know-how, it will probably do so through a wholly owned subsidiary. This rule should not be viewed as hard and fast, however. Sometimes a licensing or joint-venture arrangement can be structured to reduce the risk of licensees or joint-venture partners expropriating technological know-how. We will see how this might be achieved later in the chapter when we examine the structuring of strategic alliances. Another exception exists when a firm perceives its technological advantage to be only transitory, when it expects rapid imitation of its core technology by competitors. In such cases, the firm might want to license its technology as rapidly as possible to foreign firms to gain global acceptance for its technology before the imitation occurs.[25] Such a strategy has some advantages. By licensing its technology to competitors, the firm may deter them from developing their own, possibly superior, technology. Further, by licensing its technology, the firm may establish its technology as the dominant design in the industry (as Matsushita did with its VHS format for VCRs). This may ensure a steady stream of royalty payments. However, the attractions of licensing are frequently outweighed by the risks of losing control over technology and if this is a risk, licensing should be avoided.

Management Know-how

The competitive advantage of many service firms is based on management know-how (e.g., McDonald's). For such firms, the risk of losing control over the management skills to franchisees or joint-venture partners is not that great. These firms' valuable asset is their brand name, and brand names are generally well protected by international laws pertaining to trademarks. Given this, many of the issues arising in the case of technological know-how are of less concern here. As a result, many service firms favor a combination of franchising and subsidiaries to control the franchises within particular countries or regions. The subsidiaries may be wholly owned or joint ventures, but most service firms have found that joint ventures with local partners work best for the controlling subsidiaries. A joint venture is often politically more acceptable and brings a degree of local knowledge to the subsidiary.

PRESSURES FOR COST REDUCTIONS AND ENTRY MODE

The greater the pressures for cost reductions are, the more likely a firm will want to pursue some combination of exporting and wholly owned subsidiaries. By manufacturing in those locations where factor conditions are optimal and then exporting to the rest of the world, a firm may be able to realize substantial location and experience curve economies. The firm might then want to export the finished product to marketing subsidiaries based in various countries. These subsidiaries will typically be wholly owned and have the responsibility for overseeing distribution in their particular countries. Setting up wholly owned marketing subsidiaries is preferable to joint-venture arrangements and to using foreign marketing agents because it gives the firm tight control that might be required for coordinating a globally dispersed value chain. It also gives the firm the ability to use the profits generated in one market to improve its competitive position in another market. In other words, firms pursuing global standardization or transnational strategies tend to prefer establishing wholly owned subsidiaries.

🌐 Greenfield Venture or Acquisition?

A firm can establish a wholly owned subsidiary in a country by building a subsidiary from the ground up, the so-called greenfield strategy, or by acquiring an enterprise in the target market.[26] The volume of cross-border acquisitions has been growing at a rapid rate for two decades. Over the last decade, between 50 and 80 percent of all FDI inflows have been in the form of mergers and acquisitions. In 2001, for example, mergers and acquisitions accounted for 80 percent of all FDI inflows. In 2003 the figure was 53 percent, or some $297 billion.[27]

PROS AND CONS OF ACQUISITIONS

Acquisitions have three major points in their favor. First, they are quick to execute. By acquiring an established enterprise, a firm can rapidly build its presence in the target foreign market. When the German automobile company Daimler-Benz decided it needed a bigger presence in the U.S. automobile market, it did not increase that presence by building new factories to serve the United States, a process that would have taken years.

Instead, it acquired the number three U.S. automobile company, Chrysler, and merged the two operations to form DaimlerChrysler. When the Spanish telecommunications service provider Telefonica wanted to build a service presence in Latin America, it did so through a series of acquisitions, purchasing telecommunications companies in Brazil and Argentina. In these cases, the firms made acquisitions because they knew that was the quickest way to establish a sizable presence in the target market.

Second, in many cases firms make acquisitions to preempt their competitors. The need for preemption is particularly great in markets that are rapidly globalizing, such as telecommunications, where a combination of deregulation within nations and liberalization of regulations governing cross-border foreign direct investment has made it much easier for enterprises to enter foreign markets through acquisitions. Such markets may see concentrated waves of acquisitions as firms race each other to attain global scale. In the telecommunications industry, for example, regulatory changes triggered what can be called a feeding frenzy, with firms entering each other's markets via acquisitions to establish a global presence. These included the $60 billion acquisition of Air Touch Communications in the United States by the British company Vodafone, which was the largest acquisition ever; the $13 billion acquisition of One 2 One in Britain by the German company Deutsche Telekom; and the $6.4 billion acquisition of Excel Communications in the United States by Teleglobe of Canada, all of which occurred in 1998 and 1999.[28] A similar wave of cross-border acquisitions occurred in the global automobile industry over the same time period, with Daimler acquiring Chrysler, Ford acquiring Volvo, and Renault acquiring Nissan.

Third, managers may believe acquisitions to be less risky than greenfield ventures. When a firm makes an acquisition, it buys a set of assets that are producing a known revenue and profit stream. In contrast, the revenue and profit stream that a greenfield venture might generate is uncertain because it does not yet exist. When a firm makes an acquisition in a foreign market, it not only acquires a set of tangible assets, such as factories, logistics systems, customer service systems, and so on, but it also acquires valuable intangible assets including a local brand name and managers' knowledge of the business environment in that nation. Such knowledge can reduce the risk of mistakes caused by ignorance of the national culture.

Despite the arguments for making acquisitions, acquisitions often produce disappointing results.[29] For example, a study by Mercer Management Consulting looked at 150 acquisitions worth more than $500 million each that were undertaken between January 1990 and July 1995.[30] The Mercer study concluded that 50 percent of these acquisitions eroded shareholder value, while another 33 percent created only marginal returns. Only 17 percent were judged to be successful. Similarly, a study by KPMG, an accounting and management consulting company, looked at 700 large acquisitions between 1996 and 1998. The study found that while some 30 percent of these actually created value for the acquiring company, 31 percent destroyed value, and the remainder had little impact.[31] A similar study by McKenzie & Co. estimated that some 70 percent of mergers and acquisitions failed to achieve expected revenue synergies.[32] In a seminal study of the postacquisition performance of acquired companies, David Ravenscraft and Mike Scherer concluded that on average the profits and market shares of acquired companies declined following acquisition.[33] They also noted that a smaller but substantial subset of those companies experienced traumatic difficulties, which ultimately led to their being sold by the acquiring company. Ravenscraft and Scherer's evidence suggests that many acquisitions destroy rather than create value. While most of this research has looked at domestic acquisitions, the findings probably also apply to cross-border acquisitions.[34]

Why Do Acquisitions Fail?

Acquisitions fail for several reasons. First, the acquiring firms often overpay for the assets of the acquired firm. The price of the target firm can get bid up if more than one firm is interested in its purchase, as is often the case. In addition, the management of the acquiring firm is often too optimistic about the value that can be created via an acquisition and is thus willing to pay a significant premium over a target firm's market capitalization. This is called the "hubris hypothesis" of why acquisitions fail. The hubris hypothesis postulates that top managers typically overestimate their ability to create value from an acquisition, primarily because rising to the top of a corporation has given them an exaggerated sense of their own capabilities.[35] For example, Daimler acquired Chrysler in 1998 for $40 billion, a premium of 40 percent over the market value of Chrysler before the takeover bid. Daimler paid this much because it thought it could use Chrysler to help it grow market share in the United States. At the time, Daimler's management issued bold announcements about the "synergies" that would be created from combining the operations of the two companies. Executives believed they could attain greater scale economies from the global presence, take costs out of the German and U.S. operations, and boost the profitability of the combined entity. However, within a year of the acquisition, Daimler's German management was faced with a crisis at Chrysler, which was suddenly losing money due to weak sales in the United States. In retrospect, Daimler's management had been far too optimistic about the potential for future demand in the U.S. auto market and about the opportunities for creating value from "synergies." Daimler acquired Chrysler at the end of a multiyear boom in U.S. auto sales and paid a large premium over Chrysler's market value just before demand slumped.[36]

Second, many acquisitions fail because there is a clash between the cultures of the acquiring and acquired firm. After an acquisition, many acquired companies experience high management turnover, possibly because their employees do not like the acquiring company's way of doing things.[37] This happened at DaimlerChrysler; many senior managers left Chrysler in the first year after the merger. Apparently, Chrysler executives disliked the dominance in decision making by Daimler's German managers, while the Germans resented that Chrysler's American managers were paid two to three times as much as their German counterparts. These cultural differences created tensions, which ultimately exhibited themselves in high management turnover at Chrysler.[38] The loss of management talent and expertise can materially harm the performance of the acquired unit.[39] This may be particularly problematic in an international business, where management of the acquired unit may have valuable local knowledge that can be difficult to replace.

Third, many acquisitions fail because attempts to realize synergies by integrating the operations of the acquired and acquiring entities often run into roadblocks and take much longer than forecast. Differences in management philosophy and company culture can slow the integration of operations. Differences in national culture may exacerbate these problems. Bureaucratic haggling between managers also complicates the process. Again, this reportedly occurred at DaimlerChrysler, where grand plans to integrate the operations of the two companies were bogged down by endless committee meetings and by simple logistical considerations such as the six-hour time difference between Detroit and Germany. By the time an integration plan had been worked out, Chrysler was losing money, and Daimler's German managers suddenly had a crisis on their hands.

Finally, many acquisitions fail due to inadequate preacquisition screening.[40] Many firms decide to acquire other firms without thoroughly analyzing the potential benefits and costs. They often move with undue haste to execute the acquisition, perhaps because they fear another competitor may preempt them. After the acquisition, however, many acquiring firms discover that instead of buying a well-run business, they have purchased a troubled organization. This may be a particular problem in cross-border acquisitions because the acquiring firm may not fully understand the target firm's national culture and business system.

Reducing the Risks of Failure

These problems can all be overcome if the firm is careful about its acquisition strategy.[41] Screening of the foreign enterprise to be acquired, including a detailed auditing of operations, financial position, and management culture, can help to make sure the firm (1) does not pay too much for the acquired unit, (2) does not uncover any nasty surprises after the acquisition, and (3) acquires a firm whose organization culture is not antagonistic to that of the acquiring enterprise. It is also important for the acquirer to allay any concerns that management in the acquired enterprise might have. The objective should be to reduce unwanted management attrition after the acquisition. Finally, managers must move rapidly after an acquisition to put an integration plan in place and to act on that plan. Some people in both the acquiring and acquired units will try to slow or stop any integration efforts, particularly when losses of employment or management power are involved, and managers should have a plan for dealing with such impediments before they arise.

PROS AND CONS OF GREENFIELD VENTURES

The big advantage of establishing a greenfield venture in a foreign country is that it gives the firm a much greater ability to build the kind of subsidiary company that it wants. For example, it is much easier to build an organization culture from scratch than it is to change the culture of an acquired unit. Similarly, it is much easier to establish a set of operating routines in a new subsidiary than it is to convert the operating routines of an acquired unit. This is a very important advantage for many international businesses, where transferring products, competencies, skills, and know-how from the established operations of the firm to the new subsidiary are principal ways of creating value. For example, when Lincoln Electric, the U.S. manufacturer of arc welding equipment, first ventured overseas in the mid-1980s, it did so by acquisitions, purchasing arc welding equipment companies in Europe. However, Lincoln's competitive advantage in the United States was based on a strong organizational culture and a unique set of incentives that encouraged its employees to do everything possible to increase productivity. Lincoln found through bitter experience that it was almost impossible to transfer its organizational culture and incentives to acquired firms, which had their own distinct organizational cultures and incentives. As a result, the firm switched its entry strategy in the mid-1990s and began to enter foreign countries by establishing greenfield ventures, building operations from the ground up. While this strategy takes more time to execute, Lincoln has found that it yields greater long-run returns than the acquisition strategy.

Set against this significant advantage are the disadvantages of establishing a greenfield venture. Greenfield ventures are slower to establish. They are also risky. As with any new venture, a degree of uncertainty is associated with future revenue and profit prospects. However, if the firm has already been successful in other foreign markets and understands what it takes to do business in other countries, these risks may not be that great. For example, having already gained great knowledge about operating internationally, the risk to McDonald's of entering yet another country is probably not that great. Also, greenfield ventures are less risky than acquisitions in the sense that there is less potential for unpleasant surprises. A final disadvantage is the possibility of being preempted by more aggressive global competitors who enter via acquisitions and build a big market presence that limits the market potential for the greenfield venture.

GREENFIELD OR ACQUISITION?

The choice between acquisitions and greenfield ventures is not an easy one. Both modes have their advantages and disadvantages. In general, the choice will depend on the circumstances confronting the firm. If the firm is seeking to enter a market where there are already well-established incumbent enterprises, and where global competitors are also interested in establishing a presence, it may pay the firm to enter via an acquisition. In such circumstances, a greenfield venture may be too slow to establish a sizable presence. However, if the firm is going to make an acquisition, its management should be cognizant of the risks associated with acquisitions that were discussed earlier and consider these when determining which firms to purchase. It may be better to enter by the slower route of a greenfield venture than to make a bad acquisition.

If the firm is considering entering a country where there are no incumbent competitors to be acquired, then a greenfield venture may be the only mode. Even when incumbents exist, if the competitive advantage of the firm is based on the transfer of organizationally embedded competencies, skills, routines, and culture, it may still be preferable to enter via a greenfield venture. Things such as skills and organizational culture, which are based on significant knowledge that is difficult to articulate and codify, are much easier to embed in a new venture than they are in an acquired entity, where the firm may have to overcome the established routines and culture of the acquired firm. Thus, as our earlier examples suggest, firms such as McDonald's and Lincoln Electric prefer to enter foreign markets by establishing greenfield ventures.

Strategic Alliances

Strategic alliances refer to cooperative agreements between potential or actual competitors. In this section, we are concerned specifically with strategic alliances between firms from different countries. Strategic alliances run the range from formal joint ventures, in which two or more firms have equity stakes (e.g., Fuji Xerox), to short-term contractual agreements, in which two companies agree to cooperate on a particular task (such as developing a new product). Collaboration between competitors is fashionable; recent decades have seen an explosion in the number of strategic alliances.

THE ADVANTAGES OF STRATEGIC ALLIANCES

Firms ally themselves with actual or potential competitors for various strategic purposes.[42] First, strategic alliances may facilitate entry into a foreign market. For example, many firms feel that if they are to successfully enter the Chinese market, they need a local partner who understands business conditions, and who has good connections (or *guanxi*—see Chapter 3). Thus, in 2004 Warner Brothers entered into a joint venture with two Chinese partners to produce and distribute films in China. As a foreign film company, Warner found that if it wanted to produce films on its own for the Chinese market it had to go through a complex approval process for every film, and it had to farm out distribution to a local company, which made doing business in China very difficult. Due to the participation of Chinese firms, however, the joint-venture films will go through a streamlined approval process, and the venture will be able to distribute any films it produces. Moreover, the joint venture will be able to produce films for Chinese TV, something that foreign firms are not allowed to do.[43]

Strategic alliances also allow firms to share the fixed costs (and associated risks) of developing new products or processes. An alliance between Boeing and a number of Japanese companies to build Boeing's latest commercial jetliner, the 7E7, was motivated by Boeing's desire to share the estimated $8 billion investment required to develop the aircraft. For another example of cost sharing, see the accompanying Management Focus, which discusses the attempts of MG Rover to enter into an alliance with Chinese automobile companies.

Third, an alliance is a way to bring together complementary skills and assets that neither company could easily develop on its own.[44] In 2003, for example, Microsoft and Toshiba established an alliance aimed at developing embedded microprocessors (essentially tiny computers) that can perform a variety of entertainment functions in an automobile (e.g., run a back-seat DVD player or a wireless Internet connection). The processors will run a version of Microsoft's Windows CE operating system. Microsoft brings its software engineering skills to the alliance and Toshiba its skills in developing microprocessors.[45]

Fourth, it can make sense to form an alliance that will help the firm establish technological standards for the industry that will benefit the firm. For example, in 1999 Palm Computer, the leading maker of personal digital assistants (PDAs), entered into an alliance with Sony under which Sony agreed to license and use Palm's operating system in Sony PDAs. The motivation for the alliance was in part to help establish Palm's operating system as the industry standard for PDAs, as opposed to a rival Windows-based operating system from Microsoft.[46]

MANAGEMENT FOCUS MG Rover is a small player in the global automobile industry. A diminished descendant of Britain's venerable Rover and MG motor companies, MG Rover was spun out of BMW in 2000, when it was sold to a group of British investors for just £ 10 million. BMW had purchased the company's parent operation a few years previously, primarily for its profitable Land Rover and Mini-Cooper brands, and was happy to unload itself of MG Rover, which made Rover and MG sports cars at a single factory in Birmingham, England. At the time, the carmaker was losing some £ 780 million a year, and sales were declining.

In the four years since, sales at MG Rover have continued to slide, dropping to less than 140,000 in 2004 from 200,000 in 2000. Although losses have been narrowed, the future of the carmaker and its 6,000 employees seems in doubt. To try to ensure survival, MG Rover's managers know they need to develop a new range of car models, but the company lacks the funds—it can take up to four years and cost $1 billion to bring a new car to market. Rover's strategy, therefore, has been to seek a partner who can invest cash into MG Rover in return for access to the company's brand names and design and engineering skills.

In 2003, it looked as if the company had found a partner, China Brilliance Automotive. China Brilliance, a state-owned bus maker based in Shanghai, reportedly paid MG Rover an undisclosed sum to develop a new car that it planned to manufacture in China. For MG Rover, the partnership had the additional benefit of giving the company access to China's booming automobile market, which is among the fastest growing in the world, and if current trends continue, by 2010 will be one of the three largest. However, soon after the deal was announced, Yan Rong,

the chairman of Brilliance, was accused of fraud by the Chinese authorities, and promptly fled the country. The deal collapsed.

Shaken but not deterred, MG Rover stuck at it, and in mid-2004 the company announced it was negotiating to enter into another alliance in China, this time with Shanghai Automotive Industry Corporation (SAIC), one of the largest carmakers in China. According to news reports, SAIC would invest some £ 1.5 billion in a joint venture with MG Rover that would be 70 percent owned by SAIC. MG Rover would supply the engineering and design expertise. The venture would develop a new range of cars to be built both in Shanghai and Rover's British plant. For MG Rover, it looked like a masterstroke. The deal would pay for product development, give MG Rover access to China's market, and improve the company's bargaining position with suppliers, who were becoming increasingly hesitant to invest in business with such a marginal industry player. For its part, SIAC would get engineering technology, and ultimately access to the British and European markets through Rover.

Critics of the deal abounded, however. Some said that Rover's engineering skills were distinctly second rate and not worth anything close to the £ 1.5 billion that SIAC was putting into the venture. Others, citing SIAC skills as well, questioned the ability of either company to produce a leading-edge car. Only time will tell if the pair can prove the skeptics wrong.

Sources: E. Simpkins, "Will Rover's Drive East Go South?" *Sunday Telegraph*, November 28, 2004, p. 5; J. Griffiths, "MG Rover Thinks Big in Venture with Chinese Car Maker," *Financial Times*, September 25, 2004, p. 4; and J. Nisse, "The Lowdown: Howe Puts Foot Down on Rover's Road to Recovery," *Independent on Sunday*, February 2, 2003, p. 7.

THE DISADVANTAGES OF STRATEGIC ALLIANCES

The advantages we have discussed can be very significant. Despite this, some commentators have criticized strategic alliances on the grounds that they give competitors a low-cost route to new technology and markets.[47] For example, a few years ago some commentators argued that many strategic alliances between U.S. and Japanese firms were part of an implicit Japanese strategy to keep high-paying, high-value-added jobs in Japan while gaining the project engineering and production process skills that underlie the competitive success of many U.S. companies.[48] They argued that Japanese success in the machine tool and semiconductor industries was built on U.S. technology acquired through strategic alliances. And they argued that U.S. managers were aiding the Japanese by entering alliances that channel new inventions to Japan and provide a U.S. sales and distribution network for the resulting products. Although such deals may generate short-term profits, so the argument goes, in the long run the result is to "hollow out" U.S. firms, leaving them with no competitive advantage in the global marketplace.

These critics have a point; alliances have risks. Unless a firm is careful, it can give away more than it receives. But there are so many examples of apparently successful alliances between firms—including alliances between U.S. and Japanese firms—that their position seems extreme. It is difficult to see how the Microsoft–Toshiba alliance, the Boeing–Mitsubishi alliance for the 7E7, or the Fuji–Xerox alliance fit the critics' thesis. In these cases, both partners seem to have gained from the alliance. Why do some alliances benefit both firms while others benefit one firm and hurt the other? The next section provides an answer to this question.

MAKING ALLIANCES WORK

The failure rate for international strategic alliances seems to be high. One study of 49 international strategic alliances found that two-thirds run into serious managerial and financial troubles within two years of their formation, and that although many of these problems are solved, 33 percent are ultimately rated as failures by the parties involved.[49] The success of an alliance seems to be a function of three main factors: partner selection, alliance structure, and the manner in which the alliance is managed.

Partner Selection

One key to making a strategic alliance work is to select the right ally. A good ally, or partner, has three characteristics. First, a good partner helps the firm achieve its strategic goals, whether they are market access, sharing the costs and risks of product development, or gaining access to critical core competencies. The partner must have capabilities that the firm lacks and that it values. Second, a good partner shares the firm's vision for the purpose of the alliance. If two firms approach an alliance with radically different agendas, the chances are great that the relationship will not be harmonious, will not flourish, and will end in divorce. Third, a good partner is unlikely to try to opportunistically exploit the alliance for its own ends; that is, to expropriate the firm's technological know-how while giving away little in return. In this respect, firms with reputations for "fair play" to maintain probably make the best allies. For example, IBM is involved in so many strategic alliances that it would not pay the company to trample over individual alliance partners (in early 2003) IBM reportedly had more than 150 major strategic alliances).[50] This would tarnish IBM's reputation of being a good ally and would make it more difficult for IBM to attract alliance partners. Because IBM attaches great importance to its alliances, it is unlikely to engage in the kind of opportunistic behavior that critics highlight. Similarly, their reputations make it less likely (but by no means impossible) that such Japanese firms as Sony, Toshiba, and Fuji, which have histories of alliances with non-Japanese firms, would opportunistically exploit an alliance partner.

To select a partner with these three characteristics, a firm needs to conduct comprehensive research on potential alliance candidates. To increase the probability of selecting a good partner, the firm should:

1. Collect as much pertinent, publicly available information on potential allies as possible.
2. Gather data from informed third parties. These include firms that have had alliances with the potential partners, investment bankers who have had dealings with them, and former employees.
3. Get to know the potential partner as well as possible before committing to an alliance. This should include face-to-face meetings between senior managers (and perhaps middle-level managers) to ensure that the chemistry is right.

Alliance Structure

A partner having been selected, the alliance should be structured so that the firm's risks of giving too much away to the partner are reduced to an acceptable level. Figure 14.1 depicts four safeguards against opportunism by alliance partners. (Opportunism includes the theft of technology and/or markets.) First, alliances can be designed to make it difficult (if not impossible) to transfer technology not meant to be transferred. The design, development, manufacture, and service of a product manufactured by an alliance can be structured so as to wall off sensitive technologies to prevent their leakage to the other participant. In an alliance between General Electric and Snecma to build commercial aircraft engines, for example, GE reduced the risk of excess transfer by walling off certain sections of the production process. The modularization effectively cut off the transfer of what GE regarded as key competitive technology, while permitting Snecma access to final assembly. Similarly, in the alliance between Boeing and the Japanese to build the 767, Boeing walled off research, design, and marketing functions considered central to its competitive position, while allowing the Japanese to share in production technology. Boeing also walled off new technologies not required for 767 production.[51]

Second, contractual safeguards can be written into an alliance agreement to guard against the risk of opportunism by a partner. For example, TRW, Inc., has three strategic alliances with large Japanese auto component suppliers to produce seat belts, engine valves, and steering gears for sale to Japanese-owned auto assembly plants in the United States. TRW has clauses in each of its alliance contracts that bar the Japanese firms from competing with TRW to supply U.S.-owned auto companies with component parts. By doing this, TRW protects itself against the possibility that the Japanese companies are entering into the alliances merely to gain access to the North American market to compete with TRW in its home market.

Third, both parties to an alliance can agree in advance to swap skills and technologies that the other covets, thereby ensuring a chance for equitable gain. Cross-licensing agreements are one way to achieve this goal. Fourth, the risk of opportunism by an alliance partner can be reduced if the firm extracts a significant credible commitment from its partner in advance. The long-term alliance between Xerox and Fuji to build photocopiers for the Asian market perhaps best illustrates this. Rather than enter into an informal agreement or a licensing arrangement (which Fuji Photo initially wanted), Xerox insisted that Fuji invest in a 50/50 joint venture to serve Japan and East Asia. This venture constituted such a significant investment in people, equipment, and facilities that Fuji Photo was committed from the outset to making the alliance work in order to earn a return on its investment. By agreeing to the joint venture, Fuji essentially made a credible commitment to the alliance. Given this, Xerox felt secure in transferring its photocopier technology to Fuji.[52]

Managing the Alliance

Once a partner has been selected and an appropriate alliance structure has been agreed on, the task facing the firm is to maximize its benefits from the alliance. As in all international business deals, an important factor is sensitivity to cultural differences (see Chapter 3). Many differences in management style are attributable to cultural differences, and managers need to make allowances for these in dealing with their partner. Beyond this, maximizing the benefits from an alliance seems to involve building trust between partners and learning from partners.[53]

Managing an alliance successfully requires building interpersonal relationships between the firms' managers, or what is sometimes referred to as *relational capital*.[54] This is one lesson that can be drawn from a successful strategic alliance between Ford and Mazda. Ford and Mazda set up a framework of meetings within which their managers not only discuss matters pertaining to the alliance but also have time to get to know each other better. The belief is that the resulting friendships help build trust and facilitate harmonious relations between the two firms. Personal relationships also foster an informal management network between the firms. This network can then be used to help solve problems arising in more formal contexts (such as in joint committee meetings between personnel from the two firms).

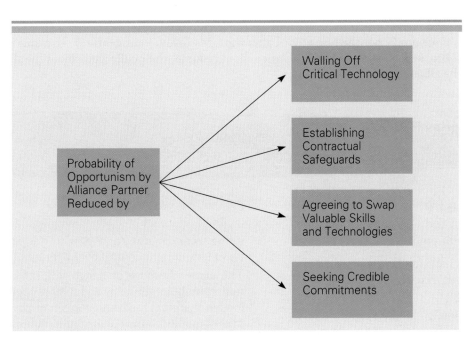

FIGURE 14.1

Structuring Alliances to Reduce Opportunism

Academics have argued that a major determinant of how much acquiring knowledge a company gains from an alliance is its ability to learn from its alliance partner.[55] For example, in a five-year study of 15 strategic alliances between major multinationals, Gary Hamel, Yves Doz, and C. K. Prahalad focused on a number of alliances between Japanese companies and Western (European or American) partners.[56] In every case in which a Japanese company emerged from an alliance stronger than its Western partner, the Japanese company had made a greater effort to learn. Few Western companies studied seemed to want to learn from their Japanese partners. They tended to regard the alliance purely as a cost-sharing or risk-sharing device, rather than as an opportunity to learn how a potential competitor does business.

Consider the alliance between General Motors and Toyota constituted in 1985 to build the Chevrolet Nova. This alliance was structured as a formal joint venture, called New United Motor Manufacturing, Inc., and each party had a 50 percent equity stake. The venture owned an auto plant in Fremont, California. According to one Japanese manager, Toyota quickly achieved most of its objectives from the alliance: "We learned about U.S. supply and transportation. And we got the confidence to manage U.S. workers."[57] All that knowledge was then transferred to Georgetown, Kentucky, where Toyota opened its own plant in 1988. Possibly all GM got was a new product, the Chevrolet Nova. Some GM managers complained that the knowledge they gained through the alliance with Toyota has never been put to good use inside GM. They believe they should have been kept together as a team to educate GM's engineers and workers about the Japanese system. Instead, they were dispersed to various GM subsidiaries.

To maximize the learning benefits of an alliance, a firm must try to learn from its partner and then apply the knowledge within its own organization. It has been suggested that all operating employees should be well briefed on the partner's strengths and weaknesses and should understand how acquiring particular skills will bolster their firm's competitive position. Hamel, Doz, and Prahalad note that this is already standard practice among Japanese companies. They made this observation:

> We accompanied a Japanese development engineer on a tour through a partner's factory. This engineer dutifully took notes on plant layout, the number of production stages, the rate at which the line was running, and the number of employees. He recorded all this despite the fact that he had no manufacturing responsibility in his own company, and that the alliance did not encompass joint manufacturing. Such dedication greatly enhances learning.[58]

For such learning to be of value, it must be diffused throughout the organization (as was seemingly not the case at GM after the GM–Toyota joint venture). To achieve this, the managers involved in the alliance should educate their colleagues about the skills of the alliance partner.

Chapter Summary

The chapter made the following points:

1. Basic entry decisions include identifying which markets to enter, when to enter those markets, and on what scale.

2. The most attractive foreign markets tend to be found in politically stable developed and developing nations that have free market systems and where there is not a dramatic upsurge in either inflation rates or private-sector debt.

3. There are several advantages associated with entering a national market early, before other international businesses have established themselves. These advantages must be balanced against the pioneering costs that early entrants often have to bear, including the greater risk of business failure.

4. Large-scale entry into a national market constitutes a major strategic commitment that is likely to change the nature of competition in that market and limit the entrant's future strategic flexibility. Although making major strategic commitments can yield many benefits, there are also risks associated with such a strategy.

5. There are six modes of entering a foreign market: exporting, creating turnkey projects, licensing, franchising, establishing joint ventures, and setting up a wholly owned subsidiary.

6. Exporting has the advantages of facilitating the realization of experience curve economies and of avoiding the costs of setting up manufacturing operations in another country. Disadvantages include high transport costs, trade barriers, and problems with local marketing agents.

7. Turnkey projects allow firms to export their process know-how to countries where FDI might be prohibited, thereby enabling the firm to earn a greater return from this asset. The disadvantage is that the firm may inadvertently create efficient global competitors in the process.

8. The main advantage of licensing is that the licensee bears the costs and risks of opening a foreign market. Disadvantages include the risk of losing technological know-how to the licensee and a lack of tight control over licensees.

9. The main advantage of franchising is that the franchisee bears the costs and risks of opening a foreign market. Disadvantages center on problems of quality control of distant franchisees.

10. Joint ventures have the advantages of sharing the costs and risks of opening a foreign market and of gaining local knowledge and political influence. Disadvantages include the risk of losing control over technology and a lack of tight control.

11. The advantages of wholly owned subsidiaries include tight control over technological know-how. The main disadvantage is that the firm must bear all the costs and risks of opening a foreign market.

12. The optimal choice of entry mode depends on the firm's strategy. When technological know-how constitutes a firm's core competence, wholly owned subsidiaries are preferred, since they best control technology. When management know-how constitutes a firm's core competence, foreign franchises controlled by joint ventures seem to be optimal. When the firm is pursuing a global standardization or transnational strategy, the need for tight control over operations to realize location and experience curve economies suggests wholly owned subsidiaries are the best entry mode.

13. When establishing a wholly owned subsidiary in a country, a firm must decide whether to do so by a greenfield venture strategy, or by acquiring an established enterprise in the target market.

14. Acquisitions are quick to execute, may enable a firm to preempt its global competitors, and involve buying a known revenue and profit stream. Acquisitions may fail when the acquiring firm overpays for the target, when the culture of the acquiring and acquired firms clash, when there is a high level of management attrition after the ac-

quisition, and when there is a failure to integrate the operations of the acquiring and acquired firm.

15. The advantage of a greenfield venture in a foreign country is that it gives the firm a much greater ability to build the kind of subsidiary company that it wants. For example, it is much easier to build an organization culture from scratch than it is to change the culture of an acquired unit.

16. Strategic alliances are cooperative agreements between actual or potential competitors. The advantage of alliances are that they facilitate entry into foreign markets, enable partners to share the fixed costs and risks associated with new products and processes, facilitate the transfer of complementary skills between companies, and help firms establish technical standards.

17. The disadvantage of a strategic alliance is that the firm risks giving away technological know-how and market access to its alliance partner.

18. The disadvantages associated with alliances can be reduced if the firm selects partners carefully, paying close attention to the firm's reputation and the structure of the alliance so as to avoid unintended transfers of know-how.

19. Two keys to making alliances work seem to be building trust and informal communications networks between partners and taking proactive steps to learn from alliance partners.

Critical Thinking and Discussion Questions

1. Review the Management Focus on ING. ING chose to enter the U.S. financial services market via acquisitions rather than greenfield ventures. What do you think are the advantages to ING of doing this? What might the drawbacks be? Does this strategy make sense? Why?

2. Licensing proprietary technology to foreign competitors is the best way to give up a firm's competitive advantage. Discuss.

3. Discuss how the need for control over foreign operations varies with firms' strategies and core competencies. What are the implications for the choice of entry mode?

4. A small Canadian firm that has developed some valuable new medical products using its unique biotechnology know-how is trying to decide how best to serve the European Community market.

Its choices are:

a. Manufacture the product at home and let foreign sales agents handle marketing.

b. Manufacture the products at home and set up a wholly owned subsidiary in Europe to handle marketing.

c. Enter into an alliance with a large European pharmaceutical firm. The product would be manufactured in Europe by the 50/50 joint venture and marketed by the European firm.

The cost of investment in manufacturing facilities will be a major one for the Canadian firm, but it is not outside its reach. If these are the firm's only options, which one would you advise it to choose? Why?

Research Task   globalEDGE™   globaledge.msu.edu

Use the globalEDGE™ site to complete the following exercises:

1. *The Entrepreneur* magazine annually publishes a list of this ranking of America's top 200 franchisors seeking international franchisees. Provide a list of the top 10 companies that pursue franchising as a mode of international expansion. Study one of these companies in detail and provide a description of its business model, its international expansion pattern, what qualifications it looks for in its franchisees, and what type of support and training it provides.

2. The U.S. Commercial Service prepares reports titled the *Country Commercial Guide* for each country of interest to U.S. investors. Utilize the *Country Commercial Guide* for Brazil to gather information on this country. Considering that your company is producing laptop computers and is considering entering this country, select the most appropriate entry method, supporting your decision with the information collected from the *Commercial Guide*.

Diebold

CLOSING CASE For much of its 144-year history, Diebold Inc. did not worry much about international business. As a premier name in bank vaults and then automated teller machines (ATMs), the Ohio-based company found that it had its hands full focusing on U.S. financial institutions. By the 1970s and 1980s, the company's growth was driven by the rapid acceptance of ATM in the United States. The company first started to sell ATM machines in foreign markets in the 1980s. Wary of going it alone, Diebold forged a distribution agreement with the large Dutch multinational electronics company Philips NV. Under the agreement, Diebold manufactured ATMs in the United States and exported them to foreign customers after Philips had made the sale.

In 1990, Diebold pulled out of the agreement with Philips and established a joint venture with IBM, called Interbold, for the research, development, and distribution of ATM worldwide. Diebold, which owned a 70 percent stake in the joint venture, supplied the machines, while IBM supplied the global marketing, sales, and service functions. Diebold established a joint venture rather than setting up its own international distribution system because the company felt that it lacked the resources to establish an international presence. In essence, Diebold was exporting its machines via IBM's distribution network. Diebold's switch from Philips to IBM as a distribution partner was driven by a belief that IBM would pursue ATM sales more aggressively.

By 1997, foreign sales had grown from the single digits to more than 20 percent of Diebold's total revenues. While sales in the United States were slowing due to a saturated domestic market, Diebold was seeing rapid growth in demand for ATMs in a wide range of developed and developing markets. Particularly enticing were countries such as China, India, and Brazil, where an emerging middle class was starting to use the banking system in large numbers and demand for ATMs was expected to surge. It was at this point that Diebold decided to take the plunge and establish its own foreign distribution network.

As a first step, Diebold purchased IBM's 30 percent stake in the Interbold joint venture. In part, the acquisition was driven by Diebold's dissatisfaction with IBM's sales efforts, which often fell short of quota. Part of the problem was that for IBM's salespeople, Diebold's ATMs were just part of their product portfolio, and not necessarily their top priority. Diebold felt that it could attain a greater market share if it gained direct control over distribution. The company also felt that during the previous 15 years it had accumulated enough international business expertise to warrant going it alone.

Diebold's managers decided that in addition to local distribution, they would need a local manufacturing presence in a number of regions because local differences in the way ATMs are used required local customization of the product. In parts of Asia, for example, many customers pay their utility bills with cash via ATMs. To gain market share, Diebold had to design ATMs that both accept and count stacks of up to 100 currency notes, and weed out counterfeits. In other countries, ATMs perform multiple functions from filing tax returns to distributing theater tickets. Diebold believed that locating manufacturing close to key markets would help facilitate local customization and drive forward sales.

To jump-start its international expansion, Diebold went on a foreign acquisition binge. In 1999 it acquired Brazil's Procomp Amazonia Industria Electronica, a Latin American electronics company with sales of $400 million and a big presence in ATMs. This was followed in quick succession by the acquisitions of the ATM units of France's Groupe Bull and Holland's Getronics, both major players in Europe, for a combined $160 million. In China, where no substantial indigenous competitors were open to acquisition, Diebold established a manufacturing and distribution joint venture in which it took a majority ownership position. By 2002, Diebold had a manufacturing presence in Asia, Europe, and Latin America as well as the United States and distribution operations in some 80 nations, the majority of which were wholly owned by Diebold. International sales accounted for some 41 percent of the company's $2.11 billion in revenues in 2003, and were forecast to grow at double-digit rates.

Interestingly, the acquisition of Brazil's Procomp also took Diebold into a new and potentially lucrative global business. In addition to its ATM business, Procomp had an electronic voting machine business. In 1999 Procomp won a $105 million contract, the largest in Diebold's history, to outfit Brazilian polling stations with electronic voting terminals. Diebold's management realized that this might become a large global business. In 2001, Diebold expanded its presence in the electronic voting business by acquiring Global Election Systems Inc., a U.S. company that provides electronic voting technology for states and countries that want to upgrade from traditional voting technology. By 2003, Diebold was the global leader in the emerging global market for electronic voting machines, with sales of more than $100 million.

Sources: H. S. Byrne, "Money Machine," *Barrons*, May 27, 2002, p. 24; M. Arndt, "Diebold," *BusinessWeek*, August 27, 2001, p. 138; W. A. Lee, "After Slump, Diebold Pins Hopes on New ATM Market

Features," *Amercian Banker,* September 15, 2000, p. 1; C. Keenan, "A Bigger Diebold, Phasing Out IBM Alliance, Will Market ATMs Itself," *American Banker,* July 3, 1997, p. 8; and Diebold *Annual Report,* 2003.

Case Discussion Questions

1. Before 1997, Diebold manufactured its ATM machines in the United States, and sold them internationally via distribution agreements, first with Philips NV and then with IBM. Why do you think Diebold chose this mode of expanding internationally? What were the advantages and disadvantages of this arrangement?

2. What do you think prompted Diebold to alter its international expansion strategy in 1997 and start setting up wholly owned subsidiaries in most markets? Why do you think the company favored acquisitions as an entry mode?

3. Diebold entered China via a joint venture, as opposed to a wholly owned subsidiary. Why do you think the company did this?

4. Is Diebold pursuing a global standardization strategy or a localization strategy? Do you think this choice of strategy has affected its choice of entry mode? How?

Notes

1. For interesting empirical studies that deal with the issues of timing and resource commitments, see T. Isobe, S. Makino, and D. B. Montgomery, "Resource Commitment, Entry Timing, and Market Performance of Foreign Direct Investments in Emerging Economies," *Academy of Management Journal* 43, no. 3 (2000), pp. 468–84, and Y. Pan and P. S. K. Chi, "Financial Performance and Survival of Multinational Corporations in China," *Strategic Management Journal* 20, no. 4 (1999), pp. 359–74. A complementary theoretical perspective on this issue can be found in V. Govindarjan and A. K. Gupta, *The Quest for Global Dominance* (San Francisco: Jossey-Bass, 2001). Also see F. Vermeulen and H. Barkeme, "Pace, Rhythm and Scope: Process Dependence in Building a Profitable Multinational Corporation," *Strategic Management Journal* 23 (2002), pp. 637–54.

2. This can be reconceptualized as the resource base of the entrant, relative to indigenous competitors. For work that focuses on this issue, see W. C. Bogenr, H. Thomas, and J. McGee, "A Longitudinal Study of the Competitive Positions and Entry Paths of European Firms in the U.S. Pharmaceutical Market," *Strategic Management Journal* 17 (1996), pp. 85–107; D. Collis, "A Resource-Based Analysis of Global Competition," *Strategic Management Journal* 12 (1991), pp. 49–68; and S. Tallman, "Strategic Management Models and Resource-Based Strategies among MNEs in a Host Market," *Strategic Management Journal* 12 (1991), pp. 69–82.

3. For a discussion of first-mover advantages, see M. Lieberman and D. Montgomery, "First-Mover Advantages," *Strategic Management Journal* 9 (Summer Special Issue, 1988), pp. 41–58.

4. J. M. Shaver, W. Mitchell, and B. Yeung, "The Effect of Own Firm and Other Firm Experience on Foreign Direct Investment Survival in the United States, 1987–92," *Strategic Management Journal* 18 (1997), pp. 811–24.

5. S. Zaheer and E. Mosakowski, "The Dynamics of the Liability of Foreignness: A Global Study of Survival in the Financial Services Industry," *Strategic Management Journal* 18 (1997), pp. 439–64.

6. Shaver, Mitchell, and Yeung, "The Effect of Own Firm and Other Firm Experience on Foreign Direct Investment Survival in the United States."

7. P. Ghemawat, *Commitment: The Dynamics of Strategy* (New York: Free Press, 1991).

8. R. Luecke, *Scuttle Your Ships before Advancing* (Oxford: Oxford University Press, 1994).

9. Isobe, Makino, and Montgomery, "Resource Commitment, Entry Timing, and Market Performance"; Pan and Chi, "Financial Performance and Survival of Multinational Corporations in China"; and Govindarjan and Gupta, *The Quest for Global Dominance*.

10. Christopher Bartlett and Sumantra Ghoshal, "Going Global: Lessons from Late Movers," *Harvard Business Review,* March–April 2000, pp. 132–45.

11. This section draws on numerous studies, including: C. W. L. Hill, P. Hwang, and W. C. Kim, "An Eclectic Theory of the Choice of International Entry Mode," *Strategic Management Journal* 11 (1990), pp. 117–28; C. W. L. Hill and W. C. Kim, "Searching for a Dynamic Theory of the Multinational Enterprise: A Transaction Cost Model," *Strategic Management Journal* 9 (Special Issue on Strategy Content, 1988), pp. 93–104; E. Anderson and H. Gatignon, "Modes of Foreign Entry: A Transaction Cost Analysis and Propositions," *Journal of International Business Studies* 17 (1986), pp. 1–26;

F. R. Root, *Entry Strategies for International Markets* (Lexington, MA: D. C. Heath, 1980); A. Madhok, "Cost, Value and Foreign Market Entry: The Transaction and the Firm," *Strategic Management Journal* 18 (1997), pp. 39–61; K. D. Brouthers and L. B. Brouthers, "Acquisition or Greenfield Start-Up?" *Strategic Management Journal* 21, no. 1 (2000), pp. 89–97; X. Martin and R. Salmon, "Knowledge Transfer Capacity and Its Implications for the Theory of the Multinational Enterprise," *Journal of International Business Studies*, July 2003, p. 356; and A. Verbeke, "The Evolutionary View of the MNE and the Future of Internalization Theory," *Journal of International Business Studies*, November 2003, pp. 498–515.

12. For a general discussion of licensing, see F. J. Contractor, "The Role of Licensing in International Strategy," *Columbia Journal of World Business*, Winter 1982, pp. 73–83.

13. See E. Terazono and C. Lorenz, "An Angry Young Warrior," *Financial Times*, September 19, 1994, p. 11, and K. McQuade and B. Gomes-Casseres, "Xerox and Fuji-Xerox," Harvard Business School Case No. 9-391-156.

14. O. E. Williamson, *The Economic Institutions of Capitalism* (New York: Free Press, 1985).

15. J. H. Dunning and M. McQueen, "The Eclectic Theory of International Production: A Case Study of the International Hotel Industry," *Managerial and Decision Economics* 2 (1981), pp. 197–210.

16. Andrew E. Serwer, "McDonald's Conquers the World," *Fortune*, October 17, 1994, pp. 103–16.

17. For an excellent review of the basic theoretical literature of joint ventures, see B. Kogut, "Joint Ventures: Theoretical and Empirical Perspectives," *Strategic Management Journal* 9 (1988), pp. 319–32. More recent studies include T. Chi, "Option to Acquire or Divest a Joint Venture," *Strategic Management Journal* 21, no. 6 (2000), pp. 665–88; H. Merchant and D. Schendel, "How Do International Joint Ventures Create Shareholder Value?" *Strategic Management Journal* 21, no. 7 (2000), pp. 723–37; H. K. Steensma and M. A. Lyles, "Explaining IJV Survival in a Transitional Economy though Social Exchange and Knowledge Based Perspectives," *Strategic Management Journal* 21, no. 8 (2000), pp. 831–51; and J. F. Hennart and M. Zeng, "Cross Cultural Differences and Joint Venture Longevity," *Journal of International Business Studies*, December 2002, pp. 699–717.

18. D. G. Bradley, "Managing against Expropriation," *Harvard Business Review*, July–August 1977, pp. 78–90.

19. J. A. Robins, S. Tallman, and K. Fladmoe-Lindquist, "Autonomy and Dependence of International Cooperative Ventures," *Strategic Management Journal*, October 2002, pp. 881–902.

20. Speech given by Tony Kobayashi at the University of Washington Business School, October 1992.

21. A. C. Inkpen and P. W. Beamish, "Knowledge, Bargaining Power, and the Instability of International Joint Ventures," *Academy of Management Review* 22 (1997), pp. 177–202, and S. H. Park and G. R. Ungson, "The Effect of National Culture, Organizational Complementarity, and Economic Motivation on Joint Venture Dissolution," *Academy of Management Journal* 40 (1997), pp. 279–307.

22. Inkpen and Beamish, "Knowledge, Bargaining Power, and the Instability of International Joint Ventures."

23. See Brouthers and Brouthers, "Acquisition or Greenfield Start-up?" and J. F. Hennart and Y. R. Park, "Greenfield versus Acquisition: The Strategy of Japanese Investors in the United States," *Management Science*, 1993, pp. 1054–70.

24. This section draws on Hill, Hwang, and Kim, "An Eclectic Theory of the Choice of International Entry Mode."

25. C. W. L. Hill, "Strategies for Exploiting Technological Innovations: When and When Not to License," *Organization Science* 3 (1992), pp. 428–41.

26. See Brouthers and Brouthers, "Acquisition or Greenfield Start-Up?" and J. Anand and A. Delios, "Absolute and Relative Resources as Determinants of International Acquisitions," *Strategic Management Journal*, February 2002, pp. 119–34.

27. United Nations, *World Investment Report, 2004* (New York and Geneva: United Nations, 2004).

28. Ibid.

29. For evidence on acquisitions and performance, see R. E. Caves, "Mergers, Takeovers, and Economic Efficiency," *International Journal of Industrial Organization* 7 (1989), pp. 151–74; M. C. Jensen and R. S. Ruback, "The Market for Corporate Control: The Scientific Evidence," *Journal of Financial Economics* 11 (1983), pp. 5–50; R. Roll, "Empirical Evidence on Takeover Activity and Shareholder Wealth," in *Knights, Raiders and Targets*, ed. J. C. Coffee, L. Lowenstein, and S. Rose (Oxford: Oxford University Press, 1989); A. Schleifer and R. W. Vishny, "Takeovers in the 60s and 80s: Evidence and Implications," *Strategic Management Journal* 12 (Winter 1991 Special Issue), pp. 51–60; T. H. Brush, "Predicted Changes in Operational

Synergy and Post-Acquisition Performance of Acquired Businesses," *Strategic Management Journal* 17 (1996), pp. 1–24; and A. Seth, K. P. Song, and R. R. Pettit, "Value Creation and Destruction in Cross-Border Acquisitions," *Strategic Management Journal* 23 (October 2002), pp. 921–40.

30. J. Warner, J. Templeman, R. Horn, "The Case against Mergers," *BusinessWeek*, October 30, 1995, pp. 122–34.

31. "Few Takeovers Pay Off for Big Buyers," *Investors Business Daily*, May 25, 2001, p. 1.

32. S. A. Christofferson, R. S. McNish, and D. L. Sias, "Where Mergers Go Wrong," *The McKinsey Quarterly* 2 (2004), pp. 92–110.

33. D. J. Ravenscraft and F. M. Scherer, *Mergers, Selloffs, and Economic Efficiency* (Washington, DC: Brookings Institution, 1987).

34. See P. Ghemawat and F. Ghadar, "The Dubious Logic of Global Mega-mergers," *Harvard Business Review*, July–August 2000, pp. 65–72.

35. R. Roll, "The Hubris Hypothesis of Corporate Takeovers," *Journal of Business* 59 (1986), pp. 197–216.

36. "Marital Problems," *The Economist*, October 14, 2000.

37. See J. P. Walsh, "Top Management Turnover Following Mergers and Acquisitions," *Strategic Management Journal* 9 (1988), pp. 173–83.

38. B. Vlasic and B. A. Stertz, *Taken for a Ride: How Daimler-Benz Drove Off with Chrysler* (New York: HarperCollins, 2000).

39. See A. A. Cannella and D. C. Hambrick, "Executive Departure and Acquisition Performance," *Strategic Management Journal* 14 (1993), pp. 137–52.

40. P. Haspeslagh and D. Jemison, *Managing Acquisitions* (New York: Free Press, 1991).

41. Ibid.

42. See K. Ohmae, "The Global Logic of Strategic Alliances," *Harvard Business Review*, March–April 1989, pp. 143–54; G. Hamel, Y. L. Doz, and C. K. Prahalad, "Collaborate with Your Competitors and Win!" *Harvard Business Review*, January–February 1989, pp. 133–39; W. Burgers, C. W. L. Hill, and W. C. Kim, "Alliances in the Global Auto Industry," *Strategic Management Journal* 14 (1993), pp. 419–32; and P. Kale, H. Singh, H. Perlmutter, "Learning and Protection of Proprietary Assets in Strategic Alliances: Building Relational Capital," *Strategic Management Journal* 21 (2000), pp. 217–37.

43. L. T. Chang, "China Eases Foreign Film Rules," *The Wall Street Journal*, October 15, 2004, p. B2.

44. B. L. Simonin, "Transfer of Marketing Know-how in International Strategic Alliances," *Journal of International Business Studies*, 1999, pp. 463–91, and J. W. Spencer, "Firms' Knowledge Sharing Strategies in the Global Innovation System," *Strategic Management Journal* 24 (2003), pp. 217–33.

45. C. Souza, "Microsoft Teams with MIPS, Toshiba," *EBN*, February 10, 2003, p. 4.

46. M. Frankel, "Now Sony Is Giving Palm a Hand," *BusinessWeek*, November 29, 2000, p. 50.

47. Kale, Singh, and Perlmutter, "Learning and Protection of Proprietary Assets."

48. R. B. Reich and E. D. Mankin, "Joint Ventures with Japan Give Away Our Future," *Harvard Business Review*, March–April 1986, pp. 78–90.

49. J. Bleeke and D. Ernst, "The Way to Win in Cross-Border Alliances," *Harvard Business Review*, November–December 1991, pp. 127–35.

50. E. Booker and C. Krol, "IBM Finds Strength in Alliances," *B to B*, February 10, 2003, pp. 3, 27.

51. W. Roehl and J. F. Truitt, "Stormy Open Marriages Are Better," *Columbia Journal of World Business*, Summer 1987, pp. 87–95.

52. McQuade and Gomes-Casseres, "Xerox and Fuji-Xerox."

53. See T. Khanna, R. Gulati, and N. Nohria, "The Dynamics of Learning Alliances: Competition, Cooperation, and Relative Scope," *Strategic Management Journal* 19 (1998), pp. 193–210, and P. Kale, H. Singh, H. Perlmutter, "Learning and Protection of Proprietary Assets in Strategic Alliances: Building Relational Capital," *Strategic Management Journal* 21 (2000), pp. 217–37.

54. Kale, Singh, Perlmutter, "Learning and Protection of Proprietary Assets in Strategic Alliances: Building Relational Capital."

55. Hamel, Doz, and Prahalad, "Collaborate with Competitors"; Khanna, Gulati, and Nohria, "The Dynamics of Learning Alliances: Competition, Cooperation, and Relative Scope"; and E. W. K. Tang, "Acquiring Knowledge by Foreign Partners from International Joint Ventures in a Transition Economy: Learning by Doing and Learning Myopia," *Strategic Management Journal* 23 (2002), pp. 835–54.

56. Hamel, Doz, and Prahalad, "Collaborate with Competitors."

57. B. Wysocki, "Cross-Border Alliances Become Favorite Way to Crack New Markets," *The Wall Street Journal*, March 4, 1990, p. A1.

58. Hamel, Doz, and Prahalad, "Collaborate with Competitors," p. 138.

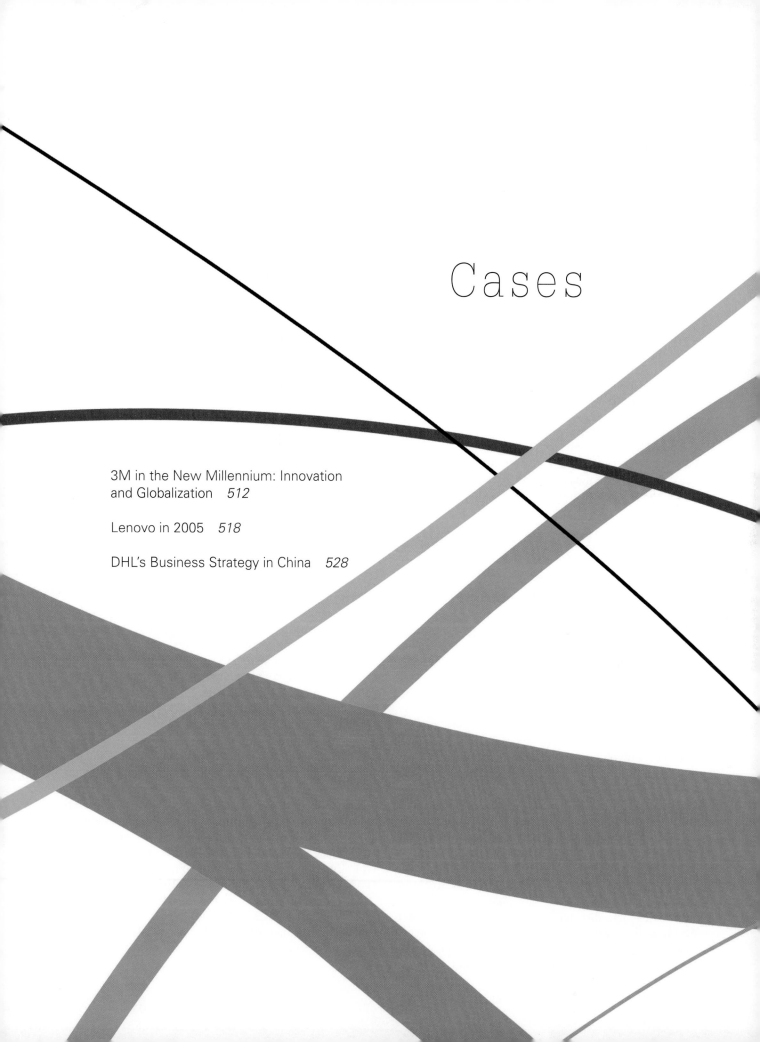

Cases

3M in the New Millennium: Innovation and Globalization

INTRODUCTION

Established in 1902, 3M by 2002 was one of the largest technology-driven enterprises in the world with annual sales of $16.4 billion, 55 percent of which were outside the United States. Throughout its history, 3M's researchers had driven much of the company's growth. In 2002 the company sold some 50,000 products, including Post-it notes, Flex circuits, Scotch tape, abrasives, specialty chemicals, Thinsulate insulation products, Nexcare bandage, optical films, fiber-optic connectors, drug delivery systems, and much more. One-third of the company's products in 2002 didn't even exist in 1997. About 7,000 of the company's 68,000 employees were technical employees. The company's annual R&D budget exceeded $1 billion, and 3M had garnered more than 6,000 patents since 1990, with some 600 new patents awarded in 2002 alone. The 40 business units covered a wide range of sectors including consumer and office products; display and graphics; electronics and telecommunications; health care; industrial; safety, security and protection services; and transportation.

A BRIEF HISTORY OF 3M: BUILDING INNOVATIVE CAPABILITIES

The story of 3M dates to 1902 when five Minnesota businessmen established the Minnesota Mining and Manufacturing Company to mine a mineral that they thought was corundum, which is ideal for making sandpaper. The mineral, however, turned out to be low-grade anorthosite, nowhere near as suitable for making sandpaper, and the company nearly failed. To try to salvage the business, 3M turned to making the sandpaper itself using materials purchased from another source.

In 1907, 3M hired a 20-year-old business student, William McKnight, as assistant bookkeeper. This turned out to be a pivotal move in the history of the company. The hardworking McKnight soon made his mark. By 1929 he was CEO of the company, and in 1949 he became chairman of 3M's board of directors, a position that he held until 1966.

It was McKnight, then 3M's president, who in 1921 hired the company's first scientist, Richard Carlton. About the same time, McKnight's interest had been roused by an odd request from Philadelphia printer Francis Okie for samples of every sandpaper grit size that 3M made. McKnight dispatched 3M's East Coast sales manager to find out what Okie was up to. The sales manager discovered that Okie had invented a new kind of sandpaper that he had patented. It was waterproof sandpaper that could be used with water or oil to reduce dust and decrease the friction that marred auto finishes. In addition, the lack of dust reduced the poisoning associated with inhaling the dust of paint that had a high lead content. Okie had a problem though; he had no financial backers to commercialize the sandpaper. McKnight and 3M quickly stepped into the breach, purchasing the rights to Okie's Wetodry waterproof sandpaper, and hiring the young printer to come and join Richard Carlton in 3M's lab. Wet and Dry sandpaper went on to revolutionize the sandpaper industry, and was the driver of significant growth at 3M.

Another key player in the company's history, Richard Drew, also joined 3M in 1921. Hired straight out of the University of Minnesota, Drew would round out the trio of scientists, Carlton, Okie, and Drew, who under McKnight's leadership would do much to shape 3M's innovative organization.

McKnight charged the newly hired Drew with developing a stronger adhesive to better bind the grit for sandpaper to paper backing. While experimenting with adhesives, Drew accidentally developed a weak adhesive that had an interesting quality—if placed on the back of a strip of paper and stuck to a surface, the strip of paper could be peeled off the surface it was adhered to without leaving any adhesive residue on that surface. This discovery gave Drew an epiphany. He had been visiting auto body paint shops to see how 3M's Wet and Dry sandpaper was used, and he noticed a problem with paint running. His idea was to cover the back of a strip of paper with his weak adhesive and use it as "masking tape" to cover parts of the auto body that were not to be painted. An excited Drew took his innovation to McKnight and explained how masking tape might create an entirely new business for 3M. McKnight reminded Drew that he had been hired to fix a specific problem and pointedly suggested that he concentrate on doing just that.

Chastised, Dew went back to his lab, but he could not get the idea out of his mind, so he continued to work on it at night, long after everyone else had gone home. Drew perfected the masking tape product, and then went to visit several auto-body shops to show them his innovation. He quickly received several commitments for orders. Drew then went to see McKnight again. He told him that he had continued to work on the masking tape idea on his own time, had perfected the product, and got several customers interested in purchasing it. This time it was McKnight's turn to be chastised. Realizing that he had almost killed a good business idea, McKnight reversed his original position, and gave Drew permission to pursue the idea.[1]

Introduced into the market in 1925, Drew's invention of masking tape represented the first significant product diversification at 3M. Company legend has it that this incident was also the genesis for 3M's famous 15 percent rule. Reflecting on Drew's work, both McKnight and Carlton agreed that technical people could disagree with management and should be allowed to experiment on their own. The company then established a norm that technical people could spend up to 15 percent of their workweek on projects that might benefit the consumer, without having to justify the project to their manager.

Over the years, other scientists followed Drew's footsteps at 3M, creating a wide range of innovative products by leveraging existing technology and applying it to new areas. The invention of Scotchgard illustrates how many of these innovations occurred.

In 1953, 3M scientist Patsy Sherman was working on a new kind of rubber for jet aircraft fuel lines. Some of the latex mixture splashed onto a pair of canvas tennis shoes. Over time, the spot stayed clean while the rest of the canvas soiled. Sherman enlisted the help of fellow chemist Sam Smith. Together they investigated polymers and soon realized they were on to something. They discovered an oil- and water-repellent substance, based on the fluorocarbon fluid used in air-conditioners, with enormous potential for protecting fabrics from stains. It took several years before the team perfected a means to apply the treatment using water as the carrier, thereby making it economically feasible for use as a finish in textile plants.

Three years after the accidental spill, the first rain and stain repellent for use on wool was announced. Experience and time revealed that one product could not, however, effectively protect all fabrics, so 3M continued working, producing a range of Scotchgard products that could be used to protect all kinds of fabrics.[2]

INSTITUTIONALIZING INNOVATION

Early on McKnight set an ambitious target for 3M—a 10 percent annual increase in sales and 25 percent profit. He also indicated how he thought that should be achieved with a commitment to plow 5 percent of sales back into R&D every year. The question, though, was how to ensure that 3M would continue to produce new products.

The answer evolved over the years from experience. A prime example was the 15 percent rule, which came out of McKnight's experience with Drew. In addition to the 15 percent rule and the continued commitment to push money back into R&D, a number of other mechanisms evolved at 3M to spur innovation.

Initially, research occurred in the business units that made and sold products, but by the 1930s, 3M had already diversified into several different fields, thanks in

large part to the efforts of Drew and others. McKnight and Carlton realized a central research function was needed. In 1937, they established a central research laboratory that was charged with supplementing the work of product divisions and undertaking long-run basic research. From the outset, the researchers were multidisciplinary, with people from different scientific disciplines working next to each other on research benches.

As the company continued to grow, some mechanism to knit together the company's diverse business operations was desired. This led to establishment of the 3M Technical Forum in 1951. The goal of Technical Forum was to foster idea sharing, discussion, and problem solving between technical employees located in different divisions and the central research laboratory. The Technical Forum sponsored problem-solving sessions at which businesses would present their most recent technical nightmares in the hope that somebody might be able to suggest a solution—and that often was the case.

During the 1970s, the Technical Forum cloned itself, establishing forums in Australia and England. By 2001 the forum had grown to 9,500 members in eight U.S. locations and 19 other countries, becoming an international network of researchers who could share ideas, solve problems, and leverage technology.

In 1999, 3M created another unit within the company, 3M Innovative Properties (3M IPC) to leverage technical know-how. The unit is charged with protecting and leveraging 3M's intellectual property around the world. At 3M, a longtime tradition holds that while divisions "own" their products, the company as a whole "owns" the underlying technology, or intellectual property. One task of 3M IPC is to find ways in which 3M technology can be applied across business units to create marketable products. Historically, the company has been remarkably successful at leveraging company technology to produce new-product ideas.

Another key to institutionalizing innovation at 3M has been the principle of "patient money." Producing revolutionary new products requires substantial long-term investments, and often repeated failure, before a major payoff occurs. Patient money doesn't mean substantial funding for long periods, however. Rather, it might imply that a small group of five researchers is supported for 10 years while they work on a technology.

More generally, if researchers create a new technology or idea, they can begin working on it using their 15 percent time. If the idea shows promise, the researchers may request seed capital from their business unit managers to develop it further. If that funding is denied, which can occur, they are free to take the idea to any other 3M business unit. Requests for seed capital do not require that researchers draft detailed business plans that are reviewed by top management. That comes later in the process. As one former senior technology manager has noted,

> In the early stages of a new product or technology, it shouldn't be overly managed. If we start asking for business plans too early and insist on tight financial evaluations, we'll kill an idea or surely slow it down.[3]

Explaining the patient money philosophy, Ron Baukol, a former executive vice president of 3M's international operations, and a manager who started as a researcher, has noted,

> You just know that some things are going to be worth working on, and that requires technological patience. . . . You don't put too much money into the investigation, but you keep one to five people working on it for 20 years if you have to. You do that because you know that, once you have cracked the code, it's going to be big.[4]

An internal review of 3M's innovation process in the early 1980s concluded that despite the liberal process for funding new-product ideas, some promising ideas did not receive funding from business units, or the central research budget. This led to the establishment in 1985 of Genesis Grants, which provide up to $100,000 in seed capital to fund projects that do not get funded through 3M's regular channels. About a dozen of these grants are given every year.

Underlying the patient money philosophy is recognition that innovation is a very risky business. The company has long acknowledged that failure is an accepted and essential part of the new-product development process. As former 3M CEO Lew Lehr once noted:

> We estimate that 60 percent of our formal new product development programs never make it. When this happens, the important thing is to not punish the people involved.[5]

In an effort to reduce the probability of failure, in the 1960s 3M started to establish a process for auditing the product development efforts in the company's business units. The idea has been to provide a peer review, or technical audit, of major development projects occurring in the company. A typical technical audit team is composed of 10 to 15 business and technical people, including technical directors and senior scientists from other divisions. The audit team looks at the strengths and weaknesses of a development program, and its probability of success, both from a technical standpoint and a business standpoint. The team then makes nonbinding recommendations, but they are normally taken very seriously by the managers of a project.

To further foster a culture of entrepreneurial innovation and risk taking, over the years 3M established a number of reward and recognition programs to honor employees who make significant contributions to the company. These in-clude the Carlton Society award, which honors employees for outstanding career scientific achievements, and the Circle of Technical Excellence and Innovation Award, which recognizes people who have made exceptional contributions to 3M's technical capabilities.

Another key component of 3M's innovative culture has been an emphasis on dual career tracks. From its early days, many of the key players in 3M's history, people such as Richard Drew, chose to stay in research, turning down opportunities to enter the management side of the business. Over the years, this became formalized in a dual career path. Today, technical employees can choose to follow a technical career path or a management career path, with equal advancement opportunities. The idea is to let researchers develop their technical professional interests, without being penalized financially for not going into management.

Although 3M's innovative culture emphasizes the role of technical employees in producing innovations, the company also has a strong tradition of emphasizing that new-product ideas often come from watching customers at work. Richard Drew's original idea for masking tape, for example, came from watching workers use 3M Wet and Dry sandpaper in auto body shops. As with much else at 3M, the tone was set by McKnight who insisted that salespeople needed to "get behind the smokestacks" of 3M customers, going onto the factory floor, talking to workers and finding out what their problems were. Over the years this theme has become ingrained in 3M's culture, with salespeople often requesting time to watch customers work, and then bringing their insights about customer problems back into their organization.

Driving the entire innovation machine at 3M has been a series of stretch goals set by top managers. The goals date back to 3M's early days and McKnight's ambitious growth targets. In 1977, the company established "Challenge 81," which called for 25 percent of sales to come from products that had been on the market for less than five years by 1981. By the 1990s, the goal had been raised to the requirement that 30 percent of sales should come from products that had been on the market less than four years.

The flip side of these goals was that over the years, many products and businesses that had been 3M staples were phased out. More than 20 of the businesses that were 3M mainstays in 1980, for example, had been phased out by 2000. Analysts estimate that sales from mature products at 3M generally fall by 3 to 4 percent a year. The company has a long history of inventing businesses, leading the market for long periods, and then shuttering those businesses, or selling them, when they can no longer meet 3M's demanding growth targets. Notable examples include the duplicating business, a business 3M invented with Thermo-Fax copiers (which were ultimately made obsolete by Xerox's patented technology) and the video and audio magnetic tape business.

The former division was sold in 1985, and the latter in 1995. In both cases the company exited these areas because they had become low-growth commodity businesses that could not generate the kind of growth that 3M was seeking.

BUILDING THE ORGANIZATION

McKnight, a strong believer in decentralization, organized the company into product divisions in 1948, making 3M one of the early adopters of this organizational form. Each division was set up as an individual profit center that had the power, autonomy, and resources to run independently. At the same time, certain functions remained centralized, including significant R&D, human resources, and finance.

McKnight wanted to keep the divisions small enough that people had a chance to be entrepreneurial and focused on the customer. A key philosophy of McKnight's was "divide and grow." When a division became too big, some of its embryonic businesses were spun off into a new division. Not only did this new division then typically attain higher growth rates, but also the original division had to find new drivers of growth to make up for the contribution of the businesses that had gained independence. This drove the search for further innovations.

At 3M the process of organic diversification by splitting divisions became known as "renewal." Examples of renewal within 3M are legion. A copying machine project for Thermo-Fax copiers grew to become the Office Products Division. When Magnetic Recording Materials was spun off from the Electrical Products Division, it grew to become its own division, and then in turn spawned a spate of divisions.

This organic process was not without its downside. By the early 1990s, some of 3M's key customers were frustrated that they had to do business with many different 3M divisions. In some cases, representatives from 10 to 20 3M divisions could be calling on the same customer. To cope with this problem, in 1992 3M started to assign key account representatives to sell 3M products directly to major customers. These representatives typically worked across divisional lines. Implementing the strategy required many of 3M's general managers to give up some of their autonomy and power, but the solution seemed to work well, particularly for 3M's consumer and office divisions.

GOING INTERNATIONAL

The first steps abroad occurred in the 1920s. There were some limited sales of Wet and Dry sandpaper in Europe during the early 1920s. These increased after 1929 when 3M joined the Durex Corporation, a joint venture for international abrasive product sales in which 3M was involved along with eight other U.S. companies. In 1950,

however, the Department of Justice alleged that the Durex Corporation was a mechanism for achieving collusion among U.S. abrasive manufacturers, and a judge ordered that the corporation be broken up. After the Durex Corporation was dissolved in 1951, 3M was left with a sandpaper factory in Britain, a small plant in France, a sales office in Germany, and a tape factory in Brazil. International sales at this point amounted to no more than 5 percent of 3M's total revenues.

Although 3M opposed the dissolution of the Durex Corporation, in retrospect it turned out to be one of the most important events in the company's history, for it forced the corporation to build its own international operations. By 2002, international sales amounted to 55 percent of total revenues.

In 1952 Clarence Sampair was put in charge of 3M's international operations and charged with getting them off the ground. He received considerable strategic and operational independence. Sampair and his successor, Maynard Patterson, worked hard to protect the international operations from getting caught up in the red tape of a major corporation. For example, Patterson recounts how

> I asked Em Monteiro to start a small company in Colombia. I told him to pick a key person he wanted to take with him. "Go start a company," I said, "and no one from St. Paul is going to visit you unless you ask for them. We'll stay out of your way, and if someone sticks his nose in your business you call me."[6]

The international businesses were grouped into an International Division that Sampair headed. From the start the company insisted that foreign ventures pay their own way. In addition, 3M's international companies were expected to pay a 5 percent to 10 percent royalty to the corporate head office. Starved of working capital, 3M's International Division relied heavily on local borrowing to fund local operations, a fact that forced those operations to quickly pay their own way.

The international growth at 3M typically occurred in stages. The company would start by exporting to a country and working through sales subsidiaries. In that way, it began to understand the country, the local marketplace, and the local business environment. Next 3M established warehouses in each nation, and stocked those with goods paid for in local currency. The next phase involved converting products to the sizes and packaging forms that the local market conditions, customs, and culture dictated. Jumbo rolls of products would be shipped from the United States, then broken up and repackaged for each country. The next stage was designing and building plants, buying machinery, and getting everything up and running. Over the years, R&D functions were often added, and by the 1980s considerable R&D was being done outside the United States.

Both Sampair and Patterson set an innovative, entrepreneurial framework that, according to the company, still guides 3M's International Operations today. The philosophy can be reduced to several key and simple commitments: (1) Get in early (within the company, the strategy is known as FIDO—"First in Defeats Others"); (2) hire talented and motivated local people; (3) become a good corporate citizen of the country; (4) grow with the local economy; (5) American products are not one size fits all around the world; tailor products to fit local needs; and (6) enforce patents in local countries.

As 3M stepped into the international market vacuum, foreign sales surged from less than 5 percent in 1951 to 42 percent by 1979. By the end of the 1970s, 3M was beginning to understand how important it was to integrate the international operations more closely with the U.S. operations and to build innovative capabilities overseas. It expanded the company's international R&D presence (there are now more than 2,200 technical employees outside the United States), built closer ties between the U.S. and foreign research organizations, and started to transfer more managerial and technical employees between businesses in different countries.

In 1978 the company started the Pathfinder Program to encourage new-product and new business initiatives born outside the United States. By 1983, products developed under the initiative were generating sales of more than $150 million a year. For example, 3M Brazil invented a low-cost, hot-melt adhesive from local raw materials; 3M Germany teamed up with Sumitomo 3M of Japan (a joint venture with Sumitomo) to develop electronic connectors with new features for the worldwide electronics industry; 3M Philippines developed a Scotch-Brite cleaning pad shaped like a foot after learning that Filipinos polished floors with their feet; and so on. On the back of such developments, in 1992 international operations exceeded 50 percent of revenues for the first time in the company's history.

By the 1990s, 3M started to shift away from a country-by-country management structure to more regional management. Drivers behind this development included the fall of trade barriers, the rise of trading blocs such as the European Union and NAFTA, and the need to drive down costs in the face of intense global competition. The first European Business Center (EBC) was created in 1991 to manage 3M's chemical business across Europe. The EBC was charged with product development, manufacturing, sales, and marketing for Europe, but also with paying attention to local country requirements. Other EBCs soon followed, such as EBCs for disposable products and pharmaceuticals.

As the millennium ended, 3M seemed set on transforming the company into an organization characterized by an integrated network of businesses that spanned the globe. The goal was to get the right mix of global scale to

deal with competitive pressures, while at the same time maintaining 3M's traditional focus on local market differences and decentralized R&D capabilities.

THE DESIMONE YEARS

In 1991, Desi DeSimone became CEO of 3M. A longtime 3M employee, the Canadian-born DeSimone was the epitome of a 21st-century manager—he had made his name by building 3M's Brazilian business and spoke five languages fluently. Unlike most prior 3M CEOs, DeSimone came from the manufacturing side of the business, rather than the technical aide. He soon received praise for managing 3M through the recession of the early 1990s. By the late 1990s, however, his leadership had come under fire from both inside and outside the company.

In 1998 and 1999, the company missed its earnings targets, and the stock price fell as disappointed investors sold. Sales were flat, profit margins fell, and earnings slumped by 50 percent. The stock had underperformed the widely tracked Standard & Poor's 500 stock index for most of the 1980s and 1990s.

One cause of the earnings slump in the late 1990s was 3M's sluggish response to the 1997 Asian crisis. During the Asian crisis, the value of several Asian currencies fell by as much as 80 percent against the U.S. dollar in a few months. The company generated a quarter of its sales from Asia, but it was slow to cut costs there in the face of slumping demand following the collapse of currency values. At the same time, a flood of cheap Asian products cut into 3M's market share in the United States and Europe as lower currency values made Asian products much cheaper.

Another problem was that for all of its vaunted innovative capabilities, 3M had not produced a new blockbuster product since Post-it notes. Most of the new products produced during the 1990s were just improvements over existing products, not truly new products.

DeSimone was also blamed for not pushing 3M hard enough earlier in the decade to reduce costs. An example was the company's supply chain excellence program. In 1995, 3M's inventory was turning over just 3.5 times a year, subpar for manufacturing. An internal study suggested that every half point increase in inventory turnover could reduce 3M's working capital needs by $700 million, and boost its return on invested capital. But by 1998 3M had made no progress on this front.[7]

Despite the criticism, 3M's board, which included four previous 3M CEOs among its members, stood behind DeSimone until he retired in 2001. However, the board began a search for a new top executive in February 2000 and signaled that it was looking for an outsider. In December 2000, the company announced that it had found the person, Jim McNerney, a 51-year-old General

Electric veteran who ran GE's medical equipment businesses and before that GE's Asian operations. McNerney was one of the front-runners in the race to succeed Jack Welch as CEO of General Electric, but lost out to Jeffrey Immelt. One week after that announcement, 3M hired him.

MCNERNEY'S 3M

In his first public statement days after being appointed, McNerney said his focus would be on getting to know 3M's people and culture and its diverse lines of business:

> I think getting to know some of those businesses and bringing some of GE here to overlay on top of 3M's strong culture of innovation will be particularly important.[8]

It soon became apparent that McNerney's game plan was exactly that: to bring the GE play book to 3M and use it to try to boost 3M's results, while simultaneously not destroying the innovative culture that had produced the company's portfolio of 50,000 products.

The first move came in April 2001 when 3M announced the company would cut 5,000 jobs, or about 7 percent of the workforce, in a restructuring effort that would zero in on struggling businesses. The job cuts were expected to save $500 million a year. In another effort to save costs, the company streamlined its purchasing processes, for example, by reducing the number of packaging suppliers on a global basis from 50 to 5, saving another $100 million a year. By 2004, McNerney stated that more than $500 million had been saved since 2000 through global sourcing by consolidating purchasing, reducing the number of suppliers, switching to lower-cost suppliers in developing nations, and introducing dual sourcing policies to keep price increases under control.

Next, McNerney introduced Six Sigma, a rigorous statistically based quality control process that was one of the drivers of process improvement and cost savings at General Electric. Six Sigma is a management philosophy, accompanied by a set of tools, rooted in identifying and prioritizing customers and their needs, reducing variation in all business processes, and selecting and grading all projects based on their impact on financial results. Six Sigma breaks every task (process) in an organization into increments to be measured against a perfect model.

McNerney called for Six Sigma to be rolled out across 3M's global operations. He also introduced a performance evaluation system at 3M under which managers were asked to rank every employee who reported to them.

In addition to boosting performance from existing business, McNerney quickly signaled that he wanted to play a more active role in allocating resources between new business opportunities. At any given time, 3M has about 1,500 products in the development pipeline. McNerney thinks that is too many; he wants to funnel more cash to the most promising ideas, those with a potential market of $100 million a year or more, while cutting funding to weaker-looking development projects.

In the same vein, he signaled that he wanted to play a more active role in resource allocation than had traditionally been the case for a 3M CEO, using cash from mature businesses to fund growth opportunities elsewhere. He scrapped the requirement that each division get 30 percent of its sales from products introduced in the past four years, noting:

> To make that number, some managers were resorting to some rather dubious innovations, such as pink Post-it notes. It became a game, what could you do to get a new SKU?[9]

Some longtime 3M watchers, however, worried that by changing resource allocation practices McNerney might harm 3M's innovative culture. If the company's history proves anything, they say, it's that it is hard to tell which of today's tiny products will become tomorrow's home runs. No one predicted that Scotchgard or Post-it notes would earn millions. They began as little experiments that evolved without planning into big hits. McNerney's innovations all sound fine in theory, they say, but there is a risk that he will transform 3M into "3E" and lose what is valuable in 3M in the process.

In general, though, securities analysts greeted McNerney's moves favorably. One noted that "McNerney is all about speed," and there will be "no more Tower of Babel—everyone speaks one language." This "one company" vision was meant to replace the program under which 3M systematically spun off successful new products into new business centers. The problem with this approach, according to the analyst, was that there was no leveraging of best practices across businesses.[10]

McNerney also signaled that he would reform 3M's regional management structure, replacing it with a global business unit structure that will be defined by either products or markets. McNerney's idea is that each business unit should be responsible for serving its market on a global basis, and should configure its assets accordingly, locating production and research facilities wherever in the world makes most sense, and customizing the final product offering to country requirements.

Case Discussion Questions

1. St. Paul–based 3M has a long history of innovation. What were the historic roots of the company's innovative culture? What are the many tenets of that culture?

2. How has innovation been formally institutionalized within 3M?

3. What were the advantages of the organization structure that developed at 3M during the second half of the 20th century? What were the disadvantages?

4. Historically, 3M has been very successful at expanding internationally. What explains 3M's success?

5. What were the drawbacks with the way 3M expanded internationally during the second half of the 20th century? How did the 1997 Asian economic crisis expose the limitations of 3M's strategy?

6. Strategically, what is McNerney trying to do with 3M?

7. During the 1990s, 3M shifted toward a regional management structure. Why?

8. In 2003 McNerney announced he wanted to replace the regional management structure with a global business unit structure? Why?

Notes

1. M. Dickson, "Back to the Future," *Financial Times*, May 30, 1994, p. 7, and www.3m.com/profile/looking/mcknight.jhtml.

2. www.3m.com/about3M/innovation/scotchgard50/index.jhtml.

3. *A Century of Innovation, the 3M Story*. (St. Paul: 3M, 2002) p. 78. Available at www.3m.com/about3m/century/index.jhtml.

4. Ibid.

5. Ibid, p. 42.

6. Ibid, pp. 143–44.

7. Michelle Conlin, "Too Much Doodle?" *Forbes*, October 19, 1998, pp. 54–56.

8. Joseph Hallinan, "3M's Next Chief Plans to Fortify Results with Discipline He Learned at GE Unit," *The Wall Street Journal*, December 6, 2000, p. B17.

9. Jerry Useem, "(Tape) + (Light bulb) = ?" *Fortune*, August 12, 2002, pp. 127–31.

10. Rick Mullin, "Analysts Rate 3M's New Culture," *Chemical Week*, September 26, 2001, pp. 39–40.

Sources

1. Collins, J. C., and J. I. Porras. *Built to Last*. New York: Harper Business, 1994.

2. Conlin, Michelle. "Too Much Doodle?" *Forbes*, October 19, 1998, pp. 54–56

3. Dickson, M. "Back to the Future." *Financial Times*, May 30, 1994, p. 7.

4. Hallinan, Joseph. "3M's Next Chief Plans to Fortify Results with Discipline He Learned at GE Unit." *The Wall Street Journal*, December 6, 2000, p. B17.

5. Von Hippel, Eric, et al. "Creating Breakthroughs at 3M." *Harvard Business Review*, September–October 1999.

6. Mullin, Rick. "Analysts Rate 3M's New Culture." *Chemical Week*, September 26, 2001, pp. 39–40.

7. *A Century of Innovation, the 3M Story*. St. Paul: 3M, 2002. Available at www.3m.com/about3m/century/index.jhtml.

8. 3M Investor Meeting, September 30, 2003. Archived at www.corporate-ir.net/ireye/ir_site.zhtml?ticker=MMM&script=2100.

9. Studt, Tim. 3M — Where Innovation Rules. *R&D Magazine*, April 2003, pp. 20–24.

10. Weimer, De Ann, "3M: The Heat Is on the Boss." *BusinessWeek*, March 15, 1999, pp. 82–83.

11. Useem, Jerry "(Tape) + (Light bulb) = ?" *Fortune*, August 12, 2002, pp. 127–31.

Lenovo in 2005

INTRODUCTION

Lenovo, formerly known as Legend, was the largest personal computer (PC) maker in China. Legend Group Holdings, which was controlled by the Chinese government, owned a majority stake in Lenovo, which offered various products including low-priced computers, servers, handheld computers, imaging equipment, and mobile phone handsets. Lenovo also provided manufacturing and IT integration and support services.

In 2004, Lenovo recorded sales of $2,971.2 million and a net income of $135 million and controlled about 2.2 percent of the global PC market and, in 2003, 27 percent of the Chinese PC market. In February 2000, Legend was ranked eighth in a survey conducted by *BusinessWeek*.[1] The following year, Legend was voted as Asia's Best Managed Company in a survey conducted by Finance Asia.

[1]The survey was called Global Information Technology 100.

On December 7, 2004, Lenovo announced that it would acquire IBM's PC Division (which has a 5.5 percent global market share) for approximately $1.75 billion, to become the world's third largest PC maker with annual sales of close to $12 billion. After a 45-day review by the Committee on Foreign Investment in the United States (CFIUS), the deal was given a green signal by the U.S. government and CFIUS on March 9, 2005.

Would the deal really take Lenovo and IBM to great heights? Could Lenovo become a global player and integrate IBM's U.S. operations? Would Lenovo be able to retain IBM's PC customers? These were the questions analysts pondered as 2005 got under way.

BACKGROUND

The Early Days

In 1984, Liu Chuanzhi, a computer scientist who became an administrative manager in the Computing Institute of the Chinese Academy of Science[2] (CAS) in Beijing, was given a mandate and $24,000 to start a company to commercialize the institute's research results in order to fund its ongoing research costs. Liu, along with 10 colleagues, formed the New Technology Development Company (NTD). They started operations in a small bungalow given by CAS free of cost. During the first two years, NTD acted as a middleman, acquiring products from large domestic distributors and selling them to government agencies and large state-owned enterprises (SOEs).

To overcome their initial funding constraints, they even tried selling television sets and electronic watches. At the time, as China had limited domestic PC manufacturing capabilities, almost all the PCs were imported. In addition to foreign products imported through formal channels, many products were also smuggled into China through gray channels. Since no tariff was paid on gray market products, they could be sold at much lower prices. As a result, many small distributors bought these products and distributor profit margins fell steeply. NTD felt the significant price pressure and realized that the company needed its own products to survive in the long run.

Almost all the operating systems (OS) were English and few Chinese spoke English. Recognizing the OS bottleneck, Liu decided to start his own product development by translating an English OS into Chinese. NTD was not alone in marketing Chinese-language solutions for PCs. But in contrast to rival software products, NTD's solution was hardware-based. NTD used a new pattern-recognition technology and developed the Legend Chinese Insertion Card (LCIC) in 1985, which was designed to be inserted into PC motherboards. Unlike software solutions, Legend's card did not occupy significant amounts of costly hard-disk space. Duplicating the hardware was also more difficult than copying competing software products. This was a significant advantage because industry experts estimated that over half of all Microsoft DOS systems installed on PCs in the People's Republic of China were pirated. An important feature of this technology was "association" or "Lian Xiang" (Legend's Chinese name). The association feature enabled the system to prompt Chinese characters which could be used to form expressions and phrases with the character input. The development of the new product also convinced a few experienced scientists in the Computing Institute of the company's future prospects and enticed them to join the sales and marketing efforts. LCIC became a huge success within a year. NTD changed its name to Legend in 1989.

By bundling LCIC with the imported PCs, Legend's distribution business also made significant progress. In 1987, Legend signed a formal agreement to distribute AST PCs and Hewlett-Packard (HP) peripheral products. With HP, Legend started by distributing CAD systems and gradually expanded into HP printers and other peripheral products. Success in the distribution business allowed Legend to accumulate capital for future development and helped a generation of young leaders gain experience in the marketing and distribution side of the business. During the 1980s, distribution itself accounted for more than 60 percent of Legend's total revenue.

In the late 1980s, the Chinese government realized the need to build an indigenous PC industry. The Ministry of Electronic Industries (MEI) granted PC manufacturing licenses to a few firms it directly owned. Not being directly owned by MEI, Legend was not granted a manufacturing license in China. Therefore, it decided to manufacture abroad. The company chose Hong Kong as its base for operations. In 1988, Legend established a joint venture with Dao Yuan[3] and China Technology Transfer Company (CTTC), which was jointly owned by the Bank of China, China Resources, and two other well-connected mainland firms.

Legend began its Hong Kong operations with distribution. It utilized Hong Kong's geographical advantage to penetrate the growing Chinese market during the 1980s. Legend's relationship with AST[4] was the most successful example of this strategy. AST distributed its products through several Chinese companies, including Legend, but experienced difficulties in communication and coordination while dealing with mainland firms. For

---

[2]A Chinese government institution in Beijing.

[3]Dao Yuan was a Hong Kong trading company.

[4]AST was a U.S.-based computer manufacturer. In the mid-1980s, AST was a second-tier PC manufacturer well behind industry leaders IBM and HP.

example, AST had to translate nearly all correspondence with its mainland Chinese distributors. Many mainland companies turned off their fax machines after work hours. After establishing a presence in Hong Kong, Legend Hong Kong took over all contract negotiations and import/export transactions with AST, while Legend Beijing carried out actual distribution, sales and service in Mainland China. Since Legend had been in the distribution business for several years by that time and its sales force had accumulated considerable experience from distributing HP, IBM, and other foreign vendors' products, Legend was instrumental to AST's success in penetrating the Chinese market. With Legend's help, AST became the number one vendor of PC products in China by the early 1990s, accounting for 29.3 percent of total unit shipments in 1992.

While the trading and distribution business grew quickly and became very profitable, Legend Hong Kong continued to look for an opportunity to enter manufacturing. In late 1988, it acquired Quantum Design International (QDI).[5] Legend aggressively marketed QDI motherboards overseas using a low-price strategy.

It was not until the 1989 World Fair held in Hanover, Germany, that Legend finally caught the attention of the Chinese government. The Chinese delegation at the fair consisted of senior officials from several ministries regulating the trading and manufacturing of electronic products in China. After Legend demonstrated its manufacturing prowess at the fair, the MEI sent a special delegation to Hong Kong to thoroughly inspect Legend's R&D and manufacturing capability. In 1990, after MEI was satisfied with the inspection, it granted Legend a license to manufacture PCs in China.

By 1995, Legend had become the fifth largest manufacturer of motherboards in the world and one of the three board manufacturers performing beta tests on each new generation of Intel CPUs (the other two were Taiwanese companies, Acer and Gigabyte). The company had established more than 30 overseas sales offices throughout the world to market its motherboards.

Reorganization

In 1994, having resolved to be in PC manufacturing, Legend conducted a detailed analysis of its PC business to identify areas that needed improvement. One such area was a misaligned incentive structure and uncoordinated internal decision-making process. Legend's PC business was organized on functional lines, such as purchasing, manufacturing, and marketing. Each area was determined by its ability to meet functional targets set in the annual planning process. To solve the problem, the

management decided to consolidate all Legend's PC-related businesses into a new PC business unit (PCBU) in 1994.

Yang Yuanqing, who was just 29 years old then, was appointed the unit's general manager. Yang had joined Legend in 1988. He had completed his master's degree in computer science from the University of Science and Technology. Most of the senior managers of the company were older than 50, and did not have much experience in working in a market environment, or in a rapidly changing PC industry. On the other hand, Yang had demonstrated his management capability in his first few years with Legend. He also had more front-line operation management experience than most other young managers.

After taking over, Yang looked after purchasing, manufacturing, and marketing of all PC products. He was given the freedom to determine new-product launches, channel selection, and pricing strategies based on market conditions. All the functional managers were evaluated on both departmental and BU results. For example, the purchasing manager was evaluated on purchasing-related performance measures, regardless of the accuracy of marketing forecasts provided by the marketing manager. Even if inventory turnover was slow due to inaccurate market forecasts, the purchasing manager had to take some responsibility.

Before 1994, Legend sold its PCs through both a direct sales force of more than 100 sales representatives and hundreds of local distributors. Channel conflicts were many. The first major marketing decision Yang took was to eliminate direct sales and switch entirely to distributor sales. Legend was the first domestic manufacturer to take this decision. Yang cut the sales force to 18 people, just enough to manage a distributor network.

The PCBU also focused on controlling costs and improving manufacturing efficiency. To ensure timely collection of receivables, Legend required all distributors initially to pay cash up front. Credit was granted only after the distributor earned a good track record with the company. Legend also tied most of its distributor incentives, such as price discounts, quarterly rebates, and co-op advertising fees, to cash collection history. This information helped Legend maintain an accounts receivable turnover of less than 30 days, compared to the industry average of around 90 days in China.

Realizing that prices were falling rapidly in the PC market, Legend also attempted to improve its inventory turnover. For the popular standard products, the company maintained abundant levels of inventory to ensure shipment within one week. For less popular products, Legend adopted a built-to-order model. Yang felt that since the national logistics and delivery system was underdeveloped in China, a complete built-to-

---

[5]Quantum Design International was a motherboard manufacturing company in Hong Kong.

order model would not work. With tightened control, Legend managed to improve inventory turnover to seven times in 1995.

The reorganization quickly paid off. In 1994, the second-quarter PC sales went up by 152 percent when compared to the same period in 1993 and the PCBU made a profit. Through its channel development efforts and improvement in management efficiency, Legend was successful in increasing the PC sales and capturing 5.7 percent of the market in 1995.

Although Legend focused more on manufacturing its own branded PCs, its separate distribution business continued to grow. Legend's agreement with HP stretched into PC products in 1994 and into servers in 1995. Legend became the unique distributor for Toshiba laptops in China. It also started distributing PCs and related peripheral products for Apple, Sun, IBM, and Canon.

By 1996, Legend had increased its manufacturing capacity to around 500,000 units a year. In addition, Legend was able to reduce overheads to about 20 percent of total unit cost. The management decided that by lowering prices, Legend could increase its sales volume, which would in turn lower unit overhead costs and improve Legend's entire cost structure.

Legend's management had noticed a mismatch between market demand for the latest technologies and the new-product introduction strategies of major players. Because of low consumption levels in China and the relatively high prices due to tariffs and transportation costs, foreign multinationals launched PC products into China about four to five months after they have been launched elsewhere.

While slashing PC prices by 30 percent, Legend also became the first to market new technologies. Early in 1996, Intel had launched its Pentium chip. In China, however, the PC makers were still selling 486s priced at around $1,800, which included a 15 percent tariff. Following a detailed analysis, Legend noted that total material cost, including tariff and transportation, for a Pentium-based PC would work out to $1,100. Falling component costs and potential lower unit overhead costs resulting from volume increases meant that Legend could break even or even make a small profit by selling Pentium-based PCs at $1,200. Legend implemented this strategy in March 1996.

Legend's sales volume increased drastically, and so the unit overhead costs fell to 16 percent of total cost. The global component costs also continued to fall and Legend reduced the prices by 25–30 percent on its latest models twice more in 1996. By early 1997, Legend sold almost 140,000 desktop PCs, capturing the number one position in China with a 9.4 percent share, slightly ahead of IBM's 8.4 percent.

By 1999, Legend felt that the Internet could pose a serious threat to the way that traditional business was conducted in China. Rapidly growing Internet portals and business-to-business (B-to-B) e-commerce start-ups were attracting large venture capital funding and going public. Even bureaucratic government agencies were moving online, spurred by a highly publicized campaign by the Beijing government.

Furthermore, potential conflicts of interest between Legend's own PC business and its distribution business became increasingly evident. Although its distribution business had commanded 30 percent annual growth in the past, it became increasingly difficult to reduce its costs while using the traditional distribution model. China's impending accession into the World Trade Organization (WTO) was apt to increase domestic competition, threatening Legend's competitive position in the domestic market.

Legend's management realized that a significant rethinking of the company's business and organization was crucial for future success. Responding to the threat from the Internet and global competition within China, Legend announced a major restructuring of its organization to take effect April 2000. Legend Holdings was restructured into two essentially independent businesses with full decision-making authorities: Legend Computing System (LCS) and Digital China. LCS became responsible for all of Legend's computers, software, and newly formed Internet businesses offering connectivity and content. Digital China took Legend's distribution business into a B-to-B marketplace and developed its new networking business.

During late 2000, Legend stepped up its efforts to capture a significant share of the corporate PC segment. In November 2000, Legend launched two models of commercial Internet PCs—Doctor of Business 6000 and Doctor of Net 2000—targeted at small and medium enterprises (SMEs) in China. The models were designed to meet the office automation requirements of SMEs. The company also launched Luna P4, China's first branded PC equipped with an Intel Pentium 4 processor.

In December 2000, Legend launched second-generation Internet PC models called Conet II and Tongxi. Conet II was equipped with an AV workstation, which allowed users to record videos. Legend launched four new models of home PCs—Tianhui for children, Future Pioneer for high school students, Tianlu for adults, and Tianle for middle-aged and elderly people. The Future Pioneer model was equipped with a multimedia and digital audio system and a 3D accelerated display card, which allowed students to play 3D video games.

In 2002, Legend entered the software consultancy business. The company acquired a 51 percent stake in Han Consulting Limited[6] to jointly offer IT consultancy

---

[6]A leading management consulting and IT services company in China.

services to medium-sized and large enterprises in China. During mid-2002, Legend entered the mobile handset business through a $150 million, 60:40 joint venture with Xiamen Overseas Chinese Electronic Company Limited.[7] The two companies agreed to integrate their research and product development efforts to develop and market mobile handsets in China.

The domestic market where Legend generated more than 90 percent of its business was proving increasingly tricky as local players such as Founder sharpened their attack. At the same time, price-cutting by international rivals such as Dell and Toshiba was eroding Legend's share of the world's fastest growing PC market.

Expanding into the international markets for Legend became inevitable with the globalization of the IT industry and to assure Legend's future. During 2002–03, about 5 percent of Legend's turnover came from overseas markets, including Europe, Asia-Pacific, and North America.

In April 2003, Legend adopted a new logo and the English brand name Lenovo. Lenovo meant innovation and creation. The Le in the name connected with Legend, while novo linked to innovation and novelty. The decision to create the new brand was also prompted by the fact that other users in a number of major markets had registered the Legend name. However, the 19-year-old company continued to trade as Legend Group, and used its Chinese brand name in combination with the Lenovo logo in its home market.

Yang remarked:

> Although our business focus is still on China, expanding into the international market is an inevitable path with the globalization of the IT industry and for Legend's self-development. Having made reference to the successful experience of well-known brands, we decided to choose a single brand structure to concentrate our resources on the accumulation of our brand value.[8]

In March 2004, Lenovo joined the Olympic Partner Program of the International Olympic Committee (IOC). Lenovo was the first Chinese company to become the computer technology equipment partner of the IOC for 2005 to 2008. Between 2004 and 2008, Lenovo would provide computing technology equipment (including desktop computers, notebooks, servers, and desktop printers) funding as well as technological support to the 2006 Turin Olympic Winter Games, the 2008 Beijing Olympic Games, and over 200 national Olympic committees around the world.

THE IBM DEAL

In December 2004, Lenovo announced it was purchasing IBM's PC manufacturing business. After the successful completion of the deal, Lenovo would locate its PC business worldwide headquarters in New York, with principal operations in Beijing and Raleigh, North Carolina, and sales offices throughout the world.

Lenovo would gain ownership of IBM's PC design facilities, including an R&D lab in Yamato, Japan. In addition, Lenovo would either acquire outright or get licensing rights to a large portfolio of IBM patents. The PC manufacturing portion of the International Information Products Company (IIPC) in Shenzhen, China, which was co-owned by IBM and Great Wall, was included in the transaction. However, IIPC's IBM eServer xSeries manufacturing was excluded.

After the merger, Lenovo would have a combined annual PC sales of approximately $12 billion and volume of 11.9 million units, based on 2003 business results—a fourfold increase in Lenovo's PC business. Lenovo's new PC business would benefit from a powerful worldwide distribution and sales network covering 160 countries.

IBM would be the preferred services and customer-financing provider to Lenovo. Lenovo would be the preferred supplier of PCs to IBM, which would offer a full range of personal computing solutions to its enterprise and small and medium business clients.

IBM's existing enterprise sales force of approximately 30,000 professionals and the Web site ibm.com would provide marketing support and demand generation services for Lenovo products, some of which would be sold through IBM PC specialists who would join Lenovo. IBM Global Financing and IBM Global Services (the number one IT services organization in the world with powerful existing enterprise channels) would be preferred providers to Lenovo for leasing and financing services and for warranty and maintenance services, respectively.

The deal, officially announced on December 7, 2004, was valued at $1.75 billion in cash, stock, and assumed liabilities. IBM would receive at least $650 million in cash and up to $600 million in Lenovo Group common stock, subject to a lock-in period expiring periodically over three years. Lenovo would assume approximately $500 million of net balance sheet liabilities from IBM. The cash portion of the consideration would be funded through internal cash and debt.

Once the agreement was finalized in early 2005, Lenovo would have three owners—the state with 46 percent, public investors with 35 percent, and IBM with 19 percent. The Chinese government owned 57 percent of Lenovo. To be managed primarily by former IBM executives working out of New York, the company would have 19,000 employees, with 10,000 of them coming from IBM. Of those 10,000, 40 percent were based in China and 25 percent in the United States.

---

[7]One of the leading electronics products companies in China.
[8]Sharon Desker Shaw, "Branding: Legend Creates Lenovo for Export," *Media Asia*, May 16, 2003, p. 10.

	2004 (HK$m)	2003 (HK$m)	Increase/ (Decrease)
Operating Results			
Turnover	23,176	20,233	14.5%
EBITDA	1,125	1,175	(4.3%)
Profit attributable to shareholders	1,053	1,017	3.5%
Earnings per share—fully diluted (HK cents)	13.99	13.54	3.3%
Financial Position			
Total assets	8,342	6,756	23.5%
Cash and cash equivalents	2,650	2,808	(5.6%)
Shareholders' fund	4,489	4,189	7.2%
Financial Ratio			
ROA (Return on assets) (%)	14.4	14.5	(0.7%)
ROE (Return on equity) (%)	24.7	25.6	(3.5%)
Current ratio (times)	1.9	2.1	(9.5%)
Others			
Interim dividend (HK cents)	2.0	1.8	11.1%
Proposed final dividend (HK cents)	3.0	3.0	–
Special dividend (HK cents)	–	5.2	N/A

EXHIBIT 1

Lenovo: Financial Highlights

Source: Lenovo Annual Report 2004.

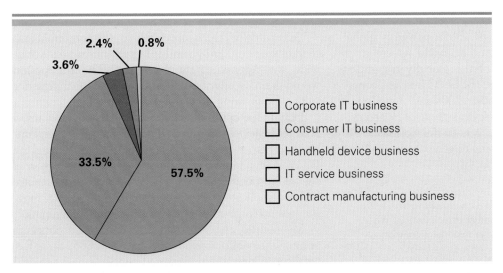

EXHIBIT 2

Lenovo: Turnover Analysis by Business Segment

Source: Lenovo Annual Report 2004.

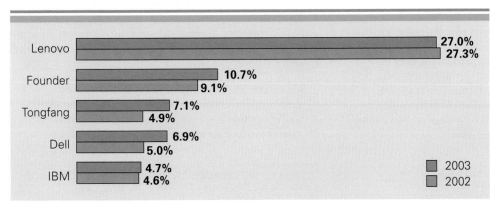

EXHIBIT 3

Market Share of Top 5 PC Brands in China

Source: Lenovo Annual Report 2004.

	2004		2003	
	Turnover (HK$'000)	Contribution to Operating Profit (HK$'000)	Turnover (HK$'000)	Contribution to Operating Profit (HK$'000)
Corporate IT	11,925,240	777,698	10,803,311	744,153
Consumer IT	7,760,668	466,814	6,822,633	363,527
Handheld device	2,050,164	(74,565)	1,440,328	29,017
IT service	547,780	(58,009)	183,800	(61,405)
Contract manufacturing	892,092	(95,208)	983,218	8,554
Gains/(losses) on disposal of investment	–	47,558	–	(26,802)
Amortization of goodwill	–	(25,274)	–	(7,463)
Others	–	(22,000)	–	–
Total	23,175,944	1,017,014	20,233,290	1,049,581

EXHIBIT 4

Lenovo: Turnover and Contribution

Source: Lenovo Annual Report 2004.

Lenovo hoped to leverage IBM's powerful global brand through a five-year brand licensing agreement as well as through ownership of the globally recognized "Think" family of trademarks. IBM's PC business generated over $9 billion in revenues in 2003 and offered a full range of desktop and notebook PC systems. The acquisition would provide Lenovo access to the worldwide PC market and enable the company to generate annual revenues of more than $12 billion.

Yang was clearly optimistic:

Lenovo of China is going to be Lenovo of the world. We won't be satisfied with the number three position. We will formally challenge the other two major competitors in the global PC market. The top management has analyzed in-depth why there is no profit for IBM's PC business. IBM is a service-oriented company, which focuses on products with high returns. But the PC business [is at a] stage where efficiency [brings] success, and that's why IBM's previous business model doesn't work . . . To reach high efficiency, there has to be big product scale. IBM only focuses on the big corporate clients, with less coverage for the middle size clients. This [hurts] IBM in the competition with rivals like Dell. Lenovo is strong where IBM is weak . . . and that is why we are confident about the future.[9]

According to IDC figures for 2003, the combined unit market share of Lenovo and IBM's PC businesses worldwide was approximately 8 percent. The transaction would dramatically strengthen Lenovo's global presence in the fast growing notebook PC marketplace.

Despite the optimism expressed by Liu and Yang, many analysts believed that the deal presented three uncertainties: acceptance of the new Lenovo by IBM's clients and the PC market; retaining IBM employees; and integration of the two corporate cultures. Lenovo would have to manage highly complicated logistics and supply chains, while moving forward in an industry with shrinking profit margins.

Meanwhile, the proposed deal had raised concerns among U.S. politicians. In mid-January 2005, three Republican congressmen expressed concerns that the deal could transfer advanced technology and corporate assets to the Chinese government, along with licensable or export-controlled technology, and might result in some U.S. government contracts involving PCs being fulfilled by the Chinese government. In the letter they stated:

Given the relationship between so-called "private companies" in communist states and their government, we believe that it is manifestly in the public interest to extend the time for review.[10]

---

[9]"The IBM/Lenovo Deal: Victory for China?" *www.knowledge.wharton.upenn.edu*, January 14, 2005.

[10]Charles Forelle, "Lawmakers Ask for More Scrutiny of IBM Unit Sale," *www.online.wsj.com*, January 27, 2005.

EXHIBIT 5

IBM: Revenue by Classes of Products or Services (dollars in millions)

Source: IBM Annual Report 2004.

	For the Year Ended December 31: Consolidated		
	2004	**2003**	**2002**
Global Services:			
Services	$ 40,517	$ 37,178	$ 31,290
Maintenance	5,696	5,457	5,070
Systems and Technology Group:			
Servers	$ 12,460	$ 11,148	$ 10,047
Storage	2,898	2,849	2,581
Microelectronics OEM	2,131	2,142	3,226
Technology services	424	325	323
Networking products	3	5	18
Enterprise Investments:			
Software	$ 1,131	$ 981	$ 916
Hardware	37	72	95
Others	12	12	11

EXHIBIT 6

IBM: Geographic Information

Source: IBM Annual Report 2004.

	For the Year Ended December 31:			
	2004	**2003**	**Year to Year Percent Change**	**Year to Year Percent Change Constant Currency**
Geographies:				
Americas	$ 40,064	$ 38,078	5.2%	4.5%
Europe/Middle East/Africa	32,068	29,102	10.2	0.8
Asia Pacific	21,276	19,317	10.1	4.2
OEM	2,885	2,634	9.6	9.3
Total	**$ 96,293**	**$ 89,131**	**8.0%**	**3.4%**

Responding to these concerns, the U.S. government decided to examine whether the deal threatened national security interests.

Lenovo's Chinese parent company and largest shareholder was closely tied to the CAS. The extended review of the deal was conducted by the U.S. Treasury Department's Committee on Foreign Investment in the U.S. (CFIUS), an interagency panel that was chaired by John W. Snow. After the review (which lasted for 45 days), a report had to be submitted to the U.S. president, who would have 15 days to announce the final decision.

In February 2005, Yang clarified that the deal would not pose a national security threat to the United States:

Probably there are more PCs sold a year than TVs throughout the world. Therefore, you know and I know of the technology content embedded in the PCs, therefore I don't think that we will pose any security

threat to the U.S. Our transaction will add a lot of benefits not only to the bilateral relationship between the two countries but also the commercial relationship between U.S. and Chinese companies. And I know that a lot of Chinese companies are also thinking about doing business in the U.S., and we hope that we can provide a good and successful example for them.[11]

He said that the deal could be "beneficial" to Sino-U.S. ties as more Chinese companies sought to grow overseas, particularly in the United States.

The committee was comforted by a plan to house Lenovo's Raleigh operations, post-acquisition, in a separate, three-building complex. Lenovo's corporate headquarters with a head count of about 100 would move to

---

[11]Hasan Jafri, "Lenovo CEO: Deal with IBM Doesn't Pose Security Threat," *www.online.wsj.com*, February 2, 2005.

EXHIBIT 7

IBM: Research, Development, and Engineering (dollars in millions)

Source: IBM Annual Report 2004.

	For the Year Ended December 31:		
	2004	**2003**	**Year to Year Change**
Research, development and engineering:			
Total	$ 5,673	$ 5,077	11.7%

EXHIBIT 8

IBM: Employees and Related Workforce

Source: IBM Annual Report 2004.

For the Year Ended December 31: Percentage Changes					
	2004	**2003**	**2002**	**2004–03**	**2003–02**
IBM wholly owned subsidiaries	329,001	319,273	315,889	3.0	1.1
Less-than-wholly owned subsidiaries	19,051	18,189	22,282	4.7	(18.4)
Complementary	21,225	17,695	17,250	19.9	2.6

New York from Beijing. Finally the deal was given a green signal by CFIUS on March 9, 2005. CFIUS did not call for any limits to be put on Lenovo's ability to sell PCs in the United States, allowing it to bid for government and military contracts.

In March 2005, there was news that Lenovo would need more funds to cope with the deal. Three private equity firms—Texas Pacific Group, General Atlantic LLC, and the Newbridge Capital LLC affiliate of Texas Pacific and Blum Capital Partners—seemed to be close to taking a stake in Lenovo.

On March 30, 2005, Lenovo officially announced that it had received a $350 million investment from Texas Pacific Group, $200 million; General Atlantic LLC, $100 million; and Newbridge Capital LLC, $50 million. Lenovo would use about $150 million towards the acquisition of the PC operations of IBM and add the remaining to its working capital.

The company would issue to the firms a total of 2.73 million unlisted Series A cumulative convertible preferred shares at HK$1,000 each and unlisted warrants for 237.4 million shares. The firms would have about 12.4 percent stake, assuming full conversion of the preferred shares and exercise of the warrants, and including the issuance of shares to IBM in the $1.25 billion PC unit transaction.

These new investors would give the company expertise in helping it carve out the IBM PC business from its former parent. In addition, they would play a role in helping merge two diverse cultures. The new investors also would take 3 out of the 12 seats on the Lenovo board.

The new investment changed the payment terms. Originally, Lenovo thought it would give IBM shares valued at $600 million and cash of $650 million, which

it obtained through bank loans. But under the changed circumstances, Lenovo had decided to use $150 million of the money from the private-equity firms to boost its cash payment to $800 million. It would issue shares valued at $450 million to IBM, which would then be left with a 13.4 percent stake in the combined firm. The remaining $200 million from the private-equity firms would be used for working capital.

THE ROAD AHEAD

Legend's diversified business portfolio included consumer and corporate IT, handheld devices, IT services, and contract manufacturing businesses. Under the Lenovo brand, it had also extended its product line to include mobile phones. To counter sluggish domestic sales, the company had shifted its customer focus to companies where it was likely to be able to charge a premium. However, Liu stressed that Legend's marketing activities would continue to be focused on the consumer market.

China, which accounted for 42 percent of PC shipments in the Asia-Pacific region excluding Japan in 2003, grew at 7.8 percent in the fourth quarter of 2002 and it was expected to continue to drive regional expansion in 2003.[12] Legend posted double-digit percentage gains year-on-year. HP retained its second spot in the region with a relatively small growth rate, while IBM, which stood at the third place, reported positive year-on-year gains. Dell, placed fourth, similarly posted year-on-year gains in most countries.

Although Lenovo faced increased competition, the multinational brands continued to lag behind. Indeed,

[12]According to IDC.

Lenovo's 27 percent market share overshadowed both local and foreign competitors—Dell and IBM, and HP at 3 percent. Even Founder lagged far behind at 9.4 percent.

Following the successful deal with IBM, both Lenovo and IBM would profit from Lenovo's access to emerging Asian markets.

Liu commented:

> In the past three years we set up a road map to achieve diversification. However, things did not go well with our plans. We were too anxious to achieve our goals, we did not think through our plans clearly, and we did not succeed. As a result, for the next three years we have developed a new strategy. We will focus on the PC industry first. Of course, this is just a three-year plan—we do not intend to focus just on PCs forever. We are now working on plans for globalization as well as new ways of diversification, but we haven't reached any conclusion yet.[13]

How the IBM/Lenovo deal would play out remained to be seen. To make the deal work, Lenovo had decided to put IBM's executives in charge. Stephen M. Ward, Jr., currently IBM senior vice president and general manager of IBM's Personal Systems Group, would serve as the CEO of Lenovo, and Yang would serve as the chairman. However, Liu, who was an extraordinarily capable person and well versed in dealing with the Chinese government, would step aside as chairman and not be part of the new management team.

Meanwhile, the average age of Lenovo employees was below 30, while IBM executives were older and more seasoned. Lenovo would have to blend executives who could manage the Chinese government and maintain a strong competitive position in the United States. Would Lenovo be able to meet these challenges?

Sources

1. "A Technology Legend in China." *Harvard Business School Case*, 9-701-052, April 5, 2001.
2. Desker Shaw, Sharon. "Branding: Legend Creates Lenovo for Export." *Media Asia*, May 16, 2003, p. 10.
3. "China's Leading Computer Manufacturer Strives for International Recognition." *World IT Report*, June 25, 2003.
4. Hargrave-Silk, Atifa. "Is Legend Ready to Go Global?" *Media Asia*, June 27, 2003, p. 21.
5. "China's IT Giant Lenovo Forms R&D Network in Major Chinese Cities." *Xinhua (China)*, August 5, 2003.
6. Fiscaldo, Donna. "IBM to Face Scrutiny in Deal to Sell PC Unit," www.online.wsj.com, January 24, 2004.
7. "Nokia, China's Lenovo Sign Licensing Agreement for Series 60 Platform." *Emerging Markets Economy*, February 23, 2004.
8. "Business China—Making a Mark." *The Economic Intelligence Unit*, April 12, 2004.
9. "Interview with Lenovo Chairman, Liu Chuanzhi," www.knowledge.wharton.upenn.edu, September 8, 2004.
10. "IBM, Lenovo Plan Joint PC Venture in US." *The Wall Street Journal*, December 7, 2004.
11. "Lenovo to Acquire IBM Personal Computing Division," www.lenovogrp.com, December 7 and 8, 2004.
12. Einhorn, Bruce. "Rethinking the China Threat." *BusinessWeek Online*, January 4, 2005.
13. "The IBM/Lenovo Deal: Victory for China?" www.knowledge.wharton.upenn.edu, January 14, 2005.
14. Wildstrom, Stephen H. "Will ThinkPads Still Be ThinkPads?" *BusinessWeek*, January 17, 2005, p. 22.
15. Croal, N'Gai. "Let Free Software Reign." *Newsweek*, January 24, 2005, p. 14.
16. Wang, Julie. "Lenovo Shareholders OK IBM PC Ops Buy in HK EGM," www.online.wsj.com, January 27, 2005.
17. Forelle, Charles. "Lawmakers Ask for More Scrutiny of IBM Unit Sale," www.online.wsj.com, January 27, 2005.
18. Lemon, Sumner. "Lenovo's IBM Deal to Face US Reviews," www.macworld.com, January 28, 2005.
19. Jafri, Hasan. "Lenovo CEO: Deal with IBM Doesn't Pose Security Threat," www.online.wsj.com, February 2, 2005.
20. Crock, Stan, and Dunham, Richard S. "Seeing Red Over Big Blue's China Deal." *BusinessWeek*, February 14, 2005, p. 45.
21. Hamm, Steve; Park, Andrew; Elgin, Ben, and Sager, Ira. "A Lemon for Lenovo?" *BusinessWeek*, February 21, 2005, p. 13.
22. Forelle, Charles, and Hitt, Greg. "IBM Discusses Security Measure in Lenovo Deal," www.online.wsj.com, February 25, 2005.
23. "Lenovo's IBM Bid Gets US Go-Ahead," news.bbc.co.uk, March 9, 2005.
24. "US Panel Clears Security Review of Lenovo-IBM Deal," news.bbc.co.uk, March 9, 2005.
25. Riordan, David. "Lenovo Still China's Biggest PC Vendor in 2004—Gartner," www.online.wsj.com, March 9, 2005.

[13]"Interview with Lenovo Chairman, Liu Chuanzhi," *www.knowledge.wharton.upenn.edu*, September 8, 2004.

26. Forelle, Charles, and Hitt, Greg. "U.S. Panel Clears IBM Sale of Unit to Chinese Firm: PC Business Will Be Moved to Separate Facility to Ease National-Security Concerns," www.online. wsj.com, March 10, 2005.

27. Burt, Jeffrey. "U.S. Committee Clears IBM-Lenovo Deal." *eWeek,* March 14, 2005, p. 22.

28. Sender, Henny. "Equity Firms to Acquire Stake in Computer Maker Lenovo," www.online.wsj.com, March 23, 2005.

29. Gale, Alastair. "China Lenovo Refuses Comment on News of Likely Stake Sale," www.online.wsj.com, March 23, 2005.

30. Stearns, Scott W. "Lenovo Gets $350M Investment from Texas Pacific-Led Grp," www.online.wsj.com, March 30, 2005.

31. "Three Firms Invest in Lenovo," www.online. wsj.com, March 31, 2005.

32. Ramstad, Evan. "New Investment in Lenovo Marks an Endorsement of IBM PC Deal," www.online. wsj.com, April 1, 2005.

33. "China's Lenovo Says Completes Purchase of IBM PC Unit," www.online.wsj.com, May 1, 2005.

34. Ramstad, Evan. "Lenovo Completes Its Acquisition of IBM's Personal-Computer Unit," www.online. wsj.com, May 2, 2005.

35. Lenovo Annual Reports.

DHL'S Business Strategy in China

"DHL intends to stay in step with the needs of our customers in China, where the industry is developing and customer expectations continue to become more sophisticated. We maintain the belief that China will become DHL's most important market in Asia Pacific within the next few years and one of the most important markets within the DHL network. The investments will provide unparalleled strength to our already comprehensive network in China, enabling us to support the growth of the market."[1]

John Mullen, CEO, DHL-Asia Pacific

THE LAUNCH

In May 2004, the Belgium-based DHL International (DHL), in collaboration with its Chinese partner, Sinotrans,[2] launched China Domestic, an international express service, in China. DHL-Sinotrans was a leading player in the Chinese express and logistics industry. The introduction of China Domestic was a part of the duo's strategy to respond to the fast-changing customer requirements in China's logistics market. The new business was a door-to-door delivery service particularly targeting parcels and freight items. The service offered shorter delivery and pick-up times, besides providing better customer service and shipment visibility via DHL's Track-and-Trace technology.[3]

Wholly owned by Deutshce Post World Net (DPWN), DHL had an established presence in over 220 countries. In April 2004, the company had over 150,000 employees globally. In China, DPWN operated through three divisions—DHL-Sinotrans, DHL-Danzas Air & Ocean, and DHL Solutions. While its core business was transporting documents and packages, DHL also offered various other services such as e-commerce fulfilment and logistics solutions for industries like automotive and life sciences. With its innovative and customized solutions, DHL emerged as the world's leading express and logistics company. It positioned itself as an integrated one-stop supply chain solutions provider, offering services in express, air and ocean freight, and overland transport.

The rapidly improving business environment in China and its entry into the World Trade Organization

[1]"DHL Announces US$ 200 Million 5-year China Expansion Programme," DHL Press Release, London. October 23, 2003.
[2]Founded in 1956 in Beijing, Sinotrans was also known as the China National Foreign Trade Transportation (Group) Corporation. Sinotrans' area of operations included cross-border regional transportation along with forwarding, shipping, chartering, shipping agency, storage and warehousing, automobile transportation, foreign trade, and economic cooperation.

[3]It is a shipment tracking service, which aims at providing customers with accurate logistics information. It helps the customers track the status of their shipment via DHL's Web site. The customers are also informed about the status of shipment delivery through SMS.

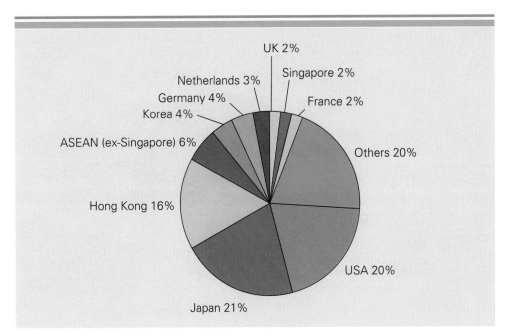

EXHIBIT I

China's Export Partners and Their Share in the Market (2001)

Source: "Sending the Right Message," www. internationalspecialreports. com, 2001.

in 2001 attracted many multinationals to the country. DHL was among those who recognized the potential for growth in the country's express logistics industry. To capitalize on growing business opportunities, DHL initiated a massive expansion program. Commenting on this, Uwe Doerken, CEO, DHL Express, said, "The logistics industry is widely recognized by the Chinese government as a critical, strategic industry and a key driver of economic progress. This wide-ranging expansion program will add significantly to DHL's ongoing investments in China, and illustrates the active role which DHL, as a leading industry partner, is committed to undertake in the country."[4]

FOREIGN LOGISTICS COMPANIES IN CHINA

Globalization offered more and more opportunities for companies operating worldwide. To realize these opportunities, global organizations shifted their production sites to low-cost developing countries like China. China's entry into the WTO led to sustained improvement of its international trade (refer to Exhibits I and II for China's export and import partners in 2001). The growth in international and domestic trade also led to the rapid growth of the Chinese logistics industry (refer to Exhibit III for the logistics industry's share in China's GDP).

A report by the Beijing Post and Telecommunication Institute in 2003 indicated that the average annual growth rate of China's express delivery market was 30 percent and that the overall logistics market was valued at US$120 billion. The improving prospects of the latter attracted significant foreign investments. The rising demand for international deliveries prompted many foreign logistics companies to expand their business in China. These companies employed modern management practices, aggressive promotion strategies, used advanced technological support, and offered high-quality services.

The expansion plans of leading foreign logistics companies also led to intensified competition with each player competing for a bigger slice of the market. Commenting on this, David Cunningham, president of FedEx Express, Asia-Pacific, said, "China is growing incredibly fast . . . it is arguably going to be the biggest and fastest-growing marketplace in the world within the next two decades. But, there is enough market for all. The cake is getting bigger all the time."[5] The four major players in the market were DHL, FedEx, UPS, and TNT.

The U.S.-based FedEx entered China in 1984. It became the first foreign express transporter to launch direct air-cargo flights in and out of China. In 1999, it formed a joint venture with the Tianjin-based Da Tian Air Services Limited.[6] The same year, FedEx launched its

---

[4]"DHL Unveils New Express and Logistics Initiatives in China," DHL press release, Shanghai, May 10, 2004.

[5]"Sending the Right Message," www.internationalspecialreports.com, 2001.
[6]Based in Tianjin, Da Tian Air Services was founded in 1992. It was ranked as one of China's top five forwarding companies in 1997. The company had branches in 16 cities in China and specialized in forwarding, charter operations, and dangerous goods handling.

EXHIBIT II

China's Import Partners and Their Share in the Market (2001)

Source: "Sending the Right Message," www.internationalspecialreports.com, 2001.

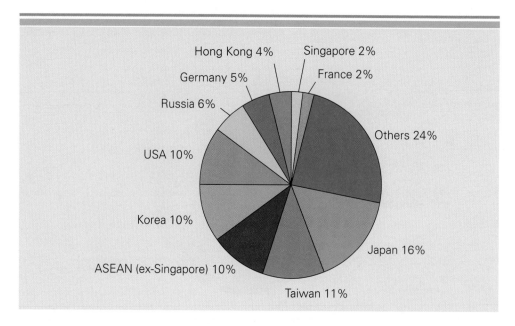

Hong Kong 4%
Singapore 2%
Germany 5%
France 2%
Russia 6%
Others 24%
USA 10%
Korea 10%
Japan 16%
ASEAN (ex-Singapore) 10%
Taiwan 11%

EXHIBIT III

Share of Logistics Industry in China's GDP

Source: "Restructuring: The Giant Leap for CMHI," *CMHI Journal*, February 2001.

Total foreign trade	Year 2000: US$474 billion Year 2010: US$800 billion (projected)
Number of foreign enterprises and amount of foreign investments	Foreign enterprises = 364,000 Foreign investments = US$677 billion
Logistics as % of GDP Infrastructure	20% of GDP (30% of total costs) Road (total 1.35 million km) Airports (total 142 airports) Rail (total 57,900 km) Navigable waterways (total 110,600 km)
Size of market	China: World's largest population with over 350 cities in 23 provinces

express handling facility in Shenzhen, which became a major revenue generator. By the end of May 2003, FedEx had a network covering 220 Chinese cities. The company also planned a separate China business unit in Shanghai to capitalize on opportunities arising in the booming airfreight market. To strengthen its position, FedEx also proposed to expand its network by 100 more cities in China by 2008.

Another U.S.-based company, UPS, entered China in 1988 through an agent partnership[7] relationship with Sinotrans. According to the agreement, UPS delivered packages or documents to China while Sino-

trans distributed them to locations within China. UPS started with express delivery of small packages and documents. After establishing itself in the market, UPS began efforts to gain approval to fly direct from the United States to China. Its first direct flight landed in Beijing in April 2000. By April 2001, the frequency rose to six flights per week between China and the United States.

The company beefed up its cargo capacity by 100 tons and cut the time-in-transit for shipments to the United States by a full day. It made all efforts to maximize its share in the market. In the fourth quarter of 2002, UPS revenues in China grew by a massive 60 percent. The company aimed at enhancing its presence from 21 to 40 cities by the end of 2003.

TNT began expanding its network in China in early 2000 by increasing its branches from 12 to 25. The num-

---

[7]A relationship between two companies in which the agent company acts on behalf of the principal company, on the basis of mutually agreed terms.

ber of gateways[8] went up from three to seven by the end of 2003. Explaining the rationale, Bryan Chan, managing director, TNT Express for China and Hong Kong, said, "China is a strategic market for us. We are very confident about China's economic development, which will churn out great business opportunities." Analyzing the implications of China's entry into the WTO, allowing foreign companies to operate independently in the country, TNT made a major move in June 2003. The company ended its 15-year collaboration with Sinotrans. After this, the company appointed Machplus Worldwide Express, a Beijing-based airfreight agency, as the main distributor of TNT Express' products and services in China.

By 2003, the four companies, FedEx, UPS, DHL, and TNT, held about 80 percent of China's international express delivery market. Before the entry of these foreign companies, Express Mail Service (EMS), owned by the China Post, enjoyed a monopoly in the domestic express market. The foreign players offered stiff competition to EMS by their better and faster delivery services. However, EMS' advantage was its vast network spread across the country, reaching small cities and rural areas, which were not touched by any foreign company. China Post also made efforts to upgrade its management and services. It hired 10 aircrafts and opened specific express airlines covering Beijing, Shanghai, Guangzhou, Chengdu, Qingdao, and Xiamen in March 2001. The company's service efficiency was improved as China's railway network became better.[9] However, its efforts were not rewarded commensurately. While the average growth rate of the international express service stood at 20 percent, EMS' growth on a year-to-year basis was just 2 percent in the early 2000s. The company's market share also declined, from 97 percent in 1995 to 40 percent in 2001.

Analysts attributed the success of foreign logistics players to their proactive use of advanced technology for distributing goods, client resources management, global communication and customs procedures, and, above all, excellent management skills. According to Fan Yimin, a researcher with the Chinese Academy of Social Sciences, "The modern express business does not only transport goods from one place to another but also involves e-business and logistics services, such as providing store houses, goods distributions, and transport solutions."[10]

---

[8]A gateway acts as a means of access, connecting various important business centers and capital cities. It helps enhance the capacity of custom clearances of express articles by allowing quick and efficient processing of shipments.
[9]In keeping with China's WTO commitments, construction and better operation of wide and extensive rail network was encouraged, thus resulting in railway services becoming faster.
[10]"Express Delivery Competition Intensifies—Expert," www.chinadaily.com, March 29, 2002.

Though the competition was heating up, analysts believed that competitive pressure would act positively to spur rapid and healthy development of the logistics industry in China.

THE ENTRY

In 1969, DHL ventured into the air express business and introduced a service between San Francisco and Honolulu. The company came up with a novel idea of sending out documentation before the cargo arrival, which speeded up importing of goods. DHL's network grew exponentially with its success in offering the best and pioneering services to customers. The company expanded its network towards the West, starting from Hawaii to the Far East and the Pacific regions. It then entered the Middle East, and thereafter Africa and Europe. By 1973, DHL expanded its customer base in the air express business to about 3000. By 1977, the company extended its range of services and started delivering small packages as well as documents. In 1982, DHL added 30 countries to its network. DHL became the first air express company to open offices in Eastern Europe in 1983. It was also the first air express company to start operations in China in 1986.

Before 1980, China was a closed economy with protectionist policies. It was tough for any foreign company to do business in the country. From the early 1980s onwards, China, under the leadership of Deng Xiaoping, initiated economic reforms, which involved opening China's economy. From the mid-1980s, China exhibited significant and sustained economic growth. The country's trade with the rest of the world grew significantly. The boom in international trade and growing domestic business attracted many foreign players.

The unprecedented industrial growth posed a challenge to the domestic logistics industry, where the demand for efficient services far exceeded supply. In the mid-1980s, China had an inefficient logistics infrastructure, insufficient and unreliable highway system, antiquated roads and ports, and overstressed civil aviation system. It was natural that China became a lucrative location for foreign express and logistics companies. These circumstances encouraged DHL to enter the Chinese market, and the only possible mode of entry then was through a joint venture with an existing domestic logistics services company. DHL identified Sinotrans as a potential partner as it had deep knowledge of the local Chinese foreign trade and export market. DHL entered into a 50:50 joint venture with Sinotrans in December 1986.

DHL's expertise in the global air express industry combined with Sinotrans' local knowledge worked well. Together, they provided international air express services to shippers in China (refer to Exhibit IV for China's air

EXHIBIT IV

China's Air Cargo
Volumes and Their
Growth

Source: "Restructuring: The
Giant Leap for CMHI," *CMHI
Journal*, February 2001.

Year	Total Air Cargo Volume (tonnage in million)	Year-on-Year Growth in Volume (%)
2000	2.24	+13.1
1999	1.98	+21.5
1998	1.63	−8.8
1997	1.79	+14.7
1996	1.56	+7.3

EXHIBIT V

Revenues of Top Five
Logistics Companies
Operating in China

Source: "Couriers in China," a
report published by *Euro Monitor*
in August 2002, executive
summary posted on
www.euromonitor.com.

Company/Revenues	2000 (RMB million)	2001 (RMB million)	Growth (%)
China Couriers Service Company	1,562	1,600	2.4
DHL-Sinotrans	510	749	46.9
Federal Express Corporation	210	299.9	42.7
UPS	160	249.7	56
TNT Skypak-Sinotrans Ltd	110	149.9	36.3

cargo volumes). The duo gradually expanded its service network throughout the country. By 2001, DHL–Sinotrans had developed the largest logistics services network among the foreign logistics companies in China (refer to Exhibit V for the top five logistics companies in China in 2001).

THE EXPANSION DRIVE

In 2001, with the global economy facing a general slowdown, China posted gross domestic product (GDP) growth of 7.3 percent. The country's trade volume in 2001 was the seventh largest in the world and significant growth was expected in the near future. With China's WTO membership, the restrictions on foreign international transportation and logistics companies were reduced. A highly conducive and transparent business environment was created. This attracted many foreign companies to invest in the Chinese mainland and expand their business too. The demand for export and import courier services increased significantly.

In early 2001, DHL–Sinotrans accounted for 36 percent of China's international express delivery market. The company sought to expand its operations fast and offer better service quality. Giving a briefing on the company's strategy, Charles Chia, GM and director of DHL–Sinotrans, said, "In the global view, the service network of DHL is capable of covering more than 20 countries and regions. In China, since its inception in

1986, DHL–Sinotrans has kept establishing branch networks throughout the country, adopting advanced technological methods and improving service quality as its principal strategy for its development, thus striving to provide customers with safer, more flexible, more accurate and highly efficient services."[11]

To further this strategy, DHL–Sinotrans increased its investments in the Chinese market and opened up several new branches to expand its domestic network. In fiscal 2000–01, the company established a number of branches in major cities like Zhengzhou, Chongquing, Nantong, Lanzhou, and Suzhou. The company gradually developed a comprehensive service network covering 318 cities throughout China by January 2004 (refer to Exhibit VI for DHL–Sinotrans's network in China in early 2004 and Exhibit VII for the growth of the network since 1986).

While DHL's major global competitors, including FedEx and UPS, launched direct flights to China, DHL decided to stick to its existing strategy. It continued to use commercial airlines instead of launching its own for delivering parcels as such alliances ensured faster delivery. DHL–Sinotrans believed that on-ground services were more important than airliner services for express delivery. The company welcomed competition and de-

---

[11]"Establishment of DHL–Sinotrans Beijing Capital Airport Gateway," www.cn.dhl.com, October 20, 2001.

EXHIBIT VI

DHL–Sinotrans'
Network in China (2004)

Source: www.asia.danzas.com.

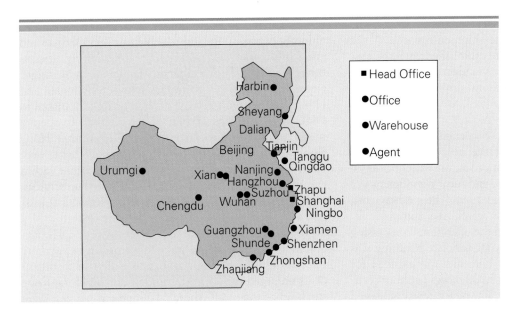

- Head Office
- Office
- Warehouse
- Agent

Harbin
Sheyang
Dalian
Beijing Tianjin
Urumgi Tanggu
Qingdao
Xian Nanjing
Hangzhou
Chengdu Suzhou Zhapu
Wuhan Shanghai
Ningbo
Guangzhou Xiamen
Shunde Shenzhen
Zhongshan
Zhanjiang

EXHIBIT VII

DHL–Sinotrans Services
Network (1986–2003)

Source: www.cn.dhl.com.

DHL–Sinotrans has developed a comprehensive service network covering 318 cities throughout China, with 50 joint venture offices and 160 facilities.

Year	Locations
1986	Beijing
1988	Shanghai, Guangzhou
1992–93	Dalian, Qingdao, Hangzhou, Shenzhen, Wuhan, Tianjin, Xiamen
1995	Ningbo, Chengdu, Nanjing, Fuzhou, Xi'an, Shijiazhuang
1996	Wuxi, Shenyang, Harbin
1997	Hefei, Suzhou
2000	Zhengzhou, Nantong, Chongqing, Lanzhou
2001	Jilin, Wenzhou, Jiaxing, Jinhua, Yangzhou, Hainan, Hunan, Zhuhai, Dongguan, Zhanjiang, Huizhou, Zhongshan, Shantou, Jiangmen
2003	Foshan, Taiyuan, Huhehaote, Kunshan, Kunming, Jinan, Changzhou, Nanning, Yantai, Shaoxing, Taizhou

nied that it was avoiding it by focusing only on specific regions. Bei Yumin, general manager, DHL–Sinotrans, Eastern Region, said, "It is to the detriment of the customer to eliminate competition in this industry. We hope there will be more competition in this market to spur its healthy development."[12]

DHL–Sinotrans also planned to add new gateways. Till 2001, the company had gateways in Beijing, Shanghai, Guangzhou, and Shenzhen. In July 2001, the Pudong Airport gateway was opened in Shanghai. This new RMB[13] 20 million gateway aimed at enhancing shipment handling capabilities in the country's eastern region. Commenting on this, Marc Duale, chief operating officer of DHL, Asia Pacific, said, "With new facilities such as the Pudong Airport Gateway, we will be able to improve our service to customers and meet their demand for shorter customs clearance and shipment

---

[12]"DHL Strives to Speed Up Growth Rate," *China Daily*, May 8, 2001.

[13]RMB (renminbi) is the Chinese currency, which means people's money. The unit of renminbi is a yuan and with smaller denominations called jiao and fen. The conversion among the three is 1 yuan = 10 jiao = 100 fen. The currency exchange rate as of November 1, 2004, was US$ 1= RMB 8.2865.

handling times, and enhanced reliability, security, and work efficiency of the whole shipment process."[14] To achieve this, direct links were established with the customs and excise departments via electronic data interchange (EDI)[15]. The maximum shipment processing capacity was also increased from 3,000 to 10,000 pieces per hour.

In October 2001, DHL–Sinotrans invested over US$1.2 million to construct the new Beijing international gateway, adopting advanced automatic control systems. They enhanced capacity and turnover efficiency of flight couriers in the north of China. The gateway consisted of a customs supervision warehouse, automatic security inspection systems, and the operational processing line. The maximum capacity for tonnage handling was hiked from 7 to 20 tons per hour and the capacity for piece handling from 3,500 to 5,000 pieces per hour compared to the previous gateway. The new gateway achieved higher operational efficiency through automatic sorting and direct loading of import commodities, enabling shorter time for customs clearances and transit of commodities. To ensure security of express articles, at various links of storage, sorting, and transit, the gateway was equipped with advanced TV monitoring systems, networked with the security monitoring system of the customs department.

In a survey conducted by AC Neilsen International Research published in the *Far Eastern Economic Review* (FEER) in January 2002, DHL was ranked 17th out of more than 200 multinational companies operating in the Asia-Pacific region. The survey was designed to identify companies regarded as leaders among the Asian business community, and DHL appeared on this list for nine consecutive years. In the survey, both multinational and local companies were ranked based on performance in key areas including product and service offerings, customer service standards, long-term vision, and financial soundness. The survey highlighted DHL's leadership position in the Asian market, especially China, which had been gained through aggressive expansion and investments in strategically located service centers, gateways, and hubs.

By mid-2002, the air express market was growing rapidly in China, particularly in the Yangtze River delta. To keep pace, DHL–Sinotrans used 182 scheduled commercial flights in Shanghai each week. Later, in October 2002, DHL acquired a 30 percent stake in Air Hong Kong, with the rest being owned by Cathay Pacific. This change in strategy was implemented to meet strong cus-

tomer demand throughout the Asia-Pacific region. To enhance connectivity and enable faster services between cities in the Yangtze River delta region and big cities in other parts of Asia, the company launched an overnight express service, Asia Overnight, between Shanghai and Hong Kong in June 2003. This helped link Shanghai to DHL's existing 13-city Asian Air Network.[16] To operate it, DHL entered into an alliance with another Hong Kong–based airline, Dragonair.[17] Dragonair flights were chartered at midnight to send packages overnight within the 13-city network. This helped DHL speed up services, making sure that its customers received packages at least half a day earlier than before.

To further strengthen the relationship, DHL acquired a 5 percent equity stake in Sinotrans in February 2003 for US$57 million. Sinotrans issued 38.5 percent of its enlarged capital to be traded on the Hong Kong stock exchange. Of these, 10 percent shares were placed with strategic investors as a part of the company's international offering. DHL acquired a 5 percent stake. Commenting on this, Jerry Hsu, regional director, Greater China and Korea, DHL Express, said, "DHL–Sinotrans has been one of our most successful joint ventures. The insights into Chinese markets brought by Sinotrans have been invaluable. The five-year expansion plan is further proof of our commitment to our partnership with Sinotrans, ensuring that DHL–Sinotrans will continue to remain a leading player for many years to come."[18]

Within three months, between September and December 2003, DHL opened 11 new branches in China, taking the number to 50. In October 2003, DHL–Sinotrans announced a US$200 million five-year China expansion program, to further expand business and capitalize on the improving prospects for the logistics industry in the country. These investments were aimed at increasing the geographical coverage of the company's services. DHL–Sinotrans planned to use the funds to expand and enhance the four existing gateways, add 14 new branches, carry out 73 new projects, buy 1,200 new vehicles, and recruit more staff, creating 2,100 new positions. Commenting on the expansion program, Doerken said, "The investments will build on our strengths in China through the expansion of our geo-

---

[14]"DHL–Sinotrans Opens Pudong Airport Gateway," www.cn.dhl.com, July 27, 2001.
[15]EDI enables the transfer of data between different companies using networks such as the Internet.

[16]DHL's Asian Air Network covers 13 major Asian cities and business centers in the region. Eleven of them are connected by air services operating specifically for DHL. The other two Chinese cities of Guangzhou and Shenzhen are served by road from the Central Asia hub in Hong Kong.
[17]Dragonair is Hong Kong's airline, founded in 1985. It serves 30 passenger destinations across Asia with one of the most advanced aircraft fleets in the region. It offers a wide variety of flexible, quality holiday packages, which cater to both business and leisure travelers.
[18]"DHL Announces US$ 200 Million 5-year Expansion Programme," www.cn.dhl.com, October 10, 2003.

graphical reach, investment in technology, people development, and enhancement of infrastructure."[19]

By May 2004, DHL's total investment in China was over US$215 million. Its initiatives helped the combination gain a 40 percent market share in China's express delivery business. In May 2004, DHL–Sinotrans had over 4,700 employees in 225 locations, four gateways, and 1,100 vehicles serving 318 cities in China. The company's growth posed a challenge to competitors, local companies as well as other foreign firms. DHL–Sinotrans had the early-mover advantage that helped it surge ahead of all other foreign logistics companies and emerge as a leader.

OFFERING INNOVATIVE SERVICES

To maintain and fortify its position, DHL–Sinotrans introduced many new services catering to both individual and corporate customers. In 2000, the company brought in a special service called Import Express, for its Chinese importers, to cater to demands arising from the growing volume of trade in the country. This service enabled importers to get their shipments picked up from the supplier's doorstep overseas and get them directly delivered anywhere in the world. This helped Chinese traders avoid hassles of arranging shipments from multiple origins using different vendors. Another new service introduced in 2000 was First in Asia. It was designed to accelerate the growth of DHL's intra-Asia business, focusing on shortening delivery time of packages within Asia.

Anticipating the growing access Chinese people would have to international products and services, DHL launched another new-look product in the market. In December 2001, the company initiated its well-known global product, DHL Jumbo Box in China. It entered with special value prices for Chinese customers, more convenience and safety in transportation during express delivery of freight shipments. The product was specially designed for sending heavy freight door to door anywhere in the world. It involved simple documentation and costs were 40 to 50 percent lower than any ordinary air express service.

Another breakthrough for DHL was using e-solutions in the logistics industry. In July 2003, the company introduced two leading e-solutions—DHL Web Shipping and DHL SMS Tracking—offering faster, easier, and more efficient shipment processing and tracking services in China. DHL Web Shipping was an Internet-based online shipment processing system. The bilingual Web site of DHL–Sinotrans provided step-by-step guidance on

airway bill completion, customs documentation, pick-up arrangement, and shipment tracking. Besides, the user could store up to 300 recipient addresses and 100 days' shipment transaction information in DHL's system database. It was designed to enable customers to print out airway bills or invoices and retrieve information from the system by a simple search. SMS tracking helped customers get their latest shipment status anytime and anywhere by entering an airway bill number as a short message and sending it to the local DHL SMS tracking service center. Due to these initiatives, DHL won its second Express and Mail Operator of the Year Award as well as the IT Innovation Award at the Asia Logistics Award Ceremony in 2003.

In March 2004, DHL–Sinotrans introduced the Time Definite Delivery (TDD) service in Shanghai. TDD comprised Start Day and Mid Day Express services, in which customers were offered the latest possible collection times for early, next-day delivery, to enhance promptness. To provide guaranteed delivery time service from Shanghai to major cities in Asia, DHL utilized its own Asian Air Network, centered on its Central Asia hub in Hong Kong. This initiative helped significantly enhance the speed of international express delivery and contributed to safer, smoother, and more efficient trade activities and exchanges among major business centers in Asia.

To secure safer delivery, the company launched its Shippers' Interest Insurance in April 2004. It was a value-added service for customers, providing them coverage against physical loss or damage due to external causes during delivery. Shipment security played an important role in meeting customer needs for protection of assets in the course of door-to-door delivery. Leveraging its rich experience in the global air express services industry, DHL–Sinotrans came up with more customized and high-tech delivery solutions to win the customers' trust and confidence.

THE ADVERTISING STRATEGY

In August 2003, DHL–Sinotrans launched an advertising campaign in China to reflect DHL's global brand image. The campaign projected DHL as the world's largest express and logistics provider, leading the market by virtue of its unparalleled capabilities in providing one-stop services, covering every key segment with its variety of logistics services.

DHL created a new bright and eye-catching company logo in which the letters "DHL" were written in red against a yellow background. The company's vehicles, office facilities, uniforms, packaging, and stationery throughout China displayed the new logo. In another advertising initiative, a new TV commercial was aired in

[19]Ibid.

15 major Chinese cities, reflecting DHL's entire range of services using the imagery of the Egyptians building the Pyramids. Print ads were also placed in over 30 leading publications nationwide.

In light of the growing importance of the Asia-Pacific region in its business portfolio, DHL launched a 360-degree advertising campaign in early 2004. The campaign was spearheaded by a new ad with a catchy tagline, "No one knows Asia Pacific like we do." The advertisements were featured across all mass media, including print, TV, radio, outdoor, and online, spreading the message that DHL knew the Asian region and the local logistics market best.

The TV commercial gave the message that organizations doing business with DHL should not worry about their logistics needs as the company would provide end-to-end supply chain solutions. The ad ran for 45 seconds with the tagline "Nothing to Do." The conceptualization was by the leading advertising agency Ogilvy & Mather. Besides this, DHL also launched a special promotion offer where selected DHL Express customers in Asia could win a pair of return flight tickets to any Asia-Pacific destination of their choice with every DHL Express shipment sent within the region from May 10 to July 31, 2004.

THE FUTURE

By the end of 2003, DHL had captured 37 percent of China's express delivery market. The company had already built up 160 delivery centers and planned to set up delivery sites in every major city in China by the end of 2005. To cement its relationship with Sinotrans, the company entered into a 50-year contract.

In 2003, China was DHL's third largest market after Japan and Hong Kong in the Asia-Pacific region. However, China was expected to become the largest market by 2006. Industry analysts forecast that the express logistics market would be the fastest growth area for DHL, thereby encouraging DHL to focus efforts in building capabilities in this segment. To intensify its express logistics activities, DHL invested US$3 million, establishing two logistics centers in Shanghai's Pudong and Jiuting areas in 2004. These two centers were established to cater to ocean freight and general warehousing requirements. The company also planned to enhance operations in the area of third-party management of spare parts inventories for companies in China. To boost its presence, DHL set out an infrastructure development program costing US$12 million that aimed to expand its logistics network to 37 cities by 2007.

By December 2004, owing to WTO implications, the Chinese government planned to liberalize its road transportation and warehousing businesses (refer to Exhibit VIII for a note on the logistics industry in China). Thus, foreign enterprises would be allowed to run their road transportation businesses independently (refer to Exhibit IX for the regulatory framework of the logistics industry in China). Analysts felt the new scenario would induce changes in the marketing strategies of foreign players, who would also review their relationships with domestic partners. Analysts feared that this might also lead to the breakup of existing joint ventures. The split up of Sinotrans and TNT in 2003 was an indicator. Except for DHL, which signed a 50-year contract with Sinotrans, other partners of Sinotrans including UPS could not explicitly clarify their intentions of carrying on their ties with it. The ties between FedEx and Da-tian Logistics also seemed to be faltering. Analysts felt that once restrictions were lifted, the foreign giants would establish wholly owned enterprises in China. Moreover, industry analysts also expected China to strengthen its macro-control on logistics infrastructure projects and guide and support enterprise investment, leading to notable changes in the business environment.

As per 2004 figures, the Chinese market was flooded with around 510,000 logistics enterprises. Of these, only 0.13 percent were foreign funded, accounting for 8 percent of the total market share. This amounted to about US$6.5 billion. The industry offered a lot of opportunities for more foreign players. Industry analysts felt that China's future hosting of the Summer Olympics in 2008 and an International Expo in Shanghai in 2010, combined with some future WTO implications would emerge as key drivers for growth. Commenting on the future scenario, Detthold Aden, chairman, consultant committee of Munich Logistics, said, "The demand for logistic services of global supply, production, and sales [is] growing progressively. The 2008 Olympic Games in Beijing, the 2010 Expo in Shanghai will be unimaginable without the strong backup of logistics services."[20]

Industry experts predicted that the courier market in China would grow at the rate of 20.5 percent per annum to RMB 27.344 billion by 2007 (refer to Exhibit X for facts and figures of the courier industry). The international delivery sector was expected to remain the largest sector in the courier market in China, with 54 percent of total sales, or RMB 14.75 billion. Considering DHL–Sinotrans' position in the market, analysts expected DHL to be well poised to meet the increasing demands.

---

[20]Zhong Jing, "Logistics Giants Snatch For Chinese Market Share," http://en.ce.cn/Insight, May 21, 2004.

In the wake of recent global developments, the traditional industry of cargo transport has transformed itself into the modern logistics industry. Logistics form a vital part of supply chain management, creating value by integrating transportation activities and other support services to facilitate smooth operation of material flow. Some subsectors include storage and warehousing, express delivery, freight forwarding and ground transportation.

Triggers of Growth

The various global forces that will trigger the growth of the logistics industry are:

- Technological developments substantially compressing the product life cycle. Make-to-order and zero inventory have become industry benchmarks.
- Changing consumer preferences require mass customization and quick response to market trends.
- Owing to price competition, reducing logistics costs is crucial to maintain the profit margin.
- The rise of e-commerce generates scattered/piecemeal orders and the consequent need for door-to-door delivery services.

Industry Scenario in China

The logistics industry in China showed rapid growth in the early 2000s. The logistics cost comprised about 20% of GDP and the related spending amounted to 190 billion yuan in 2002. Between 2001 and 2003, 70% of the logistics service providers witnessed a 30% annual increase in their business. Further, the WTO accession in the early 2000s attracted many foreign logistics providers into China. Analysts estimated China's logistics market in 2003 to be as large as 240 billion yuan, up by 26 percent over 2002. At the beginning of 2003, i.e., a year after China joined the WTO, the country's logistics market experienced accelerated growth with speedy increase of foreign capital entering the market and raising the requirement standard for logistics services.

Modes of Entry

The traditional way of entering the Chinese market was via a joint venture with a local company. However, the scenario changed with China's entry in WTO. Foreign companies that were previously allowed to own up to 49% in the local company could acquire 75% stake by the end of 2003. From 2005 onwards, there will be no ownership limitations.

Another way to enter the Chinese market that opened up in January 2003 was through a bilateral free trade agreement (Closer Economic Participation Agreement, CEPA). It allowed Hong Kong to get faster access to the mainland. This rule was particularly applicable to Hong Kong–based companies without any shareholder restrictions.

Yet another way was to be certified as a Hong Kong Service Supplier (HKSS) after being based in Hong Kong for three years.

The activities of any forwarding company operating in China are authorized through a range of freight licenses including Class-A license, road transportation, and trading licenses, etc. These licenses cover airfreight and ocean freight services, land transportation, export and import, and warehousing activities.

WTO Implications on the Chinese Logistics Market

China's decision to become a member of the WTO led to the opening up of the Chinese market to the outside world, giving an impetus to a rise in the volume of external trade and domestic distribution. It is also expected that the services trade sector would gradually open up and that international manufacturing centers would shift to China resulting in sustained heating up of international trade. Industry forecasts suggest that the logistics-outsourcing activity of large-sized multinational corporations investing in China is expected to increase significantly. As per the government's commitment, China is expected to open up its road transportation and warehousing business by December 2004, allowing foreign enterprises to independently run them.

To go back to logistics, China is making efforts to rev up the scenario. To improve efficiency, China is expected to come up with a set of new industrial standards, policies, and regulations. This should remove industrial monopoly, excessive administrative intervention and regional protectionism. China's National Development and Reform Commission is expected to come out with an outline on the development of China's logistics industry. It would possibly contain specific provisions regarding market access, tax policies, land resource policies, and transportation regulations, and encourage the development of third-party logistics enterprises. These steps would strengthen China's macro-control on logistics infrastructure projects, guide and support enterprise investment, leading to a more ordered logistics industry.

In such a scenario, logistic management is expected to become an indispensable competitive tool for China's manufacturers and exporters in the foreign market, apart from traders, wholesalers, and retailers in the domestic market. Thus, the success of any logistics company would depend on how well it integrates the entire supply chain.

EXHIBIT VIII

A Note on the Logistics Industry in China

Source: Contents for this have been adapted from the following sources:

- The executive summary of a report titled "China's WTO Accession—Enhancing Supply Chain Efficiency: Transportation and Logistics," posted on www.tdctrade.com, May 28, 2002.
- An article titled "FedEx Has Ideas for China," written by David L. Cunningham Jr. in *Nation* (Thailand), October 15, 2002.
- Executive summary of "China Logistics Industry 2004," posted on www.researchandmarkets.com in January 2004.
- An article titled "Logistics Giants Snatch For Chinese Market Share," posted on http://en.cn.ce.com, May 21, 2004.
- An article titled "DHL—Ahead of Logistics Competition in China," posted on www.eyefortransport.com, July 15, 2004.

EXHIBIT IX

Regulatory Framework for Foreign Participation in Logistics Industry in China

Source: Adapted from "People's Republic of China, Market Development Reports, China Logistics Profile, 2003," prepared by Christina Wu for GAIN Report (No. CH3833), December 18, 2003.

Subsectors	Foreign Participation	Authority for License Approval
International freight forwarding	Regulated	MOFTEC
Airfreight forwarding	Regulated	CAAC, MOFTEC
Logistics center	Encouraged	MOC, MOFTEC
Domestic trucking	Regulated	MOC, MOFTEC
Consolidation	Regulated	MOC, MOFTEC
Warehousing	Encouraged	MOC, MOFTEC
Customs brokerage	Heavily Regulated	CGA, MOFTEC
Shipping line	Regulated	MOC, MOFTEC
Airline	Heavily Regulated	CAAC, MOFTEC

EXHIBIT X

Facts and Figures on Courier Industry in China (2003)

Source: "Couriers in China," a report published by *Euro Monitor* in October 2004, executive summary posted on www.majormarketprofiles.com.

Market Size: The couriers market in China grew by 21.7% over 2002 to RMB 10,900 million (US$1,316.4 million).

Market Sectors: The international sector was the larger sector in the couriers market in China in 2003 with 68.8% of total market value. Sector value increased 50% over the previous year to RMB 7,500 million.

Share of Market: EMS was the largest courier company in China with a market share of 54.2%.

Corporate Overview: The couriers market in China was dominated by a few companies. The top three courier companies had a combined market share of 81.8%.

Federal Express Corporation (China): Turnover increased by 11.8% over 2002 to RMB 452.3 million.

EMS: Turnover increased by 18.7% over 2002 to RMB 5,800 million.

Sinotrans: Turnover increased by 52.9% over 2002 to RMB 1,760 billion.

Additional Readings and References

1. "Couriers in China," by Euro Monitor, www.majormarketprofiles.com, October 2004.
2. Deborrah Orr, "The A-List: Delivering America," www.forbes.com, September 20, 2004.
3. "DHL Plans Guangzhou Cargo Center," http://news.airwise.com, August 4, 2004.
4. "DHL—Ahead of the Logistics Competition in China," www.us.danzas.com, July 15, 2004.
5. "DHL—Ahead of Logistics Competition in China," www.eyefortransport.com, July 15, 2004.
6. "DHL Looks East—Earmarks Intra AP Trade as Growth Engine," www.domain-b.com, June 16, 2004.
7. "Problemes pour DHL en Chine??," www.eyefortransport.com, June 9, 2004.
8. "DHL Expands Investment in China with Domestic Express Service," www.supplychainbrain.com, May 25, 2004.
9. Zhong Jing, "Logistics Giants Snatch For Chinese Market Share," http://en.ce.cn.com, May 21, 2004.
10. Zhao Renfeng, "DHL Casts Its Net Further Afield," www.chinadaily.com, May 18, 2004.
11. "DHL Unveils New Express and Logistics Initiatives in China; First International Express Company to Launch Domestic Express Service in China," *Logistics Management*, May 17, 2004.
12. "DHL Unveils New Express and Logistics Initiatives in China," www.bvdp.de.com, May 13, 2004.
13. "World Express Giant DHL Begins to Provide Domestic Express Service in China," http://en.ce.cn.com, May 11, 2004.

14. Xinhua, "DHL Begins Domestic Express Service in China," www.chinadaily.com, May 11, 2004.

15. "DHL Unveils Shipper's Interest Insurance, an Extra Protection for Customer's Shipments," www.cn.dhl.com, April 2004.

16. "DHL–Sinotrans Launches DHL Time Definite Delivery Service," www.cn.dhl.com, March 2004.

17. Zhao Renfeng, "DHL Delivers 11 New Branches to China," www.chinadaily.com, February 10, 2004.

18. "DHL–Sinotrans: Leader of China's Express and Logistics Industry in 2003," www.cn.dhl.com, January 2004.

19. "China Logistics Industry 2004," www. researchandmarkets.com, January 2004.

20. "DHL Provides Supply Chain Strategies at Interlog China 2003," www.cn.dhl.com, December 5, 2003.

21. "Quality a Concern for Courier's Growth Plan," www.chinadaily.com, October 28, 2003.

22. "DHL Announces US$ 200 Million 5-Year China Expansion Program," www.cn.dhl.com, October 27, 2003.

23. "DHL Announces US$ 200 Million 5-Year Expansion Program," www.cn.dhl.com, October 10, 2003.

24. "DHL–Sinotrans Unveils the New DHL Brand as the Leader in Express and Logistics," www.cn.dhl.com, August 11, 2003.

25. Xiao Chen, "Foreign Firms Active in Chinese Market," www.chinadaily.com, July 30, 2003.

26. "DHL–Sinotrans Launches Two Leading e-Solutions," www.cn.dhl.com, July 16, 2003.

27. Zou Huilin, "DHL in Overnight Postal Service Launches," www.chinadaily.com, June 10, 2003.

28. "DHL Launched 'Asia Overnight' in Mainland China," www.cn.dhl.com, June 2, 2003.

29. "DHL–Sinotrans Launches Love Express—Free Delivery and Mobile Phones to Support Military Medical Staff in Beijing Fighting SARS," www.cn.dhl.com, May 16, 2003.

30. "DHL's China Business Grew 45%–50% in 2002," Reuters, www.thechinadma.com, April 1, 2003.

31. "DHL Acquires 5% Stake in Sinotrans," www.cn.dhl.com, February 14, 2003.

32. "Courier DHL Delivers a 5% Stake in Sinotrans," www.chinadaily.com, January 28, 2003.

33. "Competition Heats Up in China's Express Delivery Sector," www.chinadaily.com, November 17, 2002.

34. "DHL Strengthens Commitment and Development in China," press release, www.cn.dhl.com, October 16, 2002.

35. "DHL to Open 10 New Express Delivery Centers in China," www.dragonventure.com, October 13, 2002.

36. "Asia's Early Bird: A Look Back," www. worldeyereports.com, June 26, 2002.

37. "DHL Focuses on China Market with Launch of China First Campaign," www.dhl.com.sg/news, April 8, 2002.

38. "Express Delivery Competition Intensifies—Expert," www.chinadaily.com, March 29, 2003.

39. David L. Cunningham Jr., "FedEx Has Ideas for China," *Nation* (Thailand), October 15, 2002.

40. "China's WTO Accession—Enhancing Supply Chain Efficiency: Transportation and Logistics," www.tdctrade.com, May 28, 2002.

41. "DHL Staying Sturdy in Asia," www.eyefortransport. com, January 3, 2002.

42. "DHL–Sinotrans' Jumbo Box Makes Its Debut," www.cn.dhl.com, December 20, 2001.

43. "DHL Invests in Airport," www.chinadaily.com, October 26, 2001.

44. "Gateways to the World," www.chinadaily.com, October 26, 2001.

45. "Establishment of DHL Sinotrans Beijing Capital Airport Gateway," www.cn.dhl.com, October 20, 2001.

46. "DHL–Sinotrans Opens Pudong Airport Gateway," www.cn.dhl.com, July 27, 2001.

47. "Foreign Express Delivery Providers in China," www.chinadaily.com, May 8, 2001.

48. "DHL Strives to Speed Up Growth Rate," www.chinadaily.com, May 8, 2001.

49. "DHL–Sinotrans Aggressively Boosts China Network," www.cn.dhl.com, April 20, 2001.

50. "Sending the Right Message: As the Cake Gets Bigger, So Do the Number of Competitors Seeking to Expand Market Share," www. internationalspecialreports.com, 2001.

51. "DHL–Sinotrans Expands China Market," www.cn.dhl.com, December 31, 2000.

52. www.cn.dhl.com.

53. www.euromonitor.com.

54. www.chinadaily.com.

55. www.eyefortransport.com.

56. www.tdctrade.com.

Business
Operations part 6

15

Exporting, Importing, and Countertrade

FCX Systems

Founded in 1987 with the help of a $20,000 loan from the Small Business Administration, FCX Systems is an American exporting success story. FCX makes power converters for the aerospace industry. These devices convert common electric utility frequencies into the higher frequencies used in aircraft systems and are primarily used to provide power to aircraft while they are on the ground. In 2004, the West Virginia enterprise generated some 60 percent of its $20 million in annual sales from exports to more than 50 countries. FCX's prowess in opening up foreign markets has earned the company several awards for export excellence, including a 1999 presidential award for achieving extraordinary growth in export sales.

FCX initially got into exporting because it found that foreigners were often more receptive to the company's products than potential American customers. According to Don Gallion, president of FCX, "In the overseas market, they were looking for a good technical product, preferably made in the U.S., but they weren't asking questions about 'How long have you been in business? Are you still going to be here tomorrow?' They were just anxious to get the product."

In 1989, FCX signed on with an international distribution company to help with exporting, but Gallion became disillusioned with that company, and in 1994 FCX started to handle the exporting process on its own. At the time, exports represented 12 percent of sales, but by 1997 they had jumped to over 50 percent of the total, where they have stayed since.

In explaining the company's export success, Gallion cites a number of factors. One was the extensive assistance that FCX has received over the years from a number of federal and state agencies, including the U.S. Department of Commerce and the Development Office of West Virginia. These agencies demystified the process of exporting and provided good contacts for FCX. Finding a good local representative to help work through local regulations and customs is another critical factor, according to Gallion, who says, "A good rep will keep you out of trouble when it comes to customs and what you should and shouldn't do." Persistence is also very important, says Gallion, particularly when trying to break into markets where personal relationships are crucial, such as China.

China has been an interesting story for FCX. In 2004, the company booked $2 million in sales to China, but it took years to get to this point. China had been on Gallion's radar screen since the early 1990s, primarily because of the country's rapid modernization and its plans to build or remodel some 179 airports between 1998 and 2008. This constituted a potentially large market opportunity for FCX, particularly compared with the United States where perhaps only three new airports would be built during the same period. Despite the scale of the opportunity, progress was very slow. The company had to identify airports and airline projects, government agencies, customers, and decision makers, as well as work through different languages—and make friends. According to Gallion, "Only after they consider you a friend will they buy a product. They believe a friend would never cheat you." To make friends in China, Gallion estimates he had to make more than 100 trips to China since 1990, but now that the network has been established, it is starting to pay dividends.

Sources: J. Sparshott, "Businesses Must Export to Compete," *The Washington Times,* September 1, 2004, p. C8; "Entrepreneur of the Year 2001: Donald Gallion, FCX Systems," *The State Journal,* June 18, 2001, p. S10; and T. Pierro, "Exporting Powers Growth of FCX Systems," *The State Journal,* April 6, 1998, p. 1.

Introduction

In the previous chapter, we reviewed exporting from a strategic perspective. We considered exporting as just one of a range of strategic options for profiting from international expansion. This chapter is more concerned with the nuts and bolts of exporting (and importing). Here we look at how to export. As the opening case makes clear, exporting is not just for large enterprises; many small firms such as FCX Systems have benefited significantly from the moneymaking opportunities of exporting.

The volume of export activity in the world economy is increasing as exporting has become easier. The gradual decline in trade barriers under the umbrella of GATT and now the WTO (see Chapter 6) along with regional economic agreements such as the European Union and the North American Free Trade Agreement (see Chapter 9) have significantly increased export opportunities. At the same time, modern communication and transportation technologies have alleviated the logistical problems associated with exporting. Firms are increasingly using fax machines, the World Wide Web, toll-free 800 phone numbers, and international air express services to reduce the costs of exporting. Consequently, it is no longer unusual to find small companies that are thriving as exporters.

Nevertheless, exporting remains a challenge for many firms. Smaller enterprises can find the process intimidating. The firm wishing to export must identify foreign market opportunities, avoid a host of unanticipated problems that are often associated with doing business in a foreign market, familiarize itself with the mechanics of export and import financing, learn where it can get financing and export credit insurance, and learn how it should deal with foreign exchange risk. The process can be made more problematic by currencies that are not freely convertible. Arranging payment for exports to countries with weak currencies can be a problem. This brings us to the topic of countertrade, by which payment for exports is received in goods and services rather than money. In this chapter, we will discuss all these issues with the exception of foreign exchange risk, which was covered in Chapter 10. We open the chapter by considering the promise and pitfalls of exporting.

The Promise and Pitfalls of Exporting

The great promise of exporting is that large revenue and profit opportunities are to be found in foreign markets for most firms in most industries. This was true for FCX Systems, the company profiled in the opening case. The international market is normally so much larger than the firm's domestic market that exporting is nearly always a way to increase the revenue and profit base of a company. By expanding the size of the market, exporting can enable a firm to achieve economies of scale, thereby lowering its unit costs. Firms that do not export often lose out on significant opportunities for growth and cost reduction.[1]

Studies have shown that while many large firms tend to be proactive about seeking opportunities for profitable exporting, systematically scanning foreign markets to see where the opportunities lie for leveraging their technology, products, and marketing skills in foreign countries, many medium-sized and small firms are very reactive.[2] Typically, such reactive firms do not even consider exporting until their domestic market is saturated and the emergence of excess productive capacity at home forces them to look for growth opportunities in foreign markets. Also, many small and medium-sized firms tend to wait for the world to come to them, rather than going out into the world to seek opportunities. Even when the world does come to them, they may not respond. An example is MMO Music Group, which makes sing-along tapes for karaoke machines. Foreign sales accounted for about 15 percent of MMO's revenues of $8 million in the mid-1990s, but the firm's CEO admits that this figure would probably have been much higher had he paid attention to building international sales during the 1980s and early 1990s. At that time, unanswered faxes and phone messages from Asia and Europe piled up while he was trying to manage the burgeoning domestic side of the business. By the time MMO did turn its attention to foreign markets, other competitors had stepped into the breach and MMO found it tough going to build export volume.[3]

MMO's experience is common, and it suggests a need for firms to become more proactive about seeking export opportunities. One reason more firms are not proactive is that they are unfamiliar with foreign market opportunities; they simply do not know how big the opportunities actually are or where they might lie. Simple ignorance of the potential opportunities is a huge barrier to exporting.[4] Also, many would-be exporters, particularly smaller firms, are often intimidated by the complexities and mechanics of exporting to countries where business practices, language, culture, legal systems, and currency are very different from the home market.[5] This combination of unfamiliarity and intimidation probably explains why exporters still account for only a tiny percentage of U.S. firms, less than 5 percent of firms with fewer than 500 employees, according to the Small Business Administration.[6]

To make matters worse, many neophyte exporters run into significant problems when first trying to do business abroad and this sours them on future exporting ventures. Common pitfalls include poor market analysis, a poor understanding of competitive conditions in the foreign market, a failure to customize the product offering to the needs of foreign customers, lack of an effective distribution program, a poorly executed promotional campaign, and problems securing financing.[7] Novice exporters tend to underestimate the time and expertise needed to cultivate business in foreign countries.[8] Few realize the amount of management resources that have to be dedicated to this activity. Many foreign customers require face-to-face negotiations on their home turf. An exporter may have to spend months learning about a country's trade regulations, business practices, and more before a deal can be closed. The opening case, which documents the experience of FCX Systems in China, suggests that it may take years before foreigners are comfortable enough to purchase in significant quantities.

Exporters often face voluminous paperwork, complex formalities, and many potential delays and errors. According to a UN report on trade and development, a typical international trade transaction may involve 30 parties, 60 original documents, and 360 document copies, all of which have to be checked, transmitted, reentered into various information systems, processed, and filed. The United Nations has calculated that the time involved in preparing documentation, along with the costs of common errors in paperwork, often amounts to 10 percent of the final value of goods exported.[9]

🌐 Improving Export Performance

Inexperienced exporters have a number of ways to gain information about foreign market opportunities and avoid common pitfalls that tend to discourage and frustrate novice exporters.[10] In this section, we look at information sources for exporters to increase their knowledge of foreign market opportunities, we consider the pros and cons of using export management companies (EMCs) to assist in the export process, and we review various exporting strategies that can increase the probability of successful exporting. We begin, however, with a look at how several nations try to help domestic firms export.

AN INTERNATIONAL COMPARISON

One big impediment to exporting is the simple lack of knowledge of the opportunities available. Often there are many markets for a firm's product, but because they are in countries separated from the firm's home base by culture, language, distance, and time, the firm does not know of them. Identifying export opportunities is made even more complex because more than 200 countries with widely differing cultures compose the world of potential opportunities. Faced with such complexity and diversity, firms sometimes hesitate to seek export opportunities.

The way to overcome ignorance is to collect information. In Germany, one of the world's most successful exporting nations, trade associations, government agencies, and commercial banks gather information, helping small firms identify export opportunities. A similar function is provided by the Japanese Ministry of International Trade and Industry (**MITI**), which is always on the lookout for export opportunities. In addition, many Japanese firms are affiliated in some way with the *sogo shosha,* Japan's great trading houses. The *sogo shosha* have offices all over the world, and they proactively, continuously seek export opportunities for their affiliated companies large and small.[11]

German and Japanese firms can draw on the large reservoirs of experience, skills, information, and other resources of their respective export-oriented institutions. Unlike their German and Japanese competitors, many U.S. firms are relatively blind when they seek export opportunities; they are information disadvantaged. In part, this reflects historical differences. Both Germany and Japan have long made their living as trading nations, whereas until recently the United States has been a relatively self-contained continental economy in which international trade played a minor role. This is changing; both imports and exports now play a greater role in the U.S. economy than they did 20 years ago. However, the United States has not yet evolved an institutional structure for promoting exports similar to that of either Germany or Japan.

INFORMATION SOURCES

Despite institutional disadvantages, U.S. firms can increase their awareness of export opportunities. The most comprehensive source of information is the U.S. Department of Commerce and its district offices all over the country. Within that department are two organizations dedicated to providing businesses with intelligence and assistance for attacking foreign markets: the International Trade Administration and the United States and Foreign Commercial Service Agency.

These agencies provide the potential exporter with a "best prospects" list, which gives the names and addresses of potential distributors in foreign markets along with businesses they are in, the products they handle, and their contact person. In addition, the Department of Commerce has assembled a "comparison shopping service" for 14 countries that are major markets for U.S. exports. For a small fee, a firm can receive a customized market research survey on a product of its choice. This survey provides information on marketability, the competition, comparative prices, distribution channels, and names of potential sales representatives. Each study is conducted on-site by an officer of the Department of Commerce.

The Department of Commerce also organizes trade events that help potential exporters make foreign contacts and explore export opportunities. The department organizes exhibitions at international trade fairs, which are held regularly in major cities worldwide. The department also has a matchmaker program, in which department representatives accompany groups of U.S. businesspeople abroad to meet with qualified agents, distributors, and customers.

Another government organization, the Small Business Administration (SBA), can help potential exporters (see the accompanying Management Focus for examples of the SBA's work). The SBA employs 76 district international trade officers and 10 regional international trade officers throughout the United States as well as a 10-person international trade staff in Washington, D.C. Through its Service Corps of Retired Executives (SCORE) program, the SBA also oversees some 850 volunteers with international trade experience to provide one-on-one counseling to active and new-to-export businesses. The SBA also coordinates the Export Legal Assistance Network (ELAN), a nationwide group of international trade attorneys who provide free initial consultations to small businesses on export-related matters.

MANAGEMENT FOCUS

Exporting can seem like a daunting prospect, but the reality is that in the United States, as in many other countries, many small enterprises have built profitable export businesses. For example, Landmark Systems of Virginia had virtually no domestic sales before it entered the European market. Landmark had developed a software program for IBM mainframe computers and located an independent distributor in Europe to represent its product. In the first year, 80 percent of sales were attributed to exporting. In the second year, sales jumped from $100,000 to $1.4 million—with 70 percent attributable to exports. Landmark is not alone; government data suggest that in the United States nearly 89 percent of firms that export are small businesses that employ fewer than 100 people. Their share of total U.S. exports has grown steadily over the last decade and reached 21 percent by the early 2000s. Firms with less than 500 employees account for 97 percent of all U.S. exporters and almost 30 percent of all exports by value.

To help jump-start the exporting process, many small companies have drawn on the expertise of government agencies, financial institutions, and export management companies. Consider the case of Novi, Inc., a California-based business. Company President Michael Stoff tells how he utilized the services of the U.S. Small Business Administration (SBA) Office of International Trade to start exporting: "In November of 1986, when I began my business venture, Novi, Inc., I knew that my Tune-Tote (a stereo system for bicycles) had the potential to be successful in international markets. Although I had no prior experience in this area, I began researching and collecting information on international markets. I was willing to learn, and by targeting key sources for information and guidance, I was able to penetrate international markets in a short pe-

riod of time. One vital source I used from the beginning was the SBA. Through the SBA I was directed to a program that dealt specifically with business development—the Service Corps of Retired Executives (SCORE). I was assigned an adviser who had run his own import/export business for 30 years. The services of SCORE are provided on a continual basis and are free.

"As I began to pursue exporting, my first step was a thorough marketing evaluation. I targeted trade shows with a good presence of international buyers. I also went to DOC (Department of Commerce) for counseling and information about the rules and regulations of exporting. I advertised my product in "Commercial News USA," distributed through U.S. embassies to buyers worldwide. I utilized DOC's World Traders Data Reports to get background information on potential foreign buyers. As a result, I received 60 to 70 inquiries about Tune-Tote from around the world. Once I completed my research and evaluation of potential buyers, I decided which ones would be most suitable to market my product internationally. Then I decided to grant exclusive distributorship. In order to effectively communicate with my international customers, I invested in a fax. I chose a U.S. bank to handle international transactions. The bank also provided guidance on methods of payment and how best to receive and transmit money. This is essential know-how for anyone wanting to be successful in foreign markets."

In just one year of exporting, export sales at Novi topped $1 million and increased 40 percent in the second year of operations. Today, Novi, Inc., is a large distributor of wireless intercom systems that exports to more than 10 countries.

Sources: Small Business Administration Office of International Trade, "Guide to Exporting," www.sba.gov/oit/info/Guide-To-Exporting/index.html, and U.S. Department of Commerce, "A Profile of U.S. Exporting Companies, 2000–2001," February 2003. Report available at www.census.gov/foreign-trade/aip/index.html#profile.

In addition to the Department of Commerce and SBA, nearly every state and many large cities maintain active trade commissions whose purpose is to promote exports. Most of these provide business counseling, information gathering, technical assistance, and financing. Unfortunately, many have fallen victim to budget cuts or to turf battles for political and financial support with other export agencies.

A number of private organizations are also beginning to provide more assistance to would-be exporters. Commercial banks and major accounting firms are more willing to assist small firms in starting export operations than they were a decade ago. In addition, large multinationals that have been successful in the global arena are typically willing to discuss opportunities overseas with the owners or managers of small firms.[12]

UTILIZING EXPORT MANAGEMENT COMPANIES

One way for first-time exporters to identify the opportunities associated with exporting and to avoid many of the associated pitfalls is to hire an **export management company** (EMC). EMCs are export specialists who act as the export marketing department or international department for their client firms. EMCs normally accept two types of export assignments. They start exporting operations for a firm with the understanding that the firm will take over operations after they are well established. In another type, start-up services are performed with the understanding that the EMC will have continuing responsibility for selling the firm's products. Many EMCs specialize in serving firms in particular industries and in particular areas of the world. Thus, one EMC may specialize in selling agricultural products in the Asian market, while another may focus on exporting electronics products to Eastern Europe.

In theory, the advantage of EMCs is that they are experienced specialists who can help the neophyte exporter identify opportunities and avoid common pitfalls. A good EMC will have a network of contacts in potential markets, have multilingual employees, have a good knowledge of different business mores, and be fully conversant with the ins and outs of the exporting process and with local business regulations. However, the quality of EMCs varies.[13] While some perform their functions very well, others appear to add little value to the exporting company. Therefore, an exporter should review carefully a number of EMCs and check references. One drawback of relying on EMCs is that the company can fail to develop its own exporting capabilities.

EXPORT STRATEGY

In addition to using EMCs, a firm can reduce the risks associated with exporting if it is careful about its choice of export strategy.[14] A few guidelines can help firms improve their odds of success. For example, one of the most successful exporting firms in the world, the Minnesota Mining and Manufacturing Co. (3M), has built its export success on three main principles—enter on a small scale to reduce risks, add additional product lines once the exporting operations start to become successful, and hire locals to promote the firm's products (3M's export strategy is profiled in the accompanying Management Focus). Another successful exporter, Red Spot Paint & Varnish, emphasizes the importance of cultivating personal relationships when trying to build an export business (see the Management Focus at the end of this section).

The probability of exporting successfully can be increased dramatically by taking a handful of simple strategic steps. First, particularly for the novice exporter, it helps to hire an EMC or at least an experienced export consultant to help identify opportunities and navigate the paperwork and regulations so often involved in exporting. Second, it often makes sense to initially focus on one market or a handful of markets. Learn what is required to succeed in those markets before moving on to other markets. The firm that enters many markets at once runs the risk of spreading its limited management resources too thin. The result of such a shotgun approach to exporting may be a failure to become established in any one market. Third, as with 3M, it often makes sense to enter a foreign market on a small scale to reduce the costs of any subsequent failure. Most importantly, entering on a small scale provides the time and opportunity to learn about the foreign country before making significant capital commitments to that market. Fourth, the exporter needs to recognize the time and managerial commitment involved in building export sales and should hire additional personnel to oversee this activity. Fifth, in many countries, it is important to devote a lot of attention to building strong and enduring re-

MANAGEMENT FOCUS

The Minnesota Mining and Manufacturing Co. (3M), which makes more than 40,000 products including tape, sandpaper, medical products, and the ever-present Post-it notes, is one of the world's great multinational operations. In 2003, 55 percent of the firm's $16.3 billion in revenues was generated outside the United States. Although the bulk of these revenues came from foreign-based operations, 3M remains a major exporter with $1.5 billion in exports. The company often uses its exports to establish an initial presence in a foreign market, only building foreign production facilities once sales volume rises to a level that justifies local production.

The export strategy is built around simple principles. One is known as "FIDO," which stands for First In (to a new market) Defeats Others. The essence of FIDO is to gain an advantage over other exporters by getting into a market first and learning about that country and how to sell there before others do. A second principle is "make a little, sell a little," which is the idea of entering on a small scale with a very modest investment and pushing one basic product, such as reflective sheeting for traffic signs in Russia or scouring pads in Hungary. Once 3M believes it has learned enough about the market to reduce the risk of failure to reasonable levels, it adds additional products.

A third principle at 3M is to hire local employees to sell the firm's products. The company normally sets up a local sales subsidiary to handle its export activities in a country. It then staffs this subsidiary with local hires because it believes they are likely to have a much better idea of how to sell in their own country than American expatriates. Because of the implementation of this principle, just 160 of 3M's 39,500 foreign employees are U.S. expatriates.

Another common practice at 3M is to formulate global strategic plans for the export and eventual overseas production of its products. Within the context of these plans, 3M gives local managers considerable autonomy to find the best way to sell the product within their country. Thus, when 3M first exported its Post-it notes, it planned to "sample the daylights" out of the product, but it also told local managers to find the best way of doing this. Local managers hired office cleaning crews to pass out samples in Great Britain and Germany; in Italy, office products distributors were used to pass out free samples; while in Malaysia, local managers employed young women to go from office to office handing out samples of the product. In typical 3M fashion, when the volume of Post-it notes was sufficient to justify it, exports from the United States were replaced by local production. Thus, after several years 3M found it worthwhile to set up production facilities in France to produce Post-it notes for the European market.

Sources: R. L. Rose, "Success Abroad," *The Wall Street Journal*, March 29, 1991, p. A1; T. Eiben, "US Exporters Keep On Rolling," *Fortune*, June 14, 1994, pp. 128–31; 3M Company, *A Century on Innovation*, 3M, 2002; and 3M's Web site at www.mmm.com.

lationships with local distributors and/or customers (see the Management Focus on Red Spot Paint for an example). Sixth, as 3M often does, it is important to hire local personnel to help the firm establish itself in a foreign market. Local people are likely to have a much greater sense of how to do business in a given country than a manager from an exporting firm who has previously never set foot in that country. Seventh, several studies have suggested the firm needs to be proactive about seeking export opportunities.[15] Armchair exporting does not work! The world will not normally beat a pathway to your door. Finally, it is important for the exporter to retain the option of local production. Once exports reach a sufficient volume to justify cost-efficient local production, the exporting firm should consider establishing production facilities in the foreign market. Such localization helps foster good relations with the foreign country and can lead to greater market acceptance. Exporting is often not an end in itself, but merely a step on the road toward establishment of foreign production (again, 3M provides an example of this philosophy).

MANAGEMENT FOCUS

Established in 1903 and based in Evansville, Indiana, Red Spot Paint & Varnish Company is in many ways typical of the companies that can be found in the small towns of America's heartland. The closely held company, whose CEO, Charles Storms, is the great-grandson of the founder, has 500 employees and annual sales of close to $90 million. The company's main product is paint for plastic components used in the automobile industry. Red Spot products are seen on automobile bumpers, wheel covers, grilles, headlights, instrument panels, door inserts, radio buttons, and other components. Unlike many other companies of a similar size and location, however, Red Spot has a thriving international business. International sales (which include exports and local production by licensees) now account for between 15 percent and 25 percent of revenue in any one year, and Red Spot does business in about 15 countries.

Red Spot has long had some international sales and won an export award in the early 1960s. To further its international business in the late 1980s, Red Spot hired a Central Michigan University professor, Bryan Williams. Williams, who was hired because of his foreign-language skills (he speaks German, Japanese, and some Chinese), was the first employee at Red Spot whose exclusive focus was international marketing and sales. His first challenge was the lack of staff skilled in the business of exporting. He found that it was difficult to build an international business without in-house expertise in the basic mechanics of exporting. According to Williams, Red Spot needed people who understood the nuts and bolts of exporting—letters of credit, payment terms, bills of lading, and so on. As might be expected for a business based in the heartland of America, no ready supply of such individuals was in the vicinity. It took Williams several years to solve this problem. Now Red Spot has a full-time staff of two who have been trained in the principles of exporting and international operations.

A second problem that Williams encountered was the clash between the quarter-to-quarter mentality that frequently pervades management practice in the United States and the long-term perspective that is often necessary to build a successful international business. Williams has found that building long-term personal relationships with potential foreign customers is often the key to getting business. When foreign customers visit Evansville, Williams often invites them home for dinner. His young children even started calling one visitor from Hong Kong "Uncle." Even with such efforts, however, the business may not come quickly. Meeting with potential foreign customers yields no direct business 90 percent of the time, although Williams points out that it often yields benefits in terms of competitive information and relationship building. He has found that perseverance pays. For example, Williams and Storms called on a major German automobile parts manufacturer for seven years before finally landing some business from the company.

Red Spot Paint & Varnish's international business accounts for up to 25 percent of its revenue.

Sources: R. L. Rose and C. Quintanilla, "More Small U.S. Firms Take Up Exporting with Much Success," *The Wall Street Journal*, December 20, 1996, p. A1, A10, and interview with Bryan Williams of Red Spot Paint.

Export and Import Financing

Mechanisms for financing exports and imports have evolved over the centuries in response to a problem that can be particularly acute in international trade: the lack of trust that exists when one must put faith in a stranger. In this section, we examine the financial devices that have evolved to cope with this problem in the context of inter-

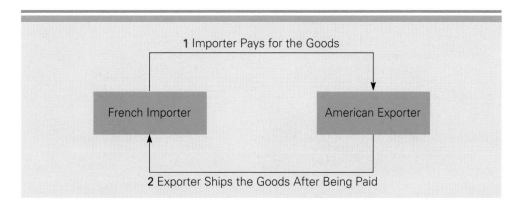

FIGURE 15.1

Preference of the U.S. Exporter

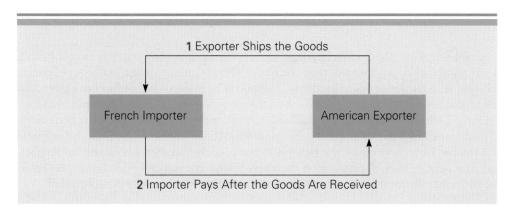

FIGURE 15.2

Preference of the French Importer

national trade: the letter of credit, the draft (or bill of exchange), and the bill of lading. Then we will trace the 14 steps of a typical export–import transaction.

LACK OF TRUST

Firms engaged in international trade have to trust someone they may have never seen, who lives in a different country, who speaks a different language, who abides by (or does not abide by) a different legal system, and who could be very difficult to track down if he or she defaults on an obligation. Consider a U.S. firm exporting to a distributor in France. The U.S. businessman might be concerned that if he ships the products to France before he receives payment from the French businesswoman, she might take delivery of the products and not pay him. Conversely, the French importer might worry that if she pays for the products before they are shipped, the U.S. firm might keep the money and never ship the products or might ship defective products. Neither party to the exchange completely trusts the other. This lack of trust is exacerbated by the distance between the two parties—in space, language, and culture—and by the problems of using an underdeveloped international legal system to enforce contractual obligations.

Due to the (quite reasonable) lack of trust between the two parties, each has his or her own preferences as to how the transaction should be configured. To make sure he is paid, the manager of the U.S. firm would prefer the French distributor to pay for the products before he ships them (see Figure 15.1). Alternatively, to ensure she receives the products, the French distributor would prefer not to pay for them until they arrive (see Figure 15.2). Thus, each party has a different set of preferences. Unless there is some way of establishing trust between the parties, the transaction might never occur.

The problem is solved by using a third party trusted by both—normally a reputable bank—to act as an intermediary. What happens can be summarized as follows (see

FIGURE 15.3

The Use of a Third Party

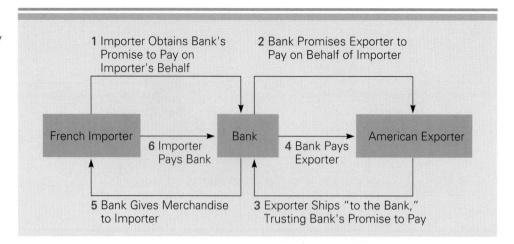

Figure 15.3). First, the French importer obtains the bank's promise to pay on her behalf, knowing the U.S. exporter will trust the bank. This promise is known as a letter of credit. Having seen the letter of credit, the U.S. exporter now ships the products to France. Title to the products is given to the bank in the form of a document called a bill of lading. In return, the U.S. exporter tells the bank to pay for the products, which the bank does. The document for requesting this payment is referred to as a draft. The bank, having paid for the products, now passes the title on to the French importer, whom the bank trusts. At that time or later, depending on their agreement, the importer reimburses the bank. In the remainder of this section, we examine how this system works in more detail.

LETTER OF CREDIT

A letter of credit, abbreviated as L/C, stands at the center of international commercial transactions. Issued by a bank at the request of an importer, the **letter of credit** states that the bank will pay a specified sum of money to a beneficiary, normally the exporter, on presentation of particular, specified documents.

Consider again the example of the U.S. exporter and the French importer. The French importer applies to her local bank, say, the Bank of Paris, for the issuance of a letter of credit. The Bank of Paris then undertakes a credit check of the importer. If the Bank of Paris is satisfied with her creditworthiness, it will issue a letter of credit. However, the Bank of Paris might require a cash deposit or some other form of collateral from her first. In addition, the Bank of Paris will charge the importer a fee for this service. Typically this amounts to between 0.5 percent and 2 percent of the value of the letter of credit, depending on the importer's creditworthiness and the size of the transaction. (As a rule, the larger the transaction, the lower the percentage.)

Assume the Bank of Paris is satisfied with the French importer's creditworthiness and agrees to issue a letter of credit. The letter states that the Bank of Paris will pay the U.S. exporter for the merchandise as long as it is shipped in accordance with specified instructions and conditions. At this point, the letter of credit becomes a financial contract between the Bank of Paris and the U.S. exporter. The Bank of Paris then sends the letter of credit to the U.S. exporter's bank, say, the Bank of New York. The Bank of New York tells the exporter that it has received a letter of credit and that he can ship the merchandise. After the exporter has shipped the merchandise, he draws a draft against the Bank of Paris in accordance with the terms of the letter of credit, attaches the required documents, and presents the draft to his own bank, the Bank of New York, for payment. The Bank of New York then forwards the letter of credit and associated documents to the Bank of Paris. If all of the terms and conditions contained in the letter of credit have been complied with, the Bank of Paris will honor the draft and will send payment to the Bank of New York. When the Bank of New York receives the funds, it will pay the U.S. exporter.

As for the Bank of Paris, once it has transferred the funds to the Bank of New York, it will collect payment from the French importer. Alternatively, the Bank of Paris may allow the importer some time to resell the merchandise before requiring payment. This is not unusual, particularly when the importer is a distributor and not the final consumer of the merchandise, since it helps the importer's cash flow. The Bank of Paris will treat such an extension of the payment period as a loan to the importer and will charge an appropriate rate of interest.

The great advantage of this system is that both the French importer and the U.S. exporter are likely to trust reputable banks, even if they do not trust each other. Once the U.S. exporter has seen a letter of credit, he knows that he is guaranteed payment and will ship the merchandise. Also, an exporter may find that having a letter of credit will facilitate obtaining preexport financing. For example, having seen the letter of credit, the Bank of New York might be willing to lend the exporter funds to process and prepare the merchandise for shipping to France. This loan may not have to be repaid until the exporter has received his payment for the merchandise. As for the French importer, she does not have to pay for the merchandise until the documents have arrived and unless all conditions stated in the letter of credit have been satisfied. The drawback for the importer is the fee she must pay the Bank of Paris for the letter of credit. In addition, since the letter of credit is a financial liability against her, it may reduce her ability to borrow funds for other purposes.

DRAFT

A draft, sometimes referred to as a **bill of exchange,** is the instrument normally used in international commerce to effect payment. A **draft** is simply an order written by an exporter instructing an importer, or an importer's agent, to pay a specified amount of money at a specified time. In the example of the U.S. exporter and the French importer, the exporter writes a draft that instructs the Bank of Paris, the French importer's agent, to pay for the merchandise shipped to France. The person or business initiating the draft is known as the maker (in this case, the U.S. exporter). The party to whom the draft is presented is known as the drawee (in this case, the Bank of Paris).

International practice is to use drafts to settle trade transactions. This differs from domestic practice in which a seller usually ships merchandise on an open account, followed by a commercial invoice that specifies the amount due and the terms of payment. In domestic transactions, the buyer can often obtain possession of the merchandise without signing a formal document acknowledging his or her obligation to pay. In contrast, due to the lack of trust in international transactions, payment or a formal promise to pay is required before the buyer can obtain the merchandise.

Drafts fall into two categories, sight drafts and time drafts. A **sight draft** is payable on presentation to the drawee. A **time draft** allows for a delay in payment—normally 30, 60, 90, or 120 days. It is presented to the drawee, who signifies acceptance of it by writing or stamping a notice of acceptance on its face. Once accepted, the time draft becomes a promise to pay by the accepting party. When a time draft is drawn on and accepted by a bank, it is called a banker's acceptance. When it is drawn on and accepted by a business firm, it is called a trade acceptance.

Time drafts are negotiable instruments; that is, once the draft is stamped with an acceptance, the maker can sell the draft to an investor at a discount from its face value. Imagine the agreement between the U.S. exporter and the French importer calls for the exporter to present the Bank of Paris (through the Bank of New York) with a time draft requiring payment 120 days after presentation. The Bank of Paris stamps the time draft with an acceptance. Imagine further that the draft is for $100,000.

The exporter can either hold onto the accepted time draft and receive $100,000 in 120 days or he can sell it to an investor, say, the Bank of New York, for a discount from the face value. If the prevailing discount rate is 7 percent, the exporter could receive $97,700 by selling it immediately (7 percent per year discount rate for 120 days for $100,000 equals $2,300, and $100,000 − $2,300 = $97,700). The Bank of New York would then collect the full $100,000 from the Bank of Paris in 120 days. The exporter might sell the accepted time draft immediately if he needed the funds to finance merchandise in transit and/or to cover cash flow shortfalls.

BILL OF LADING

The third key document for financing international trade is the bill of lading. The **bill of lading** is issued to the exporter by the common carrier transporting the merchandise. It serves three purposes: it is a receipt, a contract, and a document of title. As a receipt, the bill of lading indicates that the carrier has received the merchandise described on the face of the document. As a contract, it specifies that the carrier is obligated to provide a transportation service in return for a certain charge. As a document of title, it can be used to obtain payment or a written promise of payment before the merchandise is released to the importer. The bill of lading can also function as collateral against which funds may be advanced to the exporter by its local bank before or during shipment and before final payment by the importer.

A TYPICAL INTERNATIONAL TRADE TRANSACTION

Now that we have reviewed the elements of an international trade transaction, let us see how the process works in a typical case, sticking with the example of the U.S. exporter and the French importer. The typical transaction involves 14 steps (see Figure 15.4).

1. The French importer places an order with the U.S. exporter and asks the American if he would be willing to ship under a letter of credit.
2. The U.S. exporter agrees to ship under a letter of credit and specifies relevant information such as prices and delivery terms.
3. The French importer applies to the Bank of Paris for a letter of credit to be issued in favor of the U.S. exporter for the merchandise the importer wishes to buy.
4. The Bank of Paris issues a letter of credit in the French importer's favor and sends it to the U.S. exporter's bank, the Bank of New York.
5. The Bank of New York advises the exporter of the opening of a letter of credit in his favor.
6. The U.S. exporter ships the goods to the French importer on a common carrier. An official of the carrier gives the exporter a bill of lading.
7. The U.S. exporter presents a 90-day time draft drawn on the Bank of Paris in accordance with its letter of credit and the bill of lading to the Bank of New York. The exporter endorses the bill of lading so title to the goods is transferred to the Bank of New York.
8. The Bank of New York sends the draft and bill of lading to the Bank of Paris. The Bank of Paris accepts the draft, taking possession of the documents and promising to pay the now-accepted draft in 90 days.
9. The Bank of Paris returns the accepted draft to the Bank of New York.
10. The Bank of New York tells the U.S. exporter that it has received the accepted bank draft, which is payable in 90 days.
11. The exporter sells the draft to the Bank of New York at a discount from its face value and receives the discounted cash value of the draft in return.
12. The Bank of Paris notifies the French importer of the arrival of the documents. She agrees to pay the Bank of Paris in 90 days. The Bank of Paris releases the documents so the importer can take possession of the shipment.
13. In 90 days, the Bank of Paris receives the importer's payment, so it has funds to pay the maturing draft.
14. In 90 days, the holder of the matured acceptance (in this case, the Bank of New York) presents it to the Bank of Paris for payment. The Bank of Paris pays.

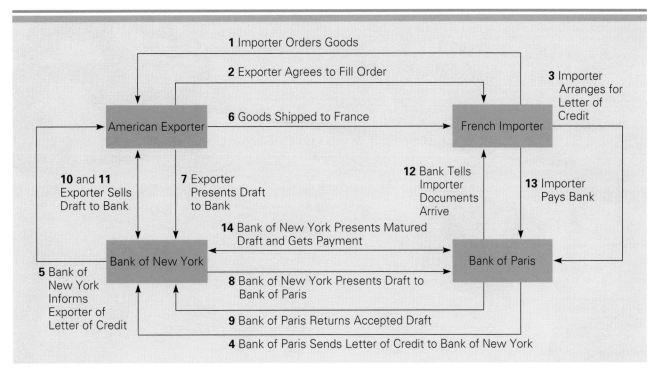

FIGURE 15.4

A Typical International Trade Transaction

Export Assistance

Prospective U.S. exporters can draw on two forms of government-backed assistance to help finance their export programs. They can get financing aid from the Export–Import Bank and export credit insurance from the Foreign Credit Insurance Association.

EXPORT–IMPORT BANK

The **Export–Import Bank,** often referred to as Eximbank, is an independent agency of the U.S. government. Its mission is to provide financing aid that will facilitate exports, imports, and the exchange of commodities between the United States and other countries. Eximbank pursues this mission with various loan and loan-guarantee programs. The agency guarantees repayment of medium and long-term loans U.S. commercial banks make to foreign borrowers for purchasing U.S. exports. The Eximbank guarantee makes the commercial banks more willing to lend cash to foreign enterprises.

Eximbank also has a direct lending operation under which it lends dollars to foreign borrowers for use in purchasing U.S. exports. In some cases, it grants loans that commercial banks would not if it sees a potential benefit to the United States in doing so. The foreign borrowers use the loans to pay U.S. suppliers and repay the loan to Eximbank with interest.

EXPORT CREDIT INSURANCE

For reasons outlined earlier, exporters clearly prefer to get letters of credit from importers. However, sometimes an exporter who insists on a letter of credit will lose an order to one who does not require a letter of credit. Thus, when the importer is in a strong bargaining position and able to play competing suppliers against each other, an exporter may have to forgo a letter of credit.[16] The lack of a letter of credit exposes the exporter to the risk that the foreign importer will default on payment. The exporter can insure against this

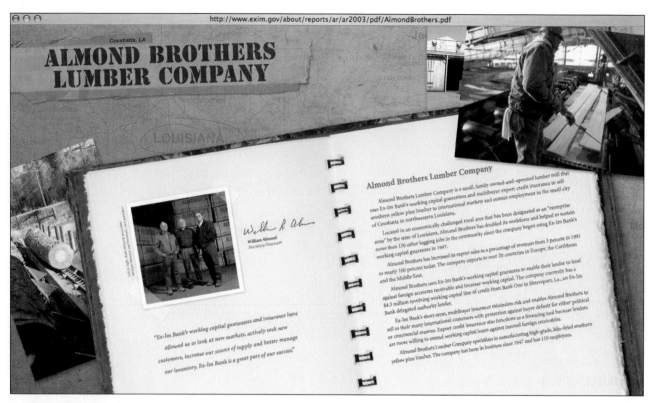

Eximbank provides financing aid to companies, such as the example above, that require assistance with imports, exports, and the exchange of commodities.

possibility by buying export credit insurance. If the customer defaults, the insurance firm will cover a major portion of the loss.

In the United States, export credit insurance is provided by the Foreign Credit Insurance Association (FCIA), an association of private commercial institutions operating under the guidance of the Export–Import Bank. The FCIA provides coverage against commercial risks and political risks. Losses due to commercial risk result from the buyer's insolvency or payment default. Political losses arise from actions of governments that are beyond the control of either buyer or seller.

Countertrade

Countertrade is an alternative means of structuring an international sale when conventional means of payment are difficult, costly, or nonexistent. We first encountered countertrade in Chapter 10 in our discussion of currency convertibility. A government may restrict the convertibility of its currency to preserve its foreign exchange reserves so they can be used to service international debt commitments and purchase crucial imports.[17] This is problematic for exporters. Nonconvertibility implies that the exporter may not be paid in his or her home currency; and few exporters would desire payment in a currency that is not convertible. Countertrade is a common solution.[18] **Countertrade** denotes a whole range of barterlike agreements; its principle is to trade goods and services for other goods and services when they cannot be traded for money. Some examples of countertrade are:

- An Italian company that manufactures power-generating equipment, ABB SAE Sadelmi SpA, was awarded a 720 million baht ($17.7 million) contract by the Electricity Generating Authority of Thailand. The contract specified that the company had to accept 218 million baht ($5.4 million) of Thai farm products as part of the payment.
- Saudi Arabia agreed to buy 10 747 jets from Boeing with payment in crude oil, discounted at 10 percent below posted world oil prices.

- General Electric won a contract for a $150 million electric generator project in Romania by agreeing to market $150 million of Romanian products in markets to which Romania did not have access.
- The Venezuelan government negotiated a contract with Caterpillar under which Venezuela would trade 350,000 tons of iron ore for Caterpillar earthmoving equipment.
- Albania offered such items as spring water, tomato juice, and chrome ore in exchange for a $60 million fertilizer and methanol complex.
- Philip Morris ships cigarettes to Russia, for which it receives chemicals that can be used to make fertilizer. Philip Morris ships the chemicals to China, and in return, China ships glassware to North America for retail sale by Philip Morris.[19]

THE INCIDENCE OF COUNTERTRADE

In the modern era, countertrade arose in the 1960s as a way for the Soviet Union and the Communist states of Eastern Europe, whose currencies were generally nonconvertible, to purchase imports. During the 1980s, the technique grew in popularity among many developing nations that lacked the foreign exchange reserves required to purchase necessary imports. Today, reflecting their own shortages of foreign exchange reserves, many of the successor states to the former Soviet Union and the Eastern European Communist nations are engaging in countertrade to purchase their imports. Consequently, according to some estimates, between 8 and 10 percent of world trade by value is now in the form of countertrade, up from only 2 percent in 1975.[20] The volume of countertrade increased notably after the Asian financial crisis of 1997. That crisis left many Asian nations with little hard currency to finance international trade. In the tight monetary regime that followed the crisis in 1997, many Asian firms found it very difficult to get access to export credits to finance their own international trade. Consequently, they turned to the only option available to them—countertrade.

Given the importance of countertrade as a means of financing world trade, prospective exporters may have to engage in this technique from time to time to gain access to certain international markets. The governments of developing nations sometimes insist on a certain amount of countertrade.[21] For example, all foreign companies contracted by Thai state agencies for work costing more than 500 million baht ($12.3 million) are required to accept at least 30 percent of their payment in Thai agricultural products. Between 1994 and mid-1998, foreign firms purchased 21 billion baht ($517 million) in Thai goods under countertrade deals.[22]

TYPES OF COUNTERTRADE

With its roots in the simple trading of goods and services for other goods and services, countertrade has evolved into a diverse set of activities that can be categorized as five distinct types of trading arrangements: barter, counterpurchase, offset, switch trading, and compensation or buyback.[23] Many countertrade deals involve not just one arrangement, but elements of two or more.

Barter

Barter is the direct exchange of goods and/or services between two parties without a cash transaction. Although barter is the simplest arrangement, it is not common. Its problems are twofold. First, if goods are not exchanged simultaneously, one party ends up financing the other for a period. Second, firms engaged in barter run the risk of having to accept goods they do not want, cannot use, or have difficulty reselling at a reasonable price. For these reasons, barter is viewed as the most restrictive countertrade arrangement. It is primarily used for one-time-only deals in transactions with trading partners who are not creditworthy or trustworthy.

Counterpurchase

Counterpurchase is a reciprocal buying agreement. It occurs when a firm agrees to purchase a certain amount of materials back from a country to which a sale is made. Suppose a U.S. firm sells some products to China. China pays the U.S. firm in dollars, but in exchange, the U.S. firm agrees to spend some of its proceeds from the sale on textiles produced by China. Thus, although China must draw on its foreign exchange reserves to pay the U.S. firm, it knows it will receive some of those dollars back because of the counterpurchase agreement. In one counterpurchase agreement, Rolls-Royce sold jet parts to Finland. As part of the deal, Rolls-Royce agreed to use some of the proceeds from the sale to purchase Finnish-manufactured TV sets that it would then sell in Great Britain.

Offset

An **offset** is similar to a counterpurchase insofar as one party agrees to purchase goods and services with a specified percentage of the proceeds from the original sale. The difference is that this party can fulfill the obligation with any firm in the country to which the sale is being made. From an exporter's perspective, this is more attractive than a straight counterpurchase agreement because it gives the exporter greater flexibility to choose the goods that it wishes to purchase.

Switch Trading

The term **switch trading** refers to the use of a specialized third-party trading house in a countertrade arrangement. When a firm enters a counterpurchase or offset agreement with a country, it often ends up with what are called counterpurchase credits, which can be used to purchase goods from that country. Switch trading occurs when a third-party trading house buys the firm's counterpurchase credits and sells them to another firm that can better use them. For example, a U.S. firm concludes a counterpurchase agreement with Poland for which it receives some number of counterpurchase credits for purchasing Polish goods. The U.S. firm cannot use and does not want any Polish goods, however, so it sells the credits to a third-party trading house at a discount. The trading house finds a firm that can use the credits and sells them at a profit.

In one example of switch trading, Poland and Greece had a counterpurchase agreement that called for Poland to buy the same U.S.-dollar value of goods from Greece that it sold to Greece. However, Poland could not find enough Greek goods that it required, so it ended up with a dollar-denominated counterpurchase balance in Greece that it was unwilling to use. A switch trader bought the right to 250,000 counterpurchase dollars from Poland for $225,000 and sold them to a European sultana (grape) merchant for $235,000, who used them to purchase sultanas from Greece.

Compensation or Buybacks

A **buyback** occurs when a firm builds a plant in a country—or supplies technology, equipment, training, or other services to the country—and agrees to take a certain percentage of the plant's output as partial payment for the contract. For example, Occidental Petroleum negotiated a deal with Russia under which Occidental would build several ammonia plants in Russia and as partial payment receive ammonia over a 20-year period.

THE PROS AND CONS OF COUNTERTRADE

Countertrade's main attraction is that it can give a firm a way to finance an export deal when other means are not available. Given the problems that many developing nations have in raising the foreign exchange necessary to pay for imports, countertrade may be the only option available when doing business in these countries. Even when countertrade is not the only option for structuring an export transaction, many countries prefer countertrade to cash deals. Thus, if a firm is unwilling to enter a countertrade agreement, it may lose an export opportunity to a competitor that is willing to make a countertrade agreement.

In addition, a countertrade agreement may be required by the government of a country to which a firm is exporting goods or services. Boeing often has to agree to counterpurchase agreements to capture orders for its commercial jet aircraft. For example, in exchange for gaining an order from Air India, Boeing may be required to purchase certain component parts, such as aircraft doors, from an Indian company. Taking this one step further, Boeing can use its willingness to enter into a counterpurchase agreement as a way of winning orders in the face of intense competition from its global rival, Airbus Industrie. Thus, countertrade can become a strategic marketing weapon.

However, the drawbacks of countertrade agreements are substantial. Other things being equal, firms would normally prefer to be paid in hard currency. Countertrade contracts may involve the exchange of unusable or poor-quality goods that the firm cannot dispose of profitably. For example, a few years ago, one U.S. firm got burned when 50 percent of the television sets it received in a countertrade agreement with Hungary were defective and could not be sold. In addition, even if the goods it receives are of high quality, the firm still needs to dispose of them profitably. To do this, countertrade requires the firm to invest in an in-house trading department dedicated to arranging and managing countertrade deals. This can be expensive and time-consuming.

Given these drawbacks, countertrade is most attractive to large, diverse multinational enterprises that can use their worldwide network of contacts to dispose of goods acquired in countertrading. The masters of countertrade are Japan's giant trading firms, the *sogo shosha*, which use their vast networks of affiliated companies to profitably dispose of goods acquired through countertrade agreements. The trading firm of Mitsui & Company, for example, has about 120 affiliated companies in almost every sector of the manufacturing and service industries. If one of Mitsui's affiliates receives goods in a countertrade agreement that it cannot consume, Mitsui & Company will normally be able to find another affiliate that can profitably use them. Firms affiliated with one of Japan's *sogo shosha* often have a competitive advantage in countries where countertrade agreements are preferred.

Western firms that are large, diverse, and have a global reach (e.g., General Electric, Philip Morris, and 3M) have similar profit advantages from countertrade agreements. Indeed, 3M has established its own trading company—3M Global Trading, Inc.—to develop and manage the company's international countertrade programs. Unless there is no alternative, small and medium-sized exporters should probably try to avoid countertrade deals because they lack the worldwide network of operations that may be required to profitably utilize or dispose of goods acquired through them.[24]

Chapter Summary

In this chapter, we examined the steps that firms must take to establish themselves as exporters. The chapter made the following points:

1. One big impediment to exporting is ignorance of foreign market opportunities.

2. Neophyte exporters often become discouraged or frustrated with the exporting process because they encounter many problems, delays, and pitfalls.

3. The way to overcome ignorance is to gather information. In the United States, a number of in-

stitutions, most important of which is the Department of Commerce, can help firms gather information in the matchmaking process. Export management companies can also help identify export opportunities.

4. Many of the pitfalls associated with exporting can be avoided if a company hires an experienced export management company, or export consultant, and if it adopts the appropriate export strategy.

5. Firms engaged in international trade must do business with people they cannot trust and people who may be difficult to track down if they default on an obligation. Due to the lack of trust, each party to an international transaction has a different set of preferences regarding the configuration of the transaction.

6. The problems arising from lack of trust between exporters and importers can be solved by using a third party that is trusted by both, normally a reputable bank.

7. A letter of credit is issued by a bank at the request of an importer. It states that the bank promises to pay a beneficiary, normally the exporter, on presentation of documents specified in the letter.

8. A draft is the instrument normally used in international commerce to effect payment. It is an order written by an exporter instructing an importer, or an importer's agent, to pay a specified amount of money at a specified time.

9. Drafts are either sight drafts or time drafts. Time drafts are negotiable instruments.

10. A bill of lading is issued to the exporter by the common carrier transporting the merchandise. It serves as a receipt, a contract, and a document of title.

11. U.S. exporters can draw on two types of government-backed assistance to help finance their exports: loans from the Export–Import Bank and export credit insurance from the FCIA.

12. Countertrade includes a range of barterlike agreements. It is primarily used when a firm exports to a country whose currency is not freely convertible and may lack the foreign exchange reserves required to purchase the imports.

13. The main attraction of countertrade is that it gives a firm a way to finance an export deal when other means are not available. A firm that insists on being paid in hard currency may be at a competitive disadvantage vis-à-vis one that is willing to engage in countertrade.

14. The main disadvantage of countertrade is that the firm may receive unusable or poor-quality goods that cannot be disposed of profitably.

Critical Thinking and Discussion Questions

1. A firm based in Washington State wants to export a shipload of finished lumber to the Philippines. The would-be importer cannot get sufficient credit from domestic sources to pay for the shipment but insists that the finished lumber can quickly be resold in the Philippines for a profit. Outline the steps the exporter should take to effect this export to the Philippines.

2. You are the assistant to the CEO of a small textile firm that manufactures quality, premium-priced, stylish clothing. The CEO has decided to see what the opportunities are for exporting and has asked you for advice as to the steps the company should take. What advice would you give the CEO?

3. An alternative to using a letter of credit is export credit insurance. What are the advantages and disadvantages of using export credit insurance rather than a letter of credit for exporting (a) a luxury yacht from California to Canada, and (b) machine tools from New York to Ukraine?

4. How do you explain the popularity of countertrade? Under what scenarios might its popularity increase still further by 2010? Under what scenarios might its popularity decline?

5. How might a company make strategic use of countertrade schemes as a marketing weapon to generate export revenues? What are the risks associated with pursuing such a strategy?

Research Task   globalEDGE™   globaledge.msu.edu

Use the globalEDGE™ site to complete the following exercises:

1. The Internet is rich with resources that provide guidance to companies that wish to expand their markets through exporting; globalEDGE provides links to these "tutorial" Web sites. Identify five of these sources and provide a description of

the services available for new exporters through each of these sources.

2. Utilize the globalEDGE™ Glossary of International Business Terms to identify the definitions of the following exporting terms: air waybill, certificate of inspection, certificate of product origin, wharfage charge, and export broker.

Megahertz Communications

CLOSING CASE Established in 1982, U.K.-based Megahertz Communications quickly became one of Great Britain's leading independent broadcasting system builders. The company's core skill is in the design, manufacture, and installation of TV and radio broadcast systems, including broadcast and news-gathering vehicles with satellite links. In 1998, Megahertz's managing director, Ashley Coles, set up a subsidiary company, Megahertz International, to sell products to the Middle East, Africa, and Eastern Europe.

While the EU market for media and broadcasting is both mature and well served by large established companies, the Middle East, Africa, and Eastern Europe are growth markets with significant long-term potential for media and broadcasting. They also were not well served by other companies, and all three regions lacked an adequate supply of local broadcast engineers.

Megahertz International's export strategy was simple. The company aimed to provide a turnkey solution to emerging broadcast and media entities in Africa, the Middle East, and Eastern Europe, offering to custom-design, manufacture, install, and test broadcasting systems. To gain access to customers, Megahertz hired salespeople with significant experience in these regions and opened a foreign sales office in Italy. Megahertz also exhibited at a number of exhibitions that focused on the targeted regions, sent mailings and e-mail messages to local broadcasters, and set up a Web page, which drew a number of international inquiries.

The response was swift. By early 2000, Megahertz had already been involved in projects in Namibia, Oman, Romania, Russia, Nigeria, Poland, South Africa, Iceland, and Ethiopia. The international operations had expanded to a staff of 75 and were generating £10 million annually. The average order size was about £250,000, and the largest £500,000. In recognition of the company's success, in January 2000 the British government picked Megahertz to receive a Small Business Export Award.

Despite the company's early success, it was not all smooth sailing. According to Managing Director Coles, preshipment financing became a major headache. Coles described his working life as a juggling act, with as much as 20 percent of his time spent chasing money. Due to financing problems, one week Megahertz could have next to nothing in the bank; the next it might have £300,000. The main problem was getting money to finance an order. Megahertz needed additional working capital to finance the purchase of component parts that go into the systems it builds for customers. The company found that banks were very cautious, particularly when they heard that the customers for the order were in Africa or Eastern Europe. The banks worried that Megahertz would not get paid on time, or at all, or that currency fluctuations would reduce the value of payments to Megahertz. Even when Megahertz had a letter of credit from the customer's bank and export insurance documentation, many lenders still saw the risks as too great and declined to lend bridging funds to Megahertz. As a partial solution, Megahertz turned to lending companies that specialize in financing international trade, but many of these companies charged interest rates significantly greater than those charged by banks, thereby squeezing Megahertz's profit margins.

Coles hoped these financing problems were temporary. Once Megahertz established a more sustained cash flow from its international operations, and once banks better appreciated the ability of Coles and his team to secure payment from foreign customers, he hoped that they would become more amenable to lending capital to Megahertz at rates that would help to protect the company's profit margins. By 2002, however, it was clear that the company's growth was too slow to achieve these goals anytime soon. As an alternative solution, in 2003 Coles agreed to sell Megahertz Communications to AZCAR of Canada. AZCAR acquired Megahertz to gain access to the expanding EU market and Megahertz's contacts in the Middle East. For Megahertz, the acquisition gave the company additional working capital that enabled it to take full advantage of export opportunities.

Sources: www.megahertz.co.uk; W. Smith, "Today Batley, Tomorrow the World?" *Director*, January 2000, pp. 42–49; and "AZCAR Acquires 80% of Megahertz Broadcast Systems," Canadian Corporate Newswire, March 31, 2003.

Case Discussion Questions

1. What was the motivation for Megahertz's shift toward a strategy of export-led growth? Why do you think the opportunities for growth might be greater in foreign markets? Do you think that developing countries are likely to be a major market opportunity for Megahertz? Why?

2. Does Megahertz's strategy for building exports make sense given the nature of the broadcast industry? Why?

3. Why do you think Megahertz found it difficult to raise the working capital required to finance its international trade activities? What does the experience of Megahertz tell you about the problems facing small firms that wish to export?

4. Megahertz solved its financing problem by selling the company to AZCAR of Canada. What other solutions might the company have adopted?

Notes

1. R. A. Pope, "Why Small Firms Export: Another Look," *Journal of Small Business Management* 40 (2002), pp. 17–26.

2. S. T. Cavusgil, "Global Dimensions of Marketing," in *Marketing,* ed. P. E. Murphy and B. M. Enis (Glenview, IL: Scott, Foresman, 1985), pp. 577–99.

3. S. M. Mehta, "Enterprise: Small Companies Look to Cultivate Foreign Business," *The Wall Street Journal,* July 7, 1994, p. B2.

4. P. A. Julien and C. Ramagelahy, "Competitive Strategy and Performance of Exporting SMEs," *Entrepreneurship Theory and Practice,* 2003, pp. 227–94.

5. W. J. Burpitt and D. A. Rondinelli, "Small Firms' Motivations for Exporting: To Earn and Learn?" *Journal of Small Business Management,* October 2000, pp. 1–14, and J. D. Mittelstaedt, G. N. Harben, and W. A. Ward, "How Small Is Too Small?" *Journal of Small Business Management* 41 (2003), pp. 68–85.

6. Small Business Administration, "The State of Small Business 1999–2000: Report to the President," 2001. Can be accessed at www.sba.gov/advo/stats/stateofsb99_00.pdf.

7. A. O. Ogbuehi and T. A. Longfellow, "Perceptions of U.S. Manufacturing Companies Concerning Exporting," *Journal of Small Business Management,* October 1994, pp. 37–59, and U.S. Small Business Administration, "Guide to Exporting," www.sba.gov/oit/info/Guide-to-Exporting/index.html.

8. R. W. Haigh, "Thinking of Exporting?" *Columbia Journal of World Business* 29 (December 1994), pp. 66–86.

9. F. Williams, "The Quest for More Efficient commerce," *Financial Times,* October 13, 1994, p. 7.

10. See Burpitt and Rondinelli, "Small Firms' Motivations for Exporting," and C. S. Katsikeas, L. C. Leonidou, and N. A. Morgan, "Firm Level Export Performance Assessment," *Academy of Marketing Science* 28 (2000), pp. 493–511.

11. M. Y. Yoshino and T. B. Lifson, *The Invisible Link* (Cambridge, MA: MIT Press, 1986).

12. L. W. Tuller, *Going Global* (Homewood, IL: Business One-Irwin, 1991).

13. Haigh, "Thinking of Exporting?"

14. M. A. Raymond, J. Kim, and A. T. Shao. "Export Strategy and Performance," *Journal of Global Marketing* 15 (2001), pp. 5–29, and P. S. Aulakh, M. Kotabe, and H. Teegen, "Export Strategies and Performance of Firms from Emerging Economies," *Academy of Management Journal* 43 (2000), pp. 342–61.

15. J. Francis and C. Collins-Dodd, "The Impact of Firms' Export Orientation on the Export Performance of High-Tech Small and Medium Sized Enterprises," *Journal of International Marketing* 8, no. 3 (2000), pp. 84–103.

16. For a review of the conditions under which a buyer has power over a supplier, see M. E. Porter, *Competitive Strategy* (New York: Free Press, 1980).

17. *Exchange Agreements and Exchange Restrictions* (Washington, DC: International Monetary Fund, 1989).

18. It's also sometimes argued that countertrade is a way of reducing the risks inherent in a traditional money-for-goods transaction, particularly with entities from emerging economies. See C. J. Choi, S. H. Lee, and J. B. Kim, "A Note of Countertrade: Contractual Uncertainty and Transactional Governance in Emerging Economies," *Journal of International Business Studies* 30, no. 1 (1999), pp. 189–202.

19. J. R. Carter and J. Gagne, "The Do's and Don'ts of International Countertrade," *Sloan Management Review,* Spring 1988, pp. 31–37, and W. Maneerungsee, "Countertrade: Farm Goods Swapped for Italian Electricity," *Bangkok Post,* July 23, 1998.

20. Estimate from the American Countertrade Association at www.countertrade.org/index.htm.

See also D. West, "Countertrade," *Business Credit* 104, no. 4 (2001), pp. 64–67, and B. Meyer, "The Original Meaning of Trade Meets the Future of Barter," *World Trade* 13 (January 2000), pp. 46–50.

21. Carter and Gagne, "The Do's and Dont's of International Countertrade."

22. Maneerungsee, "Countertrade: Farm Goods Swapped for Italian Electricity."

23. For details, see Carter and Gagne, "Do's and Dont's"; J. F. Hennart, "Some Empirical Dimensions of Countertrade," *Journal of International Business Studies*, 1990, pp. 240–60; and West, "Countertrade."

24. D. J. Lecraw, "The Management of Countertrade: Factors Influencing Success," *Journal of International Business Studies*, Spring 1989, pp. 41–59.

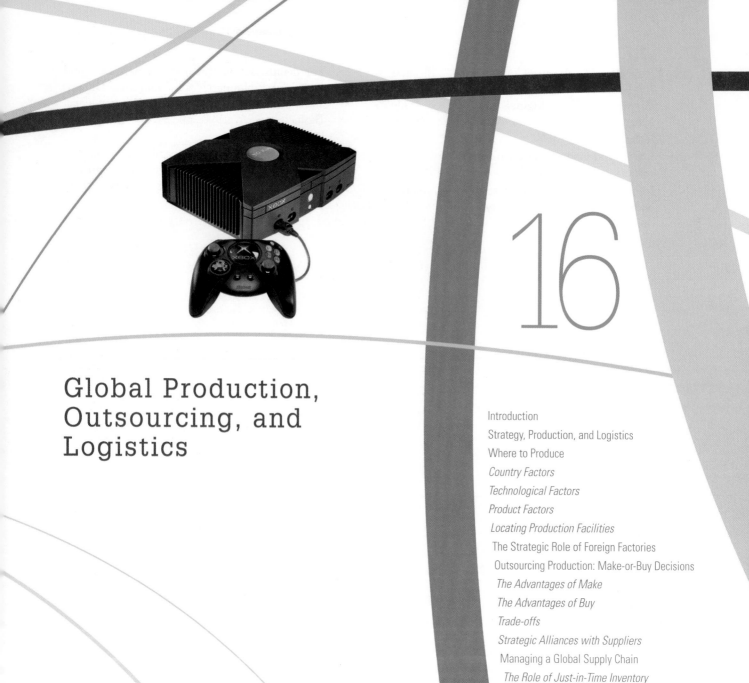

16

Global Production, Outsourcing, and Logistics

Microsoft—Outsourcing XBox Production

When Microsoft decided to enter the video game market with its Xbox gaming console it faced a crucial strategic decision: Should it manufacture the Xbox, or outsource manufacturing to a third party, and if so, whom? Although Microsoft is primarily known as a software company, it has long had a small but important hardware business selling computer mice, keyboards, and joysticks under the Microsoft brand name. However, Xbox was different. This was not a simple computer peripheral; it was a fully functional specialized computer, with multiple components including microprocessors, memory chips, graphics chips, and an internal hard drive.

Microsoft quickly decided that it lacked the manufacturing and logistics capabilities to make the Xbox itself and manage a global supply chain. After reviewing potential suppliers, it decided to outsource assembly and significant logistics functions to Flextronics, a Singapore-based contract manufacturer. Flextronics has global sales in excess of $13 billion and more than 100,000 employees. In addition to Microsoft, customers include Dell, Ericsson Telecom AB, Hewlett-Packard Company, Siemens AG, Sony-Ericsson, and Xerox Corporation. The company manufactures products for these companies in 28 countries. Its largest concentration of activities is in China, where it has 35,000 employees.

Microsoft had already contracted out the manufacture of computer mice to Flextronics, so it knew something about how the company operated and was happy with the cost and quality of Flextronics products. In looking for a supplier, Microsoft wanted a partner that could manufacture the Xbox at a low cost, maintain very high product quality, respond quickly to shifts in demand, and share detailed information on production schedules, product quality, and inventory with Microsoft on a real-time basis. Flextronics seemed to fit the bill for a number of reasons.

First, Flextronics had been pursuing an "industrial park" strategy that enabled the company to tightly manage its own supply chain, reduce the chances of supply disruptions, and lower costs, which could then be passed on to Microsoft in the form of lower prices for the Xbox. Flextronics' industrial park strategy requires key suppliers to site their factories next to a Flextronics assembly plant at low-cost locations near customers' end markets. Flextronics has large industrial parks in Brazil, China, Hungary, Mexico, and Poland. In addition to a Flextronics factory, each park contains the manufacturers of printed circuit boards, components, cables, plastics, and metal parts needed for assembly of a product such as Xbox. The co-location of Flextronics and its suppliers at an industrial park minimizes logistics costs by facilitating just-in-time inventory systems and reducing transportation costs.

Supply problems that might arise from a breakdown in globally dispersed supply chains—as occurred after September 11, 2001, and again in 2003 due to the SARS epidemic—are also minimized by the co-location.

Second, Flextronics' global presence enables the company to shift production from location to location as cost and demand conditions warrant, something that Microsoft wanted. Initially, the Xbox was produced in Hungary (for sale in Europe) and Mexico (for sale in North America and Asia). Within a year, however, Flextronics shifted production from Hungary to China, where labor costs were a fraction of those in Hungary. In 2003, it also moved Xbox production from Mexico to China, for the same reason. Today all Xbox production is in China. Flextronics can execute production shifts very quickly—the company says within three weeks—since all of the relevant manufacturing data are stored in centralized information systems. Thus, if China proves to be a suboptimal location for Xbox production in the future, Flextronics can shift production elsewhere.

Third, using Web-based information systems, Flextronics and Microsoft have the ability to share information in real time with each other. Microsoft feeds information on demand conditions to Flextronics, which enables Flextronics to configure its own production schedules to minimize inventory and closely match supply with demand. In addition, Microsoft has access to real-time information from Flextronics regarding production schedules, inventory, and product quality. This is crucially important, because Microsoft handles the overall management of about 40 strategic suppliers for Xbox, including the manufacturers of microprocessors, graphics chips, hard drives, and flash memory (Flextronics handles the supply of commodity-like inputs, such as circuit boards and plastic molding). The information exchange between Microsoft and Flextronics ensures that production schedules between all of the players in the supply chain are tightly coordinated so that inventory is minimized, shortages are avoided, and demand and supply are balanced.

Finally, Microsoft trusted Flextronics. Microsoft had worked with the company for years, and there were strong personal relationships between employees of the two companies. This helped to cement the business transaction. To facilitate joint design, which is important for reducing manufacturing costs, some Microsoft people are located at the Flextronics U.S. operations center in San Jose, California, and some Flextronics people are located at Microsoft's headquarters in Redmond, Washington. The two companies had worked together on product design before, and Microsoft knew that could be replicated with the Xbox. Microsoft also believed that Flextronics could deliver production of Xbox on time, even though assembly of the product was far more complex than the assembly of a computer mouse.

Sources: J. Carborne, "Outsourcing the Xbox," *Purchasing,* August 15, 2002, pp. 22–25; H. B. Hayes, "Outsourcing Xbox manufacturing," *Pharmaceutical Technology North America,* November 2002, pp. 88–91; "Weathering the Tech Storm," *BusinessWeek,* May 2, 2003, pp. 24–25; and Flextronics *10K Report 2003.*

Introduction

As trade barriers fall and global markets develop, many firms increasingly confront a set of interrelated issues. First, where in the world should production activities be located? Should they be concentrated in a single country, or should they be dispersed around the globe, matching the type of activity with country differences in factor costs, tariff barriers, political risks, and the like to minimize costs and maximize value added? Second, what should be the long-term strategic role of foreign production sites? Should the firm abandon a foreign site if factor costs change, moving production to another more favorable location, or is there value to maintaining an operation at a given location even if underlying economic conditions change? Third, should the firm own foreign production activities, or is it better to outsource those activities to independent vendors? Fourth, how should a globally dispersed supply chain be managed, and what is the role of Internet-based information technology in the management of global logistics? Fifth, should the firm manage global logistics itself, or should it outsource the management to enterprises that specialize in this activity?

In this chapter, we shall consider all these questions and discuss the various factors that influence decisions in this arena. The opening case provides a good example of how one company, Microsoft, approached these issues. Microsoft outsourced production of its Xbox video game console to Flextronics, a Singapore-based contract manufacturer with a global presence. Microsoft did this because it lacked the skills required to assemble a complex electronics product. Flextronics manufactures in 28 countries and moves production of products such as Xbox from location to location as demand and cost conditions change. Thus, it initially produced the Xbox in Hungary and Mexico, but shifted production to China to take advantage of lower labor costs and China's proximity to the large Asian market. Microsoft and Flextronics shared the management of global logistics, however, using Web-based information technology to exchange demand and production information in real time, thereby assuring close coordination of the global supply chain for Xbox.

Strategy, Production, and Logistics

In Chapter 12, we introduced the concept of the value chain and discussed a number of value creation activities, including production, marketing, logistics, R&D, human resources, and information systems. In this chapter, we will focus on two of these activities—**production** and **logistics**—and attempt to clarify how they might be performed internationally to (1) lower the costs of value creation and (2) add value by better serving customer needs. We will discuss the contributions of information technology to these activities, which has become particularly important in the era of the Internet. In later chapters, we will look at other value creation activities in this international context (marketing, R&D, and human resource management).

In Chapter 12, we defined *production* as "the activities involved in creating a product." We used the term *production* to denote both service and manufacturing activities, since one can produce a service or produce a physical product. Although in this chapter we focus more on the production of physical goods, one should not forget that the term can also be applied to services. This has become more evident in recent years with the trend among U.S. firms to outsource the "production" of certain service activities to developing nations where labor costs are lower (for example, the trend among many U.S. companies to outsource customer care services to places such as India, where English is widely

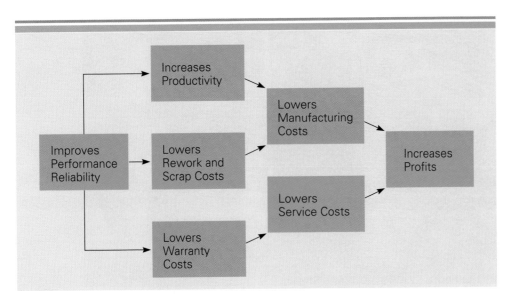

FIGURE 16.1

The Relationship between Quality and Costs

Source: Reprinted from "What Does Product Quality Really Mean?" by David A. Garvin, *Sloan Management Review* 26 (Fall 1984), Figure 1, p. 37, by permission of the publisher. Copyright 1984 by Massachusetts Institute of Technology. All rights reserved.

spoken and labor costs are much lower). Logistics is the activity that controls the transmission of physical materials through the value chain, from procurement through production and into distribution. Production and logistics are closely linked since a firm's ability to perform its production activities efficiently depends on a timely supply of high-quality material inputs, for which logistics is responsible.

The production and logistics functions of an international firm have a number of important strategic objectives.[1] One is to lower costs. Dispersing production activities to various locations around the globe where each activity can be performed most efficiently can lower costs. (As we saw in the opening case, Flextronics moved production of the Xbox from Hungary to China to reduce costs.) Costs can also be cut by managing the global supply chain efficiently so as to better match supply and demand. Efficient supply chain management reduces the amount of inventory in the system and increases inventory turnover, which means the firm has to invest less working capital in inventory and is less likely to find excess inventory on hand that cannot be sold and has to be written off.

A second strategic objective shared by production and logistics is to increase product quality by eliminating defective products from both the supply chain and the manufacturing process.[2] (In this context, *quality* means *reliability*, implying that the product has no defects and performs well.) The objectives of reducing costs and increasing quality are not independent of each other. As illustrated in Figure 16.1, the firm that improves its quality control will also reduce its costs of value creation. Improved quality control reduces costs by:

- Increasing productivity because time is not wasted producing poor-quality products that cannot be sold, leading to a direct reduction in unit costs.
- Lowering rework and scrap costs associated with defective products.
- Reducing the warranty costs and time associated with fixing defective products.

The effect is to lower the costs of value creation by reducing both production and after-sales service costs.

The principal tool that most managers now use to increase the reliability of their product offering is the Six Sigma quality improvement methodology. The Six Sigma methodology is a direct descendant of the **total quality management** (TQM) philosophy that was widely adopted, first by Japanese companies and then American companies during the 1980s and early 1990s.[3] The TQM philosophy was developed by a number of American consultants such as W. Edward Deming, Joseph Juran, and A. V. Feigenbaum.[4] Deming identified a number of steps that should be part of any TQM program. He argued that management should embrace the philosophy that mistakes, defects, and poor-

General Electric is one of the major corporations that has embraced Six Sigma. Its commitment to quality is evident in all its industries, from retail to insurance to aviation.

quality materials are not acceptable and should be eliminated. He suggested that the quality of supervision should be improved by allowing more time for supervisors to work with employees and by providing them with the tools they need to do the job. Deming recommended that management should create an environment in which employees will not fear reporting problems or recommending improvements. He believed that work standards should not only be defined as numbers or quotas, but should also include some notion of quality to promote the production of defect-free output. He argued that management has the responsibility to train employees in new skills to keep pace with changes in the workplace. In addition, he believed that achieving better quality requires the commitment of everyone in the company.

Six Sigma, the modern successor to TQM, is a statistically based philosophy that aims to reduce defects, boost productivity, eliminate waste, and cut costs throughout a company. Six Sigma programs have been adopted by several major corporations, such as Motorola, General Electric, and Allied Signal. Sigma comes from the Greek letter that statisticians use to represent a standard deviation from a mean, the higher the number of "sigmas" the smaller the number of errors. At six sigma, a production process would be 99.99966 percent accurate, creating just 3.4 defects per million units. While it is almost impossible for a company to achieve such perfection, Six Sigma quality is a goal that several strive toward. Increasingly, companies are adopting Six Sigma programs to try to boost their product quality and productivity.[5]

The growth of international standards has also focused greater attention on the importance of product quality. In Europe, for example, the European Union requires that the quality of a firm's manufacturing processes and products be certified under a quality standard known as **ISO 9000** before the firm is allowed access to the EU marketplace. Although the ISO 9000 certification process has proved to be somewhat bureaucratic and costly for many firms, it does focus management attention on the need to improve the quality of products and processes.[6]

In addition to the lowering of costs and the improvement of quality, two other objectives have particular importance in international businesses. First, production and logistics functions must be able to accommodate demands for local responsiveness. As we saw in Chapter 12, demands for local responsiveness arise from national differences in consumer tastes and preferences, infrastructure, distribution channels, and host-government demands. Demands for local responsiveness create pressures to decentralize production activities to the major national or regional markets in which the firm does business or to implement flexible manufacturing processes that enable the firm to customize the product coming out of a factory according to the market in which it is to be sold.

Second, production and logistics must be able to respond quickly to shifts in customer demand. In recent years, time-based competition has grown more important.[7] When consumer demand is prone to large and unpredictable shifts, the firm that can adapt most quickly to these shifts will gain an advantage. As we shall see, both production and logistics play critical roles here. The opening case discussed how Microsoft and Flextronics use real-time information about ordering patterns and inventory to bring demand and supply into alignment, thereby quickly satisfying customer needs and taking excess inventory out of the supply chain.

Where to Produce

An essential decision facing an international firm is where to locate its production activities to best minimize costs and improve product quality. For the firm contemplating international production, a number of factors must be considered. These factors can be grouped under three broad headings: country factors, technological factors, and product factors.[8]

COUNTRY FACTORS

We reviewed country-specific factors in some detail earlier in the book. Political economy, culture, and relative factor costs differ from country to country. In Chapter 5, we saw that due to differences in factor costs, some countries have a comparative advantage for producing certain products. In Chapters 2 and 3, we saw how differences in political economy and national culture influence the benefits, costs, and risks of doing business in a country. Other things being equal, a firm should locate its various manufacturing activities where the economic, political, and cultural conditions, including relative factor costs, are conducive to the performance of those activities (for an example, see the accompanying Management Focus, which looks at the Philips NV investment in China). In Chapter 12, we referred to the benefits derived from such a strategy as location economies. We argued that one result of the strategy is the creation of a global web of value creation activities.

Also important in some industries is the presence of global concentrations of activities at certain locations. In Chapter 7, we discussed the role of location externalities in influencing foreign direct investment decisions. Externalities include the presence of an appropriately skilled labor pool and supporting industries.[9] Such externalities can play an important role in deciding where to locate manufacturing activities. For example, because of a cluster of semiconductor manufacturing plants in Taiwan, a pool of labor with experience in the semiconductor business has developed. In addition, the plants have attracted a number of supporting industries, such as the manufacturers of semiconductor capital equipment and silicon, which have established facilities in Taiwan to be near their customers. This implies that there are real benefits to locating in Taiwan, as opposed to another location that lacks such externalities. Other things being equal, the externalities make Taiwan an attractive location for semiconductor manufacturing facilities.

Of course, other things are not equal. Differences in relative factor costs, political economy, culture, and location externalities are important, but other factors also loom large. Formal and informal trade barriers obviously influence location decisions (see Chapter 6), as do transportation costs and rules and regulations regarding foreign direct investment (see Chapter 8). For example, although relative factor costs may make a country look attractive as a location for performing a manufacturing activity, regulations prohibiting foreign direct investment may eliminate this option. Similarly, a consideration of factor costs might suggest that a firm should source production of a certain component from a particular country, but trade barriers could make this uneconomical.

Another country factor is expected future movements in its exchange rate (see Chapters 10 and 11). Adverse changes in exchange rates can quickly alter a country's attractiveness as a manufacturing base. Currency appreciation can transform a low-cost

MANAGEMENT FOCUS

The Dutch consumer electronics, lighting, semiconductor, and medical equipment conglomerate Philips NV has been operating factories in China since 1985 when the country first opened its markets to foreign investors. Then China was seen as the land of unlimited demand, and Philips, like many other Western companies, dreamed of Chinese consumers snapping up its products by the millions. But the company soon found out that one of the big reasons the company liked China—the low wage rates—also meant that few Chinese workers could afford to buy the products they were producing. Chinese wage rates are currently one-third of those in Mexico and Hungary, and 5 percent of those in the United States or Japan. So Philips hit on a new strategy; keep the factories in China but export most of the goods to the United States and elsewhere.

By 2003, Philips had invested some $2.5 billion in China. The company now operates 25 wholly owned subsidiaries and joint ventures in China. Together they employ some 30,000 people. Philips exports nearly two-thirds of the $7 billion in products that the factories produce every year. Philips accelerated its Chinese investment in anticipation of China's entry into the World Trade Organization. The company plans to move even more production to China over the next few years. In 2003, Philips announced it would phase out production of electronic razors in the Netherlands, lay off 2,000 Dutch employees, and move production to China by 2005. A week earlier, Philips had stated that it would expand capacity at its semiconductor factories in China, while phasing out production in higher-cost locations elsewhere.

The attractions of China to Philips include continuing low wage rates, an educated workforce, a robust Chinese economy, a stable exchange rate that is pegged to the U.S. dollar, a rapidly expanding industrial base that includes many other Western and Chinese companies that Philips uses as suppliers, and easier access to world markets given China's entry into the WTO. Philips has stated that ultimately its goal is to turn China into a global supply base from which the company's products will be exported around the world. In 2003, more than 20 percent of everything Philips made worldwide came from China, and executives say the figure is rising rapidly. Several products, such as CD and DVD players, are now made only in China. Philips is also starting to give its Chinese factories a greater role in product development. In the TV business, for example, basic development used to occur in Holland but was moved to Singapore in the early 1990s. Now Philips is transferring TV development work to Suzhou near Shanghai. Similarly, basic product development work on LCD screens for cell phones was recently shifted to Shanghai.

Philips is hardly alone in this process. By 2003, more than half of all exports from China came from foreign manufacturers or their joint ventures in China. China was the source of more than 80 percent of the DVD players sold worldwide, 50 percent of the cameras, 40 percent of all microwave ovens, 30 percent of the air conditioners, 25 percent of the washing machines, and 20 percent of all refrigerators.

Some observers worry that Philips and companies pursuing a similar strategy might be overdoing it. Too much dependence on China could be dangerous if political, economic, or other problems disrupt production and the company's ability to supply global markets. Some observers believe that it might be better if the manufacturing facilities of companies were more geographically diverse as a hedge against problems in China. The fears of the critics were given some substance in early 2003 when an outbreak of the pneumonia-like SARS (severe acute respiratory syndrome) virus in China resulted in the temporary shutdown of several plants operated by foreign companies and disrupted their global supply chains. Although Philips was not directly affected, it did restrict travel by its managers and engineers to its Chinese plants.

Sources: B. Einhorn. "Philips' Expanding Asia Connections," *BusinessWeek Online,* November 27, 2003; K. Leggett and P. Wonacott, "The World's Factory: A Surge in Exports from China Jolts the Global Industry," *The Wall Street Journal,* October 10, 2002, p. A1; "Philips NV: China Will Be Production Site for Electronic Razors," *The Wall Street Journal,* April 8, 2003, p. B12; "Philips Plans China Expansion," *The Wall Street Journal,* September 25, 2003, p. B13; and M. Saunderson, "Eight out of 10 DVD Players Will Be Made in China," *Dealerscope,* July 2004, p. 28.

location into a high-cost location. Many Japanese corporations had to grapple with this problem during the 1990s and early 2000s. The relatively low value of the yen on foreign exchange markets between 1950 and 1980 helped strengthen Japan's position as a low-cost location for manufacturing. Between 1980 and the mid-1990s, however, the yen's steady appreciation against the dollar increased the dollar cost of products exported from Japan, making Japan less attractive as a manufacturing location. In response, many Japanese firms moved their manufacturing offshore to lower-cost locations in East Asia.

TECHNOLOGICAL FACTORS

The type of technology a firm uses to perform specific manufacturing activities can be pivotal in location decisions. For example, because of technological constraints, in some cases it is necessary to perform certain manufacturing activities in only one location and serve the world market from there. In other cases, the technology may make it feasible to perform an activity in multiple locations. Three characteristics of a manufacturing technology are of interest here: the level of fixed costs, the minimum efficient scale, and the flexibility of the technology.

Fixed Costs

As we noted in Chapter 12, in some cases the fixed costs of setting up a production plant are so high that a firm must serve the world market from a single location or from a very few locations. For example, it now costs more than $1 billion to set up a state-of-the-art plant to manufacture semiconductor chips. Given this, other things being equal, serving the world market from a single plant sited at a single (optimal) location can make sense.

Conversely, a relatively low level of fixed costs can make it economical to perform a particular activity in several locations at once. This allows the firm to better accommodate demands for local responsiveness. Manufacturing in multiple locations may also help the firm avoid becoming too dependent on one location. Being too dependent on one location is particularly risky in a world of floating exchange rates. Many firms disperse their manufacturing plants to different locations as a "real hedge" against potentially adverse moves in currencies.

Minimum Efficient Scale

The concept of economies of scale tells us that as plant output expands, unit costs decrease. The reasons include the greater utilization of capital equipment and the productivity gains that come with specialization of employees within the plant.[10] However, beyond a certain level of output, few additional scale economies are available. Thus, the "unit cost curve" declines with output until a certain output level is reached, at which point further increases in output realize little reduction in unit costs. The level of output at which most plant-level scale economies are exhausted is referred to as the **minimum efficient scale** of output. This is the scale of output a plant must operate to realize all major plant-level scale economies (see Figure 16.2).

The implications of this concept are as follows: The larger the minimum efficient scale of a plant relative to total global demand, the greater the argument for centralizing production in a single location or a limited number of locations. Alternatively, when the minimum efficient scale of production is low relative to global demand, it may be economical to manufacture a product at several locations. For example, the minimum efficient scale for a plant to manufacture personal computers is about 250,000 units a year, while the total global demand exceeds 35 million units a year. The low level of minimum efficient scale in relation to total global demand makes it economically feasible for a company such as Dell to manufacture PCs in six locations.

As in the case of low fixed costs, the advantages of a low minimum efficient scale include allowing the firm to accommodate demands for local responsiveness or to hedge against currency risk by manufacturing the same product in several locations.

FIGURE 16.2

A Typical Unit Cost
Curve

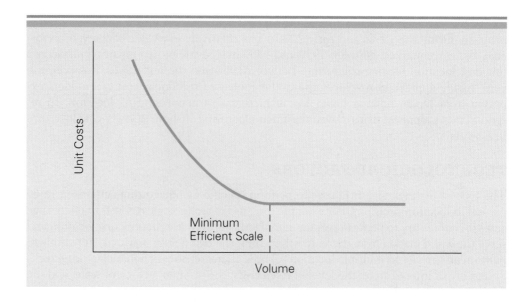

Flexible Manufacturing and Mass Customization

Central to the concept of economies of scale is the idea that the best way to achieve high efficiency, and hence low unit costs, is through the mass production of a standardized output. The trade-off implicit in this idea is between unit costs and product variety. Producing greater product variety from a factory implies shorter production runs, which in turn implies an inability to realize economies of scale. That is, wide product variety makes it difficult for a company to increase its production efficiency and thus reduce its unit costs. According to this logic, the way to increase efficiency and drive down unit costs is to limit product variety and produce a standardized product in large volumes.

This view of production efficiency has been challenged by the rise of flexible manufacturing technologies. The term **flexible manufacturing technology**—or **lean production,** as it is often called—covers a range of manufacturing technologies designed to (1) reduce setup times for complex equipment, (2) increase the utilization of individual machines through better scheduling, and (3) improve quality control at all stages of the manufacturing process.[11] Flexible manufacturing technologies allow the company to produce a wider variety of end products at a unit cost that at one time could be achieved only through the mass production of a standardized output. Research suggests the adoption of flexible manufacturing technologies may actually increase efficiency and lower unit costs relative to what can be achieved by the mass production of a standardized output, while at the same time enabling the company to customize its product offering to a much greater extent than was once thought possible. The term **mass customization** has been coined to describe the ability of companies to use flexible manufacturing technology to reconcile two goals that were once thought to be incompatible—low cost and product customization.[12] Flexible manufacturing technologies vary in their sophistication and complexity.

One of the most famous examples of a flexible manufacturing technology, Toyota's production system, has been credited with making Toyota the most efficient auto company in the world. Toyota's flexible manufacturing system was developed by one of the company's engineers, Ohno Taiichi. After working at Toyota for five years and visiting Ford's U.S. plants, Ohno became convinced that the mass production philosophy for making cars was flawed. He saw numerous problems with mass production.

First, long production runs created massive inventories that had to be stored in large warehouses. This was expensive, both because of the cost of warehousing and because inventories tied up capital in unproductive uses. Second, if the initial machine settings were wrong, long production runs resulted in the production of a large number of defects (i.e., waste). Third, the mass production system was unable to accommodate consumer preferences for product diversity.

In 2004, Ford Motor Company renovated its oldest plant in Chicago, allowing for flexible manufacturing. What other industries could benefit from flexible manufacturing?

In response, Ohno looked for ways to make shorter production runs economical. He developed a number of techniques designed to reduce setup times for production equipment (a major source of fixed costs). By using a system of levers and pulleys, he reduced the time required to change dies on stamping equipment from a full day in 1950 to three minutes by 1971. This made small production runs economical, which allowed Toyota to respond better to consumer demands for product diversity. Small production runs also eliminated the need to hold large inventories, thereby reducing warehousing costs. Plus, small product runs and the lack of inventory meant that defective parts were produced only in small numbers and entered the assembly process immediately. This reduced waste and helped trace defects back to their source to fix the problem. In sum, these innovations enabled Toyota to produce a more diverse product range at a lower unit cost than was possible with conventional mass production.[13]

Flexible machine cells are another common flexible manufacturing technology. A flexible machine cell is a grouping of various types of machinery, a common materials handler, and a centralized cell controller (computer). Each cell normally contains four to six machines capable of performing a variety of operations. The typical cell is dedicated to the production of a family of parts or products. The settings on machines are computer controlled, which allows each cell to switch quickly between the production of different parts or products.

Improved capacity utilization and reductions in work in progress (that is, stockpiles of partly finished products) and in waste are major efficiency benefits of flexible machine cells. Improved capacity utilization arises from the reduction in setup times and from the computer-controlled coordination of production flow between machines, which eliminates bottlenecks. The tight coordination between machines also reduces work-in-progress inventory. Reductions in waste are due to the ability of computer-controlled machinery to identify ways to transform inputs into outputs while producing a minimum of unusable waste material. While freestanding machines might be in use 50 percent of the time, the same machines when grouped into a cell can be used more than 80 percent of the time and produce the same end product with half the waste. This increases efficiency and results in lower costs.

The effects of installing flexible manufacturing technology on a company's cost structure can be dramatic. The Ford Motor Company is currently introducing flexible manufacturing technologies into its automotive plants around the world. These new technologies should allow Ford to produce multiple models from the same line, and to switch production from one model to another much more quickly than in the past. In total, Ford hopes to take $2 billion out of its cost structure by 2010.[14]

Besides improving efficiency and lowering costs, flexible manufacturing technologies also enable companies to customize products to the demands of small consumer groups—at a cost that at one time could be achieved only by mass-producing a standardized output. Thus, the technologies help a company achieve mass customization, which increases its customer responsiveness. Most important for international business, flexible manufacturing technologies can help a firm to customize products for different national markets. The importance of this advantage cannot be overstated. When flexible manufacturing technologies are available, a firm can manufacture products customized to various national markets at a single factory sited at the optimal location. And it can do this without absorbing a significant cost penalty. Thus, firms no longer need to establish manufacturing facilities in each major national market to provide products that satisfy specific consumer tastes and preferences, part of the rationale for a localization strategy (Chapter 12).

Summary

A number of technological factors support the economic arguments for concentrating production facilities in a few choice locations or even in a single location. Other things being equal, when fixed costs are substantial, the minimum efficient scale of production is high, and/or flexible manufacturing technologies are available, the arguments for concentrating production at a few choice locations are strong. This is true even when substantial differences in consumer tastes and preferences exist between national markets, because flexible manufacturing technologies allow the firm to customize products to national differences at a single facility. Alternatively, when fixed costs are low, the minimum efficient scale of production is low, and flexible manufacturing technologies are not available, the arguments for concentrating production at one or a few locations are not as compelling. In such cases, it may make more sense to manufacture in each major market in which the firm is active if this helps the firm better respond to local demands. This holds only if the increased local responsiveness more than offsets the cost disadvantages of not concentrating manufacturing. With the advent of flexible manufacturing technologies and mass customization, such a strategy is becoming less attractive. In sum, technological factors are making it feasible, and necessary, for firms to concentrate manufacturing facilities at optimal locations. Trade barriers and transportation costs are major brakes on this trend.

PRODUCT FACTORS

Two product features affect location decisions. The first is the product's *value-to-weight* ratio because of its influence on transportation costs. Many electronic components and pharmaceuticals have high value-to-weight ratios; they are expensive and they do not weigh very much. Thus, even if they are shipped halfway around the world, their transportation costs account for a very small percentage of total costs. Given this, other things being equal, there is great pressure to produce these products in the optimal location and to serve the world market from there. The opposite holds for products with low value-to-weight ratios. Refined sugar, certain bulk chemicals, paint, and petroleum products all have low value-to-weight ratios; they are relatively inexpensive products that weigh a lot. Accordingly, when they are shipped long distances, transportation costs account for a large percentage of total costs. Thus, other things being equal, there is great pressure to make these products in multiple locations close to major markets to reduce transportation costs.

The other product feature that can influence location decisions is whether the product serves universal needs, needs that are the same all over the world. Examples include many industrial products (e.g., industrial electronics, steel, bulk chemicals) and modern consumer products (e.g., handheld calculators, personal computers, video game consoles). Because there are few national differences in consumer taste and preference for such products, the need for local responsiveness is reduced. This increases the attractiveness of concentrating production at an optimal location.

TABLE 16.1

Location Strategy and Production

	Concentrated Production Favored	Decentralized Production Favored
Country Factors		
Differences in political economy	Substantial	Few
Differences in culture	Substantial	Few
Differences in factor costs	Substantial	Few
Trade barriers	Substantial	Few
Location externalities	Important in industry	Not important in industry
Exchange rates	Stable	Volatile
Technological Factors		
Fixed costs	High	Low
Minimum efficient scale	High	Low
Flexible manufacturing technology	Available	Not available
Product Factors		
Value-to-weight ratio	High	Low
Serves universal needs	Yes	No

LOCATING PRODUCTION FACILITIES

There are two basic strategies for locating production facilities: concentrating them in a centralized location and serving the world market from there, or decentralizing them in various regional or national locations that are close to major markets. The appropriate strategic choice is determined by the various country-specific, technological, and product factors we have discussed in this section and are summarized in Table 16.1.

As can be seen, concentration of production makes most sense when:

- Differences between countries in factor costs, political economy, and culture have a substantial impact on the costs of manufacturing in various countries.
- Trade barriers are low.
- Externalities arising from the concentration of like enterprises favor certain locations.
- Important exchange rates are expected to remain relatively stable.
- The production technology has high fixed costs and high minimum efficient scale relative to global demand, or flexible manufacturing technology exists.
- The product's value-to-weight ratio is high.
- The product serves universal needs.

Alternatively, decentralization of production is appropriate when:

- Differences between countries in factor costs, political economy, and culture do not have a substantial impact on the costs of manufacturing in various countries.
- Trade barriers are high.
- Location externalities are not important.
- Volatility in important exchange rates is expected.
- The production technology has low fixed costs and low minimum efficient scale, and flexible manufacturing technology is not available.
- The product's value-to-weight ratio is low.
- The product does not serve universal needs (that is, significant differences in consumer tastes and preferences exist between nations).

In practice, location decisions are seldom clear cut. For example, it is not unusual for differences in factor costs, technological factors, and product factors to point toward concentrated production while a combination of trade barriers and volatile exchange rates points toward decentralized production. This seems to be the case in the world automobile industry. Although the availability of flexible manufacturing and cars' relatively high value-to-weight ratios suggest concentrated manufacturing, the combination of formal and informal trade barriers and the uncertainties of the world's current floating exchange rate regime (see Chapter 11) have inhibited firms' ability to pursue this strategy. For these reasons, several automobile companies have established "top-to-bottom" manufacturing operations in three major regional markets: Asia, North America, and Western Europe.

The Strategic Role of Foreign Factories

Whatever the rationale behind establishing a foreign manufacturing facility, the strategic role of foreign factories can evolve over time.[15] Initially, many foreign factories are established where labor costs are low. Their strategic role typically is to produce labor-intensive products at as low a cost as possible. For example, beginning in the 1970s, many U.S. firms in the computer and telecommunication equipment businesses established factories across Southeast Asia to manufacture electronic components, such as circuit boards and semiconductors, at the lowest possible cost. They located their factories in countries such as Malaysia, Thailand, and Singapore precisely because each of these countries offered an attractive combination of low labor costs, adequate infrastructure, and favorable tax and trade regime. Initially, the components produced by these factories were designed elsewhere and the final product was assembled elsewhere. Over time, however, the strategic role of some of these factories has expanded; they have become important centers for the design and final assembly of products for the global marketplace. For example, Hewlett-Packard's operation in Singapore was established as a low-cost location for the production of circuit boards, but the facility has become the center for the design and final assembly of portable ink-jet printers for the global marketplace (see the accompanying Management Focus). A similar process seems to be occurring at some of the factories that Philips has established in China (see the Management Focus on Philips).

Such upward migration in the strategic role of foreign factories arises because many foreign factories upgrade their own capabilities.[16] This improvement comes from two sources. First, pressure from the center to improve a factory's cost structure and/or customize a product to the demands of consumers in a particular nation can start a chain of events that ultimately leads to development of additional capabilities at that factory. For example, to meet centrally mandated directions to drive down costs, engineers at HP's Singapore factory argued that they needed to redesign products so they could be manufactured at a lower cost. This led to the establishment of a design center in Singapore. As this design center proved its worth, HP executives realized the importance of co-locating design and manufacturing operations. They increasingly transferred more design responsibilities to the Singapore factory. In addition, the Singapore factory ultimately became the center for the design of products tailored to the needs of the Asian market. This made good strategic sense because it meant products were being designed by engineers who were close to the Asian market and probably had a good understanding of the needs of that market, as opposed to engineers located in the United States.

A second source of improvement in the capabilities of a foreign factory can be the increasing abundance of advanced factors of production in the nation in which the factory is located. Many nations that were considered economic backwaters a generation ago have been experiencing rapid economic development during the past 20 years. Their communication and transportation infrastructures and the education level of the population have improved. While these countries once lacked the advanced infrastructure required to support sophisticated design, development, and manufacturing operations, this is often no longer the case. This has made it much easier for factories based in these nations to take on a greater strategic role.

MANAGEMENT FOCUS

In the late 1960s, Hewlett-Packard was looking around Asia for a low-cost location to produce electronic components that were to be manufactured using labor-intensive processes. The company looked at several Asian locations and eventually settled on Singapore, opening its first factory there in 1970. Although Singapore did not have the lowest labor costs in the region, costs were low relative to North America. Plus, the Singapore location had several important benefits that could not be found at many other locations in Asia. The education level of the local workforce was high. English was widely spoken. The government of Singapore seemed stable and committed to economic development, and the city-state had one of the better infrastructures in the region, including good communication and transportation networks and a rapidly developing industrial and commercial base. HP also extracted favorable terms from the Singapore government with regard to taxes, tariffs, and subsidies.

At its start, the plant manufactured only basic components. The combination of low labor costs and a favorable tax regime helped to make this plant profitable early. In 1973, HP transferred the manufacture of one of its basic handheld calculators from the United States to Singapore. The objective was to reduce manufacturing costs, which the Singapore factory was quickly able to do. Increasingly confident in the capability of the Singapore factory to handle entire products, as opposed to just components, HP's management transferred other products to Singapore over the next few years including keyboards, solid-state displays, and integrated circuits. However, all these products were still designed, developed, and initially produced in the United States.

The plant's status shifted in the early 1980s when HP embarked on a worldwide campaign to boost product quality and reduce costs. HP transferred the production of its HP41C handheld calculator to Singapore. The managers at the Singapore plant were given the goal of substantially reducing manufacturing costs. They argued that this could be achieved only if they were allowed to redesign the product so it could be manufactured at a lower overall cost. HP's central management agreed, and 20 engineers from the Singapore facility were transferred to the United States for one year to learn how to design application-specific integrated circuits. They then brought this expertise back to Singapore and set about redesigning the HP41C.

The results were a huge success. By redesigning the product, the Singapore engineers reduced manufacturing costs for the HP41C by 50 percent. Using this newly acquired capability for product design, the Singapore facility then set about redesigning other products it produced. HP's corporate managers were so impressed with the progress made at the factory that they transferred production of the entire calculator line to Singapore in 1983. This was followed by the partial transfer of ink-jet production to Singapore in 1984 and keyboard production in 1986. In all cases, the facility redesigned the products and often reduced unit manufacturing costs by more than 30 percent. The initial development and design of all these products, however, still occurred in the United States.

In the late 1980s and early 1990s, the Singapore plant assumed added responsibilities, particularly in the ink-jet printer business. In 1990, the factory was given the job of redesigning an HP ink-jet printer for the Japanese market. Although the initial product redesign was a market failure, the managers at Singapore pushed to be allowed to try again, and in 1991 they were given the job of redesigning HP's DeskJet 505 printer for the Japanese market. This time the redesigned product was a success, garnering significant sales in Japan. Emboldened by this success, the plant has continued to take on additional design responsibilities. Today, it is viewed as a "lead plant" within HP's global network, with primary responsibility not just for manufacturing, but also for the development and design of a family of small ink-jet printers targeted at the Asian market.[21]

Sources: K. Ferdows, "Making the Most of Foreign Factories," *Harvard Business Review*, March–April 1997, pp. 73–88, and "Hewlett-Packard: Singapore," Harvard Business School, Case No. 694–035.

Because of such developments, many international businesses are moving away from a system in which their foreign factories were viewed as nothing more than low-cost manufacturing facilities and toward one where foreign factories are viewed as globally dispersed centers of excellence.[17] In this new model, foreign factories take the lead role for the design and manufacture of products to serve important national or regional markets or even the global market. The development of such dispersed centers of excellence is consistent with the concept of a transnational strategy, introduced in Chapter 12. A major aspect of a transnational strategy is a belief in **global learning**—the idea that valuable knowledge does not reside just in a firm's domestic operations; it may also be found in its foreign subsidiaries. Foreign factories that upgrade their capabilities over time are creating valuable knowledge that might benefit the whole corporation.

Managers of international businesses need to remember that foreign factories can improve their capabilities over time, and this can be of immense strategic benefit to the firm. Rather than viewing foreign factories simply as sweatshops where unskilled labor churns out low-cost goods, managers need to see them as potential centers of excellence and to encourage and foster attempts by local managers to upgrade the capabilities of their factories and, thereby, enhance their strategic standing within the corporation.

Such a process does imply that once a foreign factory has been established and valuable skills have been accumulated, it may not be wise to switch production to another location simply because some underlying variable, such as wage rates, has changed.[18] HP has kept its facility in Singapore, rather than switching production to a location where wage rates are now much lower, such as Vietnam, because it recognizes that the Singapore factory has accumulated valuable skills that more than make up for the higher wage rates. Thus, when reviewing the location of production facilities, the international manager must consider the valuable skills that may have been accumulated at various locations, and the impact of those skills on factors such as productivity and product design.

Outsourcing Production: Make-or-Buy Decisions

International businesses frequently face **make-or-buy decisions,** decisions about whether they should perform a certain value creation activity themselves or outsource it to another entity. Historically, most outsourcing decisions have involved the manufacture of physical products. Most manufacturing firms have done their own final assembly, but have had to decide whether to vertically integrate and manufacture their own component parts or outsource the production of such parts, purchasing them from independent suppliers. Such make-or-buy decisions are an important aspect of the strategy of many firms. In the automobile industry, for example, the typical car contains more than 10,000 components, so automobile firms constantly face make-or-buy decisions. Toyota produces less than 30 percent of the value of cars that roll off its assembly lines. The remaining 70 percent, mainly accounted for by component parts and complex subassemblies, comes from independent suppliers. In the athletic shoe industry, the make-or-buy issue has been taken to an extreme with companies such as Nike and Reebok having no involvement in manufacturing; all production has been outsourced, primarily to manufacturers based in low-wage countries. Similarly, as we saw in the opening case, Microsoft has outsourced all production of its Xbox video game terminal to Singapore-based Flextronics, which manufactures the product in China.

In recent years, the outsourcing decision has gone beyond the manufacture of physical products to embrace the production of service activities. For example, many U.S.-based companies, from credit card issuers to computer companies, have outsourced their customer call centers to India. They are "buying" the customer call center function, while "making" other parts of the product in house. Similarly, many information technology companies have been outsourcing some parts of the software development process, such as testing computer code written in the United States, to independent providers based in India. Such companies are "making" (writing) most of the code in-house, but "buying," or outsourcing, part of the production process—testing—to independent companies. India is often the focus of such outsourcing because English is widely spoken there; the nation has a well-educated workforce, particularly in engineering fields; and the pay is much lower than in the United States (a call center worker in India earns about $200 to $300 a month, about one-tenth of the comparable U.S. wage).[19]

Outsourcing decisions pose plenty of problems for purely domestic businesses but even more problems for international businesses. These decisions in the international arena are complicated by the volatility of countries' political economies, exchange rate movements, changes in relative factor costs, and the like. In this section, we examine the arguments for making products in-house and for buying them, and we consider the trade-offs involved in such a decision. Then we discuss strategic alliances as an alternative to producing all or part of a product within the company.

THE ADVANTAGES OF MAKE

The arguments that support making all or part of a product in-house—vertical integration—are fourfold. Vertical integration may be associated with lower costs, facilitate investments in highly specialized assets, protect proprietary product technology, and ease the scheduling of adjacent processes.

Lowering Costs

It may pay a firm to continue manufacturing a product or component part in-house if the firm is more efficient at that production activity than any other enterprise. Boeing, for example, has looked closely at its make-or-buy decisions with regard to commercial jet aircraft (see the accompanying Management Focus). It decided to outsource the production of some component parts but keep the design and final integration of aircraft. Boeing's rationale was that it has a core competence in large systems integration, and it is more efficient at this activity than any other comparable enterprise in the world. Therefore, it makes little sense for Boeing to outsource this particular activity.

Facilitating Specialized Investments

We first encountered the concept of specialized assets in Chapter 7 when we looked at the economic theory of vertical foreign direct investment. A variation of that concept explains why firms might want to make their own components rather than buy them.[20] When one firm must invest in specialized assets to supply another, mutual dependency is created. In such circumstances, each party fears the other will abuse the relationship by seeking more favorable terms.

Imagine Ford of Europe has developed a new, high-performance, high-quality, and uniquely designed fuel injection system. The increased fuel efficiency will help sell Ford cars. Ford must decide whether to make the system in-house or to contract out the manufacturing to an independent supplier. Manufacturing these uniquely designed systems requires investments in equipment that can be used only for this purpose; it cannot be used to make fuel injection systems for any other auto firm. Thus, investment in this equipment constitutes an investment in specialized assets.

Let us first examine this situation from the perspective of an independent supplier who has been asked by Ford to make this investment. The supplier might reason that once it has made the investment, it will become dependent on Ford for business since Ford is the only possible customer for the output of this equipment. The supplier perceives this as putting Ford in a strong bargaining position and worries that once the specialized investment has been made, Ford might use this to squeeze down prices for the systems. Given this risk, the supplier declines to make the investment in specialized equipment.

Now take the position of Ford. Ford might reason that if it contracts out production of these systems to an independent supplier, it might become too dependent on that supplier for a vital input. Because specialized equipment is required to produce the fuel injection systems, Ford cannot easily switch its orders to other suppliers who lack that equipment. (It would face high switching costs.) Ford perceives this as increasing the bargaining power of the supplier and worries that the supplier might use its bargaining strength to demand higher prices.

Nike relies on outsourcing to manufacture its products; however, the company has received worldwide criticism for turning its back on social responsibility for the sake of profit.

Thus, the mutual dependency that outsourcing would create makes Ford nervous and scares away potential suppliers. The problem here is lack of trust. Neither party completely trusts the other to play fair. Consequently, Ford might reason that the only safe way to get the new fuel injection systems is to manufacture them itself. It may be unable to persuade any independent supplier to manufacture them. Thus, Ford decides to make rather than buy.

In general, we can predict that when substantial investments in specialized assets are required to manufacture a component, the firm will prefer to make the component internally rather than contract it out to a supplier. Substantial empirical evidence supports this prediction.[21]

Protecting Proprietary Product Technology

Proprietary product technology is unique to a firm. If it enables the firm to produce a product containing superior features, proprietary technology can give the firm a competitive advantage. The firm would not want competitors to get this technology. If the firm outsources the production of entire products or components containing proprietary technology, it runs the risk that those suppliers will expropriate the technology for their own use or that they will sell it to the firm's competitors. Thus, to maintain control over its technology, the firm might prefer to make such products or component parts in-house. An example of a firm that has made such decisions is given in the accompanying Management Focus, which looks at make-or-buy decisions at Boeing. While Boeing has decided to outsource a number of important components that go toward the production of an aircraft, it has explicitly decided not to outsource the manufacture of cockpits because it believes that doing so would give away key technology to potential competitors.

Improving Scheduling

Another argument for producing all or part of a product in-house is that production cost savings result because it makes planning, coordination, and scheduling of adjacent processes easier.[22] This is particularly important in firms with just-in-time inventory systems (discussed later in the chapter). In the 1920s, for example, Ford profited from tight coordination and scheduling made possible by backward vertical integration into steel foundries, iron ore shipping, and mining. Deliveries at Ford's foundries on the Great Lakes were coordinated so well that ore was turned into engine blocks within 24 hours. This substantially reduced Ford's production costs by eliminating the need to hold excessive ore inventories.

For international businesses that source worldwide, scheduling problems can be exacerbated by the time and distance between the firm and its suppliers. This is true whether the firms use their own subunits as suppliers or use independent suppliers. However, ownership of upstream production facilities is not the issue here. By using information technology, firms can attain tight coordination between different stages in the production process. The opening case discusses how Microsoft and Flextronics use information technology to tightly coordinate the flow of inventory associated with the manufacture of the Xbox. Thus, although this argument for vertical integration is often made, it is not compelling.

THE ADVANTAGES OF BUY

Buying component parts, or an entire product, from independent suppliers can give the firm greater flexibility, can help drive down the firm's cost structure, and may help the firm capture orders from international customers.

Strategic Flexibility

The great advantage of buying component parts, or even an entire product, from independent suppliers is that the firm can maintain its flexibility, switching orders between suppliers as circumstances dictate. This is particularly important internationally, where changes in ex-

MANAGEMENT FOCUS The Boeing Company is one of the two premier manufacturers of commercial jet aircraft in the world, holding more than a 45 percent share of the global market for large commercial jet aircraft. Despite its large market share, in recent years Boeing has found it tough going. The company's problems are twofold. First, Boeing faces an aggressive competitor in Europe's Airbus Industrie. The dogfight between Boeing and Airbus for market share has enabled major airlines to play the two companies off against each other in an attempt to bargain down the price for commercial jet aircraft. Second, the airline business is quite cyclical, and airlines sharply reduce orders for new aircraft when their own business is in a downturn. This occurred in the early 1990s and again after the events of September 11, 2001, hit the airline industry hard, and resulted in slumping orders for Boeing and Airbus.

During downturns, some of which can be lengthy, intense price competition often occurs between Airbus and Boeing as they struggle to maintain market share and order volume in the face of falling demand. Given these pricing pressures, the only way that Boeing can maintain its profitability is to reduce its own manufacturing costs. With this in mind, Boeing is constantly studying make-or-buy decisions. The objective is to identify activities that can be outsourced to subcontractors, both in the United States and abroad, to reduce production costs.

When making outsourcing decisions, Boeing applies a number of criteria. First, Boeing looks at the basic economics. The central issue is whether an activity could be performed more cost-effectively by an outside manufacturer or by Boeing. Second, Boeing considers the strategic risk associated with outsourcing an activity. Boeing has decided it will not outsource any activity deemed to be part of its long-term competitive advantage, particularly design work and final integration and assembly. Third, Boeing looks at the operational risk associated with outsourcing an activity. The basic objective is to make sure Boeing does not become too dependent on a single outside supplier for critical components. Boeing's philosophy is to hedge operational risk by purchasing from two or more suppliers. Finally, Boeing considers whether it makes sense to outsource certain activities to a supplier in a given country to help secure orders for commercial jet aircraft from that country. This practice is known as offsetting, and it is common in many industries. For example, Boeing decided to outsource the production of certain components to China. This decision was influenced by forecasts suggesting that the Chinese will purchase more than $100 billion worth of commercial jets over the next 20 years. Boeing's hope is that pushing some subcontracting work China's way will help Boeing gain a larger share of this market than its global competitor, Airbus.

By 2003, Boeing was outsourcing some 64 percent of the work involved in building a commercial jet aircraft, up from 50 percent a decade earlier, with companies in Japan, Italy, and elsewhere shipping fuselage sections or even entire wings to Boeing. For its part, Boeing has decided to focus its efforts on design, final manufacturing integration and assembly, and marketing and sales. Every other activity can be potentially outsourced. There are signs that Boeing will outsource substantially more work than ever when making its latest jet, the 7E7, a "super-efficient" wide-body jet scheduled for market introduction in 2008.

Sources: D. Gates, "Boeing Buzzes about 'Source' of Work," *Seattle Times,* March 9, 2003, p. A1; S. Wilhelm, "Tough Contest Ahead over 7E7," *Puget Sound Business Journal,* April 11, 2002, p. 50; and interviews between Charles Hill and senior management personnel at Boeing.

change rates and trade barriers can alter the attractiveness of supply sources. One year Hong Kong might offer the lowest cost for a particular component, and the next year, Mexico may. Many firms source the same products from suppliers based in two countries, primarily as a hedge against adverse movements in factor costs, exchange rates, and the like.

Sourcing products from independent suppliers can also be advantageous when the optimal location for manufacturing a product is beset by political risks. Under such circumstances, foreign direct investment to establish a component manufacturing operation in that country would expose the firm to political risks. The firm can avoid many of these risks by buying from an independent supplier in that country, thereby maintaining the flexibility to switch sourcing to another country if a war, revolution, or other political change alters that country's attractiveness as a supply source.

However, maintaining strategic flexibility has its downside. If a supplier perceives the firm will change suppliers in response to changes in exchange rates, trade barriers, or general political circumstances, that supplier might not be willing to make investments in specialized plants and equipment that would ultimately benefit the firm.

Lower Costs

Although making a product or component part in-house—vertical integration—is often undertaken to lower costs, it may have the opposite effect. When this is the case, outsourcing may lower the firm's cost structure. Making all or part of a product in-house increases an organization's scope, and the resulting increase in organizational complexity can raise a firm's cost structure. There are three reasons for this.

First, the greater the number of subunits in an organization, the more problems coordinating and controlling those units. Coordinating and controlling subunits require top management to process large amounts of information about subunit activities. The greater the number of subunits, the more information top management must process and the harder it is to do well. Theoretically, when the firm becomes involved in too many activities, headquarters management will be unable to effectively control all of them, and the resulting inefficiencies will more than offset any advantages derived from vertical integration.[23] This can be particularly serious in an international business, where the problem of controlling subunits is exacerbated by distance and differences in time, language, and culture.

Second, the firm that vertically integrates into component part manufacture may find that because its internal suppliers have a captive customer in the firm, they lack an incentive to reduce costs. The fact that they do not have to compete for orders with other suppliers may result in high operating costs. The managers of the supply operation may be tempted to pass on cost increases to other parts of the firm in the form of higher transfer prices, rather than looking for ways to reduce those costs.

Third, vertically integrated firms have to determine appropriate prices for goods transferred to subunits within the firm. This is a challenge in any firm, but it is even more complex in international businesses. Different tax regimes, exchange rate movements, and headquarters' ignorance about local conditions all increase the complexity of transfer pricing decisions. This complexity enhances internal suppliers' ability to manipulate transfer prices to their advantage, passing cost increases downstream rather than looking for ways to reduce costs.

The firm that buys its components from independent suppliers can avoid all these problems and the associated costs. The firm that sources from independent suppliers has fewer subunits to control. The incentive problems that occur with internal suppliers do not arise when independent suppliers are used. Independent suppliers know they must continue to be efficient if they are to win business from the firm. Also, because independent suppliers' prices are set by market forces, the transfer pricing problem does not exist. In sum, the bureaucratic inefficiencies and resulting costs that can arise when firms vertically integrate backward and produce their own components are avoided by buying component parts from independent suppliers.

Offsets

Another reason for outsourcing some manufacturing to independent suppliers based in other countries is that it may help the firm capture more orders from that country. As noted in the Management Focus on Boeing, offsets are common in the commercial aerospace industry. For example, before Air India places a large order with Boeing, the Indian government might ask Boeing to push some subcontracting work toward Indian manufacturers. This is not unusual in international business. Representatives of the U.S. government have repeatedly urged Japanese automobile companies to purchase more component parts from U.S. suppliers to partially offset the large volume of automobile exports from Japan to the United States.

TRADE-OFFS

Clearly there are trade-offs in make-or-buy decisions. The benefits of making all or part of a product in-house seem to be greatest when highly specialized assets are involved, when vertical integration is necessary for protecting proprietary technology, or when the firm is simply more efficient than external suppliers at performing a particular activity. When these conditions are not present, the risk of strategic inflexibility and organizational problems suggest it may be better to contract out some or all production to independent suppliers. Because issues of strategic flexibility and organizational control loom even larger for international businesses than purely domestic ones, an international business should be particularly wary of vertical integration into component part manufacture. In addition, some outsourcing in the form of offsets may help a firm gain larger orders in the future.

STRATEGIC ALLIANCES WITH SUPPLIERS

Several international businesses have tried to reap some benefits of vertical integration without the associated organizational problems by entering strategic alliances with essential suppliers. For example, there is an alliance between Kodak and Canon, under which Canon builds photocopiers for sale by Kodak, an alliance between Apple and Sony, under which Sony builds laptop computers for Apple, and an alliance between Microsoft and Flextronics, under which Flextronics builds the Xbox for Microsoft (see the opening case). By these alliances, Kodak, Apple, and Microsoft have committed themselves to long-term relationships with these suppliers, which have encouraged the suppliers to undertake specialized investments. Strategic alliances build trust between the firm and its suppliers. Trust is built when a firm makes a credible commitment to continue purchasing from a supplier on reasonable terms. For example, the firm may invest money in a supplier—perhaps by taking a minority shareholding—to signal its intention to build a productive, mutually beneficial long-term relationship.

This kind of arrangement between the firm and its parts suppliers was pioneered in Japan by large auto companies such as Toyota. Many Japanese automakers have cooperative relationships with their suppliers that go back decades. In these relationships, the auto companies and their suppliers collaborate on ways to increase value added by, for example, implementing just-in-time inventory systems or cooperating in the design of component parts to improve quality and reduce assembly costs. These relationships have been formalized when the auto firms acquired minority shareholdings in many of their essential suppliers to symbolize their desire for long-term cooperative relationships with them. At the same time, the relationship between the firm and each essential supplier remains market mediated and terminable if the supplier fails to perform. By pursuing such a strategy, the Japanese automakers capture many of the benefits of vertical integration, particularly those arising from investments in specialized assets, without suffering the organizational problems that come with formal vertical integration. The parts suppliers also benefit from these relationships because they grow with the firm they supply and share in its success.[24]

In general, the trends toward just-in-time inventory systems (JIT), computer-aided design (CAD), and computer-aided manufacturing (CAM) seem to have increased pressures for firms to establish long-term relationships with their suppliers. JIT, CAD, and CAM systems all rely on close links between firms and their suppliers supported by substantial specialized investment in equipment and information systems hardware. To get a supplier to agree to adopt such systems, a firm must make a credible commitment to an enduring relationship with the supplier—it must build trust with the supplier. It can do this within the framework of a strategic alliance.

Alliances are not all good. Like formal vertical integration, a firm that enters long-term alliances may limit its strategic flexibility by the commitments it makes to its alliance partners. As we saw in Chapter 14 when we considered alliances between competitors, a firm that allies itself with another firm risks giving away key technological know-how to a potential competitor.

Managing a Global Supply Chain

Logistics encompasses the activities necessary to get materials from suppliers to a manufacturing facility, through the manufacturing process, and out through a distribution system to the end user.[25] In the international business, the logistics function manages the global supply chain. The twin objectives of logistics are to manage a firm's global supply chain at the lowest possible cost and in a way that best serves customer needs, thereby lowering the costs of value creation and helping the firm establish a competitive advantage through superior customer service.

The potential for reducing costs through more efficient logistics is enormous. For the typical manufacturing enterprise, material costs account for between 50 and 70 percent of revenues, depending on the industry. Even a small reduction in these costs can have a substantial impact on profitability. According to one estimate, for a firm with revenues of $1 million, a return on investment rate of 5 percent, and materials costs that are 50 percent of sales revenues, a $15,000 increase in total profits could be achieved either by increasing sales revenues 30 percent or by reducing materials costs by 3 percent.[26] In a saturated market, it would be much easier to reduce materials costs by 3 percent than to increase sales revenues by 30 percent.

THE ROLE OF JUST-IN-TIME INVENTORY

Pioneered by Japanese firms during the 1950s and 60s, just-in-time inventory systems now play a major role in most manufacturing firms. The basic philosophy behind **just-in-time (JIT)** systems is to economize on inventory holding costs by having materials arrive at a manufacturing plant just in time to enter the production process and not before. The major cost saving comes from speeding up inventory turnover. This reduces inventory holding costs, such as warehousing and storage costs. It means the company can reduce the amount of working capital it needs to finance inventory, freeing capital for other uses and/or lowering the total capital requirements of the enterprise. Other things being equal, this will boost the company's profitability as measured by return on capital invested. It also means the company is less likely to have excess unsold inventory that it has to write off against earnings or price low to sell.

In addition to the cost benefits, JIT systems can also help firms improve product quality. Under a JIT system, parts enter the manufacturing process immediately; they are not warehoused. This allows defective inputs to be spotted right away. The problem can then be traced to the supply source and fixed before more defective parts are produced. Under a more traditional system, warehousing parts for weeks before they are used allows many defective parts to be produced before a problem is recognized.

The drawback of a JIT system is that it leaves a firm without a buffer stock of inventory. Although buffer stocks are expensive to store, they can help a firm respond quickly to increases in demand and tide a firm over shortages brought about by disruption among suppliers. Such a disruption occurred after the September 11, 2001, attacks on the World Trade Center, when the subsequent shutdown of international air travel and shipping left many firms that relied upon globally dispersed suppliers and tightly managed "just-in-time" supply chains without a buffer stock of inventory. A less pronounced but similar situation occurred again in April 2003 when the outbreak of pneumonia-like SARS (severe acute respiratory syndrome) virus in China resulted in the temporary shutdown of several plants operated by foreign companies and disrupted their global supply chains. Similarly, in late 2004, record imports into the United States left several major West Coast shipping ports clogged with too many ships from Asia that could not be unloaded fast enough, and disrupted the finely tuned supply chains of several major U.S. enterprises.[27]

There are ways of reducing the risks associated with a global supply chain that operates on just-in-time principles. To reduce the risks associated with depending on one supplier for an important input, some firms source these inputs from several suppliers located in different countries. While this does not help in the case of an event with global ramifications, such as September 11, 2001, it does help manage country-specific supply disruptions, which are more common. As for responding quickly to increases in consumer demand, companies such as Flextronics have shown that it is possible to do this while maintaining a JIT system by using real-time information to adjust product pricing, thereby bringing demand and supply into closer alignment (see the opening case).

THE ROLE OF INFORMATION TECHNOLOGY AND THE INTERNET

As we saw in the opening case, Web-based information systems play a crucial role in modern materials management. By tracking component parts as they make their way across the globe toward an assembly plant, information systems enable a firm to optimize its production scheduling according to when components are expected to arrive. By locating component parts in the supply chain precisely, good information systems allow the firm to accelerate production when needed by pulling key components out of the regular supply chain and having them flown to the manufacturing plant.

Firms increasingly use electronic data interchange (EDI) to coordinate the flow of materials into manufacturing, through manufacturing, and out to customers. EDI systems require computer links between a firm, its suppliers, and its shippers. Sometimes customers also are integrated into the system. These electronic links are then used to place orders with suppliers, to register parts leaving a supplier, to track them as they travel toward a manufacturing plant, and to register their arrival. Suppliers typically use an EDI link to send invoices to the purchasing firm. One consequence of an EDI system is that suppliers, shippers, and the purchasing firm can communicate with each other with no time delay, which increases the flexibility and responsiveness of the whole global supply system. A second consequence is that much of the paperwork between suppliers, shippers, and the purchasing firm is eliminated. Good EDI systems can help a firm decentralize materials management decisions to the plant level by giving corporate-level managers the information they need for coordinating and controlling decentralized materials management groups.

Before the emergence of the Internet as a major communication medium, firms and their suppliers normally had to purchase expensive proprietary software solutions to implement EDI systems. The ubiquity of the Internet and the availability of Web-based applications have made most of these proprietary solutions obsolete. Less expensive Web-based systems that are much easier to install and manage now dominate the market for global supply chain management software. These Web-based systems are rapidly transforming the management of globally dispersed supply chains, allowing even small firms to achieve a much better balance between supply and demand, thereby reducing the inventory in their systems and reaping the associated economic benefits. With increasing numbers of firms adopting these systems, those that don't may find themselves at a significant competitive disadvantage.

Chapter Summary

This chapter explained how efficient production and logistics functions can improve an international business's competitive position by lowering the costs of value creation and by performing value creation activities in such ways that customer service is enhanced and value added is maximized. We looked closely at three issues central to international production and logistics: where to produce, what to make and what to buy, and

how to coordinate a globally dispersed manufacturing and supply system. The chapter made the following points:

1. The choice of an optimal production location must consider country factors, technological factors, and product factors.

2. Country factors include the influence of factor costs, political economy, and national culture on production costs, along with the presence of location externalities.

3. Technological factors include the fixed costs of setting up production facilities, the minimum efficient scale of production, and the availability of flexible manufacturing technologies that allow for mass customization.

4. Product factors include the value-to-weight ratio of the product and whether the product serves universal needs.

5. Location strategies either concentrate or decentralize manufacturing. The choice should be made in light of country, technological, and product factors. All location decisions involve trade-offs.

6. Foreign factories can improve their capabilities over time, and this can be of immense strategic benefit to the firm. Managers need to view foreign factories as potential centers of excellence and to encourage and foster attempts by local managers to upgrade factory capabilities.

7. An essential issue in many international businesses is determining which component parts should be manufactured in-house and which should be outsourced to independent suppliers.

8. Making components in-house facilitates investments in specialized assets and helps the firm protect its proprietary technology. It may improve scheduling between adjacent stages in the value chain, also. In-house production also makes sense if the firm is an efficient, low-cost producer of a technology.

9. Buying components from independent suppliers facilitates strategic flexibility and helps the firm avoid the organizational problems associated with extensive vertical integration. Outsourcing might also be employed as part of an "offset" policy, which is designed to win more orders for the firm from a country by pushing some subcontracting work to that country.

10. Several firms have tried to attain the benefits of vertical integration and avoid its associated organizational problems by entering long-term strategic alliances with essential suppliers.

11. Although alliances with suppliers can give a firm the benefits of vertical integration without dispensing entirely with the benefits of a market relationship, alliances have drawbacks. The firm that enters a strategic alliance may find its strategic flexibility limited by commitments to alliance partners.

12. Logistics encompasses all the activities that move materials to a production facility, through the production process, and out through a distribution system to the end user. The logistics function is complicated in an international business by distance, time, exchange rates, custom barriers, and other things.

13. Just-in-time systems generate major cost savings from reducing warehousing and inventory holding costs and from reducing the need to write off excess inventory. In addition, JIT systems help the firm spot defective parts and remove them from the manufacturing process quickly, thereby improving product quality.

14. Information technology, particularly Internet-based electronic data interchange, plays a major role in materials management. EDI facilitates the tracking of inputs, allows the firm to optimize its production schedule, lets the firm and its suppliers communicate in real time, and eliminates the flow of paperwork between a firm and its suppliers.

Critical Thinking and Discussion Questions

1. An electronics firm is considering how best to supply the world market for microprocessors used in consumer and industrial electronic products. A manufacturing plant costs about $500 million to construct and requires a highly skilled workforce. The total value of the world market for this product over the next 10 years is estimated to be between $10 billion and $15 billion. The tariffs prevailing in this industry are currently low. Should the firm adopt a concentrated or decentralized manufacturing strategy? What kind of location(s) should the firm favor for its plant(s)?

2. A chemical firm is considering how best to supply the world market for sulfuric acid. A manufacturing plant costs about $20 million to construct and requires a moderately skilled workforce. The total value of the world market

for this product over the next 10 years is estimated to be between $20 billion and $30 billion. The tariffs prevailing in this industry are moderate. Should the firm favor concentrated manufacturing or decentralized manufacturing? What kind of location(s) should the firm seek for its plant(s)?

3. A firm must decide whether to make a component part in-house or to contract it out to an independent supplier. Manufacturing the part requires a nonrecoverable investment in special-

ized assets. The most efficient suppliers are located in countries with currencies that many foreign exchange analysts expect to appreciate substantially over the next decade. What are the pros and cons of (*a*) manufacturing the component in-house and (*b*) outsourcing manufacturing to an independent supplier? Which option would you recommend? Why?

4. Explain how an efficient logistics function can help an international business compete more effectively in the global marketplace.

Research Task 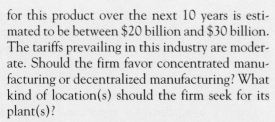 globaledge.msu.edu

Use the globalEDGE™ site to complete the following exercises:

1. The U.S. Department of Labor's Bureau of International Labor Affairs publishes the *Chartbook of International Labor Comparisons*. Given the demands of an increasingly competitive marketplace, your company is considering the construction of a manufacturing facility somewhere in Asia. Locate the latest edition of the International Labor Affairs report and identify the hourly compensation costs

for manufacturing workers in Hong Kong, Japan, South Korea, Singapore, and Taiwan. On the basis of this information, where would you locate a new manufacturing facility? Provide compelling reasons to support your decision.

2. *Industry Week* magazine ranks the world's largest manufacturing companies by sales revenue. Identify the largest Chinese manufacturing companies in the most recent ranking, noting the industries in which these companies operate.

Competitive Advantage at Dell Inc.

CLOSING CASE Michael Dell started Dell Inc. in 1984 when he was an undergraduate student at the University of Texas. Two decades later, Dell has grown to become one of the world's great computer companies, with a leading share in the personal computer and server businesses. In fiscal 2004, a year in which most computer makers lost money due to slumping global demand for PCs, Dell saw its revenues jump by $6 billion, to $41 billion, made $3.5 billion in operating profit, and gained over 2 percent in global market share. Approximately one-third of Dell's sales were made outside the United States. Dell credits much of its strong performance in a tough environment to a cost structure that is the lowest in the industry. That cost structure is in part the result of Dell's global manufacturing and supply chain management strategy.

Dell has manufacturing sites in Brazil, Ireland, Malaysia, and China, in addition to three sites in the United States (and a fourth now under construction). The sites were chosen for low labor costs, the high productivity of the local workforce, and their proximity to important regional markets. Dell prefers to manufacture

close to regional markets to reduce shipping costs and increase the speed of delivery to customers. (Dell still manufactures computers in the United States because its U.S workforce is very productive, and the United States is its largest market, so it pays to be close to U.S. customers.)

In addition to manufacturing, much of Dell's customer support operations are also performed outside of the United States with a major center in Bangalore, India (U.S. customers calling Dell's customer support are likely to be connected to a service agent in India). India was chosen not just because of low wage rates, but also because of the availability of an educated and English-speaking workforce. However, moving customer support offshore has not been all smooth sailing. Differences in accent and culture between U.S. callers and Indian employees led to a spike in complaints from customers following the 2001 opening of the Bangalore call center, and in 2004, Dell moved some of its support operations for larger corporate customers back to the United States. Dell's support operations for retail customers, however, are still located in Bangalore, and Dell's management states it is committed to maintaining its Indian calling center.

Dell's supply base is also global. Dell has some 200 suppliers, more than half of which are located outside the United States. Thirty suppliers account for about 75 percent of Dell's total purchases. Over 50 percent of its major suppliers are in Asia.

From inception, Dell's business model was based on direct selling to customers, eliminating wholesalers and retailers. The original thought was that by cutting out the middle of the distribution chain, Dell could offer consumers lower prices. Initially, direct selling was achieved through mailings and telephone contacts, but since the mid-1990s the majority of Dell's sales have been made over the Internet, and by 2004, some 85 percent of all sales were made through this medium. Internet selling has enabled Dell to offer its customers the ability to customize their orders, mixing and matching product features such as microprocessors, memory, monitors, internal hard drives, CD and DVD drives, keyboard and mouse format, and the like, to get the system that best suits their particular requirements.

While the ability to customize products, when combined with low prices, has made Dell attractive to customers, the real power of the business model is to be found in how Dell manages its global supply chain to minimize inventory while building PCs to individual customer orders within three days. Dell uses the Internet to feed real-time information about order flow to its suppliers. Dell's suppliers, wherever they are located, have up-to-the-minute information about demand trends for the components they produce, along with volume expectations for the next 4 to 12 weeks that are constantly updated as new information becomes available. Dell's suppliers use this information to adjust their own production schedules on a real-time basis, producing just enough components for Dell's needs and shipping them by the most appropriate mode, typically truck or air express, so that they arrive just in time for production. This tight coordination is pushed far down the supply chain, with Dell sharing key data with its suppliers' principal suppliers. For example, Quanta of Taiwan makes notebook computers for Dell that incorporate digital signal processing chips from Texas Instruments. To better coordinate the supply chain, Dell passes information to Texas Instruments in addition to Quanta. This allows Texas Instruments to adjust its schedules to Quanta's needs, which in turn can adjust its schedule according to data from Dell.

Dell's ultimate goal is to drive all inventories out of the supply chain apart from those in transit between suppliers and Dell, effectively replacing inventory with information. Although Dell has not yet achieved this goal, the firm has reduced inventory to the lowest level in the industry. In 2004, Dell carried only three days of inventory, compared to 30, 45, or even 90 days' worth at

competitors. This is a critical advantage in the computer industry, where component costs account for 75 percent of revenues and typically fall by 1 percent per week due to rapid obsolescence. For example, when larger, faster hard drives are introduced, which occurs every three to six months, the value of previous-generation hard drives is significantly reduced. So if Dell holds one week of inventory, and a competitor holds four weeks, this translates immediately into 3 percent worth of component cost advantage to Dell, which can mean a 2 percent advantage on the bottom line. Driving inventory out of the system also dramatically reduces Dell's need for working capital and boosts the company's profitability.

Dell's Internet-based customer ordering and procurement systems have also allowed the company to synchronize demand and supply to an extent that few other companies can. For example, if Dell sees that it is running out of a particular component, say, 17-inch monitors from Sony, it can manipulate demand by offering a 19-inch model at a lower price until Sony delivers more 17-inch monitors. By taking such steps to fine-tune the balance between demand and supply, Dell can meet customers' expectations. Also, balancing supply and demand allows the company to minimize excess and obsolete inventory. Dell writes off between 0.05 percent and 0.1 percent of total materials costs in excess or obsolete inventory. Its competitors write off between 2 percent and 3 percent, which again gives Dell a significant cost advantage.

Sources: D. Hunter, "How Dell Keeps from Stumbling," *BusinessWeek*, May 14, 2001, pp. 38–40; "Enter the Eco-system: From Supply Chain to Network," *The Economist*, November 11, 2000; "Dell's Direct Initiative," *Country Monitor*, June 7, 2000, p. 5; B. Einhorn, "Quanta's Quantum Leap," *BusinessWeek*, November 5, 2001, pp. 79–80; Dell 10K statement for fiscal 2003, April 28, 2003; J. E. Garten, "When Everything Is Made in China," *BusinessWeek*, June 17, 2002, pp. 20–22; G. Rivlin, "Who's Afraid of China?" *The New York Times*, December 19, 2004, Section 3, pp. 1, 4; and E. Corcoran, "Unoutsourcing," *Forbes*, May 10, 2004, pp. 50–51.

Case Discussion Questions

1. What are the advantages to Dell of having manufacturing sites located where they are? What are the potential disadvantages?

2. Why does Dell purchase most of the components that go into its PC from independent suppliers, as opposed to making more itself (Dell does little more than final assembly of components into PC)?

3. What are the consequences for Dell's cost structure and profitability of replacing inventories with information?

4. Do you think that Dell's model can be imitated by other PC manufacturers and manufacturers in other industries?

5. What factors might make it difficult for other PC companies firms to adopt Dell's model?

6. What is the source of Dell's competitive advantage? How secure is this advantage?

7. What are the potential risks associated with Dell's global supply chain strategy? How can these risks be mitigated?

Notes

1. B. C. Arntzen, G. G. Brown, T. P. Harrison, and L. L. Trafton, "Global Supply Chain Management at Digital Equipment Corporation," *Interfaces* 25 (1995), pp. 69–93, and Diana Farrell, "Beyond Offshoring," *Harvard Business Review*, December 2004, pp 1–8.

2. D. A. Garvin, "What Does Product Quality Really Mean," *Sloan Management Review* 26 (Fall 1984), pp. 25–44.

3. See the articles published in the special issue of the *Academy of Management Review on Total Quality Management* 19, no. 3 (1994). The following article provides a good overview of many of the issues involved from an academic perspective: J. W. Dean and D. E. Bowen, "Management Theory and Total Quality," *Academy of Management Review* 19 (1994), pp. 392–418. Also see T. C. Powell, "Total Quality Management as Competitive Advantage," *Strategic Management Journal* 16 (1995), pp. 15–37.

4. For general background information, see "How to Build Quality," *The Economist*, September 23, 1989, pp. 91–92; A. Gabor, *The Man Who Discovered Quality* (New York: Penguin, 1990); P. B. Crosby, *Quality Is Free* (New York: Mentor, 1980); and M. Elliot et al., "A Quality World, a Quality Life," *Industrial Engineer*, January 2003, pp. 26–33.

5. G. T. Lucier and S. Seshadri, "GE Takes Six Sigma beyond the Bottom line," *Strategic Finance*, May 2001, pp. 40–46.

6. M. Saunders, "U.S. Firms Doing Business in Europe Have Options in Registering for ISO 9000 Quality Standards," *Business America*, June 14, 1993, p. 7.

7. G. Stalk and T. M. Hout, *Competing against Time* (New York: Free Press, 1990).

8. Diana Farrell, "Beyond Offshoring," *Harvard Business Review*, December 2004, pp. 1–8, and M. A. Cohen and H. L. Lee, "Resource Deployment Analysis of Global Manufacturing and Distribution Networks," *Journal of Manufacturing and Operations Management* 2 (1989), pp. 81–104.

9. P. Krugman, "Increasing Returns and Economic Geography," *Journal of Political Economy* 99, no. 3 (1991), pp. 483–99, and J. M. Shaver and F. Flyer, "Agglomeration Economies, Firm Heterogeneity, and Foreign Direct Investment in the United States," *Strategic Management Journal* 21 (2000), pp. 1175–93.

10. For a review of the technical arguments, see D. A. Hay and D. J. Morris, *Industrial Economics: Theory and Evidence* (Oxford: Oxford University Press, 1979). See also C. W. L. Hill and G. R. Jones, *Strategic Management: An Integrated Approach* (Boston: Houghton Mifflin, 2004).

11. See P. Nemetz and L. Fry, "Flexible Manufacturing Organizations: Implications for Strategy Formulation," *Academy of Management Review* 13 (1988), pp. 627–38; N. Greenwood, *Implementing Flexible Manufacturing Systems* (New York: Halstead Press, 1986); J. P. Womack, D. T. Jones, and D. Roos, *The Machine That Changed the World* (New York: Rawson Associates, 1990); and R. Parthasarthy and S. P. Seith, "The Impact of Flexible Automation on Business Strategy and Organizational Structure," *Academy of Management Review* 17 (1992), pp. 86–111.

12. B. J. Pine, *Mass Customization: The New Frontier in Business Competition* (Boston: Harvard Business School Press, 1993); S. Kotha, "Mass Customization: Implementing the Emerging Paradigm for Competitive Advantage," *Strategic Management Journal* 16 (1995), pp. 21–42; and J. H. Gilmore and B. J. Pine II, "The Four Faces of Mass Customization," *Harvard Business Review*, January–February 1997, pp. 91–101.

13. M. A. Cusumano, *The Japanese Automobile Industry* (Cambridge, MA: Harvard University Press, 1989); T. Ohno, *Toyota Production System* (Cambridge, MA: Productivity Press, 1990); and Womack, Jones, and Roos, *The Machine That Changed the World*.

14. P. Waurzyniak, "Ford's Flexible Push," *Manufacturing Engineering*, September 2003, pp. 47–50.

15. K. Ferdows, "Making the Most of Foreign Factories," *Harvard Business Review*, March–April 1997, pp. 73–88.

16. This argument represents a simple extension of the dynamic capabilities research stream in the strategic management literature. See D. J. Teece, G. Pisano, and A. Shuen, "Dynamic Capabilities and Strategic Management," *Strategic Management Journal* 18 (1997), pp. 509–33.

17. T. S. Frost, J. M. Birkinshaw, and P. C. Ensign, "Centers of Excellence in Multinational Corporations," *Strategic Management Journal* 23 (November 2002), pp. 997–1018.

18. C. W. L. Hill, "Globalization, the Myth of the Nomadic Multinational Enterprise, and the Advantages of Location Persistence," Working Paper, School of Business, University of Washington, 2001.

19. J. Solomon and E. Cherney, "A Global Report: Outsourcing to India Sees a Twist," *The Wall Street Journal*, April 1, 2004, p. A2.

20. The material in this section is based primarily on the transaction cost literature of vertical integration; for example, O. E. Williamson, *The Economic Institutions of Capitalism* (New York: The Free Press, 1985).

21. For a review of the evidence, see Williamson, *The Economic Institutions of Capitalism*. See also L. Poppo and T. Zenger, "Testing Alternative Theories of the Firm: Transaction Cost, Knowledge Based, and Measurement Explanations for Make or Buy Decisions in Information Services," *Strategic Management Journal* 19 (1998), pp. 853–78.

22. A. D. Chandler, *The Visible Hand* (Cambridge, MA: Harvard University Press, 1977).

23. For a review of these arguments, see C. W. L. Hill and R. E. Hoskisson, "Strategy and Structure in the Multiproduct Firm," *Academy of Management Review* 12 (1987), pp. 331–41.

24. C. W. L. Hill, "Cooperation, Opportunism, and the Invisible Hand," *Academy of Management Review* 15 (1990), pp. 500–13.

25. See R. Narasimhan and J. R. Carter, "Organization, Communication and Coordination of International Sourcing," *International Marketing Review* 7 (1990), pp. 6–20, and Arntzen, Brown, Harrison, and Trafton, "Global Supply Chain Management at Digital Equipment Corporation."

26. H. F. Busch, "Integrated Materials Management," *IJPD & MM* 18 (1990), pp. 28–39.

27. T. Aeppel, "Manufacturers Cope with the Costs of Strained Global Supply Lines," *The Wall Street Journal*, December 8, 2004, p. A1.

Global Marketing and R&D

Notes

1. For evidence on the importance of marketing and R&D in the performance of a multinational firm, see M. Kotabe, Srini Srinivasan, and P. S. Aulakh, "Multinationality and Firm Performance: The Moderating Role of R&D and Marketing Capabilities," *Journal of International Business Studies* 33 no. 1 (2002), pp. 79–97.

2. See R. W. Ruekert and O. C. Walker, "Interactions between Marketing and R&D Departments in Implementing Different Business-Level Strategies," *Strategic Management Journal* 8 (1987), pp. 233–48, and K. B. Clark and S. C. Wheelwright, *Managing New Product and Process Development* (New York: Free Press, 1993).

3. T. Levitt, "The Globalization of Markets," *Harvard Business Review*, May–June 1983, pp. 92–102. Reprinted by permission of *Harvard Business Review*, an excerpt from "The Globalization of Markets," by Theodore Levitt, May–June 1983. Copyright © 1983 by the President and Fellows of Harvard College. All rights reserved.

4. For example, see S. P. Douglas and Y. Wind, "The Myth of Globalization," *Columbia Journal of World Business*, Winter 1987, pp. 19–29; C. A. Bartlett and S. Ghoshal, *Managing across Borders: The Transnational Solution* (Boston: Harvard Business School Press, 1989); V. J. Govindarajan and A. K. Gupta, *The Quest for Global Dominance* (San Francisco: Jossey Bass, 2001); and J. Quelch, "The Return of the Global Brand," *Harvard Business Review*, August 2003, pp. 1–3.

5. J. Tagliabue, "U.S. Brands Are Feeling Global Tension," *The New York Times*, March 15, 2003, p. C3.

6. D. B. Holt, J. A. Quelch, and E. L. Taylor, "How Global Brands Compete," *Harvard Business Review*, September 2004.

7. J. T. Landry, "Emerging Markets: Are Chinese Consumers Coming of Age?" *Harvard Business Review*, May–June 1998, pp. 17–20.

8. C. Miller, "Teens Seen as the First Truly Global Consumers," *Marketing News*, March 27, 1995, p. 9.

9. This approach was originally developed in K. Lancaster, "A New Approach to Demand Theory," *Journal of Political Economy* 74 (1965), pp. 132–57.

10. V. R. Alden, "Who Says You Can't Crack Japanese Markets?" *Harvard Business Review*, January–February 1987, pp. 52–56.

11. T. Parker-Pope, "Custom Made," *The Wall Street Journal*, September 26, 1996, p. 22.

12. "RCA's New Vista: The Bottom Line," *BusinessWeek*, July 4, 1987, p. 44.

13. N. Gross and K. Rebello, "Apple? Japan Can't Say No," *BusinessWeek*, June 29, 1992, pp. 32–33.

14. "After Early Stumbles P&G Is Making Inroads Overseas," *The Wall Street Journal*, February 6, 1989, p. B1.

15. C. Matlack and P. Gogoi, "What's This? The French Love McDonald's?" *BusinessWeek*, January 13, 2003, pp. 50–51.

16. Z. Gurhan-Cvanli and D. Maheswaran, "Cultural Variation in Country of Origin Effects," *Journal of Marketing Research*, August 2000, pp. 309–17.

17. See M. Laroche, V. H. Kirpalani, F. Pons, and L. Zhou, "A Model of Advertising Standardization in Multinational Corporations," *Journal of International Business Studies* 32 (2001), pp. 249–66, and D. A. Aaker and E. Joachimsthaler, "The Lure of Global Branding," *Harvard Business Review*, November–December 1999, pp. 137–44.

18. "Advertising in a Single Market," *The Economist*, March 24, 1990, p. 64.

19. D. Waller, "Charged Up over Competition Law," *Financial Times*, June 23, 1994, p. 14.

20. R. G. Matthews and D. Pringle, "Nokia Bets One Global Message Will Ring True in Many Markets," *The Wall Street Journal*, September 27, 2004, p. B6.

21. R. J. Dolan and H. Simon, *Power Pricing* (New York: Free Press, 1999).

22. B. Stottinger, "Strategic Export Pricing: A Long Winding Road," *Journal of International Marketing* 9 (2001), pp. 40–63, and S. Gil-Pareja, "Export Process Discrimination in Europe and Exchange Rates," *Review of International Economics*, May 2002, pp. 299–312.

23. These allegations were made on a PBS "Frontline" documentary telecast in the United States in May 1992.

24. Y. Tsurumi and H. Tsurumi, "Fujifilm-Kodak Dopoloistic competition in Japan and the United States," *Journal of International Business Studies* 30 (1999), pp. 813–30.

25. G. Smith and B. Wolverton, "A Dark Moment for Kodak," *BusinessWeek,* August 4, 1997, pp. 30–31.

26. R. Narisette and J. Friedland, "Disposable Income: Diaper Wars of P&G and Kimberly-Clark Now Heat Up in Brazil," *The Wall Street Journal,* June 4, 1997, p. A1.

27. J. F. Pickering, *Industrial Structure and Market Conduct* (London: Martin Robertson, 1974).

28. S. P. Douglas, C. Samuel Craig, and E. J. Nijissen, "Integrating Branding Strategy across Markets," *Journal of International Marketing* 9, no. 2 (2001), pp. 97–114.

29. The phrase was first used by economist Joseph Schumpeter in *Capitalism, Socialism, and Democracy* (New York: Harper Brothers, 1942).

30. S. Kotabe, S. Srinivasan, and P. S. Aulakh. "Multinationality and Firm Performance: The Moderating Role of R&D and Marketing," *Journal of International Business Studies* 33 (2002), pp. 79–97.

31. See D. C. Mowery and N. Rosenberg, *Technology and the Pursuit of Economic Growth* (Cambridge, UK: Cambridge University Press, 1989), and M. E. Porter, *The Competitive Advantage of Nations* (New York: The Free Press, 1990).

32. W. Kuemmerle, "Building Effective R&D Capabilities Abroad," *Harvard Business Review,* March–April 1997, pp. 61–70, and C. Le Bas and C. Sierra, "Location versus Home Country Advantages in R&D Activities," *Research Policy* 31 (2002), pp. 589–609.

33. "When the Corporate Lab Goes to Japan," *The New York Times,* April 28, 1991, sec. 3, p. 1.

34. D. Shapley, "Globalization Prompts Exodus," *Financial Times,* March 17, 1994, p. 10.

35. E. Mansfield. "How Economists See R&D," *Harvard Business Review,* November–December 1981, pp. 98–106.

36. Ibid.

37. G. A. Stevens and J. Burley, "Piloting the Rocket of Radical Innovation," *Research Technology Management* 46 (2003), pp. 16–26.

38. K. B. Clark and S. C. Wheelwright, *Managing New Product and Process Development* (New York: Free Press, 1993), and M. A. Shilling and C. W. L. Hill, "Managing the New Product Development Process," *Academy of Management Executive* 12, no. 3 (1998), pp. 67–81.

39. O. Port, "Moving Past the Assembly Line," *BusinessWeek Special Issue: Reinventing America,* 1992, pp. 177–80.

40. K. B. Clark and T. Fujimoto, "The Power of Product Integrity," *Harvard Business Review,* November–December 1990, pp. 107–18; Clark and Wheelwright, *Managing New Product and Process Development;* S. L. Brown and K. M. Eisenhardt, "Product Development: Past Research, Present Findings, and Future Directions," *Academy of Management Review* 20 (1995), pp. 348–78; and G. Stalk and T. M. Hout, *Competing against Time* (New York: Free Press, 1990).

41. Shilling and Hill, "Managing the New Product Development Process."

42. C. Christensen. "Quantum Corporation—Business and Product Teams," Harvard Business School Case No. 9-692-023.

43. R. Nobel and J. Birkinshaw, "Innovation in Multinational Corporations: Control and Communication Patterns in International R&D Operations," *Strategic Management Journal* 19 (1998), pp. 479–96.

44. Information comes from the company's Web site, and from K. Ferdows, "Making the Most of Foreign Factories," *Harvard Business Review,* March–April 1997, pp. 73–88.

Global Human Resource Management

18

XCO China

It had been a very bad morning for John Ross, the general manager of XCO's Chinese joint venture. He had just got off the phone with Phil Smith, his boss in St. Louis, who was demanding to know why the joint venture's return on investment was still in the low single digits four years after Ross had taken over the top post in the operation. "We had expected much better performance by now," said Smith, "particularly given your record of achievement; you need to fix this, Phil. Our patience is not infinite. You know the corporate goal is for a 20 percent return on investment for operating units, and your unit is not even close to that." Ross had a very bad feeling that Smith had just fired a warning shot across his bow. There was an implicit threat underlying Smith's demands for improved performance. For the first time in his 20-year career at XCO, Ross felt that his job was on the line.

XCO was a U.S.-based multinational electronics enterprise with sales of $2 billion and operations in more than 10 countries. XCO China specialized in the mass production of printed circuit boards for companies in the cell phone and computer industries. XCO China was a joint venture with Shanghai Electronic Corporation, a former state-owned enterprise that held 40 percent of the equity (XCO held the rest). While XCO held a majority of the equity, the company had to consult with its partner before making major investments or changing employment levels.

John Ross had been running XCO China for the past four years. He had arrived at XCO China after a very successful career at XCO, which included extended postings in Mexico and Hungary. When he took the China position, Ross thought that if he succeeded he would probably be in line for one of the top jobs at corporate headquarters within a few years. Ross had known that he was taking on a challenge with XCO China, but nothing prepared him for what he found there. The joint venture was a mess. Operations were horribly inefficient. Despite very low wage rates, productivity was being killed by poor product quality and lax inventory controls. The venture probably employed too many people, but XCO's Chinese partner seemed to view the venture as a job creation program, and repeatedly objected to any plans for cutting the workforce. To make matters worse, XCO China had failed to keep up with the latest developments in manufacturing technology, and it was falling behind competitors. Ross was determined to change this, but it had not been easy.

To improve operations, Ross had asked corporate HR for two specialists from the United States to work with the Chinese production employees. It had been a disaster. One had lasted just three months before requesting a transfer home for personal reasons. Apparently, his spouse hated China. The other had stayed for a year, but he had interacted so poorly with the local Chinese employees that he had to be sent back to the United States. Ross wished that XCO's corporate HR department had done a better job of selecting and then training these employees for a difficult foreign posting, but in retrospect he had to admit that he wasn't surprised at the lack of cultural training—after all, he had never been given any.

After this failure, Ross had taken a different tack. He had picked four of his best Chinese production employees and sent them to XCO's U.S. operations, along with a translator, for a two-month training program focusing on the latest production techniques. This had worked out much better. The Chinese had visited efficient XCO factories in the United States, Mexico, and Brazil and had seen what was possible. They had returned home fired up to improve operations at XCO China. Within a year they had introduced a Six Sigma quality control program and improved the flow of inventory through XCO's factory. Ross could now walk through the factory without being appalled by the sight of large quantities of inventory stacked on the floor or bins full of discarded circuit boards that had failed postassembly quality tests. Productivity had improved as a result, and after three tough years, XCO China had finally turned a profit.

Apparently this was not good enough for corporate headquarters. Ross knew that improving performance further would be tough. The market in China had become very competitive. XCO was vying with many other enterprises to produce printed circuit boards for large multinational customers that had assembly operations in China. The customers were constantly demanding lower prices, and it seemed to Ross that prices were falling almost as fast as XCO's costs. Also, Ross was limited in his ability to cut the workforce by the demands of his Chinese joint-venture partner. Ross had tried to explain all of this to Phil Smith, but Smith didn't seem to get it. "The man is just a number cruncher," thought Ross, "he has no sense of the market in China. He has no idea how hard it is to do business here. I have worked damn hard to turn this operation around, and I am getting no credit for it, none at all."

Source: This is a disguised case based on interviews undertaken by Charles Hill.

Introduction

This chapter continues our survey of specific functions within an international business, by looking at international human resource management (HRM). **Human resource management** refers to the activities an organization carries out to use its human resources effectively.[1] These activities include determining the firm's human resource strategy, staffing, performance evaluation, management development, compensation, and labor relations. None of these activities is performed in a vacuum; all are related to the strategy of the firm. As we will see, HRM has an important strategic component.[2] Through its influence on the character, development, quality, and productivity of the firm's human resources, the HRM function can help the firm achieve its primary strategic goals of reducing the costs of value creation and adding value by better serving customer needs.

The strategic role of HRM is complex enough in a domestic firm, but it is more complex in an international business, where staffing, management development, performance evaluation, and compensation activities are complicated by profound differences in labor markets, culture, legal systems, economic systems, and the like (see Chapters 2 and 3). For example,

- Compensation practices may vary from country to country depending on prevailing management customs.
- Labor laws may prohibit union organization in one country and mandate it in another.
- Equal employment legislation may be strongly pursued in one country and not in another.

If it is to build a cadre of managers capable of leading a multinational enterprise, the HRM function must deal with a host of issues. It must decide how to staff key management posts in the company, how to develop managers so that they are familiar with the nuances of doing business in different countries, how to compensate people in different nations, and how to evaluate the performance of managers based in different countries. HRM must also deal with a host of issues related to expatriate managers. (An **expatriate manager** is a citizen of one country who is working abroad in one of the firm's subsidiaries.) It must decide when to use expatriates, whom to send on expatriate postings, be clear about why they are doing it, compensate expatriates appropriately, and make sure that they are adequately debriefed and reoriented once they return home.

The opening case described what can happen when the HRM function does not perform as well as it might. XCO sent two expatriates to XCO China to help the beleaguered boss of that unit, John Ross, but neither expatriate was successful. Apparently the HR department had picked two employees who were well qualified from a technical perspective, but were not suited to a difficult foreign posting. This is not unusual. As we shall see, a large number of expatriates return home before their tour of duty is completed, often because while they have the technical skills to perform the required job, they lack the skills required to manage in a different cultural context, or because their spouses do not like the posting. To his credit, Ross came up with a solution to the problem—send Chinese employees to the United States and get them trained in the latest manufacturing techniques. The XCO case also illustrates another problem in international HRM—how to evaluate the performance of expatriate managers who are operating in very different circumstances from those found in the home country. It is apparent from the case that John Ross was being evaluated on the basis of the performance of his unit against corporatewide profitability criteria, but these criteria failed to account for the difficult conditions Ross inherited and the problems inherent in doing business in the Chinese market. The most skilled multinationals have found ways of dealing with this problem and adjust performance appraisal criteria to consider differences in context. XCO apparently did not do this.

In this chapter, we will look closely at the role of HRM in an international business. We begin by briefly discussing the strategic role of HRM. Then we turn our attention to four major tasks of the HRM function: staffing policy, management training and development, performance appraisal, and compensation policy. We will point out the strategic implications of each of these tasks. The chapter closes with a look at international labor relations and the relationship between the firm's management of labor relations and its overall strategy.

The Strategic Role of International HRM

A large and expanding body of academic research suggests a strong fit between human resources practices and strategy is required for high profitability.[3] You will recall from Chapters 12 and 13 that superior performance requires not only the right strategy, but also that strategy is supported by the right organization architecture. Strategy is implemented through the organization architecture. As shown in Figure 18.1 (which is based on Figure 13.1), people are the linchpin of a firm's organization architecture. For a firm to outperform its rivals in the global marketplace, it must have the right people in the right postings. Those people must be trained appropriately so that they have the skill sets required to perform their jobs effectively, and so that they behave in a manner that is congruent with the desired culture of the firm. Their compensation packages must create incentives for them to take actions that are consistent with the strategy of the firm, and the performance appraisal system the firm uses must measure the behavior that the firm wants to encourage.

As indicated in Figure 18.1, the human resource function, through its staffing, training, compensation, and performance appraisal activities, has a critical impact upon the people, culture, incentive, and control system elements of the firm's organization architecture (performance appraisal systems are part of the control systems in an enterprise). Thus, human resource professionals have a critically important strategic role. It is incumbent upon them to shape these elements of a firm's organization architecture in a manner that is consistent with the strategy of the enterprise, so that the firm can effectively implement its strategy.

In short, superior human resources can be a sustained source of high productivity and competitive advantage in the global economy. At the same time, research suggests that many international businesses have room for improving the effectiveness of their human resource function. In one study of competitiveness among 326 large multinationals, the authors found that human resources was one of the weakest capabilities in most firms, suggesting that improving the effectiveness of international human resource practices might have substantial performance benefits.[4]

In Chapter 12, we examined four strategies pursued by international businesses—a localization strategy, international strategy, global standardization strategy, and transnational strategy. Firms that emphasize localization try to create value by emphasizing local responsiveness; international firms, by transferring products and competencies overseas; global firms, by realizing experience curve and location economies; and transnational firms, by doing all these things simultaneously. In this chapter we will see that success also requires HRM policies to be congruent with the firm's strategy. For example, a transnational strategy imposes different requirements for staffing, management development, and compensation practices than a localization strategy. Firms pursuing a transnational strategy need to build a strong corporate culture and an informal management network for transmitting information and knowledge within the organization. Through its employee selection, management development, performance appraisal, and compensation policies, the HRM function can help develop these things. Thus, as we have noted, HRM has a critical role to play in implementing strategy. In each section that follows, we will review the strategic role of HRM in some detail.

FIGURE 18.1

The Role of Human
Resources in Shaping
Organization
Architecture

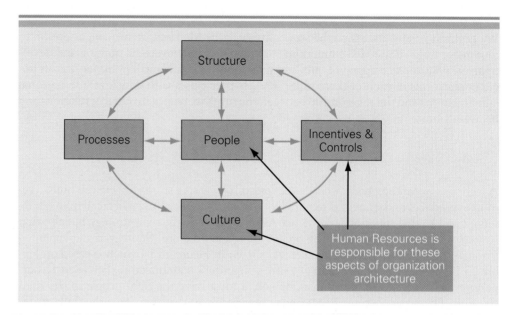

Staffing Policy

Staffing policy is concerned with the selection of employees for particular jobs. At one level, this involves selecting individuals who have the skills required to do particular jobs. At another level, staffing policy can be a tool for developing and promoting the desired corporate culture of the firm.[5] By **corporate culture,** we mean the organization's norms and value systems. A strong corporate culture can help a firm to implement its strategy. General Electric, for example, is not just concerned with hiring people who have the skills required for performing particular jobs; it wants to hire individuals whose behavioral styles, beliefs, and value systems are consistent with those of GE. This is true whether an American is being hired, an Italian, a German, or an Australian and whether the hiring is for a U.S. operation or a foreign operation. The belief is that if employees are predisposed toward the organization's norms and value systems by their personality type, the firm will be able to attain higher performance.

TYPES OF STAFFING POLICY

Research has identified three types of staffing policies in international businesses: the ethnocentric approach, the polycentric approach, and the geocentric approach.[6] We will review each policy and link it to the strategy pursued by the firm. The most attractive staffing policy is probably the geocentric approach, although there are several impediments to adopting it.

The Ethnocentric Approach

An **ethnocentric staffing** policy is one in which all key management positions are filled by parent-country nationals. This practice was very widespread at one time. Firms such as Procter & Gamble, Philips NV, and Matsushita originally followed it. In the Dutch firm Philips, for example, all important positions in most foreign subsidiaries were at one time held by Dutch nationals who were referred to by their non-Dutch colleagues as the Dutch Mafia. In many Japanese and South Korean firms, such as Toyota, Matsushita, and Samsung, key positions in international operations have often been held by home-country nationals. According to the Japanese Overseas Enterprise Association, in 1996 only 29 percent of foreign subsidiaries of Japanese companies had presidents who were not Japanese. In contrast, 66 percent of the Japanese subsidiaries of foreign companies had Japanese presidents.[7]

Firms pursue an ethnocentric staffing policy for three reasons. First, the firm may believe the host country lacks qualified individuals to fill senior management positions. This argument is heard most often when the firm has operations in less developed countries. Second, the firm may see an ethnocentric staffing policy as the best way to maintain a unified corporate culture. Many Japanese firms, for example, prefer their foreign operations to be headed by expatriate Japanese managers because these managers have been socialized into the firm's culture while employed in Japan.[8] Procter & Gamble until recently preferred to staff important management positions in its foreign subsidiaries with U.S. nationals who had been socialized into P&G's corporate culture by years of employment in its U.S. operations. Such reasoning tends to predominate when a firm places a high value on its corporate culture.

Third, if the firm is trying to create value by transferring core competencies to a foreign operation, as firms pursuing an international strategy are, it may believe that the best way to do this is to transfer parent-country nationals who have knowledge of that competency to the foreign operation. Imagine what might occur if a firm tried to transfer a core competency in marketing to a foreign subsidiary without supporting the transfer with a corresponding transfer of home-country marketing management personnel. The transfer would probably fail to produce the anticipated benefits because the knowledge underlying a core competency cannot easily be articulated and written down. Such knowledge often has a significant tacit dimension; it is acquired through experience. Just like the great tennis player who cannot instruct others how to become great tennis players simply by writing a handbook, the firm that has a core competency in marketing—or anything else—cannot just write a handbook that tells a foreign subsidiary how to build the firm's core competency anew in a foreign setting. It must also transfer management personnel to the foreign operation to show foreign managers how to become good marketers, for example. The need to transfer managers overseas arises because the knowledge that underlies the firm's core competency resides in the heads of its domestic managers and was acquired through years of experience, not by reading a handbook. Thus, if a firm is to transfer a core competency to a foreign subsidiary, it must also transfer the appropriate managers.

Despite this rationale for pursuing an ethnocentric staffing policy, the policy is now on the wane in most international businesses for two reasons. First, an ethnocentric staffing policy limits advancement opportunities for host-country nationals. This can lead to resentment, lower productivity, and increased turnover among that group. Resentment can be greater still if, as often occurs, expatriate managers are paid significantly more than host-country nationals.

Second, an ethnocentric policy can lead to "cultural myopia," the firm's failure to understand host-country cultural differences that require different approaches to marketing and management. The adaptation of expatriate managers can take a long time, during which they may make major mistakes. For example, expatriate managers may fail to appreciate how product attributes, distribution strategy, communications strategy, and pricing strategy should be adapted to host-country conditions. The result may be costly blunders. They may also make decisions that are ethically suspect simply because they do not understand the culture in which they are managing.[9] In one highly publicized case in the United States, Mitsubishi Motors was sued by the federal Equal Employment Opportunity Commission for tolerating extensive and systematic sexual harassment in a plant in Illinois. The plant's top management, all Japanese expatriates, denied the charges. The Japanese managers may have failed to realize that behavior that would be viewed as acceptable in Japan was not acceptable in the United States.[10]

The Polycentric Approach

A **polycentric staffing** policy recruits host-country nationals to manage subsidiaries while parent-country nationals occupy key positions at corporate headquarters. In many respects, a polycentric approach is a response to the shortcomings of an ethnocentric approach. One advantage of adopting a polycentric approach is that the firm is

MANAGEMENT FOCUS In 1999, two major drug firms, Zeneca and Astra, merged to form AstraZeneca. Based in the United Kingdom, in 2000 AstraZeneca had a profit of $865 million under U.S. accounting rules, but $3,318 million under British accounting rules. The largest difference between the two sets of accounts was $1,756 million, which related to amortization and other acquisition-related costs. Under rules then prevailing in the United States, the combination of Astra and Zeneca was treated as an acquisition, which required goodwill to be recognized with consequent amortization. Under British rules, any amortization was avoided as the combination was treated as a merger and so no goodwill arose.

U.S.-based SmithKline Beckman (SKB) merged with the British company Beecham Group in 1989. After the merger, SKB had quotations on both the London and New York stock exchanges, so it had to prepare financial reports in accordance with both U.S. and British standards. SKB's postmerger earnings, properly prepared in accordance with British accounting standards, were £130 million—quite a bit more than the £87 million reported in SKB's statement prepared in accordance with U.S. accounting standards. The difference resulted primarily from treating the merger as a pooling of assets for British purposes and as a purchase of assets for U.S. purposes. Even more confusing, the differences resulted in a shareholders' equity of £3.5 billion in the United States, but a negative £300 million in Great Britain! After these figures were released, SKB's stock was trading 17 percent lower on the London Stock Exchange than on the New York Stock Exchange.

In the mid-1980s, Telefonica, Spain's largest industrial company, was the first company in the world to float a multicountry stock offering simultaneously. In 1990, it reported net income under U.S. accounting standards of 176 billion pesetas, more than twice the 76 billion pesetas it reported under Spanish accounting standards. The difference was mainly due to an "add-back" of the incremental depreciation on assets carried at historic cost in the United States but reflecting more recent market value in the Spanish report. The effect of this difference on shareholders' equity was in the opposite direction; the equity reported in the U.S. accounts was 15 percent less than the equity reported in the Spanish accounts.

In 2000, British Airways reported a loss of £21 million under British accounting rules, but under U.S. rules, its loss was £412 million. Most of the difference could be attributed to adjustments for a number of relatively small items such as depreciation and amortization, pensions, and deferred taxation. The largest adjustment was due to a reduction in revenue reported in the U.S. accounts of £136 million. This reduced revenue was related to frequent flier miles, which under U.S. rules have to be deferred until the miles are redeemed. Apparently, this is not the case under British rules.

A final example is more hypothetical in nature, but just as revealing. Two college professors set up a computer model to evaluate the reported net profits of an imaginary company with gross operating profits of $1.5 million. This imaginary company operated in three different countries—the United States, Britain, and Australia. The professors found that holding all else equal (such as national differences in interest rates on the firm's debt), when different accounting standards were applied the firm made a net profit of $34,600 in the United States, $260,600 in Britain, and $240,600 in Australia.

Sources: S. F. O'Malley, "Accounting across Borders," *Financial Executive*, March–April 1992, pp. 28–31; L. Berton, "All Accountants May Soon Speak the Same Language," *The Wall Street Journal*, August 29, 1995, p. A15; and "GAAP Reconciliations," *Company Reporting*, July 2001, pp. 3–6.

www.mhhe.com/hill

a large number of Japanese investors might wish to issue reports that serve the needs of those investors. However, the lack of comparability between accounting standards in different nations can lead to confusion. For example, the German firm that issues two sets of financial reports, one set prepared under German standards and the other under U.S. standards, may find that its financial position looks significantly different in the two reports, and its investors may have difficulty identifying the firm's true worth. Some examples of the confusion that can arise from this lack of comparability appear in the accompanying Management Focus.

In addition to the problems this lack of comparability gives investors, it can give the firm major headaches. The firm has to explain to its investors why its financial position looks so different in the two accountings. Also, an international business may find it difficult to assess the financial positions of important foreign customers, suppliers, and competitors.

INTERNATIONAL STANDARDS

Substantial efforts have been made in recent years to harmonize accounting standards across countries.[12] The rise of global capital markets during the last two decades has added some urgency to this endeavor. Today, many companies raise money from providers of capital outside their national borders. Those providers are demanding consistency in the way in which financial results are reported, so that they can make more informed investment decisions. Also, adoption of common accounting standards will facilitate the development of global capital markets, since more investors will be willing to invest across borders, and the end result will be to lower the cost of capital and stimulate economic growth. Thus, it is increasingly accepted that the standardization of accounting practices across national borders is in the best interests of all participants in the world economy.

The **International Accounting Standards Board (IASB)** has emerged as a major proponent of standardization. The IASB was formed in March 2001 to replace the International Accounting Standards Committee (IASC), which had been established in 1973. The IASB has 14 members responsible for the formulation of new international financial reporting standards. By 2005, the IASB and its predecessor, the IASC, had issued 41 international accounting standards.[13] To issue a new standard, 75 percent of the 14 members of the board must agree. It can be difficult to get three-quarters agreement, particularly since members come from different cultures and legal systems. To get around this problem, most IASB statements provide two acceptable alternatives. As Arthur Wyatt, former chairman of the IASB, once said, "It's not much of a standard if you have two alternatives, but it's better than having six. If you can get agreement on two alternatives, you can capture the 11 required votes and eliminate some of the less used practices."[14]

Another hindrance to the development of international accounting standards is that compliance is voluntary; the IASB has no power to enforce its standards. Despite this, support for the IASB and recognition of its standards has been growing. Increasingly, the IASB is regarded as an effective voice for defining acceptable worldwide accounting principles. Japan, for example, began requiring financial statements to be prepared on a consolidated basis after the IASB issued its initial standards on the topic, and in 2004 Japanese accounting authorities started working closely with the IASB to try to harmonize standards. Russia and China have also stated their intention to adopt emerging international standards.

The impact of the IASB standards has probably been least noticeable in the United States because most of the standards issued by the IASB have been consistent with opinions already articulated by the U.S. **Financial Accounting Standards Board (FASB).** The FASB writes the generally accepted accounting principles (GAAP) by which the financial statements of U.S. firms must be prepared. In sharp contrast, some IASB standards have had a significant impact in many other countries because they eliminated a commonly used alternative.

Another body that is having a substantial influence on the harmonization of accounting standards is the European Union (EU). In accordance with its plans for closer economic and political union, the EU is mandating harmonization of the accounting principles of its 25 member countries. The EU does this by issuing directives that the member states are obligated to incorporate into their own national laws. Because EU directives have the power of law, we might assume the EU has a better chance of achieving harmonization than the IASB does. As noted in the opening case, the EU has required that starting January 1, 2005, financial accounts issued by some

MANAGEMENT FOCUS Switzerland does not have a history of very detailed accounting rules. As a result, published financial statements by major Swiss firms such as Novartis, Roche Group, and Nestlé often obscured as much as they revealed. The standard set of accounts from a Swiss firm was viewed as being very unusual and difficult for international investors to understand and was described as being more like a statistical summary than the result of an integrated accounting system.

Swiss firms began to move toward adoption of IASC accounting principles in the 1990s. The catalyst was increasing interest by foreign investors in the stock of major Swiss corporations. By the early 1990s, up to 40 percent of the stock of many of these firms was owned by foreign investors. As a group these investors were demanding more detailed financial statements that were comparable to those issued by other multinational enterprises.

One of the first firms to respond to these pressures was Ciba, Switzerland's largest pharmaceuticals and chemicals firm and a major multinational enterprise with operations around the globe (Ciba subsequently became Novartis after it merged with another Swiss pharmaceutical company, Sandoz, in 1998). In 1993, the company announced that its 1994 financial statements would be in accordance with IASC guidelines. At the same time, it restated its 1992 results in line with IASC guidelines. The effect was to increase post-tax profits by 18 percent while raising inventories, cash, and marketable securities. Ciba's decision was motivated by a desire to appease foreign stockholders, who in 1994 held over one-third of Ciba's stock, and to position itself for the possibility of listings on the London and New York stock exchanges.

Ciba also decided to use the same international standards for internal financial reporting. Ciba set up a small international team to develop and implement its new system. While there were some preliminary problems in development of the system, including a figure on the insurance value of fixed assets that was off by $690 million, the new system is now running smoothly and seems to have produced several major benefits.

Ciba discovered large savings as a result of the change, including tighter cash management, more efficient capital investment, a different approach to acquisitions, and more rigid asset management, which has reportedly reduced the value of inventories by 6 percent. The new system also enabled the company to benchmark its performance for the first time against its global competitors.

One big difference between the new and old systems was the move from the arguably more informative current cost accounting method, which Ciba used for more than 25 years and which regularly updates asset values to account for inflation, to historic cost accounting under international standards. However, management admits this drawback is not serious given the low inflation rate in Switzerland and given the offsetting gains produced by the switch to a new system.

In 2000, Novartis decided that it needed to become more aggressive about attracting U.S. investors. Although Novartis already listed its shares as American Depositary Receipts (ADRs) on the American Stock Exchange, it decided to switch the listing to the more visible New York Stock Exchange and to double the amount of ADRs offered. Accompanying this shift, Novartis also decided that in addition to presenting its rules based on IASC principles, it needed to adopt full U.S. accounting principles. Novartis published its first complete set of U.S. accounts in 2002.

Sources: A. Jack, "Swiss Group Moves from Night to Day," *Financial Times*, March 30, 1994, p. 22; L. Berton, "All Accountants May Soon Speak the Same Language," *The Wall Street Journal*, August 29, 1995, p. A15; and A. Beard, "Novartis Steps Up the Pace of Its U.S. Charm Offensive," *Financial Times*, May 14, 2001, p. 23.

7,000 publicly listed companies in the EU must be in accordance with IASB standards. The Europeans hope that this requirement, by making it easier to compare the financial position of companies from different EU member states, will facilitate the development of a pan-European capital market and ultimately lower the cost of capital for EU firms. Following the lead set by the EU, some 65 other countries have signaled that they too will either require or allow companies to issue accounts based on IASB standards.

Assuming that the EU is successful in achieving harmonization according to IASB standards, and that countries such as Australia, Japan, China, and Russia will follow suite as they have signaled, there soon could be only two major accounting bodies with dominant influence on global reporting: FASB in the United States and IASB elsewhere. Under an agreement reached in 2002, these two bodies will increasingly work together to align their standards, suggesting that differences in accounting standards across countries may well disappear.

In a move that indicates the trend toward adoption of acceptable international accounting standards is accelerating, the IASB has developed accounting standards for firms seeking stock listings in global markets. Also, the FASB has joined forces with accounting standard setters in Canada, Mexico, and Chile to explore areas in which the four countries can harmonize their accounting standards (Canada, Mexico, and the United States are members of NAFTA, and Chile may join in the near future). The Securities and Exchange Commission has also dropped some of its objections to international standards, which could accelerate their adoption. In 1994, the SEC started accepting three international accounting standards on cash flow data, the effects of hyperinflation, and business combinations for cross-border filings.[15] A taste of what is to come if increasing numbers of international firms jump on the bandwagon and adopt IASB principles can be found in the accompanying Management Focus, which details the impact of adopting these standards on Novartis, the Swiss pharmaceuticals and chemicals group.

Multinational Consolidation and Currency Translation

A consolidated financial statement combines the separate financial statements of two or more companies to yield a single set of financial statements as if the individual companies were really one. Most multinational firms are composed of a parent company and a number of subsidiary companies located in various countries. Such firms typically issue consolidated financial statements, which merge the accounts of all the companies, rather than issuing individual financial statements for the parent company and each subsidiary. In this section we examine the consolidated financial statements and then look at the related issue of foreign currency translation.

CONSOLIDATED FINANCIAL STATEMENTS

Many firms find it advantageous to organize as a set of separate legal entities (companies). For example, a firm may separately incorporate the various components of its business to limit its total legal liability or to take advantage of corporate tax regulations. Multinationals are often required by the countries in which they do business to set up a separate company. Thus, the typical multinational consists of a parent company and a number of subsidiary companies located in different countries, most of which are wholly owned by the parent. However, although the subsidiaries may be separate legal entities, they are not separate economic entities. Economically, all the companies in a corporate group are interdependent. For example, if the Brazilian subsidiary of a U.S. parent company experiences substantial financial losses that suck up corporate funds, the cash available for investment in that subsidiary, the U.S. parent company, and other subsidiary companies will be limited. Thus, the purpose of consolidated financial statements is to provide accounting information about a group of companies that recognize their economic interdependence.

Transactions among the members of a corporate family are not included in consolidated financial statements; only assets, liabilities, revenues, and expenses with external third parties are shown. By law, however, separate legal entities are required to keep their own accounting records and to prepare their own financial statements. Thus, transactions with other members of a corporate group must be identified in the separate statements so they can be excluded when the consolidated statements are prepared. The process involves adding up the individual assets, liabilities, revenues, and expenses reported on the separate financial statements and then eliminating the intragroup ones. For example, consider these items selected from the individual financial statements of a parent company and one of its foreign subsidiaries:

	Parent	Foreign Subsidiary
Cash	$1,000	$250
Receivables	3,000*	900
Payables	300	500*
Revenues	7,000†	5,000
Expenses	2,000	3,000†

*Subsidiary owes parent $300.
†Subsidiary pays parent $1,000 in royalties for products licensed from parent.

The $300 receivable that the parent includes on its financial statements and the $300 payable that the subsidiary includes on its statements represent an intragroup item. These items cancel each other out and thus are not included in consolidated financial statements. Similarly, the $1,000 the subsidiary owes the parent in royalty payments is an intragroup item that will not appear in the consolidated accounts. The adjustments are as follows:

			Eliminations		
	Parent	Subsidiary	Debit	Credit	Consolidated
Cash	$1,000	$250			$1,250
Receivables	3,000*	900		$ 300	3,600
Payables	300	500*	$ 300		500
Revenues	7,000†	5,000		1,000	11,000
Expenses	2,000	3,000†	1,000		4,000

*Subsidiary owes parent $300.
†Subsidiary pays parent $1,000 in royalties for products licensed from parent.

Thus, while simply adding the two sets of accounts would suggest that the group of companies has revenues of $12,000 and receivables of $3,900, once intragroup transactions are removed from the picture, these figures drop to $11,000 and $3,600, respectively.

Preparing consolidated financial statements is becoming the norm for multinational firms. Investors realize that without consolidated financial statements, a multinational firm could conceal losses in an unconsolidated subsidiary, thereby hiding the economic status of the entire group. For example, the parent company in our illustration could increase its profit merely by charging the subsidiary company higher royalty fees. Since this has no effect on the group's overall profits, it amounts to little more than window dressing, making the parent company look good. If the parent does not issue a consolidated financial statement, however, the true economic status of the group is obscured by such a practice. With this in mind, the IASB has issued two standards requiring firms to prepare consolidated financial statements, and in most industrialized countries this is now required.

CURRENCY TRANSLATION

Foreign subsidiaries of multinational firms normally keep their accounting records and prepare their financial statements in the currency of the country in which they are located. Thus, the Japanese subsidiary of a U.S. firm will prepare its accounts in yen, a Brazilian subsidiary in real, a Korean subsidiary in won, and so on. When a multinational prepares consolidated accounts, it must convert all these financial statements into the currency of its home country. As we saw in Chapter 10, however, exchange rates vary in response to changes in economic circumstances. Companies can use two main methods to determine what exchange rate should be used when translating financial statement currencies—the current rate method and the temporal method.

The Current Rate Method

Under the **current rate method,** the exchange rate at the balance sheet date is used to translate the financial statements of a foreign subsidiary into the home currency of the multinational firm. Although this may seem logical, it is incompatible with the historic cost principle, which, as we saw earlier, is a generally accepted accounting principle in many countries, including the United States. Consider the case of a U.S. firm that invests $100,000 in a Malaysian subsidiary. Assume the exchange rate at the time is $1 = 5 Malaysian ringgit. The subsidiary converts the $100,000 into ringgit, which gives it 500,000 ringgit. It then purchases land with this money. Subsequently, the dollar depreciates against the ringgit, so that by year-end, $1 = 4 ringgit. If this exchange rate is used to convert the value of the land back into U.S. dollars for preparing consolidated accounts, the land will be valued at $125,000. The piece of land would appear to have increased in value by $25,000, although in reality the increase would be simply a function of an exchange rate change. Thus, the consolidated accounts would present a somewhat misleading picture.

The Temporal Method

One way to avoid this problem is to use the temporal method to translate the accounts of a foreign subsidiary. The **temporal method** translates assets valued in a foreign currency into the home-country currency using the exchange rate that exists when the assets are purchased. Referring to our example, the exchange rate of $1 = 5 ringgit, the rate on the day the Malaysian subsidiary purchased the land, would be used to convert the value of the land back into U.S. dollars at year-end. However, although the temporal method will ensure the dollar value of the land does not fluctuate due to exchange rate changes, it has its own serious problem. Because the various assets of a foreign subsidiary will in all probability be acquired at different times and because exchange rates seldom remain stable for long, different exchange rates will probably have to be used to translate those foreign assets into the multinational's home currency. Consequently, the multinational's balance sheet may not balance!

Consider the case of a U.S. firm that on January 1, 2005, invests $100,000 in a new Japanese subsidiary. The exchange rate at that time is $1 = ¥100. The initial investment is therefore ¥10 million, and the Japanese subsidiary's balance sheet looks like this on January 1, 2004:

	Yen	Exchange Rate	U.S. Dollars
Cash	10,000,000	($1 = ¥100)	100,000
Owners' equity	10,000,000	($1 = ¥100)	100,000

Assume that on January 31, when the exchange rate is $1 = ¥95, the Japanese subsidiary invests ¥5 million in a factory (i.e., fixed assets). Then on February 15, when the exchange rate is $1 = ¥90, the subsidiary purchases ¥5 million of inventory. The balance sheet of the subsidiary will look like this on March 1, 2004:

	Yen	Exchange Rate	U.S. Dollars
Fixed assets	5,000,000	($1 = ¥95)	52,632
Inventory	5,000,000	($1 = ¥90)	55,556
Total	10,000,000		108,188
Owners' equity	10,000,000	($1 = ¥100)	100,000

Although the balance sheet balances in yen, it does not balance when the temporal method is used to translate the yen-denominated balance sheet figures back into dollars. In translation, the balance sheet debits exceed the credits by $8,188. The accounting profession has yet to adopt a satisfactory solution to the gap between debits and credits. The practice currently used in the United States is explained next.

CURRENT U.S. PRACTICE

U.S.-based multinational firms must follow the requirements of Statement 52, "Foreign Currency Translation," issued by the Financial Accounting Standards Board in 1981.[16] Under Statement 52, a foreign subsidiary is classified either as a self-sustaining, autonomous subsidiary or as integral to the activities of the parent company.[17] (A link can be made here with the material on strategy discussed in Chapter 12. Firms pursuing localization and international strategies are most likely to have self-sustaining subsidiaries, whereas firms pursuing global and transnational strategies are most likely to have integral subsidiaries.) According to Statement 52, the local currency of a self-sustaining foreign subsidiary is to be its functional currency. The balance sheet for such subsidiaries is translated into the home currency using the exchange rate in effect at the end of the firm's financial year, whereas the income statement is translated using the average exchange rate for the firm's financial year. But the functional currency of an integral subsidiary is to be U.S. dollars. The financial statements of such subsidiaries are translated at various historic rates using the temporal method (as we did in the example), and the dangling debit or credit increases or decreases consolidated earnings for the period.

⊕ Accounting Aspects of Control Systems

Corporate headquarters' role is to control subunits within the organization to ensure they achieve the best possible performance. In the typical firm, the control process is annual and involves three main steps:

1. Head office and subunit management jointly determine subunit goals for the coming year.
2. Throughout the year, the head office monitors subunit performance against the agreed goals.
3. If a subunit fails to achieve its goals, the head office intervenes in the subunit to learn why the shortfall occurred, taking corrective action when appropriate.

The accounting function plays a critical role in this process. Most of the goals for subunits are expressed in financial terms and are embodied in the subunit's budget for the coming year. The budget is the main instrument of financial control. The budget is typically prepared by the subunit, but it must be approved by headquarters management.

During the approval process, headquarters and subunit managements debate the goals that should be incorporated in the budget. One function of headquarters management is to ensure a subunit's budget contains challenging but realistic performance goals. Once a budget is agreed to, accounting information systems are used to collect data throughout the year so a subunit's performance can be evaluated against the goals contained in its budget.

In most international businesses, many of the firm's subunits are foreign subsidiaries. The performance goals for the coming year are thus set by negotiation between corporate management and the managers of foreign subsidiaries. According to one survey of control practices within multinational enterprises, the most important criterion for evaluating the performance of a foreign subsidiary is the subsidiary's actual profits compared to budgeted profits.[18] This is closely followed by a subsidiary's actual sales compared to budgeted sales and its return on investment. The same criteria were also useful in evaluating the performance of the subsidiary managers. We will discuss this point later in this section. First, however, we will examine two factors that can complicate the control process in an international business: exchange rate changes and transfer pricing practices.

EXCHANGE RATE CHANGES AND CONTROL SYSTEMS

Most international businesses require all budgets and performance data within the firm to be expressed in the "corporate currency," which is normally the home currency. Thus, the Malaysian subsidiary of a U.S. multinational would probably submit a budget prepared in U.S. dollars, rather than Malaysian ringgit, and performance data throughout the year would be reported to headquarters in U.S. dollars. This facilitates comparisons between subsidiaries in different countries, and it makes things easier for headquarters management. However, it also allows exchange rate changes during the year to introduce substantial distortions. For example, the Malaysian subsidiary may fail to achieve profit goals not because of any performance problems, but merely because of a decline in the value of the ringgit against the dollar. The opposite can occur, also, making a foreign subsidiary's performance look better than it actually is.

The Lessard-Lorange Model

According to research by Donald Lessard and Peter Lorange, a number of methods are available to international businesses for dealing with this problem.[19] Lessard and Lorange point out three exchange rates that can be used to translate foreign currencies into the corporate currency in setting budgets and in the subsequent tracking of performance:

- The **initial rate,** the spot exchange rate when the budget is adopted.
- The **projected rate,** the spot exchange rate forecast for the end of the budget period (i.e., the forward rate).
- The **ending rate,** the spot exchange rate when the budget and performance are being compared.

These three exchange rates imply nine possible combinations (see Figure 19.3). Lessard and Lorange ruled out four of the nine combinations as illogical and unreasonable; they are lighter-colored in Figure 19.3. For example, it would make no sense to use the ending rate to translate the budget and the initial rate to translate actual performance data. Any of the remaining five combinations might be used for setting budgets and evaluating performance.

With three of these five combinations—II, PP, and EE—the same exchange rate is used for translating both budget figures and performance figures into the corporate currency. All three combinations have the advantage that a change in the exchange rate during the year does not distort the control process. This is not true for the other

	Rate Used to Translate Actual Performance for Comparison with Budget		
	Initial (I)	Projected (P)	Ending (E)
Rate Used for Translating Budget — Initial (I)	(II) Budget at Initial Actual at Initial	Budget at Initial Actual at Projected	(IE) Budget at Initial Actual at Ending
Projected (P)	Budget at Projected Actual at Initial	(PP) Budget at Projected Actual at Projected	(PE) Budget at Projected Actual at Ending
Ending (E)	Budget at Ending Actual at Initial	Budget at Ending Actual at Projected	(EE) Budget at Ending Actual at Ending

two combinations, IE and PE. In those cases, exchange rate changes can introduce distortions. The potential for distortion is greater with IE; the ending spot exchange rate used to evaluate performance against the budget may be quite different from the initial spot exchange rate used to translate the budget. The distortion is less serious in the case of PE because the projected exchange rate takes into account future exchange rate movements.

Of the five combinations, Lessard and Lorange recommend that firms use the projected spot exchange rate to translate both the budget and performance figures into the corporate currency, combination PP. The projected rate in such cases will typically be the forward exchange rate as determined by the foreign exchange market (see Chapter 10 for the definition of forward rate) or some company-generated forecast of future spot rates, which Lessard and Lorange refer to as the **internal forward rate.** The internal forward rate may differ from the forward rate quoted by the foreign exchange market if the firm wishes to bias its business in favor of, or against, the particular foreign currency.

TRANSFER PRICING AND CONTROL SYSTEMS

In Chapter 12 we reviewed the various strategies that international businesses pursue. Two of these strategies, the global strategy and the transnational strategy, give rise to a globally dispersed web of productive activities. Firms pursuing these strategies disperse each value creation activity to its optimal location in the world. Thus, a product might be designed in one country, some of its components manufactured in a second country, other components manufactured in a third country, all assembled in a fourth country, and then sold worldwide.

The volume of intrafirm transactions in such companies is very high. The firms are continually shipping component parts and finished goods between subsidiaries in different countries. This poses a very important question: How should goods and services transferred between subsidiary companies in a multinational firm be priced? The price at which such goods and services are transferred is referred to as the **transfer price.**

The choice of transfer price can critically affect the performance of two subsidiaries that exchange goods or services. Consider this example: A French manufacturing subsidiary of a U.S. multinational imports a major component from Brazil. It incorporates this part into a product that it sells in France for the equivalent of $230 per unit. The product costs $200 to manufacture, of which $100 goes to the Brazilian subsidiary to pay for the component part. The remaining $100 covers costs incurred in France. Thus, the French subsidiary earns $30 profit per unit.

	Before Change in Transfer Price	After 20 Percent Increase in Transfer Price
Revenues per unit	$230	$230
Cost of component per unit	100	120
Other costs per unit	100	100
Profit per unit	$30	$10

Look at what happens if corporate headquarters decides to increase transfer prices by 20 percent ($20 per unit). The French subsidiary's profits will fall by two-thirds from $30 per unit to $10 per unit. Thus, the performance of the French subsidiary depends on the transfer price for the component part imported from Brazil, and the transfer price is controlled by corporate headquarters. When setting budgets and reviewing a subsidiary's performance, corporate headquarters must keep in mind the distorting effect of transfer prices.

How should transfer prices be determined? We discuss this issue in detail in the next chapter. International businesses often manipulate transfer prices to minimize their worldwide tax liability, minimize import duties, and avoid government restrictions on capital flows. For now, however, it is enough to note that the transfer price must be considered when setting budgets and evaluating a subsidiary's performance.

SEPARATION OF SUBSIDIARY AND MANAGER PERFORMANCE

In many international businesses, the same quantitative criteria are used to assess the performance of both a foreign subsidiary and its managers. Many accountants, however, argue that although it is legitimate to compare subsidiaries against each other on the basis of return on investment (ROI) or other indicators of profitability, it may not be appropriate to use these for comparing and evaluating the managers of different subsidiaries. Foreign subsidiaries do not operate in uniform environments; their environments have widely different economic, political, and social conditions, all of which influence the costs of doing business in a country and hence the subsidiaries' profitability. Thus, the manager of a subsidiary in an adverse environment that has an ROI of 5 percent may be doing a better job than the manager of a subsidiary in a benign environment that has an ROI of 20 percent. Although the firm might want to pull out of a country where its ROI is only 5 percent, it may also want to recognize the manager's achievement.

Accordingly, it has been suggested that the evaluation of a subsidiary should be kept separate from the evaluation of its manager.[20] The manager's evaluation should consider how hostile or benign the country's environment is for that business. Further, managers should be evaluated in local currency terms after making allowances for those items over which they have no control (e.g., interest rates, tax rates, inflation rates, transfer prices, exchange rates).

Chapter Summary

This chapter focused on financial accounting within the multinational firm. We explained why accounting practices and standards differ from country to country and surveyed the efforts under way to harmonize countries' accounting practices. We discussed the rationale behind consolidated accounts and looked at currency translation. We reviewed several issues related to the use of accounting-based control systems within international businesses. This chapter made the following points:

1. Accounting is the language of business: the means by which firms communicate their financial position to the providers of capital and to governments (for tax purposes). It is also the means by which firms evaluate their own performance, control their expenditures, and plan for the future.

2. Accounting is shaped by the environment in which it operates. Each country's accounting system has evolved in response to the local demands for accounting information.

3. Five main factors seem to influence the type of accounting system a country has: (*i*) the relationship between business and the providers of capital, (*ii*) political and economic ties with other countries, (*iii*) the level of inflation, (*iv*) the level of a country's development, and (*v*) the prevailing culture in a country.

4. National differences in accounting and auditing standards have historically resulted in a general lack of comparability in countries' financial reports.

5. This lack of comparability has become a problem as transnational financing and transnational investment have grown rapidly in recent decades (a consequence of the globalization of capital markets). Due to the lack of comparability, a firm may have to explain to investors why its financial position looks very different on financial reports that are based on different accounting practices.

6. The most significant push for harmonization of accounting standards across countries has come from the International Accounting Standards Board (IASB).

7. Consolidated financial statements provide financial accounting information about a group of companies that recognizes the companies' economic interdependence.

8. Transactions among the members of a corporate family are not included on consolidated financial statements; only assets, liabilities, revenues, and expenses generated with external third parties are shown.

9. Foreign subsidiaries of a multinational firm normally keep their accounting records and prepare their financial statements in the currency of the country in which they are located. When the multinational prepares its consolidated accounts, these financial statements must be translated into the currency of its home country.

10. Under the current rate translation method, the exchange rate at the balance sheet date is used to translate the financial statements of a foreign subsidiary into the home currency. This has the drawback of being incompatible with the historic cost principle.

11. Under the temporal method, assets valued in a foreign currency are translated into the home currency using the exchange rate that existed when the assets were purchased. A problem with this approach is that the multinational's balance sheet may not balance.

12. In most international businesses, the annual budget is the main instrument by which headquarters controls foreign subsidiaries. Throughout the year, headquarters compares a subsidiary's performance against the financial goals incorporated in its budget, intervening selectively in its operations when shortfalls occur.

13. Most international businesses require all budgets and performance data within the firm to be expressed in the corporate currency. This enhances comparability, but it distorts the control process if the relevant exchange rates change between the time a foreign subsidiary's budget is set and the time its performance is evaluated.

14. According to the Lessard-Lorange model, the best way to deal with this problem is to use a projected spot exchange rate to translate both

budget figures and performance figures into the corporate currency.

15. Transfer prices also can introduce significant distortions into the control process and thus must be considered when setting budgets and evaluating a subsidiary's performance.

16. Foreign subsidiaries do not operate in uniform environments, and some environments are much tougher than others. Accordingly, it has been suggested that the evaluation of a subsidiary should be kept separate from the evaluation of the subsidiary manager.

Critical Thinking and Discussion Questions

1. Why do the accounting systems of different countries differ? Why do these differences matter?

2. Why are transactions among members of a corporate family not included in consolidated financial statements?

3. The following are selected amounts from the separate financial statements of a parent company (unconsolidated) and one of its subsidiaries.

	Parent	Subsidiary
Cash	$ 180	$ 80
Receivables	380	200
Accounts payable	245	110
Retained earnings	790	680
Revenues	4,980	3,520
Rent income	0	200
Dividend income	250	0
Expenses	4,160	2,960

Notes:

 i. Parent owes subsidiary $70.

 ii. Parent owns 100% of subsidiary. During the year subsidiary paid parent a dividend of $250.

 iii. Subsidiary owns the building that parent rents for $200.

 iv. During the year parent sold some inventory to subsidiary for $2,200. It had cost parent $1,500. Subsidiary, in turn, sold the inventory to an unrelated party for $3,200.

Given this,

 a. What is the parent's (unconsolidated) net income?

 b. What is the subsidiary's net income?

 c. What is the consolidated profit on the inventory that the parent originally sold to the subsidiary?

 d. What are the amounts of consolidated cash and receivables?

4. Why might an accounting-based control system provide headquarters management with biased information about the performance of a foreign subsidiary? How can these biases best be corrected?

Research Task `globalEDGE™`   globaledge.msu.edu

Use the globalEDGE™ site to complete the following exercises:

1. The globalEDGE™ site offers a tool that allows for comparing countries based on statisti-

cal indicators. Utilize this tool to identify in which of the following countries the historic cost principle of accounting cannot provide accurate results: Bahrain, Bangladesh, Egypt,

India, Iran, Jordan, Lebanon, Pakistan, Qatar, and Yemen. Utilize the "rank countries" tool to identify other countries in which the historic cost principle would not provide valid results.

2. Deloitte Touche Tohmatsu hosts an International Accounting Standards Web site that provides information and guidelines regarding the accounting procedures approved by IASC. Locate the Web site's section on Standards, and prepare a short description of the international accounting standards for recording inventory levels.

China's Developing Accounting System

CLOSING CASE Attracted by its rapid transformation from a socialist planned economy into a market economy, economic annual growth rates of 10 to 12 percent, and a population in excess of 1.2 billion, Western firms over the past 10 years have favored China as a site for foreign direct investment. Most see China as an emerging economic superpower with an economy that will soon be as large as that of Japan and will surpass United States in size sometime after 2010 if current growth projections hold true.

The Chinese government sees foreign direct investment as a primary engine of China's economic growth. To encourage such investment, the government has offered generous tax incentives to foreign firms that invest in China, either on their own or in a joint venture with a local enterprise. These tax incentives include a two-year exemption from corporate income tax following an investment, plus a further three years during which taxes are paid at only 50 percent of the standard tax rate. Such incentives when coupled with the promise of China's vast internal market have made the country a prime site for investment by Western firms. However, once established in China, many Western firms find themselves struggling to comply with the complex and often obtuse nature of China's rapidly evolving accounting system.

Accounting in China has traditionally been rooted in information gathering and compliance reporting designed to measure the government's production and tax goals. The Chinese system was based on the old Soviet system, which had little to do with profit or accounting systems created to report financial positions or the results of foreign operations. Although the system is changing rapidly, many problems associated with the old system still remain.

One problem for investors is a severe shortage of accountants, financial managers, and auditors in China, especially those experienced with market economy transactions and international accounting practices. Estimates suggest that China needs some 600,000 accountants, but as of 2003 there were still only 130,000 in the country. Chinese enterprises, including equity and cooperative joint ventures with foreign firms, must be audited by Chinese accounting firms, which are regulated by the state. Traditionally, many experienced auditors have audited only state-owned enterprises, working through the local province or city authorities and the state audit bureau to report to the government entity overseeing the audited firm. In response to the shortage of accountants schooled in the principles of private-sector accounting, several large international auditing firms have established joint ventures with emerging Chinese accounting and auditing firms to bridge the growing need for international accounting, tax, and securities expertise. Still, the current lack of experienced auditors in China raises questions about how accurate the financial statements of Chinese companies actually are.

This is becoming an issue for foreigners since more and more Chinese companies have been tapping global capital markets, and more foreigners have been investing in Chinese companies through the Shanghai stock exchange. Foreign investors want to be assured that the financial picture they are getting of Chinese enterprises is reliable. So far, that has not always been the case. In December 2003, for example, China Life Insurance successfully listed its stock on the Hong Kong and New York stock exchanges, raising some $3.4 billion. However, in January 2004, the head of China's National Audit Office let it slip that a routine audit of China Life's state-owned parent company had uncovered $652 million in financial irregularities in 2003. The stock immediately fell, and China Life found itself the target of a class-action lawsuit on behalf of U.S. investors claiming financial fraud. Shortly afterward, plans to list China Minsheng Banking Corp., China's largest private bank, on the New York Stock Exchange were put on hold after the company admitted that it had faked a shareholder meeting in 2000. The stock of another successful Chinese offering in New York, that of Semiconductor Manufacturing International, slid in 2004 when its chief financial officer made statements that contradicted those contained in filings with the U.S. Securities and Exchange Commission.

Apart from weak auditing, another probable cause of problems such as these has been the somewhat halting evolution of China's emerging accounting standards. Lacking its own standards, China has signaled that it will move toward adopting international standards developed by the IASB. In 2001, China adopted a new regulation, called the Accounting System for Business Enterprises, that is largely based on ISAB standards. The system is now used to regulate both local and foreign companies operating in China. Still, the Chinese have not totally embraced IASB rules, and they may not. As recently as 2004, the chief accounting regulator in China stated that the country would follow some but not all IASB rules because international rules do not take into consideration the special situation in China. He said, "China is different from other Western markets in many areas. China still has many companies that are state-owned enterprises while overseas markets mainly have privately owned companies." He went on to note, "We would like (international) standards to be set in a way that gives more consideration to the market situations of China, or else give exceptions in accounting treatment for Chinese firms."

Sources: L. E. Graham and A. H. Carley, "When East Meets West," *Financial Executive*, July–August 1995, pp. 40–45; K. Theonnes and A. Yeung, "Playing Favorites," *Financial Executive*, July–August 1995, pp. 46–51; P. Practer, "Emerging Trends," *Accountancy*, May 2001, p. 1293; E. Yiu, "China Sees Benefits of Global Standards," *South China Morning Post*, November 20, 2004, p. 3; J. Baglole, "China's Listings Lose Steam," *The Wall Street Journal*, April 26, 2004, p. A13; and "Skills Shortage a Hurdle to IAS'," *The Standard*, December 2, 2003.

Case Discussion Questions

1. What factors have shaped the accounting system currently in use in China?

2. What problems does the accounting system currently in use in China present to foreign investors in joint ventures with Chinese companies?

3. If the evolving Chinese system does not totally conform with IASB standards, but instead to standards that the Chinese government deems appropriate to China's "special situation," how might this affect foreign firms with operations in China?

4. How might the imperfect accounting and auditing system in China affect the cost of capital of Chinese firms? What are the implications for the long-term growth rate of the Chinese economy?

Notes

1. G. G. Mueller, H. Gernon, and G. Meek, *Accounting: An International Perspective* (Burr Ridge, IL: Richard D. Irwin, 1991).

2. S. J. Gary, "Towards a Theory of Cultural Influence on the Development of Accounting Systems Internationally," *Abacus* 3 (1988), pp. 1–15, and R. S. Wallace, O. Gernon, and H. Gernon, "Frameworks for International Comparative Financial Accounting," *Journal of Accounting Literature* 10 (1991), pp. 209–64.

3. K. M. Dunne and G. A. Ndubizu, "International Acquisition Accounting Method and Corporate Multinationalism," *Journal of International Business Studies* 26 (1995), pp. 361–77.

4. D. L. Holamn, "Convergence: Hurdles Remain," *Financial Executive*, November 2004, pp. 32–35.

5. W. A. Wallace and J. Walsh, "Apples to Apples: Profits Abroad," *Financial Executive*, May–June 1995, pp. 28–31.

6. Wallace, Gernon, and Gernon, "Frameworks for International Comparative Financial Accounting."

7. P. Walton, "Special Rules for a Special Case," *Financial Times*, September 18, 1997, p. 11.

8. Gary, "Towards a Theory of Cultural Influence on the Development of Accounting Systems Internationally," and S. B. Salter and F. Niswander, "Cultural Influences on the Development of Accounting Systems Internationally," *Journal of International Business Studies* 26 (1995), pp. 379–97.

9. G. Hofstede, *Culture's Consequences: International Differences in Work Related Values* (Beverly Hills, CA: Sage Publications, 1980).

10. Salter and Niswander, "Cultural Influences on the Development of Accounting Systems Internationally."

11. Ibid.

12. R. G. Barker, "Global Accounting is Coming," *Harvard Business Review*, April 2003, pp. 2–3.

13. A current list can be accessed at www.iasb.org.uk. See also D. Tweedie, "Globalization, Here We Come," *Financial Times*, February 1, 2001, p. 2, and "Bean Counters, Unite!" *The Economist*, June 10, 1995, pp. 67–68.

14. P. D. Fleming, "The Growing Importance of International Accounting Standards," *Journal of Accountancy*, September 1991, pp. 100–06.

15. L. Berton, "All Accountants May Soon Speak the Same Language," *The Wall Street Journal*, August 29, 1995, p. A15.

16. L. Henock, "The Value Relevance of the Foreign Translation Adjustment," *The Accounting Review* 78, no. 4 (October 2003), pp. 1027–48.

17. The statement can be accessed at www.fasb.org/st/summary/stsum52.shtml.

18. F. Choi and I. Czechowicz, "Assessing Foreign Subsidiary Performance: A Multinational Comparison," *Management International Review* 4 (1983), pp. 14–25.

19. D. Lessard and P. Lorange, "Currency Changes and Management Control: Resolving the Centralization/Decentralization Dilemma," *Accounting Review*, July 1977, pp. 628–37.

20. Mueller, Gernon, and Meek, *Accounting: An International Perspective*.

Financial Management in the International Business

Country	Top Corporate Income Tax Rate
Canada	36.1%
Chile	17.0
China	33.0
France	34.33
Germany	38.29
Ireland	12.5
Japan	42.0
Mexico	33.0
Singapore	22.0
United Kingdom	30.0
United States	40.0

TABLE 20.1

Corporate Income Tax Rates, 2004

Source: KPMG Corporate Tax Rates Survey, January 2004.

varied from a high of 42 percent in Japan to a low of 12.5 percent in Ireland. However, the picture is much more complex than the one presented in Table 20.1. For example, in Germany and Japan, the tax rate is lower on income distributed to stockholders as dividends (36 and 35 percent, respectively), whereas in France the tax on profits distributed to stockholders is higher (42 percent). In the United States, the rate varies from state to state. The federal top rate is 35 percent, but states also tax corporate income, with state and local taxes ranging from 1 percent to 12 percent, hence the average effective rate of 40 percent.

Many nations follow the worldwide principle that they have the right to tax income earned outside their boundaries by entities based in their country.[15] Thus, the U.S. government can tax the earnings of the German subsidiary of an enterprise incorporated in the United States. Double taxation occurs when the income of a foreign subsidiary is taxed both by the host-country government and by the parent company's home government. However, double taxation is mitigated to some extent by tax credits, tax treaties, and the deferral principle.

A **tax credit** allows an entity to reduce the taxes paid to the home government by the amount of taxes paid to the foreign government. A **tax treaty** between two countries is an agreement specifying what items of income will be taxed by the authorities of the country where the income is earned. For example, a tax treaty between the United States and Germany may specify that a U.S. firm need not pay tax in Germany on any earnings from its German subsidiary that are remitted to the United States in the form of dividends. A **deferral principle** specifies that parent companies are not taxed on foreign source income until they actually receive a dividend.

For the international business with activities in many countries, the various tax regimes and the tax treaties have important implications for how the firm should structure its internal payments system among the foreign subsidiaries and the parent company. As we will see in the next section, the firm can use transfer prices and fronting loans to minimize its global tax liability. In addition, the form in which income is remitted from a foreign subsidiary to the parent company (e.g., royalty payments versus dividend payments) can be structured to minimize the firm's global tax liability.

Some firms use **tax havens** such as the Bahamas and Bermuda to minimize their tax liability. A tax haven is a country with an exceptionally low, or even no, income tax. International businesses avoid or defer income taxes by establishing a wholly owned, nonoperating subsidiary in the tax haven. The tax haven subsidiary owns the common stock of the operating foreign subsidiaries. This allows all transfers of funds from foreign operating subsidiaries to the parent company to be funneled through the tax haven subsidiary. The tax levied on foreign source income by a firm's home government, which might normally be paid when a dividend is declared by a foreign subsidiary, can be deferred under the deferral principle until the tax haven subsidiary pays the dividend to the parent. This dividend payment can be postponed indefinitely if foreign operations continue to grow and require new internal financing from the tax haven affiliate. For U.S.-based enterprises, however, U.S. regulations tax U.S. shareholders on the firm's overseas income when it is earned, regardless of when the parent company in the United States receives it. This regulation eliminates U.S.-based firms' ability to use tax haven subsidiaries to avoid tax liabilities in the manner just described.

Moving Money across Borders: Attaining Efficiencies and Reducing Taxes

Pursuing the objectives of utilizing the firm's cash resources most efficiently and minimizing the firm's global tax liability requires the firm to be able to transfer funds from one location to another around the globe. International businesses use a number of techniques to transfer liquid funds across borders. These include dividend remittances, royalty payments and fees, transfer prices, and fronting loans. Some firms rely on more than one of these techniques to transfer funds across borders—a practice known as **unbundling.** By using a mix of techniques to transfer liquid funds from a foreign subsidiary to the parent company, unbundling allows an international business to recover funds from its foreign subsidiaries without piquing host-country sensitivities with large "dividend drains."

A firm's ability to select a particular policy is severely limited when a foreign subsidiary is part-owned either by a local joint-venture partner or by local stockholders. Serving the legitimate demands of the local co-owners of a foreign subsidiary may limit the firm's ability to impose the kind of dividend policy, royalty payment schedule, or transfer pricing policy that would be optimal for the parent company.

DIVIDEND REMITTANCES

Payment of dividends is probably the most common method by which firms transfer funds from foreign subsidiaries to the parent company. The dividend policy typically varies with each subsidiary depending on such factors as tax regulations, foreign exchange risk, age of the subsidiary, and extent of local equity participation. For example, the higher the rate of tax levied on dividends by the host-country government, the less attractive this option becomes relative to other options for transferring liquid funds. With regard to foreign exchange risk, firms sometimes require foreign subsidiaries based in "high-risk" countries to speed up the transfer of funds to the parent through accelerated dividend payments. This moves corporate funds out of a country whose currency is expected to depreciate significantly. The age of a foreign subsidiary influences dividend policy in that older subsidiaries tend to remit a higher proportion of their earnings in dividends to the parent, presumably because a subsidiary has fewer capital investment needs as it matures. Local equity participation is a factor because local co-owners' demands for dividends must be recognized.

ROYALTY PAYMENTS AND FEES

Royalties represent the remuneration paid to the owners of technology, patents, or trade names for the use of that technology or the right to manufacture and/or sell products under those patents or trade names. It is common for a parent company to charge its foreign subsidiaries royalties for the technology, patents, or trade names it has transferred to them. Royalties may be levied as a fixed monetary amount per unit of the product the subsidiary sells or as a percentage of a subsidiary's gross revenues.

A fee is compensation for professional services or expertise supplied to a foreign subsidiary by the parent company or another subsidiary. Fees are sometimes differentiated into "management fees" for general expertise and advice and "technical assistance fees" for guidance in technical matters. Fees are usually levied as fixed charges for the particular services provided.

Royalties and fees have certain tax advantages over dividends, particularly when the corporate tax rate is higher in the host country than in the parent's home country. Royalties and fees are often tax-deductible locally (because they are viewed as an expense), so arranging for payment in royalties and fees will reduce the foreign subsidiary's tax liability. If the foreign subsidiary compensates the parent company by dividend payments, local income taxes must be paid before the dividend distribution, and withholding taxes must be paid on the dividend itself. Although the parent can often take a tax credit for the local withholding and income taxes it has paid, part of the benefit can be lost if the subsidiary's combined tax rate is higher than the parent's.

TRANSFER PRICES

In any international business, there are normally a large number of transfers of goods and services between the parent company and foreign subsidiaries and between foreign subsidiaries. This is particularly likely in firms pursuing global and transnational strategies because these firms are likely to have dispersed their value creation activities to various optimal locations around the globe (see Chapter 12). As noted in Chapter 19, the price at which goods and services are transferred between entities within the firm is referred to as the **transfer price.**[16]

Transfer prices can be used to position funds within an international business. For example, funds can be moved out of a particular country by setting high transfer prices for goods and services supplied to a subsidiary in that country and by setting low transfer prices for the goods and services sourced from that subsidiary. Conversely, funds can be positioned in a country by the opposite policy: setting low transfer prices for goods and services supplied to a subsidiary in that country and setting high transfer prices for the goods and services sourced from that subsidiary. This movement of funds can be between the firm's subsidiaries or between the parent company and a subsidiary.

Benefits of Manipulating Transfer Prices

At least four gains can be derived by manipulating transfer prices.

1. The firm can reduce its tax liabilities by using transfer prices to shift earnings from a high-tax country to a low-tax one.
2. The firm can use transfer prices to move funds out of a country where a significant currency devaluation is expected, thereby reducing its exposure to foreign exchange risk.
3. The firm can use transfer prices to move funds from a subsidiary to the parent company (or a tax haven) when financial transfers in the form of dividends are restricted or blocked by host-country government policies.
4. The firm can use transfer prices to reduce the import duties it must pay when an ad valorem tariff is in force—a tariff assessed as a percentage of value. In this case, low transfer prices on goods or services being imported into the country are required. Since this lowers the value of the goods or services, it lowers the tariff.

Problems with Transfer Pricing

Significant problems are associated with pursuing a transfer pricing policy.[17] Few governments like it.[18] When transfer prices are used to reduce a firm's tax liabilities or import duties, most governments feel they are being cheated of their legitimate income. Similarly, when transfer prices are manipulated to circumvent government restrictions on capital flows (e.g., dividend remittances), governments perceive this as breaking the spirit—if not the letter—of the law. Many governments now limit international businesses' ability to manipulate transfer prices in the manner described. The United States has strict regulations governing transfer pricing practices. According to Section 482 of the Internal Revenue Code, the Internal Revenue Service (IRS) can reallocate gross income, deductions, credits, or allowances between related corporations to prevent tax evasion or to reflect more clearly a proper allocation of income. Under the IRS guidelines and subsequent judicial interpretation, the burden of proof is on the taxpayer to show that the IRS has been arbitrary or unreasonable in reallocating income. The correct transfer price, according to the IRS guidelines, is an arm's-length price—the price that would prevail between unrelated firms in a market setting. Such a strict interpretation of what is a correct transfer price theoretically limits a firm's ability to manipulate transfer prices to achieve the benefits we have discussed. Many other countries have followed the U.S. lead in emphasizing that transfer prices should be set on an arm's-length basis.

Another problem associated with transfer pricing is related to management incentives and performance evaluation.[19] Transfer pricing is inconsistent with a policy of treating each subsidiary in the firm as a profit center. When transfer prices are manipulated by the firm and deviate significantly from the arm's-length price, the subsidiary's performance may depend as much on transfer prices as it does on other pertinent factors, such as management effort. A subsidiary told to charge a high transfer price for a good supplied to another subsidiary will appear to be doing better than it actually is, while the subsidiary purchasing the good will appear to be doing worse. Unless this is recognized when performance is being evaluated, serious distortions in management incentive systems can occur. For example, managers in the selling subsidiary may be able to use high transfer prices to mask inefficiencies, while managers in the purchasing subsidiary may become disheartened by the effect of high transfer prices on their subsidiary's profitability.

Despite these problems, research suggests that not all international businesses use arm's-length pricing but instead use some cost-based system for pricing transfers among their subunits (typically cost plus some standard markup). A survey of 164 U.S. multinational firms found that 35 percent of the firms used market-based prices, 15 percent used negotiated prices, and 65 percent used a cost-based pricing method. (The figures add up to more than 100 percent because some companies use more than one method.)[20] Only market and negotiated prices could reasonably be interpreted as arm's-length prices. The opportunity for price manipulation is much greater with cost-based transfer pricing. Other more sophisticated research has uncovered indirect evidence that many corporations manipulate transfer prices to reduce global tax liabilities.[21]

Although a firm may be able to manipulate transfer prices to avoid tax liabilities or circumvent government restrictions on capital flows across borders, this does not mean the firm should do so. Since the practice often violates at least the spirit of the law in many countries, the ethics of engaging in transfer pricing are dubious at best. Also, there are clear signs that tax authorities in many countries are increasing their scrutiny of this practice to stamp out abuses. A 2000 survey of some 600 multinationals undertaken by accountants Ernst & Young found that 75 percent of them believed that they would be the subject of a transfer pricing audit by tax authorities in the next two years.[22] Some 61 percent of the multinationals in the survey stated that transfer pricing was the number one tax issue they faced.

FRONTING LOANS

A **fronting loan** is a loan between a parent and its subsidiary channeled through a financial intermediary, usually a large international bank. In a direct intrafirm loan, the parent company lends cash directly to the foreign subsidiary, and the subsidiary repays it

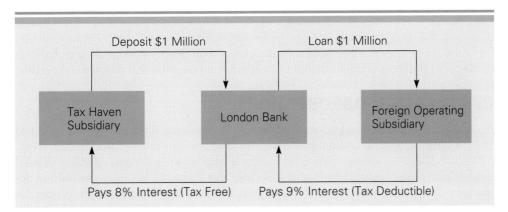

FIGURE 20.2

An Example of the Tax Aspects of a Fronting Loan

later. In a fronting loan, the parent company deposits funds in an international bank, and the bank then lends the same amount to the foreign subsidiary. Thus, a U.S. firm might deposit $100,000 in a London bank. The London bank might then lend that $100,000 to an Indian subsidiary of the firm. From the bank's point of view, the loan is risk free because it has 100 percent collateral in the form of the parent's deposit. The bank "fronts" for the parent, hence the name. The bank makes a profit by paying the parent company a slightly lower interest rate on its deposit than it charges the foreign subsidiary on the borrowed funds.

Firms use fronting loans for two reasons. First, fronting loans can circumvent host-country restrictions on the remittance of funds from a foreign subsidiary to the parent company. A host government might restrict a foreign subsidiary from repaying a loan to its parent in order to preserve the country's foreign exchange reserves, but it is less likely to restrict a subsidiary's ability to repay a loan to a large international bank. To stop payment to an international bank would hurt the country's credit image, whereas halting payment to the parent company would probably have a minimal impact on its image. Consequently, international businesses sometimes use fronting loans when they want to lend funds to a subsidiary based in a country with a fairly high probability of political turmoil that might lead to restrictions on capital flows (i.e., where the level of political risk is high).

A fronting loan can also provide tax advantages. For example, a tax haven (Bermuda) subsidiary that is 100 percent owned by the parent company deposits $1 million in a London-based international bank at 8 percent interest. The bank lends the $1 million to a foreign operating subsidiary at 9 percent interest. The country where the foreign operating subsidiary is based taxes corporate income at 50 percent (see Figure 20.2).

Under this arrangement, interest payments net of income tax will be as follows:

1. The foreign operating subsidiary pays $90,000 interest to the London bank. Deducting these interest payments from its taxable income results in a net after-tax cost of $45,000 to the foreign operating subsidiary.

2. The London bank receives the $90,000. It retains $10,000 for its services and pays $80,000 interest on the deposit to the Bermuda subsidiary.

3. The Bermuda subsidiary receives $80,000 interest on its deposit tax free.

The net result is that $80,000 in cash has been moved from the foreign operating subsidiary to the tax haven subsidiary. Because the foreign operating subsidiary's after-tax cost of borrowing is only $45,000, the parent company has moved an additional $35,000 out of the country by using this arrangement. If the tax haven subsidiary had made a direct loan to the foreign operating subsidiary, the host government may have disallowed the interest charge as a tax-deductible expense by ruling that it was a dividend to the parent disguised as an interest payment.

Techniques for Global Money Management

Firms use two money management techniques in attempting to manage their global cash resources in the most efficient manner: centralized depositories and multilateral netting.

CENTRALIZED DEPOSITORIES

Every business needs to hold some cash balances for servicing accounts that must be paid and for insuring against unanticipated negative variation from its projected cash flows. The critical issue for an international business is whether each foreign subsidiary should hold its own cash balances or whether cash balances should be held at a **centralized depository.** In general, firms prefer to hold cash balances at a centralized depository for three reasons.

First, by pooling cash reserves centrally, the firm can deposit larger amounts. Cash balances are typically deposited in liquid accounts, such as overnight money market accounts. Because interest rates on such deposits normally increase with the size of the deposit, by pooling cash centrally, the firm should be able to earn a higher interest rate than it would if each subsidiary managed its own cash balances.

Second, if the centralized depository is located in a major financial center (e.g., London, New York, or Tokyo), it should have access to information about good short-term investment opportunities that the typical foreign subsidiary would lack. Also, the financial experts at a centralized depository should be able to develop investment skills and know-how that managers in the typical foreign subsidiary might not. Thus, the firm should make better investment decisions if it pools its cash reserves at a centralized depository.

Third, by pooling its cash reserves, the firm can reduce the total size of the cash pool it must hold in highly liquid accounts, which enables the firm to invest a larger amount of cash reserves in longer-term, less liquid financial instruments that earn a higher interest rate. For example, a U.S. firm has three foreign subsidiaries—one in South Korea, one in China, and one in Japan. Each subsidiary maintains a cash balance that includes an amount for dealing with its day-to-day needs plus a precautionary amount for dealing with unanticipated cash demands. The firm's policy is that the total required cash balance is equal to three standard deviations of the expected day-to-day-needs amount. The three-standard-deviation requirement reflects the firm's estimate that, in practice, there is a 99.87 percent probability that the subsidiary will have sufficient cash to deal with both day-to-day and unanticipated cash demands. Cash needs are assumed to be normally distributed in each country and independent of each other (e.g., cash needs in Japan do not affect cash needs in China).

The individual subsidiaries' day-to-day cash needs and the precautionary cash balances they should hold are as follows (in millions of dollars):

	Day-to-Day Cash Needs (A)	One Standard Deviation (B)	Required Cash Balance (A + 3 × B)
South Korea	$10	$1	$13
China	6	2	12
Japan	12	3	21
Total	$28	$6	$46

Thus, the Korean subsidiary estimates that it must hold $10 million to serve its day-to-day needs. The standard deviation of this is $1 million, so it is to hold an additional

$3 million as a precautionary amount. This gives a total required cash balance of $13 million. The total of the required cash balances for all three subsidiaries is $46 million.

Now consider what might occur if the firm decided to maintain all three cash balances at a centralized depository in Tokyo. Because variances are additive when probability distributions are independent of each other, the standard deviation of the combined precautionary account would be:

$$\text{Square root of } (\$1,000,000^2 + 2,000,000^2 + 3,000,000^2)$$
$$= \text{Square root of } 14,000,000$$
$$= \$3,741,657$$

Therefore, if the firm used a centralized depository, it would need to hold $28 million for day-to-day needs plus (3 × $3,741,657) as a precautionary amount, or a total cash balance of $39,224,971. In other words, the firm's total required cash balance would be reduced from $46 million to $39,224,971, a saving of $6,775,029. This is cash that could be invested in less liquid, higher-interest accounts or in tangible assets. The saving arises simply due to the statistical effects of summing the three independent, normal probability distributions.

However, a firm's ability to establish a centralized depository that can serve short-term cash needs might be limited by government-imposed restrictions on capital flows across borders (e.g., controls put in place to protect a country's foreign exchange reserves). Also, the transaction costs of moving money into and out of different currencies can limit the advantages of such a system. Despite this, many firms hold at least their subsidiaries' precautionary cash reserves at a centralized depository, having each subsidiary hold its own day-to-day-needs cash balance. The globalization of the world capital market and the general removal of barriers to the free flow of cash across borders (particularly among advanced industrialized countries) are two trends likely to increase the use of centralized depositories.

MULTILATERAL NETTING

Multilateral netting allows a multinational firm to reduce the transaction costs that arise when many transactions occur between its subsidiaries. These transaction costs are the commissions paid to foreign exchange dealers for foreign exchange transactions and the fees charged by banks for transferring cash between locations. The volume of such transactions is likely to be particularly high in a firm that has a globally dispersed web of interdependent value creation activities. Netting reduces transaction costs by reducing the number of transactions.

Multilateral netting is an extension of **bilateral netting.** Under bilateral netting, if a French subsidiary owes a Mexican subsidiary $6 million and the Mexican subsidiary simultaneously owes the French subsidiary $4 million, a bilateral settlement will be made with a single payment of $2 million from the French subsidiary to the Mexican subsidiary, the remaining debt being canceled.

Under **multilateral netting,** this simple concept is extended to the transactions between multiple subsidiaries within an international business. Consider a firm that wants to establish multilateral netting among four Asian subsidiaries based in South Korea, China, Japan, and Taiwan. These subsidiaries all trade with each other, so at the end of each month a large volume of cash transactions must be settled. Figure 20.3A shows how the payment schedule might look at the end of a given month. Figure 20.3B is a payment matrix that summarizes the obligations among the subsidiaries. Note that $43 million needs to flow among the subsidiaries. If the transaction costs (foreign exchange commissions plus transfer fees) amount to 1 percent of the total funds to be transferred, this will cost the parent firm $430,000. However, this amount can be reduced by multilateral netting. Using the payment matrix (Figure 20.3B), the

FIGURE 20.3A

Cash Flows before
Multilateral Netting

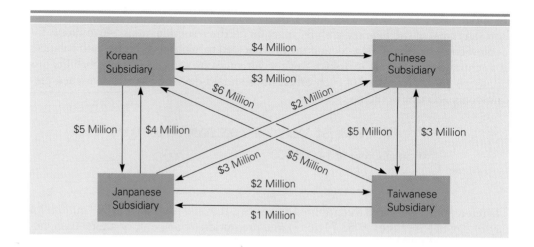

| | Paying Subsidiary | | | | | Net Receipts |
Receiving Subsidiary	**Germany**	**France**	**Spain**	**Italy**	**Total Receipts**	**(payments)**
Korean	—	$3	$4	$5	$12	($3)
Chinese	$ 4	—	2	3	9	(2)
Japanese	5	3	—	1	9	1
Taiwanese	6	5	2	—	13	4
Total payments	$15	$11	$8	$9		

FIGURE 20.3B

Calculation of Net Receipts (all amounts in millions)

FIGURE 20.3C

Cash Flows after
Multilateral Netting

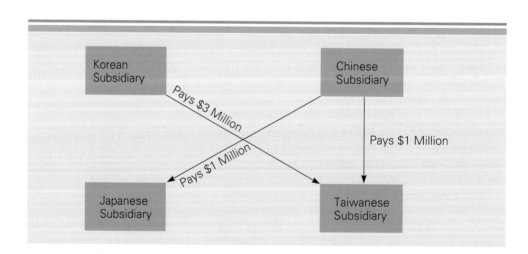

firm can determine the payments that need to be made among its subsidiaries to settle these obligations. Figure 20.3C shows the results. By multilateral netting, the transactions depicted in Figure 20.3A are reduced to just three; the Korean subsidiary pays $3 million to the Taiwanese subsidiary, and the Chinese subsidiary pays $1 million to the Japanese subsidiary and $1 million to the Taiwanese subsidiary. The total funds that flow among the subsidiaries are reduced from $43 million to just $5 million, and the transaction costs are reduced from $430,000 to $50,000, a savings of $380,000 achieved through multilateral netting.

Chapter Summary

This chapter was concerned with financial management in the international business. We discussed how investment decisions, financing decisions, and money management decisions are complicated by the fact that different countries have different currencies, tax regimes, levels of political and economic risk, and so on. Financial managers must account for all of these factors when deciding which activities to finance, how best to finance those activities, how best to manage the firm's financial resources, and how best to protect the firm from political and economic risks (including foreign exchange risk). The chapter made the following points:

1. When using capital budgeting techniques to evaluate a potential foreign project, a distinction must be made between cash flows to the project and cash flows to the parent. The two will not be the same thing when a host-country government blocks the repatriation of cash flows from a foreign investment.

2. When using capital budgeting techniques to evaluate a potential foreign project, the firm needs to recognize the specific risks arising from its foreign location. These include political risks and economic risks (including foreign exchange risk).

3. Political and economic risks can be incorporated into the capital budgeting process either by using a higher discount rate to evaluate risky projects or by forecasting lower cash flows for such projects.

4. The cost of capital is typically lower in the global capital market than in domestic markets. Consequently, other things being equal, firms prefer to finance their investments by borrowing from the global capital market.

5. Borrowing from the global capital market may be restricted by host-government regulations or demands. In such cases, the discount rate used in capital budgeting must be revised upward to reflect this.

6. The firm may want to consider local debt financing for investments in countries where the local currency is expected to depreciate.

7. The principal objectives of global money management are to utilize the firm's cash resources in the most efficient manner and to minimize the firm's global tax liabilities.

8. Firms use a number of techniques to transfer funds across borders, including dividend remittances, royalty payments and fees, transfer prices, and fronting loans.

9. Dividend remittances are the most common method used for transferring funds across borders, but royalty payments and fees have certain tax advantages over dividend remittances.

10. The manipulation of transfer prices is sometimes used by firms to move funds out of a country to minimize tax liabilities, hedge against foreign exchange risk, circumvent government restrictions on capital flows, and reduce tariff payments.

11. However, manipulating transfer prices in this manner runs counter to government regulations in many countries, it may distort incentive systems within the firm, and it has ethically dubious foundations.

12. Fronting loans involves channeling funds from a parent company to a foreign subsidiary through a third party, normally an international bank. Fronting loans can circumvent host-government restrictions on the remittance of funds and provide certain tax advantages.

13. By holding cash at a centralized depository, the firm may be able to invest its cash reserves more efficiently. It can reduce the total size of the cash pool that it needs to hold in highly liquid accounts, thereby freeing cash for investment in higher-interest-bearing (less liquid) accounts or in tangible assets.

14. Multilateral netting reduces the transaction costs arising when a large number of transactions occur between a firm's subsidiaries in the normal course of business.

Critical Thinking and Discussion Questions

1. How can the finance function of an international business improve the firm's competitive position in the global marketplace?

2. What actions can a firm take to minimize its global tax liability? On ethical grounds, can such actions be justified?

3. You are the CFO of a U.S. firm whose wholly owned subsidiary in Mexico manufactures component parts for your U.S. assembly operations. The subsidiary has been financed by bank borrowings in the United States. One of your analysts told you that the Mexican peso is expected to depreciate by 30 percent against the dollar on the foreign exchange markets over the next year. What actions, if any, should you take?

4. You are the CFO of a Canadian firm that is considering building a $10 million factory in Russia to produce milk. The investment is expected to produce net cash flows of $3 million each year for the next 10 years, after which the investment will have to close because of technological obsolescence. Scrap values will be zero. The cost of capital will be 6 percent if financing is arranged through the eurobond market. However, you have an option to finance the project by borrowing funds from a Russian bank at 12 percent. Analysts tell you that due to high inflation in Russia, the Russian ruble is expected to depreciate against the Canadian dollar. Analysts also rate the probability of violent revolution occurring in Russia within the next 10 years as high. How would you incorporate these factors into your evaluation of the investment opportunity? What would you recommend the firm do?

Research Task globaledge.msu.edu

Use the globalEDGE™ site to complete the following exercises:

1. The top management of your company requested a report regarding the tax policies of the following countries: Argentina, Belgium, Bulgaria, China, Czech Republic, Denmark, Egypt, Germany, Italy and the United Kingdom. Prepare a table including the corporate and individual income tax rates and the value-added tax rates (where applicable) for those countries.

2. One of the Marketing Potential Indicators for Emerging Markets is identified as country risk. Utilizing the ranking provided by the globalEDGE™ Web site, identify five emerging markets that exhibit the least risk for foreign investors.

Financing Gol

CLOSING CASE Brazil's Gol Linhas Aereas Inteligentes is a tropical version of JetBlue Airways and Ryanair, the low-cost, no-frills carriers in the United States and Europe. Established in 2001, Gol adopted the low-cost model pioneered by Southwest Airlines, and refined by the likes of JetBlue and Ryanair. Gol sells discount tickets, mainly over the Internet. It targets price-sensitive business travelers, who account for 70 percent of traffic in Brazil's rapidly growing market for air travel (demand for air travel in Brazil is growing at roughly twice the rate of growth in the country's gross domestic product). Gol is also going after Brazil's large bus market—in 2001, some 130 million people in Brazil traveled by interstate bus companies. Gol has standardized its fleet on a single aircraft model, Boeing's 737 series. There are no airport clubs or frequent-flier programs, cabins are a single class, and light snacks and beverages replace meals. The airline also offers Internet check-in and delivers a reliable product, with 95 percent of flights arriving on time. Gol's service has elicited a remarkable response from customers, with an independent market research survey finding that more than 90 percent of customers would continue to use the airline and recommend it to others.

From a standing start in January 2001, this business model enabled Gol to capture a 22 percent share of the Brazilian market by mid-2004. By then, Gol had a fleet of 25 aircraft and was already ranked as one of the fastest growing and most profitable airlines in the world, but its aspirations are much bigger. Gol wants to be the low-cost carrier in South America. To get to that point, it plans to expand its fleet to some 69 aircraft by 2010.

To help finance this expansion, Gol decided to tap into the global capital market. In mid-2004, the privately held company offered nonvoting preferred stock to investors on the São Paulo Bovespa and the New York Stock Exchange. The simultaneous offering was oversubscribed, with the underwriters lifting the offering price twice, and raised some $322 million. In explaining the decision to offer stock through the New York Stock Exchange, Gol's chief financial officer noted, "We wanted to get a solid group of long-term investors that understood the business. We've got that. We also wanted to get a group of research analysts that understood this sector, and we now have seven analysts covering the stock. Southwest, JetBlue, Ryanair, and Westjet are considered the tier one in terms of operating profitability and successes. We were able to put Gol right up in that group. Doing both the NYSE and Bovespa was part of our strategy to sell shares to investors that have familiarity with low-cost carriers. The strategy works. If you look at the list of major investors in the company, the majority of them have high positions in trade of the equities of JetBlue, Southwest, and Ryanair. For them, it was a very easy analysis to understand Gol's business model and how it makes money."

Sources: E. P. Lima, "Winning Gol!" *Air Transport World*, October 2004, pp. 22–26; G. Samor, "Brazil's Gol Faces Hurdles," *The Wall Street Journal*, August 9, 2004, p. C3; and "Gol Launches $322 million Flotation," *Airfinance Journal*, June 2004, p. 1.

Case Discussion Questions

1. What were the benefits to Gol of a listing on the New York Stock Exchange in addition to the São Paulo Bovespa?

2. Why do you think the Gol stock offering was oversubscribed?

3. Do you think Gol would have raised as much money if it had just listed on the São Paulo exchange?

4. How might the joint listing of the New York and São Paulo stock exchanges affect Gol's ability to raise additional capital in the future?

Notes

1. L. Quinn, "Currency Futures Trading Helps Firms Sharpen Competitive Edge," *Crain's Chicago Business*, March 2, 1992, p. 20.

2. For details of capital budgeting techniques, see R. A. Brealey and S. C. Myers, *Principles of Corporate Finance* (New York: McGraw-Hill, 1988).

3. D. J. Feils and F. M. Sabac, "The Impact of Political Risk on the Foreign Direct Investment Decision: A Capital Budgeting Analysis," *The Engineering Economist*, 45 (2000), pp. 129–34.

4. See: S. Block, "Integrating Traditional Capital Budgeting Concepts into an International Decision Making Environment," *The Engineering Economist* 45 (2000), pp. 309–25, and J. C. Backer and L. J. Beardsley, "Multinational Companies' Use of Risk Evaluation and Profit Measurement for Capital Budgeting Decisions," *Journal of Business Finance*, Spring 1973, pp. 34–43.

5. For example, see D. K. Eiteman, A. I. Stonehill, and M. H. Moffett, *Multinational Business Finance* (Reading, MA: Addison-Wesley, 1992).

6. M. Stanley and S. Block, "An Empirical Study of Management and Financial Variables Influencing Capital Budgeting Decisions for Multinational Corporations in the 1980s," *Management International Review* 23 (1983), pp. 61–71.

7. Bank for International Settlements, *BIS Quarterly Review*, December 2004.

8. T. F. Huertas, "U.S. Multinational Banking: History and Prospects," in *Banks as Multinationals*, ed. G. Jones (London: Routledge, 1990).

9. P. Dicken, *Global Shift: The Internationalization of Economic Activity* (London: The Guilford Press, 1992).

10. W. S. Sekely and J. M. Collins, "Cultural Influences on International Capital Structure," *Journal of International Business Studies*, Spring 1988, pp. 87–100.

11. J. K. Wald, "How Firm Characteristics Affect Capital Structure: An International Comparison," *Journal of Financial Research* 22, no. 2 (1999), pp. 161–87.

12. J. Collins and W. S. Sekely, "The Relationship of Headquarters, Country, and Industry Classification to Financial Structure," *Financial Structure*, Autumn 1983, pp. 45–51; J. Rutterford, "An International Perspective on the Capital Structure Puzzle," *Midland Corporate Finance Journal*, Fall 1985, p. 72; R. G. Rajan and L. Zingales, "What Do We Know about Capital Structure," *Journal of Finance* 50 (1995), pp. 1421–60; and Wald, "How Firm Characteristics Affect Capital Structure."

13. Sekely and Collins, "Cultural Influences on International Capital Structure." See also A. C. W. Chui, A. E. Lloyd, and C. C. Y. Kwok, "The Determinantion of Capital Structure: Is National Culture the Missing Piece to the Puzzle?" *Journal of International Business Studies* 33 (2002), pp. 99–127.

14. KPMG, "KPMG Corporate Tax Rate Survey—January 2003," www.us.kpmg.com/microsite/Global_Tax/CTR_Survey/2004CTRS.pdf.

15. "Taxing Questions," *The Economist*, May 22, 1993, p. 73.

16. S. Crow and E. Sauls, "Setting the Right Transfer Price," *Management Accounting*, December 1994, pp. 41–47.

17. V. H. Miesel, H. H. Higinbotham, and C. W. Yi, "International Transfer Pricing: Practical Solutions for Inter-company Pricing," *International Tax Journal*, Fall 2002, pp. 1–22.

18. J. Kelly, "Administrators Prepare for a More Efficient Future," *Financial Times Survey: World Taxation*, February 24, 1995, p. 9.

19. Crow and Sauls, "Setting the Right Transfer Price."

20. M. F. Al-Eryani, P. Alam, and S. Akhter, "Transfer Pricing Determinants of U.S. Multinationals," *Journal of International Business Studies*, September 1990, pp. 409–25.

21. D. L. Swenson, "Tax Reforms and Evidence of Transfer Pricing," *National Tax Journal*, March 2001, pp. 7–25.

22. "Transfer Pricing Survey Shows Multinationals Face Greater Scrutiny," *The CPA Journal*, March 2000, p. 10.

Cases

Merrill Lynch in Japan

Merrill Lynch is an investment banking titan. The U.S.-based financial services institution is the world's largest underwriter of debt and equity and the third largest mergers and acquisitions adviser behind Morgan Stanley and Goldman Sachs. Merrill Lynch's investment banking operations have long had a global reach. The company has a dominant presence in London and Tokyo. However, Merrill Lynch's international presence was limited to the investment banking side of its business until recently. In contrast, its private client business, which offers banking, financial advice, and stockbrokerage services to individuals, had historically been concentrated in the United States. This started to change in the mid-1990s. In 1995, Merrill Lynch purchased Smith New Court, the largest stockbrokerage in Great Britain. This was followed in 1997 by the acquisition of Mercury Asset Management, the United Kingdom's leading manager of mutual funds. Then in 1998, Merrill Lynch acquired Midland Walwyn, Canada's last major independent stockbrokerage. The company's boldest moves, however, have probably been in Japan.

Merrill Lynch started a private client business in Japan in the 1980s but met with limited success. At the time, it was the first foreign firm to enter Japan's private client investment market. The company found it extremely difficult to attract employee talent and customers away from Japan's big four stockbrokerages, which traditionally had monopolized the Japanese market. Plus, restrictive regulations made it almost impossible for Merrill Lynch to offer its Japanese private clients the range of services it offered clients in the United States. For example, foreign exchange regulations meant it was very difficult to sell non-Japanese stocks, bonds, and mutual funds to Japanese investors. In 1993, Merrill Lynch admitted defeat, closed its six retail branches in Kobe and Kyoto, and withdrew from the private client market in Japan.

Over the next few years, however, things changed. In the mid-1990s, Japan embarked on a wide-ranging deregulation of its financial services industry. This led to the removal of many restrictions that had made it so difficult for Merrill Lynch to do business in Japan. For example, the relaxation of foreign exchange controls meant that by 1998, Japanese citizens could purchase foreign stocks, bonds, and mutual funds. Meanwhile, Japan's big four stockbrokerages continued to struggle with serious financial problems that resulted from the 1991 crash of that country's stock market. In November 1997, in what was a shock to many Japanese, one of these firms, Yamaichi Securities, declared it was bankrupt due to $2.2 billion in accumulated "hidden losses" and that it would shut its doors. Recognizing the country's financial system was strained and in need of fresh capital, know-how, and the

stimulus of greater competition, the Japanese government signaled that it would adopt a more relaxed attitude to foreign entry into its financial services industry. This attitude underlay Japan's wholehearted endorsement of a 1997 deal brokered by the World Trade Organization to liberalize global financial services. Among other things, the WTO deal made it much easier for foreign firms to sell financial service products to Japanese investors.

By 1997, it had become clear to Merrill Lynch that the climate in Japan had changed significantly. The big attraction of the market was still the same: The financial assets owned by Japanese households are huge, amounting to ¥1,220 trillion in late 1997, only 3 percent of which were then invested in mutual funds (most were invested in low-yielding bank accounts and government bonds). In mid-1997, Merrill Lynch started to consider reentering the Japanese private client market.

The company initially considered a joint venture with Sanwa Bank to sell Merrill Lynch's mutual fund products to Japanese consumers through Sanwa's 400 retail branches. The proposed alliance would have allowed Merrill Lynch to leverage Sanwa's existing distribution system, rather than having to build its own distribution system. However, the long-run disadvantage of such a strategy was that it would not have given Merrill Lynch the presence that it believed it needed to build a solid financial services business in Japan. Top executives reasoned that it was important for them to make a major commitment to the Japanese market to establish the company's brand name as a premier provider of investment products and financial advice to individuals. This would enable Merrill Lynch to entrench itself as a major player before other foreign institutions entered the market—and before Japan's own stockbrokerages rose to the challenge. At the same time, given their prior experience in Japan, Merrill Lynch executives were hesitant to go down this road because of the huge costs and risks involved.

The problem of how best to enter the Japanese market was solved by the bankruptcy of Yamaichi Securities. Suddenly Yamaichi's nationwide network of offices and 7,000 employees were up for grabs. In late December 1997, Merrill Lynch announced it would hire 2,000 of Yamaichi's employees and acquire 33 of Yamaichi's branch offices. The deal, which was enthusiastically endorsed by the Japanese government, significantly lowered Merrill Lynch's costs of establishing a retail network in Japan.

The company got off to a quick start. In February 1998, Merrill Lynch launched its first mutual fund in Japan and saw the value of its assets swell to $1 billion by April. By mid-2002, Merrill Lynch announced it had $12.9 billion under management in Japan. However, the collapse in global stock markets in 2001–2002 hit Merrill Lynch's Japanese unit hard. After losing $500 million in Japan, in January 2002 the company fired 75 percent of its Japanese workforce and closed all but eight of its retail locations. Despite this costly downsizing, the company held onto almost all of the assets under management, continued to attract new accounts, and by mid-2002 was reportedly making a profit in Japan.

Case Discussion Questions

1. Given the changes that have occurred in the international capital markets during the past decade, does Merrill Lynch's strategy of expanding internationally make sense? Why?

2. What factors make Japan a suitable market for Merrill Lynch to enter?

3. Review Merrill Lynch's 1997 reentry into the Japanese private client market. Pay close attention to the timing and scale of entry and the nature of the strategic commitments Merrill Lynch is making in Japan. What are the potential benefits associated with this strategy? What are the costs and risks? Do you think the trade-off between benefits and risks and costs makes sense? Why?

4. The collapse in stock market values in 2001–2002 resulted in Merrill Lynch's Japanese unit incurring significant losses. In retrospect, was the Japanese expansion a costly blunder or did the company simply get hit by macroeconomic events that were difficult to predict and avoid?

5. Do you think Merrill Lynch should continue in Japan? Why?

Sources

1. Donlon, J. P. "Merrill Cinch." *Chief Executive*, March 1998, pp. 28–32.

2. Holley, D. "Merrill Lynch to Open 31 Offices throughout Japan," *Los Angeles Times*, February 13, 1998, p. D1.

3. "Japan's Big Bang. Enter Merrill." *The Economist*, January 3, 1998, p. 72.

4. Merrill Lynch Web site, www.ml.com.

5. Rowley, A. "Merrill Thunders into Japan." *The Banker*, March 1998, p. 6.

6. Singer, J. "Merrill Reports Profits for Operation in Japan." *The Wall Street Journal*, July 19, 2002, p. A9.

🌐 GTI in Russia IVEY

In early 2001, the president of GTI (Global Traffic, Inc.), Joe Walker, discovered an opportunity to expand his company into Russia using GTI's main product line, reflective signs for traffic control. This U.S.-based manufacturing corporation had been moderately successful with projects in Venezuela, Argentina, Finland, and Germany. Any new opportunity, however, was filled with complicated challenges since the venture involved unprecedented and uncharted experiences with Russia.

Walker asked Jeremy Granum, vice president of human resource, to recommend a human resource strategy and the personnel requirements for the venture. Granum had only four weeks to address the human resource strategic vision, including expatriate assignments, the selection and compensation procedures, the training package for all involved in the new Russian venture, and the outline of organizational culture.

WEEK 1

Unfamiliar with business in Russia, Granum was concerned about whether this venture would be profitable. But business is business, he thought. And corporate HR was his responsibility. So he started his project, determined to make it successful.

Granum discovered that Russia was rapidly moving to a free market, willing to join the World Trade Organization (WTO) and act as a reliable business partner in the global economy. Many international corporations already operating in Russia were well positioned in the local markets and were getting reasonable profits; in fact, some were even thriving, despite chaos, risk, and uncertainty. The most attractive industries for foreign investments were trade, food processing, oil and gas, and machine-building. Companies such as Microsoft and Shell, 3M and Siemens, Coca-Cola and Unilever, among others, had successfully expanded their Russian operations, some

Mikhail V. Grachev, P.C. (Peggy) Smith and Mariya A. Bobina prepared this case solely to provide material for class discussion. The authors do not intend to illustrate either effective or ineffective handling of a managerial situation. The authors may have disguised certain names and other identifying information to protect confidentiality. One time permission to reproduce granted by IVEY Management Services on September 12, 2005. Ivey Management Services prohibits any form of reproduction, storage or transmittal without its written permission. This material is not covered under authorization from CanCopy or any reproduction rights organization. To order copies or request permission to reproduce materials, contact Ivey Publishing, Ivey Management Services, c/o Richard Ivey School of Business, The University of Western Ontario, London, Ontario, Canada, N6A 3K7; phone (519) 661-3208; fax (519) 661-3882; e-mail cases@ivey.uwo.ca.

Copyright © 2003, Ivey Management Services   Version: (A) 2003-03-19

showing significant profit growth. Granum was surprised to learn that KPMG or PricewaterhouseCoopers Moscow offices listed hundreds of international companies among their clients.

Sales for reflective tapes in the Russian market were almost nonexistent. Reflective tapes are needed for several industries, such as automobiles, bicycles, safety tools, and traffic control. Certainly there was an obvious need for these products in a country that was the largest in the world with major expanses of connecting roads (in poor condition, however). Success was heavily dependent on how quickly GTI could launch the venture and start producing and distributing reflective tapes and signs. Granum was aware that his company's competitors from Italy and Taiwan were also active in Moscow, looking for contracts and creating business networks for effective operations.

GTI had already sold small stocks of reflective tape to Russia in the past, yet the sales of the product had not kept pace with the expanding needs. In addition, the rapidly changing customs and tax regulations in Russia put additional financial pressure on deliveries. Consequently, the only way to manage growth was to establish in-country operations.

Walker was exuberant after his last trip to Moscow. He signed documents with the Russian officials and contractors for their venture, including the Ministry of Transportation; with local authorities in the Greater Moscow Region to officially register GTI/Russia; and with three privatized plants that would act as subcontractors for materials. On a long-term basis, the company managed to lease factory space in Mitino, a few miles beyond the Moscow automobile circle (city line), a move which helped GTI to avoid extremely high city taxes. Now, Russian–Turkish joint-venture contractors were assembling new equipment. Upon his return, Walker informed Granum that GTI/Russia should plan to start hiring new personnel in a month.

Granum has altered his initial skepticism with cautious excitement after learning about some technological breakthroughs made by the Russians and by taking a closer look at the courage of the Russian people to foster social and economic transformation. He was becoming a believer. If the human resource policy was established correctly, GTI could build an excellent, competitive team for this new venture. Two years ago, Granum had put together competent, productive teams in Brazil and Venezuela; he was conscious that he needed to apply his knowledge of that success to this new situation.

Traditionally, within GTI, regional managers had a great deal of freedom in the development of the business in other countries. This innovative spirit provided the encouragement to adapt and be flexible in all assignments, both at home or at a multinational level.

GTI, like many companies that were globally successful, made allowance for the cultural differences in its international ventures, while at the same time accomplishing the necessary "total company culture melting pot" to speak to the GTI teamwork concept. An underlying premise of the organization was "think global, act local." Similarly, the GTI organizational culture had adhered to longer term commitments to employees than many companies, and this had helped to foster loyalty. Examples of this organizational commitment included extensive promotion from within the company and encouragement of the delegation of responsibility. HR had also established itself as an essential component in the past through transferring employees in necessary redeployment activities. This involved movement and selection of "fast trackers," and the establishment of a better mix of career goals that aided in identifying those interested in and capable of managing global assignments.

With these thoughts in mind, Granum outlined his plan: (1) to acquire current, reliable information on the Russian business environment and pertinent human resources practices; (2) to present to the board his recommendations for human resources management (HRM) policy in Russia; and (3) to administer and test the practicality of his ideas in Russia.

What was most urgent? Probably, to get current information from a variety of sources and to analyze it carefully. Granum sent a letter to the U.S. Department of Commerce with questions on the current practices of American companies in Russia. Another message was sent by e-mail to 12 GTI managers in the domestic and foreign subsidiaries. Granum asked his colleagues to share ideas on potential HRM needs in Russia. Also, he decided to informally interview managers from other multinational companies that already experienced Russian business practices. The last approach Granum designed for himself was a general information search in journals and newspapers on the current situation in Russia and on characteristics of the country's business culture.

Granum thought of the company's contacts in Moscow. He understood that people in the Ministry of Transportation, who assisted in developing technical matters on the launching stage, were not committed to GTI objectives. Instead, they were pressured to express their personal interests. The ministry staff didn't have any serious background in HRM, and they didn't speak fluent English. Previous contacts needed an interpreter.

Granum knew from different sources that personal contacts in Russia were very important. He was aware of the need to follow the Russian proverb: "Don't have a hundred roubles, but have a hundred friends." Therefore, he decided to contact his Russian acquaintance, Dr. Gleb Popov, who was an academic scholar and business consultant in Moscow and whom he had met at the International Human Resources Management Conference in St. Louis a year ago.

WEEK 2

Within a few days, a package of materials arrived from the U.S. Department of Commerce. Granum sequestered himself in his office and read the papers closely. Some of the documents focused on obstacles to trade and investments, while others tracked recent, positive developments and successes of companies operating in Russia.

In the "obstacles" papers, Granum read about instability and uncertainty in regulations and laws; the often conflicting banking system; lack of commercial, legal, and market information: the high costs of establishing offices; and severe infrastructure problems. A major difference from the United States was the loosely defined property rights in Russia. What really caught Granum's attention was the mention of Russian managers' lack of know-how about business ethics, individual job descriptions and responsibilities, arbitration in labor negotiations, and a few other traditional aspects of HRM. Conflict of interest in ethical issues and the breakdown of traditional approaches frequently placed American companies, operating under strict Foreign Corrupt Practices Act restraints, in a no-win situation. Many companies were concerned about widespread requests for bribes and payoffs.

Granum also discovered from this packet that there were professional associations, agencies, and organizations that could be contacted, such as the American Chamber of Commerce, the European Business Club, and BISNIS (Business Information Service for the Newly Independent States). U.S. government institutions such as the State Department and USAID had developed infrastructure assistance to support American business in the newly independent states and had designed internship programs for Russian managers and entrepreneurs in the United States.

The next source of information came from e-mail inquiries to Granum's colleagues in GTI. He was surprised to have such quick, forthcoming responses, which included some excellent ideas on future Russian expansion in relation to the company's overall strategy and culture, as well as advice on HRM practices. All the company managers who were contacted advised Granum "to be cautious in the move into uncharted territories." One expatriate manager with years of experience admitted he wasn't sure anything could guarantee success; yet, he felt the key ingredient was flexible thinking. As another valued colleague expressed that, "Russia is likely to pass through a period of considerable chaos. Be prepared to be flexible so as not to lose your best people."

A primary consideration for expansion into Russia was to ensure a solid understanding of global strategies among the selected future managers. In terms of communications, the company managers stressed the importance of sharing their professional and personal visions with the other members of the Russian subsidiary. GTI would need to continue to transfer its changing organizational culture as well as the historical approaches the company had undertaken to this new target expansion.

An operations manager whom Granum particularly admired stated that it would be vitally important to understand customer structures, financial and legal constraints. "The Russian society is not going to change because you (the manager) arrived," he quipped. It would be necessary to understand the local Russian specifics and customer requirements (both internal and external). Probably more than in most countries, it would be essential to combine both, ask for advice as much as necessary and make quick decisions, but remember to keep the organization involved in the decision process. This approach had to be undertaken to aid in developing a strong and cooperative local organization that guaranteed a profit in the shorter term. Because his company had a better understanding of other countries and longer periods of joint participation, thought Granum, it will be essential to ignore (as much as possible) the drawbacks of Russian society. This might be more likely to occur among the managers since the Russian culture has some rigid and often misunderstood notions about other unfamiliar cultures.

Having spent time in the library, reading and making notes, Granum designed a chart (see Exhibit 1) for Russian business and management profile. This helped him to compare characteristics of the Russian environment, firm and manager to his experience in the other countries and to design the following guidelines for analyzing information from different sources.

In order to better understand Russian management culture, Granum also utilized the Global Leadership and Organizational Behavior Effectiveness (GLOBE) research project. One hundred and seventy scholars from 62 countries participated in this international cross-cultural research. Russian project co-investigators had interviewed 450 Russian managers in the telecommunication, food processing, and finance industries and had developed the Russian cultural profile.

To measure this profile, Granum used seven-point Likert scales for GLOBE cultural dimensions and designed the radar chart (see Exhibit 2). The cultural dimensions followed in the tradition of the famous comparative research by Geert Hofstede. Granum drew the circles to display Russian managers' behaviors ("As Is"), and triangles to display managers' values and expectations ("Should Be"). The little square markers identified all-countries means for "As Is" data.

EXHIBIT 1

Russian Business and
Management Profile

Environment	• Diverse cultural background; 99.8% workforce literate; common language throughout Russia; still the largest country in the world
	• Mixture of Russian-historic and acquired-Soviet mentality
	• Strong entrepreneurship potential
	• Market economy in transition; not all institutions successfully established; business laws changing
	• New labor code favorable to business
	• Conflicting business attitudes and backgrounds among generations, lack of marketing and finance education and business ethics
	• Visible changes in putting more order into the economy not always democratic
	• Poor government/industrial policy, reliance on Western assistance
Firm	• Low respect to customers and contracts
	• Loosely defined responsibilities, in-company rules and confidentiality
	• Mission statements and strategic plans are rare; short-term vision, financial profits orientation dominates
	• Diversification strategies not developed, holdings prevail
	• Specific schemes of privatization of large companies; small businesses not favored, services largely privatized
	• Wild labor market; high quality of engineering skills, low quality of human resource management skills
	• Corruption
	• Financial and accounting practices don't fit international standards
	• Barriers for innovations
	• Low trust environment
Manager	• Respect to leadership, risk-taking, courage; visible status influence
	• Communications and information technologies not well developed (with few exceptions in former defense-oriented clusters); trust and personal relations important
	• Time is not high value
	• Group work is developed, but slow intergroup communications
	• Ability to work in highly uncertain environment ("creative survival")
	• High level of technical expertise within management ranks
	• Quickly absorb Western management techniques
	• Poor business ethics
	• Sense of humor

While analyzing the GLOBE indicators and rankings for Russia, Granum understood the realities of painful economic reforms and current business "mental models" in Russia. Extreme scores and comparative country ratings on Uncertainty Avoidance, Future Orientation, Performance Orientation "As Is" scales, as well as the gaps between values and behaviors, confirmed the Russian managers' mind-set of "creative survival" in an uncertain environment, their search for a "quick buck" rather than for long-term investments (such as investments in human resources), unpredictability, and reliance on substitutes for legal structures. The extreme uncertainty avoidance indicator and country rank could be assessed favorably for entrepreneurship unless one linked it to future orientation that was marginal as well. This could be interpreted

as lack of vision in entrepreneurship activities primarily focused on survival and not on long-term development of business. Low human orientation of behavior left little hope for long-term investments in human resources. The power distance and assertiveness numbers explained the tough (preferably administrative) measures in crisis management and in restructuring enterprises and industries.

The overall picture of "As Is" of Russian managers' behavior presented Granum with the profile that did not easily fit with internationally recognized practices. This fact could add additional challenges for Russian businesses in their interaction with foreign partners, for example, in creating strategic alliances.

There was a large gap between "As Is" and "Should Be" data on the dimensions linked directly to reforms in

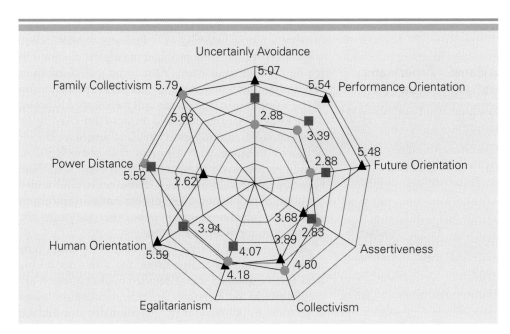

EXHIBIT 2

Globe Radar Chart for Russia

Source: Globe Project.

the economy. The "Should Be" model, however, displayed the preference for a more humanistic, ethical, democratic, and stable system. At the same time, there was no serious gap on dimensions strongly linked to historical cultural roots, such as family collectivism. Gender egalitarianism was also not part of the focus of current management concern.

Granum compared Russian and American GLOBE profiles. He underlined that uncertainty avoidance, performance orientation, assertiveness, and future orientation indicators for the United States were much higher, while family collectivism, power distance, and gender egalitarianism indicators were much lower than in Russia. These cross-cultural differences could create serious obstacles for developing an organizational culture for the Russian subsidiary.

Granum's findings conveyed a certain optimistic outlook for multinational companies that was rooted in Russian managers' willingness to launch large-scale projects, decisiveness, ability to make decisions and assume responsibility, ability to react quickly and operate in an unstable environment, increasingly common future orientation, and entrepreneurial potential. He identified dimensions on the societal level that were strongly influenced by the "transitional factor," but also those that were rooted in historic features of Russian society and resistant to this factor, i.e., visible collectivism and modest gender differentiation, high educational level of the workforce, managers' willingness to do business in more democratic and human-oriented environment.

Granum considered the recent changes in management in Russia and examples of positive corporate cultures. One could get rich on speculations and cheating on the partners and the state, thought Granum. But the

West would not build long-term cooperation with entrepreneurs who stray from business ethics, do not stand by their word, and are not responsible for their firms. "Predatory entrepreneurship" and Mafia structures frightened American business, which was based on a code of ethics and respect for the law. On the Transparency International corruption index, Russia was lower than sub-Sahara African countries.

In Babson Entrepreneurship Research database, Granum found Russian-American comparative data on business ethics. There were areas where Russians and Americans were close in their judgments and areas where the differences were striking. He sketched two tables with some questions from the survey that compared over 300 American and Russian managers. The first table displayed come similarities:

Questions	Russians: "yes" (%)	Americans: "yes" (%)
Is it ethical to use company time for noncompany benefits?	27.7	19.3
Things illegal are ethically wrong, aren't they?	51.9	52.5
Does your company need a "Code of Ethics" in decision-making?	62.7	73.5
Do you sacrifice personal ethics to business?	64.6	52.1

The second table set off serious warning signals:

Questions	Russians: "yes" (%)	Americans: "yes" (%)
Is it ethical to purchase shares using insider information?	53.8	11.1
Is it ethical to authorize violating company policy?	34.2	4.9
Is it ethical to give gifts for preferential treatment?	50.3	15.2
Is it ethical to accept gifts for preferential treatment?	32.5	7.3

However, Granum recognized that in the Russian economy, clusters of a healthy entrepreneurial culture existed: PC assemblers fostered fair competition, software developers followed the copyright convention, and several large enterprises developed and implemented principles of organizational culture, similar to the advanced Western practice. *BusinessWeek* referred to some Russian corporations such as Gazprom as "well managed and sophisticated," and "professional." It was not accidental that the international projects of such firms had significant potential for success.

A week later, Granum scheduled his Russian trip.

WEEK 3

The Delta Airlines flight was exceedingly long, with connections in Cincinnati and New York. In fact, it took Granum nearly 20 hours to get to Moscow. But he was a seasoned traveler and was glad to spend some time alone putting together ideas for the upcoming Russian venture. He understood that a lot of pressure regarding the success of this venture was riding on his own work and creativity.

At Moscow's Sheremetievo International Airport, Granum tested the "3P principle for foreigners"—patience, patience, and patience. Waiting in a long line to clear customs was also a learning experience, and Granum was surprised to observe people of different ethnic origins speaking Russian. In fact, this reminded him of the melting pot in the United States. Russian appeared to be a common language for people of different nationalities, and the acceptance of other cultures was evident.

Fortunately, Gleb was waiting at the airport to meet Granum. Their conversation while driving to a down-

town hotel was not long but was very useful. They immediately focused on the GTI business venture. Gleb was concerned with the problem of cultural compatibility, mentioning that many Americans still based their business decisions on oversimplification or politicization of the Russian situation. Some still stereotyped Russians as lacking in motivation and insisted on playing by American rules, forcing individualistic practices. He felt obligated to share with Granum that some Russians viewed Americans as invaders and didn't deal with them beyond a minimal level of trust. Fortunately, Gleb ended his litany of problems with an upbeat summary; if certain steps towards real success were to be made, they would be based on in-depth considerations.

A commitment to this deeper level of understanding might be accomplished by contracting with a consulting firm. Gleb explained that a detailed market research approach would aid managers in understanding the many differences in business terms. Additionally, it would aid the HR department in their training on cultural diversity through the generation of responsibility, reliance on trust (and if possible, matching up individuals with mentors), and how to avoid direct criticism of the country and its people. Needless to say, Granum was grateful to Gleb for these comments and ideas.

Now in Moscow, Granum referred to another Russian proverb: "It is better to see once, than hear a hundred times." Yes, Moscow was an impressive modern city. The hotel Mertopol, walking distance from the Kremlin, met global quality standards but was extremely expensive. Granum could see the Bolshoi Theatre from his window and was amazed with the beauty of Moscow architecture.

Although he would like to have the time to explore the city, Granum was aware that having dinner with Gleb and some of the Russian members of the GTI business expansion was extremely important. Granum followed his Washington friend's recommendation and invited *Wall Street Journal* Moscow correspondent John Sachs to join him for dinner. Russian cuisine—with borscht (beet soup), blini (pancakes), ikra (caviar), and hot tea with lemon—was appealing. After an exhausting and eventful but useful day, Granum followed a final Russian proverb: "Morning is wiser than evening" (sleep on it) and went to bed.

The next few days were heavily scheduled. Granum visited the facility in Mitino. The equipment was installed, leaving only the final polishing and painting to complete the site. The representative of the Russian–Turkish construction company assured him that all the work would be finished according to the plan. At the same time, he informed Granum that many people in the nearby community (housing almost 200,000 people) were asking if there would be jobs for them. The Russian economy was in the process of restructuring, and unemployment was high.

Granum thought this situation could be favorable for GTI in terms of pay policy and labor costs reduction.

An American correspondent who had joined the previous evening's dinner invited Granum to join him for the press conference at the Ministry of Labor of the Russian Federation. This press conference was rather short. From the deputy minister, Granum learned about the strategic vision of the preferred employment and labor system for Russia. It was a flexible and legalized labor market, guaranteeing acceptable unemployment of 4 percent to 5 percent and stability of economic growth of 3 percent to 5 percent, with salaries and wages rising accordingly. The key features of such a system were linked to improved legal infrastructure. It was necessary to adopt term labor contracts, destroying the long-life employment systems still formally dominating in Russia. The system of firing extra workers was intended to be quite simple.

The strategic guidelines suggested that collective agreements should be made at the enterprise level. Collective bargaining at the levels of industries or regions, and the national level as well, should not lead to obligatory decisions. This brought substantial variability into the pay levels and put quite a few otherwise healthy enterprises on the edge of bankruptcy. The right to strike should be supplemented by the effective labor arbitration and by a mechanism supporting implementation of individual and collective agreements.

Sachs advised Granum to contact one of the influential Russian business dailies, such as *The Moscow Times* or *Kommersant,* to advertise the new venture and announce the corporate requirements for new management personnel. This turned out to be easily accomplished, and Granum marked it in his notebook.

At his next appointment with the Ministry of Transportation, Granum was informed about different potential candidates for managerial jobs. The ministry was helpful, although somewhat directive. The difficulty for Granum was in determining the differences in quality and preparation between the credentials and universities the candidates had.

As his information and paperwork grew, Granum thought of leasing office space. He was shocked, however, at the high rent prices in Moscow. He also asked Elena Zotova, his interpreter, to help with some office work. From conversations with Zotova, Granum found out that the pay systems in Russian and foreign companies were very different than what he had expected. Western companies wanted to hire skilled and committed people; hence, the salaries in multinational companies were moving closer to international standards. This wage averaged 10 or more times higher than salaries in current Russian enterprises. However, successfully privatized and newly established companies also followed tough employment and pay policy approaches on the

"fewer but better" principle. The labor market of knowledgeable, skilled workers with fluent foreign language was decidedly narrow.

Granum learned that for Russian staff at multinational companies, maximum gross salary levels varied from $4,500 per month for a brand manager to $1,000 per month for an office manager. Nonsalary benefits were still unusual in Russia. According to surveys, only one-third of multinationals considered making contributions to private medical insurance. Other ideas under consideration were pension fund contributions, company cars, stock option schemes, and mortgage loans. In order to strengthen loyalty among management personnel, multinational companies were developing prospects in one- and two-year career plans, including possible expatriate positions outside Russia.

Granum was hesitant to rely on cheap labor because he had been informed about poorly motivated workers who were known to break rules and cause discipline problems. What was the right strategy for building a "Soviet-styled" HRM system? Granum spoke with other American companies' managers. They told him that they took Western models and implemented the principles of corporate organizational culture. They imposed high standards on selection, and skills were tested through the interview process. Some preferred hiring young people with the ability to learn, rather than older people. The latter, with few exceptions, seemed unable to change their mental models towards market-oriented work, competitiveness, and learning. This put a strong emphasis not only on selection but also on the training system. Evidently this approach had paid off for other companies.

Granum also learned about a survey of multinationals in Russia that showed the rapid staff turnover (up to 70 percent) as the main operational concern of multinational companies. Job-hopping was a problem for HRM. The basic skill set of the average Russian employee was higher than that of the United States or Europe. At the same time, the key skill gaps among Russian managers were in leadership, creativity, and the ability to improve, as well as in problem-solving, teamwork, and showing initiative. Western firms were spending a lot of money on training in an effort to fill the gaps. But while training wins staff loyalty, it can also make employees tantalizing targets for poachers. Russian companies for this reason did virtually no training of their own, preferring to hire staff away from other firms.

Headhunters also encouraged disloyalty. About two-thirds of multinationals used search firms. Recruitment and training costs made replacing staff in Russia pricier than in the United States or United Kingdom. Filling a clerical position in Russia would cost about twice as much as in the United States.

Granum thought of his conversation with Gleb, who commented that when American and Russian managers and executives can speak a common language and understand the content of the economic terms in the same way, both countries would advance. The current initiatives by a number of American corporations to bring educational resources to Russia or to set up internships in the United States were not purely charitable. Speaking a common language would decrease risk, both political and economic, while entering the Russian market. What were the training needs? Granum knew the greatest concern of the Russian personnel lay in the area of management skills. How should he design training for Russian personnel and, in particular, for the management staff?

The quick decision to work with Gleb's consulting firm had an immediate payoff. Information was available to Granum regarding the training needs of Russian managers and entrepreneurs, based on a current questionnaire. Russian managers felt they were least capable in the area of finance followed by marketing/sales. They also felt more positive about their management skills in dealing with people and idea generation than they felt about their skills in business operations and organizing and planning. As would be expected in a once controlled economy just starting to emerge as market-oriented, the questionnaire uncovered numerous business problems confronting Russian entrepreneurs. The most frequently mentioned problem was the lack of business training, followed by lack of experience in hiring outside services, lack of guidance and counseling, lack of experience in financial planning, demands of the company affecting personal relations, personnel problems, lack of involvement with business colleagues, and weak collateral position.

Thus, expatriates were a serious concern to Granum. In order to be successful in Russia, it became obvious that GTI had to hire, train, and motivate the right mix of local and international people. One possible option would be to find managers from other GTI subsidiaries who might be willing to relocate.

Granum was fortunate that GTI had developed a reliable HR information system. From this database search, he managed to find several managers in other countries who indicated an interest in Russia. Granum thought that it was logical to involve at least two candidates from within the Russian business expansion planning office. One of them was Fritz Bauer, the sales manager from the company's German subsidiary. Before the unification of Germany, Bauer had lived in East Berlin. He had a moderate background in Russian (which was taught in East German schools) and was familiar with socialist-type businesses, bureaucratic vehicles, and the negotiation process. The second candidate for reassignment was Aivo Pukalo from Finland. The Finnish subsidiary was the channel for previous deliveries of the company's products to Russia, and Pukalo had often traveled to St. Petersburg and Moscow.

Granum discovered that objective hiring of locals to work in the company would not be easy because reference checks and background information were difficult to obtain. Many of the employment-related tests assessed the networking ability of the individual. Also, there was great diversity across curricula in management education in Russia (opposite to well-developed technical/engineering education); therefore, it was difficult to assess a candidate's educational background with consistency.

As a minimum expectation for hiring, Granum felt that potential Russian managers should have at least five years of managerial experience, should be fluent in English, and should have socialization and communication skills. He was not concerned with the educational experience skills level since he understood that mathematical and science skills were excellent in the Russian school system.

WEEK 4

It was Monday. Using his laptop, Granum made notes during the flight back to New York. He outlined three key lessons he had learned from the other companies and from the economic history of Russia and its current practices, and he listed a page of questions that still required resolution. In three more days, Granum would have to present his plan for training, hiring, and compensation to GTI's board of directors.

Can Madison Avenue Marketing Help Developing Countries? The Case of Jordan

Marketing a product or service has long been a staple of any modern corporation's business plan. Firms of all sizes use marketing to introduce new products, increase market share of existing products, enter new markets, improve firm image, establish a brand, or even develop relationships with suppliers and vendors. According to Regis McKenna, a noted marketing expert who helped launch Apple Computer, "Marketing is everything, and everything is marketing." The quality of a firm's marketing can make the difference between the success and failure of an organization.

If marketing efforts can be so important in attracting customers to a product or service, can the same marketing tools assist entire nations in attracting foreign enterprises to invest in their economy? A few countries are answering this important question with a resounding yes and are taking important steps to use marketing to attract foreign direct investment.

Jordan, surrounded by Iraq, Israel, Saudi Arabia, and Syria in the Middle East, has not traditionally been known as a center of economic activity. Jordan has few ports and inadequate supplies of water and other natural resources. Debt and poverty are fundamental problems in Jordan, and unemployment may reach as high as 30 percent, according to unofficial estimates. Furthermore, Jordan lacks the significant oil reserves held by many Middle Eastern nations and must import rather than export oil for survival. Yet, the Jordanian government has taken significant steps toward attracting foreign direct investment to the country.

First, Jordan has established an all-important Web presence designed specifically for attracting foreign direct investment. Jordan's Web page, www.jordaninvestment.com, has a wealth of information about the economic characteristics of the Jordanian economy. Smartly, the page can be viewed in both English and Arabic so as to be accessible to a global audience. The page offers an overview of Jordan, provides facts about the Jordanian economy, and lists regulations relevant to foreign investors. More than just providing facts, the page markets these important facts in a format attractive to visitors and simple to digest. For example, at www.jordaninvestment.com/about-jordan.htm, the page lists the top 10 reasons to invest in Jordan. These reasons include a "Unique and Strategic Location," "Stable Political Environment," and a "Free Market Oriented Economy." Jordan also emphasizes its high-quality infrastructure, quality of life, and educated workforce that can staff facilities established by foreign firms.

Jordan has backed these catchphrases with specific changes to its regulatory structure specifically designed to attract and retain foreign capital. For example, Jordan's Web site advertises that selected projects are partially exempted from income and social services taxes (as high as 75 percent) for a 10-year period, depending on the location and type of project. Furthermore, Jordan provides relief from customs and income tax obligations for the expansion and development of existing projects. Finally, imported assets are completely exempt from customs obligations for foreign investors.

Jordan has even developed an investment brand. Jordan's investment brand is a Black Iris flower on a red background. The flower, native only to Jordan, is a symbol of growth and renewal, thereby representing Jordan's fertile ground for investment and growth.

Beyond a Web site, Jordanian representatives have used diplomatic and promotional efforts to attract investment from abroad. For example, in 1999 Mr. Abu Mohammed, then director general of the Investment Promotion Corporation (IPC) responsible for promoting foreign investment, traveled to Asia.[1] His goal was to initiate contacts with business interests there and lay the groundwork for a senior-level delegation of Jordanian government officials and business leaders to follow up later. Mohammed's efforts were simply another form of marketing—direct, interpersonal efforts that forge initial contacts that eventually build into mature business relationships.

Mohammed's first visit was to Taiwan. After spending a day familiarizing himself with the city, Mohammed visited Taiwan's Ministry for Foreign Affairs to promote formal diplomatic relations and to encourage a taxation agreement that would eliminate double taxation of firms doing business in both nations. Such agreements, according to Mohammed, are important for fostering trust with Taiwan's business community that Jordan is serious about receiving investment projects.

Mohammed then spoke with the director of the Taipei Computer Association, who offered to publicize an investment seminar sponsored by the Jordanian government. Mohammed then met with an executive of a computer company and encouraged him to expand his already-established Jordanian operations.

After further meetings with executives and business organizations in Taiwan, Mohammed then traveled to Hong Kong and met with Anthony Tang, secretary general of the Hong Kong Manufacturers Association. Mohammed marketed Jordan as a more competitive alternative for Hong Kong textile manufacturing than China. Responding to Tang's concerns that complex Chinese bureaucratic rules were "a mess," Mohammed cited the streamlined bureaucratic approval process that Jordan's IPC offers. Mohammed also learned that the firms that Tang represented preferred isolated locations for their factories to limit job-shopping by employees. This may be another opportunity to distinguish Jordan as an alternative location for Chinese textile operations.

By visiting business leaders, Mohammed also learned of the marketing obstacles that needed to be overcome to attract investment. For example, when Mohammed met with Chris Chan, vice president of Asian Source for Liz Claiborne International, Ltd., he learned that Chan was concerned with the high price of water in Jordan and the risk of lost productivity during the holy month of Ramadan.

---

[1]This example is adapted from Sarah Harpending, *Investment Promotion: Marketing a Nation*, available at www.iie.org/programs/emdap/CaseStudies/secondary/_cases/IIECS_10.pdf.

Mohammed also learned of the negative brand images of Jordan that might exist among potential investors. For example, when Mohammed met with S. K. Chhatwal, president of Marsalla Fabrics Limited in India, Chhatwall reported that he initially believed that Jordan was a very strict country, like Saudi Arabia, with no freedoms for women. In addition, Chhatwall expressed concerns about security in Jordan and noted that other executives would have to be reassured about safety issues before making investments there.

Mohammed also gained valuable intelligence by learning of key competitors in certain industries. Mohammed's meeting with the Northern India Textile Mills Association showed him that while Indian manufacturers are not satisfied with conditions in India, they perceived Pakistan, Turkey, and Egypt as superior investment choices because of their location to important markets. Bangladesh, Mauritius, and Nepal were all similarly courting Indian textile investments.

Although no specific investment agreements arose from Mohammed's trip, his efforts were not without purpose. Such meetings lay important groundwork that must precede any long-term relationships. Most of his meetings resulted in invitations to return again, offer seminars, and establish contacts with Jordanian representatives. These efforts, commonly described as relationship marketing, enhance relationships with potential and current customers and allow quick responses to customer needs. Efforts such as these can bear fruit for any developing nation seeking foreign direct investment.

Although Jordan has done much to establish investment promotion, it still has much to do to improve its marketing image. For example, although Jordan has established an investment logo, the black iris flower, it has apparently done little to integrate the logo into its investment operations. Also, the logo is likely not widely known. Consider, by contrast, South Africa's logo, which not only has well-developed branding[2] but has even developed brands for specific industries such as wine[3] and tourism.[4] South Africa's Web sites are well organized, graphically intensive, and well stocked with pertinent information for the foreign investor.

Jordan's efforts represent a good example of a developing country marketing a national brand to the world. Through a combination of Internet promotion, relationship marketing, and strong economic conditions in Jordan favorable to investment, this Middle Eastern nation can emerge as a strong presence in the global marketplace.

Case Discussion Questions

1. Notice that Mohammed visited both Taiwan and Hong Kong to attract investment. What kind of political challenges can arise from soliciting relationships from both Taiwan and mainland China? What can Mohammed do to circumvent these challenges and attract investments from these vibrant economies?

2. Jordan is not the only developing nation aggressively seeking foreign direct investment. How can Jordan distinguish itself from its competitors such as Bangladesh, Mauritius, and Nepal? How can Jordan make inroads against nations such as Egypt, Turkey, and Pakistan that possess inherent geographic advantages that Jordan lacks? Does the choice of investment solicited impact that decision?

3. Review and compare the national brands of South Africa and Jordan. What does each of the two brands say about its national identity? How effective is each nation in implementing its brand into its overall investment strategy? What can both nations do to better promote their respective brands to the world?

---

[2] www.imc.org.za.

[3] www.wosa.co.za.

[4] www.southafrica.info/plan_trip/holiday.

GLOSSARY

A

absolute advantage A country has an absolute advantage in the production of a product when it is more efficient than any other country at producing it.

accounting standards Rules for preparing financial statements.

ad valorem tariff A tariff levied as a proportion of the value of an imported good.

administrative trade policies Administrative policies, typically adopted by government bureaucracies, that can be used to restrict imports or boost exports.

Andean Pact A 1969 agreement between Bolivia, Chile, Ecuador, Colombia, and Peru to establish a customs union.

antidumping policies Designed to punish foreign firms that engage in dumping and thus protect domestic producers from unfair foreign competition.

antidumping regulations Regulations designed to restrict the sale of goods for less than their fair market price.

arbitrage The purchase of securities in one market for immediate resale in another to profit from a price discrepancy.

Association of South East Asian Nations (ASEAN) Formed in 1967, an attempt to establish a free trade area between Brunei, Indonesia, Malaysia, the Philippines, Singapore, and Thailand.

auditing standards Rules for performing an audit.

B

backward vertical FDI Investing in an industry abroad that provides inputs for a firm's domestic processes.

balance-of-payments accounts National accounts that track both payments to and receipts from foreigners.

balance-of-trade equilibrium Reached when the income a nation's residents earn from exports equals money paid for imports.

banking crisis A loss of confidence in the banking system that leads to a run on banks, as individuals and companies withdraw their deposits.

barriers to entry Factors that make it difficult or costly for firms to enter an industry or market.

barter The direct exchange of goods or services between two parties without a cash transaction.

basic research centers Centers for fundamental research located in regions where valuable scientific knowledge is being created; they develop the basic technologies that become new products.

bilateral netting Settlement in which the amount one subsidiary owes another can be canceled by the debt the second subsidiary owes the first.

bill of exchange An order written by an exporter instructing an importer, or an importer's agent, to pay a specified amount of money at a specified time.

bill of lading A document issued to an exporter by a common carrier transporting merchandise. It serves as a receipt, a contract, and a document of title.

Bretton Woods A 1944 conference in which representatives of 40 countries met to design a new international monetary system.

bureaucratic controls Achieving control through establishment of a system of rules and procedures.

business ethics The accepted principles of right or wrong governing the conduct of businesspeople.

buyback Agreement to accept percentage of a plant's output as payment for contract to build a plant.

C

capital account In the balance of payments, records transactions involving the purchase or sale of assets.

capital controls Restrictions on cross-border capital flows that segment different stock markets; limit amount of a firm's stock a foreigner can own; and limit a citizen's ability to invest outside the country.

capital flight Residents convert domestic currency into a foreign currency.

CARICOM An association of English-speaking Caribbean states that are attempting to establish a customs union.

caste system A system of social stratification in which social position is determined by the family into which a person is born, and change in that position is usually not possible during an individual's lifetime.

centralized depository The practice of centralizing corporate cash balances in a single depository.

channel length The number of intermediaries that a product has to go through before it reaches the final consumer.

civil law system A system of law based on a very detailed set of written laws and codes.

class consciousness   A tendency for individuals to perceive themselves in terms of their class background.

class system   A system of social stratification in which social status is determined by the family into which a person is born and by subsequent socioeconomic achievements. Mobility between classes is possible.

code of ethics   A formal statement of the ethical priorities of a business or organization.

collectivism   An emphasis on collective goals as opposed to individual goals.

COMECON   Now-defunct economic association of Eastern European Communist states headed by the former Soviet Union.

command economy   An economic system where the allocation of resources, including determination of what goods and services should be produced, and in what quantity, is planned by the government.

common law system   A system of law based on tradition, precedent, and custom. When law courts interpret common law, they do so with regard to these characteristics.

common market   A group of countries committed to (1) removing all barriers to the free flow of goods, services, and factors of production between each other and (2) the pursuit of a common external trade policy.

communist totalitarianism   A version of collectivism advocating that socialism can be achieved only through a totalitarian dictatorship.

communists   Those who believe socialism can be achieved only through revolution and totalitarian dictatorship.

comparative advantage   The theory that countries should specialize in the production of goods and services they can produce most efficiently. A country is said to have a comparative advantage in the production of such goods and services.

competition policy   Regulations designed to promote competition and restrict monopoly practices.

Confucian dynamism   Theory that Confucian teachings affect attitudes toward time, persistence, ordering by status, protection of face, respect for tradition, and reciprocation of gifts and favors.

constant returns to specialization   The units of resources required to produce a good are assumed to remain constant no matter where one is on a country's production possibility frontier.

contract   Document that specifies conditions of an exchange and details rights and obligations of involved parties.

contract law   Body of law that governs contract enforcement.

control systems   Metrics used to measure performance of subunits.

controlling interest   A firm has a controlling interest in another business entity when it owns more than 50 percent of that entity's voting stock.

Convention on Combating Bribery of Foreign Public Officials in International Business Transactions   OECD agreement to make the bribery of foreign public officials a criminal offense.

copyright   Exclusive legal rights of authors, composers, playwrights, artists, and publishers to publish and dispose of their work as they see fit.

core competence   Firm skills that competitors cannot easily match or imitate.

corporate culture   The organization's norms and value systems.

cost of capital   Price of money.

Council of the European Union   Represents the interests of EU members and has authority to approve EU laws.

counterpurchase   A reciprocal buying agreement.

countertrade   The trade of goods and services for other goods and services.

countervailing duties   Antidumping duties.

Court of Justice   Supreme appeals court for EU law.

cross-cultural literacy   Understanding how the culture of a country affects the way business is practiced.

cross-licensing agreement   An arrangement in which a company licenses valuable intangible property to a foreign partner and receives a license for the partner's valuable knowledge; reduces risk of licensing.

cultural controls   Achieving control by persuading subordinates to identify with the norms and value systems of the organization (self-control).

cultural relativism   Belief that ethics are culturally determined, and a firm should adopt the ethics of the culture in which it is operating.

culture   The complex whole that includes knowledge, belief, art, morals, law, custom, and other capabilities acquired by a person as a member of society.

currency board   Means of controlling a country's currency.

currency crisis   Occurs when a speculative attack on the exchange value of a currency results in a sharp depreciation in the value of the currency or forces authorities to expend large volumes of international currency reserves and sharply increase interest rates to defend the prevailing exchange rate.

currency speculation   Involves short-term movement of funds from one currency to another in hopes of profiting from shifts in exchange rates.

currency swap Simultaneous purchase and sale of a given amount of foreign exchange for two different value dates.

currency translation Converting the financial statements of foreign subsidiaries into the currency of the home country.

current account In the balance of payments, records transactions involving the export or import of goods and services.

current account deficit The current account of the balance of payments is in deficit when a country imports more goods and services than it exports.

current account surplus The current account of the balance of payments is in surplus when a country exports more goods and services than it imports.

current cost accounting Method that adjusts all items in a financial statement to factor out the effects of inflation.

current rate method Using the exchange rate at the balance sheet date to translate the financial statements of a foreign subsidiary into the home currency.

customs union A group of countries committed to (1) removing all barriers to the free flow of goods and services between each other and (2) the pursuit of a common external trade policy.

D

D'Amato Act Act passed in 1996, similar to the Helms-Burton Act, aimed at Libya and Iran.

debt loan Requires a corporation to repay loan at regular intervals.

deferral principle Parent companies are not taxed on the income of a foreign subsidiary until they actually receive a dividend from that subsidiary.

democracy Political system in which government is by the people, exercised either directly or through elected representatives.

deregulation Removal of government restrictions concerning the conduct of a business.

diminishing returns to specialization Applied to international trade theory, the more of a good that a country produces, the greater the units of resources required to produce each additional item.

dirty-float system A system under which a country's currency is nominally allowed to float freely against other currencies, but in which the government will intervene, buying and selling currency, if it believes that the currency has deviated too far from its fair value.

draft An order written by an exporter telling an importer what and when to pay.

drawee The party to whom a bill of lading is presented.

dumping Selling goods in a foreign market for less than their cost of production or below their "fair" market value.

E

eclectic paradigm Argument that combining location-specific assets or resource endowments and the firm's own unique assets often requires FDI; it requires the firm to establish production facilities where those foreign assets or resource endowments are located.

e-commerce Conducting business online through the Internet.

economic exposure The extent to which a firm's future international earning power is affected by changes in exchange rates.

economic risk The likelihood that events, including economic mismanagement, will cause drastic changes in a country's business environment that adversely affect the profit and other goals of a particular business enterprise.

economic union A group of countries committed to (1) removing all barriers to the free flow of goods, services, and factors of production between each other, (2) the adoption of a common currency, (3) the harmonization of tax rates, and (4) the pursuit of a common external trade policy.

economies of scale Cost advantages associated with large-scale production.

efficient market A market where prices reflect all available information.

ending rate The spot exchange rate when budget and performance are being compared.

equity loan Occurs when a corporation sells stock to an investor.

ethical dilemma Situation in which no available alternative seems ethically acceptable.

ethical strategy A course of action that does not violate business ethics.

ethical systems Cultural beliefs about what is proper behavior and conduct.

ethnocentric behavior Behavior that is based on the belief in the superiority of one's own ethnic group or culture; often shows disregard or contempt for the culture of other countries.

ethnocentric staffing A staffing approach within the MNE in which all key management positions are filled by parent-country nationals.

ethnocentrism Belief in the superiority of one's own ethnic group or culture.

eurobonds A bond placed in countries other than the one in whose currency the bond is denominated.

eurocurrency   Any currency banked outside its country of origin.

eurodollar   Dollar banked outside the United States.

European Commission   Responsible for proposing EU legislation, implementing it, and monitoring compliance.

European Council   Consists of the heads of state of EU members and the president of the European Commission.

European Free Trade Association (EFTA)   A free trade association including Norway, Iceland, and Switzerland.

European Monetary System (EMS)   EU system designed to create a zone of monetary stability in Europe, control inflation, and coordinate exchange rate policies of EU countries.

European Parliament   Elected EU body that provides consultation on issues proposed by European Commission.

European Union (EU)   An economic group of 25 European nations. Established as a customs union, it is now moving toward economic union. (Formerly the European Community.)

exchange rate   The rate at which one currency is converted into another.

exchange rate mechanism (ERM)   Mechanism for aligning the exchange rates of EU currencies against each other.

exclusive channels   A distribution channel that outsiders find difficult to access.

expatriate   A citizen of one country working in another country.

expatriate failure   The premature return of an expatriate manager to the home country.

expatriate manager   A national of one country appointed to a management position in another country.

experience curve   Systematic production cost reductions that occur over the life of a product.

experience curve pricing   Aggressive pricing designed to increase volume and help the firm realize experience curve economies.

export management company   Export specialists who act as an export marketing department for client firms.

Export–Import Bank (Eximbank)   Agency of the U.S. government whose mission is to provide aid in financing and facilitate exports and imports.

exporting   Sale of products produced in one country to residents of another country.

externalities   Knowledge spillovers.

externally convertible currency   Nonresidents can convert their holdings of domestic currency into foreign currency, but the ability of residents to convert the currency is limited in some way.

external stakeholders   All other individuals and groups, other than internal stakeholders, that have some claim on the business.

F

factor endowments   A country's endowment with resources such as land, labor, and capital.

factors of production   Inputs into the productive process of a firm, including labor, management, land, capital, and technological know-how.

Financial Accounting Standards Board (FASB)   The body that writes the generally accepted accounting principles by which the financial statements of U.S. firms must be prepared.

financial structure   Mix of debt and equity used to finance a business.

first-mover advantages   Advantages accruing to the first to enter a market.

first-mover disadvantages   Disadvantages associated with entering a foreign market before other international businesses.

Fisher Effect   Nominal interest rates (i) in each country equal the required real rate of interest (r) and the expected rate of inflation over the period of time for which the funds are to be lent (I). That is, $i = r + I$.

fixed exchange rates   A system under which the exchange rate for converting one currency into another is fixed.

fixed-rate bond   Offers a fixed set of cash payoffs each year until maturity, when the investor also receives the face value of the bond in cash.

flexible machine cells   Flexible manufacturing technology in which a grouping of various machine types, a common materials handler, and a centralized cell controller produce a family of products.

flexible manufacturing technologies   Manufacturing technologies designed to improve job scheduling, reduce setup time, and improve quality control.

floating exchange rates   A system under which the exchange rate for converting one currency into another is continuously adjusted depending on the laws of supply and demand.

flow of foreign direct investment   The amount of foreign direct investment undertaken over a given time period (normally one year).

folkways   Routine conventions of everyday life.

foreign bonds   Bonds sold outside the borrower's country and denominated in the currency of the country in which they are issued.

Foreign Corrupt Practices Act   U.S. law regulating behavior regarding the conduct of international business in the taking of bribes and other unethical actions.

foreign debt crisis Situation in which a country cannot service its foreign debt obligations, whether private-sector or government debt.

foreign direct investment (FDI) Direct investment in business operations in a foreign country.

foreign exchange exposure The risk that future changes in a country's exchange rate will hurt the firm.

foreign exchange market A market for converting the currency of one country into that of another country.

foreign exchange risk The risk that changes in exchange rates will hurt the profitability of a business deal.

foreign portfolio investment (FPI) Investments by individuals, firms, or public bodies (e.g., national and local governments) in foreign financial instruments (e.g., government bonds, foreign stocks).

forward exchange When two parties agree to exchange currency and execute a deal at some specific date in the future.

forward exchange rate The exchange rates governing forward exchange transactions.

forward vertical FDI Investing in an industry abroad that sells outputs of domestic processes.

franchising A specialized form of licensing in which the franchiser sells intangible property to the franchisee and insists on rules to conduct the business.

free trade The absence of barriers to the free flow of goods and services between countries.

free trade area A group of countries committed to removing all barriers to the free flow of goods and services between each other, but pursuing independent external trade policies.

freely convertible currency A country's currency is freely convertible when the government of that country allows both residents and nonresidents to purchase unlimited amounts of foreign currency with the domestic currency.

fronting loan A loan between a parent company and a foreign subsidiary that is channeled through a financial intermediary.

fundamental analysis Draws on economic theory to construct sophisticated econometric models for predicting exchange rate movements.

G

gains from trade The economic gains to a country from engaging in international trade.

General Agreement on Tariffs and Trade (GATT) International treaty that committed signatories to lowering barriers to the free flow of goods across national borders and led to the WTO.

geocentric staffing A staffing policy where the best people are sought for key jobs throughout an MNE, regardless of nationality.

global learning The flow of skills and product offerings from foreign subsidiary to home country and from foreign subsidiary to foreign subsidiary.

global matrix structure Horizontal differentiation proceeds along two dimensions: product divisions and areas.

global standardization strategy Strategy focusing on increasing profitability by reaping cost reductions from experience curve and location economies.

global web When different stages of value chain are dispersed to those locations around the globe where value added is maximized or where costs of value creation are minimized.

globalization Trend away from distinct national economic units and toward one huge global market.

globalization of markets Moving away from an economic system in which national markets are distinct entities, isolated by trade barriers and barriers of distance, time, and culture, and toward a system in which national markets are merging into one global market.

globalization of production Trend by individual firms to disperse parts of their productive processes to different locations around the globe to take advantage of differences in cost and quality of factors of production.

gold par value The amount of currency needed to purchase one ounce of gold.

gold standard The practice of pegging currencies to gold and guaranteeing convertibility.

greenfield investment Establishing a new operation in a foreign country.

gross domestic product (GDP) The market value of a country's output attributable to factors of production located in the country's territory.

gross national income (GNI) Measures the total annual income received by residents of a nation.

gross fixed capital formation Summarizes the total amount of capital invested in factories, stores, office buildings, and the like.

gross national product (GNP) The market value of all the final goods and services produced by a national economy.

group An association of two or more individuals who have a shared sense of identity and who interact with each other in structured ways on the basis of a common set of expectations about each other's behavior.

H

Heckscher-Ohlin theory Countries will export those goods that make intensive use of locally abundant factors of production and import goods that make intensive use of locally scarce factors of production.

hedge fund   Investment fund that not only buys financial assets (stocks, bonds, currencies) but also sells them short.

Helms-Burton Act   Act passed in 1996 that allowed Americans to sue foreign firms that use Cuban property confiscated from them after the 1959 revolution.

historic cost principle   Accounting principle founded on the assumption that the currency unit used to report financial results is not losing its value due to inflation.

home country   The source country for foreign direct investment.

horizontal differentiation   The division of the firm into subunits.

horizontal foreign direct investment   Foreign direct investment in the same industry abroad as a firm operates in at home.

host country   Recipient country of inward investment by a foreign firm.

Human Development Index   An attempt by the United Nations to assess the impact of a number of factors on the quality of human life in a country.

human resource management   Activities an organization conducts to use its human resources effectively.

I

import quota   A direct restriction on the quantity of a good that can be imported into a country.

incentives   Devices used to reward managerial behavior.

individualism   An emphasis on the importance of guaranteeing individual freedom and self-expression.

individualism versus collectivism   Theory focusing on the relationship between the individual and his or her fellows. In individualistic societies, the ties between individuals are loose and individual achievement is highly valued. In societies where collectivism is emphasized, ties between individuals are tight, people are born into collectives, such as extended families, and everyone is supposed to look after the interests of his or her collective.

inefficient market   One in which prices do not reflect all available information.

infant industry argument   New industries in developing countries must be temporarily protected from international competition to help them reach a position where they can compete on world markets with the firms of developed nations.

inflows of FDI   Flow of foreign direct investment into a country.

initial rate   The spot exchange rate when a budget is adopted.

innovation   Development of new products, processes, organizations, management practices, and strategies.

integrating mechanisms   Mechanisms for achieving coordination between subunits within an organization.

intellectual property   Products of the mind, ideas (e.g., books, music, computer software, designs, technological know-how). Intellectual property can be protected by patents, copyrights, and trademarks.

internal forward rate   A company-generated forecast of future spot rates.

internal stakeholders   Individuals or groups who work for or own the business.

internalization theory   Marketing imperfection approach to foreign direct investment.

International Accounting Standards Board (IASB)   Organization of representatives of professional accounting organizations from many countries that is attempting to harmonize accounting standards across countries.

international business   Any firm that engages in international trade or investment.

international division   Division responsible for a firm's international activities.

International Fisher Effect   For any two countries, the spot exchange rate should change in an equal amount but in the opposite direction to the difference in nominal interest rates between countries.

International Monetary Fund (IMF)   International institution set up to maintain order in the international monetary system.

international monetary system   Institutional arrangements countries adopt to govern exchange rates.

international strategy   Trying to create value by transferring core competencies to foreign markets where indigenous competitors lack those competencies.

international trade   Occurs when a firm exports goods or services to consumers in another country.

ISO 9000   Certification process that requires certain quality standards that must be met.

J

joint venture   A cooperative undertaking between two or more firms.

just distribution   One that is considered fair and equitable.

just-in-time (JIT)   Logistics systems designed to deliver parts to a production process as they are needed, not before.

K

Kantian ethics   Belief that people should be treated as ends and never purely as means to the ends of others.

knowledge network Network for transmitting information within an organization that is based on informal contacts between managers within an enterprise and on distributed information systems.

L

lag strategy Delaying the collection of foreign currency receivables if that currency is expected to appreciate, and delaying payables if that currency is expected to depreciate.

late-mover advantages Benefits enjoyed by a company that is late to enter a new market, such as consumer familiarity with the product or knowledge gained about a market.

late-mover disadvantages Handicap that late entrants to a market suffer.

law of one price In competitive markets free of transportation costs and barriers to trade, identical products sold in different countries must sell for the same price when their price is expressed in the same currency.

lead market Market where products are first introduced.

lead strategy Collecting foreign currency receivables early when a foreign currency is expected to depreciate, and paying foreign currency payables before they are due when a currency is expected to appreciate.

lean production systems Flexible manufacturing technologies pioneered at Toyota and now used in much of the automobile industry.

learning effects Cost savings from learning by doing.

legal risk The likelihood that a trading partner will opportunistically break a contract or expropriate intellectual property rights.

legal system System of rules that regulate behavior and the processes by which the laws of a country are enforced and through which redress of grievances is obtained.

Leontief paradox The empirical finding that, in contrast to the predictions of the Heckscher-Ohlin theory, U.S. exports are less capital intensive than U.S. imports.

letter of credit Issued by a bank, indicating that the bank will make payments under specific circumstances.

licensing Occurs when a firm (the licensor) licenses the right to produce its product, use its production processes, or use its brand name or trademark to another firm (the licensee). In return for giving the licensee these rights, the licensor collects a royalty fee on every unit the licensee sells.

licensing agreement Arrangement in which a licensor grants the rights to intangible property to a licensee for a specified period and receives a royalty fee in return.

local content requirement A requirement that some specific fraction of a good be produced domestically.

localization strategy Plan focusing on increasing profitability by customizing the goods or services to match tastes in national markets.

location economies Cost advantages from performing a value creation activity at the optimal location for that activity.

location-specific advantages Advantages that arise from using resource endowments or assets that are tied to a particular foreign location and that a firm finds valuable to combine with its own unique assets (such as the firm's technological, marketing, or management know-how).

logistics The procurement and physical transmission of material through the supply chain, from suppliers to customers.

M

Maastricht Treaty Treaty agreed to in 1991, but not ratified until January 1, 1994, that committed the 12 member states of the European Community to a closer economic and political union.

make-or-buy decisions Decisions a company makes about whether to perform a value creation activity itself or to outsource it to another entity.

maker Person or business initiating a bill of lading (draft).

managed-float system System under which some currencies are allowed to float freely, but the majority are either managed by government intervention or pegged to another currency.

management network A network of informal contact between individual managers.

market economy The allocation of resources is determined by the invisible hand of the price system.

market imperfections Imperfections in the operation of the market mechanism.

market makers Financial service companies that connect investors and borrowers, either directly or indirectly.

market power Ability of a firm to exercise control over industry prices or output.

market segmentation Identifying groups of consumers whose purchasing behavior differs from others in important ways.

marketing mix Choices about product attributes, distribution strategy, communication strategy, and pricing strategy that a firm offers its targeted markets.

masculinity versus femininity Theory of the relationship between gender and work roles. In masculine cultures, sex roles are sharply differentiated and traditional "masculine values" such as achievement and the effective exercise of power determine cultural ideals. In feminine cultures, sex roles are less sharply distinguished, and little differentiation is made between men and women in the same job.

mass customization   The production of a wide variety of end products at a unit cost that could once be achieved only through mass production of a standardized output.

materials management   The activity that controls the transmission of physical materials through the value chain, from procurement through production and into distribution.

mercantilism   An economic philosophy advocating that countries should simultaneously encourage exports and discourage imports.

MERCOSUR   Pact between Argentina, Brazil, Paraguay, and Uruguay to establish a free trade area.

minimum efficient scale   The level of output at which most plant-level scale economies are exhausted.

MITI   Japan's Ministry of International Trade and Industry.

mixed economy   Certain sectors of the economy are left to private ownership and free market mechanisms, while other sectors have significant government ownership and government planning.

money management   Managing a firm's global cash resources efficiently.

Moore's Law   The power of microprocessor technology doubles and its costs of production fall in half every 18 months.

moral hazard   Arises when people behave recklessly because they know they will be saved if things go wrong.

mores   Norms seen as central to the functioning of a society and to its social life.

multidomestic strategy   Emphasizing the need to be responsive to the unique conditions prevailing in different national markets.

Multilateral Agreement on Investment (MAI)   An agreement that would make it illegal for signatory states to discriminate against foreign investors; would have liberalized rules governing FDI between OECD states.

multilateral netting   A technique used to reduce the number of transactions between subsidiaries of the firm, thereby reducing the total transaction costs arising from foreign exchange dealings and transfer fees.

multinational enterprise (MNE)   A firm that owns business operations in more than one country.

multipoint competition   Arises when two or more enterprises encounter each other in different regional markets, national markets, or industries.

multipoint pricing   Occurs when a pricing strategy in one market may have an impact on a rival's pricing strategy in another market.

N

naive immoralist   Approach that accepts ignoring ethical norms if others do so too.

new trade theory   The observed pattern of trade in the world economy may be due in part to the ability of firms in a given market to capture first-mover advantages.

nonconvertible currency   A currency is not convertible when both residents and nonresidents are prohibited from converting their holdings of that currency into another currency.

norms   Social rules and guidelines that prescribe appropriate behavior in particular situations.

North American Free Trade Agreement (NAFTA)   Free trade area between Canada, Mexico, and the United States.

O

offset   Agreement to purchase goods and services with a specified percentage of proceeds from an original sale in that country from any firm in the country.

offshore production   FDI undertaken to serve the home market.

oligopoly   An industry composed of a limited number of large firms.

optimal currency area   Region in which similarities in economic activity make a single currency and exchange rate feasible instruments of macroeconomic policy.

organization culture   Norms and values shared by employees.

Organization for Economic Cooperation and Development (OECD)   A Paris-based intergovernmental organization of "wealthy" nations whose purpose is to provide its 29 member states with a forum in which governments can compare their experiences, discuss the problems they share, and seek solutions that can then be applied within their own national contexts.

organizational architecture   Totality of a firm's organization.

organizational structure   Determined by the formal division into subunits, the location of decision making, and the coordination of activities of subunits.

outflows of FDI   Flow of foreign direct investment out of a country.

output controls   Achieving control by setting goals for subordinates, expressing these goals in terms of objective criteria, and then judging performance by a subordinate's ability to meet these goals.

P

Paris Convention for the Protection of Industrial Property   International agreement to protect intellectual property; signed by 96 countries.

patent   Grants the inventor of a new product or process exclusive rights to the manufacture, use, or sale of that invention.

pegged exchange rate Currency value is fixed relative to a reference currency.

people Part of the organizational architecture that includes strategy used to recruit, compensate, and retain employees.

performance ambiguity Occurs when the causes of good or bad performance are not clearly identifiable.

personal controls Achieving control by personal contact with subordinates.

pioneering costs Costs an early entrant bears that later entrants avoid, such as the time and effort in learning the rules, failure due to ignorance, and the liability of being a foreigner.

political economy The study of how political factors influence the functioning of an economic system.

political risk The likelihood that political forces will cause drastic changes in a country's business environment that will adversely affect the profit and other goals of a particular business enterprise.

political system System of government in a nation.

political union A central political apparatus coordinates economic, social, and foreign policy.

polycentric staffing A staffing policy in an MNE in which host-country nationals are recruited to manage subsidiaries in their own country, while parent-country nationals occupy key positions at corporate headquarters.

positive-sum game A situation in which all countries can benefit even if some benefit more than others.

power distance Theory of how a society deals with the fact that people are unequal in physical and intellectual capabilities. High power distance cultures are found in countries that let inequalities grow over time into inequalities of power and wealth. Low power distance cultures are found in societies that try to play down such inequalities as much as possible.

predatory pricing Reducing prices below fair market value as a competitive weapon to drive weaker competitors out of the market ("fair" being cost plus some reasonable profit margin).

price discrimination The practice of charging different prices for the same product in different markets.

price elasticity of demand A measure of how responsive demand for a product is to changes in price.

private action Violation of property rights through theft, piracy, blackmail, and the like by private individuals or groups.

privatization The sale of state-owned enterprises to private investors.

processes Manner in which decisions are made and work is performed.

product liability Involves holding a firm and its officers responsible when a product causes injury, death, or damage.

product life-cycle theory The optimal location in the world to produce a product change as the market for the product matures.

product safety laws Set certain safety standards to which a product must adhere.

production Activities involved in creating a product.

profit Difference between revenues and costs.

profit growth The percentage increase in net profits over time.

profitability A rate of return concept.

projected rate The spot exchange rate forecast for the end of the budget period.

property rights Bundle of legal rights over the use to which a resource is put and over the use made of any income that may be derived from that resource.

public action Violation of property rights when public officials extort income, resources, or the property itself from property holders.

pull strategy A marketing strategy emphasizing mass media advertising as opposed to personal selling.

purchasing power parity (PPP) An adjustment in gross domestic product per capita to reflect differences in the cost of living.

push strategy A marketing strategy emphasizing personal selling rather than mass media advertising.

Q

quota rent Extra profit producers make when supply is artificially limited by an import quota.

R

regional economic integration Agreements among countries in a geographic region to reduce and ultimately remove tariff and nontariff barriers to the free flow of goods, services, and factors of production between each other.

relatively efficient market One in which few impediments to international trade and investment exist.

religion A system of shared beliefs and rituals concerned with the sacred.

representative democracy A political system in which citizens periodically elect individuals to represent them in government.

righteous moralist Approach that one's own ethics are appropriate in all cultures.

rights theories Ethical approaches that recognize that humans have fundamental rights that transcend national boundaries.

right-wing totalitarianism   A political system in which political power is monopolized by a party, group, or individual that generally permits individual economic freedom but restricts individual political freedom, including free speech, often on the grounds that it would lead to the rise of communism.

royalties   Remuneration paid to the owners of technology, patents, or trade names for the use of same.

S

short selling   Occurs when an investor places a speculative bet that the value of a financial asset will decline, and profits from that decline.

sight draft   A draft payable on presentation to the drawee.

Single European Act   A 1997 act, adopted by members of the European Community, that committed member countries to establishing an economic union.

Six Sigma   Statistically based philosophy to reduce defects, boost productivity, eliminate waste, and cut costs.

Smoot-Hawley Act   Enacted in 1930 by the U.S. Congress, this act erected a wall of tariff barriers against imports into the United States.

social democrats   Those committed to achieving socialism by democratic means.

social mobility   The extent to which individuals can move out of the social strata into which they are born.

social responsibility   Concept that businesspeople should consider the social consequences of economic actions when making business decisions.

social strata   Hierarchical social categories.

social structure   The basic social organization of a society.

socialism   A political philosophy advocating substantial public involvement, through government ownership, in the means of production and distribution.

society   Group of people who share a common set of values and norms.

sogo shosha   Japanese trading companies; a key part of the *keiretsu*, the large Japanese industrial groups.

sourcing decisions   Whether a firm should make or buy component parts.

specialized asset   An asset designed to perform a specific task, whose value is significantly reduced in its next-best use.

specific tariff   Tariff levied as a fixed charge for each unit of good imported.

spot exchange rate   The exchange rate at which a foreign exchange dealer will convert one currency into another that particular day.

staffing policy   Strategy concerned with selecting employees for particular jobs.

stakeholders   Individuals or groups that have an interest, claim, or stake in the company, in what it does, and in how well it performs.

state-directed economy   An economy in which the state plays a proactive role in influencing the direction and magnitude of private-sector investments.

stock of foreign direct investment   The total accumulated value of foreign-owned assets at a given time.

strategic alliances   Cooperative agreements between two or more firms.

strategic commitment   A decision that has a long-term impact and is difficult to reverse, such as entering a foreign market on a large scale.

strategic trade policy   Government policy aimed at improving the competitive position of a domestic industry and/or domestic firm in the world market.

strategy   Actions managers take to attain the firm's goals.

Structural Impediments Initiative   A 1990 agreement between the United States and Japan aimed at trying to decrease nontariff barriers restricting imports into Japan.

subsidy   Government financial assistance to a domestic producer.

swaps   The simultaneous purchase and sale of a given amount of foreign exchange for two different value dates.

switch trading   Use of a specialized third-party trading house in a countertrade arrangement.

systematic risk   Movements in a stock portfolio's value that are attributable to macroeconomic forces affecting all firms in an economy, rather than factors specific to an individual firm (unsystematic risk).

T

tariff   A tax levied on imports.

tariff rate quota   Lower tariff rates applied to imports within the quota than those over the quota.

tax credit   Allows a firm to reduce the taxes paid to the home government by the amount of taxes paid to the foreign government.

tax haven   A country with exceptionally low, or even no, income taxes.

tax treaty   Agreement between two countries specifying what items of income will be taxed by the authorities of the country where the income is earned.

technical analysis   Uses price and volume data to determine past trends, which are expected to continue into the future.

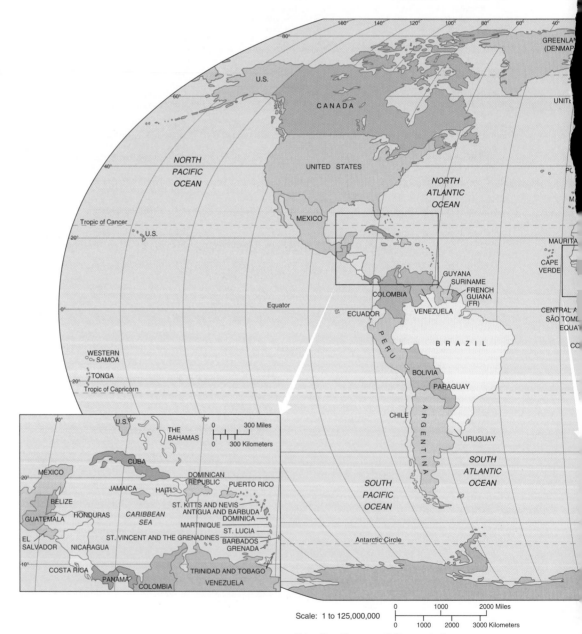

GREENLAND
(DENMARK)

U.S.

CANADA

UNITED

NORTH
PACIFIC
OCEAN

UNITED STATES

NORTH
ATLANTIC
OCEAN

PO

M

Tropic of Cancer

U.S.

MEXICO

MAURITA

CAPE
VERDE

GUYANA
SURINAME
FRENCH
GUIANA
(FR)

COLOMBIA

Equator

ECUADOR

VENEZUELA

CENTRAL A
SÃO TOMÉ
EQUATO

CO

B R A Z I L

WESTERN
SAMOA

P
E
R
U

BOLIVIA

TONGA

Tropic of Capricorn

PARAGUAY

CHILE

A
R
G
E
N
T
I
N
A

URUGUAY

SOUTH
ATLANTIC
OCEAN

SOUTH
PACIFIC
OCEAN

Antarctic Circle

90°

U.S. 80°

70°

THE
BAHAMAS

0   300 Miles

0   300 Kilometers

MEXICO

CUBA

DOMINICAN
REPUBLIC

PUERTO RICO

JAMAICA

HAITI

BELIZE

ST. KITTS AND NEVIS
ANTIGUA AND BARBUDA
DOMINICA

GUATEMALA

HONDURAS

CARIBBEAN
SEA

MARTINIQUE
ST. LUCIA

EL
SALVADOR

NICARAGUA

ST. VINCENT AND THE GRENADINES

BARBADOS
GRENADA

COSTA RICA

PANAMA

COLOMBIA

TRINIDAD AND TOBAGO

VENEZUELA

Scale: 1 to 125,000,000

0   1000   2000 Miles

0   1000   2000   3000 Kilometers

Note: All world maps are Robinson projection.

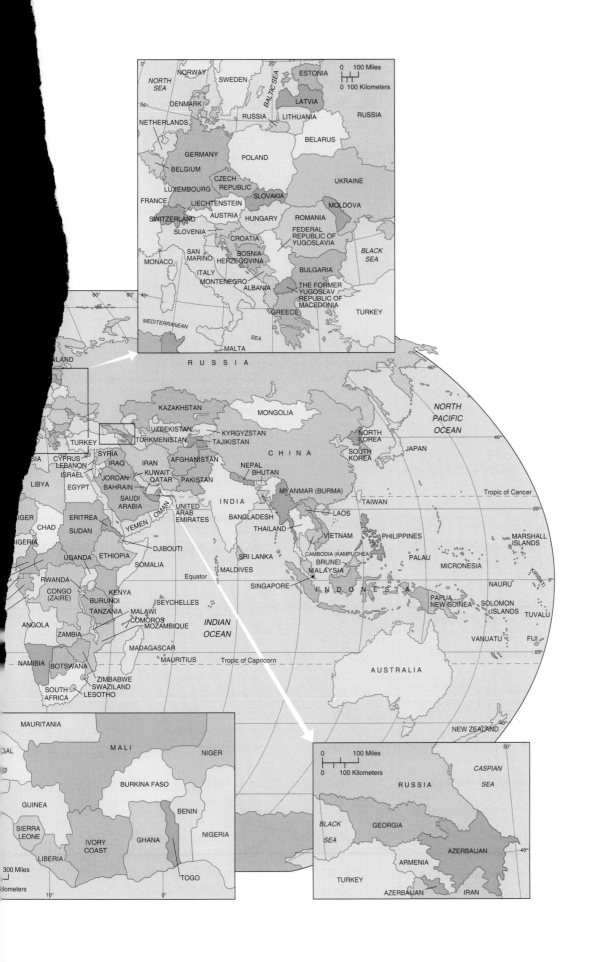

0°   20°
NORTH SEA
BALTIC SEA
0   100 Miles
0   100 Kilometers
NORWAY   SWEDEN   ESTONIA
NORTH SEA
DENMARK   LATVIA
55°   RUSSIA   LITHUANIA   RUSSIA
NETHERLANDS   BELARUS
GERMANY   POLAND
BELGIUM   UKRAINE
LUXEMBOURG   CZECH REPUBLIC
FRANCE   LIECHTENSTEIN   SLOVAKIA   MOLDOVA
SWITZERLAND   AUSTRIA   HUNGARY   ROMANIA
SLOVENIA   CROATIA   FEDERAL REPUBLIC OF YUGOSLAVIA
SAN MARINO   BOSNIA-HERZEGOVINA   BLACK SEA
MONACO   ITALY   MONTENEGRO   BULGARIA
ALBANIA   THE FORMER YUGOSLAV REPUBLIC OF MACEDONIA
60°   80°   40°   GREECE   TURKEY
MEDITERRANEAN   SEA
MALTA

60°   RUSSIA

FINLAND

KAZAKHSTAN   MONGOLIA   NORTH PACIFIC OCEAN
60°
TURKEY   UZBEKISTAN   KYRGYZSTAN   NORTH KOREA   40°
TURKMENISTAN   TAJIKISTAN   SOUTH KOREA   JAPAN
CYPRUS   SYRIA   CHINA
LEBANON   IRAQ   IRAN   AFGHANISTAN   NEPAL   BHUTAN
ISRAEL   JORDAN   KUWAIT   PAKISTAN   MYANMAR (BURMA)   Tropic of Cancer
LIBYA   EGYPT   BAHRAIN   QATAR   INDIA   LAOS   TAIWAN   20°
NIGER   SAUDI ARABIA   UNITED ARAB EMIRATES   BANGLADESH   MARSHALL ISLANDS
NIGERIA   ERITREA   YEMEN   OMAN   THAILAND   VIETNAM   PHILIPPINES
CHAD   SUDAN   DJIBOUTI   SRI LANKA   CAMBODIA (KAMPUCHEA)   PALAU   MICRONESIA   NAURU
UGANDA   ETHIOPIA   MALDIVES   BRUNEI   KIRIBATI   0°
RWANDA   SOMALIA   Equator   SINGAPORE   MALAYSIA   INDONESIA
CONGO (ZAIRE)   KENYA   SEYCHELLES   PAPUA NEW GUINEA   SOLOMON ISLANDS   TUVALU
BURUNDI   TANZANIA   MALAWI   INDIAN OCEAN   VANUATU   FIJI
ANGOLA   COMOROS   MOZAMBIQUE
ZAMBIA   MADAGASCAR   AUSTRALIA   20°
NAMIBIA   BOTSWANA   MAURITIUS   Tropic of Capricorn
ZIMBABWE   SWAZILAND
SOUTH AFRICA   LESOTHO   NEW ZEALAND

MAURITANIA
MALI   NIGER   0   100 Miles   CASPIAN SEA
SENEGAL   0   100 Kilometers   RUSSIA   50°
BURKINA FASO
GUINEA   BENIN   BLACK SEA   GEORGIA
SIERRA LEONE   IVORY COAST   GHANA   NIGERIA   AZERBAIJAN
LIBERIA   TOGO   TURKEY   ARMENIA   40°
300 Miles   AZERBAIJAN   IRAN
Kilometers   10°   0°

ACRONYM	PROPER NAME
ADB	Asian Development Bank
AfDB	African Development Bank
AFIC	Asian Finance and Investment Corporation
AFTA	Asian Free Trade Agreement
ASEAN	Association of Southeast Asian Nations
ATPA	Andean Trade Preference Act
BIS	Bank for International Settlements
BOP	Balance of Payments
CIM	Computer-Integrated Manufacturing
CIS	Commonwealth of Independent States
CISG	UN Convention on Contracts for the International Sale of Goods
CEMA	Council for Mutual Economic Assistance
CRA	Country Risk Assessment
DB	Development Bank
DC	Developed Country
DFIs	Development Finance Institutions
DISC	Domestic International Sales Corporation
EBRD	European Bank for Reconstruction and Development
ECOWAS	Economic Community of West African States
EMU	Economic and Monetary Union
EEA	European Economic Area
EFTA	European Free Trade Association
EMs	Export Management Companies
EMCF	European Monetary Cooperation Fund
EMS	European Monetary System
EPO	European Patent Organization
ETC	Export Trading Company
ETUC	European Trade Union Confederation
EU	European Union
FCPA	Foreign Corrupt Practices Act
FDI	Foreign Direct Investment
FSC	Foreign Sales Corporation
FTAA	Free Trade Agreement of the Americas
FTZ	Foreign Trade Zone
Fx	Foreign Exchange
G7	Group of Seven
GATT	General Agreement on Tariffs and Trade
GC	Global Company
GDP	Gross Domestic Product
GNP	Gross National Product
GSP	Generalized System of Preferences
IAC	International Anti-counterfeiting Coalition
IC	International Company
IDA	International Development Association

ACRONYM	PROPER NAME
IDB	Inter-American Development Bank
IEC	International Electrotechnical Commission
IFC	International Finance Corporation
IMF	International Monetary Fund
IPLC	International Product Life Cycle
IRC	International Revenue Code
ISA	International Seabed Authority
ISO	International Organization for Standardization
ITA	International Trade Administration
JIT	Just-in-Time
JV	Joint Venture
LAIA	Latin American Integration Association (formerly LAFTA)
LDC	Less Developed Country
LIBOR	London Interbank Offer Rate
LOST	Law of the Sea Treaty
MERCOSUR	Free Trade Agreement between Argentina, Brazil, Paraguay, and Uruguay
MNC	Multinational Company
MNE	Multinational Enterprise
NAFTA	North American Free Trade Agreement
NATO	North Atlantic Treaty Organization
NIC	Newly Industrializing Country
NTBs	Nontariff Barriers
OECD	Organization for Economic Cooperation & Development
OPEC	Organizational of Petroleum Exporting Countries
PPP	Purchasing Power Parity
PRC	People's Republic of China
PTA	Preferential Trade Area for Eastern and Southern Africa
SACC	Southern African Development Coordination Conference
SBA	Small Business Administration
SBC	Strategic Business Center
SBU	Small Business Unit
SDR	Special Drawing Rights
SEZ	Special Economic Zone
TQM	Total Quality Management
UN	United Nations
UNCTAD	UN Conference on Trade and Development
VAT	Value Added Tax
VER	Voluntary Export Restraint
VRAs	Voluntary Restraints Agreements
WEC	World Energy Council
WIPO	World Intellectual Property Organization
WTO	World Trade Organization

COUNTRY	CAPITAL
Afghanistan	Kabul
Albania	Tirana
Algeria	Algiers
Andorra	Andorra la Vella
Angola	Luanda
Antigua and Barbuda	St. John's
Argentina	Buenos Aires
Armenia	Yerevan
Australia	Canberra
Austria	Vienna
Azerbaijan	Baku
Bahamas	Nassau
Bahrain	Manama
Bangladesh	Dhaka
Barbados	Bridgetown
Belarus	Minsk
Belgium	Brussels
Belize	Belmopan
Benin	Porto-Novo
Bhutan	Thimphu
Bolivia	La Paz
Bosnia and Herzegovina	Sarajevo
Botswana	Gaborone
Brazil	Brasilia
Brunei	Bandar Seri Begawan
Bulgaria	Sofia
Burkina Faso	Ouagadougou
Burundi	Bujumbura
Cambodia	Phnom Penh
Cameroon	Yaounde
Canada	Ottawa
Cape Verde	Praia
Central African Republic	Bangui
Chad	N'Djamena
Chile	Santiago
China	Beijing
Colombia	Bogota
Comoros	Moroni
Congo	Brazzaville
Congo (formerly Zaire)	Kinshasa
Costa Rica	San Jose
Cote d'Ivoire	Yamoussoukro
Croatia	Zagreb
Cuba	Havana
Cyprus	Nicosia
Czech Republic	Prague
Denmark	Copenhagen
Djibouti	Djibouti
Dominica	Roseau
Dominican Republic	Santo Domingo
Ecuador	Quito
Egypt	Cairo
El Salvador	San Salvador
Equatorial Guinea	Malabo
Eritrea	Asmara
Estonia	Tallinn
Ethiopia	Addis Ababa
Fiji	Suva
Finland	Helsinki
France	Paris
Gabon	Libreville
The Gambia	Banjul
Georgia	Tbilisi
Germany	Berlin

COUNTRY	CAPITAL
Ghana	Accra
Greece	Athens
Grenada	St. George's
Guatemala	Guatemala City
Guinea	Conakry
Guinea-Bissau	Bissau
Guyana	Georgetown
Haiti	Port-au-Prince
Honduras	Tegucigalpa
Hungary	Budapest
Iceland	Reykjavik
India	New Delhi
Indonisia	Jakarta
Iran	Tehran
Iraq	Baghdad
Ireland	Dublin
Israel	Jerusalem
Italy	Rome
Jamaica	Kingston
Japan	Tokyo
Jordan	Amman
Kazakhstan	Astana
Kenya	Nairobi
Kiribati	Tarawa
Korea, North	Pyongyang
Korea, South	Seoul
Kuwait	Kuwait City
Kyrgyzstan	Bishkek
Laos	Vientiane
Latvia	Riga
Lebanon	Beirut
Lesotho	Maseru
Liberia	Monrovia
Libya	Tripoli
Liechtenstein	Vaduz
Lithuania	Vilnius
Luxembourg	Luxembourg
Macedonia, The Former Yugoslav Republic of	Skopje
Madagascar	Antananarivo
Malawi	Lilongwe
Malaysia	Kuala Lumpur
Maldives	Male
Mali	Bamako
Malta	Valletta
Marshall Islands	Majuro
Mauritania	Nouakchott
Mauritius	Port Louis
Mexico	Mexico City
Micronesia	Palikir
Moldova	Chisinau
Monaco	Monaco
Mongolia	Ulaanbaatar
Montenegro	Podgorica
Morocco	Rabat
Mozambique	Maputo
Myanmar	Rangoon
Namibia	Windhoek
Nauru	Yaren
Nepal	Kathmandu
The Netherlands	Amsterdam
New Zealand	Wellington
Nicaragua	Managua
Niger	Niamey
Nigeria	Abuja
Norway	Oslo
Oman	Muscat
Pakistan	Islamabad
Palau	Koror

COUNTRY	CAPITAL
Panama	Panama City
Papua New Guinea	Port Moresby
Paraguay	Asuncion
Peru	Lima
Philippines	Manila
Poland	Warsaw
Portugal	Lisbon
Qatar	Doha
Romania	Bucharest
Russia	Moscow
Rwanda	Kigali
Saint Kitts and Nevis	Basseterre
Saint Lucia	Castries
Saint Vincent and the Grenadines	Kingstown
San Marino	San Marino
Sao Tome and Principe	Sao Tome
Saudi Arabia	Riyadh
Senegal	Dakar
Seychelles	Victoria
Sierra Leone	Freetown
Singapore	Singapore
Slovakia	Bratislava
Slovenia	Ljubljana
Solomon Islands	Honiara
Somalia	Mogadishu
South Africa	Pretoria
Spain	Madrid
Sri Lanka	Colombo
Sudan	Khartoum
Suriname	Paramaribo
Swaziland	Mbabane
Sweden	Stockholm
Switzerland	Bern
Syria	Damascus
Taiwan	Taipei
Tajikistan	Dushanbe
Tanzania	Dar-es-Salaam
Thailand	Bangkok
Togo	Lome
Tonga	Nuku'alofa
Trinidad and Tobago	Port-of-Spain
Tunisia	Tunis
Turkey	Ankara
Turkmenistan	Ashgabat
Tuvalu	Funafuti
Uganda	Kampala
Ukraine	Kiev
United Arab Emirates	Abu Dhabi
United Kingdom	London
United States of America	Washington, DC
Uruguay	Montevideo
Uzbekistan	Tashkent
Vanuatu	Vila
Vatican City	
Venezuela	Caracas
Vietnam	Hanoi
Western Samoa	Apia
Yemen	Sanaa
Yugoslavia, Federal Republic of	Belgrade
Zambia	Lusaka
Zimbabwe	Harare

ISBN 0-07-297371-4